Diarmuid and Grania

Manuscript Materials

THE CORNELL YEATS

PLAYS

The Countess Cathleen, edited by Michael J. Sidnell and Wayne K. Chapman
The Land of Heart's Desire, edited by Jared Curtis
Diarmuid and Grania, edited by J. C. C. Mays
The Hour-Glass, edited by Catherine Phillips
Deirdre, edited by Virginia Bartholome Rohan
"The Dreaming of the Bones" and "Calvary," edited by Wayne K. Chapman
"The Only Jealousy of Emer" and "Fighting the Waves," edited by Steven Winnett
The Words Upon the Window Pane, edited by Mary FitzGerald
The Herne's Egg, edited by Alison Armstrong
Purgatory, edited by Sandra F. Siegel
The Death of Cuchulain, edited by Phillip L. Marcus

POEMS

The Early Poetry, Volume I: "Mosada" and "The Island of Statues," edited by George Bornstein
The Early Poetry, Volume II: "The Wanderings of Oisin" and Other Early Poems to 1895, edited by George Bornstein
The Wind Among the Reeds, edited by Carolyn Holdsworth
"In the Seven Woods" and "The Green Helmet and Other Poems," edited by David Holdeman
Responsibilities, edited by William H. O'Donnell
The Wild Swans at Coole, edited by Stephen Parrish
Michael Robartes and the Dancer, edited by Thomas Parkinson, with Anne Brannen
The Winding Stair (1929), edited by David R. Clark
Words for Music, Perhaps, edited by David R. Clark
"Parnell's Funeral and Other Poems" from "A Full Moon in March," edited by David R. Clark
New Poems, edited by J. C. C. Mays and Stephen Parrish
Last Poems, edited by James Pethica

Diarmuid and Grania

Manuscript Materials

BY W. B. YEATS AND GEORGE MOORE

EDITED BY

J. C. C. MAYS

Cornell University Press

ITHACA AND LONDON

The preparation of this volume was made possible in part
by a grant from The Atlantic Philanthropies.

First published 2005 by Cornell University Press

Printed in the United States of America

Library of Congress Cataloging-in-Publication Data

Yeats, W. B. (William Butler), 1865-1939.
Diarmuid and Grania : manuscript materials / by W.B. Yeats and George Moore ; edited by J.C.C. Mays.
p. cm. -- (The Cornell Yeats)
Includes bibliographical references.
ISBN 0-8014-4361-X
1. Moore, George, 1852-1933. Diarmuid and Grania--Criticism, Textual. 2. Yeats, W. B. (William Butler), 1865-1939--Criticism, Textual. 3. Mythology, Celtic, in literature. I. Moore, George, 1852-1933. II. Mays, J. C. C. III. Title.
PR5042.D53Y43 2004
823'.8--dc22

2004051266

Cornell University strives to utilize environmentally responsible suppliers and materials to the fullest extent possible in the publishing of its books. Such materials include vegetable-based, low-VOC inks and acid-free papers that are recycled, totally chlorine-free, or partly composed of non-wood fibers. For further information, visit our website at www.cornellpress.cornell.edu.

1 3 5 7 9 cloth printing 10 8 6 4 2

The Cornell Yeats

The volumes in this series present all available manuscripts, revised typescripts, proof-sheets, and other materials that record the growth of Yeats's poems and plays from the earliest draftings through to the texts published in his lifetime. Most of the materials are from the archives of Senator Michael Yeats, now in the care of the National Library of Ireland, supplemented by materials held by the late Anne Yeats; the remainder are preserved in public collections and private hands in Ireland and around the world. The volumes of poems, with a few exceptions, follow the titles of Yeats's own collections; several volumes of plays in the series contain more than one play.

In all the volumes manuscripts are reproduced in photographs accompanied by transcriptions, in order to illuminate Yeats's creative process—to show the poet at work. The remaining materials—such as clean typescripts and printed versions—are generally recorded in collated form in an apparatus hung below a finished text. Each volume contains an Introduction describing the significance of the materials it includes, tracing the relation of the various texts to one another. There is also a census of manuscripts, with full descriptive detail, and appendixes are frequently used to present related materials, some of them unpublished.

As the editions seek to present, comprehensively and accurately, the various versions behind Yeats's published poems and plays, including versions he left unpublished, they will be of use to readers who seek to understand how great writing can take shape, and to scholars and editors who seek to establish and verify authoritative final texts.

The Yeats Editorial Board

Contents

*All manuscripts and typescripts listed are transcribed in full; the titles that are marked with an asterisk appear with full photographic reproductions; all but two of the remaining typescripts are represented by sample photographs because their distinctive typing-styles can be as revealing as other features.

Act II

Act III

Acknowledgments

This edition was made possible by the generous cooperation of Michael Yeats and of the late Anne Yeats. On their behalf, A. P. Watt Ltd., literary agents, have authorized reproduction of all the Yeats texts in this edition, and the Design and Artists Copyright Society (DACS) the Jack B. Yeats sketches in Appendix V. I should also like to thank Colin Smythe, acting on behalf of the estates of George Moore and Diarmuid Russell, for his equally generous cooperation. The musical accompaniment in Appendix IV is reproduced by permission of Novello and the Elgar Estate.

I further acknowledge, for permission to reproduce and/or consult materials in their care, the Council of Trustees of the National Library of Ireland, Dublin; the Henry W. and Albert A. Berg Collection of the New York Public Library (Astor, Lennox and Tilden Foundations); the Harry Ransom Humanities Research Center, University of Texas, Austin; Special Collections, Washington University Libraries, St. Louis; Special Collections, Woodruff Library, Emory University; Special Collections, State University of New York (SUNY) at Stony Brook; the Board of Trinity College Dublin; and the Houghton Library, Harvard University.

I am specially grateful for particular assistance to the Keeper of Manuscripts at the National Library of Ireland, Gerard Lyne, and, in the reading room, Tom Desmond; Stephen Crook, librarian, and Philip Mileto, technical assistant, at the Berg; Richard Oram and Tara Wenger at the Harry Ransom Humanities Research Center; Alison Carrick at Washington University Libraries; Stephen Enniss at Emory University; Kristen Nyitray at SUNY Stony Brook; and Stuart O'Seanoir at Trinity College Dublin. Also, for help with enquiries surrounding the text, to Romaine Ahlstrom, Reader Services, and Gayle M. Barkley, Department of Manuscripts, at the Huntington Library, San Marino, California; Katie Salzmann, curator of Manuscripts at Southern Illinois University, Carbondale; David Byers, chief executive, Ulster Orchestra, Belfast; Professor D. C. Greer, University of Durham; and Dr. Catherine Morris, St. John's College, Oxford. At University College, the following colleagues have cheerfully repaired my ignorance: Kathleen Clune and Eoghan Ó hAnluain (Department of Irish); Séamas Ó Catháin and Dáithi Ó hÓgáin (Department of Irish Folklore); and Harry White (Department of Music). Silé Yeats, Annabelle Shaw, and Phil Mayer gave other kinds of assistance at crucial times.

My work on this edition and its publication have been supported by generous grants awarded to the Department of English at Cornell by the Atlantic Philanthropies; and, toward the cost of publication, by the National University of Ireland, and the Academic Publications Committee and the Faculty of Arts Revenue Committee of University College Dublin. I am indebted in every way to my fellow editors, colleagues, and friends on the Yeats Editorial Board—in particular to Jared Curtis, Declan Kiely, Phillip Marcus, Stephen Parrish, and Ann Saddlemyer.

J. C. C. Mays

University College Dublin

Abbreviations

AG	Augusta, Lady Gregory
Als	Autograph letter, signed
Aut	W. B. Yeats, *Autobiographies,* ed. William O'Donnell and Douglas N. Archibald (New York: Scribner, 1999). Same as vol. 3 of *Collected Works* (listed below).
Berg	Henry W. and Albert A. Berg Collection, New York Public Library, Astor, Lennox and Tilden Foundations
CL I	*The Collected Letters of W. B. Yeats: Volume I, 1865–1895,* ed. John Kelly and Eric Domville (Oxford: Clarendon Press, 1986).
CL II	*The Collected Letters of W. B. Yeats: Volume II, 1896–1900,* ed. Warwick Gould, John Kelly and Deirdre Toomey (Oxford: Clarendon Press, 1997).
CL III	*The Collected Letters of W. B. Yeats: Volume III, 1901–1904,* ed. John Kelly and Ronald Suchard (Oxford: Clarendon Press, 1994).
CW I (–XIV)	*The Collected Works of W. B. Yeats,* ed. Richard J. Finneran and George Mills Harper (14 vols., New York: Macmillan/Scribner, 1989–).
Diarmuid	The play, *Diarmuid and Grania,* by W. B. Yeats and George Moore.
DMag	"'Diarmuid and Grania' . . . Now first printed with an introductory note by William Becker," *The Dublin Magazine* n.s., 26, no. 2 (April–June 1951): 1–41.
EM	Edward Martyn
Foster I	R. F. Foster, *W. B. Yeats: A Life*, volume I: *The Apprentice Mage, 1865–1914* (Oxford: Oxford University Press, 1997).
Frazier	Adrian Frazier, *George Moore, 1852–1933* (New Haven: Yale University Press, 2000).
GM	George Moore
GML	Robert Stephen Becker, *The Letters of George Moore, 1863–1901* (Ph.D. diss., University of Reading, 1980). The dissertation is in three continuously paginated volumes; the letters are numbered 1–909. I have added references to Becker only in cases where letters have not been published elsewhere. Becker's text is for the most part reliable, but his dating can often be improved with reference to *CL* I–III.
GMP	*George Moore on Parnassus: Letters (1900–1933) to Secretaries, Publishers, Printers, Agents, Agents, Literati, Friends, and Acquaintances,* ed. Helmut E. Gerber with the assistance of O. M. Brack (Newark: University of Delaware Press, 1988).

GMT	*George Moore in Transition: Letters to T. Fisher Unwin and Lena Milman, 1894–1910,* ed. Helmut E. Gerber (Detroit: Wayne State University Press, 1968).
GR	George Russell (AE)
GY	Mrs. W. B. Yeats (George Yeats)
H&F	George Moore, *Hail and Farewell: Ave, Salve, Vale*, ed. Richard Allen Cave (Gerrards Cross: Colin Smythe; Washington, D.C.: Catholic University of America, 1985). The titles *Ave* and *Salve* in commentary refer to the the first and third volumes of *Hail and Farewell,* as first published in installments by Moore (1911–1914). The text quoted, however, is that of the edition last published by Moore in 1933.
Hone	Joseph Hone, *The Life of George Moore* (London: Victor Gollancz, 1936).
HRC	Harry Ransom Humanities Research Center, University of Texas at Austin
Hogan	Robert Hogan and James Kilroy, *The Irish Literary Theatre, 1899–1901*, Modern Irish Drama series, 1 (Dublin: Dolmen Press, 1975).
JBY	Jack B. Yeats
Kennedy	Eileen Kennedy, "George Moore to Edward Elgar: Eighteen Letters on *Diarmuid and Grania* and Operatic Dreams," *English Literature in Transition,* 21, no. 3 (1978): 168–187.
LGD	*Lady Gregory's Diaries, 1892–1902,* ed. James Pethica (Gerrards Cross: Colin Smythe, 1996).
LWBY	*Letters to W. B. Yeats,* ed. Richard J. Finneran, George Mills Harper, and William M. Murphy, 2 vols. (London: Macmillan; New York: Columbia University Press, 1977). Note that the dates of GM's letters in this collection have been corrected by *CL* II and Frazier.
LH	Left-hand
MS, MSS	Manuscript, manuscripts
NLI	Manuscript Collections, National Library of Ireland
RH	Right-hand
Tls	Typescript letter, signed
TS, TSS	Typescript, typescripts
VPlays	*The Variorum Edition of the Plays of W. B. Yeats,* ed. Russell K. Alspach and Catharine C. Alspach (New York: Macmillan, 1966).
VPoems	*The Variorum Edition of the Poems of W. B. Yeats,* ed. Peter Allt and Russell K. Alspach (New York: Macmillan, 1966).
Wade	Allan Wade, *A Bibliography of the Writings of W. B. Yeats*, 3d ed., rev. Russell K. Alspach (London: Rupert Hart-Davis, 1968).
WBY	William Butler Yeats
WM, WMs	Watermark, watermarks

Census of Manuscripts

Paper Types

A. White exercise paper, 22.8 by 17.5/7 cm; no watermark; chain lines 2.7/8 cm; twenty-three lines per page; some pages conjoined but no evidence of removal from an exercise book (no staple holes), others separated—includes Berg(00); Berg(09); NLI 8777(4) a, c, f; NLI 8777(8) b, c

B. White exercise paper, 23.2/3 by 18.2 cm; watermarked COMMERCIAL / BUSBRIDGE & Co.; chain lines 2.5 cm; twenty-three lines per page; some pages conjoined but no evidence of removal from an exercise book (no staple holes)—includes Berg(10), NLI 8777(3) e

C. White typing paper, 24.8/9 by 20.2 cm; watermarked JOHN McDONNEL & Co LTD / SWIFT BROOK; no chain lines—includes Berg(04), Berg(12), NLI 8777(12)

D. White typing paper, 25.3/4 by 20.2/3 cm; watermarked JOHN McDONNEL & Co LTD / SWIFT BROOK; no chain lines—includes Berg(01), Berg(06), NLI 8777(13)

E. White typing paper, 26.2/4 by 20.2/3 cm; watermarked JOHN McDONNEL & Co LTD / SWIFT BROOK; no chain lines—includes Berg(99); Berg(11); Berg(15) a, c; HRC; NLI 8777(3) a, b, c, f, g

F. White typing paper, 26.6 by 20.3 cm, watermarked "INVINCIBLE"; chain lines 2.4 cm—includes HRC(1) a, HRC(2), HRC(3)

G. White typing paper, 26.6/7 by 20.3/5 cm, watermarked "INVINCIBLE" / LINEN BOND; no chain lines—includes Berg(02); Berg(07); Berg(13); Berg(14); HRC(1) b; NLI 8777(4) g, h, j, k, l; NLI 8777(6); NLI 8777(7) b, c, d, e, f; NLI 8777(10) a, b

H. White typing paper, 26.3 by 20.2 cm, watermarked [AC monogram within five-point star] / THE ARTICLE CLUB; chain lines 2.5 cm—includes NLI 8777(4) d, NLI 8777(7) a, d

I. White typing paper, 26.7/8 by 20.2/3 cm, watermarked BRITANNIA / [Britannia head device] / PURE LINEN; chain lines 2.9 cm—includes NLI 8777(4) b, NLI 8777(11)

J. White typing paper, 25.4 by 20.3 cm; no watermark; chain lines 2.6 cm—includes NLI 8777(14); NLI 8777(15)

Measurements are given as (height) by (width) in centimeters. Measurement is taken at the center of edges that are irregularly trimmed. A difference of one centimeter in paper from the same manufacturer may reflect the difficulty of measuring exactly, but differences of more than one centimeter may indicate a different batch. The distance between chain lines can also vary by up to two centimeters on the same leaf. In palimpsest pages, underlying material is given an unqualified folio number and pasted-over material is foliated as in, for example, HRC(1), folio 13bis or folio 7tres (the suffixes indicating layers of palimpsest). In such cases, the pasted-over lines are given line numbers to match their position in the palimpsest. Covers or title pages are included in the transcription and foliation when they contain significant information.

The tendency of typists to economize on materials sometimes makes it difficult to distinguish between ribbon and carbon copies of TSS. Sometimes a ribbon is so dry that it produces an inadequate, faint image, resembling a carbon; and, in such situations, a typist can strike harder and leave an impression even on the verso of a carbon that resembles a top (ribbon) copy (e.g., on some leaves of the continuous HRC). Sometimes a fresh carbon on thin or porous paper leaves a spreading impression that can be confused with a ribbon copy (the early leaves of the continuous HRC, again). The color of both kinds of TS is black, unless blue is specified. There are no duplicates (ribbon plus carbons of the same, or duplicate carbons), and the circumstances of the collaboration explain the preponderance of single-ribbon copies.

Additions have been made to some library references in order to facilitate collation and cross-referencing. Thus, all the Berg manuscripts cited share the same shelf mark, "m.b." They are also stamped with accession numbers, running from 64B6799 to 64B6815, as illustrated in the facsimile of Berg(01), folio 1^r (Act I). These numbers do not register the position of folders or possess any meaning in present-day library arrangements, but I have supplied the last two digits, in parenthesis, to identify and separate the overlapping material, listing the folders as Berg(99) to Berg(15).[1] For the same reason, I have signalled the separately paged acts of the earlier HRC typescript as (1), (2), and (3); and have added an alphabetic suffix to register separate materials within mixed NLI folders—for example, 8777(8) a through e. I emphasize that these parenthetical supplements possess no meaning in the institutions that hold the originals; their justification is that an edition requires a different organization from a library collection. I follow library cataloguers on ribbon and carbon copies, but I have doubts about several copies designated as carbons.

The present census requires considerable rearrangement to arrive at the original configuration of TSS. Some sequences as they exist today have been constructed from materials originally composed or copied in different sequences; and materials, now separate, were originally part of larger sequences. In the latter instance, I have supplied consecutive foliation—for example, for the mixed sequence of Berg and NLI folders that make up the earliest continuous TS of Act III. This is explained in the Chronology of Composition, where some peculiarities of typing and layout are added to the descriptions given below.

There are patent gaps in the record. In addition, both Moore and Yeats make references to

---

[1]An exception to this inclusive string is the copy of *Samhaim* designated as Berg(3–4), a name based on the Berg accession numbers 62B5533–4.

copies that have not been traced: for instance, a copy Moore promised to send to Dr. Heilborn (Als [September 3, 1901], NLI 2648, folios 19^{v}–20^{v}; quoted only in part in Hone 239); a copy Moore sent Elgar, in two installments, on September 4 and 10, 1901 (Kennedy 171, 172–173); a copy Yeats gave Mrs. Patrick Campbell in December 1901 (*CL* III 135n); possibly a copy owned by James A. Reardon of St. Louis that Yeats believed was given him by Moore (*CL* III 580; but see GR quoted in 568n)—unless one of the above is Washington, whose provenance is unknown. None of the copies used in the Dublin production has been traced (the Washington copy is too clean to have come from this source).

Berg(99) One hundred and one TS pages (carbon) of the complete text, with MS corrections by WBY (pencil and blue-black ink). Paper type E. Pages numbered continuously, though renumbered by hand (ink) between pages 5–58 (fols. 7^{r}–60^{r}), quite likely due to the rewriting of the opening of the play traceable in the palimpsest of HRC. Further possible substitute pages at pages 5–6, 12, 27, 32, 38–39, 41, 69, 89 (fols. 7–8, 14, 29, 34, 40–41, 43, 71, 91); and, in spite of first appearances, the TS mixes pages in a similar format typed (not very well) on different occasions (e.g., p. 96/fol. 98^{r} and the numerous minor overtypings), as successive improvements were incorporated. Bound in a wrapping-paper cover with a pink ribbon through three roughly made holes along LH side of page. Cover endorsed in WBY's hand "From/W B Yeats/18 Woburn Buildings/Euston Road."

Berg(00) Two-page holograph synopsis of a scene from Act I in GM's hand (blue-black ink). Paper type A, conjoined. GM wrote on the outside pages of the bifolium, leaving the inside opening blank.

Berg(01) Thirty-one-page TS (carbon) of Act I, with single pencil correction on folio 6^{r} (author uncertain). Paper type D. Unnumbered pages joined by a brass split pin though hole at top LH corner. A margin has been ruled in red ink on the LH side (3.6/4.0 cm) and part ascriptions underlined in red ink. There are physical similarities with NLI 8777(13), for which see below.

Berg(02) Forty-page TS (carbon) of Act I, with MS corrections and additions by GM and WBY (both pencil and blue-black ink). Paper type G. Numbered pages with split-pin holes at top LH corner and through front brown-paper cover (no WM; chain lines 2.5 cm; rear cover not present). Cf. the similarly prepared version of Act II in Berg(07).

Berg(03) Twenty-page TS (carbon—or ribbon?) of Act I, with MS corrections by WBY (pencil and blue-black ink). Typing paper 26.7 by 20.8 cm; no WM or chain lines. Bound in a cover of blue-grey paper with a pink ribbon through three holes along LH side of page. Cover and title page stamped at bottom RH: MISS LAWRENCE, / TYPE WRITING OFFICE, / 26, WELLINGTON STREET, / STRAND, W.C. Part ascriptions and stage directions are double underlined and single underlined, respectively, in red ink.

Berg(3–4) AG's grangerized copy of *Samhain* [No. 1], 1901, containing small watercolor sketches of the first performance of the play, portraits and signatures of the actors and members of the audience, and WBY's signed holograph of the spinning song in Act I (ink).

Comments on the sketches contained in this copy are given in Appendix V: Staging. Copy 1.

Berg(04) Two-page TS (ribbon) preliminary version of Act I spinning song, part of stanza 1 canceled in pencil (by GM?). Paper type C. Unnumbered pages with a split-pin hole in top LH corner. The pages were at some time folded horizontally in three and remain slightly crumpled.

Berg(05) Two-page TS (ribbon?) of fragment from near beginning of Act I. Paper 25.3 by 20.1 cm. WM SOUTHERN CROSS [in ornate caps arranged in arching curve] / SUPERFINE; chain lines 2.5.

Berg(06) Thirty-six-page TS (carbon) of Act II, with MS corrections by WBY on folio 7ʳ (pencil). Paper type D. Three split-pin holes along top edge and through brown-paper wraparound cover, marked by WBY on front "Act II" (pencil).

Berg(07) Thirty-seven-page TS (carbon) of Act II, with MS corrections by WBY (two shades of blue-black ink) and one comment by GM on folio 22ʳ (pencil). Paper type G. Numbered pages with split-pin holes at top LH corner and through front and rear cover made of thick brown paper (no WM; chain lines 2.5 cm). There are two pages numbered 36. Cf. the similarly prepared version of Act II in Berg(02).

Berg(08) Two separate TS (both carbon) fragments of Act III, with MS corrections by WBY. Folio 1 has been trimmed from the top of a page numbered "—33—", has an uneven lower edge and measures 9.7 by 20.4 cm; folio 2 has been trimmed from the bottom of a page, has an uneven upper edge and measures 9.2 by 20.4 cm. No WMs or chain lines.

Berg(09) Two-page holograph draft of portion of Act II (miscatalogued as Act III) in GM's hand (blue-black ink). Paper type A. Separated pages numbered 11 and 12; versos blank.

Berg(10) Four-page holograph draft of close of Act III in WBY's hand (blue-black ink). Paper type B. Unnumbered separated pages, LH edge torn; versos blank. See the similar paper used by WBY to revise Act III in NLI 8777(3) e.

Berg(11) Four-page TS (carbon) of Act III with a pencil correction (perhaps by GM or AG rather than WBY). Paper type E. The carbon has a distinctive blue color. The pages are unnumbered and the second page in fact follows on Berg(15) a, folio 2 (as is confirmed by the identical folding pattern and the color of ink smudges).

Berg(12) Twelve-page TS (ribbon) of Act II (miscatalogued as Act III), with MS corrections by GM (pencil). Paper type C. Pages numbered "(18)" to "(30)"; all pages have a split-pin hole in the top LH corner. Pages (1)–(17) of the same corrected TS comprise NLI 8777(12).

Berg(13) Four-page TS (carbon) of Act III, with MS corrections by WBY (pencil) and MS title and comment by AG (also pencil). Paper type G. Pages numbered; all pages have a split-pin hole in top LH corner. All pages canceled with a vertical line (blue-black ink).

Berg(14) Seven separate pages of TS (carbon) of Act III, with MS corrections by WBY (two shades of blue-black ink). Paper type G; folio 7, numbered "–39–", has been trimmed along the bottom edge and measures 19.7 by 20.4 cm. Pages numbered but discontinuous; all have split-pin holes in top LH corners.

Berg(15) Three TS versions of close of Act III. The threefold separation needs rearranging on grounds of internal consistency and chronological development.

Berg(15) a, 1–2 Two pages (carbon) 26.3 by 20.3 cm, with corrections and an insertion by WBY (blue-black ink). Paper type E. The carbon has a distinctive blue color. The unnumbered pages have at one time been folded in six, as if to fit an envelope, and the sequence is completed by the miscatalogued Berg(11), folio 2.

Berg(15) b, 3–5 Three pages (ribbon?) 26.6 by 20.1 cm, with a few emendations by WBY (blue-black ink). No WM; chain lines 2.5 cm. The paper is of a flimsy, lightweight quality. The unnumbered pages were once folded in half.

Berg(15) c, 6–7 Two-page TS (carbon) 26.3 by 20.3 cm, with MS corrections by GM (ink). Paper type E. The carbon has a distinctive strong blue color. The unnumbered pages were at one time folded in six (though differently from Berg[15] a + [11]), as if to fit an envelope.

Emory Bifolium measuring overall 17.5 by 21.3 cm, folded to make four pages; WM [harp on shield, with crown above] / Olde Irish Vellum; no chain lines. WBY has copied out Finn's "Blood Bond" (Act II) and Laban's spinning song (Act I) on the RH pages (here given as fols. 1^r and 2^r) of the folded bifolium. Pages 2 and 4 are blank. W. B. Yeats Collection, Woodruff Library, Emory University.

Harvard(1) Microfilm reel 5 of WBY materials contains, along with much else, the larger part of the *Diarmuid and Grania* MS materials acquired by the NLI while they were still in the hands of GY. Another microfilm, in the possession of Stephen M. Parrish at Cornell, dating from about the same time, reproduces the same material in a different sequence. Houghton Library, Harvard University; catalogued as *447F-1(5).

Harvard(2) Twelve Tls and autograph cards (October 29, 1950–early February 1951) from William Becker to James Starkey, with final corrected galleys of the text of *Diarmuid and Grania* together with an offprint of the printed version of the play from *DMag*. The materials confirm Becker's awareness of how he "tidied up the punctuation a bit" and normalized the text in other ways. Catalogued as EC9.Y3455.951d; Houghton Library, Harvard University.

HRC(1) Twenty-page TS (carbon) of Act I, with MS corrections by WBY and GM, in a folder containing disbound, separately paginated TSS of all three acts and the brown leatherette binder that once contained them. Paper type F, except for paper type G on folios 7–9 (pages numbered 7, 8, and 9). The TS is composed of two or more layers. Folios 1–3, 5–6, 10–13 (pp. 1–3, 5–6, 9bis, 10+11 [both numbers on one page], 12–13) have slightly wider margins and, given that some of them carry duplicated page numbers, they may represent either an earlier level of text or substitutions; folios 7–9 (pp. 7–9), on paper type G, have centered part ascriptions, underlined stage directions, and represent a different, separate layer of text; folios 13–13bis comprise a palimpsest (paste-over text) of page 13. All Act I leaves contain three subsequently punched holes at the LH side to fit the leatherette binder. The binder is stamped in blue ink—LEATHERETTE / BY ROYAL LETTERS PATENT.—inside the rear cover.

An additional leaf preceding the first page of text—WM (a), annotated (in a later hand?) "*1st state*"—has not been included in the foliation, nor has a blank leaf between Acts I and II. The hand that appears on the leaf preceding the first page of text looks like the hand that made the penciled marginal comments in HRC(2), folios 11^r, 14^r, 28^r, 32^r, and in HRC, folios 38^r and 62^r—which are quite certainly later. This may be the same hand that made the small ticks and crosses that appear in the RH margins throughout HRC (1)–(3). Alternatively, a small detail on HCR(1), folio 19^r, suggests the ticks and crosses might have been inserted by WBY (the tick is in the same ink as his annotations on this page; ticks and crosses in the two subsequent acts are in pencil, like WBY's annotations).

HRC(2) Thirty-page TS (carbon) of Act II, with MS corrections by WBY and GM, in a folder containing disbound, separately paginated TSS of all three acts and the brown leatherette binder that once contained them. Paper type F. The TS is composed of two or more layers. Folios 1–4, 8–10, 12, 32 (pp. 1–4, 6–8, 10, 30) have wider margins and/or underlined stage descriptions, and may represent substitutions (see also editorial note on fol. 13); folios 3 and 5, 4 and 6, 12 and 13 comprise two versions of pages 3, 4, and 10. All Act II leaves contain two series of punched and stabbed holes at the LH side, the stabbed holes fitting the leatherette binder. The binder is stamped in blue ink—LEATHERETTE / BY ROYAL LETTERS PATENT.—inside the rear cover. A blank leaf between Acts I and II and two blank leaves between Acts II and III have not been included in the foliation.

HRC(3) Twenty-seven-page TS (carbon) of Act III, with MS corrections by WBY solely, in a folder containing disbound, separately paginated TSS of all three acts and the brown leatherette binder that once contained them. Paper type F. The text on folios 23^r–24^r (pp. 23–24) is set to wider margins, but stage directions are not underlined. All Act III leaves contain two series of punched and stabbed holes at the LH side, the stabbed holes fitting the leatherette binder. The binder is stamped in blue ink—LEATHERETTE / BY ROYAL LETTERS PATENT.—inside the rear cover.

Two blank leaves between Acts II and III and a further blank leaf following the close of Act III have not been included in the foliation. HRC(3) contains the largest number of the small ticks and crosses that appear in the RH margins of HRC(1)–(3).

HRC One hundred and thirteen TS pages (blue carbon) of complete text, with MS corrections by WBY and GM. Paper type E. The weight and absorbency of the paper varies. Folios 6, 7, 27 (pp. 3, [4], 24, 111–113) are palimpsests, the last two pages (the top versions of pp. 112, 113) being numbered 2 and 3; and a fold-over flap is pasted onto folio 38 (p. 35). The additions pasted onto folios 6 and 7, (pp. 3 and [4]) are blue ribbon; onto folios 27, 38, 114–116 (pp. 24, 35, 111–113) black ribbon. The whole is bound in blue-marbled card covers 27.3 by 20.9 cm, with well-rubbed edges and corners. There is no title, inscription, or sign of ownership.

This is the copy GM gave to Maud, Lady Cunard, which was published in *DMag* when it came into the possession of John Millward, and of which NLI 8777(2) is a corrected TS copy. Several years later, GY told Lennox Robinson a different story—that Millward had purchased the TS from Hatchard's of Piccadilly, and that the director, Mr. McEwen, had obtained it from Mrs. Patrick Campbell (personal note communicated to me by Ann Saddlemyer)—but GY must have misremembered. Later pencil annotations on folios 38ʳ, 62ʳ, and 77ʳ resemble marks found in HRC(1), (2), and (3) and strengthen the likelihood that such marks are later insertions; but see commentary on folio 110ʳ.

A selection of differences from Berg(99) is noted in the notes to HRC, invariably with reference to Washington—this being the other extant fair copy of the present revised TS.

NLI 8777(2) Ninety-two-page TS (carbon) of complete text, with MS corrections by William Becker; there are, in addition, three unnumbered pages containing respectively the title, list of characters, and text inserted between pages 30 and 31.

The TS was given by Becker to GY in 1950, being a copy of HRC when it was in the possession of John Millward. Becker has corrected typos throughout, but his larger MS corrections represent authorial corrections in the original TS, and these and other details confirm that he was working from HRC.

NLI 8777(3) Unfoliated TS of complete text in three separately paginated acts, each with MS corrections by WBY and GM, in both ink and pencil, followed by other related materials, the whole bound together in a brown leatherette folder, with string through the outer two of the three roughly made holes on the LH side. The folder is identical with the folder that once contained HRC(1)–(3), as is confirmed by the traces of the same rubber stamp (here "E" over "ENT.") on the inside rear cover.

The separate portions are designated "a" through "g" below, in the order in which they are contained in the folder.

NLI 8777(3) a, fols. 1–36 TS of Act I comprising an unnumbered title page, thirty-one numbered pages of text (the failure to number fol. 31ʳ as p. 26 is evidently an oversight), and three loosely inserted substitute pages (pp. 7A, 15B2, 18C at fols. 9, 16, 23)—everything on paper type E. The main body of pages is a ribbon copy of a light blue color; the title page and pages 7A, 14B, 15B2, 18C (fols. 1, 9, 16, 17, 23) are dark blue ribbon.

NLI 8777(3) b, fols. 37–80 Act II comprising forty-four TS (dark blue ribbon) pages on the same paper type E as the body of Act I above, numbered by hand in pencil.

NLI 8777(3) c, fols. 81–111 Act III comprising thirty-one TS numbered pages: the paper for the most part the same as the body of Act I above (paper type E), though some are 26.3 cm high; all but page 25 are light blue ribbon copies—page 25 (fol. 105ʳ) being dark blue ribbon. Between pages 1 and 2 (fols. 81–82) is a portion of a single page of a lighter-stock paper measuring 7.6 by 20.0 cm, lower edge irregularly trimmed. No WM, chain lines 2.5 cm; the whole being a TS (dark blue ribbon), with two small ink emendations and WBY's ink heading, "Act 111".

NLI 8777(3) d, fol. 112 Single TS (blue ribbon) page typed by AG containing a portion of Act I and of Act III above, with one pencil correction in the hand of ?GM; lighter-stock paper measuring 26.5 by 20.0 cm; WM [scroll design] / EXTRA STRONG / 3000.

NLI 8777(3) e, fols. 113–114 Holograph draft of part of Act III in the hand of WBY (blue-black ink) on page 1 of two conjoined leaves, paper type B. See the similarly treated bifoliate paper employed by WBY to revise Act III in Berg(10).

NLI 8777(3) f, fols. 114–117 Four-page TS (blue ribbon) of close of Act III, with corrections by WBY and GM; paper type E.

NLI 8777(3) g, fol. 118 Single-page TS (blue ribbon) of Act I on lighter stock of paper type E.

NLI 8777(4) Miscellaneously gathered versions of Act II; interspersed with other materials from Act II and single pages from Acts I and III. The twelve separate portions are designated "a" through "l" below, in the order in which they are contained in the folder. These portions originally continued or were continued by portions of NLI 8777(7).

NLI 8777(4) a, fols. 1–28 A version of Act II comprising twenty-eight numbered holograph pages in WBY's hand, rectos only plus a canceled insertion on folio 17^{v}; paper type A. Folios 12–13 are conjoint; folios 13–14, 15–16, and 17–18 were evidently conjoint at one time. Blue-black ink on rectos, with some rewriting and frequent blotting on versos.

NLI 8777(4) b, fols. 29–30, 33–36 The above continued by six (ribbon? dark blue) TS pages—typed by AG on her Coole Park Remington?—numbered 29–30, 33–36, with corrections by AG, GM, and WBY; paper type I. See NLI 8777(11) and 8777(3) d for other pages typed by AG.

NLI 8777(4) c, fols. 31–32 The above complemented by two separate holograph pages numbered 31 and 32 in WBY's hand on the same paper as (4) a. The continuous series (4) a+b+c has a split-pin hole in each top LH corner.

NLI 8777(4) d, fol. 37 Single-page TS (black ribbon) of part of Act I headed "—11—"; paper type A.

NLI 8777(4) e, fol. 38 Fragment of Act III on a TS fragment trimmed from the foot of a page; measuring 7.0 by 20.3 cm (upper edge irregular); no WM or chain lines. Revised in WBY's hand in two shades of blue-black ink, as in NLI 8777(10) a.

NLI 8777(4) f, fol. 39 Single holograph unnumbered page in WBY's hand—being his improved copy of GM's draft of Act II on NLI 8777(4) b, folio 36^{v}—on the same lined exercise paper as (4) a and c (paper type A); split-pin hole in top LH corner.

NLI 8777(4) g, fols. 40–45 Six numbered TS pages (black ribbon) headed by WBY (blue ink) "Moore's latest version. / Nov 27"; paper type G. Extensively revised by WBY in pencil, blue-black and blue ink. Punched hole in top LH corner. The first page (fol. 40^{r}) is soiled. The six pages were originally continued in rejected material filed in a separate folder (NLI 8777(7) c, fols. 5–11/pp. 7–13).

The six pages here make the beginning of a near-continuous text of the first half of Act II, cobbled together from TSS prepared on separate occasions when they were revised by WBY in pencil and blue-black ink, and all together in blue ink when he at the same time filled a gap in the new sequence in holograph on the verso of two black-bordered funeral cards. The new continuous sequence comprises NLI 8777(4) g+h+i+j+k+l.

The paper employed in the TSS is the same, but the body of text is set at two margin settings—here measured from the LH side of part ascriptions. The present margin measures 3.7 cm.

NLI 8777(4) h, fols. 46–49 Four TS pages (black ribbon) on the same paper, type G, as (4) g, numbered 8–11. Page 8 (fol. 46ʳ) is headed in WBY's hand (blue ink) "Insert ~~after~~ after King goes out page 6–". The TS, extensively revised in his hand in pencil and blue ink only, continues the text from the close of (4) g. Margin measures 4.0 cm; split-pin holes in top LH corner. Note that this portion of TS was originally continued in NLI 8777(7) d, folios 12–15/pages 12–15.

NLI 8777(4) i, fols. 50ᵛ–51ᵛ Two pages of text in WBY's hand (blue ink) on the versos of bifolio funeral cards measuring 22.8 by 17.7 cm overall; WM FAIRFORD VALE / JS & CO. LTD.; chain lines 2.5 cm. Split-pin holes in top LH corner. The text follows on (4) h (fol. 49/p. 11) without a break, but some TS pages appear to be missing between the close and the beginning of (4) j.

NLI 8777(4) j, fol. 52 Single TS page (black ribbon) on the same paper, type G, as (4) g above, numbered 16, corrected in WBY's hand in pencil, blue-black and blue ink, 4.0 cm margin; punched hole at top LH corner. Note that this portion of TS was originally continued in NLI 8777(7) e, folios 16–18/pages 17–19.

NLI 8777(4) k, 53–61 Nine TS pages (black ribbon) on the same paper, type G, as (4) g above, numbered 18–26, corrected in WBY's hand in pencil and blue ink only. The margin measures 3.7 cm (perhaps typed later?); split-pin holes in top LH corner. The text ends two-thirds down the page. The TS shares characteristics with NLI 8777(7) c, folios 5–11/pages 7–13.

NLI 8777(4) l, fol. 62 Single TS page (black ribbon) on the same paper, type G, as (4) g above, numbered 20, corrected in WBY's hand in pencil, blue-black and blue ink, 4.0 cm margin; punched hole in top LH corner. This page represents an earlier version of folio 55ʳ—also numbered page 20—and this in turn is the basis for supposing that pages with a 4.0 cm margin were typed at a separate, earlier session than pages with a 3.7 cm margin. Note that this page follows directly on NLI 8777(7) e, folios 16–18/pages 17–19.

NLI 8777(5) Holograph draft of Act III in WBY's hand in an exercise book labelled on the light blue cover, "THE MUSEUM NOTE BOOK. / [rule] / [sketch of British Museum] / THE BRITISH MUSEUM. / [rule and space] / CLARKE & DAVIES, / Fancy & Commercial Stationers, Photographic Publishers / 38, MUSEUM STREET, W.C." Twenty-four leaves (twelve bifolia), sewn, each of the twenty-four leaves/pages measuring 20.4 by 16.4 cm; ruled, twenty lines per page. WBY filled the rectos of each unnumbered leaf, writing continuously until partway down folio 20ʳ, where his text ends; folios 21ʳ–24ᵛ contain two revised passages keyed to the earlier TS of Act III (Berg(13), Berg(08), etc.), written in the same blue-black ink; no leaves appear to have been removed.

The ink is the same lighter shade that appears in the later revisions and the page-by-page cancellations in NLI 8777(10) and Berg(13), (14), (08).

NLI 8777(6) Twelve-page TS (black ribbon) of Act II, with MS corrections by WBY. Paper type G. Continuously numbered pages with punched holes at top LH corner. Annotated by WBY in blue ink on page 1 "mostly rejected"—his corrections being in blue-black ink and in pencil. Different shades of the blue-black ink indicate two rounds of correction, the second being much more extensive than the first.

See the continuation of the same miscellaneous collection in NLI 8777(7) b, folio 3ʳ/page 13 below, and also the complicated relation of the series to portions of NLI 8777(4) above.

NLI 8777(7) Miscellaneous TS pages of Act II, mostly rejected. The six separate groups of pages are designated "a" through "f" below, in the order in which they are contained in the folder. They represent at least two series of revised TSS, each containing substitutions, elsewhere represented by NLI 8777(4) g–l.

NLI 8777(7) a, fols. 1–2 Two TS (black ribbon) pages numbered 11 and 11a. Paper type H. Text margin set at 4.0 cm from LH of part ascriptions. Punched holes at top LH corner that are not quite congruent with punched holes in other pages in same folder. The pages appear to have been drafted to substitute for a passage beginning on 8777(6), folio 11ʳ/page 11.

NLI 8777(7) b, fols. 3–4 Two TS (black ribbon) pages numbered 13 and 14, corrected by WBY in pencil, blue-black and blue ink. Paper type G. Text margin set at 4.0 cm. Punched holes at top LH corner. These two pages originally followed on NLI 8777(6), folio 12ʳ/page 12.

NLI 8777(7) c, fols. 5–11 Seven pages of TS (black ribbon) numbered 7–13, pages 7–12 canceled, page 13 corrected by WBY, all in blue ink. Paper type G. Text margin set at 3.7 cm. Punched holes at top LH corner. These pages originally followed NLI 8777(4) g, folio 45ʳ/page 6. The TS also shares physical characteristics with NLI 8777(4) k, folios 53–61/pages 18–26.

NLI 8777(7) d, fols. 12–15 Four pages of TS (black ribbon) numbered 12–15, corrected by WBY in pencil and blue-black ink but mainly blue ink. Pages 12, 13, and 15 are paper type G. Text margin set at 4.0 cm on all pages. Split-pin holes at top LH corner. The text on page 14 begins lower down the page and the hole is not congruent with those in the pages before and after, confirming that it was inserted into the sequence later. Note that this portion of TS originally followed NLI 8777(4) h, folio 49ʳ/page 11.

NLI 8777(7) e, fols. 16–18 Three TS (black ribbon) pages numbered 17–19, lightly corrected by WBY in pencil and blue-black ink. Paper type G. Text margin set at 4.0 cm. Punched holes at top LH corner. Note that this portion of text originally followed NLI 8777(4) j, folio 52ʳ/page 16, and was in turn continued by 8777(4) l, folio 62ʳ/page 20.

NLI 8777(7) f, fols. 19–32 Fourteen pages of TS (black ribbon) numbered 28–41, with one emendation by GM in blue-black ink and several light corrections by WBY in blue-black and blue ink and pencil. Paper type G. Text margin set at 4.0 cm. Punched holes at top LH corner, all congruent. The set of pages could originally have completed the pages of the version of Act II that are now divided between NLI 8777(6) and those portions of 8777(4) and (7) that share the same paper and format.

NLI 8777(8) Materials for all three acts contributed by both GM and WBY. The five separate groups of pages are designated "a" through "e" below, in the order in which they are contained in the folder.

NLI 8777(8) a, fols. 1–2 Two-page holograph synopsis of Act II in GM's hand. Two conjoint leaves of Tillyra Castle notepaper, each page measuring 17.7 by 11.1 cm; WM [eagle-design within shield] / IMPERIAL SUPERFINE; chain lines 2.7 cm. The bifolium was used upside down, from back to front.

NLI 8777(8) b, fols. 3–11 Nine-page holograph draft of portion of Act II in GM's hand. Paper type A. Separated pages numbered 1–9; versos blank except for page 1.

NLI 8777(8) c, fol. 12 Single-page holograph draft of portion of Act II in GM's hand, numbered 13; on same paper as b above. Page half-filled.

NLI 8777(8) d, fols. 13–22 Ten-page holograph draft of portion of Act I in GM's hand, numbered 1–10; on versos of Shelbourne Hotel Dublin crested notepaper (no WM or chain lines). Final page (10/fol. 22) has an architectural doodle (of a theater auditorium?) on recto.

NLI 8777(8) e, fols. 23–24 Two-page corrected TS (ribbon, blue tinge) headed "Act 111." and endorsed on page 2 "When you send me ~~the~~ your final / 'Grania' send me this back. / WBY". Typing paper measuring 26.2 by 21.3 cm; WM Old / Royal Manufactory / [rule] / VIDALON; chain lines 2.6 cm. Versos blank. The typing is of amateur quality; some minor corrections may be by GM. Both pages were at some time folded over three times.

NLI 8777(9) TS (black ribbon) of Act II complete, with extensive MS corrections by WBY, all in pencil. Twenty-five numbered pages measuring 26.9 by 20.4 cm; WM "INVINCIBLE" / ALL LINEN; no chain lines. Bound in pale blue covers, WM "INVINCIBLE", the whole fastened at top LH corner with a brass split pin. Page 6 is a paste-up; text and corrections on rectos only. Compare NLI 30,437.

NLI 8777(10) TS (black ribbon) of parts of Acts I and III, all on paper type G; all fastened together at top LH corner with a split pin. The separate groups of pages are designated here as "a" and "b."

NLI 8777(10) a, fols. 1–17 Seventeen pages of Act III material, numbered 5–21, with extensive MS corrections by WBY on rectos and also verso of folio 2, mostly in pencil but also ink; most pages canceled with a single vertical ink line. Different shades of ink corrections suggest they were made on two separate occasions.

NLI 8777(10) b, fol. 18 Single TS page containing two substitutions, separately keyed to pages 10 and 12 of Act I; penciled headnote by WBY (possibly with GM). The substitutions connect with Berg(02).

NLI 8777(11) Sixteen-page TS (ribbon and carbon, mixed colors) of Act I, with some corrections in pencil by WBY, numbered in ink by hand. The typewriter appears to be the Remington AG kept at Coole Park, and the typing (layout) and minor ink corrections also appear to be hers. Paper type I, although it should be noted that three pages (6bis, 10, 11/fols. 7, 11, 12), have WM BRITANNIA / [Britannia-head device] / PURE LINEN; chain lines 2.9 cm; other pages lack WMs and chain lines. Versos blank. Split-pin holes at top LH corner.

The compilation is of mixed sources. Pages 1–6, 6bis, 9–15 are blue ribbon; pages 7, 5 [deleted], and 9 are black carbon. Page 6 has been trimmed away at the bottom; page 7 is a palimpsest formed by three overlapped portions; page 5 [deleted] has an extra portion glued onto the foot of the page, which has been folded over and has degraded; the typing on page 9 ends two-thirds down the page. In summary, pages 1–6bis form a connected series, as do pages 10–15, although the different kinds of paper employed (pp. 6bis, 10, 11) may signify revision; and pages 7–5[deleted]–9 represent the same or a further stage of revision. The detailed nature of MS correction is the more interesting in light of the TS itself. The carbon was rolled in upside down with pages 9 and 12 (fols. 10 and 13), leaving a black impression of the same text on the versos and proving that the carbon and ribbon copies were typed on the same occasion. The pattern of emendation suggests that the TS was first corrected by AG and then by WBY, and that AG then confirmed and added to WBY's corrections.

NLI 8777(12) Seventeen-page TS (black ribbon) of part of Act II, with MS corrections by GM (pencil) and WBY (dark blue ink). Paper type C. The cover page is blank, the following are numbered 1–17; insertions by GM on folios 4^v and 8^v; all pages have a split-pin hole in the top LH corner. Pages (18)–(30) of the same corrected TS comprise Berg(12).

NLI 8777(13) Four-page TS (black ribbon) of part of Act II, with extensive MS corrections by GM and WBY, both in different shades of blue-black ink. Paper type D. Unnumbered pages, but folio 1^r is headed (center) "Page 25." and (RH) "Act 2nd." The typing contains many small errors. A margin measuring 2.6/4.0 cm has been ruled in red ink on the LH side of each recto, and part ascriptions underlined/double-underlined in red ink—similar to Berg(01); split-pin holes at top LH corner.

The paper, layout, and appearance resemble Berg(01) and the machine appears in both cases to have been the same Imperial, which is unusual among the TSS. But the NLI typist was less practiced (frequent errors in horizontal and vertical alignment) and less careful (part ascriptions not in caps, single spaced, multiple spelling errors and typos).

NLI 8777(14) Eighteen-page TS (black ribbon) of part of Act II, numbered 8–25; single holograph intervention (blue-black ink) linking pages 14 and 15. Paper type J. Pages 14 and 25 end halfway down each page; and the sequence of pages continues the text of NLI 8777(15)—see further below. Split-pin holes in top LH corner.

NLI 8777(15) Seven-page TS (black ribbon) of part of Act II, numbered 1–7. Paper type J. Split-pin holes in top LH corner.

The verso of page 7 is clean, compared to both the recto of page 1 and the verso of NLI 8777(14) page 25, which appears to put beyond doubt that (14) and (15) were once fastened as a consecutive unit.

The half-filled pages of NLI 8777(14), combined with the change of name from Foster-Mother to Laban which takes place between pages 14 and 15 (though uncertainty remains on p. 17), suggests the two folders together contain two installments of Act II, which was being typed up in three parts. The continuous text was made by a professional typist, who was unfamiliar with WBY's handwriting, copying from his revision of "Moore's new version" (NLI 8777[4] g–l) and incorporating further improvements.

However, there are suggestions of complexity in the preparation of the continuous TS that are difficult to square with the features already noted. The bulk of the TS was typed with a new ribbon, but pages 15, 17–18, 20 were typed with a worn ribbon of the same blue-black color, suggesting they were typed later. At the same time, the margins of the text are set at three different measures: pages 1–8 at 3.8 cm, pages 9–15, 17–18, 20 at 2.8 cm; and pages 16, 19, 21–25 at 2.5 cm. Finally, while the typist was evidently following (or failing to follow) WBY's holograph, the source of the further typed revisions is unknown.

NLI 8777(16) Twenty TS pages (black ribbon) of beginning of Act II, unnumbered, with extensive MS corrections in blue-black ink by GM and WBY. Headed by GM "From George Moore / 4 Upper Ely Place / Dublin". Foolscap typing paper measuring 32.9 by 20.4 cm; WM EXCELSIOR / SUPERFINE; chain lines 2.5 cm. Folio 16^{v} contains an insertion by WBY; split-pin holes in all top LH corners. The typist's style—for example, the habitual omission of periods at the close of speeches—is unique among the MSS.

NLI 30,437 TS (black ribbon) of Act II complete, with light MS revisions by WBY (pencil, mainly cancellations) and one revision by GM (ink). Twenty-four numbered pages, thin paper measuring 26.5 by 20.0 cm; WM INDIAN / & / COLONIAL; no chain lines. Text and corrections on rectos only. Bound in pale blue covers, WM "INVINCIBLE"; no chain lines. Split-pin holes through covers and pages at top LH corner, but no pin present (disbound).

The presentation closely resembles NLI 8777(9) but the text is entirely different. The fact that it does not appear on the Cornell and Harvard microfilms of MS materials, made when the originals were still in GY's hands, might suggest, taken with the separated NLI index number, that this TS was not on hand when the larger part of the MS materials were sorted and arranged. The text lies to one side of the development of Act II, as far as this can be determined. Note that the paper type is unique, unusual among extant versions.

SUNY at Stony Brook Box 8, subseries B. Plays (unpublished) (I.1.B), together with box 9 contain microfilm and xerox copies of all the *Diarmuid and Grania* materials now held by the NLI. In the W. B. Yeats Collection, University Library, State University at Stony Brook.

Washington A 106-page TS (carbon?) of the complete text, with minor pencil corrections and queries in an unknown hand on pages 12, 17, 19, 23, 81, 101/folios 14^{r}, 19^{r}, 21^{r}, 25^{r}, 83^{r}, 103^{r}. Pages numbered continuously, with pages 74a, 81a, 92a additional to the numerical sequence, of two types. Pages 1–48 comprise typing paper measuring 27.0 by 21.0 cm.; WM JOHN M^{C}DONNEL & C^{O} L^{TD} / SWIFT BROOK; no chain lines. The title page, list of characters, and pages following page 48/folio 50 are on typing paper measuring 28.0 by 21.0 cm, with no WM or chain lines and displaying a high level of acidity. The text on pages 105, 106/folios 107^r, 108^r has been obscured in part by damage, from dampness, on the top RH side.

The Washington TS is a tidied version of the corrected HRC palimpsest. The expanded opening of the play is seamlessly incorporated, in contrast to the complicated substitutions and renumbering of Berg(99), as are both authors' several holograph improvements. The three pages additional to the numerical sequence appear to be the result of simple wrong numbering—they are not inserts containing revised material—and the change of paper also appears not to possess textual significance. The TS closely resembles HRC in format and typing style, and the relation between the two versions, and incidentally of both to Berg(99), is clarified in the notes to the full text in HRC. References are foliated 1–108, to include the unnumbered title page and page of dramatis personae. Variations of spelling and patent typos are not recorded, nor is the widespread improvement of punctuation and formatting. Differences in wording from either or both related TSS are recorded when they could relate to significant corrections, although they sometimes represent the typist's wrong guess (cf. HRC p. 90/fol. 93^r, line 16 note, and p. 103/fol. 106^r, line 13 note). Special Collections, Washington University Libraries, St. Louis.

Introduction

The introduction is in five parts. Part i describes how Yeats's collaboration with Moore evolved within a scenario of Moore's contrivance. The collaboration was generated by Moore's work on a novel, *Evelyn Innes*, in which a character based on Yeats comes to be writing an opera based on the legend of Diarmuid and Grania. At the same time, Moore's ambitions for a national theater inspired by Wagnerian ideals prompted his return to Ireland so as to realize his fictional ideal.

The writing of the play extended from November 1899 to the eve of performance in October 1901. Part ii describes the several phases of composition: nine months of discussion and dispersed effort; a period of concentrated writing and revision during September–December 1900, sometimes at cross-purposes and interrupted by two quarrels, one irritable, the other acrimonious; extended negotiations with actors and management during the earlier half of 1901, and a further period of adjustment and improvement—including the addition of Edward Elgar's music—when the play went into production. Moore simultaneously worked through to the end of the fictional project he had begun in *Evelyn Innes*.

Part iii describes the staging of the play in a double bill alongside Douglas Hyde's *Casadh an tSugáin, The Twisting of the Rope*. *Diarmuid* was recognized as the most ambitious play to have been performed by the Irish Literary Theatre;[1] *Sugáin* was welcomed as the first play the Theatre had done in Irish. But a conjunction that worked in favor of Moore and Yeats at the beginning turned against them within a very short time. *Diarmuid* fell afoul of a campaign on behalf of Irish actors for Irish theater and simultaneously of charges of historical inaccuracy and moral indecency. "People said, and not without reason, that Mr. Moore and Mr. Yeats had gone to Irish legend to find in epic tradition the plot of an average French novel."[2] Yeats stood by Moore, whom everyone held responsible for what they did not like, while Moore made provocative statements on behalf of Catholic-Irish Ireland to launch counteroffensives on different fronts. Both were meanwhile engaged with other matters—Yeats with the composition of a substitute second act, Moore with attempting to persuade Elgar to write a full-scale opera on the same theme. Within a few months, they discovered that the moderate success of their play had been written into history as a failure.

The collaboration came to an effective end in July 1902, when Yeats and Moore quarreled over a second joint venture, *Where There Is Nothing*. Thereafter, Yeats fitfully continued to entertain plans for rewriting *Diarmuid*, perhaps as a verse play, but they were finally over-

---

[1]"The Irish Literary Theatre," an unsigned review in *The Freeman's Journal*, October 22, 1901, 4; in Hogan 102–104 at 103.

[2]Stephen Gwynn, "The Irish Literary Theatre and its Affinities," *The Fortnightly Review* 76 (1901): 1050–1062 at 1055; quoted by Hogan 113.

taken with the publication of Moore's crushing account of the Irish Literary Revival in the first installment of *Hail and Farewell* (*Ave*, 1911). Moore continued to write to Elgar for some years longer, hoping to interest him in a Wagnerian opera, but could not prevail. Part iv describes how the period of collaboration engaged each writer in different ways and how the play embodies different perspectives on their shared investment. Each was helped forward in his career by the collaboration, pretty much as each hoped to be, even though their contributions did not totally merge.

Part v discusses editorial matters arising from these conditions. Authorship of the play is often unclear because so many versions of the text are typescripts, not holograph manuscripts. Their relationship and chronology are frequently difficult to establish because the two authors worked independently or at cross-purposes for much of the time. Such circumstances require that a reader take the materiality of each typescript as seriously as any other kind of document. Close attention must be paid to such features as the type of paper, the quality of typewriter ribbons, different manufacturers' typefaces and their condition (the alignment, degradation, and spacing of characters), page layout and typing styles (margins, page numbering, and part ascriptions), characteristic spellings and mistakes, even different styles of cancellation. Taken together, they help attach typescripts to different authors on different occasions and suggest different levels of authority.

Successive versions of the text never eventually came together. A chronology of manuscripts is appended to the introduction, followed by a note on this complex situation and the problems it poses for the construction of a reading text. It comments on characteristics of the available published versions and on misreadings that have entered the sequence of versions and have been perpetuated.

(i)

The seeds of George Moore's interest in the legend of Diarmuid and Grania were sown in a conversation with his cousin, Edward Martyn, in London during 1894, when Moore was engaged in finishing his novel *Esther Waters*: "I had heard of Grania for the first time that night" (*H&F* 57). The seeds germinated in a typically complicated way in the course of Moore's next novel, *Evelyn Innes*, which contains a character, Ulick Dean, who embodies themes he had begun to explore in the character of Montgomery in *A Mummer's Wife* (1885 [for 1884]) and that he now developed with reference to W. B. Yeats. Yeats served as a model of the artist as a young man because he was the emergent lyric genius of his generation and because his dramatic, occult, and nationalistic interests assimilated him, in Moore's mind, to literary Wagnerianism.[3]

Meanwhile, during the time the narrative of *Evelyn Innes* was in the process of construction, Vincent D'Indy's opera based on the last Celtic hero, *Fervaal*, premiered in Brussels on March 12, 1897, and inspired Moore with the ambition to imitate it in collaboration with Édouard Dujardin.[4] Then, Hamish MacCunn's opera *Diarmid* premiered at Covent Garden on October 23, 1897, and, reckoning he had found another Dujardin in Yeats, Moore was led to make Ulick

[3]Succinctly surveyed by William F. Blissett, "George Moore and Literary Wagnerism," *Comparative Literature* 13 (1961): 52–71; reprinted in *George Moore's Mind and Art*, ed. Graham Owens (Edinburgh: Oliver and Boyd, 1968), pp. 53–76.

[4]*Letters from George Moore to Ed. Dujardin, 1886–1922,* ed. and trans. John Eglinton (New York: Crosby Gaige,

Dean author of a scenario based on the Grania story. Yeats's evident reserve in sexual matters reinforced the Diarmuid association in Moore's mind and intrigued him equally. Moore habitually referred to the play by Grania's name alone, insisting that her character was his and that Yeats must not alter her dialogue: "You have said over and over again that you could do nothing with her. . . . Supposing I were to write psychological passages into the Countess Cathleen." This is the third factor in the equation, alongside the connection between the fictional Ulick, the real Yeats, and the legendary Diarmuid. Grania was based on Moore's mistress, Maud Cunard, as he openly confessed to her.[5] The affair went into suspension at about the time he began *Evelyn Innes*, and the elaboration of a parallel plot in which infatuation is simultaneously admitted and distanced held a particular interest for him.

The writing of the novel proved increasingly difficult for Moore because its scope widened to absorb these interests. Indeed, the incorporation of explicit reference to the Grania material signalled a crisis that forced him to assess the direction of his narrative. "The subject proved too vast to be treated in one book," he decided. "I had to break it off in the middle."[6] So, without ado and without troubling to eliminate traces of its fictional context, he removed the opera scenario and published it separately.[7] Sending the remainder of the novel to his publisher a month later, even while continuing to remove further references to the Diarmuid and Grania legend, he simultaneously embarked on a continuation of the fictional narrative under a separate title, *Sister Teresa*. *Evelyn Innes* was published in June 1898, and the role of Ulick Dean continued to be revised in four further editions. *Sister Teresa* was eventually finished in August 1900—"After *Esther Waters* it is the best thing I have done," Moore said (*GMP* 98), buoyed up by a sense of release and of a turning point in his career—and it was eventually published in July 1901.[8]

It was during the crucial period when the one novel became two that Moore began to involve Yeats personally in the revision—indeed, "entire elimination" (*GMT* 183)—of the character based upon him. Simultaneously, via his cousin, Edward Martyn, he began to insert himself into the affairs of the Irish Literary Theatre, of which his cousin was one of the founders. Moore's first recorded letter to Yeats was written on September 8, 1898 (Als NLI 8777[1]; *GML* #764), and on December 12 he suggested that Yeats should set aside *The Countess Cathleen*, which was proving difficult to write, and "start a new play Grania for example. Shall I send you my

---

1929), p. 38. While, in his April letter to Dujardin, GM cites the first part of D'Indy's *Wallenstein* trilogy, this had premiered as long before as April 1880, and his interest must have been triggered by the recent *Fervaal*, which he mentions alongside MacCunn's *Diarmid* in his November contribution to the *Musician* (Appendix III below, p. 1056). On WBY as another Dujardin for GM, see Hone 238; and further on Dujardin, GM's friend of forty years and cofounder of the *Revue Wagnérienne*, see Frazier's index under "Dujardin."

[5]For the Yeats-Moore exchange, see Als [November 16, 1900], Berg; *LWBY* I 74–75 at 75; *CL* II 589n supplies correct date). Berg also supplies GM's previous Als, written probably November 15, to which the present one is a postscript (*LWBY* I 73–74; *CL* II 589–590). *Letters to Lady Cunard, 1895–1933,* ed. Rupert Hart-Davis (London: Rupert Hart-Davis, 1957), p. 31 [*LWBY* dates GM's letter autumn 1900].

[6]GM to Maud Cunard, February 10, 1898: *Letters to Lady Cunard*, p. 26.

[7]Letter to the editor, "A Scenario for an Opera," *Musician* (London), November 17, 1897, 24—given in Appendix III below. The covering letter mentions both D'Indy and MacCunn, and the extract does not disguise the relation to *Evelyn Innes*.

[8]The complicated story of the evolution and parallel revision of the two novels is analyzed in a Ph.D. dissertation by John Denny Fischer, *"Evelyn Innes" and "Sister Teresa" by George Moore: A Variorum Edition* (University of Illinois, 1958). Frazier 416 notes GM's opinion, when he reviewed his work for the collected Liveright edition in 1921, that the two books stood outside his development—were dead ends. At the same time, GM's commentators agree, they form the pivot on which the development rests.

scenario it may break the ice of a new subject for you" (Als NLI 8777[1]; *GML* #778). In this way he began to insinuate the idea of collaboration during the period when *Evelyn Innes* was mutating into its achieved form, an idea that was finally realized at exactly the time the companion novel *Sister Teresa* was eventually published.

The collaboration on the play originated in a fiction in which Moore's version of Yeats played a formative role. Moore's restructuring of a major fictional project generated a dramatic composition, a method of proceeding characteristic of the way he worked. Like James Joyce, he went out of his way to contrive situations in life that he used as an artist. The method is selfless and shameless, and in Moore's case it was more situational: it typically involved a number of people interacting—not solitary individuals like Oliver Gogarty or Marthe Fleischmann. He left those groups he befriended in the cause of art with a sense that they had been used or mistreated or betrayed, though he treated them no less honestly than himself. "Yeats," Moore told him after their final quarrel, "a man can only have one conscience, mine is artistic" (*Aut* 334).

Not that Yeats was from the beginning uninterested in Diarmuid and Grania, or ignorant of his collaborator's proclivities before he became absorbed into Moore's scheme. The legend was part of local Sligo lore, and Katharine Tynan had introduced him to its literary dimension—it was the subject of the chief poem in her collection *Shamrocks* (1887), which he read in page proof and subsequently reviewed[9]—and it was natural that traces found their way into early texts like *John Sherman*, *Dhoya*, and *The Speckled Bird*. From the first, his colleague and sometime patron Lady Gregory made evident that she was strongly opposed to a partnership with Moore because it would impinge on Yeats's other work and complicate his contribution to the cultural revival (*H&F* 204–205; *Aut* 321). But the fact that Yeats persisted in face of good advice and, one would think, common sense suggests that he felt the collaboration could serve a purpose. He received incisive criticism of the structure of *The Countess Cathleen* from Moore during September–December 1898, and watched him and assisted him in rewriting Martyn's *The Tale of a Town* as *The Bending of the Bough* during the summer months of 1899. Is it an accident that Moore set Yeats to rewrite and enlarge the character of Jasper Dean in Martyn's play? Although Jasper is founded on a number of real-life sources, the surname is shared with the Yeats character in *Evelyn Innes*.[10] Yeats admired Moore's sense of dramatic structure, and also his practical forethought; for example, Moore had begun his pursuit of Mrs. Patrick Campbell, whom he had in mind for the part of Grania, as early as September 1897 (Als Folger; *GML* #653). Yeats did not share his father's view of Ulick Dean as a "complicated insult,"[11] and the correspondence shows that he willingly assisted in the revision of Moore's fictional construction.

This was not the seduction of innocent genius by a mischievous troublemaker, therefore. When Moore eventually proposed a formal collaboration, the move was blessed by what Yeats understood as supernatural intimation (*CL* II 461n4, citing "Visions Notebook," October 26, 1899), and he fell in with Moore's scheme of working with high hopes, excitedly, even if with circumspection (*CL* II 460–462). He felt he could learn from Moore's handling of structural problems and confidence in the face of practical issues. "I am afraid he is quite untrustworthy," he acknowledged soon afterward: "one must look upon him after all as only a mind that can be of service to ones cause" (*CL* II 537). Yeats began with reservations and advanced warily; the

[9]See also the contemporaneous letter, in which he reports going up Ben Bulben to locate the place where Diarmuid died and reveals his knowledge of local versions of the story: *CL* I 37.

[10]See WBY's comment on rewriting Dean's part in *Dramatis Personae* (*Aut* 316).

[11]*Letters from Bedford Park: A Selection from the Correspondence (1890–1901) of John Butler Yeats*, ed. William M. Murphy (Dublin: Cuala Press, 1972), p. 42 (to AG, July 29, 1898).

series of increasingly bitter disagreements that followed was entirely predictable. The collaborators failed to join at the center of the work, but, in other important respects, the play delivered what each hoped to gain.

(ii)

The plan was for Moore to settle the construction and provide a rough draft of the dialogue, and for Yeats to rewrite the dialogue in a more polished style. It was a division of labor that each agreed was suited to his own abilities, and, though Gregory always believed that one or the other should be assigned overall responsibility, there appeared to be no need. The preliminary stage of the working out of the plan is obscure, possibly because many of the earlier records are missing, and more likely because, during the first six or nine months, progress was unsystematic. Thus, Yeats refers to their completion of a first draft on November 1, 1899 (*CL* II 460–461), and Moore to having carried the play a step farther on November 6 (Als Berg; *GML* #815). Moore's rough outline of the first part of Act II is extant on writing paper from Tillyra (Martyn's home in County Galway) (NLI 8777[8] a), together with his dialogue for the middle part of Act II (NLI 8777[8] b, Berg[9], NLI 8777[8] c), but the textual evidence suggests that the draft dialogue could date from the following summer, when a version of the play by Yeats (NLI 8777[4] a+b+c) patently builds on it.

Other references during the winter and early summer of 1899–1900 are scant and phrased in general terms. The authors agreed on basic principles; for example, that the first act must be horizontal, the second perpendicular, and the third circular (*H&F* 247). In his *Beltaine* progress report, Yeats claimed the play was halfway complete; in a speech given at the Gresham Hotel during the same month, Moore referred to the joint enterprise in resounding but equally vague terms.[12] The play was frequently referred to by Moore in his dealings with his publisher, Fisher Unwin, but patently as a bargaining tool to exert pressure on arrangements for *Evelyn Innes* and *Sister Teresa* (e.g., *GMT* 194–195). Indeed, during this initial period, Moore was preoccupied with advancing and adjusting the relationship between his two novels, while Yeats was wrestling with the construction of *The Shadowy Waters*.[13] There was undoubtedly talk, and decisions must have been arrived at to compose the scenes that make up the acts; perhaps some outlines and drafts were exchanged, but such work must have been too interrupted to accumulate satisfactorily. Moore let slip to Douglas Hyde in June 1900 that he needed "to go into the country for a month to write the play" (Als NLI 8777[1]; *GML* #854) and, significantly, none of the extended manuscript records can be conclusively dated before the following month.

Moore sent a freshly typed version of *Diarmuid*, Act II, that brought together the "various M.S.S." to Yeats on July 30, 1900 (Tls, Berg; *LWBY* I 69–70), that is, before he completed *Sister Teresa* on August 16. Anticipating that he would soon have time on his hands, he characteristically began to push at what appears to have emerged, early on, as the act that would cause the most difficulty. But *The Shadowy Waters* continued to take all Yeats's time for several more

[12]For WBY, see his "Plans and Methods" in *Beltaine,* no. 2 (February 1900): 3–6 at 5. GM's speech was published in *Freeman's Journal*, February 23, 1900, 6; reprinted as "The Irish Literary Renaissance and the Irish Language" in *New Ireland Review*, April 1900, 65–72 at 65–66; and collected in *Ideals in Ireland,* ed. Lady Gregory (London: At the Unicorn, 1901), pp. 45–51 at 45. GM's phrasing becomes more specific in successive formulations.

[13]Significantly for the present story, *The Countess Cathleen*, the other play with which WBY was involved as he revised *The Shadowy Waters*, was described by Dublin critics as so Wagnerian as to be un-Irish, and Yeats subsequently planned an operatic version: Foster I 212 and also 210, 440, 574n1.

months (the play was eventually published in December). Then Hyde joined him at Gregory's home in Coole Park to be nursed through the writing of *Casadh an tSugáin* with bottles of champagne; Yeats's own lyric poems pushed to be written; and George Russell joined forces with Gregory to fend off Moore's approaches. Moore eventually took matters into his own hands and arrived at Coole in mid-September, an almost self-invited and certainly intrusive guest. There was unpleasantness, and Moore withdrew after two nights (September 15–16) to the Shelbourne Hotel in Dublin, from whence he continued to bombard Yeats with criticisms and suggestions. Moore then returned to Coole for a more productive stay that eventually stretched to six nights (September 29–October 5), during which time, though differences over an appropriate language and ultimate authority were not settled, there was an uneasy truce. Moore was teased, even got angry, but Gregory's typewriter was at the service of the enterprise for several days before and after his departure. The first stage of composition proper was brought near to completion.

The argument at Coole was about style. The high feeling at the time Moore withdrew is evidenced by the tone of heckling remonstration in a telegram sent from Merrion Row on September 21 and received at Gort Post Office the following day: "Picturesque description of the times turbulent fianni [i.e., warriors] | Moore" (Berg; *GML* #878). The terms are carefully chosen, since Yeats specifically disavowed a turbulent style and generally disliked the picturesque.[14] Moore repeated the complaint in a letter written on September 26 (Als to AG, Berg; *GML* #879), in terms that connect it unambiguously to Act I, and Russell wrote to Gregory on the same day, repeating the charge: "Dairmuid [*sic*] was supposed to be a man" (Als postmarked September 26, 1900, Berg). Russell's intervention marked the turning point, and a conciliatory—even contradictory—letter from Moore the next day (September 27, reported in *LGD* 280) prompted Gregory to invite him to return. Yeats had complained that Moore used "soldiers" for "fianna" or "fighting men," and the like, without regard for historical associations (*Aut* 322; cf. *LGD* 281). Moore had insisted that primitive man thought much as modern man does and that Galway dialect words, in particular, should be excluded (*H&F* 245–246; *Aut* 325). But the focus on words, considered historically and culturally, limited the area of disagreement, and other differences were settled with relative ease. The situation reinforces the supposition that this was Yeats's first systematic attempt to heighten the style of the material Moore had provided.

Collaboration resumed when Yeats caught up with Moore in Dublin on October 9–10, bringing progress up to the middle of Act III, and it continued on all fronts when Moore moved back to London. The play had evidently advanced to the close of Act III by October 25, when Yeats read it to Gregory,[15] and the next day Moore and Yeats visited Mrs. Patrick Campbell in her dressing room at the close of a performance of Frank Harris's *Mr and Mrs Daventry* to interest her in their play. She "begged" them to send it to her, "returning to the subject again & again. She wanted it at once, 'tomorrow' 'Monday'" (*CL* II 581). Adjustments to the plotting continued (see, e.g., *LWBY* I 71–72), while Moore also accompanied Gregory to see Mrs. Campbell as Mrs. Daventry—though he failed to persuade Gregory that *Diarmuid* should be performed in London before Dublin.[16]

---

[14]As *CL* II 570n1 remarks, supplying references to WBY's attitudes.

[15]*LGD* 283; note that the diary entry is retrospective, written on Sunday to describe an event that took place on the previous Thusday.

[16]*LGD* 285n and *CL* II 581n give different dates for GM's and AG's joint visit to the theater. GM appears to have gone to see Mrs. Campbell as Mrs. Daventry on three occasions, the second being between the visits on which he was

An enormous amount of work appears to have been done during October–November 1900. The many extant versions can be arranged in a probable sequence, but it is difficult to assign specific dates and to synchronize exactly the stage of revision of one act with the revision of another. A version of Acts I and II in what came to be called the "old version" was arrived at before October 10 (Berg[1] and [6]), and a "new version" of the same acts was therefore begun after that date (Berg[2] and [7]); but Act III appears to have developed across the same period in a continuous fashion, without a sense of stages being reached; see the composite Berg(13), NLI 8777(10) a, Berg(14), Berg(08), NLI 8777(4) e. However, even as the play appeared to be moving toward a finished state on multiple tracks, the disagreement over style flared up again.

The causes of disagreement were the same as at Coole but they now advanced beyond a level of general debate and suppressed sniggers. They concentrated on Act II, where Moore's feelings for Cunard were most involved. Moore and Yeats spelled out their differences in writing, and Gregory, who had long worked to fan the flames of an open quarrel, was more explicit in her diary entries. The "original compact" had been based on Yeats's acknowledgement of Moore's knowledge of the stage and powers of construction—"a power of inventing a dramatic crisis far beyond me"—but on the question of style Moore should give way to Yeats (WBY to GM, unsigned draft [November 15, 1900], NLI 8777[1]; *CL* II 585–586). The problem was that Yeats's rewriting changed the meaning of incident and interpretation of character that Moore intended. Moore's argument now became that revision of the style should not be in Yeats's hands entirely, but could only be managed "by mutual concession" (Als, GM to WBY [November 16, 1900], Berg; *LWBY* I 78–79, but see *CL* II 589n5, for date). But by then, Yeats had already written, "On the question of style however I <will> can make no concession. Here in your turn you must give way to me" (*CL* II 584).

The disagreement in London was serious and it brought the point at issue into the open. However, it came to be resolved—or not resolved—in a way very similar to before. Yeats's old friend the critic Arthur Symons was invited to arbitrate, but then, at that same juncture, the gesture of displacement provided the solution. The knot immediately unravelled, both sides became conciliatory, unworkable proposals—such as that Yeats should write all Diarmuid's part and Moore all Grania's—were set aside (*LGD* 289). Neither collaborator was forced to concede, since both gave up their claim to be "Master" (GM's term, according to AG: *LGD* 289). Perhaps that is the clue: the literary principle was clouded by issues of personal self-esteem that could be gratified by short-term concessions, thereby creating an illusion that the issue had been resolved. Some emendations were retained, other differences fudged. The word that caused particular trouble—the "singing" that entered Grania's breasts—was replaced by "laughter" (*LGD* 290–291)[17] but it crept back into the text very soon afterward. Events following the production reveal the fault lines that were buried over—Yeats was to restructure Grania's behavior in a completely rewritten Act II, Moore was to construct a fictional mockery of Gregory's interference—but the changed amicable mood was sufficient to allow the writing to move toward completion.

Yeats reported that Act I had been passed on November 25, 1900; Act II on December 2 or

---

accompanied by WBY and AG: see Stanley Weintraub, ed., *The Playwright and the Pirate: Bernard Shaw and Frank Harris; A Correspondence* (Gerrards Cross, UK: Colin Smythe, 1982), pp. 6–7, where Shaw mentions talking to Moore before the curtain went up. Shaw would surely have mentioned WBY or AG if either had been in GM's company.

[17]Further references to "the objectionable passage" are to be found in *LWBY* I 78; *CL* II 587, 589, 592–593; *LGD* 289.

before; Act III, finally, following further changes to the other acts, before December 12 (*CL* II 592, 594, 602). Moore "behaves now like an angel," Yeats told Gregory (*CL* II 597), and the following January Moore sent Symons two Degas lithographs as a wedding present—surely evidence that he was well satisfied (Frazier 542–543n141). Two versions of the authors' revised typescripts, the pages of each act separately numbered, were bound in identical leatherette wrappers at about this time. The slightly earlier one, belonging to Moore, now comprises HRC(1), (2), and (3); the slightly later one, belonging to Yeats, comprises NLI 8777(3) a–c. Moore gave away his copy to Maud Cunard; Yeats's copy is the only version of the complete text he retained.

The play continued to be retouched as it was successively read to people like actor-manager Johnston Forbes-Robertson, Mrs. Campbell, and Edward Martyn, each of whom heard it with different degrees of enthusiasm.[18] Mrs. Campbell's involvement would have assured financial success, and she was initially the most enthusiastic, but it emerged that she was reluctant to come to Dublin, and Lady Gregory continued to insist on the principle of opening Irish Literary Theatre plays in home surroundings. By January 4, 1901, a compromise was reached: the acting team of Mr. and Mrs. Frank Benson would do the play in Dublin and Mrs. Campbell in London, in September, the Bensons having the advantage of being a safe bet with conventional playgoing opinion. By April 3, it had been decided to present *Diarmuid* in a double bill with Hyde's *Casadh an tSugáin*, and, at about the same time, Mrs. Campbell began to think the play did not promise commercial success and began to drop out. Meanwhile, Yeats discussed seat pricing with the Bensons when he was at Stratford in April (*CL* III 63) and fiddled with the text (*CL* III 70), while Moore saw *Sister Teresa* through its proof stage. Two continuously paged versions were prepared from Yeats's copy of the leatherette-bound version, and updated in tandem throughout the period December 1900–August 1901. Moore gave his copy to Maud Cunard and it now comprises HRC; Yeats gave his copy to Gregory following the production of the play and it now comprises Berg(99). What is called here the Washington version is a derivative of the final state of HRC, which provides the basis of all versions of the play that have been published up to the present time.

On July 1, 1901, a day after receiving a copy of *Sister Teresa* from Unwin, Moore reported that *Diarmuid* was finished, "for neither Yeats nor myself can find anything to alter and we are professed re-writers" (*GMP* 98). Before the month was out, Yeats suggested a redistribution of the closing speeches and the tidying up of further details; to which Moore promptly replied with an elaboration of Yeats's suggestion and a plan to ask Augusta Holmes, an Irishwoman and former mistress of Catulle Mendès, to compose music to "exalt the end of the play" (see GM's reply, Tls dated July 27, 1901, Berg; *LWBY* I 85–86).[19] In early August, Moore spent a day with the Bensons at Brighton, on his way to Bayreuth, discussing the play in rehearsal, and acceded to Frank Benson's enthusiasm for introducing a live sheep (it became a goat) at the opening of Act III (GM to WBY, Als dated August 8, 1901, NLI 8777[1]; quoted by William Becker, *DMag* 3–4). On his way back from Bayreuth at the beginning of the next month, Moore discovered that Holmes could not oblige with music and, without delay, he put the proposal to Edward Elgar.

---

[18]Although, according to AG, Forbes-Robertson was cooler in private, Mrs. Campbell resisted committing herself to Dublin and began to raise practical difficulties, and EM changed his mind (*LGD* 294, 296, 297). Mrs. Campbell always responded more warmly to WBY than to GM, especially to WBY in person, which postponed the outcome slightly.

[19]GM's acquaintance with Mendès (1842–1909) went back to the time when Mendès was coeditor of *La République des lettres*; cf. Frazier 45–46, etc.

He hurried on to London to secure Elgar's interest, and the coup was promptly advertised in the Dublin newspapers.[20] Moore threw himself into rehearsals, sensibly insisting that the actors learn their parts during rehearsal at the same time as they got to know their positions and their business, not beforehand separately (*H&F* 315). He busied himself with publicity, he hired local actor William Fay to help rehearse the Irish play, he organized horn players from Liverpool and the loan of a harp. The actress playing Laban, Lucy Franklein, worried Benson, but she had a singing voice of which she was proud,[21] so Yeats wrote additional lyrics for Acts I and II, the first of which Elgar promptly set to music. The play opened at the Gaiety Theatre, Dublin, on October 21, 1901.

(iii)

The first night was a greater success than many anticipated. Queen Victoria's death had caused the theaters to be closed during January and February, so they were still laboring to recover capital. Mrs. Campbell's advance fee, which would have been used to bring glamour to the production with rich costumes and elaborately painted shields (see AG quoted in *CL* II 619n), had been lost. Constance Benson's "lackadaisical manner and eternal attitudinising"[22] were a poor substitute for star quality, Frank Benson's athleticism could not compensate for what was evidently a thin performance, and so on. Alongside these material constraints were other anxieties. Hyde and Gregory had long before worried that Moore's "singing of the breasts & 3 or 4 other 'fleshy' sentences" would cause trouble, and Yeats's horoscope prepared him to expect "another row" (*CL* III 82 and n).

Thus, Jack Yeats's sketches reproduced in Appendix V make evident that the production was done on a shoestring; and it is undeniable that knowing members of the audience enjoyed playing the attribution game: "Ah! that's Willie. . . . [that's] dirty George."[23] But there were no real disasters, and, by happy accident, the generosity of the Irish-language enthusiasts who came to cheer Hyde carried over to the English companion piece (as they saw it). J. M. Synge reported how they sang choruses of Irish melodies during an interval; and, when Yeats and Maud Gonne left the theater, the same crowd from the gallery wanted to pull the cab in which they travelled.[24] Again, the English actors had trouble with the pronunciation of Irish names and were given scant assistance. How were they to say Caoelte? Yeats proposed "Wheelsher"; the actors

---

[20]The exchange in the *Freeman's Journal* on September 13 and 16 anticipated criticism and advertised the coup (see Frazier 303). GM read the play to Henry Wood at Bayreuth, in the hope of interesting him in an opera, and Wood appears to have suggested Elgar—whom, GM afterward suggested, he already had in mind (*H&F* 313). GM wrote to Elgar from Paris on August 22 (Kennedy 170–171). See Appendix IV: Elgar's Musical Accompaniment.

[21]See J. C. Trewin, *Benson and the Bensonians* (London: Barrie and Rockliff, 1960), p. 129. For GM's damning description of Franklein's singing, see his letter to Elgar, October 23, 1901 (Kennedy 178–179).

[22]*Joseph Holloway's Abbey Theatre: A Selection from His Unpublished Journal,* ed. Robert Hogan and Michael J. O'Neill (Carbondale: Southern Illinois University Press, 1967), pp. 13–15 at p. 14 (October 21, 1901).

[23]J. H. and Margaret E. Cousins, *We Two Together* (Madras: Ganesh, [1950]), pp. 62–63 (quoted in Hogan 109). Cf. *The Selected Letters of Somerville and Ross,* ed. Gifford Lewis (London: Faber and Faber, 1989), pp. 253–254; also E. OE. Somerville and Martin Ross, *Wheel-Tracks* (London: Longmans, Green, 1923), pp. 231–233.

[24]For Synge, see his *Collected Works II: Prose,* ed. Alan Price (London: Oxford University Press, 1966), pp. 381–382. For WBY and Gonne, see *Aut* 327. Douglas Hyde also recorded how the good humor of those who came to see his own play extended to the English actors: diary, October 21, 1901, quoted in Dominic Daly, *The Young Douglas Hyde: The Dawn of the Irish Revolution and Renaissance, 1874–1893* (Dublin: Irish University Press, 1974), p. 135.

responded with "Wheelchair," "Coldtea," and "Quilty."[25] Despite their continued awkwardness on opening night, indeed Yeats's uncharitable apology for it at the curtain call,[26] the success of Hyde's *Sugáin* put the audience in a happy mood and all faults were forgiven. Frank Benson looked back on it as a "qualified success": "it certainly aroused a great deal of interest, and gave much pleasure to the performers, and the public who witnessed it."[27]

The unexpectedly good reception continued and led to the Monday-to-Wednesday run being extended. Moore had for some months been aware that Forbes-Robertson would be in Dublin at the same time, playing Shakespeare, which might persuade the Bensons not to compete but to extend the run of the Irish plays (GM to WBY, Als August 8, 1901, NLI 8777[1]). So, besides the additional matinee performance of *Diarmuid and Grania* on Wednesday—a matinee on this day only because the amateur actors of Hyde's play were not able to obtain leave from work on other days—a joint bill of the two plays was substituted for Benson's evening performance of *King Lear* on Friday, October 25. There were thus five performances in all—which was an extension of the run and not a curtailment—and audiences were full.[28] But the reputation of the play altered during the run of performances and even more during the weeks following, as Moore described for his brother, Maurice:

> They first of all enjoyed the play, and having enjoyed it they repented in sackcloth and ashes, and I really believe that the repentance was much greater than their enjoyment of the play. At the end of the week they all discovered that the irrelevancies of the legend (the folklore) which had collected round the essential story had been omitted. They also discovered that Grania was not as perfectly virtuous as an Irishwoman should be. (Hone 239)

This reversal of opinion confirmed the previous fears of those who steered the fortunes of the Irish Literary Theatre. And whereas *Diarmuid* was on the night, in Gregory's words, "a success, quite respectable—even Times & Irish Times blessed us—And Hyde's 'Sugan' . . . was a real & immense success" (*LGD* 308; note, another retrospective entry), the good fortune came unstuck. The negative dimension of Violet Martin's response ("Grania . . . was excessively French in her loves") had been partly muted by the Bensons' reputation for respectability,[29] but it became mixed up with even deeper prejudices. The play was criticized for historical inaccuracy and for involving English actors in quintessentially Irish theater, and these more detached-seeming topics for debate allowed prejudice a freer rein. Hyde touches on the volatile issues that were involved in an unpublished letter to Gregory, dated September 22, 1901, when he notes that Moore's relations with the Gaelic League and with William Fay and his brother

---

[25]Matheson Lang, *Mr. Wu Looks Back: Thoughts and Memories* (London: Stanley Paul, 1940), p. 48. Lang played Niall.

[26]A hurt that colored the memory of both Bensons: see Lady Benson, *Mainly Players: Bensonian Memories* (London: Thornton Butterworth, 1926), p. 213; Sir Frank Benson, *My Memoirs* (London: Ernest Benn, 1930), p. 311.

[27]Frank Benson, *My Memoirs*, p. 311.

[28]Foster I 253 says there was a single performance; Una Ellis-Fermor, *The Irish Dramatic Movement*, 2d ed. (London: Methuen, 1954), p. 212, says there were four, etc. Curtailment followed later—that is, of projected performances in Belfast and London. "By the Way," *Freeman's Journal*, October 24, 1901, 4, comments on attendance: "*Diarmuid and Grania* continues to draw large audiences to the Gaiety Theatre" (quoted Hogan 110).

[29]Trewin, *Benson and the Bensonians*, pp. 80–81, describes their Irish reputation. AG was conscious from the start of this advantage, particularly in gaining the support of Unionist Dublin, which would find anything of GM's distasteful on principle (*LGD* 296–297). For Violet Martin, see *The Selected Letters of Somerville and Ross*, p. 253.

Frank (Als, Berg) were a disaster waiting to happen.

Moore had rehearsed Hyde's play for three weeks at his home in Ely Place, and continued to rehearse it when it moved onto the Gaiety stage. His enthusiasm was immense, abstract and selfless to a point that almost beggared belief: "But our play doesn't matter, Yeats; what matters is *The Twisting of the Rope*. We either want to make Irish the language of Ireland, or we don't; and if we do, nothing else matters" (*H&F* 315; cf. *GMT* 220–221). Nobody believed him; they feared he was joking at their expense, as they were later bewildered and challenged by his Gaelic Lawn Party, and truth became a casualty. According to Hyde, William Fay turned up for only one of the Irish rehearsals, leaving Moore to preside over the rest (Als to AG, postmarked October 2, 1901, Berg). According to both Fay brothers, the success of Hyde's play followed entirely from the work that Willie put into rehearsing it.[30] It was a no-win situation, given the way politics impinged on Irish theater, and Moore was damned if he did and damned if he didn't.

The swiftly moving process is evident in the reviews and responses collected by Hogan and Kilroy. As they write, "Within days considerable opposition arose to *Diarmuid and Grania*, and even the originally sympathetic *Freeman's Journal* joined the attack" (Hogan 110). Blame was subtly mixed with praise: "To my mind, the greatest triumph of the authors lies in their having written in English a play in which English actors are intolerable," Frank Fay wrote in the *United Irishman*.[31] The inability of the imported actors to adjust to Irish idiom was remembered thirty years afterward by Dawson Byrne.[32] It was also the sole memory of the play registered by Willie Fay, who added: "I came away from the rehearsals more convinced than ever that these plays, if they were to be successful, must be played by Irish actors."[33] The inevitable result was summed up by Gerard Fay: *Diarmuid and Grania* "has this place in Irish theatre history—that it was the last time Dubliners had to call in English actors before they could see a production of an Irish play."[34]

Charlotte ("L.") MacManus, in her memoir of the Irish Literary Revival, formulates the consensus that emerged. She attacked the play because it read base modern meanings ("licentiousness of thought") into pure Irish legend and pronounced "Irish Ireland looked upon it coldly, if not with hostility."

> The essential underlying beauty of the story was ignored or not seen. The play was not altogether unlike a divorce case in a modern court. The skilful grouping of words, the distinction of style could not redeem it.[35]

---

[30]W. G. Fay and Catherine Carswell, *The Fays of the Abbey Theatre: An Autobiographical Record* (London: Rich and Cowan, 1935), pp. 114–115; Frank Fay to Joseph Holloway, letter dated 1904 quoted in *Joseph Holloway's Abbey Theatre* 33–34 (cited by Hogan 95).

[31]"The Irish Literary Theatre," October 26, 1901, collected in *Towards a National Theatre: The Dramatic Criticism of Frank J. Fay*, ed. Robert Hogan (Dublin: Dolmen Press, 1970), pp. 71–73 at p. 72.

[32]Dawson Byrne, *The Story of Ireland's National Theatre: The Abbey Theatre, Dublin* (Dublin: Talbot Press, 1929), p. 3.

[33]Fay and Carswell, *The Fays of the Abbey Theatre*, p. 115.

[34]*The Abbey Theatre: Cradle of Genius* (Dublin: Clonmore and Reynolds, 1958), p. 126. For recollections of the Yeats-Fay split, which determined the later fortunes of the Abbey Theatre, see Padraic Colum, "Early Days of the Irish Theatre (continued)," *Dublin Magazine*, n.s., 25, no. 5 (January–March 1950): 18–33.

[35]*White Light and Flame: Memories of the Irish Literary Revival and the Anglo-Irish War* (Dublin: Talbot Press, 1929), pp. 46–47.

An example of how first impressions were overtaken by local reaction is provided by Stephen Gwynn, who wrote a lengthy review shortly after the performance, but who later professed that the play "left nothing but a blank" in his memory, although he could remember vividly a scene from Hyde's play on the same program.[36] So the play found its place in history, benefiting on its first night from the success of Hyde's *Sugáin*, torn apart when sentiment cooled and it could be appraised separately, a monument to what was proclaimed as an impossible merger.

Moore's estimation of the play was highest during the period between the completion of the play and its going into rehearsal. He told his friend, Dr. Ernst Heilborn, on September 3:

> with the exception of *Esther Waters* I like it better than anything I have done. It is a play in the style of the *Walkure*, of *Tristan and Isolde* and there is no reason why it should not be a success in Germany.[37]

On the same day or before, he uttered even more strongly the same judgement of worth to Fisher Unwin (*GMT* 218), but the question of publication had been set aside since the quarrel of the year before (Als, GM to WBY [November 12, 1900], Berg; *LWBY* I 78, but see *CL* II 585n for date). When he wrote again to Unwin in October 1901, he continued to be unsure about publication and suggested that the decision rested with Yeats (*GMT* 220–221). Alongside this diffidence, there are hints that his mind had reverted to the scheme for an opera based on the Grania theme, even in the months leading up to the stage performance: his correspondence with Elgar strongly suggests this is the case. At all events, following the performances in October 1901, he threw himself into defending the play against critics and focused on matters of historical accuracy and interpretation rather than of value. He was less concerned with what he and Yeats had written than with how it was received and misunderstood.

Yeats at the same time, though he had previously registered anxiety about the trouble Moore might land them in, became outwardly more confident and busier about the play itself after it became public property. While Moore recommended ecclesiastical censorship for the new theater and complicated everybody's lives, Yeats stood firm, indeed firmer, in his support for their collaboration. He wrote and spoke repeatedly about a printed text, which he conceived would be accompanied by a preface that would dispose of its critics (*CL* III 120); he began to negotiate for publication by Unwin (*CL* III 128), and arrangements reached a stage when he hoped to deliver the text before Christmas (*CL* III 135); he met with Mrs. Campbell to discuss the possibility of her playing Grania during an American tour (*CL* III 126, 135). In the end, Mrs. Campbell's interest came to nothing, and Yeats's historical note on the various versions of the Diarmuid and Grania legend was not written. The results of his preoccupation were oblique. He afterward began *The Player Queen* for Mrs. Campbell to star in (Foster I 380). Russell's *Deirdre*, begun long before to manifest a properly "heroic" version of bardic character, was performed on January 2, 1902. The joint researches by Yeats and Gregory on Grania and Finn fed into the project that was eventually published as Gregory's *Gods and Fighting Men* (1904) (see *CL* III 141). Work on the complementary volume, *Cuchulain of Muirthemne* (2d ed., 1904), also began as early as November 1900; and her three-act *Grania* was published in *Irish Folk History Plays* (1912), although, probably for autobiographical reasons, it was not staged during her

---

36 "The Irish Literary Theatre and Its Affinities," pp. 1055, 1058 esp.; see also Hogan 113.

37 Als, "Tuesday" [September 3, 1901], NLI 2648, 19^{v}–20^{v}. NLI incorrectly dates the letter "c. 1903." GM also raised the possibility of a German production with Elgar on September 7 ("the ways are open to me"): Kennedy 172.

lifetime. And, most significantly of all, Yeats continued to work on the text itself, despite—that is, outwardly unaffected by—the controversy that raged in the Dublin newspapers.

In such circumstances, his construction of an alternative Act II in the early months of 1902 is beguiling. When the play had struggled toward completion in December 1900, he thought Act II "the most stirring and exciting," "our best stage Act," though he thought the other acts more imaginative and Act III "the most literary," "our most poetical" (*CL* II 602, 606). It is unlikely that he was directly influenced by Martyn's second thoughts about Act II (*LGD* 297, 298)—"fleshy"—that anticipated the later unhappy controversy. Instead, he engaged the same issues at a deeper level and attempted a structural resolution to what had been seen before as an argument about style. He rewrote the act as a series of episodes linked in obvious ways to the traditional narratives he had recently been rereading and, at the same time, more importantly, replaced the "foreign" psychology Moore had introduced into the Diarmuid-Grania relationship.

Moore's involvement in this reconstruction of his design is curious. In *Dramatis Personae*, Yeats described how he, Yeats, was the prime mover. He says he discovered in performance that the "second act, instead of moving swiftly from incident to incident, was reminiscent and descriptive; almost a new first act. I had written enough poetical drama to know this and to point it out to Moore" (*Aut* 322).[38] Though other sources confirm that the modification originated with Yeats in the weeks following the production,[39] the only surviving material record of Moore's thoughts is contained in his correspondence with Elgar, which, from the beginning, urges Elgar to cut and rewrite the text in any way the music demands—"for the merit of a libretto is measured by the music it inspires" (GM to Elgar, [August 22, 1901]; Kennedy 170). In short, Moore's thinking moved away from the literary text Yeats helped him produce; he was more than willing to sacrifice it. "The libretto I want you to set is prehistoric. . . . I think it will suit you better than Diarmuid and Grania. I think it will make a better opera" (GM to Elgar, January 15, 1902; Kennedy 180). However, Moore framed a new version of Act II of the existing play for Elgar in a letter dated February 26, 1902 (Kennedy 181–182), and Yeats broke the news of his own new version in a letter to Gregory dated April 3, 1902, as if the news would surprise her:

> You will be sorry to hear that I have just dictated a rough draft of a new 'Grania' second act to Moore's type writer. He is to work on it in Paris. He gave me a few ideas & I worked over them & I think got the most poetical & beautiful material that we have put into the play as yet. He is delighted & will write the act ~~in Paris~~ & then send it to me for revision. (*CL* III 167)

What appears to have happened is that Yeats took advantage of Moore's lessening commitment to the stage play to return to the center of their disagreement. He rewrote the earlier half of Act II—the part that had provoked most difficulty—and was more than content for the later half to remain as it stood (see *CL* III 621). The two versions of Act II that evolved in early 1902—Moore's in outline, Yeats's dictated to Moore's typist in continuous dialogue—were

[38]See also *Aut* 330 and Hone 238. One first-nighter recorded that "the second act was dramatically the strongest" (*Joseph Holloway's Abbey Theatre*, p. 15): WBY's reversal of opinion is oddly decided and certainly contestable.

[39]Perhaps earlier. In the first issue of *Samhain*, which was sent to the printer in July or August and went on sale at the performance, Yeats wrote, "The first scene is in the great banqueting hall of Tara, and the second and third on the slopes of Ben Bulben in Sligo" ("Windlestraws," pp. 3–10 at p. 9; the essay was collected in Ellis-Fermor, *The Irish Dramatic Movement*, in 1908 [Wade, item 78, p. 89], and cf. *CW* VIII 10)—as if the change was already in his mind.

produced by different attitudes of mind, and perhaps Yeats believed Moore's tacit assent was collaboration. Moore did indeed revise the typescript Yeats sent him, although it differed from the plot he described for Elgar, and there the matter stood at the time he took the typescript to Paris, leaving Yeats to reply to an enquiry in May 1902: "'Dermot and Grania' has not yet been published, I suppose it will be sooner or later, but I cannot say who the publisher will be" (*CL* III 182–183). He evidently returned portions of the typescript to Yeats on different occasions, one portion now being among Yeats's papers in Dublin and the other, perhaps returned later, after Yeats had lost interest, with Gregory's in New York.

At this point, in midair as it were, the situation was overtaken by another play whose shadow already loomed. Yeats and Moore had begun to collaborate on *Where There Is Nothing* in July 1901, before the finishing touches to *Diarmuid* were added, but the collaboration unravelled into a dispute exactly twelve months later for the same reasons and along the same lines as before.[40] When Yeats eventually withdrew from the venture, Moore announced that he was writing a novel based on the same plot and would get an injunction if Yeats used it. Hearing from Russell that Moore had begun not a novel but a play, Yeats went to Coole and dictated his own version to Gregory and Hyde in a fortnight. Publication was secretly arranged as a supplement to *The United Irishman* on November 1 in order to gain the copyright; Moore took no legal action, and, though the American lawyer and collector John Quinn tried to reconcile the parties, the quarrel was not patched up until November–December 1904. However, Yeats wrote, "we were never cordial again; on my side distrust remained, on his disgust. I look back with some remorse" (*Aut* 334). It was the end of the several attempts to bring the writing of *Diarmuid and Grania* to a close.

During the period of estrangement, in April 1903, Russell reported to Yeats that Moore had called to discuss the conditions on which he might continue to work on the play. "He thought them reasonable, but I think the clause empowering you also to rewrite rather took away his desire to do anything at it himself. He said then he would think it over."[41] The following year, a question arose of a pirate American production, that Moore might involuntarily have assisted, which Yeats moved to quash (*CL* III 568–571, 580). Following the rapprochement in November 1904, Yeats made clear what was on his mind in a letter to Frank Fay:

> He made up with me the other day. I also had my object, (keep it to yourself) I want to get Dermot & Grania into my hands & think I see my way to an arrangement which will leave him free to do what he likes with it in England for a certain time; I to reshape it for you—it would make a fine verse play. (*CL* III 671)[42]

However, Yeats did no further work on the play. It was not included in his 1911 collection of *Plays for an Irish Theatre*; it is unlikely to be the unnamed "new play in three acts" announced at that time that anyway never appeared.[43] He was deeply wounded by the publication of Moore's *Ave* (October 1911), and delayed his public response, in *Dramatis Personae*, until 1934/35. The mention there of York Powell's high opinion of the play, preferring it to Ibsen's *Vikings at Helgeland* (*Aut* 327), is difficult to construe. For a start, no evidence can be

---

[40] *CL* III 228n2, supplies much of the phrasing in this paragraph, along with references.

[41] *Letters from AE*, ed. Alan Denson (London: Abelard-Schuman, 1961), pp. 45–46 at p. 46.

[42] Discussion of WBY turning the play into verse had aired as early as August 1901: see GM to Elgar in Kennedy 170.

[43] The unnamed play was to have been included in a ninth volume of Bullen's Shakespeare Head Collected Edition: see Wade 94.

found that Powell attended the performance. He died in 1904 and one can only suppose he was shown Berg(99) by John Butler Yeats, who was sketching him at the time the play went into production.[44] Everything suggests that Yeats was overtaken by a sense of stalemate, and that memories and bitterness left him unable to focus. He mentioned *Diarmuid* as a possible dance play to Frederic Ashton in 1930 (Foster I 253); in 1935, he recalled moments in performance, "Benson's athletic dignity in one scene and the notes of the horn in Elgar's dirge over the dead Diarmuid" (*Aut* 327). He looked at the play with a view to reviving it on the Abbey stage, but other interests intervened. It was left for Mrs. Yeats, somewhat diffidently and protectively, to consider publication and arrange an editor among the first such projects she undertook after her husband's death—as described in part v below.

Following Moore's concentration on the play in *Ave*, it would have been nearly impossible to contrive a fair hearing. He chose to translate Yeats's replacement Act II into French as his final extended comment on the play, resituating it in the Coole quarrel of September–October 1900. It is a characteristic displacement that amounts to exactly weighted criticism. Of course, Moore withdrew to the Shelbourne in 1900, and not with this version of Act II—more likely an early version of Act I. Of course, when he took the 1902 Act II with him to France it was not to turn it into French but to improve its English, as the revisions prove. But the choice of Yeats's less sensual dramatic action rather than his own to turn into French makes an argument about Yeats's emotional evasiveness, and the notion that literary works could be improved by filtering their composition through several languages exactly frames Moore's ambivalent attitude toward style (*Aut* 323)[45]—and exactly counters Yeats's. Moore's critique is totally unfair yet it hits more bull's-eyes than any straight shot, striking idle bystanders as well as the principals.

It leaves one curious episode unexplained. A letter in an unknown hand, filed with the Moore materials at HRC, contains an opera scenario of *Diarmuid and Grania* oddly close to the original Moore-Yeats version. It is dated September 29, 1913, carries the address of W. B. Reynolds, a journalist working for the *Belfast Evening Telegraph*, is addressed to "Shamus," and the signature page is missing. The identity of "Shamus" is unknown. Seamus MacManus, a prolific popular writer who emigrated to the United States in 1899 but returned each year to Donegal, whose early plays were staged by the Abbey but who became one of its fiercest critics after the 1911 tour of Synge's *Playboy*, is one candidate. James Starkey, aka Seumas O'Sullivan, is a possibility, although he seems never to have taken a particular interest in the legend. Reynolds was also a composer and the first to set poems by Joyce to music, but he is not necessarily the author of the letter. The sequence of scenes follows the Moore-Yeats sequence nearly but not exactly, and the original Druid, Daire, replaces Laban. Even if one gives up speculating whether the letter is influenced by the Moore-Yeats plot, and about the identities of the lyrical "Shamus" and the unknown composer-author, how did the letter attach itself to the Cunard materials that found their way to Texas? One can only add that Moore found it difficult to relinquish the opera project. He wrote to Elgar in May 1914: "I can no longer believe, if I ever believed it, that you were wise in refraining from writing an opera."[46]

[44]*Letters from Bedford Park*, p. 65.

[45]Cf. *Sister Teresa* (London: Fisher Unwin, 1901), p. 17: "Harding said that he had known Hugo, Banville and Tourgueneff and that they had never spoken of style. He said that the gods do not talk theology: 'they leave theology to the inferior saints and the clergy.'" GM's view coincides with Walter Savage Landor's: "Enter into the mind and heart of your own creatures: think of them long, entirely, solely: never of style, never of self" (*The Romantics: An Anthology*, ed. Geoffrey Grigson [London: George Routledge, 1942], p. 172).

[46]Quoted by Robert Anderson, *Elgar* (London: J. M. Dent, 1993), p. 264.

The plays by Russell and Gregory that were prompted—indeed, provoked—by the Moore-Yeats collaboration have received mention above (p. xl): both attempt to liberate Irish materials from Moore's baleful influence. Another stage version of the legend was constructed in the late 1920s, independently of the Moore-Yeats initiative, by Micheál MacLíammóir.[47] Austin Clarke, again, gave it epic-poematic treatment in *The Vengeance of Fionn* (1917) and prose-romance embodiment in *The Bright Temptation* (1932). Such evidence of interest might lie behind James Starkey's request for permission to publish the play as part of a proposed series of booklets attached to *The Dublin Magazine* in 1927, but this throws no light on the Belfast mystery, and Moore responded negatively with comments about magazine publication in general rather than saying anything specific about the success or suitability of the play.[48] His comment in the preface to *The Coming of Gabrielle* (1920) should be taken at face value. He listed the play among those he was proud to acknowledge, adding in his characteristically diffident way, "the writing of *Diarmuid and Grania* was undertaken for the pleasure of collaborating with Mr. W. B. Yeats".[49] The corrosive *Ave* should be read adjacent to his earlier commitment to the play, and the play never supplanted his interest in an opera, although Moore was not an author to regret burnt bridges he left behind him.

(iv)

The story of the collaboration is one in which Yeats and Moore met a great deal but their minds did not; as Susan Mitchell wrote, "They had passed one another on the journey."[50] The disjunction is evident in the play they wrote and even more clearly, if subtly, with reference to the manuscript materials.

A good many references to revision and retouching are unspecific. For instance, when Yeats, ill in bed but working nonetheless, reports in early January 1901 that Grania "has been continually retouched" (*CL* III 5), one does not know what he did or did not do. Again, a good number of revisions/improvements were not taken forward, and there is no record of whether this is a result of accident or discussion. The prime example is a complete fair-copy typescript of Act II (NLI 8777[9]), apparently originating from Moore and extensively revised by Yeats, which is completely off the highway of transmission: it remains unclear whence it derives and why it was prepared, and it leads nowhere. One can only suppose that Moore dispatched it to Yeats to demonstrate a scenario that would not work, but that Yeats took it only too seriously before he was disabused.

At the other extreme are words and phrases that appear in a version or dated letter as subject to dispute, that are revised or disappear in a following version. The instances of Moore's

[47] A text is preserved in British Library, Department of Manuscripts, reference no. 1931/34. It was performed in Irish in Galway and in English—as a Gate Theatre Studio Production—in the Peacock Theatre attached to the Abbey, both in 1928. The English version was revived at the Mansion House for Dublin Civic Week in September 1929. MacLíammóir's and Clarke's versions might well have revived memories of his own play in WBY's mind, and prompted him to review it in the early 1930s.

[48] GM's negative response to Starkey is at the Huntington Library (Tls November 8, 1927: HM 35373). Richard Burnham, *The Development of Seumas O'Sullivan and "The Dublin Magazine"* (Ph.D. diss., University College Dublin, 1977), pp. 237–238, is the authority for Starkey having requested permission to publish *Diarmuid and Grania*.

[49] *The Coming of Gabrielle: A Comedy* (London: privately printed for subscribers only by Cumann Sean-eolais na h-Éireann, 1920), p. vi.

[50] Susan L. Mitchell, *George Moore* (Dublin: Talbot Press, [1916]), p. 102.

vocabulary that Gregory and Yeats complained of at Coole are not visible because the extant texts are already revised according to their preferences. But subsequent words and phrases—like Moore's "little mishaps of the birds" in Act III, which amused Gregory on October 25, 1900 (*LGD* 283), and was finally cut—can be exactly registered. Similarly, revisions such as the close of Act III, or the introduction of the spinning song, or the revision of the opening of Act II can all be exactly assigned and dated. Alongside these are others again that confuse the pattern that begins to emerge. Thus, Moore retrospectively described the composition of a passage involving Cairbre's two-headed chicken in Act III, but he leaves unclear whether Yeats entered his bedroom and read it to him when he was half-asleep or whether he himself composed it in his dreams (*H&F* 248). Either way, however the passage fits, it is clear that Yeats is being blamed or ridiculed, and textual and circumstantial evidence confirms Yeats's authorship.[51] In the end, the complicated fiction Moore constructs around Yeats's contribution is the only explanation of a curtailed possibility that arose and was punctured like a bubble in the linked advance toward a performative version.

If one looks beyond words or passages that can be tagged with an author's name and a specific date, one can see signatures of each author no less clearly than such tags afford and perhaps see each writer more pervasively inhabiting the characters and situations of the play. Very obviously, when one comes to the play from the direction of its grand arranger, Moore, Yeats was a version of Ulick Dean who mutates into a version of Diarmuid; that is, a Diarmuid in relation to Moore's version of Grania, in which he explored his own relation to Maud Cunard—weighed it, indulged it, philosophized on it. Yeats's complicity in the revision of Ulick's part has been noted. Moore told him he should consider Diarmuid his own,[52] and Yeats's taking of possession is acknowledged in the subtlest, strongest way in the flying white heron on Diarmuid's shield (one should note Yeats's pride in having contributed the shields: *CL* II 619). Herons, with all they represent as a talisman of the Tuatha de Danaan, inhabit Yeats's writing from stories in *The Secret Rose* (1897) to the late play *The Herne's Egg* (1938). Diarmuid's passivity perhaps comes from Moore's prompting, but the way the connections with the god Aognhus are handled was surely contributed by Yeats; and this dimension of the play, which intrigued the Wagnerian in Moore, is a dimension of the plotting he for the most part encouraged.

In traditional versions of the story available to Moore and Yeats,[53] the person who advises Grania concerning the potion in Act I is a male druid named Daire. The MacCunn opera had replaced the druid with a female figure, Freya, Norse Goddess of Love, and extended the part, along with Assistant Maidens and Shades of the Immortals, so that she exerted a supernatural influence over the whole action.[54] In turn, Moore and Yeats began by converting the traditional Irish Daire into an Old Woman or Nurse and simultaneously restricting the Viking dimension

---

[51]The two-headed chicken in Berg(13) 2/fol. 2^r is Maintain's, but NLI 8777(3) e and 8777(3) d are WBY-authored modifications of Cairbre's part. Cairbre Cinn Cait, like Forgael (Berg[01], fol. 16^r), was a Firbolg who floated in and out of early plans for *The Shadowy Waters*: see *Druid Craft: The Writing of 'The Shadowy Waters,'* ed. Michael J. Sidnell, George P. Mayhew, and David R. Clark (Amherst: University of Massachusetts Press, 1971), p. 36

[52]"Diarmuid is largely your conception and the character as it stands owes much to you. . . . Do you take the hero and leave the heroine to me": GM to WBY, Als [November 17, 1900] Berg; *LWBY* I 73–74 (see *CL* II 593n for revised date).

[53]For example, Standish Hayes O'Grady, ed., *Transactions of the Ossianic Society for the Year 1855* 3 (1857): 49; Katharine Tynan, *Shamrocks* (London: Kegan Paul, 1887), p. 7. In neither version does Daire assist with the love potion.

[54]*Diarmid: Grand Opera in Four Acts; Founded on Heroic Celtic Legends and Written by the Marquis of Lorne, K.T.; The Music Composed by Hamish MacCunn, Opus 34* (London: Boosey, 1897). Among lesser traces left by the opera is the tendency, found among GM versions, to describe Diarmuid's dwelling as a "dun" and GM's habitual spelling, "Diarmid."

of the opera to the attacks of the Lochlanders; and the figure of the Old Woman evolved into a Foster-Mother, which bound her into a closer, filial relationship with Grania. It is clear from a letter Moore wrote to Gregory on August 11, 1900, that the modifications caused disagreement at first: "Tell him I think he will find he is mistaken when he introduces the Old Woman into the middle of the act [Act II?]; the balance will be overthrown at once" (Tls, Berg; *GML* #874). Indeed, the relation between the Foster-Mother's supernatural powers and those exerted over other parts of the action—with reference to Aognhus and Diarmuid, in particular—is never coherently articulated. But following the initial spat, at the moment when talk and planning gave way to drafts and versions, Moore's silence over the development of and changes to the part are just as instructive as Yeats's protestations at Moore's interventions elsewhere. It is worth emphasizing, given the public disagreement over "style," that Moore benignly encouraged Yeats to write a good deal into the "scenario."

In the earliest continuous version of Act III (NLI 8777[10] a, fol. 2^{v}), Yeats named the Foster-Mother character as Dana, mother of Gods who has been seven years in the sea. In his Museum Notebook rewrite of the same passage (NLI 8777[5], fol. 11^{r}), he does not name her, but he extends the period she spent in the sea to 700 years. The name Laban first appears as a holograph revision to an Act I typescript, and in different states of typescript that make up a continuous version of Act II (respectively, HRC[1] and NLI 8777[14]–[15]). It first appears in continuous-typescript form in Berg(03)—a typescript of Act I that might be the "sufficient version" Yeats sent Moore on or about November 15, 1900.

There is no recorded discussion of the development of the character or the name, and this could suggest that this change dates from the time at Coole when such matters were settled in conversation. The name has nothing to do with the unpleasant male character in Genesis 31, nor with the Irish *lábán*, meaning a rotten egg; instead it appears to be Yeats's version of Líbán (literally "beauty of women"), who was the sister of Manannan McLir's wife, Fand. The written sources describing Liban are quite clear,[55] but why Liban converted to Laban is unexplained. Perhaps Yeats wanted to cover his tracks and obscured them with the place name Labane, which is close to Gort; Laban as a place name spelled thus crops up in his play *The Cat and the Moon*.[56] He incorporated Liban as Laban into his lyric "Under the Moon," which he was engaged in writing in early September 1900, in which Gregory assisted with the mythology.[57] Perhaps Gregory, at the beginning of her researches, merged Liban with the daughter of King Under-Wave who assists Diarmuid in his legendary travels.[58]

The Laban/Liban connection explains several undeveloped references to the connection between the character, the sea, and her longevity. It is also a reminder of other connections, such as with the lyric "The Danaan Quicken Tree" (1893), which grew into "The Lake Isle of Innisfree."[59] The "golden apples of the sun" that recur like a Wagnerian motif, not least in Yeats's late Act II substitution, are associated with Aognhus and the Danaan Island of the Young. The sense of absence that colors Diarmuid's character—of waiting to be called, of ultimate indifference—

---

[55]Standish Hayes O'Grady, ed., *Silva Gaedelica, I–XXXI: A Collection of Tales in Irish*, 2 vols. (London: Williams and Norgate, 1892), 1:234–237, 2:184–185.

[56]*VPlays* 797, lines 114, 122, var 115.

[57]*VPoems* 209, line 12; first published in *Speaker,* June 15, 1901. Cf. *LGD* 278–279.

[58]Cf. *Gods and Fighting Men: The Story of the Tuatha de Danaan and the Fianna,* 2d ed. (Gerrards Cross, UK: Colin Smythe, 1970 [Coole Edition III]), bk. 6, pp. 252–258.

[59]*VPoems* 742–743, 117. Both pieces of writing were based on experience of a sort: see *CL* I 321. For the phrase "golden apples of the sun," see "The Song of Wandering Aengus," *VPoems* 150.

is something Yeats experienced and wrote about in terms that connect it to the same mythology.[60] Virginia Rohan suggests a parallel between Laban and Deirdre's nurse and confidante, Lavoureen, and points to references to the sea god Mannanan as Deirdre's father.[61] Yeats threaded the play with such signatures, with Moore's tacit approval. They were rarely commented on or resisted, and the fun at Yeats's expense in *Ave* over Cairbre is an exception.

Moore instead wrote his position into the play in a manner Yeats must have noticed but also did not protest against. There is a special bond between Moore and Conan, in particular: "Well he eats when he's hungry," Niall tells the boy in the opening scene of Act I, and his tasteless realism counterpoints Diarmuid's high romanticism (HRC 5/fol. 8^r). Conan insists on the special bond that links the two characters, despite Diarmuid's denial. He has a prescience of future events that matches Laban's, such as when he tells Goll that Finn will kill him (HRC 103/fol. 106^r), though it is for the most part founded on different (realistic) premises, and indeed he replaces Laban when, in later versions, he speaks the closing words. The coincidence between his sceptical, unappreciated realism and Moore's point of view appears to be underwritten by a slyly humorous detail. Yeats and Gregory had fun at Moore's expense over his phrase "the little mishaps of the birds" in a version of Act III, describing four wild swans being blown into the trees (*LGD* 283). When the act was revised, swans and geese are deliberately muddled by Conan ("Are not swans a kind of geese" HRC 102/fol. 105^r), and ungainly, practical geese are thereby associated with Conan as the heron is with Diarmuid. In the light of this personal signature, the imagery of Yeats's bitter lines on Moore, in a 1909 diary, is likely to have been deliberately chosen:

> Moore once had visits from the muse
> But fearing that she would refuse
> An ancient lecher took to geese
> He now gets novels at his ease.[62]

One of the most interesting of these filiations that link motifs in the play with their joint authors is Moore's subsequent treatment of the golden apples theme. In the months after *Diarmuid* was performed, during the height of the controversy that it caused, he worked hard at drafting and remodelling a short story that was published in April 1902 as "The Golden Apples."[63] It was conceived from the beginning as the first of a series and, further revised under the title "Julia Cahill's Curse," was collected in *The Untilled Field* (1903). The curious circumstance of how many stories in *The Untilled Field* followed the translation process in and out of Irish proposed for *Diarmuid* in *Ave* (*H&F* 249; and cf. *Salve, H&F* 312) can simply be noted. Moore's handling of Yeats's myth converts the legendary into the contemporary, the mystical into something

---

[60] See his long essay "Away," first published in the *Fortnightly Review* (April 1902), collected in *Later Articles and Reviews: Uncollected Articles, Reviews, and Radio Broadcasts Written after 1900,* ed. Colton Johnson (New York: Scribner, 2000 [*CW* X]), pp. 64–81.

[61] Virginia Rohan, *Deirdre: Manuscript Materials* (Ithaca: Cornell University Press, 2003), pp. xxxviii–xlii; see her discussion of MS version B.

[62] *VPoems* 792, quoting William Becker's note in *DMag* 3.

[63] *English Illustrated Magazine* (April 1902): 58–65. For references to the story in letters to Unwin, see *GMT* 237–247 passim. The story, "The Wedding Gown," had been published earlier in a different form under a different title, but "The Golden Apples" has a better claim to be the beginning of the series of stories that developed into the unified collection *The Untilled Field* (1903); see *GMT* 237n and cf. Hone 242.

sensual; and Moore's story, written at the time Grania was under attack exactly because she was held to be too "fleshy" to be properly Irish, became a protest against freedom and enjoyment squashed by priest-ridden, poverty-stricken narrow-mindedness. Like the famous Gaelic Lawn Party Moore held on May 18, 1902, his story was simultaneously celebration and mockery, and was revised to become more harshly satirical as his estrangement deepened.[64]

Perhaps most interesting of all, in the shadowy dialogue that worked itself out in the construction of the drama, is the area where novelist met poet. Two kinds of writing, two kinds of understanding, engage or fail to engage; two different kinds of psychology are involved. Thus, the subtlety of Grania's attitude toward Diarmuid and Finn—her dressing for Finn in Act II alongside her genuine longing for Diarmuid and Finn to be reconciled, the question of whether she wants Diarmuid to go to the hunt in Act III, her simultaneous boredom with and attraction to pastoral life—this kind of psychology appears to me to inhabit fictional space. It assumes a kind of interior way of understanding character that is deeper than any physical way on which it can be projected; the dialogue contains meanings that resonate in a reader's head even while theatrical realization selects and changes those same meanings for an audience. At the same time, one has to acknowledge that a genuine theatrical sense is made to communicate complex meanings in this play. A good instance is contained in Conan's compressed, flat words, at the close of the play: "Grania makes a great mourning for Diarmuid, but her welcome to Finn shall be greater" (Berg[99] 98/fol. 100^{r}; see p. 1007 below). Grand funeral orations drop into an ocean of solitude, the degree of understatement makes options reverberate like a coda in Beckett—like the closing words of *Krapp's Last Tape*.

One could continue with such examples: Niall's surprising regard for Conan's unheroic position in Act I, the corrosive realism of a shepherd's view of the heroic life at the opening of Act III, Usheen's distinctive role. It is Usheen who proposes the blood bond, gives Conan his ale skin, and speaks, with Caoelte, at the end; his prominence in Jack Yeats's sketches is not accidental. The theatrical mode at times picks up with muddled motives, at other times with dimensions of satire, at times shifts from a position that comes with a novelist's advantage to exploit pure theater. It is natural to associate it with Moore, given his background and documented contributions to the play, just as it is natural to credit Yeats with tableau, romance, and the sense of poetic style that inheres in his rewriting. Tension inevitably results between the complex of interests surrounding the psychology of the characters. They move in part as inheritors of their counterparts in *Evelyn Innes* and *Sister Teresa*, in part as characters in a three-act stage performance, mixtures of Zola and Wagner. The advance from Moore's crude scenarios to Yeats's rewritten texts is truly astonishing. The problem is, while the play contains the very good things each collaborator contributed, it has never been given a fair trial on stage.

The only certainty was described by Yeats in conversation with Mrs. Campbell: "I told her that I was just a lyric poet & that Moore was a very considerable dramatist & she answered 'well you have made a very great work between you some how' & quoted Max Beerbohm who had said 'But where do they begin to come together'" (*CL* II 620). Others said the same thing in different ways: for instance, Constance Benson summed up rehearsals with "what Edmund [*sic*] Yeats liked, George Moore hated, and vice versa."[65] The collision was as much between two

[64]AG maintained the legendary Irish dimension of the story in her play for Kiltartan children, *The Golden Apple* (London: John Murray, 1916). It deals with the adventures of the King of Ireland's son, who goes in search of the Golden Apple of Healing.

[65]*Mainly Players*, 212.

kinds of writing as between two personalities who wrote. Yeats appears to have learned something about dramatic construction and gained confidence in practical management; perhaps his strong sense of Moore's avoidance of style reinforced his sense of a life constructed through style. Perhaps also, although forever wounded by his teacher's methods, he learned that Moore was right to be downbeat about curing the manners of a nation by cultural revival. Moore appears to have learned less because he entered a situation that he for a large part continued to control, but it was of great use to him in ways I have indicated. Ann Saddlemyer's conclusion is admirably balanced. "The play is neither a failure nor a success," but each collaborator got from it all anyone could reasonably have expected—everything, that is, except a jointly written masterpiece.[66]

(v)

Finally, some words on the foul papers that make up the bulk of the manuscript materials are in order. Why typescripts need to be transcribed as literally as possible may not be obvious, and how their features embody information about transmission should be explained. As I said at the opening of this introduction, the materials comprise a multilayered jigsaw puzzle. The pieces are scattered, those collected in single locations sometimes deliberately and sometimes accidentally bring together pieces that belonged elsewhere, and some pieces are missing. Some of the extant pieces were tried out by the authors in different positions and abandoned before a resting place was found for them, and others seem to have been written and taken no further. The materials can be brought into relation in a generally explicable way, but the pattern is complicated by abandoned starts, obscured by false directions, and contains gaps.

There are various indicators that help orient an investigator in this imperfectly designed labyrinth. The most obvious indicators of chronology are changes of names: from Foster-Mother to Laban in September 1900, and the emergence, in the revision of NLI 8777(3) b and c, of the three previously unnamed spearmen, Fergus, Fathna, and Criffan. The variable spelling of names is a clue in earlier stages, since the more unusual ones took a while to settle down: Caolte, Caolite, Caoltie, and Caoilte alternated until Caoelte was settled on; Aognhus similarly took a while to establish itself. In addition, particular spellings tend to be associated with one or another author. Thus, Moore prefers Diarmuid and Diarmid, while Yeats most frequently wrote Darmuid, Damud, Dairmd, Darmd, etc.—which some typescripts reflect. The blue-ink and the black-ink paste-in additions to the continuous HRC typescript tend to have the later spellings—in contrast to the body of text, which has the first spelling—which in turn bolsters the association between the revisions and Yeats or the person who typed the revisions on his behalf.

Different typing styles also help indicate different families of manuscripts. Attention is drawn to the fact that page numbers are central or ranged right, and are contained in brackets or em dashes or are freestanding. Part ascriptions are ranged left or centered, in level capitals or otherwise, underlined or not underlined; thus substitute pages in HRC(2) are detectable because part ascriptions are underlined. Similarly, stage descriptions are underlined or not underlined. Margins are set at measures ranging from 2.6 to 4 cm, which photocopying reduces and sometimes distorts, but differences can be calculated by comparing the number of type characters

[66]"'All Art Is a Collaboration'? George Moore and Edward Martyn" in *The World of W. B. Yeats: Essays in Perspective,* ed. Robin Skelton and Ann Saddlemyer (Victoria, BC: Adelphi Bookshop for the University of Victoria, 1965), pp. 203–222 at p. 221.

and blanks that fill a given page width. In addition, individual typists make different kinds of habitual mistakes. Lady Gregory typed a number of versions on the Remington she kept at Coole Park, and the mistakes they contain may be noted in versions of less certain origin. Yeats dictated his substitute Act II to Moore's "type writer" (*CL* III 167)—namely, Augusta Gill (see *CL* II 583n)—which corroborates evidence concerning the use of the same typewriter (in both senses) elsewhere.

All of the above can assist in discriminating among layers of typescript that sometimes make up a continuous run of pages. Some features provide stronger evidence than others. A typist is unlikely to change the format of part ascriptions as she moves through her job, while a margin setting can slip. An apostrophe for a period following a string of capital letters is a natural error (it occurs in HRC and Berg[99], which are patently from different typewriters), but other errors can be revealing. The spellings in the Berg(06) version of Act II suggest either a typist who typed as she repeated the words of NLI 8777(4) in her own uneducated head, or typed what a person with a strong Irish accent dictated to her. Interpreted with caution, the details can be suggestive and/or corroborative. The mixture of ribbon and carbon pages in NLI 8777(11) is a clear indication of complexity in the first complete typescript of Act I. The first half of Act II comprised by NLI 8777(4) g+h+i+j+k+l emerges like a deck of cards shuffled together from at least two packs, from which a third composite has been created by arrangement and overwriting. Another version of Act II contained in NLI 8777(14) and (15) is set at three margins on two different ribbons, which raises further possibilities of combination. Evidence of bindings and ring holes confirms relationships of other kinds; for instance, that HRC(1), (2), and (3) and NLI 8777(3) a+b+c were constructed in tandem for Moore and Yeats respectively.

Given the way in which such details forge links and help position the superabundance of closely similar versions, they are worth recording. They do not explain everything, and this is a good reason for recording some details that for the moment lead nowhere. What at present appears inconsequential could provide the necessary clue to resolving an outstanding question, and, given their importance of such details, I have thought it worth preserving as many of them as is practicable. Varying margins, missed letters, random oddities stand out with special clarity in the otherwise more uniform right-hand pages and redirect attention to the facing reproduction.

However, a final caveat. The transcriptions cannot reproduce the typefaces of distinctive typewriters or subtleties of different typewriting "hands"—both of these as distinctive as handwriting when one learns to read the signs. Nor can they reproduce overtypes or different kinds of type cancellation (by solidus "/" or by cross "x"). Nor can transcriptions reproduce different kinds of manuscript cancellation. Moore tends to use a diagonal strike through, character by character, Yeats a horizontal line through words and phrases; indeed, Moore's neat strike throughs can be confused with typed solidi in the reproductions. For anyone who returns to the original typescripts, I strongly recommend a preliminary reading of Wilson R. Harrison's *Suspect Documents: Their Scientific Examination*, 2d ed. (London: Sweet and Maxwell, 1966), chapter 8. Wilson, a former director of the Home Office Forensic Laboratory at Cardiff, describes how to identify the individual behind the technology. His analyses and demonstrations have been more helpful to the present enterprise than any handbook of traditional bibliography.

Chronology of Manuscripts

The odd mix of personal and professional maneuvering surrounding the composition of the play is sketched in the introduction. An amount of labor was expended before the outline plot was settled and, despite public references and mutual advertisement, the collaborators were preoccupied with other projects until summer 1900. There is reason to believe that serious revision began with the turning point in the dramatic construction. Moore wrote to Gregory on August 11, 1900: "[Yeats] must finish the second act. I will not touch it again, but I will write the first and third acts whenever he pleases. I can easily finish them both in a fortnight—a week for each" (Tls Berg; *GML* #874). Becker and Frazier (295) suppose Moore intended to write that Yeats must finish the first act before going on to the second and third, but it is more likely that Moore meant exactly what he wrote. His dialogue for Act I indeed appears to have been written later (September 1900), while he dispatched the first extant version of Act II to Yeats before the end of July.

A complete version of Act I was arrived at before October 1900 and a fair copy made. Disagreement over an appropriate style and working method involved Moore's withdrawal from Coole to Dublin, but a new version was prepared within weeks, and the act remained substantially the same thereafter. Act II meanwhile underwent very many rewritings, each author contributing versions that passed the other by. These were eventually cobbled together and revised in mid-November, after further brief but acrimonious disagreement. Work on Act III began last and proceeded most consistently, reaching a conclusion within three and half months. The once-identical binding of NLI 8777(3) and HRC(1)–(3) signals the overall resolution achieved in early December 1900.

Another phase of adjustment and improvement accompanied the preparation for performance, and is recorded in the continuously paginated versions prepared between December 1900 and October 1901. A different phase again followed the reception of the play, at a time when the friendship between the collaborators began to come to an end. The modifications introduced at these later times are specific and can be assigned dates. After the final quarrel in July 1902, each author took only a fitful interest in what had been jointly created.

Despite the running commentary on the composition of the play supplied by letters and diaries, it is often difficult to attach calendar dates or establish links between work on the separate acts. Again, several crucial details in the record are obscure or indeed contradictory. The change of nomenclature from Foster-Mother to Laban helps establish one of the few definite links of a "horizontal" kind between acts, although this clue does not help with Act III. Spelling and the formatting of typescripts suggest other links. Finally, the sequence contains gaps and is made to appear lopsided by Moore's lack of interest in preserving working papers, compared with Yeats.

To repeat what is obvious, for reasons given above, the manuscripts are not listed in overall chronological order. They are instead arranged chronologically within the various parts—separate acts, continuously paginated versions, and addenda—of the present edition.

Act I

> [Note that a version arrived at before summer 1900 is no longer extant. GM read a version of Act I to GR, immediately following his first short visit to Coole, that he then appears to have realized was unsatisfactory (*LGD* 280). It appears that GR inadvertently confirmed GM's belief that Diarmuid should be made to appear more manly and the fianna more heroic (see GR to AG, Als [September 26, 1900], Berg; also *LGD* 280 and telegram quoted).]

NLI 8777(8) d An Als by GM to WBY from the Shelborne Hotel (Berg [September 28, 1900]; *LWBY* I 71) describes Grania's description, apparently by anticipation, of the life she and Diarmuid will share in the woods. GM subsequently sent WBY, from 92 Victoria Street, a description of a "woman offering to a man a set of sensuous temptations" as part of his finished version of a complete act (Als Berg [*CL* II 582n dates it November 8, 1900]; *LWBY* I 71–72). *CL* supposes the act in question to be Act II, *LWBY* supposes it to be Act I: the holograph is apparently the basis for the close of NLI 8777(11) below.

The hotel stationery could suggest a date between September 17 and 28, 1900, when GM stayed over in Dublin following his first visit to Coole. Or the draft could have been sent from 92 Victoria Street more than a month later, as suggested by *CL* II 582n. If the later date is accepted, the draft is a revision of an already completed version and should be positioned later in the present sequence.

An undated Als by GM to WBY (Berg) describes the enclosure of a "rough draft" of Grania's description, by anticipation, of the life she and Diarmuid will share in the woods—a "woman offering to a man a set of sensuous temptations." *LWBY* I 71–72 understands GM to refer to a scene in Act II and *CL* I 582 to a scene in Act I; the holograph numeral can be read as a "1" with a head and foot clumsily added, or as a wobbly "2", or indeed as "1" emended to "2". However, GM's description of future temptation fits Act I and excludes Act II, and he habitually employs roman—not arabic—numerals for act-references (as correctly reproduced in, e.g., *LWBY* I 69, 79).

Also, in the same letter, GM refers to a scene involving Grania and the Foster-Mother. Since such a scene did not enter Act II until the second stage of its development, the reference appears to date the letter—and the present draft scene for Act I—at the earlier time (September 17–28). However, against the background of an altered act reference, it is just possible that GM refers to one scene he has worked over in Act I and another scene in Act II. This interpretation makes more sense of his remark that Act III is the next task to face WBY and himself.

Berg(00) Two-page outline of a scene from the middle section of Act I in GM's hand, containing the beginnings of some dialogue. Apparently the basis for the substitute middle section; see NLI 8777(11) 6bis/folio 7^{r} and surrounding pages.

Dates from around October 10, 1900, from Wales, following GM's second, longer visit to Coole (*LWBY* I 69; see *CL* II 580n for revised date). GM approves Act II but sketches a replacement scene in Act I between Grania and Foster-Mother. He has written out the scene and will send a TS copy to WBY on returning to London. Phrases in the letter overlap with Berg(00).

NB also that the Berg(00) paper is the same as that used for GM's outline pages for Act II; like NLI 8777(8) b, Berg(09), and NLI 8777(8) c below.

NLI 8777(11) Fifteen-page TS of Act I complete, with substitute TS pages in middle section, corrected by AG and WBY. Apparently based on the revised earlier version. The character of the revisions, which appear to have gone through three stages, suggests this version aimed at fair-copy status.

The pages corresponding to NLI 8777(8) d were perhaps mediated by WBY's holograph, now missing, since they contain traces of his characteristic Darmuid spelling. The typewriter appears to be AG's Remington, and the format and minor corrections also appear to be AG's.

Foster-Mother here.

Berg(01) Professionally prepared TS comprising an accurate copy of the corrected NLI 8777(11).

Foster-Mother here; Darmuid spelling appears occasionally.

The first complete copy of the "old version" (that is, before around October 10, 1900: cf. Berg[02] below).

Berg(02) TS of Act I, extensively revised and added to by WBY and GM. Is this the TS version GM promised to send WBY around October 10, 1900 (*LWBY* I 69; see *CL* II 580n for revised date)? WBY's emendations concentrate particularly on Grania and the Foster-Mother, in the way GM's letter recommends. A MS note on page 24 (fol. 25^r) refers to "the old version"—here assumed to be Berg(01).

Foster-Mother revised to Laban on TS—as in HRC(1).

[?November 1, 1900] from London: GM has read Acts I and II to a friend: cf. Berg(07) version of Act II, which shares similar paper, binding, and format (*LWBY* I 72; see *CL* II 582n for revised date.)

After [?November 17, 1900] from London: GM questions grammar of WBY's "last emendation," "The man who has come to be wed"—here made in MS revision of Berg(02) 1 (also in Berg[03] but not in subsequent texts) (*LWBY* I 74, and see *CL* II 587–588 for revised date).

Berg(05) Two-page TS variation on a passage in Act I that corresponds to Berg(02) 5–7.

Same typist as Berg(02)? Not adopted.

NLI 8777(10) b Single-page TS containing substitutions for Berg(02) 10 and 12.

Not adopted.

[?November 12, 1900] from London: GM tells WBY he has rewritten the passage about the spring spoken by Grania to the Foster-Mother (*LWBY* I 78; see *CL* II 585n for revised date). Does GM refer to the page 10 passage here? The same afterward became the site of the disputed "singing in the breasts" phrase.

NLI 8777(4) d Single-page TS containing substitution for Berg(02), folio 12^r, also numbered page 11, on unusual paper, incorporating some of GM's revisions for that page but differently developed.

Not adopted.

Foster-Mother here.

Berg(03) TS of Act I extensively but neatly revised in pencil and ink by WBY.

A selective fair copy of the revised Berg(02)—TS Laban throughout—with further modifications and the addition of a passage in which Grania speaks of springtime in the woods (fol. 12[v]).

Is this the "sufficient version" of the act that WBY sent GM on [?November 15, 1900] in the middle of their quarrel (*CL* II 586)? The circumstances might explain why it is revised by WBY alone and was largely set to one side when the collaboration resumed. The two authors picked up their exchange with HRC(1).

HRC(1) Composite TS of Act I based on Berg(02) and with reference to Berg(03), with substitute pages and further revised by GM and WBY, sometime bound into a leatherette folder with separately paginated revised TSS of Acts II and III.

Foster-Mother revised to Laban; TS Laban on substitute pages. Basis of NLI 8777(3) a.

GM's copy?

NLI 8777(3) a TS of Act I, being a modified copy of HRC(1), with substitute pages and further revised by WBY and GM, bound into a leatherette folder with separately paginated revised TSS of Acts II and III.

Laban throughout. The major rearrangements (substitute pages) are marked in WBY's hand.

The disputed phrase—"singing came into my breasts"—enters the text here on folio 10[r] (it was under dispute between November 12 and 25, 1900: see *LWBY* I 78, *LGD* 289, 291, *CL* II 592–593).

WBY's copy.

NLI 8777(3) g TS page containing single-line, keyed-in substitute for NLI 8777(3) a.

WBY to AG, [November 26, 1900]: he and GM passed Act I, but no extant version is so endorsed (*CL* II 592).

NLI 8777(3) d Single-page TS containing substitutions for Acts I and III—same typist as NLI 8777(11) but on different paper—corrected by GM.

There is slight evidence to suggest that the Act I substitution falls between HRC and Berg(99); whereas the Act III substitution appears to precede HRC, and hence the positioning of 8777(3) d here.

WBY to AG [December 9 1900] reports that GM is drafting a new scene for Act I, which he will show him that day (*CL* II 597). Not extant, unless incorporated in one of the above.

Act II

[The most extensive and confused extant record.]

NLI 8777(8) a GM's two-page scenario for Act II on Tillyra Castle writing paper.

WBY to Susan Mary ("Lily") Yeats, November 1 [1899]: he and GM have made "the first draft . . . & Moore is now writing the play out fully" (*CL* II 460–461).

GM to AG [November 6, 1899] on Shelbourne Hotel paper (Als Berg; cited in part in *CL* II 467n): "Tomorrow I will send him [WBY] Grania. I have carried the play a step further and I send it to him so that he may carry it still another step. Then I will write out a complete text."

NLI 8777(8) b, Berg(09), NLI 8777(8) c Near-continuous holograph draft by GM for a scene in the middle of Act II, on pages numbered 1–9, 11–12, and 13. WBY followed the draft fairly closely on pages 15–27 of his holograph contribution to NLI 8777(4).

NLI 30,437 Twenty-four-page professionally prepared TS of Act II in pale blue covers, with corrections by GM and WBY.

Foster-Mother here.

July 30, 1900: GM tells WBY that he has had a copy made of Act II—"It only makes twenty-four closely typed pages"—so that WBY can make his revisions more easily. "It does not differ from the last, or very slightly, but it is all together. Needs to be embellished and lengthened, but wants no new incidents" (*LWBY* I 69–70). The paper on which the original Tls is written (Berg) is identical with the unusual paper employed by NLI 30,437.

This version plays up Diarmuid and Grania's early adventures (giant, young men, apples of quicken tree), Diarmuid's awareness of Foster-Mother's controlling role, and also Grania's feelings for Finn. It may be significant that WBY's emendations are fitful.

NLI 8777(9) Twenty-five-page TS of Act II in blue covers, extensively revised by WBY.

Foster-Mother here.

This version, in a format identical with NLI 30,437, contains the structural change that GM specifically disrecommended on August 11, 1900, cited in the headnote above: the introduction of the Foster-Mother into the middle of Act II. Did GM quickly write and dispatch it to WBY in order to demonstrate a version that would not work? Both NLI 30,437 and 8777(9) employ GM's characteristic spellings: Caoilte, Diarmuid, and Aonghus.

Magic apples are revised to the berries of a quicken tree on page 4. Whoever was responsible, it might suggest that this version precedes NLI 30,437. It is unclear if the excursion represented by this pair of texts precedes or follows the composite version represented by NLI 8777(4) a+b+c, etc.

NLI 8777(4) a+b+c Composite version of Act II, made up of twenty-nine pages of WBY holograph, followed by six pages of TS revised by WBY and GM, followed by two further pages of WBY holograph.

NB the TS pages have the same format and are from the same typewriter as the first continuous TS of Act I (NLI 8777[11])—that is, are from AG's Remington typewriter at Coole.

NLI 8777(4) f Single holograph unnumbered page in WBY's hand, on the same ruled paper as NLI 8777(4) a and c, being an improved copy of GM's draft on NLI 8777(4) b, folio 36^{v}.

Berg(06) Rough TS fair copy of composite version NLI 8777(4) a+b+c+f incorporating improvements and with two pencil corrections by WBY. Evidently dictated by a person with an Irish accent (e.g "trust" for "thrust" on fols. 18, 32) who could not always read WBY's handwriting but who introduced minor substantive changes.

Foster-Mother here; Darmud/Dairmud spellings.

There are similarities in format and typing style (and revision) with Berg(01), which is the first complete copy of the "old version" of Act I (that is, dates from before about October 10, 1900).

Berg(07) Thirty-six-page TS version of Act II that derives from Berg(06), revised by WBY and with a comment and perhaps a cancellation by GM. Bound in brown-paper covers and titled in a way resembling Berg(02), the first "new version" of Act I completed before about October 10, 1900.

See above Berg(02): GM read Acts I and II to a friend [?November 1, 1900] (*LWBY* I 72; see *CL* II 582n for revised date).

Foster-Mother here.

NLI 8777(6)–(7) TS pages comprising portions of at least two versions of the complete act, plus substitute pages, the whole described by WBY as "mostly rejected." One TS version was prepared by GM before November 27, 1900, and both contain extensive corrections by WBY; both versions were cannibalized to form WBY's collage version of the beginning of Act II. See NLI 8777(4) g+h+i+j+k+l below.

Foster-Mother here.

NLI 8777(4) g+h+i+j+k+l Near-continuous text of first half of Act II cobbled together from the above sequences of revised TS pages (endorsed "Moore's latest version/Nov 27" in WBY's hand), linked by pages of WBY holograph on the reverse of funeral cards. WBY is evidently responsible for the collage, his endorsement being a description of the materials he worked with. There is evidence of at least three layers of revision.

Foster-Mother here.

WBY's insertions into NLI 8777(4) k, folio 55^r/page 20 appear to have been written in response to GM's request for the Foster-Mother to describe "what she has been doing" (e.g., "only casting a few spells taking a spell of[f] some cows which was cast upon them by etc."), so as to strengthen the "psychological" as opposed to "picturesque" aspects of play; Als from 92 Victoria Street, dated only "Sunday," though *CL* II 582n suggests October 28, 1900: NLI 8777(1). Apropos the date of NLI 8777(4) i (written on the back of funeral cards), WBY's mother died on January 3, 1900.

NLI 8777(14)–(15) Twenty-five-page TS copy of NLI 8777(4) g+h+i+j+k+l text of first half of Act II, incorporating WBY's improvements, if not always accurately.

Laban appears here, alternating with Foster-Mother. It is possible that the name changed between the different spells of typing; cf. the MS corrections in HRC(1).

NLI 8777(16) "From George Moore,/4 Upper Ely Place/Dublin" (that is, endorsed after GM took up residence in April 1901). Unnumbered TS of beginning part of Act II, poorly typed on foolscap, heavily revised by GM and WBY.

Laban here.

NLI 8777(13) Four unnumbered TS pages headed "Act 2nd" and "Page 25", revised by GM and WBY. The format resembles the professionally prepared Berg(01) version of Act I, but the typing and spelling are poor.

Does the reference to page 25 connect with a lost development of NLI 8777(16) above? There is a connection with NLI 8777(3) b, folios 30–34 below.

Laban here.

HRC(2) Thirty-page TS of Act II with corrections by GM and WBY, with some substitute and paste-over pages, at some time bound into a leatherette folder with separately paginated revised TSS of Acts I and III. A revised, improved, slightly abbreviated version of NLI 8777(14)–(15), with connections to NLI 8777(4) l and (16), that positions Laban at the beginning of the act for the first time.

Note that Foster-Mother, corrected to Laban in HRC(1), is given as Laban here in HRC(2).

NLI 8777(3) b TS of Act II, revised by WBY and GM, bound into a leatherette folder with separately paginated, revised TSS of Acts I and III. The text is connected with NLI 8777(16) and (13), that is, in part derived from them, although (16) continued to be revised afterward.

Laban here; Diarmuid/Diarmid spellings.

Act III

[Note that there are no preliminary materials in GM's hand—GM explicitly reckoned it was WBY's act more than his (see his protestation in *LWBY* I 72, and cf. 73)—and only fragmentary TSS of the act are among the materials WBY left with AG (Berg). GM did not see a copy of Act III until sometime after November 17 (*LWBY* I 73; see *CL* II 587–588 for revised date), and revisions to the TS versions of Act III up to and including HRC(3) are corrected by WBY alone.]

Berg(13), NLI 8777(10) a, Berg(14), Berg(08), NLI 8777(4) e A single, interrupted, forty-one-page TS sequence, the consecutive portions of which are made up as follows: pages 1–4 = Berg(13); pages 5–21 = NLI 8777(10) a; page 22 = Berg(14); [pp. 23–29 missing]; pages 30–32 = Berg(14); top of page 33 = Berg(08); bottom of page 34 = Berg(08); page 35 = Berg(14); [pp. 36–37 missing]; pages 38–39 = Berg(14); fragment of page 40 = NLI 8777(4) e; [p. 41 missing]. Thus, only pages 23–29, 36–37, and 41 are not represented in the continuous sequence. All pages heavily revised by WBY, in pencil exclusively up to page 10 and in ink thereafter on at least two occasions; early pages canceled with a vertical line, later pages often differently (ink). The split-pin holes (top LH corner) align through the sequence.

Did this first known TS evolve directly from discussions at Coole during and after GM's second, longer visit in September–October 1900, when "'Grania' [was] being altered a good deal" (*LGD* 281)? When GM left WBY in Dublin on October 10, WBY reported back that Act III was more than half-finished (*CL* II 575). AG continued typing versions of previous acts—"going through . . . altering Moore's words"—during the week thereafter (*LGD* 281). Although the opening page (fol. 1^r) of the present sequence is endorsed by AG, it appears not to have been put together until after WBY left Coole.

Thus, page 19 contains the phrase "I may pitch him down the stairway of the stars," also revised by WBY. This is the phrase cited *variatim* by WBY in *Aut* 322 to instance GM's insensitivity to language that was a cause of dispute at Coole. Surely, it would have been one of the phrases revised by AG as she typed? Again, page 17 contains the TS phrase, "Three wild swans were blown into the trees," deleted and revised by WBY. AG heard the passage for the first time when WBY read Act III to her as late as October 25, 1900, in London (*LGD* 283). This was also the first time she heard the end of the act (and she was disappointed by the account of Diarmuid's death)—surely the present truncated version?

NLI 8777(5) WBY's holograph version of portions of the previous revised TS version of Act

III (corresponding to pp. 1–16, 33, 34 above) in his Museum Notebook, incorporating further improvements and keyed to the previous TS. The version was made in haste: the syntax remains unresolved at many points, and several rectos have blotted onto the facing versos. The ink is the same shade of blue-black as in the page-by-page cancellations of NLI 8777(10) a, which suggests WBY canceled the TS as he progressed.

October 13, 1900: WBY reports that he and GM had worked halfway through Act III at the time GM left Dublin, three days before (*CL* II 575).

NLI 8777(8) e Improved (amateur?) TS of Museum Notebook opening of Act III, with further corrections by WBY and the instruction, "When you send me ~~the~~ your final 'Grania' send me this back./W B.Y".

Was the typist WBY himself? And the instruction addressed to AG, as she prepared her "final 'Grania'"? NLI 8777(5) and the present (8) e might have evolved alongside the previous largely canceled TS during September–October 1900.

HRC(3) TS of Act III selectively based on previous materials, with a few corrections in the hand of WBY alone, and other small marks in an unknown hand, at some time bound into a leatherette folder along with HRC(1) and (2).

Diarmuid spelling.

Basis of NLI 8777(3) c below; the several paste-over pages are also duplicated in revisions to NLI 8777(3) c.

[November 1, 1900]: GM appears not to have Act III on hand (Als Berg; *LWBY* I 72; see *CL* II 582n for date); [November 17, 1900]: GM says he has not seen Act III, which WBY is in process of writing (Als Berg; *LWBY* I 73; see *CL* II 593n for date); [December 9, 1900]: WBY tells AG that, with GM's cooperation, Act III was "finished some days ago" but still needs revision (*CL* II 597).

NLI 8777(3) c TS of Act III, revised by WBY and GM, bound into a leatherette folder with separately paginated revised TSS of Acts I and II. The text follows the corrected version of HRC(3), incorporating further revisions; and the closing sequence (Grania > Niall > Cormac > Conan) develops from HRC (3).

Diarmid spelling.

WBY's copy but revised text nonetheless closely associated with GM; the Diarmid spelling and the lines GM inserted on pages 16 and 22 appear in the later, continuously paged HRC text. The closing sequence, in particular, is revised by GM. The revised opening and closing sequence worked out below were carried forward to the first continuously paged version (HRC below).

NLI 8777(3) e Single-page holograph revision for Act III, on bifoliate lined paper, in WBY's hand.

NLI 8777(3) d Single-page TS containing substitutions for Acts I and III—apparently by AG on the Coole Park Remington, like NLI 8777(11) and 8777(4) b—corrected by GM.

[December 11, 1900]: the whole play finally "passed" that afternoon. "Now I am free again." (*CL* II 600); [December 12, 1900]: WBY reports that, though the play is "quite definately finished," Act III still "wants to be cut in one place" (*CL* II 602).

[Separate attempts to recast the ending of Act III overlap revisions of the complete act described above and revisions made to continuous versions of the play listed below. Thus, the first version listed in the present subsection may date from November–December 1900, the others from July–August 1901.]

NLI 8777(3) f Five-page unnumbered TS of closing sequence (Grania > Cormac > Conan), revised primarily by WBY but also by GM.

Berg(10) Four-page holograph by WBY on lined paper of closing sequence (Grania > Finn > Grania > Finn > Cormac etc). Copies out and develops revised NLI 8777(3) f ending.
Incorporates changes suggested by WBY around July 26, 1901: see *CL* III 95.

Berg(11) [fol. 1^{r}], Berg(15) c Three-page unnumbered TS of closing sequence (Grania > Finn > Grania > Cormac > Conan), emended by GM. Apparently based on NLI 8777(3) f.
Diarmid spelling.

Berg(15) a, Berg(11) [fol. 2^{r}] Three-page unnumbered TS of closing sequence (Grania > Finn > Grania > Cormac > Finn > Caoelte > Usheen > Finn > Cormac > Conan), expanded and revised by WBY.
Diarmid spelling.
Incorporates the further changes suggested by GM in response to WBY (Tls, July 27, 1901, Berg; *LWBY* I 85–186). The paper and distinctive ribbon color of the three-page TS are the same as in the letter. The paper and the ribbon are also the same as in the previous, Berg(11), [fol. 1^{r}], Berg(15) c, sequence, which, taken with the Diarmid spelling, suggests that both originate with GM.

Berg(15) b Three-page unnumbered TS of closing sequence (Grania > Finn > Grania > Cormac > Finn > Caoelte > Usheen > Finn > Cormac > Conan), lightly revised by WBY.
Poor quality typing (perhaps WBY on AG's Remington); Diarmuid spelling.
Clearly based on Berg(15) a, Berg(11). This is the final form.

Continuously Paginated Versions

[These versions evolve in tandem over a period extending from November–December 1900 to October 1901 that comes to overlap the revision of the ending and the incorporation of the songs.]

HRC Version sewn into card covers based on WBY's leatherette-bound version (NLI 8777[3] a+b+c), incorporating revisions, several of them on paste-up TS pages, up to about September 1901.
Diarmid spelling, except for Diarmuid on substitute leaves (fols. 7tres, 27bis, 38bis, 114bis, 116bis); also Dairmuid in WBY's holograph revisions on folios 16 and 33 [pp. 13 and 30]. Again, Caoelte spelling, except for Caoilte on substitute folio 27bis and Caolte on folio 115bis; and Aognhus, except for Angus on folio 115bis.
The original closing sequence—Grania > Niall > Cormac > Conan—follows NLI 8777(3), folios 109–111, as revised by GM. It is overlaid by the sequence: Grania > Finn > Grania > Cormac > Caolte > Usheen > Finn > Niall > Cormac > Conan.

The revisions in GM's hand made on folios 44–46 [pp. 41–43] of HRC could be the changes referred to by WBY on [December 14, 1900] (*CL* II 606–607); the revisions at the close of Act III were made during late July and early August 1901 (*LWBY* I 85) and at the opening of Act II during early August 1901 (and sent to Benson before August 27 or September 3: undated Als from GM to WBY, from Hotel Continental [Paris]: in NLI 8777[1] folder; part quoted in *CL* III 112n).

Washington Fair-copy TS of the revised HRC, unbound, incorporating the paste-over modifications and the improved ending, perhaps by the same HRC typist (early September 1901). There is only a sprinkling of minor differences that possess transmissional significance, and six minor pencil corrections and queries that are almost certainly not authorial.

Diarmid spelling.

Closing sequence: Grania > Cormac > Grania > Caoelte > Usheen > Finn > Cormac > Conan.

Berg(99) Another fair-copy TS of HRC, loosely bound, prepared while HRC was in the process of revision, amounting to a version equivalent to the tidier Washington TS. Retyped pages are inserted into the earlier part of the sequence and there is extensive repagination. Additional deletions and further revisions carried forward from HRC are made by type cancellations and inserted with a different-colored ribbon. Laban's spinning song in Act I is inserted in WBY's holograph.

Diarmuid spelling.

Closing sequence: Grania > Cormac > Grania > Caoelte > Usheen > Finn > Cormac > Conan.

The earliest state of the TS dates from sometime after December 1900, and comparison of HRC 42–43/folios 45–46 with Berg 38–39/folios 40–41 shows that the pair of TSS was revised in tandem. The final, supplemented version of Berg(99) was brought together with its present continuous pagination at about the time the Washington copy was made (early September 1901), and at this stage these two versions largely coincide. However, WBY introduced further improvements in Berg(99) during the month leading up to the first performances (October 1901).

Appendix I: Songs

Berg(04) Two-page TS substitution for Laban's spell over the ale in Act I.

The first development of the short version of the charm to be found in the HRC and Berg(99) TSS. WBY's Diarmuid spelling and same McDonnel paper as Berg(99), perhaps drafted during August–September 1901. This development proved a false start and WBY began differently on Berg(99), folio 21^{v}, improving on this different version in subsequent revisions.

Emory WBY's holograph fair copy of the new Act I Spinning Song. GM reports having received WBY's verses, and having forwarded them to Elgar, in an Als to AG dated October 10, 1901 (Berg); for his letter of the same date to Elgar, see Kennedy 177.

Accompanied in MS by the Act II song of the Blood Bond.

The Spinning Song was published with Elgar's score in 1902.

Berg(3–4) WBY's holograph fair copy of the Act I Spinning Song in AG's copy of *Samhain*, presumably written on or very soon after the opening night, October 21, 1901.

Broad Sheet Published January 1902. Printed versions of Act I Spinning Song and Act II Blood Bond, accompanied by illustrations by Pamela Colman Smith.

Appendix II: Experimental Redrafting of Act II

NLI 8777(12), Berg(12) Pages 1–17, 18–30 [for 29] of a continuous TS of three scenes for Act II. The first NLI portion contains extensive revisions by GM and a few made afterward by WBY (see note on NLI 8777[12], folio 8^v, line 10, concerning this sequence). The second, Berg portion contains revisions by GM only; note that he did not hesitate to rephrase WBY's verses. It is unclear how much of the act the rewritten scenes are intended to comprise.

Part iii of the introduction discusses how the modification of Act II originated with WBY in the weeks following the production, how GM sketched a version of the modified act in a letter to Elgar in February 1902, and how WBY afterward prepared the present, slightly different version of the same for GM to take to Paris to revise. GM's letter is given in Appendix II below prefatory to WBY's TS.

For reasons given in the introduction, part iii, the suggestion in *Ave* (*H&F* 246–254) that the original, of which NLI 8777(12) is a fair copy, was composed by GM himself, in French during September–October 1900 in the midst of negotiations with WBY and AG over an appropriate style, is mischievously misleading. The French translation in Appendix VI dates not from 1900, nor from 1902, but almost certainly from 1904 and afterward.

On Preparing an Edition of *Diarmuid and Grania*

The problem of a text that never quite came together presents a problem for an editor. The collaborators learned something from each other but the result of their collaboration is, properly speaking, an *editio interruptus*. For different reasons, largely practical or accidental, the versions that have been published are based on materials that were on hand and contain unexplained oddities and mistakes. The business of the present edition is to make the full range of textual materials available, not to construct a new edition; but, given the unusual circumstances, some observations are in order.

First, all the versions that have been published are to different degrees defective. Mrs. Yeats had shown the only complete copy she knew to Lennox Robinson, but she played down his mildly enthusiastic reaction and was disparaging about its value. She contradicted Robinson's report that Yeats said, "I think it's better than I remembered it to be,"[1] and told another correspondent, "He [WBY] looked through it in 1935 to see if it could be shaped into an Abbey production but rejected it with groans."[2] In the summer of 1946, when Mrs. Yeats asked Una Ellis-Fermor to edit the play,[3] the version Mrs. Yeats had on hand was the one arrived at in November–December 1900 (NLI 8777[3] a+b+c), and it is as well that Ellis-Fermor delayed beginning work on it, because William Becker, then a doctoral student at Lincoln College, Oxford, laid hands on the later version Moore gave to Maud Cunard (HRC) and eventually, with Mrs. Yeats's and George Moore's executor's permission, published this in the *Dublin Magazine*.[4] The Moore-Cunard version contains inconsistencies and errors, which Becker compounded and added to, while, at his instruction, the printer regularized the text.[5]

The *Dublin Magazine* version was reproduced with further patent errors in *Variorum Plays*, and later, for the first time as a separate title, with an essay-length introduction by Anthony Farrow.[6] Meanwhile, when the original on which it is based reached Austin, Texas, it was edited alongside the other version Moore gave Cunard—now HRC(1), (2), and (3)—in a doctoral dis-

---

[1]Robinson, *Ireland's Abbey Theatre*, p. 20.

[2]GY to H. O. White, Tls April 29, 1949: Trinity College, Dublin, MS 3777/118.

[3]Ellis-Fermor to H. O. White, Als April 24, 1949: Trinity College, Dublin, MS 3777/54.

[4]"Diarmuid and Grania . . . Now first printed with an introductory note by William Becker," *Dublin Magazine*, n.s., 26, no. 2 (April–June 1951): 1–41. The letter from GY to H. O. White, April 29, 1949 (Trinity College, Dublin, MS 3777/118), confirms that she had never seen a copy of the continuous typescript. She mentions proposing to have Becker make a copy for her—the copy that is now NLI 8777(2).

[5]Becker's correspondence with the editor of the *Dublin Magazine*, James Starkey, is now at Harvard: see census, Harvard(2).

[6]In *Diarmuid and Grania*, introduction by Anthony Farrow, Irish Drama Series, ed. William Feeney, vol. 10 (Chicago: De Paul University, 1974).

sertation by Ray Small.[7] The dissertation contains errors of transcription and the account of the two versions ignores their position in the larger sequence now divided between Dublin, Washington, and New York. Becker and Small failed to realize that HRC had to an extent been superseded by Yeats's additions in what is now Berg(99), and Small failed to realize how HRC(1), (2), and (3) are counterpart to the copy Yeats retained and must likewise be interpreted as part of a sequence. Finally, the most recently published version in the Scribner *Collected Works*[8] is again based on the *Dublin Magazine* text. Although it professes to be emended with reference to the Washington version, it shows no awareness of the status of this text, nor of the existence of Berg(99), nor of any other materials. The emendations in *Collected Works* are random and based on guesswork.

The narrative contained in the introduction, taken alongside the census and the chronology of manuscripts, suggests that an edited text must rest on an analysis of the three continuously paginated versions. Each developed alongside the other two, from a slightly different starting point, and each contains different improvements. At the same time, each preserves mistakes that entered at earlier times and were carried forward even while different selections of other mistakes were corrected—sometimes incorrectly! A final Moore version would be based on HRC (and Washington), the Yeats counterpart would be based on Berg(99). The names of characters would be spelled differently according to each collaborator's preference, a different selection of debated passages would be allowed if the edition was an interventionist one, vocabulary might be differently modified. Most extremely, one could argue that Yeats's version should contain a different dramatic action in the first part of Act II.

This last suggestion is not practicable because it would involve a mixed text—a patently unrevised beginning of the act connecting to the more carefully worked-over conclusion in a way constructed by an editorial stitch-up. The previous suggestions also rewind the clock too far: both authors conceded too much for anyone to separate their contributions entirely. The obvious way to produce a Yeats text is to base it on Berg(99). But then the question arises why Yeats retained a much earlier, incompletely realized version of the play for his own records and gave Berg(99), the more perfected and complete version, to Gregory. Was it elation following the play's success, or despair following open hostilities with Moore, or prudence in anticipation of a lawsuit? He seems to have buried his memory of the play, quickly and completely. He included the Laban lyric "Under the Moon" in the *Seven Woods* collection but omitted it from collections thereafter. "The Blood Bond" was to have been included in the same *Seven Woods* collection, but was canceled in proof.[9]

An edited text based on Berg(99) would require decisions to be made that Moore and Yeats were unable to reach for themselves, that they even repressed so as to avoid bad memories, and the result would likely be at odds with arguments on behalf of single-version texts that emerged during the second half of the twentieth century. In view of the use made of Washington in the most recent collation (*CW* II), one might note that, though it includes minor spelling errors, it is better punctuated than either HRC or Berg(99). The typist sometimes guesses the punctuation wrong (see census), but it is no less useful as a check and sometimes changes meaning.

---

[7]Ray Small, *Critical Edition of Diarmuid and Grania by William Butler Yeats and George Moore* (Ph.D. diss., University of Texas, Austin, 1958).

[8]*The Plays* (*CW* II), ed. David R. Clark and Rosalind E. Clark (New York: Scribner, 2001, pp. 557–607, 923–930, 955–956.

[9]*"In the Seven Woods" and "The Green Helmet and Other Poems": Manuscript Materials*, ed. David Holdeman (Ithaca: Cornell University Press, 2002), pp. xlii, 96.

The following errors are a sample of those that need to be corrected, and they make evident the work to be done.

Act I

The word "whitethorn": the second "t" dropped out halfway through the sequence of TSS, specifically at Berg(02) folio 3^{r}, HRC 2/folio 5^{r}, and Berg(99) 2/folio 4^{r} (and *DMag* 6, *VPlays* 1173, and *CW* II 558), give "whitehorn," which is nonsense. Only Washington 2/folio 4^{r} has the correct reading—perhaps on the typist's initiative.

Again, "their" for "there" in HRC 12/folio 15^{r}, line 5; Berg(99) 11/folio 13^{r}. Washington 12/folio 14^{r} adds a pencil question mark, although it does not correct.

All three complete TS versions have "peace" for "price" in Finn's opening speech—a mistake that the typist of HRC appears to have been inclined to make and that Washington and Berg(99) duplicated without noticing. See HRC 18/ folio 21^{r}, editorial note on line 7.

Laban's double exit: Yeats inserted Laban's exit into HRC(1), following her charm at page 18/folio 19^{r}, and Moore inserted the same stage direction a few lines later at page 19/folio 20^{r}. Both exits were incorporated by the typist of NLI 8777(3) a 20/folio 25^{r}, although a tentative pencil line has at some time been drawn through the first, and both were carried forward to the complete HRC and Washington TSS. Yeats canceled the first duplicated exit and then reinstated it, perhaps inadvertently when he enlarged on the charm, in Berg(99) 20 and facing folio 22^{r} and folio 21^{v}, while allowing the second exit to remain. NLI 8777(2), based on a transcript of HRC before it left London, preserves both exits, William Becker not questioning the inconsistency at this stage as he did others. The *DMag*, *VPlays*, and *CW* II printings cancel the second exit with no reference to the textual history and apparently on their own authority.

"Bristless": thus in HRC 26/folio 29^{r}, Washington 27/folio 29^{r}, Berg(99) 24/folio 26^{r}; but see Berg(02) 28/folio 29^{r}, where a penciled "e" is inserted above the word. The word contains the extra "e" up to this time, and Berg(03) 12/folio 14^{r} also gives "bristleless." Subsequent omissions therefore appear to be a mistake, although a case could be made that the authors wanted to draw attention to the word by giving it an unusual form.

The word "would" has a broken pencil underline in HRC 29/folio 32^{r}, line 10. The Berg(99) typist converted this into a firm type underline (p. 26/fol. 28^{r}). The Washington typist got it right: no underline (p. 29/fol. 31^{r}).

Act II

Even small differences between HRC and Berg should be checked with reference to Washington and also earlier TSS. Thus (1) Berg(99) 41/ folio 43^{r}, line 8, has "a", when HRC 45/folio 48^{r}, Washington 45/folio 47^{r}, and previous TSS have "the." (2) Berg(99) 42/folio 44^{r}, line 15, inserts an additional "should" which is not present in HRC 47/folio 50^{r}, Washington 47/folio 49^{r}, and earlier TSS. (3) Berg(99) 53/folio 55^{r}, line 18, mistakenly omits "are": HRC 59/folio 62^{r}, Washington 58/folio 60^{r}, and earlier TSS include it. (4) HRC 69 and 76/folios 72^{r} and 79^{r} misspell "Lochland" as "Lochlann". The first misspelling is corrected by Washington and Berg(99), but the second by Washington only.

Typists sometimes made corrections and sometimes introduced mistakes. Some errors are not patent, and some differences were not corrected by the authors; that is, the authors either missed them or allowed them, or they might even be authoritative in some way not yet understood. Differences between HRC and Berg(99) are not systematically noted, and the person who seeks to produce an edited text will have to compare all the texts assembled here in a critical manner. Such differences are for the most part noted in the apparatus attached to HRC because that text has provided the basis for all versions available up to the present time.

Act III

(1) Both HRC 82/folio 85^{r} and Berg(99) 71/folio 73^{r} have "go in search for". Washington 78/folio 80^{r} has "go in search of", which coincides with earlier versions. (2) HRC 88/folio 91^{r}, line 11, has "heard". Washington 83/folio 85^{r} corrects this to "hear" (again coincident with earlier versions); Berg(99) 76/folio 78^{r} guesses wrong and gives "heard you". (3) HRC 91/folio 94^{r} and Washington 85/folio 87^{r} have "breast" (correct); Berg(99) 78/folio 80^{r} introduces the mistaken "breasts". (4) I should emphasize that there is no evidence to suggest that Washington corrected HRC with reference to earlier TSS: in fact, the reverse is true. Thus, HRC 90/folio 93^{r} has "shen"; Washington 85/folio 87^{r} emends to "then", but Berg(99) 78/folio 80^{r} emends to "when", which coincides with NLI 8777(3) c, folio 90^{r}. Again (5), HRC 90/folio 93^{r} and Berg(99) 78/folio 80^{r} have "be come other", Washington 85/folio 87^{r} guesses "be others", but the correct emendation is probably "be some other" (cf. NLI 8777[5], folio 17^{r}; HRC[3], folio 8^{r}; NLI 8777[3], folio 90^{r}). And lastly (6), HRC 103/folio 106^{r} has the nonsensical "beatd". Washington 97/folio 99^{r} emends to "head"; Berg(99) 89/folio 91^{r} has "beard". The Berg reading coincides with earlier TSS, but this could be by chance.

Transcription Principles and Procedures

This edition is not a genetic one. Although a chronological arrangement is followed for the larger part, it is violated in three important instances. First, while the three sequences of texts beneath the headings of Acts I, II, and III are arranged chronologically beneath each heading, this does not signify that work on one act was complete before work on the next act began. Work on Act II appears to have begun early and to have interrupted and affected work on the other two acts as they in turn progressed. Second, the sequence of the pages of each text is presented as the pages appear, not in the order of composition. Yeats's addition of Laban's song to Act I of Berg(99) provides an example. Chronologically, the manuscript addition follows the typescript page into which Yeats meant it to be inserted; but here the pages follow as they appear in the text, folio 21[v] followed by the facing page, folio 22[r]. Third, a particular application of the same logic determines the presentation of typescript versions that have been shuffled together from two and, in some instances, three different sequences. These are presented as they appear in the final sequence, not as one layer of a discretely numbered series followed by a second layer, which fills in the gaps, and, in a few cases, a third layer that was imposed on the second.

In the case of palimpsests, the original version is presented first with the overlay or attachment second, numbered with "bis." Thus, the revised pages at the close of the continuously paged HRC version are presented following each of the pages they substitute for, foliated 114bis, 115bis, and 116bis. The justification of this procedure is evident where pasted-on slips cover only small parts of a page; as for instance in HRC(1), folio 13, where folio 13bis covers only four lines. The textual relationship between two of the three complete typescripts, HRC and Berg(99), is illustrated by facing the corresponding pages of transcription.

Manuscripts are transcribed literatim as far as this is compatible with sense. In particular, words are left incomplete if the authors wrote them so and the meaning is evident, but some additional characters are supplied in instances where the incomplete form is mystifying or confusing. The transcript of HRC(2), folio 22[v], supplies an example: the intention is to clarify a difficult hand while communicating the conditions under which it appears. The variations in Moore's hand—hasty or careful—do not affect his orthography in the same way. Autograph corrections in typescript are identified as pencil or ink where this is not obvious from the context. The authorship of simple deletions is frequently deducible from the way the deletions are made, but the authorship of minor corrections is not always decidable.

Typescripts are also transcribed as far as possible literatim, for reasons described in the introduction, part v. That is, the transcriptions mimic the varying format of different typists and preserve run-together words, misspellings, and typos in the originals. Nevertheless, an exact type facsimile is not attempted, and distinctions between different styles of type cancellation (by repeated "/"s or "x"s, for instance) are not preserved. The following exceptions to literal transcription of all typescripts should be specially noted:

(1) An extra line space is introduced between all speeches, whether such a space appears in the original or not, and any line space before and after stage directions is removed.
(2) The positioning of page numbers at the head of each page adjusts to the norm for each text, that is, does not mimic all minor variations of tab setting or indentation.
(3) Although words and letters that have been typed over (canceled) are reproduced when they occupy space in the text, single-letter mistypes plus overtyping are not reproduced when the resulting overtyped word makes sense.

Note that the line numbering of manuscript transcriptions—e.g., of Berg(10)—includes stage directions, but that stage directions are not included in the line numbering of typescripts.

In the transcriptions the following typographical conventions are adopted:

roman type (Times Roman)	ink in WBY's hand
roman type (Arial)	ink in AG's or GM's hand
italic type (Times Roman)	pencil in WBY's hand
italic type (Arial)	pencil in AG's or GM's hand
boldface type	typescript or print
[?]	a totally illegible word
[? ? ?]	several totally unintelligible words
[~~?~~]	a canceled and totally unintelligible word
[?and]	conjectural reading
[?this/?that]	alternative conjectural readings
ha$\left\{\begin{matrix}s\\ve\end{matrix}\right.$	"have" changed to "has" by overwriting

Cancellations of single letters, words, and sequences of words are shown by a horizontal cancellation line, ~~thus, for example.~~ When words in sequence are canceled separately the horizontal cancellation line is discontinuous, ~~thus~~ ~~and~~ ~~thus~~. When a word or phrase has been canceled, then canceled again with contiguous words, ~~the line appears thus, or thus and thus.~~ Cancellations of blocks of lines all together are shown by formalized graphic means. Type deletions are very often noted, since they can be confused with pencil or ink deletions in photographic reproduction. Though the default for holograph corrections is ink, deletions of all single characters in typed words are identified, whether in ink, pencil, or type, because such a small difference is invariably obscured in reproduction.

Yeats is manifestly inconsistent in his practice concerning the cancellation of larger groups of lines. He sometimes strikes through a whole page and is careful to include part ascriptions in the left-hand margin. At other times—most noticeably when part ascriptions are centered—his cancellation lines deliberately exclude them. The only solution appears to be to transcribe the cancellations as they stand. When cancellation lines fail to reach to the limits of a full page, though certainly intended to, they register the pressure under which he was working as clearly as missing punctuation or erratic spelling.

Finally, each transcription faces a corresponding photographic reproduction when the original materials are either holograph manuscripts or typescripts that are heavily annotated. These complete sets are signalled in the table of contents by an asterisk. Sample reproductions of all of the remaining typescripts—that is, those that are uncorrected or only lightly corrected—have also been included to display their distinctive typing styles, which can be just as revealing as holograph manuscripts.

Diarmuid and Grania

Transcriptions and Photographic Reproductions

Act I

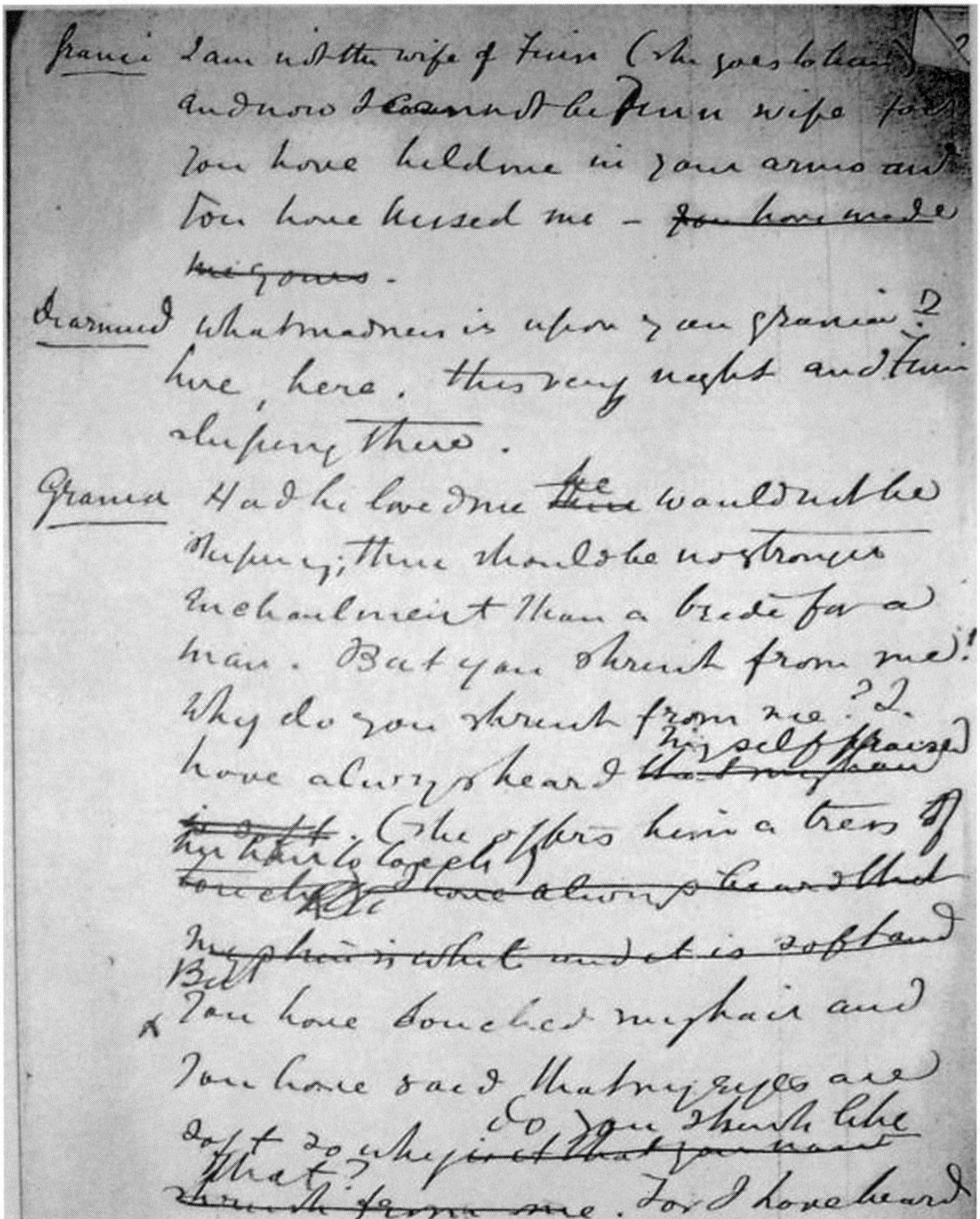

Grania I am not the wife of Finn (she goes to him)
And now I cannot be Finn's wife for
You have held me in your arms and
You have kissed me — ~~you have made me yours~~.
Diarmuid What madness is upon you Grania?
here, here, this very night and Finn
sleeping there.
Grania Had he loved me ~~there~~ he would not be
sleeping; there should be no stronger
enchantment than a bride for a
man. But you shrink from me!
Why do you shrink from me? I
have always heard ~~that my hair~~ myself praised
~~is soft~~. (She offers him a tress of her hair to touch)
~~touch it I have always heard that~~
~~my hair is white and it is soft and~~
But
You have touched my hair and
You have said that my eyes are
soft so why ~~just that you want~~ Do you think like that?
~~shrink from me~~. For I have heard

Ten-Page Draft of a Scene in George Moore's Hand

[NLI 8777(8) d, 13r]

(1

<u>Grania</u> I am not the wife of Finn (she goes to him)
{cannot F}
and now I {cant be h {inn wife for
you have held me in your arms and
you have kissed me – ~~you have made~~
~~me yours~~ –

{–
<u>Diarmuid</u> What madness is upon you Grania {?
here, here. this very night and Finn
sleeping there.

he
<u>Grania</u> Had he loved me ~~there~~ would not be
sleeping; there should be no stronger
enchantment than a bride for a
man. But you shrink from me!
Why do you shrink from me? I
my self praised
have always heard ~~that my hair~~
{of
~~is soft~~. (she offers him a tress {to
her hair to touch)
~~touch~~ ^ ~~) I have always heard that~~
~~my skin is white and it is soft and~~
But
^ You have touched my hair and
you have said that my eyes are
do you shrink like
soft so why ~~is it that you now~~
that?
~~shrink from me~~. For I have heard

[NLI 8777(8) d, 14r]

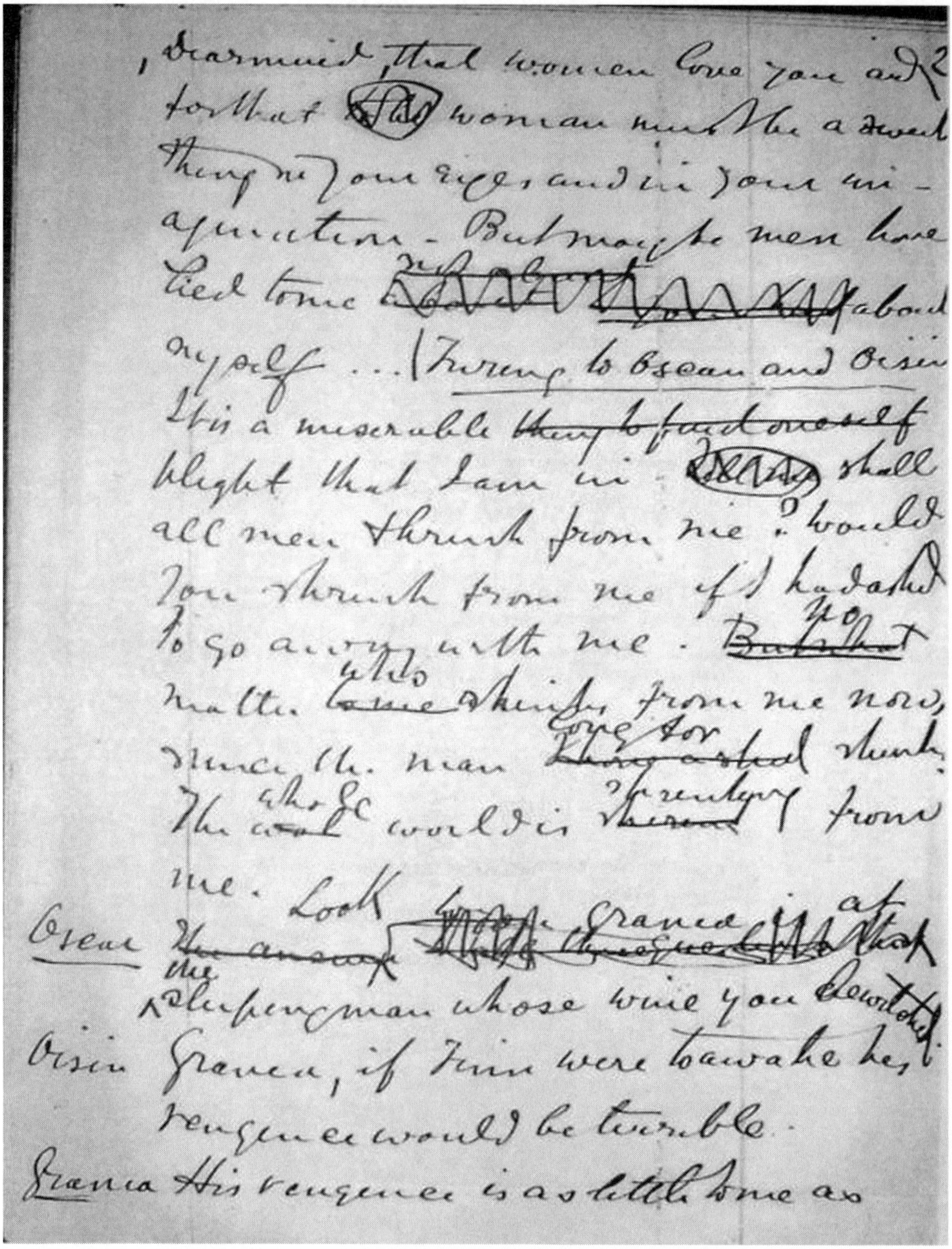

, Diarmuid, that women love you and 2
for that [circled] woman must be a sweet
thing in your eyes and in your im-
agination – But may be men have
lied to me ~~not about~~ ~~[illegible]~~ about
myself ... (Turning to Oscar and Oisin
It is a miserable ~~thing to find oneself~~
blight that I am in [circled] shall
all men shrink from me? Would
you shrink from me if I had asked
you to go away with me. ~~But what~~ not
matter ~~to me~~ who shrinks from me now,
since the man ~~I had asked~~ love for shrinks.
The ~~world~~ whole world is ~~shrink~~ shrinking from
me. Look ~~[illegible]~~ Grania ~~[illegible]~~ at that
Oscar ~~He answers~~ ~~[illegible]~~
the sleeping man whose wine you drank
Oisin Grania, if Finn were to awake his
vengeance would be terrible.
Grania His vengeance is as little to me as

[NLI 8777(8) d, 14^{r}]

(2

, Diarmuid, that women love you and
for that ~~to be~~ woman must be a sweet
thing in your eyes and in your im-
agination – But maybe men have
~~not about~~
lied to me ~~about~~ ~~you but~~ about
myself . . . (<u>Turning to Oscar and Oisin</u>
It is a miserable ~~thing to find oneself~~
plight that I am in – ~~Tell me~~ shall
all men shrink from me? Would
you shrink from me if I had asked
No
to go away with me – ~~But what~~
who s
matter ~~to me~~ w}hrinks from me now,
long for
since the man ~~I have asked~~ shrinks.
whole shrinking
The ~~wol~~ world is ~~shrunk~~ from
me.

Look ~~to you~~ Grania is at
<u>Oscar</u> ~~The answer~~ ^ ~~to all these questions that~~ ^
the
^sleeping man whose wine you bewitched.

Oisin Grania, if Finn were to awake his
vengence would be terrible.

<u>Grania</u> His vengence is as little to me as

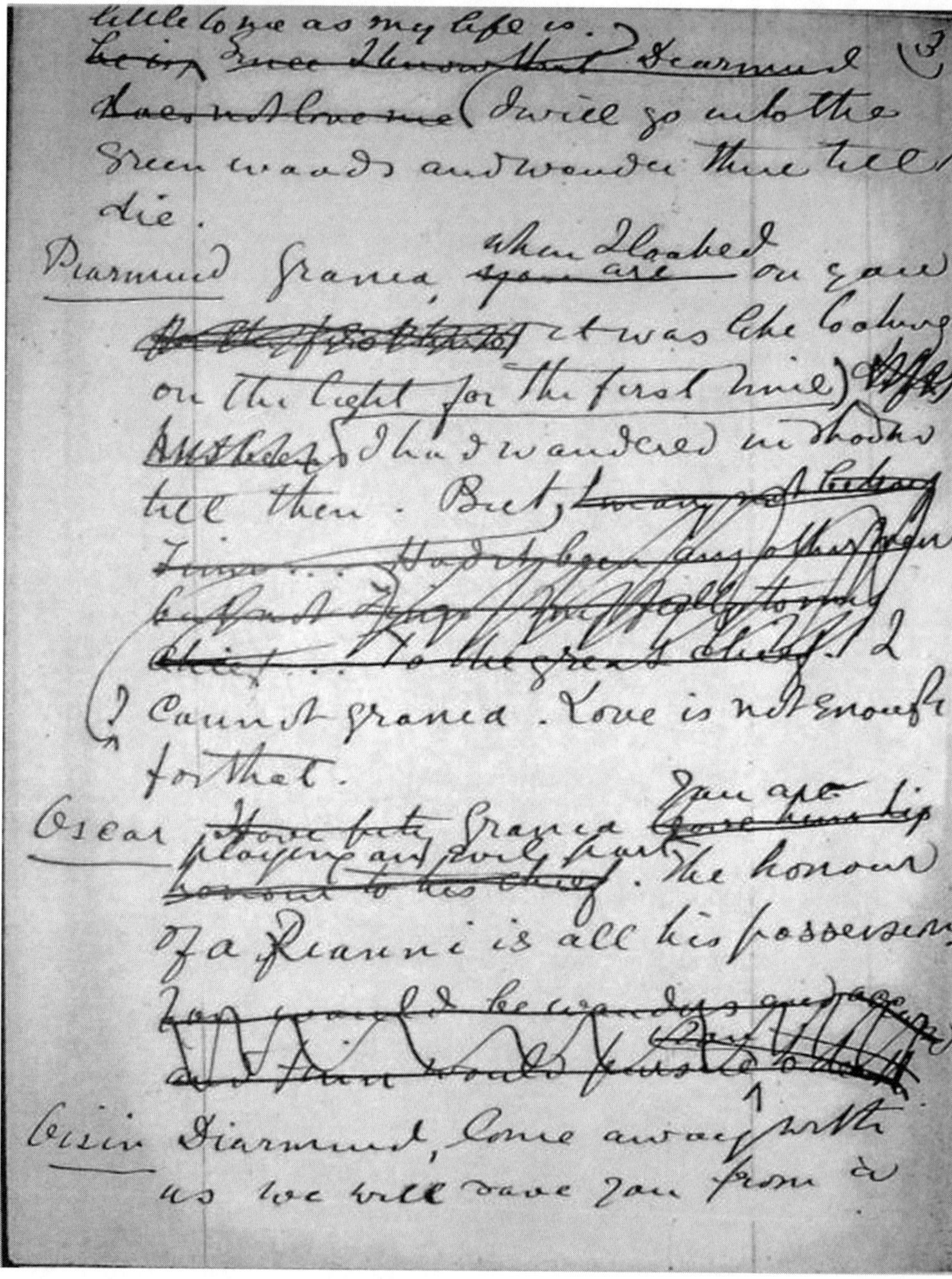
little to me as my life is.
~~being since I know that~~ Diarmuid (3
~~does not love me~~ I will go into the
green woods and wander there till I
die.
Diarmuid Grania, when I looked ~~you are~~ on your
~~[illegible]~~ it was like looking
on the light for the first time) ~~[illegible]~~
~~[illegible]~~ I had wandered in shadow
till then. But, ~~[illegible]~~
~~[illegible]~~
~~[illegible]~~
~~[illegible]~~ 2
I cannot Grania. Love is not enough
for that.
Oscar ~~[illegible]~~ Grania You are ~~[illegible]~~
playing an evil part
~~honour to his chief~~. The honour
of a Fianna is all his possession.
~~[illegible]~~ But
~~[illegible]~~
Oisin Diarmuid, come away with
us we will save you from it

[NLI 8777(8) d, 15r]

(3

little to me as my life is.
~~he is~~ ^ ~~Since I know that Diarmuid~~
~~does not love me~~ I will go into the
green woods and wander there till I
die.

when I looked
Diarmuid Grania, ~~you are~~ on you
~~for the first time~~ it was like looking
on the light for the first time) ~~but I~~
~~had been~~ ^ I had wandered in shadow
till then – But ~~I may not betray~~
~~Finn . . . Had it been any other man~~
~~but not Finn – My fealty to my~~
~~Chief . . . to the great chief~~ – L
^ I cannot Grania – Love is not enough
for that.

You are
Oscar ~~Have pity~~ Grania ~~leave him his~~
playing an evil part
~~honour to his chief~~. The honour
F
of a f }ianni is all his possession.
You would be wanderng and accursed
you
and Finn would pursue ^ to death.

Oisin Diarmuid, Come away with
us we will save you from a

1 The caret serves to cancel the dash, not the other way round.

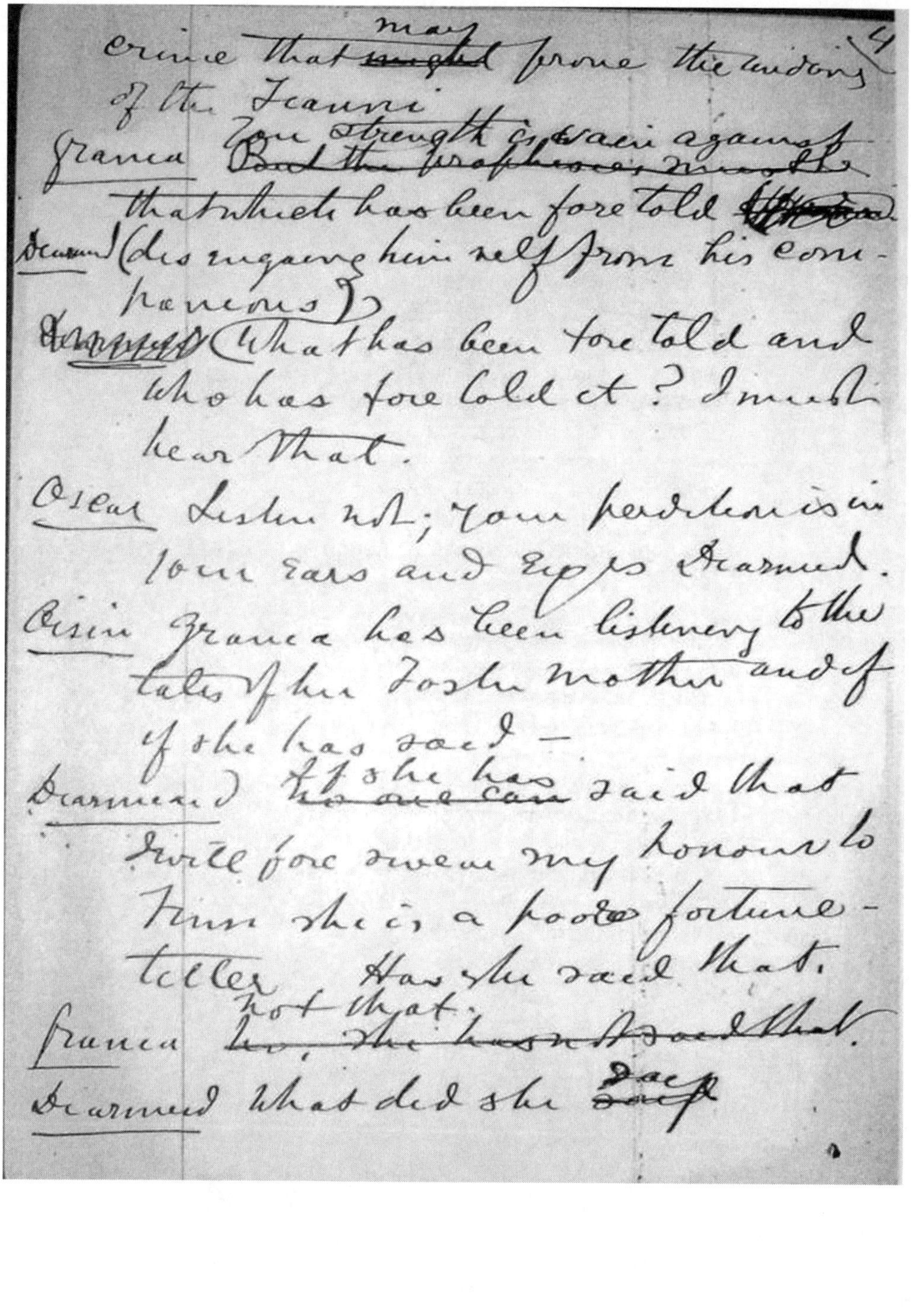

crime that ~~might~~ may prove the undoing 4
of the Feanni
Grania ~~But the prophecies must be~~ Your strength is vain against
that which has been foretold ~~[illegible]~~
Diarmuid (dis engaging him self from his companions)
~~[illegible]~~ (What has been foretold and
who has foretold it? I must
hear that.
Oscar Listen not; your perdition is in
your ears and eyes Diarmuid.
Oisin Grania has been listening to the
tales of her foster mother and if
if she has said —
Diarmuid If she has ~~no one can~~ said that
I will for swear my honour to
him she is a poor fortune-
teller. Has she said that.
Grania ~~No, she has not said that.~~ not that.
Diarmuid What did she ~~say~~ say

[NLI 8777(8) d, 16r]

(4

may
crime that ~~might~~ prove the undoing
of the Fianni

v}
You strength is a∫ain against
Grania ~~But the prophesies must be~~
that which has been fore told (~~Diarmuid~~)

Diarmuid (disengaing him self from his companions)

~~Diarmuid~~ What has been fore told and
who has fore told it? I must
hear that.

Oscar Listen not; your perdition is in
your ears and eyes Diarmuid.

Oisin Grania has been listening to the
tales of her Foster Mother and if
if she has said —

If she has
Diarmuid ~~No one can~~ said that
I will fore swear my honour to
Finn she is a poore fortune –
teller. Has she said that.

Not that.
Grania ~~No, she has not said that~~.

say
Diarmuid What did she ~~said~~

[NLI 8777(8) d, 17r]

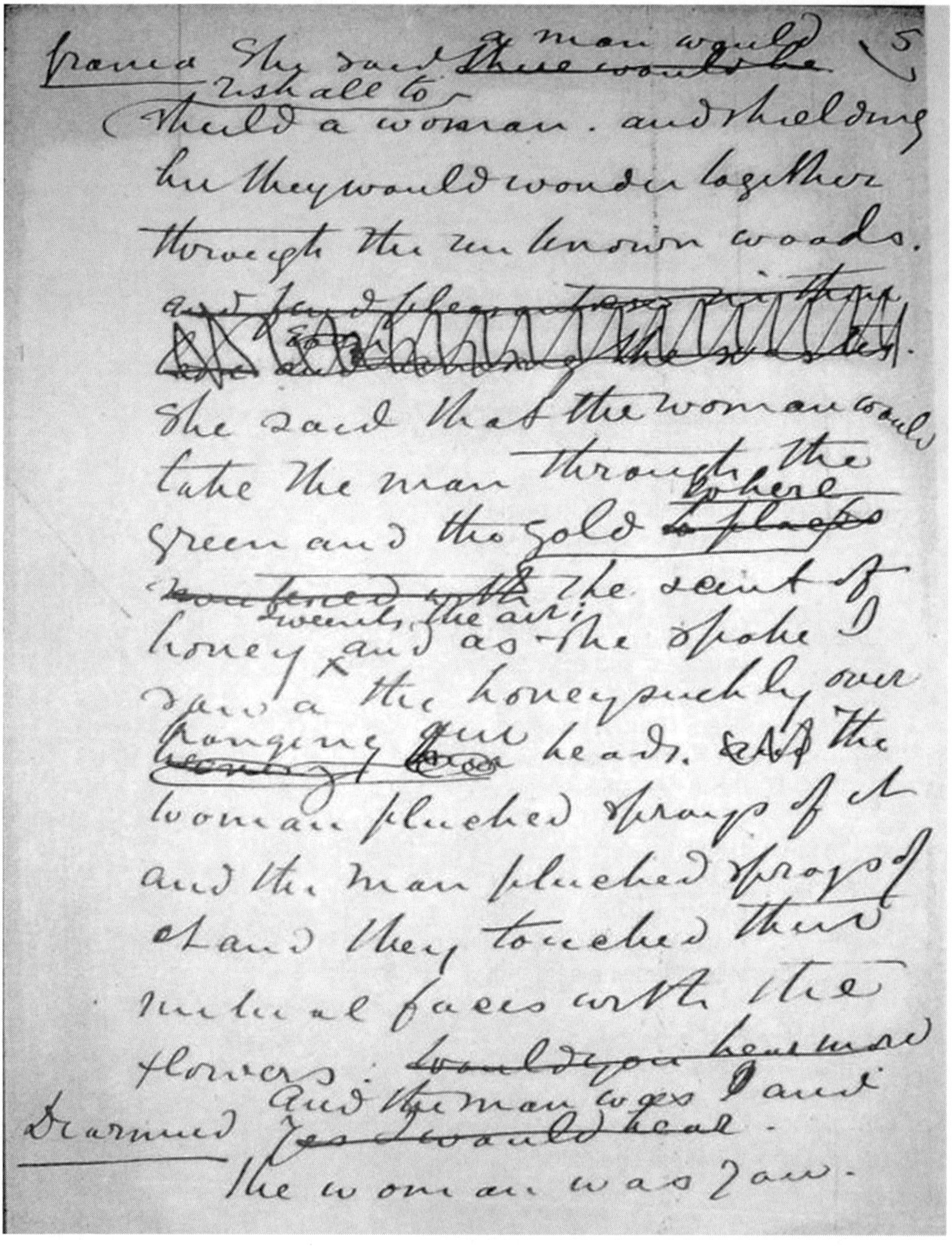
pause She said ~~there would be~~ a man would
shall to
(build a woman. and holding
her they would wander together
through the unknown woods.
~~and found pleasant [illegible] with them~~
~~[illegible] among the waters.~~
She said that the woman would
take the man through the
green and the gold ~~to places~~ where
~~[illegible] scented with~~ the scent of
sweets, the air;
honey and as she spoke I
saw a x the honeysuckle over
hanging our ~~[illegible]~~ heads. And the
woman plucked sprays of it
and the man plucked sprays of
it and they touched their
mutual faces with the
flowers: ~~would you hear more~~
Dreamed And the man was I and ~~yes I would hear~~ -
the woman was Zaw.

[NLI 8777(8) d, 17r]

(5

a man would
Grania She said ~~there would be~~
risk all to
shield a woman – and shielding
her they would wander together
through the unknown woods.
~~and find pleasantness in their~~
~~Even~~
~~love and among the wastes~~.
She said that the woman would
take the man through the
where
green and the gold ~~to places~~
~~moistened with~~ the scent of
sweets the air;
honey^ and as she spoke I
saw a the honey suck ly over
hanging our T
~~[?among] [?our]~~ heads. and t he
woman plucked sprays of it
and the man plucked sprays of
it and they touched their
mutual faces with the
flowers – ~~Would you hear more~~

And the man was I and
Diarmuid ~~Yes I would hear~~ –
the woman was you –

19–20 The substitution is written in a paler shade of ink.

[NLI 8777(8) d, 18r]

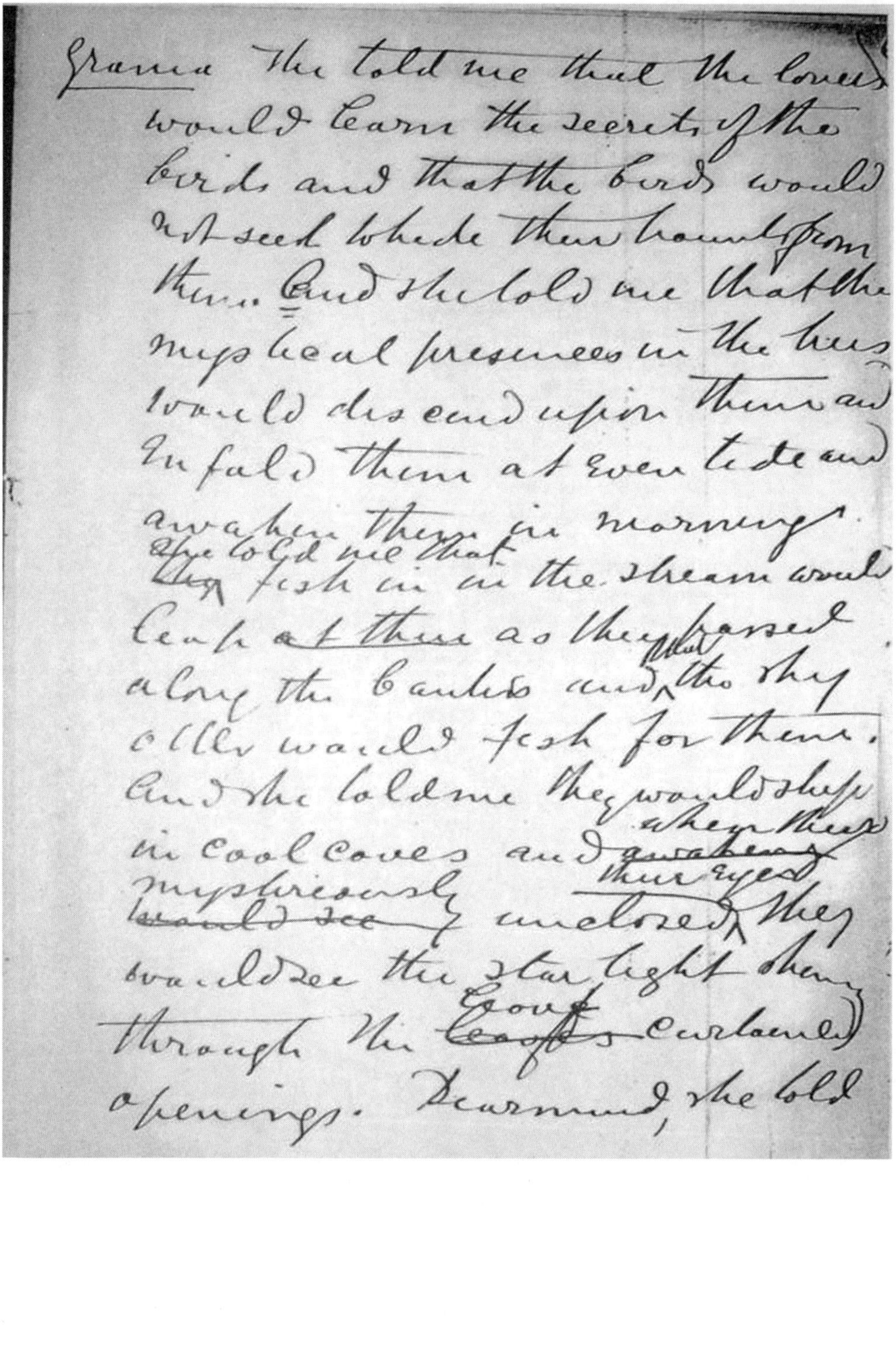

Grania She told me that the lovers
would learn the secrets of the
birds and that the birds would
not seek to hide their knowledge from
them. And she told me that the
mystical presences in the trees
would descend upon them and
enfold them at eventide and
awaken them in morning.
She told me that
~~the~~ fish in ~~in~~ the stream would
leap at them as they passed
along the banks and that the shy
otter would fish for them.
And she told me they would sleep
in cool caves and ~~awaken~~ when their
mysteriously their eyes
~~would see~~ unclosed they
would see the star light shine
through the ~~leafs~~ Grove curtained
openings. Diarmuid, she told

[NLI 8777(8) d, 18r]

(6

Grania She told me that the lovers
would learn the secrets of the
birds and that the birds would
not seek to hide their haunts from
A}
them. a}nd she told me that the
mystical presences in the trees
would descend upon them and
enfold them at even tide and
awaken them in mornings.
She told me that
~~The~~^fish in in the stream would
leap ~~at them~~ as they passed
that
along the banks and^the shy
otter would fish for them.
And she told me they would sleep
when their
in cool caves and ~~awakening~~
mystereously their eyes
~~would see~~ unclosed^they
would see the star light shining
leave
through the ~~leafves~~ curtained
openings. Diarmuid, she told

[NLI 8777(8) d, 19[r]]

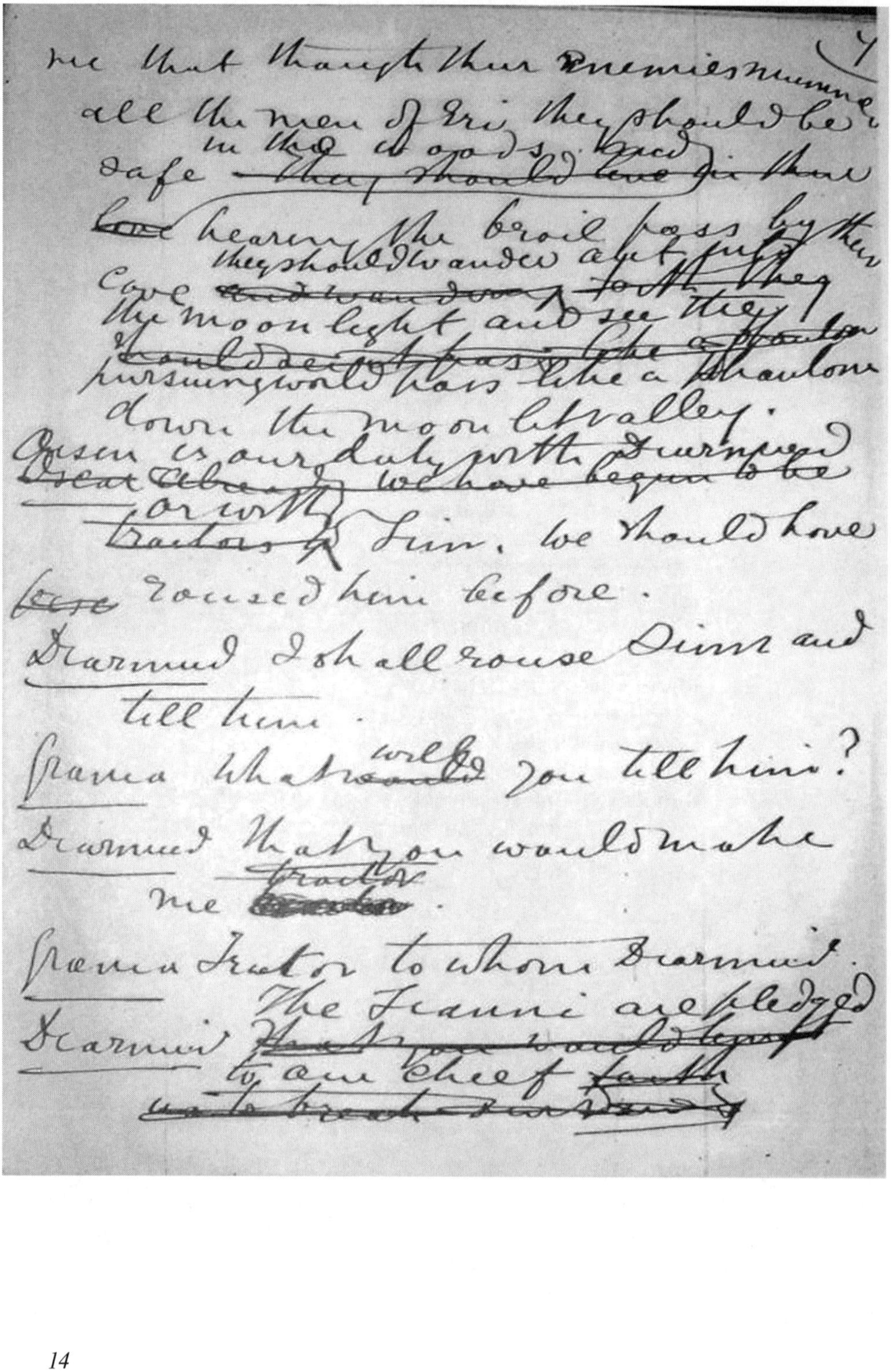
7

me that though their enemies numbered
all the men of Eri, they should be
in the woods faced
safe ~~they should live in their~~
~~love~~ hearing the broil pass by their
they should wander out into
cove ~~and wandering forth they~~
the moonlight and see they
~~should see it pass like a phantom~~
pursuing would pass like a phantom
down the moon lit valley.

Usheen Is our duty with Diarmuid
~~Great Usheen~~ we have begun to be
or with
~~traitors~~ to Finn. We should have
~~have~~ roused him before.

Diarmuid I shall rouse Finn and
tell him.

Grania What will ~~would~~ you tell him?

Diarmuid That you would make
traitor
me ~~traitor~~.

Grania Traitor to whom Diarmuid.

The Fianna are pledged
Diarmuid ~~That you would keep~~
to our Chief ~~faith~~
~~unbroken~~

[NLI 8777(8) d, 19r]

(7

1 me that though their enemies nummered
2 all the men of Eri they should be
in the woods and
3 safe – ~~They should live in their~~
4 love hearing all the broil pass by their
they should wander out into
5 cave ~~and wandering~~ ^ ~~forth they~~
the moon light and see the
6 ~~should see it pass like a phantom~~
7 pursuing world pass like a phantom
8 down the moonlit valley.

Oisin is our duty with Diurmuid
9 ~~Oscar~~ ~~Already we have begun to be~~
or with
10 ~~traitors to~~ ^ Finn. We should have
11 rousèd him before.

12 ~~Osca~~
Diarmuid I shall rouse Finn and
13 tell him.

will
14 Grania What ~~would~~ you tell him?

15 Diarmuid That you would make
traitor
16 me [?~~traitor~~].

17 Grania Traitor to whom Diarmuid.

The Fianni are pledged
18 Diarmuid ~~That you would tempt~~
to our chief ~~faith~~
19 ~~us to break our vows~~

[NLI 8777(8) d, 20^{r}]

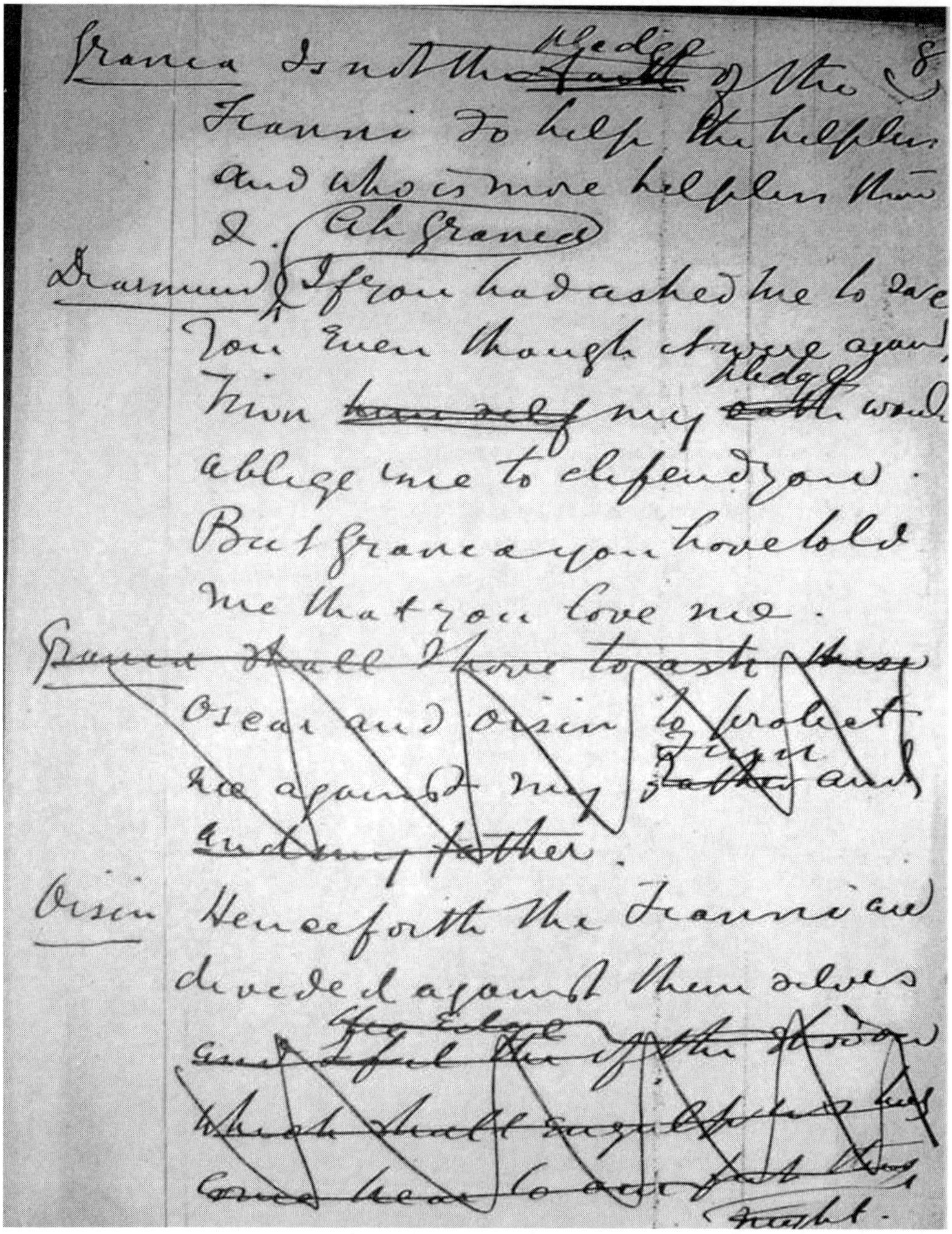

Grania Is not the ~~oath~~ pledge of the
Fianna to help the helpless
and who is more helpless than
I. (Ah Grania)
Diarmuid If you had asked me to save
you even though it were against
Finn ~~himself~~ my ~~oath~~ pledge would
oblige me to defend you.
But Grania you have told
me that you love me.
~~Grania Shall I have to ask these~~
~~Oscar and Oisin to protect~~
~~me against my father Finn and~~
~~and my father.~~
Oisin Henceforth the Fianna are
divided against themselves
~~and I feel the~~ ~~Edge~~ ~~of the sword~~
~~which shall engulf~~ [illegible]
~~come near to our~~ [illegible]
~~night.~~

[NLI 8777(8) d, 20r]

(8

pledge
<u>Grania</u> Is not the ~~faith~~ of the
Fianni to help the helpless
and who is more helpless than
I.

Ah Grania
<u>Diarmuid</u> X If you had asked me to save
you even though it were against
pledge
Finn ~~him self~~ my ~~oath~~ would
oblige me to defend you.
But Grania you have told
me that you love me.

<u>Grania</u> Shall I have to ask these
Oscar and Oisin to protect
Finn
me against my ~~father~~ and
and my father.

<u>Oisin</u> Henceforth the Fianni are
divided against them selves
the edge
and I feel the of the shadow
which shall engulph us has
come hear to our feast this
night.

[NLI 8777(8) d, 21r]

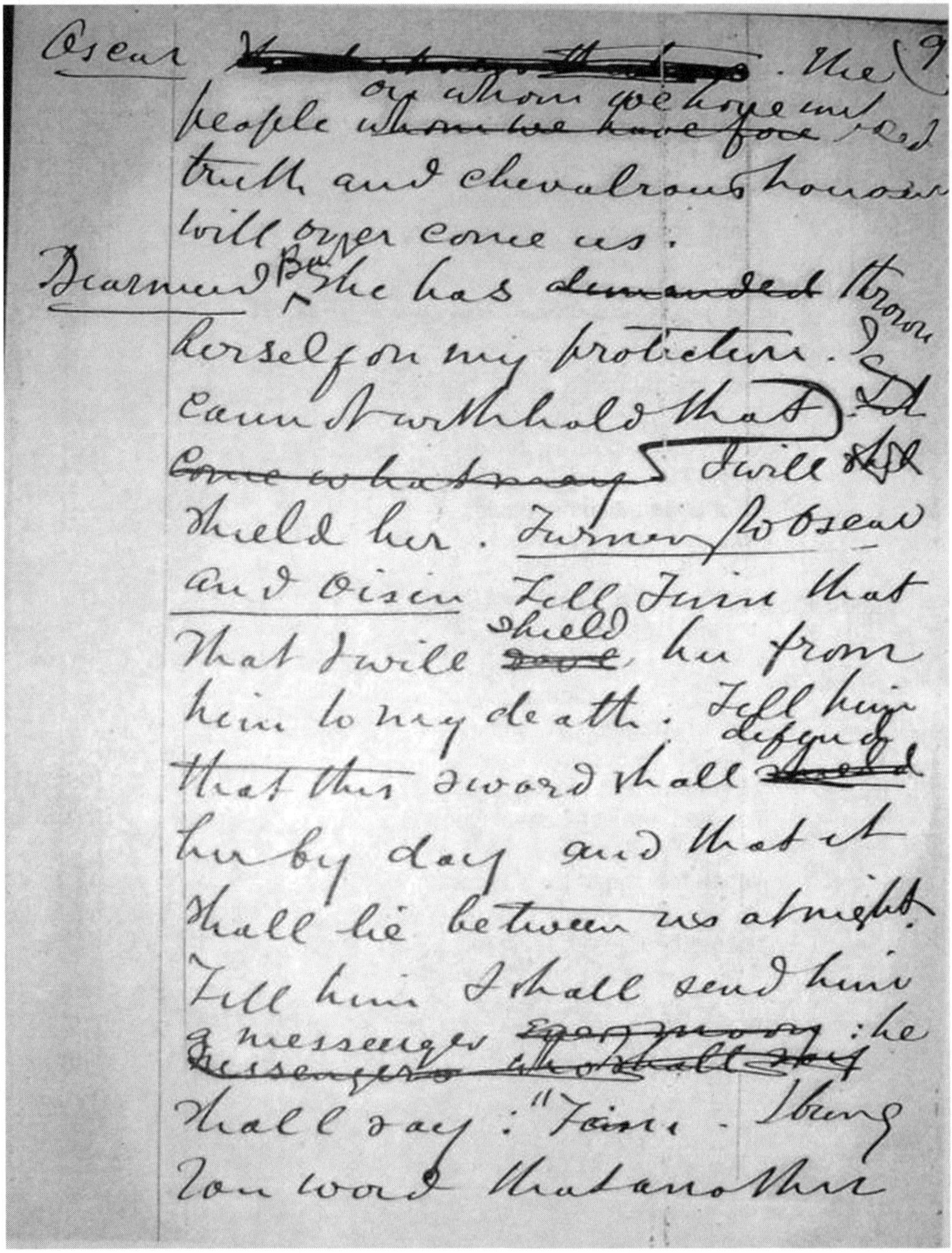

Oscar ~~[illegible]~~. The (9)
or whom we have met
people ~~whom we have fore~~ ~~sed~~
truth and chevalrous honour
will over come us.
Dearmid Be She has ~~demanded~~ thrown
herself on my protection. I
cannot withhold that ~~I~~
~~come what may~~ I will
shield her. Turning to Oscar
and Oisin Tell Finn that
that I will shield ~~[illegible]~~ her from
him to my death. Tell him
that this sword shall defend ~~guard~~
her by day and that it
shall lie between us at night.
Tell him I shall send him
a messenger ~~every moon~~: the
~~messengers who shall say~~
shall say: "Finn – bring
Your word that another

[NLI 8777(8) d, 21r]

(9

<u>Oscar</u> ~~[?The] [?darkness] [?there] [?has]~~. The
on whom we have imposed
people ~~whom we have fore~~
truth and chevalrous honour
will over come us.

But
<u>Diarmuid</u> ^She has ~~demanded~~ thrown
herself on my protection. I
cannot withhold that,– ~~Let~~
~~come what may~~ I will ~~shil~~
shield her. <u>Turning to Oscar</u>
<u>and Oisin</u> Tell Finn that
shield
that I will ~~save~~ her from
him to my death. Tell him
defend
that this sword shall ~~shield~~
her by day and that it
shall lie between us at night.
Tell him I shall send him
a messenger ~~every [?moon]~~:he
~~messengers who shall say~~
i
shall say: "Fa}nn – I bring
you word that another

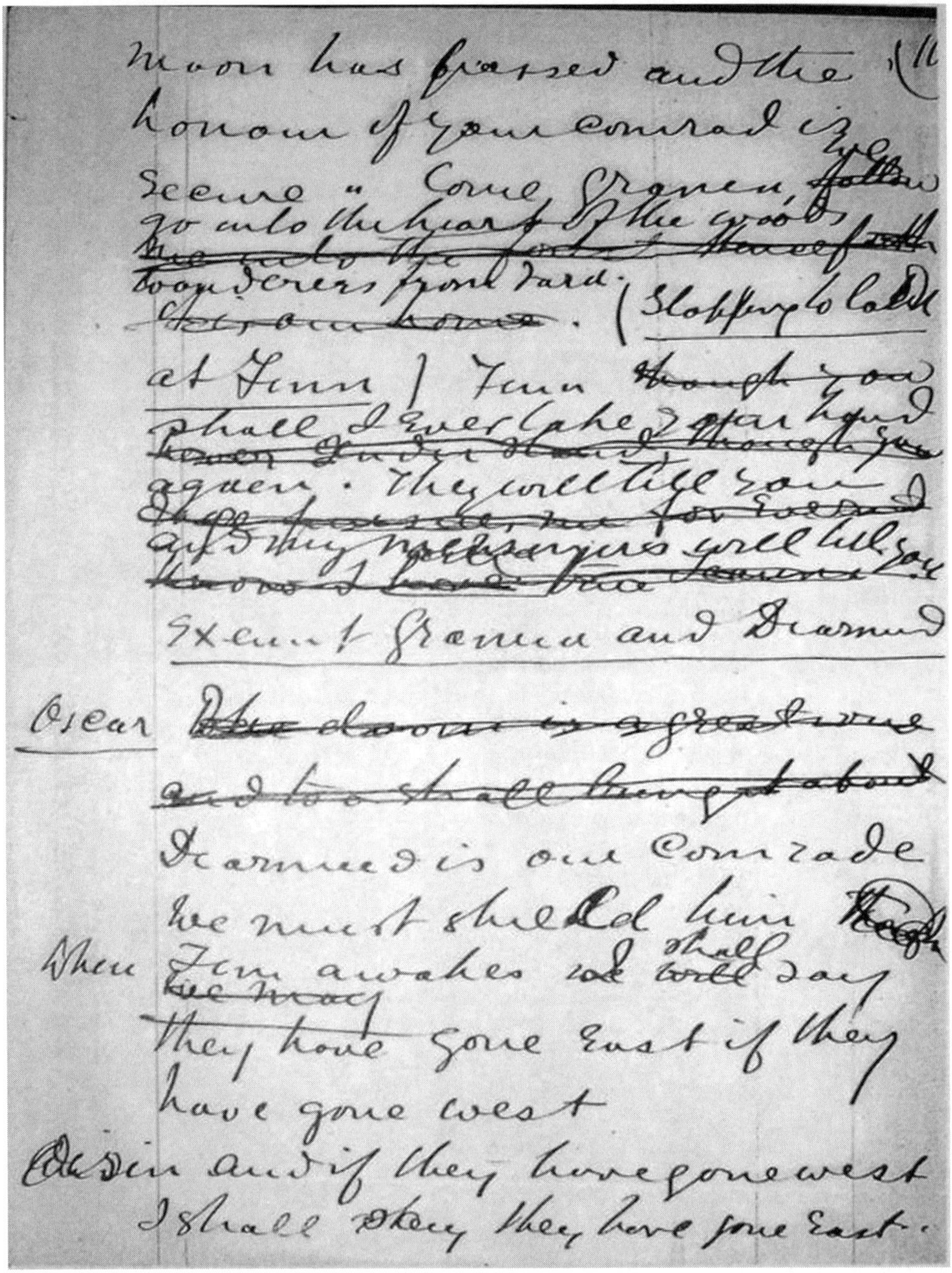

moon has passed and the (11
honour of your comrad is
secure " Come Grania, ~~follow~~ we
go into the heart of the woods
~~me into the forest~~ [illegible]
wanderers from dard.
~~[illegible]~~ . (Slipping to [illegible]
at Finn / Finn ~~though you~~
shall I ever take your hand
~~[illegible] though you~~
again. They will tell you
~~[illegible]~~
and they messengers will tell you
~~[illegible]~~
Exeunt Grania and Diarmuid

Oscar ~~The doom is a great one~~
~~and too shall [illegible]~~
Diarmuid is our comrade
we must shield him ~~though~~
When Finn awakes we ~~will~~ shall say
~~we may~~
they have gone East if they
have gone west
Oisin and if they have gone west
I shall ~~say~~ say they have gone East.

[NLI 8777(8) d, 22r]

(10

p}
1 Moon has o}assed and the
2 honour of your comrad is
we
3 secure" Come Grania, ~~follow~~
go into the heart of the woods
4 ~~me into the forest – Henceforth~~
wanderers from Tara.
5 ~~it is our home~~. (<u>Stopping to look</u>
6 <u>at Finn</u>) Finn ~~though you~~
shall I ever take your hand
7 ~~never under stand, though you~~
again. They will tell you
8 ~~shall pursue me for ever I~~
and my messengers will tell you.
9 ~~know I have true Fianni.~~
<u>Exeunt Grania and Dairmuid</u>

10 <u>Oscar</u> ~~[?The] [?charm] is a great wine~~
11 ~~and too shall bring it about~~
12 Dairmuid is our Comrade
l}
13 We must shied}d him ~~though~~
I } shall
14 When Finn awakes we} ~~will~~ say
~~we may~~
15 they have gone East if they
16 have gone west

{Oisin
17 {Osc And if they have gone west
18 I shall say they have gone East.

14 Though it may look as though GM first changed "we" to "we'l," in fact, he revised "we will" to "I shall."

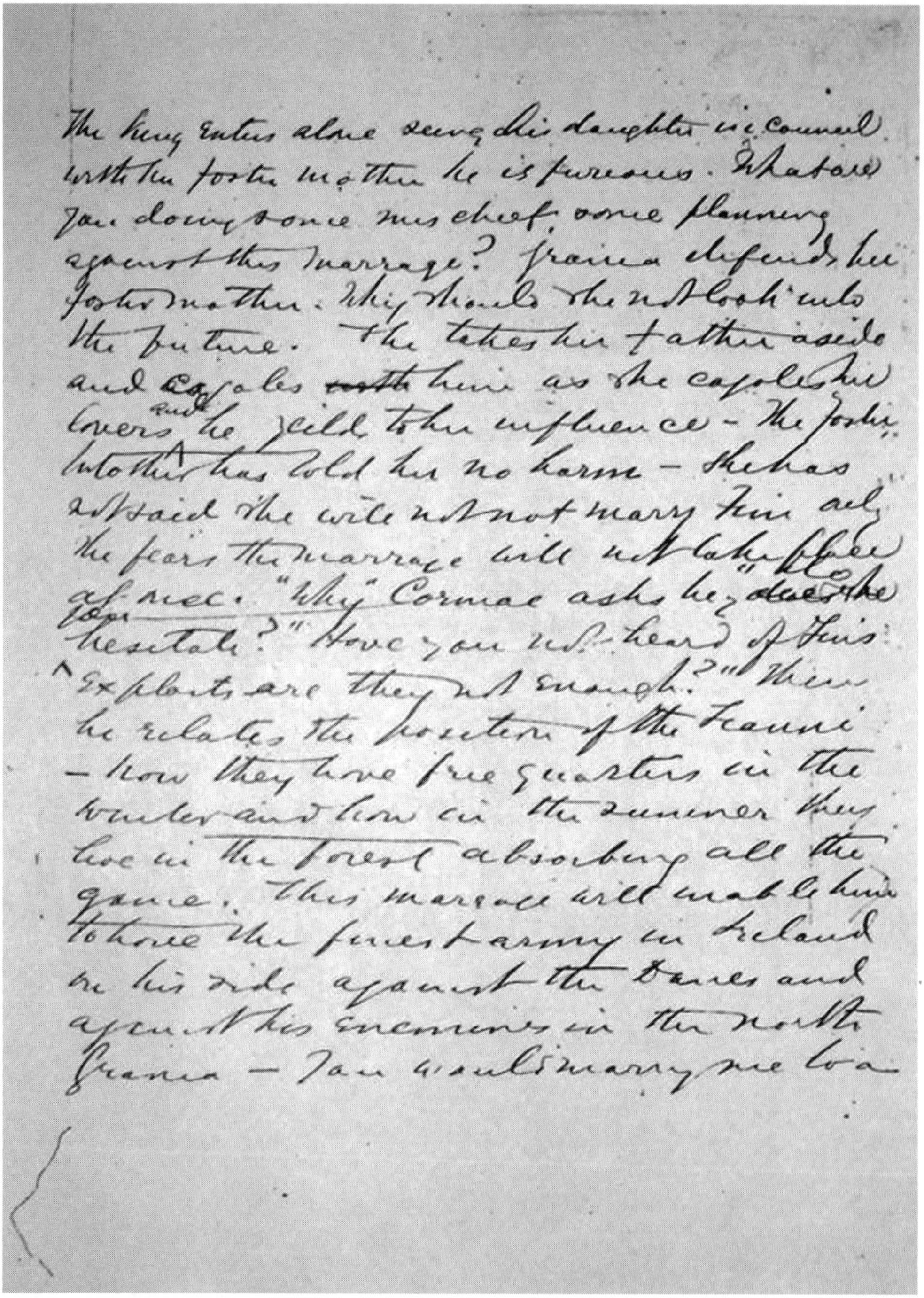

The king enters alone seeing his daughter in council with her foster mother he is furious. What are you doing some mischief, some planning against this marriage? Grania defends her foster mother. Why should she not look into the future. She takes her father aside and cajoles ~~with~~ him as she cajoles her lovers and he yields to her influence – The foster mother has told her no harm – she has not said she will not not marry him only she fears the marriage will not take place at once. "Why" Cormac asks he, "does she hesitate?" Have you not heard of Finn's exploits are they not enough?" Then he relates the position of the Fianni – how they have free quarters in the winter and how in the summer they live in the forest absorbing all the game. This marriage will enable him to have the finest army in Ireland on his side against the Danes and against his enemies in the north. Grania – You would marry me to a

Two-Page Outline of a Scene in George Moore's Hand

[Berg(00), 1r]

The King enters alone seeng his daughter in council
with her foster mother he is furious. What are
you doing some mischief some planning
against this marriage? Grania defends her
foster mother – Why should she not look into
the future. She takes her father aside
caj
and arg}oles ~~with~~ him as she cajoles her
and
lovers^he yields to her influence – The Foster
Mother has told her no harm – She has
not said she will not marry Fin only
she fears the marrage will not take place
do
at onec. "Why" Cormac asks her, "~~does she~~
you
hesitate?" Have you not heard of Fin's
^exploits – are they not enough?" Then
he relates the position of the Fianni
— how they have free quarters in the
winter and how in the summer they
live in the forest absorbing all the
game. This marriage will enable him
to have the finest army in Ireland
on his side against the Danes and
against his enemines in the north
Grania — You would marry me to a

[Berg(00), 2v]

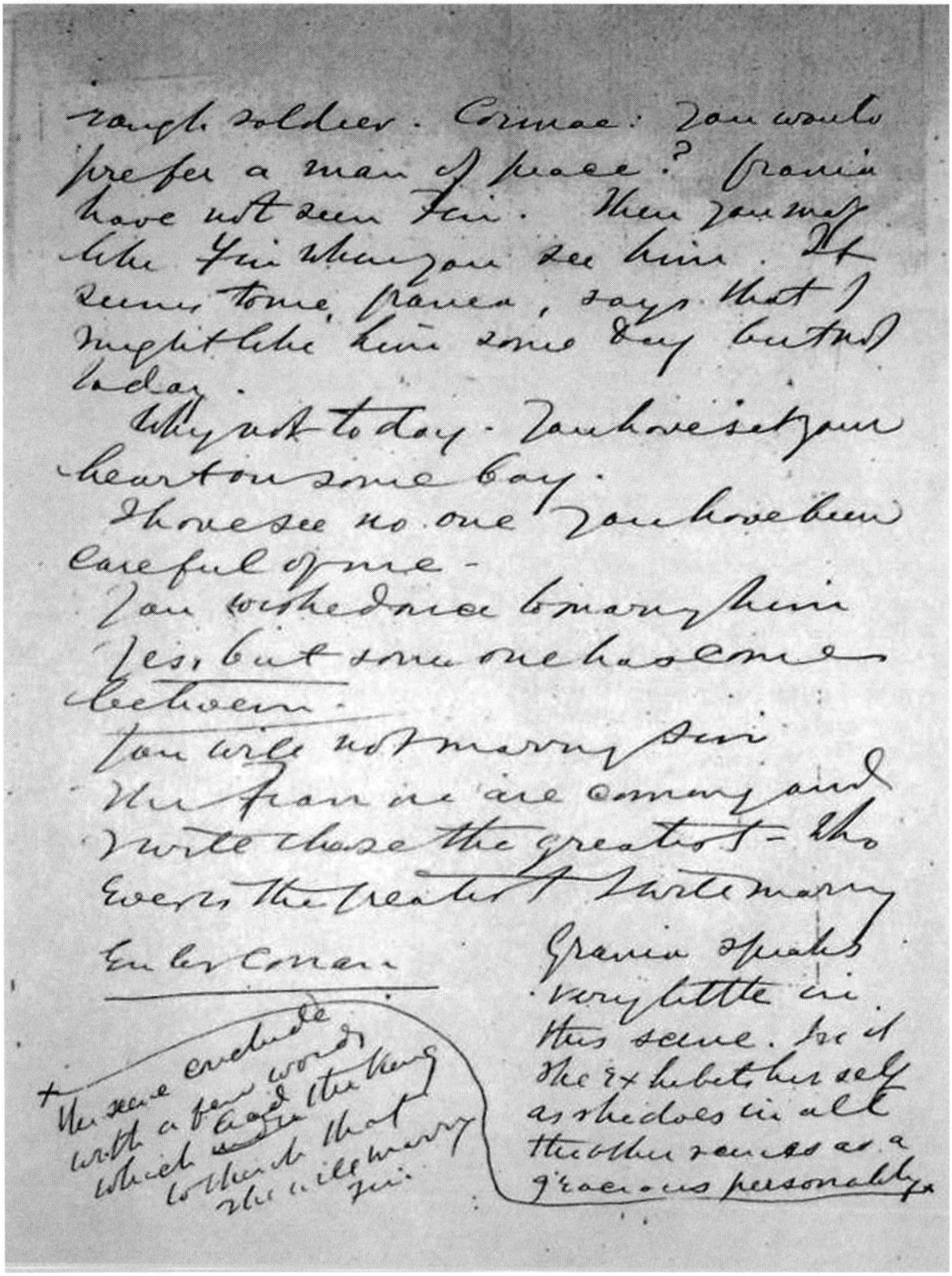
rough soldier. Cormac: You would
prefer a man of peace? Grania
have not seen Finn. Then you may
like Finn when you see him. It
seems to me, Grania, says that I
might like him some day but not
today.
Why not today. You have set your
heart on some boy.
I have see no one. You have been
careful of me -
You wished once to marry him
Yes, but some one has come
between.
You will not marry him
The Fianna are coming and
I will chose the greatest - who
ever is the greatest I will marry

Enter Conan

Grania speaks very little in this scene. Nor is she exhibit herself as she does in all the other scenes as a gracious personality +

+ The scene concludes with a few words which [illegible] agree the king to think that she will marry Finn.

[Berg(00), 2v]

rough soldier – Cormac: You would
prefer a man of peace? Grania
have not seen Fin. Then you may
like Fin when you see him. It
seems to me, Grania, says that I
might like him some day but not
today –
   Why not today – You have set your
heart on some boy –
   I have see no one You have been
careful of me –
   You wished once to marry him
   Yes, but some one has come
between.
   You will not marry him
            F
   The f }ianni are coming and
   I will choose the greatest – Who
   ever is the greatest I will marry
   Enter Conan

X The scene conclude
with a few words
lead
which ~~make~~ the King
to think that
she will marry
Fin.

Grania speaks
very little in
this scene. In it
she exhibits herself
as she does in all
the other scenes as a
gracious personality X

The curious foliation is explained by GM writing on the outside pages of a bifolium.

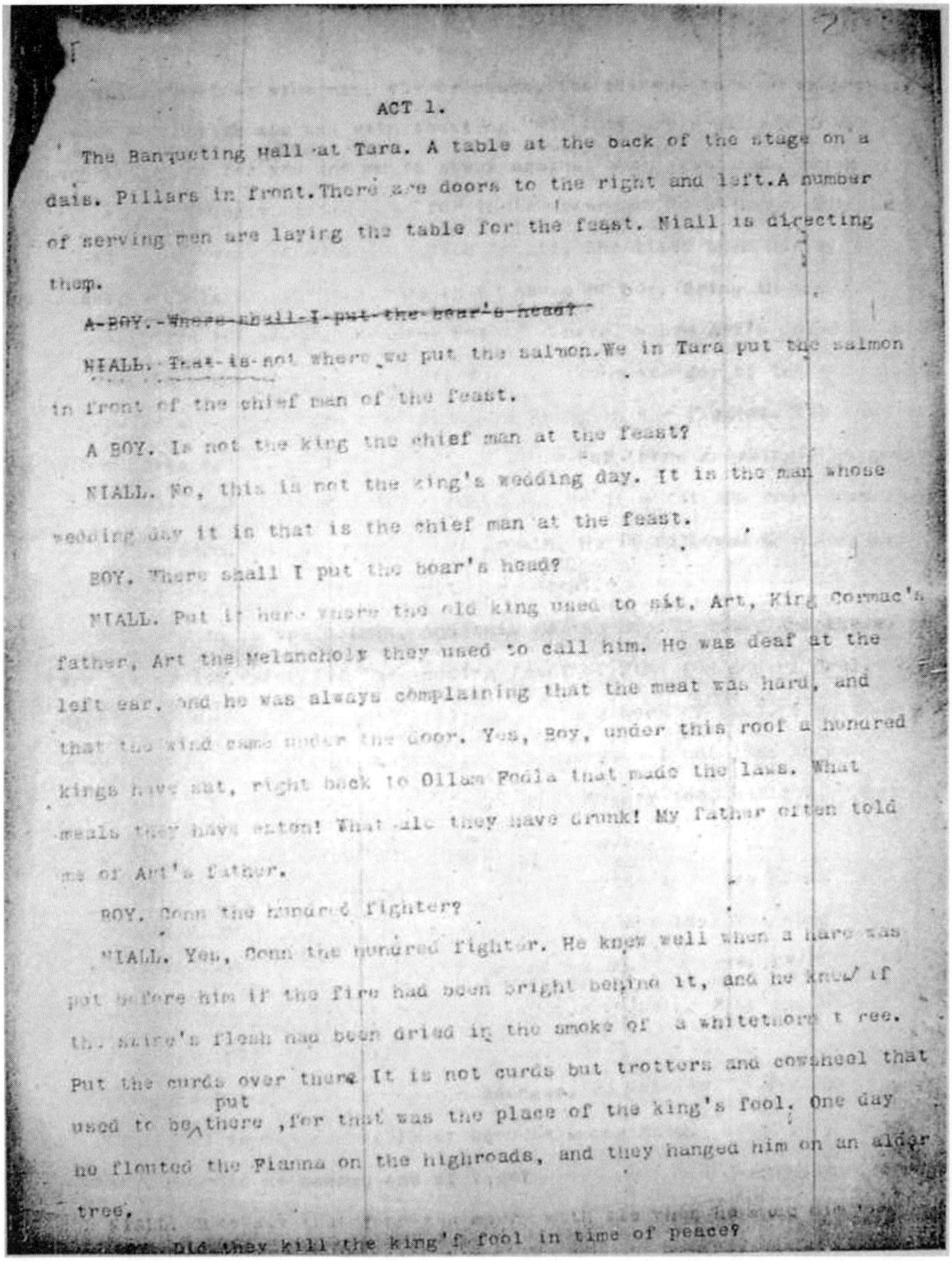

ACT 1.

The Banqueting Hall at Tara. A table at the back of the stage on a
dais. Pillars in front. There are doors to the right and left. A number
of serving men are laying the table for the feast. Niall is directing
them.

~~A BOY. Where shall I put the boar's head?~~

NIALL. ~~That is not~~ where we put the salmon. We in Tara put the salmon
in front of the chief man of the feast.

A BOY. Is not the king the chief man at the feast?

NIALL. No, this is not the king's wedding day. It is the man whose
wedding day it is that is the chief man at the feast.

BOY. Where shall I put the boar's head?

NIALL. Put it here where the old king used to sit, Art, King Cormac's
father, Art the Melancholy they used to call him. He was deaf at the
left ear, and he was always complaining that the meat was hard, and
that the wind came under the door. Yes, Boy, under this roof a hundred
kings have sat, right back to Ollam Fodla that made the laws. What
meals they have eaten! What ale they have drunk! My father often told
me of Art's father.

BOY. Conn the hundred fighter?

NIALL. Yes, Conn the hundred fighter. He knew well when a hare was
put before him if the fire had been bright behind it, and he knew if
the swine's flesh had been dried in the smoke of a whitethorn tree.
Put the curds over there. It is not curds but trotters and cowsheel that
used to be put there, for that was the place of the king's fool. One day
he flouted the Fianna on the highroads, and they hanged him on an alder
tree.

[illegible]. Did they kill the king's fool in time of peace?

The first leaf does not bear a page number but is darkened and worn.

1, 2, 17, 19, 20. The cancellation in line 1 and the underlining in line 2 are in pencil, the remaining corrections on the page in ink—in the style of the typist, AG.

Fifteen-Page Typescript of Complete Act, Revised by W. B. Yeats and George Moore

[NLI 8777(11), 1r]

ACT 1.

The Banqueting Hall at Tara. A table at the back of the stage on a dais. Pillars in front.There are doors to the right and left.A number of serving men are laying the table for the feast. Niall is directing them.

~~A BOY. -Where shall I put the bear's head?~~

~~NIALL. That is not~~ where we put the salmon . We in Tara put the salmon in front of the chief man of the feast.

A BOY. Is not the king the chief man at the feast?

NIALL. No, this is not the king's wedding day. It is the man whose wedding day it is that is the chief man at the feast.

BOY. Where shall I put the boar's head?

NIALL. Put it here where the old king used to sit , Art, King Cormac's father, Art the Melancholy they used to call him. He was deaf at the left ear, and he was always complaining that the meat was hard, and that the wind came under the door. Yes, Boy, under this roof a hundred kings have sat, right back to Ollam Fodla that made the laws. What meals they have eaten! What ale they have drunk! My father often told me of Art's father.

BOY. Conn the hundred fighter?

NIALL. Yes, Conn the hundred fighter. He knew well when a hare was put before him if the fire had been bright behind it, and he kne w if the swine's flesh had been dried in the smoke of a whitethorn t ree. Put the curds over ther e. It is not curds but trotters and cowsheel that used to be ^put^ there ,for that was the place of the king's fool. One day he flouted the Fianna on the highroads, and they hanged him on an alder tree.

BOY. Did they kill the king'f fool in time of peace?

[NLI 8777(11)]

[2^{r}]

2

NIALL. Fool or wise man, war or peace, its all one to them when their blood is up with ale and with feasting. But they are great men , B[b]oy, and it is not for you and me to speak against such great men. Bring the dishes quickly, it is time for their messenger to be here. Put th[e]d bread there, where Queen   used to sit. She liked thin barley cakes, and six men got thier death be cause of her. Bring in the flagons. (To ~~the other servants)~~ put them here, where Art's hound used to lie. (A knocking at the door). Here is the messenger of the Fianna - I knew we should not get done in time. Bring in the flagons. (To the other servants) Where are the drinking hor‿ns? (More knocking). He goes to the door and opens it. Conan comes in. He is a fat and rough man in a sheepskin, and is much out of breath. He is followed by three men who carry bundles of shields on their backs).

CONAN. This is the salmon, and this is the boar's head, and these are the barley cakes for the wedding feast of Finn the son of Cool. G[i]ove me a horn full of ale.(Niall gives him a horn of ale). I have much trouble going messages for the Fianna. Have I not legs to grow weary and body to sweat like another. I am hungry too, but I dare not put a knife in the meat till the Fianna are here.

NIALL. There will be plenty and to spare when they are here.

CONAN. You will look to the hanging of the shields. You have been in Tara these fifty years and have hung them many a time. (Turning to the men tha t are with him) Come, the sooner we bring Finn the sooner we will eat. (They go out).

B[B]OY. The Fianna have a rough messenger.

NIALL. He is the man of least account among them.

BOY. How did he become one of them?

NIALL. They say that Finn was merry with ale when he made him one

---

5 The missing name is Maeve.

7 The deletion is in pencil, the remaining corrections on the page in ink.

[3r]

3

of the Fianna. (He rushes across the stage to prevent one of the men from hangin{g}e Goll Mac Morna's shield at the lower end of the table). Would y{o}uu put Goll Mac Morna's shield below Congal's and Finmole's. Would you have the roof tree burnt over our heads ? Let me see now, let me think. It was Art the Melancholy who made this custom of the hanging up of every man's shield above his pla{c}ve, no quarrelling, everything settle{d}e. It is a bad day for Eri when the Fianna quarrel among themselves. There is no one in Tara now who is old enough but myself to remember the way things were before the coming of the Fianna. The men of Lochlann and the men of Mona and the men of Alba making us their spoil, carrying off women here and sheep there, and leaving smoke and fire behind them. Yes, yes, that is where Caoilte's shield hangs, I told you its place last time and you remember it. But I was telling yo you how the Fianna saved our women and our sheep. They fight well , but they are proud, they are very proud, it is a word and a blow with them always. I was telling you ,boy, how they hanged the High King's foll, and many and many a time they have made war on the High King himself. Finn's father, Cool, died fighting against Cormac's af{fa}ther Art the Melancholy. And because of that death,Finn kept out of the battle when Cormac was fighting against~~v~~ the men of Mona. It has been that way always, and sometimes Eri has been like a shaking sod between them. But this marriage ends all, the marriage of Finn and Grania.ends all.

){(}Enter Grania and her foater moher).

BOY. Ther e is Grania , and her foster mother.

NIALL. Quick quick, put up the rest of the shields. Come away boy, I am sorry to see that old woman come back after these many years, an old witch{,}. they say she has more shapes than one. (~~The~~ Niall and the boy go out, and are followed by the other serving men%)

GRANIA. And so you tell me that I and the man I am to marr~~y shall~~ wander fro

18 The correction appears to be by AG. The shade of blue-black ink is shared with the other minor ink corrections which appear to be in her hand.

20, 27, 28 The corrections are in ink.

[NLI 8777(11)]

[4r]

4

must wander from wood to wood and from valley to valley., and that we shall sleep under caves and under cromlechs, and that we shall seem for long as if death and change had forgotten us.

FOSTER MOTHER. Not I Grania, but Angus who spoke through me, Angus who is always busy that the harp strings may not be silent.

GRANIA. You did well to come mother, and now you will tell me who is the greatest of the Fianna.,that I may know him I am to marry.

FOSTER MOTHER. Finn is the greatest.

GRANIA. I have told you that I will not marry Finn, so tell me of another.

FOSTER MOTHER. Finn is coming to marry you tonight. There is the marriage feast,and the shields of the Fi~~n~~anna are already above theor places. Are you afraid of Finn?

GRANIA. I do not know mother. but I will not marry him. Tell me of some other who is great among the Fianna. .

Foster mother. Ther e are sevem who are greater than all others; that shield with the red otter painted upon it is the shield of Caoilte, he is taller than all the othe rs, his hair and his beard are brown, and he wears a crimson cloak over a white tunic .

GRANIA . I do not want to know the colour of his cloak or of his tunic. Is he stately and courteous and merry.?

FOSTER MOTHER. He is all these things.

GRANIA. Is he young?

FOSTER MOTHER. No child, he is as old~~as~~ as Finn. That red shield with the white deer's head painted upon it is the shiel{d}s of U s heen. He has yellow hair, and he has long white hands with fingers hard at the tips from the plucking of harpstrings, and they say no woman has refused him her love.

---

24 The correction is in ink.

[5r]

GRANIA. Is he young?

FOSTER MOTHER. He is as old as Finn. That grey shield with the raven painted upon it is the shield of Goll the son of Morna .His arms ~~and his~~ He is a great hunter, and his arms and his legs are strong as the posts of a door, and his neck is like a bulls, and his voice is like the wind, and he has the quiet of the woods in his eyes. But I see~~m~~ ~~my child that —~~m that your mind is not set upon one that is strong , but on one that is young. That wh‿ite shield with the green fish is the shield of Oscar son of Usheen. He is young and a teller of battle tales. But that silver shield with the flying white heron upon it i s the shield of Diarmuid. He is the youngest anf the comeliest of all. He has dark hair and blue eyes and light limbs and his skin is white but

ck} H}

for the frec∫les. h∫e is courteous and he is merry with women and it is said of him that he will not be~~r~~ remebered for deeds of arms but as a true lover and that he will die young.

GRANIA. It may be that I will choose Diarmuid. You must help me mother, you must not let them give me to Finn.

FOSTER MOTHER. If I am to help you , although it is your wedding night a war will be put into my mind.

GRANIA. Yes mother, you will find a way to help me. (The foster mother has sat down and begun to spin).

GRANIA. You have not told me what will come at the end of our wandering. You wave not told me what shall come to him I sill choose.

FOSTER MOTHER. It may be that I can tell you now.For tho‿se who see the beginning of a thing can tell if they watch wisely what its end will be. The flight of a raven may tell it or the chance words of a child{, . or the song of a harper, or the flax that comes from the spindle. I have seen death in a straw whirling on the road, the gods are near ~~us at the beginning of a thing.~~

6, 14, 28 The corrections are in ink.

[NLI 8777(11)]

[6r]

6

us at the beginning of all things.

GRANIA. Draw out the flax quickly ,perhaps it will tell us.

FOSTER MOTHER. It will it will, I am shivering with cold. The ~~htread~~ thread of someone I know is coming from the spindle.

(KIng Cormac comes in.)

CORMAC. How is it Grania that you have forgotten you r bracelets and your circlets and your brooch with the emeralds.

GRANIA. I do not wish to wear them father.

CORMAC. Why not child?

GRANIA. I will not wear them till I am married.

CORMAC. Yes, yes when the feast is over, when I send for you , you must wear~~s~~ them, and the chain that your mother wore.(seeing the old woman). What was that woman saying to you when I came in.? It is ~~not~~ not well to talk often with one who has so much knowledge. (To the old woman) What have you been telling my daughter?

GRANIA. I have been asking her what is going to happen.

6r The bottom portion of fol. 6 following line 15 has been trimmed off, so that the remaining leaf measures 15.8 by 20.3 cm.

3, 6, 11, 12 The corrections are in ink.

7r (opposite), ll. 10, 12 The correction in line 10 is in ink, and the first deletion in line 12 ("The men of Eri had") likewise. The second deletion in line 12 is in pencil.

[7r]

6

I am going away from this house where my mother lived, and where I have always lived. What wonder that I should ask   what is going to happen. You know that everything that she foretells happens.

CORMAC. That is true. What has she foretold you ?

GRANIA. Nothing father. She had only begun to pull out the thread.

CORMAC. I will question her. But why should I question her. You are troubled my daughter, a woman is always troubled when her marriage is
too *a man* ~~*for a husband*~~ *to marry*
at hand. Maybe you think Finn ~~a~~ rough ~~fighting man~~, I might have married you to the King of Alba ^who is a man of peace, he sent messenges ~~But~~ But Finn is more worthy to be your husband.

GRANIA. I have not seen Finn.

CORMAC. The enemies of Eri have seen him{, / .} ~~The men of Eri had~~ ~~and you~~ you know how he has held its borders against them. The men   of Eri had grown too wealthy, they had begun t{*o* / i} think of nothing but of cattle and sheep or of dancing and harp-playing, and the men of Lochlann and of Mona had begun to make us their spoil, but Finn and his Fianna have ma{*d* / ae} Eri as great as when the Red Branch was at Eman of Macha.

GRANIA. You wish me to marry as Kings and queens marry,-but I-

CORMAC,(suspiciously) You have set your heart upon some boy.

GRANI A. The f{F / }ianna are coming. I shall wed this night him who is the chief man among them in my eyes.

CORMAC. That is w{W / }ell,Finn is the chief man of Eri after the High King

(A soun{d / d} of trumpets outside. The counsellors of Cormac and the servants enter. The servants open the door. Niall stands by the door. *)*

NIALL Let Finn and his council enter.(Enter Finn,Usheen,Oscar Diarmuid &c.

Cormac. Finn is welcome to my house.

FINN. As the marriage law is, I declare the Bride price upon the threshold. I give my word to guard this kingdom against all cattle

[NLI 8777(11)]

[8r]

7

spoilers that are of the kingdoms of Eri, and to guard it before my own country from the men od Lochlann and the men of Mona,and I give my word to overthrow all kings of Eri that raise their hands against the High King. I cannot give a kings gift, for the Fianna have neither sheep not cattle nor towns nor viallges nor great store of gold or silver.

CORMAC. The bride price is worthy of Finn and of my daughter, and I give you my daughter.(Cormac takes Finn across the stage and presents him to Grania).

NIALL. (I‿n a loud voice). Let the hot meats be brought in. Let the Fianna enter.(Enter a number of men.They stand about the door.Cormac leaves Finn and Grania and goes towards the door to welcome the Finnaa.

GRANIA. There is a scar on your cheek. That is the scar made by the sword of Forgael when you overthrew the men of Aidne.

FINN. Has the tale of that battle come so for ?

GRANI . ~~I have listened for hours to my fostermother talking about your battles.~~

GRANIA. I have listened ~~for hour~~ all my life to t‿ales of your battles. (taking his hand in both her hands)This hand has overthrown many kings.

GRFINN. Grania must not praise me if she would not take my luck away.

GRANIA. Some day you will tell me about your battles. (She turns away ~~as~~ if already we‿ary of him).

FINN. Are my battles more to you than my love?
(Cormac brings Oscar,Usheen and Diarmuid towards Grania. Cormac and Finn go up the stage).

GRANIA. Ah, ~~that~~ this is Usheen. I know him by his harp. Will you sing us love songs tonight?

1–6 Folio 8 is constructed from three unequal-sized pieces of paper glued together, thereby making a larger than usual folio that required to be folded over at the foot. The first piece of paper (5.8 by 20.3 cm) contains the page number only, the second (12.9 by 20.3 cm) the present lines 1–6, and the third (21.7 by 20.3) the remaining lines 7–27.

1 In the penultimate word, the letters “m” and “y” are typed on top of each other.

12–20 Compare the alternative TS version of the same lines at NLI 8777(3), fol. 112r.

15–16, 17 The correction in lines 15–16 is in ink and, in 17, in ink over type.

OSCAR. I am Oscar, and this is Diarmuid.

GRANIA. Welcome Oscar, teller of battle tales. There is a t ale you tell - (She stands looking at Diarmuid forgetful of everything.) And

[9r]

5

This is Diarmuid .

NIALL. The meats are on the table. The King and Finn the son of Cool ~~ae re~~ are seated(The Fianna begin to take their places).

GRANIA. Let there be no sertving men at this feast. Let me pour out the ale for you and for your guests.

CORMAC. My daughter must not pour out alle for us.

GRANIA. Let me have my way father, it is the last time I will ask it. (The serving men go out, ~~adf~~Grania retirns to her foster moth er.

GRANIA. You told me mother that a way to help me would be out into your mind when the time had come. The time~~h~~ has now come. I would bid Diarmuid take me away tonight.

FOSTER MOTHER% The way has been put into your mind and into mine. Give me two flagons and I will make them sleepy.
~~FOSTER MOTHER.~~
By fire and wave and wind
Do all things to my mind
Pour sleep in cup and horn
That every sleepy head
Lie low as on i ts bed
Till the cock crow in the morn.
Give them this ale and the will sleep till the cock crows. Give it to all but Oscar Usheen and Diarmuid. (Grania passes~~a~~ along the table filling in the cups and horns. Oscar and Usheen are the last who shlo ld be served When she comes to Diarmuid she stands looking at him.

CORMAC. Why do you not fill Diarmuid's horn?

3, 8, 10, 21 The corrections are in ink (NB in line 13+ in pencil).

22–29 The lines appear on an additional piece of paper (8.3 by 20.0 cm) pasted onto the foot of the original p. 5, thereby extending the overall page size to 30.3 by 20.0/20.3 cm. Though the extended portion was folded over, several words have been lost through rubbing. The original reading is almost certainly preserved in Berg(01), fol. 19r: "Tell us a story, Oscar, and put the spilling of the ale / out of our minds. (Oscar rises from his place and takes his harp). He stands" (cf. also HRC(1), fol. 20r). Note that Oscar is made the harpist in the earlier texts, contradicting what was previously said of him—a mistake that was subsequently corrected.

[NLI 8777(11)]

GRANIA. The ale is all spilled. I will bring another flagon.

CORMAC. I do not like the spilling of ale at a marriage feast.

CONAN. It never happens but it brings ill luck.

DIARMUID. Conan sees ill luck everywhere. When will Finn take away his favour from Conan and let the Fianna give him his deserts.

FINN. Tell us a s Oscar, the s illing of the r minds. (Oscar ha

[10r]

9

touching his harp as i f uncertain what story he is going to tell)

FINN Tell us the story of the house of the quicken trees.

Oscar. Yes, I will tell the story of the house of the quicken trees. (A pause). It is gone- it went out of my mind ~~like~~ of a sudden. A new tale is coming to me. It is coming to me---I see a man lying dead- and his w{i}ife is going away with another.

FINN. What quarrel have you with me that you sho{u}ld t{e}ell such a tale at my marriage.

USHEEN. Finn, Finn, the gods are in the room,the ale has been spilled and a stramge tale has been out into Oscar's mind. Our luck is being tak taken away. (They all start to their feet).

FINN. Let us all sit down again. Let us drink and forget our thoughts of ill luck. (They all drink-

CORMAC. (suddenly sleepy and trying to rouse himself(. Let somebody else tell a story, I am growing sleepy.

USHEEN. I cannot remember any story. I too have had my thoughts taken away.

10r A mirror image of the same text appears on the verso, a result of the (black) carbon paper being rolled in upside down. Cf. fol. 13v.

3 The deletion is ink over type.

16 Note that the text ends two-thirds of the way down the page.

[11[r]]

10

CONAN. Darmuid Oscar and Usheen have forgotten their boasting stories but Conan has many a pleasant story and no one asks him for one. I will tell a pleasant story, I will tell of the death of Darmuid.

FINN. I will have no tale of death at my marriage feast. To speak of Darmuid's death may be to bring death upon him. <u>Be silent or you may take his luck away.</u>

GRANIA. (coming nearer to the table). Will Darmuid die by the sword or will he be made captive ?

~~GRANIA. Wi~~CONAN. Thank you beautiful Grania for being kind to the bald Conan. The Fianna are becoming like children, they fear everything

{ei
will take away th{ier luck, but I should not speak of Darmuid's death for it makes Darmuid afraid.

it has not made
DIARMUID. I have long known what my death is to be, and ~~I have not~~
me afraid
~~feared it~~. Tell on.

{({a
CONAN {9obsequiously) O my beautifl Grania, this is the way it w{as. Darmuid was put out to foster with a shepherd, and nobody was so beautiful as Darmuid when he w‿as a child, except the shepherds son. The shepherd's son was much more beautiful than Darmuid, ~~se~~ and his beuty made Darmuid's father jealous, and one day he crushed him to death between his knees.

GRANIA. Tell me of Diarmuid, tell me of Diarmuid.

CONAN. The shepherd wept and wept, O how he wept. And after a while he took his second son into the woods, and made a spell over him with a Druid hazel stick., and changed him into a black and bristleless boar. And some day that boar is to break out of the woods and to kill many men and many women. All the Fianna are to gather for the hunting of him, they are to hunt him round Eri and through Eri from kingdom to kingdom. O what a hunting! O what a hunting!

5–6 The underlining and the circling are in pencil.
9, 13–14 The deletions are in pencil.

[NLI 8777(11)]

[12r]

GRANIA, Tell me more of Diarmuid, tell me quickly !

CONAN. I must drink I am thirsty again.{(/)}**He drinks). Diarmuid must go out against that boar and must be killed. It was to kill him that the shepherd made the spell over his second son. He shall be torn by the tusks, he shall be bloody. His face shall be foul because it will be bloody. I would that the women of Eri could see him when he is all foul- and bloody.(He staggers). I am growing sleepy, because I have to run the messages of the Fianna.(He recoveres himself) I shall** ^*live to*^ **see him when the tusks hav**{e/e}**e torn him, ~~o~~for it has been foretold of him also that he shall not be remembered for deeds of arms, but as a lover of women. that he shall live as a lover of women and that his life shall be soon over.--Who has put witchcraft into my ale ? Who among the Fianna has done this ? (He falls).**

USHEEN. He said there was witchcraf{t/ }**in the ale, and look, they are all sleeping. Who was it that put witchcraft into the ale Grania. ?**

GRANIA. I ordered the witchcraft to be put into the ale. I ha{d/d}**d neve**{r/ }**a mind to marry Finn. But why does not Darmuid come to us ? (Darmuid comes from the table) It was for you that I ordered witchcraft to be put into the ale.**

DARMUID. For me Grania ?

GRANIA. I had never a mind to marry Finn. I am going away with you tonight, we are going away before they awake.

DIARMUID. You and I ?and you did not see me before this night %

~~I DIARMUID~~GRANIA, I desired you and you were in my thoughts before I saw you Diarmuid. You were in my thoughts Diarmuid. *(She takes him in her arms.)*

DIARMUID. I too desired you and you were in my thoughts ~~Grania.~~0 beautiful womwn! You were in my thoughts Grania. Let me look at you- Let me put back your hair- Your eyes are gray Grania, your eyes are gray ! --and your hands-

9 The deletion—like all other deletions and emendations on this page—is in pencil.

20 The pencil mark beneath the part ascription might be the beginning of an underline or accidental.

[13r]

12

but Finn, -but Finn,-but Finn. Grania,wife of Finn, why have you played with me !

GRANIA. I am not the wife of Finn. ~~S~~ (She goes towards Darmuid~~(~~.) And now I cannot be Finn's wife, for you have held me in your arms and you have kissed me.

DIARMUID. What is this madness Grania ? Here, here- this night--- and Finn sleeping there.

GRANIA. If he had loved me his love would have been stronger than witchcraft. (a pause). You shrink from me,-why do you shrink from me? Am I not desirable ? I have heard men praise me.(She holds out her hair towards him) You have touched my hair and have looked into my eyes.Why do you shrink away? I have heard Diarmuid that womwn love you, and certainly a woman must be desirable in your eyes. It may be that men ha{v}e lied to me me, and that this hair is not soft, this body delicate. (To Oscar and Usheen). Is not my plight miserable ? Shall men shrink from me ? Would you shrink from me ~~iif~~— if it was you I had asked to {*g*}to away with me? No matter who shrinks from me now, since the man I long for shrinks. The whole world shrinks from me.

OSCAR. Look Grania at the sleeping man whose ale you have bewitched.

USHEEN. If Finn were to awake he would take some terrible vengeance on this.

GRANIA, His vengeance is as little to me as my life is. I will go into the green woods and I will wander alone there till I die.

DIARMUID. When I looked into your eyes Grania it was as though~~t~~ I had been *in* ~~wandering through~~ the dark night and that I saw the dawn. But I cannot, I cannot- there are stronger,-ther e are stronger things than love.

OSCAR. You are doing an evil work Grania. The Fianna live poor and

---

A mirror image of the first six words appears on the verso, a result of the (black) carbon paper being rolled in upside down. Cf. fol. 10v.

3, 16, 24 The deletions (like the second closing bracket in line 3) are in ink.

[NLI 8777(11)]

[14r]

13

live near to death always that they may have honour. You wo{u/ }ld take Diarmuid's honour from him.

USHEEN. Come with us Diarmuid.Co Turn your eyes away from her Diarmud

GRANIA. ~~You have more~~ Your stren{gth/ }th is no more than the strength of a leaf upon a stream., for that which is to be has been foretold.

DIARMUID.(disengaging himself from Usheen and Oscar) What has been foretold? Who has foretold it?

USHEEN Do not listen to her Diarmuid. Your eyes and your ears will be your undoing.

OSCAR. Grania has been listening to the tales of her foster mothe, and if she has said{—/)}

DIARMUID. If she has said I will break my oath to Finn– if she has said I will be dishonoured ,she is no fort{u/ }ine teller. Has she said this?

GRANIA. She has not said it.

DIARMUID. Then what has she said ?

GRANIA. She has said that a man would give up all he once held dear to guard a woman from the thing she most feared and hated. She said they would wander through unploughed valleys and through unpeople{d/ }s woods,and that this woman would ~~leave~~ lead this man by the rushy margin of many streams where the ouzel flies and the otter hunts ,and that they would smell wild honey of a sudden on paths worn bythe feet of deer.

DIARMUID. And the man was I and the woman was you{?/%}

GRANIA. She told me that the ouzel and the otter w ould not fly from them, and that it would seem for a long time as if men had forgotten

---

14r, ll. 4, 19 The deletions are in ink.
11 The emendation is in pencil.

she
them. She told me that if they who are called the seven creatures,the sun
and the moon and the stars and the sea and the fire and the wind and
the dew,would love them; but it would seem for a long time as if change
and death had forgotten them.(She goes nearer to him). And she told me
Diarmuid that we would make our beds with the skins of deer under grey

[15r]

14

cromlechs and in cool ⁄ caves, and that we would wake from sleep we knew
secret *the divine*
not why, as though the ~~divine~~ people ^ of the rocks had called to us,
that we might see the starlight shining among the leaves. And she told
me Diarmuid that though our enemies were all the men of Eri they would
not find us, but that we would lie under the cromlechs and in the caves
us
watching them passing away from ^ seeking us.

USHEEN. Is our love of Diarmuid greater than our love of Finn ?
We should have awakened him before this.

DIARMUID. I will awake Finn and tell him.

GRANIA. What will you tell him?

DIARMUID. That you would make me traitor.

GRANIA. Traitor to whom DIARMUID ?

I *my*
DIARMUID. ~~The Fianna~~ have sworn to uphold ~~their~~ chief and the honour
my
of ~~their~~ chief.

you
GRANIA. Have ~~they~~ not sworn to help the helpless, and who us mo re
helpless than I?

DIARMUID. And I would have helped you even against my chief if you
had asked me, - but Grania you have said that you love me.

GRANIA. Help me Diarmuid.

USHEEN. From this night the Fianna are rent in two. The people ~~on~~

15r, l. 1 The deletion is in ink.

her but stops and looks at Finn) Finn, shall I ever look upon your face in friendship again. They will tell you, my messengers will [illegible]
(He goes out- . (b)
USHEEN (Goes to the door and looks out after them) They have gone westward towards ~~into~~ the woods ~~of the west~~
OSCAR. When Finn wakes we must tell him that they have gone into [illegible] ~~hills of the south.~~ eastward towards the sea.

[NLI 8777(11), 15[r] (continued)]

overthrown
~~whom~~ we have ~~laid the burden of upholding truth and honour will~~ tun
{*u* throw {u
upon{os and over~~come~~{os.

DIARMUID. She asked me for my help and I must give it. (To Oscar and Usheen) I will ~~guard her~~, keep her from him until my death. Tell him that this sword will guard her ~~her~~ by day, and will lie between us
him {,
at night. Tell^I will send him some messenger{m some token which will say to him,Finn I bring you word that so many hours or so many moons have passed by , and that Diarmuid's oath is unbroken. (Grania runs out through the door)We go wanderers from Tara.(He is about to follow

[NLI 8777(11), 16[r]]

15

her but stops and looks at Finn) Finn, shall I ever look upon your face in friendship again. They will tell you, my messengers will t‿ell you- (He goes out- . ~~U~~

{m *westward*
USHEEN (Goes to the door and looks out after the{.) They have gone^
towards
~~into~~^the woods ~~of the west.~~

toward
OSCAR. When Finn wakes we must te‿ll him that they have gone into the ~~hills of the south.~~ *eastward towards the sea—*

15[r], ll. 21, 22 The deletions in both lines are in pencil; the words written above each line are ?AG's ink over WBY's pencil.
24, 25 The deletions are in pencil.

16[r], l. 2[+] The deletion is in ink.
3–4 The deletions and the words written above and alongside the lines are all ?AG's ink over WBY's pencil.
6 The deletion is in pencil, and the substitution ?AG's ink over WBY's pencil.

[Berg(01), 1r]

ACT 1.

The Banqueting Hall at Tara. A table at the back of the stage on a dais. Pillars in front. There are doors to the right and left. A number of serving men are laying the table for the feast. Niall is directing them.

NIALL That is not where we put the salmon. We in Tara put the salmon in front of the chief man of the feast.

A BOY. Is not the King the chief man at the feast ?

NIALL. No, this is not the King's wedding day. It is the man whose wedding day it is that is the chief man at the feast.

BOY. Where shall I put the boar's head ?

NIALL. Put it here where the old king used to sit, Art, King Cormac's father, Art the Melancholy they used to call him. He was deaf at the left ear, and he was always complaining

64B680

The underlining of part ascriptions and the vertical margin on the LH side of each page in the present TS are inserted by hand in red ink.

Professionally Prepared Typescript of Complete Act—the "Old Version"

[Berg(01), 1r]

ACT 1.

The Banqueting Hall at Tara. A table at the back of the stage on a dais. Pillars in front. There are doors to the right and left. A number of serving men are laying the table for the feast. Niall is directing them.

NIALL **That is not where we put the salmon. We in Tara put the salmon in front of the chief man of the feast.**

A BOY. **Is not the King the chief man at the feast ?**

NIALL. **No,this is not the King's wedding day. It is the man whose wedding day it is that is the chief man at the feast.**

BOY. **Where shall I put the boar's head ?**

NIALL. **Put it here where the old king used to sit,Art,King Cormac's father,Art the Melancholy they used to call him. He was deaf at the left ear, and he was always complaining**

[Berg(01), 2r]

that the meat was hard,and that the wind came under the door. Yes,Boy, under this roof a hundred kings have sat, right back to Ollam Fodla that made the laws. What meals they have eaten! What ale they havc drunk! My father often told me of Art's father.

BOY **Conn the hundred fighter ?**

NIALL **Yes, Conn the hundred fighter. He knew well when a hare was put before him if the fire had been bright behind it, and he knew if the swine's flesh had been dried in the smoke of a whitethorn tree. Put the curds over there,it is not curds but trotters and cowsheel that used to be put there,for that was the place of the king's fool. One day he flouted the Fianna on the highroads,and they hanged him on an alder tree.**

[Berg(01)]

[3^{r}]

<u>BOY.</u> **Did they kill the king's fool in time of peace ?**

<u>NIALL</u> **Fool or wise man,war or peace, its all one to them when their blood is up with ale and with feasting. But they are great men,boy, and it is not for you and me to speak against such great men. Bring the dishes quickly, it is time for their messenger to be here. Put the bread there,where Queen used to sit. She liked thin barley cakes,and six men got their death because of her. Bring in the flagons. (To) Put them here, where Art's hound used to lie. (A knocking at the door). Here is the messenger of the Fianna– I knew we should not get done in time. Bring in the flagons. (To the other servants). Where are the drinking horns ? (More knocking). He goes to the door and opens it. Conan comes in. He is a fat and rough man in a sheepskin,and is much out of breath. He is followed by three men who carry bundles of**

[4^{r}]

of shields on their backs).

<u>CONAN</u> **This is the salmon, and this is the boar's head,and these are the barley cakes for the wedding feast of Finn the son of Cool. Give me a horn full of ale. (Niall gives him a horn of ale). I have much trouble going messages for the Fianna. Have I not legs to grow weary and body to sweat like another. I am hungry too,but I dare not put a knife in the meat till the Fianna are here.**

<u>NIALL</u> **There will be plenty and to spare when they are here.**

<u>CONAN</u> **You will look to the hanging of the shields. You have been in Tara these fifty years and have hung them many a time. (Turning to the men that are with him) Come,the sooner we bring Finn the sooner we will eat (They go out).**

<u>BOY</u> **The Fianna have a rough messenger.**

<u>NIALL</u> **He is the man of least account among them.**

[5^{r}]

<u>BOY</u> **How did he become one of them ?**

3^{r}, l. 6 Queen Maeve. Compare the gaps in NLI 8777(11), fol. 2^{r}, which the typist is copying.

NIALL They say that Finn was merry with ale when he made him one of the Fianna. (He rushes across the stage to prevent one of the men from hanging Goll MacMorna's Shield at the lower end of the table). Would you put Goll MacMorna's shield below Congal's and Finmole's. Would you have the roof tree burnt over our heads ? Let me see now, let me think – It was Art the Melancholy who made this custom of the hanging up of every man's shield above his place, no quarrelling, everything settled. It is a bad day for Eri when the Fianna quarrel among themselves. There is no one in Tara now who is old enough but myself to remember the way things were before the coming of the Fianna. The men of Lochlann and the men of Mona and the men of Alba making us their spoil,carrying off women here and sheep there,and leaving smoke and fire behind

[6^{r}]

them. Yes,yes, that is where Caoilite's shield hangs, I told you i ts place last time and you remember it. But I was telling you how the Fianna saved our women and our sheep. They fight well,but they are proud, they are very proud, it is a word and a blow with them always. I was telling you,boy, how they hanged the High King's fool, and many and many a time they have made war on the High King himself. Finn's father,Cool, died fighting against Cormac's father,Art the Melancholy. And because of that death,Finn kept out of the battle when Cormac was fighting against the men of Mona. It has been that way always,and sometimes Eri has been like a shaking sod between them. But this marriage ends all,the marriage of Finn and Grania, ^*m* ends all. (Enter Grania and her foster mother).

[7^{r}]

BOY There is Grania,and her foster mother.

NIALL Quick,quick, put up the rest of the shields. Come away, boy, I am sorry to see that old woman come back after these many years, an old witch,they say she has more shapes than one. (Niall and the boy go out,and are followed by the other serving men).

GRANIA. And so you tell me that I and the man I am to marry must

---

6^{r}, l. 13 The hand that made the insertion remains uncertain.

[Berg(01)]

wander from wood to wood and from valley to valley,and that we shall sleep under caves and under cromlechs,and that we shall seem for long as if death and change had forgotten us.

FOSTER MOTHER Not I Grania,but Angus who spoke through me, Angus who is always busy that the harp strings may not be silent.

GRANIA You did well to come mother,and now you will tell me who is the greatest of the Fianna,that I may know him I am to marry.

[8^r]

FOSTER MOTHER Finn is the greatest.

GRANIA I havetold you that I will not marry Finn,so tell me of another.

FOSTER MOTHER Finn is coming to marry you to-night. There is the marriage feast,and the shields of the Fianna are already above their places. Are you afraid of Finn ?

GRANIA I do not know mother,but I will not marry him. Tell me of some other who is great among the Fianna,

FOSTER MOTHER There are seven who are greater than all others;that shield with the red otter painted upon it is the shield of Caolite, he is taller than all the others,his hair and his beard are brown,and he wears a crimson cloak over a white tunic.

GRANIA I do not want to know the colour of his cloak or of his tunic. Is he stately and courteous and merry ?

[9^r]

FOSTER MOTHER He is all these things.

GRANIA Is he young ?

FOSTER MOTHER No child,he is as old as Finn. That red shield with the white deer's head painted upon it is the shield of Usheen. He has yellow hair,and he has long white hands with fingers hard at the tips from the plucking of harpstrings, and they say no woman has refused him her love.

GRANIA Is he young ?

FOSTER MOTHER He is as old as Finn. That grey shield with the raven painted upon it is the shield of Goll the son of Morna He is a great hunter,and his arms and his legs are strong as the posts of a door,and his neck is like a bull's,and his voice is like the wind,and he has the quiet of the woods in his eyes. But I see,that your mind is not set upon one that is strong, but on one that is young. That white shield

[10r]

with the green fish is the shield of Oscar son of Usheen. He is young and a teller of battle tales. But that silver shield with the flying white heron upon it is the shield of Diarmuid. He is the youngest and the comeliest of all. He has dark hair and blue eyes and light limbs and his skin is white but for the freckles. He is courteous and he is merry with women and it is said of him that he will not be remembered for deeds of arms but as a true lover and that he will die young.

GRANIA It may be that I will choose Diarmuid. You must help me mother,you must not let them give me to Finn.

FOSTER MOTHER If I am to help you,although it is your wedding night a way will be put into my mind.

GRANIA Yes mother,you will find a way to help me. (The foster mother has sat down and begun to spin).

[11r]

GRANIA You have not told me what will come at the end of our wandering. You have not told me what shall come to him I will choose.

FOSTER MOTHER It may be that I can tell you now. For those who see the beginning of a thing can tell if they watch wisely what its end will be. The flight of a raven may tell it or the chance words of a child, or the song of a harper,or the flax that comes from the spindle. I have seen death in a straw whirling on the road,the gods are near us at the beginning of all things.

[Berg(01)]

GRANIA Draw out the flax quickly,perhaps it will tell us.

FOSTER MOTHER It will,it will,I am shivering with cold. The thread of someone I know is coming from the spindle.

[12r]

(King Cormac comes in)

CORMAC How is it Grania that you have forgotten your bracelets and your circlet and your brooch with the emeralds.

GRANIA I do not wish to wear them father.

CORMAC Why not child ?

GRANIA I will not wear them till I am married.

CORMAC Yes,yes when the feast is over,when I send for you,you must wear them,and the chain that your mother wore,(seeing the old woman). What was that woman saying to you when I came in ? It is not well to talk often with one who has so much knowledge. (To the old woman) What have you been telling my daughter ?

GRANIA I have been asking her what is going to happen.

[13r]

I am going away from this house where my mother lived,and where I have always lived. What wonder that I should ask what is going to happen. You know that everything that she foretells happens.

CORMAC That is true. What has she foretold you ?

GRANIA Nothing father, she had only begun to pull out the thread.

CORMAC I will question her. But why should I question her. You are troubled my daughter,a woman is always troubled when her marriage is at hand. May be you think Finn too rough a man to marry; I might have married you to the King of Alba who is a man of peace, he sent messengers,but Finn is more worthy to be your husband.

GRANIA I have not seen Finn.

CORMAC The enemies of Eri have seen him,you know how he has

[14r]

has held its borders against them. The men of Eri had grown too wealthy,they had begun to think of nothing but of cattle and sheep or of dancing and harp playing,and the men of Lochlann and of Mona had begun to make us their spoil. But Finn and his Fianna have made Eri as great as when the Red Branch was at Eman of Macha.

GRANIA You wish me to marry as kings and queens marry,but I--

CORMAC (suspiciously) You have set your heart upon some boy.

GRANIA The Fianna are coming. I shall wed this night him who is the chief man among them in my eyes.

CORMAC That is well,Finn is the chief man of Eri after the High King (a sound of trumpetsoutside. The counsellors of Cormac and the servants enter. The servants open the door. Niall stands by the door).

[15r]

NIALL Let Finn and his council enter. (Enter Finn,Usheen,Oscar, Diarmuid &c.,

CORMAC Finn is welcome to my house.

FINN As the marriage law is, I declare the bride price upon the threshold. I give my word to guard this kingdom against all cattle spoilers that are of the kingdoms of Eri,and to guard it before my own country from the men of Lochlann and the men of Mona,and I give my word to overthrow all kings of Eri that raise their hands against the High King. I cannot give a King's gift,for the Fianna have neither sheep norcattle nor towns nor villages nor great store of gold or silver.

CORMAC The bride price is worthy of Finn and of my daughter, and I give you my daughter. (Cormac takes Finn across the stage and presents him to Grania).

NIALL (In a loud voice) Let the hot meats be brought in.

[Berg(01)]

[16r]

1 **Let the Fianna enter (Enter a number of men, they stand about the door, Cormac leaves Finn and Grania and goes towards the door to welcome the Fianna.)**

2 GRANIA **There is a scar on your cheek. That is the scar made by**
3 **the sword of Forgael when you overthrew the men of Aidne.**

4 FINN **Has the tale of that battle come so far ?**

5 GRANIA **I have listened all my life to tales of your battles.**
6 **(taking his hand in both her hands) This hand has overthrown**
7 **many kings.**

8 FINN **Grania must not praise me if she would not take my**
9 **luck away.**

10 GRANIA **Some day you will tell me about your battles–. (She turns away as if already weary of him).**

11 FINN **Are my battles more to you than my love ? (Cormac brings Oscar, Usheen and Diarmuid towards Grania. Cormac and Finn go up the stage).**

[17r]

1 GRANIA **Ah, this is Usheen.I know him by his harp. Will you**
2 **sing us love songs to-night ?**

3 OSCAR **I am Oscar,and this is Diarmuid.**

4 GRANIA **Welcome Oscar,teller of battle tales. There is a tale**
5 **you tell – (She stands looking at Diarmuid forgetful of**
6 **everything) And this is Diarmuid.**

7 NIALL **Themeats are on the table. The king and Finn the son**
8 **of Cool are seated (The Fianna begin to take their places).**

9 GRANIA **Let there be no serving men at this feast. Let me pour**
10 **out the ale for you and for your guests.**

11 CORMAC **My daughter must not pour out ale for us.**

12 GRANIA **Let me have my way father,it is the last time I will**
13 **ask it. (The serving men go out, Grania returns to her foster mother).**

<u>GRANIA</u> You told me mother that a way to help me would be out into your mind when the time had come. The time has now come. I would bid Diarmuid take me away to-night.

[18r]

<u>FOSTER MOTHER</u> The way has been put into your mind and into mine. Give me two flagons and I will make them sleepy.

By fire and wave and wind
Do all things to my mind
Pour sleep in cup and horn
That every sleepy head–
Lie low as on its bed,
Till the cock crow in the morn.

Give them this ale and they will sleep till the cock crows. Give it to all but Oscar Usheen and Diarmuid. (Grania passes along the table filling the cups and horns. Oscar and Usheen are the last who should be served. When she comes to Diarmuid she stands looking at him.)

<u>CORMAC</u> Why do you not fill Diarmuid's horn ?

<u>GRANIA</u> The ale is all spilled. I will bring another flagon.

<u>CORMAC</u> I do not like the spilling of ale at a marriage feast.

[19r]

<u>CONAN</u> It never happens but it brings ill luck.

<u>DIARMUID</u> Conan sees ill luck everywhere. When will Finn take away his favour from Conan and let the Fianna give him his deserts.

<u>FINN</u> Tell us a story Oscar,and put the spilling of the ale out of ourminds (Oscar rises from his place and takes his harp). He stands touching his harp as if uncertain what story he is going to tell.

<u>FINN</u> Tell us the story of the house of the quicken trees.

<u>OSCAR</u> Yes, I will tell the story of the house of the quicken trees. (A pause) It is gone, it went out of my mind of a sudden. A new tale is coming to me. It is coming to me– I see a man lying dead – and his wife is going away with another.

[Berg(01)]

FINN What quarrel have you with me that you should tell such a tale at my marriage.

[20r]

USHEEN Finn,Finn, the gods are in the room,the ale has been spilled and a strange tale has been out into Oscar's mind. Our luck is being taken away (They all start to their feet)

FINN Let us all sit down again. Let us drink and forget our thoughts of ill luck. (They all drink)–

CORMAC (Suddenly sleepy and trying to rouse himself) Let somebody else tell a story,I am growing sleepy.

USHEEN I cannot remember any story. I too have had my thoughts taken away.

CONAN Diarmuid Oscar and Usheen have forgotten their boasting stories but Conan has many a pleasant story and no one asks him for one. I will tell a pleasant story,I will tell of the death of Darmuid.

FINN I will have no tale of death at my marriage feast. To speak of Darmuid's death may be to bring death upon him. Be silent or you may take his luck away.

[21r]

GRANIA (Coming nearer to the table). Will Darmuid die by the sword or will he be made captive ?

CONAN Thank you beautiful Grania for being kind to the bald Conan. The Fianna are becoming like children. They fear everything will take away their luck,but I should not speak of Darmuid's death for it makes Darmuid afraid.

DARMUID I have long known what my death is to be,and it has not made me afraid; Tell on.

CONAN (obsequiously) Oh my beautiful Grania,this is the way it was. Darmuid was put out to foster with a shepherd,and nobody was so beautiful as Darmuid when he was a child,except the shepherd's son. The shepherd's son was much more beautiful than Darmuid, and his beauty made Darmuid's father jealous,and one day he crushed him to death between his knees.

GRANIA **Tell me of Diarmuid, tell me of Diarmuid.**

[22r]

CONAN **The shepherd wept and wept, Oh how he wept. And after a while he took his second son into the woods,and made a spell over him with a Druid hazel stick,and changed him into a black and bristleless boar. And some day that boar is to break out of the woods and to kill many men and many women. All the Fianna are to gather for the hunting of him,they are to hunt him round Eri and through Eri from kingdom to kingdom. O what a hunting! O what a hunting !**

GRANIA **Tell me more of Diarmuid, tell me quickly ?**

CONAN **I must drink I am thirsty again (He drinks) Diarmuid must go out against that boar and must be killed. It was to kill him that the shepherd made the spell over his second son. He shall be torn by the tusks, he shall be bloody, his face shall be foul because it will be bloody. I would that the women of Eri could see him when he is all foul,**

[23r]

and bloody. (He staggers). I am growing sleepy,because I have to run the messages of the Fianna. (He recovers himself) I shall live to see him when the tusks have torn him,for it has been foretold of him also that he shall not be remembered for deeds of arms,but as a lover of women. That he shall live as a lover of women and that his life shall be soon over. Who has put witchcraft into my ale? Who among the Fianna has done this ? (he falls)

USHEEN **He said there was witchcraft in the ale,and look, they are all sleeping. Who was it that put witchcraft into the ale Grania ?**

GRANIA **I ordered the witchcraft to be put into the ale.I had never a mind to marry Finn.But why does not Darmuid come to us ? (Darmuid comes from the table) It was for you that I ordered witchcraft to be put into the ale.**

[24r]

DARMUID **For me Grania ?**

GRANIA **I had never a mind to marry Finn.I am going away with**

[Berg(01)]

you tonight, we are going away before they awake.

DIARMUID You and I ? and you did not see me before this night ?

GRANIA I desired you and you were in my thoughts before I saw you Diarmuid. You were in my thoughts Diarmuid.(She takes him in her arms)

DIARMUID I too desired you and you were in my thoughts. O beautiful woman! You were in my thoughts Grania. Let me look at you – Let me put back your hair – Your eyes are grey Grania,your eyes are grey ! and your hands – but Finn, but Finn. Grania,wife of Finn,why have you played with me !

GRANIA I am not the wife of Finn, (She goes towards Darmuid) And now I cannot be Finn's wife,foryou have held me in your arms and you have kissed me.

[25^{r}]

DIARMUID What is this madness Grania ? Here,here – this night-- and Finn sleeping there.

GRANIA If he had loved me his love would have been stronger than witchcraft. (a pause) You shrink from me,why do you shrink from me ? Am I not desirable ? I have heard men praise me. She holds out her hair towards him) You have touched my hair and have looked into my eyes. Why do you shrink away? I have heard Diarmuid that women love you,and certainly a woman must be desirable in your eyes. It may be that men have lied to me, and this hair is not soft,this body delicate. (To Oscar and Usheen) Is not my plight miserable? Shall men shrink from me ? Would you shrink from me,if it was you I had asked to go away with me ? No matter who shrinks from me now,since the man I long for shrinks. The whole world shrinks from me.

[26^{r}]

OSCAR. Look Grania at the sleeping man whose ale you have bewitched.

USHEEN If Finn were to awake he would take some terrible vengeance for this.

GRANIA His vengeance is as little to me as my life is.I will go into the green woods and I will wander alone there till I die.

DIARMUID When I looked into your eyes Grania it was as though I had been in the dark night and that I saw the dawn. But I cannot,I cannot, there are stronger,there are stronger things than love.

OSCAR You are doing an evil work Grania. The Fianna live poor and live near to death always that they may have honour. You would take Diarmuid's honour from him.

USHEEN Come with us Diarmuid, Come turn your eyes away from her Diarmuid.

[27r]

GRANIA Your strength is no more Than the strength of a leaf upon a stream, for that which is to be has been foretold.

DIARMUID (Disengaging himself from Usheen and Oscar) What has been foretold ? Who has foretold it ?

USHEEN Do not listen to her Diarmuid, Your eyes and your ears will be your undoing.

OSCAR Grania has been listening to the tales of her foster mother, and if she has said –

DIARMUID If she has said I will break my oath to Finn– if she has said I will be dishonoured,she is no fortune- teller. Has she said this ?

GRANIA She has not said it.

DIARMUID Then what has she said ?

GRANIA She has said that a man would give up all he once held dear to guard a woman from the thing she most feared and hated. She said they would wander through unploughed

[28r]

valleys and through unpeopled woods,and that this woman would lead this man by the rushy margin of many streams

[Berg(01)]

where the ouzel flies and the otter hunts,and that they would smell wild honey of a sudden on paths worn by the feet of deer.

DIARMUID And the man was I and the woman was you ?

GRANIA She told me that the ouzel and the otter would not fly from them,and that it would seem for a long time as if men had forgotten them. She told me that they who are called the seven creatures,the sun and the moon and the stars and the sea and the fire and the wind and the dew, would love them; but it would seem for a long time as if change and death had forgotten them. (She goes nearer to him) And she told me Diarmuid that we would make our beds with the skins of deer under grey cromlechs and in cool

[29r]

caves,and that we would wake from sleep we knew not why, as though the secret people the divine of the rocks had called to us, that we might see the starlight shining among the leaves. And she told me Diarmuid that though our enemies were all the men of Eri they would not find us,but that we would lie under the cromlechs and in the caves watching them passing away from us seeking us.

USHEEN Is our love of Diarmuid greater than our love of Finn? We should have awakened him before this.

DIARMUID I will awake Finn and tell him.

GRANIA What will you tell him ?

DIARMUID That you would make me traitor.

GRANIA Traitor to whom Diarmuid ?

DIARMUID I have sworn to uphold my chief and the honour of my chief.

[30r]

GRANIA Have you not sworn to help the helpless,and who is more helpless than I?

DIARMUID And I would have helped you even against my chief if

you had asked me, but Grania you have said that you love me.

__GRANIA__ **Help me Diarmuid.**

__USHEEN__ **From this night the Fianna are rent in two. The people we have overthrown turn upon us and overthrow us.**

__DIARMUID__ **She asked me for my help and I must give it. (To Oscar and Usheen) I will keep her from him until my death. Tell him that this sword will guard her by day,and will lie between us at night. Tell her I will send him some messenger some token which will say to him, Finn I bring you word that so many hours or so many moons have passed by,and that Diarmuid's oath is unbroken. (Grania runs out through the door) We go wanderers from Tara (He is about to follow her but stops and looks at Finn) Finn,shall I ever look upon**

[31r]

upon your face in friendship again. They will tell you my messengers will tell you – (He goes out)

__USHEEN__ **(Goes to the door and looks out after them) They have gone westward towards the woods.**

__OSCAR__ **When Finn wakes we must tell him that they have gone into the eastward towards the sea.**

[Berg(02), 1r, 2r]

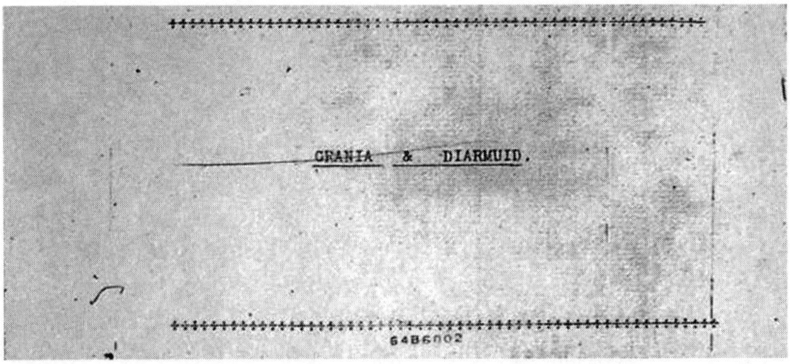

GRANIA & DIARMUID.

6486002

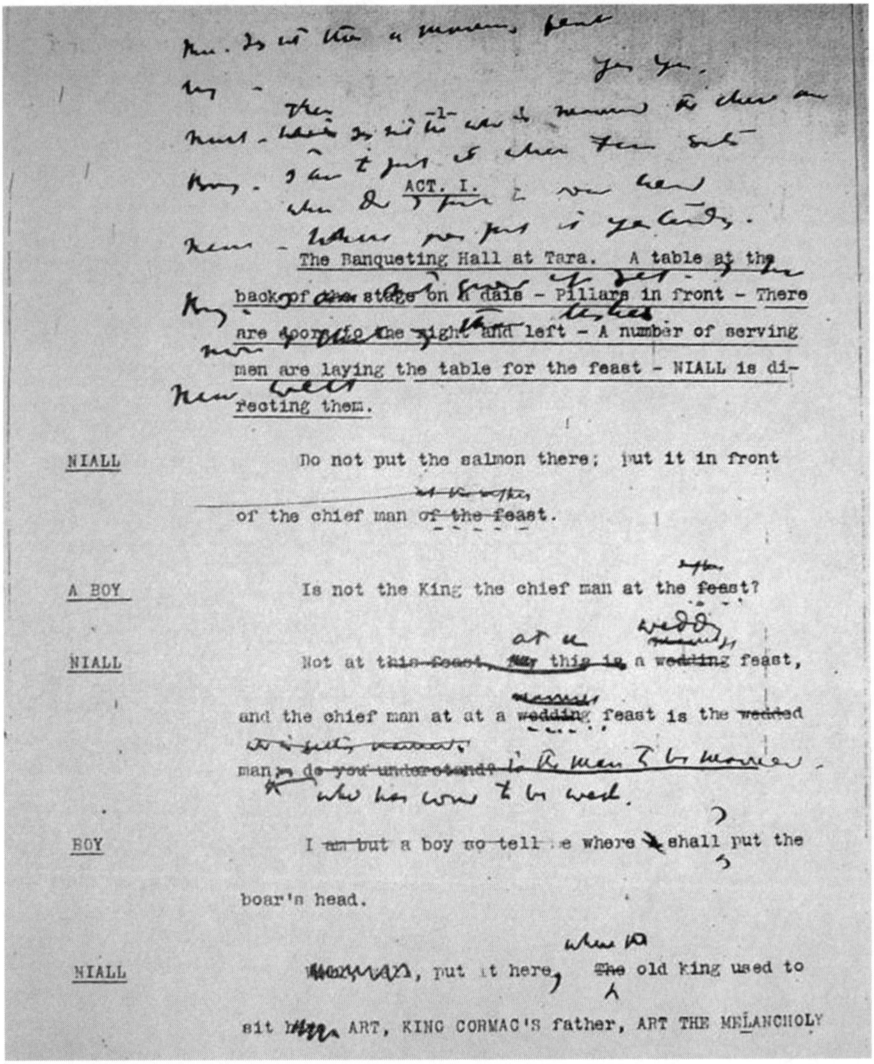

-1-

ACT. I.

The Banqueting Hall at Tara. A table at the back of the stage on a dais - Pillars in front - There are doors to the right and left - A number of serving men are laying the table for the feast - NIALL is directing them.

NIALL Do not put the salmon there; put it in front of the chief man of the feast.

A BOY Is not the King the chief man at the feast?

NIALL Not at this feast, for this is a wedding feast, and the chief man at at a wedding feast is the wedded man, do you understand?

BOY I am but a boy so tell me where I shall put the boar's head.

NIALL ..., put it here, The old king used to sit ... ART, KING CORMAC'S father, ART THE MELANCHOLY

2r, -1 Note that the position of WBY's entry has been separated from the text it overwrites, for reasons of clarity.

Typescript of Complete Act, Extensively Revised by W. B. Yeats and George Moore—the New Version?

[Berg(02), 1r]

~~:::~~

GRANIA & DIARMUID.

~~:::~~

[Berg(02), 2r]

Nia. Is not this a marriage feast
Boy – Yes Yes.
Then
Niall – ~~Who~~ is Is not he who is married the chief one
Boy – I am to put it wher Fin sits
wher I do I put it th boar head
Niall – Where you put it yesterday.
Boy – I am not given up yet – I hav
now to think of those fishes.
Niall Well

–1–

ACT. I.

The Banqueting Hall at Tara. A table at the back of the stage on a dais – Pillars in front – There are doors to the right and left – A number of serving men are laying the table for the feast – NIALL is directing them.

NIALL **Do not put the salmon there; put it in front**
~~at the supper~~
of the chief man ~~of the feast~~.

~~supper~~
A BOY **Is not the King the chief man at the ~~feast~~?**

wedding
at a ~~marriage~~
NIALL **Not at ~~this feast, for this is~~ a ~~wedding~~ feast,**
~~marriage~~
and the chief man at a ~~wedding~~ feast is the ~~wedded~~
~~who is getting married.~~
man; -- ~~do you understand?~~ ~~is the man to be married~~ –
who has come to be wed.

I
BOY **I ~~am but a boy so tell me~~ where ~~I~~ shall put the**
boar's head. ^

{, where the
NIALL **~~Well, well,~~ put it here{. ~~The~~ old king used to**
sit ~~here,~~ ART, KING CORMAC'S father, ART THE MELANCHOLY

[Berg(02), 3r, 4r]

-2-

they used to call him. He was deaf at the left ~~ear~~, side

and he was always complaining that the meat was hard,

and that the wind came under the door. Yes, BOY, under

this roof a hundre' kings have sat, right back to OLLAM

FODLA that made the laws. What meals they have eaten!

What ale they have drunk! Before CORMAC was ART, and

before ART was CONN.

BOY	~~Tell me about him.~~ He ~~was a great fighter~~.
NIALL	~~He was~~ CONN ~~the~~ hundred ~~fighter~~; and he knew when a hare was put before him if the fire had been bright behind it; and he knew if the swine's flesh had been dried in the smoke of a whitehorn tree. Put the curds over there; it is not curds but trotters and cows-heel that used to be put there, for that was the place of the king's fool. One day he flouted the Fianna on the high road, and they hanged him on an alder tree.

-3-

BOY	Did they kill the king's fool in time of peace?
NIALL	Fool or wise man, war or peace, its all one to them when their pride is up. But they are great men, BOY. It is not for ~~and~~ you and me to speak against ~~them~~. Bring the dishes quickly, it is time for their messenger to be here. Put the bread there, ART'S wife, QUEEN MAIVE used to sit there, the HALF RUDDY they called her ~~[illegible]~~ she liked thin barley cakes, and six men got their death because of her - Bring in the flagons (To) Put them here, where ART'S hound used to lie - (A knocking at the door) Here is the messenger of the Fianna - I knew we should not get done in time. Bring in the flagons - (To the other servants). Where are the drinking horns? (More knocking)- He goes to the door and opens it - CONAN comes in. He is a fat and

4r, l. 8 The cancellations in and above the line are all in pencil.

9 "He was", "of the", and "battles" are all canceled in pencil; and the broken underline beneath "the" is in pencil.

10 The words "if the" are typed over an erasure with different (black) ribbon.

16 The "s" is deleted in pencil.

5r, l. 3 The line is drawn loosely beneath the words in pencil.

4, 8 Pencil cancellations.

[Berg(02), 3r]

–2–

side
they used to call him. He was deaf at the left ~~ear~~,
and he was always complaining that the meat was hard,
and that the wind came under the door. Yes, BOY, under
this roof a hundred kings have sat, right back to OLLAM
FODLA that made the laws. What meals they have eaten!
there
What ale they have drunk! Before CORMAC ^ was ART, and
there
before ART ^ was CONN.
n
Was that Con ^ the hundred fighter
~~fought many battles~~

BOY ~~Tell me about him. He was a great fighter.~~

Yes ~~of the~~ ~~battles~~ *they used to call him*
NIALL ~~He was~~ CONN the hundred ~~fighter~~; and he knew when a
hare was put before him if the fire had been bright behind it; and he knew if the swine's flesh had been
dried in the smoke of a whitehorn tree. Put the curds
over there; it is not curds but trotters and cows-heel
that used to be put there, for that was the place of
the king's fool. One day he flouted the Fianna on the
high road~~s~~, and they hanged him on an alder tree.

[Berg(02), 4r]

–3–

BOY Did they kill the king's fool in time of peace?

NIALL Fool or wise man, war or peace, its all one to them
when their pride is up. But they are great men, BOY.
such great men.
It is not for ~~and~~ you and me to speak against ~~them.~~ ^
Bring the dishes quickly, it is time for their messenger
to be here. Put the bread there, ART'S wife, QUEEN
Maeve
MAIVE – used to sit there, ^ the HALF RUDDY they called
her , ~~then, and~~ she liked thin barley cakes, and six
men got their death because of her – Bring in the flagons
(To) Put them here, where ART'S hound used
to lie – (A knocking at the door) Here is the messenger
of the Fianna – I knew we should not get done in time.
Bring in the flagons – (To the other servants). Where
are the drinking horns? (More knocking)– He goes to the
door and opens it – CONAN comes in. He is a fat and

[Berg(02), 5r]

-4-

rough man in a sheepskin, and is much out of breath – He is followed by three men who carry bundles of shields on their backs.)

CONAN This is the salmon, and this is the boar's head, and these are the barley cakes for the [illegible] ~~wedding feast~~ of FINN the son of COOL. Give me a horn full of ale – (NIALL gives him a horn of ale.) I have much trouble going messages for the Fianna. Have I not legs to grow weary & body to sweat like another. I am hungry too, but I dare not [illegible] ~~put a knife~~ in the meat till the Fianna are here.

NIALL There will be plenty and to spare when they are here.

CONAN Well, look to the hanging of the shields. I've seen you before, (now) I remember you, you have been in Tara [illegible] fifty years, and have hung ~~them~~ the shields many a time – (Turning

[Berg(02), 5[r]]

~~-4-~~

rough man in a sheepskin, and is much out of breath –
He is followed by three men who carry bundles of shields
on their backs.)

CONAN This is the salmon, and this is the boar's head, and

~~marriage feast~~

stet **these are the barley cakes for the ~~wedding feast~~ of**
FINN the son of COOL. Give me a horn full of ale –
(NIALL gives him a horn of ale.) I have much trouble
going messages for the Fianna. Have I not legs to grow

a

weary and ^ body to sweat like another. I am hungry too,

~~make a whole~~

Stet **but I dare not ~~put a knife~~ in the meat till the Fianna**
are here.

NIALL **There will be plenty and to spare when they are here.**

CONAN **Well, look to the hanging of the shields. I've seen**
you before, (now) I remember you ^, you have been in Tara these

the shields

fifty years, and have hung ~~them~~ many a time – (Turning

2, 7 The broken underlining, together with the cancellation of the revisions above lines 2 and 7, is in pencil.
11 The transposition is made in ink.
12 Ink deletion.

-5-

to the men that are with him) Come, the sooner we bring FINN, the sooner we shall ~~meal~~ eat - (They go out)

BOY The Fianna have a rough messenger.

NIALL ~~Say not that I have~~ said it, but he is a man of ~~common~~ little account among them.

BOY ~~Being but a boy I know little of dress, but~~ a sheepskin is a rough ~~dress, even in a boy's eyes, for a great man.~~ They ~~do~~ are not all ~~dress~~ like that?

NIALL No, BOY ~~his sheepskin is~~ part of ~~his business. He is their fool,~~ and 'tis said FINN made him one of the ~~when he~~ was merry with ~~wine one night~~ - (He rushes across the stage to prevent one of the men from hanging COLL MAC.MORNA'S shield at the lower end of the table.) Would you put COLL MACMORNA'S shield below CONGAL'S and FINNOLE'S. Would you have the roof tree burnt

[Berg(02), 6r]

–5–

to the men that are with him) Come, the sooner we

eat

bring FINN, the sooner we shall ~~meal~~ – (They go out)

BOY **The Fianna have a rough messenger.**

~~Do not~~ I would have none say that I have *little*

NIALL ^ **~~Say not that I have~~ said it, but he is a man of ~~common~~** ^

account among them.

~~littl~~ *~~of the clothes great men~~*

~~the way great men~~

BOY **~~Being but a boy I know little of dress, but~~ a sheepskin** ^ ^

{ing

~~cloak~~ cloth{*es* ~~wear.~~

is a rough ~~dress,even in a boy's eyes,for a great man.~~

are *cloathed*

They ~~do~~ not all ~~dress~~ like that? ^ ^

the Feanna make him wear it. The ar alwy floutng

NIALL **No, BOY ~~his sheepskin is part of his business.~~ ~~He is~~**

him when he *Fianna*

~~their fool,~~ ~~and~~ ^ **'tis said FINN** ^ **made him one of the** ^

ale

~~when he~~ was merry with ~~wine~~ ~~one night~~ – (He rushes across the stage to prevent one of the men from hanging GOLL MAC.MORNA'S shield at the lower end of the table.)

Would you put GOLL MACMORNA'S shield below CONGAL'S and FINMOLE'S. Would you have the roof tree burnt

---

2, 4 ("Do not" and "common"), 6, 7, 8, 9, 9–10, 11 ("wine" and "one night") pencil deletions; 4 ("Say not that I have"), 11 ("when he") ink deletions.

6 The passage down to fol. 8r line 8 is separately developed in a two-page typescript—Berg(05)—which stands to one side of the evolution of the text.

7 When WBY deleted "wear." he also canceled the remainder of the type line with ink.

10–11 The transposition is made in pencil.

[Berg(02), 7[r], 8[r]]

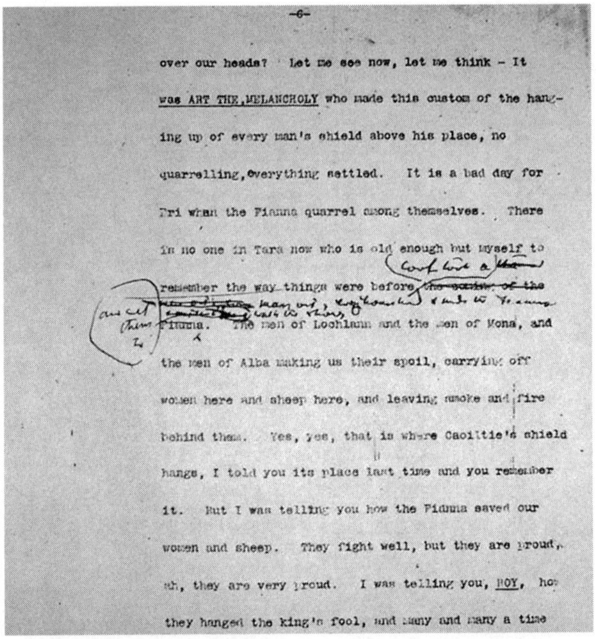

-6-

over our heads? Let me see now, let me think - It was ART THE MELANCHOLY who made this custom of the hanging up of every man's shield above his place, no quarrelling, everything settled. It is a bad day for Eri when the Fianna quarrel among themselves. There is no one in Tara now who is old enough but myself to remember the way things were before the coming of the Fianna. The men of Lochlann and the men of Mona, and the men of Alba making us their spoil, carrying off women here and sheep here, and leaving smoke and fire behind them. Yes, yes, that is where Caoiltie's shield hangs, I told you its place last time and you remember it. But I was telling you how the Fianna saved our women and sheep. They fight well, but they are proud, ah, they are very proud. I was telling you, BOY, how they hanged the king's fool, and many and many a time

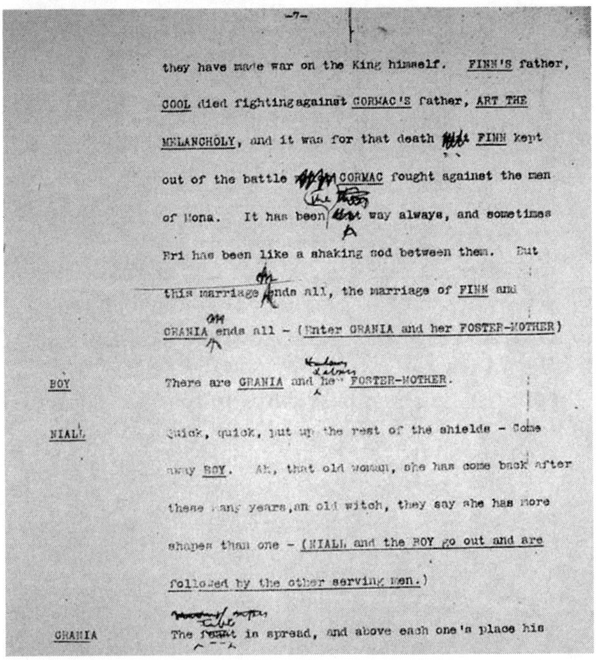

-7-

they have made war on the King himself. FINN'S father, COOL died fighting against CORMAC'S father, ART THE MELANCHOLY, and it was for that death FINN kept out of the battle CORMAC fought against the men of Mona. It has been that way always, and sometimes Eri has been like a shaking sod between them. But this marriage ends all, the marriage of FINN and GRANIA ends all - (Enter GRANIA and her FOSTER-MOTHER)

BOY There are GRANIA and her FOSTER-MOTHER.

NIALL Quick, quick, put up the rest of the shields - Come away BOY. Ah, that old woman, she has come back after these many years, an old witch, they say she has more shapes than one - (NIALL and the BOY go out and are followed by the other serving men.)

GRANIA The feast is spread, and above each one's place his

7[r], l. 4 everything] The initial "e" is inserted with different (black) ribbon.

8[r], l. 2 against] Inserted later with a different (black) ribbon.

3 that] The broken underlining of "that" is in pencil.

3, 4, 5 Pencil deletions. "Their" inserted above line 5, and the caret mark beneath, are also deleted in pencil.

8 The inserted "m" and the caret mark beneath appear to be ink over or under pencil. The same insertion in the previous line is straightforwardly smudged ink.

[Berg(02), 7r]

–6–

over our heads? Let me see now, let me think – It <u>was ART THE,MELANCHOLY</u> who made this custom of the hanging up of every man's shield above his place, no quarrelling,everything settled. It is a bad day for Eri when the Fianna quarrel among themselves. There is no one in Tara now who is old enough but myself to remember the way things were before Cool took a ~~thousand~~ **~~the coming of the~~** ~~men out of every~~ man out of every household & made the Feanna ~~& [?set them] to [?guar]~~ watch the shores (and set them to) **~~Fianna~~. The men of Lochlann and the men of Mona, and the men of Alba making us their spoil, carrying off women here and sheep here, and leaving smoke and fire behind them. Yes, yes, that is where Caoiltie's shield hangs, I told you its place last time and you remember it. But I was telling you how the Fianna saved our women and sheep. They fight well, but they are proud, ah, they are very proud. I was telling you, <u>BOY</u>, how they hanged the king's fool, and many and many a time**

[Berg(02), 8r]

–7–

they have made war on the King himself. <u>FINN'S</u> father, <u>COOL</u> died fightingagainst <u>CORMAC'S</u> father, <u>ART THE MELANCHOLY</u>, and it was for that death ~~that~~ <u>FINN</u> kept out of the battle ~~which~~ <u>CORMAC</u> fought against the men of Mona. It has been the ~~their~~ **~~that~~ way always, and sometimes Eri has been like a shaking sod between them. But this marriage** m **ends all, the marriage of <u>FINN</u> and <u>GRANIA</u>** m **ends all – (<u>Enter GRANIA and her FOSTER-MOTHER</u>)**

<u>BOY</u> **There are <u>GRANIA</u> and** ~~Laban~~ Laban **her <u>FOSTER-MOTHER</u>.**

<u>NIALL</u> **Quick, quick, put up the rest of the shields – Come away <u>BOY</u>. Ah, that old woman, she has come back after these many years,an old witch, they say she has more shapes than one – <u>(NIALL and the BOY go out and are followed by the other serving men.</u>)**

<u>GRANIA</u> **The** [?~~banquet~~]/~~supper~~ table **~~feast~~ is spread, and above each one's place his**

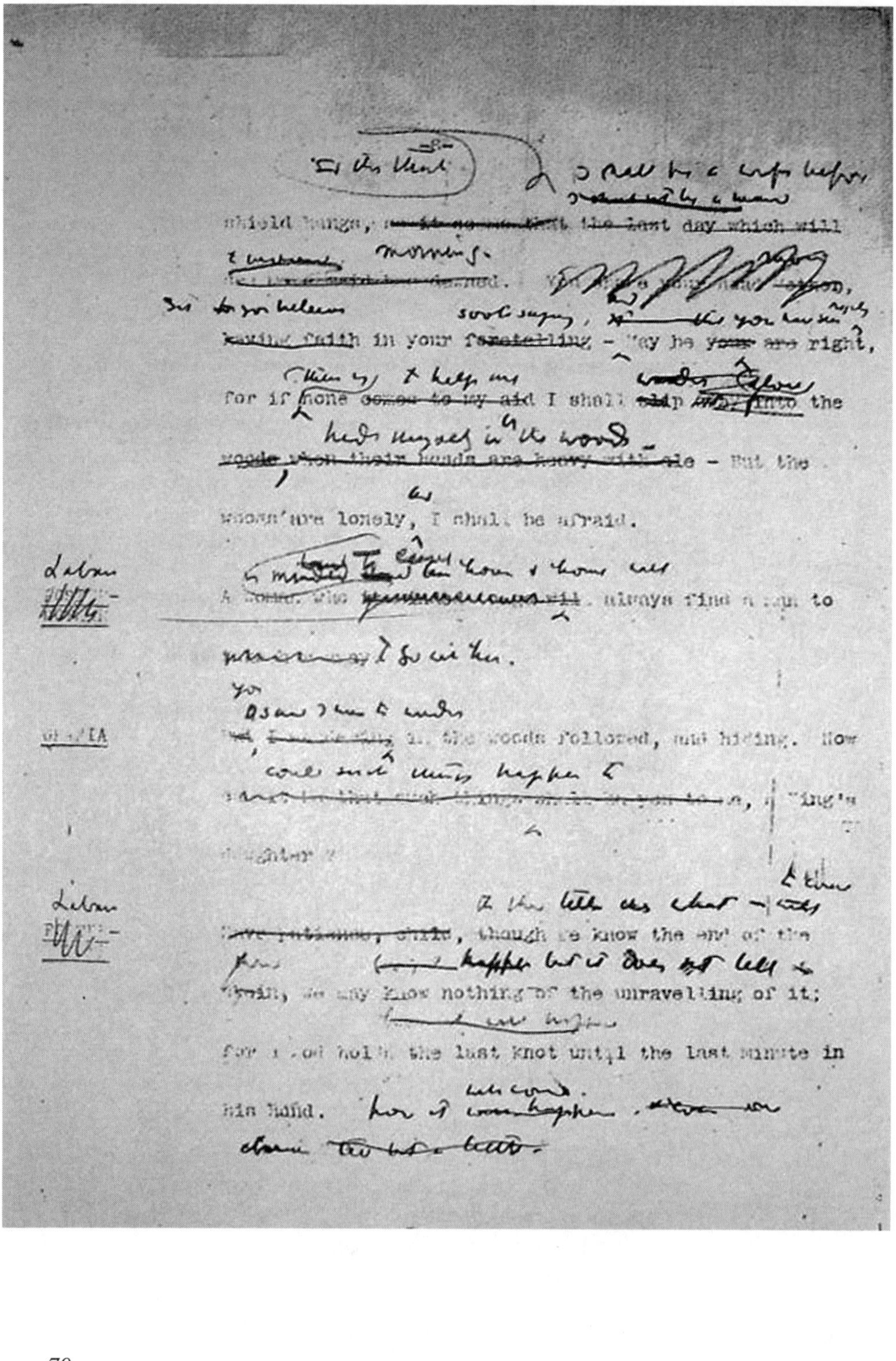
shield hangs, ... the last day which will
...ned. You ... upon,
having faith in your foretelling - May be you are right,
for if none comes to my aid I shall slip into the
woods when their heads are heavy with sleep - But the
woods are lonely, I shall be afraid.
LABAN
A woman who ... will always find a man to
OLIVIA
... in the woods followed, and hiding. How
... King's
daughter ?
LABAN
Have patience, child, though we know the end of the
skein, we may know nothing of the unravelling of it;
for God holds the last knot until the last minute in
his hand.

[Berg(02), 9r]

~~-8-~~

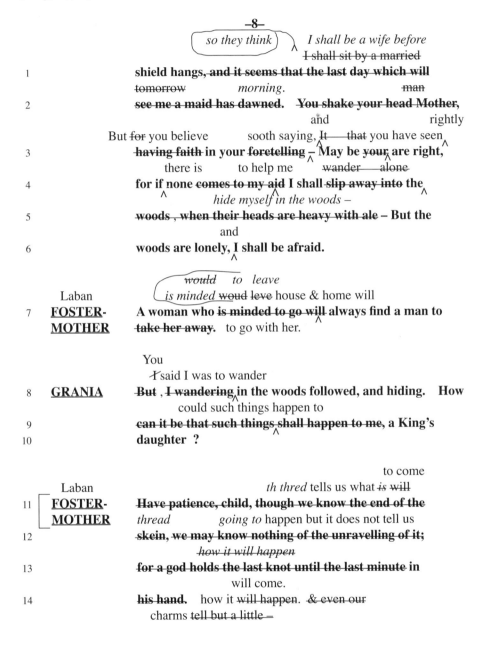

(so they think) ^ *I shall be a wife before*

~~I shall sit by a married~~

shield hangs, ~~and it seems that the last day which will~~

~~tomorrow~~ *morning.* ~~man~~

~~see me a maid has dawned.~~ ~~You shake your head Mother,~~

and rightly

But ~~for~~ you believe sooth saying, ~~It~~ ~~that~~ you have seen ^

~~having faith~~ **in your ~~foretelling~~ – ^ May be ~~your~~ ^ are right,** ^

there is to help me ~~wander~~ ~~alone~~

for if none ~~comes to my aid~~ I shall ~~slip away into~~ the ^

^ *hide myself ^ in the woods –*

~~woods , when their heads are heavy with ale~~ – But the

and

woods are lonely, ^ I shall be afraid.

~~would~~ to leave

(*is minded* ~~woud~~ ~~leve~~) house & home will

Laban

<u>FOSTER-MOTHER</u> **A woman who ~~is minded to go will~~ ^ always find a man to**

~~take her away.~~ to go with her.

You

~~I~~ said I was to wander

<u>GRANIA</u> **~~But~~ , ~~I wandering~~ ^ in the woods followed, and hiding. How**

could such things happen to

~~can it be that such things~~ ^ ~~shall happen to me~~, a King's

daughter ?

to come

Laban *th thred* tells us what ~~is~~ ~~will~~

<u>FOSTER-MOTHER</u> **~~Have patience, child, though we know the end of the~~**

thread *going to* happen but it does not tell us

~~skein, we may know nothing of the unravelling of it;~~

~~*how it will happen*~~

~~for a god holds the last knot until the last minute~~ in

will come.

~~his hand.~~ how it ~~will happen~~. ~~& even our~~

charms ~~tell but a little –~~

The process of revision on this page is particularly complicated. In the first ten lines, it appears that WBY first made substitutions in ink, and revised his substitutions in pencil, and that the process is reversed in lines 11–14 (here first pencil, then ink). The insertions above lines 11 and 12 are ink over pencil, and the pencil insertion above line 13 is canceled with ink.

[Berg(02), 10r]

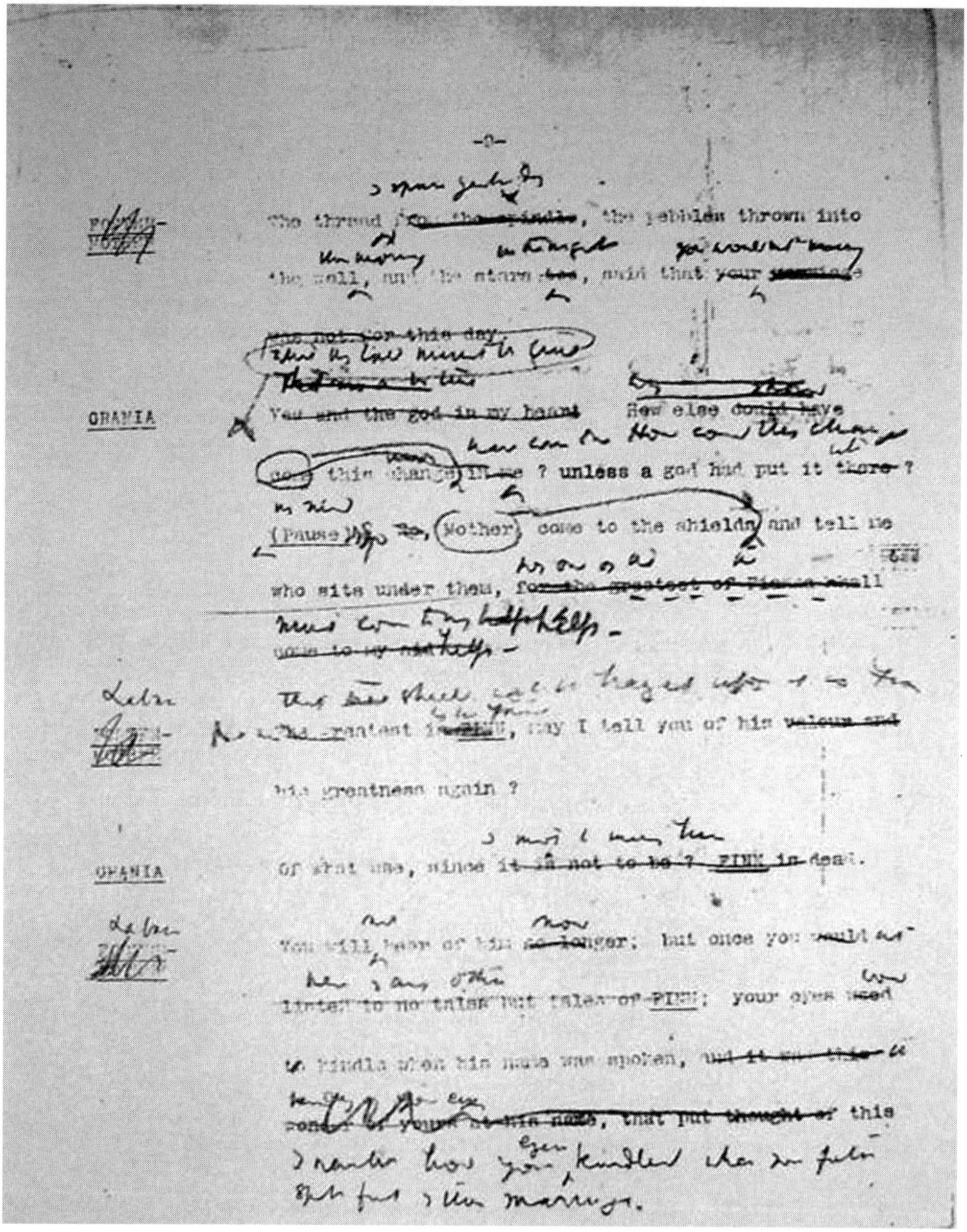

-2-

FOSTER-MOTHER

The thread from the spindle, the pebbles thrown into the well, and the stars too, said that your marriage was not for this day.

GRANIA

You and the god in my heart How else could have come this change in me ? unless a god had put it there ? (Pause) No, Mother, come to the shields and tell me who sits under them, for the greatest of Fianna shall come to my help.

FOSTER-MOTHER

The greatest is FINN, may I tell you of his valour and his greatness again ?

GRANIA

Of what use, since it is not to be ? FINN is deaf.

FOSTER-MOTHER

You will hear of him no longer; but once you would not listen to no thing but tales of FINN; your eyes used to kindle when his name was spoken, and it was this tender of yours in his name, that put thought of this

[Berg(02), 10r]

–9–

I spun yesterday
FOSTER-MOTHER **The thread , ~~from the spindle~~, the pebbles thrown into**
this morning *in the night* you would not marry
the well, and the stars ~~too~~, said that ~~your marriage~~
~~was not for this day.~~

What they told must be true
~~That~~ ~~*must be*~~ *true* ~~*Why*~~ ~~*should*~~
GRANIA **~~Yes and the god in my heart~~ How else ~~could have~~**
have come on How could this change
[?~~*have*~~] *into*
~~come~~ this change ~~in me~~ ? unless a god had put it ~~there~~ ?
my mind
(Pause) [?*So*] **So, Mother, come to the shields and tell me**
for one of the *the*
who sits under them, ~~for the greatest of Fianna shall~~
must come to my ~~*help*~~ *help –*
~~come to my aid –~~ ~~*help*~~ *–*

That ~~*tall*~~ *shield with th hazel upon it is Fins*
Laban *of the Fianni*
~~FOSTER-MOTHER~~ ~~*He is*~~ **~~The~~ greatest ~~is FINN~~, may I tell you of his ~~valour and~~**
his greatness again ?

I must to marry him
GRANIA **Of what use, since ~~it is not to be ? FINN is dead.~~**

Laban *not* *now*
~~FOSTER-MOTHER~~ **You will hear of him ~~no longer~~; but once you ~~would~~** *not*
hear of any other *woud*
~~listen to no tales but tales of FINN~~; your eyes ~~used~~
to kindle when his name was spoken, ~~and it was this~~ *th*
kindlng in your eyes
~~wonder of yours at his name, that put thought of~~ this
eyes
I remember how your kindled when your father
spoke first of this marriage.

1, 9, 12 The cancellation of "Foster-Mother" and the insertion of "Laban", along with the ink-over-pencil substitutions in lines 2 and 4, are the only ink revisions on the present page.

2 you would not marry] Ink over pencil.

4 That] Ink over pencil.

5 unless a] Typed in afterward with different (black) ribbon.

7 Pencil broken-underlining.

11 Berg(03), fol. 6r, line 18, has "since I am not to marry him?" which of course makes better sense.

[Berg(02), 10v]

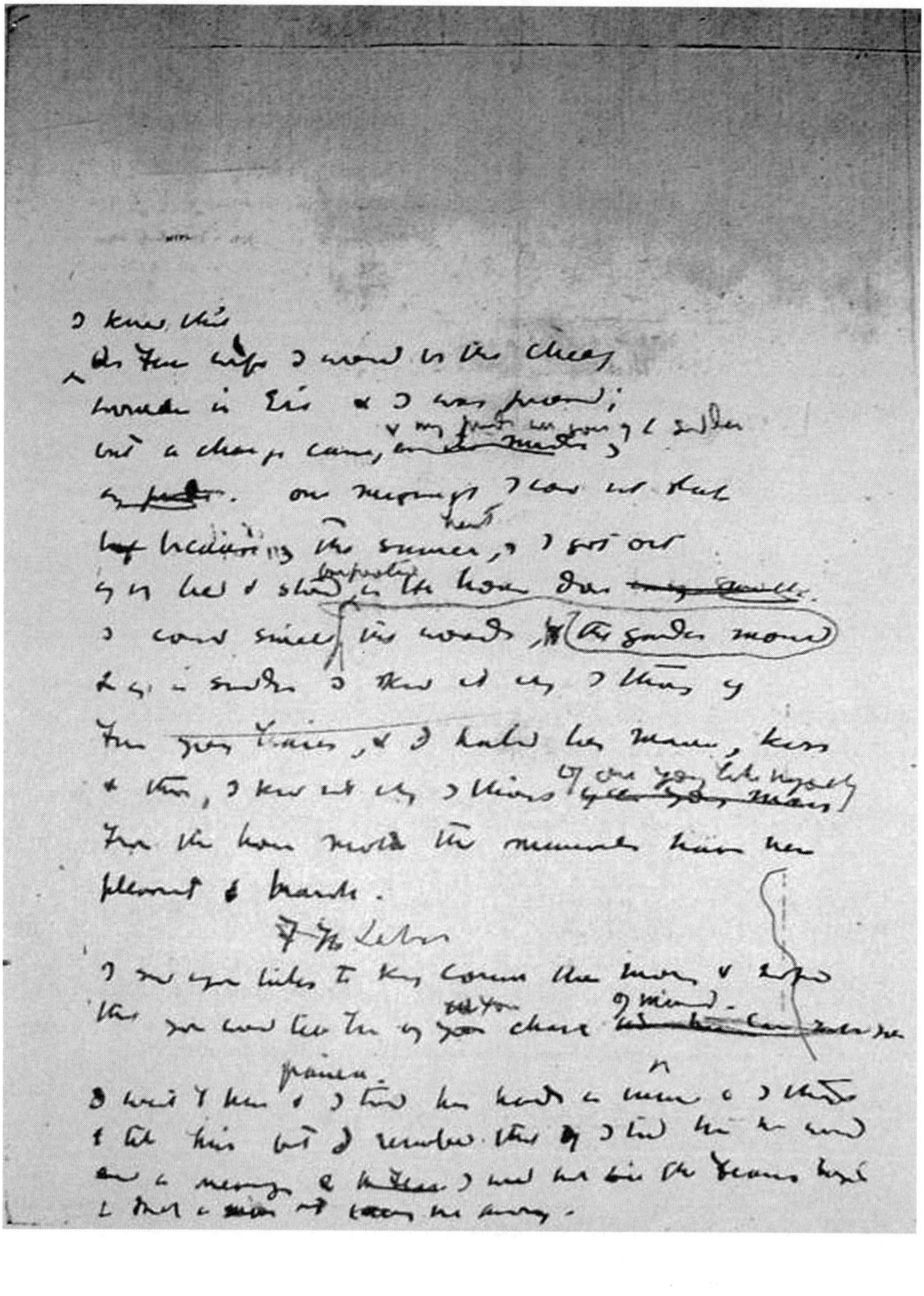

[Berg(02), 10v]

I knew that
a }
A{s Fins wife I would be the cheaf
^woman in Eri & I was proud *;*
& my pride was gone of a sudden
but a change came , ~~and the~~ ~~murder~~ of
~~my pride.~~ One morning I coud not sleep
heat
~~bef~~ because of the summer, & I got out
barfooted
of my bed & stood^in the house door ~~in my smock~~.
I could smell^(the woods, ~~&~~)(the garden mould)
& of a sudden I knew not why I thoug of
Fin grey hairs, & I hated his marrag kiss
of one young like myself
& the*n ,* I knew not why I though ~~of the young man~~
From tha hour mothr the minutes have been
pleasant & harsh.

~~F M~~ Laban

I saw you talkng to Kng Cormac this mornng & hoped
~~the~~ *your* *of mind –*
that you woud tell him of ~~you~~ change ~~and he can tell~~ me

Grania.

I went t him and I took his hands in mine & I thougt
to tell him but I remembrd that if I told him he woud
send a mesnger [?~~to~~] ~~the Feann~~ I woud not see the Feann toghr
to pick a man to carry me away –

3, 4, 6, 7, 10, 14 Pencil cancellations; the remainder are in blue-black ink.
7 The transposition is made in pencil.

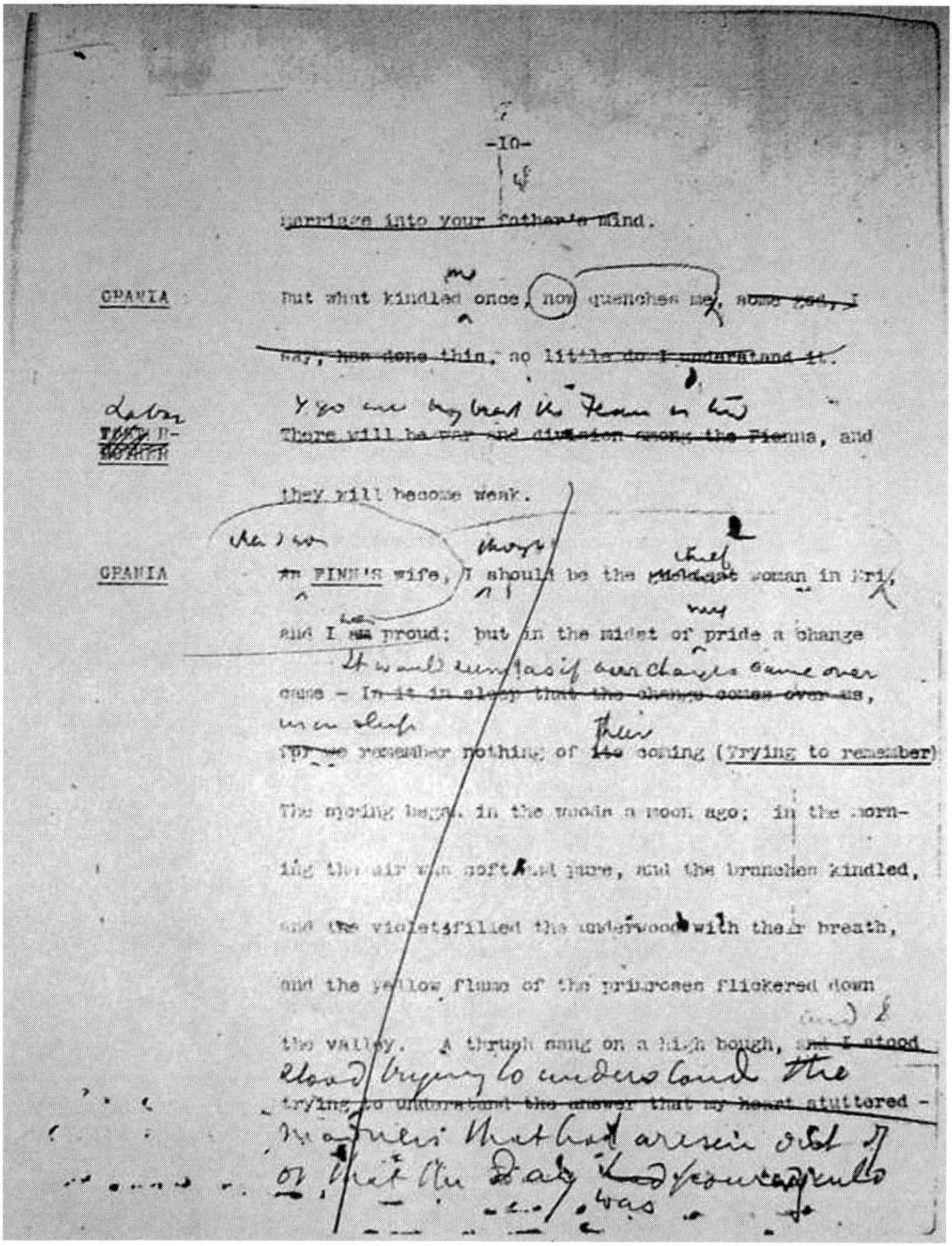

-10-

marriage into your father's mind.

GRANIA But what kindled once, now quenches me, some god, I say, has done this, so little do I understand it.

There will be war and division among the Fiannas, and they will become weak.

GRANIA An FINN'S wife, I should be the proudest woman in Eri, and I am proud: but in the midst of pride a change came – Is it in sleep that the change comes over us, for we remember nothing of its coming (Trying to remember) The spring began in the woods a moon ago; in the morning the air was soft and pure, and the branches kindled, and the violets filled the underwood with their breath, and the yellow flame of the primroses flickered down the valley. A thrush sang on a high bough, and I stood trying to understand the answer that my heart stuttered –

stood trying to understand the madness that had arisen out of

[Berg(02), 11r]

–10–

~~marriage into your father's mind~~.

me
GRANIA **But what kindled ^ once, (now) quenches me, ^ ~~some god, I~~ ~~say, has done this, so little do I understand it.~~**

Laban *Y. yo will ~~bring~~ break the Fean in two*
FOSTER-MOTHER **~~There will be war and division among the Fianna~~, and they will become weak.**

When I was *thought I* chief
GRANIA **~~As~~ ^ FINN'S wife, ^ I should be the ~~greatest~~ woman in Eri, ^**
was *my*
and I ~~am~~ proud; but in the midst of ^ pride a change
It would seem as if our changes came over
came – ~~Is it in sleep that the change comes over us~~,
us in sleep *their*
~~for we~~ remember nothing of ~~its~~ coming (Trying to remember) The spring began in the woods a moon ago; in the morning the air was soft and pure, and the branches kindled, and ~~the~~ violet*s* filled the underwood with their breath, and the yellow flame of the primroses flickered down
and I
the valley. A thrush sang on a high bough, ~~and I stood~~
stood trying to understand the
~~trying to understand the answer that my heart stuttered –~~
madness that had arisen out of
or that the {sun / day} ~~had~~ pour{ing / ed} into
was

6ff. Revisions of Grania's lines, here and on the next page (12r), were made in a clean TS version—NLI 8777(10) b, fol. 18r—but were not carried forward (see pp. 124–125).

6–15 The cancellation is in blue-black ink—like the alteration of the Foster-Mother's name in line 4 and in line 6 (and some ink smudges elsewhere). The remaining revisions on this page are in pencil.

8–9 The author of this pencil insertion might be GM. The revisions at the beginning of Grania's speech are certainly by WBY, and at the foot of the page certainly by GM.

9 Broken pencil underlining.

12 the] Pencil deletion.

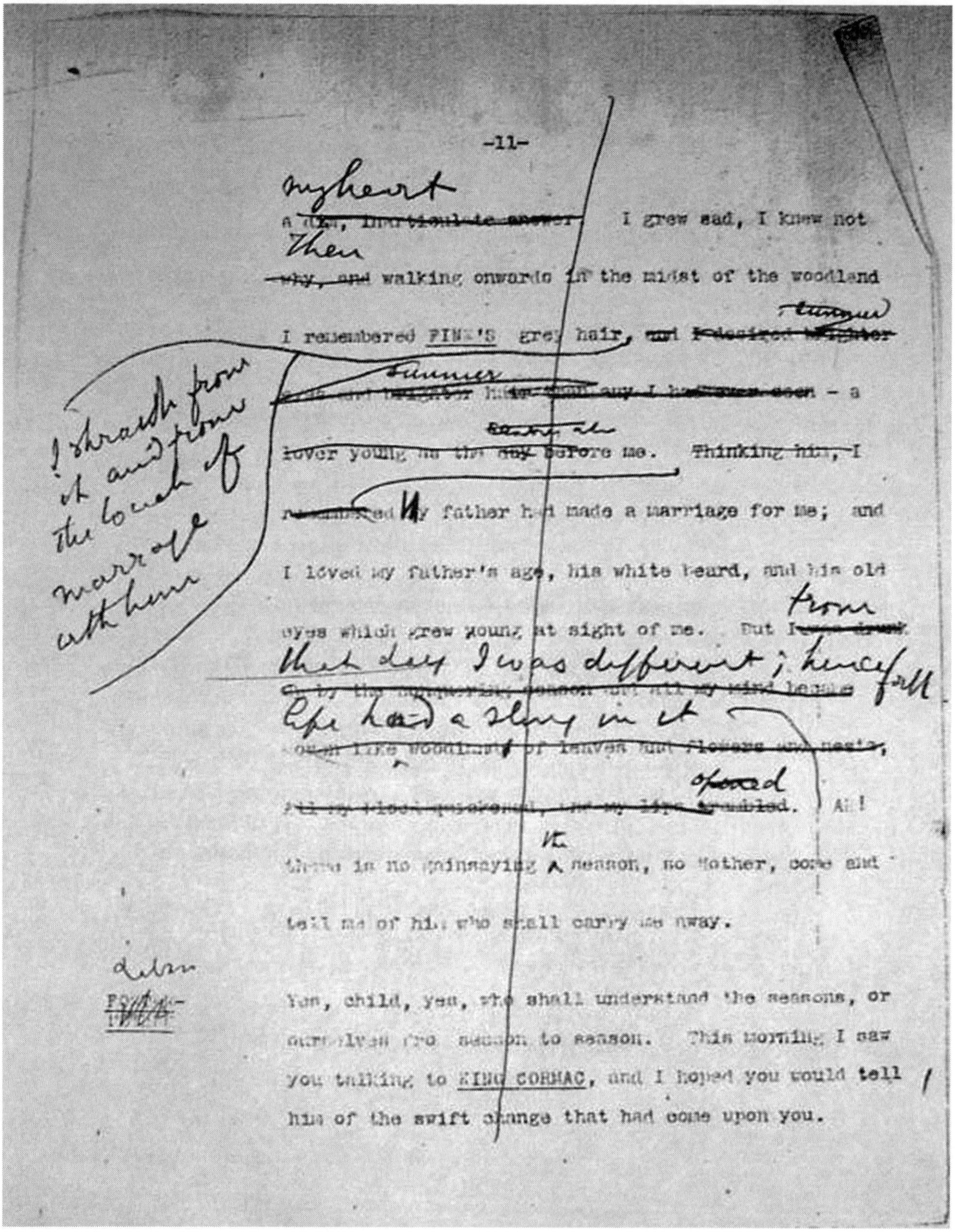

-11-

my heart
a ~~dim, inarticulate answer~~ I grew sad, I knew not
Then
~~why, and~~ walking onwards in the midst of the woodland
turned
I remembered FINN'S grey hair, ~~and I desired brighter~~
summer
~~hair and brighter hair than any I had ever seen~~ - a
~~lover young as the day before me.~~ ~~Thinking him,~~ I
~~remembered~~ my father had made a marriage for me; and
I loved my father's age, his white beard, and his old
from
eyes which grew young at sight of me. But I ~~have drunk~~
that day I was different; hence fall
~~of the quickening season and all my mind became~~
life had a sting in it
~~[illegible] like woodlands of leaves and flowers and nests,~~
opposed
~~All my blood quickened, and my life troubled~~. Ah!
the
there is no gainsaying season, no Mother, come and
tell me of him who shall carry me away.

I shrank from it and from the touch of marriage with him

Lebn
~~FOTHAD~~

Yes, child, yes, we shall understand the seasons, or
ourselves from season to season. This morning I saw
you talking to KING CORMAC, and I hoped you would tell
him of the swift change that had come upon you.

[Berg(02), 12r]

–11–

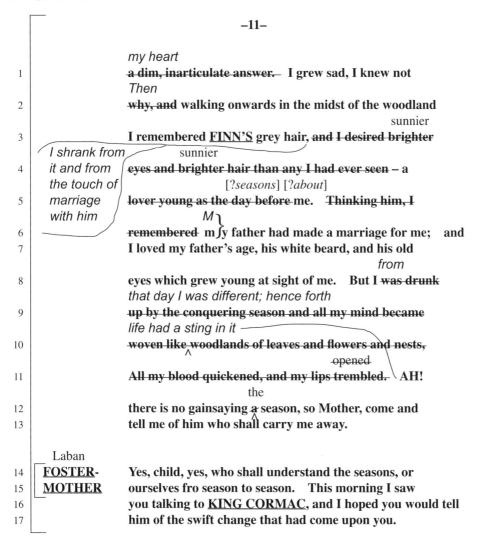

my heart
~~a dim, inarticulate answer.~~ I grew sad, I knew not
Then
~~why, and~~ walking onwards in the midst of the woodland
sunnier
I remembered FINN'S grey hair, ~~and I desired brighter~~
I shrank from it and from the touch of marriage with him
sunnier
~~eyes and brighter hair than any I had ever seen~~ – a
[?*seasons*] [?*about*]
~~lover young as the day before~~ me. ~~Thinking him, I~~
M
~~remembered~~ my father had made a marriage for me; and
I loved my father's age, his white beard, and his old
from
eyes which grew young at sight of me. But I ~~was drunk~~
that day I was different; hence forth
~~up by the conquering season and all my mind became~~
life had a sting in it
~~woven like woodlands of leaves and flowers and nests,~~
~~opened~~
~~All my blood quickened, and my lips trembled.~~ AH!
the
there is no gainsaying ~~a~~ season, so Mother, come and
tell me of him who shall carry me away.

Laban
FOSTER-MOTHER **Yes, child, yes, who shall understand the seasons, or**
ourselves fro season to season. This morning I saw
you talking to KING CORMAC, and I hoped you would tell
him of the swift change that had come upon you.

The page is canceled with a blue-black ink vertical line. Apart from the revisions in lines 3, 4, 11, 14–15, the remainder of revisions on this page are in pencil.

NLI 8777(4), fol. 37r, also headed "–11–" and in the same typing style, is a TS fair copy of this page, with modifications.

10 woodlands] Note that the terminal "s" was first canceled independently (in pencil).

16 The vertical mark in the RH margin is made with either an indelible pencil or blue carbon paper.

-12-

GRANIA This morning I sought him, and I took his hands in mine that I might tell him, but my lips shrank from speech as from a flame.

FOSTER-MOTHER When CORMAC went against the men of Alba I foretold his defeat. Why did he not come to me about this marriage, why did he not come to me? Of what use to shut his mind against my foretelling, why walk in the dark when a lamp is by you? I have seen the end of many things, but of this feud neither DIARMUID nor FINN shall see the end.

GRANIA Am I then a feud sent by the gods? Even so must I do their will, I can but obey them, so tell me MOTHER of the men I shall see to-night.

FOSTER-MOTHER There will be feuds and flights, ruin and death, and neither you nor I can do anything. The lust of life

[Berg(02), 13ʳ]

But
^It shall be long before men come to an end of
this mischief. – the Fean shall be broken in
two because of it.

–12–

GRANIA **This morning I sought him, and I took his hands in mine that I might tell him, but my lips shrank from speech as from a flame.**

Laban
FOSTER-MOTHER **When CORMAC went against the men of Alba I foretold his defeat, Why did he not come to me about this marriage,**
why does he shut
~~**why did he not come to me**~~**?** ~~**Of what use to shut his**~~
his ears to my sooth saying
~~**mind against my foretelling, why walk in the dark when**~~
It will be long befor th Fean are at one again.
~~**a lamp is by you? I have seen the end of many things**~~
~~it will be long~~ until ~~Eri~~ sees
~~**but of this feud neither DIARMUID nor FINN shall see the**~~
~~the end of them~~
~~**end.**~~^ *th Fean will be long broken in two –*

~~undyng ones~~
If th ~~gods~~ have plannd that & ~~decided~~ break the
GRANIA **Am** ~~**I then a feud sent by the gods**~~**?** ~~**Even so must I do**~~
may help
Fean in two — break them I must. Neithr I nor you
~~**their will, I can but obey them**~~**, so tell me MOTHER of the men I shall see to-night.**

Yes — yes
Laban
flights & fights
FOSTER-MOTHER ~~**There will be feuds and flights, ruin and death,**~~ **and**
help it. I have foreseen it all clearly
neither you nor I can ~~**do anything**~~**. The lust of life**

1–3 Canceled with blue-black ink. Revisions made in a clean typescript version of Grania's lines—NLI 8777(10) b, fol. 18ʳ—were not carried forward.

4 men] Inserted with new (black) ribbon.

6–7 The phrases inserted above these lines are in pencil overwritten with blue-black ink.

7–10, 11–12, 14, 15 Pencil cancellations. Lines 7–9 are canceled all together in blue-black ink.

-13-

is upon you, child. [illegible]

GRANIA Tell me, MOTHER, tell me of these men

Laban ~~FOSTER-MOTHER~~ That shield with the red otter painted upon it is the shield of ~~Caoilte~~ Fergus. He is taller than all others, his hair and his beard are brown, ~~and he wears a crimson cloak over a white tunic~~.

GRANIA ~~Such a man would look well in such a dress. Is his walk stately,~~ [illegible] . Is he strong and stately? would he make my heart beat. will he bewitch me?

Laban ~~FOSTER-MOTHER~~ He ~~His walk~~ is stately, but there is grey in his beard. ~~[illegible]~~ ~~I think you would like a younger man.~~ That red shield with the white deer's head painted upon it is the shield of USHEEN. He has yellow hair, and he has long white hands with fingers hard at the tips from the plucking of harp-strings, and they say no woman has refused him her love.

[Berg(02), 14r]

–13–

is upon you, child. ~~*& I must do your will.*~~

GRANIA **Tell me, MOTHER, tell me of these men**

Laban
FOSTER-MOTHER **That shield with the red otter painted upon it is the**
Fergus
~~Finmole~~
shield of ~~Caoltie~~. He is taller than all others, his hair and his beard are brown, ~~and he wears a crimson cloak over a white tunic.~~

strong
~~*Do not stop among his clothes*~~. Is he ~~strong~~ and
GRANIA **~~Such a man would look well in such a dress. Is his~~**
stately? would he make my heart beat –
~~walk stately, will he bewitch~~ me?

Laban
He *enough*
FOSTER-MOTHER **~~His walk~~ is stately, but there is grey in his beard.**
It may be ~~that you long for~~ that your longing is for a younger man
~~I think you would like a younger man.~~ That red shield with the white deer's head painted upon it is the shield of USHEEN. He has yellow hair, and he has long white hands with fingers hard at the tips from the plucking of harp-strings, and they say no woman has refused him her love.

1 The pencil insertion is canceled with blue-black ink.
5–6, 7–8, 9, 10 The lines are canceled in pencil. The line 6 cancellation is overwritten with blue-black ribbon.
7–8 The ink insertions are over pencil.

[Berg(02), 15r]

-14-

Is he young?

GRANIA ~~OISIN, it is not [illegible]~~ [illegible]

Laban ~~FOSTER-MOTHER~~ cut ~~There [illegible]~~; there are younger than he is.

That grey shield with the raven painted upon it is the shield of GOLL the son of MORNA. He is a great hunter, and his arms and legs are strong as the posts of a door.

GRANIA Is there ~~delight~~ merriment in his eyes?

Laban ~~FOSTER-MOTHER~~ He has the quiet of the woods in his eyes. But I see that your mind is not set ~~upon one that is~~ [illegible] strong, but on ~~one that is~~ [illegible] young. That white shield with the green fish is the shield of ~~OSGAR son of USHEEN~~ Caolte, his swift [illegible]. He is young and a teller of battle tales. But that silver shield with the ~~a~~ flying white heron upon it is the shield of DIARMUID. He is the youngest and comliest of all. He has dark hair and blue eyes, and light limbs, and his skin is white but for the freckles. He

[Berg(02), 15[r]]

–14–

Is he young —?
<u>GRANIA</u> ~~**<u>OISIN</u>, it is not he?** th man I am to choose.~~

Laban stet ~~There is grey in his hair~~; there are younger than he ~~;~~.
<u>FOSTER</u>- <u>MOTHER</u> ^**That grey shield with the raven painted upon it is the shield of <u>GOLL</u> the son of <u>MORNA</u>. He is a great hunter, and his arms and legs are strong as the posts of a door.**

mirth
<u>GRANIA</u> **Is there ~~delight~~ in his eyes?**

Laban
<u>FOSTER</u>- <u>MOTHER</u> **He has the quiet of the woods in his eyes. But I see**
~~on a~~ *~~man~~*
that your mind is not set ~~upon one that is~~ strong, but ^
~~a~~ *~~man~~*
on ~~one that is~~ young^ **That white shield with the green**
footed
Caolte, the swift ~~pointed~~
fish is the shield of ~~<u>OSCAR</u> son of <u>USHEEN</u>~~^**. He is young and a teller of battle tales. B**^**ut that silver shield with the e flying heron upon it is the shield of <u>DIARMUID</u>. He is the youngest and comliest of all. He has dark hair and blue eyes, and light limbs, and his skin is white but for the freckles. He**

---

2 "he" was followed by a semicolon, which WBY deleted in pencil in favor of a period.
8–9 Pencil underlining.
12 Type deletion.

-15-

is courteous and he is merry with women. It is said of him that he will not be remembered for deeds of arms but as a true lover, and that he will die young.

GRANIA DIARMUID, DIARMUID, ~~how sweetly the syllables sound~~ a pleasant sounding name

~~and~~ ~~that is the name~~, DIARMUID. a sweet sounding name, 2

Laban ~~FOSTER-MOTHER~~ But child, how think you ~~the wishes of your blood is~~ these things are to

~~planning will be brought~~ come about. The blood ~~finds~~ will find its way, ~~and this time~~ ~~the way will be terrible~~. ~~But~~ it will all happen, though FINN is coming with his army

~~he shall not carry you off~~.

GRANIA You are sure of ~~that~~ it will happen MOTHER ?

Laban ~~FOSTER-MOTHER~~ I am sure of that, but the way, the way.

GRANIA When the time comes the way will be put into your mind.

Laban ~~FOSTER-MOTHER~~ Child, love has made you wise as the bird that desires a mate in ~~the heart of~~ the woods (She sits down to spin)

[Berg(02), 16r]

–15–

is courteous and he is merry with women. It is said of him that he will not be remembered for deeds of arms but as a true lover, and that he will die young.

a pleasant sounding name
<u>GRANIA</u> **<u>DIARMUID</u>, <u>DIARMUID</u>, ~~how sweetly the syllables sound~~**
a <u>sweet</u> sound*ing* name,
~~flow~~ – ~~that is the name~~, <u>DIARMUID</u>. ^

Laban ~~th~~ these things are to
<u>FOSTER-MOTHER</u> **But child, how think you ~~the mischief your blood is~~**
come will
~~planning will be brought~~ about. The blood ^ finds its
but it shall be some terrible way, ah
way, ~~and this time the way will be terrible.~~ ~~But~~ it will al *l* happen, though <u>FINN</u> is coming with his army
& ~~th~~ his marriage ~~has~~ table has been spread.
~~he shall not carry you off.~~

it will happen
<u>GRANIA</u> **You are sure of ^ ~~that~~ <u>MOTHER</u> ?**

Laban
<u>FOSTER-MOTHER</u> **I am sure of that, but the way, the way.**

<u>GRANIA</u> **When the time comes the way will be put into your mind.**

Laban
<u>FOSTER-MOTHER</u> **Child, love has made you wise as the bird ^ that desires a mate in ~~the heart of~~ the woods (<u>She sits down to spin</u>)**

4–5 "sound" is a type deletion, then "how sweetly . . . flow" is canceled with pencil, then with blue-black ink; "that is the name" is canceled with ink only. The inserted word "sweet" is underlined in pencil.

6–7 The inserted words, "these things are to" and "come", are ink over pencil—like the accompanying cancellation.

8, 10, 15 Ink cancellations.

9 all] Note that the second "l" is inserted in pencil.

14–15 The Foster-Mother's speech (not the part ascription) is typed in later with a different (black) ribbon. The transposition is made in ink.

[Berg(02), 17r]

-16-

GRANIA	I must not think of him yet Mother, I ~~can see him - his eyes and his freckles~~. I'm ~~drawn deliciously, but I must not think of it~~ - thinking of love makes the heart giddy - Spin MOTHER - after my You have not told me what ~~I shall find at the end of~~ ~~the woods - PINK~~ will follow us. not then
~~FOSTER-MOTHER~~ Lab[illegible]	(Pulling out a long thread) ~~And there~~ shall ~~be mar-~~ ~~vellous~~ escape[s], and the end ~~[illegible]~~ - many [illegible]
GRANIA	Shall be what, MOTHER?
~~FOSTER-MOTHER~~ Lab[illegible]	It shall be like the beginning. (Enter CORMAC and two COUNSELLORS)
CORMAC	This is the wisest marriage, I might have made a greater I might have married her to one, the King of Alba, but this one will keep our king- dom safe (He turns and sees GRANIA) - My ~~[illegible]~~ daughter I have been seeking you. Let us sit together and ~~have~~ to one another a ~~little~~ talk; to-night you go away, but you go with

[Berg(02), 17r]

–16–

I must not think of him yet
GRANIA **Mother, ~~I can see him – his eyes and his freckles.~~**
~~I'm drawn deliciously, but I must not think of it~~ –
thinking of love makes the heart giddy – Spin <u>MOTHER</u> –
~~after~~ my
You have not told me what ~~I shall find at the end of~~
will happen after my ~~wa~~ wandering ~~in the woods~~ –
not Finn
~~the woods – <u>FINN</u>~~ will^follow us.

Laban
<u>FOSTER-MOTHER</u> You
<u>(Pulling out a long thread)</u> ~~And there~~ shall ~~be mar-~~
many times
~~vellous~~ escape~~s~~^, and the end ~~shall be~~ –

<u>GRANIA</u> **Shall be what, <u>MOTHER?</u>**

Laban
<u>FOSTER-MOTHER</u> I cannot understand it yet but —
^It shall be like the beginning. <u>(Enter CORMAC and two</u>
<u>COUNSELLORS)</u>

<u>CORMAC</u> **This is the wisest marriage, I might have made a greater**
I might have married her to
one,^the King of Alba, but this one will keep our king-
dom safe <u>(He turns and sees GRANIA)</u> – My ~~dearest~~ daughter
I have been seeking you. Let us sit together and have
to one another from me
a ~~little~~ talk^; to-night you go away^, but you go with

1–2, 4, 13, 14 Ink deletions.

4+ "in the woods –" is canceled in pencil.

5 "the woods" is canceled with blue-black ink; "<u>FINN</u>" with pencil.

6–7 "And there", "be", and "shall be" are canceled with blue-black ink; "marvellous" and the second "s" in "escapes" with pencil.

9+ COUNSELLORS] The first "S" is inserted in new (black) ribbon.

12 Pencil deletion. The partial double-underline is made with either an indelible pencil or through blue carbon paper.

-17-

the chief man in Eri (<u>The Counsellors withdraw</u>)-

daughter

Come, ~~dearest~~, let us sit together, why ~~do~~ you ~~stand~~

with ~~fixed~~ eyes, ~~and~~ ... ornaments

~~...you~~ why have you not put on your ornaments -

<u>GRANIA</u> I have forgotten them.

<u>CORMAC</u>. I shou d ~~like to have seen you~~ wear your bracelets,

and your brooch with the emeralds - will you not wear

them?

Then

<u>GRANIA</u> I can send for ~~the ornaments and wear them for you~~, but

I am not minded to wear them.

<u>CORMAC</u>. Why are you not minded to wear them (<u>Pause</u>) What has

~~the~~ <u>FOSTER-MOTHER</u> told you, she was telling you some-

thing when I came in?

<u>GRANIA</u> ~~These ornaments~~, father, you have often seen me wear,

and ~~thou love~~ me without them, ~~as can any other man whose~~

[Berg(02), 18[r]]

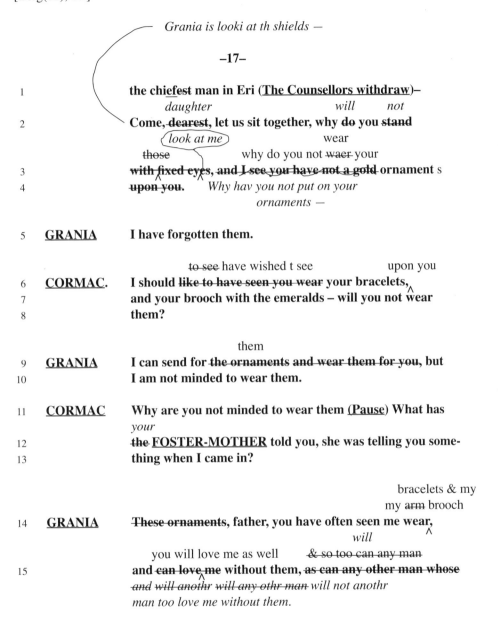

Grania is looki at th shields –

–17–

the chiefest man in Eri (<u>The Counsellors withdraw</u>)–

daughter *will* *not*

Come, ~~dearest~~, let us sit together, why ~~do~~ you ~~stand~~

look at me wear

~~those~~ why do you not ~~waer~~ your

~~with fixed eyes~~, ~~and I see you have not a gold~~ ornament s

~~upon you.~~ *Why hav you not put on your ornaments –*

<u>GRANIA</u> **I have forgotten them.**

~~to see~~ have wished t see upon you

<u>CORMAC</u>. **I should ~~like to have seen you wear~~ your bracelets, and your brooch with the emeralds – will you not wear them?**

them

<u>GRANIA</u> **I can send for ~~the ornaments and wear them for you~~, but I am not minded to wear them.**

<u>CORMAC</u> **Why are you not minded to wear them (<u>Pause</u>) What has**

your

~~the~~ <u>FOSTER-MOTHER</u> told you, she was telling you something when I came in?

bracelets & my

my ~~arm~~ brooch

<u>GRANIA</u> **~~These ornaments~~, father, you have often seen me wear,**

will

you will love me as well ~~& so too can any man~~

and ~~can love me~~ without them, ~~as can any other man whose~~

~~and will anothr will any othr man~~ will not anothr man too love me without them.

---

1 chiefest] The partial underline is made with either an indelible pencil or through blue carbon paper.

The cancellations in lines 2, 3 ("fixed eyes" and the two ink insertions above the line), 12 ("the"), the second insertion above line 15, and 15+ are all in pencil. The remaining cancellations on this page are in blue-black ink.

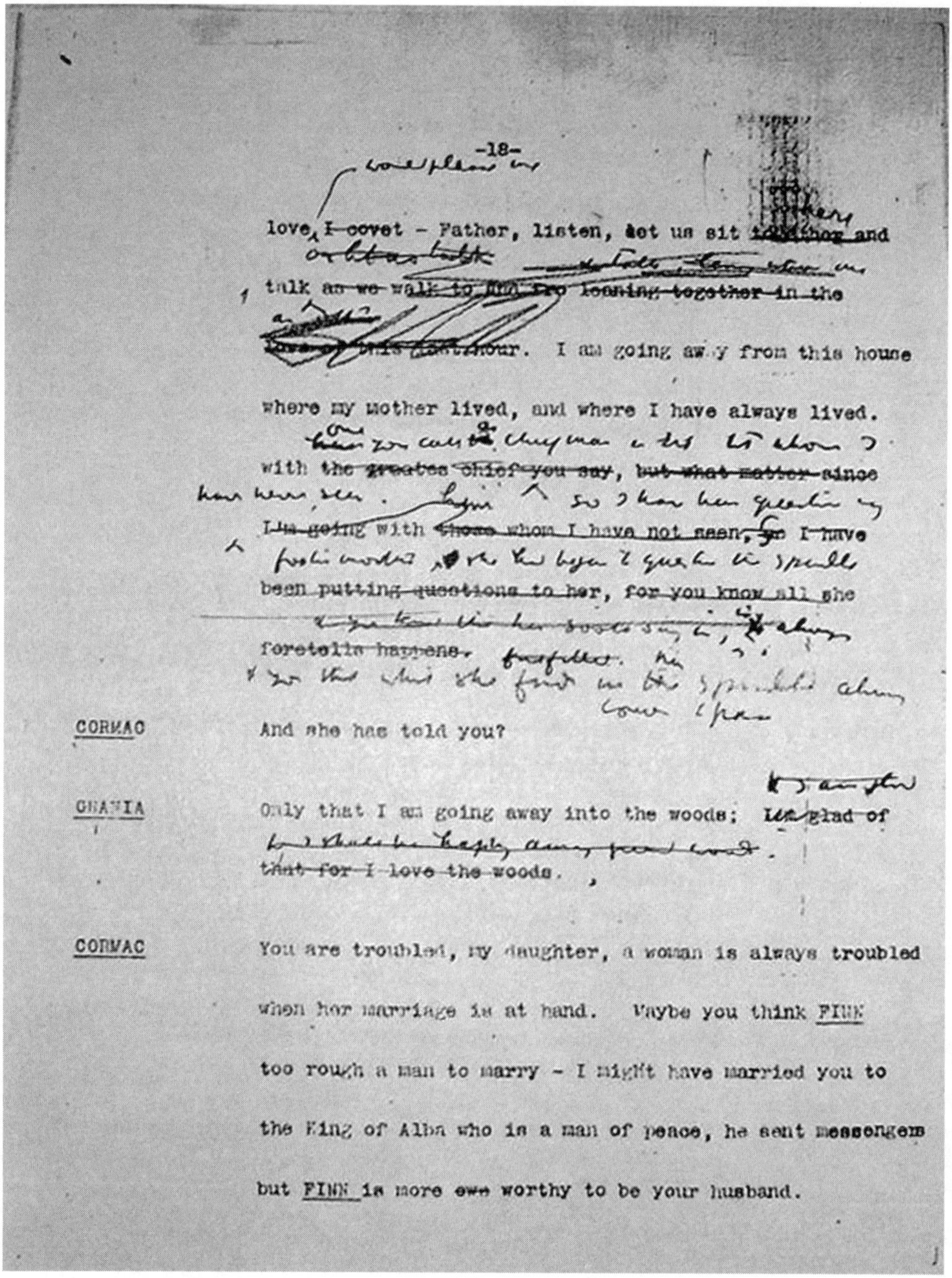

-18-

love, ~~I covet~~ [would please me] - Father, listen, let us sit ~~together and~~ [or listen]

talk ~~as we walk to and fro leaning together in the~~

~~heavy of this last~~ hour. I am going away from this house

where my mother lived, and where I have always lived.

with ~~the greatest chief you say~~, ~~but what matter since~~

~~I'm going~~ with ~~those~~ whom I have not seen, ~~so~~ I have

been ~~putting questions to her~~, ~~for you know all she~~

~~foretells happens.~~ [foretells]

CORMAC And she has told you?

GRANIA Only that I am going away into the woods; ~~I'm glad of~~

~~that for I love the woods.~~

CORMAC You are troubled, my daughter, a woman is always troubled

when her marriage is at hand. Maybe you think FINN

too rough a man to marry - I might have married you to

the King of Alba who is a man of peace, he sent messengers

but FINN is more ~~ewe~~ worthy to be your husband.

[Berg(02), 19r]

–18–

would please me

here

love^ I covet – Father, listen, let us sit ~~together and~~

~~*or let us talk*~~ ~~& talk, leanng upon one~~

(**talk^ ~~as we walk to and fro leaning together in the~~**

~~an other?~~

~~love of this last hour~~. I am going away from this house
where my mother lived, and where I have always lived.

one a

~~him~~ you call ~~the~~ chief man in Eri but whom I

with ~~the greates chief^ you say, but what matter since~~

have never seen. so I have been question my

~~him~~ {. {S

^**~~I'm going with those whom I have not seen{, {so I have~~**

foster mother{. {, ~~&~~ she had begun to question the spindle

~~been putting questions to her, for you know all she~~

~~is~~

~~& you know that her sooth saying^ tr always~~

~~foretells happens.~~ ~~fulfilled.~~ *her*

& you that what she finds in ~~the~~ spindle always comes to pass

CORMAC **And she has told you?**

~~& I am glad~~

GRANIA **Only that I am going away into the woods; ~~I'm glad of~~**

~~and I shall be happy among great woods~~.

~~that for I love the woods.~~

CORMAC **You are troubled, my daughter, a woman is always troubled when her marriage is at hand. Maybe you think FINN too rough a man to marry – I might have married you to the King of Alba who is a man of peace, he sent messengers but FINN is more ~~owo~~ worthy to be your husband.**

2, 10 The marks alongside line 2 in the LH margin and beneath "I'm" (line 10) are both made with either an indelible pencil or through blue carbon paper.

2–3 WBY recast the phrasing in blue-black ink (with a query), then recast it in pencil, and finally canceled the whole passage—including the recast versions—in pencil. That is, the first stage of cancellation—of separate phrases in TS—is in ink.

7 The inserted comma is converted into a period and the inserted ampersand deleted—both with pencil.

10–11 Canceled in pencil, before the subsequently canceled ink substitution was inserted.

16 Type deletion.

-19-

GRANIA I have not seen FINN.

CÒRMAC The enemies of Eri have seen him; you know how he has held its borders against them. ~~The men of Eri had~~ forgotten every thing but ~~grown too wealthy, they had ~~begun to think of nothing~~ but of~~ ~~cattle and sheep, or ~~of~~ dancing and harp playing, and the men of Lochlann and of Mona had begun to make us their spoil.~~ ~~But~~ FINN and his Fianna have made Eri great as when the Red Branch was at Eman of Macha.

GRANIA You wish me to marry as Kings and Queens marry – but I–

CORMAC (Suspiciously) You have set your heart upon some boy

GRANIA The Fianna are coming. I shall wed this night ~~he~~ him who~~m~~ is the chief man among them in my eyes.

CORMAC That is well, FINN is the chief man of Eri after the

-20-

High King (a sound of trumpets outside,)the Counsell[illegible] of CORMAC and the Servants enter – The servants open the door – NIALL stands by the door)

NIALL Let FINN and his Council enter (Enter FINN USHEEN, Caoilte ~~OSCAR~~ DIARMUID etc)

CORMAC FINN is welcome to my house.

FINN As the marriage law is, I declare the bride price upon the threshold. I give my word to guard this kingdom against all cattle spoilers that are of the kingdoms of Eri, and to guard it before my own country from the men of Lochlann and the men of Mona; and I give my word to overthrow all Kings of Eri that raise their hands against the High King. I cannot give a King's gift, for the Fianna have neither sheep nor cattle nor towns nor villages nor great store of gold or silver.

19r, ll. 3–7 Canceled with a blue-black ink line. The separate deletion in line 7 is also in blue-black ink. 4–5, 5 ("of"), 12 (last letter of "whom") are all pencil deletions.

20r, l. 6 are] The word is typed in later with a different (black) ribbon—as is the "g" of "give" in line 10.

[Berg(02), 20r]

–19–

GRANIA I have not seen FINN.

CORMAC The enemies of Eri have seen him;, you know how he has held its borders against them. ~~The men of Eri have~~ [d] grown too wealthy, they had ~~begun to think of nothing~~ [*forgotten every thing but*] but of cattle and sheep, or of dancing and harp playing, and the men of Lochlann and of Mona had begun to ~~make us their spoil. But~~ FINN and his Fianna have made Eri great as when the Red Branch was at Eman of Macha.

GRANIA You wish me to marry as Kings and Queens marry – but I –

CORMAC (Suspiciously) You have set your heart upon some boy

GRANIA The Fianna are coming. I shall wed this night ~~he~~ [him] whom is the chief man among them in my eyes.

CORMAC That is well, FINN is the chief man of Eri after the

[Berg(02), 21r]

–20–

High King (a sound of trumpets outside,) the Counsellors of CORMAC and the Servants enter – The servants open the door – NIALL stands by the door)

NIALL Let FINN and his Council enter (Enter FINN USHEEN, ~~OSCAR~~ [Caolt] DIARMUID etc)

CORMAC FINN is welcome to my house.

FINN As the marriage law is, I declare the bride price upon the threshold. I give my word to guard this kingdom against all cattle spoilers that areof the kingdoms of Eri, and to guard it before my own country from the men of Lochlann and the men of Mona; and I give my word to overthrow all kings of Eri that raise their hands against the High King. I cannot give a King's gift, for the Fianna have neither sheep nor cattle nor towns nor villages nor great store of gold or silver.

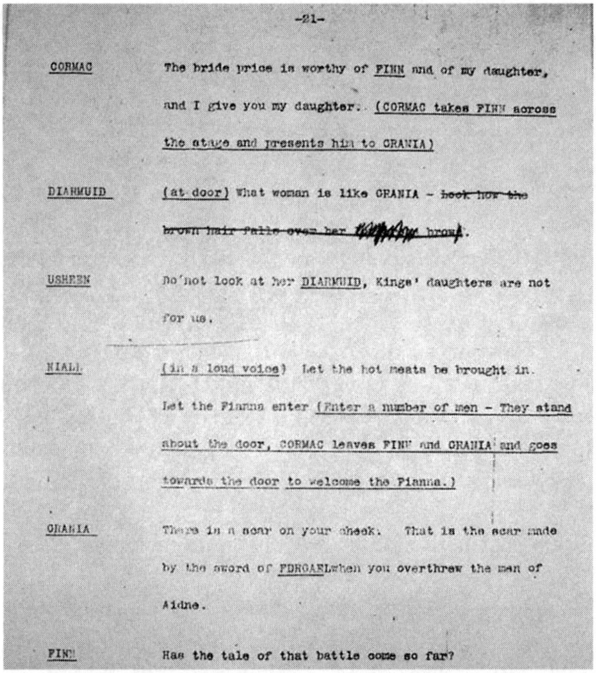

-21-

CORMAC The bride price is worthy of FINN and of my daughter, and I give you my daughter. (CORMAC takes FINN across the stage and presents him to GRANIA)

DIARMUID (at door) What woman is like GRANIA - ~~look how the brown hair falls over her low brown brows~~.

USHEEN Do not look at her DIARMUID, Kings' daughters are not for us.

NIALL (in a loud voice) Let the hot meats be brought in. Let the Fianna enter (Enter a number of men - They stand about the door, CORMAC leaves FINN and GRANIA and goes towards the door to welcome the Fianna.)

GRANIA There is a scar on your cheek. That is the scar made by the sword of FDRGAELwhen you overthrew the men of Aidne.

FINN Has the tale of that battle come so far?

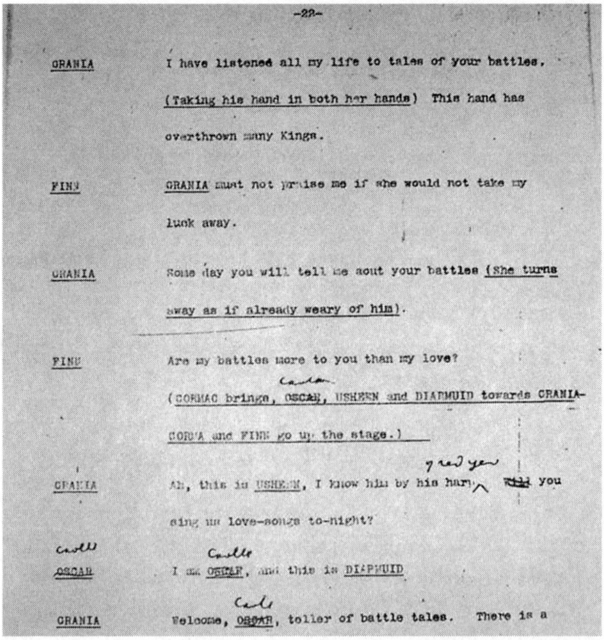

-22-

GRANIA I have listened all my life to tales of your battles. (Taking his hand in both her hands) This hand has overthrown many Kings.

FINN GRANIA must not praise me if she would not take my luck away.

GRANIA Some day you will tell me aout your battles (She turns away as if already weary of him).

FINN Are my battles more to you than my love?

(CORMAC brings, OSCAR, USHEEN and DIARMUID towards GRANIA- CORMA and FINN go up the stage.)

GRANIA Ah, this is USHEEN, I know him by his harp, ~~Will~~ you sing us love-songs to-night?

OSCAR I am OSCAR, and this is DIARMUID

GRANIA Welcome, OSCAR, teller of battle tales. There is a

22r, l. 2 daughter] The last five characters are typed in with a different (black) ribbon.

3–4 Pencil cancellation. Note that "low brown" and the terminal "s" of "brows" were canceled first.

23r, l. 8 Pencil deletion. The remaining emendations on this page are in blue-black ink. The inserted caret mark has a blue tinge, as if it had been written with indelible pencil or typed through blue carbon paper.

[Berg(02), 22r]

–21–

CORMAC — The bride price is worthy of FINN and of my daughter, and I give you my daughter. (CORMAC takes FINN across the stage and presents him to GRANIA)

DIARMUID — (at door) What woman is like GRANIA – ~~Look how the brown hair falls over her low brown brows.~~

USHEEN — Do not look at her DIARMUID, Kings' daughters are not for us.

NIALL — (in a loud voice) Let the hot meats be brought in. Let the Fianna enter (Enter a number of men – They stand about the door, CORMAC leaves FINN and GRANIA and goes towards the door to welcome the Fianna.)

GRANIA — There is a scar on your cheek. That is the scar made by the sword of FORGAELwhen you overthrew the men of Aidne.

FINN — Has the tale of that battle come so far?

[Berg(02), 23r]

–22–

GRANIA — I have listened all my life to tales of your battles. (Taking his hand in both her hands) This hand has overthrown many Kings.

FINN — GRANIA must not praise me if she would not take my luck away.

GRANIA — Some day you will tell me aout your battles (She turns away as if already weary of him).

FINN — Are my battles more to you than my love?

(CORMAC brings, ~~OSCAR~~ [Caolte], USHEEN and DIARMUID towards GRANIA– CORMA and FINN go up the stage.)

GRANIA — Ah, this is USHEEN, I know him by his harp. [^ of red yew] ~~Will~~ you sing us love-songs to-night?

~~OSCAR~~ [Caolte] — I am ~~OSCAR~~ [Caolte], and this is DIARMUID

GRANIA — Welcome, ~~OSCAR~~ [Caolte], teller of battle tales. There is a

-25-

tale you tell - (She stands looking at DIARMUID, forgetful of everything) And this is DIARMUID.

NIALL The King, and FINN, the son of COOL are seated, and the guests at this table, ~~are - DIARMUID, OSCAR, USHEEN CAOLTE GALL, son of MORNA, CONAN THE BALD, CONGAL~~ and ~~FINMOLE~~ - (The Fianna and Serving Men ~~withdraw, leaving NIALL and one Serving Man to wait at the King's table.~~)

[Handwritten insertions: "Conchubar & Finn are" / "at table & the rest" / "& the Fianna have been spread beyond the arras." / "[illegible] in the western half." / "go out &" / "except Diarmuid, Caoilte, Goll, Usheen, Oscar"]

CORMAC My daughter, why do you not take your place beside FINN ~~son of COOL~~?

GRANIA Every night I have poured out your ale, father, I would do so this last time, and this night I would pour out my husband's for the first time.

CORMAC If this be your wish.

FINN GRANIA must not pour out our ale.

[Berg(02), 24r]

–23–

**tale you tell – (She stands looking at DIARMUID, for-
getful of everything) And this is DIARMUID.**

Concillors of Fin are

NIALL **The King , and FINN, the son of COOL are seated , and the**

the tables for the rest

guests at this table , ~~are – DIARMUID, OSCAR, USHEEN~~

of th Feann have been spread beyond the arras

~~CAOLTE GALL, son of MORNA, CONAN THE BALD, CONGAL~~ and

~~in the west of the h~~ in the western hall!

& all go out &

~~FINMOLE –~~ (The Fianna and Serving Men ~~withdraw~~ , ~~leaving~~

Conan, who sit at a table –

except Darmd ~~N~~ Caolt Ushen, Goll, Alvin, & Fergus

NIALL and one Serving Man ~~to wait at the King's table.~~)

CORMAC **My daughter, why do you not take your place beside FINN
~~son of COOL~~ ?**

GRANIA **Every night I have poured out your ale, father, I would
do so this last time, and this night I would pour out
my husband's for the first time.**

CORMAC **If this be your wish.**

FINN **GRANIA must not pour out our ale.**

3–6 and stage direction Subsequent versions display how the tangled revisions join to make sense.

8 Pencil deletion. The remaining emendations on this page are in blue-black ink.

[Berg(02), 25r]

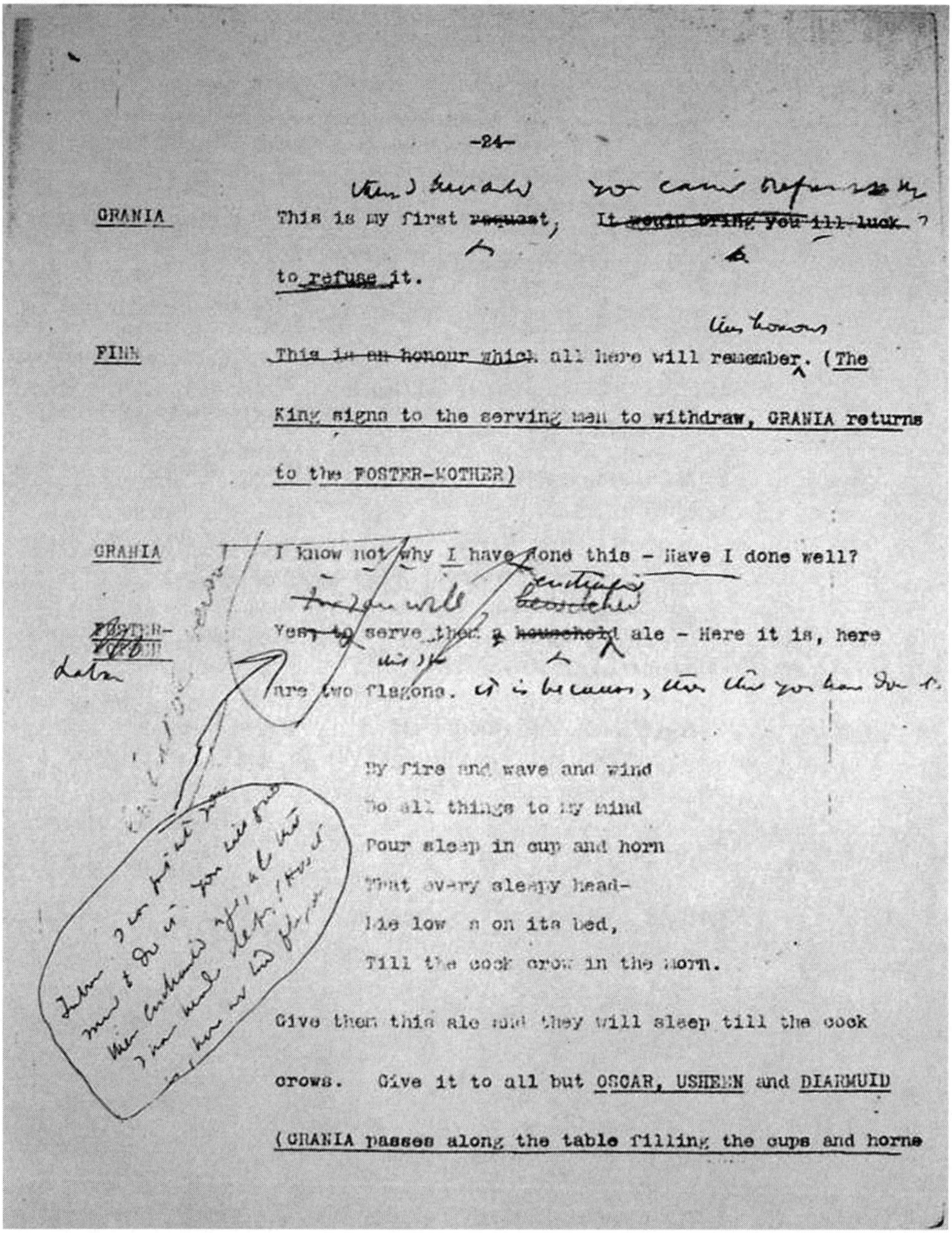
-24-

GRANIA This is my first ~~request~~, ~~It would bring you ill luck~~ to ~~refuse~~ it.

FINN ~~This is an honour which~~ all here will remember. (The King signs to the serving men to withdraw, GRANIA returns to the FOSTER-MOTHER)

GRANIA I know not why I have done this - Have I done well?

FOSTER-MOTHER Yes, ~~to~~ serve them a ~~household~~ ale - Here it is, here are two flagons.

My fire and wave and wind
Do all things to my mind
Pour sleep in cup and horn
That every sleepy head-
Lie low n on its bed,
Till the cock crow in the morn.

Give them this ale and they will sleep till the cock crows. Give it to all but OSCAR, USHEEN and DIARMUID (GRANIA passes along the table filling the cups and horns

[Berg(02), 25r]

–24–

thing I have asked *you cannot refuse me.*

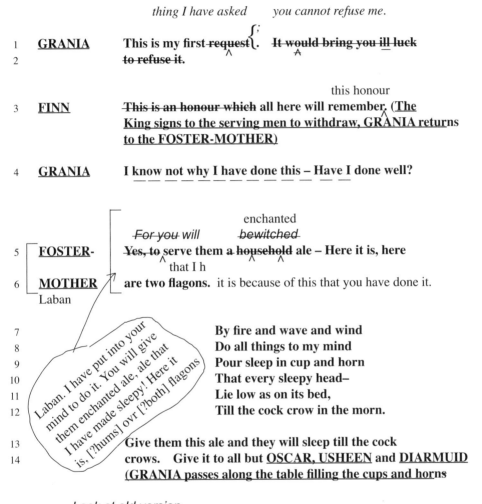

GRANIA This is my first ~~request~~ {; . ~~It would bring you ill luck to refuse it.~~

this honour

FINN ~~This is an honour which~~ all here will remember. (The King signs to the serving men to withdraw, GRANIA returns to the FOSTER-MOTHER)

GRANIA I know not why I have done this – Have I done well?

enchanted

~~*For you*~~ *will* ~~*bewitched*~~

FOSTER-MOTHER ~~Yes, to~~ serve them ~~a household~~ ale – Here it is, here are two flagons. it is because of this that you have done it.

that I h

Laban

Laban. I have put into your mind to do it. You will give them enchanted ale, ale that I have made sleepy! Here it is, [?hums] ovr [?both] flagons

By fire and wave and wind
Do all things to my mind
Pour sleep in cup and horn
That every sleepy head–
Lie low as on its bed,
Till the cock crow in the morn.

Give them this ale and they will sleep till the cock crows. Give it to all but OSCAR, USHEEN and DIARMUID (GRANIA passes along the table filling the cups and horns

Look at old version

1–2, 5 Pencil deletions.

1 ill] The underline has a blue tinge, as if it had been written with indelible pencil or through blue carbon paper.

3 Ink deletion.

4 Ink underlining.

4–6 For the "old version" in the holograph cross-reference, cf. Berg(01), fol. 18r. It might be remarked that GM's authorship of the comment is uncertain.

14+ Type deletion.

-25-

OSCAR and USHEEN are the last who should be served – When she comes to DIARMUID she stands looking at him.)

CORMAC Why do you not fill DIARMUID'S horn?

GRANIA The ale is all spilled – I will bring another flagon.

CORMAC I do not like the spilling of ale at a marriage feast.

CONAN It never happens but it brings ill luck.

DIARMUID CONAN sees ill luck everywhere. When will FINN take away his favour from CONAN and let the Fianna give him his deserts.

FINN Tell us a story OSCAR, and put the spilling of the ale out of our minds (OSCAR rises from his place and takes his harp. He stands touching his harp as if uncertain what story he is going to tell.

FINN Tell us the story of the house of the quicken trees.

-26-

[Caoilte] ~~OSCAR~~ Yes, I will tell the story of the house of the quicken trees –(A pause) – It is gone, it went out of my mind of a sudden – A new take is coming to me – It is coming to me – I see a man lying dead – and his wife is going away with another.

FINN What quarrel have you with me that you should tell me such a tale at my marriage?

USHEEN FINN, FINN, the gods are in the room, the ale has been spilled and a strange tale has been [bit] into [Caoilte's] ~~OSCAR'S~~ mind. Our luck is being taken away (They all start to their feet.)

FINN Let us all sit down again. Let us drink and forget our thoughts of ill luck – (They all drink)

CORMAC (Suddenly sleepy and trying to rouse himself) Let

[Berg(02), 26^r]

–25–

OSCAR and USHEEN are the last who should be served – When she comes to DIARMUID she stands looking at him.)

CORMAC **Why do you not fill DIARMUID'S horn?**

GRANIA **The ale is all spilled – I will bring another flagon.**

CORMAC **I do not like the spilling of ale at a marriage feast.**

CONAN **It never happens but it brings ill luck.**

DIARMUID **CONAN sees ill luck everywhere. When will FINN take away his favour from CONAN and let the Fianna give him his deserts.**

FINN **Tell us a story OSCAR, and put the spilling of the ale out of our minds (OSCAR rises from his place and takes his harp. He stands touching his harp as if uncertain what story he is going to tell.**

FINN **Tell us the story of the house of the quicken trees.**

[Berg(02), 27^r]

–26–

Caolte
~~OSCAR~~ **Yes, I will tell the story of the house of the quicken trees –(A pause) – It is gone, it went out of my mind of a sudden – A new tale is coming to me – It is coming to me – I see a man lying dead – and his wife is going away with another.**

FINN **What quarrel have you with me that you should tell me such a tale at my marriage?**

USHEEN **FINN, FINN, the gods are in the room, the ale has been spilled and a strange tale has been ~~out~~** *put* **into ~~OSCAR'S~~** Caolte. **mind. Our luck is being taken away (They all start to their feet.)**

FINN **Let us all sit down again. Let us drink and forget our thoughts of ill luck – (They all drink)**

CORMAC **(Suddenly sleepy and trying to rouse himself) Let**

27^r, l. 9 Oscar] The name was deleted in pencil before the ink substitution was made.

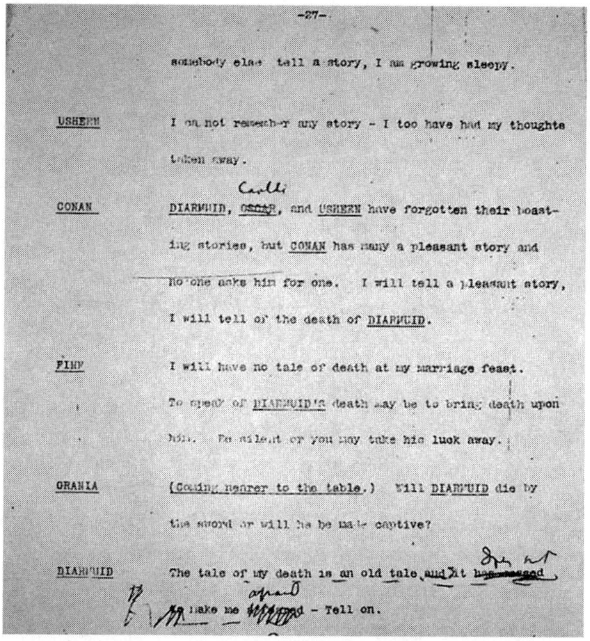

-27-

somebody else tell a story, I am growing sleepy.

USHEEN I can not remember any story - I too have had my thoughts taken away.

CONAN DIARMUID, ~~OSCAR~~ [Caolte], and USHEEN have forgotten their boasting stories, but CONAN has many a pleasant story and no one asks him for one. I will tell a pleasant story, I will tell of the death of DIARMUID.

FINN I will have no tale of death at my marriage feast. To speak of DIARMUID'S death may be to bring death upon him. Be silent or you may take his luck away.

GRANIA (Coming nearer to the table.) Will DIARMUID die by the sword or will he be made captive?

DIARMUID The tale of my death is an old tale, and it ~~has passed~~ [does not] to make me ~~afeared~~ [afeard] - Tell on.

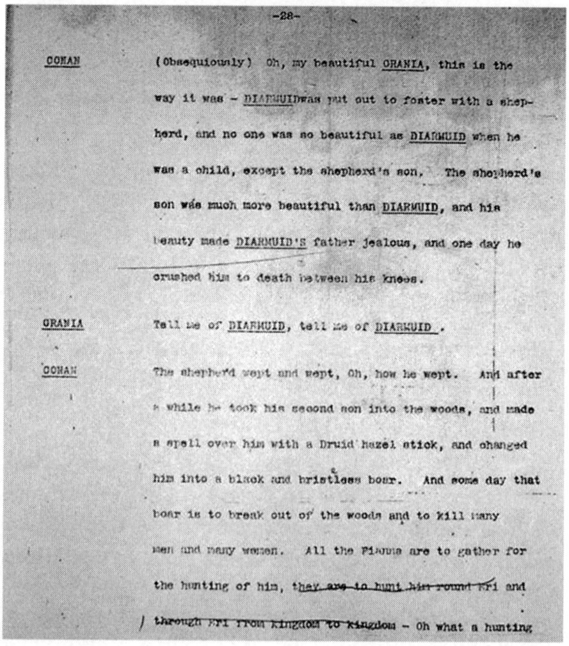

-28-

CONAN (Obsequiously) Oh, my beautiful GRANIA, this is the way it was - DIARMUID was put out to foster with a shepherd, and no one was so beautiful as DIARMUID when he was a child, except the shepherd's son. The shepherd's son was much more beautiful than DIARMUID, and his beauty made DIARMUID'S father jealous, and one day he crushed him to death between his knees.

GRANIA Tell me of DIARMUID, tell me of DIARMUID.

CONAN The shepherd wept and wept, Oh, how he wept. And after a while he took his second son into the woods, and made a spell over him with a Druid hazel stick, and changed him into a black and bristless boar. And some day that boar is to break out of the woods and to kill many men and many women. All the Fianna are to gather for the hunting of him, ~~they are to hunt him round Eri and through Eri from kingdom to kingdom~~ - Oh what a hunting

28r, ll. 13–14 Pencil underlining. The underline beneath "a'feared" is different: it has a blue tinge, as if made with an indelible pencil or through blue carbon paper.

29r, ll. 12, 16 The "e" inserted above line 12 and the mark in the LH margin of line 16 both have a blue tinge, as if written with an indelible pencil or through blue carbon paper.

15, 16 Pencil cancellations.

[Berg(02), 28r]

–27–

somebody else tell a story, I am growing sleepy.

USHEEN I cannot remember any story – I too have had my thoughts taken away.

Caolte

CONAN **DIARMUID, ~~OSCAR~~, and USHEEN have forgotten their boasting stories, but CONAN has many a pleasant story and no one asks him for one. I will tell a pleasant story, I will tell of the death of DIARMUID.**

FINN **I will have no tale of death at my marriage feast. To speak of DIARMUID'S death may be to bring death upon him. Be silent or you may take his luck away.**

GRANIA **(Coming nearer to the table.) Will DIARMUID die by the sword or will he be made captive?**

{I does not

DIARMUID **The tale of my death is an old tale . and {it has ceased**

afraid

? **to make me ~~a'feared~~ – Tell on.**

[Berg(02), 29r]

–28–

CONAN **(Obsequiously) Oh, my beautiful GRANIA, this is the way it was – DIARMUIDwas put out to foster with a shepherd, and no one was so beautiful as DIARMUID when he was a child, except the shepherd's son. The shepherd's son was much more beautiful than DIARMUID, and his beauty made DIARMUID'S father jealous, and one day he crushed him to death between his knees.**

GRANIA **Tell me of DIARMUID, tell me of DIARMUID .**

CONAN **The shepherd wept and wept, Oh, how he wept. And after a while he took his second son into the woods, and made a spell over him with a Druid hazel stick, and changed**

e

him into a black and bristless boar. And some day that boar is to break out of the woods and to kill many men and many women. All the Fianna are to gather for the hunting of him, ~~they are to hunt him round Eri~~ and

(**~~through Eri from kingdom to kingdom~~ – Oh what a hunting**

-29-

Oh, what a hunting !

GRANIA Tell me more of DIARMUID, tell me quickly.

CONAN I must drink I am thirsty again (He drinks) DIARMUID must go out against that boar and must be killed. It was to kill him that the shepherd made the spell over his second son. He shall be torn by the tusks, he shall be bloody, his face shall be foul because it will be bloody. I would that the women of Eri could see him when he is foul, and bloody - (He staggers). I am growing sleepy, because I have to run the messages of the Fianna (He recovers himself) I shall live to see him when the tusks have torn him, for it has been foretold of him also that he shall not be remembered for deeds of arms, but as a lover of women. That he shall live as a lover of women and that his life shall be

-30-

be soon over. Who has put witchcraft into my ale? Who among the Fianna has done this? -(He falls)

USHEEN He said there was witchcraft in the ale, and look, they are all sleeping. Who was it that put witchcraft into the ale, GRANIA?

GRANIA My foster mother has done this for me ~~I ordered the witchcraft to be put into the ale~~. I had never a mind to marry FINN. But why does not DIARMUID come to us? (DIARMUID comes from the table) It was for you that She ~~I ordered~~ witchcraft ~~to be~~ was put into the ale.

DIARMUID For me, GRANIA?

GRANIA I had never a mind to marry FINN; I am going away with you to-night, we are going to leave without before they awake.

30r, l. 9 There is a faint pencil tick across the stage-direction in this line.

15 women] The word has been inserted later, using a different (black) ribbon.

[Berg(02), 30r]

–29–

Oh, what a hunting !

GRANIA Tell me more of **DIARMUID**, tell me quickly.

CONAN I must drink I am thirsty again (He drinks)DIARMUID must go out against that boar and must be killed. It was to kill him that the shepherd made the spell over his second son. He shall be torn by the tusks, he shall be bloody, his face shall be foul because it will be bloody. I would that the women of Eri could see him when he is foul, and bloody – (He staggers). I am growing sleepy, because I have to run the messages of the Fianna (He recovers himself)I shall live to see him when the tusks have torn him, for it has been fore-told of him also that he shall not be remembered for deeds of arms, but as a lover of women. That he shall live as a lover of women and that his life shall be

[Berg(02), 31r]

–30–

be soon over. Who has put witchcraft into my ale? Who among the Fianna has done this? –(He falls)

USHEEN He said there was witchcraft in the ale, and look, they are all sleeping. Who was it that put witchcraft into the ale, GRANIA?

My foster mother has done this for me

GRANIA ~~I ordered the witchcraft to be put into the ale.~~ I had never a mind to marry FINN. But why does not DIARMUID come to us? (DIARMUID comes from the table)

the *was*

It was for you that I ~~ordered~~ ^ witchcraft ~~to be~~ put in-to the ale.

DIARMUID For me, GRANIA?

GRANIA I had never a mind to marry FINN; I am going away

this house

with you to-night, we are going to leave ^ before they awake.

31r, l. 2 among] The first character has been inserted later with a new (black) ribbon.

6, 9 The substitutions on this page provide a good example of the particular difficulty of attributing handwriting in this TS.

-31-

DIARMUID You and I ? and you did not see me before this night ?

GRANIA I desired you, and you were in my thoughts before I saw you, DIARMUID. You were in my thoughts, DIARMUID (She takes him in her arms)

DIARMUID I too desired you, and you were in my thoughts - Oh, beautiful woman ! You were in my thoughts, GRANIA - Let me look at you - Let me put back your hair - Your eyes are grey, GRANIA, your eyes are grey ! and your hands - but FINN, but FINN, but FINN - (he disengages them softly) GRANIA, wife of FINN, why have you played with me !

GRANIA I am not the wife of FINN (She goes towards DIARMUID) And now I cannot be FINN'S wife, for you have held me in your arms and you have kissed me.

DIARMUID What is this madness, GRANIA ? Here, here, this night - and FINN sleeping there.

-32-

GRANIA If he had loved me, his love would have been stronger than witchcraft (A pause)- You shrink from me, why do you shrink from me ? Am I not desirable ? I have heard men praise me. (She holds out her hair towards him) You have touched my hair and looked into my eyes. Why do you shrink away ? I have heard, DIARMUID, that women love you, and certainly a woman must be desirable in your eyes. It may be that men have lied to me, and this hair is not soft, this body delicate - (To OSCAR and USHEEN). Is not my plight miserable ? Shall all men shrink from me ? Would you shrink from me, if it ~~with~~ were you I had asked to go away with me ? No matter who shrinks from me now/ since the man I long for shrinks. The world that ~~is shrinking~~ shrinks from me - ~~It has shrunk till it is like a little nut.~~

~~OSCAR~~ Conan. Look, GRANIA, at the sleeping man whose ale you have bewitched.

33r, l. 13 If the circled period is meant to substitute for the deleted comma—and what other meaning can it have—it is an uncharacteristic mark of revision by either author.

14–15 Ink cancellation.

[Berg(02), 32r]

–31–

DIARMUID **You and I ? and you did not see me before this night ?**

GRANIA **I desired you, and you were in my thoughts before I saw you, DIARMUID. You were in my thoughts, DIARMUID (She takes him in her arms)**

DIARMUID **I too desired you, and you were in my thoughts – Oh, beautiful woman ! You were in my thoughts, GRANIA – Let me look at you – Let me put back your hair – Your eyes are grey, GRANIA, your eyes are grey ! and your**

(He disengages himself)

hands – But FINN, but FINN, but FINN – ^ GRANIA, wife of FINN, why have you played with me !

GRANIA **I am not the wife of FINN (She goes towards DIARMUID) And now I cannot be FINN'S wife, for you have held me in your arms and you have kissed me.**

DIARMUID **What is this madness, GRANIA ? Here, here, this night – and FINN sleeping there.**

[Berg(02), 33r]

–32–

GRANIA **If he had loved me, his love would have been stronger than witchcraft (A pause)– You shrink from me, why do you shrink from me ? Am I not desirable ? I have heard men praise me. (She holds out her hair towards him) You have touched my hair and looked into my eyes. Why do you shrink away ? I have heard, DIARMUID, that women love you, and certainly a woman must be desirable in your eyes. It may be that men have lied to me, and this hair is not soft, this body delicate – (To OSCAR and USHEEN). Is not my plight miserable ? Shall**

all

^ men shrink from me ? Would you shrink from me, if it

were

~~was~~ you I had asked to go away with me ? No matter ⊙ **who shrinks from me me now ; since the man I long for shrinks.**

whole shrinks from me

The ^ ~~world is shrinking – It has shrunk till it is like a little nut.~~

Caolt

~~OSCAR~~. **Look, GRANIA, at the sleeping man whose ale you have bewitched.**

-33-

USHEEN If ~~FINN~~ were to awake he would take some terrible vengeance for this.

[What is his vengeance to me? Has not my world withered?]

GRANIA The ~~world has withered, so away with his vengeance~~. I will go into the green woods, and I will wander alone there till I die.

DIARMUID When I looked into your eyes, GRANIA, it was as though [I had been in the dark & I saw the dawn] ~~life had begun to dawn~~, ~~and your eyes were the heart~~ of ~~the dawn~~ - But [no-no-I cannot I cannot.] ~~for you and I, GRANIA, that can never be, for~~ there ~~are~~ [is a] stronger thing~~s~~ than love.

[Conall] ~~OSCAR~~ GRANIA, GRANIA - The Fianna live poor and live near to death always that ~~there may be nothing stronger than~~ [honour may be the strongest thing] ~~honour~~ among them.

USHEEN DIARMUID, ~~you would do well to~~ turn your eyes [away] from her.

GRANIA He looks ~~on~~ [at] me, because ~~I have~~ [it has] been foretold - foretold ~~for him~~ [that by ...].

[Berg(02), 34r]

–33–

USHEEN **If FINN were to awake he would take some terrible vengeance for this.**

What is his vengeance to me? Has not my world withered?

GRANIA **~~The world has withered, so away with his vengeance~~. I will go into the green woods, and I will wander alone there till I die.**

DIARMUID **When I looked into your eyes, GRANIA, it was as though**
I had been in the dark & I saw the dawn
~~life had begun to dawn, and your eyes were the heart~~
no – no – I cannot, I cannot.
of ~~the dawn~~ – But ~~for you and I, GRANIA, that can never~~
is a
~~be, for~~ there ~~are~~ stronger thing~~s~~ than love.

Caolte
~~OSCAR~~ **GRANIA, GRANIA – The FIanna live poor and live near to**
honour may be the strongest thing
death always that ~~there may be nothing stronger than~~
st
~~honour~~ among them.

away
USHEEN **DIARMUID~~, you would do well to~~ turn your eyes from her.**

at it has
GRANIA **He looks ~~on~~ me, because ~~I have~~ been forctold – foretold ~~for him.~~** that he & I.

3, 11 The fragmentary underlinings appear as if made with an indelible pencil or through blue carbon paper.
9 The second and third emendations in this line (substitution of "is a" and deletion of "s") are in pencil. The remaining emendations on this page are all in blue-black ink.

-34-

DIARMUID (Disengaging himself from USHEEN and OSCAR) What has been foretold - Who has foretold ~~this of~~ me? ~~Oh, what a strange foretelling~~.

USHEEN DIARMUID, look ~~at your sleeping friend~~.

Caolte
~~OSCAR~~ Think of your battle ~~tales~~, DIARMUID, and your ~~tale of fealty~~.

DIARMUID If ~~the~~ fortune-telling has ~~foretold~~ ~~that I must die and save my honour, having lost~~ it - What did she ~~tell you, oh, what did she tell you~~ ?

GRANIA She ~~said~~ of a woman pledged to a man whom she ~~could~~ not love, and of ~~one sent to help her from this dismal bridal~~. It ~~is~~ foretold that the man will ~~forego~~ all things and that the woman ~~will forego~~ all things ~~for the sake of their love~~. It is foretold that they will go away in the ~~midst of the bridal feast into~~ the un-

[Berg(02), 35[r]]

–34–

DIARMUID **~~(Disengaging himself from USHEEN and OSCAR)~~ What has**
it
been foretold – Who has foretold ~~you for me~~? ~~Oh, what~~
~~a sweet foretelling.~~

where Finn sleeps
USHEEN **DIARMUID, look ~~on your sleeping friend.~~**

Caolte fame in of *oath*
~~OSCAR~~ **Think of your^ battle ~~tales~~, DIARMUID, and^ your ~~talk of~~**
~~fealty~~.

The *er* lied if she has said
DIARMUID **~~If the~~ fortune-telling has ~~foretold dishonour to me I~~**
that I shall break my oath to Finn ~~he she has spoken falsehood~~
~~must die and save my honour, having lost~~ it – What did
Has she said [?~~it was~~] this. ~~Has she said that~~ I
~~Grania~~ ~~she has not Dairmd~~.
~~she tell you, oh, what did she tell you~~ ?
has she said
Darmd What ~~did she tell you~~, O what did she tell you.

spoke did
GRANIA **She ~~told~~ of a woman pledged to a man , whom she ~~could~~ not**
will
a man, who be her friend & her helper.
love, and of ~~one sent to help her from this dismal~~
She *for* leave
~~bridal.~~ ~~It is~~ ~~fore~~told that the man will ~~forego~~ all
will leave
things and that the woman ~~will forego~~ all things ~~for~~
for
~~but their~~ loves sake. She
~~the sake of their love.~~ ~~It is~~ foretold that they will
a ~~it~~
middle^of marriage feast & wander in
go away in the ~~midst of the bridal feast into~~ the un-

---

5 battle, 6 fealty The lines beneath the two words are instances of the several indelible pencil or blue carbon underlines and marks to be found scattered through the present TS. In the first instance here, the underline has been canceled by WBY (in ink).

5 oath, 12 for With accompanying cancellations, the only two pencil emendations on this page.

[Berg(02), 36r]

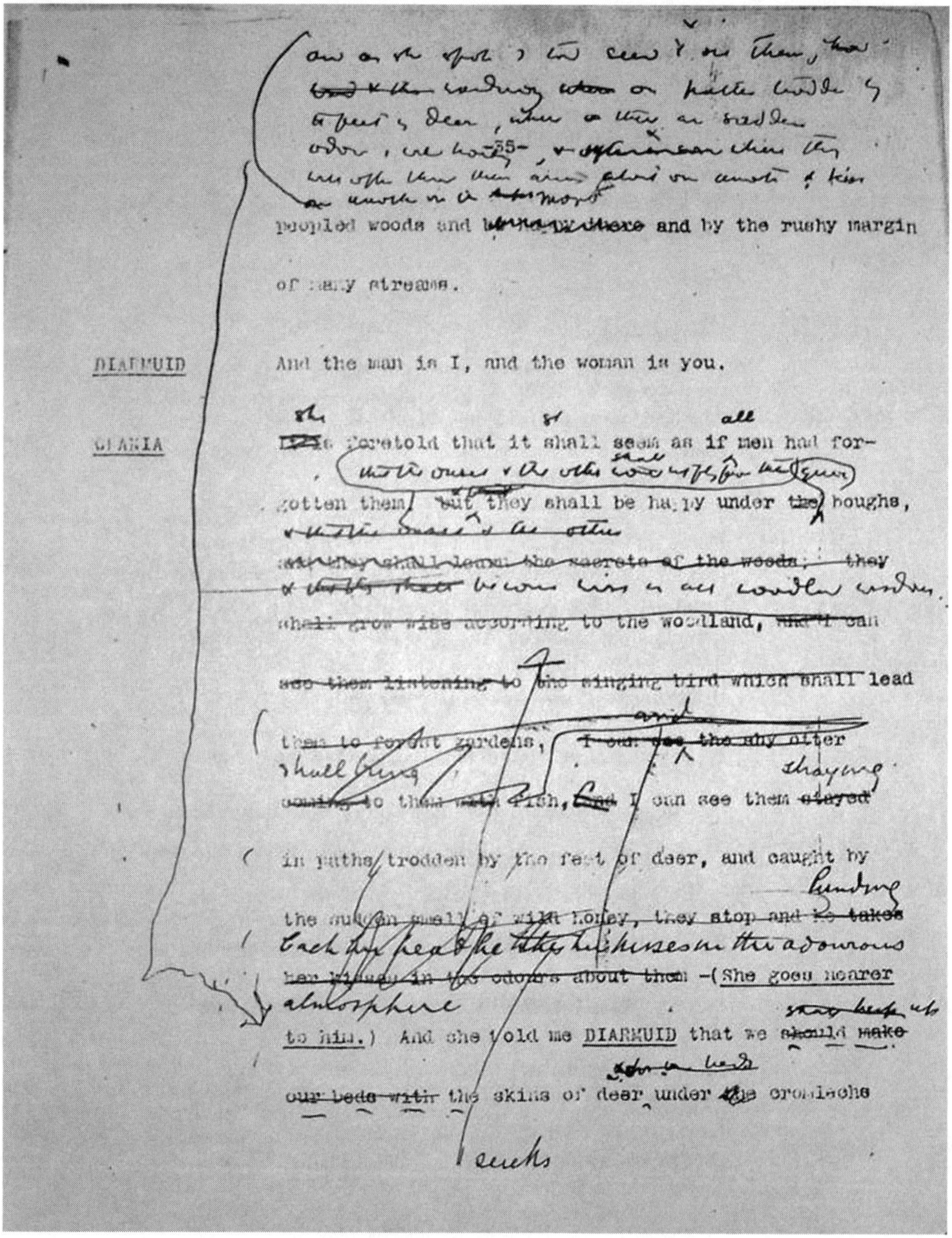

peopled woods and by the rushy margin

of many streams.

DIARMUID And the man is I, and the woman is you.

GRANIA ... foretold that it shall seem as if men had for-

gotten them, but they shall be happy under the boughs,

and they shall learn the secrets of the woods; they

shall grow wise according to the woodland, and I can

see them listening to the singing bird which shall lead

them to forest gardens, I can see the shy otter

coming to them with fish, and I can see them stayed

in paths trodden by the feet of deer, and caught by

the sudden smell of wild honey, they stop and he takes

her hand in the odours about them -(She goes nearer

to him.) And she told me DIARMUID that we should make

our beds with the skins of deer under the cromlechs

[Berg(02), 36r]

and as she spoke I too seemd to see them, [?~~home~~]
~~ward & thro~~ wandering ~~where~~ on paths trodden by
th feet of deer, where a ther are sudden

–35– &

odour f wild honey, & ~~often some~~ where they
will often throw their arms about one anothr & kiss
on anothr on th ~~lips~~ *mouth*

peopled woods and ~~be happy there~~ and by the rushy margin of many streams.

<u>DIARMUID</u> **And the man is I, and the woman is you.**

She sh all

<u>GRANIA</u> **~~It is~~ foretold that it shall seem as if men had for-**

shall

(that the ousel & the otter ~~would~~ not fly from them) (green)

& ~~that~~

gotten them, but that they shall be happy under ~~the~~ boughs,

~~& that the ousel & the otter~~

~~and they shall learn the secrets of the woods; they~~

& ~~that they shall~~ become wise in all woodland wandrng.

~~shall grow wise according to the woodland,~~ ~~and I can~~

T

~~see them listening to~~ ~~the singing bird which shall~~ lead

, *and*

(them to forest gardens. I can see the shy otter

shall bring ~~A~~ *straying*

~~coming to~~ them ~~with~~ fish, ~~and~~ I can see them ~~stayed~~

(in paths trodden by the feet of deer, and caught by

bending

the sudden smell of wild honey, they stop and ~~he takes~~

(back her head he ~~takes~~ her kisses in the odourous

~~her kisses in the odours about them~~ –(<u>She goes nearer</u>

(atmosphere ~~shall heap~~ up

(><u>to him.</u>) And she told me <u>DIARMUID</u> that we ~~should make~~

~~& for our beds~~

~~our beds with~~ the skins of deer under ~~the~~ cromlechs

sucks

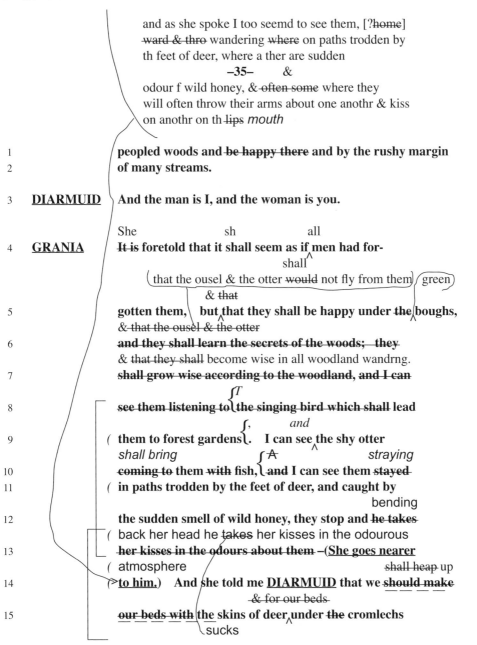

GM's revision of "lips" to "mouth" (l. -1), cancellation of "that they shall" and of "and I can" (l. 7), plus the revisions in lines 8–10, are in pencil. The remaining emendations on this page are in ink.

1 and] Inserted later with a (new) black ribbon.

9, 11, 13, 14 The accompanying marks in the LH margin appear as if drawn with a an indelible pencil or through blue carbon paper.

-36-

and in cool caves, and awaking from sleep, we knew not why, we should see the same light shining through the leaves. She told me that we should know the secret people of the glades and rocks, and that if al. the men in Eri were their enemies they would not snatch our love could never be snatched from us.

DIARMUID I must not listen, for listening my eyes fill with mist, and swooning I shall fall into thine arms; or I shall awaken FINN - FINN, FINN, awake (she puts her hand on his mouth)

GRANIA What would you tell him ?

DIARMUID That the world vanishes; that I see nothing but you.

GRANIA Have you not sworn to help the helpless, and who is more helpless than I ?

DIARMUID Had you not told me that you loved me, I would have

[Berg(02), 37[r]]

pull
they coo could not ~~take~~ us out eac othrs a arms.

–36–

~~we will~~ awake
and in cool caves, and ~~awaking~~ from sleep, we knew not
though the dwarfs of ^the rocks had calld to us [?then]
why, we ~~should see the same light shining through~~ the
that we may fee see the starlight fallng throug th leaves
~~leaves.~~ She told me that ~~we should know the secret~~
the dwarfs of the rocks & the secret peopl of th trees shal
~~people of the glades and rocks, and that if all~~ the
watch over us & thoug all the men of Eri were
our
~~men in Eri were their enemies they could not snatch~~
our enemies, ~~they shoud not find us~~ ~~they coud not~~
~~our love could never~~ be ~~snatched from us.~~
they [?~~should~~] they shoud not find us amng th green woods

~~or I shall~~ ~~*fall*~~ *or I will take*
DIARMUID **I must not listen, ~~for listening my eyes fill with mist~~,**
her in my arms —
~~thoug for seeng~~ ~~*her*~~ *I will*
(**~~and swooning I shall fall into thine arms; or I shall~~**
awaken FINN – FINN, FINN, awake ~~(She puts her hand on~~
~~his mouth)~~ I will awake him (He goes ner to Fin)

GRANIA **What would you tell him ?**

DIARMUID **That the world vanishes; that I see nothing but you.**

GRANIA **Have you not sworn to help the helpless, and who is more helpless than I ?**

DIARMUID **Had you not told me that you loved me, I would have**

---

5 our, 6 our, 6 us, 12 sworn All typed in later with a different (black) ribbon.
6+–8 The ink revisions are canceled and overwritten with pencil in this passage.
7–8 The type lines are first canceled with ink.
7–9 Another passage where the authorship of the revisions is manifestly disputable.
8 The mark in the LH margin is drawn as if with an indelible pencil or through blue carbon paper.
9–9+ stage direction The cancellation is made as if drawn with indelible pencil or through blue carbon paper.

-37-

helped you.

GRANIA Help me, DIARMUID.

DIARMUID My ~~friends here witness my distress~~; ~~and~~ tell FINN of ~~it~~; ~~and tell him that~~ ~~until she came on a helpless~~ ~~she I refused her~~

she has asked me for my help.

GRANIA (Standing at the door which she has thrown open)

Come DIARMUID to the woods, the birds of AONGHUS, the birds of love, the birds that the eye cannot see, sing joyously, singing fiercely, they clap their wings and sing.

DIARMUID She asked for my help and I must give it.

USHEEN From this night the Fianna are ~~rent~~ broken in two.

Conall ~~OSCAR~~ And the kingdom that was ~~to be safe~~ ~~besides~~ and DIARMUID'S honour is taken away.

[Berg(02), 38r]

–37–

helped you.

<u>GRANIA</u> **Help me, <u>DIARMUID</u>.**

Caolt
~~D~~ Oscar & Usheen hav seen my trouble *they will*
<u>DIARMUID</u> **~~My friends here witness my distress;~~ ~~and~~ tell <u>FINN</u>**)
[?~~*they*~~])
my trouble [?~~*th*~~] *now* ~~& will show him~~ till she)
of ~~it~~; ~~and~~ ~~tell him~~ that ~~until she came as a helpless~~)
~~asked for~~ ~~bid me help her –~~ ~~asked for my help~~.)
~~one I refused her~~
she has asked me for my help.)

<u>GRANIA</u> **(<u>Standing at the door which she has thrown open</u>)**)
Come <u>DIARMUID</u> to the woods, the birds of <u>AONGHUS</u>, the)
birds of love, the birds that the eye cannot see, sing)
joyously, singing fiercely , they clap their wings and)
sing.

has me
<u>DIARMUID</u> **She ^ asked ^ for my help and I must give it.**

broken
<u>USHEEN</u> **From this night the Fianna are ~~rent~~ ^ in two.**

Caolte to be [?~~fu~~] safe is in danger
~~<u>OSCAR</u>~~ **And the kingdom that was ~~to be made safe~~ ~~trembles~~ ^ and**

<u>DIARMUID'S</u> honour is taken away.

---

3 The word "and" is deleted in pencil; the remaining cancellations in Diarmuid's speech are in blue-black ink.
3–5, 6–8 The two sets of broken lines in the RH margin are drawn as if with an indelible pencil or through blue carbon paper.
11 night] Typed in later with a different (black) ribbon.

-38-

DIARMUID My honour is without stain; tell FINN that - Tell him that this sword will guard ~~him~~ [her] by day and it will lie between us at night. Tell ~~him~~ [him] I will send some messenger, some token, which will say to him - FINN, I bring you word that so many hours, or so many moons, have passed by and ~~[illegible]~~ DIARMUID'S oath is unbroken.

GRANIA The woods are sad with ~~the~~ [their summer] sadness ~~of summer~~, and the ~~love~~-birds [of love] have ~~deserted the hazel boughs trees~~ [become silent, [illegible]] which ~~once were their trees~~. [illegible] (She goes out)

DIARMUID Good-bye - Upon whose face [of all things] shall I look in friendship again (He goes out)

USHEEN (Goes to the door and looks out after them) They have gone westward to the woods.

~~OSCAR~~ [Caolte] When FINN wakes we must tell him that they have gone ~~into the~~ eastward, towards the sea.

[Berg(02), 39[r]]

–38–

<u>DIARMUID</u> **My honour is without stain; tell <u>FINN</u> that – Tell him**
her
that this sword will guard ~~him~~ by day and it will lie
~~*her*~~ him
between us at night. Tell ~~him~~ ^ I will send some
messenger , some token , which will say to him – <u>FINN,</u> I
bring you word that so many hours , or so many moons , have
&
passed by ~~and that~~ ^ DIARMUID'S oath is unbroken.

their summer
<u>GRANIA</u> **The woods are sad with ~~the~~ ^ sadness ~~of summer~~, and the**
of love become silent, but they are not
~~love~~-birds ^ have ~~deserted the hazel boughs trees~~ which
sleeping – Their eyes are bright among the boughs.
~~once were their trees~~. (<u>She goes out</u>)

of all these
<u>DIARMUID</u> **Good-bye – Upon whose face ^ shall I look in friendship**
again <u>(He goes out)</u>

<u>USHEEN</u> **<u>(Goes to the door and looks out after them</u>) They have**
gone westward to the woods.

Caolte
~~<u>OSCAR</u>~~ **When <u>FINN</u> wakes we must tell him that they have gone**
~~into the~~ eastward, towards the sea.

9 "their", plus stage direction] Typed in later with a different (black) ribbon.
15 The cancellation is made as if with an indelible pencil or through blue carbon paper.

[Berg(05), 1r]

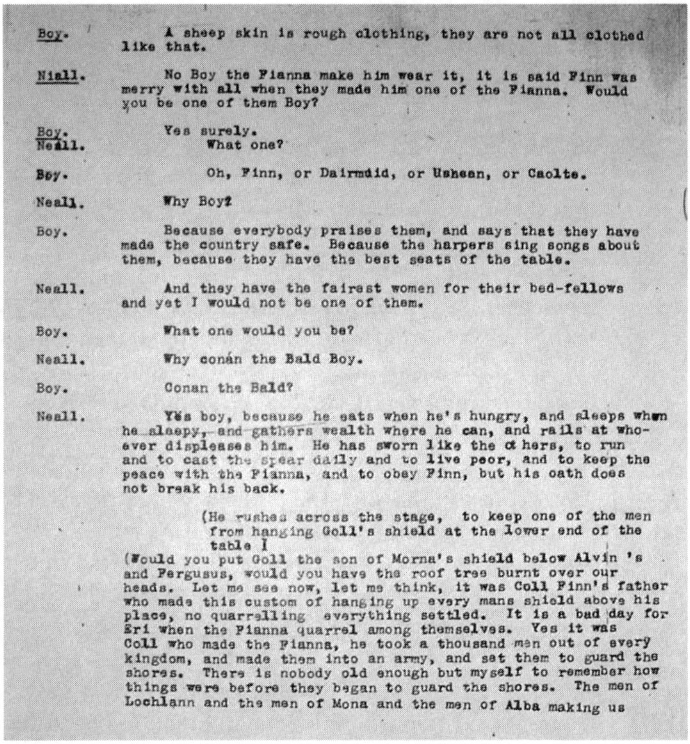

Boy. A sheep skin is rough clothing, they are not all clothed like that.

Niall. No Boy the Fianna make him wear it, it is said Finn was merry with all when they made him one of the Fianna. Would you be one of them Boy?

Boy. Yes surely.
Neall. What one?

Boy. Oh, Finn, or Dairmdid, or Usheen, or Caolte.

Neall. Why Boy?

Boy. Because everybody praises them, and says that they have made the country safe. Because the harpers sing songs about them, because they have the best seats of the table.

Neall. And they have the fairest women for their bed-fellows and yet I would not be one of them.

Boy. What one would you be?

Neall. Why conán the Bald Boy.

Boy. Conan the Bald?

Neall. Yës boy, because he eats when he's hungry, and sleeps whwn he sleepy, and gathers wealth where he can, and rails at whoever displeases him. He has sworn like the ot hers, to run and to cast the spear daily and to live poor, and to keep the peace with the Fianna, and to obey Finn, but his oath does not break his back.

(He rushes across the stage, to keep one of the men from hanging Goll's shield at the lower end of the table I
(Would you put Goll the son of Morna's shield below Alvin 's and Fergusus, would you have the roof tree burnt over our heads. Let me see now, let me think, it was Coll Finn's father who made this custom of hanging up every mans shield above his place, no quarrelling everything settled. It is a bad day for Eri when the Fianna quarrel among themselves. Yes it was Coll who made the Fianna, he took a thousand men out of every kingdom, and made them into an army, and set them to guard the shores. There is nobody old enough but myself to remember how things were before they began to guard the shores. The men of Lochlann and the men of Mona and the men of Alba making us

[Berg(05), 1r]

Boy.		**A sheep skin is rough clothing, they are not all clothed like that.**
Niall.		**No Boy the Fianna make him wear it, it is said Finn was merry with all when they made him one of the Fianna. Would you be one of them Boy?**
Boy.		**Yes surely.**
Neall.		**What one?**
Boy.		**Oh, Finn, or Dairmuid, or Usheen, or Caolte.**
Neall.		**Why Boy?**
Boy.		**Because everybody praises them, and says that they have made the country safe. Because the harpers sing songs about them, because they have the best seats of the table.**
Neall.		**And they have the fairest women for their bed-fellows and yet I would not be one of them.**

The typescript represents a variant development of a passage in Berg(02)—from fol. 6r, line 6, to fol. 8r, line 8—that was not adopted. Compare the spur-of-the-moment holograph addition at the beginning of Berg(02), fol. 2r, and the difficulty with the same passage evident in Berg(03), fol. 5r. Note that the typing here is draft quality and that patent mistakes are uncorrected.

4 all] The misreading of WBY's inserted "ale" in Berg(02), fol. 6r/p. 5, confirms the typist was following this version.

Two-Page Typescript Variant

Boy. What one would you be?

Neall. Why conan the Bald Boy.

Boy. Conan the Bald?

Neall. Yes boy, because he eats when he's hungry, and sleeps when he sleepy, and gathers wealth where he can, and rails at who-ever displeases him. He has sworn like the ot hers, to run and to cast the spear daily and to live poor, and to keep the peace with the Fianna, and to obey Finn, but his oath does not break his back.

(He rushes across the stage, to keep one of the men from hanging Goll's shield at the lower end of the table)

(Would you put Goll the son of Morna's shield below Alvin 's and Fergusus, would you have the roof tree burnt over our heads. Let me see now, let me think, it was Coll Finn's father who made this custom of hanging up every mans shield above his place, no quarrelling everything settled. It is a bad day for Eri when the Fianna quarrel among themselves. Yes it was Coll who made the Fianna, he took a thousand men out of every kingdom, and made them into an army, and set them to guard the shores. There is nobody old enough but myself to remember how things were before they began to guard the shores. The men of Lochlann and the men of Mona and the men of Alba making us

[Berg(05), 2[r]]

their spoil, carrying off women here and sheep there, and leaving smoke and fire behind them, and nobody to meet them but men taken from the sheep fold, and from the plough and from the smithy. Yes, yes, that is where Caoltie shield hangs I told you its place last time and you remembered it, and that is Conan's shield, no that one with the blue dog painted upon it But I was telling you how the Fianna saved our women and sheep. They fight well but they are proud, ah they are very proud. I was telling you Boy, how they hang the King's fool and many and many a time they have made war on the King himself. Finn's father Coll, died fighting against Cormac's father after the melancholy, and it was for that death Finn kept out of the battle. Cormac fought against the men of Mona. It has been this way always, and sometimes Erie has been like a shaking sod between them, but this marriage mends all, the marriage of Finn and of Grannia the king's daughter mends all

[NLI 8777(10) b, 18r; NLI 8777(4) d, 37r]

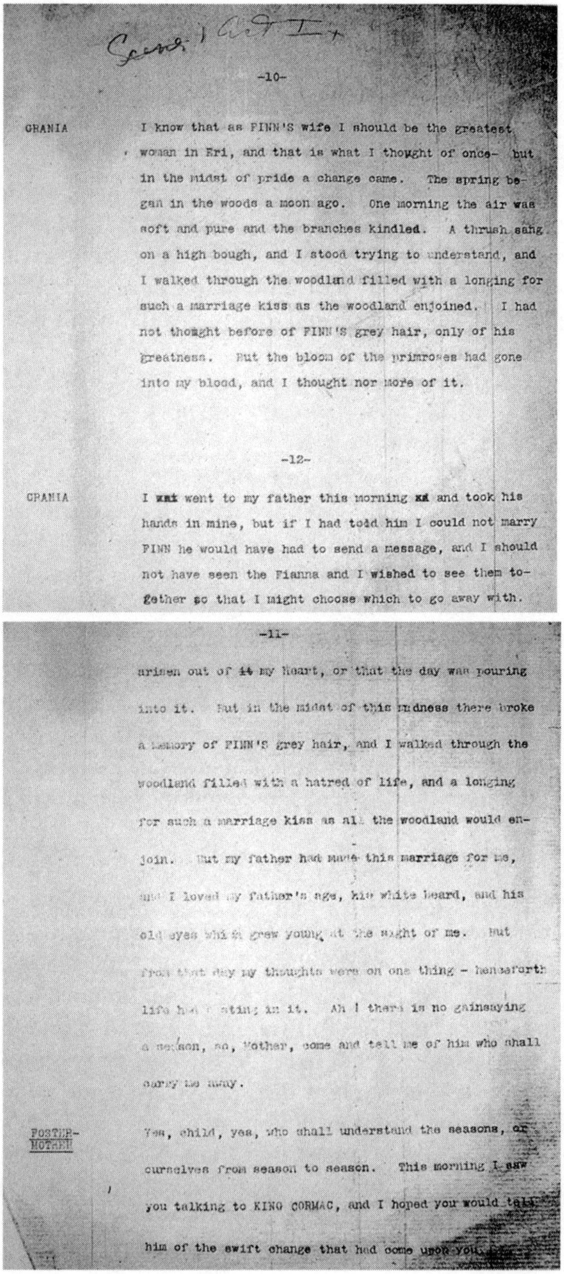

Scene 1 Act I x

-10-

GRANIA I know that as FINN'S wife I should be the greatest woman in Eri, and that is what I thought of once- but in the midst of pride a change came. The spring began in the woods a moon ago. One morning the air was soft and pure and the branches kindled. A thrush sang on a high bough, and I stood trying to understand, and I walked through the woodland filled with a longing for such a marriage kiss as the woodland enjoined. I had not thought before of FINN'S grey hair, only of his greatness. But the bloom of the primroses had gone into my blood, and I thought nor more of it.

-12-

GRANIA I ~~wat~~ went to my father this morning ~~xx~~ and took his hands in mine, but if I had told him I could not marry FINN he would have had to send a message, and I should not have seen the Fianna and I wished to see them together so that I might choose which to go away with.

-11-

arisen out of ~~it~~ my heart, or that the day was pouring into it. But in the midst of this madness there broke a memory of FINN'S grey hair, and I walked through the woodland filled with a hatred of life, and a longing for such a marriage kiss as all the woodland would enjoin. But my father had made this marriage for me, and I loved my father's age, his white beard, and his old eyes which grew young at the sight of me. But from that day my thoughts were on one thing - henceforth life had nothing in it. Ah ! there is no gainsaying a season, so, Mother, come and tell me of him who shall carry me away.

FOSTER-MOTHER Yes, child, yes, who shall understand the seasons, or ourselves from season to season. This morning I saw you talking to KING CORMAC, and I hoped you would tell him of the swift change that had come upon you.

[NLI 8777(10) b, 18r]

~~Scene 1~~ Act I x

–10–

GRANIA **I know that as FINN'S wife I should be the greatest woman in Eri, and that is what I thought of once– but**

[NLI 8777(10) b, 18r, continued]

in the midst of pride a change came. The spring began in the woods a moon ago. One morning the air was soft and pure and the branches kindled. A thrush sang on a high bough, and I stood trying to understand, and I walked through the woodland filled with a longing for such a marriage kiss as the woodland enjoined. I had not thought before of FINN'S grey hair, only of his greatness. But the bloom of the primroses had gone into my blood, and I thought nor more of it.

–12–

GRANIA **I ~~wet~~ went to my father this morning ~~ad~~ and took his hands in mine, but if I had told him I could not marry FINN he would have had to send a message, and I should not have seen the Fianna and I wished to see them together so that I might choose which to go away with.**

[NLI 8777(4) d, 37r]

–11–

arisen out of ~~it~~ my heart, or that the day was pouring into it. But in the midst of this madness there broke a memory of FINN'S grey hair, and I walked through the woodland filled with a hatred of life, and a longing for such a marriage kiss as all the woodland would enjoin. But my father had made this marriage for me, and I loved my father's age, his white beard, and his old eyes which grew young at the sight of me. But from that day my thoughts were on one thing – henceforth life had a sting in it. Ah ! there is no gainsaying a season, so, Mother, come and tell me of him who shall carry me away.

FOSTER-MOTHER **Yes, child, yes, who shall understand the seasons, or ourselves from season to season. This morning I saw you talking to KING CORMAC, and I hoped you would tell him of the swift change that had come upon you.**

NLI 8777(10) b The two passages supply variant readings for pages 10 and 12 (fols. 11r, 13r) of Berg(02)—readings not carried forward. Some doubt hangs over the attribution of the penciled headnote. (Is the substitution in GM's hand?)

NLI 8777(4) d The typescript represents a modified fair copy of the heavily revised TS Berg(02), fol. 12r, which is also headed "–11–". Note that the paper is unique among extant Act I materials, although it was in use for rejected TS versions of Act II; cf. NLI 8777(7) a and d.

[Berg(03), 1r, 2r, and 3r]

ACT. 1.

6486003

MISS LAWRENCE,
TYPE WRITING OFFICE,
2[illegible] WELLINGTON STREET,
STRAND, W.C.

Persons

Finn

Cormac.

Dearmuid

Usheen

Caoilte

Goll.

ACT. 1.

SCENE: Banqueting Hall at Tara. Table back of stage on a dais. There are pillars in front of table. doors R. & L. A number of serving men are laying table for feast, NIALL is directing them.
[illegible]

NIALL: Do not put the salmon there; put in front of the chief man ~~of~~ at the feast.

BOY: Is not the king the chief man at the feast?

NIALL: Not at a wedding feast. The chief man at a wedding feast is the man who has come to be wed.

BOY: Where shall I put the boar's head?

NIALL: ~~Put it here~~ where the old king used to sit. Art King Cormac's father, Art the Melancholy, they used to call him. He was deaf at the left side and he was always complaining that the meat was hard, and that the wind came under the door. Yes, boy, under this roof a hundred kings have sat, right back to Ollam Fodla that made the laws. What meals they have eaten; what ale they have drunk. Before Cormac there was Art, and before Art there was Conn.

BOY: Was that Conn the hundred fighter?

NIALL: Yes! Conn the Hundred fighter they used to call him. And he knew when a hare was put before him if the fire had been bright behind it, and he knew the swine's flesh had been dried in the smoke of a white-thorn tree. Put the curds over there; it is not curds but trotter and cows heel that used to be put there, for that was the place of the King's Fool. One day he flouted the Fianna on the high road and they hanged him on an elder tree.

BOY: Did they hang the King's Fool in time of peace?

NIALL: Fool or wise man, war or peace, it is all one to them when their pride is up. But they are great men, boy. It is not for you and me to speak against such great men. Bring the dishes quickly, it is time for their messenger to be here. Put the bread there. Art's wife Queen Maive used to sit there, Maive the half-ruddy they called her. She liked thin barley cakes, and six men got their death because of her. (To one of the serving men)

Typescript of Complete Act, Extensively Revised by W. B. Yeats— W. B. Yeats's "Sufficient Version"?

[Berg(03), 1^r^]

ACT. 1

[2^r^]

Person

Finn
Cormac.
Dairmuid
Usheen
Caolte
Goll.

[3^r^]

ACT. 1

SCENE: Banqueting Hall at Tara. Table back of stage on a dais. There are pillars in front of table, doors R. & L. A number of serving men are laying table for feast, NIALL is directing them.
There is a spinning-wheel t left side of stage

NIALL: **Do not put the salmon there; put in front of the chief** *at* **man ~~of~~ the feast.**

BOY: **Is not the king the chief man at the feast ?**

NIALL: **Not at a wedding feast. The chief man at a wedding feast is the man who has come to be wed.**

BOY: **Where shall I put the boar's head?**

NIALL: **Put it here where the old king used to sit. Art King Cormac's father, Art the Melancholy, they used to call him. He was deaf at the left side and he was always complaining that the meat was hard, and that the wind came under the door. Yes, boy, under this roof a**

Berg(03) The underlining throughout this TS is in red ink, sometimes (as here) double. Double lines in the text are reproduced in the transcription except for those beneath the part ascriptions.

[Berg(03)]

hundred kings have sat, right back to Ollam Fodla that made the laws. What meals they have eaten; what ale they have drunk. Before Cormac there was Art, and be fore Art there was Conn.

BOY: Was that Conn the hundred fighter?

NIALL: Yes! Conn the Hundred fighter they used to call him. And he knew when a hare was put before him if the fire had been bright behind it; and he knew^the swine's flesh *if* had been dried in the smoke of a white-thorn tree. Put the curds over there; it is not curds but trotter and cows heel that used to be put there, for that was the place of the King's Fool. One day he flouted the Fianna on the high road and they hanged him on an elder tree.

BOY: Did they hang the King's Fool in time of peace?

NIALL: Fool or wise man, war or peace, it is all one to them when their pride is up. But they are great men, boy. It is not for you and me to speak against such great men. Bring the dishes quickly, it is time for their messenger to be here. Put the bread there. Art's wife Queen Maive used to sit there, Maive the half-ruddy they called her. She liked thin barley cakes, and six men got their death because of her. (To one of the serving men)

[4^r]

2.

Put them here where Art's hound used to lie.

(Knocking at door)

Here is the messenger of the Fianna. I knew we should not get done in time. Bring in the flagons. (To the other servan ts) Where are the drinking horns?

(More knocking)

(He goes to the door and opens it. Conan the Bald comes in. He is a fat and rough man in a sheep skin, and is much out of breath. He is followed by THREE MEN who carry bundles of shields on their backs.)

CONAN: **This is the salmon, and this is the boar's head, and these are the barley cakes for the wedding feast of Finn the son of Cool. Give me a horn full of ale.**

(NIALL gives him a horn of ale)

I have much trouble going messages for the Fianna. Have I not legs to grow weary and a body to sweat like another. I am hungry too, but I dare not put a knife in the meat till the Fianna are here.

NIALL: **There will be plenty and to spare when they are here.**

CONAN: **Well look to the hanging of the shields. I have seen you before. I remember you now. You have been in Tara these fifty years and hung the shields many a time. (Turning to the men that are with him) Come, the sooner we bring Finn, the sooner we shall eat.**

(They go out)

BOY: **The Fianna have a rough messenger.**

NIALL: **I would have none say that I have said it, but he is a man of little account among them.**

BOY: **A sheep skin is rough clothing; they are not all clothed like that?**

NIALL: **No, boy, the Fianna make him wear it. They are always flouting him. It is said Finn was merry with ale when he made him one of the Fianna. (He rushes across the**

3

stage to keep one of the men from hanging Goll the son of Morna's shield at the lower end of the table) Would you put Goll the son of Morna's shield below Alvin's and Fergus's. Would you have the roof-tree burnt over our heads? Let me see now, let me think. It was Art the Melancholy who made this custom of the hanging up of every man's shield above his place. No quarrelling, everything settled! It is a bad day for Erie when the Fianna quarrel among themselves. There is no one in Tara now but myself who is old enough to remember the way things were before Cool took a man out of every household and made the Fianna and set them to watch the shores. A The men of Lochlann and the men of Mona, and the men of Alba making us their spoil, carrying off women here and sheep there, and leaving smoke and fire behind them. B Yes! Yes! that is where Caoilte's shield hangs; I told you it's place last time and you remember it. But I was telling you how the Fianna saved our women and sheep. They fight well, but they are proud. Ah! they are very proud. C I was telling you, boy, how they hanged the King's Fool and many and many a time they have made war on the King himself. Finn's father Cool died fighting against Cormac's father Art the Melancholy, and it was for that death Finn kept out of the battle, Cormac fought against the men of Mona. It has been this way always, and sometimes Eri has been like a shaking sod between them. But this marriage mends all. The marriage of Finn and Grania mends all.

(ENTER GRANIA and LABAN)

BOY: There is Grania and Laban her foster-mother.

NIALL: Quick, quick, put up the rest of the shields. Come away boy. Ah! that old woman, she has come back after these many years, an old witch. They say she has more shapes than one.

(NIALL and the BOY go out and are followed by the other serving men)

GRANIA: The table is spread, and above each man's place his shield hangs. So they think. I shall be a wife before morning; but you, Mother, believe in your sooth saying. And it may be that you have seen rightly, for if there is none to help me I shall hide myself in the woods. But the woods are lonely and I shall be afraid.

7–11, 9, 12, 19, 26 The passage is canceled, and the following letters and the word "of" inserted, in a distinctive shade of bright blue ink. The other ink insertions, here and throughout the TS, are blue-black.

7–11 It would appear that the sentence in lines 8–11 was deleted first, and that the previous sentence in lines 7–8 was included in the same deletion afterward.

9, 12, 19 If the letters refer to substituted passages labelled A, B, and C, the substitutions have not been recovered; but compare the rewritten version of the passage in Berg(05).

[Berg(03), 5r]

& commd them with an oath **3.**

stage to keep one of the men from hanging Goll the son of Morna's shield at the lower end of the table) Would you put Goll the son of Morna's shield below Alvin's and Fergus's. Would you have the roof-tree burnt over out heads? Let me see now, let me think. It was ~~Art~~ Cumhall Finns father ~~the Melancholy~~ who made th is cus tom of the hanging up of every man's shield above his place. No quarrelling, everything settled! ~~It is a bad day for Erie when the Fianna quarrel among themselves.~~ There is no one in ~~Tara now but myself who is old enough to remember the way things were before Cool took a man out of every house-hold and made the Fianna and set them to watch the shores.~~ A The men ^ of Lochlann and the men of Mona, and the men of Alba making us th eir spoil, carrying off women here and sheep there, and leaving smoke and fire behind them. ^ B ~~Yes! Yes! that is where Caoiltie's shield hangs; I told you it's place last time and you remember it.~~ ^ ~~But I was telling you how the Fianna saved our women and sheep. They fight well, but they are proud. Ah! they are very proud.~~ C I was telling you, boy, how they hanged the King's Fool and many and many a time they have made war on the King himself. Finn's father Cool died fighting against Cormac's father Art the Melancholy, and it was for that death Finn kept out of the battle, Cormac fought against the men of Mona. It has been this way always, and sometimes Eri has been like a shaking sod between them. But this marriage mends all. The marriage of Finn and ^ of Grania ^ the Kings daughter, mends all.

(ENTER GRANIA and LABAN)

BOY: There is ~~Grania~~ ^ the Kings daughter and Laban her foster-mother.

NIALL: Quick, quick, put up the rest of the shields. Come away boy. Ah! that old woman, she has come back after these many years, an old witch. They say she has more shapes than one.

(NIALL and the BOY go out and are followed by the other serving men)

GRANIA: The table is spread, and above each man's place his shield hangs. So they think I shall be a wife before morning; but you, Mother, believe in your sooth saying. And it may be that you have seen rightly, for if there is none to help me I shall hide myself in the woods. But the woods are lonely and I shall be afraid.

[Berg(03)]

[6r]

4.

LABAN: A woman who is minded to leave house and home will always find a man to go with her.

GRANIA: You said I was to wander in the woods, followed and hiding. How could such things happen to a King's daughter?

LABAN: The thread tells what is to come, but it does not tell how it will come. The thread I span yesterday, the pebbles thrown into the well this morning and the stars in the night, said that you would not marry.

GRANIA: What they said must be true. How could this change have come upon me unless a God had put it into my mind. Come to the shields mother, and tell me who sit under them, for one of the greatest of the Fianna must come to my help.

LABAN: That shield with the hazel upon it is Finn's. He is the greatest of the Fianna. May I tell you of his greatness again?

GRANIA: Of what use since I am not to marry him?

LABAN: You will not hear of him now; but once you would not hear of any other. Your eyes would kindle when his name was spoken. I remember how your eyes kindled when your father spoke first of this marriage.

GRANIA: But what kindled me once quenches me now.

LABAN: You will break the Fianna in two.

GRANIA: I knew that as Finn's wife I would be the chief woman in Eri, and I was proud, but a change came and my pride was gone of a sudden. One midnight I could not sleep because of the summer heat, and I got out of my bed and stood barefooted in the house door. I could smell the garden mould and the woods, and of a sudden I do not know why, I thought of Finn's grey hair and I hated his marriage kiss, and then I cannot tell why, I thought of one young like myself. From that hour, mother, the

minutes have been pleasant and harsh.

<u>LABAN:</u> **I saw you talking to King Cormac this morning, and I hoped that you would tell him ~~of~~ ~~this~~ that you had changed your mind.**

him of the change

[7r]

The Fianna
~~They~~ ^ are bound together by an oath to uphold one anothers
no injury to one another to
rights, to do one ~~another no~~ ~~injury~~ & obey Finn that all
may be like
their swords ~~may be as~~ ^ one sword

5.

<u>GRANIA:</u> **I went to him, I took his hands in mine and I though t to tell him, but I remembered that I if I told him he would send a message, and I would not see the Fianna together to pick a man who would carry me away.**

<u>LABAN:</u> **When Cormac went against the men of Alba I foretold his defeat. Why did he not come to me about this marriage . It shall be long before men come to an end of this mischief. ^ ~~The Fianna shall be~~ broken in two ~~because of it~~.**
*O^* ^ **Why does Cormac shut his ears ~~to my~~ sooth saying?** *will*
& now they ~~shall~~

<u>GRANIA:</u> **If the gods have planned that I break the Fianna in two, break them I must. Neither I nor you can help it, so tell me mother of the men I shall see to-night.**

<u>LABAN:</u> **Yes, yes, neither you nor I can help it. I have forseen it all clearly. The lust of life is upon you child.**

<u>GRANIA:</u> **Tell me mother, tell me of these men.**

<u>LABAN:</u> **That shield with the red otter painted upon it, is the shield of Fergus. He is taller than all others, and his hair and his beard are brown.**

<u>GRANIA:</u> **Is he strong and stately? Would he make my heart beat?**

strong &
<u>LABAN:</u> **He is ^ stately enough, but there is grey in his beard.**

6r, l. 36 Type deletions.

[Berg(03)]

That red shield with the white deer's head painted upon it is the shield of Usheen. He has yellow hair, and he has long white hands, with fingers hard at the tips from the plucking of harp str ings, and they say no woman has refused him her love.

GRANIA: **Is he young?**

LABAN: **There are younger than he. That grey shield with the raven painted upon it is the shield of Goll , the son of Morna. He is a great hunter and his arms and legs are strong as the posts of a door.**

GRANIA: **Is there mirth in his eyes?**

LABAN: **He has the quiet of the woods in his eyes. But I see that your mind is not set upon one that is strong, but upon one that is young. That white shield with the green fish is the shield of Caolte, they call him Caolte the**

[8^{r}]

6.

Swift-footed . He is young and a teller of battle tales. But that silver shield with the flying white heron upon it is the shield of Diarmuid. He is the youngest and comeliest of all. He has dark hair and blue eyes, and light limbs, and his skin is white but for the freckles. He is courteous and he is merry with women. It is said of him that he will not be remembered for deeds of arms but as a true lover, and that he will die young.

GRANIA: **Diarmuid, Diarmuid! A pleasant sounding name. Diarmuid, a sweet sounding name.**

LABAN: **But child, how think you these things are to come about? The blood will find its way, but it shall be some terrible way. Ah! it will all happen, though Finn is coming with his army, and though his marriage table has been spread.**

GRANIA: **You are sure it will happen mother?**

LABAN: **I am sure of that, but the way , the way.**

GRANIA: **When the time comes, the way will be put into your mind.**

LABAN: Child, love has made you wise as the bird in the woods that desires a mate. (She sits down to spin)

GRANIA: Mother, I must not think of him yet; thinking of love makes the heart giddy. Spin mother, you have not told me what will happen after my wanderings. Will not Finn follow us?

? head

LABAN: (Pulling a thread out of the spindle) You shall escape many times, and the end –

GRANIA: Shall be what mother?

LABAN: I cannot understand it yet, but it shall be like the beginning.

(ENTER CORMAC and TWO COUNSELLORS)

CORMAC: This is the wisest marriage, though I might have made a greater one. I might have married her to the King of Alba, but this marriage will keep our kingdom safe. (He turns and sees GRANIA) I have been looking for you

[9r]

7.

Let us sit together and talk to one another. To-night you go away from me, but you go with the chief man in Eri.

(The Two Counsellors withdraw. GRANIA stands looking dreamily at the shields.)

Come, daugh ter, let us sit together. Why will you not look to me? Why have you not put on your ornaments.

GRANIA: I have forgotten them.

? gems

CORMAC: I should have wished to see your bracelets upon you, and your ~~brooch~~ with the emeralds. Will you not wear them?

clasp –

GRANIA: I can send for them, but I am not minded to wear them.

CORMAC: Why are you not minded to wear them? (Pause) What has your foster-mother told you. She was telling you something when I came in.

[Berg(03)]

GRANIA: **Father, you have often seen me wear my bracelets and my brooch, and you will love me as well without them. Cannot another man too love me without them? Father, let us sit here and talk, I am going away from this house, where my mother lived and where I have always lived with one yo u call the chief man in Eri, but whom I have never seen. So I have been questioning my foster-mother and** *been/ing/* **she has ~~begun to~~ question^her spindle, ~~as~~ you know that** *and/* **all that she finds in her spindle comes to pass.**

CORMAC: **And she has told you?**

GRANIA: **Only that I am going away into the woods.**

CORMAC: **You are troubled my daughter. A woman is always troubled when her marriage is at hand. May be you think Finn too rough a man to marry; I might have married you to the King of Alba who was a man of peace. He sent messengers. But Finn is more worthy to be your husband.**

GRANIA: **I have not seen Finn.**

CORMAC: **The enemies of Eri have seen him. You know how he has held his borders against them. Finn and his Fianna have made Eri great as when the Red Branch was at Eman of Macha.** *The oath that binds the Feanni together has made him more powerful than any king –*

[10r]

8.

GRANIA: **You wish me to marry as kings and queens marry but I –**

CORMAC: **(Suspiciously)** **You have set your heart upon some boy.**

GRANIA: **The Fianna are coming. I shall wed this night him who is the chief man among them in my eyes.**

CORMAC: **That is well. Finn is the chief man in Eri after the High King.**

(A sound of trumpets outside. THE COUNSELLORS of CORMAC and the SERVANTS ENTER. The SERVANTS open

---

9r, l. 20 A slight doubt exists as to whether WBY is the author of these and a few other small emendations in this TS (for example, "clasp" at line 6 above). The revised line is meant to read "she has been questioning her spindle, and you know that".

<u>the door</u>. <u>NIALL stands by the door.)</u>

<u>NIALL</u>: **Let Finn and his Counsellors enter.**

<u>(ENTER FINN, USHEEN, CAOLTIE, DIARMUID, FERGUS, ALVIN and CONAN the Bald .</u> , } <u>)</u> *Usheen & Caoltie carry harps –*

<u>CORMAC:</u> **Finn is welcome to my house.**

<u>FINN:</u> **As the marriage law is I declare the bride price upon the threshold. I give my word to guard this kingdom against all cattle spoilers that are of the kingdoms of Eri, and to guard as before my own country from the men of Lochland and the men of Mona. And I give my word to overthrow all kings of Eri that raise their hands against the high king. I cannot give a king's gift for the Fianna have neither sheep nor cattle nor towns nor villages, nor great store of gold or silver.**

<u>CORMAC:</u> **The bride price is worthy of Finn and of my daughter, and I give you my daughter.**

<u>(CORMAC takes FINN across the stage and presents him to GRANIA.)</u>

<u>DIARMUID</u>: **(<u>At door)</u> What woman is like Grania.**

<u>USHEEN:</u> **Do not look at her Diarmuid. Kings daughters are not for us.**

<u>NIALL:</u> **(In a loud vo ice) Let the hot meats be brought in. Let the Fianna enter.**

<u>(ENTER a number of MEN.</u> <u>They stand about the door</u>. <u>CORMAC leaves FINN and GRANIA and goes towards</u>

[11r]

9.

<u>the door to welcome the FIANNA)</u>

<u>GRANIA:</u> **There is a scar on your cheek. That is the scar made by the sword of Forgael when you overthrew the men of Uladh.**

<u>FINN:</u> **Has the tale of that battle come so far.**

<u>GRANIA</u>: **I have listened all my life to tales of your battles.**

[Berg(03)]

(Taking his hand in both her hands) This hand has overthrown many kings.

FINN: Grania must not praise me if she would not take my luck away.

GRANIA: Some day you will tell me about your battles. (She turns away as if already weary of him.)

FINN: Are my battles more to you than my love?

(CORMAC brings CAOLTIE, USHEEN and DIARMUID towards GRANIA. CORMAC and FINN go up the stage)

GRANIA: Ah! this is Usheen, I know him by his harp of red yew. You will sing us love songs to-night.

COAOLTIE: I am Caoltie and this is Diarmuid.

GRANIA: Welcome Caoltie teller of battle tales. ~~I would have known you by your harp on which there are sea creatures.~~ There is a tale you tell. (She stands looking at DIARMUID forgetful of everyt hing) And this is Diarmuid.

NIALL: (At the table) The King and Finn son of Cool are seated. The Counsellors of Finn are guests at th is table. The tables for the rest of the Fianna have been spread beyond the arras in the western hall.

(DIARMUID, USHEEN, CAOLTIE, FERGUS, GOLL, ALVIN and CONAN seat themselves at the table. The rest of the FIANNA and the Servants except NIALL and one serving man go out.

CORMAC: My daughter, why do you not take your place beside Finn?

GRANIA: Every night I have poured out your ale father, and I

[12r]

10.

would pour it out th is last time, and I would pour out my husband's for the first time.

CORMAC: If th is be your wish.

11r, ll. 16–17 Pencil deletions.

FINN: Grania must not pour out our ale.

GRANIA: This is the fir st thing I have asked. You cannot refuse me.

FINN: All here will remember this honour.
(The KING signs to the serving men to withdraw. GRANIA returns to her foster-mother.)

GRANIA: I cannot tell why I have done this. Have I done well? Have you found a way to help me,

LABAN: The way has been put into your mind.
(She has taken two flagons of ale in her hand.)

You will give them enchanted ale. Here it is. Here are two flagons that I have made sleepy. (She mutters over the flagons)

By fire and wave and wind
Do all things to my mind
Pour sleep in cup and horn
That every sleepy head
Sleep as upon a bed
Till the cock crow in the morn.

Give them this ale and they will sleep till the cock crow. Give it to all but Caoltie, Usheen and Diarmuid.
(GRANIA passes along the table filling the cups and horns, and while she does so LABAN goes out. CAOLTIE USHEEN and DIARMUID are the last who should be served. When GRANIA comes to DIAR: she stands looking at him)

CORMAC: Why do you not fill Diarmuid's horn?

GRANIA: The ale is all spilt; I will bring another flagon.
(She has dropped the flagon)

CORMAC: I do not like the spilling of ale at a marriage feast.

12r, l. 9 "Laban?" has been erased at the end of the line—which explains the comma.

[Berg(03), 12v]

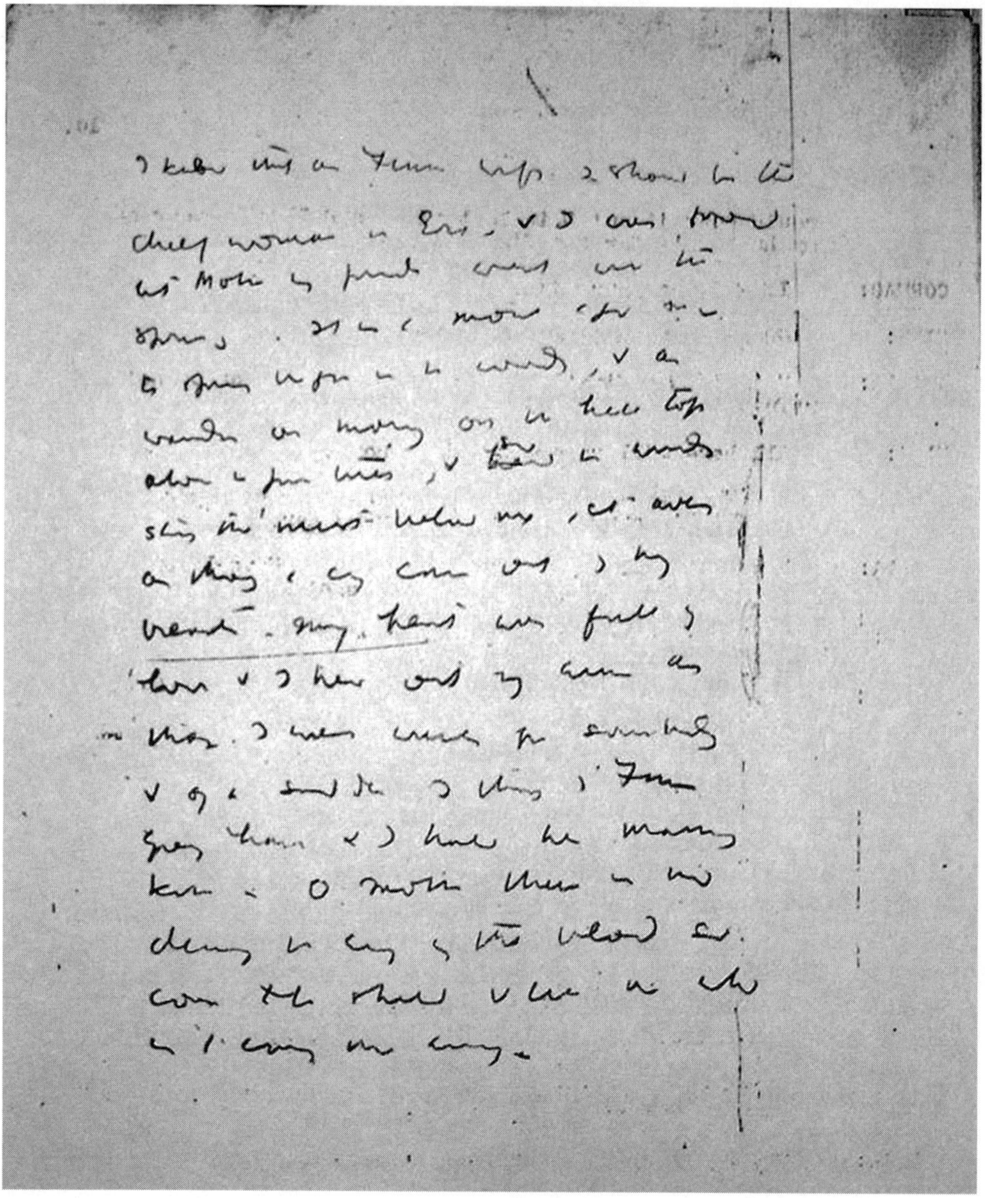

[Berg(03), 12^{v}]

e
I kn{ow that as Finns wife I shoud be the
chief woman in Eri – & I was proud
but Mothr my pride went in the
spring. It is a mont ago since
th spring began in th woods, I [?*was/am*]
wanderng on mornng on th hill top
saw
alone in fir trees, and ~~heard~~ in woods
still thro mist below me, it was
as thog a cry came out of my
breasts – my heart was full of
love & I held out my arms as
thogh I was waitng for somebody
& of a sudden I thoght of Finns
grey hair & I hated his marriage
kiss – O Mother ther is no
denying the cry of the blood so
turn the wheel & tell me who
is t carry me away –

12^{v} The pencil is either blue indelible lead, different from WBY's pencil revisions elsewhere, or has been traced through blue carbon. The TS version of these lines contained in NLI 8777(10) b, fol. 18^{r}, supplies several difficult readings.

[Berg(03)]

[13r]

11.

CONAN: It never happens but it brings ill luck.

DIARMUID: Conan sees ill luck everywhere. When will Finn take away his favour from Conan, and let the Fianna give him his deserts.

FINN: Tell us a story Caoltie, and put th e spilling of th e ale out of our minds.

(CAOLTIE rises from his place and takes his harp. He stands touching his harp as if uncerta in what story he is go ing to tell)

FINN: Tell us the story of the House of the Quicken Trees.

CAOL: Yes, I will tell you the story of the House of the Quicken Tree. (A pause) It is gone! It went out of my mind of a sudden. A new tale has come into me. It has come in to me. I see a man lying dead, and his wife is going away with another.

FINN: What quarrel have you with me that you should tell me such a tale at my marriage.

USHEEN: Finn, Finn, the gods are in the room. The ale has been spilt, and a strange tale has been put into Caoltie's mind. Our luck is being taken away.

(They all start to their feet.)

FINN: Let us all sit down again. Let us drink and forget our though ts of ill luck.

(They all drink)

CORMAC: (Suddenly sleepy and tr ying to rouse himself) Let someb ody else tell a story, I am gr owing sleepy .

USHEEN: I cannot remember any story; I too have had my thoughts taken away.

CONAN: Diarmuid, Caoltie and Usheen have forgotten their boasted stories, but Conan has many a pleasant story, and nobody asks him for one. I will tell a pleasant story I will tell of the death of Diarmuid.

FINN: I will have no tale of death at my marriage feast. To speak of Diarmuid's death may be to bring death upon him. Be silent or you may take his luck away.

[14^{r}]

12.

GRANIA: (Coming nearer to the table) Will Diarmuid die by the sword or will he be made captive.

DIAR: The story of my death is an old story. It does not make me afraid. Tell on!

CONAN: (Obsequiously) Oh! my beautiful Grania this is the way it was. Diarmuid was put out to foster with a shepherd and no one was so beautiful as Diarmuid when he was a child, except the shepherd's son. He was much more beautiful than Diarmuid, and his beauty made Diarmuid's father jealous, and one day he crushed the shepherd's son to death be tween his knees.

GRANIA: But tell me of Diarmuid. Tell me of Diarmuid.

CONAN: The shepherd wept and wept, oh! how he wept, and after a while he took his second son into the woods and made a spell over him with a Druid hazel stick, and changed him into a black and bristleless boar. And some day that boar is to break out of the woods and to kill many men and many women. All the Fianna are to gather for the hunting of him. Oh! what a hunting, what a hunting.

GRANIA: Tell me more of Diarmuid. Tell me quickly!

CONAN: I must drink, I am thirsty again. (He drinks) Diarmuid must go out against that boar and must be killed. It was to kill him that the shepherd made this spell over his second son. He shall be torn by the tusks; he shall be all bloody. His face shall be foul because it will be bloody. I would that the women of Eri could see him when he is foul and bloody. (He staggers) I am growing sleepy because I have to run the messages of the Fianna. (He recovers himself) I shall live to see him when the

---

14^{r}, l. 19 The pencil circle around the comma is not characteristic of WBY's annotation.

[Berg(03)]

tusks have torn him for it has been foretold of him also that he shall not live long, that he shall not be remember-ed for deeds of arms, but as a lover of women. That he shall live as a lover of women and that his life shall be soon over. Who has put witchcraft into my ale; who among the Fianna has do ne this. (He falls)

USHEEN: He said there was witchcraft in the ale, and look they are all sleeping. Who was it that put witchcraft into the ale ~~of~~ Grania.

GRANIA: My foster-mother has done this for me. I had never a mind to marry Finn. But why does not Diarmuid come to us?

[15^r]

(DIARMUID comes from the table)

It was for you that the witchcraft was put into the ale.

DIAR: For me, Grania?

GRANIA: I had never a mind to marry Finn. I am going away with you to-night. We are going to leave this house before they awake.

DIAR: You and I? And you did not see me be fore this night!

GRANIA: I desired you and you were in my thoughts before I saw you Diarmuid. You were in my thoughts DIARMUID. (She throws her arms about him)

DIAR: I, too, desired you, and you were in my thoughts, oh! beauti ful woman. You were in my thoughts Grania. Let me look at you, let me put back your hair. Your eyes are grey Grania, your eyes are grey, and your hands – but Finn, but Finn, but Finn – (He breaks away from her) Grania, wife of Finn, why have you played with me?

GRANIA: I am not the wife of Finn. (She goes towards DIARMUID) And now I cannot be Finn's wife, for you have held me in your arms and you have kissed me.

DIAR: What is th is madness Grania? Here, here this night and

---

14^r, l. 38 Pencil deletion.

Finn sleeping there.

GRANIA: **If he had loved me his love would have been stronger than wi tchcraft. (A pause) You shrink from me! Why do you shrink from me? Am I not desirable. I have heard men praise me. (She holds out her hair towards him) You have touched my hair and looked into my eyes; why do you shr ink away. I have Diarmuid that women love you and certainly a woman must be desirable in your eyes. It may be that men have lied to me, and this hair is not soft this bo dy delicate. (To CAOLTIE and USHEEN) ~~Is~~** *Am I* **not ~~my plight~~ miserable. Shall all men shrink from me? Would you shrink from me if it were you I had asked to go away with me? No matter who shr inks from me now. Since the man I longed for, the whole world sh rinks from me.**

CAOL: **Look Grania at the sleeping man whose ale you have bewitched.**

[16[r]]

there may be nothing stronger
amonst them than their oath. **14.**

USHEEN: **If Finn were to awake he would take some terrible vengeance for this.**

GRANIA: **What is his vengeance to me? Has not my world withered! I will go into the green woods and I will wander alone there till I die.**

DIAR: **When I looked into your eyes Grania it was as though I had been in the dark and I saw the dawn. But no, no! I cannot, I cannot. There is a stronger thing than love.**

CAOL: **Grania, Grania, the Fianna live poor and live near to death always, that ~~honour~~ may be the strongest thing amongst them.**
their oath

USHEEN: **Turn your eyes away from her, ~~Grania~~.** *Darmud*

GRANIA: **He looks at me because it has been foretold, foretold that he and I.**

15[r], ll. 28, 29 Pencil deletions.

16[r], l. ⁻1 The pencil draft supplies an alternative for lines 10–11 below.

<u>DIAR:</u> **(<u>Breaking away from USHEEN and CAOLTIE)</u> What has been foretold? Who has foretold it?.**

<u>USHEEN:</u> **Diarmuid look where Finn sleeps.**

<u>CAOL:</u> **Think of your fame in battle.**

~~<u>DIAR:</u>~~ *Ushn* **And of your oath.**

<u>DIAR:</u> **The fortune-teller has lied, if she has said that I shall break my oath to Finn. What did she tell you? What has she said? Has she said th is.**

<u>GRANIA:</u> **She spoke of a woman pledged to a man whom she did not love, and of a man who would be her friend and her helper.** *would/* **She foretold that th e man ~~will~~ leave all things and that** *would/* **the woman ~~will~~ leave all things for love's sake. She** *would/* **foretold that they ~~will~~ go away in the middle of a marriage feast, and wander in the unpeopled woods, and by the rushy margin of many streams.**

<u>DIAR:</u> **And the man is I, and the woman is you.**

~~and~~

<u>GRAN:</u> **She foretold that it shall seem as if all men had forgotten them, ~~that the Ousel and the Otter shall not~~ fly ~~from them.~~ They shall be happy under green boughs and become wise in all woodland wisdom, and as she spoke I**

They shall have no friend & their mates be
th ousel & the otter –

16r, ll. 32–33 Pencil deletion.

[Berg(03), 16[v]]

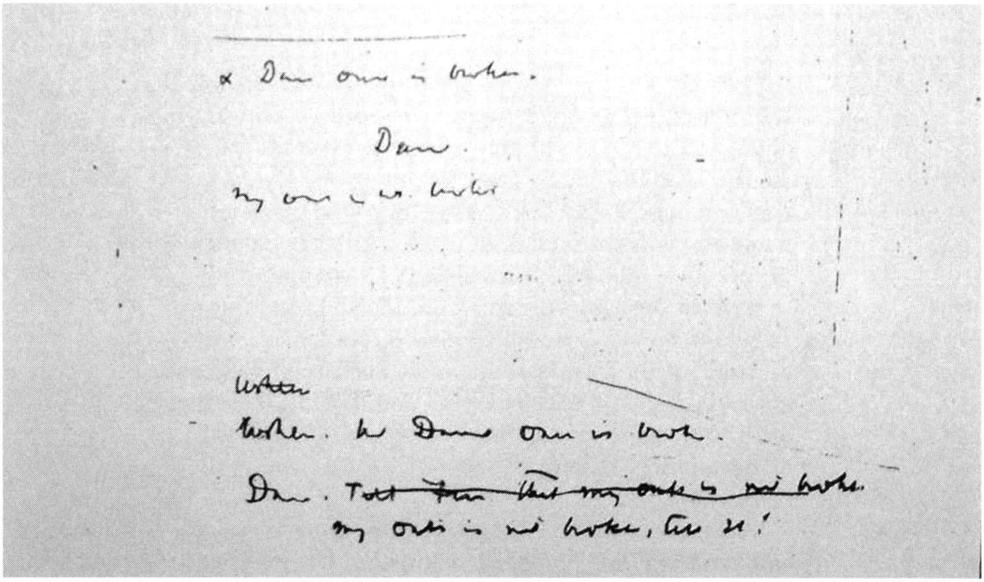

[Berg(03), 16[v]]

1 & Darm oath is broken.

Darm
2 my oath is now broken

~~*Usheen*~~
3 *Usheen. And Darms oath is brokn.*

4 *Darm.* ~~*Tell Fin that my oath is not broken*~~
My oath is not broken, tell [?*Fi*]*!*

16[v] The lines were written to substitute for ll. 32–34 on the facing page (fol. 17[r]). The first two lines (in blue-black ink) were entered after the second two.

[Berg(03)]

[17r]

~~wr~~ *often*/

too seemed to see them wandering on paths trodden by the feet of deer, where there are sudden odours of wild honey and where they will ~~also~~ throw their arms about one another and kiss one ano ther on th e mouth. <u>(She goes nearer to him)</u> And she told me Diarmuid that we should make our beds with the skins of deer under cromlecs and in ~~cool~~ caves, and awake from sleep we knew not why, as though the dwarfs of the rocks had called to us , that we might see the starlight falling through the leaves.
She told me the dwarfs of the rocks, and the secret people of the trees should watch over us, and though all the men of Eri were our enemies, they should not pluck us out of one anoth er's arms.

<u>DIAR:</u> I must not listen or I will take her in my arms. I will awaken Finn. Finn, Finn, awake. <u>(He goes nearer to FINN)</u>

<u>GRANIA:</u> What would you tell him?

<u>DIAR:</u> That the world vanishes, that I see nothing but you.

<u>GRANIA</u>: Have you not sworn to help the helpless, and who is more he lpless than I?

<u>DIAR</u>: Had you not told me that you loved me I would have helped you.

<u>GRAN:</u> Help me, Diarmuid.

<u>DIAR:</u> Caoltie and Usheen have s een my trouble, they will tell Finn of my tro uble, she has asked me for my help and I must gi ve it.

<u>GRAN:</u> (<u>Standing at the door which he has thrown open</u>) Come Diarmuid to th e woods, the birds of Aengus, the birds of love, the birds of the eye cannot see, sing joyously, sing fie rcely: they clap their wings and sing

<u>DIAR:</u> She has asked me for my help and I must gi ve it.

USHEEN: **From th is night the Fianna are broken in two.**

CAOL: **And the kingdom that was to be safe is in danger, ~~and Diarmuid's honour is taken away.~~**

Ushen ~~a~~

DIAR: **My honour is not taken away, tell Finn that, tell him**
The oath of the Fianna is broken
~~oath~~

[18r]

16.

that this sword will guard her by day, and lie between us at night. Tell him I will send some messenger, some token that will say to him, "Finn I bring you word that so many hours, or so many moons have passed by and Diarmuid's oath is unbroken.

GRAN: **The woods are sad with their summer sadness and the birds of love have become silent, but they are not sleeping, their eyes are bright among the boughs.**

(She goes out)

I must follow her *faces*

DIAR: **~~Good-bye!~~ Upon whose face of all these ^ shall I look in friendship again?**

(He goes out)

USHEEN: **(Going to the door and looking out after them) They have gone westward to the woods.**

CAOL: **When Finn wakes we must tell him, that they have gone eastward to the sea.**

End of Act. 1

17r, ll. 32–33 Pencil underlining and cancellation.

[HRC(1), 1r]

-1-

DIARMUID & GRANIA.

ACT I.

The banquetting hall in Tara - A table at the back of the stage on a dais - Pillars in front - There are doors to the right and left - A number of serving men are laying the table for the feast - NIALL is directing them. There is a spinning wheel to Left.

NIALL Do not put the sal on there; put it in front of the chief man ~~of~~ at the feast.

BOY Is not the King the chief man at a feast ?

NIALL Not at a wedding feast - the chief man at a wedding feast is the man come to be wed.

BOY Where shall I put the boar's head ?

NIALL Put it here where the old king used to sit, Art, KING CORMAC's father, Art the Melancholy they used to call him. He was deaf at the left ear, and he was always complaining that the meat was hard, and that the wind came under the door. Yes, BOY, under this roof an hundred kings have sat, right back to Ollam Fodla

Composite Typescript of Complete Act, Revised by George Moore and W. B. Yeats—George Moore's Copy?

[HRC(1), 1r]

–1–

DIARMUID & GRANIA.

ACT I.

The banquetting hall in Tara – A table at the back of the stage on a dais – Pillars in front – There are doors to the right and left – A number of serving men are laying the table for the feast – NIALL is directing them. There is a ~~p~~spinning wheel to L. eft –

NIALL **Do not put the salmon there; put it in front of the chief man** ~~**of**~~ at **the feast.**

BOY **Is not the King the chief man at a feast ?**

NIALL **Not at a wedding feast – the chief man at a wedding feast is the man come to be wed.**

BOY **Where shall I put the boar's head ?**

NIALL **Put it where the old king used to sit, Art, KING CORMAC'S father, Art the Melancholy they used to call him. He was deaf at the left ear, and he was always complaining that the meat was hard, and that the wind came under the door. Yes, BOY, under this roof an hundred kings have sat, right back to Ollam Fodla**

-1 WBY first wrote "L." to stand alone, then added "eft".

[HRC(1)]

[2^{r}]

–2–

that made the laws. What meals they have eaten ! What ale they have drunk ! Before CORMAC there was Art, and before Art there was CONN.

BOY Was that CONN the hundred fighter ?

NIALL Yes, Conn, the hundred fighter they used to call him, and he knew when a hare was put before him if the fire had been bright behind it; and he knew if the swine's flesh had been dried in the smoke of a whitehorn tree. Put the curds over there; it is not the curds, but the trotters and cows'-heel that used to be put there, for that was the place of the king's fool. One day he flouted the Fianna on the high road, and they hanged him on an alder tree.

BOY Did they hang the king's fool in time of peace ?

NIALL Fool, or wise man, war or peace, its all one to them when their pride is up. But they are great men, BOY . It is not for you and me to speak against such great men. Bring the dishes quickly, it is time for their messenger to be here. Put the bread there, Art's wife, Queen Maive, used to sit there, Maive the Half Ruddy they called her, and she liked thin barley cakes, and six men got their death because of her – Bring

[3^{r}]

–3–

Bring in the flagons (To   ), put them here, where Art's hound used to lie – (A knocking at the door), Here is the messenger of the Fianna – I knew we should not get done in time. Bring in the flagons – (To the other servants). Where are the drinking horns ? (More knocking – He goes to the door and opens it – CONAN comes in; he is a fat and rough man, and is much out of breath – He is followed by three men who carry bundles of shields on their backs).

CONAN This is the salmon, and this is the boar's head, and these are the barley cakes for the wedding feast of FINN the son of Cool. Give me a horn full of ale – (NIALL gives him a horn of ale.) I have much trouble, going messages for the Fianna. Have I not legs to grow weary and body to sweat like another. I am hungry too; but I dare not put a knife in the meat till the Fianna are here.

NIALL There will be plenty and to spare when they are here.

CONAN Well, look to the hanging of the shields. I've seen you before, now I remember you; you have been in Tara fifty years, and have hung them many a time – (Turning to the men that are with him.) Come, the sooner we bring FINN, the sooner we shall ~~meal~~ *Eat*

[4r]

–4–

(They go out).

BOY The Fianna have a rough messenger.

NIALL I would have none say that I have said it, but he is a man of little account among them.

BOY Men wear sheep skins in my country, but I had thought that the Fianna wore fine clothes.

NIALL I will tell you why the Fianna made him wear it one of these days, and why FINN made him one of the Fianna. Would you be one of them ?

BOY Yes, if I might be FINN or DIARMUID or CAOELTE.

NIALL They are famous for their battles: they are great *men* ones, but would you not be CONAN THE BALD if you could ?

BL That man with the sheepskin ?

NIALL Well, he eats when he is hungry, and sleeps when he is sleepy, and rails at whomever displeases him. Th~~e~~*o*se great men have the best seats at the table, and the^

4r, ll. 10, 14 The two insertions are written in a wobbly hand that is not certainly GM's.

[HRC(1)]

fairest women for their bed-fellows, and yet I would not. (He rushes across the stage to keep one of the men from hanging GOLL'S shield at the lower end of

[5r]

–5–

the table.) Would you put GOLL the son of Morna's shield below Alvin's and Fergus'; would you have the roof tree burnt over our heads. It is the third shield from FINN'S. Let me see now, let me think, it was COOL, Finn's father who made this custom of the hanging up of every man's shield above his place. No quarrelling, everything settled. I was going to tell you who made the Fianna, Boy; it was Cool. He took a thousand men out of every kingdom, and made them into an army, and set them to watch the shores. No one is old enough but myself to remember those times
~~things~~. The men of Lochland and the men of Mona and the men of Alba carrying off women here and sheep there, and leaving smoke and fire behind them, and nobody to meet them but men taken from the sheep-fold, and from the plough and from the smithy. Yes,

[6r]

–6–

yes, that is where CAOELTE's shield hangs. I told
(Returning to the Boy)
you its place last time and you remembered ~~it~~. But
have
I was telling you how the Fianna saved our women and sheep. They fight well, but they are proud – ah, they are very proud. I was telling you, BOY, how they hanged the king's fool, and many and many a time they have made war on the king himself. FINN'S father, Cool, died fighting against CORMAC'S father after Art the Melancholy, and it was for that death FINN kept out of the battle{,/.} CORMAC fought against

---

5r, l. 11 The pencil substitution is again not certainly in GM's hand.

6r, l. 2 The cancellation is in pencil and presumably by WBY.

10 The comma is in pencil and again presumably by WBY.

the men of Mona. It has been this way always, and sometimes Erie has been like a shaking sod between them; but this marriage mends all, and the marriage of FINN and of GRANIA the king's daughter mends all.

(Enter Grania & Laban)

is that old Laban and that

BOY ^**There is the king's daughter ~~and LABAN her foster-mother.~~**

NIALL **Quick, quick, put up the rest of the shields – Come away BOY. Ah, that old woman, she has come back after these many years, an old witch; they say she has more shapes than one (NIALL and the BOY go out and are followed by other serving-men.)**

T

GRANIA **I see that the table is spread, and above each one's**

shield s

Every man's ~~Should~~ hang above his place

6[r], l. 21[+] The "'s" following "man" and "s" following "hang" are part of WBY's revision of GM's substitution.

[HRC(1), 7^{r}]

-7-

GRANIA

They must have brought the shields - (Looking round). They have brought them, mother - You have promised to tell me of the Fianna - (LABAN breaks from her) If you will not NIALL will.

LABAN

Do not call him, let nobody know what is in your mind.

GRANIA

My father sits here, FINN son of Cool, sits next to him, and here is my place next to FINN - But it will be empty.

LABAN

Hush, no man matters to you now but FINN.

GRANIA

You have wearied me with tales of his battles... You have told me that his hair is grey.

LABAN

Hush, you have always known that his hair is grey.

GRANIA

Till a month ago I never knew whether a man's hair was grey or brown. I only knew that as FINN'S wife I should be the chief woman in Eri. But the spring took my pride away

Note that fols. 7–9 are inserted (different paper, different typing style, Laban for Foster-Mother, etc.).

[HRC(1), 7r]

–7–

GRANIA

They must have brought the shields – (Looking round). They have brought them, mother – You have promised to tell me of the Fianna – (LABAN breaks from her) If you will not NIALL will.

LABAN

Do not call him, let nobody know what is in your mind.

GRANIA

My father sits here, FINN son of Cool, sits next to him, and here my place is next to FINN – But it will be empty.

LABAN

Hush, no man matters to you now but FINN.

GRANIA

You have wearied me with tales of his battles... You have told me that his hair is grey.

LABAN

Hush, you have always known that his hair is grey.

GRANIA

Till a month ago I never knew whether a man's hair was grey or brown. I only knew that as FINN'S wife I should be the chief woman in Eri. But the spring took my pride away

[8r]

–8–

one morning when I climbed by the little path where the trees grew sparer, and stood looking into the mist; something was moving over the world; it came into my breasts and my arms seemed full. But there was nobody, nobody came, nothing came, but a thought

[HRC(1)]

of FINN'S grey hair. That night I shrank from his marriage kiss in a dream. Come to the shields, Mother, and tell me of the men who will sit under them.

LABAN

I dare not, I dare not.

GRANIA

But you said that to-night would not be my marriage night.

LABAN

No, no, child, I never said such a thing. Hush, lest they should hear you.

GRANIA

They who are wiser than you said it Mother. The thread that you spun yesterday – the stars that we watched last night, the pebbles that we threw into the well this morning.

[9r]

–9–

LABAN

Hush,you father will be here; there is no time now. I saw you talking to KING CORMAC this morning. Why did you not tell him of this change ?

GRANIA

I took his hands in mine and thought to tell him.

LABAN

You should have told him.

GRANIA

But he would have sent a messenger, and I wis hed to see the Fianna together.

LABAN

So that you might pick a man who would carry you away.

[10r]

–9–

It shall be long before men come to the end of this mischief. The Fianna shall be broken in two because of it. Oh, why did CORMAC shut his ears to what I told him. There will be flights and battles, ruin on ruin, and neither you nor I can do anything.

GRANIA **I would not be a trouble if I could help it. I would not set FINN against any man. I would have FINN and my man friends. I would stand between them. I would hand them their ale.** Whose shield is that Mother, that one with the Red Otter ^painted upon it. **~~Come Mother to the shields and tell me of the men I shall see to-night~~.**

Laban **~~FOSTER-MOTHER~~** **That shield with the red otter painted upon it is the shield of Fergus. He is taller than all others, his hair and his beard are brown, and he wears a crimson cloak over a white tunic.**

GRANIA **Is he strong and stately – Would he make my heart beat ?**

[HRC(1)]

Laban ~~**FOSTER-MOTHER**~~ **He is strong and stately, but there is grey in his beard. That red shield with the white deer's head painted upon it is the shield of USHEEN. He has yellow hair, and he has long white hands, with fingers hard at the tips from plucking of harp strings, and they say no woman has refused him her love.**

[11r]

–10– & –11–

GRANIA **Is he young ?**

~~**FOSTER-MOTHER**~~ Laban **There are younger than he. That grey shield with the raven painted upon it is the shield of Goll, the son of Mona. He is a great hunter and his arms and legs are as strong as the posts of a door.**

GRANIA **Is there mirth in his eyes ?**

Laban ~~**FOSTER-MOTHER**~~ **He has the quiet of the wood in his eyes. But I see that your mind is not set upon one that is strong, but on one that is young. That white shield with the green fish is the shield of CAOELTE. They call him CAOELTE the swift footed, and he is young and a teller of battle tales. But that silver shield with the flying white heron upon it is the shiled of DIARMUID. He is the youngest and comeliest of all. He has dark hair and blue eyes, and light limbs, and his skin is white but for the freckles. He is courteous and he is merry with women. It is said of him that he will not be remembered for deeds of arms but as a true lover, and that he will die young.**

GRANIA **DIARMUID, DIARMUID, a pleasant sounding name – DIARMUID a sweet soundung name.**

[12r]

–12–

Laban ~~**FOSTER-MOTHER**~~ **But child how think you that these things will come about ?**

GRANIA I believe in your soothsaying Mother, and a man as young as I am will come and carry me away.

Laban
~~FOSTER-MOTHER~~ No, no, DIARMUID will not break his oath to FINN.

GRANIA ~~Then it will be DIARMUID~~ ! You said that his hair was ~~dark~~ *brown*, and his eyes blue, and his limbs ~~straight~~ light; and his skin white but for the freckles. It was for such a man that I looked into the mist. But thinking of love makes the brain giddy.

Laban
~~FOSTER-MOTHER~~ What can he do ? He cannot overthroww FINN and his army ?

GRANIA (Waking from a reverie) You must find a way – Mother, it is for you to find a way.

Laban
~~FOSTER-MOTHER~~ They would hang me from the rafters, child, they would hang me.

GRANIA You will baffle them; that will not be difficult for you. But how shall I escape from FINN'S marriage bed ? Shall I run into the woods ?

Laban
~~FOSTER-Mother~~ But the woods are full of wolves; they are lonely

12r, l. 7 Type deletion.

[HRC(1), 13r, 13bisr]

-13-

GRANIA A woman who is minded to leave her home will always find a man to go with her.

Laban ~~FOSTER-MOTHER~~ Child, love has made you wise as the bird in the wood that seeks a mate. There is a way - listen ! The greatest among the Fianna sit at that table with CORMAC and FINN; and NIALL and another serving man will wait upon them. But do you say that you will pour out their ale for them, and let them not deny you this. You must say that there could be no denying you anything on your marriage night. Then come to me and I will find a way - Then I will bewitch the ale, I will put a pale dust ~~in it~~ into it, and will make a spell over it (Enter CORMAC with two Councillors.) Hush ! here is your father.

(Laban sits down to & begins to spin)

FOSTER-MOTHER I cannot understand it yet, but [illegible] be like the beginning - (Enter CORMAC and [illegible]cillors.)

CORMAC This is the wisest marriage, though I might have made a greater one - I might have married her to the king ov Alba, but this marriage will keep our kingdom safe (He turns and sees GRANIA) My dear daughter, I have

[HRC(1)]
[13^{r}]

–13–

GRANIA **A woman who is minded to leave her home will always find a man to go with her.**

Laban
~~FOSTER-MOTHER~~ **Child, love has made you wise as the bird in the wood that seeks a mate. There is a way – listen ! The greatest among the Fianna sit at that table with CORMAC and FINN; and NIALL and another serving man will wait upon them. But do you say that you will pour out their ale for them, and let them not deny you this. You must say that there could be no denying you anything on your marriage night. Then come to me and I will find a way – Then I will bewitch the ale, I will put a pale dust ~~in it~~ into it, and will make a spell over it (Enter CORMAC with two Councillors.) Hush ! here is your father.**

(Laban sits down ~~to~~ & begins to spin)

FOSTER-MOTHER **I cannot understand it yet, but it shall be like the beginning – (Enter CORMAC and two Counsellors.)**

[13bis^{r}]

CORMAC **This is the wisest marriage, though I might have made a greater one – I might have married her to the king ov Alba, but this marriage will keep our kingdom safe (He turns and sees GRANIA) My dear daughter, I have**

[14^{r}]

–13–

been looking for you. Let us sit together and talk to one another. To-night you go away from me, but you go with the chief man in Eri (The Counsellors withdraw) – Come, dear daughter, let us sit together. Why do you stand with fixed eyes, and I see you have not an ornament upon you.

13^{r}, ll. 15–16 The lines are covered by a slip of paper—here fol. 13bis—measuring 5.6 by 17.6 cm and on which the typing is set to the narrower margin.

[HRC(1)]

GRANIA — **I have forgotten them.**

you in
CORMAC — **I should have wished to have seen^your bracelets and your clasp with the emeralds – Will you not wear them?**

GRANIA — **I can send for them, and wear them for you, but I am not minded to wear them.**

CORMAC — **Why are you not minded to wear them (Pause) – What has**
~~your~~ Laban
~~the FOSTER-MOTHER~~^told you, she was telling you something when I came in ?

GRANIA — **Father, you have often seen me wear my bracelets, and my clasp, and can love me without them, as can any other man. Father, listen, let us sit together, or let us talk as we walk hither and thither. I am going ~~away~~ from this house,where my mother lived, and where I have always lived, with one you call the chief man in Eri, but whom I have never seen, so I have**

[15r]

–14–

been questioning her spindle, and you know that all she finds in her spindle is true.

CORMAC — **And she has told you ?**

GRANIA — **Only that I am going away into the woods.**

CORMAC — **You are troubled, my daughter, a woman is always troubled when her marriage is at hand. Maybe you think FINN too rough a man to marry – I might have married you to the king of Alba who is a man of peace; he sent messengers, but FINN is more worthy to be your husband.**

GRANIA — **I have not seen FINN.**

CORMAC — **The enemies of Eri have seen him; you know how he has**

14r, l. 13 The word "your" was first substituted for "the", and then both were canceled together with the two following words in a different ink.

19 The cancellation is in pencil.

its

held ~~his~~ borders against them. ~~The men of Eri have grown too wealthy, they had begun to think of nothing but of cattle and sheep, or of dancing and harp playing, and the men of Lochlann and of Mona had begun to make us their spoil.~~ But FINN and his Fianna have made Eri great as when the Red Branch was at Eman of Macha.

GRANIA **You wish me to marry as kings and queens marry – but I –**

[16r]

–15–

CORMAC **(Suspiciously) You have set your heart upon some boy.**

GRANIA **The Fianna are coming. I shall wed this night him who is the chief man among them in my eyes.**

CORMAC **That is well, FINN is the chief man of Eri after the high king (A sound of trumpets outside – the Counsellors of CORMAC and the servants enter – the servants open the door – NIALL stands by the door.)**

Way for Way for.

NIALL **~~Let~~ FINN and his Council ~~enter~~ (Enter FINN, USHEEN, CAOELTE, DIARMUID etc.)**

CORMAC **FINN is welcome to my house.**

FINN **As the marriage law is, I declare the bride price upon the threshold. I give my word to guard this kingdom against all cattle spoilers that are of the kingdoms of Eri, and to guard it before my own country from the men of Lochlann and the men of Mona; and I give my word to overthrow all kings of Eri that raise their hands against the high king. I cannot give a king's gift, for the Fianna have neither sheep nor cattle, nor towns nor villages nor great store of gold and or silver.**

CORMAC **The bride price is worthy of FINN and of my daughter,**

15r, ll. 13–17 The cancellation is in pencil.

16r, l. 6 It looks as if WBY meant to confirm GM's revision, not redouble it. The cancellations in the same line are in ink.

[HRC(1)]

[17^{r}]

Way for the heads of the four troops
of the Feanna

–16–

(CORMAC takes FINN across the stage and presents him to GRANIA.)

DIARMUID **(At the door). And this is GRANIA.**

USHEEN **Do not look at her DIARMUID, King's daughters are not for us.**

NIALL **(In a loud voice.) Let the hot meats be brought in.**

~~heads of the four parts of the~~
^~~Let the~~ ^~~Fianna enter~~ (Enter a number of men – They stand about the door, CORMAC leaves FINN and GRANIA and goes towards the door to welcome the Fianna.)

GRANIA **There is a scar on your cheek. That is the scar made by the sword of Forgael, when you overthrew the men of Aidne.**

FINN **Has the tale of that battle come so far.**

GRANIA **I have listened all my life to tales of your battles. (Taking his hand in both her hands.) This hand has overthrown many kings.**

FINN **GRANIA must not praise me if she would not take my luck away.**

GRANIA **Some day you will tell me about your battles (She turns away as if already weary of him.)**

17^{r}, l. 5 WBY first wrote a substitution for "the Fianna" above the line. This revision was canceled when the different substitution was looped in from the head of the page.

[18r]

The tables for the rest

–17–

FINN **Are my battles more to you than my love ? (CORMAC brings CAOELTE, USHEEN and DIARMUID towards GRANIA – CORMAC and FINN go up the stage.)**

Of red yew

GRANIA **AH, this is USHEEN, I know him by his harp. Will you sing us love songs to-night ?**

CAOELTE **I am CAOELTE, and this is DIARMUID.**

GRANIA **Welcome, CAOELTE, teller of battle tales. There is a tale you tell – (She stands looking at DIARMUID, forgetful of everything) And this is DIARMUID.**

NIALL **The king, and FINN, the son of COOL are seated and the guests at this table are – ~~DIARMUID, CAOELTE, USHEEN, GALL, son of MONA, CONAN THE BALD, CONGAL and FINMOLE,~~**
The tables for the rest of the Feanna have been ~~pre~~ spread before the arras in the western Hall
The Fianna and serving men withdraw, leaving NIALL and one serving man to wait at the king's table.)

CORMAC **My daughter, why do you not take your place beside FINN, son of COOL ?**

GRANIA **Every night, father, I have poured out your ale, I would do so this last time, and this night I would pour out my husband's for the first time.**

CORMAC **GRANIA must not pour out our ale.**

18r, l. 9–10 The deletion within the stage direction and the vertical line in the LH margin are in pencil.

[HRC(1), 19^{r}]

-12-

FINN But if this be her wish ?

GRANIA This is the first favour I have asked.

FINN All here will remember, this is my honour (The King signs to the serving men to withdraw, GRANIA returns to the FOSTER-MOTHER)

GRANIA I ~~cannot tell why I have done this~~ - Has this been done ~~Have I done~~ well ? Have ~~you found a way of helping me~~ given them the ale. —

FOSTER-MOTHER ~~The way has been put into your mind; you will give them enchanted ale~~ - Here are two flagons that I have made sleepy — but now I will make a spell over them.

~~By fire and wave and wind~~
~~Do all things to my mind~~
~~Pour sleep in cup and horn~~
~~That every sleepy head~~
~~Lie low as on its bed~~
~~Till the cock crow in the morn.~~

Do all as I bid you
Pour sleep in the ale horns
That all who have drunk them
May sleep as on pillow
Till cocks crow at morning

Give them this ale and they will sleep till the cock crows. Give it to all but CAOELTE, USHEEN and DIARMUID

Laban goes out.
(GRANIA passes along the table filling the cups and horns - CAOELTE and USHEEN are the last who should be served - When she comes to DIARMUID she stands looking

[HRC(1)]
[19r]

–18–

1 **FINN** **But if this be her wish ?**

2 **GRANIA** **This is the first favour I have asked.**

3 **FINN** **All here will remember ,this ~~is an~~ honour (The King signs to the serving men to withdraw, GRANIA returns to the FOSTER-MOTHER)**

Has this been done

4 **GRANIA** **~~I cannot tell why I have done this~~ – ~~Have I done~~ well ?**

give me the ale.

5 **Have ~~you found a way of helping me ? Ar yo~~**

6 **FOSTER-**
7 **MOTHER** **~~The way has been put into your mind; you will give them enchanted ale~~ – Here are two flagons that I have** √

8 **made sleepy{—** / **.** but now I will make a spell over them.

9 Do all as I bid you	**By fire and wave and wind**
10 Pour sleep in the ale horns	**Do all things to my mind**
11 That all who have drunk	**Pour sleep in cup and horn**
12 them	**That every sleepy head**
13 May sleep as on pillow	**Lie low as on its bed**
14 Till cock crow at morning	**Till the cock crow in the morn.**

15 **Give them this ale and they will sleep till the cock**
16 **crow ~~s~~. Give it to all but CAOELTE, USHEEN and DIARMUID**
Laban goes out.
(^GRANIA passes along the table filling the cups and horns – CAOELTE and USHEEN are the last who should be served – When she comes to DIARMUID she stands looking

[20r]

–19–

1 **at him.)**

2 **CORMAC** **Why do you not fill DIARMUID'S cup ?** *(Grania drops the flagon)*

19r, l. 3 All the emendations in this line are in pencil; the remainder of the emendations on this page are in ink.
7 The only tick in the RH margin to appear in HRC(1) and in the same colored ink as WBY's emendations on this same page.

3 **GRANIA** **The ale is all spilled – I will bring another flagon.**

—

4 **CORMAC** ^**I do not like the spilling of ale at a marriage feast.**

5 **CONAN** **It never happens but it brings ill luck.**
(<u>Ex. Laban</u>)

6 **DIARMUID** **CONAN sees ill luck everywhere. When will FINN**
7 **take away his favour from CONAN, and let the Fianna**
8 **give him his deserts.**

9 **FINN** **Tell us a story, CAOELTE, and put the spilling of**
our
10 **the ale out of ~~your~~ minds (CAOELTE rises from his**
place and takes his harp) – He stands touching his
harp as if uncertain what story he is going to tell.)

11 **FINN** **Tell us the story of the house of the quicken trees.**

12 **CAOELTE** **Yes, I will tell the story of the house of the quicken**
13 **trees – (A pause) It is gone, it went out of mind of**
story
14 **a sudden. A new ~~tale~~ is coming to me – It is coming**
15 **to me – I see a man lying dead, and his wife is going**
16 **away with another.**

17 **FINN** **What quarrel have you with me that you should tell**

[21[r]]

–20–

story
1 **me such a ~~tale~~ at my marriage ?**

2 **USHEEN** **FINN, FINN, the gods are in the room, the ale has been**
put
3 *(<u>Starting to</u>* **spilled, and a strange tale has been ~~but~~ into CAOELTE' S**
4 *<u>his feet)</u>* **mind. Our luck is being taken away^ (They all start**
to their feet.)

5 **FINN** **~~Let us all sit down again.~~ Let us drink and forget**

20[r], l. 4 Both marks are in pencil. The insertion at line 5+ is ink over pencil.
21[r], l. 5 The cancellation is in pencil.

their
~~**our**~~ **thoughts of ill luck – They all** ~~**drink.)**~~ <u>Sit & drink except Laban & Cormac who remain standing</u>)

CORMAC **(Suddenly sleepy, and trying to rouse himself) Let somebody else tell a story, I am growing sleepy.**

USHEEN **I cannot remember any story – I too have had my thoughts taken away.**

CONAN **DIARMUID, CAOELTE, and USHEEN have forgotten their boasting stories, but CONAN has many a pleasant story and no one asks him for one. I will tell a pleasant story, I will tell of the death of DIARMUID.**

FINN **I will have no tale of death at my marriage feast. To speak of DIARMUID'S death may be to bring death upon him. Be silent or you may take his luck away.**

GRANIA **(Coming nearer to the table.) Will DIARMUID die by the sword, or will he be made captive ?**

[22^r]

–21–

FINN **I forbid this story.**

story
DIARMUID **The story of my death is an old** ~~**tale,**~~ **and it no longer makes me a'feared – Tell on.**

Coming from table)
CONAN **(Obsequiously** ⋏ **Oh, my beautiful GRANIA, this is the way it was – DIARMUID was put out to foster with a xhepherd, and no one was so beautiful as DIARMUID when he was a child, except the shepherd's son. The shepherd's son was much more beautiful than DIARMUID, and his beauty made DIARMUID'S father jealous, and one day he crushed the shepherd's son to death between his knees.**

21^r, l. 6 GM's insertion appears to be written over some pencil marks.

22^r, l. 4 The caret cancels the typed right parenthesis.

5–6 Some indecipherable pencil marks between brackets appear, half-erased, beneath the part ascription. They have the same configuration as the beginning of the pencil addition beneath Usheen's name on fol. 21^r.

[HRC(1)]

GRANIA Tell me of DIARMUID, tell me of DIARMUID.

CONAN The shepherd wept and wept, Oh, how he wept. And after a while he took his second son into the woods, and made a spell over him with a Druid hazel stick, and changed him into a black and bristless boar. And some day that boar is to break out of the woods and to kill many men and many women. All the Fianna are to gather for the hunting of him; they are to hunt him round through Eri and through Eri from kingdom to kingdom – Oh what a hunting – Oh, what a hunting !

[23r]

–22–

GRANIA Tell me more of DIARMUID, tell me quickly.

CONAN I must drink, I am thirsty again (He drinks) DIARMUID must go out against that boar and must be killed. It was to kill him that the shepherd made the spell over his second son. He shall be torn by the tusks, he shall be bloody, his face shall be foul because it will be bloody. I would that the women of Eri could see him when he is foul and bloody (He staggers.) I am growing sleepy, because I have to run the messages of the Fianna (He recovers himself) I shall live to see him when the tusks have torn him, for it has been foretold of him also that he shall not live long. He shall not be remembered for deeds of arms, but as a lover of women; he shall live as a lover of women and his life shall be soon over. Who has put witchcraft into my ale ? who among the Fianna has done this (He falls)

USHEEN He said there was witchcraft in the ale, and look, they are all sleeping. Who was it that put witchcraft into the ale, GRANIA ?

~~My FOSTER-MOTHER~~ [Laban *the Druidess*] has done this for me. I had never a mind to marry FINN. But why does not DIARMUID come to us ? (DIARMUID comes from the table) It was

[24r]

–23–

for you that I ordered witchcraft to be put into the ale.

DIARMUID For me, GRANIA ?

GRANIA I had never a mind to marry FINN; I am going away with you to-night, we are going ~~to leave~~ *away* before they awake.

DIARMUID You and I, and you did not see me before this night ?

GRANIA I desired you, and you were in my thoughts before I saw you, DIARMUID. You were in my thoughts, DIARMUID (She takes him in her arms.)

DIARMUID I too desired you, and you were in my thoughts – Oh, beautiful woman ! You were in my thoughts, GRANIA – Let me look at you – Let me put back your hair – Your eyes are grey, GRANIA, your eyes are grey ! and your hands – But FINN, but FINN, but FINN – GRANIA, wife of FINN, why have you played with me !

GRANIA I am not the wife of FINN (She goes towards DIARMUID) And now I cannot be FINN'S wife, for you have held me in your arms and you hav e kissed me.

DIARMUID What is this madness, GRANIA ? Here, here this night – and FINN sleeping there.

[25r]

–24–

GRANIA If he had loved me, his love would have been stronger than witchcraft (A pause) – You shrink from me; why do you shrink from me ? Am I not desirable ? I have heard men praise me. You have touched my hair and looked into my eyes. Why do you shrink from ^*me* ? I have heard, DIARMUID, that women love you, and cer-

25r, l. 5 The pencil insertion is in a wobbly hand.

tainly a woman must be desirable in your eyes. It may be that men have lied to me, and this hair is not soft, this body delicate (To CAOELTE and USHEEN) – Am I not miserable ? Will men shrink from me ? Would you shrink from me, if it were you I had asked to go away with me ? No matter who shrinks from me now, since the man I long for shrinks. The world shrinks from me.

CAOELTE **Look, GRANIA, at the sleeping man whose ale you have bewitched.**

USHEEN **If FINN were to awake he would take some terrible vengeance for this.**

GRANIA **~~In a withered world~~ what is his vengeance to me. Has not my world withered ? I will go into the woods, and will wander alone there till I die.**

DIARMUID **When I looked into your eyes, GRANIA, it was as though**

[26r]

–25–

out of
I had come ~~from~~ ^ a cave into the dawn. But no, no, I cannot, for there is a stronger thing than love.

CAOELTE **GRANIA, GRANIA, the Fianna live poor and live near to**
their oath
death always that honour may be the strongest thing among them.

USHEEN **Turn your eyes away from her, DIARMUID.**

at it has
GRANIA **He looks ~~on~~ ^ me, because ~~I have~~ ^ been foretold – ~~foretold for him.~~**

DIARMUID **(Disengaging himself from USHEEN and CAOELTE) What has been foretold – Who has foretold it ?**

25r, l. 19 The cancellation is in ink.
26r, l. 4 WBY entered the alternate “their oath” without cancelling “honour.”
7–8 The cancellation is in pencil.

USHEEN **DIARMUID, look where FINN sleeps.**

CAOELTE **Think of your fame in battle.**

USHEEN **And of your oath.**

er
DIARMUID **If the fortune-tell~~ing~~ has lied, if se she has said that I will break my oath ~~(~~To FINN~~)~~ What did she tell you ? What has she said, has she said this ?**

GRANIA **She spoke of a woman pledged to marry a man whom she did not love, ~~and she foretold that the man would leave all things and that the woman would leave all things~~**

[27[r]]

–26–

and of a man who would come and take her away from that marriage bed. She foretold that the man would leave all things and that the woman would leave all things for love's sake. She foretold that they would go away in the middle of the marriage feast, and wander in the unpeopled woods and be happy , by the rushy margin of many streams.

DIARMUID **And the man is I, and the woman is you.**

GRANIA **She foretold that it shall seem as if all men had forgotten them, that the ousel and the otter shall not fly from them. They shall be happy under green boughs and become wise in all woodland wisdom, and as she spoke I too seemed to see them wandering on paths trodden by the feet of deer, where there are sudden**
often
odours of wild honey and where they will throw their arms about one another and ~~will~~ kiss one another on the mouth. (She goes nearer to him). And she told me, DIARMUID that we should make our beds with the skins of deer under cromlechs and in caves, and awake from sleep we know not why, as though the dwarfs of the rocks had called to us, that we might see the star-

---

26[r], l. 15 The parentheses are canceled in pencil.

[HRC(1)]

light falling through the leaves. She told me the
of the trees
dwarfs of the rocks and the secret people should watch

[28r]

–27–

over us, and though all the men of Eri were our enemies they should not pluck us out of one another's arms.

DIARMUID **I must not listen, or I will take her in my arms. I will awaken FINN – FINN, FINN, awake (~~She puts her hand on his mouth~~.)**

GRANIA **What would you tell him ?**

DIARMUID **That the world vanishes, that I see nothing but you.**

GRANIA **Have you not sworn to help the helpless, and who is more helpless than I ?**

DIARMUID **Had you not told me that you loved me, I would have helped you.**

GRANIA **Help me, DIARMUID.**

DIARMUID **CAOELTE and USHEEN have seen my trouble; they will tell FINN of my trouble. She has asked me for my help and I must give it.**

GRANIA **(Standing at the door which she has thrown open) Come DIARMUID to the woods, the birds of AONGHUS, the birds of love, the birds that the eye cannot see, sing joy-ously, singing fiercely they clap their wings and sing.**

[29r]

–28–

DIARMUID **She asks for my help and I must give it.**

USHEEN **From this night the Fianna are broken in two.**

28r, ll. 4–4+ The cancellation is in faint pencil.

is in danger
CAOELTE **And the kingdom that was to be made safe ~~trembles,~~ and**
Oath is broken
DIARMUID'S honour is ~~taken away~~.

broken
DIARMUID **My honour is not ~~taken away,~~ tell FINN that – Tell him that this sword will guard her by day, and it will lie between us at night. Tell him I will send some**
that
messenger, some token ~~which~~ ~~I~~ shall say to him – FINN, I bring you word that so many hours or so many moons have passed by and that DIARMUID'S oath is unbroken.

GRANIA **The woods are sad with their summer sadness, and the birds of love have become silent, but they are not sleeping, their eyes are bright among the boughs – (She goes out.)**

after this
DIARMUID **I must follow her. Upon whose face shall I look in friendship again, (He goes out.)**

USHEEN **(Goes to the door and looks after them.) They have gone westward to the woods.**

CAOELTE **When FINN awakes, we must tell him that they have gone ~~into the~~ eastward, towards the sea.**

[NLI 8777(3) a, 1r, 2r]

DIARMID AND GRANIA.

ACT I.

1

DIARMID AND GRANIA.

ACT I.

The banqueting hall in Tara - A table at the back of the stage on a dais - Pillars in front - There are doors to the right and left - A number of Serving Men are laying the table for the feast - Niall is directing them. There is a spinning wheel to left.

Niall.

Do not put the salmon there; put it in front of the chief man at the feast.

Boy.

Is not the King the chief man at a feast.

Niall.

Not at a wedding feast - the chief man at a wedding feast is the man come to be wed.

Boy.

Where shall I put the boar's head?

Niall.

Put it where the old King used to sit, Art, King Cormac's

Complete Typescript of Complete Act, Revised by W. B. Yeats and George Moore—W. B. Yeats's Copy?

[NLI 8777(3) a, 1r]

DIARMID AND GRANIA.

ACT I.

[2r]

1

DIARMID AND GRANIA.

ACT I.

The banquetting hall in Tara – A table at the back of the stage on a dais – Pillars in front – There are doors to the right and left – A number of Serving Men are laying the table for the feast – Niall is directing them. There is a spinning wheel to left.

Niall.

Do not put the salmon there; put it in front of the ch{ie/eff} man at the feast.

Boy.

Is not the King the chief man at a feast.

Niall.

Not at a wedding feast – the chief man at a wedding feast is the man come to be wed.

Boy.

Where shall I put the boar's head?

Niall.

Put it where the old king used to sit, Art, King Cormac's

[NLI 8777(3) a]

[3r]

2

father, Art the Melancholy they used to call him. He was deaf at the left ear, and he was always complaining that the meat was hard, and that the wind came under the door. Yes, Boy, under this roo{f/d an hundred kings have sat, right back to Ollam Fodla that made the laws. What meals they have eaten! What ale they have drunk! Before Cormac there was Art, and before Art there was Conn.

Boy.

Was that Conn the hundred fighter?

Niall.

Yes, Conn the hundred fighter they used to call him, and he knew when a hare was put before him if the fire had been bright *t behind* ~~under~~ it; and he knew if the swine's flesh had been dried in the smoke of a whitehorn tree. Put the curds over there; it is not ~~the~~ curds, but ~~the~~ trotters and cows'-heel that used to be put there, for that was the place of the king'sfool. One day he flouted the Fianna on the high road, and they hanged him on an alder tree.

Boy.

Did they hang the king's fool in time of peace?

Niall.

Fool, or wise man, war or peace, its all one to them when their pride is up. But they are great men, Boy. It is not for you and me to speak against such great men. Bring the

[4r]

3

dishes quickly, it is time for their messenger to be here. Put the bread there, Art's wife. Queen Maive used to sit there Maive the Half Ruddy they called her, and she liked thin barley cakes, and six men got their death because of her – Bring in

---

3r, l. 11 Cancellation of a word letter by letter is characteristic of GM; the correction is in heavy pencil.
13 The deletions are in pencil

the flagons (To the servants ____); put them here, where Art's hound used to lie – (A knocking at the door) Here is the messenger of the Fianna – I knew we should not get done in time. Bring in the flagons – (To the ~~other~~ servants) Where are the drinking horns? (More knocking – he goes to the door and opens it – Conan comes in; he is a fat rough man and is much out of breath – He is followed by three men, who carry bundles of shields on their backs.)

Conan. *(going to table)*

This is the salmon, and this is the boar's head, and these are the barley cakes for the wedding feast of Finn, the son of Cool. Give me a horn full of ale – (Niall gives him a horn of ale.) I have much trouble going messages for the Fianna. Have I not legs to grow weary and body to sweat like another. I am hungry too; but I dare not put a knife in the meat till the Fianna are here.

Niall.

There will be plenty, and to spare when they are here.

Conan.

Well look to the hanging of the shields. I've seen you

[5r]

4.

yes, now

before, ~~now~~ I remember you; you have been in Tara fifty years and have hung them many a time –(Turning to the men that are with him) Come, the sooner we bring Finn, the sooner we shall eat – (They go out)

Boy.

The Fianna have a rough messenger.

Niall.

I would have none say that I have said it, but he is a man of little account among them.

Boy.

Men wear sheep skins in my country, but I had thought that the Fianna wore fine clothes.

4r, l. 8 The deletion by GM is in the same shade of ink as his insertion into line 5 above.

[NLI 8777(3) a]

Niall.

I will tell you why the Fianna made him wear it one of these days, and why Finn made him one of the Fianna. Would you be one of them?

Boy.

Yes, if I might be Finn, or Diarmid or Caoelte.

Niall.

They are famous for their battles; they are great men, but would you not be Conan the Bald if you could?

[6^{r}]

5

Boy.

That man with the sheepskin?

Niall.

Well, he eats when he is hungry, and sleeps when he is sleepy, and rails at whomever displeases him. Those great men have the best seats at the table, and the fairest women for their bed-fellows, and yet I would not. (He rushes across the stage to keep one of the men from hanging Goll's shield at the lower end of the table.) Would you put Gool the son of Morna's shield below Alvin's and Fergus's; would you have the roof tree burnt over our heads. It is the third shield from Finn's. Let me see now, let me think, it was Cool, Finn's father who made this custom of the hanging up of every man's shield above his place. No quarreling everything settled. I was going to tell you who made the Fianna, Boy; it was Cool. He took a thousand men out of every kingdom, and made the into an army, and set them to watch the shores. No one is old enough but myself to remember those times. The men of Lochland and the men of Mona, and the men of Alba carrying off ~~the~~ women here and sheep there, and leaving smoke and fire behind them, and nobody to meet them but men taken from the sheep-fold, and from the plough and from the smithy. Yes, that is where Caoelte's shield hangs. I told you its place last time and you remembered it – (Returning to the Boy) But I was telling you how the Fianna saved the women and sheep. They fight well but they are proud – Ah, they

6^{r}, l. 16 GM's deletion is in ink.

[7r]

6

are very proud. I was telling you, Boy, how they hanged the king's fool, and many and many a time they have made war on the king himself. Finn's , father, Cool, died fighting against *that* Cormac's father ~~after~~ Art the Melancholy, and it was for {~~*this*~~ that} death Finn kept out of the battl{*e* o}, Cormac fought against the men of Mona. It has been this way always, and sometimes Eri has been like a shaking sod between them; but this marriage mends all – (<u>Enter Grania and Laban</u>)

Boy.

There is that old Laban and the King's daughter.

Niall.

Quick, quick, put up the rest of the shields – Come away Boy. Ah, that old woman, she has come back after these many years, an~~d~~ old witch; they say she has more shapes than one – (<u>Niall and the Boy go out and are followed by other Serving men</u>.

Grania.

You cannot persuade me. I will not marry Finn.

Laban.

Hush! Hush!

Grania.

But the Fianna are coming too, you will tell me about them, about the young men. Yes their shields are here already.

[8r]

7

Laban.

Conan has brought them.

Grania.

You have promised to tell me about the Fianna. If you

7r, ll. 3, 4 The inserted comma in line 3 and GM's deletion in line 4 are both in ink.

12 The deletion is in ink.

[NLI 8777(3) a]

will not Niall will.

Laban. slip A.

[**Do not call him, let nobody know what is in your mind.**

Grania.

(<u>Going tothe table)</u> My father sits here, Finn son of Cool sits next to him, and here is my place next to Finn – but it will be empty.

Laban.

Hush! No man matters to you now but Finn.

Grania.

You told me his hair was grey.

Laban.

You have always known that his hair was grey.

Grania.

Grey hair and brown hair were the same to me a month ago. A month ago I was in the woods –

[9r]

7

A.

Laban.

You have been in the woods with Niall lately, and he has shown you where the bees make their nests and you have come home with honey-comb and birds eggs and flowers!

Grania.

there is in

But it was you who taught me ~~to know~~ the magic ~~of~~ ^ the herbs. You took me to a place where ~~the~~ earth breathes

a cave

out of ~~the abysseses.~~

Laban.

I am too old to go far, now.

8r, l. 4 The substitution appears in NLI 8777(3) g, fol. 118r.

9r Headed "A" because the page is inserted into the sequence as a replacement page 7.

4, 5, 6, etc. All the deletions on this page are in WBY's ink.

Grania.

There are some that say
Mother, ^ you will never be older than you are, and now
we go over
~~you~~ ^ will ~~come~~ ^ to the shields because you will not refuse me
not ~~not~~ anything
anything I ask. Niall would ^ refuse me ~~nothing~~.

[10r]

8

Laban.

It was spring time when the young find many things among the woods.

Grania,

I had climbed the little path, and stood on the hill, where the trees grow sparer,looking into the mist.

Laban.

And it was then that you thought about a young man.

Grania.

The mist was hanging on the brow of the hill, and something seemed to be moving over the world and to come out of the mist. It was beautiful mother. The world was singing and the singing came into my breasts, but come to the shields and tell me of the men who are to sit under them.

Laban.

I dare not, I dare not.

Grania.

But you said that to-night would not be my marriage night.

Laban.

No, no child, I never said such a thing. Hush, lest they should hear you.

10r, ll. 8–9 The earliest appearance of a phrase originating from GM and a cause of considerable dispute: references are given in the introduction, note 16.

[NLI 8777(3) a]

[11r]

9

Grania.

They who are wiser than you said it, Mother. The thread
that you spun yesterday – the stars that we watched last night,
the pebbles that we threw into the well~~s~~ this morning.

Laban.

Hush, your father will be here; there is no time now.
I saw you talking to King Cormac this morning, why did you not
tell him of this change?

Grania.

I took his hands in mine, and thought to tell him.

Laban.

You should have told him.

Grania.

But he would have sent a messenger, and I should not have
seen the Fianna together.

Laban.

So that you might pick a man who would carry you away.
will
It ~~shall~~ be long before men come to the end of this mischief.
The Fianna shall be broken in two because of it. Oh, why did
Cormac shut his ears to what I told him. There will be flights
and battles, ruin on ruin, and neither you nor I can do anything.

[12r]

10.

Grania.

I would not be a trouble if I could help it. I would not
set Finn against any man. I would have Finn and my man friends.
I would stand between them. I would hand them their ale.
shield
Whose ~~sword~~ is that, mother? That one with the red otter paint-
ed upon it.

11r, l. 3 The deletion is in ink.

Laban.

That shield with the red otter is the shield of Fergus.
He is taller than all the others, his hair and his bread are
brown, and he wears a crimson cloak over a white tunic.

Grania.

Is he tall and stately – would he make my heart beat.

Laban.

He is strong and stately, but there is grey in his beard.
{e , {d
That red shield with the whit{ ' { eer 's **painted upon it is**
the shield of Usheen. He has yellow hair and he has long white
hands, with fingers hard at the tips from plucking of harp string *s*
that no {wom
and they say ~~not~~ {woman has refused him her love.

Grania.

Is he young?

Laban.

There are younger than he. That grey shield with the

[13r]

11.

r
raven painted upon it is the shield of Goll, the son of Mona.
He is a great hunter and his arms and legs are as strong^as the
posts of a door.

Grania.

Is there mirth in his eyes?

Laban.

He has the quiet of the wood in his eyes. But I see your
on
mind is not set upon one that is strong, but^one that is young.
That white shield with the green fish is the shield of Caoelte.
They call him Caoelte the swift-footed, and he is young and a
teller~~s~~ of battle tales. But that silver shield withthe flying
white heron upon it is the shield of Diarmid. He is the young-
est and comeliest of all. He has dark hair and blue eyes, and
light limbs, and his~~s~~ skin is white but for the freckles. He

13r, l. 9 Type deletion.

[NLI 8777(3) a]

is courteous and he is merry with women. It is said of him that he will not be remembered for deeds of arms but as a true lover, and that he will die young.

Grania.

Diarmid, Diarmid, a pleasant sounding name – Diarmid a sweet sounding name.

Laban.

But, child, how think you that these things will come about?

Grania.

I believe in your soothsaying Mother, ~~and~~ that ^ **a man as young**

[14r]

12

as I am will come and carry me away.

Laban.

No, no, Diarmid will not break his oath to Finn.

Grania.

You said his hair was brown, and his eyes blue, and his limbs light; and his skin white but for the freckles. It was for such a man that I looked into the mist. But thinking of love makes the brain giddy.

Laban.

What can he do? He cannot overthrow Finn and his army.

Grania.

(<u>Waking from a reverie</u>) You must find a way, Mother, it is for you to find a way.

Laban.

They would hang me from the rafters, child, they would hang me.

Grania.

You would baffle them; that will not be difficult for

13r, l. 19 The cancellation and the caret mark are in pencil—although the substitution is in ink.

you. But how shall I escape from Finn's marriage bed? Shall I run into the woods?

Laban.

But the woods are full of wolves; they are lonely.

[15r]

13. B.

Child, love has made you wise as the bird in the wood that seeks a mate. There is a way – listen! The greatest among the Fianna sit at table with Cormac and Finn; and Niall and another serving man will wait upon them But do you say that you will pour out their ale for them, and let them not deny you this. You must say that there could be no denying you anything on your marriage night. Then come to me and I will find a way Then I will bewitch the ale, I will put a pale dust into it, and will make a spell over it (Enter Cormac with two Councillors Hush! here is your father. (Laban sits down and begins to spin)

Cormac.

This is the wisest marriage, though I might have made a greater one – I might have married her to the King of Alba, but this marriage will keep our kingdom safe – (He turns and sees Grania) My dear daughter, I have been looking for you. Let us sit together and talk to one another. To-night you go away from me, but you go with the cheif man in Eri – (The councillors withdraw) Come, dear daughter, let us sit together. Why do you ~~sit~~ stand with fixed eyes, and I see you have not an ornament upon you.

Grania.

I have forgotten them.

15r, l. -1 Note that, although the page is lettered as if it were an insertion, the color of the TS ribbon is light blue, as in the majority of pages.

-18 The underlining and cancellation are in pencil.

[NLI 8777(3) a]

[16r]

14. (B.)

Laban.

There are wolves in the wood.

Grania.

I do not fear the wolves.

Laban.

would You could not escape them –
They ~~will~~ follow you. ~~I can see them about you.~~ I
They would tear you in pieces
~~can hear your screams, Oh, Grania, your screams growing~~ faint
~~as they tear you.~~

Grania.

would
If you ~~will~~ not have me go ~~away~~ into the woods, find a ~~way~~
~~of escape.~~ some other way.

Laban.

Why will you not marry Finn, you will be the greatest
woman in Eri.

[17r]

15 (B2)

Grania.

I will not marry Finn; and you mother, who have cared
for me since I stood no taller than your knee, you will not
alone
see me run away ^ ~~alone~~ into the ~~lonely~~ woods.

Laban.

The woods are lonely, Grania, you must not go.

Grania.

~~There is~~ ^ a herb (you have told me of) that makes men sleep.

16r Though headed "B", this and the following page (fols. 16–17) enlarge on the final line of fol. 14r—that is, they were intended to be inserted *before* the intervening page marked "B" by Yeats.

17r, l. -1 The smudged inserted page number could be read as "B?"

Laban.

Hush! (Taking her aside)

[18r]

14.

Cormac.

I should have wished to have seen you in your bracelets and your clasp with the emeralds – Will you wear them?

Grania.

I can send for them and wear them for you, but I am not minded to wear them.

Cormac.

Why are you not minded to wear them? (Pause) What has Laban told you? She was telling you something when I came in.

Grania.

Father, you have often seen me wear my bracelets, and my clasp, and can love me without them, as can any other man. Father listen, ~~Letten~~ let us sit together, or let us talk as we walk thither and hither. I am going from this house where my mother lived, and where I have always lived, with one you call the chief man in Eri, but whom I have never seen, so I have been questioning her spindle, and you know all that she finds in her spindle is true.

Cormac.

And she has told you?

Grania.

Only that I am going away into the woods.

[19r]

15.

Cormac

You are troubled my daughter, a woman is always troubled when her marriage is at hand. Maybe you think Finn too rough a man to marry – I might have married you to the King of Alba

18r, l. 9 Type deletion.

10 The correction is in faint pencil.

[NLI 8777(3) a]

who is a man of peace; he sent messengers but Finn is more worthy to be your husband.

Grania.

I have not seen Finn.

Cormac.

The enemies of Eri have seen him; you know how he has held its borders against them. But Finn and his Fianna have made Eri great, as when the Red Branch was at Eman of Macha.

Grania.

You wish me to marry as kings and queens marry – but I –

Cormac.

(Suspiciously) You have set your heart upon some boy.

Grania.

The Fianna are coming. I shall wed this night him who is the chief man among them in my eyes.

Cormac.

That is well, Finn is the chief man of Eri after the high king – (A sound of trumpets outside – The Councillors of Cormac

[20r]

16.

and the servants enter – The servants open the door – Niall stand by the door.)

Niall.

Way for Finn and his council. (Enter Finn, Usheen Caoelte, Diarmid, etc.,)

Cormac.

Finn is welcome to my house.

Finn.

As the marriage law is, I declare the bride ~~peace~~ price upon the threshold. I give my word to guard this kingdom against all cattle spoilers that are of the kingdoms of Eri, and to guard it before my own country from the men of Lochland and the men of Mona; and I give my word to overthrow all kings of Eri that

raise their hand against the high king. I cannot give a king's gift for the Fianna have neither sheep nor cattle, nor towns nor villages nor great store of gold or silver.

Cormac.

The bride price is worthy of Finn and of my daughter – (<u>Cormac takes Finn across the stage and presents him to Grania</u>.)

Diarmid.

(<u>At the door</u>) And this is Grania?

[21r]

17.

Usheen.

Do not look at her Diarmid, King's daughters are not for us.

Niall.

(<u>In a loud voice</u>) Let the hot meats be brought in – Way for the heads of the four troops of the Fianna – (<u>Enter a numbe r of men, they stand about the door, Cormac leaves Finn and Grania and goes towards the door to welcome the Fianna.)</u>

Grania.

There is a scar on your cheek. That is the scar made by the sword of Forgael, ~~and~~ when you overthrew the men of Aidne.

Finn.

Has the tale of that battle come so far.

Grania.

i

I have listened all my l~~o~~fe to tales of your battles. (<u>Taking his hand in both her hands)</u> This hand has overthrown many kings.

Finn.

Grania must not praise me if ahe would not take my luck away

Grania.

Some day you will tell me about your battles–() <u>She turns away as if already weary of him.</u>)

21r, l. 7 The correction is in ink.

[NLI 8777(3) a]

[22r]

18.

Finn.

Are my battles more to you than my love? (Cormac brings Caoelte, Usheen and Diarmid towards Grania – Cormac and Finn go up the stage)

Grania.

Ah, this is Usheen, I knew him by his harp of red yew. Will you sing us love songs to-night?

Caoelte.

I am Caoelte, and this is Diarmid.

Grania.

Welcome Caoelte, teller of battle tales. There is a tale you tell – (She stands looking at Diarmid, forgetful of everything.) And this is Diarmid.

Niall. C.

The king, and Finn the son of Cool are seated, the guests at this table ^ are Usheen Caoelte Goll son of Morna Diarmid Fergus & Fath~~e~~na ? The tables for the rest of the Fianna are spread beyond the arras in the western hall. (The Fianna and serving men withdraw, leaving Niall and one serving Man to wait at the king's table.

Cormac.

My daughter why do you not take your place beside Finn son of Cool?

Grania.

[23r]

18

Grania.

Has Diarmid nothing to say to me{?.

Diarmid.

So this is your wedding night, Grania.

Grania.

The wedding feast is spread and I shall be wedded if
body does   I know your shield   It
some ~~does~~ not carry me away. ~~But~~ Diarmid . ~~your shield~~ has a flying white heron upon it and this is your sword.

Usheen.

Diarmid!

[24^{r}]

19.

Grania.

Every night father, I have poured out your ale, I would
~~the~~
do so this last time, and this night pour out my husband's for the first time.

Cormac.

Grania must not pour out our ale.

Finn.

But if this be her wish?

Grania.

It is the first favour I have asked.

Finn.

as a
All here will remember, this ~~is my~~ honour – (<u>The king signs to the serving men to withdraw, Grania returns to Laban.)</u>

Grania.

Has this been done well? Give me the ale.

Laban.

Here are two flagons that I have made sleepy – but no – I will make a spell over them.

Do all that I bid you
Pour sleep in the ale horns
That all who have drunk them
May sleep as on pillows
Till cock crow at morning

[NLI 8777(3) a]

[25r]

20.

Give them this ale and they will sleep till cockcrow. Give it to all but Caoelte, Usheen and Diarmid. (~~Laban goes out – Grania~~ passes along the table filling the cups and horns – Caoelte and Usheen are the last who should be served When she comes to Diarmid she stands looking at him.)

Cormac.

Why do you not fill Diarmid's cup? (Grania drops the flagon,)

Grania.

The ale is all spilled; I will bring another flagon.

Cormac.

Daughter, I do not like the spilling of ale at a marriage feast.

Conan.

It never happens but it brings ill luck. (Exeunt Laban)

Diarmid.

Conan sees ill luck everywhere. When will Finn take away his favour from Conan, and let the Fianna give him his deserts?

Finn.

Tell us a story Caoelte, and put the spilling of the ale out of our minds – (Caoelte rises from his place, and takes his

[26r]

21.

harp – He stands touching his harp as if uncertain what story he is going to tell.) Tell us the story of the house of the quicken trees.

Caoelte.

Yes, I will tell you the story of the house of the quicken trees – (A pause) It is gone, it went out of my mind of a

---

25r, l. 2+ The tentative deletion is in pencil.

sudden – A new story is coming to me – It is coming to me – I see a man lying dead and his wife is going away with another.

Finn.

What quarrel have you with me, that you should tell me such a story at my marriage?

Usheen.

(Starting to his feet) Finn, Finn, the gods are in the
the
room, ~~that~~ ale has been spilled, and a strange tale has been put into^Caoelte's mind. Our luck is being taken away- (They all start to their feet.)

Finn.

our
? **Let us drink, and forget ~~their~~** thoughts of ill luck.
Caoelte and Usheen {who
(They all sit and drink, except ~~Laban and Conan~~ {who remain standing.)

Cormac.

(Suddenly sleepy and trying to rouse himself.) Let somebody else tell a story I am growing sleepy.

[27r]

22.

Usheen.

I cannot remember any story; I too have had my thoughts taken away.

Conan.

Diarmid, Caoelte, and Usheen have forgotten their boasting stories, but Conan has many a pleasant story and no one asks him for one. I will tell a pleasant story; I will tell of the death of Diarmid.

Finn.

I will have no tale of death at my marriage feast. To

26r, l. 10 The deletion and the caret mark, like the question mark to the LH of line 12, are in pencil.

12 It is unclear if the insertion within the line overwrites faint type.

13 The deleted names might each be supposed to made up of five characters, reckoning from GM's style of deletion: here, therefore, Laban and Conan. However, GM wrote Laban and Cormac into HRC(1), fol. 21r.

15 The faint inverted characters above "am gro" are "21.", the consequence of a typist's false start.

[NLI 8777(3) a]

speak of Diarmid's death may be to bring death upon him. Be silent or you may take his luck away.

Grania.

(Coming nearer to the table) Will Diarmid die by the sword or will he be made captive?

Finn.

I forbid this story.

Diarmid.

The story of my death is an old story, and it no longer makes me ~~a'feard~~ afraid ' Tell on.

Conan.

(Obsequiously – coming from the table) Oh my beautiful Grania, this is the way it was – Diarmid was put out to foster

[28^{r}]

23

with a shepherd, and no one was so beautiful as Diarmid when he was a child, except the shepherd's son. The shepherd's son was much more beautiful than Diarmid, and his beauty made Diarmid's father jealous and one day he crushed the shepherd's son to death between his knees.

Grania.

Tell me of Diarmid, tell me of Diarmid.

Conan.

The shepherd wept and wept – Oh, how he wept. And after a while he took his second son into the woods, and made a spell over him with a Druid hazel stick, and changed him into a black and bristless boar. And some day that boar is to break out of the woods and to kill many men and many women. All the Fiann are to gather for the hunting of him; they are to hunt him round Eri and through Eri from kingdom to kingdom – Oh what a hunting, what a hunting!

28^{r}, l. ⁻1 The page number has been inserted in dark blue ribbon TS over a very faint impression of lines 18–19 below, crowded at the head of the page.

Grania.

Tell me more of Diarmid, tell me quickly.

Conan.

I must drink again, I am thirsty again – (He drinks) Diarmid must go out against that boar and must be killed. It was to kill him that the shepherd made the spell over his second son. He shall be torn by the tusks, and his face shall be foul

[29r]

24.

because it will be bloody. I would that the women of Eri could see him when he is foul and bloody (He staggers) I am growing sleepy, because I have to run the messages of the Fianna – (He recovers himself.) I shall live to see him when the tusks have torn him, for it has been foretold of him also that he shall not live long. He shall not be remembered for deeds of arms, but as a lover of women. He shall live as a lover of women and his life shall be soon over. Who has put witchcraft into my ale? Who among the Fianna has done this? (He falls)

Usheen.

He said there was witchcraft in the ale, and look, they are all sleeping. Who was it that put witchcraft into the ale Grania?

Grania.

Laban, the Druidess has done this for me. I had never a mind to marry Finn. But why does not Diarmid come to us? (Diarmid comes from the table) It was for you that I ordered witchcraft to be put into the ale.

Diarmid.

For me, Grania!

[30r]

25.

Grania.

I never had a mind to marry Finn; I am going away with

shall be far away

you to-night, we ~~are going to leave~~ ^ before they awake.

[NLI 8777(3) a]

Diarmid.

You and I, and you did not see me before this night!

Grania.

I desired you, and you were in my thoughts before I saw you, Diarmid. You were in my thoughts, Diarmid. (She takes him in her arms.)

Diarmid.

I too desired you and you were in my thoughts – Oh, beauti-ful woman! You were in my thoughts, Grania – Let me look at you – Let me put back your hair – Your eyes are grey, Grania, Your eyes are grey and your hands – But Fin, but Finn, but Finn – Grania wife of Finn why have you played with me?

Grania.

I am not the wife of Finn (She goes towards Diarmid) And now I cannot be Finn's wife, for you have held me in your arms and you have kissed me.

Diarmid.

What is this madness, Grania? Here, here this night and Finn sleeping there.

[31r]

Grania.

If he had loved me his love would have been stronger than witchcraft – (A pause) But why do you go away? Is not my hair soft, are not my cheeks red, is not my body shapely? Your held my hair in your hands, but now, and your lips were on my cheek and lips. Were not my lips soft? You see that he shrin-ks from me. It may be that no man will take me because he wants me, but only because I am a king's daughter. Would you shrink

Caoelte

from me if it were you I had asked to go away with me. Would you, Usheen?

Caoelte.

Look Grania, at the sleeping man whose ale you have bewitch-ed.

31r, l. 8 The second caret, in ink like GM's substitution above, is deleted in pencil, and the substitution is linked by pencil to the new caret in pencil inserted before "if".

Usheen.

If Finn were to wake he would take some terrible vengeance for this.

Grania.

What is his vengeance to me now. I will go into the woods and will wander alone there till I die.

Diarmid.

When I looked into your eyes, Grania, it was a s though I had come out of a cave into the dawn. But I cannot I cannot we have sworn an oath to Finn. We swore it upon the rock where

Con son of Filmy were

the earth screamed under^ ~~King Bocha~~. If the oath ~~was~~ broken

[32r]

27.

the earth would send famine, the corn would wither, the Fianna would be divided, an enemy would come.

Usheen.

Take down your shield and begone from her, Diarmid.

Grania.

He looks at me because it has been foretold.

Diarmid.

(<u>Disengaging himself from Usheen and Caoelte)</u> What has been foretold? Who has foretold it?

Usheen.

(<u>Putting his hand on Diarmid's shoulder</u>) Diarmid.

Caoelte.

You will be the first of the Fianna to break his oath.

Diarmid.

{T {if

~~If~~ { the fortune teller has lied { – if she has said that I will break my oath to Finn. What did she tell you? What has she said? Has she said this?

32r, l. 9 The emendations are probably GM's but may be in WBY's hand. The dash was canceled by the inked "if."

[NLI 8777(3) a]

Grania.

She spoke of a woman pledged to marry a man whom she did not love, and of a man who would come and take her away from that marriage bed. She foretold that the man would leave all things, and that the woman would leave all things for love's sake

[33r]

28.

She foretold that they would go away in the middle of the marria ge feast, andwander in the unpeopled woods , and be h{a appy, by the ꝯ rushy margin of many streams.

Diarmid.

And the man is I and the woman is you.

Grania.

She foretold that it shall seem as if all men had forgotten them, but the wild creatures shall not fly from them. They shall be happy under green boughs and become wise in all woodland wisdom, and as she spoke I too seemed to see them wandering on paths untrodden by the feet of deer, where there are sudden odours of wild honey, and where they will often throw their arms about one another and kissone another on the mouth. <u>(She goes nearer to him)</u> And she told me, Diarmid that we should make our beds with the skins of deer under cromlechs and in caves, and awake from sleep we know not why, as though the dwarfs of the rocks had called to us, that we might see the starlight falling through the leaves. She told me the dwarfs of the rocks and the secret people of the trees should watch over us, and though all the men of Eri were our enemies they should not pluck us out of one another's arms.

Diarmid.

I must not listen, or I will take her in my arms. I will

[34r]

29.

awaken Finn –Finn, Finn, awake.

33r, l. 2 While the inserted comma following "woods" is in ink, and the deleted typed comma following "happy" is in pencil—like the deletion indicator to the RH of the line.

Grania.

What would you tell him?

Diarmid.

That the world vanishes, that I see nothing but you.

Grania.

{Is it
{**It is not said that Diarmid never refused help to a woman, and who is more helpless than I?**

Diarmid.

Had you not told me that you loved me, I would have helped you.

Grania.

Help me Diarmid.

Diarmid.

Caoelte and Usheen have seen my trouble; they will tell~~l~~ Finn of my trouble. She has asked me for my help and I must give it.

Grania.

(<u>Standing at the door which she has thrown open)</u> Come, Diarmid to the woods, the birds of Aonghus, the birds of love, the birds that the eye cannot see, sing joyously, sing~~ing~~ fiercely , they clap their wings and sing.

[35^{r}]

30.

Diarmid.

She asks for my help and I must give it.

Usheen.

From this night the Fianna are broken in two.

{**Usheen.**
{**Diarmid.**

And the kingdom that was to be made safe is in danger,

34^{r}, l. 9 Type deletion.

14, 15 Both emendations are in pencil.

35^{r}, l. $^{-}$3 Usheen's name in the part ascription is a dark blue ribbon insertion over hardly discernible light blue carbon. It was typed in error for Caoelte, but the mistake does not carry forward to later versions.

[NLI 8777(3) a]

and Diarmid's oath is broken.

Diarmid.

My oath is not broken, tell Finn that – Tell him that this sword will guard her by day, and will lie between us at night. Tell him I will send some messenger, some token that shall say to him – Finn, I bring you word that so many hours, or so many moons have passed by and that Diarmid's oath is unbroken.

Grania.

The woods are sad with their summer sadness, and the birds of love have become silent, but they are not sleeping, their eyes are bright among the boughs – (She goes out)

Diarmid.

I must follow her. Upon whose face shall I, after this

He takes his shield from the wall and

look in friendship again – (~~He~~ goes out)

Usheen.

(Goes to the door and looks after them) They have gone westward to the woods.

[36r]

31.

Caoelte.

When Finn awakes, we must tell him that they have gone eastward, towards the sea.

Single-Page Typescript Containing Substitution

[NLI 8777(3) g, 118^{r}]

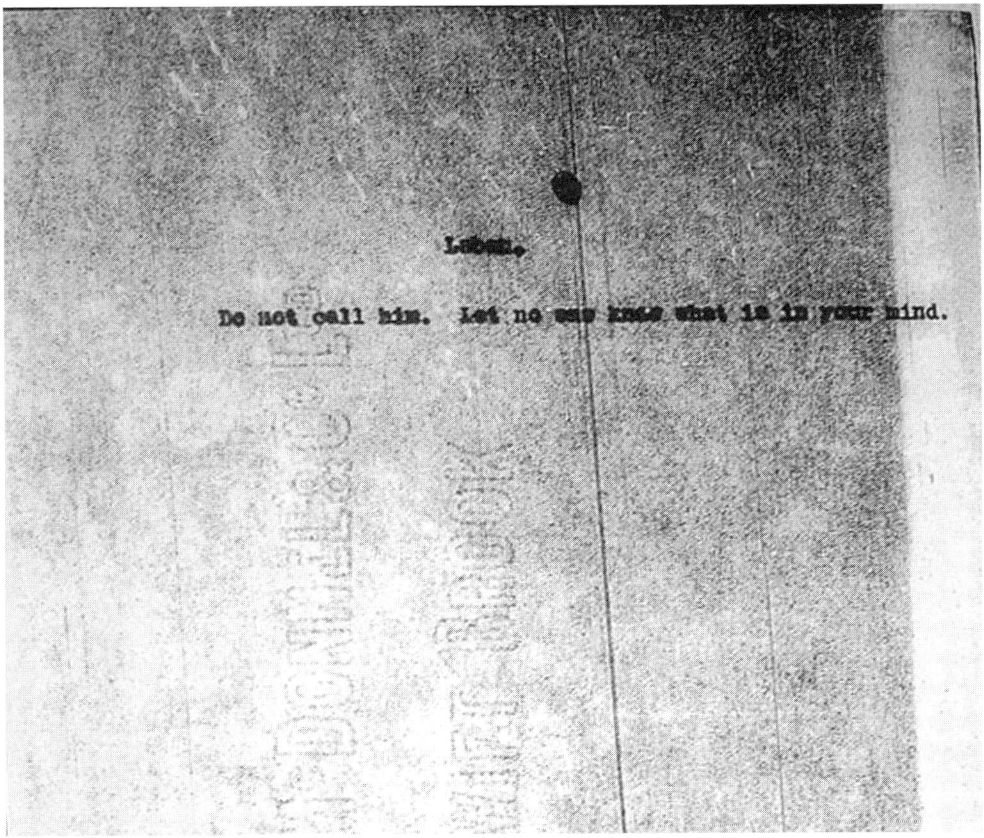
Laban.

Do not call him. Let no one know what is in your mind.

[NLI 8777(3) g, 118^{r}]

Laban.

Do not call him. Let no one know what is in your mind.

118^{r} The leaf appears to be the substitute "slip A" referred to in NLI 8777(3) a, fol. 8^{r}.

[NLI 8777(3) d, 112r]

ACT11

GRANIA. There is a sca on your cheek, that is where you were wounded when you burned the ships of the Lochlanders at Inver Colpa.

FINN. Was the tale of that fighting battle come so far ?

GRANIA. I have been hearing about you since I was a child. (Taking his hand in both her hands) This hand has overcome many kings.

Act III

FINN. To praise a man overmuch takes his luck away.

GRANIA. Some day you will tell me of your other battles against the Northern ships. (She turns away as if already weary of him).

FINN. Are my battles more to you than I am?

ACT 111. OLD MAN That was the god Angus. He watches over Darmuid. I have heard that the deaths of all those men have been foretold. I think there is to be a battle by the sea, a great battle. Maybe that some common man will gather the people against ~~them~~ the Fianna, as Cairbre that was called Cathead gathered them against their forefathers .

BOY ~~Tell-me-about-him~~ I have heard about him, I have heard a song about him,- It begins, I cannot remember how it begins.

OLD MAN. Come boy, we must go find our sheep. If I have lost my &,

Single-Page Typescript Containing Substitution

[NLI 8777(3) d, 112^{r}]

ACT1.

GRANIA. There is a scar on your cheek, that is where you were wounded when you burned the ships of the Lochlanders at Inver Colpa.

fighting

FINN. Has the tale of that battle come so far ?

GRANIA. I have been hearing about you since I was a child. (Taking his hand in both her hands) This hand has overcome many kings.

FINN% To praise a man overmuch takes his luck away.

GRANIA. Some day you will tell me of your other battles against the Northern ships. (She turns away as if already weary of him).

FINN. Are my battles more to you than I am?

112^{r} An unused substitution on a paper type unique among the TSS. The typist is AG on her Coole Park Remington; cf. NLI 8777(11) TS of Act I and the six closing TS pages of Act II in NLI 8777(4) a, both relatively early. The beginning of the equivalent passage in HRC 19/fol. 22^{r} is marked with two unexplained pencil crosses, and the usual "men of Aidne" is revised to "men of Lochland" in Berg(99) 18/fol. 20^{r}.

3 Above the end of the line, the word "fighting" may be an alternative for "battle."

Line 9 is followed by an eight-line substitution for the beginning of Act III (see p. 797 below). This also appears to represent a late substitution into that sequence and was likewise not fully incorporated.

Act II

[NLI 8777(8) a, 1r, 2r]

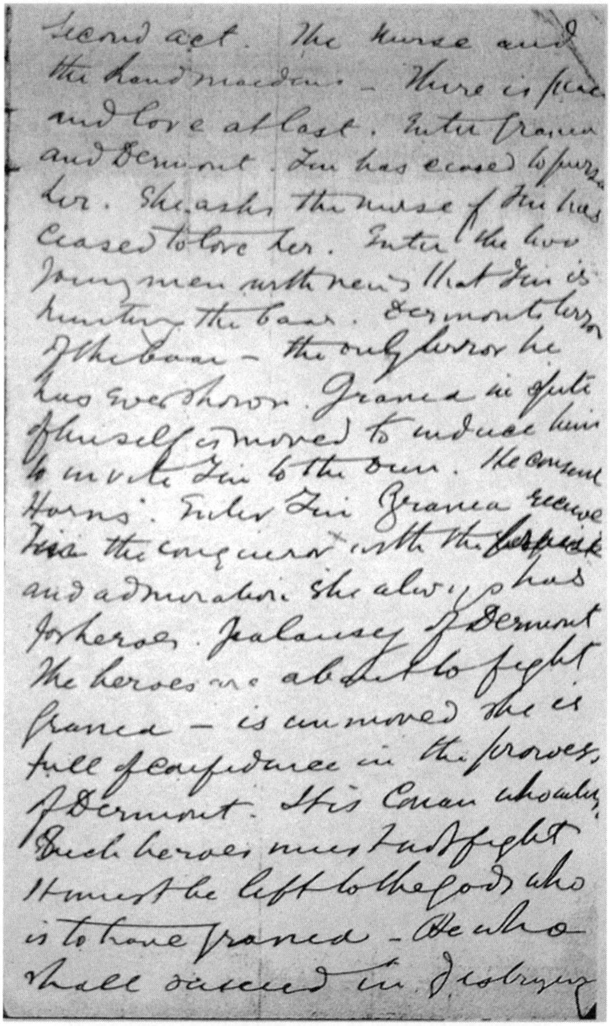

Second act. The Nurse and
the hand maidens – There is peace
and love at last. Enter Grania
and Dermont. Finn has ceased to pursue
her. She asks the nurse if Finn has
ceased to love her. Enter the two
young men with news that Finn is
hunting the boar. Dermont's terror
of the boar – the only terror he
has ever known. Grania in spite
of herself is moved to induce him
to invite Finn to the dun. He consents
Horns. Enter Finn Grania receives
him the conqueror with the surprise
and admiration she always had
for heroes. Jealousy of Dermont
The heroes are about to fight
Grania – is unmoved she is
full of confidence in the prowess
of Dermont. It is Conan who says
Such heroes must not fight
It must be left to the gods who
is to have Grania – He who
shall succeed in destroying

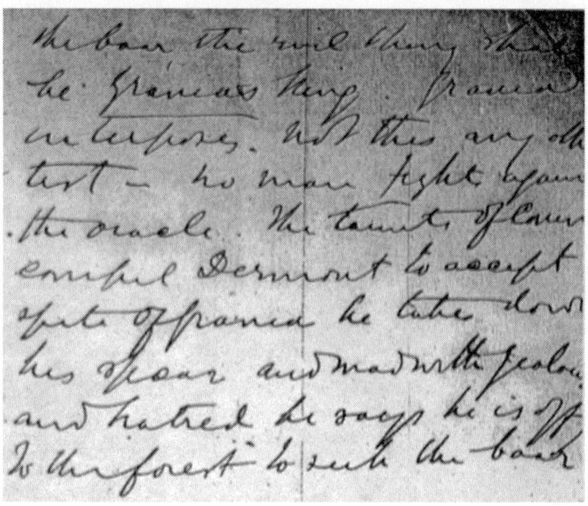

the boar the evil thing shall
be Grania's king. Grania
interposes. Not this any other
test – no man fight against
the oracle. The taunts of Conan
compel Dermont to accept
in spite of Grania he takes down
his spear and mad with jealousy
and hatred he says he is off
to the forest to seek the boar

Two-Page Scenario in George Moore's Hand

[NLI 8777(8) a, 1r]

Second act. The Nurse and the handmaidens – There is peace and love at last. Enter Grania and Dermout. Fin has ceased to pursue her. She asks the nurse if Fin has ceased to love her. Enter the two young men with news that Fin is hunting the boar. Dermouts terror of the boar – the only terror he has ever shown. Grania in spite of herself is moved to induce him to invite Fin to the Dun. He consents Horns. Enter Fin Grania receives {Fin / him} the conqueror with the {praise / respect} and admiration she always has for heroes. Jealousy of Dermout. The heroes are about to fight Grania – is unmoved she is full of confidence in the prowess of Dermout. It is Conan who interferes Such heroes must not fight It must be left to the gods who is to have Grania – He who shall succeed in destroying

[2r]

the boar, the evil thing shall be Granias king. Grania interposes. Not this any other test – no man fights against the oracle. The taunts of Conan compel Dermout to accept. In spite of Grania he takes down his spear and mad with jealousy and hatred he says he is off to the forest to seek the boar.

[NLI 8777(8) b, 3r]

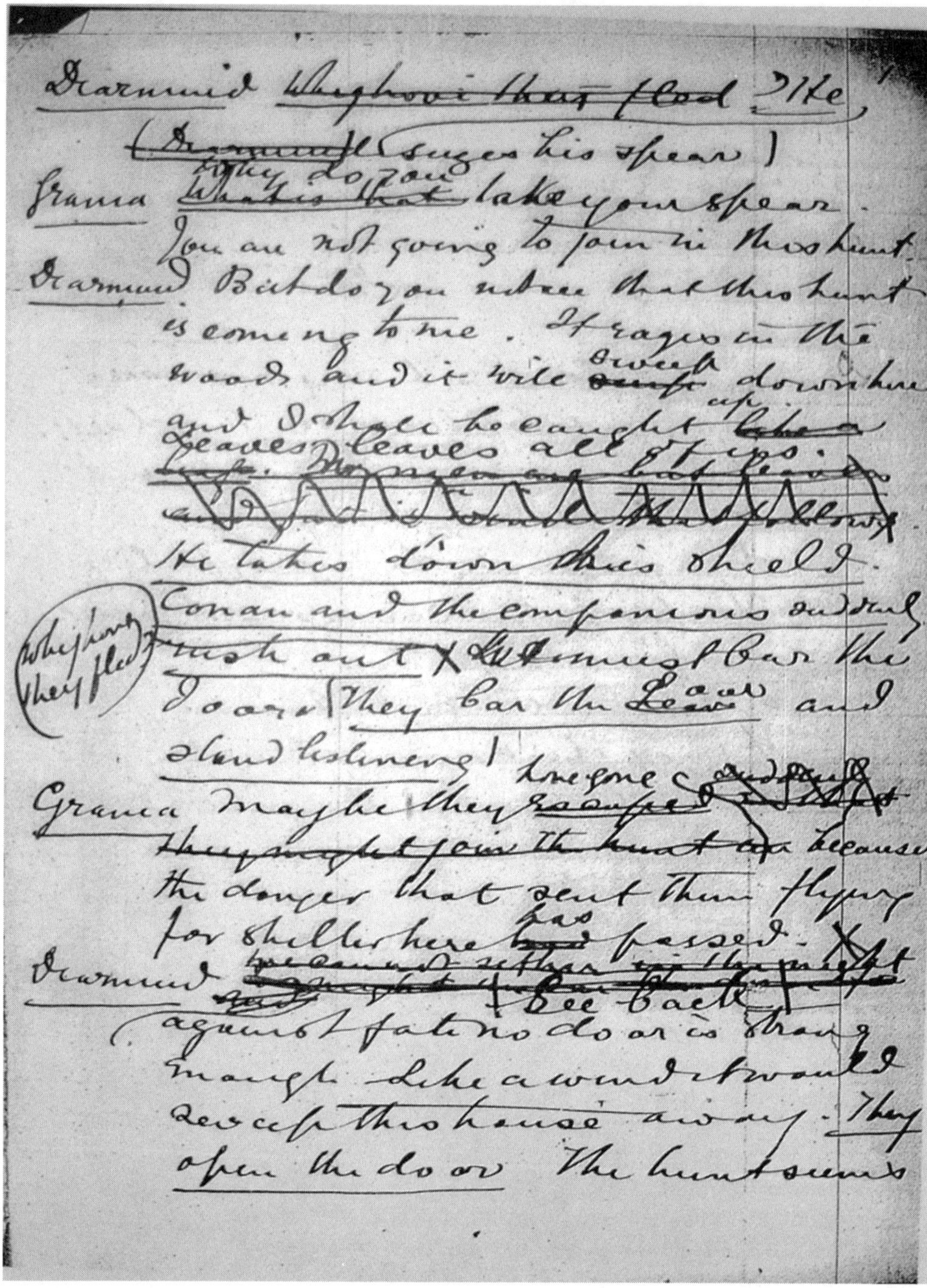

16 GM deleted "in the night for" before continuing; and then deleted the improved line(s) after writing an expanded version on fol. 3v.

Near-Continuous Ten-Page Draft in George Moore's Hand

[NLI 8777(8) b, 3r]

(1

Diarmuid ~~Why have thy fled~~? He
~~(Diarmuid~~ seizes his spear)

Why do you
Grania ~~What is that~~ take your spear.
You are not going to join in this hunt.

Diarmuid But do you not see that this hunt
is coming to me. It rages in the
sweep
woods and it will ~~swep~~ down here
up
and I shall be caught ~~like a~~
Leaves leaves all of us.
~~leaf~~. ~~We men are but leaves~~
~~a~~
~~and~~ ^ ~~fate is wind that follows~~. ^
his
He takes down the shield.
Conan and the companions suddenly
Why have they fled?
We
rush out X ~~Let~~ must bar the
door
door. (They bar the ~~leave~~ and
stand listening)

have gone suddenly
Grania Maybe ~~they escaped~~ ~~so that~~
~~they might join the hunt an~~ because
the danger that sent them flying
has
for shelter here ~~had~~ passed. X

~~We cannot sit here in the night~~
Diarmuid ~~[?At] night unbar the door~~ ~~for~~
~~and~~ X See back
against fate no door is strong
enough Like a wind it would
sweep this house away. They
open the door The hunt seems

[NLI 8777(8) b, 3v]

house
Diarmuid Come sit by me and
So we sit together in the dark
There is no sound now and
yet the silence is full of
the
danger and the darkness full of
no:
shape - we cannot sit here;
we bar the door and let
the light whatever danger
I may discover would be
more bearable than the night

[NLI 8777(8) b, 3^{v}]

pause
<u>Diarmuid</u> Come sit my me^–and
So we sit together in the dark.
There is no sound now and
yet the silence is full of
the ~~is~~
danger and^the darkness^~~^~~full of
No
shape –^We cannot sit here;
Unbar the door and let
the light ~~in~~ whatever danger
it may discover ~~it~~ will be
more bearable than the night

3^{v} GM's draft is to be inserted at the beginning of Diarmuid's speech at fol. 3^{r}, line 16.
5 full] GM added the second "l" when he inserted "is".

[NLI 8777(8) b, 4r]

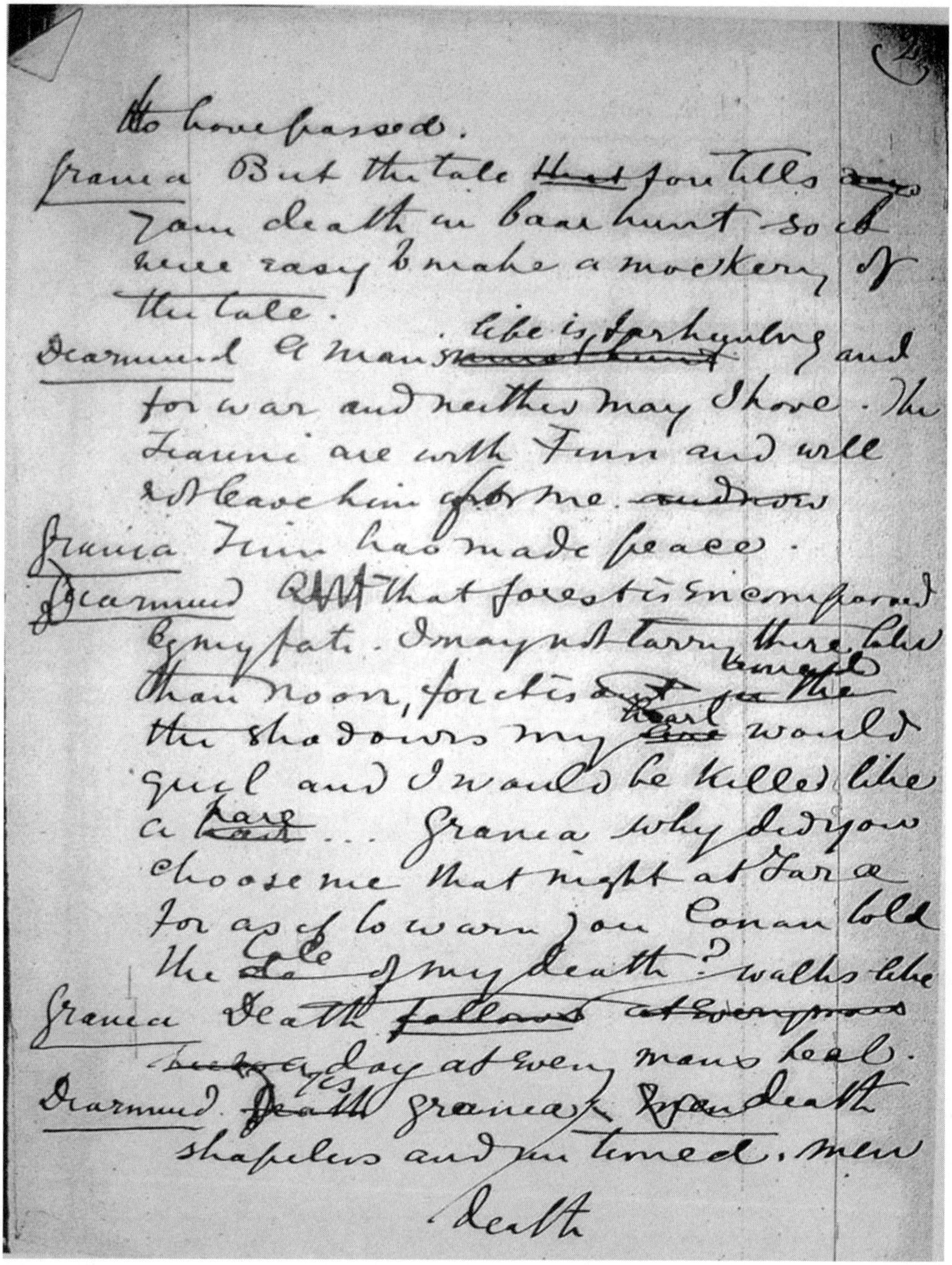
(2)

to have passed.

Grania But the tale ~~that~~ foretells ~~any~~
your death in boar hunt. So it
were easy to make a mockery of
the tale.

Diarmuid A man ~~[illegible]~~ like is for hunting and
for war and neither may I have. The
Fianna are with Finn and will
not leave him for me. ~~and now~~

Grania Finn has made peace.

Diarmuid ~~All~~ that forest tis encompassed
by my fate. I may not tarry there later
than noon, for it is ~~at~~ ~~in the~~ twilight
the shadows my ~~[illegible]~~ heart would
quail and I would be killed like
a ~~[illegible]~~ hare ... Grania why did you
choose me that night at Tara
for as if to warn you Conan told
the ~~[illegible]~~ tale of my death? walks like

Grania Death ~~follows~~ ~~at every mans~~
~~heels~~ a day at every mans heel.

Diarmuid. ~~Death~~ yes Grania ~~[illegible]~~ death
shapeless and untimed. mere
death

[NLI 8777(8) b, 4r]

(2

to have passed.

Grania But the tale ~~that~~ foretells ~~says~~
your death in boar hunt so is
never easy to make a mockery of
the tale.

's life is for hunting
Diarmuid A Man ~~must hunt~~ and
for war and neither may I have. The
Fianni are with Finn and will
for
not leave him ~~and~~ me. ~~and now~~

Grania Finn has made peace.
D} T}
G}iarmuid ~~And~~ t}hat forest is encompassed
by my fate. I may not tarry there later
amongst
than noon, for it is ~~out in the~~
heart
the shadows my ~~arm~~ would
quail and I would be killed
hare
a ~~hair~~ . . . Grania why did you
choose me that night at Tara
for as if to warn you Conan told
tale
the ~~do~~ of my death?
walks like
Grania Death ~~follows~~ ~~at everymans~~
~~heels~~ a dog at every mans heel.
Yes
Diarmuid ~~Death~~ Grania ^ ~~Men~~ death
shapeless and untimed. Men
death

[NLI 8777(8) b, 5r]

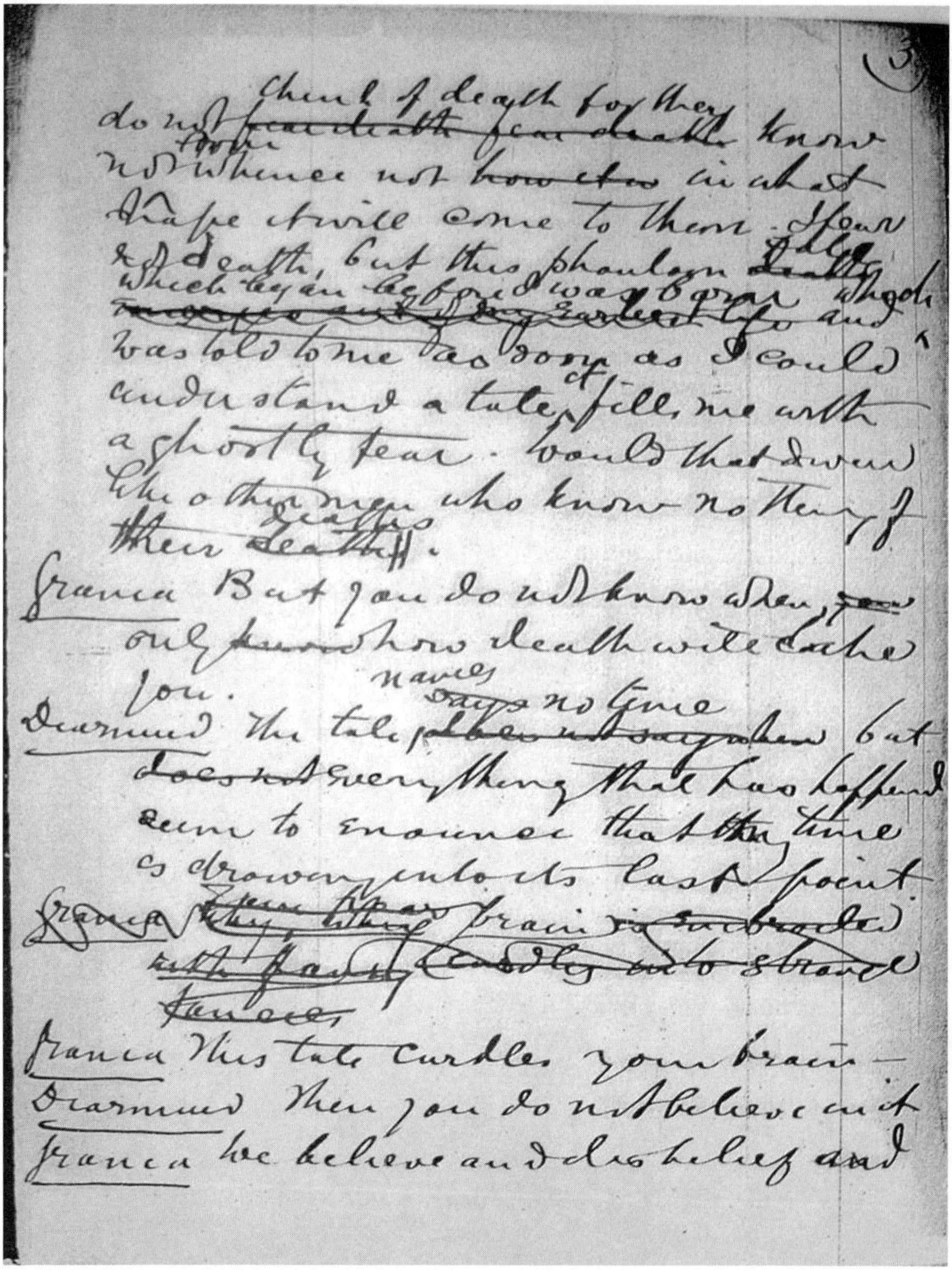
3

do not ~~fear death fear death~~ think of death for they know
not whence nor ~~how etc~~ in what
shape it will come to them. Fear
of death, but this phantom ~~death~~ fate
~~which began before I was born~~ which
~~[illegible] my earliest life~~ and
was told to me as soon as I could
understand a tale, fills me with
a ghostly fear. Would that I were
like other men who know nothing of
their ~~deaths~~ fates.

Grania But you do not know when, ~~you~~
only ~~know~~ how death will take
you.

Diarmuid The tale ~~does not say when~~ names no time but
~~does not~~ everything that has happened
seem to announce that the time
is drawing into its last point.

~~Grania Your brain is [illegible] with [illegible] curdles into strange fancies~~

Grania This tale curdles your brain—

Diarmuid Then you do not believe in it

Grania We believe and disbelief and

[NLI 8777(8) b, 5r]

(3

think of death for they
do not ~~fear death fear death~~ know
from
not^whence not know how it is in what
shape it will come to them. I fear
pale
not death, but this phantom ~~death~~
which began before I was born which
~~emerges out of my earliest life~~ and ^
was told to me as soon as I could
it
understand a tale^fills me with
a ghostly fear. Would that I were
like other men who know nothing of
deaths
their ~~deaths~~.

<u>Grania</u> But you do not know when ~~you~~
ta }
only ~~know~~ how death will ca }ke
you.

names
~~says~~ no time
<u>Diarmuid</u> The tale^~~does not say when~~ but
~~does not~~ everything that has happened
seem to enounce that ~~the~~ time
as drawing into its last point.

I fear
<u>Grania</u> ~~Why, where~~ brain is embroiled
with fancy curdling into strange
fancies

<u>Grania</u> This tale curdles your brain –

<u>Diarmuid</u> Then you do not believe in it

<u>Grania</u> We believe and disbelief ~~and~~

10 GM first wrote "deaths" and canceled the "s". He subsequently canceled the whole word and rewrote "deaths" above it.

[NLI 8777(8) b, 6r]

there is a time between when
~~sound as the wind passes~~ we know
not what we think.

I earned for seven years I have overcome
all dangers: dangers that no single
man could overcome. Why should
such strength have been given me except
to keep me for the ~~save me for ever long~~ doom ~~things~~ the
gods created for me. Why this
aptent glory feast of love
~~feast of happiness~~ and meditation
To eat and drink of happiness at every
hour? The gods know our appetites
and give us more than ~~more than~~ we can eat
when they are about to slake our
appetites away. A silent valley
has been prepared with peace and ~~for~~
I am told to love you as if I had
never loved you and ~~and~~ we were new
to one another and needed inducement
other than ourselves. I am told
that Fergus has foresworn ~~many~~ his quest
as if this hundred time ~~defeated~~ defeated
quest mattered. A whetstone it
has been and those moments snatched

[NLI 8777(8) b, 6r]

(4

there is a time between when
~~easily as the wind passes~~ we know
we
not what^ ~~to~~ think.

Diarmuid For seven years I have over come
all dangers: dangers that no single
man could over come. Why should
such strength have been given me except
keep me for the the
to ~~save^me from my~~ doom ^ ~~Why is~~
gods created for me. Why this
ostentatious feast of love
~~feast of happiness~~^and invitation
to eat and drink of happiness at every
hour? The gods know our appetites
more than we
and give us ~~much when~~ can eat
when they are about to take our
appetites away. A silent valley
and
has been prepared with peace ~~for~~
I am told to love you as if I had
and
never loved you, ~~and~~ we were new
to one another and needed inducement
other than ourselves. I am told
foresworn
that Finn has ~~renou~~ his quest
th} hundred time
as if h}is ~~defeated~~ defeated
quest mattered. A whetstone it
has been and those moments snatched

---

2 The caret mark is written over the word "to".
7 The caret mark is written over the period.

(5)

beneath the oaks were sweeter than
all this time. I'm told to make
you happy." (Starting up) This valley
is a trap and you are the bait in it.
Grania What is your meaning Diarmuid?
Diarmuid (with a vague gesture) I do not
know, the words suddenly flashed
into my mind but from whence
they came or what they mean I
know nothing. I said "this valley
is a trap" that I understand, but
how you should be the bait I can
tell you nothing. You must ask
the gods. ~~I~~ nor can I tell you why
Finn should have been at pains to
contrive this valley and its cursed
peacefulness. ~~I only~~ know it is
not because he hates me less. ~~He has~~
~~failed so~~ Force has failed him
so often that ~~now may be~~ he may be now ~~driven~~ strained
to employ a ruse. Then why has
he come into my country upon the
quest of some unnatural beast

[NLI 8777(8) b, 7r]

(5

wer}
beneath the oaks ar{e sweeter than
all this time. I'm told to make
you happy! (Starting up) This valley
is a trap and you are the bait in it.

Grania What is your meaning Diarmuid?

Diarmuid (with a vague gesture) I do not
know. The words suddenly started
P}
into my mind F{ut from whence
they came or what they mean I
know nothing. I said 'this valley
is a trap' that I understand, but
how you should be the bait I can
tell you nothing. You must ask
Nor {can
the gods. ~~No,~~ ^ {[?te] I tell you why
Finn should have been at pains to
contrive this valley and its cursed
peacefulness. I ~~only~~ know it is
not because he hates me less. ~~He has~~
~~faild so~~ Force has faild him
he may be now strained
so often that ^ ~~now may be~~ ^ ~~determined~~
to employ a ruse. Then why has
he come into my county upon the
quest of some unnatural beast

[NLI 8777(8) b, 8r]

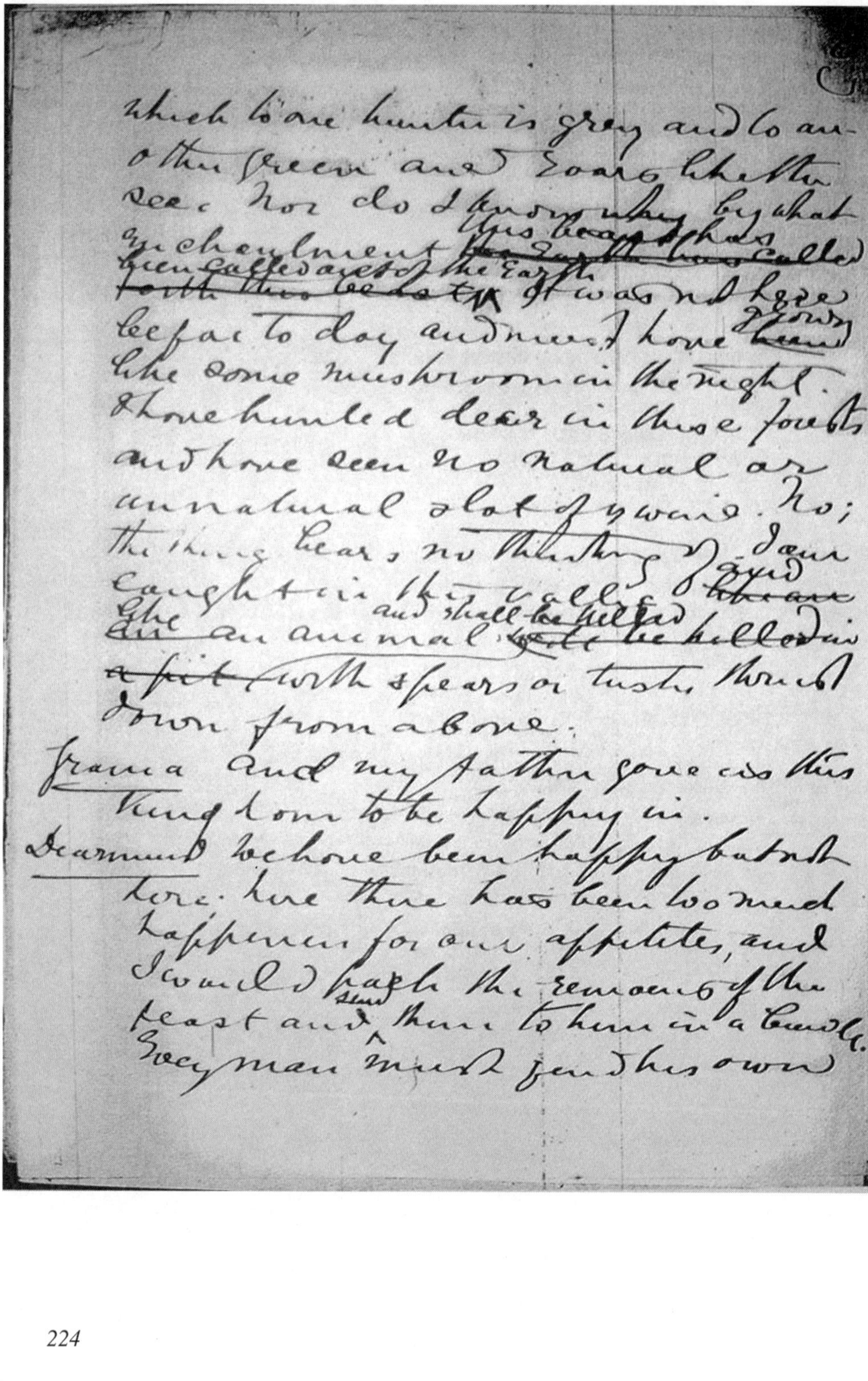

which to one hunter is grey and to another green and roars like the sea. Nor do I know why by what enchantment ~~[illegible]~~ this beast has been called out of the earth ~~[illegible]~~ It was not here before to day and must have ~~been~~ grown like some mushroom in the night. I have hunted deer in these forests and have seen no natural or unnatural slot of swine. No; the thing bears no likeness of swine caught in this valley ~~[illegible]~~ and ~~the~~ an animal ~~will be killed in a pit~~ and shall be killed with spears or tusks thrust down from above.

Grania And my father gave us this kingdom to be happy in.

Diarmuid We have been happy but not here. Here there has been too much happiness for our appetites, and I would pack the remnants of the feast and send them to him in a bundle. Every man must find his own

[NLI 8777(8) b, 8^r]

(6

which to one hunter is grey and to another green and roars like the
sea. Nor do I know ~~why~~ by what
this beast has
enchantment ~~the Earth has called~~
been called out of the Earth
~~forth this beast~~ ^It was not here
grown
before today and must have ~~been~~
like some mushroom in the night.
e
I have hunted dea}r in these forests
and have seen no natural or
unnatural slot of swine. No;
the thing bears no thinking of. I am
and
caught in this valley ~~like an~~
like and shall be killed
~~an~~ an animal ~~will be killed in~~
~~a pit~~ with spears or tusks thrust
down from above.

<u>Grania</u> And my father gave us this
Kingdom to be happy in.

<u>Diarmuid</u> We have been happy but not
here; here there has been too much
happiness for our appetites, and
I would pack the remains of the
send
feast and ^them to him in a bundle.
Every man must find his own

[NLI 8777(8) b, 9r]

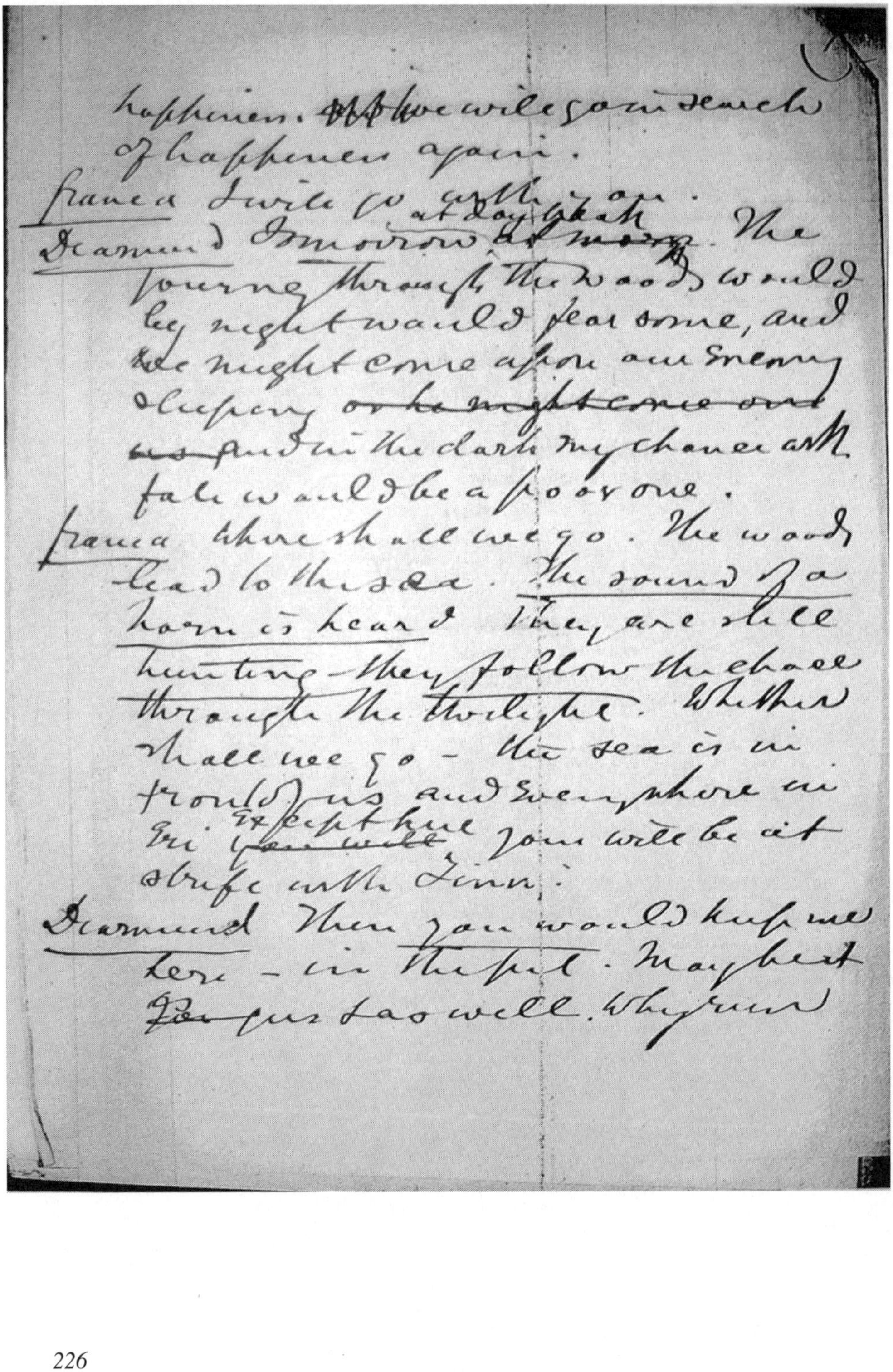
happiness. ~~[illegible]~~ we will go in search
of happiness again.
Grania I will go with you.
Diarmuid Tomorrow at daybreak ~~at morn~~. The
journey through the woods would
by night would be fearsome, and
we might come upon an enemy
sleeping ~~or he might come on~~
~~us~~ and in the dark my chance with
fate would be a poor one.
Grania Where shall we go. The woods
lead to the sea. The sound of a
horn is heard They are still
hunting – they follow the chase
through the twilight. Whither
shall we go – the sea is in
front of us and everywhere in
Eri except here ~~you will~~ you will be at
strife with Finn.
Diarmuid Then you would keep me
here – in the pit. Maybe it
~~[illegible]~~ [illegible] as well. Why [illegible]

[NLI 8777(8) b, 9r]

(7

W}
happiness. ~~and w~~ }e will go in search
of happiness again.

Grania I will go with you.

at daybreak
Diarmuid Tomorrow ^ ~~at morn~~. The
journey through the woods would
by night would fear some, and
we might come upon our enemy
sleeping ~~or he might come on~~
~~us p~~ and in the dark my chance with
fate would be a poor one.

Grania Where shall we go. The woods
lead to the sea. The sound of a
horn is heard They are still
hunting – they follow the chase
through the twilight. Whither
shall we go – the sea is in
front of us and everywhere in
except here
Eri ~~You will~~ you will be at
strife with Finn.

Diarmuid Then you would keep me
here – in the pit. May best
as
~~for~~ just as well. Why run

[NLI 8777(8) b, 10r]

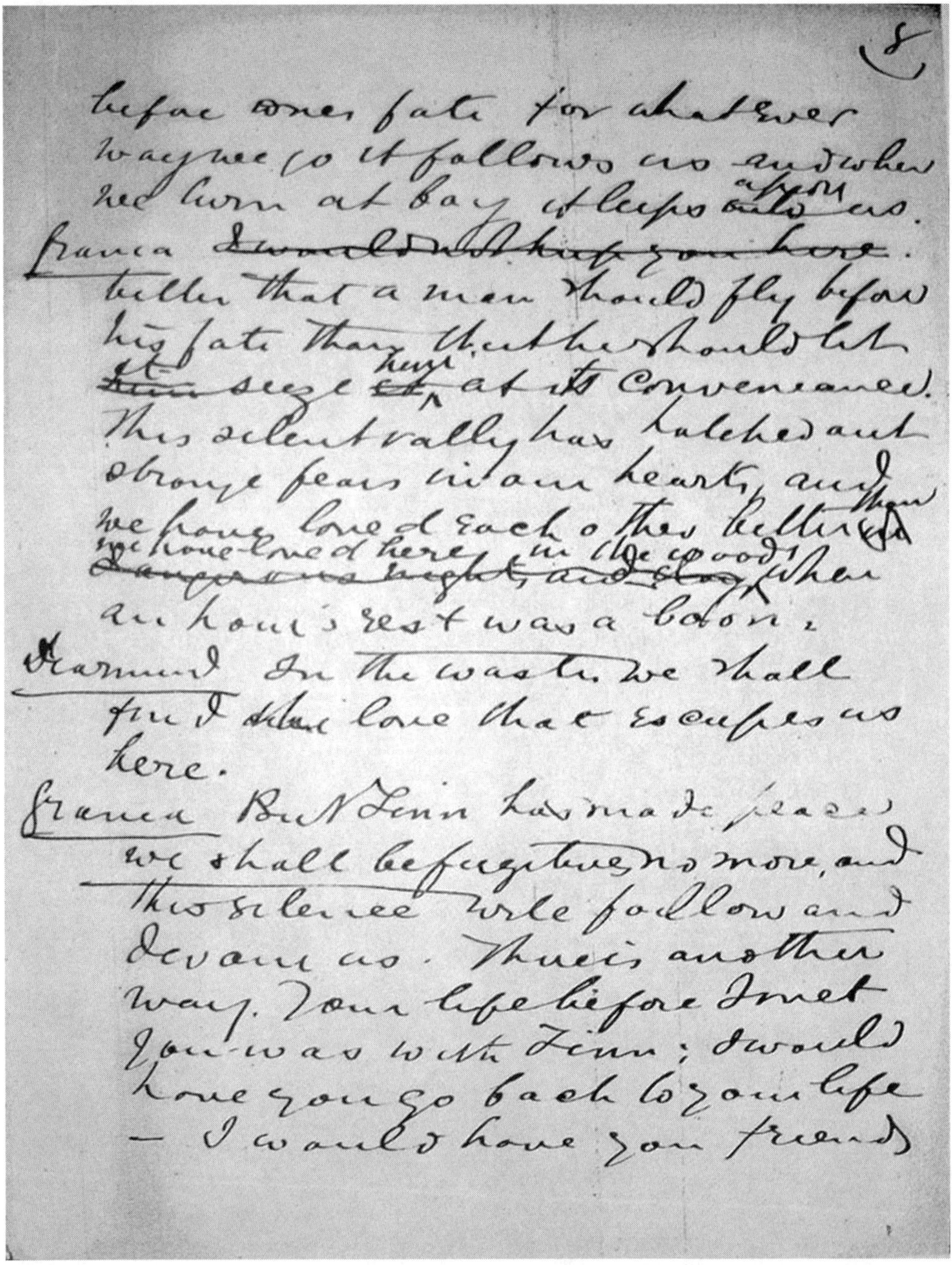
(8)

before ones fate for whatever
way we go it follows us and when
we turn at bay it leaps ~~into~~ upon us.
Grania ~~I would not keep you here~~.
better that a man should fly before
his fate than that he should let
~~him~~ it seize ~~on~~ him at its convenience.
This silent valley has hatched out
strange fears in our hearts, and
we have loved each other better ~~(than)~~ than
~~we have loved here~~ in the woods when
~~dangerous night, and day~~
an hour's rest was a boon.
Diarmuid In the waste we shall
find that love that escapes us
here.
Grania But Finn has made peace
we shall be fugitives no more, and
this silence will follow and
devour us. There is another
way. Your life before I met
you was with Finn; I would
have you go back to your life
— I would have you friends

[NLI 8777(8) b, 10r]

(8

before ones fate for whatever
way we go it follows us and when
upon
we turn at bay it leeps ~~onto~~ us.
Grania ~~I would not keep you here~~.
better that a man should fly before
his fate than that he should let
it him
~~him~~ sieze ~~it~~ ^ at its convenience.
This silent vally has hatched out
strange fears in our hearts, and
than
we have loved each other better ~~in~~
we have loved here in the woods
~~dangerous nights and days~~ ^ when
an hour's rest was a boon.

Diarmuid In the wastes we shall
{the
find {[?our] love that escapes us
here.

Grania But Finn has made peace
we shall be fugitives no more, and
this silence will follow and
devour us. There is another
way. Your life before I met
you was with Finn; I would
have you go back to your life
– I would have you friends

[NLI 8777(8) b, 11r]

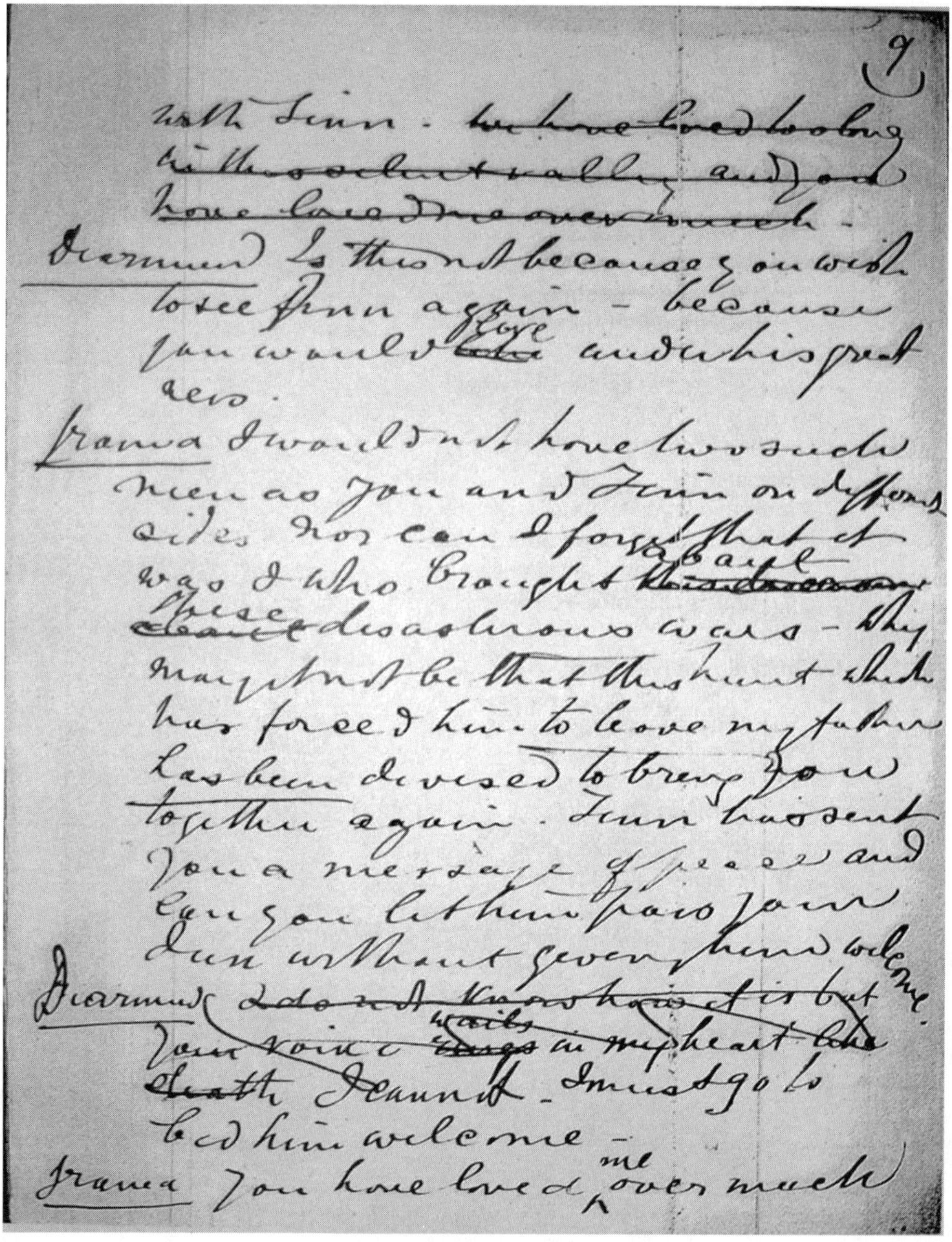

9

with Finn. ~~we have lived too long with those that wallow and you have loved me over much~~ -

Diarmuid Is this not because you wish to see Finn again — because you would ~~like~~ love and whisper great ears.

Grania I would not have two such men as you and Finn on different sides nor can I forget that it was I who brought ~~this discovery~~ about ~~about~~ these disastrous wars — Why may it not be that this hunt which has forced him to leave my father has been devised to bring you together again. Finn has sent you a message of peace and can you let him pass your door without giving him welcome.

Diarmuid ~~I do not know how it is but your voice ~~rings~~ wails in my heart like death~~ I cannot — I must go to bid him welcome —

Grania You have loved me over much

[NLI 8777(8) b, 11r]

(9

with Finn – ~~We have lived too long~~
~~in this silent valley and you~~
~~have loved me overmuch~~ –

Diarmuid Is this not because you wish
F
to see f}inn again – because
love
you would ~~like~~ and in his great
ness.

Grania I would not have two such
men as you and Finn on different
sides. Nor can I forget that it
about
was I who brought ~~this disaster~~
these
~~about~~ disasterous wars – Why
may it not be that this hunt which
has forced him to leave my father
has been devised to bring you
together again. Finn has sent
you a message of peace and
can you let him pass your
dun without giving him welcome.

Diarmuid ~~I do not know how it is but~~
~~wails~~
~~your voice rings in my heart like~~
~~death~~ I cannot – I must go to
bid him welcome –

me
Grania You have loved ^ over much

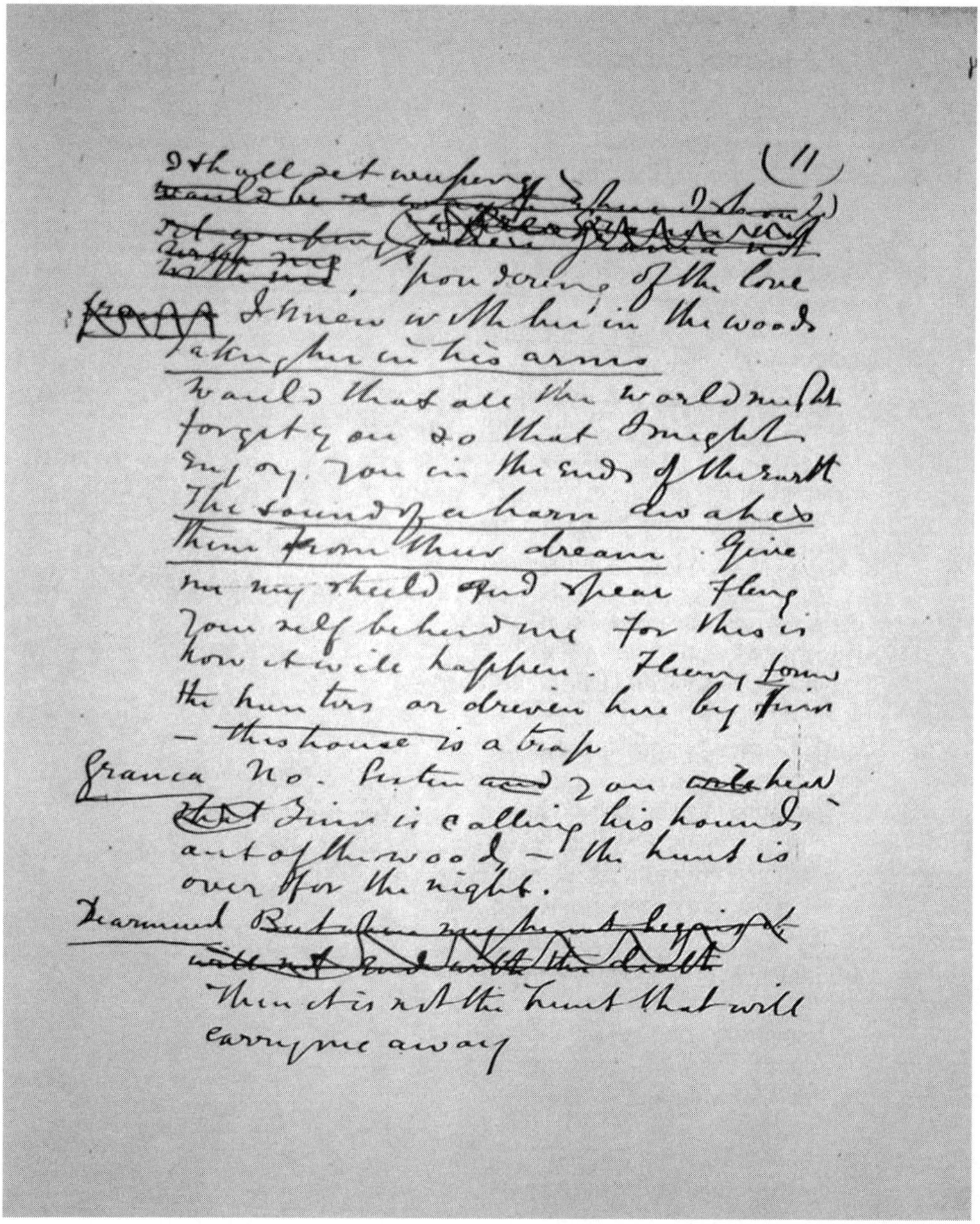

(11)

I shall set weeping

[illegible]

[illegible] pondering of the love

[illegible] I knew with her in the woods

taking her in his arms

Would that all the world might forget you so that I might enjoy you in the ends of the earth

The sound of a horn awakes them from their dream. Give me my shield and spear. Fling yourself behind me for this is how it will happen. Fling [illegible] the hunters are driven here by Finn — this house is a trap

Grania No. Listen [illegible] you will hear [illegible] Finn is calling his hounds out of the wood — the hunt is over for the night.

Diarmuid [illegible]

Then it is not the hunt that will carry me away

[Berg(09), 1r]

(11

I shall sit weeping
~~would be a [?wraith] where I should~~
~~were Grania not~~
~~sit weeping were Grania not~~
~~with me~~ ^
~~with me~~. pondering of the love

~~Grania~~ I knew with her in the woods.
taking her in his arms
Would that all the world might
forget you so that I might
enjoy you in the ends of the earth
The sound of a horn awakes
them from their dream Give
me my shield and spear Fling
your self behind me For this is
how it will happen. Fleeing from
the hunters or driven here by Finn
– this house is a trap

Grania No– Listen ~~and~~ you ~~will~~ hear
~~that~~ Finn is calling his hounds
out of the woods – the hunt is
over for the night.

Diarmuid ~~But when my hunt begins it~~
~~will not end with the death~~
Then it is not the hunt that will
carry me away

GM's draft appears to be the basis of WBY's holograph development in NLI 8777(4) a, between fol. 25r, line 8, and fol. 27r, line 7. Compare also Berg(06), fols. 25r–26r, and Berg(07), fols. 24r–25r.

3–4 GM ended Diarmuid's speech with "me" and wrote the part ascription "Grania"; then deleted both and inserted "pondering of the love" before continuing.

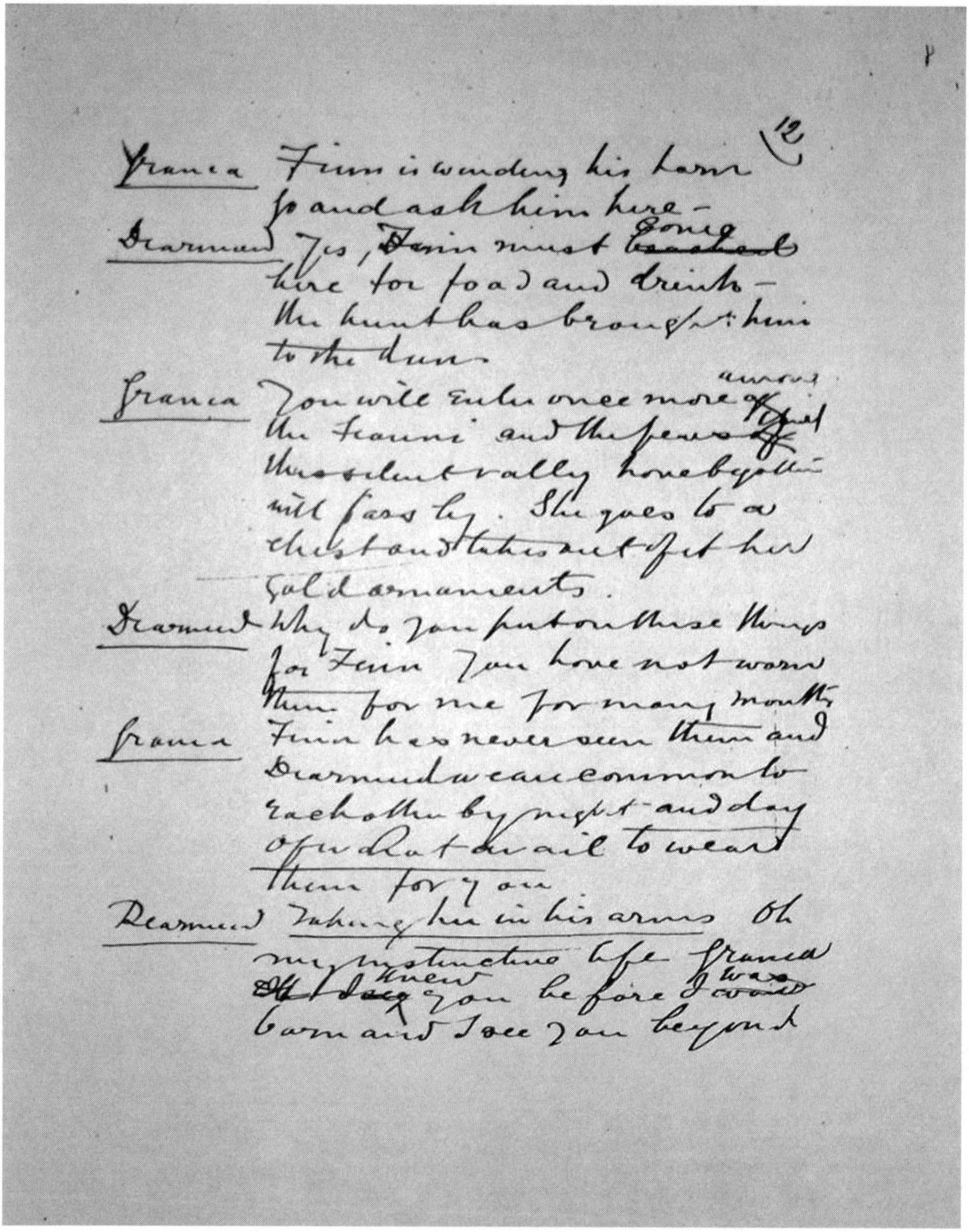

(12

Grania Finn is winding his horn
go and ask him here –
Diarmuid Yes, ~~Finn~~ must ~~have reached~~ come
here for food and drink –
the hunt has brought him
to the dun.
Grania You will enter once more ~~of~~ among
the Fianna and the fears ~~of~~ that
this silent valley have begotten
will pass by. She goes to a
chest and takes out of it her
gold ornaments.
Diarmuid Why do you put on these things
for Finn You have not worn
them for me for many months
Grania Finn has never seen them and
Diarmuid we are common to
each other by night and day
of what avail to wear
them for you
Diarmuid Taking her in his arms Oh
my instinctive life Grania
~~It I saw~~ knew you before I ~~was~~ was
born and I see you beyond

[Berg(09), 2r]

(12

Grania Finn is winding his horn
Go and ask him here –

{Finn come
Diarmuid Yes, {He must ~~be asked~~
here for food and drink –
the hunt has brought him
to the dun.

among
Grania You will enter once more ~~of~~
that
the Fianni and the fears ~~of~~
this silent vally have begotten
will pass by. She goes to a
chest and takes out of it her
gold ornaments.

Diarmuid Why do you put on these things
for Finn You have not worn
them for me for many months

Grania Finn has never seen them and
Diarmuid we are common to
each other by night and day
Of what avail to wear
them for you

Diarmuid Taking her in his arms Oh
my instinctive life Grania
knew was
~~Oh I see~~ ^ you before I [?~~would~~]
born and I see you beyond

[NLI 8777(8) c, 12r]

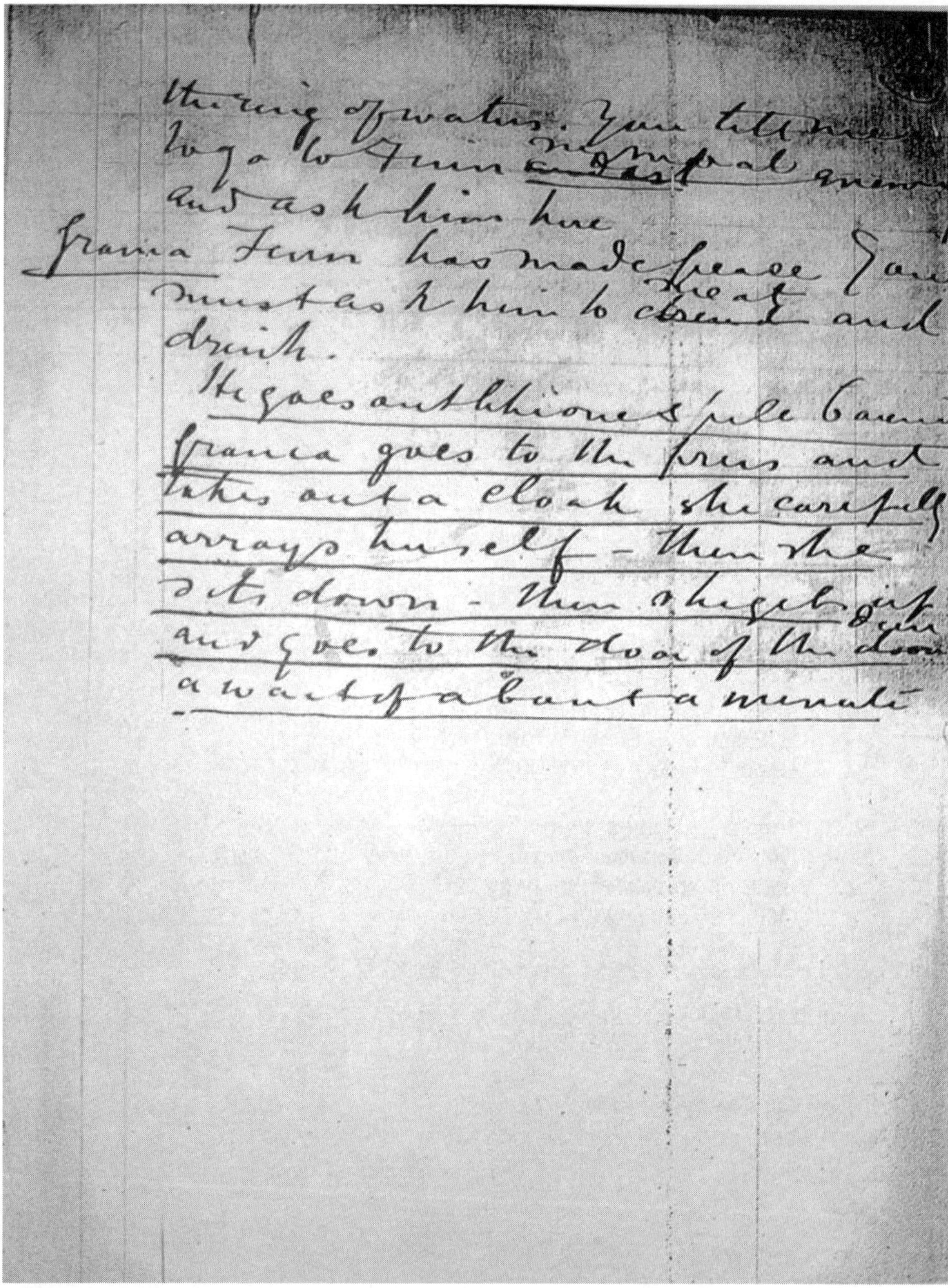

the ring of waters. You tell me
to go to Finn ~~and ask~~ at once
and ask him here
Francia Finn has made peace You
must ask him to ~~?~~ eat and
drink.
He goes out ... Carrie
Francia goes to the press and
takes out a cloak she carefully
arrays herself – then she
sits down – then she gets up
and goes to the door of the door
a waits about a minute

[NLI 8777(8) c, 12r]

(13

the ring of waters. You tell me
my mortal
to go to Finn ~~and as~~ enemy
and ask him here

Grania Finn has made peace You
meat
must ask him to ~~drink~~ and
drink.

He goes out like one spell bound
Grania goes to the press and
takes out a cloak she carefully
arrays herself – Then she
sits down – Then she gets up
dun
and goes to the door of the ~~doon~~
a wait of about a minute

[NLI 30,437, 1[r], 2[r]]

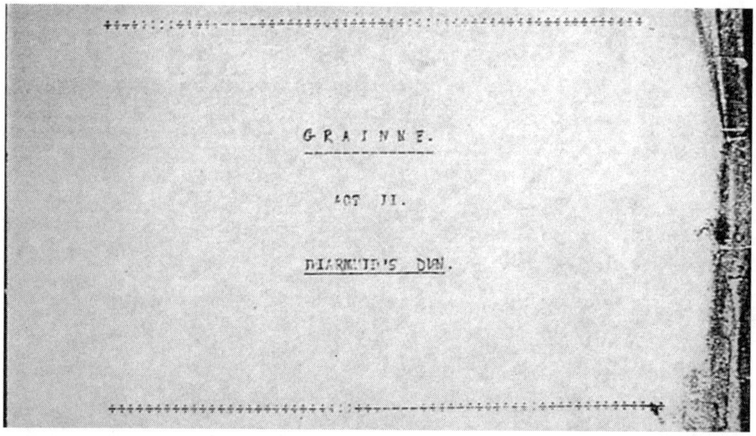

G R A I N N E.

ACT II.

DIARMUID'S DUN.

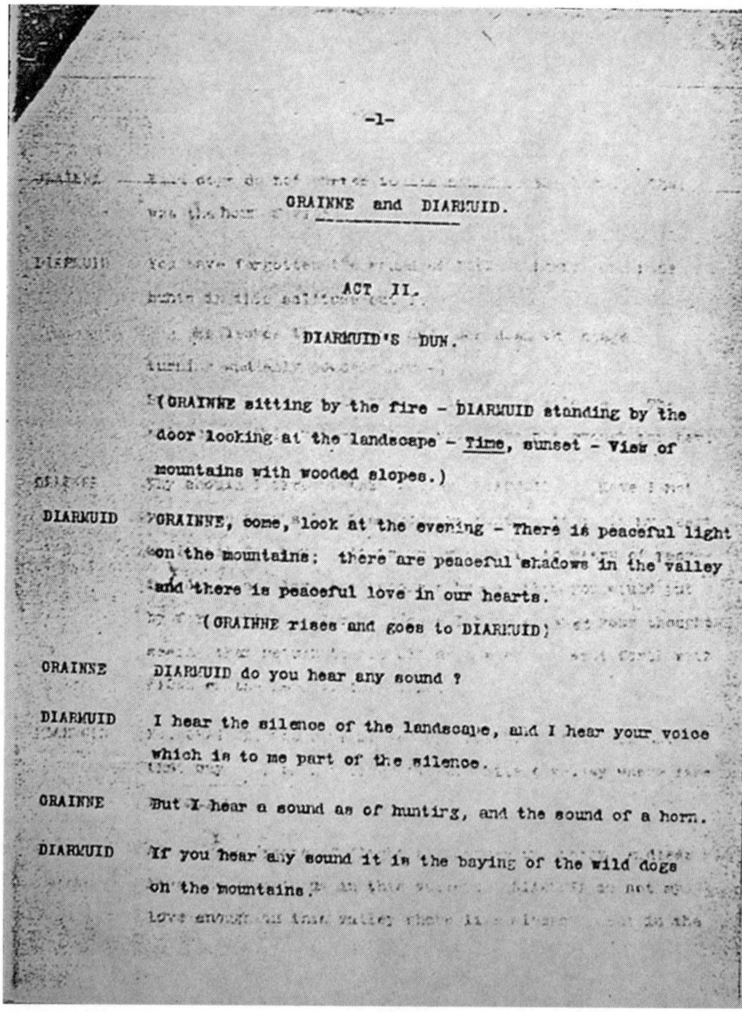

-1-

GRAINNE and DIARMUID.

ACT II.

DIARMUID'S DUN.

(GRAINNE sitting by the fire – DIARMUID standing by the door looking at the landscape – Time, sunset – View of mountains with wooded slopes.)

DIARMUID GRAINNE, come, look at the evening – There is peaceful light on the mountains; there are peaceful shadows in the valley and there is peaceful love in our hearts.

(GRAINNE rises and goes to DIARMUID)

GRAINNE DIARMUID do you hear any sound ?

DIARMUID I hear the silence of the landscape, and I hear your voice which is to me part of the silence.

GRAINNE But I hear a sound as of hunting, and the sound of a horn.

DIARMUID If you hear any sound it is the baying of the wild dogs on the mountains.

Twenty-four-Page Professionally Prepared Typescript of Complete Act, Revised by George Moore and W. B. Yeats

[NLI 30,437, 1r]

G R A I N N E.

ACT II.

DIARMUID'S DUN.

[2r]

–1–

GRAINNE and DIARMUID.

ACT II.

DIARMUID'S DUN.

(GRAINNE sitting by the fire – DIARMUID standing by the door looking at the landscape – Time, sunset – View of mountains with wooded slopes.)

DIARMUID **GRAINNE, come, look at the evening – There is peaceful light on the mountains; there are peaceful shadows in the valley and there is peaceful love in our hearts.**

(GRAINNE rises and goes to DIARMUID)

GRAINNE **DIARMUID do you hear any sound ?**

DIARMUID **I hear the silence of the landscape, and I hear your voice which is to me part of the silence.**

GRAINNE **But I hear a sound as of hunting, and the sound of a horn.**

DIARMUID **If you hear any sound it is the baying of the wild dogs on the mountains.**

The light-card front cover is transcribed above as fol. 1.

[NLI 30,437]

[3^{r}]

–2–

GRAINNE Wild dogs do not answer to the sound of the horn. That was the horn of FIONN.

DIARMUID You have forgotten the sound of FIONN'S horn; and none hunts in this solitude but I.

He leaves the doorway and goes down the stage – turning suddenly towards her –)

But GRAINNE has not learned to love this silence. The silence of this valley and my voice are not enough for her.

GRAINNE Why should I tire of this valley, DIARMUID ? Have I not your love always ? When you are hunting it is in my heart as I wait for you. It is you who begin to weary of peace-ful days, and love has become a burden that you would put by for a while. For many days I have watched your thoughts, seeing them return to the old days when you went forth with FIONN at the head of the Fiani.

DIARMUID No, GRAINNE, you have missed my thoughts; they did not go that way. I am not tired of this silent valley where life is only you.

GRAINNE After seven years of flight and danger and foray, endless love has come to us in this valley. DIARMUID is not my love enough in this valley where life sleeps. But in the

[4^{r}]

–3–

seven years that FIONN followed us life was always awake. Life in this valley passes like a single minute. Yester-day has passed like a little vapour, but yester-year is bright in our memory. Seven years of memory have we.

DIARMUID Of these days, you remember which, GRAINNE ?

(GRAINNE thinks)

Of what are you thinking now ?

GRAINNE One midnight when the trees were like carven stones, and the moon shed a mysterious light upon the plain. We had been dreaming in each others' arms and had been awaked by the baying of a hound, and lifting our heads from the cromlech, we saw FIONN and the Fiani passing away in pursuit of us, their wolf hounds straining in the leash.

DIARMUID Yes, I remember that night. We could not have escaped from FIONN then; he was coming towards us, but some sudden thought seemed to turn him aside.

GRAINNE Since I have told my memory, tell me yours; of what are you thinking ?

DIARMUID When FIONN had passed by, how we stole away into the great forest in which we lived many days, and where we should

[5r]

–4–

have starved had we not met an old man who fished for us. And he divided the fish which we would not undertake to divide equally.

GRAINNE Keeping the smallest fish for himself, he being very old, and giving the second largest fish to me, I being a woman, and giving the largest fish to you, for it was for you to shield me against the perils of the forest. But of what are you thinking now DIARMUID ?

DIARMUID Of the two young men whom we met when we had passed safely out of the perils of the forest.

GRAINNE Of they whom FIONN had sent to slay you, but whom you conquered easily and bound with thongs.

DIARMUID And whom I undbound so that they might see me fight the giant who guarded the magic apples on which your desire was set. The apples of the quicken tree.

GRAINNE You would not give me those apples, fearing they should give me longer life than yours; but I feigned illness for eight days so that you might go against the giant.

DIARMUID But when I brought you the apples your thirst was cooled after eating one of them. The others I sent by the two young men whom FIONN had sent to kill me, as a present to

[NLI 30,437]

[6r]

–5–

FIONN telling them that they were to tell FIONN that it was they who had killed the giant, and that the deed should admit them among the Fiani.

GRAINNE **But DIARMUID laughed, and didnot believe the young men. He said – It was DIARMUID who killed the giant and gave you these apples. So I was right DIARMUID, I knew there was no danger you could not overcome, and did not fear to send you against the giant. But of what are you thinking now DIARMUID ?**

DIARMUID **Of nothing, GRAINNE.**

GRAINNE **I pray you tell me DIARMUID of what you are thinking.**

DIARMUID **Of how I overcame FIONN when he set guards at the seven doors of the dun.**

GRAINNE **Ah ! but behind your thoughts of these things there is something of which you will not speak. DIARMUID tell me of the trouble which I read in your eyes.**

DIARMUID **I am thinking ~~of~~ why I have escaped all these perils – if it be that I may fall a prey to the peril from which none may escape – The peril that when we bite life through and through we find like the core in an apple.**

GRAINNE **And have you bitten life through in this valley ?**

[7r]

–6–

DIARMUID **I bite the apple through to the core which is bitter sweet, but the apple never grows less.**

GRAINNE **But the peril that you dread is –**

DIARMUID **You heard it told by CONAN THE BALD the day I escaped with**

6r, l. 17 Type deletion.

you from Tara.

GRAINNE	I thought that tale long forgotten DIARMUID. These seven years I have not heard you speak of it.

DIARMUID	In the silence of this valley it has waked again, and I fear this death, for why, GRAINNE ?

GRAINNE	For why, DIARMUID ?

DIARMUID	Though the boar's tusks shall carry me among the gods, you will remain here, and for whom, GRAINNE ?

GRAINNE	There is danger in the silence of this valley.

DIARMUID	This day you heard the baying of hounds on the mountains, and you fancied that you heard the horn of FIONN.

GRAINNE	Tell me, DIARMUID, what has befallen you on the mountains. You have seen something in the woods. Not FIONN, for you said it was not FIONN'S horn that I heard calling, and not the boar, for on the mountains there are but harmless deer. Yesterday, DIARMUID, you were late, it was the moon that

[8r]

–7–

brought you home, and your face was as white as it.

DIARMUID	For seven years we have wandered over Erie, and we have met with all things that may be met with in life, except she who bewitched the wine the night we escaped from Tara.

GRAINNE	DIARMUID, you do not mean my old Nurse, you have not met her in the mountains, and you do not think her to be part of the enchantment about you.

DIARMUID	She who had so much share in the beginning must have some share in the end.

GRAINNE	Then it was she whom you met yesterday in the forest ?

DIARMUID	I don't know if it were she, but as I followed my hounds I saw an old woman with a spinning wheel stealing across the green hollow in the woods.

[NLI 30,437]

GRAINNE She is on her way here, and will tell me many things.

DIARMUID I lost sight of the deer suddenly – my hounds threw up their noses at fault, and I saw her pass out of the bracken through the bushes. But how could one so old find her way through the forest alone ? And where could she have been all these many years.

GRAINNE She is very old, and could not have followed us through all our wanderings. But news of our peace with FIONN must have

[9r]

–8–

reached her, and she is hurrying to us.

DIARMUID IS she your Foster-Mother, GRAINNE ? or one of the wood wives ?

GRAINNE It is said she came out of the woods the night I was born, but they say many things about her and about us, DIARMUID, so it is difficult to know.

(At that moment CONAN THE BALD and TWO COMPANIONS rush into DIARMUID'S dun.)

CONAN It is well for you to sit here by the fireside, DIARMUID, but we have been hunting for three months the great boar that has escaped from KING CORMAC'S country and has laid waste the wood and fields.

GRAINNE Welcome, CONAN, to the house of DIARMUID and GRAINNE.

CONAN DIARMUID, we have been hunting a boar; maybe the boar you would not let me speak of that day in Tara. You have seen him in the woods and that is why you sit by the fire.

DIARMUID I have met no boar in the woods. . . In these woods there are but harmless deer. This cannot be for I should have seen it.

CONAN A boar has come from KING CORMAC'S country and has harried three hundred sheep on the hills, and in the valley he has

[10r]

–9–

killed one thousand men. Some say he had the sun for father and the moon for mother. It is certain that he is no mortal beast. For three months we have hunted him in the woods and wastes of Erie, and all men but DIARMUID know of this hunt.

DIARMUID **Did you say he was a black boar without bristles ?**

CONAN **The boar of the story is black and without bristles – In the heart of DIARMUID and CONAN there is one terror**

(He stands by DIARMUID)

CONAN and DIARMUID are brothers – Look on us GRAINNE, we are in terror.

DIARMUID **Did you say he was a black boar and without bristles ?**

1st.COMPANION **I saw him but once, and I thought he was grey.**

DIARMUID **(To the second) And you ?**

2nd. COMPANION **I saw him pass by me and I thought he was green like the sea, and he made a sound like the sea in a storm.**

(CONAN and the TWO COMPANIONS go up the stage and watch the hunt.)

GRAINNE **So FIONN is hunting in our woods, and there is nothing on earth or in heaven which he cannot overcome.**

DIARMUID **If it be a black boar without bristles he may not overcome**

[11r]

–10–

it. I am drawn along like a fish in a net. For many nights I have dreamed of this fiercely tusked fate of mine and for many days its dark shadow has floated in front of me. Now, yesterday, I saw the SPINNING WOMAN in the forest. And now there comes news of this boar from KING CORMAC'S country.

GRAINNE **We should not have lingered in this silent valley, DIARMUID,**

[NLI 30,437]

its silence has hatched out strange fears. You remember and dream too much. But why should you fear my old Nurse. Why should you not remember it was she who cast sleep upon FIONN'S eyes so that we might escape together ?

DIARMUID She enchanted FIONN and I was glad; but even as I watched him in sleep I knew that the day would come when she would cast her spells upon me. It is turn and turn about always.

GRAINNE FIONN has made peace.

DIARMUID Better war than that he should come hunting the boar in my country – Maybe it was she who has woven a spell to bring FIONN and the boar together.

GRAINNE This boar is but a phantom – Why believe in it, DIARMUID ?

DIARMUID Purge me of my belief, for it is belief that makes the hand tremble and dims the eye. The boar is nothing, if fear

[12r]

–11–

of it were dead in my heart I should conquer it. My life has been made weak by this omen.

CONAN This is our time to join the hunt. We can slip back and FIONN will not know we have been away.

1st COMPANION If we could bring back DIARMUID with us.

2nd. COMPANION FIONN would bid him welcome. He would like to join with his old comrade with whom he is now at peace. Will DIARMUID hunt this black boar with us.

DIARMUID There is no boar on this mountain. You are hunting in your dreams (laughter)

(FIONN'S horn is heard far away)

CONAN Now let us go (Exeunt)

DIARMUID They are gone, or soon will be. If they are hunting such boar as they tell of he will lead them back whence they came. Our love shall begin again, GRAINNE, in this silent valley.

GRAINNE You have loved me over much, and it is my love which has begotten fear in a heart that once knew no fear.

DIARMUID I have no comrades in arms now – The Fiani are with FIONN. They will not leave him – Nor can I leave you, GRAINNE.

[13r]

–12–

GRAINNE Forget my love for a while. I will help you to forget it. I will take up shiled and spear and follow you to battle
(She goes to the wall where the weapons hang)
And you and FIONN shall be friends again.

DIARMUID Can I be friends with FIONN ?

GRAINNE I said to my father, KING CORMAC, that there could be no right on me except my desire. FIONN has made peace, he has forgotten his desire – You need fear FIONN no longer.

DIARMUID (Taking her in his arms) Would that all the world should forget you, so that I might enjoy you for ever in the ends of the earth – You and I alone – and for ever.

GRAINNE You must win my love in battle.

DIARMUID Have I not won you ?

GRAINNE I must be won again and again.

DIARMUID It was not by feats of arms that I won your love, but by the desire of the eye.

GRAINNE Now you must win it by great feats of arms.

DIARMUID GRAINNE is not made for the peace of the hearth and for love of children, nor simple comforts and homeliness.

[14r]

–13–

GRAINNE What do you see in me GRAINNE ?

DIARMUID **The blown flame which quickens and consumes the world.**
It is ~~strange to~~ have known you so long without knowing you at all.

(FIONN'S horn is heard again)

GRAINNE **FIONN is winding his horn and gathering his huntsmen together – Go and ask him here.**

DIARMUID **Is this a wise thing to do ? When he sees you the broil will begin again.**

GRAINNE **Other men see me and think of other things – You cannot let FIONN pass your dun without giving him welcome. Why do you tarry ? You must not fear FIONN and the boar or both will overcome you DIARMUID.**

DIARMUID **Would you have me friends with FIONN ?**

GRAINNE **I would not have two such heroes as you and FIONN on different sides. I would have you friends as you were before either of you felt the weakening spell of GRAINNE.**

DIARMUID **GRAINNE is right. FIONN has made peace with me and it is**
go to
certain I must bid him welcome.

(GRAINNE goes to the chest and takes out her gold ornaments, and puts on the land.)

[15r]

–14–

DIARMUID **Is it for FIONN, GRAINNE,you put on these things ? For me you have not worn them this many a day.**

GRAINNE **We two are common to each other by night and by day; but FIONN I have not seen since I left him asleep at my father's table.**

DIARMUID **GRAINNE, oh my instinctive life – Oh strange craving which tears and then pursues me like a hound.**

14r, l. 3 The cancellation is in pencil, its casual character indicating discontent with Diarmuid's whole speech. This and subsequent cancellation marks in pencil are presumably by WBY: cf. his pencil insertions on fol. 21r below.

GRAINNE **FIONN has gathered his huntsmen and his hounds together – Go bid him welcome.**

DIARMUID **You said I was to put fear aside and that there would be no boar to kill me.**

(He goes out)

GRAINNE **But you must go without fear.**

(She goes to the chest and takes out the boretto and the cloak)

So she is coming through the woods{., ~~home.~~ While she is on my side I have nothing to fear. She came out of the woods when I was born, she came again when KING CORMAC would have married me to FIONN, and she is coming now when I have sent for FIONN

(Pause, during which she completes her dressing)

But this time she is late.

[16r]

–15–

(GRAINNE crosses the stage getting down to the Right – FIONN enters, followed by the COMPANIONS – They enter like tired men who have been hunting many days – They are armed with bows and spears, and they rest on their spears and lean against the door post – FIONN goes down the stage and speaks to GRAINNE).

FIONN **We meet after a long betrayal. But, GRAINNE, I have made peace with you.**

GRAINNE **~~This peace has not come too soon~~. Too long have two such chiefs as FIONN and DIARMUID been foes. That is why I sent for you FIONN.**

FIONN **Right glad am I to be friends with my old comrade though he took GRAINNE from me.**

GRAINNE **I give you back your comrade, and your love of me is dead and your heart light again. But I would know now FIONN that you have seen me if I were worth all these wars.**

15r, l. 13 The revision of "woods, home." to "woods." was made by erasure.

16r, l. 3 Cancellation is in pencil.

[NLI 30,437]

FIONN **I would begin them again, GRAINNE, if I could get you. . . . I have done you wrong by this peace – ~~For your hand's sake I should have dared to the end of time.~~**

(He takes her hand)

DIARMUID **GRAINNE, all are weary here and want food and drink – Let**

[17r]

–16–

us to wine.

(Wine is brought in and GRAINNE gives some to FIONN and DIARMUID and USHEEN go to the table and drink together)

OSCAR **You should have been with us DIARMUID in this hunt – There has been no such hunt known as this – For three months we have been hunting and have crossed the woods and hills of Erie. Once the boar hid himself in the mountains of ACTAR and we surrounded the mountain for a week, hunting the boar, till the herdsmen came to tell us the boar was not there but on the ACTAR hills where he had killed one thousand sheep.**

1st COMPANION **Yes, to-day fifty of the Fiani are slain.**

USHEEN **It is certainly a god we are hunting sent among us for the destruction of Erie. If we do not kill it,it will not leave any living men or cattle.**

DIARMUID **I know nothing of these things – I have been long out of ~~the~~ earshot of the voices of Erie. Here I have hunted the deer for many months, and guarded my flocks and herds.**

(CONAN enters accompanied by many men carrying horns and deer skins.)

CONAN **I, CONAN, ~~Master of the household goods~~, and of the Fiani, bring deer skins as a peace offering from FIONN to this**

16r, ll. 12–13 The cancellations are in pencil.
17r, ll. 3–9, 17 Pencil cancellations.
15 Type deletion.

[18r]

–17–

great house – This deer skin with its great antlers is a peace offering from FIONN to GRAINNE that it may be soft under her feet.

(To the crowd)

What woman would not have been glad to see FIONN kill that deer upon the slopes of Ben Gualbin, and to see him pull his great bow that no man, no, not even DIARMUID, could pull. The boar was three bow shots distant from any bow but his, and the stag went so quickly that no other arrow could overtake it.

(DIARMUID, FIONN and USHEEN go up the stage and look at the boar skin – FIONN and GRAINNE walk down the stage)

FIONN I made peace for your sake, GRAINNE.

You were a long time – about the flight

GRAINNE FIONN, I did not reproach you, but if I went away with DIARMUID it does not mean that the great deeds of FIONN, son of CUHL, have not always filled me with wonder. DIARMUID was young, and I loved him for his youth and beauty.

FIONN Now seven years have passed and his youth and beauty have passed with them; ~~but I too am seven years older~~.

GRAINNE ~~I love DIARMUID always, FIONN, and~~ I would have you friends, that is why I sent for you.

FIONN I made peace for your sake, GRAINNE, DIARMUID was young

[19r]

–18–

~~and beautiful~~ and you loved him for his youth ~~and beauty;~~ and in Tara I thought it was valour and renown that would have won you.

GRAINNE If I went away with DIARMUID it does not mean that the great deeds of FIONN, son of CUHL, have not filled me with wonder.

18r, ll. 4–9, 16, 17 Pencil cancellations.
19r, l. 1 Pencil cancellation.

[NLI 30,437]

Here, in this gentle valley, we talk of your deeds often.
I know well of your journey to Alba, and of your valour
there, and that is why I sent for you. I would have you
and DIARMUID friends.

FIONN Then why did not you send for me before ?

GRAINNE Until now you were DIARMUID'S foe.

FIONN Now think you I am DIARMUID'S foe no longer.

GRAINNE You have come to kill the boar which is laying waste
DIARMUID'S country. But DIARMUID says that you hunt this
if
boar in vain it be a black boar without bristles.

FIONN DIARMUID says that ?
(Aside)
The boar is black and without bristles.
(Aloud)
This peace is a false peace! There can never be peace be-
tween me and DIARMUID. Years had hidden from me the wrong
he did me, but the sight of you, GRAINNE, has made it leap

[20r]

–19–

like a flame.
(Turning from her to DIARMUID)
And I say this to DIARMUID now.

DIARMUID What says FIONN to me – That he who took my hand this day
is my foe again.

GRAINNE Let there be no more war, FIONN, I beseech you, for my
heart is bidden to both.

FIONN The question is now, as it was before – the question is
ever the same – Which is the better a man's hand or a woman's
breast.

DIARMUID Then, FIONN, the peace you made with me was perfidious ?

19r, ll. 13–17 Pencil cancellations.

FIONN GRAINNE is free to choose now, as she was before; it is not my desire or yours, DIARMUID, it is GRAINNE who knows no law but her desire.

GRAINNE Then, if war there must be, I am with DIARMUID.
(She goes to him)
Alas, I am an evil thing in these men, and DIARMUID you saw clearly when you saw me as a flame that consumes. Yet ~~I think no evil~~, but would see you friends again, ~~standing shoulder to shoulder against the foes of Erie~~.

DIARMUID (With exaltation) GRAINNE have no fear. You have brought about my escape from it – ~~You have saved me from the mysterious forest, and its lurking danger~~. FIONN I shall

[21ʳ]

Fin – I or this Diarmd, or [?both] shall die this day –

–20–

overcome – Oh FIONN is as nothing at all !
(To FIONN)
FIONN has said this peace is a false peace in him as in me. He speaks well – only our swords can bring peace.

GRAINNE Now we shall witness the finest feats of arms in Erie. Happy is he who lives to see such swordsmen matched against each other, and to watch the combat.
(Advancing between them)
But no, this cannot be – for one of the greatest men must fall, and that would be a sorrowful peace indeed.
(The men cross their swords)

CONAN One of Erie's greatest chiefs shall be slain, so that there may be peace – Hear her say it – Then, who shall rid your fields of the pestilence that has come out of the forest, and has laid waste your fields, and harried your flocks.

1st COMPANION Yes, who shall rid the country of the boar if FIONN and DIARMUID slay each other. We want DIARMUID'S hounds.

20ʳ, ll. 16–17, 17–18, 20–21 Pencil cancellations.

21ʳ, ll. 4–6 Pencil cancellations.

4–6, 19+ Grania presumably speaks the line added at the foot of the page in place of her canceled lines. Finn's lines added at the head of the page presumably come in here, also.

[NLI 30,437]

	There mus be no fight here [?*while*] [?*he*] *is ours*
ALL	**~~We want their hounds~~.**
2nd. COMPANION	**DIARMUID sits by the fire and has not yet raised his spear to free his country of the boar. He sits by the fire and dreams.**
	There is only [?*one*] [?*way*] *for Finn now he has* [?*drawn*] his *sword.*

[22r]

–21–

ALL	**DIARMUID is craven.**
CONAN	**Who shall kill the boar if DIARMUID and FIONN kill one another. GRAINNE is the most beautiful woman in Erie – let AONGHUS the god of hunters bestow her upon him who kills the boar – Then, when the boar is killed, GRAINNE shall watch the flocks feeding upon the hillside, and the green corn growing in the fields, and FIONN and DIARMUID shall be friends.**
	(DIARMUID turns to strike CONAN)
GRAINNE	**He is not worthy of your arm – Give me your sword, not you, but I, shall strike him.**
CONAN	**DIARMUID, would strike me because I speak of the great boar of which he lives in great fear.**
FIONN	**DIARMUID has sat too long by the fireside and the Old Woman has scared him with her tales.**
	(DIARMUID'S Henchmen intervene)
	Who are these ? His henchmen who would save him from the combat.
DIARMUID	**FIONN lies. He knows why I do not against the boar, and would force me to my fate rather than he would dare my sword. See how he shrinks from it.**
	(FIONN advances to the combat; as he does so the
	e
	Crowd intervene, det‸rmined that there may be no fight.)

21r, l. 16 Pencil cancellation.

19+ See the note on p. 365.

22r, l. 19+ The ink insertion appears to be in a fourth hand (neither WBY, GM, nor AG).

[23r]

–22–

DIARMUID to GRAINNE – You see there is no way for men except the way of the gods, but if I fear it not I may conquer it still.

OSCAR — **DIARMUID cannot accept this ordeal – FIONN you must not press it upon him.**

USHEEN — **DIARMUID must not join this hunt – CONAN this day you have done a wicked thing.**

1st COMPANION — **If DIARMUID refuses to hunt , DIARMUID is craven.**

2nd. COMPANION — **AONGHUS god of hunters shall decide it.**
(Uproar among the hunters)

DIARMUID — **Every man has his time – A spear is to kill FIONN, an arrow waits for CAOILTE and a mysterious old age for USHEEN. I will hunt the boar with FIONN – FIONN is right. Let us begin this hunt for it shall not be soon ended.**
(He takes from the wall his light spear and shield)

GRAINNE — **Take BROAD-EDGE your heavy spear, which has served you so well**
(FIONN and the hunters go out, and the others follow)

DIARMUID — **This spear will do well enough against the boar, he is but a mortal beast, and my fate is not in this hunt.**
(He takes his light shield from the wall)

[24r]

–23–

GRAINNE — **Take your great shield for this boar's tusks are keen, and he has killed many men.**

DIARMUID — **This shield will do for any boar that is not black, and without bristles.**

GRAINNE — **DIARMUID, DIARMUID, forego this hunt.**

[NLI 30,437]

DIARMUID Have no fear for me GRAINNE, for there is no fear in my heart.

(DIAMUIRD breaks away and GRAINNE is left alone – She stands looking, lost in thought – The FOSTER-MOTHER enters with her spinning wheel.)

GRAINNE MOTHER, so you have come at last, but you have come too late. DIAMUID has gone to hunt the boar which has escaped from KING CORMAC'S country.

FOSTER-MOTHER I passed DIARMUID on his way; he was winding his horn, and his dogs were leaping around him.

GRAINNE Have you seen or heard of the boar which has laid waste our country ?

FOSTER-MOTHER I have been away in Alba where the KING was dying; and I
of
have come here, because news of the peace that FIONN has made with you.

GRAINNE But, MOTHER you have come out of the forest and should have

[25^{r}]

–24–

seen the boar. MOTHER, I love DIARMUID with the love that wedlock brings; but DIARMUID has gone, and you who have come out of the woods can tell me if this be DIARMUID'S doom ?

FOSTER-MOTHER It is said that DIARMUID is but an earthly shadow of the god AONGHUS which is in heaven, and many boars shall he hunt and slay; some may be without bristles and some may be black, but none shall slay him till his father calls him away.

GRAINNE MOTHER, you have come too late ! too late. But, MOTHER, you who are wise, you who have come out of the woods, tell me if there is no way to save DIARMUID. Sit down and spin, and make the flax prophesy.

(The FOSTER-MOTHER begins to spin)

Ah, see how the thread tangles; see how it breaks.

FOSTER-MOTHER It was your desire to see FIONN that has sent DIARMUID to hunt this boar.

GRAINNE Spin, MOTHER, spin, make the flax prophesy. Tell me if my heart shall be purged of FIONN, and if I may save DIARMUID by making of FIONN a foe again. Why are you not spinning ?

FOSTER-MOTHER There is no more flax on the distaff.

The light-card rear cover (disbound) is blank and not foliated here.

[NLI 8777(9), 1r, 2r]

G R A I N N E.

ACT II

DIARMUID'S DUN.

-1-

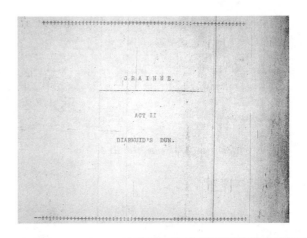

GRAINNE and DIARMUID.

ACT II.

DIARMUID'S DUN.

(GRAINNE sitting by the fire – DIARMUID standing by the door looking at the landscape – Time, sunset – View of mountains with wooded slopes.)

DIARMUID GRAINNE, come, look at the evening – There is peaceful light on the mountains; there are peaceful shadows in the valley ~~and there is peaceful love in our hearts.~~

(GRAINNE rises and goes to DIARMUID)

GRAINNE DIARMUID do you hear any sound ?

DIARMUID [There is] ~~I hear~~ the silence ~~of the landscape~~ [in the valley], and I ~~hear~~ your voice ~~which~~ is ~~to me~~ part of the silence.

GRAINNE But I hear a sound as of hounds hunting, and the sound of a horn.

DIARMUID If you hear any sound it is the baying of the wild dogs on the mountains.

Twenty-five-Page Professionally Prepared Typescript of Complete Act, Extensively Revised by W. B. Yeats

[NLI 8777(9), 1^{r}]

G R A I N N E.

ACT II

DIARMUID'S DUN.

[2^{r}]

–1–

GRAINNE and DIARMUID

ACT II.

DIARMUID'S DUN.

(GRAINNE sitting by the fire – DIARMUID standing by the door looking at the landscape – Time, sunset – View of mountains with wooded slopes.)

DIARMUID **GRAINNE, come, look at the evening – There is peaceful light on the mountains; there are peaceful shadows in the valley ~~and there is peaceful love in our hearts.~~**

(GRAINNE rises and goes to DIARMUID)

GRAINNE **DIARMUID do you hear any sound ?**

DIARMUID *There is* **~~I hear the~~ silence** *in the valley* **~~of the landscape~~, and I ~~hear~~ your voice ~~which~~ is ~~to me~~ part of the silence.**

GRAINNE **But I hear a sound as of horns hunting, and the sound of a horn.**

DIARMUID **If you hear any sound it is the baying of the wild dogs on the mountains.**

The light-card front cover is transcribed above as fol. 1.

2^{r}, l. 3 The cancellation, like all other MS revisions of the TS, is in pencil.

-2-

GRAINNE Wild dogs do not answer to the sound of the horn. That was the horn of FIONN.

DIARMUID You have forgotten the sound of FIONN's horn; and none hunts in this solitude but I.

(He leaves the doorway and goes down the stage – turning suddenly towards her)

But GRAINNE has not learned to love this silence. The silence of this valley and my voice are not enough for her.

GRAINNE Why should ~~I tire of~~ I not love this valley if you were DIARMUID. Have I not your love always ? ~~When you are hunting it is in my heart as I wait for you.~~ It is you who begin to weary of peaceful days, and love has become a burden ~~that~~ to you ~~would put by for a while~~. For many days I have ~~watched~~ understood your thoughts, ~~seeing them~~ They return to the old days when you went ~~forth~~ with FIONN at the head of the Fiani.

DIARMUID No, GRAINNE, you have ~~missed my~~ not understood thoughts; they do not go that way. I am not tired of this ~~silent~~ valley where ~~life is only~~ you make up the whole of life.

GRAINNE After seven years of flight and danger ~~and foray~~, ~~endless~~ we have found unending love ~~has come~~ to us in this valley. DIARMUID is not ~~my~~

[NLI 8777(9), 3r]

–2–

GRAINNE **Wild dogs do not answer to the sound of the horn. That was the horn of FIONN.**

DIARMUID **You have forgotten the sound of FIONN's horn; and none hunts in this solitude but I.**
(He leaves the doorway and goes down the stage – turning suddenly towards her)
But GRAINNE has not learned to love this silence. The silence of this valley and my voice are not enough for her.

I not love *& your voice*
GRAINNE **Why should ~~I tire of~~ this valley^ DIARMUID. Have I not**
your love always ^? ~~When you are hunting it is in my heart~~
~~as I wait for you.~~ It is you who begin to weary of peace-
to
ful days, and love has become a burden ~~that~~ you ~~would put~~
understood
~~by for a while~~. For many days I have ~~watched~~ ^ your thoughts .
They
~~seeing them~~ return to the old days when you went ~~forth~~ with
FIONN at the head of the Fiani.

not understood
DIARMUID **No, GRAINNE, you have ~~missed my~~ ^ thoughts; they do not go**
that way. I am not tired of this ~~silent~~ valley where ~~life~~
~~is only~~ you . *make up the whole of life.*

we have
GRAINNE **After seven years of flight and danger ~~and foray, endless~~**
found unending
^ love ~~has come~~ to us in this valley. DIARMUID is not ~~my~~

14 WBY probably did not mean to extend the cancel line through "my.".

-3-

love ~~enough in this valley where~~ life sleeps. ~~But~~ in the seven years that FIONN followed us life was always awake - Life in this valley passes like a single minute - Yester-day has perished like a little ~~vapour~~, but yester-year is ~~bright~~ in our memory. Seven years of memory ~~have we~~.

DIARMUID Of those days, you remember (which) GRAINNE ?

(GRAINNE thinks)

Of what are you thinking now ?

GRAINNE ~~Of the madness of yester year~~. Do you remember the silence which seemed to touch the very stars ? and the trees were like carven stones, and the moon shed ~~a shadowy mysteri~~ous light upon the ~~plain~~. We had been dreaming in each others' arms, and had been awaked by the baying of a hound, and ~~lifting our heads from~~ the cromlech we saw FIONN and the Fiani passing away ~~in pursuit~~ ~~of us~~, their wolf hounds straining in the leash.

DIARMUID Yes, I remember that night. We could not have escaped from FIONN then; he was coming towards us, but ~~some~~ sudden thought ~~seemed~~ to turn him aside.

GRAINNE ~~Since~~ I have told my memory, tell me yours; of what are you thinking ?

[NLI 8777(9), 4^{r}]

–3–

enough that my love should wake while
~~love enough in this valley where~~ ^ life sleeps. ~~But~~ in the
seven years that FIONN followed us life was always awake –
Life in this valley passes like a single minute – Yester-
smoke
day has perished like a little ~~vapour~~ ^, but yester-year is
vivid the We have
~~bright~~ ^ in ~~our~~ ^ memory. ^ Seven years of memory ~~have we~~.
do
DIARMUID ^ **Of those days, ^ you remember (which) GRAINNE ?**
(GRAINNE thinks)
Of what are you thinking now ?

GRAINNE **~~Of the madness of yester year~~. Do you remember the silence**
which seemed to touch the very stars ? and the trees were
an opal
like carven stones, and the moon shed ~~a shadowy mysterious~~
grass
light upon the ~~plain~~. We had been dreaming in each others'
arms, and had been awaked by the baying of a hound, and
looking out from under
~~lifting our heads from~~ the cromlech we saw FIONN and the
from where we were
Fiani passing away ~~in pursuit of us~~ ^, their wolf hounds
straining in the leash.

DIARMUID **Yes, I remember that night. We could not have escaped from**
a
FIONN then; he was coming towards us, but ^ ~~some~~ sudden
some thing may be a friend [?~~*that*~~] [?*we*/?*are*] *among the hidden people*
thought ~~seemed to~~ ^ turn him aside.

GRAINNE **~~Since~~ I have told my memory, tell me yours; of what are**
you thinking ?

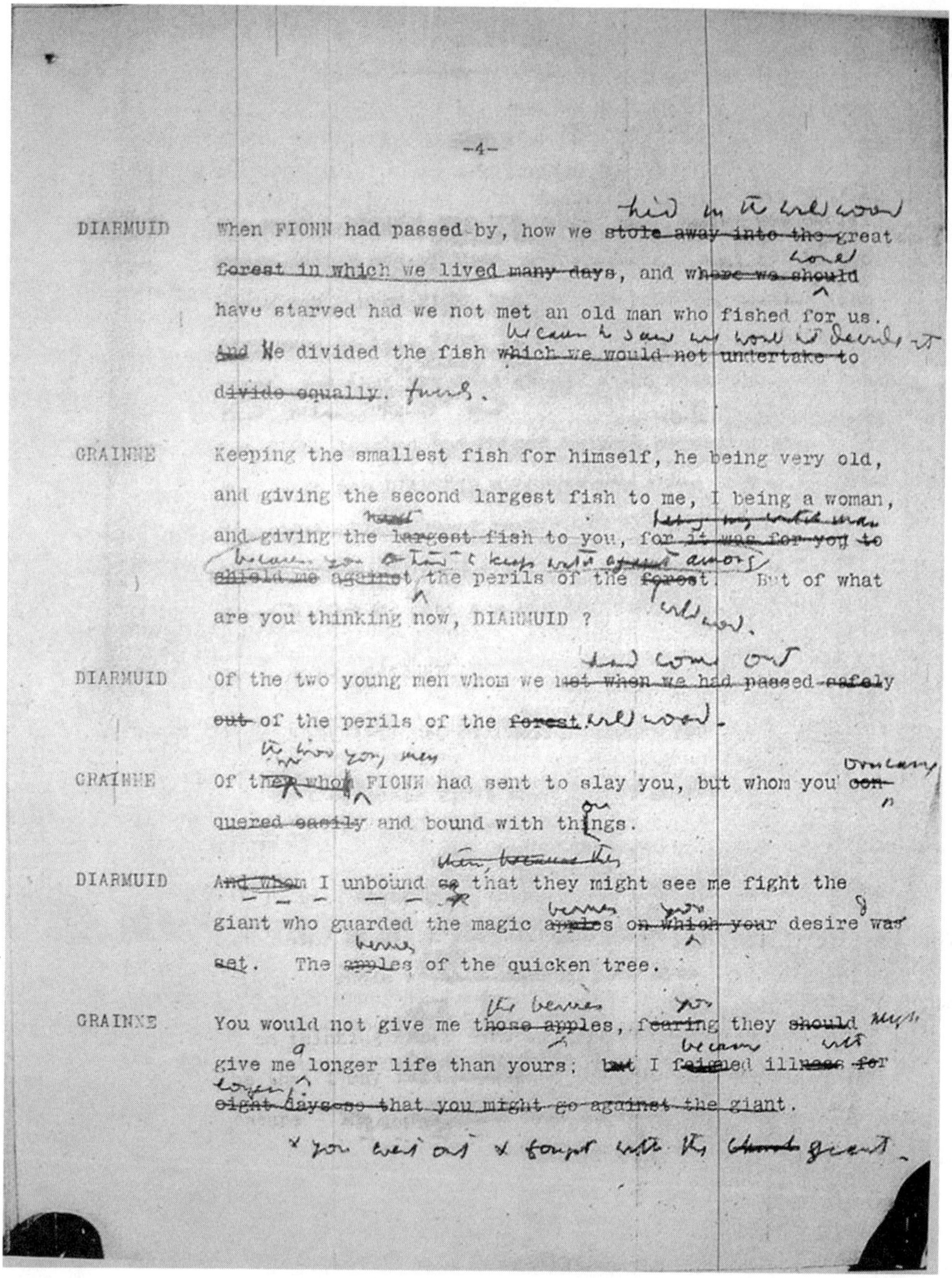

-4-

DIARMUID When FIONN had passed by, how we ~~stole away into the~~ great ~~forest in which~~ we lived ~~many days~~, and wh~~ere we should~~ have starved had we not met an old man who fished for us. ~~And~~ We divided the fish ~~which we would not undertake to divide equally~~.

GRAINNE Keeping the smallest fish for himself, he being very old, and giving the second largest fish to me, I being a woman, ~~and giving~~ the ~~largest fish~~ to you, ~~for it was for you to shield me against~~ the perils of the ~~forest~~. But of what are you thinking now, DIARMUID ?

DIARMUID Of the two young men whom we ~~met when we had passed safely out~~ of the perils of the ~~forest~~.

GRAINNE Of ~~those whom~~ FIONN had sent to slay you, but whom you ~~conquered easily~~ and bound with things.

DIARMUID ~~And whom~~ I unbound ~~so~~ that they might see me fight the giant who guarded the magic ~~apples~~ ~~on which your~~ desire was ~~set~~. The ~~apples~~ of the quicken tree.

GRAINNE You would not give me ~~those apples~~, ~~fearing~~ they ~~should~~ give me longer life than yours; ~~but~~ I ~~feigned~~ ill~~ness for eight days so that you might go against the~~ giant.

[NLI 8777(9), 5r]

–4–

hid in the wild wood
DIARMUID **When FIONN had passed by, how we ~~stole away into the great~~**
would
~~forest in which we lived many days~~, and ~~where we should~~
have starved had we not met an old man who fished for us.
H *because he saw we would not devide it*
~~And~~ h~~e~~ divided the fish ~~which we would not undertake to~~
~~divide equally.~~ *fairly.*

GRAINNE **Keeping the smallest fish for himself, he being very old,**
and giving the second largest fish to me, I being a woman,
~~*next*~~ ~~*being my watch man*~~
and giving the largest fish to you, ~~for it was for you to~~
because you had to keep watch ~~against~~ among
~~shield me against~~ the perils of the ~~forest~~. But of what
are you thinking now, DIARMUID ? *wild wood.*

had come out
DIARMUID **Of the two young men whom we ~~met when we had passed safely~~**
~~out~~ of the perils of the ~~forest.~~ *wild wood.*

the two young men
m overcame
GRAINNE **Of ~~the~~ ~~y whom~~ FIONN had sent to slay you, but whom you ~~con-~~**
on
~~quered easily~~ and bound with th~~i~~ngs.
~~*them, because they*~~
DIARMUID **~~And whom~~ I unbound ~~so~~ that they might see me fight the**
berries *you* *d*
giant who guarded the magic ~~apples on which your~~ desire ~~was~~
berries
~~set~~. The ~~apples~~ of the quicken tree.

the berries *you*
GRAINNE **You would not give me ~~those apples~~, ~~fearing~~ they ~~should~~** *might*
a *became* *with*
give me longer life than yours; ~~but~~ I ~~feigned~~ ~~illness for~~
longing.
~~eight days so that you might go against the giant~~.
& you went out & fought with the ~~Churl~~ giant.

18 *you*] WBY surely intended to write *for*.

-5-

DIARMUID But when I brought you the apples your thirst was cooled after eating one of them. The others I sent by the two young men , whom FIONN had sent to kill me, telling them they were to tell FIONN it was they who had killed the giant, and that the deed should admit them among the Fiani.

GRAINNE But FIONN laughed and did not believe the young men. He said -"It was DIARMUID who gave you these apples." So I was right, DIARMUID, I knew there was no danger you could not overcome, and did not fear to send you against the giant. But O what are you thinking now, DIARMUID ?

DIARMUID Of nothing, GRAINNE.

GRAINNE I pray you tell me, DIARMUID, of what you are thinking.

DIARMUID Of how I overcame FIONN when he set guards at the seven doors of the dun.

GRAINNE Ah ! but behind your thoughts of these things there is something of which you will not speak. DIARMUID tell me of the trouble which I read in your eyes.

DIARMUID I am thinking why I have escaped all these perils if it be that I may fall a prey to the peril from which none may escape - The peril that when we bite life through and

[NLI 8777(9), 6r]

–5–

berries *eat one of them*

DIARMUID **But when I brought you the ~~apples~~ your ~~thirst was cooled~~**

& would have thrown the rest away. I gave them to

~~after eating~~ one of them. ~~The others I sent by~~ ^ the two

I told

young men, whom FIONN had sent to kill me ~~, telling~~ ^ them

that

~~they were~~ to tell FIONN ~~it was~~ ^ they ~~who~~ had killed the

so hardy

giant, and that ~~the~~ ^ deed should admit them among the Fiani.

But I have heard that *them*

GRAINNE **~~But~~ FIONN laughed and did not believe ~~the young men~~. He**

o

said – "It was DIARMUID who gave you th ^ ese apples." ~~So I~~
~~was right, DIARMUID, I knew there was no danger you~~ could
~~not overcome, and did not fear to send you against the~~

O

~~giant.~~ ^ ~~But~~ of what are you thinking now, DIARMUID ?

DIARMUID **Of nothing, GRAINNE.**

GRAINNE **I pray you tell me, DIARMUID, of what you are thinking.**

DIARMUID **Of how I overcame FIONN when he set guards at the seven doors of the dun.**

GRAINNE **Ah ! but behind your thoughts of these things there is something of which you will not speak. DIARMUID tell me**

that is

of the trouble ~~which I read~~ ^ in your eyes.

that

DIARMUID **I am thinking ~~why~~ I have escaped all these perils ~~, If it~~**

be as overcome by

be that I may ~~fall a prey to~~ ^ the peril ~~from which~~ none may
escape – ~~The peril, that when we bite life through and~~

[NLI 8777(9), 7[r]]

through we find like the core in an apple

GRAINNE And have you biten life through in this valley.

DIARMUID Daily I bite throu the apple through to the core which is bitter sweet, but the apple never grows less.

GRAINNE But the peril that you dread is -

DIARMUID You heard of the death which waits for me from CONAN THE BALD the day I escaped with you from Tara.

GRAINNE But that is a tale you have long forgotten, DIARMUID, These seven years I have not heard you speak of it.

DIARMUID In the silence of our lives it has awaked again, and I fear this death, GRAINNE,

GRAINNE For why, DIARMUID ?

DIARMUID Though the boar's tusks shall carry me among the gods, you will remain here, and for whom, GRAINNE ?

GRAINNE There is danger in this silence and not in the boar at all.

DIARMUID For whom, GRAINNE ? This you heard the baying of the hounds on the mountains, and you fancied that you heard the horn of FIONN.

GRAINNE But something you have seen on the mountain - Not FIONN for you said it was not FIONN's horn that I heard calling, and not the boar, for on the mountain there are but harmless

1–5 A scrap of paper measuring 6.8 (h) by 20.3 (w) cm was pasted over the head of the original page. The two lines in the typescript beneath read: "though we find like the core of an apple. / GRAINNE And have you bitten life through in this valley?"

21+ Did WBY intend the phrase "on the mountain" to be inserted at the end of the present sentence, inserting the pointer when the sentence ended on the following page?

[NLI 8777(9), 7r]

The peril the gods keep for every man ~~who [?has]~~
*~~had the best~~ **~~–6–~~** ~~of life~~ they be friend lest he become as the*
that *gods.*
~~through~~ we find like the core in an apple *when we have*
bitten life through & through. ~~The peril the gods keep~~ in
~~every man~~.

& through
GRAINNE **And have you bitten life through ^ in this valley.**
have bitten *through & through*
DIARMUID **~~Daily~~ I ~~bite~~ ^ ~~throu~~ the apple ~~through~~ ~~to the core which~~ is**
& **~~bitter sweet, but~~ the apple ~~never~~ grows less.**
What *do* *does not*
GRAINNE **~~But the~~ peril ~~that~~ you dread ~~is~~ –**
what *a* *me*
DIARMUID **You heard ~~of the~~ death ~~which~~ waits for me from CONAN THE**
brought out of
BALD the day I ~~escaped with you from~~ Tara.
That will not be for a long time
GRAINNE **~~But that is a tale you have long forgotten~~, DIARMUID,**
these
~~These~~ seven years I have not heard you speak of it. ^
between us ^
DIARMUID **In the silence of our lives it has awaked again, and I**
fear this death, GRAINNE, ~~for why~~ ? *~~[?then] [?I]~~*
Why should you fear death Dairmud. The gods are not
GRAINNE **~~For why, DIARMUID~~ ?** *evil.*
Though I ~~shou~~ shall go *I*
DIARMUID **~~Thought the boar's tusks shall carry~~ ^ me among the gods, ~~you~~**
shall leave you here
~~will remain here, and for whom~~, GRAINNE ? *For whom shall*
I leave you Grainia –
~~GRAINNE There is danger in this silence and not in the boar at~~ all.

DIARMUID **~~For whom, GRAINNE~~ ? ~~This day~~ you heard the baying of the**
thoght of
hounds on the mountains, ^ and you ~~fancied that you heard~~ the
horn of FIONN.
You have heard or seen *It was not*
GRAINNE **~~But~~ something ~~you have seen~~ on the mountain – ~~Not~~ ^ FIONN**
^ *could not be*
for you said it ~~was not~~ FIONN'S horn that I heard ~~calling~~,
It was *deer*
~~and~~ ^ not the boar, for on the mountain there are but harmless

[NLI 8777(9), 8r]

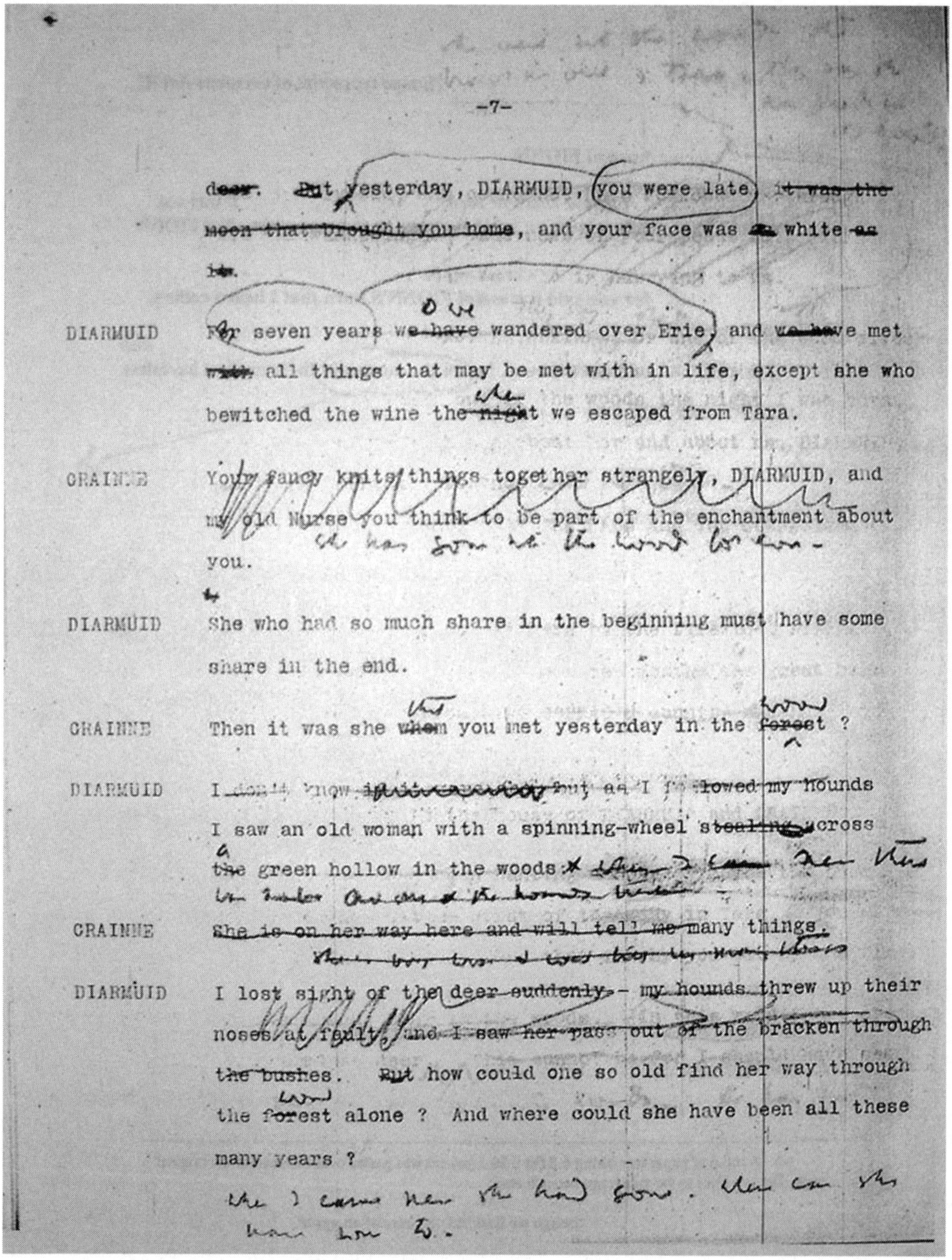

-7-

d~~ear~~. ~~But~~ yesterday, DIARMUID, you were late, ~~it was the moon that brought you home~~, and your face was ~~as~~ white ~~as it~~.

DIARMUID ~~For~~ seven years ~~we have~~ O we wandered over Erie, and ~~we have~~ met ~~with~~ all things that may be met with in life, except she who bewitched the wine the ~~night~~ the we escaped from Tara.

GRAINNE ~~Your fancy knits things together strangely, DIARMUID, and my old Nurse you think to be part of the enchantment about you.~~ she has gone into the wood for — you.

DIARMUID She who had so much share in the beginning must have some share in the end.

GRAINNE Then it was she ~~whom~~ that you met yesterday in the ~~forest~~ wood ?

DIARMUID I ~~don't know~~ ~~if it was~~ but as I followed my hounds I saw an old woman with a spinning-wheel ~~stealing~~ across ~~the~~ a green hollow in the woods. [illegible]

GRAINNE ~~She is on her way here and will tell me many things.~~ ~~[illegible]~~

DIARMUID I lost sight of the ~~deer suddenly~~ — my hounds threw up their noses at fault, ~~and I saw her pass out of the bracken through the bushes~~. ~~But~~ how could one so old find her way through the ~~forest~~ wood alone ? And where could she have been all these many years ?

When I came there she had gone. Where can she have been to.

[NLI 8777(9), 8r]

–7–

~~deer.~~ ~~But~~ yesterday, DIARMUID, you were late, ~~it was the~~
~~moon that brought you home~~, and your face was ~~as~~ white ~~as~~
~~it.~~

O we

DIARMUID ~~For~~ seven years ~~we have~~ wandered over Eric, and ~~we have~~ met
~~with~~ all things that may be met with in life, except she who
when
bewitched the wine ~~the night~~ we escaped from Tara.

GRAINNE Your fancy knits things together strangely, DIARMUID, and
my old Nurse you think to be part of the enchantment about
you. *She has gone to the woods for ever –*
[?~~O~~]

DIARMUID She who had so much share in the beginning must have some
share in the end.

that *wood*
GRAINNE Then it was she ~~whom~~ you met yesterday in the ~~forest~~ ?

DIARMUID I don't know ~~if it were she~~ but as I followed my hounds
I saw an old woman with a spinning-wheel ~~stealing~~ across
a
the green hollow in the woods. *& when I came near there*
was [?~~*number*~~] ~~*And she & the hounds became*~~

GRAINNE ~~She is on her way here and will tell me many~~ things.
~~*She is very wise & could tell me many things*~~

DIARMUID I lost sight of the deer suddenly – my hounds threw up their
noses at fault, and I saw her pass out of the bracken through
~~the bushes.~~ ~~But~~ how could one so old find her way through
wood
the ~~forest~~ alone ? And where could she have been all these
many years ?
When I came near she had gone. When can she
have gone to.

---

13 WBY first canceled the whole line of type with a single stroke, then erased his cancellation, leaving several TS letters indistinct and some of his cancellation line in place, and finally canceled "if it were she" with an irregular line.

[NLI 8777(9), 9r]

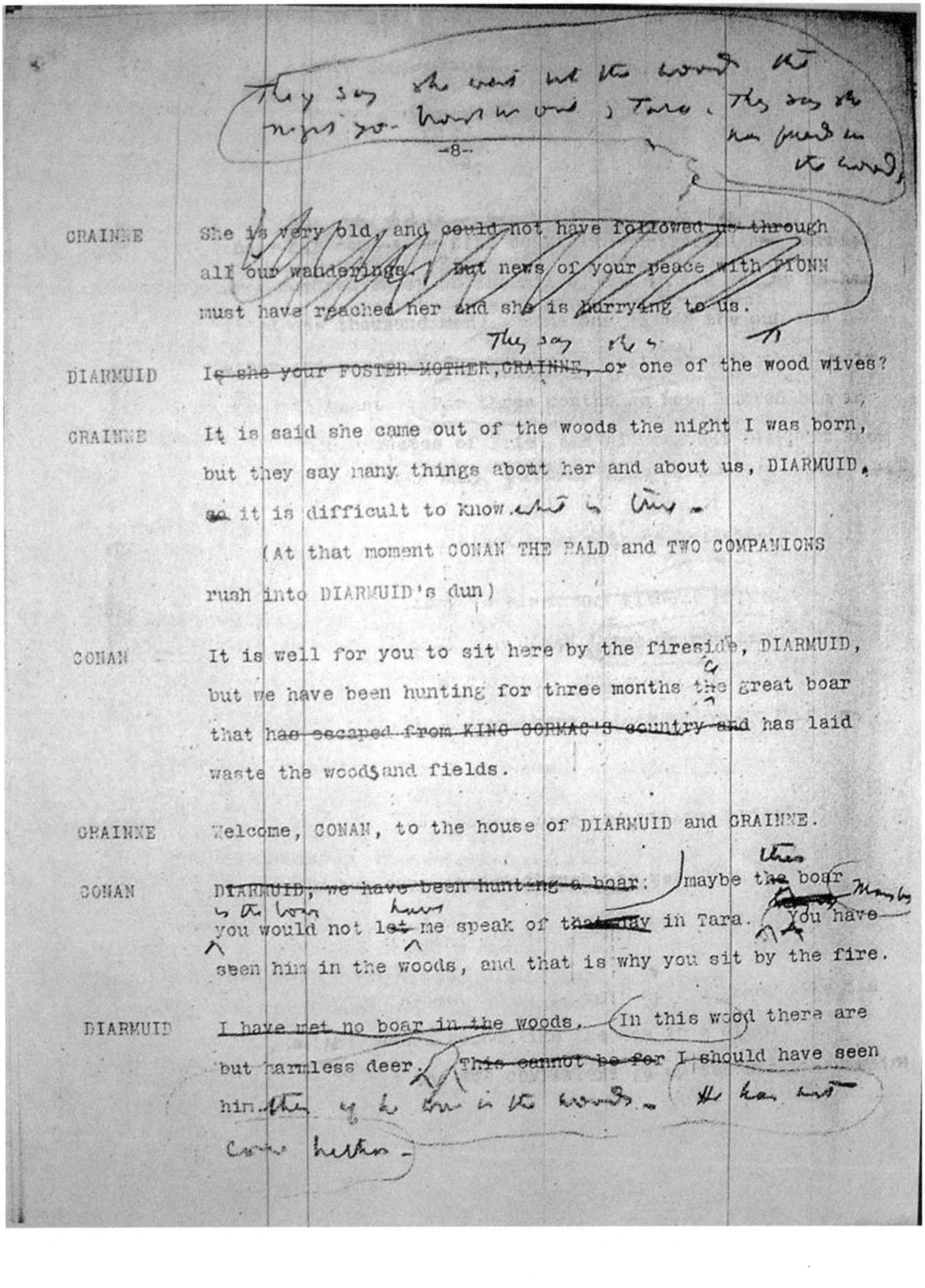

They say she went out the woods the night you were born in Tara. They say she has friends in the woods,

-8-

GRAINNE She is very old, ~~and could not have followed us through all our wanderings. But news of your peace with FIONN must have reached her and she is hurrying to us.~~

DIARMUID ~~Is she your FOSTER-MOTHER, GRAINNE,~~ They say she is or one of the wood wives?

GRAINNE It is said she came out of the woods the night I was born, but they say many things about her and about us, DIARMUID, ~~so~~ it is difficult to know what is true.

(At that moment CONAN THE BALD and TWO COMPANIONS rush into DIARMUID's dun)

CONAN It is well for you to sit here by the fireside, DIARMUID, but we have been hunting for three months ~~the~~ a great boar that ~~has escaped from KING CORMAC'S country and~~ has laid waste the woods and fields.

GRAINNE Welcome, CONAN, to the house of DIARMUID and GRAINNE.

CONAN ~~DIARMUID, we have been hunting a boar:~~ maybe ~~the~~ there ~~boar~~ is the boar you would not ~~let~~ have me speak of ~~that day~~ in Tara. You have seen him in the woods, and that is why you sit by the fire.

DIARMUID ~~I have met no boar in the woods.~~ In this wood there are but harmless deer. ~~This cannot be for I should have seen him.~~ there is no boar in the woods. He has not come hither.

[NLI 8777(9), 9r]

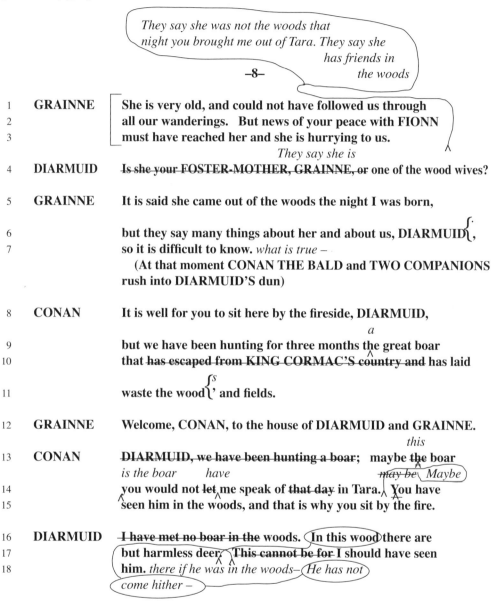

They say she was not the woods that night you brought me out of Tara. They say she has friends in the woods

–8–

GRAINNE **She is very old, and could not have followed us through all our wanderings. But news of your peace with FIONN must have reached her and she is hurrying to us.**

They say she is

DIARMUID **~~Is she your FOSTER-MOTHER, GRAINNE, or~~ one of the wood wives?**

GRAINNE **It is said she came out of the woods the night I was born,**

but they say many things about her and about us, DIARMUID {. ,

so it is difficult to know. *what is true –*

(At that moment CONAN THE BALD and TWO COMPANIONS rush into DIARMUID'S dun)

CONAN **It is well for you to sit here by the fireside, DIARMUID,**

a

but we have been hunting for three months ~~the~~ great boar that ~~has escaped from KING CORMAC'S country and~~ has laid

waste the wood {s ' **and fields.**

GRAINNE **Welcome, CONAN, to the house of DIARMUID and GRAINNE.**

this

CONAN **~~DIARMUID, we have been hunting a boar~~; maybe ~~the~~ boar**

is the boar *have* ~~*may be*~~ *Maybe*

you would not ~~let~~ me speak of ~~that day~~ in Tara. ~~You~~ You have seen him in the woods, and that is why you sit by the fire.

DIARMUID **~~I have met no boar in the~~ woods. In this wood there are but harmless deer. ~~This cannot be for~~ I should have seen him.** *there if he was in the woods– He has not come hither –*

-9-

CONAN A ~~boar has~~ ~~come from~~ KING CORMAC'S country ~~and~~ ~~has~~ harried three hundred sheep on the hills, and in the valley ~~he has~~ killed one thousand men. Some say he had the sun for father and the moon for mother. It is certain that he is no mortal beast. For three months we have hunted him in the woods and wastes of Erie, and all men but DIARMUID know of this hunt. we have followed him to the edge of the wood

DIARMUID Did you say he was a black boar without bristles ?

CONAN ~~The boar of the story is black and without bristles~~ - In the heart of DIARMUID and CONAN there is one terror.

(He stands by DIARMUID)

CONAN and DIARMUID are brothers - Look on us, GRAINNE, we are in terror.

DIARMUID Did you say he was a black boar and without bristles ?

1st. COMPANION I saw him but once, and I thought he was grey.

DIARMUID (To the second) And you ?

2nd. COMPANION I saw him ~~pass by me,~~ but once and I thought he was green like the sea, ~~and~~ he made a sound like the sea in a storm.

(CONAN and the TWO COMPANIONS go up the stage and watch the hunt).

[NLI 8777(9), 10r]

–9–

He ~~ap~~/ appear in *He*
CONAN **~~A boar has come from~~ KING CORMAC'S country – ~~and has~~ harried**
^ *he*
three hundred sheep on the hills and in the valley ~~he has~~
killed one thousand men. Some say he had the sun for
father and the moon for mother. It is certain that he is
a
no *t* **mortal beast. For three months we have hunted him in**
the woods and wastes of Erie, and all men but DIARMUID know
of this hunt. *We have followd him to the edge of thes woods*

DIARMUID **Did you say he was a black boar without bristles ?**

CONAN **~~The boar of the story is black and without bristles~~ – In**
the heart of DIARMUID and CONAN there is one terror.
(He stands by DIARMUID)
CONAN and DIARMUID are brothers – Look on us,GRAINNE, we
are in terror.

DIARMUID **Did you say he was a black boar and without bristles ?**

1st. COMPANION **I saw him but once, and I thought he was grey.**

DIARMUID **(To the second) And you ?**
but once
2nd. COMPANION **I saw him ~~pass by me~~, and I thought he was green like the**
{. *H}*
sea, and h{e made a sound like the sea in a storm.
(CONAN and the TWO COMPANIONS go up the stage and watch the hunt).

[NLI 8777(9), 11r]

-10-

GRAINNE So FIONN is hunting in our woods, and there is nothing on earth or in heaven which he cannot overcome.

DIARMUID If it be a black boar without bristles he may not overcome it. I am drawn along like a fish in a net. For many nights I have dreamed of this fiercely-tusked fate of mine and for many days its dark shadow has floated in front of me. Then, yesterday, I saw the SPINNING WOMAN in the forest. And now there comes news of this boar from KING CORMAC's country.

GRAINNE We should not have lingered in this silent valley, DIARMUID, its silence has hatched out strange fears . You remember and dream too much. Why why should you fear my old Nurse Why should you not remember that it was she who cast sleep upon FIONN's eyes so that we might escape together ?"

DIARMUID She enchanted FIONN, and I was glad; but even as I watched him in sleep I knew that the day would come when she would cast her spells upon me. It is turn and turn about always.

GRAINNE FIONN has made peace.

DIARMUID Better war than that he should come hunting the boar in my country - Maybe it was she who has woven a spell to bring

[NLI 8777(9), 11r]

Grania Fin wl kil it whet it is grey or green or
I ~~will can kill th~~ black for he is a gret hunter
~~Grania – Fin will kill it wheth it is~~
^

–10–

Great Fion is hunting *There*
GRAINNE **~~So~~ FIONN is hunting in our woods, ~~and there~~ is nothing on**
Fion
earth or in heaven ~~which he~~ cannot overcome.
^

is
DIARMUID **If it ~~be~~ a black boar without bristles he may not overcome**
it. I am drawn ~~along~~ like a fish in a net. ~~For many~~ *I*
have [?*thence*] [?] *my* [?*death*]
~~nights I have~~ dreamed , **~~of this fiercely tusked fate of mine~~**
~~and for many days its dark shadow has floated in front~~ of
~~me~~. ~~Then,~~ (yesterday), I saw the SPINNING WOMAN in the wood
~~forest~~. And now ~~there comes news of this boar from KING~~
~~CORMAC'S country.~~ *you bring me the news.*

GRAINNE **We should not have lingered in this silent valley, DIARMUID,**
it is full of fears
~~its silence has hatched out strange fears~~ . You remember
and dream too much. ~~But~~ why should you fear my ~~odl~~ Nurse
~~Why should you not remember that~~ it was she who cast sleep
upon FIONN'S eyes ~~so~~ that we might escape together ?"

cast spell on
DIARMUID **She ~~enchanted~~ FIONN, and I was glad; but even as I watched**
him in sleep I knew that the day would come when she would
cast her spells upon me. It is turn and turn about always.

GRAINNE **FIONN has made peace.**

this
DIARMUID **Better war than ~~that he should come~~ hunting ~~the boar in my~~**
~~country~~ – Maybe it was she who has woven a spell to bring

[NLI 8777(9), 12r]

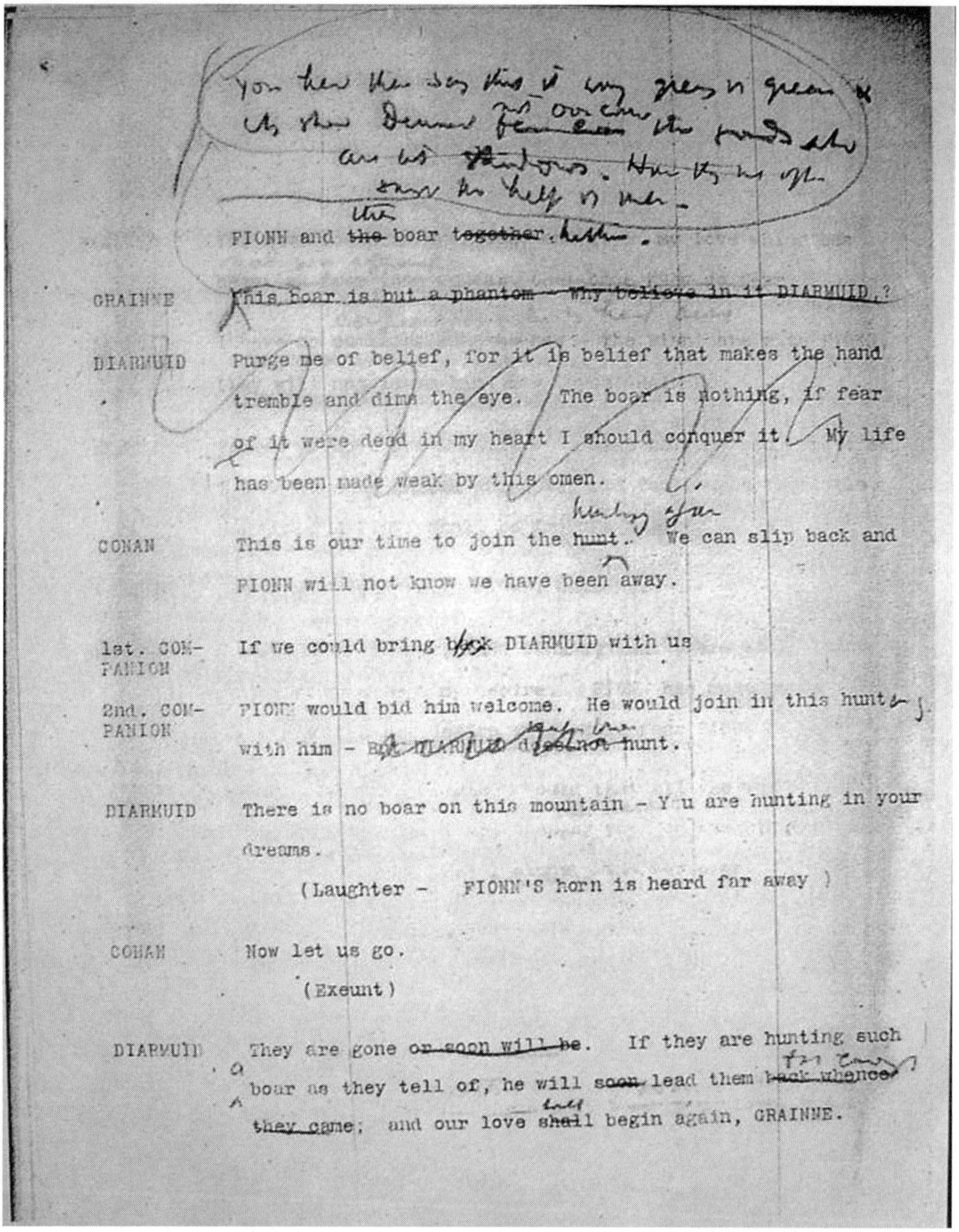

FIONN and ~~the~~ boar ~~together~~.

GRAINNE ~~This boar is but a phantom - Why believe in it DIARMUID ?~~

DIARMUID Purge me of belief, for it is belief that makes the hand tremble and dims the eye. The boar is nothing, if fear of it were dead in my heart I should conquer it. My life has been made weak by this omen.

CONAN This is our time to join the hunt. We can slip back and FIONN will not know we have been away.

1st. COMPANION If we could bring back DIARMUID with us

2nd. COMPANION FIONN would bid him welcome. He would join in this hunt with him - ~~But DIARMUID does not~~ hunt.

DIARMUID There is no boar on this mountain - Y u are hunting in your dreams.

(Laughter - FIONN'S horn is heard far away)

CONAN Now let us go.

(Exeunt)

DIARMUID They are gone ~~or soon will be~~. If they are hunting such boar as they tell of, he will ~~soon~~ lead them ~~back whence they came~~; and our love shall begin again, GRAINNE.

[NLI 8777(9), 12r]

You heard them say that it was grey or green &
not over come
why shoud Dermuid ~~fear even~~ the gods who
are but **–11–** *shadows. Hav they not oftn*
sought the help of men –
this

FIONN and ~~the~~ boar ~~together.~~ *hither.*

GRAINNE **~~This boar is but a phantom – Why believe in it DIARMUID, ?~~**

DIARMUID **Purge me of belief, for it is belief that makes the hand tremble and dims the eye. The boar is nothing, if fear of it were dead in my heart I should conquer it. My life has been made weak by this omen.**

hunting again
CONAN **This is our time to join the ~~hunt~~. We can slip back and FIONN will not know we have been away.**

1st. COMPANION **If we could bring ~~back~~ DIARMUID with us**

2nd. COMPANION **FIONN would bid him welcome. He would join in this hunt** *ing*
[?~~*keeps*~~] [?*from*]
with him – ~~But DIARMUID does not hunt~~.

DIARMUID **There is no boar on this mountain – You are hunting in your dreams.**

(Laughter – FIONN'S horn is heard far away)

CONAN **Now let us go.**

(Exeunt)

DIARMUID **They are gone ~~or soon will be~~. If they are hunting such**
a *far enough*
boar as they tell of, he will ~~soon~~ lead them ~~back whence~~
will
~~they came~~; and our love ~~shall~~ begin again, GRAINNE.

-1 WBY first wrote and circled the first sentence at the head of the page, then added the second sentence and circled both together, to substitute for line 2.

11 WBY clearly intended to cancel the second word of his trial substitution, also.

-12-

GRAINNE You have loved me overmuch, and it is my love which has {made you afraid.} ~~begotten fear into a heart that once knew no fear~~.

DIARMUID I have no c~~omrades in arms now~~ {companions to watch by my [illegible]} - The Fiani are with FIONN, they will not leave him, nor I you GRAINNE.

GRAINNE Forget my love for a while. I will help you to forget it. I will take up shield and spear and follow you to battle, and you and FIONN shall be friends again.

DIARMUID Can I be friends with FIONN, GRAINNE?

GRAINNE I said to my father, KING CORMAC, that there could be no right ~~on~~ {over} me except my desire. FIONN has made peace - He has forgotten his desire - You need fear FIONN no longer.

DIARMUID (Taking her in his arms) Would that all the world should forget you so that I might en~~joy~~ {the kindred} you for ever in the ends of the earth - ~~You and I alone - and for ever~~.

GRAINNE You ~~must win my love~~ {I am of those that are won} in battle.

DIARMUID Have I not won you ?

GRAINNE I must be won again and again

DIARMUID It was not by ~~feats of arms~~ {battle} that ~~I won your~~ {won} love, but by the desire {[illegible]} of the eyes

[NLI 8777(9), 13r]

–12–

GRAINNE **You have loved me overmuch, and it is my love which has**
made you afraid.
~~**begotten fear into a heart that once knew no fear.**~~

companions to make my heart [?*rise*]
DIARMUID **I have no ~~comrades in arms now~~ – The Fiani are with FIONN,**
they will not leave him, nor I you GRAINNE.

GRAINNE **Forget my love for a while. I will help you to forget it.**
I will take up shield and spear and follow you to battle,
and you and FIONN shall be friends ~~again~~.

DIARMUID **Can I be friends with FIONN, GRAINNE?**

GRAINNE **I said to my father, KING CORMAC, that there could be no**
over
right ~~on~~ me except my desire. FIONN has made peace – He
has forgotten his desire – You need fear FIONN no longer.

DIARMUID **(Taking her in his arms) Would that all the world should**
[?*still*] [? *know*]
forget you so that I might ~~enjoy~~ you for ever in the ends
of the earth – ~~You and I alone – and for ever~~.

I am of those that are won
GRAINNE ~~**You must win my love**~~ **in battle.**

DIARMUID **Have I not won you ?**

GRAINNE **I must be won again and again**

battle *your*
DIARMUID **It was not by ~~feats of arms~~ that I ~~won your love~~, but by**
that is in
the desire ~~of~~ the eye~~,~~ *s*

18 WBY evidently did not intend to cancel "love".

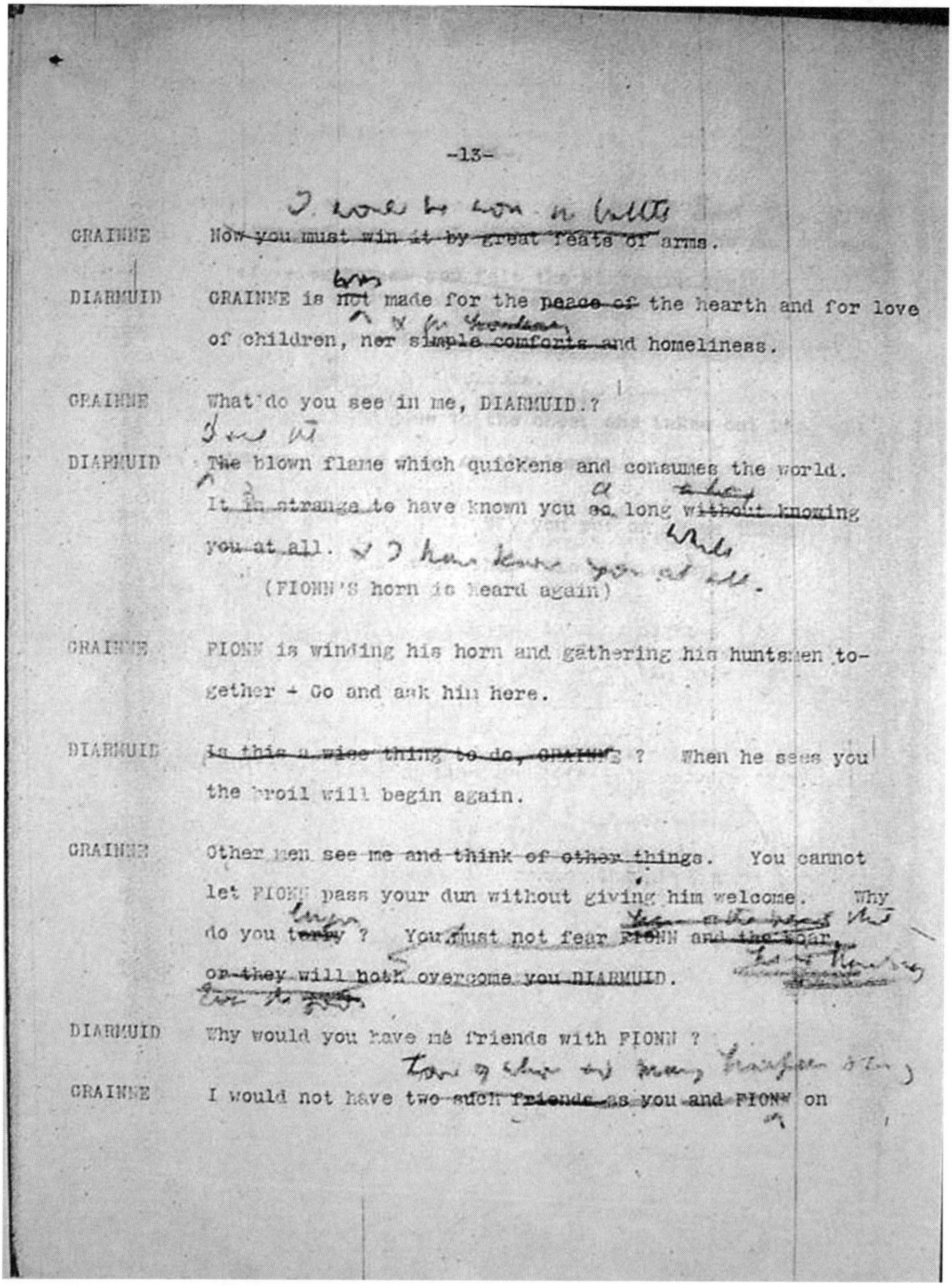

-13-

GRAINNE ~~Now you must win it by great feats of~~ arms.

DIARMUID GRAINNE is ~~not~~ made for the ~~peace of~~ the hearth and for love of children, ~~nor simple comforts a~~nd homeliness.

GRAINNE What do you see in me, DIARMUID.?

DIARMUID The blown flame which quickens and consumes the world. It ~~is strange to~~ have known you ~~so~~ long ~~without knowing you at all~~.

(FIONN'S horn is heard again)

GRAINNE FIONN is winding his horn and gathering his huntsmen together + Go and ask him here.

DIARMUID ~~Is this a wise thing to do, GRAINNE~~ ? When he sees you the broil will begin again.

GRAINNE Other men see ~~me and think of other things~~. You cannot let FIONN pass your dun without giving him welcome. Why do you ~~tarry~~ ? You must not fear ~~FIONN~~ and ~~the boar,~~ ~~or they will both overcome you DIARMUID~~.

DIARMUID Why would you have me friends with FIONN ?

GRAINNE I would not have two ~~such friends as you and FIONN~~ on

[NLI 8777(9), 14r]

–13–

I would be won in battle
GRAINNE **~~Now you must win it by great feats of~~ arms.**
was
DIARMUID **GRAINNE is ~~not~~ made for the ~~peace of~~ the hearth and for love**
^ *& for ~~homelines~~*
of children, ~~nor~~ ~~simple comforts and~~ homeliness.

GRAINNE **What do you see in me, DIARMUID ?**
I see the
DIARMUID ^**~~The~~ blown flame which quickens and consumes the world.**
I *a* *~~[?a] [?time]~~*
~~It is strange to~~ have know you ~~so~~ long ~~without knowing~~
~~you at all.~~ *while*
& I have known you at all.
(FIONN'S horn is heard again)

GRAINNE **FIONN is winding his horn and gathering his huntsmen to-**
gether – Go and ask him here.

DIARMUID **~~Is this a wise thing to do, GRAINNE~~ ? When he sees you**
the broil will begin again.

GRAINNE **~~Other men see me and think of other things.~~ You cannot**
let FIONN pass your dun without giving him welcome. Why
linger *~~Finn or the boar that~~*
do you ~~tarry~~ ? ~~You must not fear FIONN and the boar,~~
~~he is hunting~~
~~or they will both overcome you DIARMUID.~~
~~Even the gods~~
DIARMUID **Why would you have me friends with FIONN ?**
two of whom so many harpers sing
GRAINNE **I would not have ~~two such friends as you and FIONN~~ on**
^

---

2 WBY evidently canceled the word following the one he intended.

14–15 WBY evidently intended to cancel "FIONN" when he first revised the TS. He afterward canceled what he had substituted.

[NLI 8777(9)]

[15r]

[?said/say] you wer
different sides. I would have you friends as you ~~were~~ ^
~~before either of you felt the weakening spell of~~ GRAINNE.

you
DIARMUID **FIONN has made peace with me, ~~and it is certain that~~ I**
&
must go ~~to~~ bid him welcome.

(GRAINNE goes to the chest and takes out her gold ornaments, and puts on the land)

DIARMUID **Is it for FIONN, GRAINNE, you put on these things ? For me you have not worn them this many a day.**

GRAINNE **We two are common to each other by night and by day, but FIONN I have not seen since I left him asleep at my father's table.**

DIARMUID **GRAINNE, oh my instinctive life – Oh strange craving which tears and then pursues me like a hound.**

GRAINNE **FIONN has gathered his huntsmen and his hounds together – Go bid him welcome.**

DIARMUID **You said I was to put fear aside, and that there would be no boar to kill me.**

(He goes out)

GRAINNE **But you must go without fear.**

[16r]

–15–

(She goes to the chest and takes out the boretto and the cloak – A long pause, at the end of which the FOSTER: MOTHER enters with her spinning wheel)

Oh MOTHER, so you have come again, and I knew you were
wood
coming. DIARMUID saw you in the ~~forest~~ yesterday – Much
much is
has happened, ~~things are~~ happening now, and you have come to tell me what they mean.

FOSTER-MOTHER ~~I have been away in Alba where the King~~ was dying. I have come a long way dear child.

GRAINNE You are tired, MOTHER, and must rest. But presently we will talk, over the fire.

FOSTER-MOTHER I have come but for a little while – for a night's rest, and after daybreak will be gone again.

GRAINNE DIARMUID has gone to bid welcome to FIONN who is hunting ~~a great boar, which has escaped from KING CORMAC'S country.~~

FOSTER-MOTHER You have loved DIARMUID, and now you are waiting for FIONN.

GRAINNE MOTHER, I love DIARMUID, and DIARMUID and FIONN have made peace. ~~Will you come in here~~ ? But put your wheel away; you have come here to rest. Will you comein here

(pointing to a door)

and wait till the FIani who are coming here for food and

[NLI 8777(9)]

[17r]

–16–

drink ~~and rest have gone~~.

FOSTER-MOTHER They are coming, I ~~suppose~~, to take DIARMUID with them. He cannot refuse to hunt with them since he has asked them to his dun.

GRAINNE He must not hunt this boar with FIONN. This is so ? Tell me MOTHER.

FOSTER-MOTHER If you love DIARMUID as you did he will have no fear of the boar.

GRAINNE MOTHER that is what I told him. The Fiani are on their way here – Tell me before they come why I love DIARMUID and yet would see FIONN. Will FIONN see me with the same eyes he saw me when I used witchcraft over the wine in Tara – Will the pursuit begin again ?

(She goes to the door)

Hasten,MOTHER, to tell me these things for they are coming. Tell me above all things if this boar you say DIARMUID will go away to hunt is the boar of the story ?

FOSTER-MOTHER It is said that DIARMUID is but an earthly shadow of the god AONGHUS which is in heaven, and many boars shall he hunt and slay – Some may be without bristles and some may

5–8 The vertical line at the LH margin of the text, after the part ascriptions, may signal a questioning like the underlining of lines 2–4.

[18^{r}]

–17–

be black, but none shall slay him till his father shall call him away.

(The FOSTER-MOTHER goes through a doorway into another room – GRAINNE crosses the stage getting down to the Right – FIONN enters, followed by the COMPANIONS – They enter like tired men who have been hunting many days – They are armed with bows and spears and they rest on their spears and lean against the door post – FIONN goes down the stages and speaks to GRAINNE)

FIONN **We meet after a long betrayal. But, GRAINNE, I have made peace with you.**

GRAINNE **This peace has not come too soon. Too long have such chiefs as FIONN and DIARMUID been foes. That is why I sent for you FIONN.**

FIONN **Right glad I am to be friends with my old comrade, though he took GRAINNE from me.**

GRAINNE **I give you back your comrade, and your love of me is dead, and your heart light again. But I would** *know* **now, FIONN, that you have seen me if I were worth all these wars.** *tr*

FIONN *It may be that* ~~**I would begin them again, GRAINNE.**~~ **I have done you wrong by this peace – For your** ~~**hand's**~~ **sake I should** ~~**have dared**~~ *not have* [?*waited*]

[NLI 8777(9)]

[19^{r}]

–18–

to the end of time.

(He takes her hand)

DIARMUID GRAINNE, all are weary her and want food and drink – Let us to wine.

(Wine is brought in and GRAINNE gives some to FIONN, and DIARMUID and USHEEN go to the table and drink together)

OSCAR You should have been with us, DIARMUID, ~~in this hunt~~ – There has been no such hunt known as this – For three months we have been hunting and have crossed the woods and hills of Erie. Once the boar hid himself in the mountains of ^ ~~Actar~~, and we surrounded the mountain for a week ~~hunting the boar~~, till the herdsman came to tell us the boar was not there, but on the Actar hills where he had killed one thousand sheep.

1st. COMPANION Yes, to-day fifty of the Fiani are slain.

USHEEN It is certainly a god we are hunting, sent among us for the destruction of Erie. If we do not kill it, it will not leave any living men or cattle.

DIARMUID ~~I know nothing of these things~~ – I have been long out of earshot of the voices of Erie. Here I have hunted the deer for many months, and guarded my flocks and herds.

7–11 A single stroke cancels the second half of line 7 through line 11.

8 Was it WBY's intention to replace the canceled word "Actar" with a long dash?

[20r]

–19–

(CONAN enters accompanied by many men carrying horns and deer skins.)

CONAN **I, CONAN, Master of the household goods and of the Fiani bring deer skins as a peace offering from FIONN to this great house – This deer skin with its great antlers is a peace offering from FIONN to GRAINNE that it may be soft under her feet.**

(To the Crowd)

What woman would not have been glad to have seen FIONN kill that deer upon the slopes of Ben Gualbin, and to see him pull his great bow that no man, no, not even DIARMUID could pull. The boar was three bow shots distant from any bow but his, and it went so quickly that no other arrow could overtake it.

(DIARMUID, FIONN and USHEEN go up the stage and look at the boar skin – FIONN and GRAINNE walk down the stage.)

FIONN **I made peace for your sake GRAINNE. DIARMUID was young**
for his
and you loved him for his youth and ^ beauty, ~~and in Tara~~ I
[?*only*/*once*] [?] *that it* [?*may*]
thought ^ it was valour and renown that would have won you.

GRAINNE **If I went away with DIARMUID, it does not mean that the**
fame [?*has*]
~~great deeds~~ of FIONN, son of CUHL, have not always filled

[NLI 8777(9)]

[21r]

–20–

Harpers have told of you

e

me with wonder. ^Her{, in this gentle valley, we talk of your deeds often. ^I know well of your journey to Alba and of your valour there, and that is why I sent for you.

[?*Here*] *is why*

I would have you and DIARMUID friends.

FIONN Then why did you not send for me before ?

GRAINNE Until now you were DIARMUID'S foe.

FIONN ~~Now~~ think you I am DIARMUID'S foe no longer.

GRAINNE Now DIARMUID says that you hunt this boar, which has laid this country waste, in vain if it be a black boar without bristles.

FIONN DIARMUID says that ?

(Aside)

The boar is black and without bristles.

(Aloud)

This peace is a false peace. Ther *e* can never be peace between me and DIARMUID. Years had hidden from me the wrong he did me, but the sight of you, GRAINNE, has made it leap like a flame.

(Turning from her to DIARMUID)

And I say this to DIARMUID now.

[22r]

–21–

DIARMUID **What says FIONN to me – that he who took my hand is already my foe again?**

GRAINNE **Let there be no more war, FIONN, I beseech you for my heart is bidden to both.**

FIONN **That is why there must be war. All the world loves GRAINNE, DIARMUID I love GRAINNE as I loved her when she deserted me for you. I have loved her all these years, but I would not wage war against a friend, even a friend who has betrayed me, longer than seven years. If you expected otherwise you were wrong to ask me to your dun. The question is now, as it was before – the question is ever the same – Which is the better a man's hand or a woman's breast.**

DIARMUID **Then, FIONN, the peace you made with me was peridious.**

FIONN **GRAINNE is free to choose now, as she was before; it is not my desire or yours, ~~FIONN~~ DIARMUID, it is GRAINNE who knows no law but her desire.**

GRAINNE **Then, if war there must be I am with DIARMUID**
(She goes to him)
Alas, I am an evil thing in these men, and DIARMUID you

16 Type deletion.

[NLI 8777(9)]

[23^{r}]

–22–

	saw clearly when you saw me as a flame that consumes. Yet I think no evil, but would see you friends, standing shoulder to shoulder against the plains of Erie. *foes*
DIARMUID	**(With exaltation) GRAINNE have no fear. You have brought about my escape from it – You have saved me from the mysterious forest, and its lurking danger. FIONN I shall overcome – Oh FIONN is as nothing at all !**
	(To FIONN)
	FIONN has said this peace is a false peace in him as ~~in~~ *it is* **me. He speaks well, and only our swords can bring peace.**
GRAINNE	**Now we shall witness the finest feats of arms in Erie. Happy is he who lives to see such swordsmen matched against each other, and to watch the combat.**
	(Advancing between them)
	But no, this cannot be – for one of the greatest men must fall and that would be a sorrowful peace indeed.
	(The men cross their swords)
CONAN	**One of Erie's greatest chiefs shall be slain, so that there may be peace – Hear her say it – Then, who shall rid your fields of the pestilence that has come out of the forest, and has laid waste your fields, and harried your flocks.**

[24r]

–23–

1st COMPANION — **Yes, who shall rid the country of the boar if FIONN and DIARMUID slay each other. We want DIARMUID'S hounds.**

ALL — **We want their hounds.**

2nd. COMPANION — **DIARMUID sits by the fire and has not yet raised his spear to free his country of the boar. He sits by the fire and dreams.**

ALL — **DIARMUID is craven.**

CONAN — **Who shall kill the boar if DIARMUID and FIONN kill one another. GRAINNE is the most beautiful woman in Erie – Let AONGHUS the god of hunters bestow her upon him who kills the boar – Then, when the boar is killed, GRAINNE shall watch the flocks feeding upon the hillside, and the green corn growing in the fields, and FIONN and DIARMUID shall be friends.**

(DIARMUID turns to strike CONAN)

GRAINNE — **He is not worthy of your arm – Give me your sword, not you but I shall strike him.**

CONAN — **DIARMUID would strike me because I speak of the great boar of which he lives in great fear.**

FIONN — **DIARMUID has sat too long by the fireside and the Old Woman has scared him with her tales.**

[NLI 8777(9)]

[25^{r}]

–24–

(DIARMUID'S Henchmen intervene.)

Who are these ? Hs henchmen who would save him from the combat.

DIARMUID — FIONN lies. He knows why I do not go against the boar, and would force me to my fate rather than he would dare my sword. See how he shrinks from it.

(FIONN advances to the combat; as he does so the Crowd intervene, determined that there may be no fight.)

DIarmuid to GRAINNE – You see there is no way for men except the way of the gods, but if I fear it not I may conquer it still.

OSCAR — DIARMUID cannot accept this ordeal – FIONN you must not press it upon him.

USHEEN — DIARMUID must not join this hunt – CONAN this day you have done a wicked thing.

1st. COMPANION — If DIARMUID refuses to hunt DIARMUID is craven,

2nd. COMPANION — AONGHUS god of hunters shall decide it.

(Uproar among the hunters)

DIARMUID — Every man has his time – A spear is ~~for~~ to kill FIONN, an arrow waits for CAOILTE and a mysterious old age for USHEEN. I will hunt the boar with FIONN – FIONN is right. let us begin this hunt for it shall not be soon ended.

15 Type deletion.

[26r]

–25–

(He takes from the wall his light spear and shield)

GRAINNE **Take BROAD-EDGE your heavy spear, which has served you so well.**

(FIONN and the Hunters go out, and the others follow)

DIARMUID **This spear will do well enough against the boar, he is but a mortal beast and my fate is not in this hunt.**

(He takes his light shield from the wall)

GRAINNE **Take your great shield for this boar.'s tusks are keen, and he has killed many men.**

DIARMUID **This shield will do for any boar that is not blac *k* and without bristles.**

GRAINNE **DIARMUID, DIARMUID, forego this hunt.**

DIARMUID **Have no fear for me GRAINNE, for there is no fear in my heart.**

(DIARMUID breaks away and GRAINNE is left alone – She stand *s* looking, lost in thought – The FOSTER-MOTHER enters and sits down and begins to spin – After a moment ' s pause GRAINNE sees the FOSTER-MOTHER)

GRAINNE **MOTHER, how will all this end ? What end of the thread are you spinning now ?**

(The Old Woman rises from her seat)

FOSTER-MOTHER **I have done, see there is no more flax on the distaff.**

The rear cover (blank) is still attached and follows on directly.

[NLI 8777(4) a, 1r]

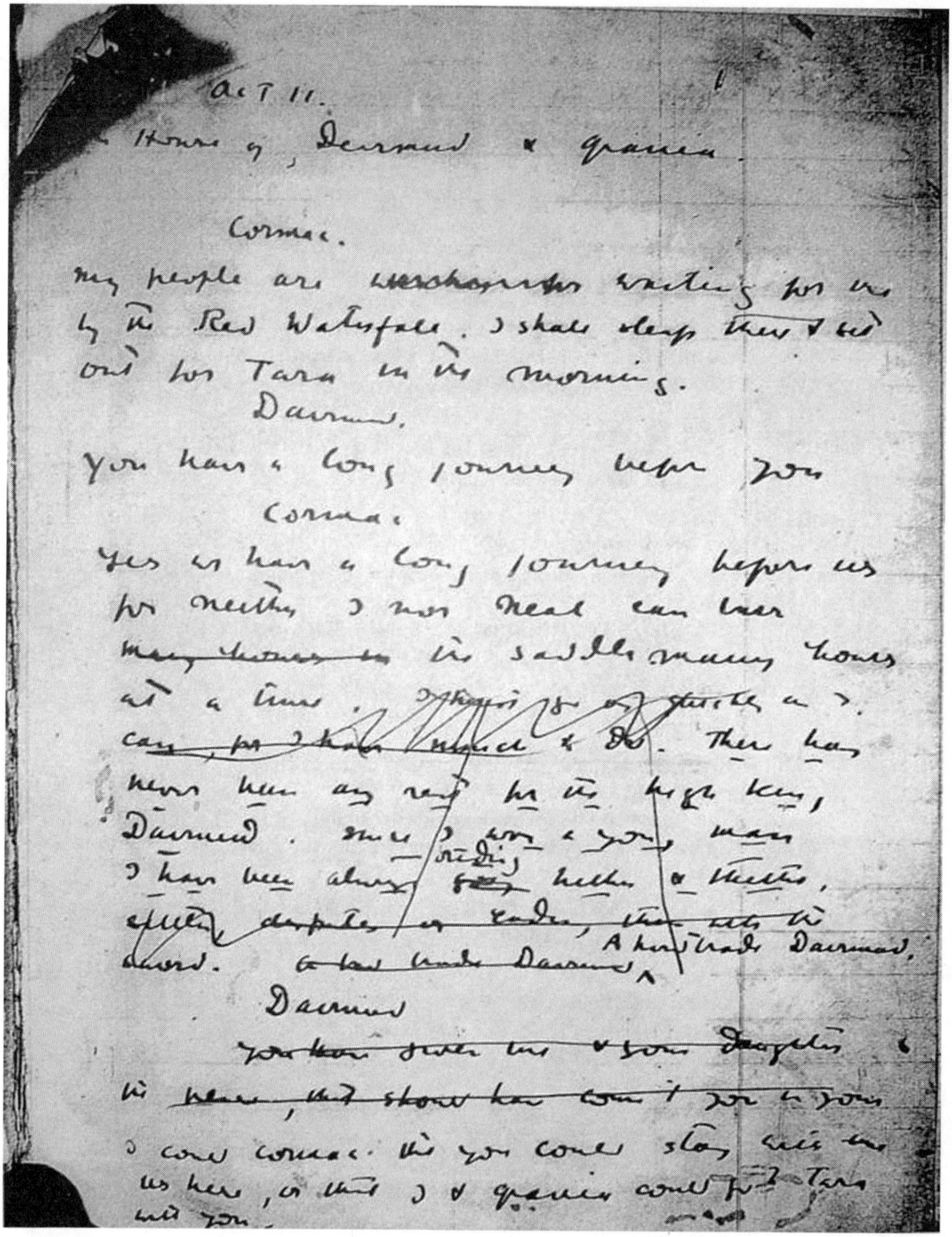

Act II.

House of Dermot & Grania.

Cormac.

My people are ~~[illegible]~~ waiting for us by the Red Waterfall. I shall sleep there & set out for Tara in the morning.

Dairmuid.

You have a long journey before you

Cormac.

Yes we have a long journey before us for neither I nor Neal can bear ~~many [illegible] in~~ the saddle many hours at a time. ~~[illegible] as I can, for I have [illegible] & do~~. There has never been any rest for the high king, Dairmuid. Since I was a young man I have been always riding ~~[illegible]~~ hither & thither, settling disputes ~~or [illegible], [illegible] the sword. [illegible] Dairmuid~~ A hundred trade Dairmuid,

Dairmuid

~~You have [illegible] me & your daughter~~ to the ~~[illegible], [illegible] should [illegible] you to [illegible]~~ your

I come Cormac. Will you come stay with us here, or shall I & Grania come to Tara with you.

Composite Text of Complete Act, Made Up of W. B. Yeat's Holograph and Typescript, Revised by W. B. Yeats and George Moore

[NLI 8777(4) a, 1r]

1

Act II.

The House of Deirmud & Grania.

Cormac.

My people are ~~waiting for~~ waiting for me
by the Red Waterfall. I shall sleep there & set
out for Tara in the morning.

Darmuid.

You have a long journey before you

Cormac

Yes we have a long journey before us
for neither I nor Neal can bear
~~many hours in~~ the saddle many hours
at a time. ~~I must go as quickly~~ as I
~~can, for I have much to do~~. There has
never been any rest for the high king
Darmuid.. since I was a young man
riding
I have been always ~~going~~ hither & thither,
~~settling disputes or ending them with the~~
A hard tradc Dairmuid.
~~sword~~. ~~A law under Dairmuid~~ ^

Darmuid

~~You have given me & your daughter~~
the ~~peace, that should have come to you in your~~
I could Cormac that you could stay with ~~me~~
us here, or that I & Grania could go to Tara
with you

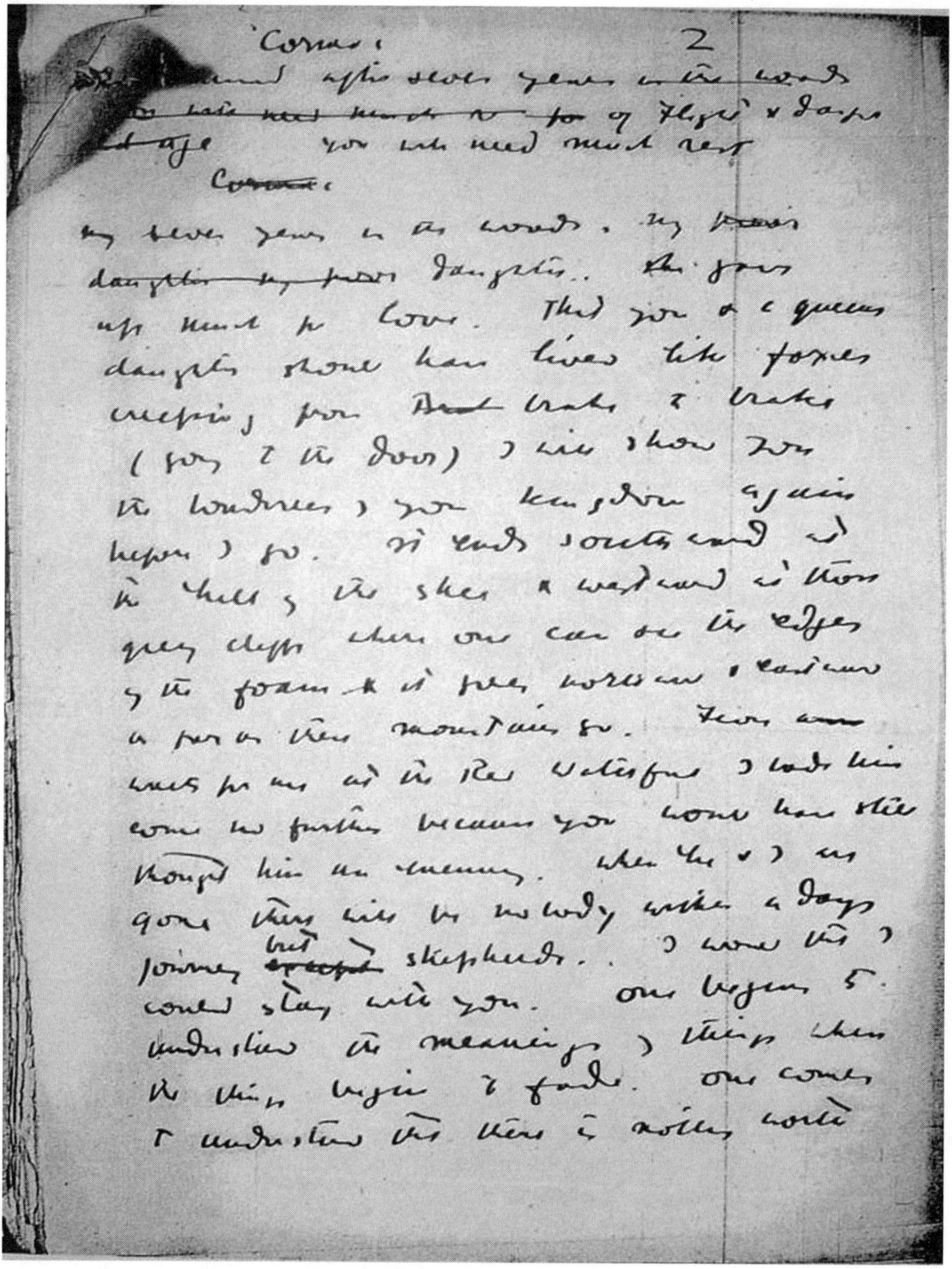

Conar: 2

~~[illegible]~~ after seven years in the woods ~~[illegible]~~ of flight & days ~~[illegible]~~ age you will need much rest

~~Conar~~:

My seven years in the woods. My ~~[illegible]~~ ~~daughter my poor~~ daughter.. ~~the~~ years upon years of love. That you a queens daughter should have lived like foxes creeping from ~~[illegible]~~ brake to brake (going to the door) I will show you the wonders of your kingdom again before I go. To the southward is the hill of the skies & westward is those grey cliffs where one can see the edges of the foam & to the northward & eastward a peak on these mountains go. Then [illegible] was for me at the Red Waterfall I could have come no further because you would have still thought him an enemy. When he & I are gone there will be nobody within a days journey but ~~[illegible]~~ shepherds. I would that I could stay with you. One begins to understand the meanings of things when the things begin to fade. One comes to understand that there is nothing worth

[NLI 8777(4) a, 2r]

2

Cormac
No Darmuid after seven years ~~in the woods~~
~~You will need much r to~~ of Flight & dangr
~~old age~~ You will need much rest

~~Cormac~~
~~my~~ seven years in the woods. My ~~poor~~
~~daughter my poor~~ daughter. ~~She~~ gave
up much for love. That you & a queens
daughter should have lived like foxes
creeping from ~~Break~~ brake to brake
(going to the door) I will show you
the boundaries of your kingdom again
before I go. It ends southward at
the hill of the Shee & westward at those
grey cliffs where one can see the edges
of the foam & it goes northward & eastward
as far as these mountains go. Fion ~~awai~~
waits for me at the Red Waterfal I bade him
come no further because you would have still
thought him an enemy. When he & I are
gone there will be nobody within a days
but
journey ~~except~~ shepherds. I would that I
could stay with you. One begins to
understand the meanings of things when
the things begin to fade. One comes
to understand that there is nothing worth

3 my] The typist who copied WBY's manuscript read, or supplied, "from"; cf. Berg(06), fol. 2r.

[NLI 8777(4) a, 3r]

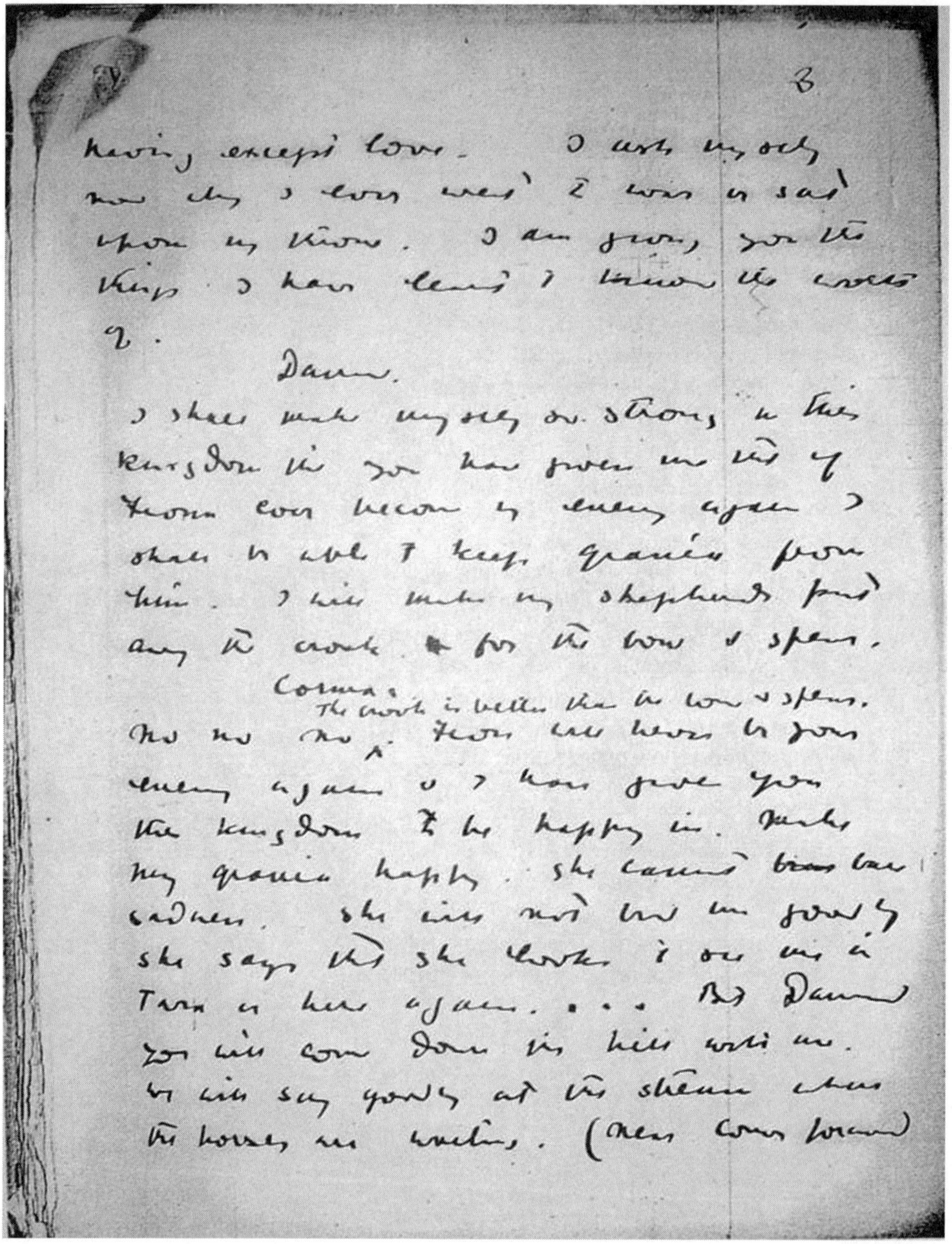
3

having except love. I ask myself
now why I lover wast & was so sad
upon my throne. I am going, for the
things I have learned I know the world
of.

Darm.

I shall make myself so strong in this
kingdom that you have given me that if
Fionn ever become my enemy again I
shall be able to keep Grania from
him. I will make my shepherds fight
and the crook for the bow & spear.

Cormac.

The crook is better than the bow & spear.
No no no. ^ Fionn will never be your
enemy again & I have given you
the kingdom to be happy in. Make
my Grania happy. She cannot bear live
sadness. She will not bid me goodbye
she says that she looks to see me in
Tara or here again. . . . But Darm
you will come down the hill with me.
We will say goodbye at the stream where
the horses are waiting. (they come forward)

[NLI 8777(4) a, 3^{r}]

3

having except love. I ask my self now why I ever went to war or sat upon my throne. I am giving you the things I have learnt to know the worth of.

Darmuid.

I shall make myself so strong in this kingdom that you have given me that if Fionn ever becomes my enemy again I shall be able t keep Grania from him. I will make my shepherds put away the crook ~~&~~ for the bow & spear.

Cormac.

The crook is better than the bow & spear.

No no no^. Fion will never be your enemy again & I have given you the kingdom to be happy in. Make my Grania happy. She cannot ~~brear~~ bare sadness. She will not bid me good by she says that she looks t see me in Tara or here again. . . . But Darmuid you will come down the hill with me. We will say good by at the stream where the horses are waiting. (Neal comes forward

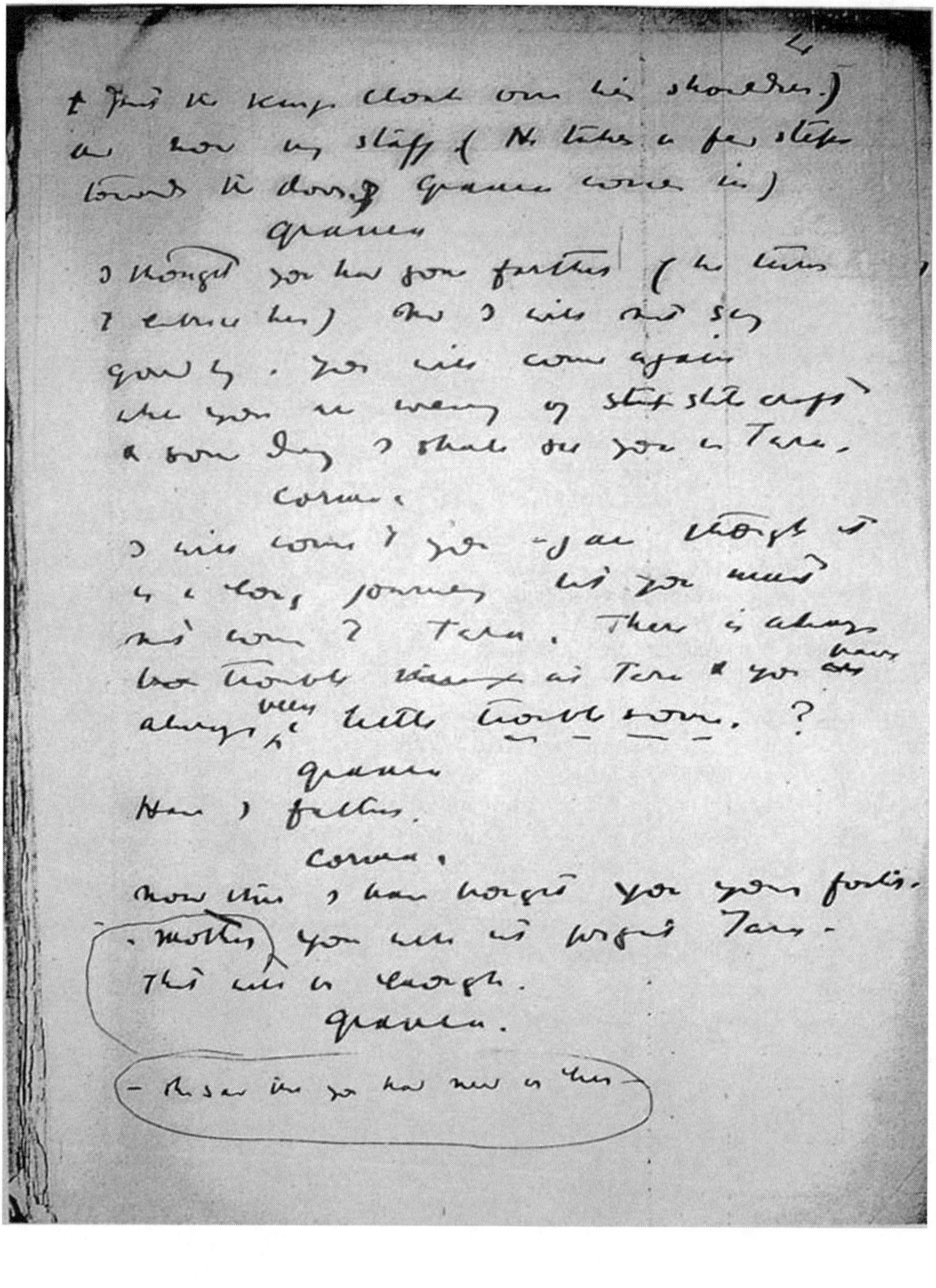
4

& puts the kings cloak over his shoulders)
and now my staff (He takes a few steps
towards the door & Grania comes in)
Grania
I thought you had gone farther (he turns
to embrace her) Then I will not say
good by. You will come again
when you are weary of strife & camps
& some day I shall see you in Tara.
Cormac.
I will come to you when I have thought
of a long journey but you must
not come to Tara. There is always
too much trouble at Tara & you have always
very little trouble now. ?
Grania
Have I father.
Cormac.
Now that I have brought you your father
mother you will not forget Tara.
This will be enough.
Grania.
– the same you have never in this –

[NLI 8777(4) a, 4r]

4

to put the kings cloak over his shoulder.)
and now my staff. (He takes a few steps
towards the door.)(Grania comes in)

Grania

I thought you had gone farther (he turns
to embrace her) No I will not say
good by. You will come again
when you are weary of ~~stat~~ state craft
& some day I shall see you in Tara.

Cormac

I will come t you again though it
is a long journey but you must
not come to Tara. There is always
have
~~tro~~ trouble ~~there~~ at Tara & you ~~are~~
been
always ^ a little trouble some. ?

Grania

Have I father.

Cormac.

Now that I have brought you your foster-

-mother ^ you will not forget Tara –
That will be enough.

Grania.

– she said that you had need of her –

[NLI 8777(4) a, 5r]

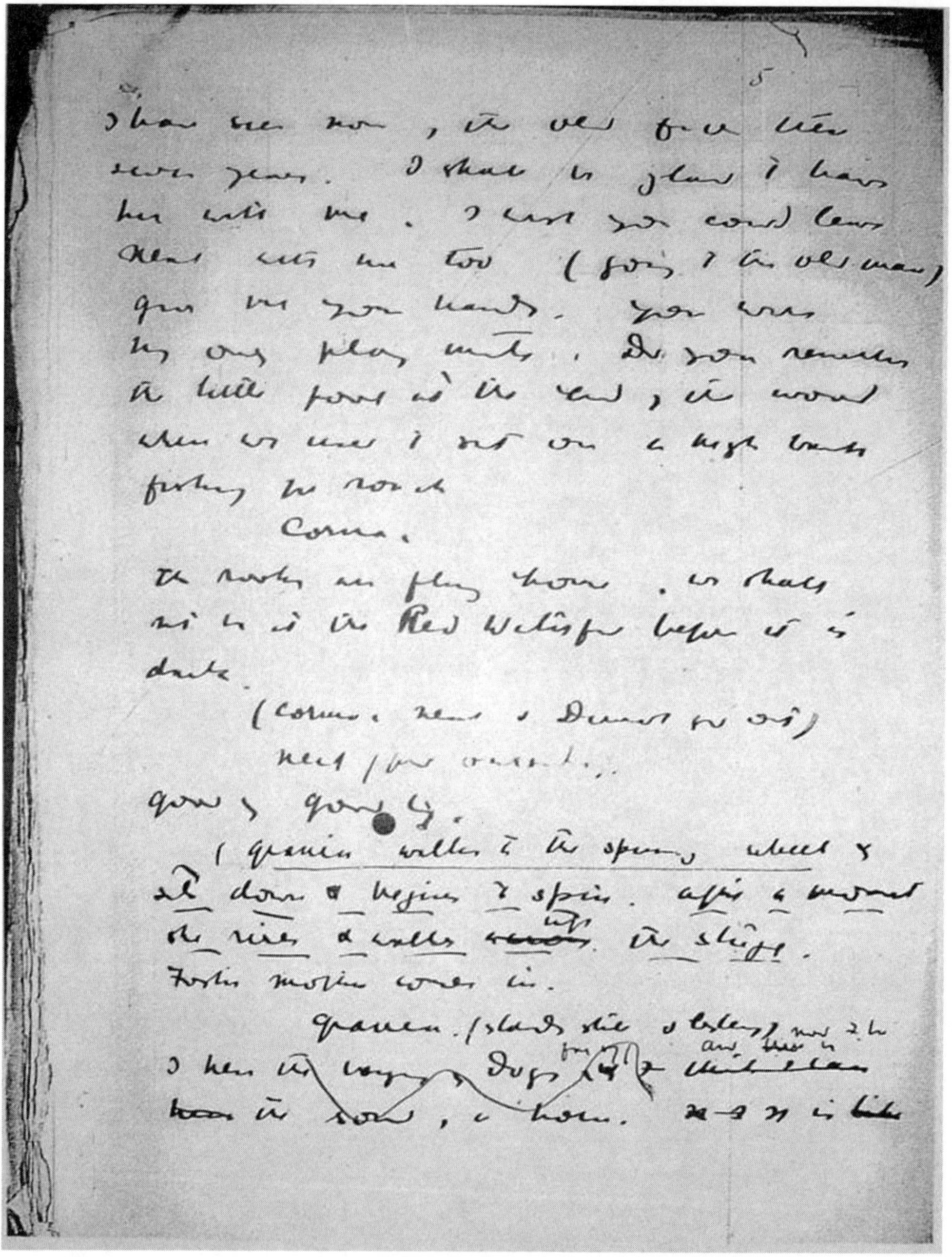

5

I have seen now, the old face these seven years. I shall be glad to have her with me. I wish you could have Aleel with me too (going to the old man) give me your hand. You were my only playmate. Do you remember the little pool in the wood, the wood where we used to sit on a high bank fishing for roach

Comma.

The rooks are flying home. We shall not be in the Red Wolf before it is dark.

(Comma, Aleel & Dermot go out)

[illegible]

Going & going [illegible].

(Grania walks to the spinning wheel & sits down & begins to spin. After a moment she rises & walks up the stage.

Foster mother comes in.

Grania. (stands still & listens [illegible]

I hear the baying of dogs [illegible]

[illegible] the road, a horn. [illegible]

[NLI 8777(4) a, 5[r]]

5

I have seen none of the old faces these seven years. I shall be glad t have her with me. I wish you could leave Neal with me too (going t the old man) give me your hands. You were my only play mate. Do you remember the little pond at the end of the wood where we used to sit on a high bank fishing for roach.

Cormac.

The rooks are flying home. We shall not be at the Red Waterfal before it is dark.

(Cormac, Neal & Darmid go out)

Neil (from outside).

good by good by.

(Grania walks to the spinning wheel & sits down & begins to spin. After a moment
up
she rises & walks ~~across~~ the stage. Foster mother comes in.

Grania. (stands still & listens) now F. M
far off and ~~there~~ is
I hear the baying of dogs. ~~& I think I can hear~~ the sound of a horn. ~~It I~~ It is ~~like~~

[NLI 8777(4) a, 6r]

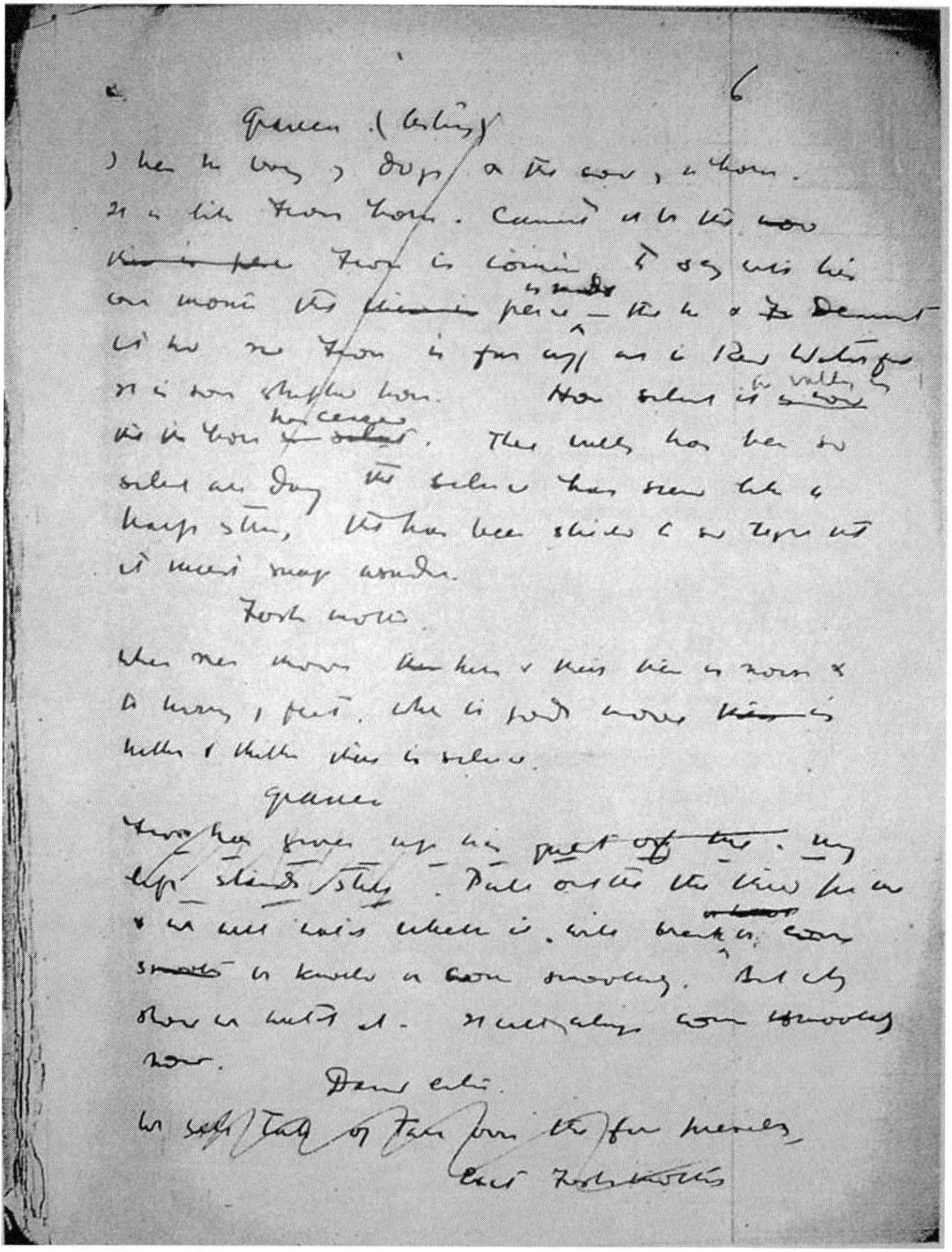

[NLI 8777(4) a, 6r]

6

Grania (listning)
I hear the baying of dogs & the sound of a horn.
It is like Fions horn. Cannot it be that ~~now~~
~~this is ple~~ Fion is coming to say with his
is made
own mouth that ~~this is~~ peice^ – that he & ~~Fi~~ Dermont
but [?how] [?since] Fion is far [?off] at th Red Waterfal
the valley is
It is some shepherd horn. How silent it ~~is now~~
has ceased
that the horn ~~is silent~~. The valley has been so
silent all day the silence has been like a
harp string that has been stretched to so tight that
it must snap asunder.

Foster mother.
When men move ~~thi~~ hithr & thithr their is noise &
th hurring of feet. When th gods move ~~there~~ is
hither & thither their is silence.

Grania
{f
Fion has given up his quest o{n me. My
life stands still. Pull out the thread for me
~~or knotted~~
& we will watch whethr it will break^ or ~~come~~
~~smooth~~ or knotted or com smoothly. But why
should we watch it. It will always com smoothly
now.
Darmd enters
We will talk of Tara over the fire [?presntly].
Exit Foster mother

1–7, 6, 14–15, 20–20^{+} The cancellations, and also the broken underlining of 14–15, are in pencil.

[NLI 8777(4) a, 7r]

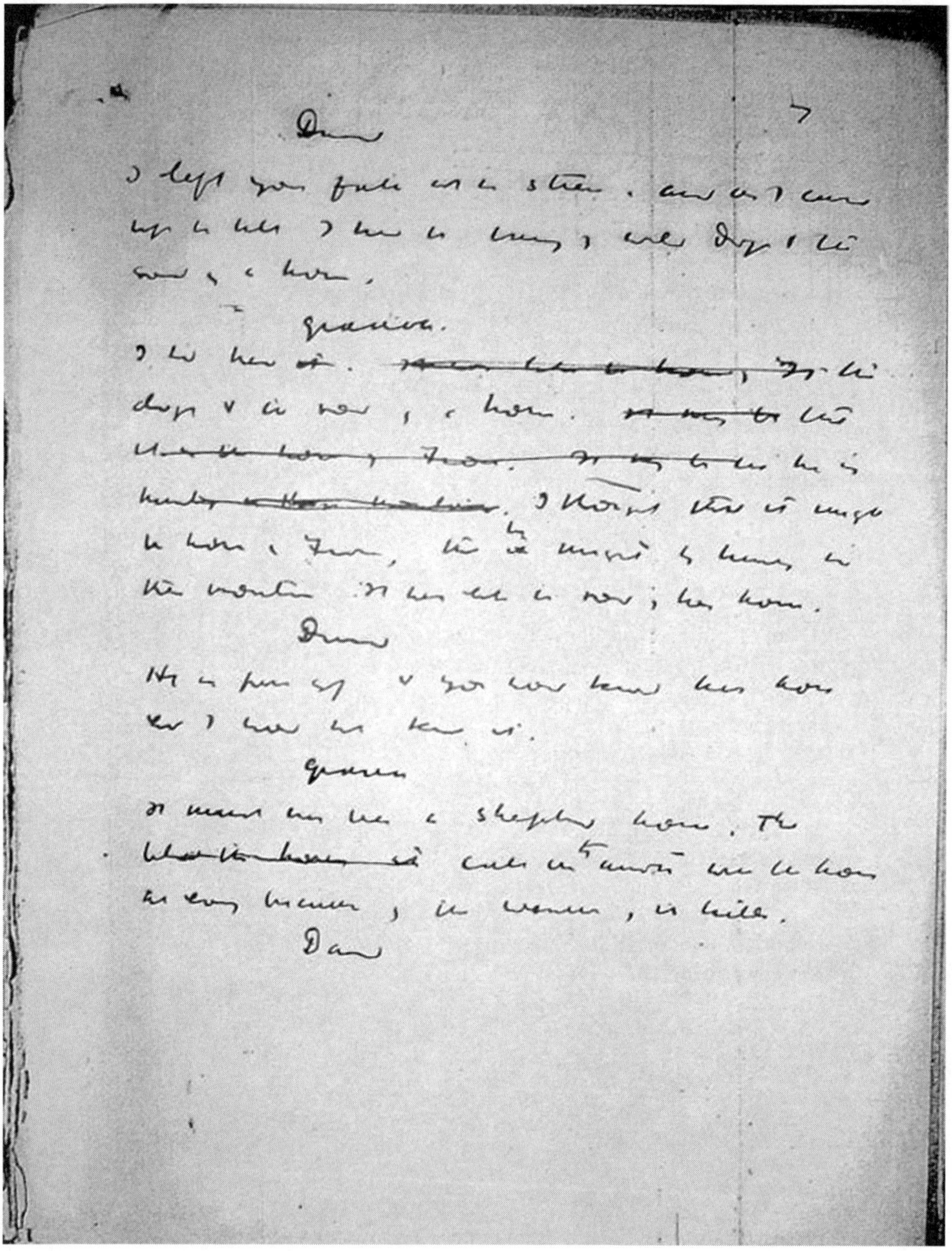

[NLI 8777(4) a, 7r]

7

Darmd

I left your father at th stream, and as I came
up th hill I heard th baying of wild dogs & the
sound of a horn.

Grania.

I had heard ~~it~~. ~~It was like a horn, It~~ the
dogs & th sound of a horn. ~~It may be~~ that
~~it is the horn of Fion. It may be his~~ he is
~~hunting in these mountains~~. I thought that it might
he
be horn of Fion, that ~~it~~ might be hunting in
the mountains. It was like th sound of his horn.

Darmd

He is far off & you never knew his horn
even I woud not know it.

Grania

It must have been a shepherd horn. The
to
~~blow thr hornes at~~ call on another with thr horns
at evning because of of the wolves in th hills

Darmd

[NLI 8777(4) a, 8r]

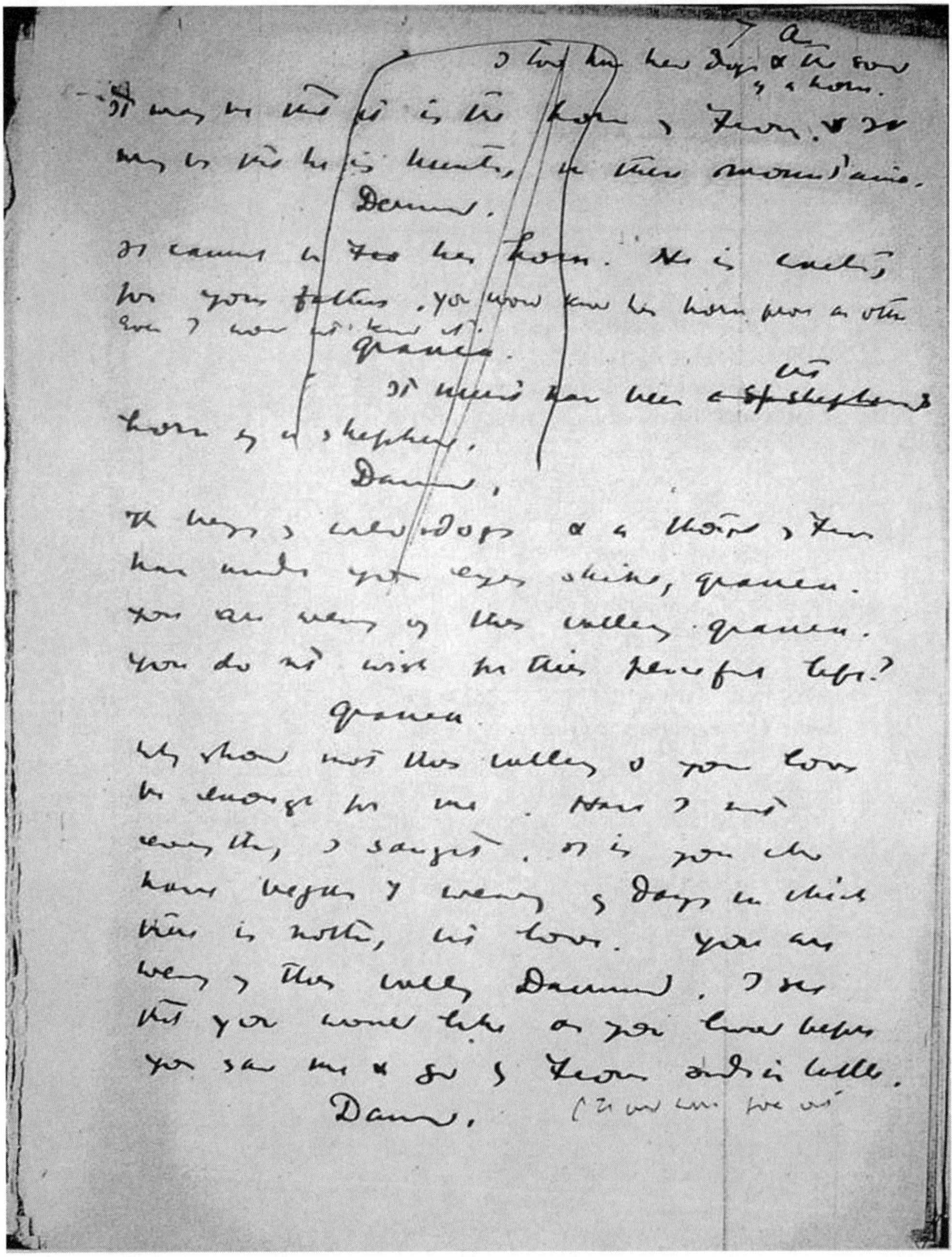

I [illegible] her days & the [illegible] of a horn.

It may be that it is the horn of Finn. & it may be that he is hunting in these mountains.

Diarmuid.

It cannot be Finn's horn. He is calling, for your father, you would know his horn from another even I [illegible] it.

Grania.

It must have been a shepherd's horn of a shepherd.

Diarmuid.

The [illegible] of [illegible] days & a horn of Finn has made your eyes shine, Grania. You are weary of this valley Grania. You do not wish for this peaceful life?

Grania

Why should not this valley & your love be enough for me. Have I not everything I sought. It is you who have begun to weary of days in which there is nothing but love. You are weary of this valley Diarmuid. I see that you would like as you lived before you saw me & [illegible] of Finn and his battles.

Diarmuid. [illegible]

[NLI 8777(4) a, 8r]

7 a

I too have heard dogs & the sound
of a horn.
It may be that it is the horn of Fion. ~~&~~ so
may be that he is hunting in these mountains.

Dermuid
It cannot be ~~Fin~~ his horn. He is waiting
for your father. You woud knew his horn from an other
Even I woud not know it.

Grania.
the
It must hav been ~~a sp shepherds~~
horn of a shepherd.

Darmuid
The baying of wild dogs & a thought of Fion
has made your eyes shine, Grania.
You are weary of this valley Grania.
You do not wish for this peaceful life?

Grania
Why should not this valley & your love
be enough for me. Have I not
every thing I sought. It is you who
have begun to weary of days in which
there is nothing but love. You are
weary of this valley Dairmuid. I see
that you would like as you lived before
you saw me & go by Fion and in battle.
(Fostr mothr goe out

Dairmd.

The typescript copy of the manuscript diverges at this point—cf. Berg(06), fol. 7r—which might suggest that a second page of manuscript following fol. 7 has been lost. Here, page and folio numbers do not coincide again.

4–5 "You woud know . . . know it" was inserted later. In his haste, WBY omitted "not" following "would".

18 like] Sense requires "live".

[NLI 8777(4) a, 9r]

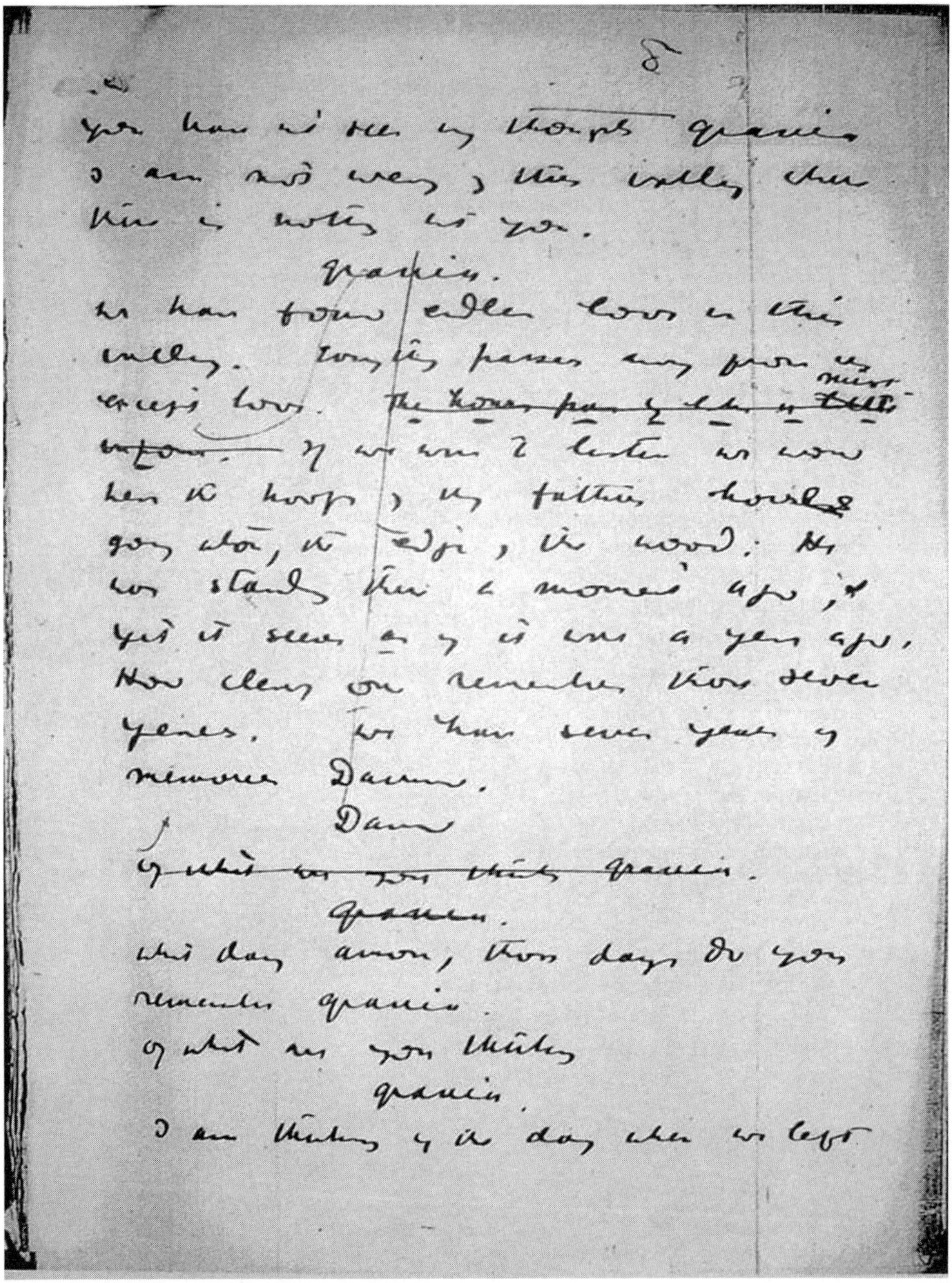

[NLI 8777(4) a, 9r]

8

You have not seen my thoughts Grania
I am not weary of this valley where
there is nothing but you.

Grania.

We have found endless love in this
valley. Every thing passes away from us
mist.
except love. ~~The hours pass by like a little~~
[?~~onpour~~.] If we were to listen we would
hear the hoofs of my fathers horses
going along the edge of the wood. He
was standing there a moment ago, &
yet it seems as if it was a year ago.
How clearly one remembers those seven
years. We have seven years of
memories Darmuid.

Darmuid

~~Of what are you thinkng Grania.~~

~~Grania.~~

What day among those days do you
remember Grania.
Of what are you thinking

Grania.

I am thinking of the day when we left

4–14 The cancellation lines are in pencil. The longer stroke is intersected by four short horizontals, as if it, in turn, was meant to be canceled; or possibly these short horizontals are intended as midline underlinings.

4–17 The typescript fair copy—Berg(06), fols. 8r–9r—substitutes different text.

[NLI 8777(4) a, 10r]

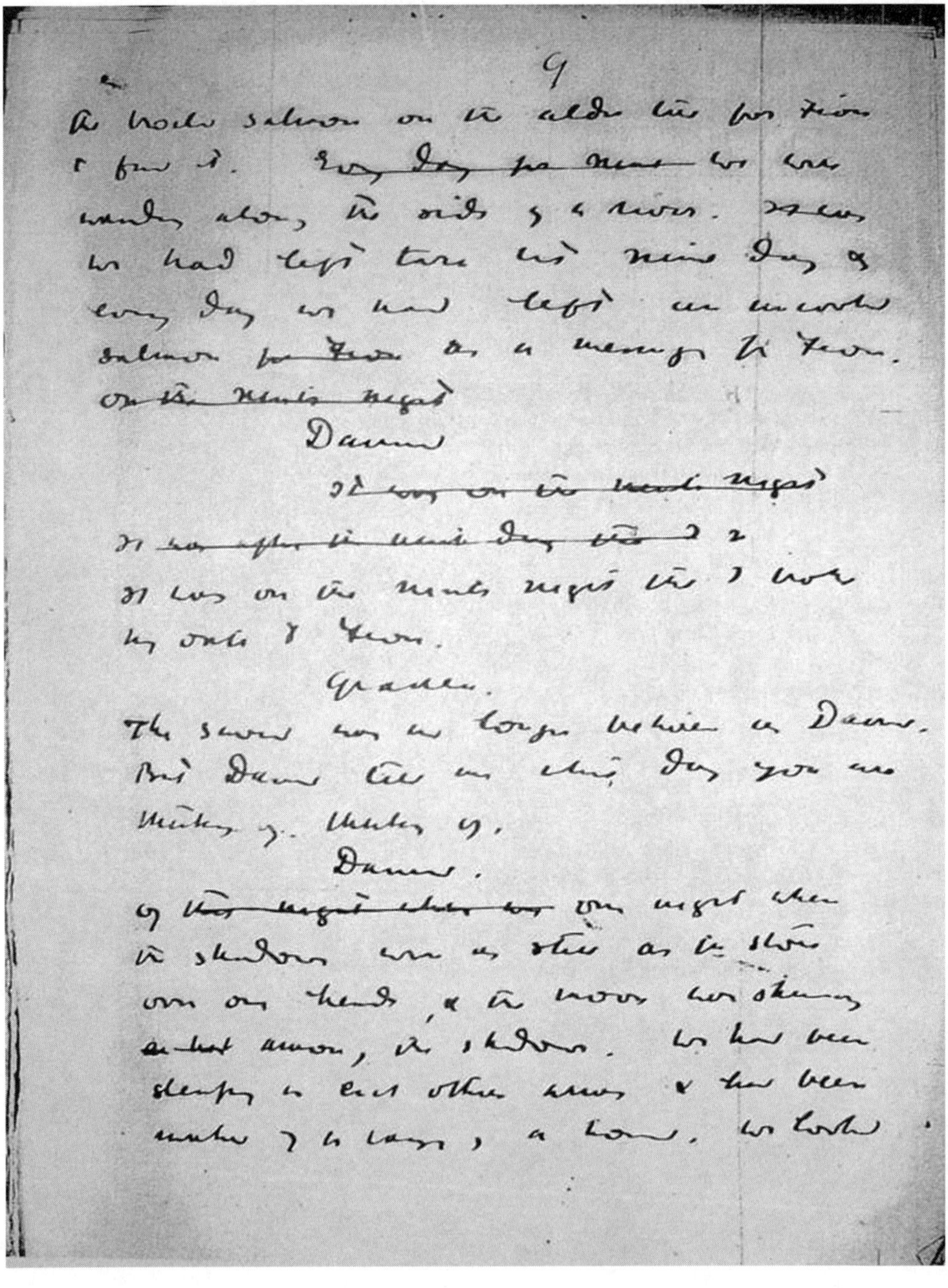

[NLI 8777(4) a, 10^{r}]

9

a broiled salmon on the alder tree for Fion t find it. ~~Evry day for nine~~ we were wandring along the side of a river. ~~It was~~ We had left tara but nine day & evry day we had left an uncooked salmon ~~for Fion~~ as a message for Fion. ~~On the ninth night~~

Dairmud

~~It was on the ninth night~~ ~~It was after the ninth day that I~~ & It was on the ninth night that I broke my oath t Fion

Grania.

The sword was no longer between us Diarmd. But Diarmd tell me what day you are ~~thinking of~~. thinking of.

Diarmud.

Of ~~that night when we~~ One night when the shadows were as still as the stars over our heads, & the moon was shining [?~~at best~~] among the shadows. We had been sleeping in each others arms & had been waked by th bayng of a hound. We looked

[NLI 8777(4) a, 11r]

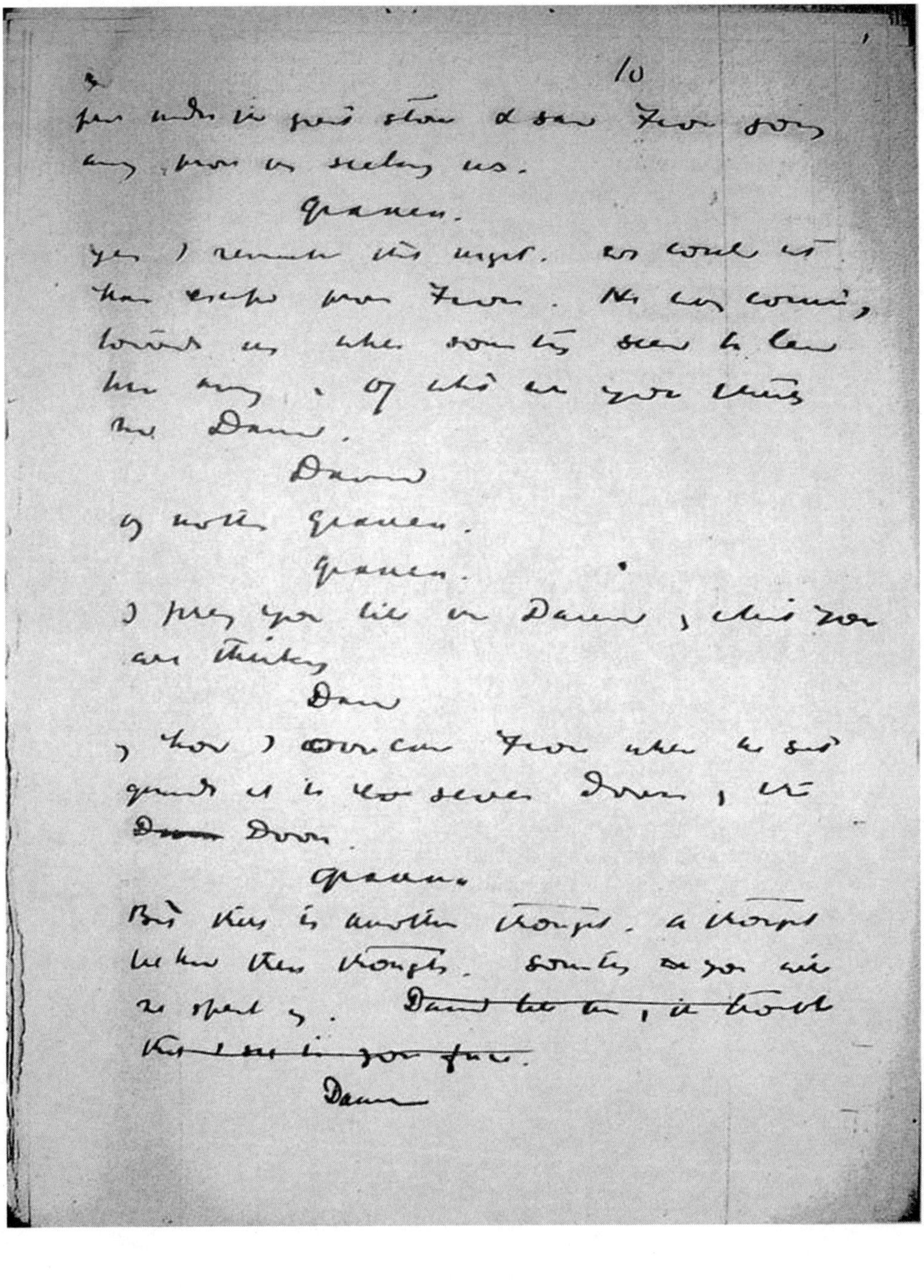

[NLI 8777(4) a, 11[r]]

10

from under the great stone & saw Fion going away from [?his]seeking us.

Grania.

Yes I remember that night. We could not have escaped from Fion. He was coming towards us when some thing seemd to lead him away. Of what are you thinkng now Diarmd.

Diarmud

Of nothing Grania.

Grania.

I prey you tell me Diarmd of what you are thinking

Diarmd

of how I overcame Fion when he set guards at th ~~ev~~ seven doors of the ~~Dun~~ Doon.

Grania

But their is another thought, a thought behind these thoughts. Somethg ~~we~~ you will not speak of. ~~Diarmd tell me of th troubl that I see in your face.~~

Diarmd

[NLI 8777(4) a, 12r]

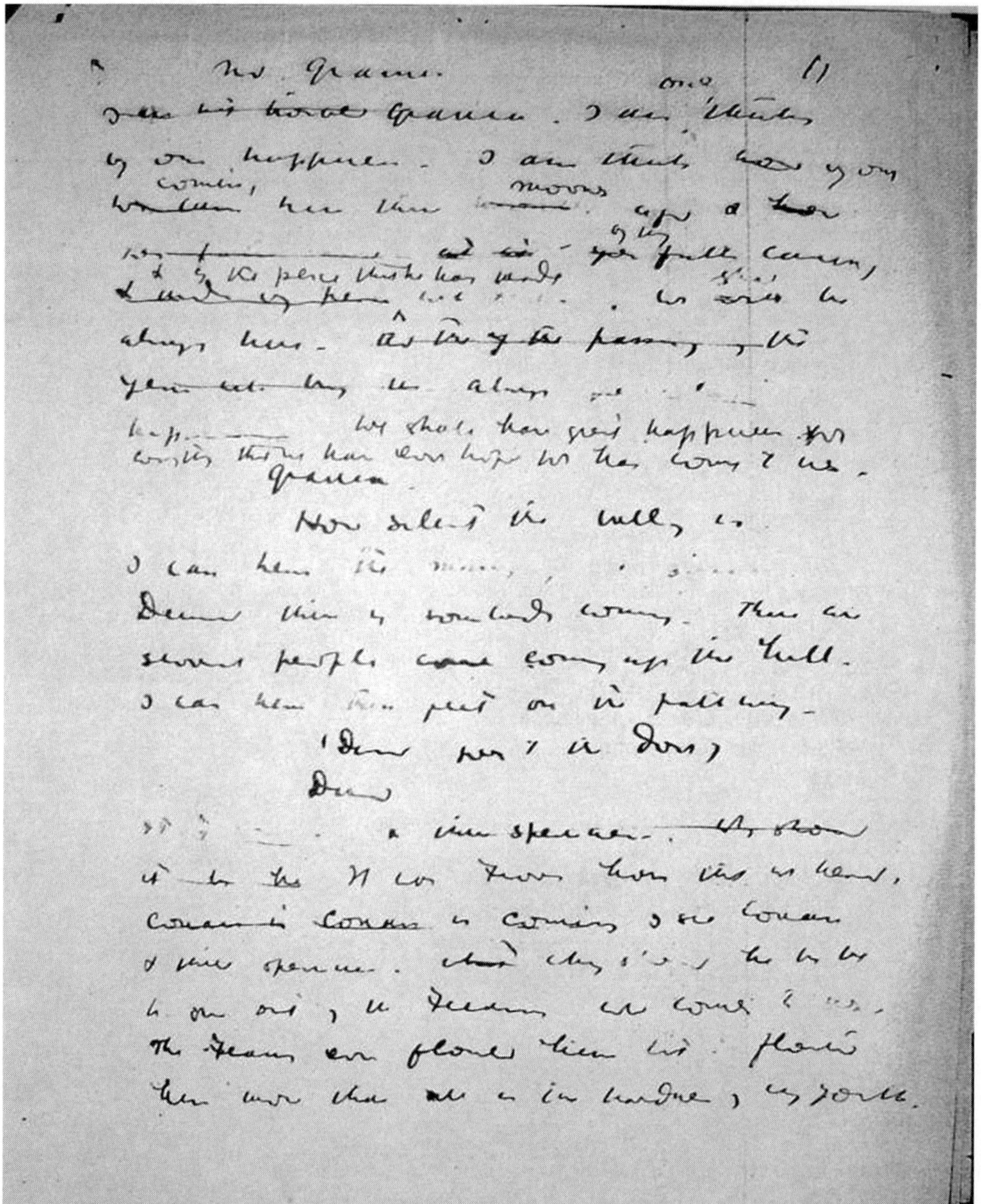

[NLI 8777(4) a, 12[r]]

11

No, Grania   only
~~I am in trouble Grania.~~ I am ^thinking
of our happiness. I am thinking ~~how~~ of our
coming   moons
~~we came~~ here three ~~months~~ ago & ~~how~~
of thy
~~your father came [?out] in~~ – your fathrs coming
& of the peice that he has made shall
~~& under my peice~~ ^with Fion.   We ~~will~~ be
always here – ~~And then of the passing of~~ the
~~years will bring us always greater & greater~~
~~happiness.~~ We shall have great happiness for
everything that we hav ever hopd for has come t us –

Grania.
How silent the valley is.
I can hear the mumur of the stream
Dermud there is somebody coming. There are
several people ~~come~~ coming up the hill –
I can hear their feet on the pathway –
(Dermd goes t th door)

Dermud
~~It is Conan & three spearmen. Why should~~
it be hi It was Fions horse tht we heard,
~~Cona is Conan is coming~~ I see Conan
& three spearmen – ~~that~~ why should he be be
th one out of th Feannna who comes to us –
The Feanna cver floutd him but I flouted
him more than all in the hardness of my youth.

---

8 The sentence following "happiness" was inserted later.

19 So WBY wrote. The Berg(06) typescript, fol. 11[r], interprets this as "never flouted him but I flouted".

[NLI 8777(4) a, 13r]

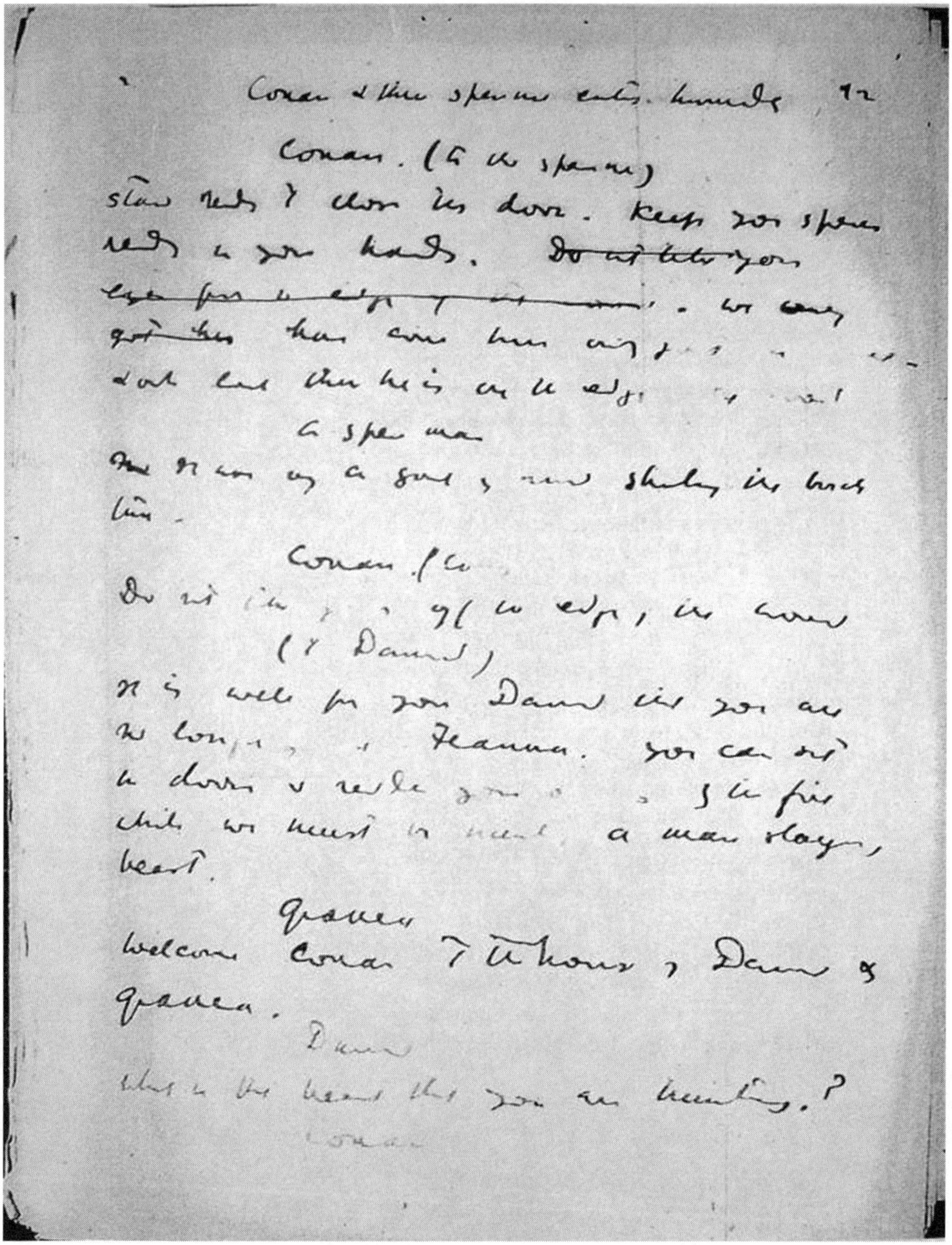

[NLI 8777(4) a, 13^{r}]

12

Conan & the spear men enter hurriedly

Conan (to the spear mn)
Stand ready t close the door. Keep your speres
ready in your hands. ~~Do not lift your~~
~~eyes from the edge of the wood~~ – we ~~only~~
~~got his~~ has come here only just in time –
Look but there he is on th edge of the wood.

A spear man
~~No~~ It was only a gush of wind shaking the birch
tree –

Conan (coming int the house)
Do not take your ey of the edge of the wood

(t Diarmud)
It is well for you Diarmd that you are
no longer of th Feanna. You can sit
in doors & redden your shins by th fire
while we must be hunting a man slaying
beast.

Grania
Welcome Conan t the house of Darmd &
Grania.

Darmd
What is the beast that you are hunting?

Conan.

[NLI 8777(4) a, 14r]

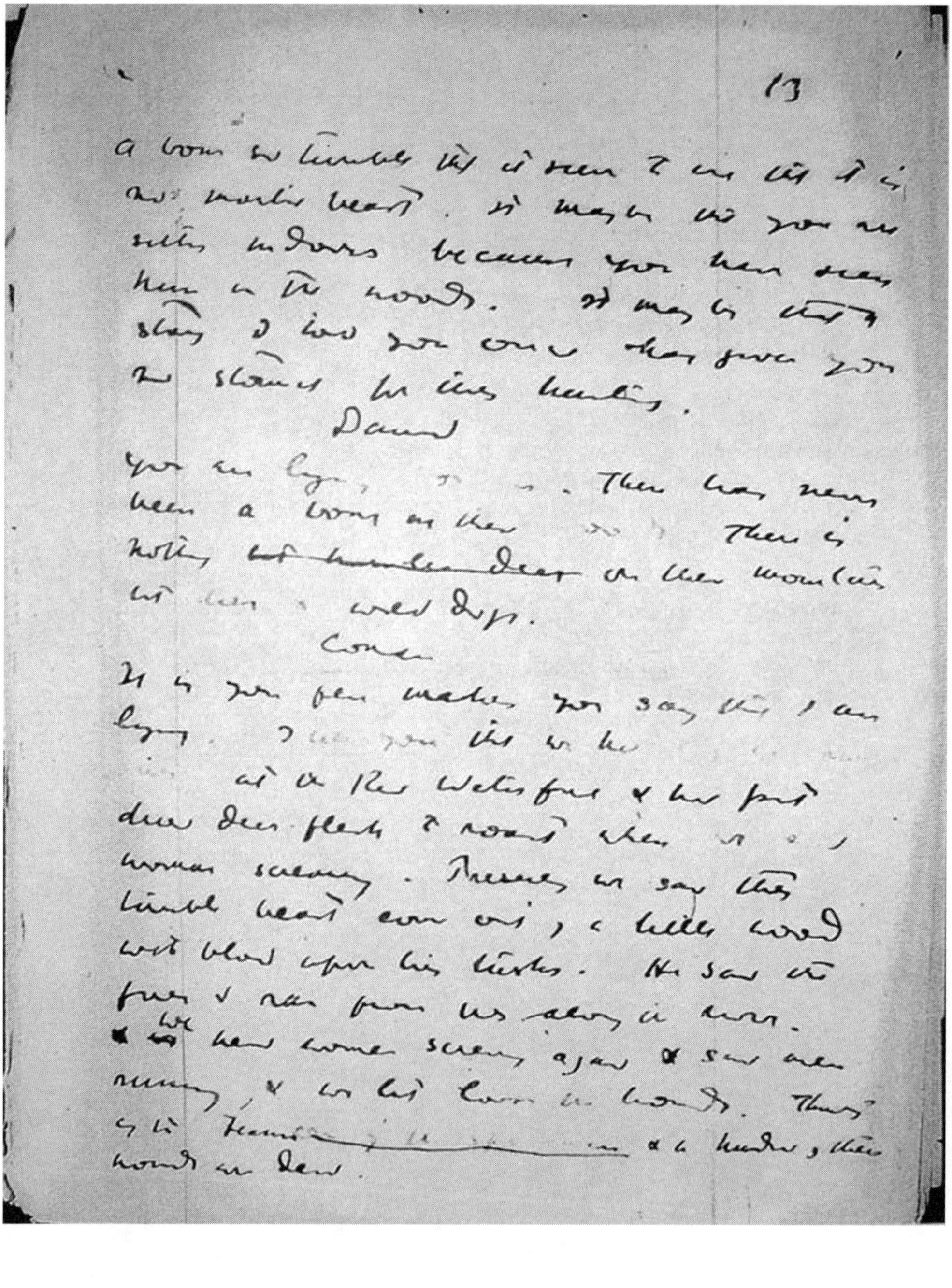

[NLI 8777(4) a, 14r]

13

A boar so terrible that it seems to us tht it is
no mortal beast. It may be that you are
sitting indoors because you have seen
him in the woods. It may be that a
story I told you once has given you
no stomach for this hunting.

Darmud

You are lying Conan – There has never
been a boar in these woods. There is
nothing ~~but harmless deer~~ on these mountains
but deer & wild dogs.

Conan

It is your fear makes you say that I am
lying. I tell you that we hav lighted our
fires at the Red Waterfal & had put
dried deer-flesh to roast when we heard
women screaming. Presently we saw this
terrible beast come out of a little wood
with blood upon his tusks. He saw the
fires & ran from us along th river –
We
~~& as~~ heard women screaming again & saw men
running, & we let loose th hounds. Thirty
of th Feana ~~[?com] of the spear men~~ & a hundred of their
hounds are dead.

21 The phrase "[?com] of the spear men" was written as a stage direction following "loose the hounds." WBY deleted it when he added the surrounding words ("Thirty . . . dead.").

[NLI 8777(4) a, 15r]

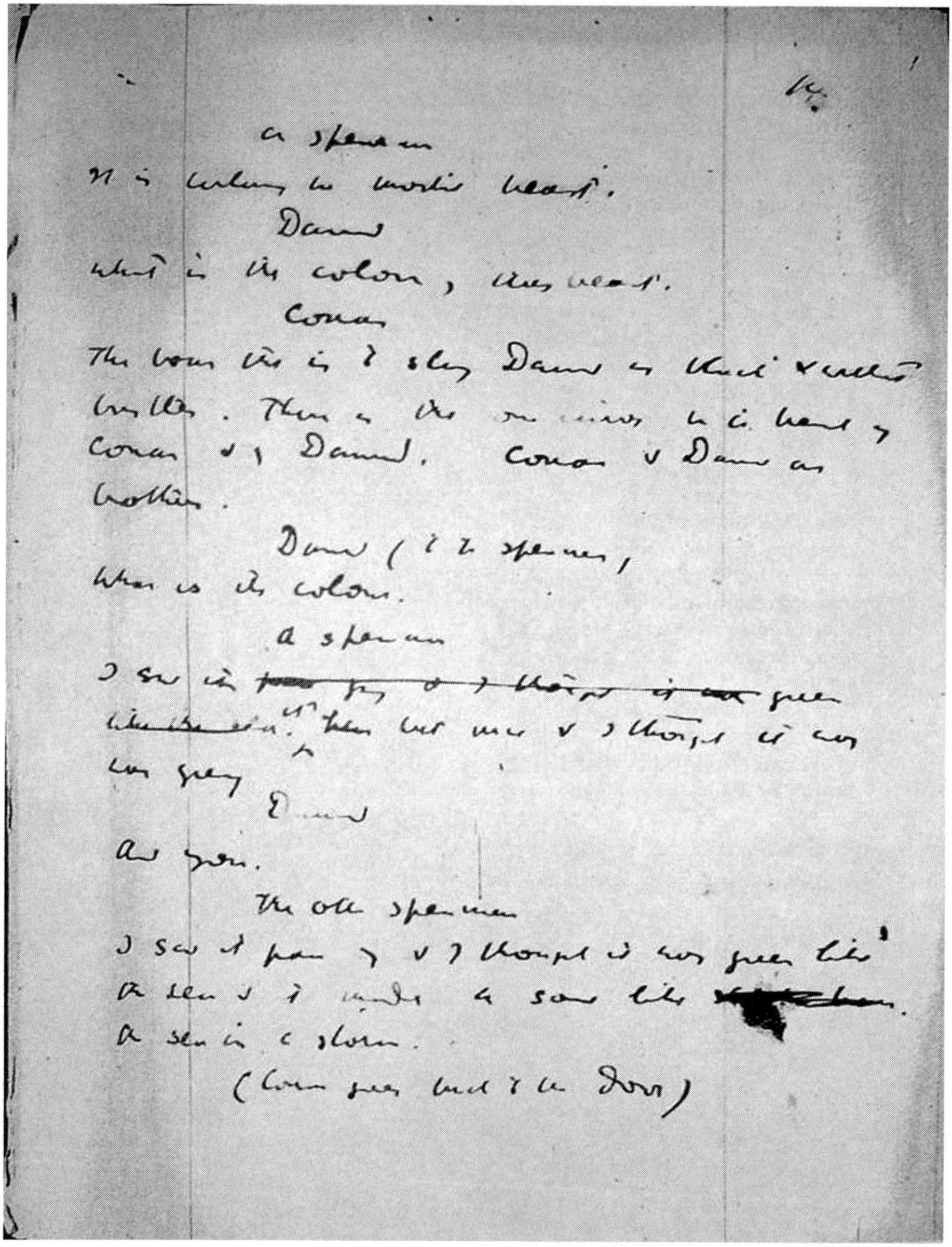

[NLI 8777(4) a, 15r]

14

A Spearman
It is certainly no mortal beast.

Darmd
What is the colour of this beast.

Conan
The boar that is to slay Darmd is black & without
bristles. There is this one terror in th heart of
Conan & of Darmud. Conan & Darmd ar
brothers.

Darmd (t th spear men)
What is its colours.

A sperman
I saw ~~it~~ ~~pass by & I thought it was green~~
it
~~like the sea.~~ ^ ~~have~~ but once & I thought it was
was grey

Darmd
And you.

The other spear man
I saw it pass by & I thought it was green like
the sea & it made a sound like ~~storm leaves~~.
th sea in a storm.

(Conan goes back t th door)

[NLI 8777(4) a, 16r]

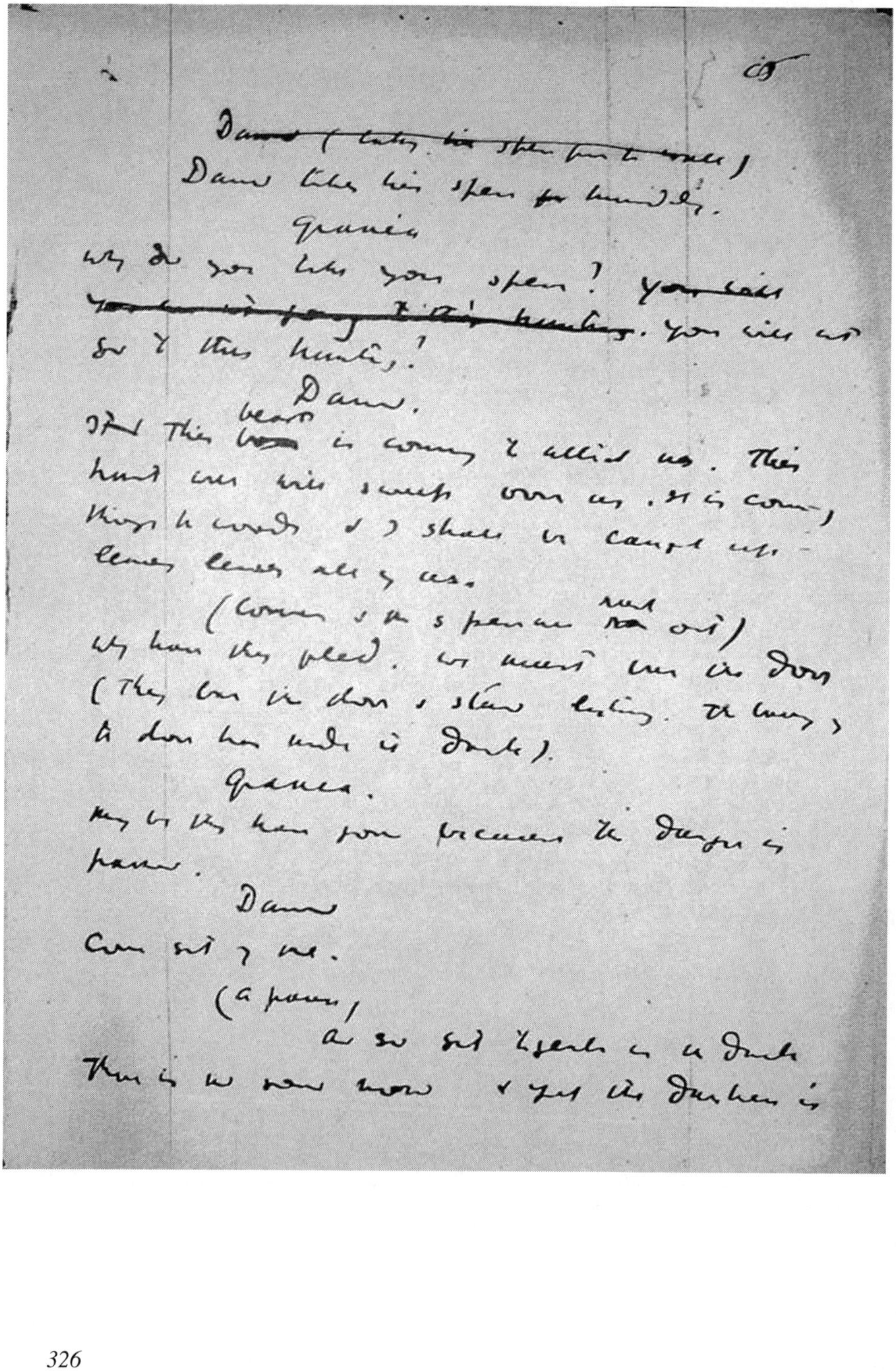
~~Dermot (takes his spear from the wall)~~
Dermot takes his spear [illegible].
Grania
Why do you take your spear? ~~Your [illegible]~~. You will not go to this hunting?
Dermot.
I feel this beast is coming to attack us. This hunt will sweep over us. It is coming through the woods & I shall be caught up. [illegible] all of us.
(Conan & the 5 persons run out)
Why have they fled. We must bar the door
(They bar the door & stand listening. The [illegible] the door has made it dark).
Grania.
May be they have gone because the danger is passed.
Dermot
Come sit by me.
(a pause)
As we sit together in the dark
There is no [illegible] & yet this darkness is

[NLI 8777(4) a, 16^{r}]

15

~~Darmd (taking his spear from th wall~~)
Darmd takes his spear ~~fr~~ hurredly.

Grania

Why do you take your spear? ~~You will~~ ~~You are not going t this hunting~~. You will not go t this hunting?

Damd.

beast
~~It r~~ This ~~boar~~ is coming t attack us. This hunt ever will sweep over us. It is coming through th woods & I shall be caught up – leaves leaves all of us.

rush
(Conan & th spear men ~~run~~ out)
Why have they fled. We must bar the door (They bar the door & stand listeng. The baring of th door has made it dark).

Grania

May be they have gone because the danger is passed.

Darmd

Come sit by me.
(a pause)
And so sit togeatr in th dark
There is no sound now & yet the darkness is

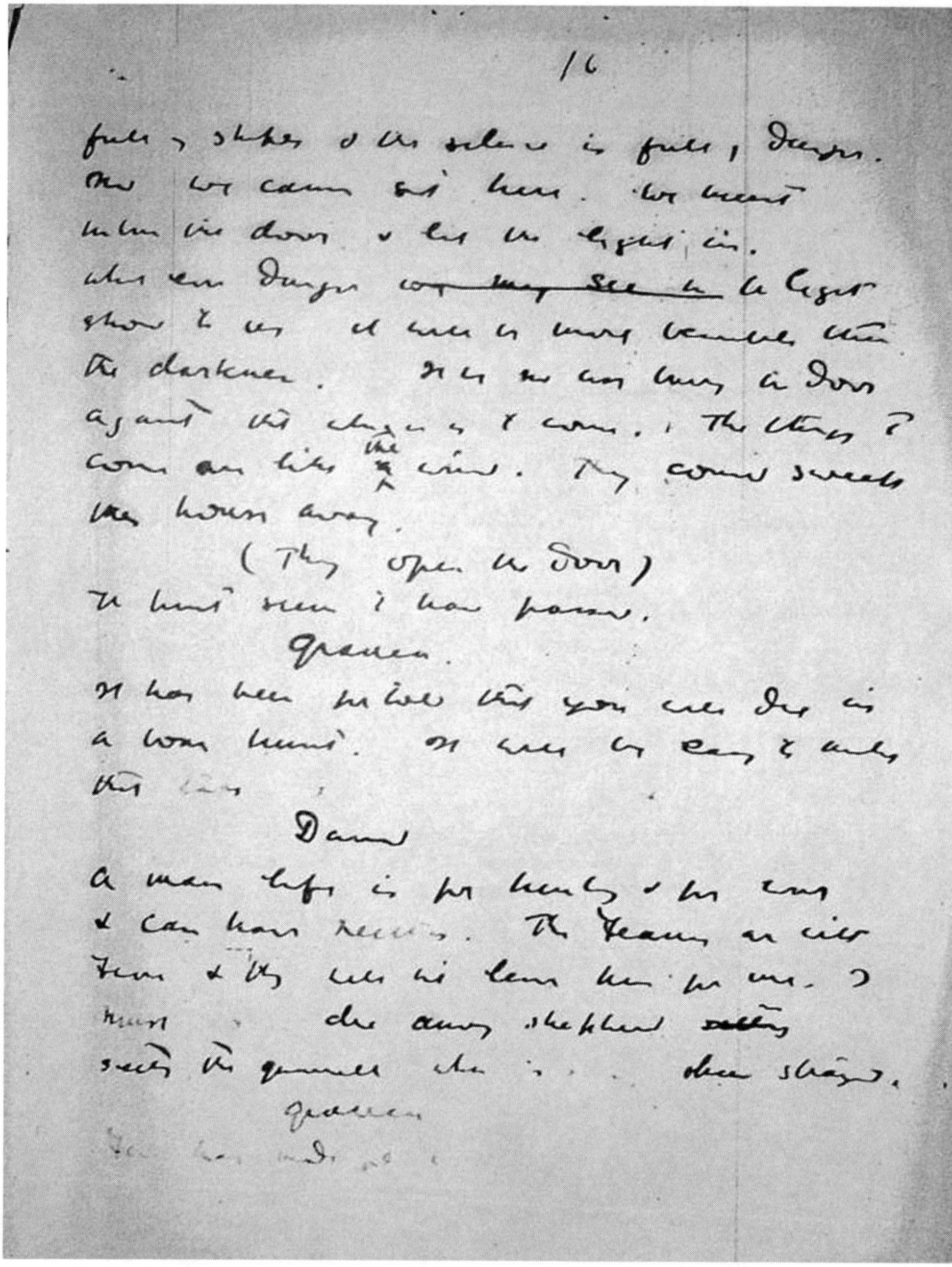

16

full of shapes & the silence is full of dangers.
When we came out here. We must
[illegible] the door & let the light in.
What ever dangers ~~we may see in~~ the light
show to us it will be more beautiful than
the darkness. It is no use [illegible] the door
against the dangers & [illegible] come, & the things ?
come are like the wind. They come & sweep
the house away.
(They open the door)
It hasn't seen I have passed.
Grania
It has been foretold that you will die in
a boar hunt. It will be easy to [illegible]
that [illegible]
Diarmuid
A man's life is for heroes & his [illegible]
& can have [illegible]. The Fianna are all
[illegible] & they will not leave him for me. I
must [illegible] among shepherds ~~[illegible]~~
seeing the quarrels [illegible] strange.
Grania
[illegible]

[NLI 8777(4) a, 17^{r}]

16

full of shapes & this silence is full of danger. No we cannt sit here. We must unbar the door & let the light in. what ever danger ~~we may see in~~ th light show t us it will be more bearable than the darkness. It is no use baring th door against that which is t come. The things t come are like ^the ~~a~~ wind. They could sweep this house away.

(They open the door)

The hunt seem t have passed.

Grania.

It has been fortold that you will die in a boar hunt. It will be easy to make that tale nothing.

Darmd

A mans life is for hunting & for war & can have neither. The Feanni ar with Fion & they will not leave him for me. I must live & die among shepherd ~~setting~~ setling thir quarrell when thir sheep have strayed..

Grania

Finn has made peace

[NLI 8777(4) a, 17^{v}, 18^{r}]

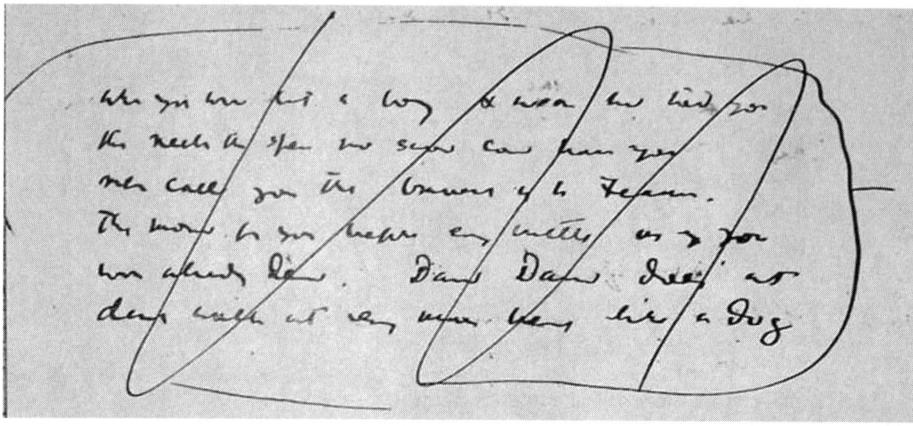

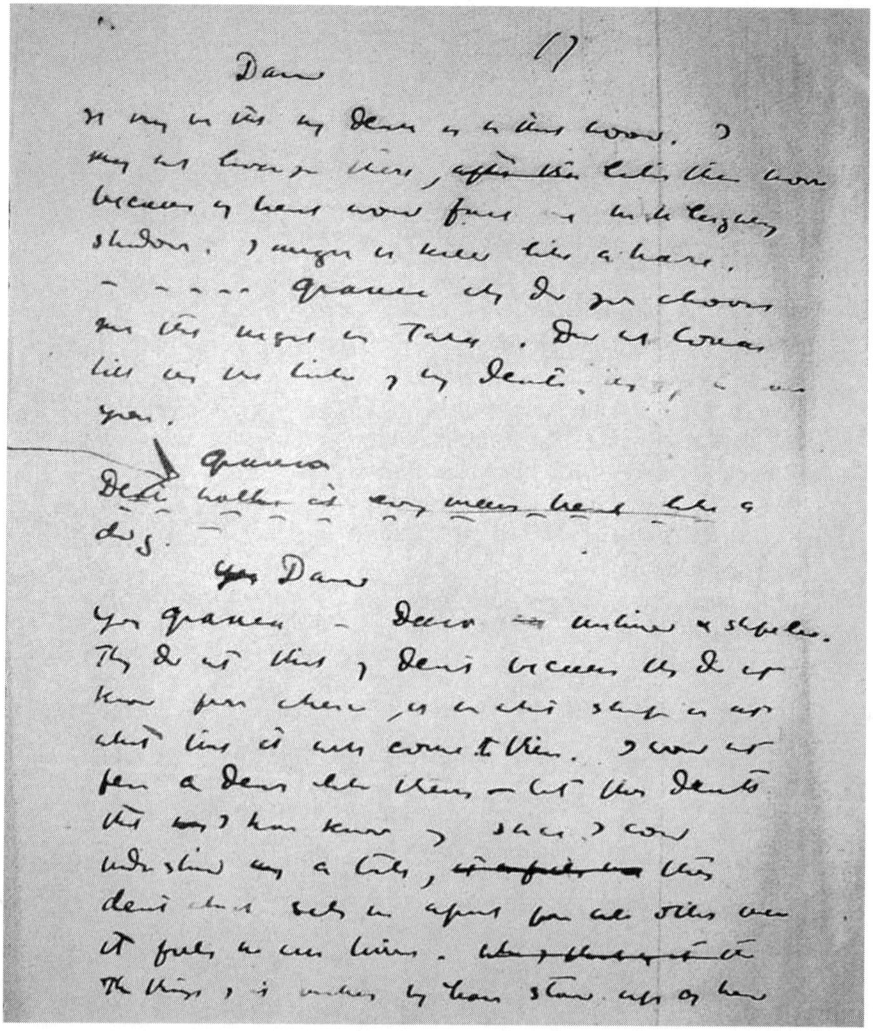

[NLI 8777(4) a, 17v]

When you were but a boy & in a but kid you
the neck the spear no score coud have you
men calld you the bravest of the Feanna.
They mournd for you before every battle as if you
were already dead. Dairmd Dairmd does not
death walk at evry mans heels like a dog

[NLI 8777(4) a, 18r]

17

Diarmuid

It may be that my death is in that wood. I
may not linger there, ~~after the~~ later than noon
because my heart woud fail me in th lengthng
shadows. I might be killd like a hare.
– – – – – Grania why di you choose
me that night in Tara. Did not Conan
tell us the tale of my death, as if to [?warn]
you.

Grania
~~Death walks at every in every mans heal like a~~
~~dog.~~

~~Gra~~ Damd
Yes Grania – Death ~~that~~ untimed & shapeles.
They do not think of death becaus they do not
know from whence, or in what shape or at
what time it will come to them. I would not
fear a death like theirs – but this death
that ~~my~~ I have known of since I coud
understand ~~my~~ a tale, ~~it a fills me~~ this
deat which sets me apart from all other men
it fills me wth terror – ~~When I think of it the~~
The thougt of it makes by hair stand up on head

17v The lines are keyed to lines 9–10 of the facing page 17 (here fol. 18r). WBY's enlargement of the GM draft from which he was working was clearly opportunistic; cf. NLI 8777(8) b, fol. 4r; also Berg(06), fol. 16r.

[NLI 8777(4) a, 18v, 19r]

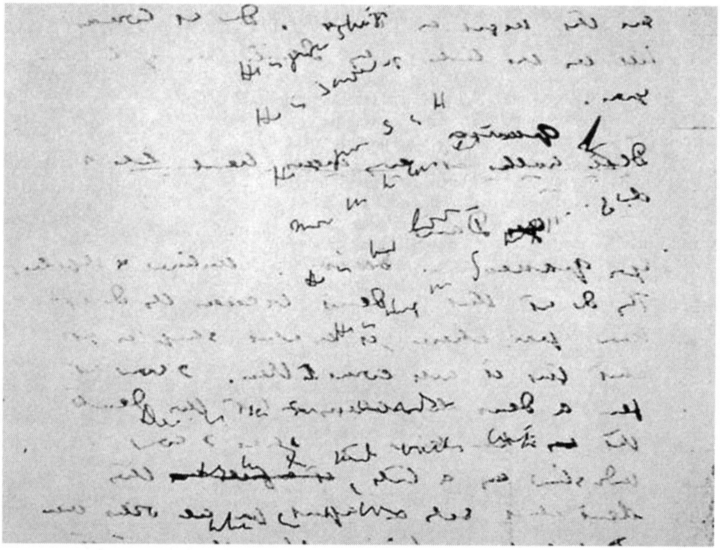

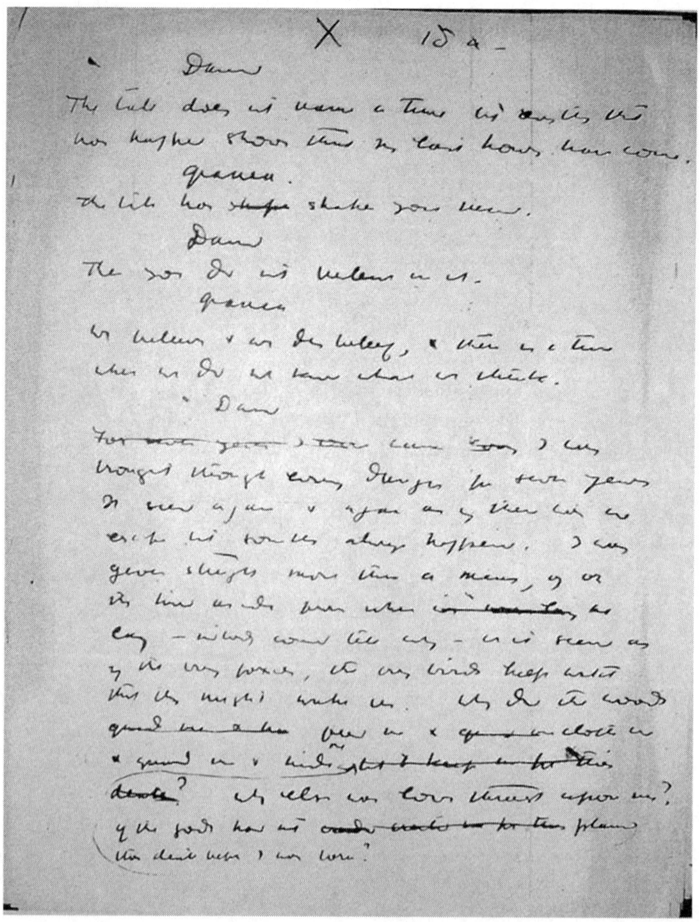

[NLI 8777(4) a, 18[v]]

He is given strength
He is saved –
He is given G by H
More [?than] he can [?eat] –
He is her lover-
He is [?alive] in G [?heart] –

Diar is the Sun towards –
[?*try*] [?*be*] *Finn* [?*turnd*] *back but*
When he [?*is*] [?*lover/living*]

[NLI 8777(4) a, 19[r]]

18a

Darmd
The tale does not name a time but evry thng that
has happend shows that my last hours have come.

Grania.
The tale has ~~shape~~ shake your nerves.

Darmd
Then you do not believe in it.

Grania
We believe & we disbelief, & there is a time
when we do not know what we think.

Darmd
~~For seven years I over came every~~ I was
brought through every danger for seven years
It seemd again & again as if there was no
escpe but troubles always happend. I was
given strength more than a mans, of or
they turnd aside from where ~~we were layng~~ we
lay – no body coud tell why – or it seemd as
if the very foxes, the very birds keep watch
that they might wake us. Why did the woods
~~guard me & hi~~ feed us & ~~guard me~~ clothe us
me
& guard me & hide, ~~but t keep me for this~~
~~death~~? Why else was love thrust upon me?

if the gods had not ~~orderd created me for this~~ plannd
this death before I was born?

18[v] WBY's faint pencil jottings are not everywhere possible to decipher. Lines 1–6 were written at an angle; lines 7–9 were subsequently added on the level. They appear to be related to the opposite, substituted page (fol. 19[r]).

[NLI 8777(4) a, 20r]

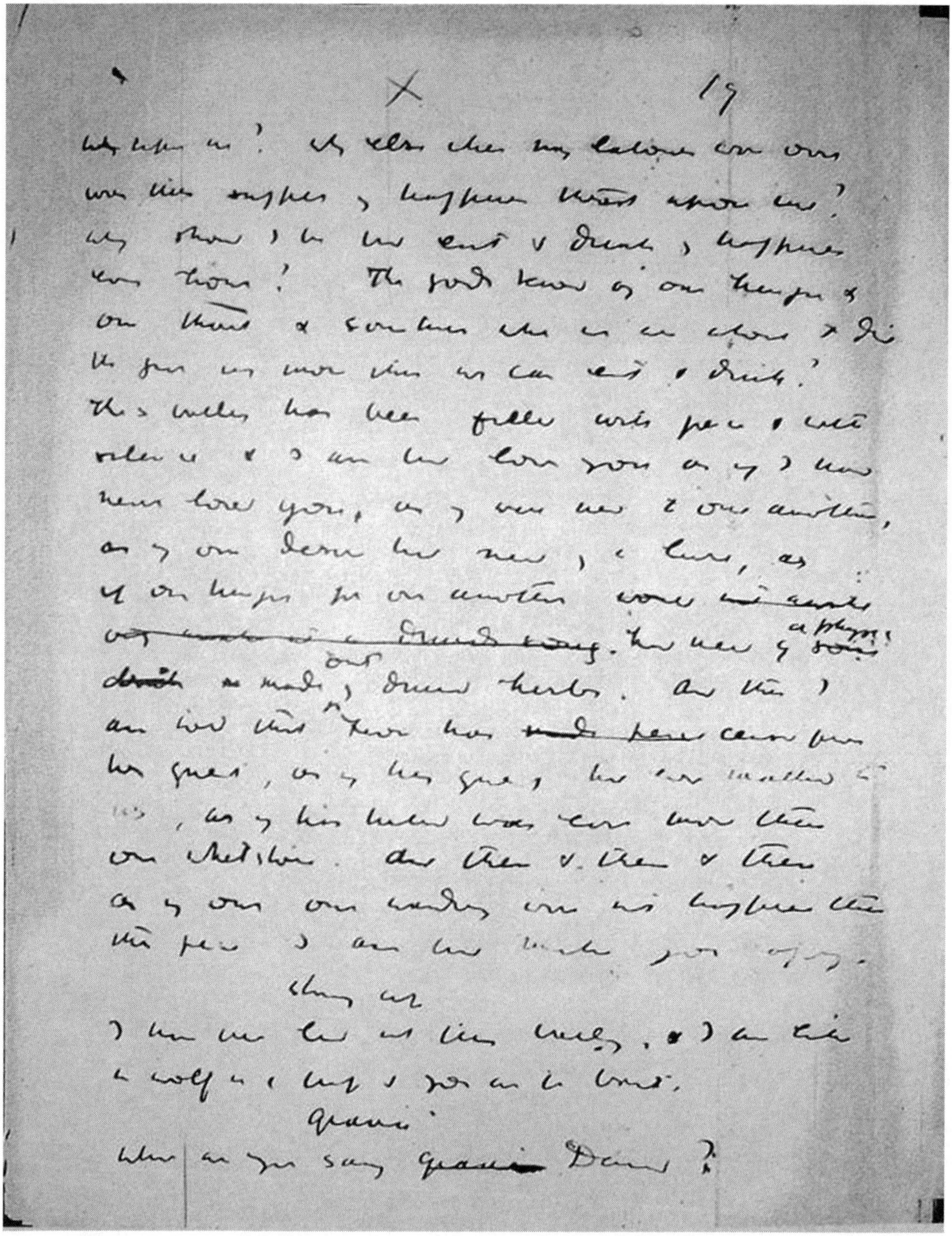

[NLI 8777(4) a, 20^{r}]

X 19

Why upon us? Why else when my labours were over
were this supper of happines thrust upon me?
Why should I be bid eat & drink of happines
every hour? The gods know of our hunger &
our thirst & sometimes whn we are about t die
th give us more than we can eat & drink?
This valley has been filled with peice & with
silence & I am bid love you as if I had
,
never loved you.} as if were new t one another,
as if our desire had need of a lure, as
if our hunger for on another ~~would~~ ~~not awake~~
a physic
~~only awake at a druids song~~. had need of ~~some~~
out
~~drink~~ ~~in~~ made of ^ druid herbs. And then I
am told that Fion has ~~made peace~~ ceasd from
his quest, as if his quest had ever matterd to
us, as if his hatred was ever more than
our whetstone. And then & then & then
as if our own wandring were not happier than
this peice I am bid make you happy.

staing up

I hav been led int this vally. ~~&~~ I am like
a wolf in a trap & you ar th bait.

Grania

What ar you saing ~~Grania~~ Darmd?

Patterns of blotting on the facing page (fol. 19^{v}) show that the two pages marked "X" (fols. 19, 20) were written out continuously.

[NLI 8777(4) a, 21r]

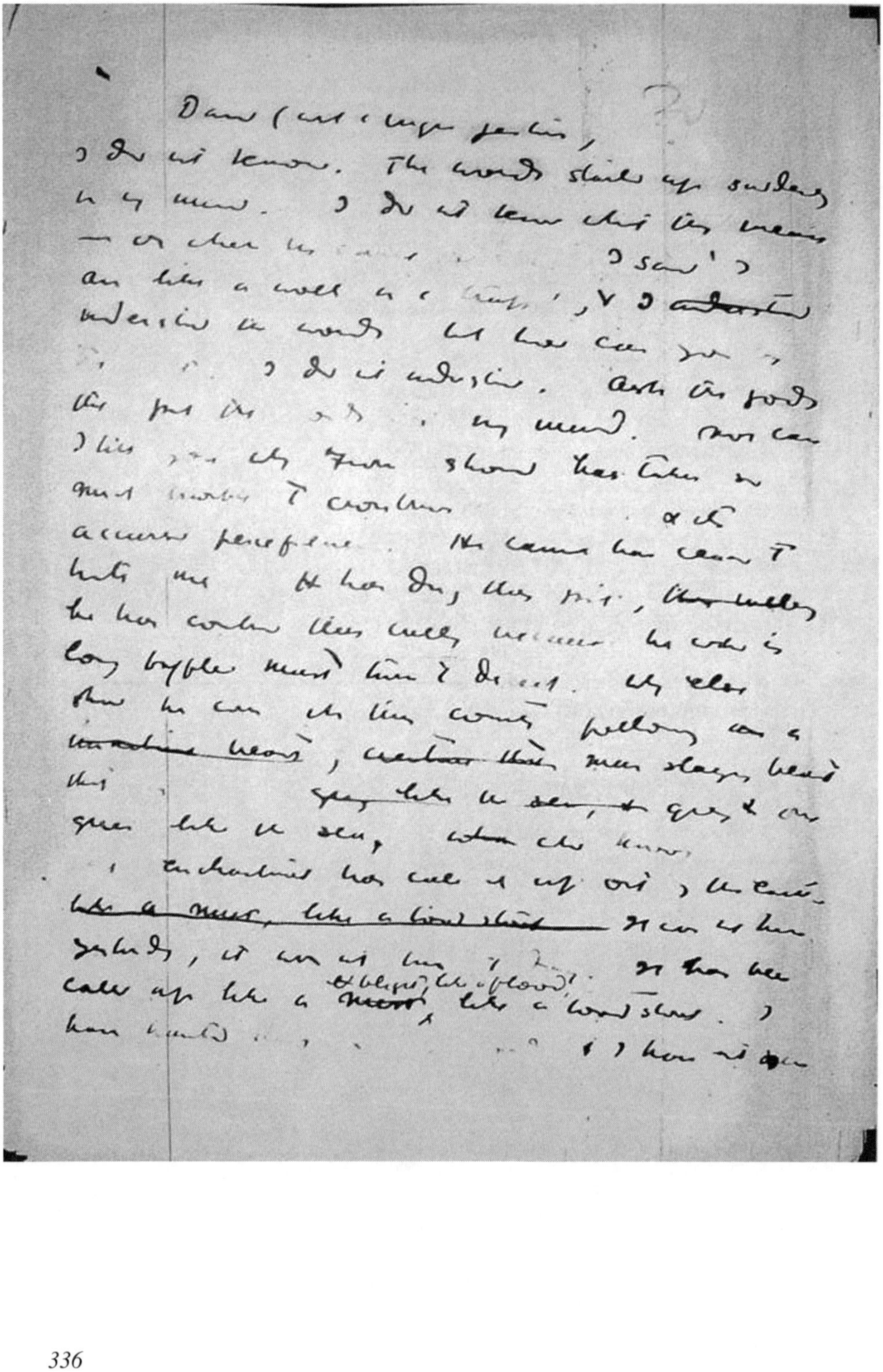

[NLI 8777(4) a, 21^{r}]

20

Diarmuid (with a vague gesture)
I do not know. The words started up suddenly
in my mind. I do not know what they mean
— or where they came from   I said 'I
am like a wolf in a trap' & I ~~understand~~
understand th words but how can you be
the bait. I do not understand. Ask the gods
that put the words into my mind. Nor can
I tell you why Fion should has taken so
much trouble t contrive this valley & its
accursed peacefulness. He cannot hav ceasd t
hate me He has dug this pit, ~~this valley~~
he has contrivd this vally because he who is
long baffled must turn to deceit. Why else
shld he come into this country following ~~us~~ a
~~unatural beast~~, ~~creature that~~ man slaying beast
that one calls ~~grey like~~ th ~~sea, &~~ grey & one
green like th sea, ~~when~~ who knows
what enchantment has cald it up out of the earth –
~~like a mist, like a toad stool.~~ It was not here
yesterday, it was not here to day. It has been
a blight! like a flood!
calld up like a ~~mist~~^like a toad stool. I
have hunted deer in these woods & I have not seen

Note that pencil numbering begins on this page.

[NLI 8777(4) a, 22r]

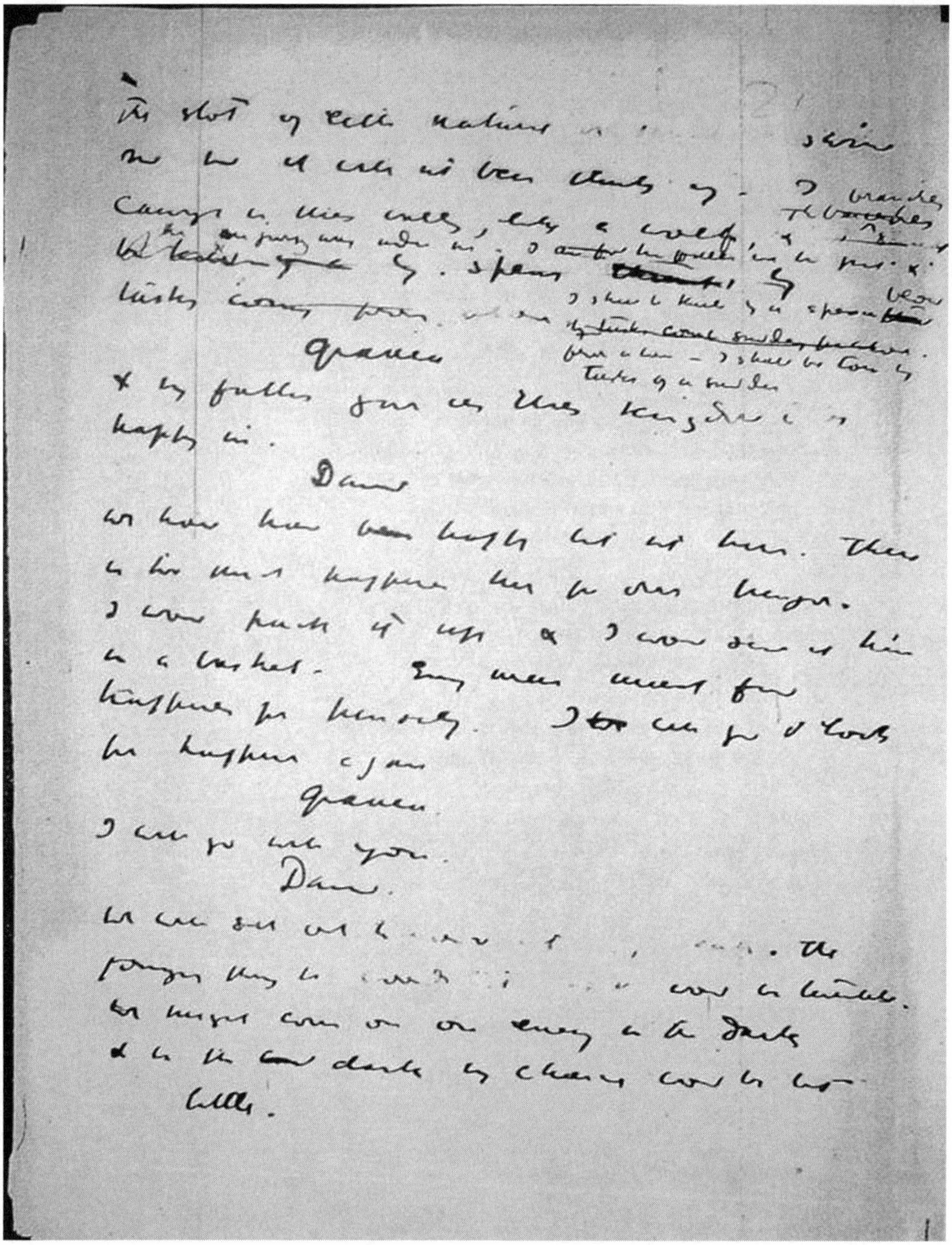

[NLI 8777(4) a, 22r]

21

the slot of eithr natural or unatural swine
no no it will not bear thinking of – I
caught in this vally, like a wol{f/l}, ~~& I shall~~
~~the~~ are giving way under me – I ~~am fal~~ hav fallen int th pit & [branches / Th ~~branches~~ / blow]
~~be held~~ ~~by a by spears thrust, by~~ I shall be killd by a spear ~~thrust~~
tusks ~~coming from~~ above. ~~by tusks comg suddenly frm above.~~
from above – I shall be torn by
tusks of a sudden

Grania
& my father gave us this kingdom to be
happy in,

Diarmd
We have been happy but not here. There
is too much happines here for our hunger.
I would pack it up & I would send it him
in a basket. Every man must find
happines for himself. I ~~we~~ will go & look
for happinss again

Grania
I will go with you.

Dard.
We will set out tomorow at day break. The
journeying throug th woods at night woud be terrible.
We might come on our enemy in the dark
& in the ~~cou~~ dark my chance woud be but
little.

[NLI 8777(4) a, 23r]

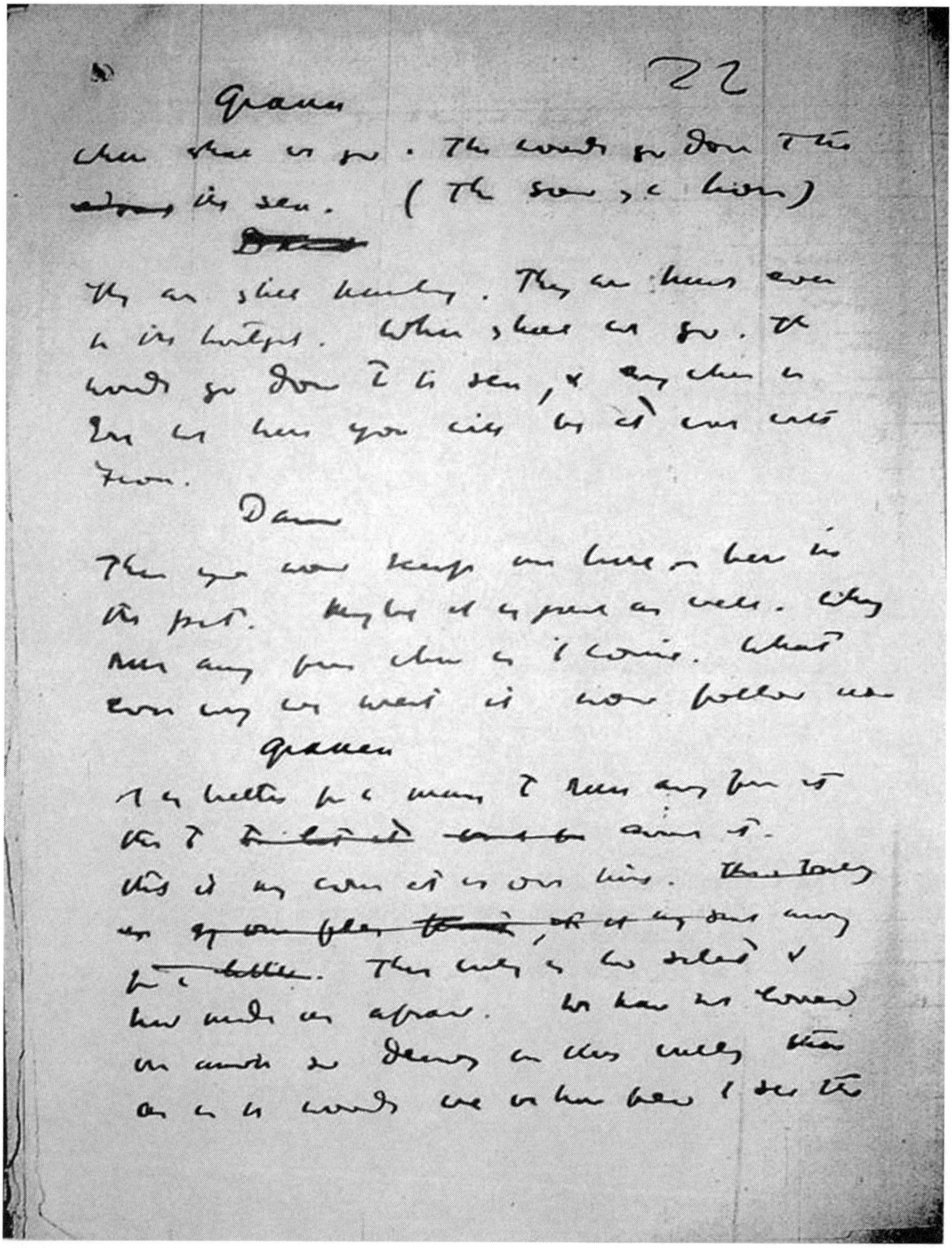

[NLI 8777(4) a, 23^{r}]

22

Grania

Where shall we go. The woods go down t the ~~edge of~~ the sea (The sound of a horn)

~~Diarmd~~

They are still hunting. They are huning even in the twilght. Wher shal we go. The woods go down to th sea, & evry wher in Eri but here you will be at war with Fion.

Dard

Then you would keep me here. – here in the pit. May be it is just as well. Why run away from when is to come. What ever way we went it now follow us.

Grania

It is better for a man t run away from it than to ~~to let it come to~~ await it – that it may come at its own time. ~~This valey is If our [?fears] [?toward], [?or] if my sent~~ away ~~for a little~~. This valy is too silent & had made us afraid. We hav not loved on anothr so dearly in this vally ~~than~~ as in th woods we or hav feard t see the

---

10 WBY omits the words "ones fate" from the manuscript by GM he is following; cf. NLI 8777(8), fol. 10^{r}, linc 1.

[NLI 8777(4) a, 24r]

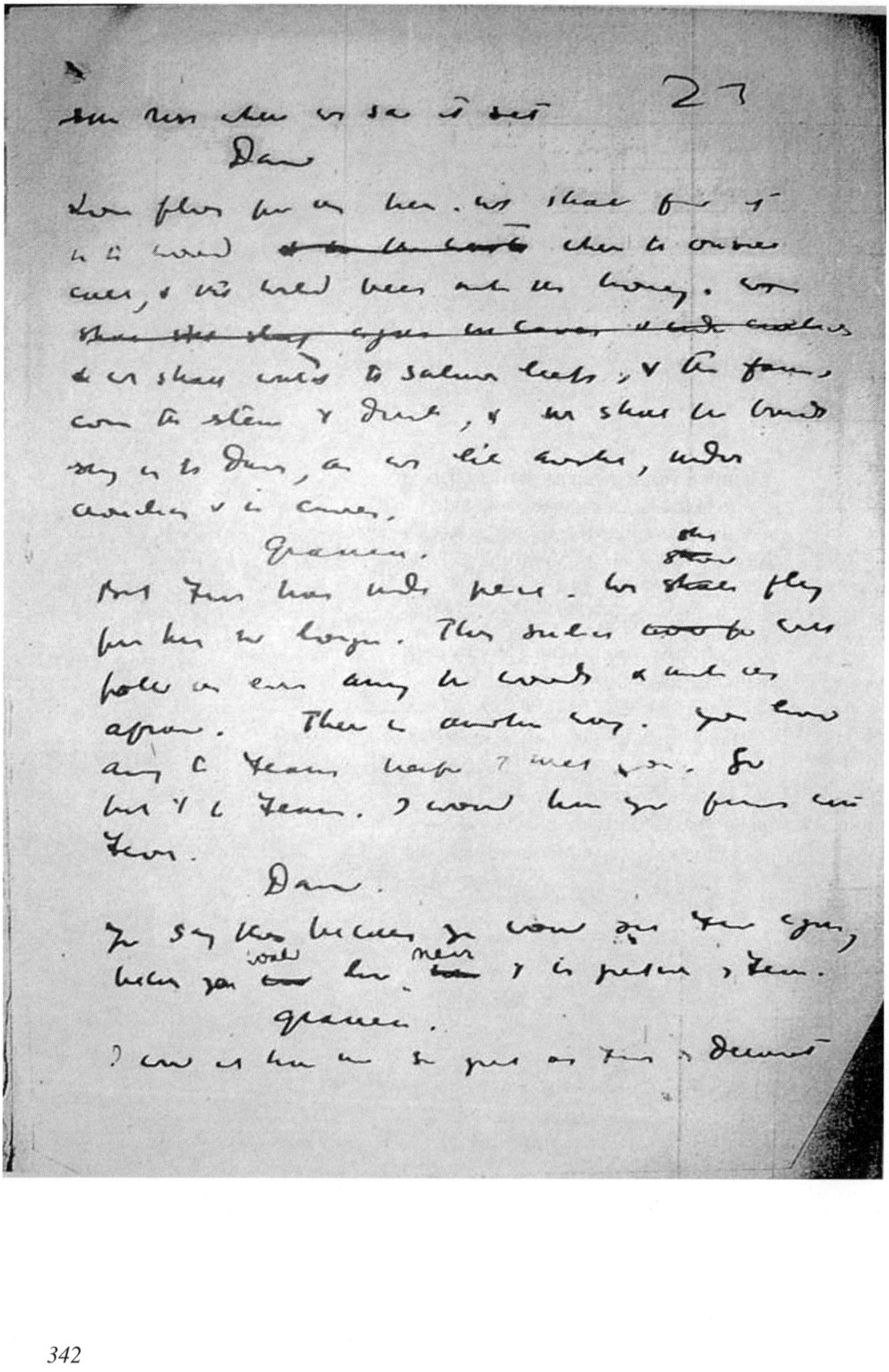

[NLI 8777(4) a, 24r]

23

sun rise where we saw it set.

Dard
Love flies from us here – We shall find it
in th wood ~~& in the waste~~ when th ousels
call, & the wild bees make thr honey. ~~We~~
~~shall [?still] sleep again in caves & under cromlecs~~
~~&~~ we shall watch th salmon leap, & the fauns
come th stream & drink, & not shall hr birds
sing in th dawn, as we lie awake, under
cromlecs & in caves.

shal
Grania. ~~shoud~~
But Fin has made peace – We ~~shall~~ fly
from him no longer. This silence ~~woud fo~~ will
follw us even amng th woods & make us
afraid. There is another way. You livd
amng th Feani befor I met you. Go
back t th Fean. I would have you friens wit
Feon.

Darm.
You say this because you woud see Fin again,
would near
because you ~~co~~ liv ~~sit~~ & in presence of Fin.

Grania.
I woud not hav men so gret as Fin & dermot

[NLI 8777(4) a, 25r]

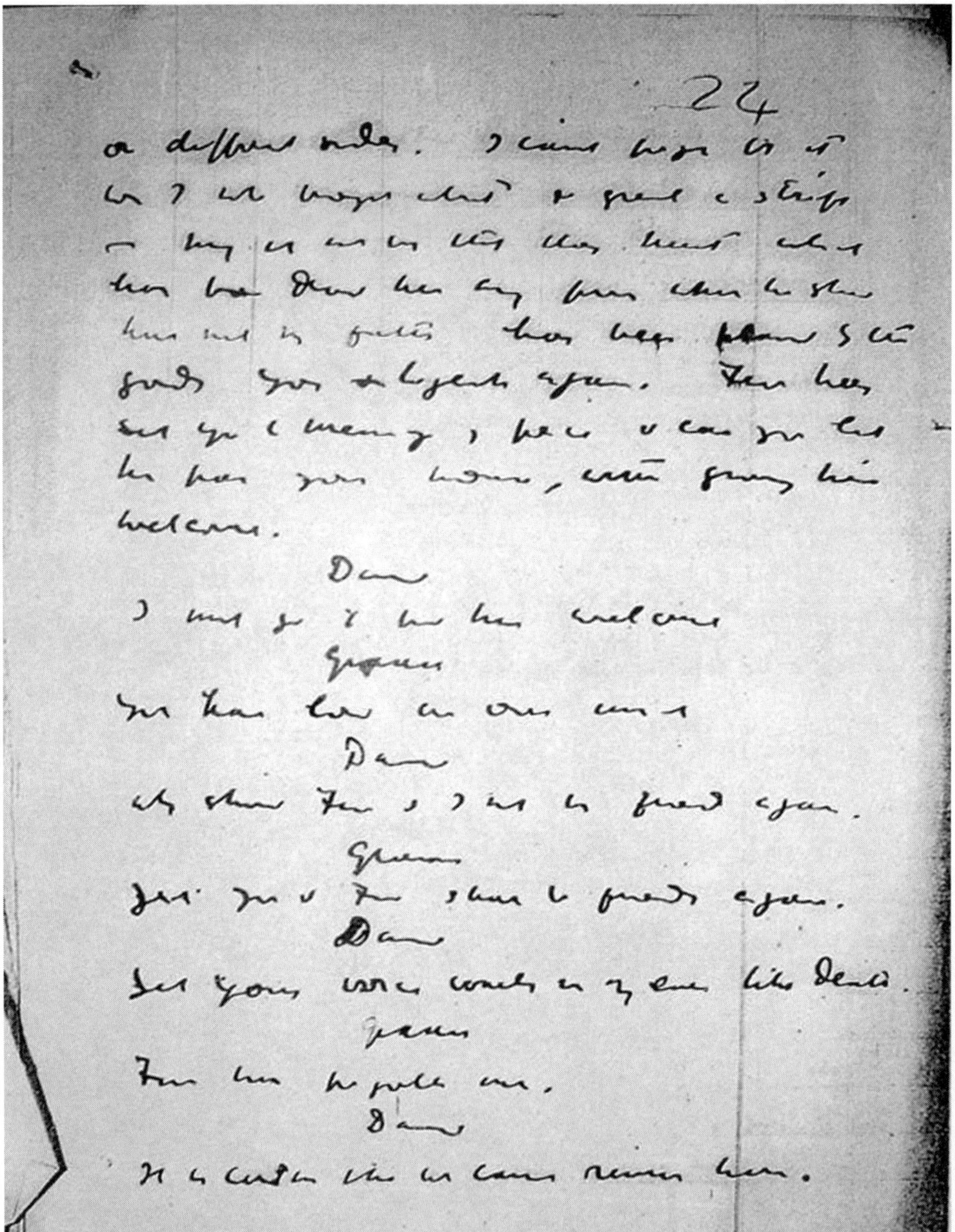

[NLI 8777(4) a, 25^{r}]

24

on different sides. I canot forget th it
was I wh broght about so great a strife
– may it not be tht this hunt which
has [?~~fo~~] drivn him awy from wher he shd
hav met my fathr has been plannd by th
gods you ~~&~~ togethr again. Fin has
sent you a messag of peice & can you let
him pas your house, withou giving him
welcome.

Darmd
I must go to bid him welcome

Grania
You hav lovd me over much

Darmd
Why shoud Fin & I not be friends again.

Grania
Yes. You & Fin shall be friends again.

Darmd
Yet your voice wails in my ears like death.

Grania
Fin has forgottn me.

Darmd
It is certain tht we cannot remain here

---

16 The mark at the end of the line appears to be an ink blob, not a period.

[NLI 8777(4) a, 26r]

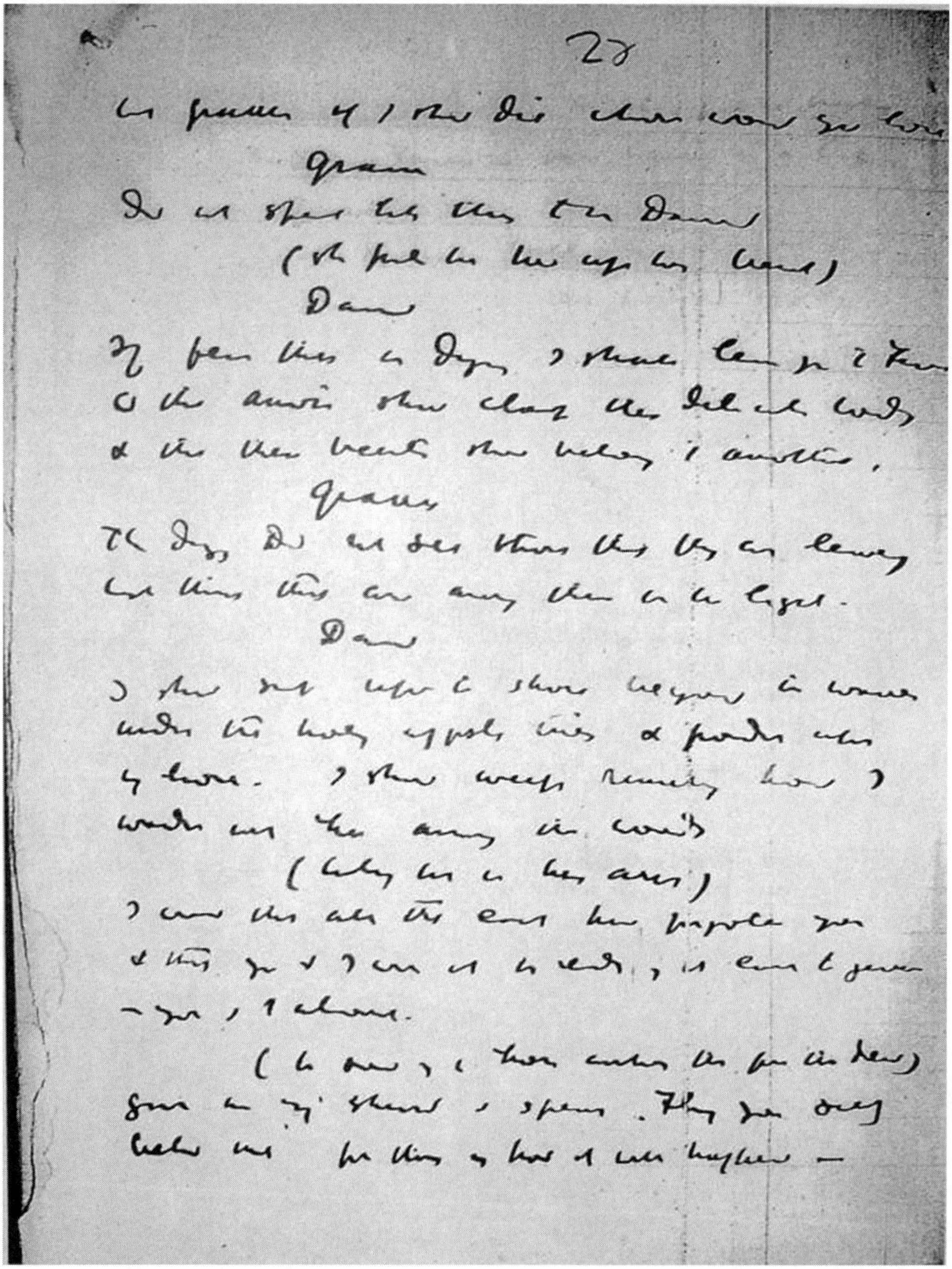

[NLI 8777(4) a, 26[r]]

25

but Grania if I shd die whom would you love

Grania
Do not speak like this t me Diarmd
(sh puts hr hnd upn his breast)

Diarmd
I fear that in dying I shall leav you t Finn
O tht anothr shd clasp this delicate body
& that these breasts shd belong t another.

Grania
The dyng do not see those that they ar leaving
but those that are awaitng them in th light.

Dard
I shall sit upon th shore beyond th waves
under the holy apple trees & ponder upon
my love. I shall weep remebring how I
wanderd wth her among the woods
(taking her in his arms)
I would that all the earth had forgoten you
& that you & I wer at its ends, at even to [?given]
– you & I alone.
(A sound of a horn awakns thm frm thir dream)
Give me my shield & spear. Fling your self
behnd me for this is how it will happen –

[NLI 8777(4) a, 27r]

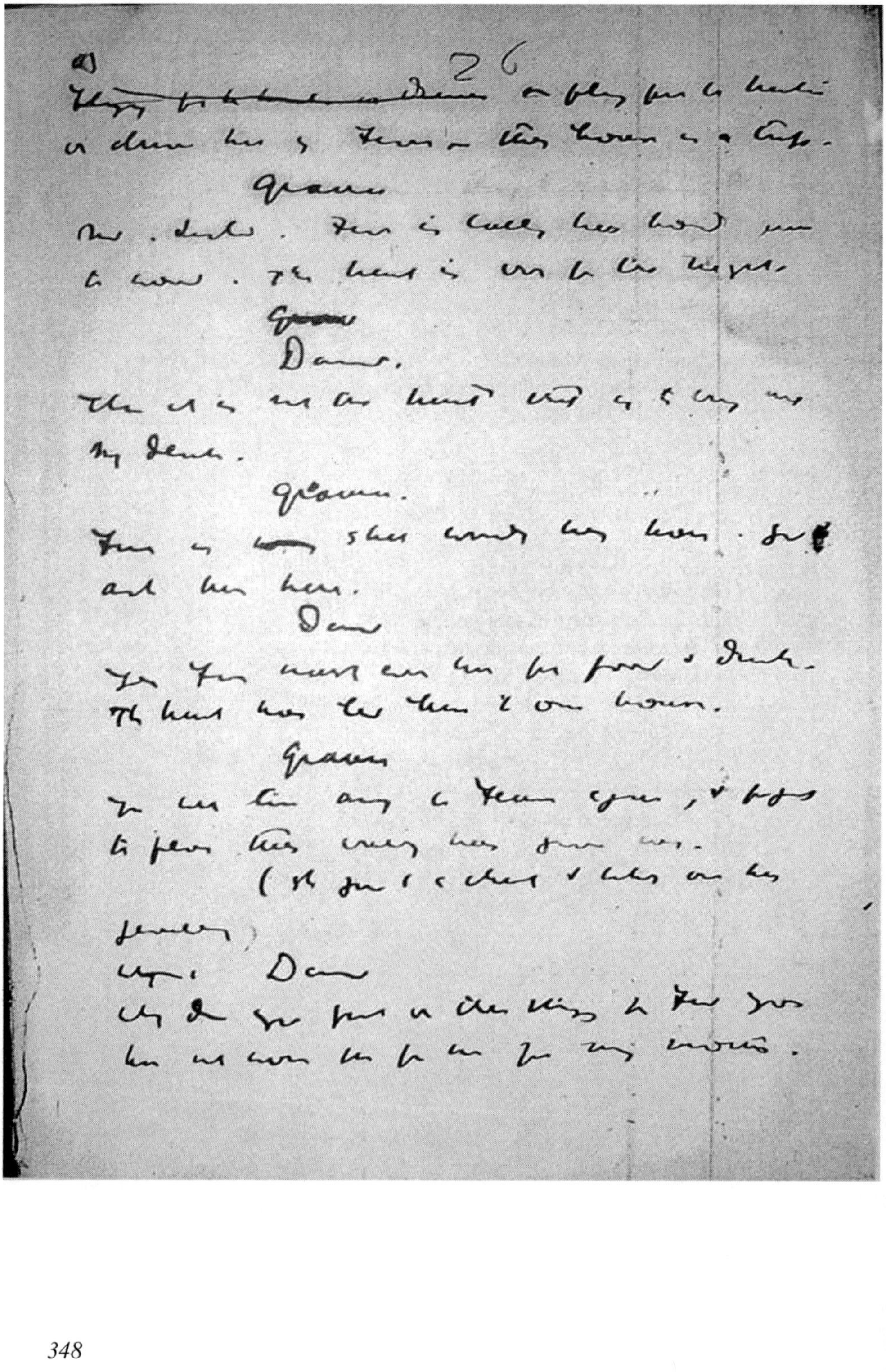

[NLI 8777(4) a, 27^{r}]

26

~~Flying fr th hunters or driven~~ – or flyng frm th hunters
or drivn her by Fin – this house is a trap.

Grania
No. Listen. Fin is callng his hounds from
th wood. The hunt is ovr for the night

~~Grania~~
Darmd.
Then it is not the hunt that is to bring me
my death.

Grania.
Fin is ~~wing~~ still windng his horn. go &
ask him here.

Damd
Yes Fin must come here for food & drink.
The hunt has led him t our house.

Grania
You will live amng th Feana again, & forget
th fears this vally has givn us.

(sh goes to a chest & takes out her
jewelry)

~~Why~~. Damd
Why do you put on these things for Fin you
have not worn thm for me for mny months.

[NLI 8777(4) a, 28r]

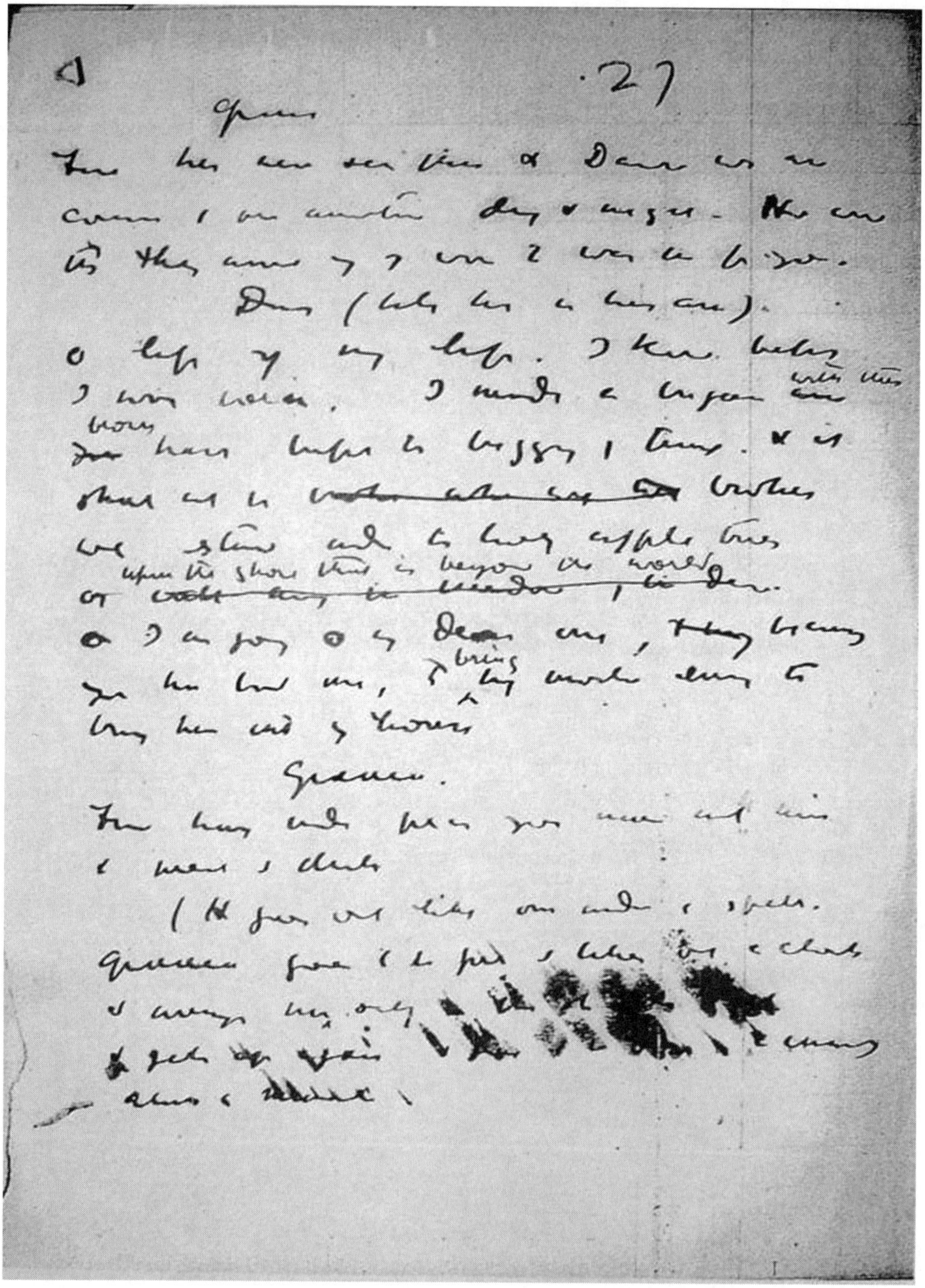

[NLI 8777(4) a, 28^{r}]

27

Grania
Fin has nevr seen them & Dairmd we are
common tot one anoter day & night. How wld
ths they [?avail] if I wer t wear thm for you.

Darm (takng her in his arm)
O life of my life. I knew before
with this
I was born. I made a bargain [?~~with~~]
brown
[?~~your/fair~~] hair before th beggng of time. & it
shal not be ~~brokn when we wa~~ broken
we stand under th holy apple trees
upon the shore that is beyond the world
or ~~walk among th meadow, in death~~.
O I am going O my dear one, ~~t my~~ because
bring
you have bid me, to‸my mortal enemy to
bring him into my house

Grania.
Fin has made piece you must set him
to meat & drink

(He goes out like one under a spell.
Grania goes t th press & takes out a cloak
& arrays her self & then she sits down
& gets up again & goes to th door & [?waits]
about a minute.

[NLI 8777(4) a, 29r]

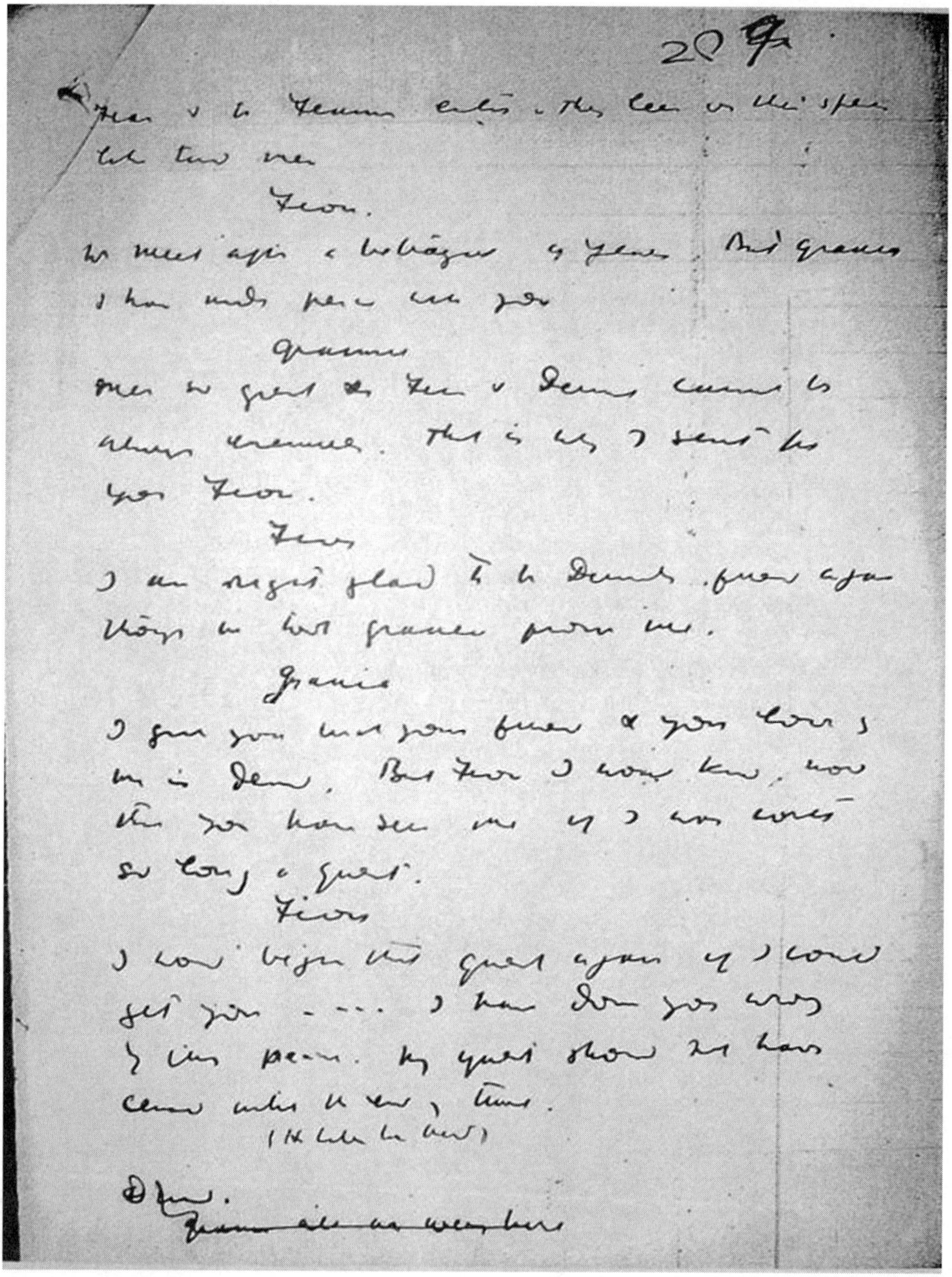

[NLI 8777(4) a, 29^{r}]

28 ~~9~~

Fean & th Feanna enter. They lean on their spears like tired men

Fion.

We meet after a betrayal of years. But Grania I have made peice with you

Grania

Men so great as Fin & Dermt cannot be always enemies. This is why I sent for you Fion.

Fion

I am right glad to be Diarmds friend again though he took Grania from me.

Grania

I gave you back your friend & your love of me is dead. But Fion I would know, now that you have seen me if I was worth so long a quest.

Fion

I would begin that quest again if I could get you . . . . I have done you wrong by this peace. My quest shoud not have ended until the end of time.

(He takes her hand)

Diard.

Grania all ar weary here.

The numeral "9" at the head of the page was canceled when "28" was substituted. Compare the canceled "10" on fol. 31^{r} below. Also note that the remaining subsequently revised numerals (9–14) on these closing pages of the act are in pencil.

[NLI 8777(4) b, 30r]

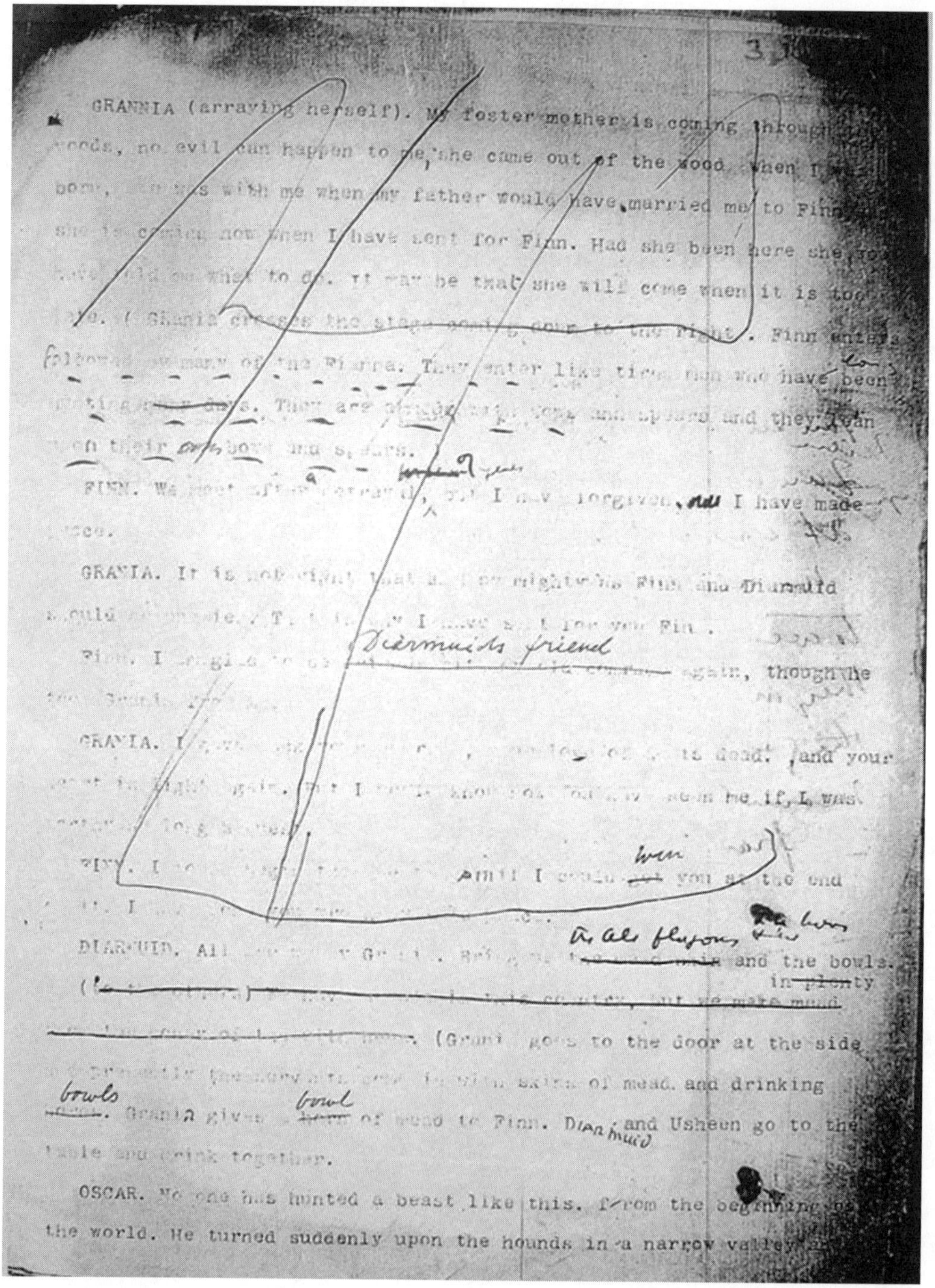

3

GRANNIA (arraving herself). My foster mother is coming through the woods, no evil can happen to me, she came out of the wood when I was born, [illegible] with me when my father would have married me to Finn [illegible] coming now when I have sent for Finn. Had she been here she [illegible] what to do. It may be that she will come when it is too late. (Grania crosses the stage [illegible] to the right. Finn enters followed by many of the Fianna. They enter like tired men who have been [illegible] days. They are [illegible] and they lean on their [illegible])

FINN. We [illegible] I have forgiven, I have made [illegible]

GRANIA. It is not right [illegible] mighty [illegible] Finn and Diarmuid [illegible] I have sent for you Finn.

FINN. I [illegible] Diarmuid's friend [illegible] again, though the [illegible]

GRANIA. [illegible] is dead, and your [illegible] me if I was [illegible]

FINN. I [illegible] until I could were you at the end [illegible]

DIARMUID. All [illegible] and the bowls. in plenty [illegible] (Grania goes to the door at the side [illegible] of mead and drinking bowls. Grania gives bowl of mead to Finn. Diarmuid and Usheen go to the table and drink together.

OSCAR. No one has hunted a beast like this, from the beginning of the world. He turned suddenly upon the hounds in a narrow valley [illegible]

The numeral at the head of the page was made by adding an ink "2" to an existing pencil "9". The small corrections on this and following pages of NLI 8777(4) b were almost certainly made by the typist, AG.

1–6, 1–9, 1–20 comprise three enlarging areas of cancellation.

[NLI 8777(4) b, 30r]

2 9

GRANNIA (arraying herself). My foster mother is coming through the woods, no evil can happen to me , she came out of the wood when I was born, she was with me when my father would have married me to Finn, and she is coming now when I have sent for Finn. Had she been here she would have told me what to do. It may be tha t she will come when it is too late. (GRania crosses the stage coming down to the right . Finn enters

fo   long

f llowed by many of the Fianna. They enter like tired men who have been ^ hunting ~~many days~~. They are armed with bows and spears and they lean upon their own bows and spears.   of

a   ~~for seven~~ years

FINN. We meet after betrayal,^ but I hav forgiven . ~~and~~ I have made peace.

GRANIA. It is not right that men so mighty as Finn and Dairmuid should be enemies. That is why I have sent for you Fin

Diarmuids friend

Finn. I am glad to be ~~friends with my old comrade~~ again, though he took Grania from me.

GRANIA. I gave back your friend, your love of me is dead. , and your heart is light again. But I would know now you have seen me if I was worthy so long a quest.

ain   win

FINN. I would begin the quest ag in if I could ~~get~~ you at the end of it. I have done you wrong by this peace.

& th horns

the ale flagons ~~& his~~

DIARMUID. All are weary Grania. Bring us ~~the mead skin~~ and the bowls.

~~in plenty~~

~~(to the others) We have no ale in this country, but we make mead from the honey of the wild bees.~~ (Grania goes to the door at the side and presently the servants come in with skins of mead and drinking

bowls   bowl

~~horns~~. Grani a gives a ~~horn~~ of mead to Finn. Diarmuid and Usheen go to the table and drink together.

OSCAR. No one has hunted a beast like this. f rom the beginning of the world. He turned suddenly upon the hounds in a narrow valley and a

[NLI 8777(4) b, 30v]

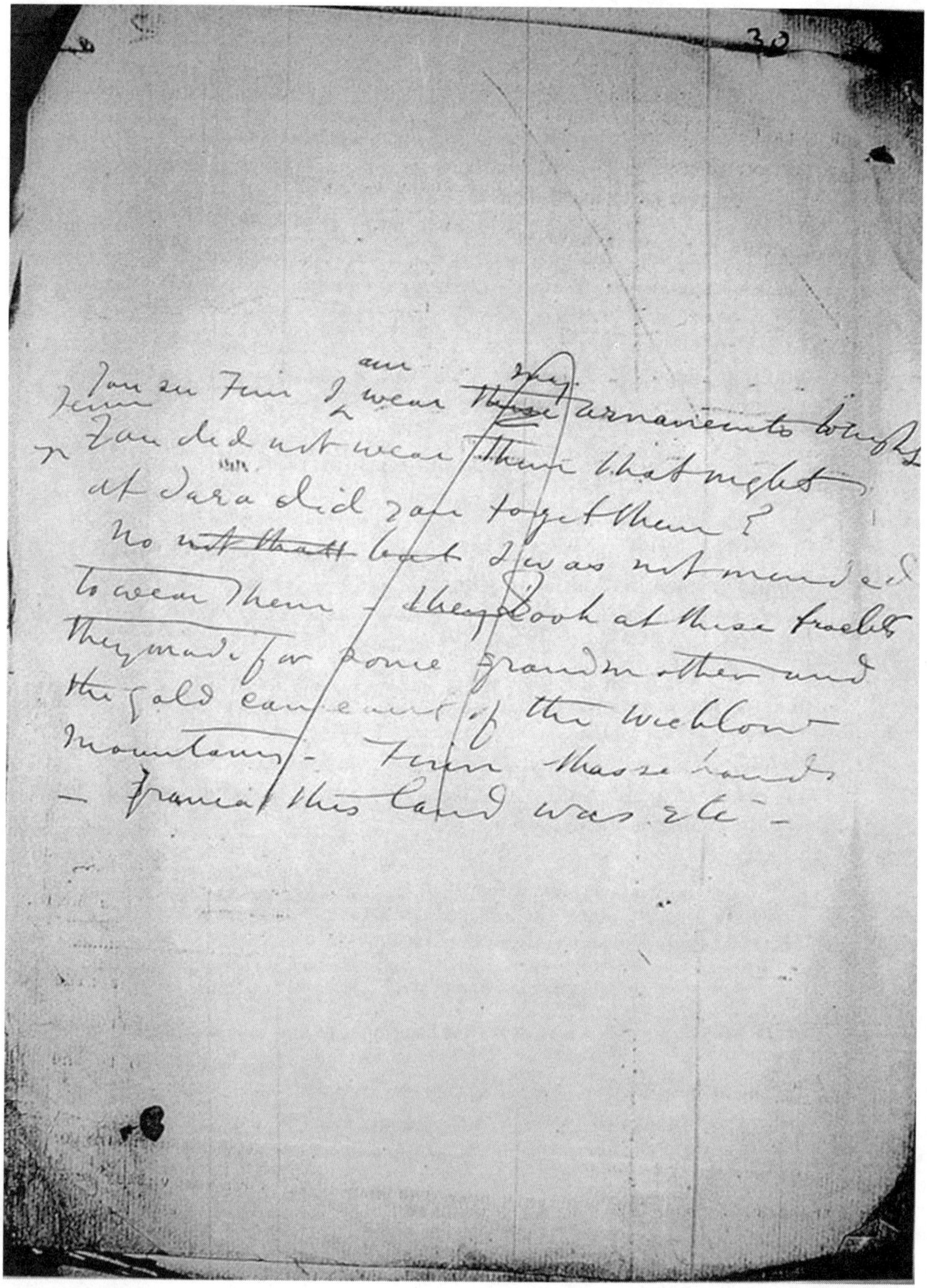

Fergus You see Fergus I am wear ~~these~~ my ornaments tonight
? You did not wear them that night
at Dara did you forget them?
No ~~not that~~ but I was not minded
to wear them — ~~they~~ Look at these bracelets
they made for some grandmother and
the gold came out of the Wicklow
mountains — From these hands
— fram at this land was etc —

[NLI 8777(4) b, 30v]

am my
You see Finn I ^ wear ~~these~~ ornaments to night
Finn
^You did not wear them that night
at Tara did you forget them?
No ~~not thatt~~ but I was not minded
L}
to wear them – ~~they~~ l}ook at these frocks
they made for some grandmother and
the gold came out of the Wicklow
Mountains – Finn those hounds
– Grania this land was etc –

[NLI 8777(4) b, 31r]

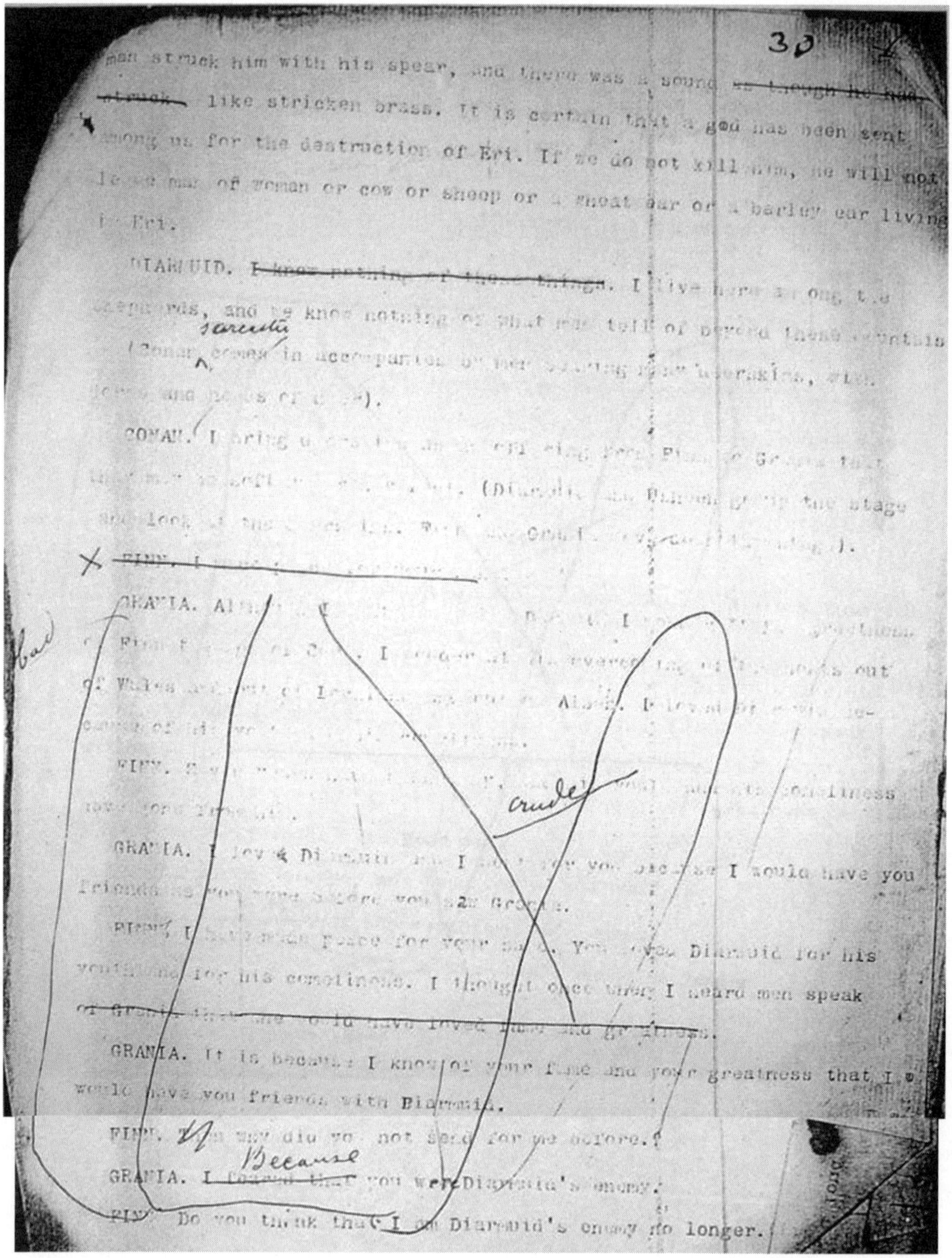

30

man struck him with his spear, and there was a sound ~~as though he had struck~~ like stricken brass. It is certain that a god has been sent among us for the destruction of Eri. If we do not kill him, he will not le[illegible] man of woman or cow or sheep or a wheat ear or a barley ear living in Eri.

DIARMUID. ~~I know nothing of these things~~. I live here among the shepherds, and we know nothing of what may tell of beyond these mountains.

(Conan sarcastic comes in accompanied by men [illegible] skins, with [illegible]).

CONAN. I bring [illegible] (Diarmuid and [illegible] up the stage and look [illegible]).

X ~~FINN. [illegible]~~

GRANIA. Al[illegible] of Finn [illegible]. I [illegible] out of Wales [illegible] Almhuin. I [illegible] because of his [illegible].

bad

FINN. [illegible] crude [illegible] comeliness [illegible].

GRANIA. I love Diarmuid [illegible] I [illegible] you because I would have you friends [illegible] Grania.

FINN. I [illegible] peace for your sake. You love Diarmuid for his youth and for his comeliness. I thought once when I heard men speak ~~of Grania that she would have loved fame and greatness.~~

GRANIA. It is because I know of your fame and your greatness that I would have you friends with Diarmuid.

FINN. Why did you not send for me before.

GRANIA. Because ~~I feared that~~ you were Diarmuid's enemy.

FINN. Do you think that I am Diarmuid's enemy no longer.

10 GM's large cross marks the beginning of the passage for which fols. 32–33 in WBY's holograph are a substitution; cf. also Berg(06), fol. 29r, line 7–fol. 31r, line 6.

17, 18, 25 The repairs to the typing (17: deletion; 18 and 25: overwriting) are likely to be in the hand of the typist, AG.

[NLI 8777(4) b, 31r]

30 ~~10~~

man struck him with his spear, and there was a sound ~~as though he had struck~~ like stricken brass. It is certain that a god has been sent among us for the destruction of Eri. If we do not kill him, he will not leave man or woman or cow or sheep or a wheat ear or a barley ear living in Eri.

DIARMUID. ~~I know nothing of these things.~~ I live here am ong the shepherds, and we know nothing of what men tell of beyond those mountais

(Conan [sarcastic] **comes in accompanied by men bearing many deerskins, with horns and heads of deer).**

CONAN. I bring deerskins as an offering from Finn to Grania that they may be soft under her feet. (Diarmuid and Usheen go up the stage and look at the deerskins. Finn and Grania move down the stage).

X **~~FINN. I made peace for your sake.~~**

[bad] **GRANIA. Although I went away with Darmuid I wonder at the greatness of Finn the son of Cool. I wonder at his overcoming of the hosts out of Wales and out of Lochlann and out of Alban. I loved Diarmuid because of his youth and his comeliness.**

FINN. Seven years have passed by, and his youth and his comeliness have gone from him.

[crude]

GRANIA. I love d Diarmuid and I sent for you because I would have you friends as you were before you s a w Grania.

FINN% I have made peace for your sake. You loved Diarmuid for his youth and for his comeliness. I thought once when I heard men speak ~~of Grania that she would have loved fame and greatness.~~

GRANIA. It is because I know of your fame and your greatness that I would have you friends with Diarmuid.

FINN. ~~Then~~ why did you not send for me before.?

GRANIA. ~~I feared that~~ [Because] **you w**[ere]**re Diarmuid's enemy.**

FINN. Do you think that I am Diarmuid's enemy no longer. (in a loud

[NLI 8777(4) c, 32r]

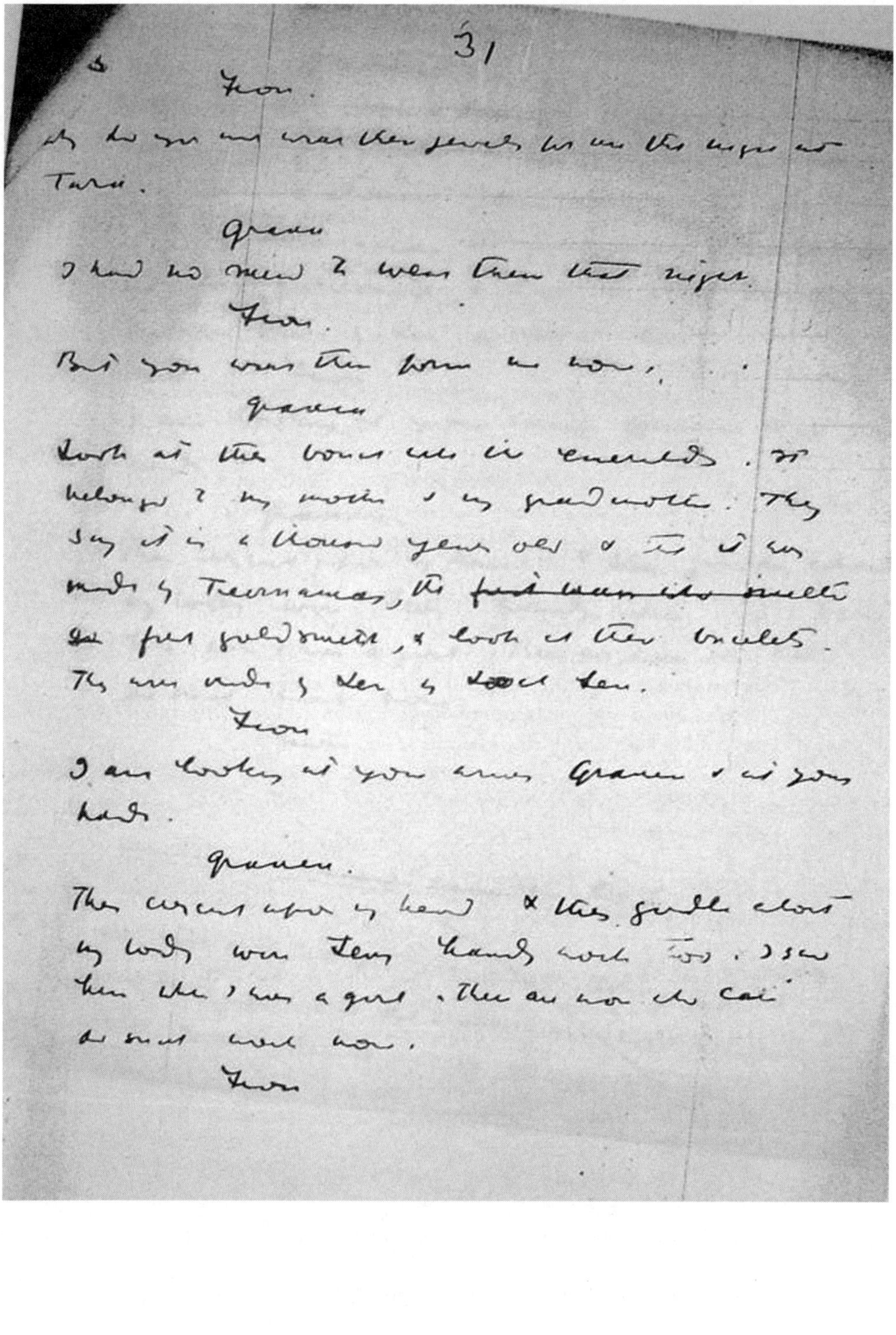

3 31

Fion.

Why do you not wear these jewels [illegible] on this night at Tara.

Grania

I had no need to wear them that night.

Fion.

But you wear them for me now.

Grania

Look at the bronze [illegible] in emeralds. It belonged to my mother & my grandmother. They say it is a thousand years old & that it was made by [illegible], the ~~first man who smelt~~ first goldsmith, & look at these bracelets. They were made by [illegible] of ~~[illegible]~~ [illegible].

Fion

I am looking at your arms Grania & at your hands.

Grania.

These circlets upon my head & this girdle about my body were [illegible] hands work too. I saw him when I was a girl. There are none who can do such work now.

Fion

[NLI 8777(4) c, 32r]

31

Fion.

Why did you not wear those jewels on tht night at Tara.

Grania

I had no mind to wear them that night.

Fion.

But you wear them for me now.

Grania

Look at the brace lets in emeralds. It belonged t my mother & my grandmother. They say it is a thousand years old & tht it was made by Teernamas, the ~~first man who smelted go~~ first goldsmith, & look at these bracelets – This was made by Len of Loch Len.

Fion

I am looking at your arms Grania & at your hands.

Grania.

This circlet upon my head & this girdle about my body were Lens handy work too. I saw him when I was a girl. There are non who can do such work now.

Fion

[NLI 8777(4) c, 33r]

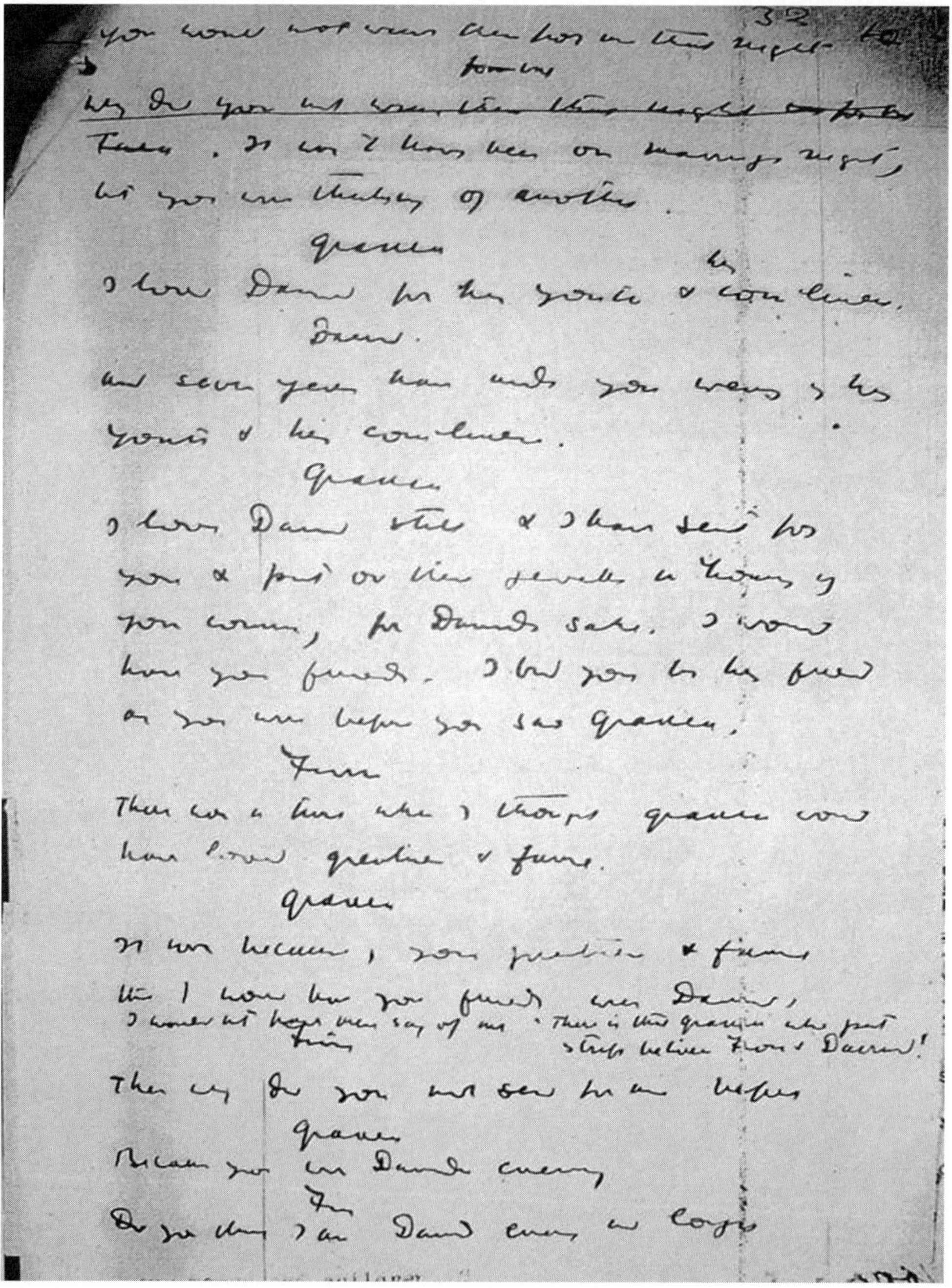
32

you would not wear them [illegible] on this night
Finn
~~Why do you not wear them this night [illegible]~~
Finn. It was to have been our marriage night;
but you are thinking of another.

Grania
I love Diarmuid for his youth & comeliness.

Diarmuid.
And seven years hence until you weary of his
youth & his comeliness.

Grania
I love Diarmuid still & I have sent for
you & put on these jewels in honour of
your coming, for Diarmuid's sake. I would
have you friends. I bid you be his friend
as you were before you saw Grania.

Finn
There was a time when I thought Grania would
have loved greatness & fame.

Grania
It was because of your greatness & fame
that I would have you friends with Diarmuid,
I would not have men say of me 'There is the Grania who put
strife between Finn & Diarmuid'!

Then why do you not send for me before

Grania
Because you were Diarmuid's enemy

Finn
Do you think I am Diarmuid's enemy no longer

[NLI 8777(4) c, 33[r]]

32 ~~10~~

You would not wear them for me that night
~~for~~ me
~~Why did you not wear them that night at for me~~
~~Tara~~. It was to have been our marriage night,
but you were thinking of another.

Grania his
I lovd Darmd for his youth & com liness

Darmd
And seven years hav made you weary of his
youth & his com liness.

Grania
I love Darmd still & I have sent for
you & put on these jewells in honour of
you coming for Darmds sake. I woud
have you friends. I bid you be his friend
as you were before you saw Grania.

Finn
There was a time when I thougt Grania woud
have lovd greatnes & fame.

Grania
It was because of your greatness & fame
that I would hav you friends with Darmd,
I would not have men say of me 'There is that Grania who put
strife between Fion & Dairmd.'

Finn
Then why did you not send for me before.

Grania
Because you wer Darmds enemy

Fin
Do you think I am Darmd enemy no longer

1–2 WBY first wrote "at Tara", then deleted both words and substituted "for me", and finally deleted the entire first sentence.

16–17 The lines were squeezed in after the surrounding lines were written.

[NLI 8777(4) b, 34[r]]

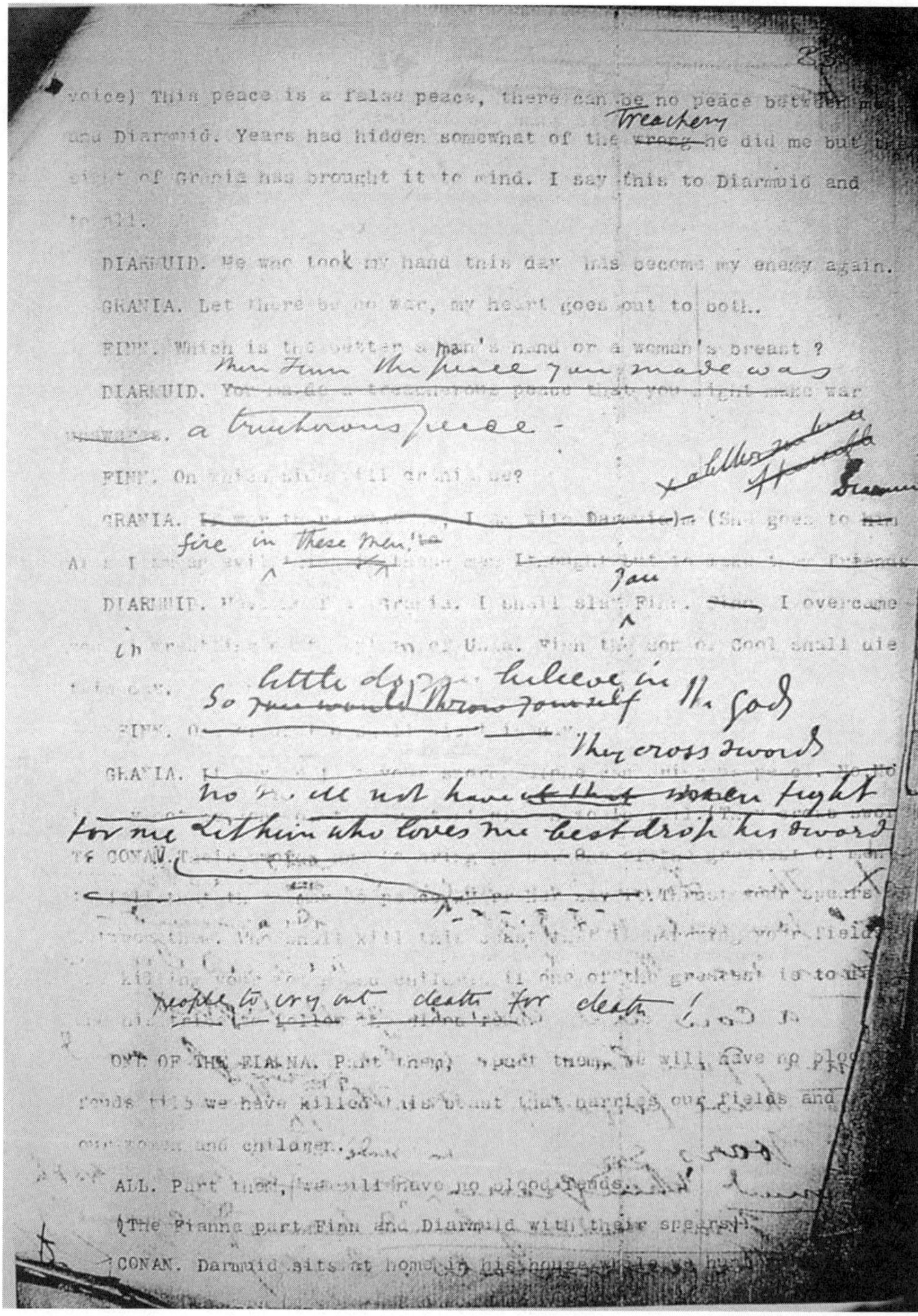

voice) This peace is a false peace, there can be no peace between me and Diarmuid. Years had hidden somewhat of the ~~wrong~~ treachery he did me but the sight of Grania has brought it to mind. I say this to Diarmuid and to all.

DIARMUID. He who took my hand this day has become my enemy again.

GRANIA. Let there be no war, my heart goes out to both.

FINN. Which is the better a man's hand or a woman's breast ?

DIARMUID. Then Finn the peace you made was ~~You made a treacherous peace that you might make war unawares~~. a treacherous peace –

FINN. On which side will Grania be?

GRANIA. ~~[illegible] I am with Diarmuid~~ (She goes to ~~him~~ [illegible]

And I [illegible] fire in these men ~~[illegible]~~

DIARMUID. [illegible] Grania. I shall slay you Finn. ~~[illegible]~~ I overcame [illegible] in wrestling [illegible] of Ulla. When the son of Cool shall die [illegible]

So ~~you would throw yourself~~ little do you believe in the gods

FINN. ~~[illegible]~~

They cross swords

GRANIA. ~~[illegible]~~ No I will not have ~~[illegible]~~ men fight for me Let him who loves me best drop his sword

CONAN. ~~[illegible]~~

~~[illegible]~~ Thrust your spears between them. We shall kill this beast [illegible] your fields killing your [illegible] children if one of the greatest is to [illegible] people to cry out death for death!

ONE OF THE FIANNA. Part them, part them, we will have no blood feuds till we have killed this beast that harries our fields and our women and children.

ALL. Part them, we will have no blood feuds.

(The Fianna part Finn and Diarmuid with their spears.)

CONAN. Diarmuid sits at home in his house while we hunt

[NLI 8777(4) b, 34r]

33 ~~11~~

voice) This peace is a false peace, there can be no peace between me
treachery
and Diarmuid. Years had hidden somewhat of the ~~wrong~~ he did me but the
sight of Grania has brought it to mind. I say this to Diarmuid and
to all.

DIARMUID. He who too k **my hand this day has become my enemy again.**

GRANIA. Let there be no war, my heart goes out to both.

FINN. Which is the better a ma **n's hand or a woman's breast?**

Then Finn the peace you made was
DIARMUID. ~~You ma de a treacherous peace that you might make~~ war
~~unawares~~. a treacherous peace –

FINN. On which side will Grania be? × ~~a letter [?you] [?have] if possible~~

Diarmuid
GRANIA. ~~If war there must be, I am with Darmuid)m~~ (She goes to ~~him~~
fire in these men! ~~**to**~~
Alas I am an evil‸**~~thing in~~**‸**these men. I thought but to make them friends**
you
DIARMUID. Have no fear Grania. I shall slay‸ **Finn. ~~Finn,~~ I overcame**
{in {n
you {**ni wrestling on the plai** {**n of Usna. Finn the son of Cool shall die**
this day.
little do you believe in the Gods
So ~~you would throw yourself~~
FINN. ~~One of of the two shall die this day~~.
They cross swords
GRANIA. ~~It may be that your swords alone can bring us peace. No, No~~
No no ill not have ~~at that~~ men fight
~~it may not be, one of the greatest of men would fall. (They cross swords~~
for me Let him who loves me best drop his sword
{o {N
T {**h CONA** {**n. ~~Their swords are to bring peace. One of the greatest of men~~ is**
~~to fall that there may be peace.~~‸ – **~~Hear her say it.~~ Thrust your spears**

The repairs of faint typing in lines 5, 7, 14, and 19 are likely to have been made by AG. The authorship of some of the other insertions and comments on this page is uncertain. The last nine lines are transcribed on p. 367.

[NLI 8777(4) b, 34r continued, 34v]

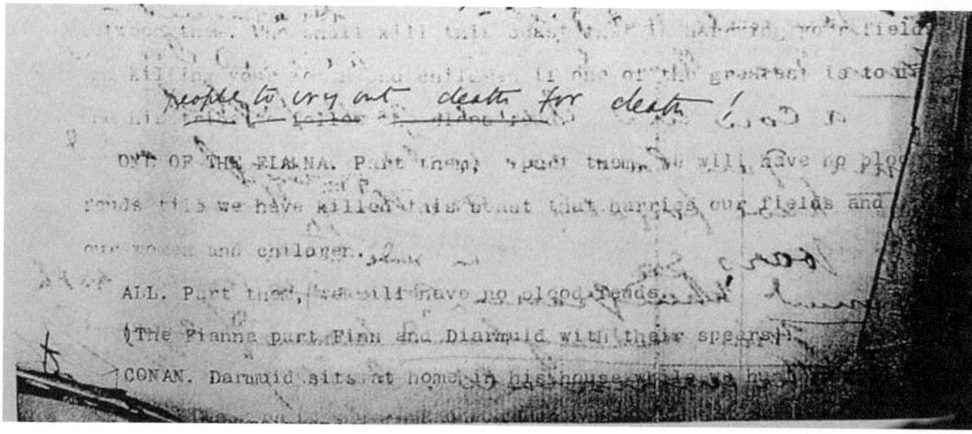

kill this beast ... your fields

... is one of the greatest ... is to ...

people to cry out death for death!

ONE OF THE FIANNA. Part them; part them. We will have no blood feuds till we have killed this beast that harries our fields and our ... and cattle.

ALL. Part them, we will have no blood feuds.

(The Fianna part Finn and Diarmuid with their spears.)

CONAN. Diarmuid sits at home in his house while we hunt

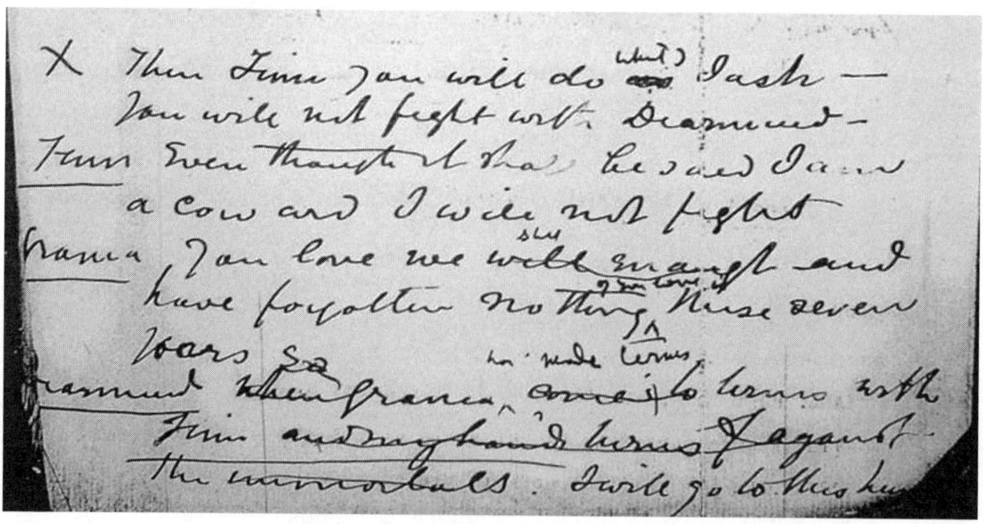

X Then Finn you will do what I ask —
You will not fight with Diarmuid —
Finn Even though it was he said I am
a coward and I will not fight
Grania You love me still with angst and
have forgotten nothing these seven
years
Diarmuid Grania made terms to terms with
Finn and ... against
the immortals. I will go to his h

[NLI 8777(4) b, 34r continued]

between them. Who shall kill this beast that is harrying your fields

{,
and killing your women and children if one of the greatest is to fall{.
people to cry out death for death!
and his ~~tribe to follow the blood feud~~.

ONE OF THE FIANNA. Part them, part them, we will have no blood feuds till we have killed this beast that harries our fields and killes our women and children.

ALL. Part them, we will have no blood feuds.

(}
)}The Fianna part Finn and Diarmuid with their spears).

CONAN. Darmuid sits at home in his house while we hunt in the <u>wind</u> hail and the rain and

[NLI 8777(4) b, 34v]

what I
X Then Finn you will do ~~as~~ I ask –
You will not fight with Diarmuid –

<u>Finn</u> Even though it shall be said I am
a coward I will not fight

still
<u>Grania</u> You love me ~~well enough~~ and
of your love
have forgotten nothing ^ these seven
years

~~So~~ has made terms
<u>Diarmuid</u> ~~When~~ Grania ~~comes to terms~~ with
Finn ~~and my ^hands turns to against~~
~~the immortals~~. I will go to this hunt

34v, l. 1 The lines are keyed to lines 18–19 on the facing page (here fol. 35r).
8 WBY appears to have inserted "has" after he made the other insertion

[NLI 8777(4) b, 35r]

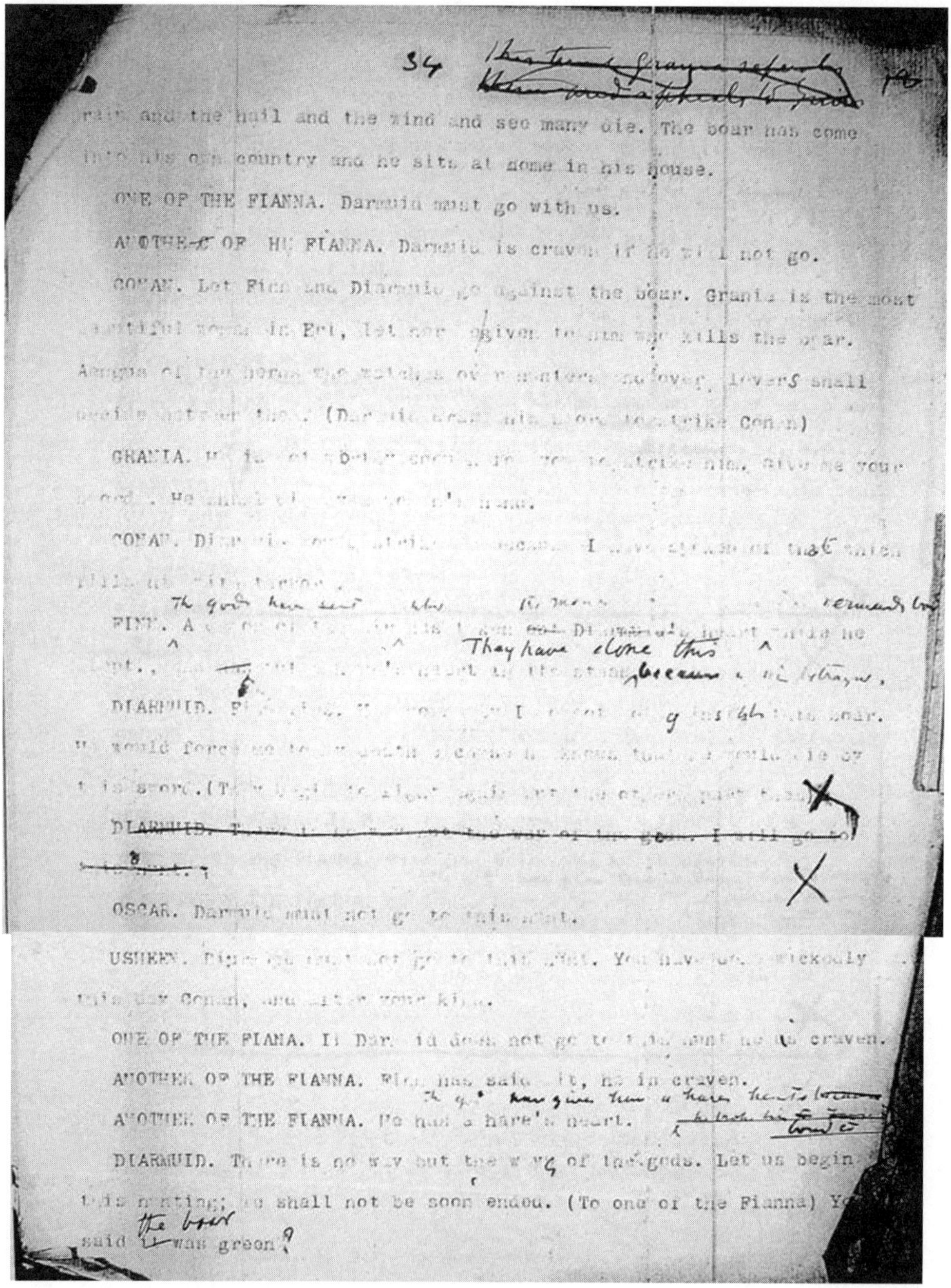

34

rain and the hail and the wind and see many die. The boar has come into his own country and he sits at home in his house.

ONE OF THE FIANNA. Darmuid must go with us.

ANOTHER OF THE FIANNA. Darmuid is craven if he will not go.

CONAN. Let Finn and Diarmuid go against the boar. Grania is the most beautiful woman in Eri, let her be given to him who kills the boar. [illegible] lovers shall [illegible] (Diarmuid draws his sword to strike Conan)

GRANIA. [illegible] Give me your sword. [illegible]

CONAN. [illegible] I [illegible] that [illegible]

FINN. A [illegible] Diarmuid's heart [illegible] They have done this because [illegible]

DIARMUID. [illegible] I [illegible] this boar. [illegible] sword. [illegible]

~~DIARMUID. [illegible] I will go to [illegible]~~

OSCAR. Darmuid must not go to this hunt.

USHEEN. [illegible] You have [illegible] wickedly [illegible] Conan, [illegible]

ONE OF THE FIANNA. If Darmuid does not go to this hunt he is craven.

ANOTHER OF THE FIANNA. Who has said it, he is craven.

ANOTHER OF THE FIANNA. He has a hare's heart.

DIARMUID. There is no way but the way of the gods. Let us begin this hunting; it shall not be soon ended. (To one of the Fianna) You said the boar was green?

The repairs of faint typing and corrections of typos in lines 4, 6, 7, 9, 11, 14, 15, 18, 25, and 27 are likely to have been made by AG. Images of the top and bottom of the page are combined to show all of the text.

[NLI 8777(4) b, 35r]

34 ~~this time Grania separates them and appeals to Finn~~ ~~*12*~~

rain and the hail and the wind and see many die. The boar has come into his own country and he sits at home in his house.

ONE OF THE FIANNA. Darmuid must go with us.

ANOTHER ~~C~~ OF THE FIANNA. Darmuid is craven if he will not go.

CONAN. Let Finn and Diarmuid go against the boar. Grania is the most beautiful woman in Eri, let her be/given to him who kills the boar. Aengus of the herds who watches over hunters and over lover s shall decide between them. (Darmuid draws his sword to strike Conan)

GRANIA. He is not not w{o/i}rthy enough for you to strike him. Give me your sword. He shall die by a woman's hand.

CONAN. Diarmuid would strike me because I have spoken of th{at/ey} which fills him with terror.

The gods have sent who this mans out of Dermuids body

FINN.^A demon of the air^has taken ~~out~~ ~~Diarmuids~~ heart^while he

They have done this

slept., and ~~has~~ put put a hare's heart in its stead.^because [?of] [?his] betrayal.

DIARMUID. Finn lies. He knows why I do not go a{g}ains{t}bt this boar. He would force me to my death because he knows that he would die by this sword. (They begin to fight again but the others part them). X

~~**DAIRMUID. There is no way but the way of the g{o}ods. I will go to this hunt.**~~ X

OSCAR. Darmuid must not go to this hunt.

USHEEN. Diarmuid must not go to this hunt. You have done wickedly this day Conan, and after your kind.

ONE OF THE FIANNA. If Diarmid does not go to this hunt he u{i}s craven

The gods have given him a hares heart. ~~because~~

ANOTHER OF THE FIANNA. He has a hare's heart.~~he broke his to Fion Finn bond to~~

DIARMUID. There is no way but the wayb of the gods. Let us begin this hunting; we shall not be soon ended. (To one of the Fianna) You

the boar

said ~~it~~ was green{?/%}

[NLI 8777(4) b, 36r]

35 13

ONE OF THE FIAnna. It was green like the sea.

DARMUID (excitedly) I have no fear, it is green like the sea. (He takes a light spear from the wall) Why should it matter to you which spear I take

GRANIA. Take Broad-edge, your heavy spear.

DIARMUID. ~~This spear is heavy enough.~~ (He takes down a light shield)

GRANIA. Take your heavy shield. ~~[illegible]~~

DIARMUID. No man shall say that Diarmuid went to that hunting with his battle harness upon him.

GRANIA. ~~Diarmuid~~ Diarmuid, do not go to this hunting.

DIARMUID. Have no fear ~~Grania~~ I do not fear this beast. He is green like the sea. 4 (The Fianna have been going out of the door, & Diarmuid rushes after them. ~~[illegible]~~

Grania alone — After a pause the old foster mother comes in, carrying her spindle.) × They have all gone what there is ~~[illegible]~~ all quiet again

FOSTER MOTHER. ~~It was your desire to [illegible] Finn that sent Diarmuid to this hunting.~~ (She sits down & begins to spin)

GRANIA. Mother, [illegible] you could tell me what is coming to Diarmuid. You know the [illegible] of the [illegible].

FOSTER MOTHER. You [illegible] pleasure out to [illegible] or love.

GRANIA. Mother, I love Diarmuid with the love that marriage brings. ~~My father has told me that [illegible]~~ When I was a child you had still those wrinkles under your eyes, you were no younger then than you are today. You who know so much of the past must know of what is to come. You will tell me what is coming to Diarmuid.

FOSTER MOTHER. When last I saw Finn he slept and it was for your happiness. It may be that if Darmuid [he] sleeps it will be for your happiness.

Grania — What does the ~~thread~~ flax say ~~to~~ [to] mother ? Is the thread that is coming from the distaff Darmuid's [thread], or mine ?

FOSTER MOTHER. It is not yours thread —

[NLI 8777(4) b, 36r]

35 *13*

ONE OF THE FIAnna. It was green like the sea.

DARMUID{( )excitedly) I have no fear, it is green like the sea. (He takes a light spear from the wall) Why should it matter to you which spear I take

GRANIA. Take Broad-edge, your heavy spear.

DIARMUID. ~~This spear is heavy enough.~~ (He takes down a light shield)

GRANIA. T{ake he your heavy shield. ~~Forgive me Diarmuid~~

DIARMUID. No man shall say that Diarmuid went to thsi hunting with his battle harness upon him.

GRANIA. ~~Dermot,~~ Diarmuid, do not go to this hunting.

DIARMUID. Have no fear ~~Grania.~~ I do not fear this beast. He is green like the sea. ✗(The Fianna have been going out of the door,

+

Diarmuid rushes after them). ———
Grania alone – **After a pause the old foster mother comes in, carrying her spindle.)** ✗ They have all gone ~~what~~ there is ~~bad sentence~~ quiet again

FOSTER MOTHER. ~~It was your desire to see Finn that sent Diarmuid to this hunting.~~ (She sits down & begins to spin)

GRANIA. Mother, mother you are wise, you will tell me what is coming to Diarmuid. You know the counsels of the gods.

FOSTER MOTHER. The gods measure out to every man his time for love.

GRANIA. Mother, I love Diarmuid with the love that marriage brings. ~~My father has told me that when~~ When I was a child you had still those wrinkles under your eyes, you were no younger then than you are today. Y}ou who know so much of the past must know of what is to come. You will tell me what is coming to Diarmuid.

The repairs of faint typing and corrections of typos in lines 2, 5, 10, 10+, 19, 22, 23, and 25 are likely to have been made the typist, AG. The last five lines are transcribed on p. 373.

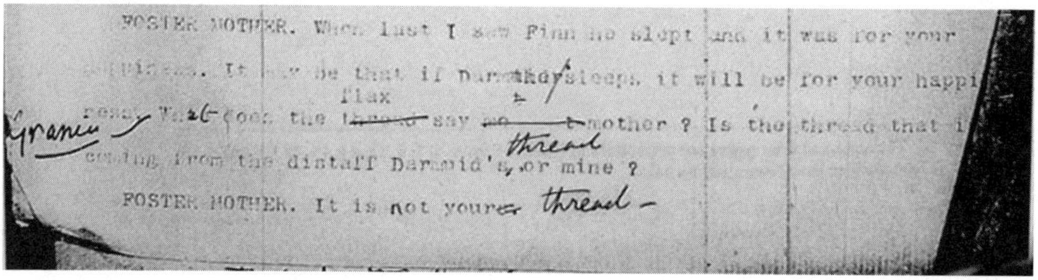

FOSTER MOTHER. When last I saw Finn he slept and it was for your happiness. It may be that if ~~Darmuid~~ they sleeps it will be for your happiness.

Grania — What does the ~~thread~~ flax say ~~mo~~ mother ? Is the thread that is coming from the distaff Darmuid's thread, or mine ?

FOSTER MOTHER. It is not yours thread —

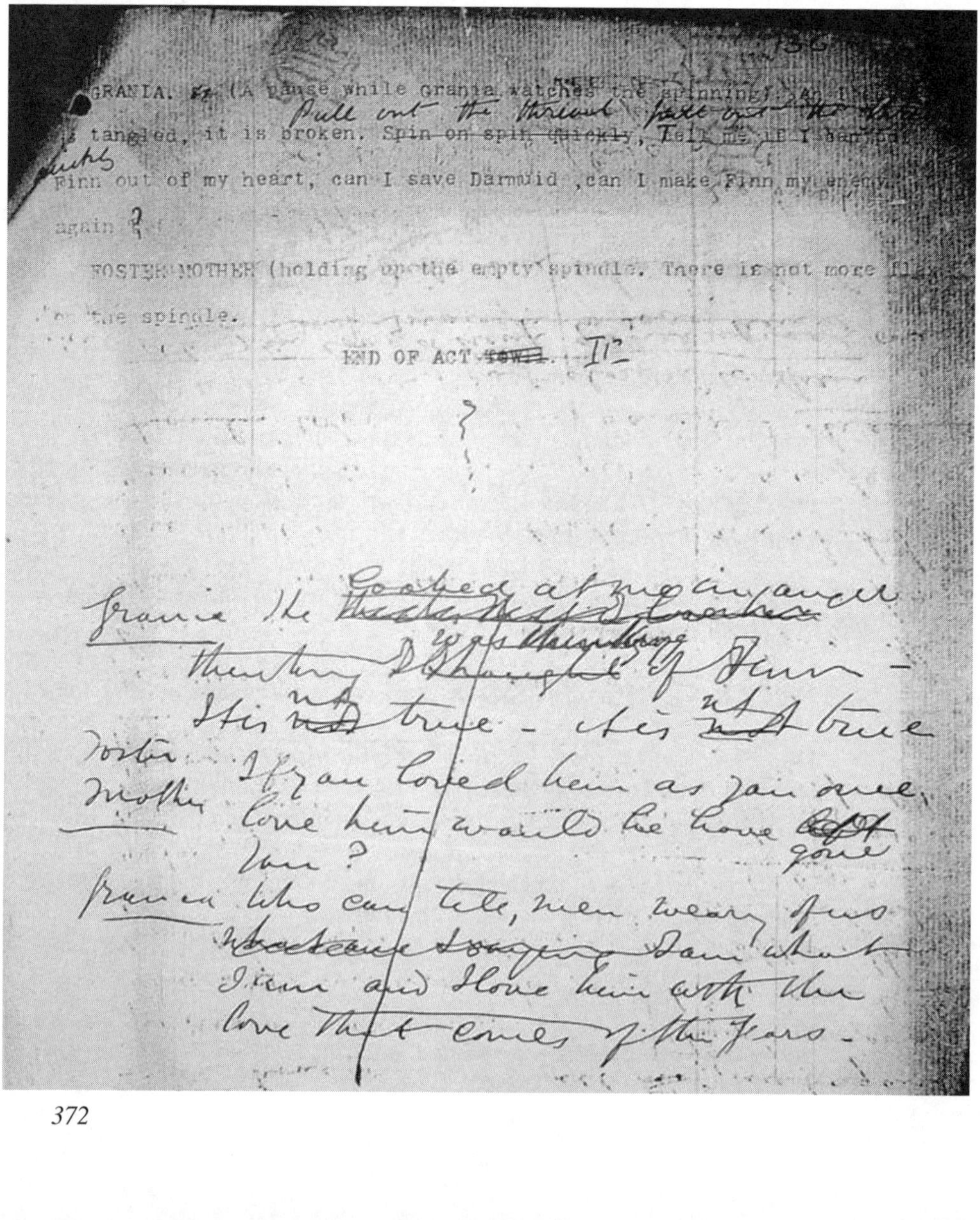

GRANIA. (A pause while Grania watches the spinning) Pull out the thread ... is tangled, it is broken. ~~Spin on spin quickly.~~ ~~Tell me if I can put~~ quickly Finn out of my heart, can I save Darmuid, can I make Finn my enemy again ?

FOSTER MOTHER (holding up the empty spindle. There is not more flax on the spindle.

END OF ACT ~~TWO~~. II

?

Grania He looked at me in anger ~~...~~ was ... then ~~I thought~~ of Finn —
It is not true — it is not true

Foster Mother If you loved him as you once love him would he have ~~left~~ gone from you?

Grania Who can tell, men weary of us ~~...~~ I am what I am and I love him with the love that comes of the years —

[NLI 8777(4) b, 36r continued]

FOSTER MOTHER. When last I saw Finn he slept and it was for your
happiness. It may be that if Darmuid~~r~~ sleeps it will be for your happi-
{ at flax ~~t~~
ness. Wh{ te does the ~~thread~~ say ~~mo t~~ mother ? Is the thread that is
Grania thread
coming from the distaff Darmuid's ,or mine ?
^

n}
FOSTER MOTHER. It is u}ot your~~s~~. thread –

[NLI 8777(4) b, 37r]

36 ~~14.~~

GRANIA. ~~Sp~~ (A pause while Grania watches the spinning). Ah I see it
Pull out the thread pull out the thread
T}
is tangled, it is broken. ~~Spin on spin quickly~~, t}ell me if I can put
quickly
Finn out of my heart, can I save Darmuid , can I make Finn my enemy
{?
again{%

FOSTER MOTHER (holding up the empty spindle. There is not more flax
on the spindle.

END OF ACT ~~TOWH~~ II

looked at me in anger
Grania He ~~thinks that I love Finn~~
was ~~thinking~~
thinking I ~~thought~~ of Finn –
not not
It is ~~not~~ true – it is ~~not~~ true

Foster Mother If you loved him as you once
love him would he have ~~left~~
you? gone

Grania Who can tell, men weary of us
~~what am I saying~~ I am what
I am and I love him with the
love that comes of the years –

37r The typos in lines 1 and 4 are likely to have been corrected by AG.

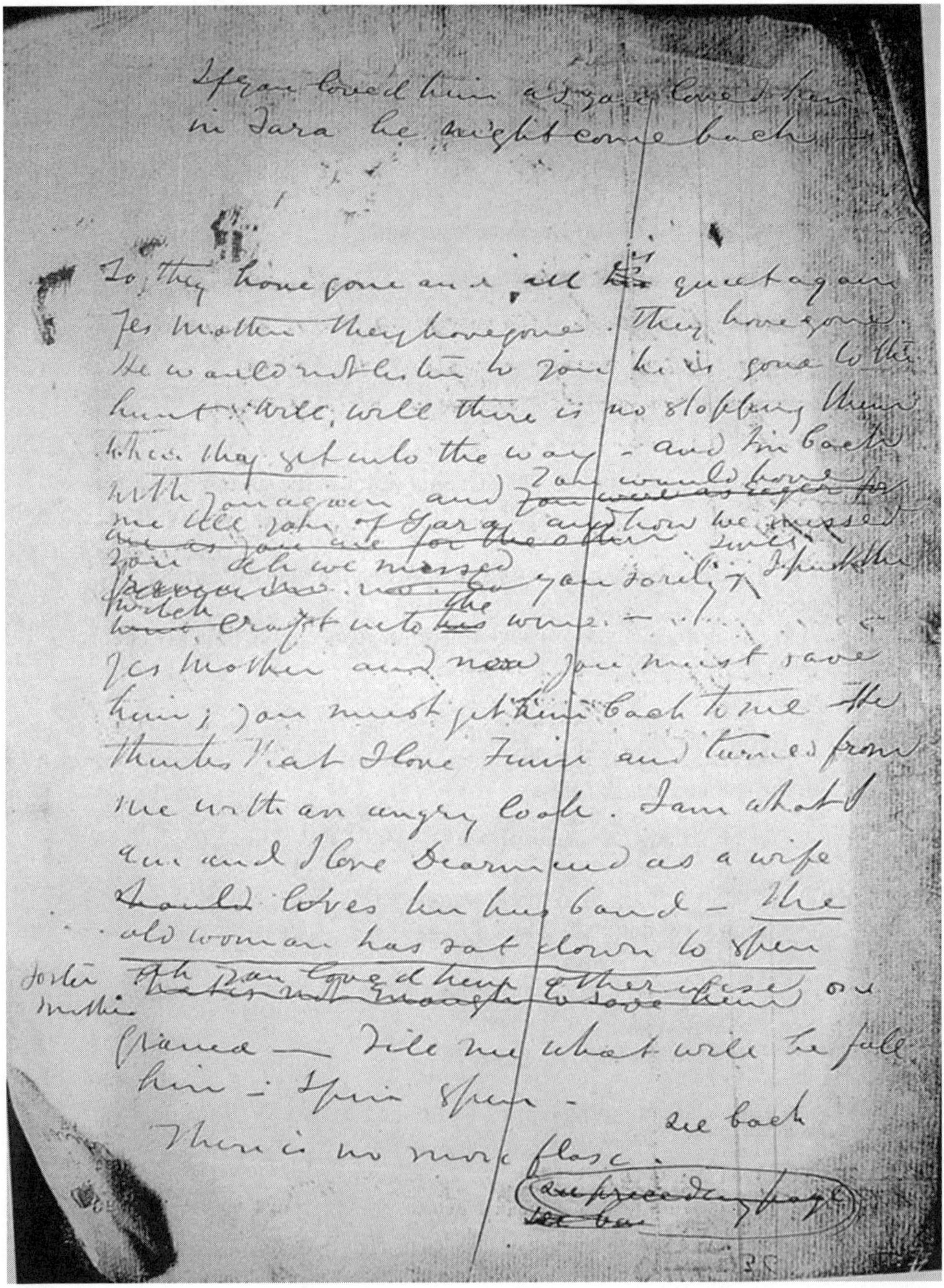
If you loved him as you love him
in Tara he might come back

So they have gone and all is quiet again
Yes mother they have gone. They have gone.
He would not listen to you he is gone to the
hunt. Well, well there is no stopping them
when they get into the way — and I'm back
with you again and ~~you were as eager~~ you would have
me all [illegible] of Tara and how we missed
~~me as you are for the other~~ [illegible]
you. Ah we missed you sorely ~~[illegible]~~ I put the
witch craft into the wine. —
Yes mother and now you must save
him; you must get him back to me. He
thinks that I love Finn and turned from
me with an angry look. I am what I
am and I love Diarmuid as a wife
~~should~~ loves her husband — The
old woman has sat down to spin
Foster mother ~~Ah you loved him otherwise~~
~~[illegible]~~ or
Grania — Tell me what will befall
him — Spin spin —
There is no more flax. see back
(see preceding page
~~see back~~)

[NLI 8777(4) b, 37v]

If you loved him as you loved him
in Tara he might come back –

is
~~is~~
So they have gone and all ~~has~~ quiet again

Yes Mother they have gone. They have gone.

He would not listen to you he is gone to the
hunt. Well, well there is no stopping them
when they get into the way – and I'm back
you would have
with you again and ~~you were as eager for~~
me tell you of Tara and how we missed
~~one as you are for the other~~
you   Ah we missed   since
~~Grania. No. No. [?bu]~~ you sorely ^ – I put the
witch   the
~~wine~~ craft into ~~his~~ wine. –

Yes Mother and now you must save
him; you must get him back to me He
thinks that I love Finn and turned from
me with an angry look. I am what I
am and I love Dearmuid as a wife
should loves her husband – <u>The</u>
<u>old woman has sat down to spin</u>

Ah you loved him otherwise once
Foster ~~That is not enough to save him~~
Mother

Grania – Tell me what will be fall
him – Spin spin –
see back
There is no more flax
~~see preceding page~~
~~see ba~~

GM turned the leaf upside down before writing on the verso. WBY transcribed and improved GM's draft on a separate unnumbered page (NLI 8777[4] f, fol. 40r).

17 The last word in the revised line appears to be in WBY's hand, in a slightly different ink.

[NLI 8777(4) f, 40r]

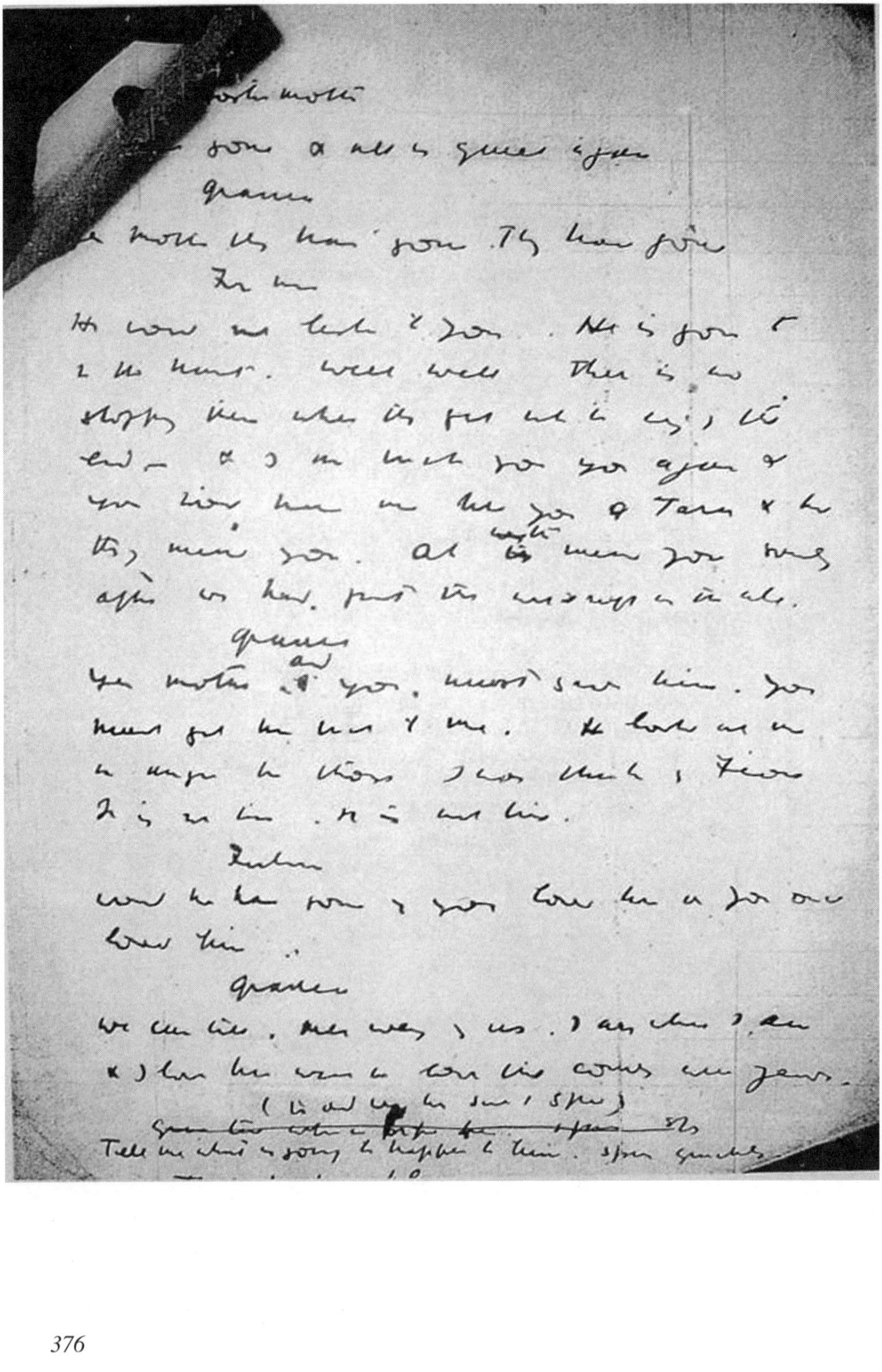

Single-Page Holograph by W. B. Yeats to Fit Act II

[NLI 8777(4) f, 40^{r}]

Foster Mother
They have gone & all is quiet again

Grania
Yes Mother they have gone. They have gone

For Mo
He woud not listen to you. He is gone t
to the hunt. Well well. There is no
stopping them when they get int th way of the
end – & I am with you you again &
you woud have me tell you of Tara & how
~~we~~ th
they missd you. Ah ~~the~~ missd you sorely
after we had put the witch craft in th ale.

Grania
and
Yes Mother – ~~O~~ you must save him. You
must get him back t me. He lookd at me
in anger he thoug I was think of Fion
It is not him. It is not him.

Fosterm
Would he hav gone if you lovd him as you once
loved him.

Grania
We can tell. Men weary of us. I am what I am
& I love him with a love that comes with years.
(to and [?wher] she [?sits] & spins)
(~~Goes to where a [?sits] her~~ ~~spins [?sits]~~)
Tell me what is going to happen to him. Spin quickly.

There is no more flax

Yeats transcribes and improves upon GM's holograph draft in NLI 8774(4) b, fol. 37^{v}.
19 The line is present in the original manuscript; the camera did not capture the full page.

ACT II.

House of Darmuid at Grania

Cormac My people are waiting for me by the Red Waterfall I shall sleep there and set out for Tara in the morning

Darmuid You have a long journey before you

Cormac Yes we have a long journey before us for neither I nor Neil can bear the saddle many hours at a time

Darmuid I would Cormac that you could stay with us here or that I and Grania could go to Tara with you

Cormac No Darmuid after 7 years of flight and danger you will need much rest from 7 years in the woods my daughter gave up much for love,Thatyou and a Queen's daughter should have lived like foxes creeping from break to break

6486[illegible]06

Rough Typescript Fair Copy of Complete Act, Lightly Revised by W. B. Yeats

[Berg(06), 2^{r}]

ACT II.

House of Darmud at Drania

Cormac **My people are waiting for me by the Red Waterfall I shall sleep there and set out for Tara in the morning**

Darmud **You have a long journey before you**

Cormac **Yes we have a long journey before us for neither I nor Neil can bear the saddle many hours at a time**

Darmud **I would Cormac that you could stay with us here or that I and Grania could go to Tara with you**

Cormac **No Darmud after 7 years of flight and danger you will need much rest from 7 years in the woods my daughter gave up much for love,thatyou and a Queen's daughter should have lived like foxes creeping from break to break**

[3^{r}]

Going to the door - I will show you the boundaries of your Kingdom again before I go It ends southward of the Hill of the Shee and westward of those gray cliffs where one can see the edges of the foam and it goes northward eastward as far as these Mountains go. Finn waits for me at the Red Waterfall I bade him come no further because you would have still thought him an enemy. When he and I are gone there will be nobody within a days journey but shepherds I wish that I could stay with you. One begins to understand the meanings of things when the things begin to fade. One comes to understand that there is nothing worth having except love. I ask myself now why I ever went to War or sat upon my throne. I am giving you the things I have learned to know the worth of.

The first leaf, 1^{r}, is an otherwise blank sheet on which WBY has written "Act II" in pencil.

[Berg(06)]

[4r]

Darmud I shall make myself so strong in this Kingdom that you have given me that if Finn never become my enemy again I shall be able to keep Grania from him. I will make my shepherds put away the Crook for the Bow and Spear.

Cormac No, No, No, the crook is better than the bow and spear Finn will never be your enemy again, and I have given you this Kingdom to be happy in. Make my Grania happy. She cannot bear sadness. She will not bid me good bye. She says she looks to see me in Tara or here again. But Dermud you will come down the hill with me, we will say good bye at the stream where the horses are waiting (Neal comes forward to put the Kings cloak over his shoulders) and now my staff (He takes a few steps towards the door Grania comes in)

[5r]

Grania I thought you had gone father (Returns to embrace her) You know I will not say good bye you will come again when you are weary of statecraft and someday I shall see you in Tara.

Cormac I will come to you again though it is a long journey but you must not come to Tara . There is always trouble at Tara, and you might make a little trouble there.

Grania Would I father

Cormac Now they have brought you your foster-mother she said you had need of her you will not forget Tara that would be enough.

Grania I have seen none of the old faces these seven years I shall be glad to have her with me I wish you would leave Neil with me too (Going to Neal) Give me your hand you were my only playmate, do you remember the little pool

[6r]

at the end of the wood where we used to sit on a high bank

5r, l. 8 Would] WBY's holograph (NLI 8777[4] a, fol. 4r, line 14) has "Have".
9 they] WBY's holograph (NLI 8777[4] a, fol. 4r, line 15) has "that I".

2 fishing for roach

3 **Cormac** The rooks are flying home we shall not be atthe Red Water-
4 fall before dark (Cormac, Neil and Darmud go out)

5 **Neil** (from outside) Good bye Good bye
(Grania walks to the spinning wheel sits down and begins
to spin after atime she risesand goes up the stage for
her foster mother comes in)

6 **Grania** How silent the valley is, it has been so silent all day
7 the silence has been like a harp string that is stretched
8 so tightly that it mustsnap asunder

9 **Foster** When men move hither and thither there is noise and hurry -
10 **Mother** ing of feet, when the gods move hither and thither there is
11 silence

12 **Grania** Finn has given up his quest of me .my life stands still, pull
13 out the thread for me ,we will watch whether it will break.,

[7^{r}]

1 or be knotted or come smoothly Butwhy should we watch it?
2 It will always come smoothly now (Dairmud enters)

3 **Dairmud** What were you and that old woman saying, Grania?

4 **Grania** We spoke of the silence of the valley and I asked her what
5 is going to happen and then I told her that it was no use
6 because nothing will happen here

7 **Dairmud** You are weary of this valley Grania, you do not wish for
8 this peaceful life

9 **Grania** Why should not this valley and your love be enough for me?
10 Have I not everything I have sought? It is you who have begu
11 begun to weary of days in which there was nothing of love.

6^{r}, ll. 12, 13 The period and the comma are lightly inserted after each occurrence of "me", in blue-black ink, perhaps by the typist.

7^{r}, ll. 3–6 The typescript departs from NLI 8777(4) a here, unless a page of manuscript is missing. In the holograph, the Foster-Mother exits at the end of fol. 6^{r} (subsequently revised to the end of fol. 8^{r}) and Dairmud's speech, "You are weary of this valley" is on fol. 8^{r} (lines 10–11). The stage description WBY wrote into the present typescript at line 14 repairs the omission. The identical stage description he inserted into NLI 8777(4) a, fol. 8^{r}, is also in pencil, which might suggest he consulted the earlier text to repair the later one.

[Berg(06)]

Maybe Dairdmd

You are weary of the valley Dairmud . ~~I see that~~ you would live as you have lived before you saw me and go by^ Finn's side in battle *(Foster mothr goes out)*

Dairmud **You have not seen my thoughts, Grania, I am not weary of this**

[8^{r}]

valley where there is nothing but you (Going to door) Your foster mother is looking out over the wood as though she was waiting for somebody or something and now she is gone round to the other side of the house.

Grania **She will go in by the other door and sit looking into the fire, she often sits that way for hours she is so old she has much to remember**

Dairmud **She has spun a great deal of flax since she came**

Grania **I shall have need for all her flax and of all that the shepherds wives spin for me for I am going to send it to the weavers to be made into a web colored like the leaves. I shall hang the web round these walls and embroider upon it our wanderings in the woods. I shall be many years embroidering but at last we shall see all round us birds and beasts and trees and rivers and you and I wandering among them**

[9^{r}]

Dairmud **Of what are you thinking now, Grania**

Grania **xxxxxxxxxxxxxxxxxxxxxx I am thinking how everything passes away from us except love. The hour pass by like the mist if we were to listen we would hear the hoofs of my fathers horses going along the edge of the wood. He was standing there a moment ago and yet it seems as if it were a year ago. How clearly one remembers those seven years We have seven years of memories Darmud.**

Darmud **What day among those days do you remember Grania. Of what are you thinking.**

8^{r}, ll. 2–15 A passage substituted for the largely canceled lines at NLI 8777(4) a, fol. 9^{r}, lines 4–17.

9^{r}, ll. 1–2 The first part ascription and the two lines of text are typed in over an erasure with black ribbon.

1–9 The lines interpolate a passage that is not present in NLI 8777(4) a, fol. 9^{r}. The texts rejoin at the second part of line 9 here.

Grania I am thinking of the day when we left the broiled salmon on the elder tree for Finn to find it, we were wandering by the side of a river we had left Tara but nine days and every day we had hung an uncooked salmon on a tree as a message for Finn

[10r]

Darmud It was on the ninth night that I broke my oath to Finn

Grania The sword was no longer between us Darmud, but Darmud tell me what day you are thinking of

Darmud Of one night when the shadows were as still as the cromlec over our heads and the moon was shining among the shadows We had been sleeping in each others arms and had been awakened by the baying of a hound. We looked from under the great stone and saw Finn going away from us seeking us

Grania Yes I remember that night, we could not have escaped from Finn He was coming towards us but something seemed to lead him away. Of what are you thinking now Darmud

Darmud Of nothing Grania

Grania I pray you tell me Darmud of what you are thinking

Darmud Of how I overcame Finn when he set guards at the seven doors of the Dun

[11r]

Grania But there is another thought, a thought behind these thoughts something you will not speak of

Darmud No Grania, I am only thinking of pur happiness I am thinking of our coming here three moons ago and of your fathers coming and of the peace he has made with Finn. We shall be always here. We shall have great happiness for everything we hoped for has come to us.

Grania How silent the valley is I can hear the murmur of the stream Darmud there is somebody coming, there are several people coming up the hill I can hear their feet on the pathway (Darmud goes to the door)

[Berg(06)]

Darmud **It was Finn's horn that we heard I see Conan and three Spear Men why should he be the one out of Feanna who comes to us The Feanna never flouted him but I flouted him more than all in the hardness of my youth. (Conan and Three Spear men enter hurriedly)**

[12r]

Conan to the (Spear men) Stand well in to close the door keep your Spears ready in your hands wehave come here only just in time, look, look there he is on the edge of the wood

The Spearman **It was only gush of wind shaking the Birch Tree**

Conan **(Coming into the house) Do not take your eyes off the edge of the wood It is well for you Darmud that you are no longer of the Feanna you can sit indoors and redden your shins by the fire while we must be hunting a man slaying beast**

Grania **Welcome Conan to the house of Darmud and Grania**

Darmud **What is the beast you are hunting - a Boar so terrible that it seems to me that it is no mortal beast. I may be that you are sitting indoors because you have seen it in the woods, it may be that a story I told you once has given**

[13r]

you no stomach for this hunting

Darmud **You are lying Conan, there has never been a Boar in these woods there is nothing on these Mountains but deer and wild dogs.**

Conan **It is your fear makes you say that I am lying I tell you that we had lighted our fires at the Red Waterfall and had put dry deer flesh to roast when we heard women screaming Presently we saw this man slaying beast coming out of a little wood with blood upon his tusks. It saw the fires**

11r, l. 13 never] The word appears to have been inserted later with black ribbon.

12r, l. 12 NLI 8777(4) a, fol. 14r, lines 1–6, gives Darmud's speech from "a Boar so terrible" onward to Conan—as the sense requires. The correct part ascription comes at the foot of the previous holograph page (NLI 8777[4] a, fol. 13r), which is perhaps why the mistake appears here.

10 **and ran from us arong the river. We heard women screaming**
11 **again and saw men running and we let loose the hounds.**
12 **Thirty of the Feanna and 100 of their hounds are dead.**

13 **Spear man** **It is certainly no mortal beast**

14 **Darmud** **What is the color of this beast**

15 **Conan** **The Boar that is to slay Darmud is black and without**

[14r]

1 **brissels.(He goes over and stands beside Darmud He**
2 **imitates Darmud's gestures) There is the one terror in**
3 **the heart of Conan and Darmud Conan and Darmud are brothers**

4 **Darmud** **(To the Spearmen) What is its color**

5 **Spearman** **I saw it but once and I thought it was gray Darmud and you**

6 **Other Spear-** **I saw it pass by and I thought it was green like the sea**
7 **man** **and it made a sound like the sea in a storm (Conan goes**
back to the door) Darmud takes his spear hurriedly

8 **Grania** **Why do you take your spear you will not go to this hunting**

9 **Darmud** **This beast is coming to attack us this hunt will sweep over**
10 **us it is coming through the woods and I shall be caught up**
11 **like a leaf, leaves,leaves all of us . (Conan and the Spear-**
12 **men rush out) Why have they fled we must bar the door**
13 **(They bar the door and stand listening) the barring of the**
door has made the room dark

[15r]

1 **Grania** **May be there gone because the danger has passed**

2 **Darmud** **Come sit by me, (a pause) and so we sit together in the**
3 **dark, there is no sound now and yet the darkness is full**
4 **of shapes and the silence is full of danger. No we**
5 **cannot sit here. We must unbar the door and let the light**

14r, l. 5 NLI 8777(4) a, fol. 15r, lines 9–11, makes evident that the last two words of this line are a separate line of dialogue spoken by Darmud.

13 NLI 8777(4) a, fol. 16r, lines 9–10, makes clear that the last two lines on this page are a stage direction (that is, the closing parenthesis should follow "dark").

in whatever danger the light shows to us it will be more bearable than this darkness. It is no use barring the door against that which has to come. The things to come are at the wind. They could sweep this house away. They open the door, the hunt seems to have passed.

Grania It has been foretold that you will die in a Boar hunt it will be easy to make that tale nothing.

Darmud A man's life is for hunting and for war and I can have neither. The Feanna are with Finn and they will not leave him for me I must live and die among shepherds I must live

[16r]

and die settling their quarrels,

Grania Finn has made peace,

Darmud It may be that my death is in that wood I may not linger there later than noon because my heart would fail me in the lengthening shadows I might be killed like a hare Grania what made you choose me that nighr in Tara did not Conan tell us the tale of my death as if to warn you

Grania Death walks at every mans heel like a dog.

Darmud Yes, Grania death untied and shapeless, they do not think of death because they do not know ~~what~~from whence or in what shape or at what time it will come to then I would not fear a death like theirs but this death that I have known of since I could understand the tale this death which sets me apart from all other men it fills me with terror. The thought of it makes my hair stand up on my head

[17r]

Grania The tale tells how you will die but not the time of your death.

Darmud The tale does not tell the hour but everything that has

---

15r, ll. 9–10   NLI 8777(4) a, fol. 17r, line -10, confirms that "They open the door," is a parenthetical stage direction.

16r, l. 9   untied] A mistake for "untimed"; cf. NLI 8777(4) a, fol. 18r, line 11. Again, "then" (below, line 11) is mistakenly for "them" (cf. ibid., line 14).

10   Type deletion.

happened shows that my last hours have come, Grania this tale has shaken your mind.

Darmud Then you do not believe in it

Grania We believe and we diabelieve and there is a time when we do not know what we think.

Darmud I was brought through every danger for 7 years it seemed again and again as if there was no escape but something always happened. I was given strength more than a man or they turned aside from where we lay nobody could tell why or it seemed as if the very birds kept watch that they might wake us. Why did the woods feed me and clothe me and guard me and hide me if the Gods had not planned this death before

[18r]

I was born why else was love trust upon me why else when my labours were over was this supper of happiness spread before me Why should I be bid to eat and drink of happiness every hour the Gods know of our hunger and our thirst and sometimes when we are about to die they give us more than we can eat and drink this valley has been filled with peace and silence and I am bid love you as if I had never loved you as if we were new to one another, as if our desire had need of a lure as if our hunger for one another had need of a physic made of druid herbs and then I am told that Finn has ceased from his quest as if his quest had ever mattered to us as if his hatred was ever more than our whet-stone and then, and then, and then as if our wanderings were not happier than this peace I am bid make you happy. (Starting up) I have been led into this valley I am like a wolf in a

[19r]

trap and you are the bait

Grania What are you saying Darmud

Darmud With ague gesture I do not know the words started up suddenly in my mind I do not know what they mean or whence they came from I said I am like a wolf in a trap and I understood those words but how can you be the bait I do not understand

19r, l. 3 With ague gesture] A stage direction; cf. NLI 8777(4) a, fol. 20r, line -1.

[Berg(06)]

ask the gods they put the words into my mind nor can I tell why Finn should have taken so much trouble to contrive this valley and its accursed peacefulness he cannot have ceased to hate me. He has dug this pit he has contrived this valley because one who was long baffled must turn to deceit Why else should he come into this country following a man slaying beast that one calls Gray and one Green like the Sea who knows what enchantement has called it up out of the earth It was not here yesterday it was not here to-day it has been

[20ʳ]

called up like a blight, like a flood, like a toad-stool I have hunted deer in these woods and I have not seen the slot of either natural or un-natural swine no, no it will not bear thinking of I am caught in this valley like a wolf the branches are giving way under me I am falling into the pit and I shall be killed by a spear blow from above I shall be torn by tusks of a sudden.

Grania — **And my father gave us this kingdom to be happy in**

Darmud — **We have been happy but not here there is too much happiness here for our hunger Iwould roll it up and I would send it to him in a sack. Every man must find happiness for himself I will go and look for happiness again.**

Grania — **I will go with you**

Darmud — **We shall set out tomorrow at day break and journey through**

[21ʳ]

the woods at night would be terrible, we might come on our enemy in the dark, and in the dark my chance would be but little.

Grania — **Where shall we go, the woods go down to the Sea (the sound of a horn) The're still hunting they are hunting even in the twilight where shall we go the woods go down to the sea and everywhere an eri but here, you will be at war with Finn.**

Darmud — **Then you would keep me here, here in the pit maybe it is**

21ʳ, l. 7 an eri] That is, "in Eri", as NLI 8777(4) a, fol. 22ʳ, lines 5–6, makes clear.

just as well while we are away from what has to come

[22r]

Maybe it is just as well why run away from what is to come whatever way we went it would follow us

Grania **It is better for a man to run away from it than await it that it may come at its own time. This valley is too silent that has made us afraid. We have not loved one another so dearly in this valley as in the woods when we feared to see the sun rise where we had seen him set.**

Dairmud **Love flies from us here. You shall find it in the woods where the ousal calls, and the wild bees make their honey We shall watch the salmon leaping and the fawns coming to the stream to drink and we shall hear the birds sing at the dawn as we lie awake under cromlecs and in caves.**

Grania **But Finn has made peace with us we shall fly from him no longer. This silence will follow us even in the woods**

[23r]

and make us afraid. There is another way. You lived upon the Feanna before I met you. Go back to the Feanna. I will have you friends with Finn.

Dairmud **You say this because you would see Finn again because you would live near the greatness of Finn.**

Grania **I would not have men so great as Finn and Dairmud at strife with one another. I cannot forget it was I who brought about so great a strife. May it not be that this hunt which has drawn him away from where he should have met my father has been planned by the Gods to bring you together again. Finn has sent you a message of peace and can you let him pass your house without bidding him welcome.**

Dairmud **I must go and bid him welcome**

Grania **You have loved me over much.**

21r, l. 10 There is no reason in NLI 8777(4) a, fol. 22r, why the typescript should not be continued to the foot of the present page, unless the last nine words—which have no counterpart in the holograph—were the result of mishearing and the following page of typescript was begun afresh with the correct reading.

[Berg(06)]

[24r]

Dairmud Why should Finn and I not be friends again.

Grania Yes you and Finn shall be friends again.

Dairmud Yet your voice wails in my ears like death

Grania Finn has forgotten me.

Dairmud It is certain that we cannot remain here but Grania if I should die whom would you love,

Grania Do not speak like this to me Dairmud (She lays her head upon his breast)

Dairmud I fear that in dying I shall leave you to Finn. Oh, but another should clasp this delicate body and that these breasts should belong to another.

Grania The dying do not see those they are leaving but those that are awaiting them in the light.

[25r]

Dairmud I shall sit upon the shore beyond the waves under the holy apple tree and ponder upon my love. I shall weep remembering how I wandered with her among the woods. (Taking her in his arms) I would that all the earth had forgotten you and that you and I were at the ends of the earth together you and I alone. (A sound of a horn awakens them from their dream) Give me my shield and spear fling yourself behind me for this is how it will happen - Flying from the hunters or driven here by Finn - This house is a trap.

Grania No. Listen. Finn is calling his hounds from the wood . The hunt is over for the night.

Dairmud Then it is not the hunt that is to bring my death.

Grania Finn is still winding his horn. Go and ask him here

Dairmud Yes Finn must come here for food and drink. The hunt has led him to our house.

[26r]

Grania You will live among the Feanna again and forget the fears this valley has given us. (She goes to a chest and takes out her jewellery)

Dairmud Why do you put on these things for Finn you have not worn them for me for many months.

Grania Finn has not seen them and you and I Dairmud are come unto one another day and night. How would it avail if I were to wear them for you.

Dairmud (Taking her in his arms) Oh light of my life. I knew you before I was born. I made a bargain with this brown hair before the beginning of time. I shall not be broken when we stand under the holy apple tree upon the shore that is beyond the world. I am going oh my dear one, because you have bid me to my mortal enemy to bring him into this house

[27r]

Grania Finn has made peace you must bring him to eat and drink (He goes out like one under a spell Grania goes to the press and takes out her cloak and arrays herself. She sits down and gets up again and goes to the door. (a pause for about a minute) Finn and the Feanna and many Spearmen enter. They lean upon their bows and spears like tired men.

Finn We meet after a betrayal of years but Grania I have made peace with you.

Grania Men so great as Finn and Dairmud cannot be always enemies That is why I sent for you Finn.

Finn I am right glad to be Dairmud's friend again though he took Grania from me.

Grania I give you back your friend and your love of me is dead.

[28r]

But Finn I would know now that you have seen me if I was worth so long a quest.

[Berg(06)]

Finn I will begin that quest again if I could get you - I have done you wrong by this peace. My quest should not have ended until the end of time. (He takes her hand)

Dairmud All are weary Grania bring us the Ale flaggons and the drinking horns. (Grania goes to the door at the sideand presently the servants come in with skins of ale and drinking horns. Grania gives a horn of ale to Finn. Dairmud and Oisin go to the table and drink to-gether.).

Oscar No-one has hunted a beast like this from the beginning of the world. He turned suddenly upon the hounds in a narrow valley and the man struck him with a Spear and there was a sound like stricken brass. It is certain that a God has been sent among us for the destruction of the Eri. If we do not kill

[29ʳ]

him he will not leave man or woman or cow or sheep or wheat ear or barley ear living in Eri (Conan comes in accompanied by men bearing many deer skins with horns and heads of deer)

Conan I bring dear skins in offering from Finn to Grania that they may be soft under her feet (Dairmud and Oisin go up the stage and look at the deer skins. Finn and Grania move down the stage).

Finn Why did you not wear these jewels for me that night in Tara

Grania I had no mind to wear them that night.

Finn But you wear them for me now.

Grania Look at this brooch with the emeralds. I belonged to my mother and my grand-mother. They say it is 1000 years old and that it was made by Tergimaus the first Gold- Smith and

[30ʳ]

look at these bracelets. They were made by Len of Lough Len.

Finn I am looking at your arms Grania and your hands.

29ʳ, l. 3 dear] An incomplete overtype onto "bear" (properly "deer").

Grania **This crescent upon my head and this girdle about my body were Lens handy work too. I saw him when I was a girl. There are none who can do such work now.**

Finn **You would not wear them for me that night. It was to have been our marriage night but you were thinking of another**

Grania **I loved Dairmud for his youth and his comeliness**

Grania **I love Dairmud still and I have sent for you and put on these jewels in honour of your coming for Dairmud's sake. I would have you be friends I bid you be his friend as you were before you saw Grania.**

Finn **There was a time when I thought Grania would have loved greatness and fame.**

[31r]

Grania **It is because of your greatness and fame that I would have you friends with Dairmud. I would not have men say of me "There is that Grania who put strife between Finn and Dairmud" Finn then why did you not send for me before.**

Grania **Because you were Dairmud's enemy**

Finn **You think I am Dairmud's enemy no longer (In a loud voice) This peace is a false peace there can be no peace between me and Dairmud. Years has hidden somewhat of the treachery he did me but the sight of Grania has brought it to mind . I will say this to Dairmud and to all.**

Dairmud **He who took my hand this day as become my enemy.**

Grania **Let there be no more strife my heart goes out to both .**

Finn **Which is the better a mans hand or a woman's breast.**

Dairmud **Then Finn the peace you made was a treacherous piece.**

30r "This crescent" and "girdle" (4), "comeliness" (9) and "Grania would" (14), are all inserted with blue ribbon.

9–10 The consecutive speeches by Grania omit a speech by Finn that appears in WBY's holograph in the copy text, NLI 8777(4) c, fol. 33r, lines 5–6, possibly because on 33r WBY mistakenly assigned the speech to Diarmuid (cf. NLI 8777[4] c, fol. 31r, lines 15–16, where the speech is correctly assigned).

31r, l. 4 The line is a separate piece of dialogue spoken by Finn. The holograph has an insertion immediately beforehand that crowds the part ascription (cf. NLI 8777[4] c, fol. 33r, lines 16–18), which could have proved distracting.

[Berg(06)]

Finn **On which side will Grania be (She goes to Dairmud)**

[32^{r}]

Grania **Alas I am the evil fire in these men.**

Dairmud **Have no fear Grania. I shall slay you Finn. I overcame you in wrestling on the plain of Usna. Finn the son of Cool shall die this day.**

Finn **So little do you believe in the Gods(They cross their swords)**

Grania **No,No, I will not have men fight for me let him who loves me best drop his sword.**

Conan **Hear her said. Trust your Spier between them. Who shall kill this beast that is hurrying your fields and killing your woman and children if one of the greatest is to fall and his people to cry out "death for death". One of the Feanna, part them part them. We will have no blood fused till we have killed this beast that hurries our fields and kills our women and children. All,part them we will have no blood fused. (The Feanna and Spearmen part Finn**

[33^{r}]

and Dairmud with their spears.

Conan **Dairmud sits at home in his house while we hunt in the wind and the hail and the rain and see many die. .The Boar has come into his own country and he sits at home in his house.**

One of the Spearman **Dairmud must go with us**

Another of the Spearmen **Dairmud is craving if he will not go.**

Conan **Let Finn and Dairmud go against the Boar and let Grania be given to him who kills it. Aengus are the herds who watches over hunters over lovers shall decide between them**

32^{r}, l. 8 "Hear" was typed over "Here". Possibly, for whatever reason, the underword was meant to be uppermost. In the earlier TS from which the present TS derives, the sentence "Hear her say it." was deleted and afterward restored with WBY's characteristic broken line; cf. NLI 8777(4) b, fol. 34^{r}, line 20.

(Dairmud draws his sword to strike Conan)

Grania — He is not worthy enough for you to strike him. Give me your sword he shall die by womans hand. (Conan slinks behind the Spearmen)

[34r]

Conan — Dairmud would strike me because I have spoken of that which fills him with terror. (Dairmuds spearmen pour into the room) Dairmud will not go to this hunt and his Spearmen have come but they may stand between him and me

Dairmud — Finn lies. He knows why I will not go against this Boar. He would force me to my death, because he knows that he would die by this sword. (They begin to fight again but the others part them) There is confusion for some time)
(Finn and Grania are seen talking together.)

Grania — Then Finn you will do what I ask, you will not fight with Dairmud.

Finn — Even though it will be said I am a coward I will not fight.

Grania — You love me still and have forgotten nothing of your love these seven years.

[35r]

Dairmud — So Grania has made terms with Finn. I will go to this Hunt

Oscar — Darmuid must not go to this hunt

Oisin — Dairmud must not go to this hunt. You have done wickedly this day Conan and after your kind.

One of the Spearmen. — If Dairmud does not go to this hunt he is craven. .

Another of the Spearmen — Finn has said it he is craven.

Another of the spear-men — He has a hares heart. The Gods have given him a hares heart.

35r, l. 8 spear-] The word is inserted in blue ribbon.

9 **Dairmud** There is no way but the way of the Gods. Let us begin
10 this hunting; we shall not be soon ended (To one of the
11 Spearmen) You said this Boar was green

12 **One of the Spearmen** It was Green like the sea

[36^{r}]

1 **Dairmud** (Excitedly) I have no fear it is green like the sea (He takes a light spear from the wall

2 **Grania** Take broad edge your heavy spear.

3 **Dairmud** Why should it matter to you what spear I take (He takes down a light shield)

4 **Grania** Take your heavy shield

5 **Dairmud** No man shall say that Dairmud went to this hunting with
6 his battle harrows upon him.

7 **Grania** Dairmud do not go to this hunting.

8 **Dairmud** Have no fear. I do not fear this beast, He is green like
9 the sea. (Finn the Feanna and the Spearmen have gone out) He rushes out after them) (Grania alone, after a pause her Foster mother comes in)

10 **Foster Mother** They have gone and all is quiet again.

[37^{r}]

1 **Grania** Yes mother they have gone, they have gone.

2 **Fostermother** He would not listen to you. He is gone to the hunt. Well,
3 well. There is no stopping them, when they get into the way
4 of the end - and I am back with you again and you will have
5 me tell you of Tara and how they missed you. Ah they missed
6 you surely after we had put the witch-craft in the ale.

7 **Grania** Yes, mother. And you must save him. You must get him
8 back to me. He looked at me in anger. He thought I was
9 thinking of Finn. It is not true. It is not true.

Fostermother **Would he have gone if you loved him as you once loved him**

Grania **Who can tell. Men weary of us. I am what I am, and I love him with a love that comes with years. (Foster-mother has begun to spin) Tell me what is going to happen to him. Spin quickly..**

Fostermother **There is no more flax in the spindle.**

[Berg(07), 2^{r}]

-1-

ACT II.

Scene: House of DIARMUID and GRANIA.

CORMAC My people are waiting for me at the Red Waterfall; I shall sleep there, and ~~set out for Tara~~ begin my journey in the morning.

DIARMUID You have ~~four~~ five days' journey before you.

CORMAC ~~Not less than five~~ It will be the sixth day before I come to Tara. Neither I nor NIALL can ~~bear the~~ ride to ~~saddle~~ on a horseback for many hours at a time.

DIARMUID I would, DIARMUID, that you could stay with us here, or that I and GRANIA could go to Tara with you.

CORMAC Have you not wandered enough ? and my daughter, does she not need rest after seven years in the woods, you two together, creeping like foxes from break to break. (Going to the door) - I will show you the boundaries of the kingdom I have given you. It ~~ends~~ ends a league southwards of the Hill of Shee and [illegible] westward of those grey cliffs

Thirty-six-Page Typescript Version of Complete Act, Revised by W. B. Yeats

[Berg(07), 1r]

ACT II.

[2r]

–1–

<u>ACT II.</u>

Scene: House of DIARMUID and GRANIA.

CORMAC **My people are waiting for me at the Red Waterfall; I**
begin my journey
shall sleep there, and ~~set out for Tara~~ in the morning.

five
DIARMUID **You have ~~four~~ days' journey before you.**

It will be the sixth day before I come to Tara ride [?or]
CORMAC **~~Not less than five.~~ ^ Neither I nor NIALL can ~~bear the~~**
be a-horse back for
~~saddle~~ ^ many hours at a time.

DIARMUID **I would, DIARMUID, that you could stay with us here, or that I and GRANIA could go to Tara with you.**

CORMAC **Have you not wandered enough ? and my daughter, does she not need rest after seven years in the woods, you two together, creeping like foxes from break to break. (Going to the door) – I will show you the boundaries**
ends a leage
of the kingdom I have given you. It ~~ends~~ ^ southwards
three leagues
of the Hill of Shee and ^ westward of those grey cliffs

2r WBY's emendations on this page are in a brighter shade of blue-black ink.

6 WBY, intent on improving and adding, missed the error of DIARMUID for CORMAC in this line—as he missed other typos later.

You must push your borders beyond the Red Waterfall
things the land there is good, for the [illegible] the sons of
begin there, a strong people — ~~[illegible]~~ a strong people.

& it ends between south & west at the dunes of [illegible] shepherd.

where one can see the edges of the foam ~~and~~ it goes

northward and eastward as far as the Red Waterfall –
and it ends between east & south on the huge ridges of the
mountains of the birds.

FINN waits for me there, I bade him come no further :

because you would have still thought him an enemy.

When he and I are gone there will be nobody within a

day's journey but shepherds. I wish that I could stay

with you. One begins to understand the meanings of

things when things begin to fade. One comes to understand that there is nothing worth having except love.

I ask myself now why I ever went to war or sat upon my

throne. I am giving you the things I have learned to

know the worth of. I was afraid of love when I was
young. I said of I love my ~~[illegible]~~ shield [illegible] the
[illegible] to [illegible], ~~[illegible]~~.

DIARMUID I shall make myself so strong in this Kingdom that I

shall have no fear of FINN should he become my enemy

again. I shall teach my shepherds to pull the bow and

and to kneel behind the spear.

I shall [illegible] in the battle like the lapwing, when [illegible]
hears a footstep [illegible] her nest among the grass, & I shall be
afraid to die because my beloved is upon the earth & the
[illegible] [illegible] the gods.

[Berg(07), 3r]

not
You must ^ push your borders beyond the Red [~~Cr~~]Waterfal
though the land there is good, but the power of the sons of
a strong people.
begins there, a strong people — ~~Fionn waits at~~

–2–

& it ends between south & west at the dun of Finmole the shepherd.

I
where one can see the edges of the foam ^ ~~and~~ i }t goes
northward and eastward as far as the Red Waterfall –
and it ends between east & south on the high ridges of the
mountain of the birds.
FINN waits for me there, I bade him come no further
because you would have still thought him an enemy.
When he and I are gone there will be nobody within a
day's journey but shepherds. I wish that I could stay
with you. One begins to understand the meanings of
things when things begin to fade. One comes to un-
derstand that there is nothing worth having except love.
I ask myself now why I ever went to war or sat upon my
throne. I am giving you the things I have learned to
know the worth of. I was afraid of love when I was
young. I said if I love my ~~spear~~ shield will have too
much to guard, ~~& it may be that I shall fear to die~~ –

DIARMUID **I shall make myself so strong in this Kingdom that I**
shall have no fear of FINN should he become my enemy
again. I shall teach my shepherds to pull the bow and
and to kneel behind the spear.
in the battle
I shall tremble ^ like the lap wing, when ~~it hears~~ she
among
hears a footstep ~~in~~ near her nest ~~in~~ ^ the grass. ~~&~~ I shall be
afraid to die because my beloved is upon the earth & the
gods are but the gods.

---

1 The last phrase of WBY's insertion—"Finn waits at"—is written and deleted in duller blue-black ink. The remaining emendations on this page are in the brighter shade.

[Berg(07)]

[4^{r}]

–3–

CORMAC **No, no, no, the crook is better than the bow and spear; and FINN will never be your enemy again. I have given you this kingdom to be happy in – Make my GRANIA happy. She cannot bear sadness. She will not bid me good-bye. She says she looks to see me in Tara or here again. But, DIARMUID, you will come down the hill with me, we will say good-bye at thes stream where the horses are waiting (NIALL comes forward to put the King's cloak over his shoulders) And now my staff – He takes a few steps towards the door – GRANIA comes in).**

GRANIA **I thought you had gone father(CORMAC returns to embrace her) You know I will not say good-bye; you will come again when you are weary of statecraft, or I shall see you in Tara.**

CORMAC **I will come to you again, though it is a long journey; but do not come to Tara yet awhile – There is always**

[5^{r}]

–4–

trouble in Tara, and you might raise a little trouble there again.

GRANIA **Should I, father, FINN has forgotten me.**

CORMAC **I hope so; and that you may not be lonely I have brought you your FOSTER-MOTHER; she said you had need of her.**
a
She will talk to you of Tar‸ over the fire.

GRANIA **I have seen none of the old faces these seven years. I shall be glad to have her with me, and I wish you would leave NIALL with me too (Going to NIALL) – Give me your hands, you were my only playmate; ~~it was you who taught me to love the woods, who showed me the nests in the branches, and~~ do you remember the little pool at the end of the wood where we used to sit on a high bank fishing for roach.**

CORMAC **The rooks are flying home, we shall not be at the Red**

5^{r}, l. 5 It is not certain that the insertion is by WBY; the ink is the brighter shade.
9–11 The cancellation is in the duller shade of blue-black ink.

[6r]

–5–

Waterfall before dark (CORMAC, NIALL and DIARMUID go out)

NIALL **(From outside) Good-bye, good-bye. (GRANIA walks to the spinning-wheel, sits down and begins to spin; after a time she rises and goes up the stage for her FOSTER-MOTHER comes in).**

seems like a harpstring that is has been stretched so

GRANIA **The stillness ~~is wound~~ ^ ~~as~~ ^ tightly ~~as a harp string~~**

that it must break asunder.

~~across this valley, so tightly that we can hear it.~~

T } when there is quiet stillness

FOSTER-MOTHER **~~Where there is silence~~ t } he gods are afoot ^ ~~, they move with soundless feet.~~**

GRANIA **Pull out the thread for me; I would see whether it**

will

~~would~~ break, or be knotted or come smoothly – But why should we watch it? It will always come smoothly now (DIARMUID enters)

DIARMUID **GRANIA, I would speak with you (She goes to him) What**

[7r]

–6–

is she telling you ?

GRANIA **A sudden stillness came up the valley and into the house, so I asked her if anything were going to happen to us.**

DIARMUID **And she said ?**

gods are by when there is great stillness.

GRANIA **That the ~~silence was~~ ^ the passing ~~feet of the~~ ^ ~~gods~~ – You are weary of this valley, DIARMUID.**

DIARMUID **Not I, GRANIA, but you.**

GRANIA **You would live as you lived before you saw me, and go by FINN'S side in battle (FOSTER-MOTHER goes out)**

imagine

DIARMUID **You ~~guess~~ ^ my thoughts badly, GRANIA, I am not weary of this valley where there is nothing but you (Going to door) Your FOSTER-MOTHER is looking out over the wood, as though waiting for somebody or something and now she**

6r, 7r WBY's emendations on these two pages are in the brighter shade of blue-black ink.

[Berg(07)]

[8^r]

–7–

is gone round to the other side of the house.

GRANIA She will go in by the other door and sit looking into the fire; she often sits that way for hours, she is so old she has much to remember.

DIARMUID She has spun a great deal of flax since she came.

GRANIA I shall have need of all her flax, and of all that the shepherds' wives spin for me, for I am going to send it to the weavers to be made into a web, coloured like the leaves. I shall hang the web round these walls, and embroider upon it our wanderings in the woods. I shall be many years embroidering, but at last we shall see ~~,~~ all round us birds and beats and trees and rivers, and you and I wandering among them!

DIARMUID Of what are you thinking now, GRANIA ?

GRANIA I am thinking how everything passes away from us except

[9^r]

–8–

love. The hours pass by like ~~thistledown.~~ a smoke. If we listen we would hear the hoofs of my father's horses in the valley ~~on~~ the edges ~~beside~~ the river ~~brow of the hill.~~ He was standing there a moment ago, and yet it seems as if it were a year ago. How clearly one remembers those seven years. We have seven years of memory, DIARMUID.

DIARMUID What day among those days do you remember, GRANIA ? Of what are you thinking ?

GRANIA I am thinking of the day when we left the broiled salmon on the elder tree for FINN to find it; we were wandering by the side of the river. We had left Tara but nine days, and every day we had hung an uncooked slamon on a tree as a message for FINN.

DIARMUID It was on the ninth day that I broke my oath to FINN.

GRANIA The sword was no longer ~~with~~ between us, DIARMUID. But

8^r, l. 11 The comma was both added and deleted in the same brighter ink.

9^r WBY's emendations on this page are in the brighter shade of ink. The cancel in line 15 is a type deletion.

[10^{r}]

–9–

DIARMUID, tell me what day you are thinking of.

DIARMUID **Of one night when the shadows were as still as the cromlech over our heads, and the moon was shining among the shadows. We had been sleeping in each others' arms , and had been awakened by the baying of a hound. We looked from under the great stone and saw FINN going**
from us,
away^ ~~from~~ seeking us.

GRANIA **Yes, I remember that night, we could not have escaped from FINN; he was coming towards us, but something seemed to lead him away. Of what are you thinking now, DIARMUID ?**

DIARMUID **Of nothing, GRANIA.**

GRANIA **I pray you tell me, DIARMUID, of what you are thinking.**

DIARMUID **Of how I overcame FINN when he set guards at the seven doors of the dun.**

[11^{r}]

–10–

GRANIA **But there is another thought, a thought behind these thoughts, something you will not speak of.**

DIARMUID **No, GRANIA, I am thinking of our coming here three moons ago, and of your fathers coming, and of the peace he has made with FINN. We shall be always here. We shall have great happiness,for everything we hoped for has come to us.**

GRANIA **How still the valley is, I can hear the murmur of the stream,someone is near, DIARMUID, ~~thir~~ I can hear their feet on the pathway – There are people moving about the the house –(DIARMUID goes to the door)**

DIARMUID **It is CONAN and ~~the~~ three SPEAR MEN, why should he be the one out of the Fianna who comes to us. The Fianna**
were always flouting
~~ever flouted~~^ him, but I flouted him more than all , in the hardness of my youth (CONAN and THREE SPEARMEN enter

---

10^{r}, 11^{r} WBY's emendations on these pages are in the brighter shade of ink.

11^{r}, ll. 9, 12 Type deletions.

[Berg(07)]

[12r]

–11–

hurriedly)

CONAN (To the SPEARMEN) Stand ready to close the door. Keep your spears ready in your hands; we're here only just in time, look, look, there he is on the edge of the wood.

THE SPEARMEN It was only a gust of wind shaking the birch tree

CONAN (Coming into the house) Do not take your eyes off the edge of the wood; it is well for you DIARMUID that you are no longer of the Fianna, you can sit in-doors and redden your shins by the fire, while we must be hunting a man-slaying beast.

GRANIA Welcome, CONAN, to the house of DIARMUID and GRANIA.

DIARMUID What is the beast you are hunting?

CONAN It may be that you are sitting in-doors because you

[13r]

–12–

have seen it in the woods. It may be that a story I told you once has given you no stomach for this hunting

DIARMUID You are lying, CONAN, there has never been a boar in these woods, there is nothing on these mountains but deer and wild dogs.

CONAN It is your ~~father~~ fear makes you say that I am lying, I tell you that we had lighted our fires at the Red Waterfall and had put dry deer flesh to roast when we heard women screaming, and soon we saw this man-slaying beast coming out of a shaw, with blood upon its tusks. It saw the fires and ran from us along the river. We heard women screaming again, and saw men running, and we let loose the hounds. Ten of the Fianna and twenty of their hounds are dead.

SPEARMEN It is certainly no mortal beast.

13r, l. 6 WBY's emendation is in the brighter shade of ink.

[14r]

–13–

DIARMUID **What is the colour of this beast.**

CONAN **The boar that is to slay DIARMUID is black and without bristles (He goes over and stands besides DIARMUID – He imitates DIARMUID'S gestures) There is the one terror in the heart of CONAN and DIARMUID, CONAN and DIARMUID are brothers.**

DIARMUID **(To the Spearmen) What is its colour.**

far off
SPEARMEN **I saw it but once ^ and I thought it was gray.**

DIARMUID **And you ?**

& near enough
2nd.SPEARMAN **I saw it pass by ^, and I thought it was green like the sea, and it made a sound like the sea in a storm (CONAN goes back to the door – DIARMUID takes his spear hurriedly.)**

GRANIA **Why do you take this spear ? You will not go to this**

14r WBY's emendations on this page are in the brighter shade of ink.

I thought I be with you among the dead Dream[s], the gods after my death but I shall be swept up over darkness ~~begun~~, below the world -14-, I shall be swept away. ~~sweeping along like a [rotting] leaf.~~

hunt ?

DIARMUID This beast is coming to attack us; this hunt will sweep over us, it is coming through the woods, and I shall be caught up like a leaf ~~, leaves, leaves, all of us.~~ (CONAN and the SPEARMAN rush out) Why have they fled ? We must bar the door. (They bar the door and stand listening ~~.~~ ~~Now~~ The moon is very dark.) ^now^

GRANIA Maybe they are gone because the danger has passed.

DIARMUID Come, sit by me (A pause), and so we sit together in the dark, there is no sound now, and yet the darkness is full of shapes, and the silence is full of danger. No, we cannot sit here - We must unbar the door and let the light in, whatever danger the light shows to us it will be more bearable than this darkness. Why bar the door against that which has to come - The things

[Berg(07), 15[r]]

I thought to be with you among the ~~do~~ duns of the
after my deaht
gods^but I shall be swept into some darkness ~~beyond~~ &
I shall be swept away.
below that world **–14–** , ~~swept away like a rolling leaf~~.

hunt ?

DIARMUID **This beast is coming to attack us; this hunt will sweep over us, it is coming through the woods, and I shall be caught up like a leaf ~~–~~ ~~leaves, leaves, all of us.~~ (CONAN and the SPEARMAN rush out) Why have they fled ? We must bar the door. (They bar the door and stand listening)/ ~~Now~~ t** T } room **he ~~moon~~ is very dark.**)

GRANIA **Maybe they are gone because the danger has passed.**

DIARMUID **Come, sit by me (A pause), and so we sit together in the dark, there is no sound now, and yet the darkness is full of shapes, and the silence is full of danger. No, we cannot sit here – We must unbar the door and let the light in, whatever danger the light shows to us it will be more bearable than this darkness. Why bar the door against that which has to come – The things**

15[r], l. ⁻1 WBY's insertion at the head of the page is written and looped in using the duller shade of ink. His other emendations on this page are in the brighter shade.

[Berg(07)]

[16^{r}]

–15–

to come are like the wind – They could sweep this house away; (They open the door), the hunt seems to have passed.

GRANIA **It has been foretold that you will die in a boar hunt, for we are hunting and make an idle tale of it.**

DIARMUID **Should I foreswear war and hunting, as well might I die living by your side; you would cease to love me**

GRANIA **Forget my love for a while. I will help you to fight I will take up shield and spear and will follow you to battle.**

DIARMUID **The Fianna are with FINN and will not leave him – And now I dare not follow a deer lest – GRANIA, what made you choose me that night In Tara, for as if to warn you, CONAN told the tale of my death.**

[17^{r}]

–16–

GRANIA **Death treads at every man's heel like a hound.**

DIARMUID **But other men know nothing of death, except that they will die; to all other men death is unnatural and shapeless, but the image of my death I have seen since a little child – a black and bristless phantom, and a thing that will come out of the unknown woods.**

GRANIA **The tale tells how you will die, but not the time of your death.**

DIARMUID **The tale does not tell the hour, but everything that happens foretells the hours.**

GRANIA **This tale has shaken your mind.**

DIARMUID **Do you not believe in it? Tell me.**

GRANIA **We believe and we disbelieve, and there is a time when we do not know what we think.**

16^{r}, ll. 4–13 [for 14] The cancellation line is in pencil (like GM's comment on p. 21/fol. 22^{r}).

17^{r}, ll. 1–14 Pencil cancellation.

10 hours] The final letter may have been intended to be erased.

13 The part ascription and line of text appear oddly fresh, as if they had been typed in afterward but with the same ribbon.

[18r]

–17–

DIARMUID **I was brought through every danger:for seven years dangers crowded upon me, but the miracle happened and I escaped – I was given strength more than a man, and men passed us by as blind men might have passed:the foxes barked to warn us, and the birds sang till we awoke. Why did the woods feed me and clothe and guard me and hide me if the gods had not planned this death before I was born. Why else was love thrust upon me, why else when our flight was over was the supper of happiness spread before us ? Why should I be bid to eat and drink~~f~~of happiness every hour? The gods know of our hunger and our thirst, and sometimes when we are about to die they give us more than we can eat and drink – This valley has been filled with peace and silence, and I am bid love you as if I had never loved you, as if we were new to one another, as if our hunger**

[19r]

–18–

for one another had need of a physic made of Druid herbs, as if the bread of our desire had need of And then I am told that FINN has ceased from his quest as if his quest had ever mattered to us, as if his hatred were ever more than whet-stone; and then, and then – and then, as if our wanderings were not happier than this peace I am bidden to make you happy (Starting up) I have been led into this valley; I am like a wolf in a trap, and you are the bait.

GRANIA **What are you saying, DIARMUID ?**

DIARMUID **(With a vague gesture) I do not know; the words started up suddenly in my mind, I do not know what they mean or whence they came from. I said I am like a wolf in a trap, and I understood those words, but how can you be the bait ? I do not understand – Ask the gods, they put those words into my mind, nor can I**

18r, l. 11 Type deletion.

19r, l. 11 The part ascription looks as if was typed in later—but with the same ribbon.

[Berg(07)]

[20^{r}]

–19–

tell you why FINN should have taken so much trouble to contrive this valley and its accursed peacefulness. He cannot have ceased to hate me – He has dug this pit, he has contrived this valley, because one who is long baffled must turn to deceit. Why else should he come into this country following a man-slaying beast, that one calls gray and one green like the sea. Who knows what enchantment has called it up out of the earth ? It was not here yesterday – it was not here to-day – it has been called up like a blight, like a flood, like a toadstool – I have hunted deer in these woods, and I have not seen the slot of either natural or unnatural swine ; no it will not bear thinking of. I am caught in this valley like a wolf; the branches are giving way under me; I am falling into the pit, and I shall be killed by a spear blow from above – I shall be torn by tusks of a sudden.

[21^{r}]

–20–

GRANIA **And my father gave us this kingdom to be happy in.**

DIARMUID **We have been happy, but not here; there is too much happiness here for our hunger, I would roll it up and I would send it to him in a sack. Every man must find happiness for himself. I will go and look for happiness again.**

GRANIA **I will go with you.**

DIARMUID **We will set out to-morrow at daybreak. The journey through the woods at night would be terrible; we might come on our enemy sleeping, and in the dark my chance would be but little.**

GRANIA **Where shall we go ? The woods go down to the sea (The sound of a horn) They're still hunting; they are hunting even in the twilight – Where shall we go ? The woods go down to the sea, and everywhere in Eri but here you will be at war with FINN.**

20^{r}, l. 2 its] Typed in later with a different (black) ribbon.
7 gray] The first two letters were typed in later.
21^{r}, l. 16 The line was typed in later with a different (black) ribbon.

[22r]

–21–

DIARMUID Then you would keep me here, here in the pit; every man lives in a pit, and he may run round it for a while.

GRANIA We have grown afraid of ourselves in this valley – Ah, for the woods! We have not loved so dearly in this valley as in the woods when we feared to see the sun rise where we had seen him set. *this is weak and impersonal.*

DIARMUID Love flies from us here. ~~You shall find it in the woods, where the ousel calls, and the wild bees make their honey,~~ we will go where the salmon leap and the fawns come to the stream to drink; and we shall hear the birds sing again at the dawn, as we lie awake under cromlechs and in caves.

GRANIA But FINN has made peace with us, we shall fly from him no longer, and this silence will follow us even in the woods and ~~a~~ make us afraid. There is another

[23r]

–22–

way. You lived upon the Fianna before I met you. Go back to the Fianna; I will have you friends with FINN.

DIARMUID You say this because you would see FINN again, because you would live near the greatness of FINN.

GRANIA Men so great as FINN and DIARMUID should not strife with one another, and it was I who brought about the strife. This hunt which has drawn him away from where he should have met my father may have been planned by the gods to bring you together again. FINN has sent you a message of peace. Can you let him pass your house without bidding him welcome.

DIARMUID I must go and bid him welcome. We cannot stay here. Now that FINN has made peace we might meet him in friendship.

22r, l. 15 Type deletion.

23r, l. 6 The sense requires the gap to be filled with "be at". The gap might arise from altering the syntax in the previous version (cf. Berg[06], fol. 23r, lines 6–7).

[Berg(07)]

[24r]

–23–

GRANIA Yes, DIARMUID, you and FINN.

DIARMUID But if the broil should begin again on seeing you.

GRANIA Even so.

DIARMUID GRANIA, if I should die would you be FINN'S wife.

GRANIA Say it not DIARMUID

DIARMUID My life began with you and it ends with you – Oh that another should clasp this delicate body, and that these breasts should belong to another.

GRANIA The dying do not see those they are leaving, but those that are awaiting them in the light.

DIARMUID When I sit upon thd shore beyond the waves, I shall ponder upon my love. I shall weep, remembering how I wandered with her among the woods. (Taking her in his arms.) I would that all the earth had forgotten you, and that you and I were at the ends of the earth together–

[25r]

–23–

you and I alone (A sound of a horn awakens them from their dream) – Give me my shield and spear, fling yourself behind me for this is how it will happen – Flying from the hunters or driven here by FINN – This house is a trap.

GRANIA No, listen, FINN is calling his hounds from the wood. The hunt is over for the night; go and ask him here.

DIARMUID The hunt has led him to our house. It is for my sake you would have us friends.

GRANIA You must sit by the fire and dream of me no longer – You must win my love in battle.

DIARMUID It was not in battle that I won your love, but by the desire of the eye (GRANIA goes to the chest and takes out her jewellry) Why do you put on these things for FINN, you have not worn them for me for many months.

25r, l. -1 There appears to be no good reason (e.g., revision, substitution) for numbering the two pages 23.

[26^{r}]

–24–

GRANIA FINN has not seen them,and you and I DIARMUID are common to one an other by day and night.

DIARMUID (Taking her in his arms) Oh light of my life. I knew you before I was born. I made a bargain with this brown hair before the beginning of time, it shall not be broken when we stand upon the shore that is beyond the world. I am going oh my dear one, because you have bid me to my mortal enemy to bring him into this house.

GRANIA FINN has made peace, you must bring him to eat and drink –(He goes out like one under a spell, GRANIA goes to the press and takes out her cloak and arrays herself– She sits down, get up and goes to the door – a pause for about a minute, FINN and the FIanna and many spearmen enter – They lean upon their bows and spears like tired men.)

[27^{r}]

–25–

FINN We meet after a betrayal of years; but, GRANIA, I have made peace with you.

GRANIA Men so great as FINN and DIARMUID cannot be always enemies, that is why I sent for you FINN.

FINN I am right glad to be DIARMUID'S friend again though he took GRANIA from me.

GRANIA I give you back your friend, and your love of me is dead.

FINN I would begin that quest again if I could get you – I have done you wrong by this peace. My quest should not have ended until the end of time (He takes her hand)

now

GRANIA But, FINN, I would know, that you have seen me, if I was worth so long a quest.

DIARMUID All are weary; GRANIA, bring us the ale flaggons and

---

27^{r}, ll. 5, 12 The words "glad" and "now" are inserted later with a different (black) ribbon.

[Berg(07)]

[28r]

–26–

1 the drinking horns. (GRANIA goes to the door at the
side and presently the servants come in with skins of
ale and drinking horns – GRANIA gives a horn of ale
to FINN. DIARMUID and USHEEN go to the table and
drink together.)

2 **OSCAR** No one has hunted a beast like this from the beginning
3 of the world. He turned suddenly upon the hounds in
4 a narrow valley, and the man struck him with a spear,
5 and there was a sound like stricken brass. It is
6 certain that a god has been sent among us for the de-
7 struction of Eri. If we do not kill him he will not
8 leave man or woman, cow or sheep, wheat or barley ear
9 living in Eri –(CONAN comes in accompanied by men bearing many deer skins with horns and heads of deer.)

10 **CONAN** I bring deer skins in offering from FINN to GRANIA that

[29r]

–27–

1 they may be soft under her feet – (DIARMUID and USHEEN
go up the stage and look at the deer skins – FINN and
GRANIA move down the stage.)

2 **FINN** Why did you not wear these jewels for me that night in
3 TARA?

4 **GRANIA** I had no mind to wear them that night.

5 **FINN** But you wear them for me now.

6 **GRANIA** Look at this brooch with the emeralds. It belonged
7 to my mother and my grand-mother; they say it is a
8 hundred years old and that it was made by Tergimaus the
9 first goldsmith – and look at these bracelets they
10 were made by Len of Lough Len.

11 **FINN** I am looking at your arms, GRANIA, and your hands.

12 **GRANIA** This crescent upon my head and this girdle about my

[30r]

–28–

body were Lens handywork too. I saw him when I was a girl; there are none who can do such work now.

FINN You would not wear them for me that night. It was to have been our marriage night, but you were thinking of another.

GRANIA I loved DIARMUID for his youth and his comeliness, and I love him still. I sent for you and put on these jewels in honour of ~~e~~ your coming for DIARMUID'S sake. I would have you be friends, I bid you be his friend as you were before you saw me, GRANIA.

FINN There was a time when I thought GRANIA would have loved greatness and fame.

GRANIA It is because of your greatness and fame that I would have you friends with DIARMUID. I would not have men say of me – There is GRANIA who put strife between FINN

[31r]

–29–

and DIARMUID.

FINN Then why did you not send for me before.

GRANIA Because you were DIARMUID'S enemy.

FINN You think I am DIARMUID'S enemy no longer (In a loud voice) This peace is a false peace, there can be no peace between me and DIARMUID. Years have hidden some – what of the treachery he did me, but the sight of GRANIA has brought it to mind. I will say this to DIARMUID and to all.

DIARMUID He who took my hadnt this day has become my enemy.

GRANIA Let there be no more strife.

FINN Which is the better a man's hand or a woman's breast.

DIARMUID Then, FINN, the peace you made was a treacherous peace.

FINN On which side will GRANIA be (She goes to DIARMUID)

30r, l. 8 Type deletion.

[Berg(07)]

[32^{r}]

–30–

GRANIA Alas, I am the evil fire in these men.

DIARMUID Have no fear, GRANIA. I shall slay you, FINN. I overcame you in wrestling on the plain of Usna – FINN, the son of COOL shall die this day.

FINN So little do you believe in the gods (They cross their swords)

GRANIA No, no, I will not have men fight for me; let him who loves me best drop his sword.

CONAN Hear her say it; thrust your spear between them. Who shall kill this beast that is harrying your fields and killing you women and children if one of the greatest is to fall, and his people to cry out "death for death"

A SPEARMAN Part them part them; we will have no blood shed till we have killed this beast that harries our fields and

[33^{r}]

–31–

kills our women and children.

ALL Part them we will have no blood shed (The Fianna and SPEARMEN part FINN and DIARMUID with their swords)

CONAN DIARMUID sits at home in his house while we hunt in the wind, and the hail, and the rain, and see many die. The boar has come into his own country and he sits at home in his house.

1st. SPEARMAN DIARMUID must go with us

2nd. SPEARMAN DIARMUID is craven if he will not go.

CONAN Let FINN and DIARMUID go against the boar, and let GRANIA be given to him who kills it. AONGHUS who watches over hunters, over lovers shall decide between them. (DIARMUID draws his sword to strike CONAN)

GRANIA He is not worthy eno gh for you to strike him. Give

[34r]

–32–

me your sword, he shall die by a woman's hand (CONAN slinks behind the SPEARMEN)

CONAN **DIARMUID would strike me because I have spoken of that which fills him with terror. (DIARMUID'S Spearmen pour into the room) DIARMUID will not go to this hunt, and his Spearmen have come but that they may stand between him and me.**

DIARMUID **FINN lies, he knows why I will not go ~~g~~ against this boar. He would force me to my death, because he knows that he would die by this sword. (They begin to fight again, but the others part them. There is confusion for some time – FINN and GRANIA are seen talking together.)**

GRANIA **Then FINN you will do what I ask, you will not fight with DIARMUID.**

[35r]

–33–

FINN **Even though it will be said that I am a coward I will not fight.**

GRANIA **You love me still, and have forgotten nothing of your love these seven years.**

DIARMUID **So, GRANIA, has made terms with FINN. I will go to this hunt.**

OSCAR **Diarmuid must not go to this hunt. You have done wickedly this day CONAN, and after your kind.**

1st SPEARMAN **If DIARMUID does not go to this hunt he is craven.**

2nd. SPEARMAN **FINN has said it, he is craven.**

3rd.SPEARMAN **He has a hare's heart; the gods have given him a hare's heart.**

DIARMUID **There is no way but the way of the gods. Let us begin hunt; it shall not be soon ended (To one of the Spearmen) You said this boar was green.**

34r, l. 7 Type deletion.

[Berg(07)]

[36r]

–34–

1 **DIARMUID** **(Excitedly) I have no fear, it is green like the sea,**
(He takes a light spear from the wall)

2 **GRANIA** **Take Braod-Edge, your heavy spear.**

3 **DIARMUID** **Why should it matter to you what spear I take (He takes down a light shield.)**

4 **GRANIA** **Take your heavy shield.**

5 **DIARMUID** **No man shall say DIARMUID went to this hunt with his**
6 **battle gear upon him.**

7 **GRANIA** **Do not go to this hunt.**

8 **DIARMUID** **I do not fear this beast; he is green like the sea.**
(FINN, the Fianna and the Spearmen have gone out – He rushes out after them – GRANIA is left alone; after a pause her FOSTER-MOTHER comes in.)

9 **FOSTER-MOTHER** **They have gone and all is quiet again.**

36r, ll. -9, 9 The words "a pause" and "They have gone and all is quiet again." are inserted later with a different (black) ribbon

[37^{r}]

–35–

GRANIA Yes, Mother, they have gone, they have gone.

FOSTER-MOTHER He would not listen to you. He is gone to the hunt. Well, well. There is no stopping them, when they get in the way of the end – and I am back with you again, and you will have me tell you of Tara, and how they missed you. Ah, they missed you sorely after we had put witchcraft into the ale.

GRANIA (Rising) But you must save him – You must get him back to me. He looked at me in anger. He thought I was thinking of FINN; it is not true, it is not true.

FOSTER-MOTHER Would he have gone if you loved him as you once loved him.

GRANIA Who can tell. Men weary of us, and I love him with a love that comes with years. (FOSTER-MOTHER has begun to spin) Tell me what is going to happen – spin

[38^{r}]

–36–

quickly. What end of the thread are you spinning.

FOSTER-MOTHER There is no more flax on the spindle.

38^{r} 1 "What . . . spinning." was inserted later, with a different (black) ribbon.

[NLI 8777(6), 1r]

-1-

ACT II .

[mostly Rejected]

DIARMUID'S HOUSE - CORMAC and GRANIA seated.

CORMAC I have been here three days and my errand ~~is~~ [is] press~~ing~~[es].

GRANIA ~~There is a grieved look in your eyes, father;~~ you are leaving [us] disappointed.

CORMAC [There is some] ~~In all things there is a measure of~~ disappointment [in everything].

GRANIA But you were glad to see me again ?

CORMAC ~~My~~ [my], daughter, and my only child.

GRANIA Three days to ~~see you in~~ ~~is~~ [are] not a long while after seven years [of absence]

CORMAC [Who made that absence] ~~Whose choosing was it~~ ? ~~Seven years in the woods and mountains~~ ~~My~~ [my] daughter and DIARMUID, her lover, followed, hiding, [and] ~~and escaping like~~ [—] foxes [creeping] from brake to [brake]

Typescript Pages Relating to Act II, Described by W. B. Yeats as "Mostly Rejected"

[NLI 8777(6), 1r]

–1–

<u>ACT II</u> .

(mostly rejected)

DIARMUID'S HOUSE – CORMAC and GRANIA seated.

es
CORMAC **I have been here three days and my errand ~~is~~ press~~ing.~~**

GRANIA **~~There is a grieved look in your eyes, father~~; you arC**
us
leaving^disappointed.
There^is some in everything
CORMAC **~~In all things there is a measure of~~ disappointment^.**

GRANIA **But you were glad to see me again ?**
My
CORMAC **~~Why~~, daughter, and my only child.**
are
GRANIA **Three days ~~to see you in is~~ not a long while after**
{o
seven years {. f absence
Who made that absence
CORMAC **~~Whose choosing was it~~ ? ~~Seven years in the woods and~~**
my
M}
~~mountains~~ m}y^daughter and DIARMUID , her lover ,
and creeping
followed, hiding, ~~and escaping like~~ foxes^from brake to^
brake

WBY's note at the head of the page is in blue ink. All his corrections are in blue-black ink, unless indicated otherwise as pencil.

1–6 The vertical cancellation is in pencil.

7–8 The corrections in these lines—along with "that absence" in line 9—are in a paler shade of blue-black ink and appear to be earlier than the surrounding corrections—indeed the vast majority of corrections in the present TS—which are in a darker shade. Cf. note on fol. 2, line 12, below.

[NLI 8777(6), 2r]

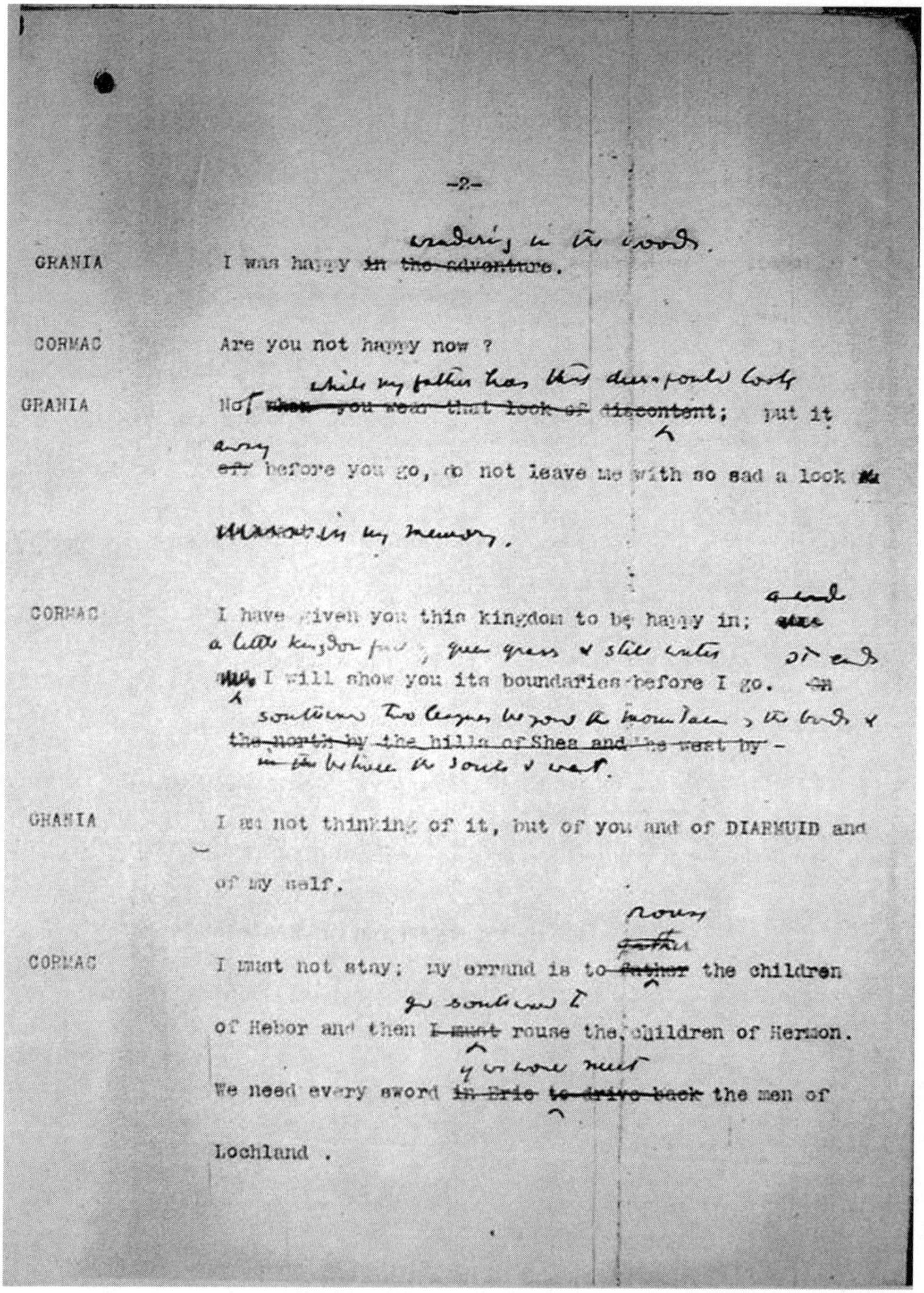

-2-

GRANIA I was happy ~~in the adventure~~ wandering in the woods.

CORMAC Are you not happy now ?

GRANIA No, ~~when you wear that look of discontent~~ while my father has this discontented look; put it ~~off~~ away before you go, do not leave me with so sad a look ~~[illegible]~~ in my memory.

CORMAC I have given you this kingdom to be happy in; ~~[illegible]~~ a land a little kingdom full of green grass & still waters or lands ~~[illegible]~~ I will show you its boundaries before I go. ~~On the north by the hills of Shea and the west by~~ southward two leagues beyond the mountains, the lands & in the between the south & west.

GRANIA I am not thinking of it, but of you and of DIARMUID and of my self.

CORMAC I must not stay; my errand is to ~~gather~~ rouse the children of Hebor and then ~~I must~~ go southward to rouse the children of Hermon. We need every sword ~~in Erie to drive back~~ if we would meet the men of Lochland .

[NLI 8777(6), 2[r]]

–2–

wandering in the woods.
GRANIA **I was happy ~~in the adventure~~.**

CORMAC **Are you not happy now ?**

{t while my father has that disappointed look
GRANIA **No{, ~~when you wear that look of discontent~~; ^ put it**
away
~~off~~ before you go, do not leave me with so sad a look in
~~my heart.~~ in my memory.

~~a word~~
CORMAC **I have given you this kingdom to be happy in; ~~come~~**
a little kingdom full of green grass & still waters It ends
~~and~~ I will show you its boundaries before I go. ~~On~~
southward two leagues beyond the mountains by the [?woods] &
~~the north by the hills of Shea and the west by~~ –
~~in the~~ between the south & west.

GRANIA **I am not thinking of it, but of you and of DIARMUID and**
of my self.

rouse
~~gather~~
CORMAC **I must not stay; my errand is to ~~father~~ the children**
go southward to
of Hebor and then ^~~I must~~ rouse the children of Hermon.
if we would meet
We need every sword ~~in Erie~~ ^~~to drive back~~ the men of
Lochland .

---

3 The first revision in the line (to "Not") is made in paler ink.

6 word] WBY clearly intended "world".

12 WBY's first revision—"gather"—is written in paler ink than his second thought (and the remaining revisions on this page), which proves the paler revisions are earlier.

[NLI 8777(6), 3ʳ]

-3-

GRANIA But their ~~vessels~~ galleys have been ~~driven back~~ scattered by storms.

CORMAC A few ~~fair~~ weeks ~~and they will collect again~~ of fair weather will gather again.

GRANIA ~~Not now that~~ not now they know that the Fianna are no longer divided.

CORMAC May be, so, maybe so but a wise king ~~is always safe guarding himself~~ must be ever on the watch.

~~and his kingdom,~~ and my councillors tell me that ~~never~~ neither Conan the melancholy nor Conal the hundred fights Caoilte [illegible]

~~were~~ uses so many cunning wiles, ~~and~~ as I ~~used to forswear him~~

~~his quest of you.~~ ~~when~~ to make Finn give up his quest of you.

GRANIA Has Finn ~~forsworn~~ given up his quest, ~~or is~~ or does he only wait his time to begin again.

CORMAC Had he not, would I have come here ~~to~~ to be bidding DIARMUID to be his

friend ~~again~~. My Councillors tell me that the words

~~which~~ that ~~swore~~ won him ~~away from you~~ were ~~deftly~~ subtly chosen, and

I think they were. They said I had a mouth of honey But ~~all those~~ wiles and words

were ~~used in vain.~~ [illegible]

[NLI 8777(6), 3r]

–3–

galleys scatterd
GRANIA **But their ~~vessels~~ have been ~~driven back~~ by storms.**
of fair weather will gather again
CORMAC **A few ~~fair~~ weeks ~~and they will collect again.~~**
Not now {~~for~~ that
GRANIA **~~Not now~~ {~~that~~ they know the Fianna are no longer divided.**
so, may be so must be ever on the watch.
CORMAC **May be but a wise king ~~is always safe guarding himself~~**
neithr
~~and his kingdom,~~ and my councillors tell me that ~~never~~
~~Con~~, Art the melancholy nor Con the hundred fighter
used turn Finn
~~wore~~ so many cunning wiles , ~~used~~ as I ~~used to forswear~~
~~from~~ up
~~his quest of you.~~ ~~when~~ to make Finn give us his quest
of you.
~~given~~ given up his
GRANIA **Has FINN ~~foresworn his~~ quest , ~~of me~~** or does he only wait
his time to begin again.
~~d~~ bidding
have hither ~~for~~
CORMAC **Had he not , would I come ~~here to beg~~ DIARMUID ~~to~~ be his**
friend ~~again~~. My councillors tell me that the words
that won subtly
~~which swore~~ him ~~away from you~~ were ~~deftly~~ chosen, and
They said I had a mouth of honey
I think they were. But ~~all these~~ wiles and words
~~were used in vain.~~ were alike in vain.

3 The inserted "for" is written in paler ink; that is, the alteration was made earlier.
6–7 The inserted "turn Finn from" is written in paler ink.
12 The inserted "won" is written in paler ink.

[NLI 8777(6), 4r]

-4-

GRANIA Not in vain, for though DIARMUID will not ask FINN to his house, he promises not to make war on FINN, and he he will counsel his friends among the Fianna to forget him; and if FINN has forgotten me is not that enough ?

CORMAC The Fianna, would have DIARMUID, their old comrade back again.

GRANIA DIARMUID that at the sight of me FINN would begin the broil again. He would live at peace in this pleasant valley kingdom which of shepherds which you have given us to be happy in telling the ten times told tale of our love he would live and die.

CORMAC After seven years of flight he needs rest, and you need rest too; but I would not have him end his days in rest. FINN waits for me at the Red Waterfall, he would have DIARMUID back again; he would have DIARMUID arm

[NLI 8777(6), 4r]

~~-4-~~

No call
GRANIA ^**Not in vain, for though DIARMUID will not ~~ask~~ FINN to**
his house, he promises ~~not to make war on FINN, and he~~
to
~~he will~~ counsel his friends among the Fianna to forget
him; and if FINN has forgotten me is not that enough ?
~~love deeds~~ love and could have
CORMAC **The Fianna, ~~would have~~ DIARMUID, ~~their old comrade~~**
him with
~~back again.~~ ~~him among~~ them again.
fear~~ed~~ s if saw me
GRANIA **~~But~~ DIARMUID ^ that ~~at the sight of me~~ FINN ~~would begin~~**
old would begin Dairmud coud
the ^ broil ^ ~~again.~~ ~~He would~~ ^ live at peace in this ~~plea-~~
grass green
~~sant valley~~ kingdom ~~which~~ of shepherds ~~which you have~~
talking of our love
~~given us~~ ~~(to be happy in)~~ ^ ~~Telling the ten times told~~
~~tale of our love~~ (he would live and die.)
have worn him out
CORMAC **~~After~~ seven years of flight ~~he needs rest~~, and you ~~need~~**
~~he must~~ he must take sword & shield from
~~rest~~ too; but ^ ~~I would not have him end his days~~ in
the wall many times again
a in the valley
~~re^st~~. FINN waits ~~for~~ me ~~at the Red Waterfall~~, he would
in th Feani
have DIARMUID ~~back~~ again; he would have DIARMUID arm

Fin waits in th vally
But I woud hav him end

1–6, 12–15 The two large cancellations are made with pencil strokes.
7 The correction to "fears" and the caret mark below are in paler ink.

Cor
tells him

-5-

~~advise~~ the shepherds in this valley, so that we ~~could~~ can
out shone the [illegible] can come.
cal them ~~to against the enemy if needful~~. You
never slain by Finn [illegible]
shake your head - Will DIARMUID'S ~~faith and FINN'S faith~~
~~may [illegible] be pledged~~ again.

~~GRANIA~~ ~~[illegible]~~
~~[illegible]~~
~~[illegible]~~ (Enter DIARMUID)

DIARMUID
do you — You are still thinking how you can break [illegible]
~~Still thinking~~, oh you foolish ones ~~[illegible] interrupt~~
which this — that even the [illegible]
~~the perfect~~ peace ~~which the forgetful~~ gods have ~~forgotten~~
not broken — or — your fathers
~~to interrupt~~. Turn you ear, Grania, from ~~the~~ wisdom
They call him Cormac the wise — ~~[illegible]~~. I think all the wise are very foolish.
~~of the world and listen to the wisdom that speaks out~~
~~of the heart~~. Come ~~with us down~~ into the valley, CORMAC,
to ~~that high~~ rock ~~from whence~~ where we sat yesterday, we shall see miles of
rooks coming home ~~to the tall shaws along the hillside~~.

[NLI 8777(6), 5[r]]

Con
tell him

–5–

can
~~and train~~ **the shepherds in this valley, so that we** ~~could~~
out should the men of Lochlan come.
call them ~~up against the enemy if needful.~~ **You**
never stand by Finns side
shake your head – Will DIARMUID'S ~~faith and FINN'S faith~~
~~never be pledged~~ **again.**
I will speak to him –
~~GRANIA~~ ~~You have heard him speak; it is said that FINN has~~
~~that~~
~~made peace,with FINN will follow us no more ; but he~~
~~will not ask FINN to this house~~ **(Enter DIARMUID)**

so you two are still ~~talk~~ thinking. how can you break ~~in to~~
~~thinking~~
DIARMUID ~~Still think, oh you foolish ones how you can interrupt~~
~~upon~~ this that even the unresting
~~the perfect~~ **peace** ~~which the forgetful~~ ^ **gods have** ~~forgotten~~
not broken your fathers
~~to interrupt~~**. Turn your ear, Grania, from** ~~the~~ **wisdom**
They call him Cormac the wise
~~He is~~ ^ ~~wise~~. I think all the wise are very foolish.
~~of the world and listen to the wisdom that speaks out~~
into
~~of the heart~~**. Come** ~~with us down~~ **the valley, CORMAC,**
the where we sat yesterday
to ~~that high~~ **rock** ~~from whence~~ ^ **we shall see miles of**
rooks coming home ~~to the tall shaws along the hillside~~**.**

6, 8 The cancellations of "with" and "think" are type deletions.
14 The cancel line extends, lightly, through "hill" of "hillside."

-6-

and presently the herdsman will be driving their herds up the valley. I have two white heifers
~~We shall meet some shepherd returning with his flock,~~
with black horns & hoofs that I would show you.
~~and we will talk with him till it is bed~~-time.

CORMAC Tell him, GRANIA, that the men of Lochland have fifty scores of galleys upon the seas.

DIARMUID The storms have ~~long ago dispersed~~ scattered their galleys - Mannanan has done this ~~ug~~ that we may be happy in this valley - in this valley ~~which~~ that you have given us to be happy in. I shall fling some great offering into his waves.

CORMAC Must I tell Finn that you will not make peace
~~that I go back with the tale of failure to FINN. Must~~
I ~~tell him~~ that you will not.

DIARMUID Tell him to ~~withdraw across the~~ go beyond the borders ~~which you have~~ of my kingdom.
~~Reached for...~~.

CORMAC Would you have men say that
~~Shall it be said that~~ the man you wronged ~~stretched out~~ has forgiven
you, & offered peace & you have refused it.
~~his hand to you~~ and that you refused it. FINN waits.

[NLI 8777(6), 6r]

–6–

and ~~pre~~ presenty the herdman will be driving their
herds up the valley. I have two white heffers
1 **~~We shall meet some shepherd returning with his flock~~**,
with black horns and hoofs that I would show you.
2 **~~and we will talk with him till it is bed-time~~**.

3 **CORMAC** **Tell him, GRANIA, that the men of Lochland have fifty**
4 **scores of galleys upon the seas.**

scatterd
5 **DIARMUID** **The storms have ~~long ago dispersed~~ their galleys –**
6 **Mananon has done this so that we may be happy in this**
that
7 **valley – in this valley ~~which~~ you have given us to be**
some
8 **happy in.** I shall fling ^ ~~a~~ great offering int his waves.

Must I tell ~~Feon~~ Fin that you will not make peace
9 **CORMAC** **~~Must I go back with the tale of failure to FINN~~. ~~Must~~**
10 **I ~~tell him that you will not~~.**

go beyond the
11 **DIARMUID** **Tell him to ~~withdraw across the~~ borders ~~which you have~~**
of my kingdom.
12 **~~marked for me~~.**

"Would you have men say that" has forgiven
13 **CORMAC** **~~Shall it be said that~~ ^ the man you wronged ~~stretched out~~**
you, & offered peace & you have refused it. waits
14 **~~his hand to you~~ and that you refused it. FINN await~~s~~**

13 WBY presumably meant to position his quotation marks around the latter part of the sentence, "the man . . . refused it."

[NLI 8777(6), 7r]

-7-

Think well upon it.

for your answer. I have made peace between you for my kingdom's sake and for my daughter's sake, but if you send ~~hand~~ him such an answer the ~~ashes may be blown into~~ sod ~~hot~~ sod may be blown at flame again.
~~flame again.~~

Let it flame up when it will

DIARMUID I have fought FINN and overthrown him; I ~~escaped~~ have Did not escape from the ~~den~~ house of seven doors when ~~there were guards~~ he had set guards at all the doors. I was there alone & how I have been, tell me, ~~I have no fear~~ of FINN.

CORMAC Do not send me back with this message.

DIARMUID ~~Most likely it~~ It would be is for GRANIA'S sake that FINN ~~will~~ & not for my sake [here?] who knows what would happen when come here, ~~and not at all for the grasp~~ of my hand. he saw her face again. What would Grania have me do ~~But GRANIA says nothing~~. Would GRANIA have me friends with FINN - She says nothing - She stands ~~apart~~ there saying nothing.

GRANIA If I say yes to you I shall say no to my father.

[NLI 8777(6), 7r]

–7–

Think well upon it.
for **your answer.^ I have made peace between you for my**
kingdom's sake and for my daughter's sake, but if you
him ~~sod~~
send ~~back~~^ such an answer the ~~ashes may be blown into~~
~~half~~ sod may be blown into flame again.
~~flame again.~~

I
Let it flame up when it will I have Did^not escape
DIARMUID ^ **I have fought FINN and^overthrown him; I ~~escaped~~ from**
house he had set guards
the ~~dun~~^of seven doors when ~~there were guards~~ at all
I was then alone & now I have many with me.
the doors. ~~I have no fear of FINN.~~

CORMAC **Do not send me ~~back~~ with this message.**

It would be & not for my sake
DIARMUID **~~Most likely it~~ is for GRANIA'S sake^that FINN ~~will~~** would
{. who knows what would happen when
come here{, ~~and not at all for the grasp of my hand.~~
he saw her face again. What woud Grania have me do
~~But GRANIA says nothing.~~^ Would GRANIA have me friends
there
with FINN – She says nothing – She stands ~~apart~~ saying
nothing.

GRANIA **If I say yes to you I shall say no to my father.**

Enter Niall & [illegible] [illegible] [illegible] [illegible] to [illegible].

-8-

DIARMUID So you say nothing.

GRANIA It may be that desires are equal either way.
~~If my desires fall equally either way.~~

DIARMUID Here we have everything we ^have^ sought for; I have you, ~~and I have~~ this peaceful valley where I can hide you away. Here we shall live and die, and our children shall grow up about us, if the ^mother of^ gods hear my prayer and accept my offerings, and give us children.

GRANIA Here we may spend our lives ~~at~~ settling the quarrels of the shepherds when the sheep go astray.

DIARMUID You are weary of this valley, GRANIA.

GRANIA Are fame has made you so weary
~~Are you so weary of fame~~, DIARMUID, that you would be a king of shepherds.

DIARMUID I have in you, GRANIA, ^& your love.^
~~My kingdom is~~ in you, GRANIA, ~~and that cannot be~~ taken

[NLI 8777(6), 8r]

Enter Nial & Cormac [?*to*] [?*goes*] [?*him*] *and counselers –*

–8–

DIARMUID **So you say nothing.**

It may be that desires are equal either way.
GRANIA ~~**If my desires fall equally either way**~~**.**

hav
DIARMUID **Here we have everything we ^ sought for; I have you,**
~~**and I have**~~ **this peaceful valley where I can hide you**
away. Here we shall live and die, and our children
mothers of
shall grow up about us, if the ^ gods hear my prayer and
accept my offering s **and give us children.**

GRANIA **Here we may spend our lives** ~~**at**~~ **settling the quarrels**
of the shepherds when the sheep go astray.

DIARMUID **You are weary of this valley, GRANIA.**

And fame has made you get weary
GRANIA ~~**Are you so weary of fame**~~**, DIARMUID, that you would be**
a king of shepherds.

I have & your love.
DIARMUID ~~**My kingdom is**~~ **in you, GRANIA,** ~~**and that cannot be**~~ **taken**

-1 Compare the loosely written words with the entrance of Niall and the Councillors on fol. 10r below.
8 Type deletion.

[NLI 8777(6), 9^r]

-8-

~~away from me.~~ No one can take your love from me.

ORANIA For you will win me again and again. ~~Love's kingdom, like other kingdoms, must be won again and again.~~ I am weary of the shadows ~~of~~ these mountains and of the smell of the fold, ~~and~~ I shall love you better ~~if you~~ when you ~~come to my arms with the reek of battle upon you.~~ come reeking from the battle.

DIARMUID When I won you at Tara, seven years ago, it was not by the sword, but by the desire of the eye.

ORANIA ~~That was once~~, but now ~~I would hear the rattling of your war gear~~. I would hold your spear for you ~~and give you your shield~~; for seeing ~~you so~~, I should thirst for you as in ~~those first moons of~~ that first wandering by the river-side. Battle was your trade ~~until I took you away with me~~ into the woods. ~~That season is~~ over, ~~and~~

[NLI 8777(6), 9r]

–9–

~~away from me.~~ No one can take your love from me.

No one

GRANIA ^ **For you will win me again and again. ~~Love's kingdom,~~**
~~like other kingdoms, must be won again and again.~~ I

& on

am weary^ of the shadows ~~of~~^ these mountains and of the

when you

smell of the fold, ~~and~~ I shall love you better ~~if you~~

~~me~~ ~~blood upon~~ spears

~~come to my arms with^ the reek of battle upon you.~~
come reeking from the battle.

DIARMUID **When I won you at Tara, seven years ago, it was not by**
the sword, but by the desire of the eye.

Yes a ~~so~~ Yes once – once

GRANIA **~~That was^ once,^~~ but now – ~~I would hear the rattle of~~**

in battle &

& your shield ~~I would~~

your war gear. I would hold your spear^ for you^ ~~and give~~

when you pull the bow string

~~& your bow~~. you pulling your bowstring

~~you^ your shield~~;^ for seeing ~~you^ so~~, I should thirst

that first

for you as in ~~those first moons of~~ wandering by the

You went from battle to before I called

river-side. ^ Battle ~~was your trade until^ I took~~ you

Our wandering was

~~away with me~~ into the woods. ~~That season is~~ over, ~~and~~

9 The correction to "so" and the caret mark below are in paler ink.

[NLI 8777(6), 10r]

-10-

another ~~season~~ kind of life has begun, and I would have you friends with FINN.

DIARMUID You fear lest you ~~might~~ will may lose your love of ~~the warrior~~ me ~~in the love of the~~ shepherd. You would ~~that I should~~ have me put away the crook ~~for~~ the spear. There is a ~~strange~~ ~~restlessness~~ light in your eyes and it ~~is many days since you have sought me these many days~~.

GRANIA ~~Yet so great an DIARMUID and FINN should not be at strife. It was I who brought about this strife.~~

There is the security of ~~my father's kingdom to think of, and my love security~~. FINN has sent his message of peace, and you have let him pass your house without bidding him welcome. (Enter NIALL - the King goes to him and some Councillors who appear in the doorway, GRANIA and DIARMUID are therefore practically alone)

[NLI 8777(6), 10r]

–10–

kind of life
another ~~season~~ has begun, and I would have you friends
with FINN.

~~will~~ may
~~would~~ me
DIARMUID **You fear lest you ~~might~~ lose your love of ~~the warrior~~**
~~wh~~ now that I have turned and have me
~~in the love of the~~ shepherd. ^ You would ~~that I should~~
fire in your
& take to again ~~fiery~~
put away the crook ~~for~~^ the spear.^ There is ~~a strange~~

~~light~~ you have not saught his
~~restlessness~~ in your eyes and ~~it is many days since you~~
have com t sit by me –
~~have sought~~ me. ~~these many days.~~

I woud you were at peace
with Fin
is that
I would not have me say always there Grania who [?put/first]
[?to/th] strife between Fin & Dairmd!
GRANIA **~~Men so great as DIARMUID and FINN should not be at~~**
^ **~~strife. It was I who brought about this strife.~~**
~~There is the security of my father's kingdom to think~~
~~of, and my love security~~. FINN has sent his message
of peace, and you have let him pass your house with-
out bidding him welcome. (Enter NIALL – the King
goes to him and some Councillors who appear in the door-
way, GRANIA and DIARMUID are therefore practically alone)

---

1 The ink marks on and below "you" appear to be adventitious.
5, 6 The substituted words "fiery light" are canceled in pencil.
6 The broken underlining is in pencil.
7 The ink addition is canceled in pencil, and the following line connecting with the beginning of Grania's speech is also in pencil.

[NLI 8777(6), 11r]

-11-

DIARMUID But if the broil should begin again ?

GRANIA FINN has forgotten me.

DIARMUID ~~None~~ no one forgets GRANIA - ~~Every man seeks GRANIA and some FINN was for a while.~~ Every man remembers Grania. Every man ~~would seek~~ desires Grania.

GRANIA ~~Yes, DIARMUID~~, you and FINN.

DIARMUID ~~You are~~ It has been foretold that my life shall be soon over; ~~for~~ if I should die would you be FINN's wife ?

GRANIA [illegible] ~~Say it not~~, DIARMUID (She goes to him)

DIARMUID ~~My life began with you and it ends with you~~ - Oh that another should clasp this delicate body and that these breasts should belon to another.

GRANIA The dying do not see those they are leaving, but those that are awaiting ~~for~~ them in the light.

[NLI 8777(6), 11r]

–11–

DIARMUID **But if the broil should begin again ?**

GRANIA **FINN has forgotten me.**

No one
DIARMUID **~~None~~ forgets GRANIA – ~~Every man seeks GRANIA and some find her for a while.~~** I Every Man remembrs Grania –
desires
Every man ~~would seek~~ Grania.

GRANIA **~~Yes, DIARMUID~~, you and FINN.**

I
DIARMUID **~~You know~~ it has been foretold that my life shall be**
. I
soon over; ~~for~~ if I should die would you be FINN'S wife ?

~~O do not say that~~ *What have you said*
GRANIA ? **~~Say it not~~, DIARMUID (She goes to him)**
x

DIARMUID **~~My life began with you and it ends with you~~ – Oh that another should clasp this delicate body and that these breasts should belong to another.**

GRANIA **The dying do not see those they are leaving, but those**
a
that are waiting ~~for~~ them in the light.

4 "would seek" is canceled in pencil.
7 Type deletion. The substituted period and capital letter in the same line are in paler ink.
8 The first substitution is canceled in pencil.

[NLI 8777(6), 12r]

-12-

DIARMUID When I stand in a meadow beyond the waves I shall ponder upon my love. I shall weep, remembering how I wandered with her among the woods (Taking her in his arms). I wish that all the world had forgotten you and that you and I were at the ends of the earth together- you and I alone.

GRANIA You must sit by the fire dreaming of me no longer. You must win new love from me in battle.

DIARMUID I can think of no other love except the love which you have given me, and without it the shore beyond the waves will be a barren shore (Taking her in his arms) Light of my life, I knew you before I was born. I made a bargain with this brown hair before the beginning of time, and it shall not be broken when we stand upon the shore beyond the world - I am going, my dear one be-

[NLI 8777(6), 12r]

–12–

beyond the waves
stand *in the meadow ~~of the dead~~*
DIARMUID **When I ~~stood~~ ~~upon the shore beyond the waves~~ I shall**
upon love
ponder ~~upon~~ my ~~life~~. I shall weep, remembering how I
wandered with her^ among the woods (Taking her in his
arms). I wish that all the world had forgotten you and
that you and I were at the ends of the earth together–
you and I alone.

GRANIA **You must^sit by the fire dreaming of me(no longer). You**
from
must win new love ~~of~~ me in battle.

DIARMUID **I can think of no other love except the love which you**
it
have given me, ~~and without the shore beyond the waves~~
O life
~~will be a barren shore~~ (Taking her in his arms) ~~Light~~
of my life, I knew you before I was born . I made
a bargain with this brown hair before the beginning of
time, and it shall not be broken when we stand upon the
shore beyond the world – I am going, ~~oh~~ my dear one ~~be-~~

1 The first substitution ("stand") is in paler ink.
7 The transposition is in pencil.
9–11 The first part of the sentence is canceled in pencil ("and without . . . barren shore" is canceled in ink)

[NLI 8777(7)]

[a, 1^{r}]

–11–

DIARMUID **But if the broil should begin again ?**

GRANIA **FINN has forgotten me.**

DIARMUID **None forgets GRANIA, and every man seeks her, and some find her for a while.**

GRANIA **Yes, DIARMUID, you and FINN.**

DIARMUID **You know that it has been foretold that I shall die soon. You heard the tale from CONAN THE BALD the night we escaped from Tara.**

GRANIA **Death treads at every man's heels like a hound.**

DIARMUID **Not in the image of a hound do I see my death, but as a black and bristless phantom which will come out of the unknown woods.**

[a, 2^{r}]

–11– a.

GRANIA **I have not heard you speak of it this long while. I thought it forgotten.**

DIARMUID **The silence of this valley has waked it in my heart, and I fear this death, for why, GRANIA ?**

GRANIA **For why, DIARMUID ?**

DIARMUID **If I were to die, GRANIA would you become FINN'S wife ?**

GRANIA **Say it not, DIARMUID (She goes to him)**

DIARMUID **My life began with you, and it ends with you – Oh that another should clasp this delicate body, and that these breasts should belong to another.**

GRANIA **The dying do not see those they are leaving; but those who are waiting for them in the light.**

1^{r}, 2^{r} These leaves appear to have been drafted to substitute for NLI 8777(6), fols. 11^{r}–12^{r}. See also 8777(7) c, fols. 5^{r}–10^{r}, where the same passage is developed differently again.

[b, 3r]

–13–

be **cause you have bidden me to my mortal enemy, to bring him into this house.**

GRANIA **FINN has made peace, you must bring him here to eat and drink.**

DIARMUID **Come hither, CORMAC; since GRANIA wishes it I will make peace with FINN.**

CORMAC **You have done well, DIARMUID, FINN and the Fianna are waiting in the valley; we will go to them and we will give them meat and drink in this house, so that all men may know that DIARMUID and FINN are no longer at** strife **~~enmity~~. I will bring them hither.**

GRANIA **~~You will come back with them, I will not say goodbye, father, for~~ I shall see you ~~again~~ in Tara in a little while, or you will come here when you are weary of**

3r, l. 1 The line follows directly on the last line of NLI 8777(6), fol. 12r/p.12

1, 11, 13 The transposition, substitution, and deletion (of “again”) are all in blue-black ink.

1–11 The large cancellation is in blue ink.

12–13 “I will not say goodbye” was deleted in pencil. Line 11 and the first two words of line 12 were then canceled in blue ink.

[NLI 8777(7) b, 4[r]]

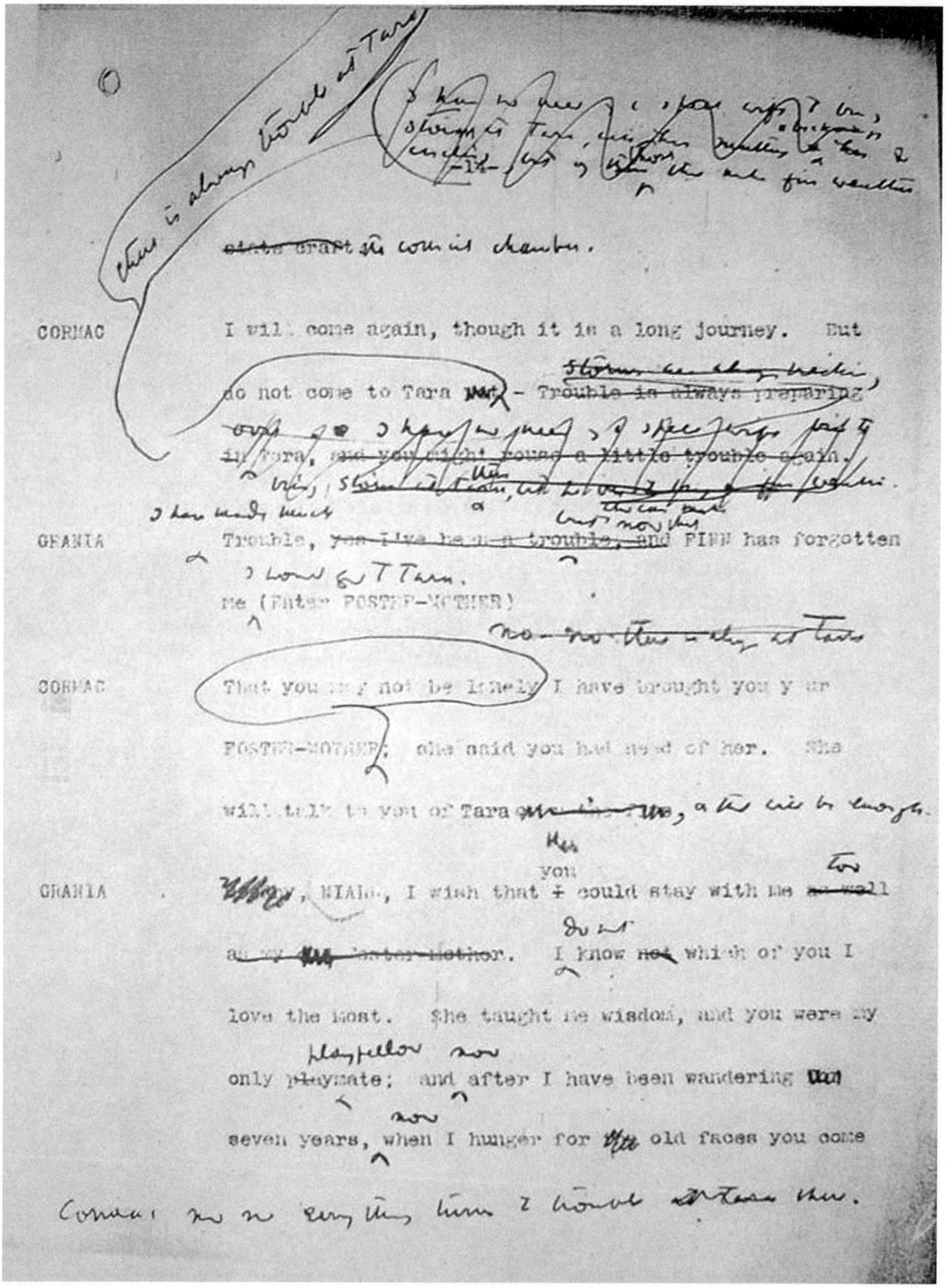

CORMAC I will come again, though it is a long journey. But do not come to Tara - Trouble is always preparing in Tara, and you might found a little trouble again.

GRANIA Trouble, you I've been in trouble, and FINN has forgotten me (Enter FOSTER-MOTHER)

CORMAC That you may not be lonely I have brought you your FOSTER-MOTHER; she said you had need of her. She will talk to you of Tara

GRANIA Goodby, NIALL, I wish that you could stay with me as well as my foster-mother. I know not which of you I love the most. She taught me wisdom, and you were my only playmate; and after I have been wandering seven years, when I hunger for the old faces you come

---

9 "Goodby" is deleted in pencil. The pencil word written above "you" is mysterious. "Ŧ" is a type deletion.
13, 13[+] The deletion and the insertion are in blue ink.

[NLI 8777(7) b, 4ʳ]

there is always trouble at Tara

~~I have no need of a spell wife to bring~~
~~& backwardgs~~
~~storm at Tara, with her mutterng & her~~ ~~7~~
~~those~~
~~circling but of them that make fine weather~~

–14–

~~state craft.~~ the council chamber.

CORMAC **I will come again, though it is a long journey. But**
Storms are always brecking
do not come to Tara ~~yet~~ – ~~Trouble is always preparing~~
over . ~~&~~ I have no need of a spell wifs vist to
~~in~~ Tara, ~~and you might rouse a little trouble again~~.
there
bring ~~storm at Tara~~, ~~but her visit to bring~~ a fair weather.
& who can make

I have made much but now that
GRANIA **Trouble, ~~yes, I've been a trouble, and~~ FINN has forgotten**
I would go to Tara.
me (Enter FOSTER-MOTHER)
~~*No – no – that is always at Tara*~~
CORMAC **That you may not be lonely I have brought you your FOSTER-MOTHER; she said you had need of her. She**
will talk to you of Tara ~~over the fire~~ {, . & that will be enough.
[?*that*]
you too
GRANIA **~~Goodby~~, NIALL, I wish that ~~I~~ could stay with me ~~as well~~**
do not
~~as my old foster-mother~~. I know ~~not~~ which of you I
love the most. She taught me wisdom, and you were my
playfellow now
only ~~playmate~~; and after I have been wandering ~~for~~
now
seven years, when I hunger for ~~the~~ old faces you come
Cormac. No no every thing turns to trouble ~~at Tara~~ there.

-1 The insertion at the top RH corner is in blue-black ink, but WBY went over the word "storm", deleted "her", and substituted "those" for "them" all in blue ink—before cancelling the whole and substituting the insertion at the top LH corner. The remainder of the emendations on this page are in blue-black ink unless noted.

3–4 The larger cancellation is in blue ink.

5–6 The words "now that" and "I would go to Tara." are in blue ink.

6 It is unclear who is meant to speak the penciled insertion. Is it yet another draft of Cormac's complaint, that there is always trouble at Tara? The insertion is canceled in blue ink.

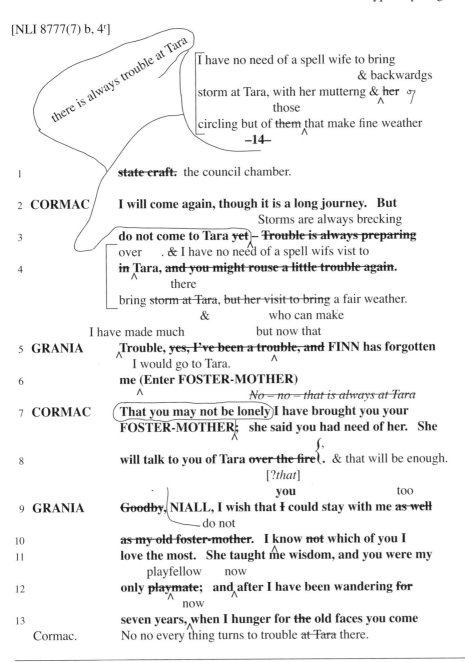

[NLI 8777(7)]

[c, 5r]

–7–

should you now wish to see him ? Do you love FINN ? I do not love FINN, but I always admired FINN. I admire his greatness.

DIARMUID **I remember seeing you speaking to him at Tara. You turned from him wearily it is true, but you seemed to like him. You told me you chose me because I was younger. FINN is seven years older than he was then. He would seem very old now.**

GRANIA **I would like to see you, who are as great as FINN, friends with FINN.**

DIARMUID **But if the broil should begin again ?**

GRANIA **FINN has forgotten me.**

DIARMUID **None forgets GRANIA; every man seeks her and some find her for a while.**

[c, 6r]

–8–

GRANIA **I should like to see Finn and the Fianna, OSCAR, USHEEN, and CAOILTE. And you, would you not like to meet your old comrades ? Peace has been made, and of what good is this peace if they remain estranged from us ?**

DIARMUID **My old comrades, USHEEN, OSCAR, CAOILTE, what should I say to them ? Seven years have sundered us – It is as if the sea sundered us – Here we have everything we sought for. I have you, and I have this peaceful valley where I can hide you away. Here we shall live and die, and our children shall grow up about us, if the gods hear my prayer and accept my offering and give us children. I often wonder now why I ever took up a sword, why I desire to excell any one – Love has come to seem enough.**

GRANIA **Here we must spend our lives settling the quarrles of the shepherds when the sheep go astray. But do you**

5r The page follows directly on NLI 8777(4) g, fol. 45r/p. 6, where the overall cancellation line is in blue ink, as it is here.

6r The overall cancellation line is in blue ink.

[c, 7r]

–9–

think we can live here seeing each other with the same eyes, and desiring each other with the same desire – Will this valley never grow weary of our love ?

DIARMUID **Not in my life time. In my life it has been foretold there is but one – Have I already outlived that season; and has the beast roused in his lair in the unknown woods, and is he on his way to rend me ?**

GRANIA **I have not heard you speak of that tale these many moons. You have seen no trace in the forest yesterday or to-day ? Tell me DIARMUID.**

DIARMUID **So there is a little love for me still in your heart ? I have seen nothing in the forest – I have seen nothing in the forest – It is the silence of this valley which has waked the thought of it (looking round) Did FINN contrive this valley because one who is long baffled must**

[c, 8r]

–10–

turn to deceit ? Is your father in league with him against us ?

GRANIA **Why should we stay in this valley ? I will set out with you to-morrow at daybreak, or this very night.**

DIARMUID **The journey through the woods at night would be terrible – We might come on our enemy sleeping,and in the dark my chance would be but little. But of what use to leave this valley – No man wanders very far from his grave sod. If I were to die, GRANIA, would you be FINN'S wife ?**

GRANIA **Say it not, DIARMUID (She goes to him.)**

DIARMUID **My life began with you, and it ends with you. Oh that another should clasp this delicate body, and that these breasts should belong to another.**

7r The overall cancellation line is in blue ink. The verso contains a jettisoned beginning of the same page in which the typist set the part ascription at the text margin.

8r The overall cancellation line is in blue ink.

[NLI 8777(7)]

[c, 9r]

–11–

GRANIA The dying do not see those they are leaving, but those who are waiting for them in the light.

DIARMUID When I stand upon the shores beyond the waves I shall ponder ^*upon* my love – I shall weep, remembering how I wandered with her among the woods.

GRANIA You must sit by the fire dreaming of me no longer. You must win new love of me in battle.

DIARMUID (Taking her in his arms). Light of my life, I knew you before I was born. I made a bargain with this brown hair before the beginning of time, and it shall not be broken when we stand upon the shore beyond the world. But you say nothing, GRANIA.

GRANIA Are you so weary of fame that you would be a king among shepherds ?

9r The overall cancellation line is in blue ink.

4 WBY's authorship of the inserted word is not certain.

[c, 10^{r}]

–12–

DIARMUID **My kingdom is in you, GRANIA, and that cannot be taken away from me.**

GRANIA **For you will win me again and again. Love's kingdom, like other kingdoms, must be won again and again – I am weary of the shadows of this mountain, and the smell of the fold. I shall love you better if you come to me with the reek of battle upon you.**

DIARMUID **When I was at Tara seven years ago, it was not by the sword but by the desire of the eye I won you.**

GRANIA **That was so once; now, I would hold your spear and give you your shield.**

DIARMUID **You fear, GRANIA, lest you might lose your love of the warrior in the shepherd. You would I should put away the crook for the spear. There is a strange restless-ness in your eyes, and it is many days since you have**

10^{r} The overall cancellation line is in blue ink.

[NLI 8777(7) c, 11r]

-13-

hair come to
~~sought~~ my bed - (She goes to a chest and takes out ~~her~~ a gold ornament~~s~~.)

Here
~~[illegible]~~ tis an ~~[illegible]~~ for another day & night

GRANIA But seeing you in your war gear I shall thirst for you as ~~I used to in the noons~~ when we wandered by the river-side.

DIARMUID You have not worn an ornament for me this many a day; but you think I may become new to you, and that in ~~the camp amid the clang of arms and the sound of trumpets~~ we may be happier than here, when we cook our food over the [illegible] [illegible] the [illegible] -

CORMAC Your cattle are coming this way, DIARMUID, and their ~~heavy~~ sides are heavy because of the rich grass of ~~those~~ these valleys which I have given you to be happy in. The day is darkening & I must go ~~I have given you this kingdom~~ ~~to be happy in~~ [illegible] I [illegible] [illegible] stay [illegible] [illegible] [illegible] [illegible] [illegible] [illegible] [illegible] [illegible] the Druid - [illegible] will [illegible] [illegible] the [illegible] Dawn

[NLI 8777(7) c, 11r]

–13–

have come to a

~~sought~~ my bed – (She goes to a chest and takes out ~~her~~
gold ornament~~s~~.)

Here
~~He~~ we are common to one anothr day & night

GRANIA **But seeing you in your war gear I shall thirst for you as ~~I used to in the moons~~ when we wandered by the river-side.**

DIARMUID **You have not worn an ornament for me this many a day; but you think I may become new to you, and that ~~in the camp amid the clang of arms and the sound of trumpets~~**
we may be happier than here{,. where we cook our food over the watch fire or hear arrows whiz in the air –

CORMAC **Your cattle are coming this way, DIARMUID, and their**
are heavy because of this
~~heavy~~ sides ~~tell me of~~ the rich grass of ~~these~~ valley ~~s~~
The day is darkenng & I must go
to be happy in – ~~valley~~
which I have given you. ~~I have given you this kingdom~~
~~to be happy in. I cannt wait~~ I woud I coud
stay with you but I cannot. I cannt wait any longer
if I woud cross the stepping stone in th river before it
is dark – You will come with me to the stone Darmud

1–2 The revision from "her gold ornaments" to "a gold ornament" was first made in pencil, and WBY went over the revision in blue ink.

The remaining emendations on this page are in blue ink.

[NLI 8777(7)]

[d, 12r]

–12–

~~**would you be FINN'S wife ?**~~
what have you said
GRANIA ~~**Say it**~~‸~~**not**~~**, DIARMUID (She goes to him)**

DIARMUID **My life began with you, and it ends with you. Oh that**
another should clasp this delicate body, and that these
breasts should belong to another.

GRANIA **The dying do not see those they are leaving, but those**
who are waiting for them in the light.

DIARMUID **When I stand upon the shore beyond the waves I shall**
upon
ponder‸**my love – I shall weep remembering how I wandered**
with her among the woods.
not any
GRANIA **You must**‸**sit by the fire dreaming of me** ~~**no**~~‸ **longer. You**
must win new love of me in battle.

DIARMUID **(Taking her in his arms) Light of my life, I knew you**
before I was born. I made a bargain with this brown

12r The present page follows on NLI 8777(4) h, fol. 49r/p. 11. The emendations are in blue ink.

[d, 13r]

–13–

hair before the beginning of time, and it shall not be broken when we stand upon the shore beyond the world.

You do not speak to me
~~But you say nothing~~, GRANIA.
^

GRANIA **Are you so weary of fame that you would be ~~a king among shepherds~~.** a shepherd always.

I have everything that I have ever desired. I have you
DIARMUID **~~My kingdom is in you~~, GRANIA, ~~and that cannot be taken~~**
^
you will never leave ^ me. You will never be taken from
~~away from me.~~ me.

GRANIA **For you will winn me again and again. ~~Love's kingdom, like other kingdoms,~~ must be won again and again – I am**
upon the
~~these~~ of
weary of the shadows ~~of this~~ ^ mountains, and ^ the smell
when you
of the fold. I shall love you better ~~if you~~ ^ come to me with the reek of battle upon you.

DIARMUID **When I was at Tara seven years ago, it was not by the sword but by the desire of the eye that I won you.**

carry I would
GRANIA **That was so once, now, I would ~~hold~~ ^ your spear and ^ give**

13r The emendations on this page are in blue ink.

[NLI 8777(7)]

[d, 14r]

–14–

{,
you your shield{**.** when you grow weary of pulling the bow string.

that may me
DIARMUID **You fear, GRANIA, ~~lest~~ you ~~might~~ lose your love of ~~the~~**
if seem but a shepherd ^ ^
~~warrior in the shepherd~~. Y<u>**o**</u>**u would I should put away**
^ fire
the crook for the spear. There is a strange ~~restless-~~
~~ness~~ in your eyes, and it is many days since ~~yl~~ you
hv have sought me (<u>**She goes to a chest and takes out**</u>
<u>**her gold ornaments)**</u>

GRANIA <u>**But seeing you in your war gear I shall thirst for you**</u>
<u>**as I used to in the moons when we wandered by the**</u>
<u>**river-side.**</u>

DIARMUID **You have not worn an ornament for me for many a day;**
and you wear it now because you are thinking of FINN.

[d, 15r]

–15–

GRANIA **Here we are common to each other by day and night.**
I}
~~But~~ i}n my war gear I shall be new to you again?
DIARMUID **~~You wear them for FINN. You know that~~ I shall go to**
fetch him for you have bidden me

GRANIA **~~Is he not our guest~~ – FINN has made peace you must**
bring him to eat and drink.

14r The emendations on this page are in blue ink.

5 "~~yl~~" is a type deletion.

15r, ll. 2, 4, etc. The revision of line 2 is in blue-black ink and of line 4 in pencil. The large cancellation is in blue ink.

[d, 15r continued]

DIARMUID **Come, hither, CORMAC; since GRANIA wishes it I will make peace with FINN.**

CORMAC **You have done well, DIARMUID, FINN and the Fianna are waiting in the valley. We will go to them and we will give them meat and drink in this house, so^that all men may know that DIARMUID and FINN are no longer at enmity. I will bring them hither.**

GRANIA **And I shall see you again in Tara in a little while, or you will come here when you are weary of. state craft.**

[e, 16r]

–17–

~~valley, so tightly~~ that it must snap asunder, and I felt all day that something was going to happen.

FOSTER-MOTHER **The gods are afoot when there is great silence.**

see

GRANIA **I had come to think that I should never ~~see the face~~ ~~of~~ a stirring day** s **again**{. **,** **~~and~~ I had thought to send all the thread you will spin to ~~the weaver~~ be woven into a grass green web, on which to embroider my wanderings with DIARMUID among the woods. I should have been many years embroidering it, but when it was done and hung all round this room I should have seen beasts and birds and leaves which ever way I looked, and DIARMUID and myself wandering amongst them.**

stet

FOSTER-MOTHER **But now you have thrown the doors wide open and the days are streaming in upon you ~~again~~.**

16r The present page follows on NLI 8777(4) j, fol. 52r/p. 16. The revisions are in blue-black ink.
6, 14 Type deletions.

[NLI 8777(7) e, 17r]

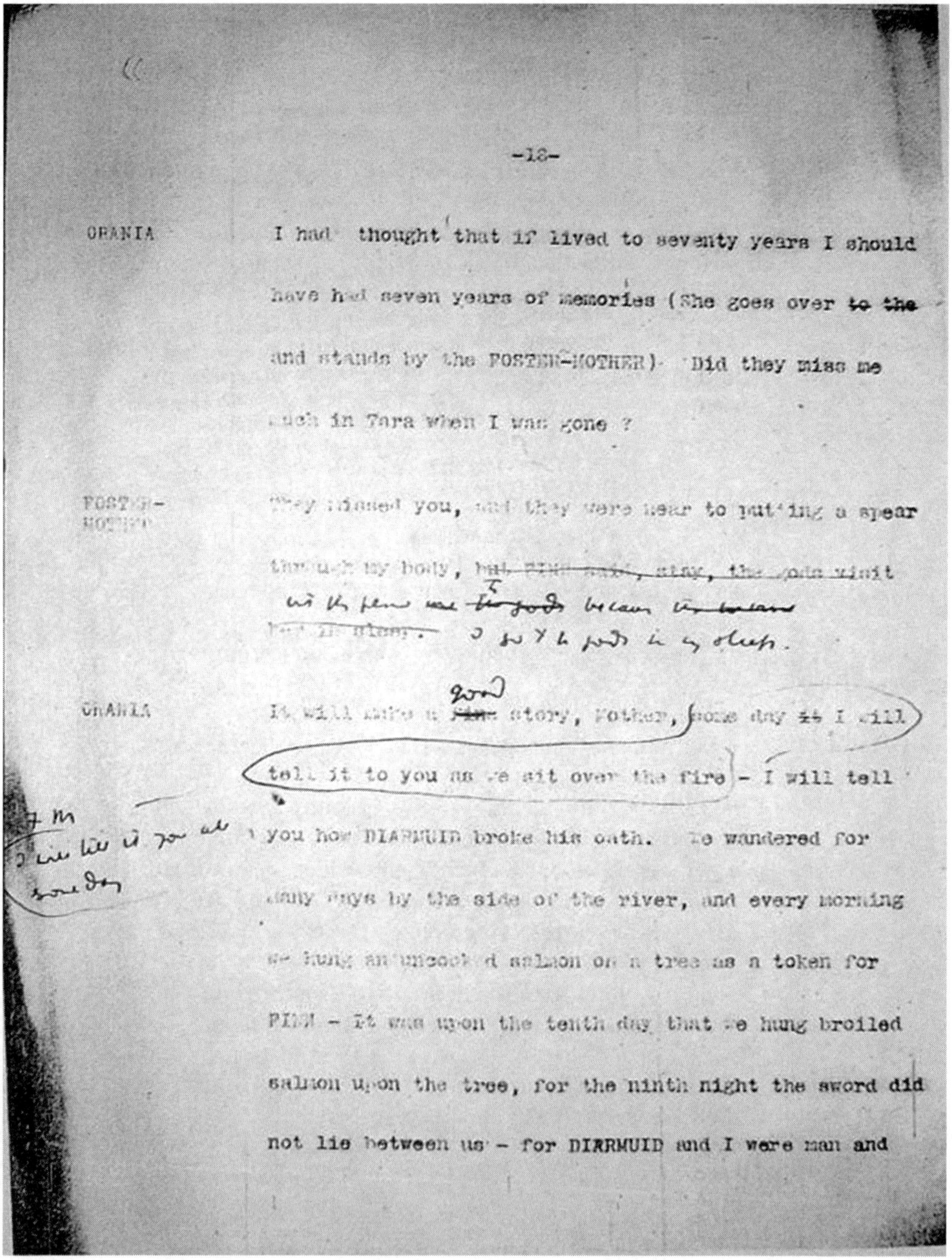

-18-

ORANIA — I had thought that if lived to seventy years I should have had seven years of memories (She goes over ~~to the~~ and stands by the FOSTER-MOTHER) Did they miss me much in Tara when I was gone ?

FOSTER-MOTHER — They missed you, and they were near to putting a spear through my body, ~~but FINN said, stay, the gods visit her in sleep.~~ with the spear ~~but the gods~~ because ~~[illegible]~~ I saw the gods in my sleep.

ORANIA — It will make a ~~fine~~ good story, Mother, some day ~~it~~ I will tell it to you as we sit over the fire - I will tell you how DIARMUID broke his oath. We wandered for many days by the side of the river, and every morning we hung an uncooked salmon on a tree as a token for FINN - It was upon the tenth day that we hung broiled salmon upon the tree, for the ninth night the sword did not lie between us - for DIARMUID and I were man and

[margin:] I'm / I will tell it you at some day

17r The revisions are in blue-black ink.

2, 8 (it) Type deletions.

18r Note that this page is continued in NLI 8777(4) l, fol. 62r/p. 20.

1, 3, 15 Pencil deletions.

8 The ink insertion is deleted in pencil.

[NLI 8777(7) e, 17r]

–18–

GRANIA **I had thought that if I lived to seventy years I should have had seven years of memories (She goes over ~~to the~~ and stands by the FOSTER-MOTHER) Did they miss me much in Tara when I was gone ?**

FOSTER-MOTHER **They missed you, and they were near to putting a spear through my body, ~~but FINN said, stay, the gods visit~~**

to

but they [?feard/persued] ~~me the gods~~ because ~~they because~~

~~her in sleep .~~ I go to th gods in my sleep.

good

GRANIA **It will make a ~~fine~~ story, Mother, some day ~~it~~ I will tell it to you as we sit over the fire – I will tell you you how DIARMUID broke his oath. We wandered for many days by the side of the river, and every morning we hung an uncooked salmon on a tree as a token for FINN – It was upon the tenth day that we hung broiled salmon upon the tree, for the ninth night the sword did not lie between us – for DIARMUID and I were man and**

FM I will tell it you [?all/at] some day

[NLI 8777(7) e, 18r]

–19–

wife; and we went northwards among the ~~stony~~ woods

[?Echti]

of ^ – and it was there that FINN nearly overtook us. As we lay under a cromlech ~~tree~~ we were awakened by the baying of the hounds coming towards us in the faint moonlight; it seemed that we could not escape then. And I will tel to you in the long evenings all about the old man who fished for us in the wood, and how he

~~& of much else I~~ [?~~knw~~] [?not] ^

divided the fish he caught between us. ~~But the best~~

tell *& of many other things*

tale of all is of the apples – the magic apples which DIARMUID would not get for me – I had to feign illness before I could get DIARMUID to go against the giants that guarded them, and I will tell you of the two young men whom FINN sent to kill DIARMUID, but who were overcome by DIARMUID. He sent them back with some of the apples to FINN ~~and you know what FINN~~ and you know what FINN said – The Fianna will be here in a moment, and I

See the facing page for notes to e, 18r.

[NLI 8777(7)]

[f, 19r]

–28–

FINN What is this beast that has filled you with so much terror ?

CONAN A boar so terrible that I think it has come for the ending of all men.

DIARMUID What is its color ?

CONAN It may be that you are sitting indoors because DIARMUID has seen it in the woods. It may be that a story I told him once has given him no stomach for this hunting and that he has filled you with his terror.

DIARMUID You are lying, CONAN, there has never been a boar in these woods – There is nothing in these woods but deer and wild dogs.

CONAN It is DIARMUID'S fear that makes him say I am lying. I was watching the horses at the mouth of the valley.

[f, 20r]

–29–

I had made a fire and I had put deer flesh to roast, when I heard women and children screaming – This man - slaying beast came out of a little thicket and ran into the wood on the mointain-side.

SPEARMAN It is certainly no mortal beast.

2nd. SPEARMAN It is bigger than any beast I ever saw, and it made a strange sound.

DIARMUID What is its colour? Was it covered with bristles.

CONAN The beast that is to slay DIARMUID is balk and without bristles (He goes over and stands by DIARMUID and imitates his gestures). FINN, CAOILTE, USHEEN, look at us; look at us, GRANIA, there is one terror in the heart of CONAN and DIARMUID.

DIARMUID (To the Spearman) What is its colour ?

[f, 21r]

–30–

SPEARMAN I saw it but once, far off and I thought it was gray.

DIARMUID (To the second SPearman) And you ?

2nd. SPEARMAN I saw it pass by, and near enough, and I thought it was green like the sea, and it made a noise like the sea in a storm.

CAOILTE Why do we listen to the foolish tales of the Spearmen who have been made deaf and blind with terror ? Take your spears in your hands (He goes to the door) – Come hither, CONAN, where did you last see it, shew us where it went into the wood (The Fianna go outside the door, DIARMUID following them.)

DIARMUID Did you say that it came out of a little thicket – Did it come out of the ground suddenly (He follows them out, GRANIA and FINN are left alone on the stage)

[f, 22r]

–31–

FINN If this were indeed a beast sent from the gods to overthrow all mankind, yet would I stand awhile looking on your beauty, GRANIA – Though this were the last day that I or you, or any one should breathe the air, maybe it was sent so ^has risen out of the earth ~~to~~ that we might speak together.

GRANIA You speak like one who loves; but there has been a time when you would have thrust your spear through my body.

FINN You fled from me seven years; and to-day you have put on your jewellry to welcome me.

GRANIA Who, among women, does not put on her jewellry and her many-colored cloak to welcome a guest, and you are more than a guest, for you have come to make peace with DIARMUID.

FINN Was I not more than a guest at Tara, and yet you did

[NLI 8777(7)]

[f, 23r]

–32–

not wear your jewels for me then ?

GRANIA **I had no mind to wear them that night.**

FINN **But you wear them for me now.**

Yes yes I wear them for you now.

GRANIA ^**Look at this brooch with the emeralds; it belonged to my mother and my grandmother; they say it is an hundred years old, and that it was made by Tergamos, the first goldsmith, and look at these bracelets, they were made by Len of Loch Len.**

FINN **You would have me look upon your treasures now; you would not wear them for me then – I am looking at your arms, GRANIA, and at your hands.**

GRANIA **Look rather upon this crescent upon my head and this girdle about my body; they were Len's handiwork too. When I, who have made so much strife in Eri, have been**

[f, 24r]

–33–

dust for a long while they will make the body and the head of some princess beautiful.

FINN **You would not wear them for me that night: it was to have been our marriage night, but you were thinking of another.**

GRANIA **I loved DIARMUID because of his youth and comeliness, and I love him still. I wear them to do you honour, because you have made peace with DIARMUID.**

FINN **There was a time when I thought GRANIA would have loved greatness and fame (DIARMUID comes slowly down the stage)**

DIARMUID **What have you two to say to one another, what were you saying to GRANIA, FINN, I can see by GRANIA'S face**

little at seeing me

that she is^ **~~mis~~pleased ~~to see me again~~ (To GRANIA) – Did you think I had already gone against this boar to**

23r, l. 14 The line is canceled with diagonal pencil strokes through most of the words.
24r, l. 1–2 The lines are canceled in pencil.

[f, 25r]

–34–

meet my death ?

FINN This is a false peace; there can be no peace between you and me, DIARMUID – Years had hidden some^thing^ of the treachery you had done me, but the sight of GRANIA has brought it to mind.

GRANIA Let there be no more strife.

FINN Which is the better a man's hand or a woman's breast ?

GRANIA Alas, I am ~~the~~ ^an^ evil fire in these men.

FINN On which side will GRANIA be (She goes over to DIARMUID They draw their swords.)

DIARMUID Nothing but the sword can decide between us – I shall slay you, FINN.

FINN One of us two shall die (The Fianna rush in)

OSCAR FINN and DIARMUID cannot fight – fling up their swords,

[f, 26r]

–35–

thrust the spear between them – Has FINN forgotten the blood bond – He who raises his hand against the blood-bond, raises his hand against the gods.

CONAN (Coming forward) FINN and DIARMUID cannot fight with one another, let FINN and DIARMUID go against the boar, and let GRANIA be given to him who kills it. AONGHUS who watches over lovers and over hunters shall decide between them.

OSCAR DIARMUID cannot go to this hunting.

USHEEN He cannot go to this hunt, nor to any boar hunt, for no man should run to meet his own death.

CONAN FINN and DIARMUID love GRANIA, and GRANIA does not know whom she loves. They have sworn the blood-bond. Who but AONGHUS can decide between them (DIARMUID lifts his sword to strike CONAN)

[NLI 8777(7)]

[f, 27^{r}]

–36–

GRANIA **He is not worthy enough for you to strike him. Give me your sword, he shall die by a woman's hand.**

FINN **(Standing in front of CONAN). No, GRANIA, he shall not die – He has spoken truth, FINN and DIARMUID love one ~~another~~ woman.**

CONAN **DIARMUID would strike me because I have spoken of that which fills him with terror.**

FINN **Take up your spears, throw your shields before you, we will go against this beast, let him who will stay**
& Co
behind (All but DIARMUID and GRANIA go out.)

DIARMUID **We must bar the door – I shall be caught up like a leaf Quick, quick, let us bar the door.**

GRANIA **They said they saw the boar go into the woods; it**
before
will have passed into the mountains ~~ere~~ this (They bar the door)

[f, 28^{r}]

–37–

DIARMUID **The darkness is full of shapes, and the silence is full of danger. No, we cannot sit here, we must unbar the door and let the light in. Why bar the door against that which has to come – The things ~~n~~ to come are like the winds – They could sweep this house away (They open the door – DIARMUID looks out of the door – I see nothing – I am not afraid of FINN. I should have killed him, he would have lain dead before you. But this image of my death which I have seen since a**
was
~~little~~ child – who knows what enchantment has called it out of the earth – It was not here yesterday, it was not here at noon. I have hunted deer in these woods and have not seen the slot of natural or unnatural swine – No, it will not bear thinking of – I am caught

---

27^{r}, l. 5 Type deletion.
28^{r}, l. 4 Type deletion.

this in a pit
in ~~the~~^valley like a wolf; ^ the branches are giving way
under me; I am falling into the pit, and I shall be

[f, 29r]

–38–

killed by a spear blow from above; I shall be torn
by tusks of a sudden (Pause) There, CORMAC, you sit
there like a stone, why did you do this ? In all
for all your wisdom
~~your wisdom~~ you do not know^why you came here; you came
here with a tale about the men of Lochland, and in your
wisdom you sought to leagye us against them. You
thought, like another, you were doing your own work,
can have done
but you^can see now that you ~~were doing~~ the ~~work of the~~
~~gods.~~ work of the gods.

CORMAC **My son-in-law I gave you this valley to be happy in.**

You spread it before us like a supper [?knew]
DIARMUID **~~An you laid it out like a feast~~; the gods ~~knew~~ all**
it
about ~~that~~. Sometimes when we are about to die they
give us more than we can eat and drink. There has
been too much happiness here for our hunger, and I
meets
would roll up the broken ~~meas~~ in a sack, and throw
them on your shoulder for ^you to carry ~~them~~ away.

[NLI 8777(7)]

[f, 30r]

GRANIA **This tale has shaken your mind .**

DIARMUID **You do not believe in it, tell me.**

GRANIA **We believe and we disbelieve, and there is a time when we do not know what we think.**

DIARMUID **What we think ? Much worth there is in thinking**
one is
when ~~we are~~ doing the work of the gods. He in state
They
craft, you in lust – ~~the gods~~ put lust into women's
bodies that men not defy the gods who made them
~~hearts lest~~ man ~~should~~ defy the ~~gods utterly~~; ~~and~~ I shall
soon over take this hunt & then I too shall
~~shall~~ ^ be doing the work of the gods ~~in this boar hunt~~
~~which I shall soon overtake~~.

GRANIA **You are not going to this hunt**

DIARMUID **I am going to this hunt because I would give you to FINN.**

[f, 31r]

~~O Darmud Darmud~~.
GRANIA **~~My life subders~~** My life is broken in pieces.

DIARMUID **Like ice on a river when a new season begins.**

GRANIA **(Distractedly) Take Borad-Edge your heavy spear**

DIARMUID **I see many ornaments upon you – How long is it since you have worn them for me. We are common to each other by day and night.**

GRANIA **(as if she had not heard) Take your he avy shield.**

not
DIARMUID **No man shall ^ say DIARMUID went to this hunt with his battle gear upon him.**

[f, 31r continued]

GRANIA **Gone – He is gone ! (She goes to her Father) Who is**
planned
to blame, you or I. Or was all this ~~written~~ before we
were born.

CORMAC **These are questions which the young are fond of asking.**
If you love DIARMUID –

[f, 32r]

–41–

he give
GRANIA **He said he was going to this hunt so that ~~I~~ might ~~be~~**
me to Finn
~~FINN'S some day~~. Men weary of us and I love DIARMUID
with a love that comes with years.

CORMAC **Then follow him and bring him back**

into
GRANIA **I will follow him ~~to~~ the forest. I shall overtake**
him. He will take the path, under the oak trees
(as GRANIA goes out the FOSTER-MOTHER comes in – She sits down and begins to spin)

was raising a host against
CORMAC **You told me what would happen when I ~~went among~~**^**the men**
of Alba – Tell me what is going to ~~hp~~ happen now. Spin
quickly, mother – What end of the thread are you spinni ng
now.

FOSTER-MOTHER **There is no more flax on the spindle.**

32r, l. 8 Type deletion.

[NLI 8777(4) g, 40r]

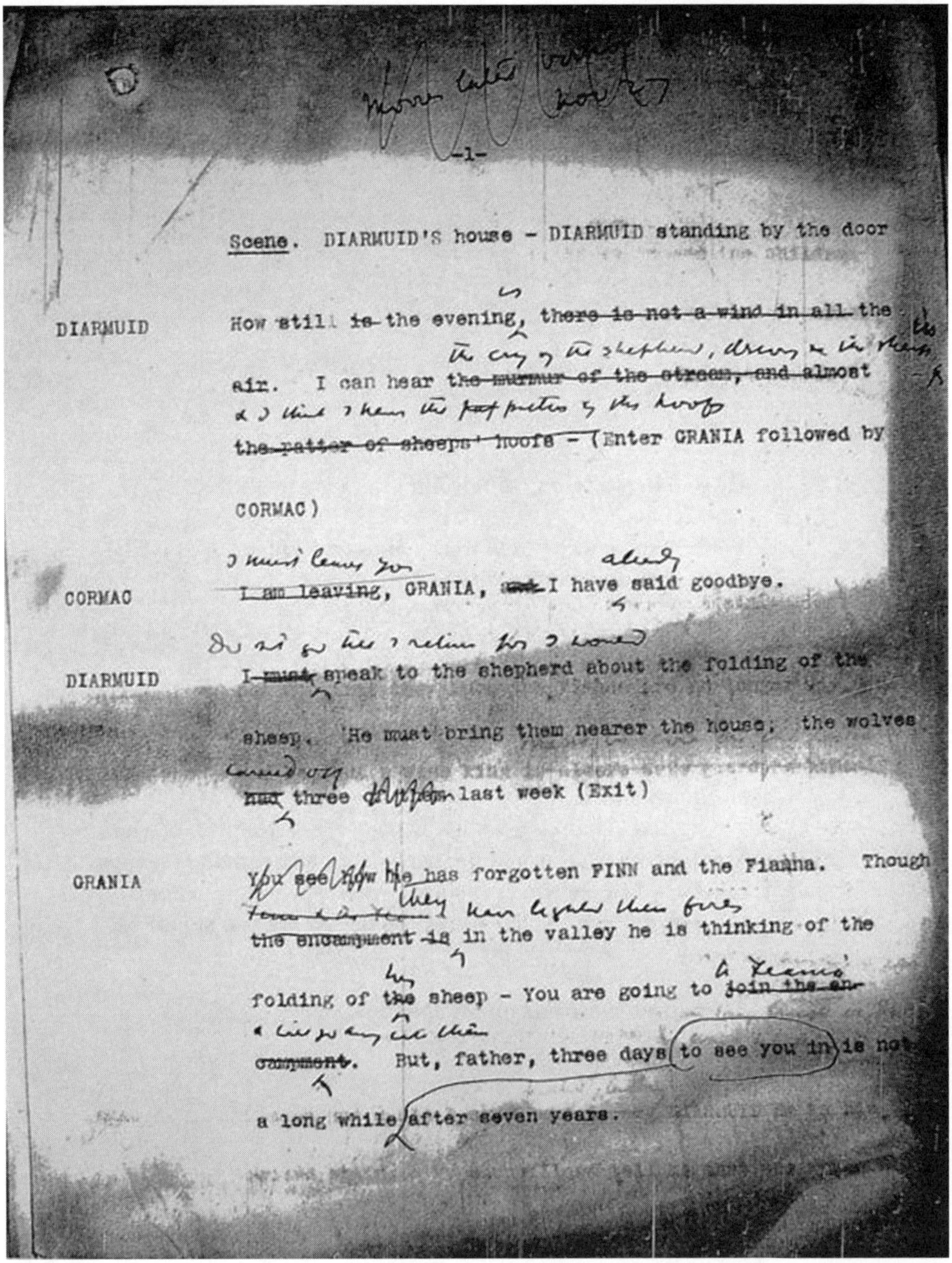

-1-

Scene. DIARMUID'S house - DIARMUID standing by the door

DIARMUID How still ~~is~~ the evening, ~~there is not a wind in all the~~
the cry of the shepherd, drowsy in the sheep
air. I can hear ~~the murmur of the stream, and almost~~
& I think I hear the patter of the hoofs
~~the patter of sheeps' hoofs~~ - (Enter GRANIA followed by CORMAC)

CORMAC I must leave you already
~~I am leaving~~, GRANIA, ~~and~~ I have said goodbye.

DIARMUID Do not go till I return for I would
~~I must~~ speak to the shepherd about the folding of the sheep. He must bring them nearer the house, the wolves
carried off
~~had~~ three ~~sheep~~ last week (Exit)

GRANIA You see how he has forgotten FINN and the Fianna. Though
they have lighted their fires
~~the encampment is~~ in the valley he is thinking of the
his
folding of ~~the~~ sheep - You are going to ~~join the en-~~
the Fianna
a king's way till then
~~campment~~. But, father, three days to see you in is not a long while after seven years.

Composite Text of First Half of Act, Endorsed by W. B. Yeats "Moore's Latest Version"

[NLI 8777(4) g, 40r]

Moores latest version
Nov 27

–1–

<u>Scene</u>. DIARMUID'S house – DIARMUID standing by the door

is
DIARMUID How still ~~is~~ the evening, ~~there is not a wind in all~~ the
in
the cry of the shepherd, driving ~~in~~ the sheep
~~air.~~ I can hear ~~the murmur of the stream, and almost~~ — ^
& I think I hear the ~~pat~~ patter of the hoofs
~~the patter of sheeps' hoofs –~~ (Enter GRANIA followed by CORMAC)

I must leave you already
CORMAC ~~I am leaving~~, GRANIA, ~~and~~ I have said goodbye.

Do not go till I return for I would
DIARMUID ~~I must~~ speak to the shepherd about the folding of the sheep. He must bring them nearer the house; the wolves
carried off
~~had~~ three ~~of them~~ last week (Exit)

H
GRANIA ~~You see how~~ h e has forgotten FINN and the Fia~~n~~na. Though
they
~~Fionn & the Fian~~ have lighted their fires
~~the encampment~~ ~~is~~ in the valley he is thinking of the
his th Feania
folding of ~~the~~ sheep – You are going to ~~join the en-~~
& will go away with them
~~campment~~. But, father, three days to see you in is not a long while after seven years.

-1 WBY's note at the head of the page is in blue ink; that is, following the time when he brought together the different TS sequences comprising NLI 8777(4) g+h+i+j+k+l and revised them as a single unit. All his other MS interventions on this and following pages of NLI 8777(4) are in blue-black ink unless recorded otherwise (as either pencil or blue ink).

2 WBY's insertions at the very end of the line ("in" above, the dash and caret below) are in blue ink.

7 WBY's cancellation of "of them" is in blue ink.

8 All WBY's revisions in this line are in blue ink.

9 WBY's revision of his own revision is in blue ink.

-2-

CORMAC I must not stay; ~~my errand is to gather~~ [I have to rouse] the children of Hebor, and then ~~I must rouse~~ the children of Hermon. We need every sword ~~[illegible]~~ [we have] to drive ~~[illegible]~~ the men of Lochland ~~[illegible]~~ [from our coast].

GRANIA But their vessels have been driven ~~back~~ [away] by storms.

CORMAC A few ~~[illegible]~~ weeks [of fair weather] and they will ~~collect~~ [gather] again.

GRANIA Not now that they know the Fianna are no longer divided.

CORMAC May be, but a wise king [so] ~~is always safe guarding himself and his kingdom, and~~ [must be, even on the edge] my councillors tell me that ~~never~~ [neither] [But the melancholy, nor even the thunder of galleys,] ~~were so many cunning wiles used as I used to turn FINN~~ [Can use so many wiles, so great cunning as I to] ~~from his quest of you.~~ [Can Finn from his hunting of you.]

GRANIA Has FINN ~~forsworn his quest of me~~ [he given up his hunting of me by truth or deed / he and his men to hope again.]

CORMAC Had he not would I come ~~here~~ ~~to beg~~ [hither, bidding] DIARMUID ~~to~~ be his friend again. My councillors tell me that the words

[NLI 8777(4) g, 41r]

–2–

I have to rouse
CORMAC **I must not stay; ~~my errand is to gather~~ the children**
of Hebor, and then ~~I must rouse~~ the children of Hermon.
if we are
We need every sword ~~in Eri~~ to drive ~~back~~ the men of
from
Lochland~~.~~ ~~frm~~ our coast.

away
GRANIA **But their vessels have been driven ~~back~~ by storms.**
of fair weather (gather)
CORMAC **A few ~~fair~~ weeks and they will ~~collect~~ again.**

GRANIA **Not now that they know the Fianna are no longer divided.**

so must be ever on the watch
CORMAC **May be, but a wise king ~~is always safe guarding himself~~**
neithr
~~and his kingdom, and~~ my councillors tell me that ~~never~~
Art the melancholy, nor Con the hundred fighter,
~~were so many cunning wiles used as I used to turn FINN~~
evr used so many wiles, so great a cunning as I to
~~from his quest of you.~~ turn Finn from his hunting of you.

{th
~~hi~~ given up his hunt of me in very tru{e or does
GRANIA **Has FINN ~~foresworn his quest of me~~** he wait his time to begin
again –

hither, bidding
CORMAC **Had he not would I come ~~here to beg~~ DIARMUID ~~to~~ be his**
friend again. My councillors tell me that the words

4 WBY's revision of his own revision is in blue ink.
12 WBY first wrote "true" (in blue-black ink) and inserted "th" in blue ink.

[NLI 8777(4) g, 42r]

men this conj great blood must be as it was or then were not

-3-

which swore him away from you were deftly chosen, and I

think they were. But all these wiles and words were

alike in vain.

GRANIA DIARMUID fears that at the sight of me FINN will begin

old broil would again begin.

not

CORMAC But I would have him end his days among. FINN waits

me in the valley

for me at the Red Waterfall, he would have DIARMUID back

among the Fenians. (x 2)

again; he would have DIARMUID arm among the shep-

herds in this valley, so that we could call them up out

against the enemy if needful. You shake your head -

Will DIARMUID'S faith and FINN'S faith never be pledged

again ?

You have

GRANIA For three days I have striven with him.

(for three days in vain)

CORMAC But you have said little - Tell him that my kingdom and

that the men of Lochland -

GRANIA I will tell him none of these things but I will persuade him

[NLI 8777(4) g, 42r]

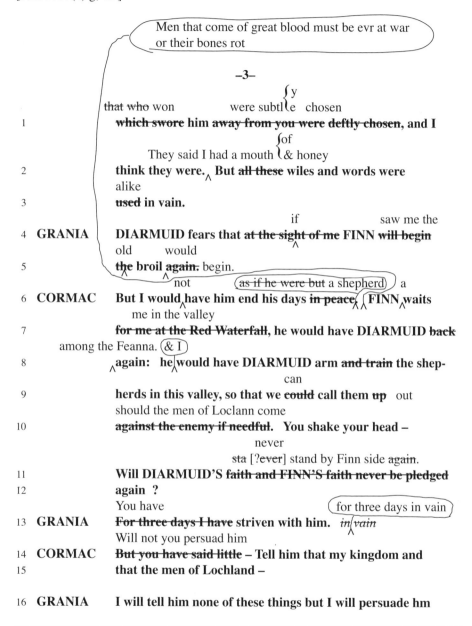

Men that come of great blood must be evr at war
or their bones rot

~~–3–~~

{y
~~that who~~ won were subtl{e chosen
~~which swore~~ him ~~away from you were deftly chosen~~, and I
{of
They said I had a mouth {& honey
think they were.^ But ~~all these~~ wiles and words were
alike
~~used~~ in vain.

if saw me the
GRANIA DIARMUID fears that ~~at the sight of me~~ FINN ~~will begin~~
old would
~~the~~ broil ~~again.~~ begin.

not (~~as if he were but~~ a shepherd) a
CORMAC But I would^have him end his days ~~in peace~~^^ FINN^waits
me in the valley
~~for me at the Red Waterfall~~, he would have DIARMUID ~~back~~
among the Feanna. (& I)
^again: he^would have DIARMUID arm ~~and train~~ the shep-
can
herds in this valley, so that we ~~could~~ call them ~~up~~ out
should the men of Loclann come
~~against the enemy if needful~~. You shake your head –
never
~~sta~~ [?~~ever~~] stand by Finn side ~~again~~.
Will DIARMUID'S ~~faith and FINN'S faith never be pledged~~
again ?
You have (for three days in vain)
GRANIA ~~For three days I have~~ striven with him. ~~*in*~~^~~*vain*~~
Will not you persuad him
CORMAC ~~But you have said little~~ – Tell him that my kingdom and
that the men of Lochland –

GRANIA I will tell him none of these things but I will persuade hm

---

1 WBY's revisions of his own revision are in blue ink. He also added the final letter of "chosen".

2 WBY clarified the final letters of his "said" and "mouth" at the same time that he corrected "&" to "of"—all in blue ink.

6 WBY deleted "in peace" and also his inserted "as if he were but" in blue ink.

11 WBY's cancellation of "[?ever]" and substitution of "never" is in blue ink; and he went over the last two letters of "stand" in blue ink at the same time.

13–14 The ink revisions are written over pencil.

[NLI 8777(4) g, 43[r]]

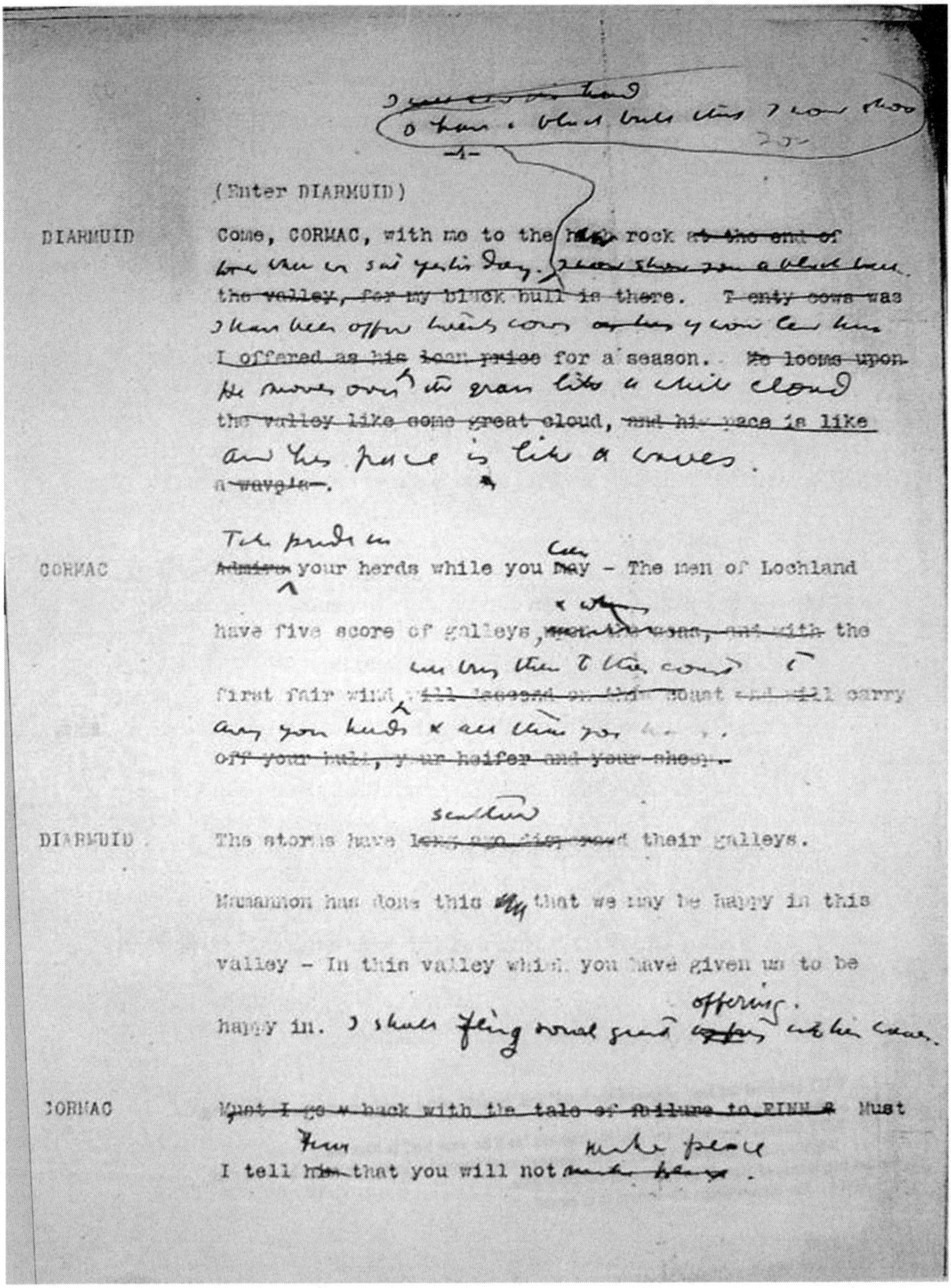

-1-

(Enter DIARMUID)

DIARMUID Come, CORMAC, with me to the ~~high~~ rock ~~at the end of~~ ~~the valley, for my black bull is there. Twenty cows was~~ ~~I offered as his loan price~~ for a season. ~~He looms upon~~ ~~the valley like some great cloud, and his pace is like~~ a ~~wave~~.

CORMAC ~~Admire~~ your herds while you may - The men of Lochland have five score of galleys, ~~upon the seas, and with the~~ first fair wind ~~will descend on this coast and will carry~~ ~~off your bull, your heifer and your sheep~~.

DIARMUID The storms have ~~long ago dispersed~~ their galleys. Mananmon has done this that we may be happy in this valley - In this valley which you have given us to be happy in.

CORMAC ~~Must I go back with the tale of failure to FINN?~~ Must I tell ~~him~~ that you will not ~~make peace~~.

[NLI 8777(4) g, 43[r]]

~~I will show the herd~~
I have a black bull that I woud show
~~-4-~~ you

(Enter DIARMUID)

DIARMUID **Come, CORMAC, with me to the ~~high~~ rock ~~at the end of~~**
~~We a~~ where we sat yesterday. ~~I woud show you a black bull~~
~~the valley, for my black bull is there.~~ ~~Twenty cows was~~
I have been offered twenty cows [?~~of~~] ~~his~~ if woud lend him
~~I offered as his~~ ~~loan price~~ for a season. ~~He looms upon~~
He moves over the grass like a white cloud
~~the valley like some great cloud~~, ~~and his pace is like~~
and his pace is like a waves.
~~a wave's~~ .
Take pride in can
CORMAC **~~Admire~~ your herds while you ~~may~~ – The men of Lochland**
& ~~when~~
have five score of galleys , ~~upon the seas, and with~~ the
will bring them to this coast to
first fair wind ~~will descend on this coast~~ ~~and will~~ carry
away your herds & all that you have.
~~off your bull, your heifer and your sheep.~~
scattered
DIARMUID **The storms have ~~long ago dispersed~~ their galleys.**
Mamannon has done this ~~so~~ that we may be happy in this
valley – In this valley which you have given us to be
offering.
happy in. I shall fling some great ~~of fring~~ into his waves.

CORMAC **~~Must I go back with the tale of failure to FINN ?~~ Must**
Finn make peace
I tell ~~him~~ that you have not ~~made peace~~.

4–5 WBY's insertions are in blue ink—although only the cancellation of line 5 is also in blue ink.

13 WBY's cancellation of "of fring" and substitution of "offering" is in blue ink; and he went over the first and last letters of "fling" and last letters of both "some" and "into" in blue ink at the same time.

15 WBY's revision of his second revision is in blue ink.

-5-

beyond out of my valley.

DIARMUID Tell him to ~~withdraw across the borders which you have marked for me.~~

Would you have men say that … forgiven

CORMAC ~~Shall it be said that~~ the man you wronged ~~stretched out his hand to you and that you~~ refused it. FINN ~~awaits~~ waits

your answer. I have made peace between you, for my kingdom's sake, and for my daughter's sake, but if you send ~~back~~ him such an answer the ~~a ashes may be blown in~~to flame again.

Let it flame up when it will.

DIARMUID I have fought FINN and overthrown him; ~~I escaped from the dun~~ out of the house of seven doors when ~~there were~~ guards at all the doors. ~~I have no fear of FINN.~~

CORMAC Do not send me ~~back~~ with this message.

DIARMUID ~~It is~~ for GRANIA'S sake that FINN will come here, ~~and not at all for the grasp of my hand.~~ But ~~GRANIA says nothing.~~ Would GRANIA have me friends with FINN - She

[NLI 8777(4) g, 44r]

–5–

begone out of my valley.

DIARMUID Tell him to ~~withdraw across the borders which you have~~
~~marked for me.~~

forgiven
Would you have men ~~to hav~~ say that has ~~go forgave~~
CORMAC ~~Shall it be said that~~ ^ the man you wronged ^ ~~stretched out~~
offered you and that
you & ~~offerd you~~ peace ~~& tht~~ ^ you have waits
~~his hand to you and that you~~ ^ refused it. FINN ~~awaits~~
Think well upon it.
your answer. ^ I have made peace between you , for my
kingdom's sake, and for my daughter's sake, but if you
him sod may be blown
send ~~back~~ such an answer the ~~e~~ ~~ashes may be blown into~~
into
^ flame again.
Let it flame up when it will Did I not break
(I have)
DIARMUID ^ I have fought FINN and ^ overthrown him; ~~I escaped from~~ ^
out of the house he had set
~~the dun~~ ^ of seven doors when ~~there were~~ ^ guards at all the
many with me
I was then alone & now I have ~~many~~ [?~~with~~] ^ ~~me~~.
doors. ~~I have no fear of FINN.~~

CORMAC Do not send me ~~back~~ with this message.
It would be (& not for my sake)
DIARMUID ~~It is~~ ^ for GRANIA'S sake ^ that FINN ~~will~~ come here, ~~and~~
woud
when
we know that would happen ~~whe~~ ^ he saw
her face again what woud
~~not at all for the grasp of my hand~~. But ~~GRANIA says~~
~~Gar~~ grania have me do?
~~nothing~~. ^ Would GRANIA have me friends with FINN – She

3–4 The following corrections are made in blue ink: the cancellation of "go forgave" and the substitution of "forgiven", the cancellation of "out", the cancellation of "offerd you" and the substitution of "offered you", the cancellation of "& tht" and the substitution of "and that" (with the caret beneath).

7 The second cancellation—of "e"—is a type cancellation. The words following are canceled in both blue-black and blue ink.

11 WBY's revision of his own revision is in blue ink.

14 In WBY's revision, "whe" is canceled in blue ink, and the substitution of "when" and the caret are in blue ink; and WBY went over "he" in blue ink at the same time. Also, "hand" is canceled in blue ink.

15 WBY went over "me" and the final letter of "do" in his own revision in blue ink.

[NLI 8777(4) g, 45r]

-6-

says nothing - She stands then saying nothing.

GRANIA If I say yes to you I shall say no to my father.

DIARMUID So you say nothing.

GRANIA If my desires fall equally either way. (Enter NIALL; the King goes to him - Some Councillors appear and engage him in conversation.)

DIARMUID For three days GRANIA I have fought your father's reasons, and you have sat listening taking neither side. But this morning you said you would like to see FINN again.

GRANIA My father has brought about peace, and you heard him say that if you refused the hand which FINN stretched to you the broil might begin again.

DIARMUID Did you not choose me ? Did you not serve him bewitched ale ? Have you not fled from for seven years ? Why

[NLI 8777(4) g, 45r]

–6–

there

1 **says nothing – She stands ~~apart~~ saying nothing.**

2 **GRANIA** **If I say yes to you I shall say no to my father.**

3 **DIARMUID** **So you say nothing.**

It may be that (are equal) & Finmole

4 **GRANIA** **~~If~~ my desires ~~fall equally~~ either way. (Enter NIALL; the King goes to him – Some Councillors appear and engage him in conversation.)**

5 **DIARMUID** **(For three days GRANIA) I have fought your father's reasons, **

6 **and you have sat listening taking neither side. But**

(that) it would please you

7 **(this morning) you said ~~you would like~~ to see FINN again.**

8 **GRANIA** **My father has brought about peace, and you heard him**

9 **say that if you refused the hand which FINN stretched to**

10 **you the broil might begin again.**

11 **DIARMUID** **Did you not choose me ? Did you not serve him bewitched**

12 **ale ? Have you not fled from for seven years ? Why**

---

4 The last of WBY's insertions in the line—"& Finmole"—is in blue ink.

5–12 The overall cancellation is in blue ink—in the same style as the rejected material that originally followed the present TS at NLI 8777(7) c, fol. 5r/p. 7.

[NLI 8777(4) h, 46r]

Quiet after agony Keys goes out night.

DIARMUID So you ~~say~~ nothing.

GRANIA If my desires fail equally either way. (Enter NIALL; the KING goes to him – Some Councillors appear and engage him in conversation.)

DIARMUID Tell, GRANIA, ~~[illegible]~~ ~~why you [illegible]~~ do call why would you call FINN here.

GRANIA I should like to see FINN again.

DIARMUID But ~~Do~~ you not ~~[illegible]~~ me ? Did you not serve him bewitched ale ? Have you not fled from him for seven years ? Why should you now wish to ~~love~~ see him ? Do you love FINN ?

GRANIA I do not love FINN, but ~~[illegible] FINN – I [illegible]~~ I have not forgotten that he is great & famous.
~~[illegible] his greatness.~~

DIARMUID I saw, when you were speaking to him at Tara
~~I remember you seeing you speaking to him at Tara.~~
You turned from him wearily ~~it is true~~ indeed, ~~but you~~ and yet it seemed

[NLI 8777(4) h, 46ʳ]

Insert ~~after~~ after
–8– King goes out
page 6 –

DIARMUID **So you say nothing.**

GRANIA **If my desires fall equally either way. (Enter NIALL; the King goes to him – Some Councillors appear and engage him in conversation.)**

XX
~~do~~
DIARMUID **But, GRANIA, ~~I should like to know~~ ~~why you wish to~~ call** ^
why would you call
^**FINN here.**

GRANIA **I should like to see FINN again.**

But
DIARMUID **~~Did~~ you ~~not~~ choose me ? Did you not serve him beweitched ale ? Have you not fled from him for seven years ?**
see
Why should you now wish to ~~love~~ him ? Do you love FINN ? ^
I have not forgotten that
GRANIA **I do not love FINN, but ~~I always admired FINN. I ad-~~**
he is great & famous.
~~mire his greatness~~.
I saw, when you were speaking to him at Tara
DIARMUID **~~I remember you seeing you speaking to him at Tara~~.**
indeed and yet it
You turned from him wearily ~~it is true~~, ~~but you~~ seemed ^

1–2⁺ The lines are canceled with blue ink and the subsequent overall cancellation is in pencil. WBY's interventions throughout this portion of text—NLI 8777(4) h—are in blue-black ink unless they are shown or noted as being in pencil.

3 The text is revised to pick up with the revised TS—NLI 8777(4) g—on fol. 45ʳ.

6, 8 The revisions in these lines are all in pencil.

11 The first "you" was deleted with type before being deleted in ink.

[NLI 8777(4) h, 47r]

-9-

~~[illegible]~~ like him - There are fruits which ripen late.

GRANIA I would ~~[illegible]~~ see you, who are as great as FINN,

friends with FINN.

DIARMUID [illegible] if the [illegible] should begin again ?

GRANIA FINN has forgotten me.

no one

DIARMUID ~~[illegible]~~ forgets GRANIA; ~~and~~ every [illegible] ~~[illegible]~~ her, ~~[illegible]~~

desires

~~[illegible] for a while.~~

would

GRANIA I ~~[illegible]~~ see FINN and the Fianna, ~~[illegible]~~, [illegible]

[illegible] CAOILTE. And you, would you not ~~[illegible]~~ [illegible] your

companions

old ~~comrades~~ [illegible] has been made, and of what good is

you & they do not [illegible]

this peace if ~~[illegible]~~.

companions Goll, Fergus, Usheen

DIARMUID My old ~~comrades~~ - ~~[illegible]~~, ~~[illegible]~~, CAOILTE, what (I) should

~~[illegible]~~ say to them ? Seven years have sundered us - it is

though had

as ~~if~~ the sea sundered us - Here

[NLI 8777(4) h, 47r]

–9–

	~~to~~ like d **him – There are fruits which ripen late.**
GRANIA	**I would ~~like to~~ see you, who are as great as FINN,** **friends with FINN.**
DIARMUID	**But if all the broil should begin again ?**
GRANIA	**FINN has forgotten me.**
	No one desires
DIARMUID	**~~None~~ ^ forgets GRANIA; ~~and~~ every man ~~seeks~~ ^ her, ~~and some~~** **~~find her for a while.~~**
	would Goll, Fergus &
GRANIA	**I ~~should like~~ ^ ~~to~~ see FINN and the Fianna, ~~Oscar~~, USHEEN** **and CAOILTE. And you, would you not ~~like to~~ meet your** companions **old ~~comrades~~. Peace has been made, and of what good is** you & they do not meet **this peace ~~if they remain estranged from us~~.**
	companions (Goll, Fergus, Usheen)
DIARMUID	**My old ~~comrades~~ ^ – ~~USHEEN~~, ~~OSCAR~~ ^, CAOILTE, what [I] should ^** **~~I~~ say to them ? Seven years have sundered us – it is** though had **as ^ ~~if~~ the sea ^ sundered us –** **Here**

---

6 and] Type deletion.

[NLI 8777(4) h, 48r]

-10-

we have everything [have] we sought for. I have you, and I have this peaceful valley where I can hide you away. Here we shall live and die and our children shall grow up about us, if the gods hear my prayer[s] and accept my offering[s] and give us children.

GRANIA Here we must spend our lives settling the quarrels of shepherds when the sheep go astray.

DIARMUID ~~This is the [illegible] way of life.~~ I often wonder now why I ever took up a sword, why I desire[d] to excell any one - Love has come to seem enough.

GRANIA ~~Do~~ [and do] you think - we can live here seeing ~~each other~~ [one another] with the same eyes, desiring ~~each other~~ [one another] with the same desire - will this valley never grow weary of our love ?

DIARMUID In some lives there are many seasons[, of love & joy] but ~~in my life it~~

[NLI 8777(4) h, 48r]

–10–

have
we have everything we^sought for. I have you, and I
have this peaceful valley where I can hide you away.
Here we shall live and die,^and our children shall grow
s
up about us, if the gods hear my prayer^ and accept my
s
offering^and give us children.

GRANIA **Here we must spend our lives settling the quarrels of**
shepherds when the sheep go astray.

~~**DIARMUID**~~ ~~**What is the wiser way of life.**~~ **I often wonder now**
ever ed
why I ever took up a sword, why I^desire^to excell any
one – Love has come to seem enough.
And do. one another
~~**GRANIA**~~ ~~**But do**~~^ **you think e we can live here seeing** ~~**each other**~~^
one another
with the same eyes, ~~**and**~~ **desiring** ~~**each other**~~^ **with the**
same desire – will this valley never grow weary of our
love ?
of love & of joy
DIARMUID **In some lives there are many seasons,^but** ~~**in my life it**~~

8–10 WBY deleted the first sentence of Diarmuid's speech and looped the remainder of the speech to the end of line 5 all in pencil. He then made further revisions to the passage, which include the deletion of the part ascription and retracing the loop line, in blue ink.

11 The part ascription and the second word in the line ("do") are canceled in pencil; "e" is a type delction.

[NLI 8777(4) h, 49r]

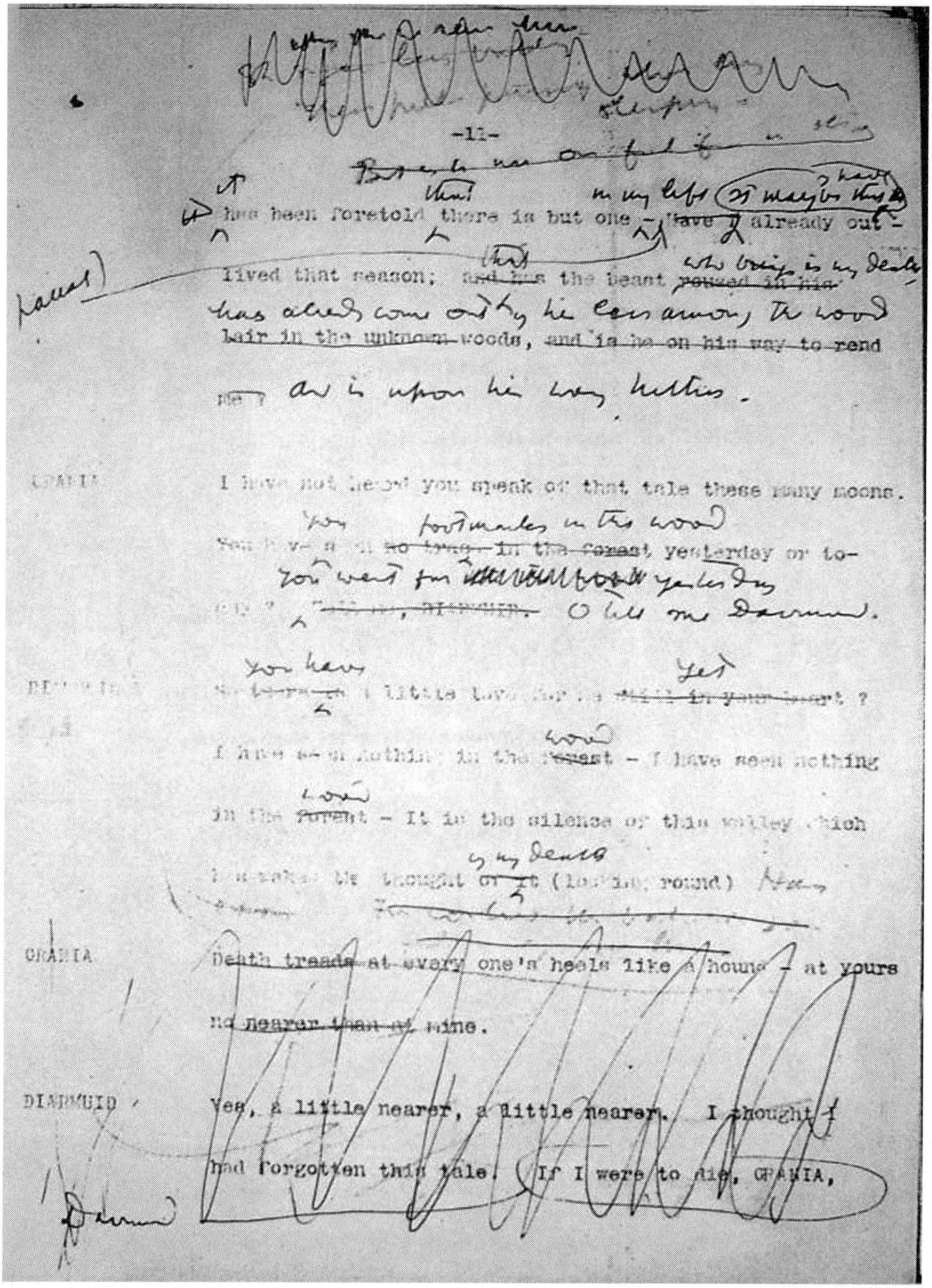
-11-

has been foretold there is but one - have I already out-

lived that season; and his the beast roused in his

lair in the unknown woods, and is he on his way to rend

me?

GRANIA I have not heard you speak of that tale these many moons.

You have seen no track in the forest yesterday or to-

day? Tell me, DIARMUID.

DIARMUID ... a little ... still in your heart?

I have seen nothing in the forest - I have seen nothing

in the forest - It is the silence of this valley which

has awaked the thought of it (looking round)

GRANIA Death treads at every one's heels like a hound - at yours

no nearer than at mine.

DIARMUID Yes, a little nearer, a little nearer. I thought I

had forgotten this tale. If I were to die, GRANIA,

[NLI 8777(4) h, 49^r]

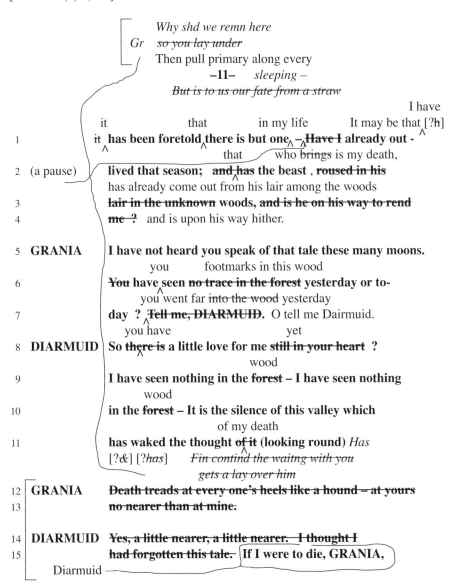

Why shd we remn here
Gr *~~so you lay under~~*
Then pull primary along every
–11– *sleeping –*
~~But is to us our fate from a straw~~

I have
it that in my life It may be that [?~~h~~]
~~it~~ ^ **has been foretold ^ there is but one ^ – ^ ~~Have I~~ already out -** ^
that who ~~brings~~ is my death,
(a pause) **lived that season; ~~and ^ has~~ the beast , ~~roused in his~~**
has already come out from his lair among the woods
~~lair in the unknown~~ woods, ~~and is he on his way to rend~~
~~me ?~~ and is upon his way hither.

GRANIA **I have not heard you speak of that tale these many moons.**
you footmarks in this wood
~~You~~ have ^ seen ~~no trace in the forest~~ yesterday or to-
you went far ~~into the wood~~ yesterday
day ? ^ ~~Tell me, DIARMUID.~~ O tell me Dairmuid.
you have yet
DIARMUID **So ~~there ^ is~~ a little love for me ~~still in your heart~~ ?**
wood
I have seen nothing in the ~~forest~~ – I have seen nothing
wood
in the ~~forest~~ – It is the silence of this valley which
of my death
has waked the thought ~~of ^ it~~ (looking round) *Has*
[?~~&~~] [?*~~has~~*] *~~Fin contind the waitng with you~~*
~~gets a lay over him~~

GRANIA **~~Death treads at every one's heels like a hound – at yours~~**
~~no nearer than at mine.~~

DIARMUID **~~Yes, a little nearer, a little nearer. I thought I~~**
~~had forgotten this tale.~~ If I were to die, GRANIA,
Diarmuid

The pencil draft is particularly obscure.

12–13, 14–15 WBY first continued Diarmuid's speech following line 11 and then at the head of the page, all in pencil. At the same time, he canceled Grania's and Diarmuid's speeches at lines 12–15. Subsequently, in ink, after clarifying that the saved phrase in line 15 is to be spoken by Diarmuid, he canceled the pencil revisions and confirmed the cancellation of lines 12–15 in toto (all in ink).

15+ The rejected material that originally followed the present TS is continued at NLI 8777(7) d, fol. 12^r/p. 12.

[NLI 8777(4) i, 50v, 51v]

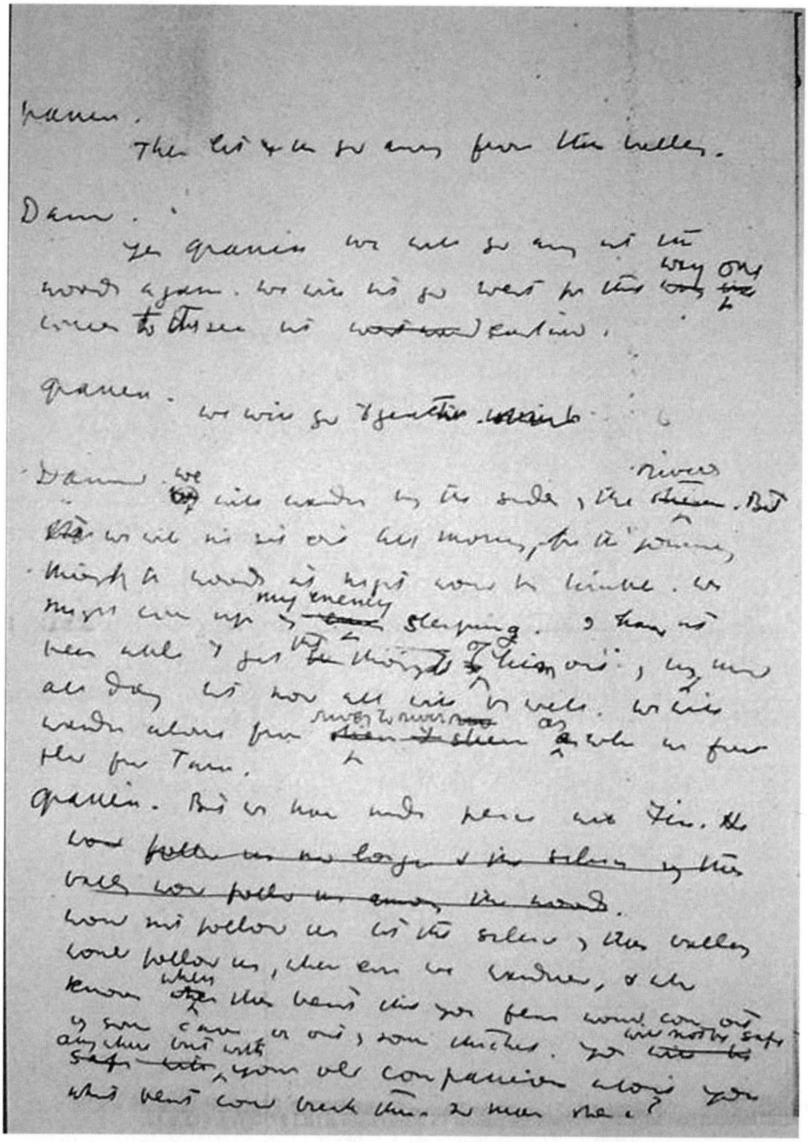

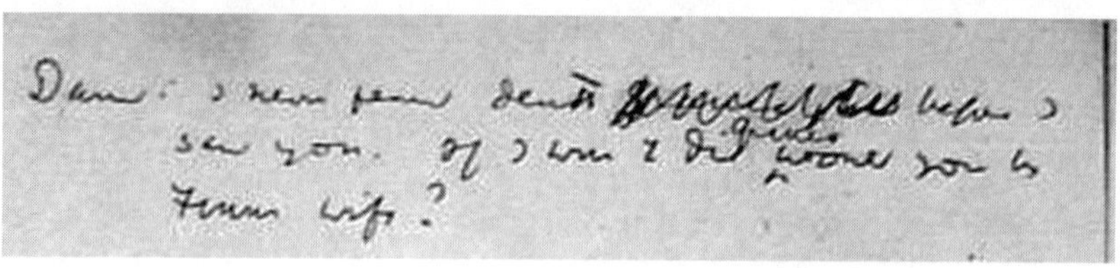

50v The holograph text follows on NLI 8777(4) h, fol. 49r.

4 to the] The words are written over other words or letters which are obscure.

51v 3 A connecting loop, not visible in the cropped illustration, points to a missing page; the present text picks up, after a gap (for which cf. NLI 8777[14] fols. 3r–8r), with NLI 8777(4) j, fol. 52r.

[NLI 8777(4) i, 50ᵛ]

Grania.
Then let us go away from this valley.

Darm.
Yes Grania we will go away int the
way one
woods again. We will not go west for that ~~way~~ ^ ~~we~~
comes to the sea but ~~west ward~~. eastward.

Grania.
We will go togeathr – ~~we will to~~

Darmuid.
We rivers
~~We~~ will wander by the sides of the ~~stream~~. But
^ ^
~~but~~ we will not set out till morning, for the journey
through th woods at night woud be terrible. We
my enemy
might come upn ~~my enmy~~ sleeping. I have not
that ^ of { m
been able to get ~~th~~ thought ~~so~~ hi{ s out of my mind
^
all day but now all will be well. We will
river to river ~~riv~~ as
wander alone from ~~stream t stream~~ ~~as~~ when we first
^
fled from Tara.

Grania. But we hav made peace with Fin. He
~~woud follow us no longer & the silence of this~~
~~vally woud follow us among the woods~~.
would not follow us but the silence of this valley
would follow us, where ever we wandred, & who
when
knows ~~wher~~ this beast that you flee would come out
^ will not be safe
of some cave or out of some thicket. You ~~will be~~
any where but with
~~safe with~~ ^ your old companions around you
what beast could break through so many spears?

[NLI 8777(4) i, 51ᵛ]

Darmd. I never feard death ~~Grania till~~ before I
Grania
saw you. If I were to die ^ would you be
Finns wife?

[NLI 8777(4) j, 52r]

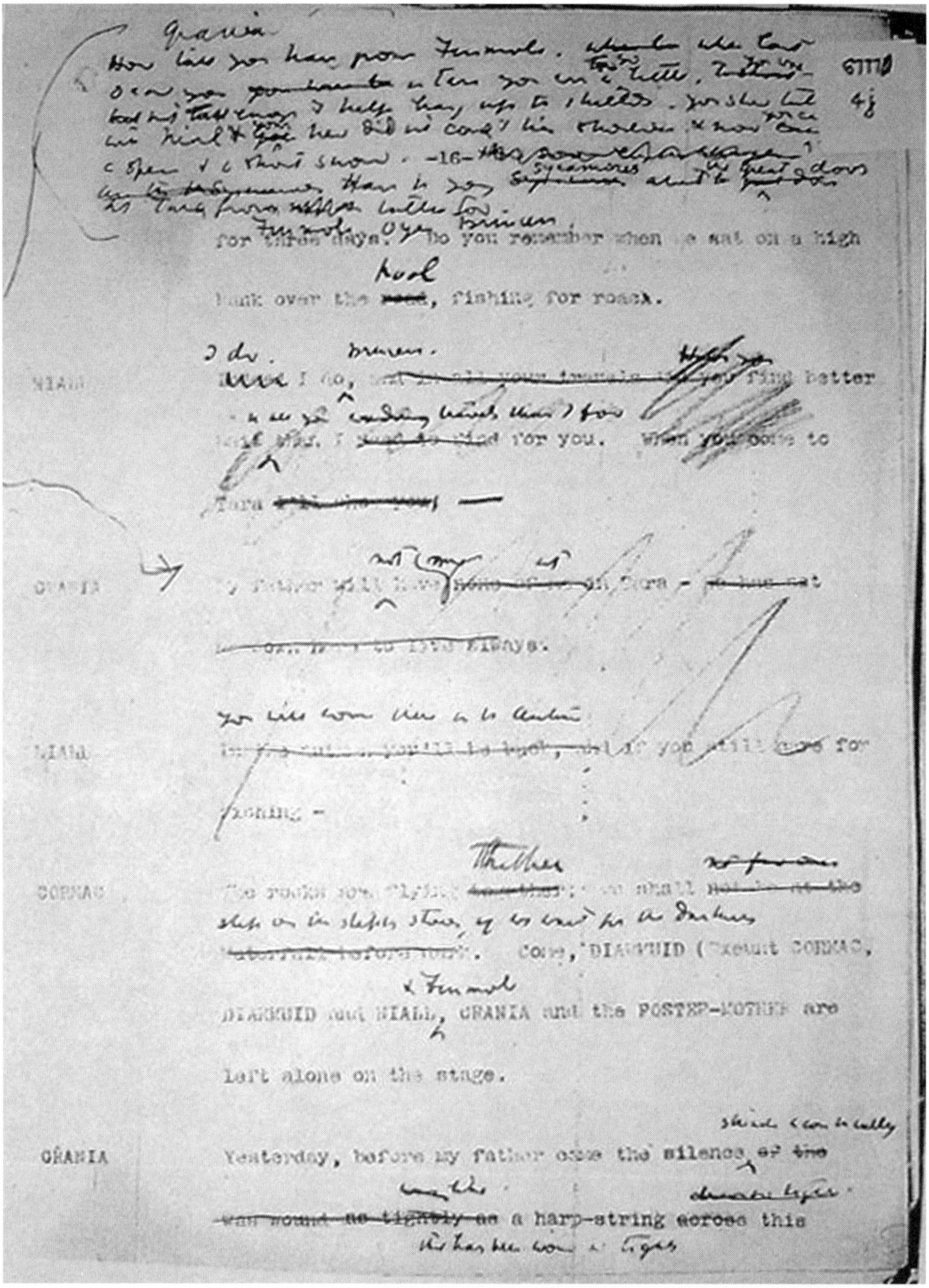
for three days. Do you remember when we sat on a high

bank over the , fishing for roach.

NIALL I do, better

half way. for you. When come to

Tara

GRANIA My father will have Tara -

always.

NIALL fishing -

CORMAC The rooks are flying . Come, DIARMUID (Exeunt CORMAC,

DIARMUID and NIALL, GRANIA and the FOSTER-MOTHER are

left alone on the stage.

GRANIA Yesterday, before my father came the silence

a harp-string across this

[NLI 8777(4) j, 52[r]]

Grania
How tall you have grown Finmole. ~~When la~~ When last
~~too~~ so you were not
I saw you ~~you were ta~~ in Tara you wer ~~a~~ little, ~~to short~~ t ^
~~hel~~ not tall enogh to help hang up th shields – You stood talkng
your you carry
with Nial & ~~you~~ head did not come to his shoulder. & now ~~cary~~ ^
a spear & a short sword. **–16–** ~~How soon evrythng changes?~~
sycamores the great doors
~~Are the Sycamores~~ Have th young ~~sycamores~~ about th ~~great doors~~ ^
at Tara grown ~~much~~ taller too –
Finmole. O yes princess.

1 **for three days. Do you remember when we sat on a high**
pool
2 **bank over the ~~reed~~, fishing for roach.**
I do. princess. Have you
3 **NIALL** **~~Indeed~~ I do, ^ ~~and in all your travels did you~~ find better**
in all your ~~wanderng~~ travels than I found
4 **bait ^ than I ~~used to find~~ for you. When you come to**
5 **Tara ^ ~~I'll show you.~~** –
not me at
6 **GRANIA** **My father will ^ have ^ ~~none of me~~ at Tara – ~~He has set~~**
7 **~~me down here to live always~~.**
You will come there in th autumn
8 **NIALL** **~~In the autumn you'll be back, and~~ if you still care for**
9 **fishing –**

thither ~~not find our~~
10 **CORMAC** **The rooks are flying ~~together~~; we shall ~~not be at the~~**
step on the stepping stones, if we wait for the darkness
11 **~~Waterfall before dark~~. Come, DIARMUID (Exeunt CORMAC,**
& Finmole
DIARMUID and NIALL ^, GRANIA and the FOSTER-MOTHER are left alone on the stage.

stretched a continually
12 **GRANIA** **Yesterday, before my father came the silence ^ ~~of the~~**
~~was~~ like ~~drawn so tight~~.
13 **~~was wound as tightly as~~ a harp-string ~~across~~ this**
that has been wound as tight

The cancellation of lines 3–5, 6–9, is in pencil; WBY's addition at the head of the page is in blue ink, together with his insertion into line 11⁺ ("& Finmole"); his remaining revisions are in blue-black ink.

12 The last two words of the line are canceled with a type cancellation.

13⁺ This portion of TS was originally continued in NLI 8777(7) e, fols. 16[r]–18[r]/pp. 17–19.

[NLI 8777(4)]

[k, 53^{v}]

–18– ^

valley so tightly that it must snap asunder. I felt all day that something was going to happen.

FOSTER-MOTHER **Something is always happening, child; here as much as in Tara – life is nothing else but a happening, among shepherds as much as among the Fianna. Yes, something is happening, I can hear it. DIARMUID has gone out with CORMAC; they are now drawing near the encampment where DIARMUID will meet FINN and make friends with him.**

GRANIA **They have not met yet (She goes to the door) In a few minutes they will meet (Returning to the FOSTER-MOTHER) Now that we are alone we can talk together. I would hear if they missed me much in Tara when I was gone. I would hear of FINN'S anger when he awoke from the ale which you bewitched. What did they say when they awoke**

Note that this page is typed on the verso. Typed on the recto is an abandoned start to the same passage:

–18–

valley, so tight that it must snap asunder. I have
felt all day that somehi

1–9 The lines are canceled in blue ink. The caret at the head of the page beside the page number is also in blue ink. The substitute for the canceled lines appears to be the revised typescript page 16 (fol. 52^{r}).

[k, 54r]

–19–

and found I was gone.

hanging me from the rafters
FOSTER-MOTHER **They were near ~~putting a spear through my body~~, but**
they feard becaus
~~FINN said, stay~~, the gods visit her in sleep.

tell ^me of Fins anger –
GRANIA **Yes, yes, I ~~can see him rising from the table, his~~ head**
~~still heavy with the ale~~.

& more calld the Feanna
FOSTER-MOTHER **He raged ~~for many~~ an hour,^ and then he ~~said the quest~~**
about him & began his hunt of you
~~should begin~~;^ and it has lasted for seven years.

me
GRANIA **He said he would never forgive,^ and yet he has forgiven**
and forgotten me. But my father, KING CORMAC, ~~what did~~
~~he say ?~~ was he too very angry.

FOSTER-MOTHER **He did not speak to me for many ~~weeks~~months, and then**
his cattle began to die; someone had thrown a spell
upon them, and I had to remove it.

GRANIA ^ **And so you have lived all this time in Tara making**

All WBY's revisions on this page are in blue ink.

[NLI 8777(4) k, 55^{r}]

-20-

Druid's spells, and prophesying victories and defeats.

FOSTER-MOTHER There have been no great battles ~~with the enemies of Eri~~ the enemies have come across the sea. ~~and happily for Diarmuid~~ since ~~you left Tara~~. ~~Likely enough~~ since you defeated (as it has been well for since you / in his time there has been none to meet the enemy) the Fianna ~~there was none to oppose the enemy~~. ~~Making~~ I have cured cattle, & have put spells on swords & I ~~spells off cattle, and making spells for swords, and~~ have gathered the little white root that I put on the eyes of lovers & [illegible] sleep, & I have gathered a ~~giving love potions~~ little red flower to make love drinks for women that love, & at last CORMAC came to me. He came ~~life passed for me until KING CORMAC came~~ and asked me ~~what he should do to put a stop to~~ every ~~after~~ [illegible] how he could stop Finn from his hunting of you. ~~FINN's pursuit of you.~~

GRANIA It ~~will make a fine story~~ some day, Mother, ~~and some day I will~~ you will tell me of all these things ~~tell it to you, all~~; but now I am thinking of the meeting of DIARMUID and FINN in the valley ~~below~~ under us. I can think of nothing else.

FOSTER-MOTHER It is not worth while thinking of it, child, it will be all here soon enough. ~~Tell me all that~~ sit beside me here & tell me what happened to you when you left Tara – ~~of the first man you met, and of~~ (in a low voice) Tell me of the first man you met & of

[NLI 8777(4) k, 55r]

–20–

~~**Druid's spells, and prophesying victories and defeats.**~~

No enemies have come
FOSTER-MOTHER **There have been no great battles** , ~~**with the enemies of Eri**~~
across the sea, ~~*and happily for*~~ ~~*divided*~~
~~**since you left Tara.**~~ ~~**Likely enough**~~ ^ ~~**since you**~~ ~~**defeated**~~
and that has been ^well for since you
in two that has been to ~~me~~ meet the enemy
broke **the Fianna** ~~**there was**~~ ^ ~~**none to oppose the enemy.**~~ ~~**Taking**~~
I have cured cattle, & have put spirits int swords & I
~~**spells off cattle, and making spells for swords, and**~~
have gatherd the little white root that I put int the ~~ag~~ ale
& given it t sick men who coud not sleep, & I hav gatherd a
~~**giving love potions life passed for me until KING CORMAC**~~
little red flowrs to make love drinks for women that coud
not love; & at last Cormac came to me. He came one
~~**came and asked me what he should do to put a stop to**~~
evening ~~after th sun~~ when th sun was going down, & he asked
~~**FINN'S pursuit of you**~~.
how he coud stop Fin from his hunting in you –
some day you will tell me of
GRANIA **It** ~~**will make a fine story**~~, **Mother,** ~~**and some day I will**~~
all these things
~~**tell it to you,all**~~: **but now I am thinking of the meet-**
under us
ing of DIARMUID and FINN in the valley ~~**below**~~. **I can**
think ~~**f**~~ **of nothing else.**
not
FOSTER-MOTHER **It is** ^ **worth while thinking of it, child, it will be all**
~~se~~ sit beside me here & tell me what
here soon enough. ~~**Tell me all that**~~ ^ **happened to you**
when you left Tara – ~~**of the first man you met, and of**~~
(in a low voice)
Tell me of the first man you met & of

---

3 The cancellations of "Likely enough" and "defeated", along with their replacements and the caret, are all written in pencil, although WBY's authorship is in doubt. The remainder of the alterations on this page —including the cancellation of the pencil substitutions in line 3—are in his hand in blue ink.

12 The canceled letter ("f") is a type deletion.

[NLI 8777(4)]

[k, 56^{r}]

–21–

the breaking of DIARMUID'S ~~vow~~ oath.

of

GRANIA **But you know^these things, Mother.**

Not all, not all

FOSTER-MOTHER **~~Yes, I know them in part~~, ~~but~~ I would hear you tell** of

Tell me of

~~Tell~~ ~~Tell~~

them – ~~I would hear~~ ~~of~~^the young man you met as you passed over the hill.

GRANIA **Yes, we met a young man, but it was not as we were crossing the hill, but as e we crossed the moor at the bottom of the hill. The features and form of that youth were good, but he had neither arms nor armour. DIARMUID greeted him, asking him tidings of him – He said he was a young warrior seeking a lord, and DIARMUID took him into his service, but I doubt not that he was greater than DIARMUID or I, so good was the counsel he gave us, and so well he served us. He told us in flying before FINN never to go into a tree having ~~two trunks~~ but one**

[k, 57^{r}]

–22–

trunk, nor to go into a cave to which there was but one mouth, and not to go into an island in a sea to which there is but one channel, and in whatever place we should cook our meals he said that we should eat it not in that place,and in whatever place we should eat we should lie not; and we should never lie down many hours in one place, but in the middle of the night change our resting place for another.

FOSTER-MOTHER **He told you his name was MUADHAN, very often a god takes the name of a mortal. DIARMUID kept his oath to FINN for nine days, and that was a long time for a man to keep it.**

GRANIA **For nine days we wandered by the banks of a river, and the youth fished for us, and he divided the fish between us, and every day we hung an uncooked salmon on a tree**

56^{r}, ll. 1, 7, 15 The cancellations in all three lines are type deletions. The remaining alterations on this page are in blue ink.

[k, 58r]

–23–

as a token for FINN – On the tenth day we hung a broiled salmon as a token, for on the ninth night the sword did not lie between us. But, mother, I can tell you no more, I would have ~~yl~~ you tell me what is passing in the valley – if FINN and DIARMUID have made friends, or if DIARMUID has passed the encampment of the Fianna without speaking.

FOSTER-MOTHER **They have spoken; they are on their way hither, so forget them for a while and tell me of what happened to the youth.**

GRANIA **(To herself) They have spoken, they are on their way hither (To the FOSTER-MOTHER) But, mother, you ask what had become of the youth. He fished for us and he served us many days, he served us by day and he watched over us by night; and then one day, after DIARMUID had**

[k, 59r]

–24–

overthrown two young men whom FINN had sent to kill him. Oh, it was a deadly battle, one after the other they rushed upon each other like wrestlers, like men making mighty efforts, ferocious and straining their arms and their swollen sinews like savage bulls or two raging lions, or two hawks upon the edge of a cliff. ~~DIARMUID came back the victor; he bound these two men with thongs and sent them back to FINN~~. It was after that night that murder took leave and farewell of us, and we stood on a high hill gloomy and grieved. ~~Other warriors pursued us; when they were too numerous we escaped from them by flight, but when they came singly or in couples DIARMUID overtook them~~. We were pursued by their hounds, and DIARMUID received the hounds upon his spear, and dashed their brains against the rocks. FINN did well to make peace for he would never have overcome DIARMUID.

58r, l. 4 Type deletion.

59r, ll. 6–8, 10–13 These two sentences are canceled in pencil. The page as a whole is canceled in ink.

[NLI 8777(4)]

[k, 60r]

–25–

It was three moons ago that ~~FINN agreed~~ he promised to follow us no longer, and‸so my father gave us this valley to be happy in – to tend our sheep and‸to love one another ~~in~~ for ever.

FOSTER-MOTHER In ~~these~~ three moons a great deal has happened ~~though you have not perceived it my child~~.

GRANIA Nothing has happened. I have stood by the door of this house, seeing the hours wane, and waiting for DIARMUID to come home from his hunting. Nothing has happened until to-day, and now DIARMUID and FINN are walking up the valley together – reconciled at last. I had come to think that I should never ~~see the face of~~ look on a stirring day again, and I had thought to send all the thread you will spin to be woven into a grass-green web on which to embroider my wanderings with DIARMUID among the woods. I should have been many years embroidering

[k, 61r]

–26–

it, but when it was done and hung all round this room I should have seen beasts and birds and leaves which ever way I looked, and DIARMUID and myself wandering among them.

FOSTER-MOTHER But now you have thrown the doors wide open and the days are streaming in upon you again.

GRANIA I had though t that if I lived to seventy years I should have had seven years of memories. I must put on my jewels, the Fianna will be here in a moment, and FINN has never seen me in my jewels.

60r All WBY's revisions on this page are in blue ink.

[l, 62r]

–20–

~~**must put on my jewels, FINN has never seen me in my**~~
~~**jewels.**~~ ~~*I do not put them on for him that night*~~ *in*
~~*tar*~~
You would not wear them for him that night in Tara
now

FOSTER-MOTHER ^**Shall I spin a thread for you,^ and tell you whether**
it is thick or whether it breaks or comes smoothly –
Shall I tell you what is going to happen. I am sure
that your thread is on the spindle, for I am shivering
with cold. I ~~**have**~~ **become as cold as the sea when the**
I care for *is*
is
thread of anybody that ~~**I knew**~~ ~~**was**~~ **on the spindle.**

GRANIA **Spin for me, mother, spin for me, while I am putting**
on my jewels. No, no. they are coming, I can hear
their footsteps. Go to the serveing-men and bid them
take the drinking horns and the ale skins from the
cupboard (Exeunt FOSTER-MOTHER – Grania alone on the
stage – She stands before a long steel mirror that
hangs upon the wall, and puts the gold circlet about
her head, and the heavy bracelets upon her arms, and

This page originally followed directly on NLI 8777(7), fol. 18r/p. 19. The alterations are all in pencil, except for the cancellations of the TS portion of lines 1–2, in blue ink, and in lines 7 and 8 ("was" deleted, "is" substituted), in blue-black ink.

[NLI 8777(15), 1^{r}]

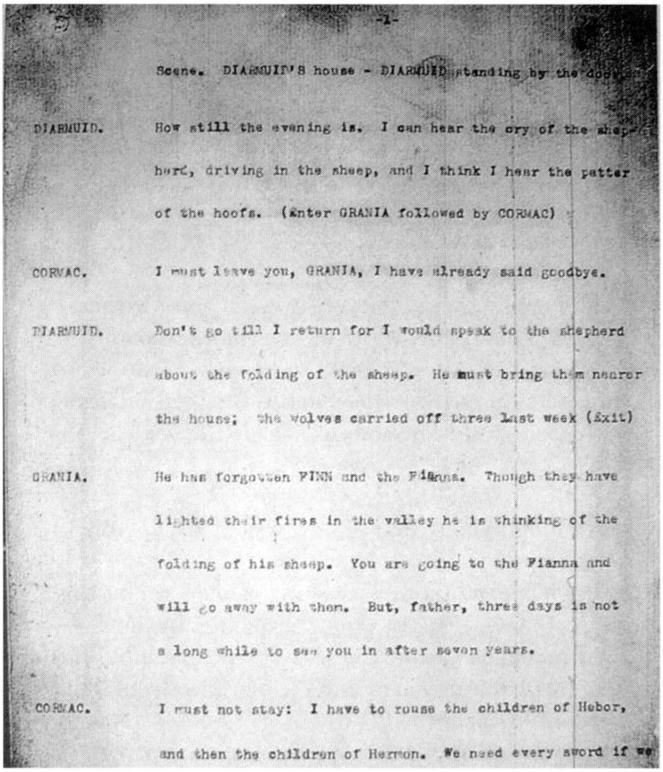

-1-

Scene. DIARMUID'S house - DIARMUID standing by the door.

DIARMUID. How still the evening is. I can hear the cry of the shep- herd, driving in the sheep, and I think I hear the patter of the hoofs. (Enter GRANIA followed by CORMAC)

CORMAC. I must leave you, GRANIA, I have already said goodbye.

DIARMUID. Don't go till I return for I would speak to the shepherd about the folding of the sheep. He must bring them nearer the house; the wolves carried off three last week (Exit)

GRANIA. He has forgotten FINN and the Fianna. Though they have lighted their fires in the valley he is thinking of the folding of his sheep. You are going to the Fianna and will go away with them. But, father, three days is not a long while to see you in after seven years.

CORMAC. I must not stay: I have to rouse the children of Hebor, and then the children of Hermon. We need every sword if we

[NLI 8777(15), 1^{r}]

–1–

Scene. DIARMUID'S house – DIARMUID standing by the door.

DIARMUID. **How still the evening is. I can hear the cry of the shep-herd, driving in the sheep, and I think I hear the patter of the hoofs. (Enter GRANIA followed by CORMAC)**

CORMAC. **I must leave you, GRANIA, I have already said goodbye.**

DIARMUID. **Don't go till I return for I would speak to the shepherd about the folding of the sheep. He must bring them nearer the house; the wolves carried off three last week (Exit)**

GRANIA. **He has forgotten FINN and the Fianna. Though they have lighted their fires in the valley he is thinking of the folding of his sheep. You are going to the Fianna and will go away with them. But, father, three days is not a long while to see you in after seven years.**

CORMAC. **I must not stay: I have to rouse the children of Hebor, and then the children of Hermon. We need every sword if we**

Twenty-five-Page Typescript of First Half of Act

[NLI 8777(15), 2^{r}]

–2–

are to drive the men of Lochland from our coast.

GRANIA. But their vessels have been driven away by storms.

CORMAC. A few weeks of fair weather and they will gather again.

GRANIA. Not now that they know the Fianna are no longer divided.

CORMAC. May be so, but a wise king must be ever on the watch, my councillors tell me that neither Art the melancholy, nor Con the hundred fighter, ever used so many wiles, so great a cunning as I to turn Finn from his hunting of you.

GRANIA. Has FINN given up his hunt of me in very truth, or does he wait his turn to begin again.

CORMAC. Had he not would I come hither bidding DIARMUID be his friend again. My councillors tell me that the words won him were subtly chosen, and I think they were. They said I had a mouth of honey. But wiles and words were alike in vain.

[3^{r}]

–3–

GRANIA. DIARMUID fears that if FINN saw us the old broil would begin.

CORMAC. But I would not have him end his days a shepherd. Men that come of great blood must be ever at war or their bones rot. FINN awaits me in the valley, he would have DIARMUID among the Fianna; he and I would have DIARMUID arm the shepherds in this valley, so that we can call them out s men, and Conn. You shake your head – Will DIARMUID'S never stand by FINN'S side again?

GRANIA. You have striven with him for three days in vain.

CORMAC. Will not you persuade him. Tell him that my kingdom and that the men of Lochland –

GRANIA. I will tell him none of these things but I will persuade him.

(Enter DIARMUID)

3^{r}, ll. 7–8 The TS corrected by WBY that the typist was copying—NLI 8777(4) g, fol. 42^{r}, line 10—reads "should the men of Lochlann come".

[NLI 8777(15)]

[4^{r}]

–4–

DIARMUID. **Come CORMAC, with me to the rock where we sat yesterday. I have a black bull that I would show you. I have been offered twenty cows He moves over the grass like a white cloud, and his pace is like a wave's.**

CORMAC. **Take pride in your herds while you can. The men of Lochland have five score of galleys, and the first fair wind will bring them to these coasts to carry away your herds and all that you have.**

DIARMUID. **The storms have scattered their galleys. Mamannon has done this that we may be happy in this valley. In this valley which you have given us to be happy in. I shall fling great offerings into his**

CORMAC. **Must I tell FINN that you will not make peace?**

DIARMUID. **Tell him to be gone out of my valley.**

[5^{r}]

–5–

CORMAC. **Would you have men say that the man you wronged has forgiven you and offered you peace and that you have refused it. FINN waits your answer. Think well upon it. I have made peace between you, for my kingdom's sake, and for my daughter's sake, but if you send him such an answer the sod may be blown into flame again.**

DIARMUID. **Let it flame up when it will. I have fought FINN and I have overthrown him. Did I not break out of the house of seven doors when he had set guards at all the doors. I was then alone and now I have many with me.**

CORMAC. **Do not send me with this message.**

DIARMUID. **It would be for GRANIA'S sake and not for my sake, that FINN would come here, We know what would happen when he saw her face again. But what would GRANIA have me do? Would GRANIA have me friends with FINN. She says nothing. She stands there saying nothing.**

4^{r}, l. 3 The TS corrected by WBY—NLI 8777(4) g, fol. 43^{r}, line 3—supplies "if woud leave him".

12 The TS corrected by WBY—NLI 8777(4) g, fol. 43^{r}, line 13—supplies "some great offering into his waves".

[6r]

–6–

GRANIA. If I say yes to you I shall say no to my father.

DIARMUID. So you say nothing.

GRANIA. It may be that my desires are equal either way. (Enter NIALL and FINMOL: the King goes to him. Some Councillors appear and engage him in conversation.)

DIARMUID. But, GRANIA, why would you call FINN here.

GRANIA. I should like to see FINN again.

DIARMUID. But you chose me? Did you not serve him bewitched ale? Have you not fled from him for seven years? Why should you now wish to see him? Do you love FINN?

GRANIA. I do not love FINN, but I have not forgotten that he is great and famous.

DIARMUID. I saw, when you were speaking to him at Tara you turned from him wearily indeed, and yet it seemed you liked him.

[7r]

–7–

There are fruits which ripen late.

GRANIA. I would see you, who are as great as FINN, friends with FINN.

DIARMUID. But if the broil should begin again?

GRANIA. FINN has forgotten me.

DIARMUID. No one forgets GRANIA; every man desires her.

GRANIA. I would see FINN and the Fianna, GOLL and FERGAS and USHEEN and CAOILTE. And you, would you not meet your old companions? Peace has been made, and of what good is this peace if you and they do not meet.

DIARMUID. My old companions. Goll, Fergus, Usheen Caoilte, what should I say to them? Seven years have sundered us – it is as though the sea had sundered us. Here we have everything we have sought for. I have you, and I have this peaceful valley where I can hide you away. We shall

[NLI 8777(14), 1r]

-8-

live and die here, and our children shall grow up about us if the gods hear my prayers and accept my offerings and give us children. I often wonder now why I ever took up a sword, why I ever desired to excel any one. Love has come to seem enough.

GRANIA. Here we must spend our lives settling the quarrels of Shepherd when the sheep go astray. And do you think we can live here seeing one another with the same eyes, desiring one another with the same desire - will this valley never grow weary of our love?

DIARMUID. In some lives there are many seasons of love and of joy. It has been foretold that there is but one (a pause) in my life. It may be that I have already out-lived that season: that the beast who is my death, has already come out of his lair among the woods and is upon his way hither.

[NLI 8777(14), 1^{r}]

–8–

live and die here, and our children shall grow up about us if the gods hear my prayers and accept my offerings and give us children. I often wonder now why I ever took up a sword, why I ever desired to excel any one. Love has come to seem enough.

GRANIA. **Here we must spend our lives settling the quarrels of Shepherd when the sheep go astray. And do you think we can live here seeing one another with the same eyes, desiring one another with the same desire – will this valley never grow weary of our love?**

DIARMUID. **In some lives there are many seasons of love and of joy. It has been foretold that there is but one (a pause) in my life. It may be that I have already out-lived that season: that the beast who is my death, has already come out of his lair among the woods and is upon his way hither.**

[2^{r}]

–9–

GRANIA. **I have not heard you speak of that tale these many moons. Have you seen footmarks in the wood yesterday or to-day? You went far yesterday. O tell me Diarmuid.**

DIARMUID. **So you have a little love for me yet? I have seen nothing in the wood – I have seen nothing in the wood – It is the silence of this valley which has waked the thought of my death (looking round.)**

GRANIA. **Then let us go away from this valley.**

DIARMUID. **Then Grania we will go away into the woods again. We will not go west for that way one crosses to the sea but eastward.**

GRANIA. **We will go together.**

DIARMUID. **We will wander by the sides of the rivers. But we will not sit   till morning, for the journey through the woods at night would be terrible. We might come upon my enemy sleeping. I have not been able to get the thought of him out**

2^{r}, l. 13 The holograph MS by WBY that the typist was copying—NLI 8777(4) i, fol. 50^{v}, line 7—reads "set out".

[NLI 8777(14)]

[3r]

–10–

of my mind all day but now all will be well. We will wander alone from river to river as when we first fled from Tara.

GRANIA. **But we have made peace with Finn. He would not follow us but the silence of the valley would follow us, where ever we wander, and who knows when the beast that you fear would come out of some cave, or out of some thicket. You will not be safe any where but with your old companions you what beast could break through so many spears?**

DIARMUID. **I never feared death before I saw you. If I were to die Grania would you be Finn's wife?**

GRANIA. **What have you said, DIARMUID (She goes to him.)**

DIARMUID. **My life began with you, and it ends with you. Oh that another should clasp this delicate body, and that these breasts would belong to another.**

GRANIA. **The dying do not see those they are leaving, but those who are waiting for them in the light.**

[4r]

–11–

DIARMUID. **When I stand upon the shore beyond the waves I shall ponder upon my love – I shall weep remembering how I wandered with her among the woods.**

GRANIA. **You must not sit by the fire dreaming of me any longer. You must win new love of me in battle.**

DIARMUID. **(Taking her in his arms) Light of my life, I knew you before I was born. I made a bargain with this brown hair before the beginning of time, and it shall not be broken when we stand upon the shore beyond the world. You do not speak to me, GRANIA.**

GRANIA. **Are you so weary of fame that you would be a shepherd always?**

DIARMUID. **I have everything that I have ever desired. I have you, you will never leave me. You will never be taken from me.**

GRANIA. **For you will win me again and again. Love must be won again and again – I am weary of the shadows upon the mountains,**

3r, l. 7 The holograph manuscript by WBY—NLI 8777(4) i, fol. 50v, line 21—supplies "around".

[5^{r}]

–12–

and of the smell of the fold. I shall love you better when you come to me with the reek of battle upon you.

DIARMUID. **When I was at Tara seven years ago, it was not by the sword but by the desire of the eye that I won you.**

GRANIA. **That was so once, now, I would carry your spear and I would give you your shield, when you grew weary of pulling the bowstring.**

DIARMUID. **You fear, GRANIA, that you may lose your love of me if I seem but a shepherd. You would I should put away the crook for the spear. There is a strange fire in your eyes, and it is many days since you have come to my bed – (She goes to a chest and takes out a gold ornament.)**

GRANIA. **Here we are common to one another day and night. But seeing you in your war gear I shall thirst for you as when we we wandered by the river-side.**

[6^{r}]

–13–

DIARMUID. **You have not worn an ornament for me this many a day; but you think I may become new to you, and that we may be happier than here, when we cook our food over the watch fire and hear arrows whizzing in the air.**

CORMAC. **Your cattle are coming this way, DIARMUID, and their sides are heavy because of the rich grass of this valley which I have given you to be happy in. The day is darkening and I must go.**

GRANIA. **I shall see you in Tara in a little while, or you will come here when you are weary of the council chamber**

CORMAC. **I will come again, though it is a long jounrey. But do not come to Tara, there is always trouble at Tara.**

GRANIA. **I have already much trouble, but now that FINN has forgotten me I would go to Tara. (Enter FOSTER-MOTHER.)**

[NLI 8777(14)]

[7r]

CORMAC. **I have brought you your FOSTER-MOTHER that you may not be lonely; she said you had need of her. She will talk to you of Tara, and that will be enough.**

GRANIA. **NIALL, I wish that you could stay with me too. I do not know which of you I love the most. She taught me wisdom, and you were my only playfellow; and now after I have been wandering seven years, now when I hunger for old faces you come.**

~~**CORMAC.** **No, no, everything turns to trouble there.**~~

[8r]

for three days. Do you remember when we sat on a high bank over the pool fishing for roach.

NIALL. **I do, I do, Princess.**

GRANIA. **How tall you have grown Finmole. When last I saw you you were not tall enough to hang up the shield. You stood talking with NIALL and your head did not come to his shoulder, and now you carry a spear and a short sword. Have the young sycamores about the great door at Tara grown taller too, Finmole?**

FINMOLE. **Oh, yes, Princess.**

CORMAC. **The rooks are flying hither, we shall slip on the stepping stones if we wait for the darkness. Come Diarmuid (Exit Cormac,Diarmuid, NIALL and FINMOLE.GRANIA and LABAN are left alone.)**

7r, ll. 8, 9 The line connecting with the lower RH corner and the cancellation are both in blue-black ink.

[9^{r}]

–16–

GRANIA. **The day before my father came, the silence was stretched across the valley like a harp string, that has been wound so tightly that it must snap asunder. I felt all day that something was going to happen.**

LABAN. **The Gods are near when there is great silence. It is very silent now, because something is going to happen.**

GRANIA. **Can anything happen in this valley?**

LABAN. **DIARMUID has gone out with CORMAC, and they are getting near the fires of FIANNA and DIARMUID and FINN will meet and make friends with another.**

GRANIA. **(Going to the door.) They have not yet met. In a few minutes they will meet (returning to LABAN) Now that we are alone we can talk together. I would hear if they missed me much in Tara when I was gone. I would hear of FINN'S anger when he awoke from sleep. What did he say when he**

[10^{r}]

–17–

awoke and found I was gone.

FOSTER-MOTHER. **They were near hanging me from the rafters, but FINN said NO, the gods visit her in sleep.**

GRANIA. **Yes, yes, tell me of FINN'S anger.**

FOSTER **He raged an hour or more, and then he called the FIANNA about him and began this hunt of you and it has lasted for seven years.**

GRANIA. **He said he would never forgive me, and yet he has forgiven and forgotten me, but my father King CORMAC was he too very angry?.**

LABAN. **He did not speak to me for many months, and then his cattle began to die and his herdsmen cried out for me to cure them and I began gathering herbs again.**

GRA NIA. **And men came to you as before, and you foretold their**

10^{r}, ll. 2, 11 Note the muddled alternation of Foster-Mother and Laban in the part ascriptions. It may be significant that this page is one of four that were typed later with a worn ribbon (the others are pp. 15, 18, 20)—the bulk of the pages having been typed with a new ribbon.

[NLI 8777(14)]

[11r]

–18–

battles and defeats.

LABAN. **There have been no great battles, no enemies have come across the sea and that has been well, for since you broke the Fianna in two there has been nobody to meet the enemy. I have cured cattle and have put spirits into swords and have gathered the little white root that I put into the ale and I have given it to sick men who could not sleep and I have gathered a little red flower to make a physic for men that would not love, and so the seven years have passed by. At last CORMAC came to me. He came one evening when the sun was going down and he asked how he could turn FINN from this hunting ofyou.**

GRANIA. **Some day Mother, you will tell me of all these things, but now now I am thinking of the meeting of DIARMUID with FINN in the valley under us, I can think of nothing else.**

LABAN. **It is not worth thinking of, child, it will be here soon enough. Sit beside me here, and tell me what happened to**

[12r]

–19–

you when you left Tara (in a low voice) Tell me of the first man you met and of the breaking of DIARMUID'S oath.

GRANIA. **But you know of these things Mother.**

LABAN. **Not all, not all, I would hear you tell of them. Tell me of the young man you met when you passed over the hill.**

GRANIA. **We came to a little glade on the hill-side and we heard there of a sudden a beautiful singing of birds and saw a red fox creeping in the grass and presently we saw a young man sitting among the long grass, he had dark hair and eyes that were grey as glass and there was an old wolf's skin about his body, but he had neither spear nor bow.**

LABAN. **What did he say? What did he say?**

GRANIA. **DIARMUID spoke first, and asked him whence he had come, and he answered that he was but a herdsman's son, that he sought a master and so DIARMUID took him into his service and yet**

[13r]

–20–

Mother I think that he was greater than DIARMUID or I for he gave us such good service and so much good counsel.

It was he who told us never to hide in a tree that stood alone by itself or in a cave that had not two mouths, or in an island that had not two harbours, and never to eat our food where we had cooked it, or sleep where we had eaten it and never to lie for many hours in one place but to change our sleeping-place in the middle of the night.

LABAN. **What name did he bid you call him?**

GRANIA. **He bid us call him MUDHAM. But I think he had some great and beautiful name did we but know it, have you ever seen him, Mother?**

LABAN. **It is said that ANGUS wanders in that wood with his birds of love singing about him and that he can take many shapes. It has been said too that none have seen him have been long**

[14r]

–21–

content with any mortal lover.

GRANIA. **You also have seen him.**

LABAN. **I am very old, I am very old and I have gathered much wisdom, but there was a time, child, when my hair was brown and soft, and my eyes and my heart hard, the hardness of youth. You have not told me all if that was the only time you heard the singing of his birds that the eye cannot see.**

GRANIA. **I hear them when DIARMUID broke an oath to FINN.**

LABAN. **He kept his oath nine days and that was a long time for a man to keep it.**

GRANIA. **We wandered by the banks of the river nine days and MUDHAM fished for us, and every day we hung an uncooked salmon on a tree as a token to FINN. On the tenth day we hung a cooked**

[NLI 8777(14)]

[15^{r}]

–22–

salmon, for on the ninth night the sword had not lain between us – but Mother I can tell you no more. I would have you tell me, you who know all things what is passing in the valley. Have FINN and DIARMUID made friends? Has DIARMUID passed the fires of the FIANNA without shrinking.

LABAN. They have spoken, they are on their way hither, so forget them for a while and tell me of the youth and when he left you.

GRANIA. (to herself) They have spoken, they are on their way hither (to LABAN) But, Mother, you asked me when he left us? He fished for us and served us for many days, he served us by day and watched over us by night, but one day FINN beset us in the House of Seven Doors and we escaped and fled over the plains westward, and the night after MUDHAM, said farewell to us and went away we were sad and sorry. The day after he had gone FINN'S hounds overtook us and DIARMUID

[16^{r}]

–23–

killed them one after another with his spear. FINN did well to make peace for he would never have overcome DIARMUID. It was three moons ago that he promised to follow us no longer and so my father gave us this valley to be happy in to tend our sheep and to love one another for ever.

LABAN. In three moons a great deal has happened.

GRANIA. Nothing has happened. I have stood by the door of this house seeing the hours wane waiting for DIARMUID to come home from his hunting, nothing has happened until to-day and now DIARMUID and FINN are walking up the valley together reconciled at last. I had come to think that I should never look on a stirring day again and I had thought to send all the thread you would spin to be woven into a grass-green web on which to embroider my wandering with DIARMUID among the woods. I should have been many years embroidering it but when it was done and hung all round this room I should have

[17r]

–24–

seen birds, beats and leaves which ever way I looked and DIARMUID and myself wandering amongst them.

LABAN. But now you have thrown the doors wide open and the days are streaming in upon you again.

GRANIA. I had thought that if I lived for seventy years I should have had seven years of memories. I must put on my jewels the Flanna, the Fianna will be here in a moment and Finn has never seen me in my jewels.

LABAN. You would not wear them for him that night in Tara. Shall I spin a thread for you now, and tell you whether it is thick or whether it breaks or whether it comes smoothly or easily Shall I tell you what is going to happen I am sure that your thread is on the spindle for I am shivering I become as cold as the sea when the thread of anybody that I care for is on the spindle.

[18r]

–25–

GRANIA. Spin for me, Mother, spin for me, when I am putting on my jewels, oh no they are coming I can hear their footsteps go to the serving men and bid them take the drinking horns and the flagons from the cupboard (Exit Laban)

GRANIA (stands before a long steel mirror that hangs upon the wall and puts the gold circlet about her head and the heavy bracelets upon her arm and the great many coloured cloak upon her which she fastens with an emerald clasp, she puts a gold girdle about her waist

[NLI 8777(16), 1r]

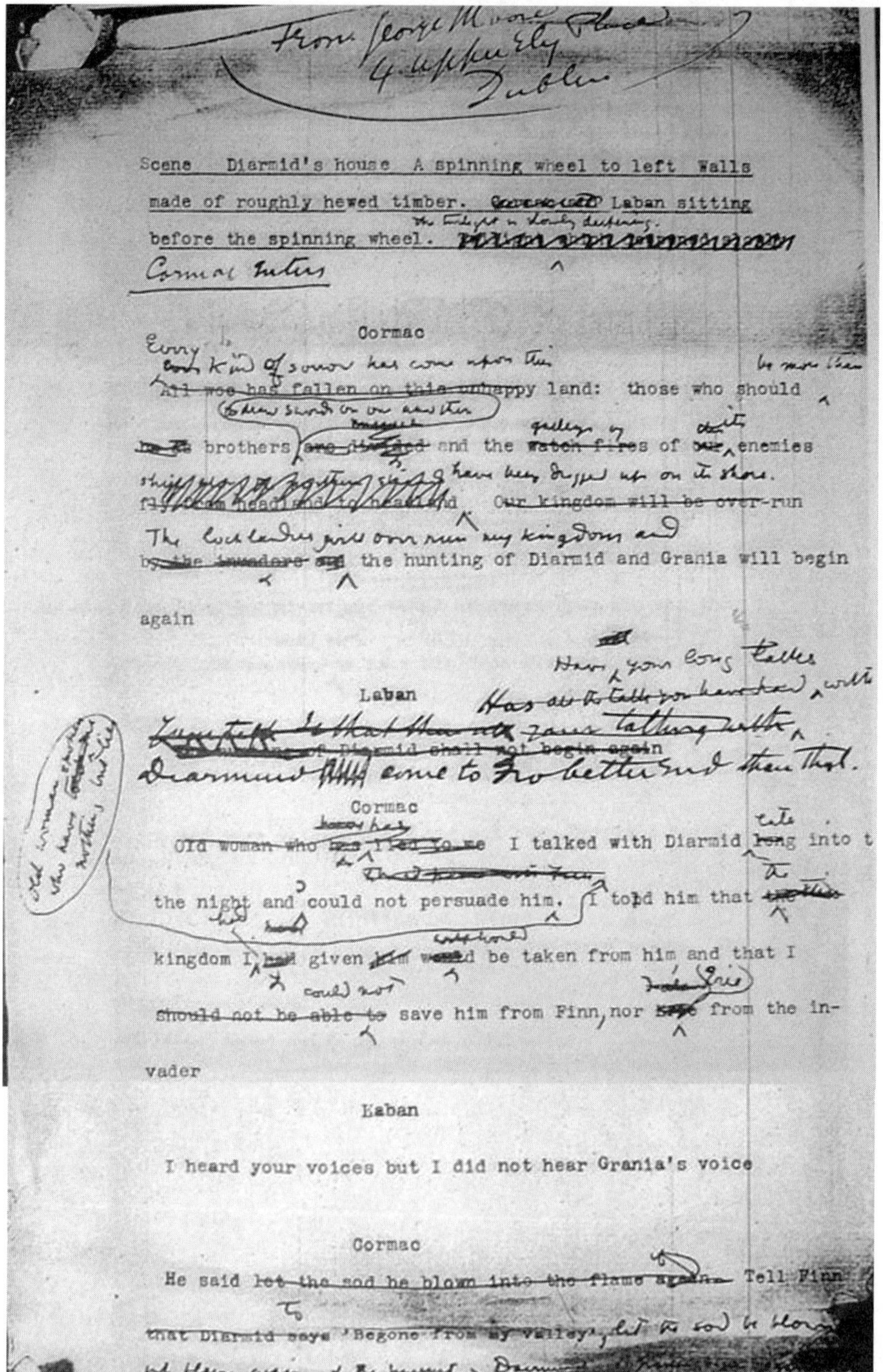

From George Moore
4 Upper Ely Place
Dublin

Scene Diarmid's house A spinning wheel to left Walls made of roughly hewed timber. [illegible] Laban sitting before the spinning wheel. [illegible] the twilight is slowly deepening.

Cormac enters

Cormac

Every kind of sorrow has come upon this
All woe has fallen on this unhappy land: those who should be more than brothers are divided and the watch fires of our enemies [illegible] have been dragged up on its shore.
Our kingdom will be over-run
The Lochlanders will over run my kingdom and
by the invaders and the hunting of Diarmid and Grania will begin again

Laban

Have your long talks
I foretell [illegible] Has all the talk you have had with
The hunting of Diarmid shall not begin again
Diarmuid [illegible] come to no better end than that.

Cormac

Old woman who has lied to me I talked with Diarmid long into the night and could not persuade him. I told him that the kingdom I had given him would be taken from him and that I should not be able to could not save him from Finn, nor save from the invader

Old woman [illegible] who have [illegible] nothing but [illegible]

Laban

I heard your voices but I did not hear Grania's voice

Cormac

He said let the sod be blown into the flame again Tell Finn that Diarmid says 'Begone from my valley', let the sod be blown into flame again [illegible]

These foolscap sheets are in some cases illustrated by splicing two images of one sheet to show the whole.

Typescript of Beginning Part of Act, Belonging to George Moore

[NLI 8777(16), 1r]

From George Moore
4 Upper Ely Place
Dublin

Scene Diarmid's house A spinning wheel to left Walls
made of roughly hewed timber. ~~Cormac and~~ Laban sitting
The twilight is slowly deepening.
before the spinning wheel. ~~Twilight which deepened slowly~~ ^
Cormac enters

Cormac

Every
^ ~~Ever~~ kind of sorrow has come upon this be more than
~~All woe has fallen on this unhappy~~ land: those who should ^
~~a~~ draw swords on one another its
~~enemies~~ galleys of ~~their~~
~~be as~~ brothers ^ ~~are divided~~ ^ and the ~~watch fires~~ of ~~our~~ ^ enemies
~~shine along the northern strands~~ have been dragged up on its shore.
~~fly from headland to headland~~ . ~~Our kingdom will be over~~-run
The lochlanders will over run my ^ kingdom and
~~by the invaders~~ ^ ~~and~~ ^ the hunting of Diarmid and Grania will begin
again ~~all~~ t }

Laban Have your long l }alks
~~Has all the^talk you have had~~ with ^
~~You talk Is that then all your talking with~~
~~The hunting of Diarmid^shall not begin^again~~
Diarmuid ~~has~~ come to no bett^er end than that.

Cormac

[?~~have~~] ~~has~~ late
~~Old woman who has lied to me~~ I talked with Diarmid ^ ~~long~~ into th
Old woman who have ~~told me~~ spoken ^ nothing but lies
I ~~^~~ ^ ~~that peace with Finn~~ the
the night and could not persuade him, ^ I told him that ~~the~~ ~~this~~
had ~~have~~ ~~will~~ would
kingdom I ^ ~~had~~ ^ given ~~him~~ ~~would~~ ^ be taken from him , and that I
could not ~~Ireland~~ Erie
~~should not be able to~~ ^ save him from Finn , nor ~~Erie~~ ^ from the in-
vader

Laban

I heard your voices but I did not hear Grania's voice

Cormac [?~~to~~]

He said ~~let the sod be blown into the flame again.~~ Tell Finn
to { ,
~~that Diarmid says 'Begone from my valley'~~ { . let the sod be blown
into flame again & th pursuit of Dairmuid & Grania begin again.

[NLI 8777(16), 2r]

Laban

And Grania stood by the door ~~[illegible]~~ post watching the moon shining down the valley: looking to where Diarmid's cattle were feeding and towards the ~~Finn's~~ encampment of Finn . . .

Cormac

Yes she stood there saying nothing. I ~~hurried~~ turned to her ~~and said~~ after [illegible] "If I take ~~Diarmid's~~ this message to Finn you will have to fly to the woods again"

Laban

And she answered nothing?

Cormac

~~Nothing~~ Only this - 'where will Laban go if we are driven from this valley?' She said "Father you brought her here to be near me and if we are driven into the woods you will see that no harm comes to her. But remember ~~that~~ how near the Fianna were ~~near~~ to hanging you from ~~the~~ a rafter that night at Tara, and if I bring Diarmid's message to Finn I may not know how to save you from them.

Laban

~~Grania would not have you take Diarmid's message to Finn~~

~~The rope slipped out of their hands & they said, we cannot hang him except with a rope that she ~~Grania~~ has spun ~~[illegible]~~ out of her own flax. And they tried to unspin the [illegible] a rope for them~~

The rope ~~burned their hands~~ became like a fire in their hands; & Conan tied them then ~~[illegible]~~ [illegible] with a rope [illegible] they [illegible] made [illegible] upon [illegible] rope, & they [illegible] [illegible] till I began to spin [illegible] they [illegible] [illegible].

[NLI 8777(16), 2r]

Laban

post

And Grania stood by the door ~~post~~ watchingthe moon shining down the valley: looking to where Diarmid's cattle were

and the of Finn

feeding , towards ~~Finn's~~ encampment . . .

Cormac

turned often, saying

Yes she stood there saying nothing. I ~~hurried~~ to her ~~and said~~

"If I this

~~I~~ take ~~Diarmid's~~ message to Finn you will have to fly to the again "

Laban

And she answered nothing?

Cormac

O

~~Nothing~~ only this – 'where will Laban go if we are driven from this valley?' She said "Father you brought her here to be near me and if we are driven into the woods you will see

how near

that no harm comes to her. ' But remember ~~that~~ the Fianna

a

were ~~near~~ to hanging from ~~the~~ rafter that night at Tara , and if I bring Diarmid's message to Finn I may not know how to save you from them .

The rope ~~burned their hand~~ became like a fire in their hands; and Conan told them that ~~I could~~ they could not hang me but with a rope that I had spung. They tried to make me spin ~~them a rope~~ one, & they ~~gatherd~~ would have beaten me till I began to spin but they were afraid.

Laban

~~Graniawould not have you take Diarmid's message to Finn~~

T

~~The rope fell out of their hands &~~ they said, We cannot hang her except with a rope that she ~~spun out~~ has spun ~~herself~~ out of her own flax. And they tried to tempt me to spin a rope for them

---

8, 11, 12, 14 Small emendations by GM are often distinguishable from WBY's by the shade of ink, here and on following leaves of this MS.

[NLI 8777(16), 3[r]]

Cormac

Eis, Yes but Finn has waited ~~Finn agreed to wait~~ for three days. ~~till~~ This sunset to-night ends ~~the~~ of the the third day (going to the door) The horses are waiting and Niall is at their heads. If you have found any meaning in the thread Speak

Laban

~~You see how~~ The thread ~~breaks~~ keeps breaking as it runs from the spindle.

Cormac

Then ~~the death~~ the end of somebody is at hand ~~the end of someone is nigh~~: the end of Diarmid ~~of~~ or Grania or ~~of~~ Finn - or the end of ~~Eire~~ ~~Fin~~ Eire. You must tell me before I go for I ~~may not~~ cannot wait any longer .

Laban

It may be a long while before I can tell you anything You must wait until the flax runs unbroken from the spindle. Words will be put into my mouth -

Cormac

Then spin, then spin.

Laban

The thread is breaking I cannot find a whole thread in the flax

[NLI 8777(16), 3r]

Cormac

Yes, yes but Finn has waited T} is the of
~~**Finn agreed to wait**~~^ **for three days** . ~~**and**~~ **t**} **his su**^**nset**^**end** ~~**s**~~ **the**
the third day (going to the door) The horses are waiting and
{if
Niall is at their heads. {**If you have found any meaning in the**
S}
thread s}**peak**

Laban

T} keeps breaking
~~**You see how**~~ **t**}**he thread** ~~**breaks**~~^ **as it runs from the spindle.**

Cormac

~~the death~~ the end of somebody is at hand or {of
~~**Then the end of someone is nigh:**~~^ **the end of Diarmid**^ {**or Grania**
{of ~~Ireland~~
or {**or Finn – or the end or** ~~**Erie**~~**.** ^ Erie. **You must tell me**
cannot
before I go for I ~~**may not**~~^ **wait any longer .**

Laban

It may be a long while before I can tell you anything
You must wait until the flax runs unbroken from the
spindle. Words will be put into my mouth .

Cormac

Then spin,then spin.

Laban

The thread is breaking I cannot find a whole thread
in the flax

Cormac

You have lied to me old woman. You brought me this long way because you never be near Grania. (she gets up from the wheel. Cormac puts her back again) But spin since there is flax in the spindle. Though you know nothing the earth knows all things and the flax comes out of the earth. So spin while there is yet time.

Laban

What would you know? You would know if there be forgiveness in Finn's heart?

Cormac

Or if he would have Diarmid back, because the men of Lockland have 70 galleys on the beach at Rury

Laban

You are troubled would know of it because Caoelte and Usheen have threatened that if Finn did not cease to make war upon Diermid that they will ask him to join them against the men of Lockland

Cormac

Old woman, full of wisdom for all but the danger that waits I have to carry with Diarmid's answer to Fin and would know what will happen to Diarmid and to my daughter. You sit silent Will you not answer me (a long pause. The king walks up the stage slowly and when he turns Laban rises from the

[NLI 8777(16), 4[r]]

Cormac

way

You have lied to me old woman. You brought me this long ~~journey~~

that might

~~because~~ you ~~wanted to~~ be near Grania.

~~from^Tara~~ (<u>she^gets up from the wheel. Cormac puts her back a-</u>

since ~~while~~

<u>gain</u>) But spin ~~since~~ there is flax in the spindle. ~~Though you~~

T

~~know nothing~~ the earth knows all ~~thigs~~ things and the flax comes out of the earth. So spin while there is yet time.

Laban

What would you know ? .

~~You would know~~^if there be forgiveness in Finn’s heart?

Cormac

~~Will he~~ ~~make peace with Diarmuid~~ (The) Lochlanrs

~~Or if he would have Diarmid back~~ ~~because the~~^men of ~~Lockland~~^

(dragged up) ~~(these)~~ onto

have^70 galleys ~~(drawn up)~~ ~~on~~ the beach at Rury

Laban

being Usheen

are troubled ~~you are~~ afraid that Caoilte & ~~Usheen~~

You ~~would know of it~~^~~because Caoelte and Usheen have threa^tened~~

may not fight against the men of Lochlann because they are angry

war

~~that if Finn did not cease to make war upon Diarmid that~~ they

y

with Finn. ~~because of Dairmuid~~. You fear that Finn ma n ~~leave~~

~~will ask him to join them against the men of Lockland~~

~~the fiann~~ forget the Lochlanders to ~~p~~ pursue Darmid & Grania? You

fear^~~fear~~ that Dairmuid & Grania –

Cormac

about everything

Old woman, full of wisdom ~~for all~~^but the danger that waits us

carry I

~~me~~ I have to ~~go now with~~ Diarmid’s answer to Finn and^would know what would^happen to Diarmid and to my daughter. You sit silent Will you not answer me (<u>a long pause. The king walks up</u> th<u>e stage slowly and when he turns Laban rises from the</u>

4 thigs] Type deletion.

[NLI 8777(16), 5r]

wheel)

Laban

I see Diarmid standing by Finn and his hand is on Finn's shoulder

Cormac

Then they are friends

Laban

I see Diarmid drawing his sword,

Cormac

Against ~~his~~ [whom] Laban? And then — -

Laban

I can see Finn drawing his dagger

Cormac

His dagger – his sword – look again.

Laban

It is a dagger that I see

Cormac

~~That cannot be/~~ Now wind the thread round the forefinger tightly. Now hold the thread ~~flat~~ [tightly] and look for the earth knows all and ~~the secret~~ [his knowledge] is in the flax

Laban

The vision has ~~passed~~ [gone from my], I see ~~no more~~ nothing; else

[NLI 8777(16), 5r]

wheel)

Laban

I see Diarmid standing by Finn and his hand is on Finn's shoulder

Cormac

Then they are friends

Laban

I see Diarmid drawing his sword .

Cormac

whom
Against ~~him~~ Laban? And then – –

Laban

I can see Finn drawing his dagger

Cormac

His dagger – his sword – look again .

Laban

It is a dagger that I see

Cormac

{i
~~That cannot be.~~ Now w{end the thread round the forefinger
tightly
tightly. Now hold the thread ~~fast~~ ^ and look for the earth knows
her knowledge
all and ~~the secret~~ ^ is in the flax

Laban

(gone from my)
The vision has ~~passed~~ ^, I see ~~no more~~ nothing else

[NLI 8777(16), 6r]

Cormac

Spin again, spin another thread

Laban

I {cannot be more than once, and} ~~should not see twice and~~ the thread is broken {again —} you have broken it.

Cormac

{There is ill luck in my hands} ~~Ill luck from my people always~~ If the thread had not broken we should know all. {You say} ~~You say~~ you saw Finn ~~draw~~ {pull out} his dagger, but was not Diarmid standing by his side with his hand on Finn's shoulder? What is the meaning of this? If you do not tell me I will have you beaten and your wheel thrown into the lake (Enter Grania)

Grania

Ah, my father she can tell you nothing if you speak so loud.

Cormac

She has told me strange things , things without meaning.

Grania

You never believe her words, father, when she speaks them, but afterwards you find that she had spoken truly.

Cormac

True or ~~fls~~ false it matters not since they do not help me

[NLI 8777(16), 6r]

Cormac

Spin again, spin another thread

Laban

cannot see more than once, and again –

T

I ~~should not see twice~~ ~~and~~ t he thread is broken you have broke en it.

Cormac

There is ill luck in my hands

~~was in my feet.~~

~~Ill luck led my feet astray~~ If the thread had not broken we

You say Y pull out

should know all. ~~You say~~ y ou saw Finn ~~draw~~ his dagger , but was not Diarmid standing by his side with his hand on Finn's shoulder? What is the meaning of this? If you do not tell me I will have you beaten and your wheel thrown into the lake (Enter Grania)

Grania

Ah, my father she can tell you nothing if you speak so loud.

Cormac

She has told me strange things , things without meaning .

Grania

You never believe her words, father, when she speaks them, but afterwards you find that she had spoken truly .

Cormac

True or ~~fls~~ false it matters not since they do not help me

---

14 Type deletion.

~~The moment has come now for me to~~ go [redacted]
It is time that I were gone.

Where is Diarmid? ^ [redacted]

[redacted]. I have not seen him all

day. Does he speak to day as he spoke last night?

Grania

He has said nothing to me and I would not speak to him

of Finn, (a night and) ~~and~~ nearly a day have ~~passed~~ gone by since you have,

spoken to him, ~~..~~ ~~The mind changes in a night~~ His mind may have changed. (Going up the stage) This is

the hour when the flock comes home Diarmid has forgotten us all,

he is thinking of the folding of his sheep You will find him with

the shepherd, or shall I send ~~Laban~~ ~~to him~~ Laban to bring him? (Laban gets up and

goes out) The fold is not far from the house, it ~~is~~ was brought n

nearer for the wolves carried off three of our sheep last week ...

Ah, I see him coming up the path Laban is going to meet him.

(Grania comes down the stage to Cormac) But father dear, three

days are not a long while to see you in after 7 years. You will

come here again and forget the troubles that kingdoms bring.

You are lonely at Tara. ~~Will miss my singing in the evening~~ I used to sing ~~to you~~ to you.

Shall I come to Tara t~~o sing~~ to your door and sing for you again.

[NLI 8777(16), 7r]

~~The moment has come now for me to~~ go ~~to Finn with Diarmid’s message~~
It is time that I were gone.
Where is Diarmid?^ ~~I could not go without seeing him even~~
~~though he sends me on an errand like this~~. I have not seen him all
day. Does he speak to day as he spoke last night?

Grania

He has said nothing to me and I would not speak to him
{. and gone ~~by~~
of Finn{, (~~a~~^night) ~~and~~ nearly^a day^have ~~passed~~ since you have ,
(Going up the stage
T} His mind may have changed.
spoken to him . ~~and~~ t}~~he mind changes in a night~~ ^ This is
the hour when the flock comes ho^me Diarmid has forgotten us all,
he is thinking ofthe folding of his sheep You will find him with
Laban to bring him.
the shepherd, or shall I send ~~Laban to him~~? (Laban gets up and
^ was
goes out) The fold is not far from the house, it ~~is~~^brought
nearer for the wolves carried off three of our sheep last week . . .
Ah, I see him coming up the path Laban is going to meet him.
(Grania comes down the stage to Cormac) But^father (dear), three
days are not a long while to see you in after 7 years. You will
come here again and forget the troubles that kingdoms bring.
I used to sing ~~to you~~ for you.
You are lonely at Tara. ~~You miss my^singing in the evening~~.
Shall I come to Tara ~~to sing to you?~~ and sing to you again.

[NLI 8777(16), 8[r]]

Cormac

Our troubles ~~increase~~ grow greater as we grow older, ~~and I doubt if~~ & it may be that your singing could not make me forget my troubles now. These last troubles seem the worst. I have ~~brought Finn here to~~ persuaded Finn to make peace and I have brought him here.. But ~~you. In these things~~ we ~~do but say the same things again~~ - - we go on saying ~~the same things again~~ this one thing again & again.

Grania

~~For seven years we have fled from the South to the North from the East to the West.~~ through north & south & east and west.

Cormac

For seven years Finn has hunted you, he ~~warred against you~~ did not cease till the Fionna had deserted him

Grania

Do not pity me ~~for~~ because of those years, ~~…~~ The blood beats in my vains when I think of ~~our many awakenings to the sound of Finn's horn in the woods~~ them.

Cormac

There is a ~~[illegible]~~ fire in your eyes and your eyes were lighted like this when you poured ~~bewitched~~ out the enchanted ale ~~into the cups~~ at Tara

Grania

Seven ~~[illegible]~~ years ~~in~~ amongst the woods should have quenched those fires

You would always set it somehow

Cormac

When your heart was set on you would always have. Who but Grania would have gone ~~away~~ out to the woods with a man she had never seen before,

[NLI 8777(16), 8r]

Cormac

grow greater
Our troubles ~~increase~~ as we grow older , ~~and I doubt if~~ & it may be that
not
your singing could make me forget my troubles now . These
persuaded Finn to make
last troubles seem the worst . I have ~~brought Finn here to~~
peace and I have brought him here . . . But
~~you. In these things~~ ~~we do but say the same things again~~ – –
we go on saying ~~the same things again~~ this one thing
again & again.

Grania

f W
F or seven years w e have fled ~~from the South to the North~~
~~from the East to the West~~ though north & south & east
and west.

Cormac

f did not cease
F or seven years Finn has hunted you, he ~~warred against you~~
had
till the Fionna deserted him

Grania

because of , T
Do not pity me ~~for~~ those years . ~~they were stirring years,~~ t he
them.
blood beats in my vains when I think of ~~our many awakenings~~
~~to the sound of Finn's horn in the woods~~

Cormac

There is a ~~strange~~ fire in your eyes and your eyes
out of the enchanted
were lighted like this when you poured ~~bewitched~~ ale
~~into our cups~~ at Tara

Grania

among
Seven ~~wild~~ years ~~in~~ the woods should have quenched those
fires

Cormac You would always get it
What you heart was set on you would always have. somehow
~~**Cormac**~~ into the woods
Who but Grania would have gone ~~away~~ with a man she
had never seen before?

[Grania.
I think I had seen him many times – I saw him once on a hill when I ~~stood~~ stood looking at the mist]

Cornac

Dear daughter, always true to your desire, ~~are you tired of this pleasant valley I have given you to be happy in?~~ It was indeed a strange freak ~~the~~ [that] putting to sleep of your father and his councillors and the man you were to marry What other woman in Erie would have run away into the woods with a man whom she had seen for the first time.

Grania

I had seen Diarmid many times before that night ~~I had seen him in my mind~~ [once on the hill, where I stood looking into the ~~mist~~ mist and often in my mind.]

Cormac

~~Never a did~~ [not so many] men sleep ~~over their ale~~ as we slept that [one and all] night. We sat at that table like stones till the cock crew. ~~the crowing of the cock woke us together and Finn cried out "I have dreamt that the Fionna are divided that Graniahas been taken from me".~~

~~Grania~~

~~[illegible] I was very young [illegible]~~ ~~[I thought that Finn did not love me and that you might be stronger than any other king, stronger than the [illegible]]~~

~~Cormac~~

~~He said I would follow them as long as a god sits on his throne.~~ [Cormac] Ah, Grania, you have your mother's eyes Your mother was very beautiful, Grania.

[Grania I thought that Finn did not love me, that you had made the marriage that you might be stronger than any of the kings [illegible]]

[NLI 8777(16), 9[r]]

Grania
I think I had seen him many times – I saw him once
on a hill when I ~~shod~~ stood looking into the mist

Cormac
Dear daughter, always true to your desire, ~~are you tired ofthis~~
~~pleasant valley I have given you to be happy in?~~ It was indeed
that
a strange freak ~~the~~ putting to sleep of your father and his coun-
cillors and the man you were to marry What other woman in
Erie would have run away into the woods with a man whom she had
seen for the first time.

Grania
once
I had seen Diarmid many times before that night ~~I had seen~~
~~standing~~ on the hill where I often stood looking into the
mist
~~him in my mind.~~ ~~mist.~~ and often in my mind.
top

Cormac
~~most~~ not many ~~men have~~
~~Never m did~~ men sleep ~~over their ale~~ as we slept that
over our ale
night, We sat at that table like stones till the cock crew, ~~the~~
crowing of the cock woke us together and Finn cried out "I
have dreamt that the Fionna are divided that Graniahas been
taken from me".

Grania the marriage was made
I thought that Finn did not love me and that you
~~Do not reproach me father I was very young then~~
might be stronger than any other King stronger
than the invader.

Cormac
He said "I will follow them as long as a god sits on his
Cormac
~~throne.~~ Ah, Grania you have your mother's eyes Your mother
was very beautiful, Grania.

Grania
I thought that Fin did not love me, that you had made this
marriage that you might be stronger than any other ~~K~~ king
or than any invader

9 m] Type deletion.

Grania

~~Diarmid was young and comely, and then~~ I thought ~~only that~~ of nothing but ~~that~~ this—that

a man should love me ~~in~~ among the woods, far away ~~in~~ among the woods

Cormac

And Diarmid has loved ~~[illegible]~~ you well.

Grania

~~Love is a sweet thing in the woods amid the dangers of flight, but~~ love in this valley has become terrible and we are sometimes afraid of one another. But now I ~~That is why I say~~ I would have Diarmid arm the shepherds and lead them against ~~[illegible] of the galleys,~~ the Lochlanders and ~~[illegible]~~ drive them into their galleys.

Cormac

If you ~~[illegible]~~ think like this

~~Then~~ why did you stand looking ~~at the moonlight~~ down the valley & ~~[illegible]~~ saying nothing? Diarmid asked you and I asked you

Grania

If I had said yes to you I should have said ~~If I say yes to you I say~~ no to Diarmid. I would say nothing but leave things to ~~ax~~ work out ~~the~~ whatever will ~~there is~~ maybe in them

(Enter Niall and the King's councillors councillors stand in the background Niall advances.)

Cormac

Yes, Niall, I have delayed too long

[NLI 8777(16), 10r]

Grania

~~Diarmid was young and comely, and then~~ I thought ~~only that~~
of nothing but ~~that~~ this – that
among among
^**a man should love me ~~in~~**^ **the woods, far away** ~~in~~^ the woods

Cormac

you well.
has { ~~this sweet~~
And Diarmid loved { **~~you well~~** ~~face for seven years~~.

Grania

Love is a sweet thing in the woods , amid the dangers
of flight, but (love) in this valley^ **has become terrible and**
But now I
we are sometimes afraid of one another . ~~That is why I say~~ I
the
would have Diarmid arm the shepherds and lead them against ~~our~~
~~enemies~~ ~~at the galleys & the~~ Lochlanders and ~~burn kill~~
drive them into their galleys.

Cormac
{If you think like this
{ **Cormac**

down the valley &
^**~~Then~~ why did you stand looking ~~at the moonlight~~**^ **saying**
~~what you thought~~
nothing? Diarmid asked you^ **and I asked you**

Grania

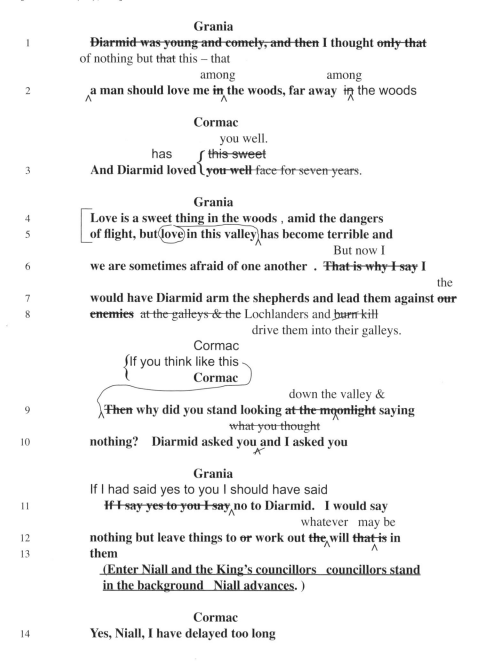

If I had said yes to you I should have said
~~If I say yes to you I say~~^ **no to Diarmid. I would say**
whatever may be
nothing but leave things to ~~or~~ work out ~~the~~^ **will ~~that is~~**^ **in**
them

<u>(Enter Niall and the King's councillors councillors stand in the background Niall advances.</u>)

Cormac

Yes, Niall, I have delayed too long

---

3 GM attempted to obliterate "sweet" with particular emphasis.
12 or] Type deletion.

[NLI 8777(16), 11r]

Grania

(going to Niall)   You are going now, Niall, and I have had little time to speak with you and I would have spoken to you about the days at Tara, when you were my only ~~[illegible]~~ playfellow.

How well ~~Do~~ you I ~~[illegible]~~ remember going with you, one spring morning ~~[illegible]~~ to a little pool at the edge of the wood, ~~and~~ we sat on the high bank fishing for roach Have you forgotten?

Niall

No, Princess, I have not forgotten. That same day I showed you a blackbird sitting on her nest You had never seen a bird sitting on her nest before. But many ~~[illegible]~~ things have happened since then; ~~[illegible]~~ you know the woodland now better than I

Grania

Shall I ever see Tara again? I have wandered a long way.

Cormac

Five days' journey from here, Grania. We must hurry ~~hasten;~~ Neither Niall nor I can keep the saddle for many hours at a time; ~~but where is Diarmid?~~ Diarmuid's cattle are coming this way and their sides are heavy with the rich grass of the valley I have given you, and the rooks are flying home.

(enter Diarmid)

Cormac.

In half an hour I shall be with Finn and I would not say to him the words you bade me say last night. Do not send

[NLI 8777(16), 11r]

Grania

(going to Niall) You/are going now, Niall, and I have
had little time to speak with you and I would have spoken
play fellow
to you about the days at Tara, when you were my only ~~playmate~~ , ^
How well spring
~~Do~~ ^ I ~~not~~ remember going with you , one ^ morning ~~in early Spring~~
W}
to a little pool at the edge of the wood . ~~and~~ w}e sat on the
high bank fishing for roach Have you forgotten?

Niall

No, Princess, I have not forgotten. That same day I showed yo
you a blackbird sitting on her nest You had never seen a bird
But many
sitting on her nest before. ~~Many~~ ^ things have happened
since then ; ~~and~~ you know the woodland now better than I

Grania

Shall I ever see Tara again? I have wandered a long way –

Cormac hurry

Five days’ journey from here, Grania. We must ~~hasten~~.
Neither Niall nor I can keep in the saddle for many hours
Diarmud’s cattle are coming this way
at a time ; ~~but where is Diarmid?~~ and their sides are
heavy with the rich grass of the valley I have
(<u>enter Diarmid)</u> given you, and the
rooks are flying home.

Cormac

(In half an hour) I shall be with Finn) ^ and I would not say
to him the words you bade me say last night. Do not send

1 The merged “Youare” is separated with a pencil line.

I went out of
~~I drew~~ the door where the hungry host the waited, ~~[illegible]~~
& I smote the sword out of his hand.

me to the man you wronged with the words you spoke last night

Diarmid

Tell him to be gone out of my valley

Cormac

Then farewell dear daughter

Grania

Father stay with us, Diarmid do you not hear? Do you not understand?

Cormac

Diarmid knows ~~what~~ how great Finn ~~angered~~ 's anger will be when I bring

him this answer

Diarmid

(fought Finn & overthrown him)
~~outwitted & out fought Finn & him now.~~
I have ~~fought Finn and overthrown him~~ Did I not break out

of the house with the sevendoors when he had ~~[illegible]~~ a sentinel s

at all the doors?

Cormac

~~Your cattle have are coming this way Diarmid and their~~

~~sides are heavy with the rich grass of this valley that I have~~

~~given you and the rooks are flying home~~ ~~Do not send me~~ If you will send me

with this answer, .. which is all can say no more. Farewell to all here. ~~Farewell to all here~~

(Exeunt Cormac Neill and Councillors)

Diarmid

We thought we should weary of the silence of this valley but

it is of their voices that we weary! why should we listen to

[NLI 8777(16), 12r]

I went out of the
I ~~close~~ ^ the door where he himself held ^ watch, ~~& he & others~~
& I smote the sword out of his hand.

me to the man you wronged with the words you spoke last night

Diarmid

Tell him to be gone out of my valley

Cormac

Then farewell dear daughter

Grania

Do you not understand?
Father stay with us . Diarmid do you not hear? ^

Cormac

how great 's anger
Diarmid knows ~~what~~ ^ Finn ^ ~~angered~~ will be when I bring him this answer

faught Finn & overthrown him

Diarmid

~~out-witted & out-fought Finn before now~~.
I have ^ ~~fought~~ ^ ~~Finn and overthrown him~~ Did I not break out

a
set ~~th~~ ^ watch
of the house with the sevendoors when he had ~~put guards~~ at|all the doors?

Cormac

~~**Your cattle have are coming this way Diarmid and their sides are heavy with the rich grass of this valley that I have**~~
If you will send me
~~**given you and the rooks are flying home**~~ ~~**Do not send me**~~
so be it – I can say no more. Fare well to all
~~**back**~~ **with this answer** ^ **. . .** ~~**Farewell to all**~~ ^ ~~**here**~~ here.

(<u>Exeunt Cormac Neill and Councillors</u>)

Diarmid

We thought we should weary of the silence s of this valley but it is of their voices that we are weary: why should we listen to

---

9 The mark separating the merged "atall" is in ink.

10 have] Type deletion beneath continuous ink line.

[NLI 8777(16), 13r]

anything except to one another But they are gone at last

and care is gone with them ~~and~~we are alone again with

ourselves and our flocks and herds Come to the door Grania and see my black bull pacing in the meadow His pace is like a ~~xxxxxx~~ wave's (coming down the stage to her)

Do you not believe that care is gone with them?

Grania

You saw my fathers face as he went out ~~overcome with care~~ ~~his~~ ~~and~~ His look ~~as he turned to go~~ has put a deep care into my ~~xxxx~~ heart

Diarmid

These northern raiders will not dare ~~to leave~~ now [illegible] ~~and would~~ their galleys, they will soon sail away. ~~A few cattle or few sheep should we rish our happiness for these things~~ ~~be a fuel to a few sheep and cattle~~

As others in giving up our happiness because we were weary [illegible] they may carry off a few score of cattle.

Grania

Let it be ~~this~~ as you wish it Diarmid.

Diarmid

But oath upon oath is broken. I broke my oath to Finn and now I break the oath which binds me to take up arms against ~~the enemies of Erie~~ all invaders. ~~Grania, you would see Finn again~~ Grania you are weary of this valley; you would see Tara again. You would see Finn again.

Grania

I gave up Tara ~~I have given up all things~~ for your sake Diarmid ~~but~~ and that was easier than to ~~live~~ live in this little valley. ~~Easier than to give up a [illegible]. Here you are but Diarmid a shepherd king~~

Diarmid

Finn and I are divided, Grania, as by the ~~[illegible]~~

[NLI 8777(16), 13r]

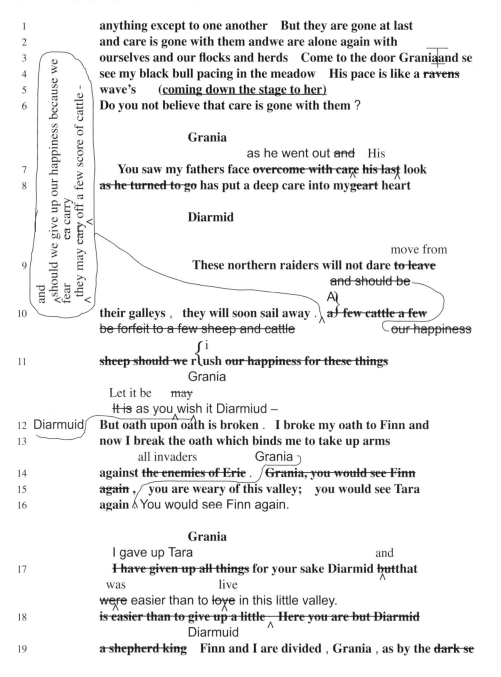

anything except to one another But they are gone at last
and care is gone with them andwe are alone again with
ourselves and our flocks and herds Come to the door Graniaand se
see my black bull pacing in the meadow His pace is like a ~~ravens~~
wave's (<u>coming down the stage to her)</u>
Do you not believe that care is gone with them ?

[left margin, written vertically:] and ^should we give up our happiness because we fear they may ~~cary~~ ~~ca~~ carry off a few score of cattle - ^

Grania

as he went out ~~and~~ His
You saw my fathers face ~~overcome with care his last~~ look
~~as he turned to go~~ has put a deep care into my~~geart~~ heart

Diarmid

move from
These northern raiders will not dare ~~to leave~~
~~and should be~~
A)
their galleys , they will soon sail away . ~~a) few cattle a few~~
~~be forfeit to a few sheep and cattle~~ ~~our happiness~~
i
~~sheep should we~~ rush ~~our happiness for these things~~

Grania

Let it be ~~may~~
~~It is~~ as you wish it Diarmiud –
Diarmuid **But oath upon oath is broken . I broke my oath to Finn and**
now I break the oath which binds me to take up arms
all invaders Grania
against ~~the enemies of Erie~~ . ~~Grania, you would see Finn~~
~~again~~ , you are weary of this valley; you would see Tara
again You would see Finn again.

Grania

I gave up Tara and
~~I have given up all things~~ for your sake Diarmid ~~but~~that
was live
~~were~~ easier than to ~~love~~ in this little valley.
~~is easier than to give up a little Here you are but Diarmid~~
Diarmuid
~~a shepherd king~~ Finn and I are divided , Grania , as by the ~~dark se~~

---

3 The mark separating the merged "Graniaand" is in ink.
4, 8 (~~geart~~) Type deletions.
11 rish] Did GM intend "wish"?

[NLI 8777(16), 14r]

sea and if the peace your father has made between us is not to be broken ~~is to be kept~~ Finn must leave my valley. It is for your sake, Grania, that he would have me ~~be~~ ~~[illegible]~~ ~~amongst~~ among his ~~the~~ Fianna again.

Grania

He has not seen me for seven years

Diarmid

To see you once is enough Grania

Grania

I think that ~~[illegible]~~ it is for Eri's sake he would have you among the Fianna ~~back~~ again He does not think of women Why should a woman think of him? Have I not loved you for seven years" Diarmid? And my father has told you that Finn is bound by an oath and that he has said "Diarmid has her love let him keep her"

Diarmid

He will not break his oath but he will find some way out of it There is always treachery behind his peacemaking

Grania

He made peace with Gall and that peace is still unbroken Yet it was Gall's father who plundered Finn's country and murdered his people

Diarmid

Gall does Finn's bidding although he might be chief man

[NLI 8777(16), 14[r]]

sea and if the peace your father has made between us is not to be
broken
~~is to be kept~~ Finn must leave my valley. It is for your
have me
sake, Grania, that he would ~~be born again amongst~~ among his
{a
~~the~~ Fi{ onna again.

Grania

He has not seen me for seven years

Diarmid

To see you once is enough Grania

Grania

I think that i
~~Finn is old and~~ it is for E^ri’s sake he would have you
among the Fianni
~~back~~^again He does not think of women Why should a woman think
of him? Have I not loved you for seven years Diarmid? And
my father has told you that Finn is bound by an oath and that he
has said “Diarmid has her love let him keep her”

Diarmid

He will not break his oath but he will find some way out of
it There is always treachery behind his peacemaking

Grania

He made peace with Gall and that peace is still unbroken
Yet it was Gall’s father who plundered Finn’s country and
murdered his people

Diarmid

Gall does Finn’s bidding although he might be chief man

himself But ~~he~~ Finn has not forgiven, Usheen saw a look in his eyes at Tara .

Grania

Ah, how well you remember That was seven years ago

Diarmid

And when I am dead it will be Gall's turn

Grania

Unhappy brooding man you will neither believe in Finn's oath nor in my love

Diarmid

Here we have everything we sought for But in return for this kingdom your father would have me ~~amongst~~ among the Fionna, again I thought we should live and die here, I thought ~~out~~ our children would grow up about us here, if the gods ~~will~~ accept my offering and give us children (He goes up the stage) Come look at the sleepy evening These evenings are better than battle the evenings of ~~…~~long ago, and were I to go back ~~…~~ among my ~~…~~ old companions again, Usheen, Gall, Caelte, I should look back upon these quiet evenings when the flock came home and you gave me my supper in the dusk (comes down the stage) If I were to die, Grania, would you be Finn's wife?

[NLI 8777(16), 15[r]]

Finn
himself But ~~he~~ has not forgiven . Usheeen saw a look in his eyes at Tara .

Grania

Ah, how well you remember That was seven years ago

Diarmid

And when I am dead it will be Gall's turn

Grania

Unhappy brooding man you will neither believe in Finn's oath nor in my love

Diarmid

Here we have everything we sought for But in return for
among again
this kingdom your father would have me ~~back amongst~~ the Fionna ^ **.** ^
our
I thought we should live and die here , I thought ~~out~~ children
{ if
would grow up about us here , { **If the gods ~~would~~ accept my offering and give us children (He goes up the stage) Come look**
the evenings of
at the sleepy evening These evenings are better than battle
~~again~~ among my
~~days of~~ long ago , and were I to go ~~back to my battle~~
again, o
~~days of~~ old companions^**Usheen, Gall, Ca**^**elte, I should look back upon these quiet evenings when the flock came home and you gave me my supper in the dusk (comes down the stage) If I were to die, Grania, would you be Finn's wife?**

12 The revision in this line is evidence that GM revised the MS first.

13 battle] Type deletion.

and yet I shall sit alone upon the shore that is beyond the world — though all the gods are there the shore shall be empty because one is not there and I shall weep remembering

Grania

~~What a strange thought that is~~ How did such a thought come into your mind?

Diarmid

My life began with you and it ends with you Oh, that these breasts should belong to another, and the sacred usage of this body Life of my life I knew you before I was born I made a bargain with this brown hair before the beginning of time and it shall not be broken through unending time.

~~[illegible] and yet I shall sit alone~~

~~When [illegible]~~ upon the shore beyond ~~the world~~ pondering on my ~~love I shall weep [illegible] empty because she is not [illegible] delight excepting the sadness of [illegible]~~, ~~[illegible] remembering~~ our wanderings ~~and~~ among the ~~[illegible]~~ woods. But you say nothing Grania You are weary of the shadows of these mountains and of the smell of the fold. It is many days since you came to my bed and it is many weeks since I have seen an ornament upon you. Your love is slipping from me, it slips away like water in ~~the~~ the brook You do not answer ~~[illegible] silences within the heart.~~ These silences have made me afraid.

Granăa

Then Diarmid go to your old companions

Diarmid

My old companions? What shall I say to them

[NLI 8777(16), 16r]

and yet I shall sit alone upon the shore that is beyond
the world – though all the gods are there the shore shall be
empty because one is not there and I shall weep remembering

Grania

~~What a strange thought that is –~~ How did such a thought
come into your mind ?

Diarmid

My life began with you and it ends with you Oh,that
these breasts should belong to another, and the sacred usage
of this body Life of my life I knew you before I was born
I made a bargain with this brown hair before the beginning
of time and it shall not be broken through unending time .
~~were I to sit~~ ~~When I shall~~ ~~And yet I shall sit alone~~
that is
~~When I sit~~ upon the shore beyond the world , pondering on my
and remembering
love I shall weep for the shore will be empty because she is
not with me and there shall be no delight excepting the sadness
of remembrance, among
~~of remembrance remembering~~ our wanderings ~~amid~~ the ~~old~~ woods . But
you say nothing Grania You are weary of the shadows of these
mountains and the smell of the fold . It is many days since
you came to my bed and it is many weeks since I have seen an
ornament upon you. Your love is slipping from me, it slips away
~~a~~ the
like water in ~~the~~ brook You do not answer ~~Ah those silences~~
~~wring the heart.~~ ~~Th~~ These silences ~~have~~ make me afraid.

Grania

Then Diarmid go to your old companions

Diarmid

My old companions? What shall I say to them

---

11 of remembrance] Type deletion.

Who is the shepherd Grania? Where has he come from?
I have never seen him before.

Grania
What shepherd do you speak of

Diarmuid
There, there in the doorway

Grania
There is no body there.

Grania

You will fight shoulder to shoulder with Finn and Caelte You will listen to Usheens harpmplaying and I shall love you better when you come to me with the reek of battle upon you.

Diarmid

We shall ~~discover new selves in each~~ be again what we were to one another You are not ~~longer the~~ that Grania ~~that you were~~ a wanderer with Diarmid in thewoods

Grania

You are no ~~longer the~~ not that Diarmid that ~~you were when you overth~~ ~~threw~~ who overthrew Finn ~~and~~ at the house of the seven doors.

Diarmid

You speak the truth Grania ~~[illegible]~~ I should have gone to the Fianna. (how it is so late)

Grania

Cormac ~~has not~~ cannot have reached the ford ~~by the path across the~~ and ~~[illegible]~~ you will overtake him (she goes to her chest and takes out an ornament)

Diarmid

Who is this shepherd Grania?

~~There is a mist in my eyes or is this mist from the~~ ~~valley [illegible] of the [illegible] upsubstantial~~ ~~shapes hangs (He goes towards the door)~~

What do I ask him [illegible]?

Diarmuid

He beckons ~~Grania~~ me - I must follow - He goes towards the door

~~Diarmid I will go withyou a little way. But~~

I see him no longer. a

[NLI 8777(16), 17ʳ]

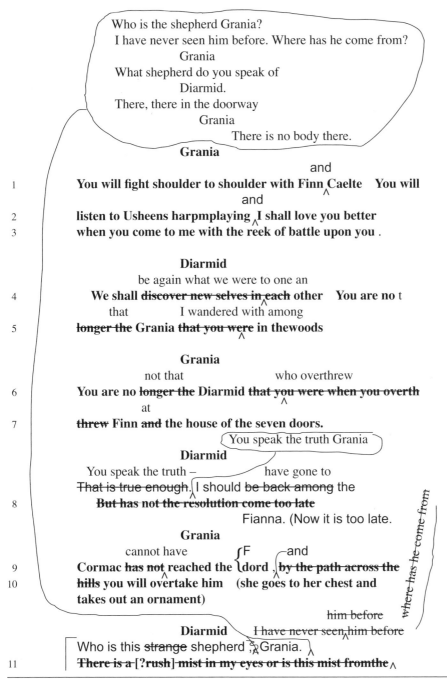

Who is the shepherd Grania?
I have never seen him before. Where has he come from?
Grania
What shepherd do you speak of
Diarmid.
There, there in the doorway
Grania
There is no body there.

Grania

and
1 **You will fight shoulder to shoulder with Finn ^ Caelte You will**
and
2 **listen to Usheens harpmplaying ^ I shall love you better**
3 **when you come to me with the reek of battle upon you .**

Diarmid

be again what we were to one an
4 **We shall ~~discover new selves in ^ each~~ other You are no** t
that I wandered with among
5 **~~longer the~~ Grania ~~that you were~~ ^ in thewoods**

Grania

not that who overthrew
6 **You are no ~~longer the~~ Diarmid ~~that you were when you overth~~ ^**
at
7 **~~threw~~ Finn ~~and~~ the house of the seven doors.**

You speak the truth Grania

Diarmid

You speak the truth – have gone to
~~That is true enough~~. ^ I should ~~be back among~~ the
8 **~~But has not the resolution come too late~~**
Fianna. (Now it is too late.

Grania

cannot have F and
9 **Cormac ~~has not~~ ^ reached the {dord , ^ ~~by the path across the~~**
10 **~~hills~~ you will overtake him (she goes to her chest and takes out an ornament)**

~~him before~~
~~where has he come from~~

Diarmid ~~I have never seen ^ him before~~

Who is this ~~strange~~ shepherd ; ^ Grania. ^
11 **~~There is a [?rush] mist in my eyes or is this mist fromthe~~** ^

11 The caret mark in the RH margin might refer to a passage Yeats wrote at the head of the facing page (NLI 8777(16), fol. 16ᵛ), perhaps before the insertion at the head of the present page : "Dar / There, There in the door way. / Grania. / There is no body there."

[NLI 8777(16), 17r continued]

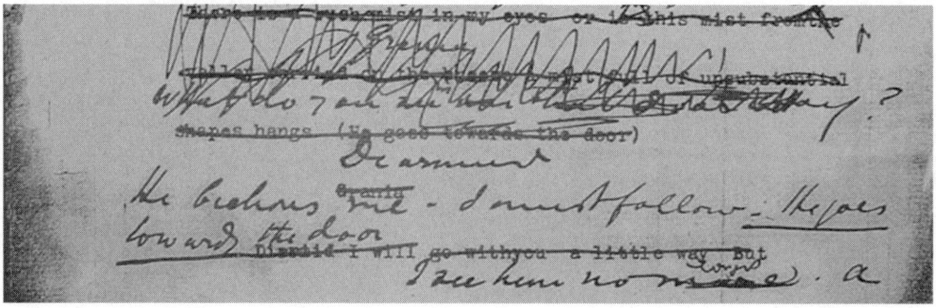
There is not such mist in my eyes or is this mist from the
chilly [illegible] of the [illegible] full of unsubstantial
What do I see [illegible] ?
Shapes hangs (He goes towards the door)
Diarmuid
He beckons me - I must follow. He goes towards the door
Diarmuid I will go with you a little way. But
I see him no longer. a

[NLI 8777(16), 17^{r} continued]

Grania

12 ~~valley carried on the breeze a mist full of unsubstantial~~

in

What do you see the hall door way?

13 ~~shapes hangs (He goes towards the door~~)

Diarmuid

~~Grania~~

He beckons me – I must follow<u> – He goes towards the door</u>

14 ~~Diarmid I will go withyou a little way But~~

longer

I see him no ~~more~~. A

[NLI 8777(16), 18r]

must had ~~fathered~~ ~~in~~ my eyes. I see clearer now and no one is there. But I must follow!

Grania

~~whom do you follow~~
Whom would you follow?

Diarmid

I see no ~~me~~ one now ~~but just now or a long while ago in~~ and yet there was

~~a~~ sudden darkening of the light ~~a strange~~ a shepherd ~~came~~ into
in a grey skin with its ears & hair upon his cap came to into the

the doorway and beckoned me He is waiting,

Grania

No Diarmid no ~~one~~ body has come into that door

way ~~None came for~~ no body came for you but one

Diarmid

Came for me

Let me go Grania ~~for I keep ghostly company~~

Grania

No no ~~there has been~~ it is a
~~You must not go to Finn For you have had~~ a warning ~~that~~ you must not go.

Diarmid

This is not how

I understand the warning ~~of~~ , I am ~~signed to~~ bid

leave this valley (they go out Enter Laban who sits down

at her wheel and begins to spin ~~Enter~~ Grania She ~~sits~~ at

the door looking after Diarmid)

Enters shortly after

[NLI 8777(16), 18r]

came int my eyes
~~before~~
mist had ~~gathered in my eyes~~. I see clearer now
now and no one is there. But I must
follow.

Grania
~~**whom do you follow**~~
Whom would you follow?

Diarmid

one and yet there was
I see ~~ne~~ now ~~but just now or a long while ago in~~
and a ~~whom I have never seen~~
a sudden darkening of the light ~~a strange~~ shepherd ~~came~~ into
in a grey skin with the ears of a hair upon his cap came ~~to~~ into the
~~a~~ doorway and beckoned me He is waiting .

Grania

body
No Diarmid no ~~one~~ has come into that door
no body came for ~~somebody~~
a
way ~~None c come for~~ you but one

Diarmid

Came for me
Let me go Grania ~~for I keep a ghostly company~~

Grania

No no ~~there has been~~ It is a that you
~~You must not go to Finn For you have had~~ a warning not to go
must not go.

Diarmid

That is not how bound
I understand the warning ~~otherwise~~ . I am ~~signed to~~
He beckons me
leave this valley (they go out Enter Laban who sits down
stands
at her wheel and begins to spin ~~Enter~~ Grania She ~~sits~~ at
the door looking after Diarmid)
Enters shortly after

[NLI 8777(16), 19r]

His thoughts are far away & I did not know that they are

Grania

He is like one whose mind is shaken ~~misgives him~~, ~~His thoughts~~ ~~have been far away and I am not there to ask himself what~~ ~~he is thinking~~

~~Diarmid~~ Laban

~~His thoughts have gone back to the~~ He is brooding over that story ~~that~~ Conan told him ~~that night in~~ at Tara — It has been in his thoughts all day —

Grania

Mother he had forgotten that story ~~and it is~~ It is the silence of this valley ~~that has waked it in his heart~~ that has brought it into his mind. It is better that he ~~should join his old comrades~~ should live among his old companions. He talks now of Finn ~~He suspects Finn of~~ crookedness; ~~and he speaks~~ of my love as ~~a waning season~~ if it were waning . . .

In a few minutes Diarmid and Finn will meet

Laban

In a few minutes Finn will stand with his hand on Diarmids shoulder

Grania

Then I have done well in sending him to Finn ~~for my~~ I did it for Diarmid's sake and for my father's ~~sake~~, and for the sake of ~~his~~ my father's kingdom, I chose Diarmid because he was young and comely, but ~~I have not~~ O how can I forget forgotten the greatness of Finn In a few minutes Finn and his Fionna will stand under this roof

[NLI 8777(16), 19r]

His thoughts are far away & I do not know that they are

Grania

is shaken

He is like one whose mind ~~misgives him~~ ^ **~~His thoughts~~**
have been far away and I am not there to ask him of what
he is thinking

~~Diarmid~~ Laban

~~It may be that his thoughts~~ He is moody over that
~~His thoughts have gone back to the~~ ^**story ~~that~~ Conan told him ~~tha~~**
at my mind
~~that night in~~ Tara – It has been in ~~the~~ ^ ~~thoughts~~ ^ all day –

Grania

It is the
T
Mother he had forgotten that story ~~and it is~~ t} he silence ^
~~hi~~ that has brought int int his mind.
of this valley ~~that has waked it in his heart~~ It is better
now
shoud live among his old companions. He talks ^ of Finns
that he ~~should join his old~~ ^ ~~comrades~~ ~~He suspects Finn of~~
now if it were wanting
crookedness ; **~~and he speaks~~ ^ of my love as ~~a waning season~~ ^ . . .**
In a few minutes Diarmid and Finn will meet

Laban

In a few minutes Finn will stand with his hand on Diarmids
shoulder

Grania

I did it for Diarmids sake
~~I did it Diarmids sake~~

Then I have done well in sending him to Finn ^ ~~but~~ ^ ~~for my~~
and for my and my fathers
^**father's ~~sake~~ ^, for the sake of ~~his~~ kingdom . I chose**
O how can I forget
Diarmid because he was young and comely , **but ~~I have ^ not forgotten~~**
the greatness of Finn In a few minutes Finn and his Fionna
will stand under this roof

[20r]

Laban

That is true, my daughter, sit beside me here and tell
me what happened to you when you left Tara .

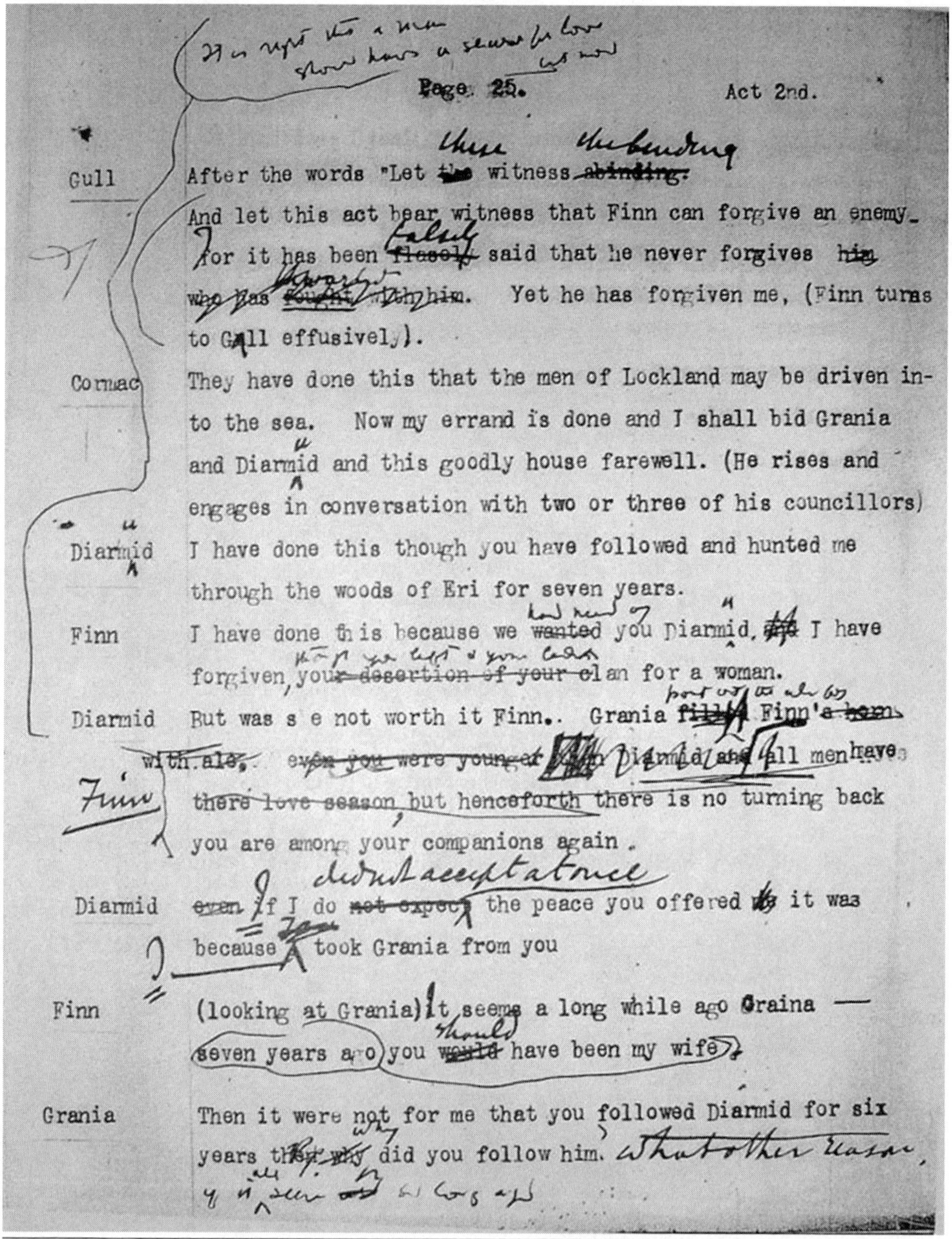

It is right that a man should have a season for love but not

Page. 25. Act 2nd.

Gull After the words "Let ~~the~~ these witness ~~abinding.~~ the bending

And let this act bear witness that Finn can forgive an enemy.

For it has been ~~flasely~~ falsely said that he never forgives ~~him~~

~~who has fought with him.~~ Yet he has forgiven me, (Finn turns

to Gall effusively).

Cormac They have done this that the men of Lockland may be driven in-

to the sea. Now my errand is done and I shall bid Grania

and Diarmid and this goodly house farewell. (He rises and

engages in conversation with two or three of his councillors)

Diarmid I have done this though you have followed and hunted me

through the woods of Eri for seven years.

Finn I have done this because we ~~wanted~~ had need of you Diarmid. ~~and~~ I have

forgiven your ~~desertion of your clan~~ that you left your clan for a woman.

Diarmid But was she not worth it Finn.. Grania ~~filled~~ Finn's ~~a horn~~

~~with ale.~~ ~~even you were younger~~ Diarmid all men have

~~there love season~~, but henceforth there is no turning back

you are among your companions again.

Diarmid ~~even~~ If I do ~~not expect~~ didn't accept at once the peace you offered ~~it~~ it was

because I took Grania from you

Finn (looking at Grania) It seems a long while ago Graina —

seven years ago you ~~would~~ should have been my wife?

Grania Then it were not for me that you followed Diarmid for six

years ~~then why~~ why did you follow him. What other reason

if it seem so long ago

1 and following The underlining beneath the part ascriptions and the rule down the LH margin of the text are drawn in red ink.

⁻1, 3–4, etc. WBY's emendations are in a paler shade of blue-black ink. In line 4, GM began to write "thwa" and WBY completed the word.

10 and] WBY's deletion.

12–14 The cancellations within lines 12–13 appear to have been made by GM and in line 14 by WBY.

19 The transposition was made by WBY.

Four-Page Typescript of Pages for Act II

[NLI 8777(13), 1r]

It is right that a man
should have a season for love
but now

Page 25. Act 2nd.

these the binding

Gull **After the words "Let ~~the~~ witness ~~abinding.~~**
And let this act bear witness that Finn can forgive an enemy_
F falsely
f or it has been ~~flasely~~ said that he never forgives ~~him~~
~~thwarted~~
~~**who has fought with him**~~**. Yet he has forgiven me, (Finn turns**
a
to G ull effusively).

Cormac **They have done this that the men of Lockland may be driven in-**
to the sea. Now my errand is done and I shall bid Grania
u
and Diarmid and this goodly house farewell. (He rises and
engages in conversation with two or three of his councillors)

u
Diarmid **I have done this though you have followed and hunted me**
through the woods of Eri for seven years.

had need of u
Finn **I have done this because we ~~wanted~~ you Diarmid . ~~and~~ I have**
though you left & your [?leader]
forgiven , ~~your desertion of your clan~~ for a woman.

pord out the ale [?into]
Diarmid **But was she not worth it Finn. Grania ~~filled~~ Finn's ~~horn~~**
~~**with ale.**~~ ~~**even you were younger then Diarmid and all men have**~~
Finn ~~**there love season**~~ , ~~**but henceforth**~~ **there is no turning back**
you are among your companions again.

I did not accept at once
Diarmid ~~**even**~~ **i f I do ~~not expect~~ the peace you offered ~~me~~ it was**
~~you~~
because ~~I~~ took Grania from you

I I
Finn **(looking at Grania) i t seems a long while ago Grania —**
should
seven years ago you ~~would~~ have been my wife —

Grania **Then it were not for me that you followed Diarmid for six**
why
years ~~then why~~ did you follow him ? what other reason ,
all
if it seems ~~all~~ so long ago

[NLI 8777(13), 2r]

Finn Our marriage Grania was to have mended all ~~our~~ ~~difficulties~~ divisions ~~for the~~ high King~~dom of~~ the Fianni ~~werenot always united~~,
~~and~~ I followed Diarmid for ~~seven~~ seven years ~~and left him not~~
~~peace~~ because he had broken his oath to the Fianni.

Diarmid For the breaking of my oath I shall make attonment with fifty head of ~~my best~~ cattle, ~~you can claim~~ my black bull ~~if you will~~, come to the door- way and you will see him in the valley .. With what a noble ~~stride~~ stride he grazes, ~~and then~~ ~~on~~ at the ~~skirts~~ edges of the herd, but who is this rough fat man in the sheep skin with two Spearsmen. It is my ~~old~~ enemy Conan, I shall be glad to ~~see him this day and~~ drink with him in, a horn of Ale, forgetfullne ss ~~in our fueds~~ (turn to the others) I have not seen you ~~all~~ for seven years have changed some ~~of you~~ here a little. I would drink with every one ofyou. I would that ~~then were a common~~ hand ~~among you~~ that I might hold it this day, ~~This happy day of peacemaking~~

(Enter ~~Colan~~ Conan the Bald with two Spearsmen and a Shepherd)

Colan keep your spears in your hands we are only just in time come, come again, we will be in time to get in front of him at the side of the woods of you ~~hasten~~ hurry (Exuent ~~colon~~ Conan followed by Fianni)

Diarmid Last week the wolves carried off three of my sheep this

[NLI 8777(13), 2[r]]

~~with~~ [?~~th~~]
divisions
Finn **Our marriage Grania was to have mended all ~~our difficulties~~**
to have united the and for ever
~~for the~~ ^ high King~~dom of~~ ^ the Fianni ^ ~~werenot always united~~ ,
Finn seven
~~and~~ I followed Diarmid for ~~seven~~ years ~~and left him now~~
~~peace~~ because he had broken his oath to the Fianni.

Diarmid **(For the breaking of my oath) I shall make attonment ^**
and I will give you
with fifty head of ~~my best~~ cattle. ^ ~~you can claim~~ ^ my black
~~if~~ C
bull~~, if you will~~ . c}ome to the door-way and you will see him
{t stride
in the valley . With wha{rt a noble ~~straid~~ he grazes~~, and~~ there
at edge B
~~on~~ ^ the ~~skirts~~ ^ of the herd . b}ut who is this rough fat man in
the sheep skin with two Spearsmen. It is my ~~old~~ enemy
Conan . I shall be glad to ~~see him this day and~~ drink with
of all our enmity
him in , a horn of Ale , forgetfullne ss ~~in our fueds~~ ^ (turn to
for and seven years
the others) I have not seen you ~~all~~ seven years ^ have changed
here
some ~~of you~~ a little. I would drink with every one ofyou .
~~there~~ you had ~~all~~ but a single
I would that ~~thou were a common~~ ^ hand ~~among you~~ that I might
– this happy day
hold it this day, ~~This happy day of peacemaking~~
Conan
(Enter ~~Colan~~ the Bald with two Spearsmen and a Shepherd)

Colan **keep your spears in your hands we are only just in time**
come, come again, we will be in time to get in front of him
hurry Conan
at the side of the woods of you ~~hasten~~ (Exuent ~~Colon~~ ^ followed by Fianni)

Diarmid **Last week the wolves carried off three of my sheep this**

1 The part ascription is written in again by hand because the type version is damaged by a staple hole—which proves that the pages were stapled before the revisions were made.
5 The transposition was made by WBY.
7 The character GM inserted above the line appears to be "f", but it may be intended to signify cancellation.

[NLI 8777(13), 3r]

D one shall pay for them (he snatches up his spear) (exit Diarmid) there are now on the stage only Cormac Grania Finn and the Shephard

Shephard It is not a wolf they are hunting it is not a wolf who broke out at the Stepping Stones and has gored twenty of my sheep (he goes towards the door)

Grania (To Finn) the Shephard said it was not a wolf ask him.

Finn He said that the beast has gored twenty of his sheep it must be a boar that I heard of on my way hither ~~here who was reported in a strange wood eastward~~ He has come out of the wood in the [illegible]

Grania ~~The~~ Then Daiarmid.must not go to the hunt I must call him back (she goes to the door) Diarmid is standing on the hill side He is coming back, ~~this~~ that is well. (coming down the stage to Finn) so Finn it was not for my sake that you followed Diarmid, for seven years, ~~and~~ for all these ~~wars had~~ wars there is no better reason than the breaking of ~~Diarmid's~~ an Oath ~~to the Fianna~~.

Finn ~~There are many reasons in a man's heart~~ I followed Diarmid because I hated him.

Grania But you have forgiven Diarmid you are friends again. Yes Finn I would have you friends but my wish is nothing to you. I was proud to think that for me that you followed Diarmid but you ~~have said~~ You have said that it was all ~~to revenge~~ because of the breaking of an oath. ~~A oath~~ This is a trial among men which a woman has no part.
This is a man's broil, no woman has part in it.

[NLI 8777(13), 3[r]]

one shall pay for them (he snatches up his spear) (exit
C
Diarmid) there are now on the stage only cJormac Grania Finn
and the Shephard

__Shephard__ **It is not a wolf e they are hunting it is not a wolf e**
who broke out at the Stepping Stones and has gored twenty of
my sheep (he goes towards the door)

__Grania__ **(To Finn) the Shephard said it was not a wolf e ask him.**

Finn – **He said that the beast has gored twenty of his sheep**
hither
it must be a boar that I heard of on my way ~~here who was~~
He has come out of the wood in the North.
~~reported in a strange wood eastward~~

Then
__Grania__ **~~The~~ Daiarmid.must not go to the hunt I must call him back**
(she goes to the door) Diarmid is standing on the hill side
t ~~at~~ That
He is coming ~~back~~ , ~~t/h is~~ is well. (coming down the stage to
Finn) so Finn it was not for my sake that you followed
for wars there is
Diarmid , for seven years , ~~and~~ all these ~~wars had~~ no better
an
reason than the breaking of ~~Diarmid's~~ Oath ~~to the Fianni~~ .

__Finn__ **~~There are many reasons in a man's heart.~~ I followed Diarmid**
because I hated him .

__Grania__ **But you have forgiven Diarmid you are friends again.** Yes Finn
I would have you friends but my wish is nothing to you .
I was proud to think ~~that~~ for me you followed Diarmid
you have said all because of
but ~~you have said~~ that it was ~~to revenge~~ the breaking of an
This is a broil in
oath. ~~A call~~ among men which a woman has no part.
This is a mans broil, no woman has part in it.

12–14 Both transpositions were made by WBY.
19 The revision was made by WBY.

[NLI 8777(13), 4r]

Finn Cormac told me ~~that~~ it was you ~~who~~ persuaded Diarmid to bring me to this house ~~there~~ could have been no peace

Grania

Grania ~~It seemed to me~~ that ~~two~~ men ~~as~~ great as Finn and Diarmid must be friends ~~and~~ my father ~~feared invasion by~~ the men of Lockland and ~~then~~ I ~~was weary~~ of this valley where there is nothing but the rising and setting of the sun and the grazing of ~~the~~ flocks and herds

Finn ~~Was this why you sent for me?~~

Grania And I ~~wished~~ to see you because of your greatness

[NLI 8777(13), 4r]

and but for this
I would have made
peace
~~otherwise there~~
that

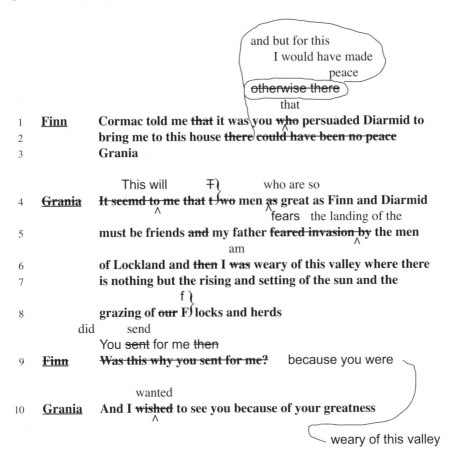

Finn Cormac told me ~~that~~ it was you ~~who~~ persuaded Diarmid to
bring me to this house ~~there could have been no peace~~
Grania

This will T who are so
~~Grania~~ ~~It seemd to me that~~ ~~t~~wo men ~~as~~ great as Finn and Diarmid
fears the landing of the
must be friends ~~and~~ my father ~~feared invasion by~~ the men
am
of Lockland and ~~then~~ I ~~was~~ weary of this valley where there
is nothing but the rising and setting of the sun and the
f
grazing of ~~our~~ Flocks and herds

did send
You ~~sent~~ for me ~~then~~
~~Finn~~ ~~Was this why you sent for me?~~ because you were

wanted
Grania And I ~~wished~~ to see you because of your greatness
weary of this valley

5 and] Deleted by GM.

[HRC(2), 1r]

DIARMUID AND GRANIA.

ACT II.

SCENE: DIARMUID'S house - A spinning wheel to left - Walls made of roughly hewn timber - CORMAC and LABAN alone on the stage - LABAN sitting at her spinning wheel. Firelight which deepens slowly.

CORMAC What have you seen in your spindle ? The wheel has become silent - You do not speak.

LABAN I have learnt but little. I have felt the thread with my fingers, and I have closed my eyes and looked into the darkness under my lids, but I have seen little.

CORMAC What have you seen ?

LABAN If I were to tell you all, some that are wiser than men and women would make my tongue like a stone.

CORMAC You know, but you will not tell me - It is a king who asks you. I will have you beaten, old as you are, and your wheel broken and thrown into the lake - You have seen some evil; you were always foreboding evil. (A pause.)

Composite Typescript of Complete Act, Revised by George Moore and W. B. Yeats—George Moore's Copy?

[HRC(2), 1r]

DIARMUID AND GRANIA.

ACT II.

SCENE: DIARMUID'S house – A spinning wheel to left – Walls made of roughly hewn timber – CORMAC and Laban alone on the stage – LABAN sitting at her spinning wheel. Twilight which deepens slowly.

CORMAC **What have you seen in your spindle ? The wheel has become silent – You do not speak.**

LABAN **~~I have learnt but little~~. I have felt the thread with my fingers, and I hav e closed my eyes and looked into the darkness under my lids, but I have seen little.**

CORMAC **What have you seen ?**

LABAN **If I were to tell you all, some that are wiser than men and women would make my tongue like a stone.**

CORMAC **You know, but you will not tell me – It is a king who asks you. I will have you beaten, old as you are, and your wheel broken and thrown into the lake – You have seen some evil; you were always foreboding evil. (A pause.)**

[HRC(2)]

[2^{r}]

–2–

LABAN I have seen FINN standing with his hand upon DIARMUID'S shoulder.

CORMAC Then I will make some great offering to the Dagda, and to AONGHUS his son, and to all the gods. When will it be ? When will they make friends ? (LABAN remains silent.) You know all things because you are so old. When I was a boy you had still those wrinkles about your eyes – Nobody knows when you were born, or where you came from. You shall tell me – (Pause) Will you tell me. . . I have come a long journey to make peace. I have given DIARMUID this valley to make my daughter happy in, and persuaded FINN to be friends with DIARMUID again. But it all comes to nothing because DIARMUID will not be friends with FINN. (Enter GRANIA. . . Turning to GRANIA) I am telling her that I must not stay, I have to rouse the children of Hebor and the children of Hermon. For we need every sword if we are to drive the men of Lochland from our coasts.

GRANIA But their vessels have been driven away by storms.

CORMAC A few weeks fair weather and they will gather again.

GRANIA You are going, father, and three days to see you in

[3^{r}]

–3–

~~is not a long while after seven years.~~

CORMAC Seven years FINN has hunted you – for seven years you and DIARMUID have fled from FINN, and now when there might be peace it is DIARMUID who will not have it.

GRANIA You will come here again, father, when you are weary of statecaraft, or shall I see you in Tara.

CORMAC I will come to you again, though it is a long journey, but do not come to Tara yet a while – there is always trouble in Tara.

GRANIA Trouble, yes, I have made trouble.

CORMAC I have brought you LABAN ~~that you may not be lonely~~. ~~She said that you had need of her, and she will talk to you of Tara over the fire.~~ Stet

GRANIA And that was kindly done, and there is NIALL waiting for you – (Going to NIALL) Goodbye, NIALL, I wish you could stay with me as well as LABAN. She taught me wisdom and you were my only playmate. ~~Do you remember the little pool on the edge of the wood where we used to sit on a high bank fishing for roach ?~~ Stet

CORMAC My people are waiting for me beyond the mountain~~s~~.

[4r]

–4–

I shall sleep there and we will begin our ride to Tara before dawn.

GRANIA It will be a journey of many days.

CORMAC Not less than five. Neither I nor Niall can keep the saddle many hours at a time. Where is DIARMUID ?

GRANIA (Going to the door) This is the hour when the flock comes home. DIARMUID has forgotten us all, he is thinking of the folding of the sheep. You will find him with the shepherd, or shall I send LABAN to tell him ? (Exit LABAN) The fold is not far from the house, it was brought nearer for the wolves carried off three of the sheep last week. Ah, I see him coming up thepathway – LABAN is going to meet him (Going to CORMAC) What has she told you ? or what has she not told you – your voice was loud when I came in.

CORMAC She has seen FINN standing with his hand on DIARMUID'S

4v carries a (carbon) false start, the page being headed "–4–", followed by "I shall sl"

[HRC(2)]

shoulder; but she has not told me when they will be friends.

GRANIA Stay a little while longer, and you will persuade him.

CORMAC I have striven with him for three days. But you have said nothing – Speak a word before I leave you. Tell him that he must arm and train the shepherds of this valley, for the men of Lochland –

GRANIA I will tell him none of these things, but I will per suade him – (Enter DIARMUID.)

[5^{r}]

–3–

them up against the enemy if needful. You shake your head – Will DIARMUID'S faith and FINN'S faith never be pledged again ?

GRANIA For three days you have striven with him, for three days in vain.

CORMAC Will you not persuade him – Tell him that my kingdom and that the men of Lochland –

GRANIA I will tell him none of these things, but I will per- suade him – (Enter DIARMUID.)

Stet

~~**DIARMUID**~~ ~~CORMAC, come with me to the end of the valley~~; my black bull is there. I have been offered twenty cows if I would lend him. He is like a black cloud and his pace is like a wave's.

CORMAC Take pride in your herds while you can. The men of Lochland have five score of galleys, and the first fair wind will bring them to these coasts, to carry away your herds and all that you have.

DIARMUID The storms have scattered their galleys. Mamannon has done this so that we may be happy in this valley.

5^{r}, ll. 1–9, 10 The cancellation, together with the subsequent underlining and cancellation, is in pencil. The revision positions this version at a point between NLI 8777(4) g and NLI 8777(14).

The revised text links with Diarmuid's entrance at the foot of fol. 4^{r}.

kneel beside his
that you have given us. I shall ~~fling~~ ~~some~~ ~~great~~
~~offering into his waves~~. waves & thank him

[6r]

–4–

CORMAC **Must I tell FINN that you will not make peace ?**

DIARMUID **Tell him to begone out of my valley.**

CORMAC **Would you have men say that the man you wronged has forgiven you and offered you peace and that you have refused it. I have made peace between you for my kingdom's sake; but if you send him such an answer the sod may be blown into flame again.**

DIARMUID **Let it flame when it will, I have fought FINN and overthrown him. Did I not break out of the house of seven doors when he had put guards at all the doors.**

CORMAC **Do not send me back with this message.**

DIARMUID **It would be for GRANIA's sake and not for my sake, who knows what would happen when he saw her face again. But what would GRANIA have me do ? Would GRANIA have me friends with FINN ? She saysnothing – She stands apartsaying nothing.**

my father you
GRANIA **If I say yes to ~~you~~, I shall say no to ~~my father~~.**

DIARMUID **So you say nothing.**

equal
GRANIA **It may be that my desires are either way – (Enter NIALL – the King goes to him – Some Councillors appear**

[7r]

–5–

DIARMUID **I have fought your father's reasons for three days, GRANIA, and you have sat listening, taking neither side. But this morning you said you would like to**

[HRC(2)]

see FINN again.

Finn has offered you my
GRANIA ~~My father has brought about~~ peace, and you heard ~~him~~
Father do
say that if you ~~would~~ not take it the broil ~~would~~ begin s again.

DIARMUID Did you not choose me ? Did you not serve him bewitched ale ? Have you not fled from him for seven years ? Why should you now wish to see him ? Do you love FINN ?

GRANIA I do not love FINN, but I have not forgotten his greatness.

saw
DIARMUID I ~~remember seeing~~ you speaking to him at Tara. You
turned from him wearily ~~it is true~~, but you seemed to
Y
like him. ~~You told me~~ y}ou chose me because I was
and now will
younger. FINN is seven years older ~~now~~. He ~~would~~
seem very old now.

GRANIA I would see you, who are great like FINN, friends with FINN.

DIARMUID But if the broil should begin again ?

GRANIA FINN has forgotten me.

[8r]

–6–

DIARMUID Here we have everything we sought for. I have you and I have this peaceful valley where I can hide you away. Here we shall live and die, and our children shall grow up about us, if the gods hear my prayer and accept my offering and give us children. I often wonder why I desired to excel any one. Love has come to seem enough.

GRANIA Sometimes I think we were happier when we had nothing.

got
When we slept under cromlechs and in caves, and ~~fished~~
our food from the hills & the streams
~~in the streams.~~

DIARMUID **We cannot go back to the woods. We have a kingdom here and flocks and herds.**

GRANIA **And a house where we can welcome the Fianna. I would see FINN and the Fianna, CAOELTE, GOLL and USHEEN. And would you not ~~like to~~ see your old companions ? Peace has been made and what is the good**
you
of peace if ~~we~~ remain apart ?

DIARMUID **My old companions, USHEEN, GOLL, CAOELTE, what should**
come between
I say to them ? Seven years have ~~sundered~~ us; it
a had
is as if ~~the~~ sea sundered us.

GRANIA **What would you say to them ? That the past is ~~the~~ past; that you go again, as brothers united, against**

[9r]

–7–

the enemies of Eri – (Pause.) You would fight shoulder to shoulder with CAOELTE and USHEEN – (Pause) You would hear CAOELTE tell his battle tales, and hear USHEEN'S harp playing.

DIARMUID **Oh, but amid it all I shall look back and sigh, think-**
came
ing of these quiet evenings when the flock ~~comes~~ home ,
dusk
and you give me my supper in the ~~twilight~~. (He goes up the stage and looks at the evening.) Come look at the ~~evening~~ sleepy evening – the sheep are folded
green
under a ~~quiet~~ hill, and the wolf dogs are lounging about the fold. (He comes down the stage.)

8r, l. 21 The cancellation is in ink (GM's?).
9r, l. 9 Type deletion.
10 The substitution is ink over pencil; the cancellation beneath remains pencil only.

[HRC(2)]

GRANIA **You hunted the wolves yesterday, but I saw you did not follow them far.**

DIARMUID **The wolves went eastward, and eastward there is an unknown wood.**

GRANIA **I thought you had forgotten that story.**

DIARMUID **What story ?**

GRANIA **The story that CONAN told you.**

DIARMUID **I had forgotten it in our wanderings; and we passed ~~by and~~ through many unknown woods. But here –**

[10[r]]

–8–

GRANIA **You have not come upon a strange track ?**

DIARMUID **I have seen nothing.**

GRANIA **Then it is the silence of this valley that has waked the thought of it.**

DIARMUID **~~Maybe.~~ It is a ~~strange~~ trap-like place, with a lake at one end, and narrow at the other, where a man might ~~easily~~ be driven to his death. Why did CORMAC choose it ? or did FINN contrive this valley, because one who is long baffled must turn to deceit ? Is your father in league with him against us ?**

GRANIA **~~It is strange you should think such a thing even for a moment.~~ If you suspect this place ~~leave it this very moment.~~** let us begone this very night.

DIARMUID No, not now, not till morning: the beast may **~~We might stumble on my enemy sleeping, and in the dark my chances would be but little.~~** be in that wood, we might stumble on him sleeping.

GRANIA **All our flocks and herds are in this valley.**

9[r], l. 20 The faint cancellations appear to be by GM.

DIARMUID **We cannot leave them, and of what use to leave this
valley ? As the saying is – no man wanders far from
his grave-sod. (Pause.) If I were to die, GRANIA,
would you be FINN'S wife?**

[11r]

–9–

GRANIA **Why do you ask me this, DIARMUID ?**

DIARMUID **My life began with you, and it ends with you. ~~Oh~~,** That
breasts
~~that another should clasp this delicate body, and~~
[?y'r hand] thear ^ ~~usage~~ should belong to another, and the
~~that these breasts should belong to another~~.
sacred usage of this body.

GRANIA **You must sit by the fire, dreaming of me no longer.
You must win new love of me in battle.**

DIARMUID **(Taking her in his arms.) Life of my life. I knew
you before I was born. . I made a bargain with this
brown hair before the beginning of time, and it shall
not be broken through unending time. I shall sit upon**
up*on*
the shore beyond the world pondering ^ my love, and I
{we
**shall weep, remembering how {I wandered ~~with her~~ among
the woods. But you say nothing, GRANIA.**

GRANIA **Are you so weary of fame, DIARMUID, that you would
be a king among shepherds.**

DIARMUID **I am a king ~~only~~ when you love me.**

GRANIA **Then go to your companions for I shall love you better
when you come to me with the reek of battle upon you.**

DIARMUID **When I was at Tara seven years ago it was not by the
fame that the sword gives, but by the desire of the**

11r, ll. 3–4 The words written in the LH margin, alongside GM's revision, are in pencil. The writing is small, and could just possibly be by WBY (certainly not GM); cf. fol. 14r below, editorial note on line 16.

11 That is, GM adds to WBY's pencil revision in ink

[HRC(2)]

[12r]

–10–

eye that I won you.

GRANIA **That was so once. Now, I am weary of the shadows on these mountains, and of the smell of the fold.**

Would you lose your love of me G if I
DIARMUID **~~You fear, GRANIA, that you may lose your love of me~~**
but bid me
if I had seen ~~like~~ a shepherd. You ~~would that I~~ put away the crook for the spear. There is a strange
I is
fire in your eyes, ~~and~~ i t many days since you have come to my bed – (GRANIA goes to a chest and takes out an ornament.)

GRANIA **But seeing you in your war gear I shall thirst for you,**
slept
as when we ~~wandered~~ by the river side.

DIARMUID **You have not worn an ornament for metthis many a day. But you think I may become new to you, ~~and that we may be happier than here~~, when we cook our food over a watch fire.**

CORMAC **Your cattle are coming this way, DIARMUID, and their**
are heavy with
heavy sides ~~tell me of~~ the rich grass of these valleys which I have given you ~~this kingdom~~. Come, and I'll show you its boundaries before I go. On the north by the hills of Shea, GRANIA, on the west by –

GRANIA **I am not thinking of it, but of you who are going;**

[13r]

–10–

CORMAC **Your cattle are coming this way, DIARMUID, and their**

12r The present page is singular in that it has a wide margin but the stage description is not underlined at l. 8.
4 The free-floating "G" in GM's substitution probably signifies "Grania".
15–20 The swirling cancellation is in pencil.

13r The page number "–10–" is repeated; there is no page marked "11." This is the only page in the HRC(2)

sides are heavy with the rich grass of this valley that I have given you, and the rooks are flying home. Are you going to FINN, DIARMUID ? (DIARMUID goes up the stage – CORMAC to GRANIA) Have you persuaded him ?

GRANIA I do not know.

DIARMUID I will go down the hill with you.

You will tell me on the way

CORMAC Yes, yes, ^ ~~if we do not hurry,~~ we shall not be at the stepping-stones before dark; ~~you will tell me on the way (Exeunt.)~~ (Ex & Enter Laban

Alone

GRANIA (~~Standing~~ at the door) In a few minutes they will meet (Returning to LABAN) Now that we are alone, Mother, you can finish this story. FINN said he would never forgive me, and yet he has forgiven me and forgotten me. You have told me of his awaking from sleep, and of his anger that night in Tara.

[14^{r}]

–12–

LABAN ~~Then~~ they were near hanging me from the rafters.

GRANIA Some day, Mother, you will tell me of all these things, but now I am thinking of the meeting of DIARMUID with FINN in the valley under us. I did right in sending DIARMUID to FINN. I sent him for my father's sake, for the sake of the kingdom, that it might be safe against the men of Lochlann – Tell me, Mother, that *this* is why I sent DIARMUID to FINN – ~~that is the truth~~.

LABAN That is the truth.

GRANIA I have said everything.

LABAN No tongue, child is ~~long enough or~~ nimble enough to

---

TS that begins with a narrower LH margin and has underlined stage directions; but note that the width of the margin increases in Grania's second speech. Line 1 picks up with the canceled line 15 on the previous page (fol. 12^{r}).

14^{r}, ll. 1, 8, 11, 12, 13 All the cancellations are in pencil—that is, here, by WBY.

[HRC(2)]

say every thing. When everything is said ~~some~~ *there is* still ~~remains~~ *something* in the heart – Sit beside me here and tell me what happened to you when you left Tara – that will be easier.

GRANIA When we left Tara ? We came to a little glade *[?here]** on the hill-side, and we heard there a sudden and a beautiful singing of birds, and we saw a red fox creeping in the grass.

LABAN And then ?

[15r]

–13–

GRANIA And then we saw a young man sitting in the long grass.

LABAN What did he say ?

GRANIA He was but a herdsman's son seeking a master, and so DIARMUID took him into his service and yet, Mother, I think that he was greater than DIARMUID or I for he gave us such good service, and so much good counsel He never put us into a cave that had not two mouths, or let us take refuge in an island that had not two harbours, nor ~~did he let us~~ eat our food where we had cooked it, ~~or~~ *nor* sleep where we had eaten it. He never let us lie for many hours in one place, and often he changed our sleeping place in the middle of the night.

LABAN What name did he bid you call him ?

GRANIA He bid us call him MUDHAM. But I think he had some great and beautiful name did we but know it; have you ever seen him, MOTHER ?

LABAN It has been said that none who have seen him have been

14r, l. 16 The underlined pencil word is in the same small hand that appears on fol. 11r; it is followed by a pencil asterisk.

15r, l. 9 The cancellation is in pencil.

long content with any mortal lover.

GRANIA I have been content with DIARMUID nigh on seven years.

LABAN Did you ever hear that beautiful singing of birds again ?

[16r]

–14–

GRANIA Yes, I heard them sing by the banks of a river; ~~and~~ I heard them when DIARMUID broke his oath to FINN. We had wandered by the banks of a river nine days, and MUDHAM fished for us, and every day we hung an uncooked salmon on a tree as a token to FINN. On the tenth day we hung a cooked salmon, for on the ninth night the sword had not lain between us – but Mother I can tell you no more. I would have you tell me, you who know all things, what is passing in the valley. Have FINN and DIARMUID made friends ? Has DIARMUID passed *by* the fires of the Fianna without speaking ?

LABAN They have spoken, they are on their way hither so forget them for a while, and tell me if you are happy in this valley.

GRANIA I stand by the door of this house, seeing the hours wane, waiting for DIARMUID to come home from his hunting. Nothing has happened until to-day, and now DIARMUID and FINN are walking up the valley together, reconciled at last. I had come to think I should never look on a stirring day again, and I had thought to send all the thread you would spin to be woven into a grass-green web on which to embroider my wanderings with DIARMUID among the woods. I should have been

[17r]

–15–

many years embroidering it, but when it was done and hung all round this room I should have seen birds, *and* beasts and leaves which ever way I turned and DIARMUID

16r, l. 1 The cancellation is in pencil.

[HRC(2)]

and myself wandering amongst them.

LABAN **But now you have thrown the doors wide open and the days are streaming in upon you again.**

{?

GRANIA **Yes, yes, but I have done rightly**{. **Had I not sent DIARMUID to FINN the broil would have begun again. . . I must put on my jewels. The Fianna~~, the Fianna~~ will be here in a moment, and FINN has never seen me in my jewels. Spin for me, Mother, spin for me; tell me I have done rightly. ~~I am putting on my jewels~~. ~~Oh~~** *But* **no, they are coming, I can hear their footsteps.' Go to the serving-men and bid them take the drinking horns and the flagons from the cupboard – (Exit LABAN – GRANIA stands before a long steel mirror that hangs upon** √ **the wall, and puts the gold circlet about her head and the heavy bracelets upon her arm, and the great many-coloured cloak upon her which she fastens with an emerald clasp; she puts a gold girdle about her waist.** ⋏ **Enter CORMAC, FINN, CAOELTE, DIARMUID etc. – DIARMUID is talking to FINN.) Welcome USHEEN, welcome CAOELTE, welcome GOLL and all the noble Fianna into my house.**

Enter Servants with flagons of wine & drinking horns & torches)

[18^{r}]

–16–

I am happy that such men should stand under my roof. The shepherds of Ben Bulben will tell each other many years after we are dead that FINN, USHEEN, CAOELTE, and GOLL stood once under this roof. (GRANIA goes to her father and leads him to a high seat.) You

glad for leave-

cannot go from us now for I am too ~~happy~~ ~~to say good-bye~~. taking.

17^{r}, l. 12 The deletion in this line—like all the emendations on this page apart from GM's addition at the foot—are in pencil.

15–16 The pencil tick in the RH margin is the only such mark to appear in the present act. No such ticks appear in HRC(1), and HRC(3) contains a good many—which might reinforce the possibility that the separate HRC acts were used to work through a continuous sequence of revision. As well as cuing the insertion, the caret also cancels the closing parenthesis.

CORMAC I ~~am happy too, and would~~ will stay a little while, and will drink a horn of ale with this noble company who will defend Erie against the ~~noble~~ men of Lochland if they should come to our coasts again.

DIARMUID We have been here but three moons and have not had time to ~~to~~ build a house great enough for ourselves and for our people. This winter we shall build a house of oak wood great enough for two hundred people to sleep under its pillars. All the Fianna who come shall sleep under our roof.

GRANIA When you speak of their coming you makeus think of their leave taking, and I ~~now~~ would forget that they shall ever leave us.

CORMAC Eri is safe now that her great men are united.

[19r]

–17–

CAOELTE For a long while when we lighted our fires at night there was no fire at which some did not side with FINN, some with DIARMUID – But at last those that were of FINN'S party, and those that were of DIARMUID'S party gathered about the different fires{, .} {a And} this year the fire‸s were lighted far apart.

USHEEN It needed but a little to bring the words out of their scabbards, and make the earth red under our feet.

FINN If all Eri were red under our feet, it were but GRANIA'S due that men in coming times might know of the love which she had put into men's hearts (He puts his hand on DIARMUID'S shoulder – Two serving men go round with ale, GRANIA stops them and takes the flagons from them.)

18r, l. 10 The cancellation is in pencil.

[HRC(2)]

GRANIA **It is right that I should serve the ale on such a day as this.**

CORMAC **My daughter must not pour out the ale.**

USHEEN **If GRANIA pours out the ale we shall sleep sound to-night.**

CORMAC **You have spoken folly, USHEEN – I – I spoke out of a dream.**

[20ʳ]

there are
Let us wait before we drink ~~&~~ till ~~Darmuid~~
[?*to*]
~~[?*has*] [?*made*] [?*the*] [?*hospitalities*]~~ *beds for us all*

–18–

CAOELTE ~~**DIARMUID has said that this winter he will build a bigger house, build big enough to hold us all.**~~

~~Not~~ Not a word more – the past is the past

CORMAC ~~**It were better if DIARMUID thought how he will teach the shepherds to hurl the spear and pull the bow.**~~
GRANIA , since you have taken the flagons from your serving-men, serve us. But I would you had not done this. (GRANIA goes round filling each one's horn with ale – DIARMUID and FINN are still standing together on the right – She pauses, considering for an instant, and then fills FINN'S horn.)

CAOELTE **DIARMUID, we have not spoken to you nor seen you this seven years.**

GOLL **Have you no word for us.**

USHEEN **We would drink with you (DIARMUID goes up the stage an d joins the group who are standing half way up the stage, near to where the king is sitting.)**

GRANIA **Are you not afraid to drink the ale that I pour out for you ?**

FINN **Why did you do this ? Did you think of it ?**

GRANIA **I had not thought of it.**

20ʳ, ll. 14–15 The cancellation, like all emendations on this page—with the exception of the comma inserted into line 5—is in pencil.

[21r]

–19–

~~**FINN**~~ ~~**But it has happened.**~~

~~**GRANIA**~~ **In this ale you will not drink of sleep but you will drink of forgetfulness of me, and of friendship for DIARMUID**

FINN **Had I known that you would speak like this I would not have come to your house.**

GRANIA **But you have come here for this.**

USHEEN **It is not enough for FINN and DIARMUID to drink together, they must be bound together by the blood-bond. They must be made brothers before the gods – They must be bound together.**

CAOELTE **Yes, yes, they must be bound together by the blood-bond.**

~~**ALL**~~ ~~**Yes, yes, they must be brothers.**~~

DIARMUID **(Coming down the stage) Take out your dagger FINN, draw blood out of your arm, as I draw blood out of mine – (FINN bares his arm and pricks it with his dagger and goes towards DIARMUID.) Speak the holy words FINN –**

[22r]

–20–

Finn
This bond has bound us
Like brother to brother,
Like son to father.
Let him who breaks it ,
Be driven from the threshold *s*
Of God-kind and man-kind.

DIARMUID **Let the sea bear witness,**

21r, ll. 1–2, 14 The cancellations are in pencil.
22r, l. 1 Or was the part ascription inserted by WBY?

[HRC(2), 22^{v}]

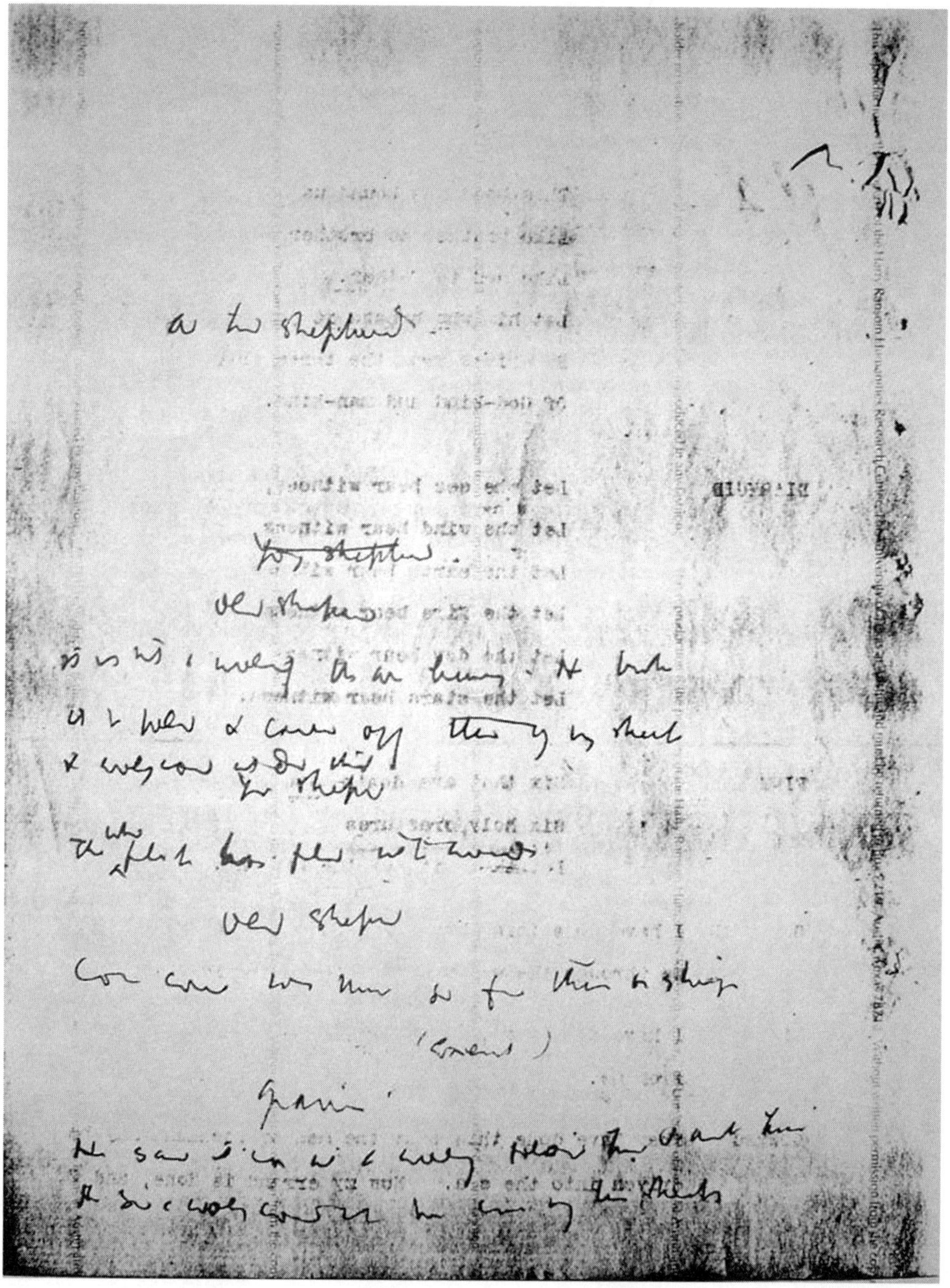

Let the wind bear witness
Let the earth bear witness
Let the fire bear witness
Let the dew bear witness
Let the stars bear witness.

FINN **Six that are death-less**
Six holy creatures
~~Have~~ ~~ed~~
~~Let them~~ witness the binding.
^

DIARMUID **I have done this though you followed me and hunted me through the woods of Eri for seven years.**

FINN **I have done this, DIARMUID , though you took GRANIA from me.**

CORMAC **They have done this that the men of Lochlann may be driven into the sea. Now my errand is done, and I**

[22v]

And two shepherds –

~~Young shepherd~~ –
Old shephrd
It is not a wolf thy ar huntng. It broke
in t fold & carred off three of my sheep
& wolf coud not do that

Yn shephd
whle
The flock has fled with hounds
^

Old sheperd
Com come we must go for [?*these*] [?*our*] *sheep*
(Exent)

Grania
He said it is nt a wolf follow him & ask him
He said a wolf could not hav carrd of his sheep

22v The unnumbered line at the head of the page is presumably meant to fit into the stage direction opposite at fol. 23r, line 2+, though it is unclear if the subsequent pencil draft was written to replace or to supplement the TS dialogue.

[HRC(2)]

[23r]

–21–

shall bid GRANIA and DIARMUID and this house farewell, and all this goodly company farewell (He rises and engages in conversation with two or three of his

& shepherds

councillors – CONAN THE Bald and two Spearmen^ enter hurriedly)

at Stepping Stones

CONAN **He broke out ~~of~~ the ~~Red Waterfall~~, and has fallen upon the sheepfold (To the Spearmen) Keep your spears in your hand, we are only just in time – Look, there he is at the edge of the wood – Come, come – You will**

{him

be in time to get in front of {it on the other side of the wood if you hasten (Exit of CONAN followed by the Fianna.)

DIARMUID **Last week the wolves carried off three of my sheep – This one shall pay for them ~~with its death~~ – (He snatches up his spear) Come FINN (Exit – There are**

Cormac

now on the stage, only CONAN, GRANIA, FINN and the Shepherd.)

SHEPHERD **It is not a wolf they are hunting, it is not a wolf.**

Stepping Stones gored

He broke out of the ~~Red Waterfall~~, and has ~~carried off~~

out)

twenty of my sheep (~~Moving towards the door~~) ~~Ah ! they have got him (CONAN goes to the shepherd and speaks to him in dumb show~~) (He goes towards the door

[24r]

–22–

GRANIA **(To FINN) The shepherd said it was not a wolf, ask him; ~~a wolf could not have carried off twenty sheep~~.**

23r, ll. 10, 14–15+ The cancellations are in pencil.

23v A false start, in typed carbon; the page is headed "–21–", followed by the words, "shall bid GRANIA and DIARMUID farewell, and"

24r, l. 2 The cancellation is in ink (that is, by GM).

FINN **Maybe this beast has come that we may speak together.**

I will go see

GRANIA **~~Let me~~ ^ see what is happening – ~~the shepherd has told my father~~ (Turning suddenly towards him) What can you have to say to me after seven years ? You have forgotten me.**

FINN **I would know why you sent for me – CORMAC told me you had persuaded DIARMUID to bring me to this house.**

GRANIA **I did not wish two great men to be in enmity, and it was I who put you at strife.**

FINN **Was this why you sent for me ?**

GRANIA **Yes, that was why, and ~~because~~ I wished to see you ~~in~~**
because of your
~~your fame and~~ greatness.

Enchanted

FINN **Then why did you give me ~~bewitched~~ ale in Tara ? Why did you fly from me for seven years ?**

GRANIA **I loved DIARMUID – He was young and comely, and you seemed to me to be old, you were grey.**

FINN **I am seven years older now, and my hair is greyer – I must seem very old to you now.**

[25r]

–23–

there as you

GRANIA **No, you seem younger, as you stand lean~~ing~~ on your spear you seem to me a young man. I do not think of your grey hairs any longer.**

FINN **Thay day in Tara you would not wear your ornaments, but now you wear them.**

24r, ll. 4, 5, 13, 14 These cancellations are in pencil (by WBY).
15 The cancellation is in ink (that is, by GM).
25r, l. 3 The cancellation is in pencil.

[HRC(2)]

GRANIA **I wear them to do you honour, because you have made peace with DIARMUID.** ×

FINN **There was a time when I thought GRANIA would have loved greatness ~~and~~ fame (DIARMUID comes slowly down the stage.)** ×

DIARMUID **What have you to say to one another; what were you saying to GRANIA, FINN, I can see by GRANIA'S face that she is but little pleased to see me again.**

GRANIA **Why do you say ~~that~~** *this* **? What has happened, DIARMUID ? the shepherd said the wolf had killed twenty sheep.**

DIARMUID **There is no wolf in the thicket, they do not know what they are hunting.**

GRANIA **~~What have you seen in the thicket~~, DIARMUID ?**

<u>Enter Conan</u>

DIARMUID **No matter whether it be a wolf or a boar that is hiding there, I have come** *in* **to find you and FINN talking ~~in a~~** *~~togeather~~* *~~that~~* **~~way I do not like~~.** *stet*

[26r]

–24–

FINN **Was it to watch me, DIARMUID, that you have come back ? (Enter the Fianna.)**

CONAN **So GRANIA ~~broods~~** *plans* **mischief.**

FINN **This is a false peace, there can be no peace between you and me DIARMUID – Years ~~have~~** had **hidden something of the wrong you had done me ~~at~~ but the sight of GRANIA has brought it to mind.**

25r, ll. 9, 13, 19–20 The cancellations in these lines are in pencil.

26r, l. 6 at] Type cancellation.

GRANIA — **To you, FINN, I say that I would not have sent for you had I thought the broil would begin again – To you, DIARMUID, I say that I will speak to what man I please, that no man shall thwart me – Where is my father ? (Turning suddenly towards them) No, I will**
Forbid them father
not have you fight for me, ~~what is happening~~ ^ ? (She goes to CORMAC.)

DIARMUID — **Our swords shall decide between us, I shall slay you FINN.**

FINN — **One of us two shall die (They draw their swords and the Fianna rush ~~in.)~~** *between them)*

GOLL — **FINN and DIARMUID cannot fight – fling up their swords, thrust the spears between them. Has FINN forgotten the blood bond; he who raises his hand against the**

[27r]

–25–

blood bond, raises his hand against the gods.

CONAN — **(Coming towards them) If FINN and DIARMUID cannot**
hunt this
fight with one another let them ~~go against the~~ boar, and let GRANIA be given to him who kills it – AOGNHUS who watches over lovers and hunters shall decide between them (DIARMUID lifts up his sword to strike him; leaving her father GRANIA comes forward.)

GRANIA — **He is not worthy enough for you to strike him – give me your sword – ~~he shall die by a woman's hand~~.**

FINN — **(Standing in front of CONAN) No, GRANIA, he shall not die, he has spoken the truth – FINN and DIARMUID**
woman
love one ~~another~~, ~~and a woman's breast is better than a friend's ha^nd~~.

CONAN — **~~DIARMUID would strike me because I have spoken of what fills him with terror.~~ It may that a tale I once told**

27r, ll. 8, 13–14, etc All the cancellations on this page are in pencil.

[HRC(2)]

~~it~~ the *{of*

him has given him no stomach for ~~this~~ hunting *{.* *a boar*

This boar

1. SPEARMAN ~~It is~~ ^ bigger than any beast I ever saw, ~~and it made a strange sound~~.

2. SPEARMAN It is certainly no mortal beast.

DIARMUID What was it its colour was it covered with bristles ?

[28r]

–26–

CONAN I saw it; it was balck and bristleless (He goes over and stands by DIARMUID) FINN, CAOELTE, USHEEN, look at us; there is one terror in the heart of DIARMUID and CONAN.)

~~**DIARMUID** What is the colour of this beast~~ ?

too, It was dark like the sea

2. SPEARMAN I saw it~~, it passed by~~, ^ ~~and I saw thought that it was green like the sea,~~ and it made a noise like the sea in a storm.

FINN We listen to the idle tales of Spearmen – Whatever the colour of the beast may be we shall slay it (The Fianna move up the stage) CONAN has spoken well, DIARMUID has little stomach for this hunting. Why did he ask for the blood bond ? It was not I who went to him – It was he who came to me with his arm pricked *14* with his dagger. These are the only wounds he will dare. This blood bond keeps him from my sword, and he speaks of an old tale that he may not go to the hunt – DIARMUID is craven.

27r, l. 15 Compare the wobbly handwriting that appears in HRC(1), fols. 4r and 5r. Could that also be in WBY's hand?

28r, ll. 5, etc. All the cancellations on this page are in pencil.

14 The small numeral at the RH end of the line is perhaps in the same hand as on fols. 11r, 14r above.

DIARMUID	**FINN lies; he knows why I will not go to the hunt, ~~and~~ he seeks my death ~~because he loves GRANIA~~.** *stet*
1.SPEAR-MAN	**If DIARMUID does not go to this hunt DIARMUID is craven.**

[29ʳ]

–27–

2. SPEAR-MAN	**FINN has said it, he is craven.**
CAOELTE	**DIARMUID must not go to this hunt. You have done wickedly this day, CONAN, and after your kind.**
3.SPEAR-MAN	**He has a hare's heart. The gods have given him a hare's heart.**
FINN	**Take up your spears, throw your shields before you. We will go against this beast, let him who will stay behind.**
DIARMUID	**Go against the boar, but it shall be as if you hunted the sea or the wind. Your spear**^*s*^ **shall break, and your hounds fly and whimper at your heels (Exeunt all except GRANIA, CORMAC and DIARMUID – After a moment's pause a horn is heard in the distance – DIARMUID takes a spear from the wall.)**
GRANIA	**Why do you take this spear – You will not go to this hunt ?**
DIARMUID	**This beast came to slay us. This hunt will sweep over us. It is coming through the woods, and I shall be caught up like a leaf – ~~We must bar the door~~ (They bar the door and stand listening.)**
GRANIA	**They said the boar ran into the woods – It will have**

29ʳ, l. 16 The cancellation is in pencil.

[HRC(2)]

[30r]

–28–

gone into the mountain before this.

DIARMUID. **The things to come are like the wind; they could**
This is coming like the wind
sweep this house away. ~~but this~~ image of my death ^
heard of ~~I was a~~
~~which I have~~^~~seen since a lit^tle child~~ – who knows what enchantment has called it out of the earth ? It was not here yesterday; it was not here at noon. I have hunted deer in these woods and have not seen the slot of natural or unnatural swine – No, it will not bear thinking of. I am caught in the valley like a wolf in a pit. (Pause.) CORMAC, you sit there like a stone, why did you do this ? You came here with a tale about the men of Lochlann. ~~You thought~~,
{B
~~like another, you were doing your own work~~. {but you were doing the gods' work.

[31r]

–29–

CORMAC **DIARMUID, I gave you this valley to be happy in.**

DIARMUID **When we are about to die the gods give us more than** we ask **~~we can eat and drink~~. There has been too much happiness here for our hunger, and I would roll up the broken meats in a sack for you to carry them away.**

GRANIA **This tale has shaken your mind.**

DIARMUID **Then you do not believe in it.**

GRANIA **We believe, and we disbelieve, and there is a time when we do not know what we think.**

We are always on the Gods' business.
DIARMUID **~~Are we not always doing the gods' work~~. CORMAC in his craftiness – you in your lust; and the gods put lust into women's bodies that men may not defy the gods**
made
who ~~are under~~ ^ them – and I shall do their work in this

hunting.

GRANIA You are not going to this hunting.

DIARMUID I see many ornaments upon you – How long is it since you have worn them for me ? You have not worn them – we are common t one another day & night.

GRANIA My life is broken.

DIARMUID Like the ice on a river when a new season has begun.

[32r]

–30–

GRANIA Take Broad Edge, your heavy spear, take your heavy shield.

DIARMUID No man shall say DIARMUID went to this hunting with his battle gear upon him – (Exit.)

GRANIA He is gone to this hunting. . . he is gone that he may give me to FINN – (She turns her face towards the wall and weeps.)

CORMAC Have you ceased to love him ? (GRANIA walks a few xteps towards her father as if she were going to speak but her emotion overpowers her and she returns to the same place.) If you hav e not ceased to love him follow him and bring him back.

GRANIA I will follow him in the woods; he will take the path under the oak trees. (Exit GRANIA.)

CORMAC (Coming down the stage) LABAN, LABAN, (He goes to-wards the wheel, and takes the spindle in his hand) There is no more flax on the spindle – LABAN, LABAN ! (Going to the door at the side) They have all followed the hunters – There is nobody in the house – But LABAN must be about – LABAN , LABAN. (Exit and curtain.) *copy*

31r, ll. 18–19 The cancellation is in pencil.

32r, l. 12 The word "*copy*" at the RH of the line appears to be in the same hand as on fols. 11r, 14r, 28r, above.

[NLI 8777(3) b, 37r]

/

Scene. Diarmid's house. A spinning wheel to left. Walls made of roughly hewed timber. Laban sitting before the spinning wheel. The twilight is slowly deepening. Cormac enters.

Cormac.

Every kind of sorrow has come upon this land: the Fianna ~~those who should be our brothers~~ are divided and the galleys of our ~~watch fires of our~~ enemies are drawn up ~~upon~~ upon the shore. ~~fly from headland to headland~~. Our kingdom will be over-run by the Lochlanders ~~invaders~~ and the hunting of Diarmid and Grania ~~will~~ begin again.

Laban.

Have your long talks with Diarmid come to no better end than that?

Cormac.

I talked with Diarmid late into the night and I could not persuade him. Old woman who has spoken nothing but lies, I told him that the Kingdom I had given him would be taken from him, and that I could not save him from Finn, or Erie from the invader.

Laban.

I heard your voices but I did not hear Grania's voice.

Cormac.

He said "Tell Finn to begone from my valley," "let the sod be blown into flame again and the pursuit of Diarmid and

Typescript of Complete Act, Revised by W. B. Yeats and George Moore—W. B. Yeats's Copy?

[NLI 8777(3) b, 37r]

1

**<u>Scene. Diarmuid's house, A spinning wheel to left</u>.
<u>Walls made of roughly hewed timber. Laban sitting before</u>
<u>The spinning wheel. The twilight is slowly deepening.</u>
<u>Cormac enters</u>.**

Cormac.

the ~~fi~~
Every kind of sorrow has come upon this land: ~~those who~~
Feanna ~~and~~ the galleys of ~~its~~ *our*
~~should be as brothers~~ are divided and ~~watch fires of^our^enemies~~
are drawn up ~~upt~~ upon the shore.
~~fly from headland^to headland~~. Our kingdom will be over-run
Loch landers
by the ~~inva^ders~~ and the hunting of Diarmid and Grania ~~will~~ begin again.

Laban.

Have your long talks with Diarmid come to no better end than that?

Cormac.

I talked with Diarmid late into the night and I could not persuade him. Old woman who has spoken nothing but lies, I told him that the Kingdom I had given him would be taken from him, and that I could not save him from Finn, or Erie from the invader.

Laban.

I heard your voices but I did not hear Grania's voice.

Cormac.

He said, "Tell Finn to begone from my valley," "let the sod be blown into flame again and the pursuit of Diarmid and

-1 The numbering is throughout in a firmer hand and blacker lead than the other pencil corrections in this act.
4 "Will" is canceled in pencil.

NLI 8777(3) b]

[38^{r}]

2

Grania begin again."

Laban.

And Grania stood by the door post watching the moon shining down the valley: looking to where Diarmid's cattle were feeding, and towards the encampment of Finn.

Cormac.

Yes she stood there saying nothing. I turned to her often saying "If I take this message to Finn you will have to fly to the woods again."

Laban.

And she answered nothing?

Cormac.

Only this – "where will Laban go if we are driven from this valley?" She said "Father you brought her here to be near me and if we are driven into the woods you will see that no harm comes to her." But remember how near the Fianna were to hanging you from a rafter that night at Tara, and if I bring Diarmid's message to Finn I may not know how to save you from them.

[39^{r}]

3

They did ~~dare~~ [?~~to~~] not dare. **Laban.**

The rope fell out of Gall's hand; and Conan told them ~~that~~ they could not hang me but with a rope that I had spun, and they

make

tried to ~~tempt~~ me ~~to~~ spin one ~~for them~~.

Cormac.

Yes, yes but Finn has waited for three days. This sunset ~~is the~~ end s **~~of~~ the third day (going to the door). The horses are waiting and Niall is at their heads. Speak if you have found any meaning in the thread.**

Laban.

The thread keeps breaking as it runs from the spindle.

Cormac

Then the end of somebody is ^near ~~by~~: the end of Diarmid or of Grania or of Finn – or the end of Erie. You must tell me before I go for I cannot wait any longer.

Laban.

It may be a long while before I can tell you anything. You must wait until the flax runs unbroken from the spindle. Words will be put into my mouth.

Cormac.

Then spin, then spin.

[40r]

4

Laban.

The thread is breaking, I cannot find a whole thread in the flax.

Cormac.

You have lied to me old woman. You brought me this long way that you might be near Grania. (<u>She gets up from the wheel. Cormac puts her back again</u>) But spin since there is flax in the spindle, the earth knows all things and the flax comes out of the earth. So spin while there is yet time.

Laban.

What would you know? If there be forgiveness in Finn's heart?

Cormac.

The men of Lochlann have dragged up 70 galleys on to the beach of Rury.

Laban.

You are troubled being afraid that Caoilte and Usheen may not fight against the men of Lochlann because they are angry

---

39r, l. 5 The style of cancellation is GM's and the revision is in a paler shade of blue-black ink than that of WBY's pen.

NLI 8777(3) b]

are afraid begin the hunting of
with Finn. You ~~fear~~ ^ that Finn may ~~urge the Lochlanders to~~ ~~pursue~~
again are afraid
?18 **Diarmid and Grania? ^ You ~~fear~~ ^ that Diarmid and Grania -------**

[41r]

5

Cormac

Old woman, full of wisdom about everything but the danger that waits us, I have to carry Diarmid's answer to Finn and I would know what will happen to Diarmid and to my daughter. You sit silent. Will you not answer me? (<u>a long pause</u>. <u>The king walks up the stage slowly and when he turns Laban rises from the wheel</u>.)

Laban

I see Diarmid standing by Finn and his hand is on Finn's shoulder.

Cormac.

Then they are friends.

Laban.

I see Diarmid drawing his sword.

Cormac.

Against whom,Laban? And then -----

Laban.

I can see Finn drawing his dagger.

Cormac.

His dagger – his sword – look again.

40r, l. 13 The second cancellation line is in pencil.

13–14 The ink insertions are in a paler shade of blue-black ink, like other of GM's interventions, although the character formation bears some resemblance to WBY's.

14 The meaning of the marginal annotation is obscure—unless what appears to be a numeral is a scribbled line, simply drawing attention to a passage to be revised. Cf. the marginal pencil marks on fols. 47r and 55r below.

[42^{r}]

6

Laban.

It is a dagger that I see.

Cormac.

Now wind the thread round the forefinger tightly. Now hold the thread tightly and look for the earth knows all and her knowledge is in the flax.

Laban.

The vision has passed from me, I see nothing else.

Cormac.

Spin again, spin another thread.

Laban.

I cannot see more than ~~one~~ once**, and the thread is broken again – you have broken it.**

Cormac.

Then is ill luck in my hands. If the thread had not broken we should know all. You say you saw Finn pull out his dagger, but was not Diarmid standing by his side with his hand on Finn's shoulder? What is the meaning of this? If you do not tell me I will have you beaten and your wheel thrown into the lake. (Enter Grania.)

Grania.

[43^{r}]

7

Grania.

Ah! my father she can tell you nothing if you speak so loud.

Cormac.

She has told me strange things, things without meaning.

Grania.

You never believe her words, father, when she speaks them,

42^{r}, l. 7 The caret was canceled by erasure.

but afterwards you find that she had spoken truly.

Cormac.

True or false it matters not since they do not help me. where is Diarmid? It is time that I were gone. I have not seen him all day. Does he speak to-day as he spoke last night?

Grania.

He has said nothing to me and I would not speak to him of Finn. Nearly a day and night have gone since you have spoken to him. His mind may have changed. (Going up the stage.) This is the hour when the flock comes home, Diarmid has forgotten us all, he is thinking of the folding of his sheep. You will find him with the shepherd, or shall I send Laban to bring him? (Laban gets up and goes out.) The fold is not far from the house, it was brought nearer for the wolves carried off three of our sheep last week . . . . Ah, I see him coming up the path, Laban is going to meet him. (Grania comes down the stage

[44r]

8

to Cormac) But dear father, three days are not a long while to see you in after 7 years. You will come here again and forget the troubles that knigdoms bring. You are lonely at Tara. I used to sing for you. Shall I come to Tara and sing for you again?

Cormac.

Our troubles grow greater as we grow older, and it may be that your singing could not ma~~l~~ke me forget my troubles now. These last troubles seem the worst. I have persuaded Finn to make peace and I have brought him here , . . . But we go~~n~~ on saying this one thing again and again.

Grania.

~~We have fled for seven years through north and south and east and west.~~ How will it all end?

Cormac.

Finn has hunted you for seven years, he did not cease till the Fionna had deserted him.

44r, l. 9 The correction is ink over pencil.

Grania.

Do not pity me because of those years. The blood beats in my veins when I think of them.

[45^{r}]

9

Cormac.

There is a fire in your eyes and your eyes were lighted like this when you poured out the enchanted ale at Tara.

Grania.

Seven years among the woods should have quenched those fires.

Cormac.

What your heart was set on you would always have, you would always get it somehow. What other woman in Erie would have gone into the woods with a man she had never seen before.

Grania.

I think I had seen him many times.. I saw him once on a hill when I stood looking into the mist.

Cormac.

Never did men sleep as we slept that night over our ale.
We woke
We sat at that table like stones till the cock crew. **~~The~~**
togeather at the
^ **crowing of the clock ~~woke us together~~ and Finn cried out ~~"I have~~**
{a
~~dreamt that the Fionna are divided that~~ " **Grani{o has been taken from me."**

[46^{r}]

10

Grania.

I thought that Finn did not love me, that you had made the marriage that you might be stronger than any other king or than any invader.

Cormac.

Ah, Grania, you have your mother's eyes. Your mother was very beautiful,Grania.

Grania.

I thought of nothing but this – that a man should love me among the woods, far away among the woods.

Cormac.

And Diarmid has loved this fair face very dearly.

Grania.

But in this valley love has become terrible and we are sometimes afraid of one another. And now I would have Diarmid arm the shepherds and lead them against the Lochlanders and drive them into their galleys.

Cormac.

If you think like this why did you stand looking down the valley and saying nothing? Diarmid asked you, and I asked you.

Grania.

If I had said "yes" to you I should have said "no" to

[47r]

11

Diarmid. I would say nothing but leave things to work out whatever will may be in them.

(Enter Niall and the King's councillors. Councillors stand in the background. Niall advances.)

Cormac.

Yes, Niall, I have delayed too long.

Grania.

(Going to Niall.) You are going away now, Niall, and I have had little time to speak with you and I would have spoken to you about the days at Tara, when you were my only play-fellow. How well I remember going with you, one spring morning to a littl pool at the edge of the wood. We sat on the high bank fishing

---

47r, ll. 7–13+ The loosely scribbled cancellation is in pencil.

for roach. Have you forgotten?

Niall.

No, Princess, I have not forgotten. That same day I showed you a blackbird sitting on her nest. You had never seen a bird sitting on her nest before. But many things have happened since then; you know the woodland now better than I.

Grania.

Shall I ever see Tara again? ~~I have wandered a long way~~. *?*

[48^{r}]

12

Cormac.

Five days' journey from here, Grania. We must hurry. Neither Niall not I can keep the saddle for many hours at a time; Diarmid's cattle are coming this way and their sides are heavy with the rich grass of the valley I have given you, and the rooks are flying home.

(Enter Diarmuid.)

Cormac.

I shall be with Finn in half an hour and I would not say to him the words you bade me say last night. Do not send me to the man you wronged with the words you spoke last night.

Diarmid.

Tell him to be gone out of my valley.

Cormac.

Then farewell, dear daughter.

Grania.

Father stay with us, Diarmid do you not hear? Do you not understand?

Cormac.

Diarmid knows how great Finn's anger will be when I bring him this answer.

47^{r}, l. 14 The ink cancellations of each word (GM's?) are over a faint, continuous pencil cancellation, made at the same time as the pencil query.

NLI 8777(3) b]

[49r]

13

Diarmid.

I have fought Finn and overthrown him. Did I not break out of the house with the seven doors when he had set a watch at all the doors? I went out of the door where he himself held the watch and my sword struck the sword out of his hand. .

Cormac.

If you will send me with this answer so be it – I can say no more – Farewell to all here.

(Exeunt Cormac Neill and Councillors.)

Diarmid.

We thought we should weary of the silence of this valley but it is of their voices that we weary. Why should we listen to anything except one another. But they are gone at last, and care is gone with them and we are alone again with ourselves and our flocks and herds. Come to the door Grania and see my black bull in the meadow. ~~His pace is like a wave's~~. (Coming down the stage to her) Do you not believe that care is gone with them?

Grania.

You saw my father's face as he went out. His look has put a deep care into my heart.

[50r]

14

Diarmid.

These northern raiders will not dare to move from their galleys, they will soon sail away and should we give up our happiness because we fear they may carry off a few score of cattle.

Grania.

Let it be as you wish it Diarmid.

49r, l. 12 The ink cancellations (GM's?) are over faint pencil.

Diarmid.

But oath upon oath is broken. I broke my oath to Finn and now I break the oath which binds me to take up arms against all invaders. Grania, ~~you are weary of this valley~~; you would ~~like to~~ see Tara again. You would see Finn again.

Grania.

I gave up Tara for your sake Diarmid and that was easier than to live in this little valley.

Diarmid.

Ah you are weary of this valley.
But **Finn and I are divided, Grania, as by the sea and if the peace your father has made between us is not to be broken Finn must leave my valley. It is for your sake Grania, that he would have me among his Fionna again.**

[51r]

15

Grania.

He has not seen me for seven years.

Diarmid.

To see you once is enough, Grania.

Grania.

I think that it is for Eiri's sake he would have you among the Fianna again. He does not think of women. Why should a woman think of him? Have I not loved you for seven years Diarmid? And my father has told you that Finn is bound by an oath and that he has said "Diarmid has her love let him keep her".

Diarmid.

He will not break his oath but he will find some way out of it. There is always treachery behind his peace-making.

Grania.

He made peace with Gall and that peace is still unbroken. Yet it was Gall's father who plundered Finn's country and murdered his people.

50r, l. 9 The cancellation is in pencil.

NLI 8777(3) b]

Diarmid.

Gall does Finn's bidding although he might be chief man himself. But Finn has not forgiven, Usheen saw a look in his eyes at Tara.

[52r]

16

Grania.

Ah, how well you remember. That was seven years ago.

Diarmid.

And when I am dead it will be Gall's turn.

Grania.

Unhappy brooding man you will neither believe in Finn's oath nor in my love.

Diarmid.

Here we have everything we sought for. But in return for this kingdom you father would have me among the Fianna again. I thought we should live and die here, I thought our children would grow up about us here, if the gods accept my offering and give us children. (He goes up the stage.) Come look at the sleepy evening. These evenings are better than the even-ings of battle long ago, and were I among my old companions again, Usheen, Gall, Caoelte, I should look back upon these quiet evenings when the flock came home and you gave me my supper in the dusk (comesdown the stage). If I were to die, Grania, would you be Finn's wife?

Grania.

How did such a thought come into your mind?

[53r]

17

Diarmid.

My life began with you and it ends with you. Oh, that these breasts should belong to another, and the ~~sacred~~ usage of this body. Life of my life I knew you before I was born, I made a bargain with this brown hair before the beginning to time and it shall not be broken through unending time. And yet I shall sit alone upon that shore that is beyond the world – though all the gods are there the shore shall be empty because one is not there and I shall weep remembering how we wandered among the woods. But you say nothing, Grania. You are weary of the shadows of these mountains and of the smell of the fold. It is many days since you came to my bed and it is many weeks since I have seen an ornament upon you. Your love is slipping from me, it slips away like water in the brook! You do not answer. These silences make me afraid.

Grania.

Then Diarmid go to your old companions.

Diarmid.

My old companions? What shall I say to them?

Grania.

You will fight shoulder to shoulder with Finn and Caoelte. You will listen to Usheen's harp playing and I shall love you

NLI 8777(3) b]

[54r]

18

better when you come to me with the reek of battle upon you.

Diarmid.

We shall be again what we were to one another. You are not that Grania I wandered with among the woods.

Grania.

You are no longer that Diarmid who overthrew Finn at the house of the seven doors.

Diarmid.

You speak the truth, Grania. I should have gone to the Fianna. Now it is too late.

Grania.

Cormac cannot have reached the Ford, and you will overtake him. (she goes to her chest and takes out an ornament.)

Diarmid.

Who is the shepherd, Grania? I have never seen him before. Where has he come from?

Grania.

What shepherd do you speak of?

Diarmid.

There, there in the door way.

[55r]

19

Grania.

There is nobody there.

Diarmid.

He beckons me – I must follow – (<u>He goes towards the door)</u> I see him no longer. A mist must have come in my eyes. I see clearer now and there is no one. But I must follow.

Grania.

Whom would you follow?

Diarmid.

I see no one now and yet there was a sudden darkening of
carrying a hazel stick
the light and a shepherd ~~in a grey skin with the ears of a hare~~ *X*
~~upon his cap~~ came into the doorway and beckoned me. ~~He is waiting~~.

Grania.

No, Diarmid nobody has come into that doorway.

Diarmid.

Nobody came for you, but one came for me. Let me go,Grania

Grania.

No, no it is a warning that you must not go.

Diarmid.

den
That is not how I understand the warning. I am bid to
^

55r, ll. 7–8 The ink cancellations of each word in these two lines (GM's?) are over a faint, continuous pencil cancellation, the partial erasure of which smudged the type characters, that was made at the same time as the pencil cross still visible in the RH margin of line 7.

20

Grania
Gr. and ~~just~~ before he left me he saw a shepherd
where there was no body
Laban—
a shepherd with a dried hazel stick.

leave this valley. He beckoned me. I am bidden to the Fianna (They go out. Enter Laban who sits down at her wheel and begins to spin. Grania enters shortly after, she stands at the door looking after Diarmid.)

Grania.

He is like one whose mind is shaken. His thoughts are far away and I do not know what they are,

Laban.

He is brooding over that story Conan told him at Tara — it has been in his mind all day.

Grania.

~~Mother he had forgotten that story. It is the silence of this valley that has brought it into his mind again.~~ It is better that he should live among his old companions. He talks one moment of Finn's crookedness; and at another of my love as if it were waning . . . In a few minutes Diarmid and Finn will meet.

Laban.

In a few minutes Finn will stand with his hand on Diarmid's shoulder.

[NLI 8777(3) b, 56r]

20

Grania

~~D~~ and ~~just~~ before he left me he saw a shepherd where there was no body

Laban –

A shepherd with a druid hazel stick.

I am bidden to the Fianna

leave this valley. He beckoned me.^ (<u>They go out. Enter Laban who sits down at her wheel and begins to spin. Grania enters shortly after, she stands at the door looking after Diarmid</u>.)

Grania.

He is like one whose mind is shaken. His thoughts are far away and I do not know what they are,

Laban.

He is brooding over that story Conan told him at Tara – it has been in his mind all day.

Grania.

Mother he had forgotten that story. It is the silence of this valley that has brought it into his mind again. It is better that he should live among his old companions. He talks one moment of Finn's crookedness; and at another of my love as if it were waning . . . In a few minutes Diarmid and Finn will meet.

Laban.

In a few minutes Finn will stand with his hand on Diarmid's shoulder.

56r, ll. 6–7 The cancellation is in pencil.

NLI 8777(3) b]

[57r]

Grania.

Then I have done well in sending him to Finn. I did it for Diarmid's sake and for my father's sake and for the sake of my father's kingdom! I chose Diarmid because he was young

He has gone to bring

and comely, but oh, how can I forget the greatness of Finn ^ Finn to me.
In a few minutes Finn and his Fianna will stand under this roof.

Laban.

That is true,my daughter, sit beside m,e here and tell me what happened to you when you left Tara.

Grania.

When we left Tara we came to a little glade on the hill-side,and we heard there a sudden and a beautiful singing of birds, and we saw a red fox creeping in the grass.

Laban.

And then?

Grania

And then we saw a young man sitting in the long grass.

Laban.

What did he say?

Grania.

He was but a herdsman's son seeking a master, and so

[58r]

22

Diarmid took him into his service and yet, Mother, I think that he was greater than Diarmid or I, for he gave us such good service, and so much good counsel. He never put us into a cave that had not two mouths, or let us take refuge in an island that had not two harbours, nor eat our food where we had cooked it, nor sleep where we had eaten it. He never let us lie for many hours in one place, and he often changed our sleeping places in the middle of the night.

Laban.

What name did he bid you call him?

Grania.

He bid us call him Mudham. But I think he had some great and beautiful name did we but know it. Have you ever seen him, Mother?

Laban,

It has been said that none who have seen him have been long content with any mortal lover.

Grania.

I have been content with Diarmid nigh on seven years.

[NLI 8777(3) b, 59r]

23

Laban.

Did you ever hear that beautiful singing of birds again?

Grania.

Yes, I heard them sing by the banks of a river; I heard them when Diarmid broke his oath to Finn, We had wandered by the banks of a river nine days, and Mudham fished for us, and every day we hung an ~~uncooked~~ salmon on a tree as a token to Finn. On the tenth day we hung a cooked salmon, for on the ninth night the sword had ~~not lain~~ between us - But, Mother, I can tell you no more. I would have you tell me, you who know all things, what is passing in the valley. Have Finn and Diarmid made friends? Has Diarmid passed the fires of the Fianna without speaking?

Laban.

They have spoken, they are on their way hither, so forget them for a while, and tell me if you are happy in this valley.

Grania.

I stand by the door of this house, seeing the hours ~~wane~~ pass, waiting for Diarmid to come home from his hunting. Nothing has happened until to-day and now Diarmid and Finn are walking up the valley together, reconciled at last. I had come to think I should never look on a stirring day again, and I had thought to send all the thread you would spin to be woven into

[NLI 8777(3) b, 59^{r}]

23

the samon we hung up had been
laid on the fire

Laban.

Did you ever hear that beautiful singing of birds again?

Grania.

Yes, I heard them sing by the banks of a river; I heard
them when Diarmid broke his oath to Finn, We had wandered by
the banks of a river nine days, and Mudham fished for us, and
? a raw or fresh –
every day we hung ~~an uncooked~~ salmon on a tree as a token to
that had bee laid on the fire
Finn. On the tenth day we hung a ~~cooked~~ salmon, ^ for on the
there had been no
ninth night ~~the~~ ^ sword ~~had not lain~~ between us – But, Mother,
I can tell you no more. I would have you tell me, you who
know all things, what is passing in the valley. Have Finn
and Diarmid made friends? Has Diarmid passed the fires of
the Fianna without speaking?

Laban.

They have spoken, they are on their way hither, so forget
them for a while, and tell me if you are happy in this valley.

Grania.

pass
I stand by the door of this house, seeing the hours ~~wane~~,
waiting for Diarmid to come home from his hunting. Nothing
has happened until to-day and now Diarmid and Finn are walking
up the valley together, reconciled at last. I had come to
think I should never look on a stirring day again, and I had
thought to send all the thread you would spin to be woven into

NLI 8777(3) b]

[60ʳ]

24

a grass-green web on which to embroider my wanderings with Diarmid among the woods, I should have been many years embroidering it, but when it was done and hung round this room I should have seen birds beasts and leaves which ever way I turned and Diarmid and myself wandering among them.

Laban.

But now you have thrown the doors wide open and the days are streaming in upon you again.

Grania.

Yes, yes, have I done rightly? Had I not sent Diarmid to Finn the broil would have begunagain . . . . I must put on my jewels. The Fianna will be here in a moment, and Finn has never seen me in my jewels. Spin for me, Mother, spin for me: tell me I have done rightly. But no, they are coming, I can hear their footsteps. Go to the serving men and bid them take the drinking horns and the flagons from the cupboard. (Exit Laban, Grania stands before a long brazen mirror that hangs upon the wall, and puts the gold circlet about her head and the heavy bracelets upon her arm, and the great many-coloured cloak
her
upon which she fastens with an emerald clasp–she puts a gold girdle about her waist – Enter Cormac, Finn, Caoelte, Diarmid,
& others of the Fianna
~~etc.,~~ – Diarmid is talking to Finn,– Enter servant with flagons

[61ʳ]

25

of ale, drinking horns, and torches) Welcome, Usheen, welcome Caoelte, welcome Goll and all the noble Fianna into my house. I am happy that such men should stand under my roof. The shepherds of Ben Bulben will tell each other many years after we are dead that Finn, Usheen, Caoelte, and Goll stood under this roof. (Grania goes to her father and leads him to a high seat.) You cannot go from us now, for I am too glad for leave taking.

Cormac.

I will stay a little while, and will drink a horn of ale

with this noble company who will defend Eri against the men of Lochland, ~~and if they should come to our coasts again~~.

Diarmid.

We have been here but three moons and have not had time to build a house great enough for ourselves and for our people. This winter we shall build a house of oak wood great enough for two hundred people to sleep under its pillars. All the Fianna who ~~shall~~ come shall sleep under our roof.

Grania.

When you speak of their coming you make us think of their leave-taking, and I would forget that they shall ever leave us.

Cormac.

Eri is safe now that her great men are united.

[62r]

26

Caoelte.

For a long while when we lighted our fires at night there was no fire at which some did not side with Finn some with Diarmid – But at last those that were of Finn's party, and those that were of Diarmid's party gathered about ~~the~~ different fires. And this year the fires were lighted far apart.

Usheen

And time wore on until one day the swords were out and the earth red under foot.

Finn.

If all Eri were red under foot, it was but Grania's due that men in coming times might know of the love she had put into men's hearts (He puts his hand on Diarmid's shoulder – Two serving men go round with ale, Grania stops them and takes the flagons from them.)

61r, l. 11 "and" is a type cancellation; the ink cancellations of the following word are over a faint, continuous pencil cancellation.

16 The deletion is in pencil.

62r, l. 4 The word is canceled in pencil.

NLI 8777(3) b]

Grania

It is right that I should serve the ale on such a day as this.

Cormac

My daughter must not pour out the ale

~~**Cormac.**~~ *Usheen*

If Grania pours out the ale we shall ~~all~~ sleep sound to-night.

[63r]

27

Cormac.

You have spoken folly Usheen – I,I spoke out of a dream. Grania since you have taken the flagons from your serving men serve us. But I would you had not done this. (Grania goes round filling each one's horn with ale – Diarmid and Finn are still standing together on the right – she pauses, considering for an instant, and then fills Finn's horn.)

Caoclte.

Diarmid, we have not spoken to you nor seen you these seven years.

Goll

Have you no word for us?

Usheen.

We would drink with you (Diarmid goes up the stage and joins the group who are standing half way up the stage, near to where the king is sitting.)

Grania.

In this ale you will not drink sleep but you will drink forgetfulness of me, and friendship for Diarmid.

Finn.

Had I known that you would speak like this I would not have come to your house.

62r, l. 13 Type deletion.

[64^r]

28

Grania.

1 **But you have come here for this.**

Usheen.

2 **It is not enough for Finn and Diarmid to drink together,**
3 **they must be bound together by the blood-bond. They must be**
4 **made brothers before the gods – They must be bound together.**

Caoelte

5 **Yes, yes, one of you there by the door – you Finmole –**
6 **cut a sod of Grass with your sword. They must be bound toge-**
7 **ther.**

Diarmid.

As he comes he draws his sword.
8 **(~~Coming~~ down the stage.) ~~Take out your dagger~~, Finn.**
d
9 **Draw blood out of your hand as I draw blood out of mine. (Finn pricks his hand with his dagger and goes towards Diarmid and lets blood from his hand drop into Diarmid's cup. Diarmid lets the blood from his hand drop into the cup also. He gives the cup to Finn.) Speak the holy words Finn.**

Finn.
(Having drunk out of the cup)

10 **This bond has bound us**
11 **like brother to brother**

[65^r]

29

1 **Like son to father**
2 **Let him who breaks it**
3 **Be driven from the thresholds.**
4 **Of God-kind and man-kind.**

64^r, l. 8 The cancellations and insertions are made over pencil revisions, which have been largely erased; hence the two pencil carets (the second canceled). One can only say that the pencil revisions were not quite identical with the final revisions.

9 Ink over pencil.

NLI 8777(3) b]

(Diarmid takes the cup and drinks)

Diarmid

Let the sea bear witness,
Let the wind bear witness,
Let the earth bear witness,
Let the fire bear witness,
Let the dew bear witness,
Let the stars bear witness,

(Finn takes the cup and drinks)

Finn

Six that are deathless
Six holy creatures,
Have witnessed the binding.

(A sod of grass is handed in through the door and from man to man till it comes to Usheen and Caoelte who holds it up one on each side. First Finn and then Diarmid passunder it.

Caoelte

They are of one blood

[66ʳ]

30

Usheen

They have been born again out of the womb of earth.

Caoelte

Give back the sod to the ground. Give the holy sod to the Goddess. (The Fianna pass the sod from one to another and out through the door, each one speaking these words over it in a monotonous and half audible muttering "Blessed is the Goddess. May the ground be blessed.")

Goll.

This bond has shown that Finn can forgive. It has been said falsely that he never forgives although he has forgiven me. (Finn turns to Goll effusively.)

65ʳ, l. 13⁺ The correction of "holds" is in pencil.

Cormac.

Now my errand is done and I shall bid Grania and Diarmid and all this goodly company farewell. (He rises but lingers talking with certain of his councillors.)

Diarmid.

I have done this though you have followed me and hunted through the woods of Eri for seven years.

[67ʳ]

31

Finn.

I forgave because we had need of you, Diarmid. (Turning away) Although you left the Fianna for a woman.

Diarmid

Grania pour out the ale for Finn.

Finn.

It is right for a man to have a time for love but now you are with your old companions again.

Diarmid.

I did not accept the peace you offered me at once , because I had taken Grania from you.

Finn.

(Looking at Grania) It seems a long while ago, Grania, you should have been my wife seven years ago.

Grania

Then it was not for me that you followed Diarmid so many years. Why did you follow him? What reason could you have had , if it all seems so long ago.

[68ʳ]

32

Finn.

Our marriage was to have mended an old crack ~~that it~~ in the land. It was to have joined the Fianna to the high king

68ʳ, l. 1 Pencil cancellations.

for ever, But it was not for this marriage sage that I followed Diarmid. I followed him because he had broken his oath.

Diarmid

I shall make atonement for the breaking of my oath with
head
herds
fifty ~~hers~~ ^ of cattle and I will give you my black bull. Come to the door, and you will see him in the valley. He is grazing on the edge of the herd and you will see what a noble stride
[~~—?—~~]
he has. But who is this with ~~the two~~, ~~the~~ Fianna this fat man
[~~-?-~~]
two of the
in a sheep skin. It is my enemy Conan. I shall be glad to drink a horn of ale with him to the forgetfulness of all enimity (to the others) I have not seen you for seven years and seven
D
years have changed some here a little. I would drink with every one of you. I would that you had but a single hand that I might hold it this day – this happy day. (Enter Conan with
Creffan & Fergus
~~two of the Fianna~~ and a shepherd.)

Conan.

only
Keep your spears in your hands! We are ~~inly~~ just in time – a great beast – come – come – we will be in front ^ of him before he can run into the wood. (Exeunt Conan and all the Fianna except Finn.~~)~~ *~~& Diarmid~~)*

[69r]

33

Diarmid.

I thought I had driven off the last of the wolves. (Diarmid goes out. There are only Cormac, Finn, Grania and the Shepherd on the stage.)

68r, l. 6 "herds" is written over pencil, and a pencil caret has been partly erased beneath.
9 The indecipherable insertion above the line is in pencil; there is also pencil writing under the deleted "the".

Shepherd.

He He
~~It~~ is not a wolf! ~~It~~ is not a wolf! He has gored twenty of my sheep. He broke out by the stepping stones. (<u>He goes out.</u>)

Grania

The shepherd said it was not a wolf. Ask him.

Finn

He said it has gored twenty of his sheep. It must be the Boar that I heard of as I came hither. It has come out of a dark wood to the east ward – A wood men are afraid of.

Grania

Then Diarmid must not go to this hunting. I will call him (<u>she goes to the door</u>) He is standing on the hillside. He is coming towards us. That is well. (<u>coming down the stage to Finn</u>) So it was not for my sake that you followed Diarmid. This flight and this pursuit for sevenyears were for no better reason than the breaking of an oath.

~~**Finn.**~~

~~I followed Diarmid because I hated him.~~

[70r]

34

Finn.

I followed ~~him~~ Diarmid because I hated him.

Grania

But now you have forgiven him. You are friends again. Yes, Finn, I would have you friends but my wish can be nothing to you. I was proud to think you followed Diarmid for me, but you said it was to avenge the breaking of an oath.
a
This is man's broil. No woman has part in it.

Finn

Cormac told me that it was you who persuaded Diarmid to

69r, l. 2 The second substitution is ink over pencil.
14 (and previous part ascription) The cancellation is ink over pencil.
70r, l. 1 Type deletion.

NLI 8777(3) b]

bring me to this house and but for this I would not have come.

Grania.

It was well that you came. Men who are so great as Finn and Diarmid must be friends. My Father fears a landing of the men of Lochlann, and I am weary of this valley where there is nothing but the rising and setting of the sun and the grazing of flocks and herds.

Finn.

Did you send for me because you are weary of this valley.

Grania.

I wanted to see you because of your greatness. I loved Diarmid – he was young and comely, and you seemed to me to be old, you were grey.

[71r]

35

Finn.

I am seven years older now, and my hair is greyer – I must seem very old to you now.

Grania.

~~*Then*~~ *you looked older then. Now you look young.*

~~No, you seem younger~~, as you stand there as you lean upon your spear you seem ^ to me a young man. I do not think of your grey hair any longer.

Finn.

That day in Tara you would not wear your ornaments, but now you wear them.

(Diarmid comes slowly down the stage.)

Diarmid.

What have you to say to one another; what were you saying to Grania, Finn, I can see by Grania's face that she is but little pleased to see me again.

Grania.

Why do you say this? What has happened, Diarmid? That shepherd said the wolf had killed twenty sheep.

Diarmid.

There is no wolf in the thicket; they do not know what they are hunting.

[72^{r}]

36

(<u>Enter Conan)</u>

Diarmid.

No matter whether it be a wolf or a boar that is hiding there, I have come in to find you and Finn talking together. in a way that is not to my liking.

Finn.

Was it to watch me Diarmid that you came back again? And would you not have me speak to Grania? As you will then. (<u>Turning to Conan</u>) Conan is listening. What has he to say about this beast that has gored twenty sheep.

Conan.

And Diarmid has come back again because he saw it was a boar and not a wolf, and he remembered that day in Tara, when I told him he is to go out hunting a ~~bar~~ *boar* **and be killed by it, and Diarmid is to be torn by the tusks, he is to be bloody, his face shall be foul because it shall be bloody. I told him these things in Tara, and he remembers them, that is why he has not gone hunting.**

Diarmid.

~~Dinn~~ *Finn* **has contrived the trap for me, but I shall not fall into it. There can be no peace between Finn and me.**

[73^{r}]

37

Finn.

<u>(Who draws his sword)</u> By the drawing of his sword, Diarmid has broken the peace I gave him, and the sight of Grania has brought to mind the wrongs he has done me.

Grania.

To you Finn, I say that I would not have sent for you had I thought that the broil would begin again – To you, Diarmid, I say that I will speak to what man I please, that no man shall thwart me– Where is my father? (Turning suddenly towards them) No, I will not have you fight for me, forbid them father – (She goes to Cormac)

Diarmid.

Our swords shall decide between us, I shall slay you Finn.

Finn.

One of us two shall die. – (They draw their swords, and the Fianna rush between them.)

Goll.

Finn and Diarmid cannot fight – fling up their swords, thrust the spears between them. Has Finn forgotten the blood bond? He who raises his hand against the blood bond raises his hand against the gods.

[74r]

38

Conan.

(Coming towards them) If Finn and Diarmid cannot fight with one another let them hunt the boar, and lat Grania be given to him who kills it – Aonghus, who watches over lovers and hunters **shall decide between them – (Diarmid lifts his sword to strike Leaving her father Grania comes forward.)**

Grania.

He is not worthy enough for you to strike him – give me your sword.

Finn.

(Standing in front of Conan) No, Grania he shall not die, he has spoken the truth – Finn and Diarmid love the one woman.

Conan.

a once

~~It may be that a~~ tale I ~~once~~ told him has given him no

74r, l. 9 The first five words were canceled in pencil, and the first four canceled again in ink; "once" is also canceled in pencil and the ink "once" above it is written over a now-indecipherable pencil word.

stomach for the hunting of a boar.

Fergus
~~First Spearman~~.

This boar is bigger than any beast I ever saw.

Creffan
~~Second Spearman~~.

It is certainly no mortal beast.

Diarmid.

What was its colour, was it covered with bristles?

[75r]

39

Conan.

I saw it; it was black and bristles – (<u>He goes over and stands by Diarmid)</u> Finn, Caoelte, Usheen look at us; there is one terror in the heart of Diarmid and Conan.

Creffan
~~Second Spearman~~.

I saw it too, it was dark like the sea, and it made a noise like the sea in a storm.

Finn.

We listen to the idle tales of Spearmen – whatever the colour of the beast may be we shall slay it – (<u>The Fianna move up the stage)</u> Conan has spoken well. Diarmid has little stomach for this hunting. Why did he ask for the blood bond? It was

hand
[~~—?—~~]

not I who went to him – it was he who came to me with his ~~arm~~ ^ **pricked with his dagger. These are the only wounds he will dare. This blood bond keeps him from my sword and he speaks of an old tale that he may not go to the hunt – Diarmid is craven.**

Diarmid.

Finn lies; He knows why I will not go to this hunt. He seeks my death because he loves Grania.

75r, l. 10 "arm" is canceled in pencil and an erased word, traces of which are still visible, is written in pencil above it; hence the pencil caret.

Fergus
~~First Spearman~~.

If Diarmid does not go to this hunt Diarmid is craven.

[76r]

40

Creffan
~~Second Spearman~~.

Finn has said it, he is craven.

Caoelte.

to
Diarmid must not go ^ this hunt. You have done wickedly
and
this day, Conan ^ after your kind.

~~Third Spearman~~. Fathna

He has a hare's heart. The gods have given him a hare's heart.

Finn.

Take up your spears. We will go against this beast, let him who will stay behind.

Diarmid.

Go against the boar, but it shall be as if you hunted the sea or the wind. Your spears shall break, and your hounds fly and whimper at your heels – (<u>Exeunt all except Grania, Cormac and Diarmid – after a moment's pause a horn is heard in the distance – Diarmid takes a spear from the wall.)</u>

Grania.

your
Why do you take ~~this~~ ^ spear – you will not go to this hunt?

[77r]

41

Diarmid.

This beast came to slay us. This hunt will sweep over

76r, ll. 2, 3, 11 All three insertions are ink over pencil; hence the pencil caret in line 11.

us. It is coming through the woods, and I shall be caught up like a leaf. (They ~~stand~~ bar the door and stand listening.)

Grania.

They said the boar ran into the woods – it will have gone into the mountain before this.

Diarmid.

The things to come are like the wind; they could sweep this house away. This image of my death is coming like the wind – who knows what enchantment has called it out of the earth? It was not here yesterday; it was not here at noon. I have hunted deer in these woods and have not seen the slot of natural or unnatural swine – No it will not bear thinking of. I am caught in this valley like a wolf in a pit – (Pause) Cormac you sit there like a stone, why did you do this? You came here with a tale about the men of Lochland, but you were on the gods business.

Cormac.

I gave you this valley to be happy in.

[78r]

42

Diarmid.

When we are about to die the gods give us more than we ask. There has been too much happiness here for our hunger, and I would roll up the broken meats in a sack for you to carry them away.

Grania.

That tale has shaken yourr mind.

Diarmid.

Then you do not believe in it?

Grania.

We believe,we disbelieve, and there is a time when we do not what we think.

77r, l. 3 Type deletion.
12 The dash was probably underlined by mistake.
78r, l. 5 Type deletion.

NLI 8777(3) b]

Diarmid.

9 **We are always on the gods business. Cormac in craftiness–**
10 **you in lust; They put lust into women's bodies that men may**
their
11 **not defy the gods who made them – I too, shall be on ~~the gods~~**
12 **business in this hunting.**

Grania.

13 **You are not going to this hunting.**

[79r]

43

Diarmid.

1 **I see many ornaments upon you – How long is it since you**
2 **have worn them for me?– You have not worn them . . . .**
3 **we are common to one another day and night.**

Grania.

shield
4 **Take Broad Edge, your heavy spear – Take your heavy ~~spea~~**

Diarmid.

5 **No man shall say Diarmid went to this hunting with his**
6 **battle gear upon him. (Exit)**

Grania

7 **He is gone to this hunting . . . he is gone that he may**
8 **give me to Finn – (She turns her face towards the wall and weeps**

Cormac.

9 **Have you ceased to love him? (Grania walks a few steps**
towards her father as if she were going to speak but her emotion
10 **overpowers her, and she returns to the same place.) If you have**
11 **not ceased to love him follow him and bring him back.**

Grania.

12 **I will follow him in the woods; he will take the path**
13 **under the oak trees. (Exit Grania)**

79r, l. 4 Type deletion.

[80r]

44

Cormac.

(Coming down the stage) Laban. Laban, (He goes towards the wheel, and takes the spindle in his hand) There is no more flax on the spindle – Laban, Laban! (Going to the door at the side) They have all followed the hunters – there is nobody in the house – But Laban must be here – Laban,Laban! (Exit and curtain.)

Act III

[Berg(13), 1[r]]

-1-

ACT III.

Scene: the wooded slopes of Ben Culpin - DIARMUID discovered sleeping under a tree - Enter two peasants and an old and youn man.

What a storm! What a storm

OLD MAN The ~~wind is in the branches, letting them up and down,~~ and all the world's a-tossing.

YOUNG MAN Maybe you have seen wilder nights.

There has been no

OLD MAN ~~No~~ such night ~~has come~~ these fifty years, ~~and well for us, for we could not bear many such~~.

YOUNG MAN Did you see anything; did you see anything about in the air.

OLD MAN a Man sees much in his life; but ~~very~~ little to think on. Never before did I give a thought to yesterday, and now I am thinking how ~~I may~~ T forget it - a Wild night,

Interrupted Forty-one-Page Typescript of Complete Act, Extensively Revised by W. B. Yeats

[Berg(13), 1r]

–1–

ACT III.

Scene: the wooded slopes of Ben Gulpin – DIARMUID discovered sleeping under a tree – Enter two peasants and an old and young man.

What a storm! What a storm

OLD MAN ~~**The wind is in the branches, letting them up and down**~~**, and all the world's a-tossing.**

YOUNG MAN **Maybe you have seen wilder nights.**

There has been no

OLD MAN ~~**No**~~ ^ **such night** ~~**has come**~~ **these fifty years,** ~~**and well for us, for we could not bear many such**~~**.**

YOUNG MAN **Did you see anything; did you see anything about in the air.**

A

OLD MAN ^ **Man sees much in his life; but** ~~**very**~~ **little to think on. Never before did I give a thought to yesterday,**

to *a*

and now I am thinking how ~~**I may**~~ **forget it –** ^ **Wild night,**

Yeats & Moores Grania & Diarmd

The vertical cancellations on this and the following three pages are in the same light shade of blue-black ink that continues on the canceled sequence of pages in NLI 8777(10) a.

2 tossing] Inserted with a new (black) ribbon.

10 The "a" and caret are written with a different pencil and perhaps a different hand from WBY's corrections on the same page.

10+ The pencil title description is in AG's hand.

[Berg(13), 2r]

-2-

as ~~strange~~ a night as ever I heard tell of; many of the beasts of ~~the forests~~ broke out of their byres last night, and drowned themselves, ~~it is said, in the~~ lake ~~on the top of the mountain.~~

YOUNG MAN And a two-headed chicken was hatched ~~out last night~~.

OLD MAN Did you see it.

YOUNG MAN ~~They had burnt it fe~~ before I came, but I saw what I wished to see on the mountain side.

OLD MAN I ~~could see but~~ a grey figure ~~which came~~ at the rising of the moon, ~~driving the~~ beast that the Fianna are hunting ~~before him~~. (DIARMUID rouses himself up to listen)

YOUNG MAN And you heard what ~~the shepherd~~ saw ? ~~he who followed the tracks~~; they ~~grew~~ wider and wider apart going to-

[Berg(13), 2r]

Dairmid & Grania
(Wrong

–2–

wild
as ~~strange~~ a night as ever I heard tell of; many of
the b^easts ~~of the forests~~ broke out of their byres
I met a shepherd but now who said that fifty had
last night, and^drowned themselves, ~~it is said, in the~~ *in the*
lake ~~on the top of the mountain.~~
~~at Mauntian~~

last night
YOUNG MAN **And a two-headed chicken was hatched ~~out last night~~.**
at [?~~Moun~~] the house of [?Montain] the wood cutter –

OLD MAN **Did you see it.**

seen
YOUNG MAN **They had burnt it ~~fo~~ before I came, but I saw what** *I had*^
I wished to see on the mountain side.

Old Man. *What did you see.*

Young *saw a quaint* *ragged man*
~~OLD~~ MAN **I ~~could see^but~~ a grey^~~figure which came~~ at the rising**
& he drove this
of the moon,^~~driving the~~ beast that the Fianna are
he prodded before him with a spear.
hunting , ~~before him~~. (DIARMUID rouses himself up to
listen)

~~Old~~ *one eyed [?Callbrie]* *He cam up th slope*
~~YOUNG~~^MAN **And you heard what ~~the^shepherd~~ saw ? ~~he who followed~~**
foot marks grew *& wider*
~~the tracks~~; they ~~grew~~ wider and wider^apart going to-
was
befor th storn^up. He ~~follwd~~ had been trapping otters
& knew nothing of this hunting & so he must needs
follow I found out this beast is very

–1 The pencil description is in AG's hand.
7 Type deletion.

-3-

wards the heart of the woods where ~~nobody goes because of the gods and the~~ evil spirits.

OLD MAN Hush ! (He points to DIARMUID)

YOUNG MAN If we do not awaken him ~~the strange~~ beast sent out of heaven may come upon him sleeping.

OLD MAN Better do nothing, for if all that is said about ~~the~~ beast is true it is a god. ~~In all~~ strange and ~~exciting~~ ~~things the gods~~ descend upon the earth. Come away, ~~these are affairs~~ of the gods.

YOUNG MAN But ~~every~~ man should have his chance.

OLD MAN What manner of chance ~~may it be~~ if the gods ~~are in it~~? What are the misfortunes of such men to such as we. These great men ~~go about killing one another~~ and no one knows what it is all about. The seasons are none the

[Berg(13), 3r]

I found a [?*slot*] *on my threshold & I ~~lift up my foot~~*
think I will find my foot in him. What is his
[?*creat*]
chance of life – **–3–** *We* [?~~*have*~~] *gods themselves*
& some times we make them angry – Come away
there are
wards the heart of the woods where ~~nobody goes because~~
~~of the gods and the~~ evil spirits.

OLD MAN **Hush ! (He points to DIARMUID)**

this
YOUNG MAN **If we do not awaken him ~~the strange~~ beast sent out of**
heaven may come upon him sleeping.

OLD MAN **Better do nothing, for if all that is said about ~~the~~** *this*
at *troublous*
beast is true it is a god. ~~In all~~ strange and ~~exciting~~
times *they* *~~they come~~ in what shape pleases them*
~~things~~ ~~the gods~~ descend upon the earth{, . Come away,
this is the business
~~these are affairs~~ of the gods.
not hav Darmd
I would die with no chance of life
YOUNG MAN **~~But every man should~~ have his chance.**
can he have *strive against him*
OLD MAN **What manner of chance ~~may it be~~ if the gods ~~are in it~~?**
What are the misfortunes of such men to such as we.
put on fine clothes
These great men ~~go about killing one another and~~ no one
knows what it is all about. The seasons are none the

put on fine clothes.[?~~*I*~~] [?~~*tell*~~] *~~go here & there~~ on horse back*
or & make war one anothr a horse back, or ~~they~~ is swords out
& blood on the grass

[Berg(13), 4r]

-4-

better; the cows have no more milk in their udders than before (exeunt peasants).

DIARMUID ~~How they~~ croak - like ravens ~~scenting a carrion~~ - A man I am now, a carrion I may be before evening, and a god in heaven to-morrow. (Enter GRANIA)

GRANIA All this night I have not seen you; I have been wandering in the forest since the moon set.

DIARMUID What have you come for ?

GRANIA I ~~am~~ a'weary; give me time to ~~catch~~ my breath.

DIARMUID Your hair is down, and your hands are torn with brambles.

GRANIA Yes, look at my hands, and I am so weary, DIARMUID, I am so weary that I could lie down and die here, that mossy bank ~~will~~ do; lay me down there, DIARMUID. Oh, DIARMUID, I have come to beg you to ~~fore~~go ~~this~~ hunt.

[Berg(13), 4r]

I saw one but now & it is that puts ravens
int my head. I cannot think. I am a man
~~**4**~~
now & I may be ravens food befor night

better; the cows have no more milk in their udders
than before (exeunt peasants).

Croak *what does it mean*
DIARMUID ~~**How they**~~ **croak – like ravens** ~~**scenting a carrion**~~ **– A**
hears
When one ~~hear~~ ~~sees~~ a raven ovr ones left shouldr
~~**man I am now, a carrion I may be before evening**~~**, and**
a god in heaven to-morrow. (Enter GRANIA)

GRANIA **All this night ^I have^ not seen you; I have been wander**
ing in the forest since the moon set.

DIARMUID **What have you come for ?**

I was afraid &
have been musing *gain*
GRANIA ^**I** ~~**am a'weary**~~^**;** **Give me time to** ~~**catch**~~ **my breath.**

DIARMUID **Your hair is down, and your hands are torn with brambles.**

GRANIA **Yes, look at my hands, and I am so weary, DIARMUID,**
I ~~will~~
I am so weary that I could lie down and die here– that
is like a bed
mossy bank ~~**will do**~~^**;** **lay me down there, DIARMUID. Oh,**
~~turn from~~
DIARMUID, I have come to beg you to ~~**forego**~~^ ~~**this hunt**~~**.**
~~turn from this hunt~~ng
give up this hunting

---

6 There are pencil lines above and below the revised "I have", almost as if the two words were to be deleted.
13 Oh,] Inserted with a new black ribbon, over a nearly erased "HO,".
14+ The TS is continued by NLI 8777(10) a, fol. 1r.

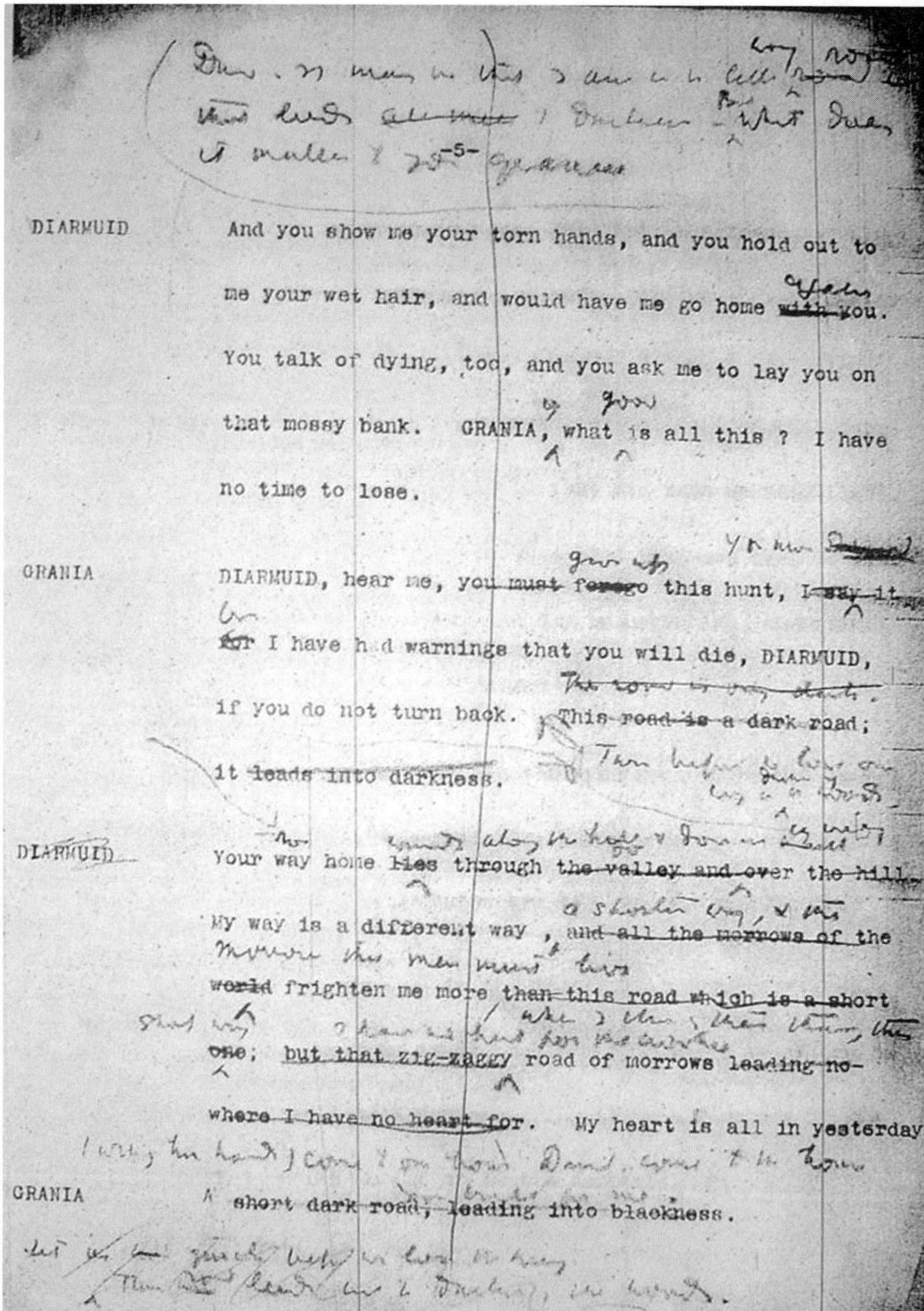

-5-

DIARMUID And you show me your torn hands, and you hold out to me your wet hair, and would have me go home with you. You talk of dying, too, and you ask me to lay you on that mossy bank. GRANIA, what is all this ? I have no time to lose.

GRANIA DIARMUID, hear me, you must forego this hunt, I say it for I have had warnings that you will die, DIARMUID, if you do not turn back. This road is a dark road; it leads into darkness.

DIARMUID Your way home lies through the valley and over the hill. My way is a different way, and all the morrows of the world frighten me more than this road which is a short one; but that zig-zaggy road of morrows leading nowhere I have no heart for. My heart is all in yesterday.

GRANIA A short dark road, leading into blackness.

[NLI 8777(10) a, 1ʳ]

wrong road
Damd – It may be that I am in a little ^ ~~road~~ ~~way~~
But
that leads ~~all men~~ to darkness – ^ What does
–5–
it matter to you Grania

DIARMUID **And you show me your torn hands, and you hold out to**
again
me your wet hair, and would have me go home ~~with you~~.
You talk of dying, too, and you ask me to lay you on
of good
that mossy bank. GRANIA, ^ what ^ is all this ? I have
no time to lose.

give up You [?must] ~~Diarmud~~
GRANIA **Diarmuid, hear me, ~~you must~~ ^ ~~forego~~ this hunt, ~~I say it~~**
for
~~for~~ I have had warnings that you will die, DIARMUID,
The road is very dark.
if you do not turn back. ^ ~~This road is a dark road~~;
Turn before we lose our
it ~~leads into darkness~~. *darknss of*
way in ^ th woods.
th valey
roa winds along the hill & down int ~~th hill~~
[?]
~~DIARMUID~~ **Your way home ~~lies~~ ^ ~~through the valley and~~ ^ ~~over the hill~~.**
a shorter way, & the
My way is a different way , ^ ~~and all the morrows of the~~
morrows that men must live
~~world~~ ^ frighten me more ~~than this road which is a short~~
when I think of these there, this
short way I have no heart for the crooked
^ ~~one~~; ~~but that zig-zaggy~~ ^ road of morrows ~~leading no-~~
~~where I have no heart for~~. My heart is all in yesterday.
(wringng her hands) come to our house Darmd come to th house
You will for me.

GRANIA **~~A short dark road, leading into blackness~~.**
Let us [?~~turn~~] quickly before we lose the way
road
^ This [?~~way~~] leads into th darkness of the woods.

The TS continues Berg(13), fol. 4ʳ. The vertical cancellation line down the center of fols. 1ʳ–13ʳ is in blue-black ink of a slightly lighter shade than WBY's ink corrections on the same and subsequent leaves.

⁻1, 8–10 The line drawn from the head of the page originally connected the additional holograph text to a position following line 9. WBY then redirected the link to the beginning of line 10 and inserted a further addition to line 8 (following "back.").

[NLI 8777(10) a, 2r; a, 2v]

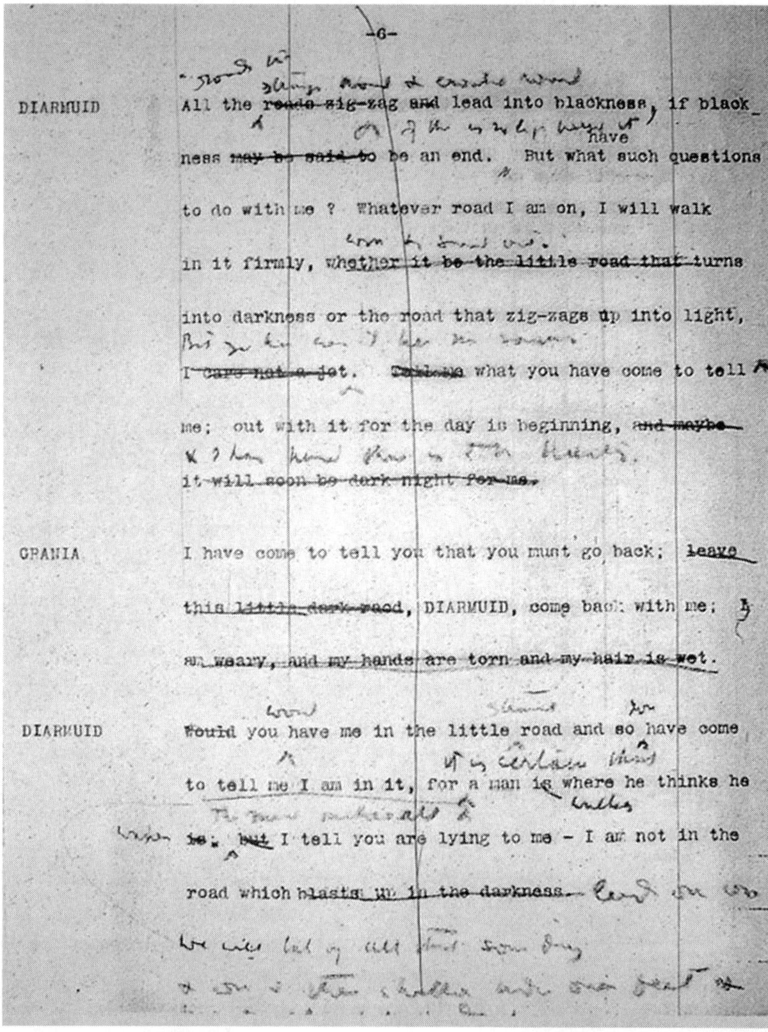

-6-

DIARMUID All the roads zig-zag and lead into blackness, if blackness may be said to be an end. But what such questions have to do with me ? Whatever road I am on, I will walk in it firmly, whether it be the little road that turns into darkness or the road that zig-zags up into light, I care not a jot. Tell me what you have come to tell me; out with it for the day is beginning, and maybe it will soon be dark night for me.

GRANIA I have come to tell you that you must go back; leave this little dark road, DIARMUID, come back with me; I am weary, and my hands are torn and my hair is wet.

DIARMUID Would you have me in the little road and so have come to tell me I am in it, for a man is where he thinks he is; but I tell you are lying to me - I am not in the road which blasts up in the darkness.

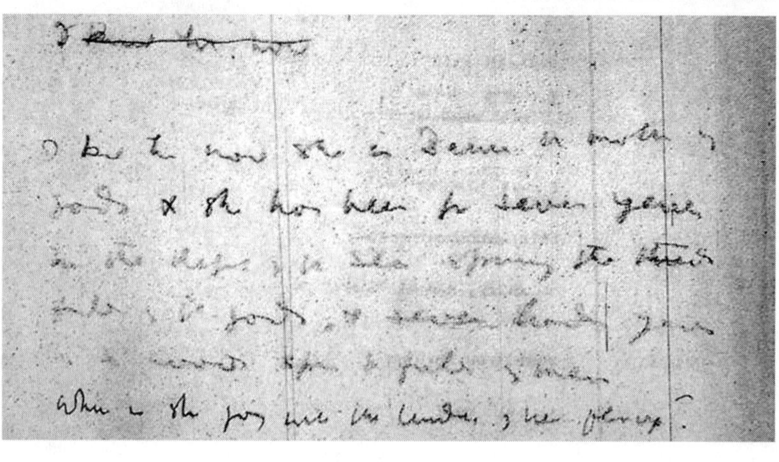

[NLI 8777(10) a, 2[r]]

–6–

roads the straigh road & crooked road
DIARMUID **All the ^ ~~roads zig-zag~~ ^ ~~and~~ lead into blackness, if black_**
& there is no light beyond it!
have
ness ~~may be said to~~ be an end. ^ But what such questions
to do with me ? Whatever road I am on, I will walk
with my sword out.
in it firmly, ~~whether it be the little road that turns~~
~~into darkness or the road that zig-zags up into light~~,
But you have come to tell me somthng.
~~I care not a jot~~. ^ ~~Tell me~~ what you have come to tell ^
me; out with it for the day is beginning, ~~and maybe~~
& I have heard there is to be hunting.
~~it will soon be dark night for me.~~

GRANIA **I have come to tell you that you must go back; ~~leave~~**
~~this little dark road~~, DIARMUID, come back with me; ~~I~~
~~am weary, and my hands are torn and my hair is wet.~~

would *straight* *you*
DIARMUID **~~Would~~ you ^ have me in the little ^ road and so ^ have come**
it is certain that
to tell me I am in it, for ^ a man ~~is~~ where he thinks he
. The mind makes all ^ *walks*
wishes **~~is~~ ; ^ ~~but~~ I tell you are lying to me – I am not in the**
road which ~~blasts up in the darkness.~~ *leads on on*

We will talk of that some day

& on & then shatters under one's feet &
becomes flyng bits of darkness

[NLI 8777(10) a, 2[v]]

~~I know her now~~

I knw her now she is Dana or mother of
gods & she has been for seven years
in the depths of the sea spinning the ~~threads~~
fates of the gods, & seven hundrd years
in the woods spin th fates of men
Where is she going with the bundles of her flax?

2[v], l. 2 Dana] The earliest naming of the previously anonymous Foster-Mother. See introduction, part iv.
7 Added after the other lines were written.

[NLI 8777(10) a, 3r]

-7-

GRANIA DIARMUID you ~~are in it~~, ~~and~~ you can come back with me.

DIARMUID What do you know of all this - You come like a sooth-sayer. Who has been whispering in your ear; who has sent you to me ?

GRANIA A warning came last night.

DIARMUID From that old woman who spins. I ~~thought I saw her~~ carrying her spinning-wheel last night through the woods ~~out of which she came years ago.~~

GRANIA No, DIARMUID, I left her spinning - No, I am forgetting. She has spun all the flax.

DIARMUID That is the warning you have come to tell me.

GRANIA Maybe, but I had not thought of all that; it was ~~last~~ night ~~that a dream came to me out of the darkness.~~

DIARMUID What did the dream say ?

[NLI 8777(10) a, 3r]

carryng a bundle of new flax
throug th wood –

–7–

are going strght upon death
GRANIA **DIARMUID you ~~are in it~~, ~~and~~ you can come back with me.**
^

DIARMUID **What do you know of all this – You come like a sooth-**
sayer. Who has been whispering in your ear; who
has sent you to me ?

GRANIA **A warning came last night.**

I tell you I have
DIARMUID **From that old woman who spins. ~~I thought I saw her~~**
had enough of her warnings – I saw her
~~carrying her spinning-wheel~~ last night through the
woods ~~out of which she came years ago~~.

GRANIA **No, DIARMUID, I left her spinning – No, I am forgetting –**
She has spun all the flax.

DIARMUID **That is the warning you have come to tell me.**

but of a dream
GRANIA **Maybe, but I had not thought of all that; ~~it was last~~**
that came to me last
^**night ~~that a dream came to me out of the darkness.~~**

DIARMUID **What did the dream say ?**

[NLI 8777(10) a, 4r]

-8-

GRANIA I dreamed I was sitting by FINN.

DIARMUID I do not think much of such a dream, for I saw you yesterday walking with FINN and holding his hands.

GRANIA That was yesterday. You did not dream that last night

DIARMUID I have no time for dreaming; my dreams end, or maybe they are about to begin.

GRANIA But I dreamed I was sitting by FINN and that your ~~arms~~ were hanging on ~~the walls~~ over our heads.

DIARMUID I have heard worse dreams than that, ~~this morning come home and dream no more.~~

GRANIA I have come to tell you of the dream I had last night. Everyone who passes here has dreams to tell - two peasants came by just now and they told of tragedies and omens, and went out seeking , telling of the cattle

[NLI 8777(10) a, 4[r]]

–8–

GRANIA **I dreamed I was sitting by FINN.**

DIARMUID **I do not think much of such a dream, for I saw you yesterday walking with FINN and holding his hands.**

GRANIA **That was yesterday. You did not dream that last night**

DIARMUID **I have no time for dreaming; my dreams end, or maybe they are about to begin.**

shield

GRANIA **But I dreamed I was sitting by Finn and that your ~~arms~~ ^**

among the shields of the slain

were hanging ^ ~~on the walls~~ over our heads.

Did you not say it was a bad dream –

DIARMUID **I have ~~heard~~ worse dreams than that, ~~this morning~~ ^~~come home and dream no more.~~**

GRANIA **I have come to tell you of the dream I had last night. Everyone who passes here has dreams to tell – two peasants came by just now and they told of tragedies and omens, and went out seeking, telling of the cattle**

4–6, 10–14 The lines are canceled with pencil.

[NLI 8777(10) a, 5r]

that had climbed the mountain to drown ~~themselves~~ in the lake at the top of ~~it~~.

GRANIA Put I ~~came to tell~~ you that this hunt ~~you must~~ forego, for the old shepherd whose sheep had fled from him came knocking at my door and asked me to come and see what was passing in the air; and among the phantoms which passed he pointed out DIARMUID[s] father and DIARMUID'S grandfather who has been dead these fifty years. The shpeherd said that he was there and with the phantoms, and he said that these phantoms were living among the dead, fighting whether FINN should live or die.

DIARMUID Is it ~~with such a dream as this that~~ you would lead me ~~from this hunt~~ - AH! impotent gods, can you [from] ~~provide~~ nothing better than the dreams of an unfaithful wife to vex and [shake] ~~undermine~~ my will.

[NLI 8777(10) a, 5ʳ]

–9–

that had climbed the mountain to drown themselves in
the lake at the top of it.

I woke & when *but* [*?hardly/?huntng*] *gone*
~~But I came to tell you that this hunt you must forego~~,
for the old shepherd whose sheep had fled from him came
knocking at my door and asked me to come and see what
was passing in the air; and among the phantoms which
passed by he pointed out DIARMUID ' *S* father and DIARMUID'S
grandfather who has been dead these fifty years. The
shpeherd said that he was there and with the phantoms,
and he said that these phantoms were living among the
dead, fighting whether FINN should live or die.

DIARMUID **Is it ~~with such a dream as this that you would lead me~~**
find
~~from this hunt~~ – AH! impotent gods, can you ~~provide~~
nothing better than the dreams of an unfaithful wife
shake
to vex and ~~undermine~~ my will.

1–2 The lines are canceled with pencil (like lines 3, 12–13).

3 I have divided the words of WBY's insertion into two groups, supposing each group to be the beginning of an inconclusive revision.

-10-

GRANIA Blaspheme ~~not~~ against the gods, for they are very near you now, ~~and you may be one of them to-morrow~~. I ~~begged them as I stumbled through the hole in the~~ ~~hedge to spare you.~~

DIARMUID Yes, every man is a god in heaven and on earth ~~we are~~ the playthings ~~of the gods~~. All night I have heard ~~their pitiless laughter as they watched our little~~ ~~antics here~~ - Do you not hear ? do you not hear ?

GRANIA I hear, but ~~what am I to say to all this~~ - Take my hands, and take my hair, they may bring some softness to your heart,

DIARMUID ~~Your~~ hands and hair were sweet to ~~me once, but now~~ ~~they are my loathing.~~ Let me see your hands; they are beautiful hands, torn as they are, no wonder I loved them; and this hair too; you loved me once

[NLI 8777(10) a, 6r]

I tell you I have heard them laughing.

–10–

Do not *us*
GRANIA **Blaspheme ~~not~~ against the gods, for they are very near ^**
^ ~~you~~ now, ~~and you may be one of them to-morrow~~. I
I have been [?*prayng*] *to them to spare* [?*you*], *I have*
~~begged them as I stumbled through the hole in the~~
[?*prayng*] *to them all night, whil I lookd for you –*
~~hedge to spare you~~.

DIARMUID **Yes, every man is a god in heaven and on earth we are**
the They drive us hither & thither – O they are great [?*hurley*] *players –*
~~the~~ playthings ~~of the gods~~. All night I have heard
their laughtr – ~~They are~~ ~~[?laughng] [?at] th world~~
~~their pitiless~~ ^ ~~laughter as they watched our little~~
me me
~~antics here~~ – Do you not hear ^ ? do you not hear ?

O Dairmud
GRANIA **I hear, but ~~what am I to say to all this~~ – Take my**
hands, and take my hair, they may bring ^ some softness
to your heart{, . some memory in your mind

O yes yes. I remember wel enough. Those
once
DIARMUID **^ ~~Your~~ hands and hair were sweet to ~~me once, but now~~**
long ago , ~~a long~~ ~~time ago~~ – no no yesterday – yes day
~~they are my loathing.~~ Let me see your hands; they
are beautiful hands, torn as they are, no wonder I
loved them; and this hair too; you loved me once

-1, etc. The blue-black ink of WBY's insertions is a slightly darker shade than that of the vertical cancellation lines.

-11-

[illegible]

GRANIA, you loved me better than FINN.

GRANIA I love you still, DIARMUID.

DIARMUID I would know how all this came about; how you who fled with me at Tara should turn now with longing eyes to FINN – Why did you chose me ?

GRANIA You were young, and FINN seemed like an old man to me then, that was why I chose you.

[illegible]

DIARMUID Why did you send me to FINN yesterday. ~~Stand quietly~~.

[illegible]

GRANIA I sent you to FINN because you longed to be among [illegible] ~~your comrades~~, and my love was become a burden to you.

[illegible]

DIARMUID All you say is true, ~~but it is not all the~~ truth. ~~Yesterday I asked you to come into the wastes with me~~ .

[illegible]

GRANIA I wished you to be friends with FINN because our love had become a madness, you know that it was driving us mad.

[NLI 8777(10) a, 7^{r}]

–11–

~~But, but no~~ I remember it all – yesterday

GRANIA, you loved me better than FINN.^

GRANIA **I love you still, DIARMUID.**

DIARMUID **I would know how all this came about; how you who fled with me at Tara should turn now with longing eyes to FINN – Why did you chose me ?**

GRANIA **You were young, and FINN seemed like an old man to me then, that was why I chose you.**

~~O~~ my dear one

DIARMUID **Why did you send me to FINN yesterday.** ~~Speak quickly~~.
^ It may be that my words hav been a little wild. Speak quickly do not be afraid

GRANIA **I sent you to FINN because you longed to be among**
the fianna
~~your comrades~~, and my love was become a burden to you.

Our love was too great –

DIARMUID **All you say is true, ~~but it is not all the truth~~.** ~~**Yes–**~~
It was our love that made th road so [?envious].
~~**terday I asked you to come into the wastes with me**~~**.**

GRANIA **I wished you to be friends with FINN because our love had become a madness, you know that it was driving us mad.**

3–7 The cancellation is in the same (darker) shade of blue-black ink as the rest of WBY's corrections.

-12-

DIARMUID All that was long ago, before we came to live in this country. It is a long while, GRANIA, since ~~you have~~ [by him] spoken to you. [illegible] days – [illegible] ~~sought me [illegible]~~; I ~~would ping this secret from you,~~ and [illegible] ~~I will~~ – There was a thought of FINN in your mind when you sent me to him.

GRANIA There is no secret in me, ~~unless my simplicity be a secret~~. I have told you everything – ~~I loved you and I admired FINN~~; and I have come through this forest by night, to beg you to leave this hunt, as a wife comes to her husband.

DIARMUID Wifely love is a little thing in GRANIA'S eyes – GRANIA was not meant to sit by the fireside with children, [She was not meant to [illegible]] and she wearied of me, when peace came she longed for me to go to battle again.

GRANIA You must win me again and again in battle.

[illegible]

[NLI 8777(10) a, 8[r]]

–12–

DIARMUID **All that was long ago, before we came to live in this**
we have
country. It is a long while, GRANIA, since ~~you have~~
spoken to gether. Many days – There may be no othr time
~~sought me out~~; ~~I would ring this secret from you~~, ~~and~~
so good to wring this secret out of you.
~~I will~~ – There was a thought of FINN in your mind when
you sent me to him.

GRANIA **There is no secret in me, ~~unless my simplicity be~~ a**
~~secret~~. I have told you everything – ~~I loved you~~
~~and I admired~~ FINN; and I have come through this forest
by night,to beg you to leave this hunt, as a wife comes
to her husband.

DIARMUID **Wifely love is a little thing in GRANIA'S eyes –**
GRANIA was not meant to sit by the fireside with child-
She was no meant to hav childrn
ren, and she wearied of me;when peace came she longed
for me to go to battle again.

GRANIA **You must win me again and again in battle.**

upn her knees. The gods made her womb barren
because she was not ment to hold childrn upn her knees –

13–15 The cancellation is in (darker) blue-black ink.

-13-

DIARMUID ~~But it was not by feats of arms that I won you,~~ GRANIA,

it was ~~by the desire of the eye - Ah, GRANIA, a woman~~

~~looks~~ from the red apple in her hand to the green

apple on the ~~topmost~~ bough - So ~~did you~~ look from me

to FINN ~~that night in Tara;~~ ~~and the malignant gods~~

~~have had their way in the~~ end. ~~Your hair is~~ very

~~soft~~ (Takes her by the hair) As easily as I could

kill ~~pluck~~ a flower by the wayside I could kill you.

GRANIA Kill me with your sword here in my breast.

DIARMUID You would have ~~e~~ me kill you - maybe if I kill ~~in killing~~ you ~~I~~

~~would undo the bondage of the gods.~~

GRANIA Hold fast my hair, draw back my head and kill me ~~cut my throat~~

~~across~~ - I would have you do it - Why do you not do it ?

(Pause) If you would go to this hunt you must do it,

for while I live you shall not go.

[NLI 8777(10) a, 9r]

–13–

~~she was not~~ The gods gave her a lustful
DIARMUID **~~But it was not by feats of arms that I won you,~~ GRANIA,**
barren womb – She looked
it ~~was by the desire of the eye – Ah, GRANIA, a woman~~
~~looks~~ from the red apple in her hand to the green
apple on the ~~topmost~~ bough – So ~~did you~~ look from me
even when she first lusted after me
to FINN^ **~~that night in Tara~~;** **~~and the malignent gods~~**
& after Fin will be some others. The malignan gods made
your beauty grania
~~have had their way in the~~ end.^ **~~Your hair is~~ very**
Your hand is very week, this arm is week & fragile
^ **~~soft~~ (Takes her by the hair)** **As easily as I could**
This hair is vry soft.
kill
~~pluck~~ a flower by the wayside I could kill you.

Kill me if you will.
GRANIA ^ **Kill me with your sword here in my breast.** what does
life matter to me now.

if I killd
DIARMUID **You would have e me kill you – maybe ~~in killing~~ you ~~I~~**
all would be well.
~~would undo the bondage of the gods.~~

kill me
GRANIA **Hold fast my hair, draw back my head and ~~cut my throat~~**
~~across~~ – I would have you do it – Why do you not do it ?
(Pause) **If you would go to this hunt you must do it,**
for while I live you shall not go.

-14-

DIARMUID, I know your wheedling ways, GRANIA, and would have none of them; nor would I waste time in seeking to undo my fate in your death, or by returning home with you like a peaceable peasant with his wife. Let go my spear I say, let go my spear if you would have your life. I see that you are thinking of FINN in this very moment; I ~~read~~ [illegible] thoughts of FINN in your eyes; let me go, or I will get the lust out of you with this sword point.

GRANIA Kill me, DIARMUID, I would have you do it.

DIARMUID And leave this white body, like a cut flower by the wayside.

GRANIA Kill me, DIARMUID

[illegible]

DIARMUID ~~Did~~ [illegible] I kill you ~~my sweet thing, I should~~ go mad, and [illegible] wander in the forest, seeing ~~strange flowers~~ white and

[NLI 8777(10) a, 10r]

–14–

DIARMUID, **I know your wheedling ways, GRANIA, and would have none of them; nor would I waste time in seeking to undo my fate in your death, or by returning home with you like a peaceable peasant with his wife. Let go my spear I say, let go my spear if you would have your life. I see that you are thinking of FINN in this**

see

very moment; I ~~read~~ thoughts of FINN in your eyes; let me go, or I will get the lust out of you with this sword point.

GRANIA **Kill me, DIARMUID, I would have you do it.**

DIARMUID **And leave this white body, like a cut flower by the wayside.**

GRANIA **Kill me, DIARMUID**

I have heard th gods laugh & I hav been merry.

~~If~~ But if I would remember everything,

DIARMUID ^**~~Did~~**^ **I kill you ~~my sweet thing I should go~~ mad, and** I

woud

wander in the forest, seeing ~~strange flowers~~ white and

1–4 The cancellation is in (darker) blue-black ink.

[NLI 8777(10) a, 11r]

-15-

red, ~~a~~ after killing you I might kill myself - that would be a good thing to do. But seeing you there, your soft hair clotted with blood, and your white hands stained with blood I might not ~~have the a sanity~~ which ~~the suicide has when he rids himself~~ of his burden -

Instead, I might go questioning the wayfarer about some half-remembered ~~facts~~ faces. I cannot kill you, go - I would not see your blood nor touch ~~yt~~ your hands ~~living or dead~~ - Your lips and teeth and all the beauty I have loved seem in mine eyes, ~~like pestilence~~, ~~and if I kissed you now, the kiss would taste like ashes -~~

GRANIA, GRANIA, out of my sight, ~~day has begun~~ (He goes out driving her before him - a moment after he enters from another side) ~~The day has begun and this~~ beast ~~will be upon the move.~~ ~~I do require all my courage~~ and coolness ~~to attack him; if he were to spring upon~~

[NLI 8777(10) a, 11r]

–15–

flowers.
red ^ ~~**or**~~ **after killing you I might kill myself – that**
would be a good thing to do. But seeing you there,
your soft hair clotted with blood, and your white hands
~~for~~ remember to do it
stained with blood I might not ~~**have the a sanity which**~~
I must remembr nothng but yesterd & today.
~~**the suicide has when he rids himself of his burden**~~ **–**
~~I might~~
Instead, I might go questioning the wayfarer about
some half-remembered ~~**facts**~~ **faces. I cannot kill you,**
go – I would not see your blood nor touch ~~**yl**~~ **your hands**
~~**living or dead**~~ **– Your lips and teeth and all the beauty**
no better than th yellow pestilence
I have loved seem in mine eyes , ~~**like pestilence**~~**,** ~~**and if**~~
~~**I kissed you now, the kiss would taste like ashes –**~~ ^

GRANIA, GRANIA, out of my sight { . , ~~**day has begun**~~ **(He goes**
out driving her before him – a moment after he enters
That is errr – let me think – yes yes. There is a beast comng tht I am
from another side) ~~**The day has begun and this**~~ **beast**
to slay
~~**will be upon the move. I do require all my courage**~~
and ~~**coolness to attack him; if he were to spring upon**~~

6–7 The cancellation is in (darker) blue-black ink.

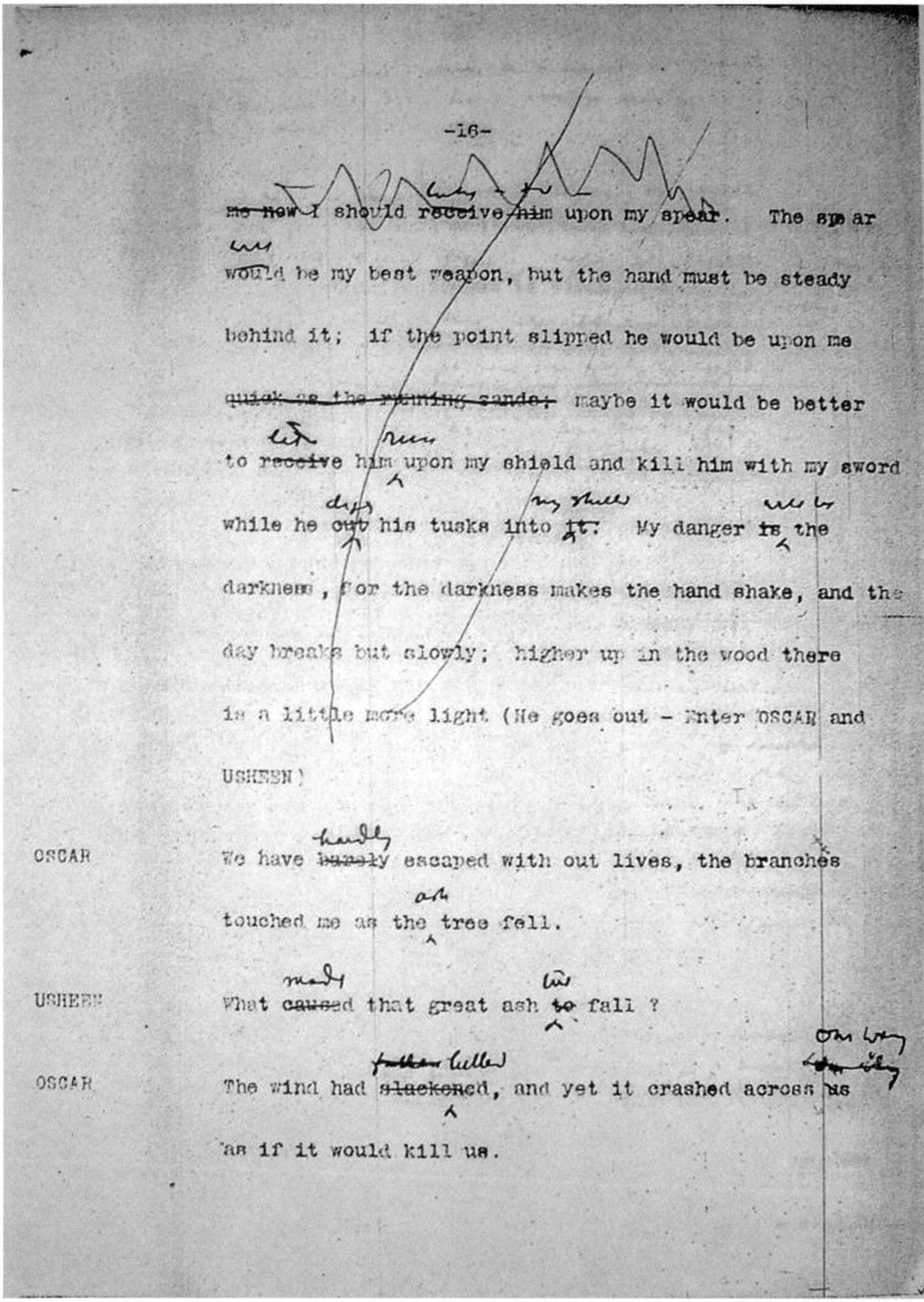

-16-

~~me now~~ I should ~~receive~~ ~~him~~ upon my ~~spear~~. The spear would be my best weapon, but the hand must be steady behind it; if the point slipped he would be upon me ~~quick as the running sands;~~ maybe it would be better to ~~receive~~ him upon my shield and kill him with my sword while he ~~cut~~ his tusks into ~~it.~~ My danger ~~is~~ the darkness, for the darkness makes the hand shake, and the day breaks but slowly; higher up in the wood there is a little more light (He goes out - Enter OSCAR and USHEEN)

OSCAR We have ~~barely~~ escaped with out lives, the branches touched me as the tree fell.

USHEEN What ~~caused~~ that great ash ~~to~~ fall ?

OSCAR The wind had ~~slackened~~, and yet it crashed across us as if it would kill us.

[NLI 8777(10) a, 12r]

–16–

take – so –
~~me now~~ I should ~~receive~~ ~~him~~ upon my spear. The spear
will
~~would~~ be my best weapon, but the hand must be steady
behind it; if the point slipped he would be upon me
~~quick as the running sands;~~ maybe it would be better
let run
to ~~receive~~ him ^ upon my shield and kill him with my sword
digs my shield will be
while he ~~cut~~ his tusks into ~~it.~~ My danger ~~is~~ the
darkness ^, for the darkness ^ makes the hand ^ shake, and the
day breaks but slowly; higher up in the wood there
is a little more light (He goes out – Enter OSCAR and
USHEEN)

hardly
OSCAR **We have ~~barely~~ escaped with out lives, the branches**
ash
touched me as the ^ tree fell.

made tree
USHEEN **What ~~caused~~ that great ash ~~to~~ ^ fall**

our way
~~fallen~~ lulled ^[?~~our way~~]
OSCAR **The wind had ~~slackened~~, and yet it crashed across ~~us~~**
as if it would kill us ^.

1 The cancellation of the first nine words together is in the same blue-black ink as the larger vertical cancel—a lighter shade than in WBY's other corrections on this same page.

-17-

I heard a thud & a cracking of branches

USHEEN ~~The tree was old, and its roots may have been~~ strained ... began to fall, as though ~~by the wind; but~~ what is stranger than ~~the falling~~ a great stone had been thrown against it ~~of the tree is what~~ ~~passed over the mountain-tops at midnight - a great hunt seemed to be going on~~ in the ~~sky,~~ ~~a greater quarry~~ seemed to be ~~pursued there~~ than ~~we are pursuing in the wood.~~

OSCAR Never was such a night before, ~~clamour and rain and fly-~~ ~~ing shadows, and the purpose of it all only the gods~~ ~~know.~~

USHEEN ~~Three wild swans were~~ blown into the trees, ~~but I~~ ~~hurried on, and why~~ think ~~you that FINN'S hounds~~ should have come back crying from the thicket.

OSCAR They ~~run at FINN'S heels~~, whimpering and ~~crying~~ for ~~his hand to cheer them;~~ they would not follow him at all were they not ~~fearful to be~~ left alone - ~~See how~~ ~~the day begins in the dark;~~ that must be the beginning

[NLI 8777(10) a, 13r]

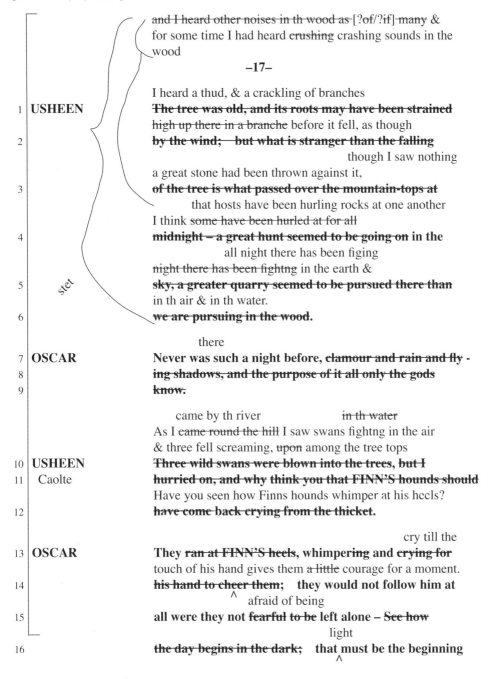

~~and I heard other noises in th wood as~~ [?~~of~~/?~~if~~] ~~many~~ &
for some time I had heard ~~crushing~~ crashing sounds in the
wood

–17–

I heard a thud, & a crackling of branches
USHEEN ~~**The tree was old, and its roots may have been strained**~~
~~high up there in a branche~~ before it fell, as though
~~**by the wind; but what is stranger than the falling**~~
though I saw nothing
a great stone had been thrown against it,
~~**of the tree is what passed over the mountain-tops at**~~
that hosts have been hurling rocks at one another
I think ~~some have been hurled at for all~~
~~**midnight – a great hunt seemed to be going on**~~ **in the**
all night there has been figing
~~night there has been fightng~~ in the earth &
~~**sky, a greater quarry seemed to be pursued there than**~~
in th air & in th water.
~~**we are pursuing in the wood**~~**.**

stet

there
OSCAR **Never was such a night before,** ~~**clamour and rain and fly**~~ **-**
~~**ing shadows, and the purpose of it all only the gods**~~
~~**know.**~~

came by th river ~~in th water~~
As I ~~came round the hill~~ I saw swans fightng in the air
& three fell screaming, ~~upon~~ among the tree tops
USHEEN ~~**Three wild swans were blown into the trees, but I**~~
Caolte ~~**hurried on, and why think you that FINN'S hounds should**~~
Have you seen how Finns hounds whimper at his heels?
~~**have come back crying from the thicket**~~**.**

cry till the
OSCAR **They** ~~**ran at FINN'S heels**~~**, whimpering and** ~~**crying for**~~
touch of his hand gives them ~~a little~~ courage for a moment.
~~**his hand to cheer them**~~**; they would not follow him at**
^ afraid of being
all were they not ~~**fearful to be**~~ **left alone –** ~~**See how**~~
light
~~**the day begins in the dark;**~~ **that must be the beginning**
^

1–6 WBY's marginal instruction ("stet", at line 5) and large LH bracket are in the same blue-black ink as his (joined) vertical cancellation line—a lighter shade than in his other ink corrections on the same page.

[NLI 8777(10) a, 14r]

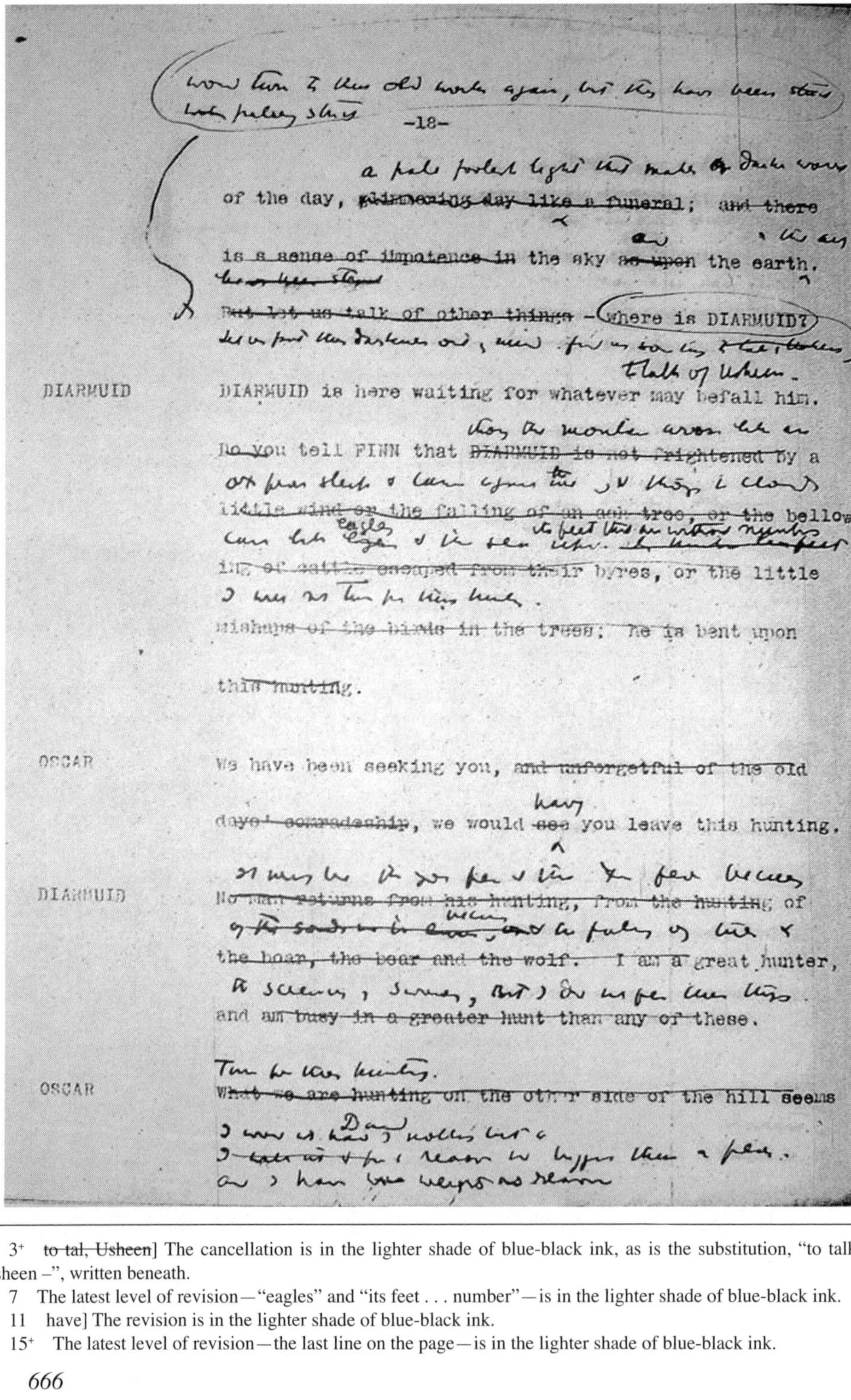
-18-

of the day, ~~glimmering day like a funeral~~; ~~and there~~ is ~~a sense of impatience in~~ the sky ~~as upon~~ the earth.

~~But let us talk of other things~~ - where is DIARMUID?

to talk of Usheen –

DIARMUID DIARMUID is here waiting for whatever may befall him. ~~Do you~~ tell FINN that ~~DIARMUID is not frightened~~ by a ~~little wind or the falling of an ash tree, or the~~ bellow- eagles its feet that are without number ~~ing of cattle escaped from their~~ byres, or the little ~~mishaps of the birds in the trees~~; he is bent upon this ~~hunting~~.

OSCAR We have been seeking you, ~~and unforgetful of the old days' commradeship~~, we would ~~see~~ have you leave this hunting.

DIARMUID ~~No man returns from his hunting, from the hunting~~ of ~~the boar, the bear and the wolf.~~ I am a great hunter, and am ~~busy in a greater hunt than any of these~~.

OSCAR ~~What we are hunting on the other side of the hill seems~~

3+ ~~to tal, Usheen~~] The cancellation is in the lighter shade of blue-black ink, as is the substitution, "to talk of Usheen –", written beneath.

7 The latest level of revision—"eagles" and "its feet . . . number"—is in the lighter shade of blue-black ink.

11 have] The revision is in the lighter shade of blue-black ink.

15+ The latest level of revision—the last line on the page—is in the lighter shade of blue-black ink.

[NLI 8777(10) a, 14r]

would turn to their old work again, but they have been ~~struck~~
~~with~~ palsy struck

–18–

a pale foolish light that makes ~~th~~ dark worse
of the day, ~~glimmering day like a funeral~~; ~~and there~~
and & the air
~~is a sense of impotence in~~ the sky ~~as upon~~ the earth.
~~have been struck~~
~~But let us talk of other things~~ – where is DIARMUID?
Let us put this darkness out of mind. find us someting ~~to tal, Usheen~~
to talk of Usheen –

DIARMUID **DIARMUID is here waiting for whatever may befall him.**
thoug the mountain arose like an
~~Do you~~ tell FINN that ~~DIARMUID is not frightened by~~ a
[?~~th~~]
ox from sleep & came against me, & thoug th clouds
~~little wind or the falling of an ash tree, or the~~ bellow-
eagles its feet that are without number
cam like ~~egles~~ & the sea upon ~~its number less feet~~
~~ing of cattle escaped from their byres, or the~~ little
I will nt turn frm this huntng –
~~mishaps of the birds in the trees;~~ ~~he is~~ bent upon
~~this hunting~~.

OSCAR **We have been seeking you, ~~and unforgetful of the old~~**
have
~~days' comradeship~~, we would ~~see~~ you leave this hunting.

It may be th you fear & tht Fin fear becaus
DIARMUID **~~No man returns from his hunting, from the hunting~~ of**
becaus
~~of the sounds in th evening on~~ & th falng of trees &
~~the boar, the bear and the wolf.~~ ~~I am a~~ great hunter,
th screaming of swans, But I do not fear thes thngs.
and ~~am busy in a greater hunt than any of these~~.
Turn from this hunting.
OSCAR **~~What we are hunting on the other side of the hill seems~~**
Darmd
I would nt had I nothng but a
~~I would not & for~~ a reason no bigger than a pea –
and I have a ~~wre~~ weight as reason

[NLI 8777(10) a, 15r]

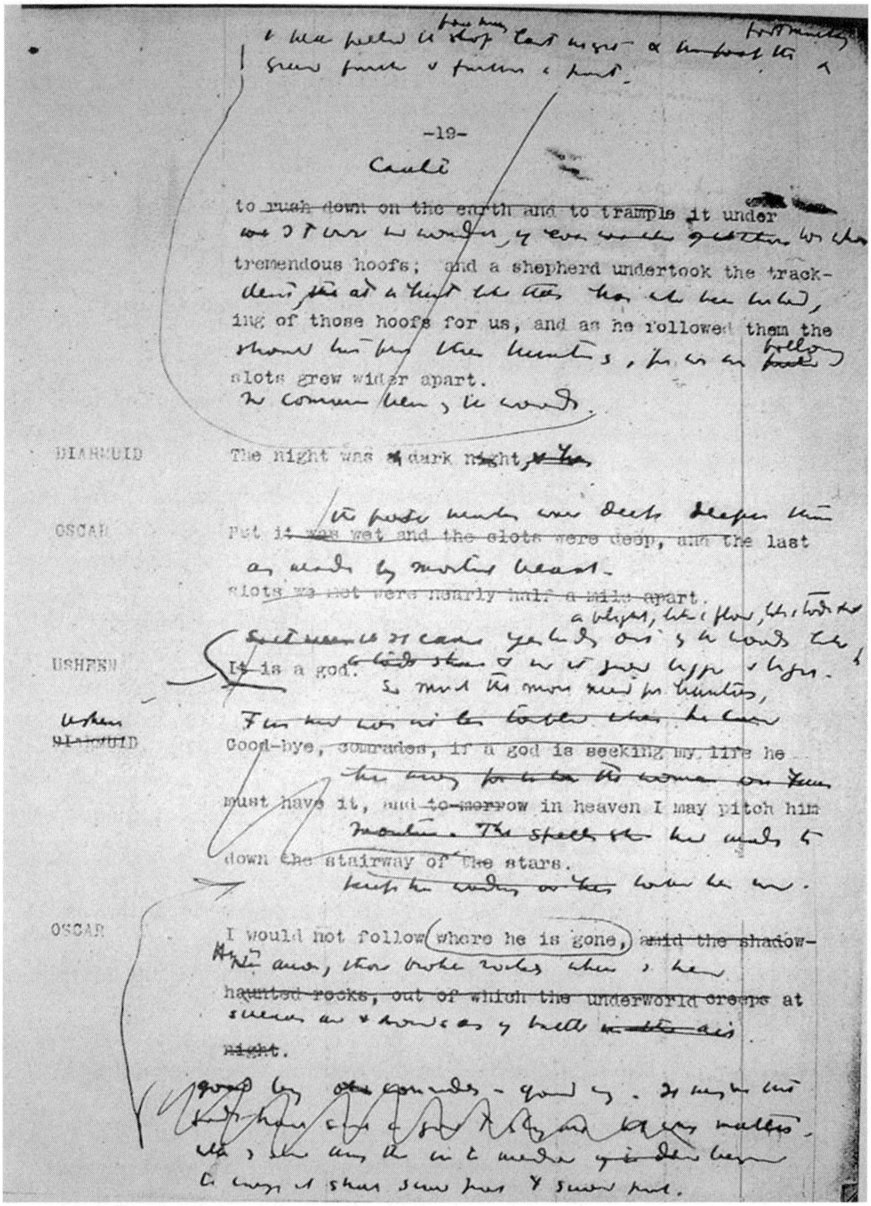
-19-

to rush down on the earth and to trample it under
tremendous hoofs; and a shepherd undertook the track-
ing of those hoofs for us, and as he followed them the
slots grew wider apart.

DIARMUID The night was a dark night,

OSCAR But it was wet and the slots were deep, and the last
slots we met were nearly half a mile apart.

USHEEN It is a god.

DIARMUID Good-bye, comrades, if a god is seeking my life he
must have it, and to-morrow in heaven I may pitch him
down the stairway of the stars.

OSCAR I would not follow where he is gone, and the shadow-
haunted rocks, out of which the underworld creeps at
night.

---

2 we whose] The words are inserted in a paler shade of blue-black ink.

3 foretold,] The comma is canceled in a paler shade of blue-black ink.

4 following] The final revision is in a paler shade of blue-black ink.

−8 a blight, . . . toad stol] The insertion and the caret are in a paler shade of blue-black ink.

8 So much . . . hunters,] The insertion is in a paler shade of blue-black ink.

12 The words are circled in a paler shade of blue-black ink.

13 He is] The inserted words are in a paler shade of blue-black ink.

14+ The lines are to be ascribed to Diarmuid. The second and third lines are canceled in a paler shade of blue-black ink, while the sense remains fragmentary.

[NLI 8777(10) a, 15r]

foot marks foot marking
a man follwd th ~~slot~~ last night & ~~th foot~~ the ^
grew further & further a part –

–19–
Caolt
~~to rush down on the earth and to trample~~ it under
~~we~~ It were no wonder, if even ~~we who if we~~ those we whose
tremendous hoofs; and a shepherd undertook the track-
[?death], ~~the~~ at a hunt like this has also been foretold
ing of those hoofs for us, and as he followed them the
following
should turn from this hunting, for we are [?~~foulow~~]
slots grew wider apart.
no common [?beast/being] of th woods.

DIARMUID **The night was ~~a~~ dark ~~night~~{, .** ~~& has~~

the fo{o tt marks were deep deeper than
OSCAR **But ~~it was wet and the slots were deep, and the~~ last**
any made by mortal beast –
~~slots we met were nearly half a mile apart.~~
a blight, like a flood, like a toad stol
~~So it seems~~ th It came yesterday out of the woods like ^
~~a toad stoo~~ & now it grows bigger & biger –
USHEEN **~~It is a god.~~** So much the more need for hunters,
Usheen ~~Fin now was not less troubled when he came~~
~~DIARMUID~~ **Good-bye, ~~comrades, if a god is seeking my life~~ he**
~~here~~ [?~~among~~] ~~for in an that woman on Finns~~
must have it, and ~~to-morrow~~ in heaven I may pitch him
~~mountain. The spells she~~ had made to
down the stairway of the stars.
~~keep him wandrng or his~~ woud her now.
OSCAR **I would not follow where he is gone, ~~amid the shadow-~~**
He is
~~He~~ among those broken rocks where I heard
~~haunted rocks, out of which the underworld creeps~~ at
screams and & sounds as of battle ~~in the air~~.
~~night~~.
good by ~~old~~ comrades – good by – It may be that
gods have sent a god to slay me but [?what/?nothng] matters,
when I shall amng th in to merder ~~of in dear~~ beyond
to image it shall sword point to sword point.

[NLI 8777(10) a, 16^{r}]

They say that the dwarfs ~~have their house~~
& worse than they have their house among the
rocks.

-20-

He is the only one among us who has
not been shaken by this night of terror.

USHEEN He ~~is one who seems untouched by the broiling horrors of the night, and now the crescent light is ghastlier than the dark~~ - ~~see, see~~, something is coming up this way.

Look - Look -

OSCAR A tall staff in his hand, and he moves noiselessly.
& there is another following him.

USHEEN Draw your sword, OSCAR.

OSCAR It will not come out of its sheath, it is but a shepherd ~~a peasant~~.

We are craven, and no better than CONAN ~~clinging to~~ a ~~[illegible]~~ ~~tree and thinking he was clasping a god~~.

OLD MAN Be of good heart great deliverer of Eri; I am but a shepherd looking for ~~peasant seeking~~ his sheep and not ~~a spectre from~~ the some bad & evil things out of the rocks ~~caves~~.

YOUNG MAN Can you tell me, noble sirs, of any strayed sheep, or what is troubling ~~wrong~~ with the waters & with the air over our heads. ~~why the night has been such a mad one~~.

OLD MAN We must go on sirs ~~Excuse, us sir~~, we must find our sheep or starve (exeunt)

[NLI 8777(10) a, 16r]

They say that the dwarfs ~~have their house~~
& worse than that have thir houses among those
rocks.

–20–

He is the only one among us who has
USHEEN **He ~~is one who seems untouched by the broiling horrors~~**
not been shaken by this night of terrors –
of ~~the night, and now the crescent light is ghastlier~~
– look – look – up
~~than the dark~~ – ~~see, see,~~ something is coming ^ this way.

OSCAR **A tall staff in his hand, and he moves noiselessly.**
& there is another pulling him.

USHEEN **Draw your sword, OSCAR.**

come out of a shepherd.
OSCAR **It will not ~~leave~~ ^ its sheath, it is but ~~a peasant~~.**
We are craven, and no better than CONAN ~~clinging to~~ a
~~who is half out of his wits with terror~~.
~~tree and thinking he was clasping a god~~.

OLD MAN **Be of good heart great deliverer of Eri; I am but a**
a shepherd looking for as well might be
~~peasant~~ ~~seeking~~ ^ his sheep and not ~~a spectre from~~ the
bad the
some ~~evil~~ thing out of ~~those~~ rocks.
~~caves~~.

YOUNG MAN **Can you tell me, noble sirs, of any strayed sheep, or**
troubling
what is ~~wrong with~~ the water & ~~with~~ the air over our
~~why the night has been such a mad one~~.
heads.

~~on~~
We must go sirs
OLD MAN **~~Excuse, us sir~~, we must find out sheep or starve (exeunt)**

[NLI 8777(10) a, 17r]

-21-

USHEEN ~~We are no better than strayed sheep~~; maybe ~~he~~ was laughing at us – ~~Here we must wait, to seek them~~ would ~~be but to lose them~~. We must wait here till we hear FINN'S horn.

OSCAR ~~Better get up on higher ground~~.

USHEEN Who is this coming ? ~~The wood is~~ as full of shadows as of leaves. Now, ~~these are the people from the caves,~~ ~~see them rise up from~~ the rocks,

OSCAR ~~That one seems~~ to be pushed along, and if it is a shadow ~~it is a thin~~ one. It is CONAN, I ~~recognise~~ the sheepskin; ~~let us look as if the night had~~ no fear for ~~us, as though we could brave the people of the~~ ~~caves~~ (Enter CAOLITE and four SPEARMEN)

Goll

~~CAOLITE~~ The night is ~~gone~~ over at last.

[NLI 8777(10) a, 17r]

–21–

~~We are little better~~ than their sheep. Were they

USHEEN ~~**We are no better than strayed sheep**~~**;** **maybe he was**

laughing at us because we are afraid.

laughing at us – ~~**Here we must wait, to seek them**~~ **would**

~~**be but to lose them**~~**.** **We must wait here till we hear**

~~ne~~ were to seek

FINN'S horn. If ~~we~~ ^ ~~saught for~~ him, we woud lose ~~our~~

~~way~~ him; & it may be nevr come alive out of this wood.

OSCAR ~~**Better get upon higher ground**~~**.**

We had better go further up th hill.

Since dawn began the wood has been as

USHEEN **Who is this coming ?** ~~**The wood is**~~ ^ **as full of shadows as**

They are coming out of the ~~caves~~ [?~~comng~~]

of leaves. ~~**Now, these are the people from the caves,**~~

~~**see them rise up from the**~~ **the rocks**{, / .} how they rise up

out of the rocks.

There is one who seems ~~to be~~ to

OSCAR ~~**That one seems to**~~ **be pushed along and if it is** ~~**a**~~ but a

it is ~~a~~ a heavy one. can see

shadow ~~**it is a thin one**~~**.** **It is CONAN, I** ~~**recognise**~~

~~Do not let us show~~ any

the sheepskin; ~~**let us look as if the night had**~~ **no fear**

~~fear before him~~ I am glad he has not seen

for ~~**us, as though we could brave the people of**~~ **the**

our fear

~~**caves**~~ **(Enter CAOLITE and four SPEARMEN)**

Goll over

~~**CAOLITE**~~ **The night is** ~~**done**~~ **at last.**

14+ The TS is continued by Berg(14), fol. 1r.

-22-

CONAN The night is ~~done~~ [over] and the last day has begun; give me a drink for I can go no further without one.

~~OSCAR~~ [Cailte] The day has begun and we must ~~get~~ [hurry] on, ~~and fall in with the hounds~~. Have you seen ~~FINN~~ [him] ? Have you heard his horn ?

CAOLITE [Goll] No, he has not sounded it, but the beast will be stirring with the day.

1st. SPEARMAN The last I saw of FINN ~~was on yonder hill-top~~; he stood facing the dawn and ~~bellowing to us~~ [shouting to his hounds].

2nd SPEARMAN Yes, ~~bellowing~~ like a bull for its heifer.

CONAN Sit down, I will go no further. When a man has got to die is it not better for him to die sitting down than walking about; it is better to die on ~~dry~~ [clean] ground than in the mire ~~or in the~~ river - Give me your ~~flagon~~, CAOILTE

[Berg(14), 1[r]]

–22–

over
CONAN **The night is ~~done~~ and the last day has begun; give me a drink for I can go no further without one.**

go further up the hill we hurry if we woud find
~~OSCAR~~ Caole **The day has begun and we ^ must ~~get~~ on, ~~and fall in with~~**
Fin again him
~~the hounds~~. Have you seen ~~FINN~~ ? Have you heard his horn ?

~~CAOLITE~~ Goll **No, he has not sounded it, but the beast will be stirring with the day.**

great rock
time he was on [?~~this~~] the ~~cliff~~ ^ yonder
1st. SPEARMAN **The last ^ I saw of FINN ~~was on yonder hill-top~~; he**
shouting to his hounds
stood facing the dawn and ~~bellowing to us~~. ~~He~~ When he saw us he shouted that we were to climb up to him.

He bellowed
2nd SPEARMAN **~~Yes~~, ~~bellowing~~ like a bull for its heifer{, .** but I have had climbing enough.

CONAN **Sit down, I will go no further. When a man has got to die is it not better for him to die sitting down than**
clean
walking about; it is better to die on ~~dry~~ ^ ground than
or up to his middle in water leathr bottle
in the mire ~~or in the river~~ ^ – Give me your ~~flagon~~, CAOILTE

The TS continues NLI 8777(10) a, fol. 17[r]. The vertical cancellation of lines 11–14 on this page is in a lighter shade of blue-black ink than the remainder of WBY's emendations.

-30-

GRANIA I would you had left me to be trampled and gored by it. I am ~~overworn~~, ~~so it seems to me that I am even what I say.~~ ~~If~~ you have ~~decided~~ that the death of this boar is to put me on one side or the other, give me ~~either~~ to DIARMUID or give me to you; but I am no man's ~~spoil~~, weary as I am I know ~~that~~. You have ~~settled~~ it all between you, ~~men that you are~~, but I do not accept your ~~account~~. ~~You waste your time here, FINN~~, go to the hunt and kill the boar, or make a fire for me here to warm myself by, it is all the same.

FINN I ~~must stay to defend you even to losing~~ my chance of killing the beast ~~of this hunt~~.

GRANIA It does not matter, leave me here, go to the hunt; so long as I have a fire I do not mind.

FINN I dare not leave - If it were to spring upon you from

[Berg(14), 2[r]]

–30–

GRANIA I would you had left me to be trampled and gored by
~~worn out~~ & cold (pause)
it. I am ~~overworn~~, ~~so it seems to me that I am even~~
planned
~~what I say.~~ ~~So~~ you have ~~decided~~ that the death of
to
this boar is to put me on one side or the other, give
to
me ~~either~~ to DIARMUID or give me to you; but I am no
no mans spoil.
spoil ~~chattel~~? this. I am ~~not any mans chattel~~.
man's ~~spoil~~, weary as I am I know ~~that~~. You have
plannd
~~settled~~ it all between you, ~~men that you are~~, but I
plan Go from me Fin
do not accept your ~~account~~. ~~You waste your time here~~,
this
~~FINN~~, go to thes hunt and kill ~~the~~ boar, or make a fire
for me here to warm myself by, it is all the same.

– I ~~must stay with~~ all though I lose
FINN **~~I must stay to defend you, even to forego~~ my chance of**
this I must stay with you – I must stay
killing ~~the~~ beast ~~of this hunt~~. to defend you.

or
GRANIA **It does not matter, leave me here, go to the hunt; so**
long as I have a fire I do not mind.

you
FINN **I dare not leave – If it were to spring upon you from**

Pages 23–29 are missing from the TS sequence.

6 The inserted words, "spoil", "this", and "no man's spoil", are in the same lighter shade of blue-black ink as the vertical cancellation lines.

-31-

the thicket -

GRANIA It might be better, for I have caused mischief enough in this world, and I am weary of the part I play in it. Yet FINN, there is no evil in me, there was none when I left you in Tara, there is none now. You seemed to me an old man then, and my thoughts turned to a younger one; I felt like that then. Yesterday when I sent DIARMUID to fetch you, I did so because I saw he could not live in estrangement from the Fianna, and had not this evil thing broken out of the earth as it was prophesied that it should, DIARMUID and you would have been friends again. You would have fought shoulder to shoulder against the men of Eri, against the men of Lockland and the men of Fiona.

FINN DIARMUID and I could never be friends ; the peace we

[Berg(14), 3r]

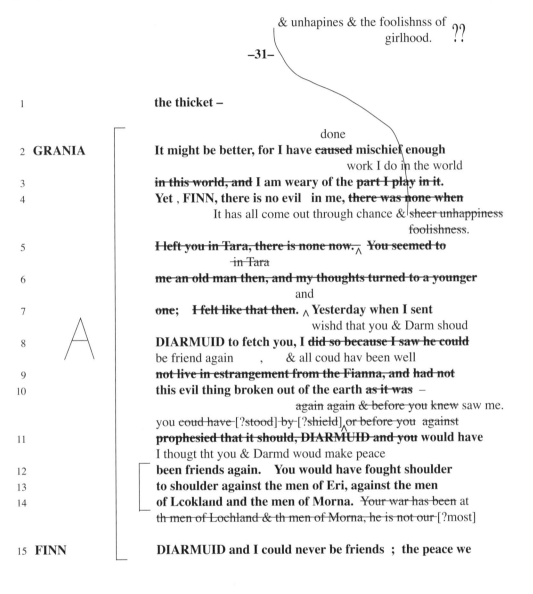

& unhapines & the foolishnss of girlhood. ??

–31–

the thicket –

done
GRANIA **It might be better, for I have ~~caused~~ mischief enough**
work I do in the world
~~in this world, and~~ I am weary of the ~~part I play in it~~.
Yet , FINN, there is no evil in me, ~~there was none when~~
It has all come out through chance & ~~sheer unhappiness~~ ~~foolishness~~.
~~I left you in Tara, there is none now.~~ ^ ~~You seemed to~~
~~in Tara~~
~~me an old man then, and my thoughts turned to a younger~~
and
~~one~~; ~~I felt like that then.~~ ^ Yesterday when I sent
wishd that you & Darm shoud
A
DIARMUID to fetch you, I ~~did so because I saw he could~~
be friend again , & all coud hav been well
~~not live in estrangement from the Fianna, and had not~~
this evil thing broken out of the earth ~~as it was~~ –
~~again again & before you knew~~ saw me.
you ~~coud have~~ [?stood] ~~by~~ [?shield] ^ ~~or before you~~ against
~~prophesied that it should, DIARMUID and you~~ would have
I thougt tht you & Darmd woud make peace
been friends again. You would have fought shoulder
to shoulder against the men of Eri, against the men
of Lcokland and the men of Morna. ~~Your war has been~~ at
~~th men of Lochland & th men of Morna, he is not our~~ [?most]

FINN **DIARMUID and I could never be friends ; the peace we**

-1 What is transcribed here as two question marks could be WBY's version of "my".

8 The large "A" in the left-hand margin refers to WBY's revised fair copy in NLI 8777(5), fol. 21r. It is drawn in the same lighter shade of blue-black ink as the vertical cancellations.

[Berg(14), 4r]

111

-32-

made was a false peace, ~~and I, as much as he, was de-~~

~~ceived by it~~ ~~That peace was one of the tricks the~~

gods ~~play upon us~~ (Hunting horns are heard in the dis-

tance)

FINN (Listening) ~~The~~ boar ~~is being~~ ~~followed~~ ~~closely~~, I

can hear my hounds - yes, it is Bran ~~and~~ now Siegleolan

AND now it is Lomair, they have ~~recovered~~ their courage

and are driving him ~~hither and thither~~ from ~~covert~~ to

~~covert~~.

GRANIA FINN, I ~~beg you to forego your desire of me~~ - be

DIARMUID'S friend and save him - kill the boar and save

him.

FINN If I kill the boar, what then ? You will ~~be mine~~ ?

GRANIA I am no man's ~~though a man may be mine~~.

[Berg(14), 4r]

–32–

made was a false peace, ~~and I, as much as he, was de-~~
~~ceived by it.~~ ~~That peace was one of the tricks the~~
~~gods play upon us~~ (Hunting horns are heard in the distance)

The th boars
{ ~~is~~ ~~has the~~ hounds at [?~~his~~] heels now.
FINN (Listening) ~~Th~~{ ~~e boar is being followed closely~~, I
it is
can hear my hounds – yes, it is Bran , and now^ Siegleolan
~~got~~ their
and now it is Lomair, they have^ ~~recovered~~ their courage
^found

cover
and are driving him ~~along and across~~ from ~~covert~~^ to
cover.
~~covert.~~

beseech put the desire of me out of your heart
GRANIA FINN, I ~~beg you to forego your desire of me~~ – be
DIARMUID'S friend and save him – kill the boar and save
him.

belong to me
FINN If I kill the boar, what then ? You will ~~be mine~~^ ?

chattel
GRANIA I am no man's ~~though a man may be mine.~~

The vertical cancellation is in the lighter shade of blue-black ink. The significance of the three vertical pencil marks in the top RH corner of the page is unknown.

13+ The next two pages of the TS are represented by the two fragments constituting Berg(08).

[Berg(08), 1[r], 2[r]]

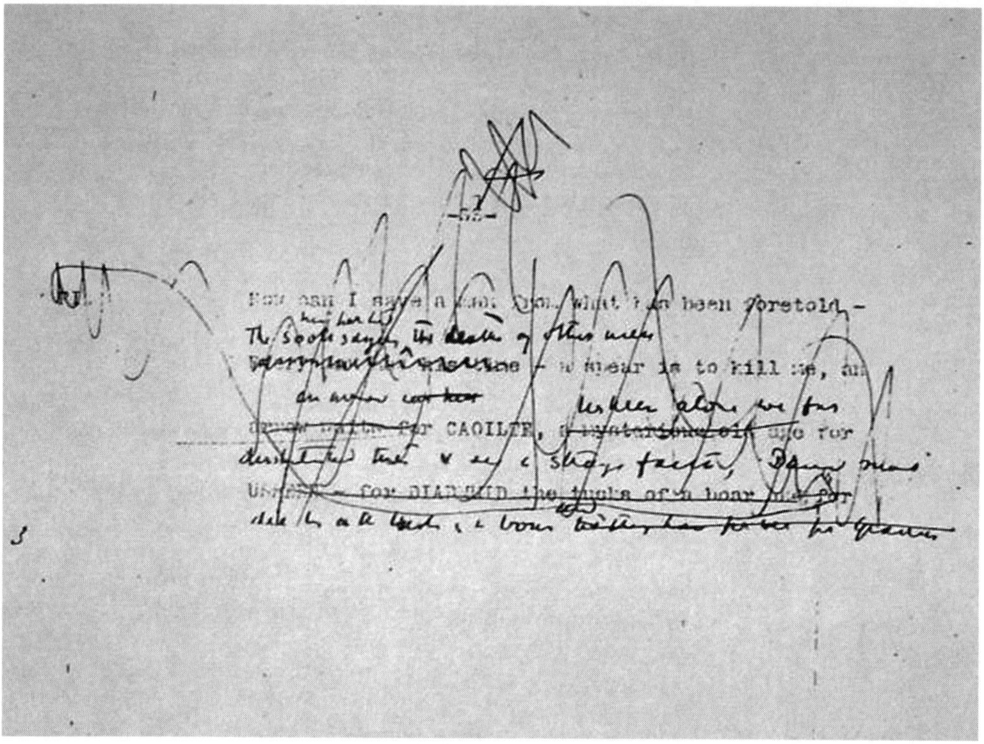

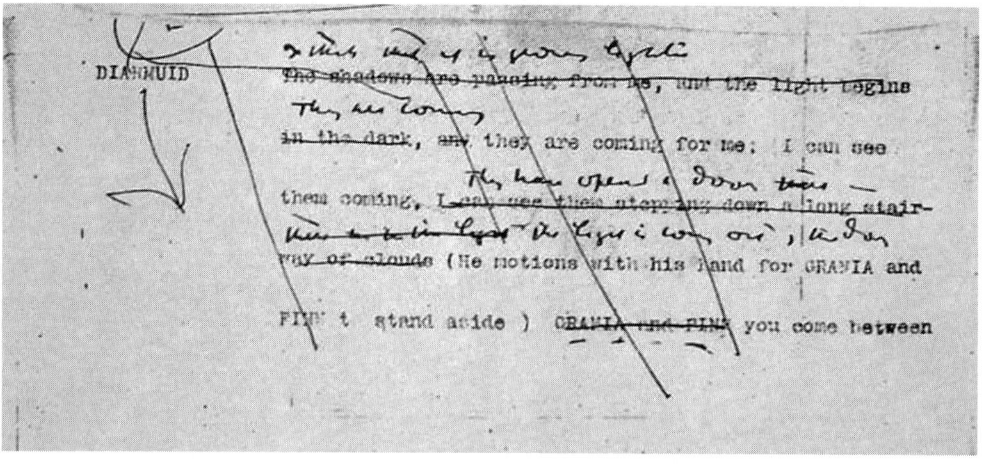

The images of the two pages are cropped to display only the text

[Berg(08), 1^{r}]

-33-

FIN **How can I save a man from what has been foretold -**
has for told
The sooth sayer ^ the deaths of other men
~~Every man has his time~~ - a spear is to kill me, an
an arrow ~~will kill~~ Usheen alone [?we/live] for
~~arrow waits for~~ CAOILTE, ~~a mysterious old age~~ for
^ [?disstant][?land] times & see a strange [?faith], Darmd must
USHEEN - for DIARMUID the tusks of a boar and for
and
die by ~~&~~ the tusks of a boar ~~but they have for seen for Grania~~

[Berg(08), 2^{r}]

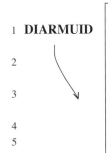

I think ~~that~~ it is growing lighter
DIARMUID **~~The shadows are passing from me, and the light begins~~**
They are coming
~~in the dark~~, ~~and~~ they are coming for me; I can see
They have opened a door ~~there~~ —
them coming , ~~I can see them stepping down a long stair~~-
~~there in in the light~~ the light is coming out of the door
~~way of clouds~~ (He motions with his hand for GRANIA and
FINN to stand aside) ~~GRANIA and FINN~~ you come between

1^{r} The content follows directly on p. 32 of Berg(14), fol. 4^{r}. WBY rewrote the same passage in NLI 8777(5), fol. 23^{r}. The overall cancellation on this page is in a lighter shade of blue-black ink than the other revisions.

2^{r} The fragment immediately precedes p. 35 of Berg(14), fol. 5^{r}, and is therefore the bottom of p. 34 of the continuous revised typescript. WBY rewrote the same passage in NLI 8777(5), fol. 24^{r}, heading it "B". The portion of a character in the top LH corner of the fragment could be the remnant of a corresponding "B".

The overall cancellation on fol. 2^{r}, along with the arrow in the LH margin, is in a lighter shade of blue-black ink than the other revisions.

[Berg(14), 5r]

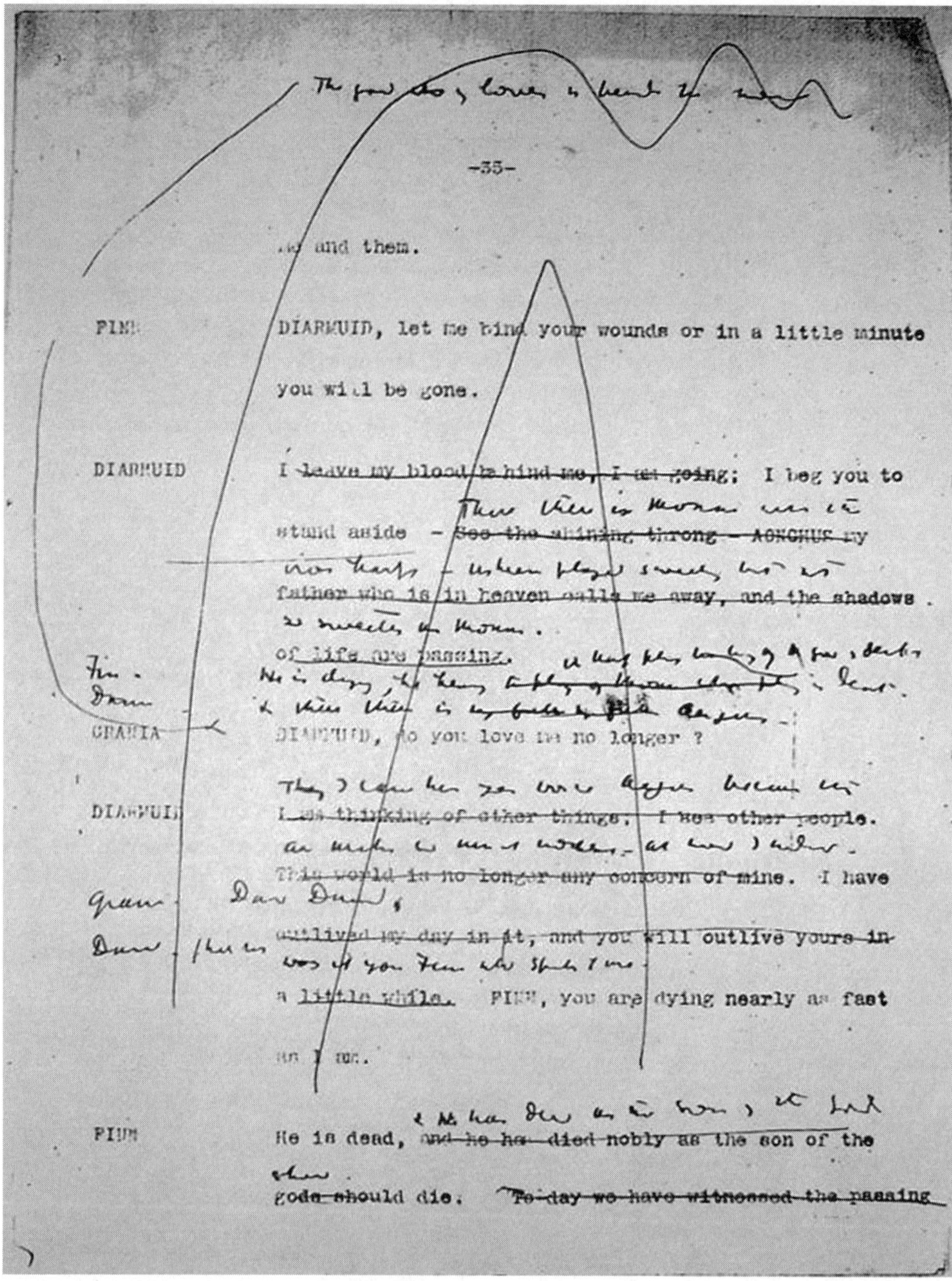

-35-

me and them.

FINN DIARMUID, let me bind your wounds or in a little minute you will be gone.

DIARMUID I leave my blood behind me, I am going; I beg you to stand aside - See the shining throng - AONGHUS my father who is in heaven calls me away, and the shadows of life are passing.

GRANIA DIARMUID, do you love me no longer ?

DIARMUID I am thinking of other things, I see other people. This world is no longer any concern of mine. I have outlived my day in it, and you will outlive yours in a little while. FINN, you are dying nearly as fast as I am.

FINN He is dead, and he has died nobly as the son of the gods should die. To-day we have witnessed the passing

[Berg(14), 5r]

The god ~~who~~ of lovers is [?leadg] his [?men]

–35–

me and them.

FINN **DIARMUID, let me bind your wounds or in a little minute you will be gone.**

DIARMUID **~~I leave my blood behind me, I am going~~; I beg you to**
Then there is Morna with the
stand aside – ~~See the shining throng – AONGHUS my~~
iron harp – Usheen played sweetly but not
~~father who is in heaven calls me away, and the shadows~~
so sweetly as Morna.
~~of life are passing.~~

th harp playg [?~~lo long~~] of the god of death
Fin – He is dying, his hearing ~~th playng of Morna whose playg~~ is death –
Dairm & that there is ~~my father~~ ~~my fath~~ Aengus –

GRANIA **DIARMUID, do you love me no longer ?**

~~They~~ I cannt hear your voice Aengus because they
DIARMUID **~~I am thinking of other things; I see other people~~.**
ar makng to much noises – [?but] now I under–
~~This world is no longer any concern of mine~~. I have
Gran – Dar Darmd
Dar – (he has **~~outlived my day in it, and you will outlive yours in~~**
was it you Finn who spoke to me –

~~a little while.~~ FINN, you are dying nearly as fast as I am.

& he has died as the son of the gods
FINN **He is dead, ~~and he has died nobly as the son of the~~**
should.
~~gods should die.~~ ~~To-day we have witnessed the passing~~

The TS continues following the fragmentary Berg(08), fol. 2r. The vertical cancellations here are in the lighter shade of blue-black ink.

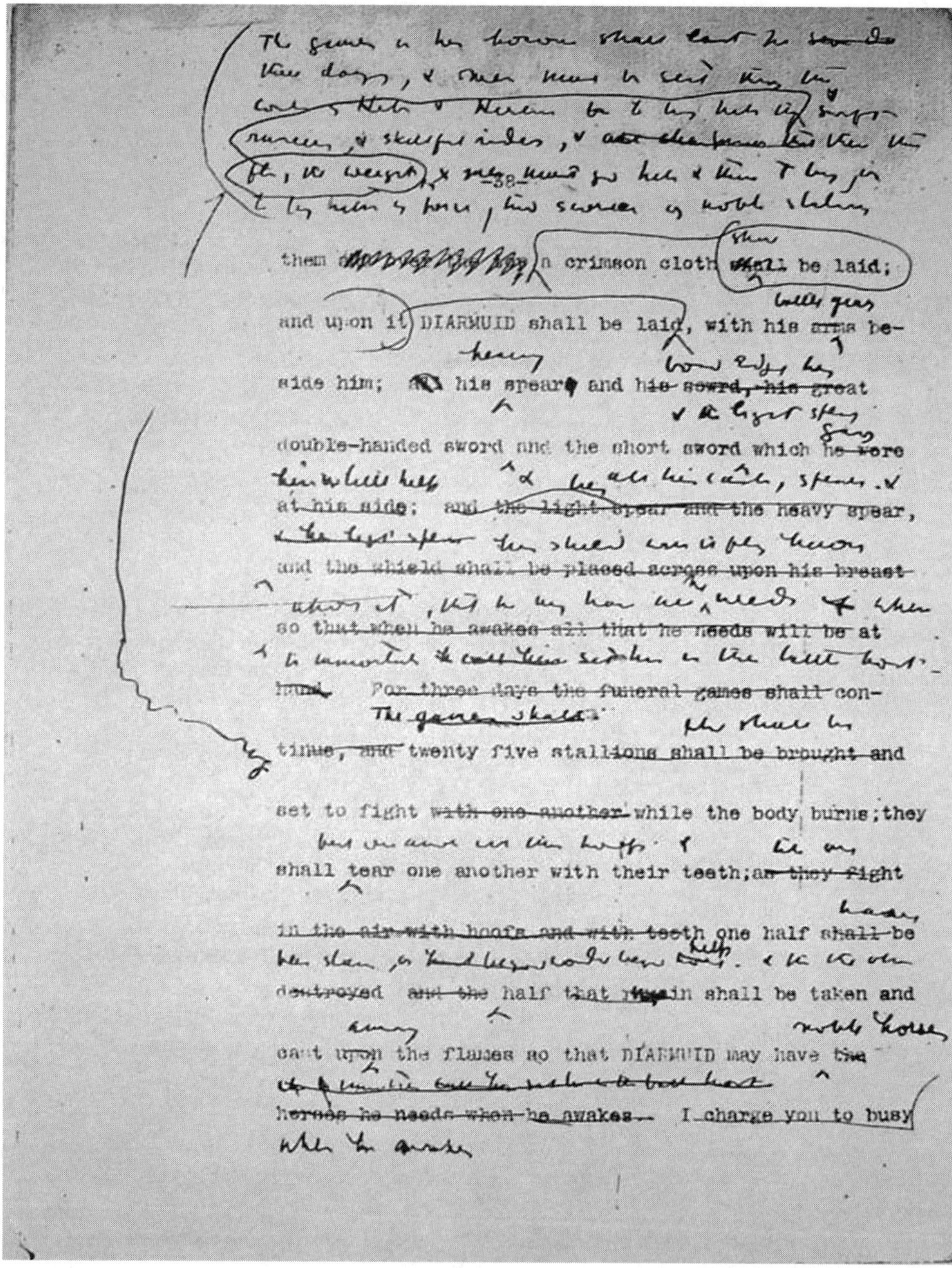
-38-

them a crimson cloth shall be laid;

and upon it DIARMUID shall be laid, with his arms beside him; his spear and his sowrd, his great double-handed sword and the short sword which he wore at his side; and the light spear and the heavy spear, and the shield shall be placed across upon his breast so that when he awakes all that he needs will be at hand. For three days the funeral games shall continue, and twenty five stallions shall be brought and set to fight with one another while the body burns; they shall tear one another with their teeth; as they fight in the air with hoofs and with teeth one half shall be destroyed and the half that remain shall be taken and cast upon the flames so that DIARMUID may have the horses he needs when he awakes. I charge you to busy

Pages 36–37 are missing from the TS sequence.

-1 and 1 The cancellation is in the lighter shade of blue-black ink—like the transposition in the same line and in line 2.

[Berg(14), 6r]

The games in his honour shall last for ~~seve da~~
three days, & men must be sent throug the
&
countries of Hebr & Hermon ~~for~~ to to bring back th^ swift
runners, & skillful riders, & ~~all champions that~~ then those
fling the weight, & men must go here & there to buy, or
–38–
to brng hither by force, two scores of noble stalions
shoud
them ~~and over the top~~^a crimson cloth ~~shall~~^ be laid;
battle gear
and upon it DIARMUID shall be laid, with his ~~arms~~^ be-
heavy broad edge his
side him; ~~all~~ his^ spears and ~~his sowrd, his great~~
& the light spear
gave
double-handed sword^ and the short sword ^which ~~he wore~~
him ~~no~~ little help all his casting spears – &
& ~~his~~
~~**at his side;**~~ ~~**and the light spear and the heavy spear,**~~
~~& the light spear~~ his shield with th flyng heron
^**and ~~the shield shall be placed across upon his breast~~**
he
upon it, that he may have all^needs ~~if~~ when
^ **so ~~that when he awakes all that he needs will be~~ at**
th immortals ~~h call him~~ set him in the battle host –
~~**hand.**~~ ~~**For three days the funeral games shall**~~ **con-**
~~The games shall~~ who shall be
~~**tinue, and twenty five stallions shall be brought and**~~
set to fight ~~with one another~~ while the body burns;they
beat one anothr with their hoofs & till one
shall^tear one another with their teeth;~~as they fight~~
have
~~**in the air with hoofs and with teeth**~~ **one half ~~shall be~~**
help
been slain, or ~~hurt beyond~~ wounded beyond [?~~horses~~] – & thn the other
~~**destroyed**~~ ~~**and the**~~^**half ~~that remain~~ shall be taken and**
among noble horses
cast ~~upon~~^ the flames so that DIARMUID may have ~~the~~^
~~when th immortals call him set him in the battl host~~
~~**horses he needs when he awakes.**~~ ~~**I charge you to busy**~~
when he awakes

7 if when] The first word is deleted, and the second word inserted, in the lighter shade of blue-black ink.

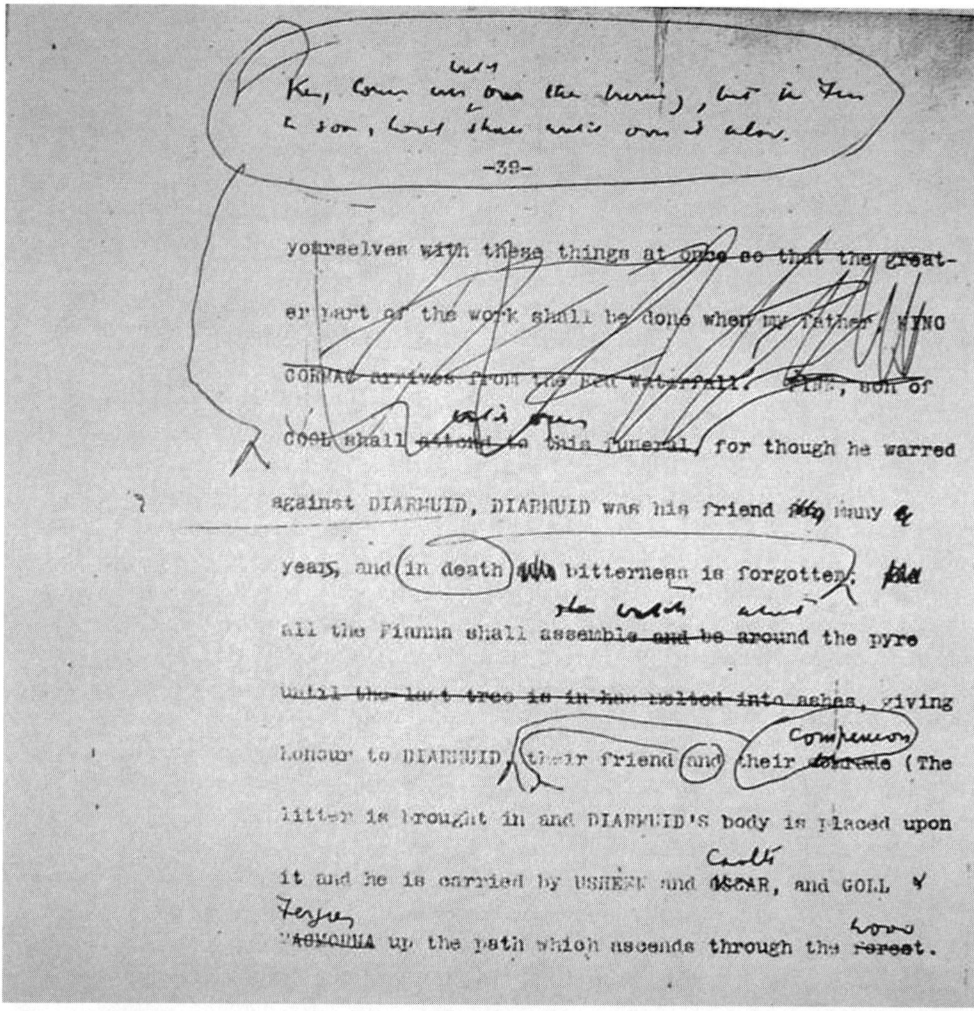

-38-

yourselves with these things at once so that the greater part of the work shall be done when my father, KING CORMAC arrives from the Red Waterfall. FINN, son of COOL shall attend to this funeral, for though he warred against DIARMUID, DIARMUID was his friend many years, and in death all bitterness is forgotten. All all the Fianna shall assemble and be around the pyre until the last tree is in has melted into ashes, giving honour to DIARMUID, their friend and their comrade (The litter is brought in and DIARMUID'S body is placed upon it and he is carried by USHEEN and OSCAR, and GOLL MACMORNA up the path which ascends through the forest.

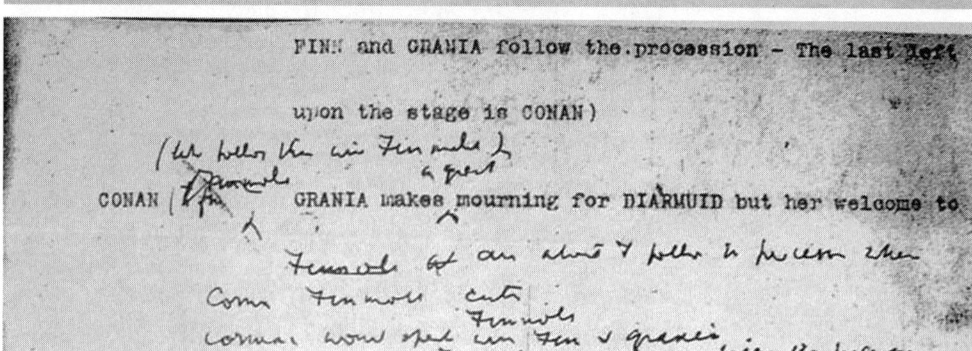

FINN and GRANIA follow the procession - The last left upon the stage is CONAN)

CONAN GRANIA makes mourning for DIARMUID but her welcome to

38[r] When the fragment was clipped from a larger sheet, which does not survive, in the last line of holograph some of the letters of "Finn" and "Grania" were cut off at the bottom.

[Berg(14), 7[r]]

watch
King Cormac will ^ over the burning, but then Fin
the son of Cool shall watch over it also.

–39–

yourselves with these things at once so that the great-
er part of the work shall be done when my father, KING
CORMAC arrives from the Red Waterfall. FINN, son of
watch over
COOL shall ~~attend to~~ this funeral, for though he warred
against DIARMUID, DIARMUID was his friend ~~for~~ many ~~a~~
years, and in death ~~all~~ bitterness is forgotten; ~~and~~
~~sha~~ watch about ^
all the Fianna shall ~~assemble and be around~~ the pyre
~~until the last tree is in has melted into ashes~~, giving
companions
honour to DIARMUID, ^^ their friend and their ~~comrade~~ (The
litter is brought in and DIARMUID'S body is placed upon
Caolte
it and he is carried by USHEEN and ~~OSCAR~~, and GOLL &
Fergus wood
~~MACMORNA~~ up the path which ascends through the ~~forest~~.

[NLI 8777(4) e, 38[r]]

FINN and GRANIA follow the procession - The last left
upon the stage is CONAN)

(Ushn follows them with Finmole)
~~Finmole~~ a great
CONAN (~~to fin~~ ^ **GRANIA makes ^ mourning for DIARMUID but her welcome to**

~~Finmole~~ ~~a~~ are about to follow th procession when
Corma Finmole enter

Finmole
Cormac would speak with Fin & Grania
& Finn & Grania & Cormac follw the processn

7[r], ll. 1–4 are canceled, and the replacement lines at the top of the page are looped in, with the lighter shade of blue-black ink. The emendations in lines 9–9+ are also in the lighter shade of ink.

38[r] The page of TS follows Berg(14), fol. 7[r], although some intervening lines of text have been lost.

1 The insertions "(to fin" and "great" are in a darker shade of blue-black ink than the other revisions on this page, and are therefore almost certainly earlier. See annotation concerning the different shades in the revision of NLI 8777(10), etc.

The following page in the TS sequence (p. 41) is missing.

[NLI 8777(5), 1[r]]

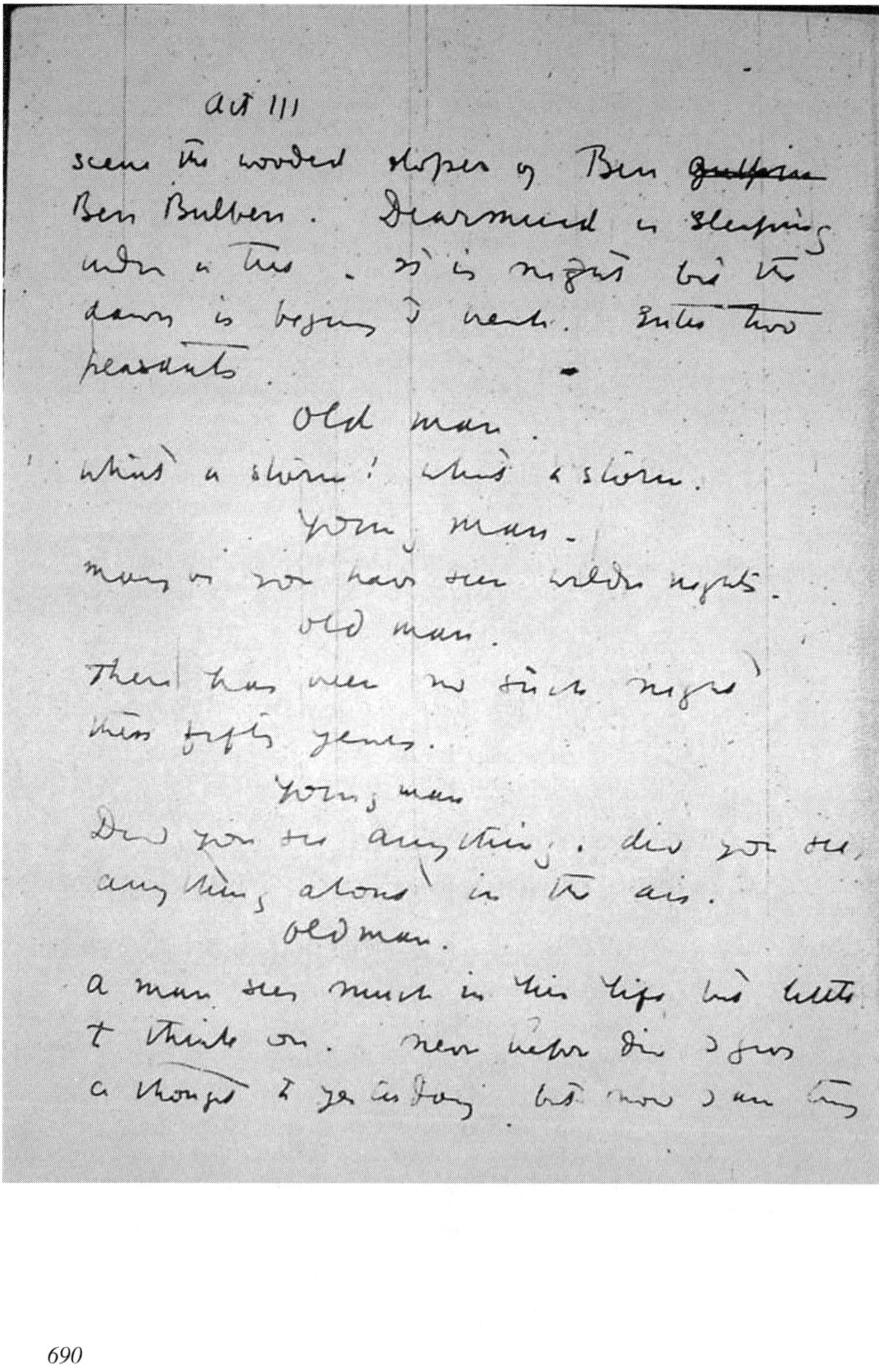

Act III

scene the wooded slopes of Ben ~~Gulban~~
Ben Bulben. Diarmuid is sleeping
under a tree. It is night but the
dawn is begining to break. Enter two
peasants.

Old man.

What a storm! what a storm.

Young man.

Many a you have seen wilder nights.

Old man.

There has been no such night
these fifty years.

Young man

Did you see anything, did you see
anything, above in the air.

Old man.

A man sees much in his life but little
to think on. Never before did I give
a thought to yesterday but now I am tiry

W. B. Yeats's Holograph Rewriting of Extensive Passages in a Notebook

[NLI 8777(5), 1^{r}]

Act III

Scene the wooded slopes of Ben ~~Gulpin~~
Ben Bulben. Diarmuid is sleeping
under a tree – It is night but the
dawn is begining to break. Enter two
peasants.

Old Man.
What a storm! What a storm.

Young Man –
May be you have seen wilder nights –

Old Man.
There has been no such night
these fifty years.

Young Man
Did you see any thing. did you see
any thing about in the air.

Old Man.
A man sees much in his life but little
to think on. Never before did I give
a thought to yesterday but now I am trying

[NLI 8777(5), 2r]

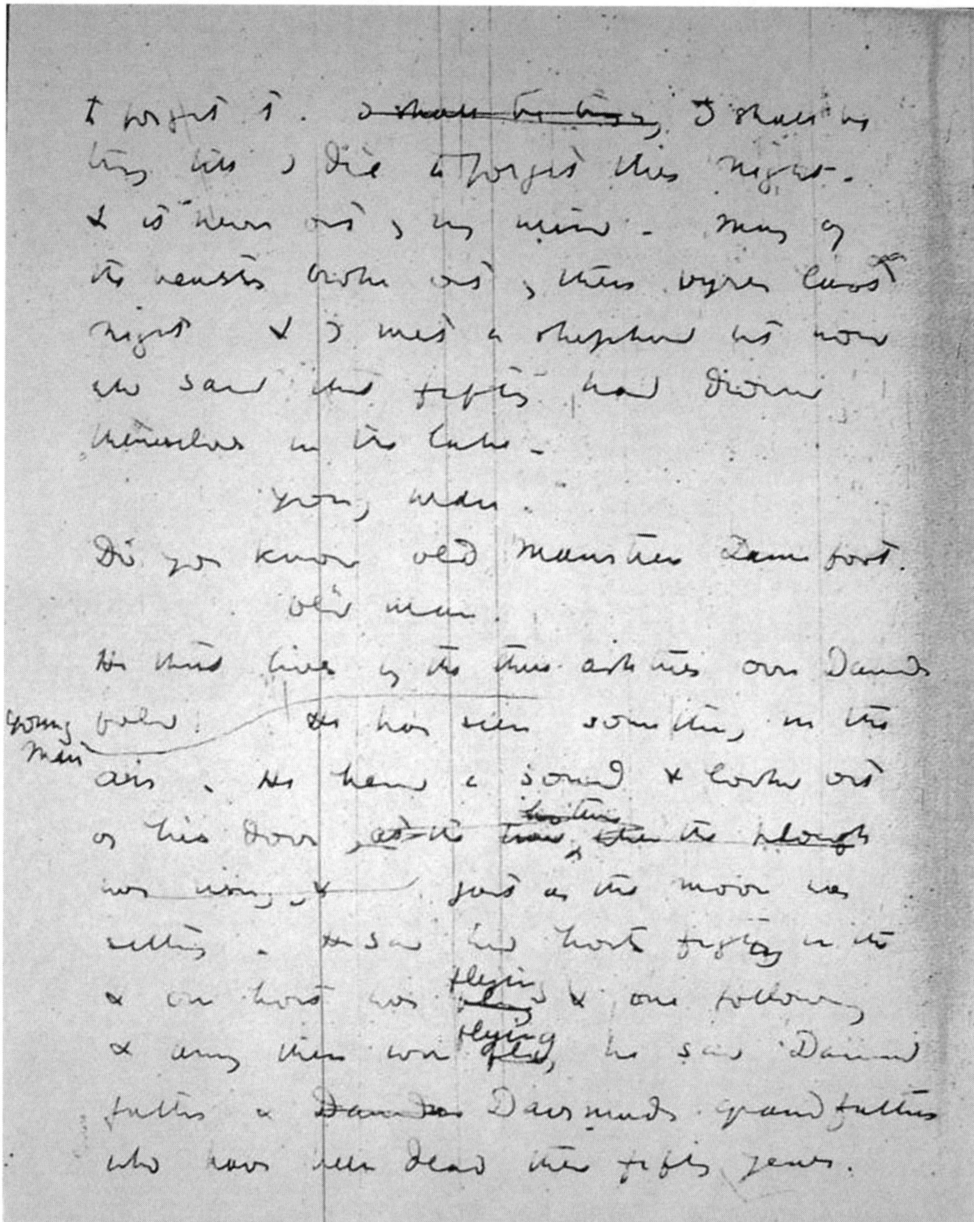
to forget it. ~~I shall be long~~, I shall be long till I die to forget this night. It is driven out of my mind. Many of the vessels broke out of their vigil last night & I met a shepherd who now he saw the fifty had driven themselves in the lake.

Young Man.

Do you know old Manister Dermott.

Old Man.

He that lives at the ... over Dermots [Young Man] ... He has seen something in the air. He heard a sound & looked out of his door ... was rising & just as the moon was setting. He saw two hosts fighting in the air & one host was flying & one following & among them that were flying, he saw Dermots father & ~~Dermots~~ Dermots grandfather who were all dead these fifty years.

[NLI 8777(5), 2r]

to forget it. ~~I shall be trying~~ I shall be
tring till I die to forget this night –
& it never out of my mind – Many of
the beasts broke out of their byres last
night & I met a shepherd but now
who said that fifty had drownd
themselves in the lake –

Young Man.

Do you know old Maintian Lame foot.

Old Man.

He that lives by the three ash trees over Darmds
Young fold! / He has seen some thing in the
Man air – He heard a sound & looked out
~~his time~~
of his door, ~~at the time~~ ^ ~~when the plough~~
~~was rising, &~~ just as the moon was
{ing
setting – He saw two hosts fight{g in the
flying
& one host was ~~fling~~ & one following
flying
& among thos were ~~fling~~ he saw Dairmuid
father & ~~Dairmds~~ Dairmuds grandfather
who have been dead these fifty years

8 Properly, Mhantáin. The English version, Lame Foot, appears in HRC(3), fol. 2r, line 1—indeed, only in these two texts.

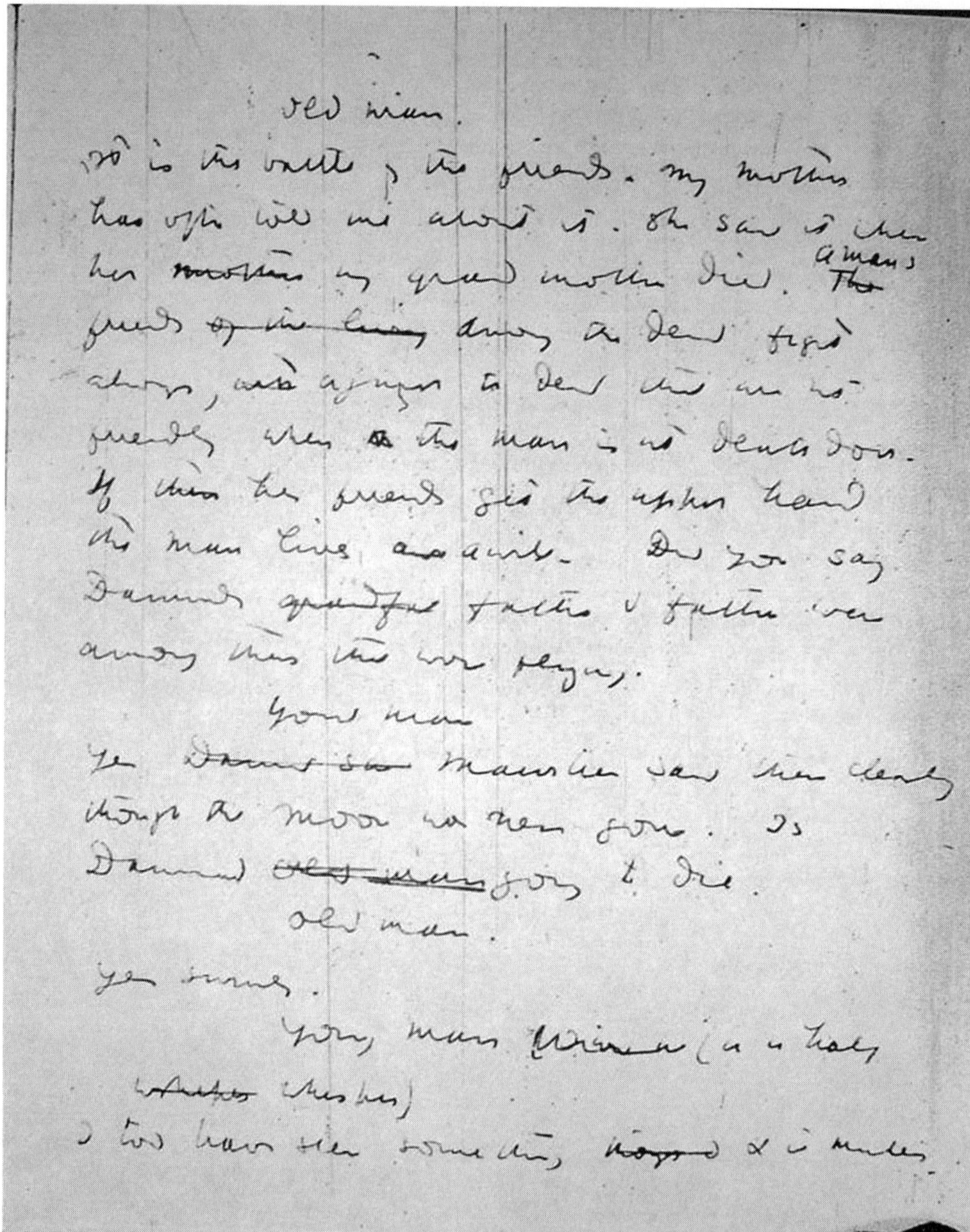

Old man.
It is the battle of the friends. My mother
has often told me about it. She saw it when
her ~~mother~~ my grand mother died. ~~The~~ A man's
friends ~~of the living~~ among the dead fight
always, and against the dead that are not
friendly when ~~a~~ the man is at death's door.
If then her friends get the upper hand
the man lives a saint. Do you say
Damned ~~grandfa~~ father & father were
among those that were playing.

Young man
Yes ~~Damned saw~~ Mauslee saw them clearly
through the moon was then gone. Is
Damned ~~Old man~~ going to die.

Old man.
Yes soon.

Young man ~~Whim~~ (in a holy
~~whisper~~ whisper)
I too have seen something ~~through~~ & it makes

[NLI 8777(5), 3^{r}]

Old Man.
It is the battle of the friends. My mother
has often told me about it – She saw it when
A man s
her ~~mother~~ my grand mother died. ~~The~~
friends ~~of the living~~ among the dead fight
always, ~~with~~ against th dead that are not
friendly when ~~a~~ the man is at deats door –
If ~~their~~ his friends get the upper hand
that man lives ~~awi~~ awhile – Did you say
Darmuids ~~grandfat~~ father & father wer
among those that were flying.

Young Man
Yes ~~Darmd saw~~ Maintian saw them clearly
though the moon was then gone. Is
Darmuid ~~Old Man.~~ going to die.

Old Man.
Yes surely.

Young Man ~~(I too h~~ (in a half
~~whisper~~ whisper)
I too have seen something ~~thogh I~~ & it makes

12–13 "Is . . . die." was added to the previous sentence after the part ascription was written.

me shake him now I speak of it.
The moon had ~~got~~ gone in hours when I
saw a giant grey ragged man & he
drove the beasts that the Feanna
are hunting; He made with a spear
along the top of the ~~moun~~ mountain

(Dairmuid rouses himself & listens
& then lies down again)

Old Man

That too means Dairmuid's death. He
will die in these hunting.

Hush

(He points to Dairmuid)

~~But~~ Young Man.

If we do not waken him the beast
may come upon him sleeping.

Old man.

Better do nothing, for if all that is
said about these beasts is true it is
some god. I have heard that
it is strange, & troubles wise things come

[NLI 8777(5), 4r]

me shake even now to speak of it.
The moon had ~~but~~ gone an hour when I
saw a quaint grey ragged man & he
drove this beast that the Feanna
are hunting – He proded with a spear
along the ~~hi~~ top of the ~~mon~~ mountain
(Darmud rouses himself to listen ~~)~~
~~& the~~ but lies down again)

Old Man
That too means Dairmuids death. He
will die in this hunting.
Hush
(He points to Dairmuid)

~~You~~ Young Man –
If we do not waken him this beast
may com upon him sleeping.

Old Man.
Better do nothing for if all that is
said about this beast is true it
some god. ~~I have heard that~~
at strange, & troubled times they come

[NLI 8777(5), 5^r]

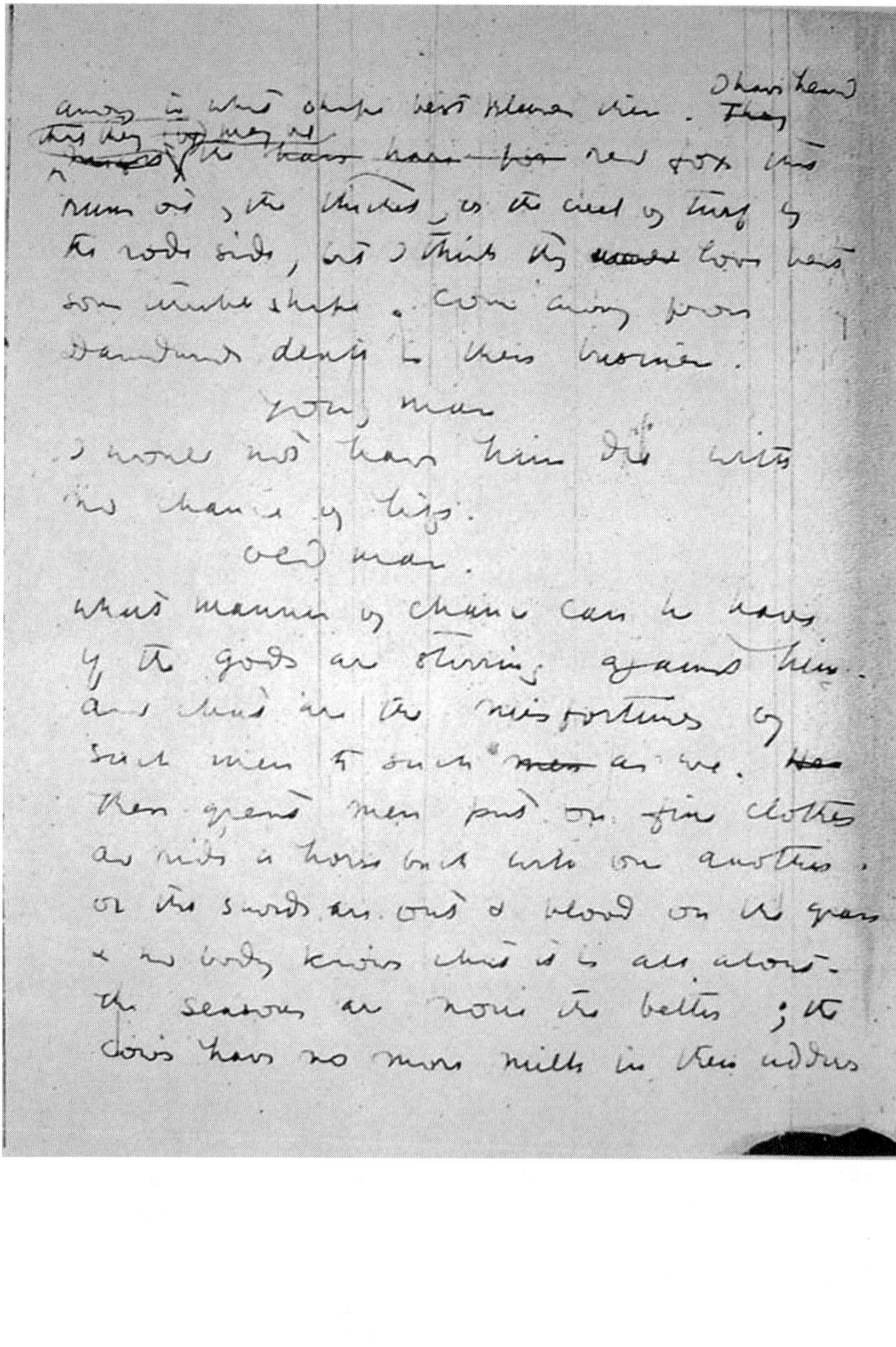

away in what shape best pleases him. They I have heard
this day may at
[illegible] the hare has for red fox this
run out of the thicket, or the curl of turf of
the roadside, but I think they would love best
some invisible shape. Come away from
Dandund [?] dealing in their business.

Young man

I would not have him die without
no chance of life.

Old man.

What manner of chance can he have
if the gods are striving against him.
And what are the misfortunes of
such men to such as we. [illegible]
When great men put on fine clothes
and ride a horseback into one another,
or the swords are out & blood on the grass
& no body knows what it is all about.
the seasons are none the better; the
cows have no more milk in their udders

[NLI 8777(5), 5^r]

I have heard
among in what shape best pleases them – ~~They~~
that they (~~be~~) may be
^~~might~~ the ~~hars~~ ~~hare~~ ~~for~~ red fox that
runs out of the thicket, in the creel of turf by
the rode side, but I think they ~~would~~ love best
some terribl shape . Come away from
Dairmuids death is their business.

Young Man
I would not have him die with
no chance of life.

Old Man.
What manner of chance can he have
if the gods are stirring against him.
And what are the misfortunes of
such men to such ~~men~~ as we. ~~He~~
These great men put on fine clothes
and ride a horse back with one another.
or the swords are out & blood on the grass
& no body knows what it is all about –
The seasons are none the better ; the
cows have no more milk in their udders

them now (exeunt peasants)

Dairmuid.

Croak croak: what does it mean
when one hears a raven over one's
left shoulder. I saw one but now
& it put ravens into my head.

(enter Grania)

Grania.

I have not seen you all this night.
I have been wandering amo^n^g the woods
since the moon went down.

Dairmuid

What have you come for?

Grania.

I was afraid & have been running.
give me time to draw my breath.

Dairmuid.

Your hair is down & your hands
are torn with brambles

[NLI 8777(5), 6^r]

than before (exeunt peasants)

Dairmuid.

Croak croak : What does it mean
when one hears a raven over one's
left shoulder . I saw one but now
and it put ravens into my head.
(enter Grania)

Grania.

I have not seen you all this night.

in
I have been wandring ~~among~~ the wood~~s~~
since the moon went down –

Dairmuid

What have you come for?

Grania.

I was afraid & have been running –
give me time to draw my breath.

Dairmuid.

Your hair is down & your hands
are torn with brambles

[NLI 8777(5), 7^r]

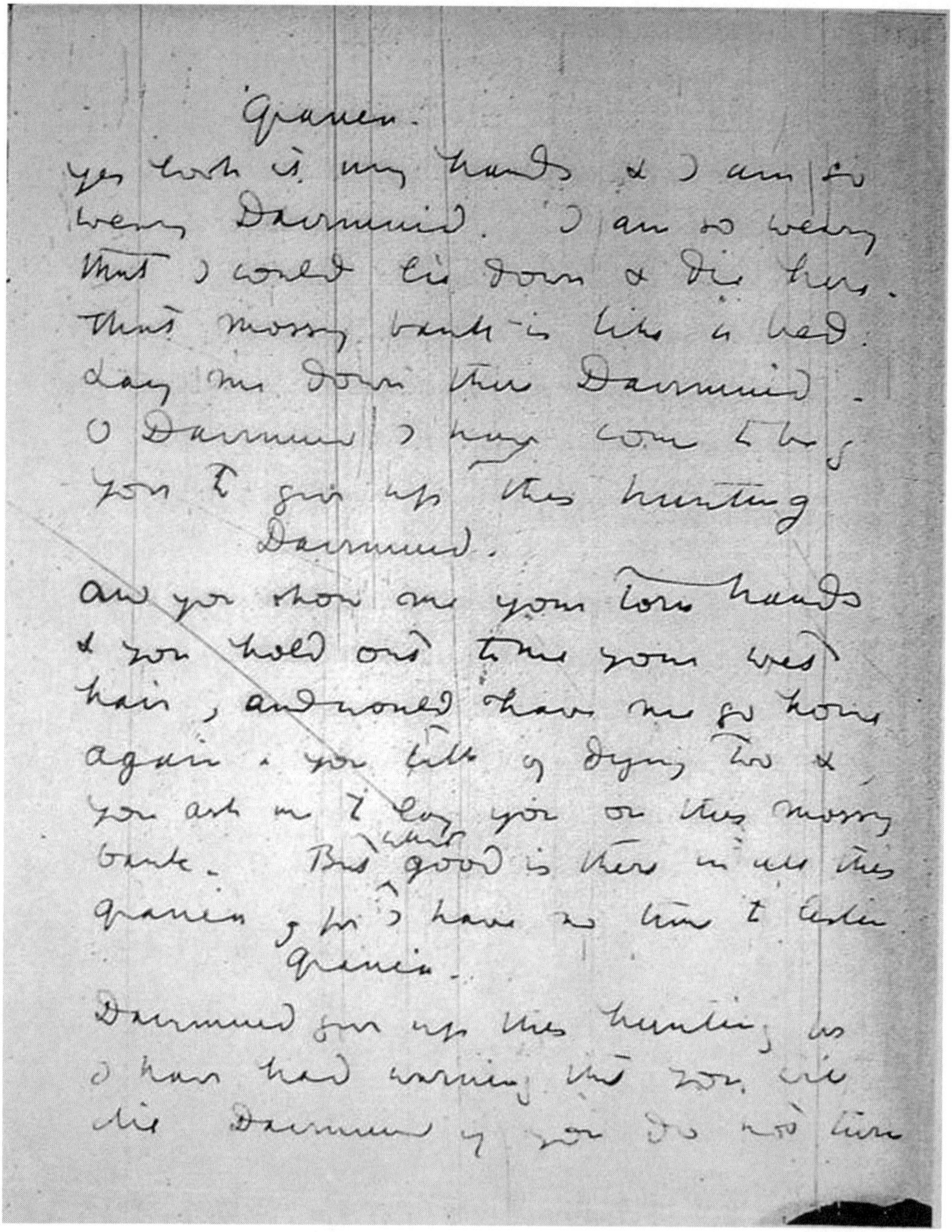
Grania.
yes look at my hands & I am so
weary Diarmuid. I am so weary
that I could lie down & die here.
That mossy bank is like a bed.
Lay me down there Diarmuid.
O Diarmuid I have come to beg
you to give up this hunting
Diarmuid.
and you show me your torn hands
& you hold out to me your wet
hair, and would have me go home
again. you talk of dying too &
you ask me to lay you on this mossy
bank. But what good is there in all this
grania, for I have no time to listen.
Grania.
Diarmuid give up this hunting, for
I have had warning that you will
die Diarmuid if you do not turn

[NLI 8777(5), 7r]

Grania

Yes look at my hands & I am so
weary Dairmuid. I am so weary
that I could lie down & die here –
That mossy bank is like a bed.
Lay me down there Dairmuid –
O Dairmuid I have come to beg
you to give up this hunting

Dairmuid.

And you show me your torn hands
& you hold out to me your wet
hair, and would have me go home
again – you talk of dying too &
you ask me lay you on this mossy
what
bank – But ^ good is there in all this
Grania{, . for I have no time to listen.

Grania –

Dairmuid give up this hunting for
I have had warning that you will
die Dairmuid if you do not turn

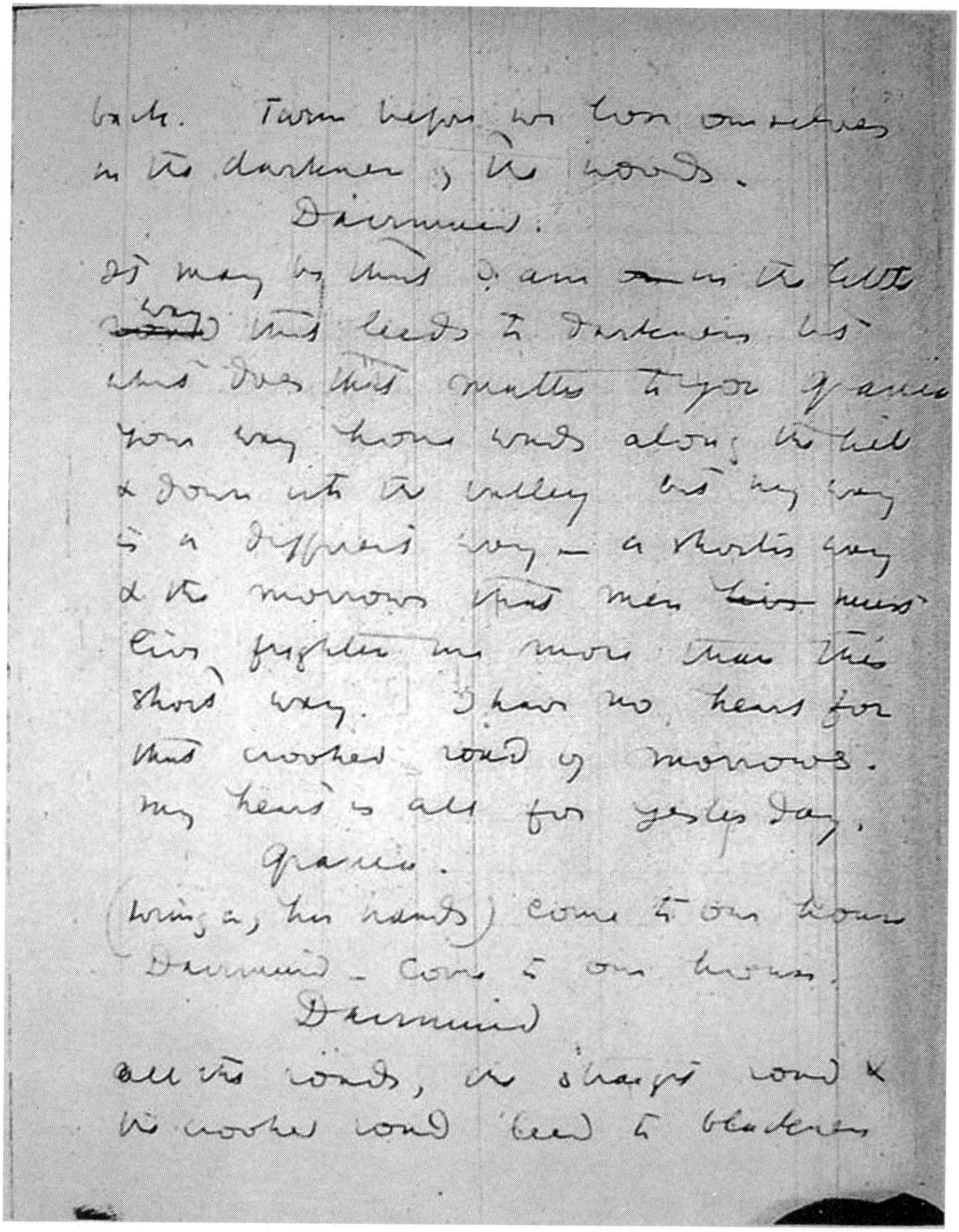

back. Turn before we lose ourselves
in the darkness of the woods.

Diarmuid:

It may be that I am ~~am~~ in the little
~~road~~ way that leads to darkness but
what does that matter to you Grania
Your way homeward along the hill
& down into the valley but my way
is a different way — a shorter way
& the morrows that men ~~live~~ must
live frighten me more than this
short way. I have no heart for
that crooked road of morrows.
My heart is all for yesterday.

Grania.

(wringing her hands) Come to our house
Diarmuid — Come to our house.

Diarmuid

all the roads, the straight road &
the crooked road lead to blackness

[NLI 8777(5), 8^{r}]

back. Turn before we lose our selves
in the darkness of the woods.

Dairmuid.

It may be that I am ~~on~~ in the little
way
~~road~~ that leads to darkness but
what does that matter to you Grania
Your way home winds along the hill
& down into the valley but my way
is a different way — a shorter way
& the morrows that men ~~live~~ must
live frighten me more than this
short way. I have no heart for
that crooked road of morrows.
My heart is all for yester day .

Grania.

(Wringing her hands) Come to our house
Dairmuid – Come to our house.

Dairmuid

All the roads, the straight road &
the crooked road lead to blackness

[NLI 8777(5), 9r]

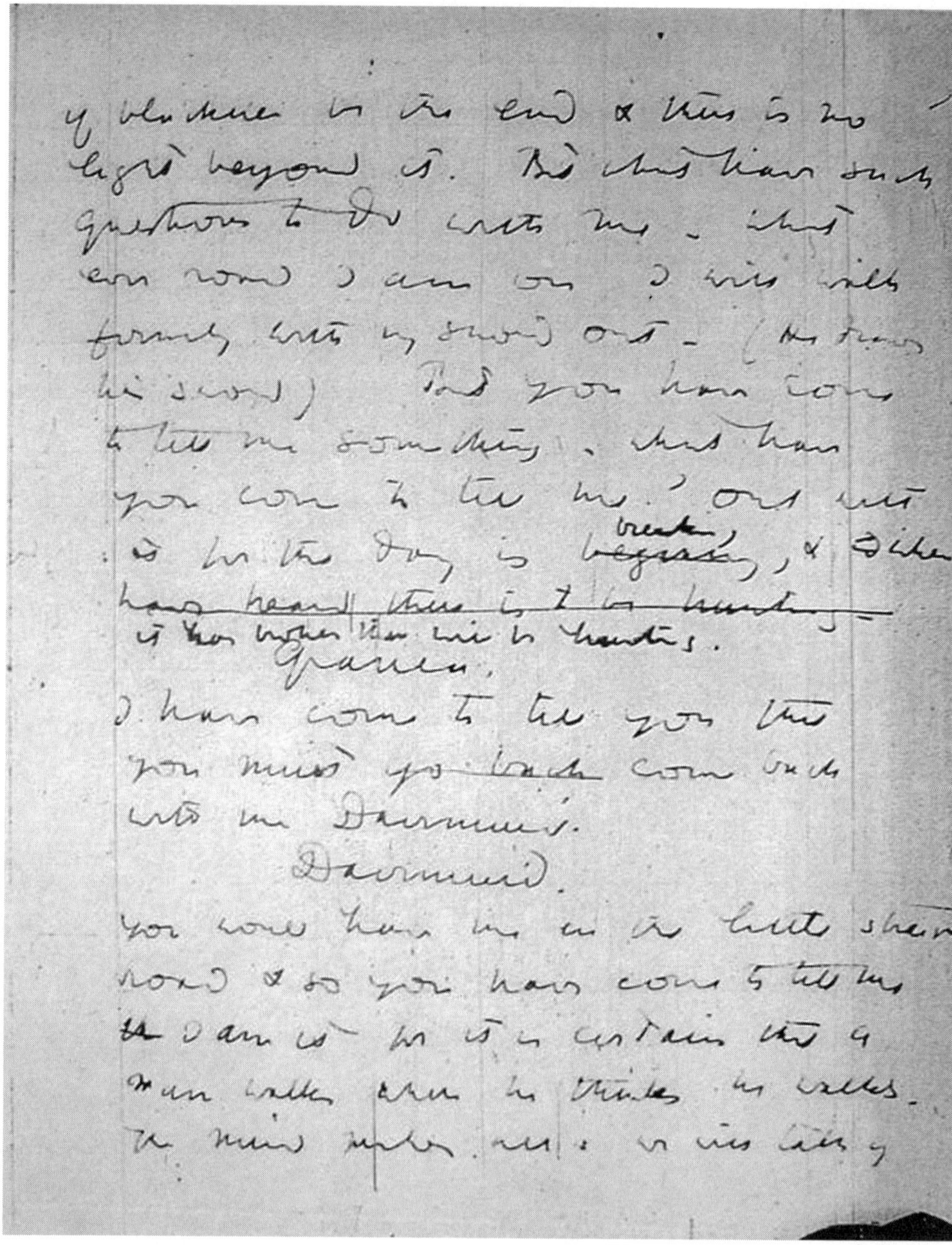

of blackness to the end & there is no
light beyond it. But what have such
questions to do with me. What
[illegible] I am on I will [illegible]
[illegible] my sword out. (He draws
his sword) And you have come
to tell me something. What have
you come to tell me? Out with
it for the day is ~~beginning~~ breaking, & I have
~~have heard there is to be hunting~~
it has better than [illegible] be hunting.
Grania.
I have come to tell you that
you must go ~~back~~ come back
with me Diarmuid.
Diarmuid.
You would have me in the little [illegible]
round & so you have come to tell me
~~th~~ I am it for it is certain that a
man walks where he thinks he walks.
The mind makes all: it [illegible] of

[NLI 8777(5), 9r]

if blacknes is the end & there is no
light beyond it. But what have such
questions to do with me – What
ever road I am on I will walk
firmly with my sword out – (He draws
his sword) But you have come
to tell me something – What have
you come to tell me ? Out with
breaking
it for the day is ~~beginning~~, & ~~I~~ when
~~have heard there is to be hunting —~~
it has broken there will be hunting .

Grania
I have come to tell you that
you must ~~go back~~ come back
with me Dairmuid.

Dairmuid.
You would have me in the little straight
road & so you have come to tell me
~~th~~ I am it for it is certain that a
man walks where he thinks he walks –
The mind makes all : we will talk of

[NLI 8777(5), 10r]

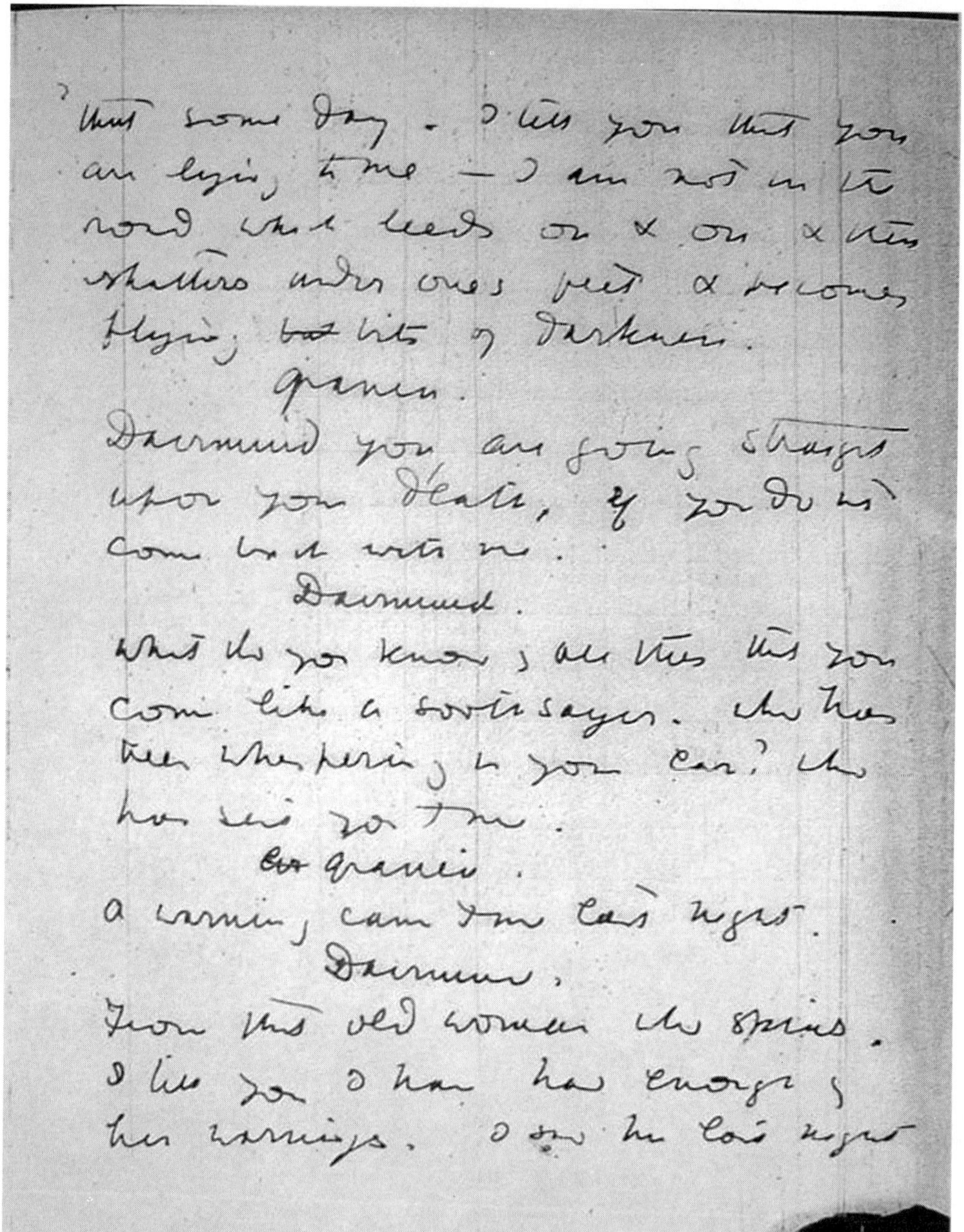
that some day. I tell you that you are lying to me — I am not on the road which leads on & on & then shatters under ones feet & becomes flying bits of darkness.

Grania.

Diarmuid you are going straight upon your death, if you do not come back with me.

Diarmuid.

What do you know, all this that you come like a soothsayer. Who has been whispering to your ear? who has said so to you.

~~Gr~~ Grania.

A warning came to me last night.

Diarmuid.

From that old woman who spins. I tell you I have had enough of her warnings. I saw her last night

[NLI 8777(5), 10^{r}]

that some day – I tell you that you are lying to me — I am not in the road which leeds on & on & then shatters under one s feet & becomes flying ~~bul~~ bits of darkness.

Grania.

Dairmuid you are going straight upon your death{, / .} {I / if} you do not come back with me.

Dairmuid.

What do you know of all this that you come like a sooth sayer. Who has been whispering in your ear? Who has sent you to me.

~~Gr~~ Grania.

A warning came to me last night.

Dairmuid.

From that old woman who spins. I tell you I hav had enough of her warnings. I saw her last night

[NLI 8777(5), 11r]

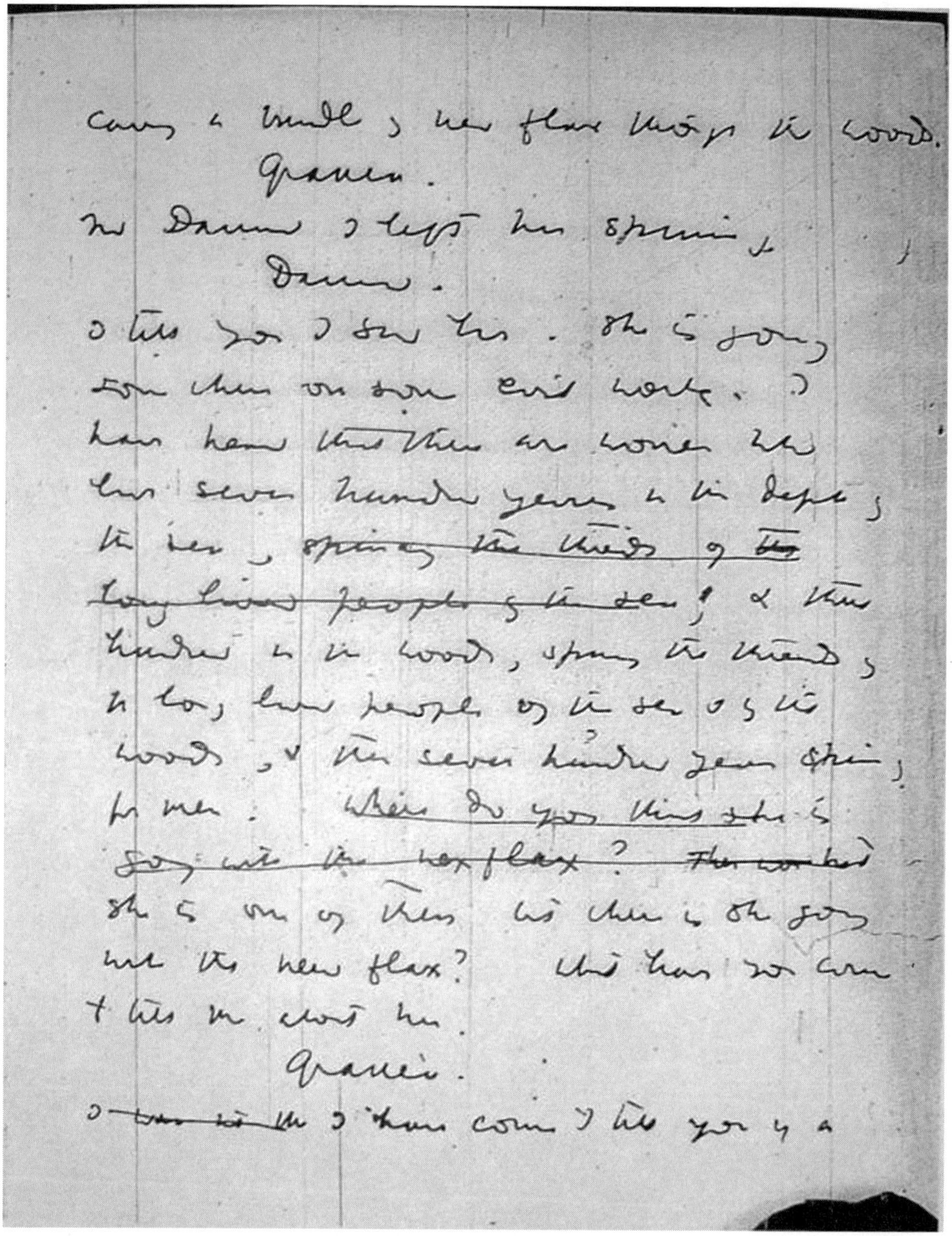

carry a bundle of new flax through the wood.

Grania.

the Dawn I left her spinning

Dawn.

O tell you I saw her. She is going
some where on some evil work. I
have heard that there are women who
live seven hundred years in the depths of
the sea, ~~spinning the threads of the~~
~~long lived people of the sea~~; & three
hundred in the woods, spinning the threads of
the long lived people of the sea & of the
woods, & three seven hundred years spinning
for men. ~~Where do you think she is~~
~~going with the new flax? The women~~
She is one of these. Where then is she going
with the new flax? Where have you come
& tell me about her.

Grania.

~~O have not all~~ I have come to tell you of a

[NLI 8777(5), 11r]

carring a bundle of new flax through the woods.

Grania.

No Dairmud I left her spinning.

Dairmd.

I tell you I saw her – She is going some where on some evil work – I have heard that there are women who live seven hundred years in the depth of the sea, ~~spinning the threads of the long lived people of the sea~~, & three hundred in the woods, spinning the threads of th long lived people of the sea & of the woods, & then seven hundred years spinng for men – ~~Where do you think she~~ is ~~going with the new flax ? Ther was but~~ She is one of them but where is she going with the new flax? What have you come to tell me about her.

Grania.

~~I was not the~~ I have come to tell you of a

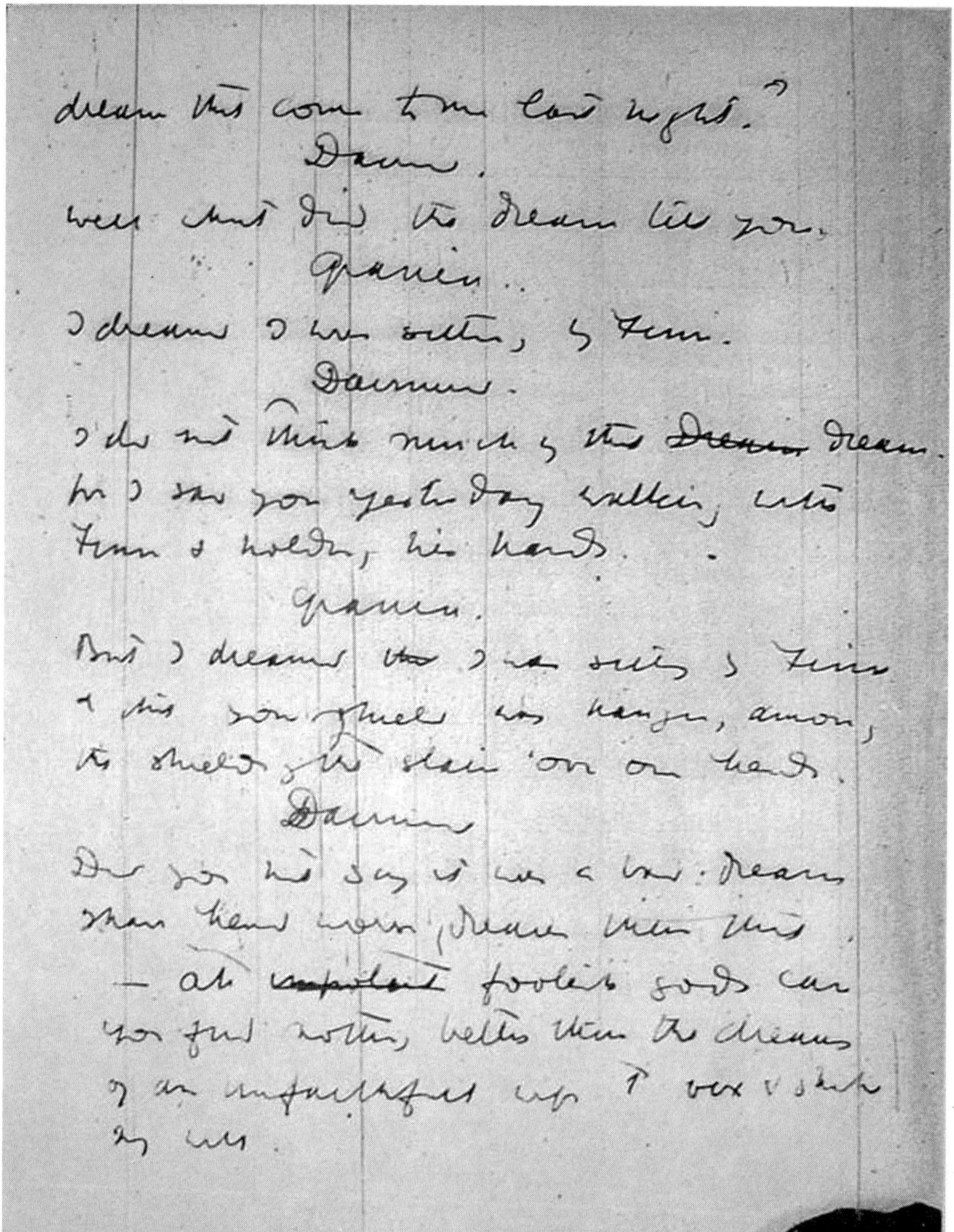
dream that came to me last night?
Diarm.
well what did the dream tell you.
Grania.
I dreamed I was sitting by Finn.
Diarmuid.
I do not think much of the ~~Dream~~ dream.
for I saw you yesterday walking with
Finn & holding his hands.
Grania.
But I dreamed that I was sitting by Finn
& his son shield was hanging among
the shields of the slain over our heads.
Diarmuid
Did you not say it was a bad dream
I have heard worse dreams than this
— ah ~~impotent~~ foolish gods can
you find nothing better than the dreams
of an unfaithful wife to vex & shake
my will.

[NLI 8777(5), 12r]

dream that came to me last night?

Dairmd.

Well what did the dream tell you.

Grania. .

I dreamd I was sitting by Finn.

Diarmuid.

I do not think much of that ~~Dream~~ dream.
for I saw you yesterday walking with
Finn & holding his hands.

Grania.

But I dreamed ~~that~~ I was sitting by Finn
& that your shield was hanging among
the shields of the slain over our heads.

{ D
{ diarmuid

Did you not say it was a bad dream
I have heard worse dreams than that
— Ah ~~important~~ foolish gods can
you find nothing better than the dreams
of an unfaithfull wife to vex & shake
my will.

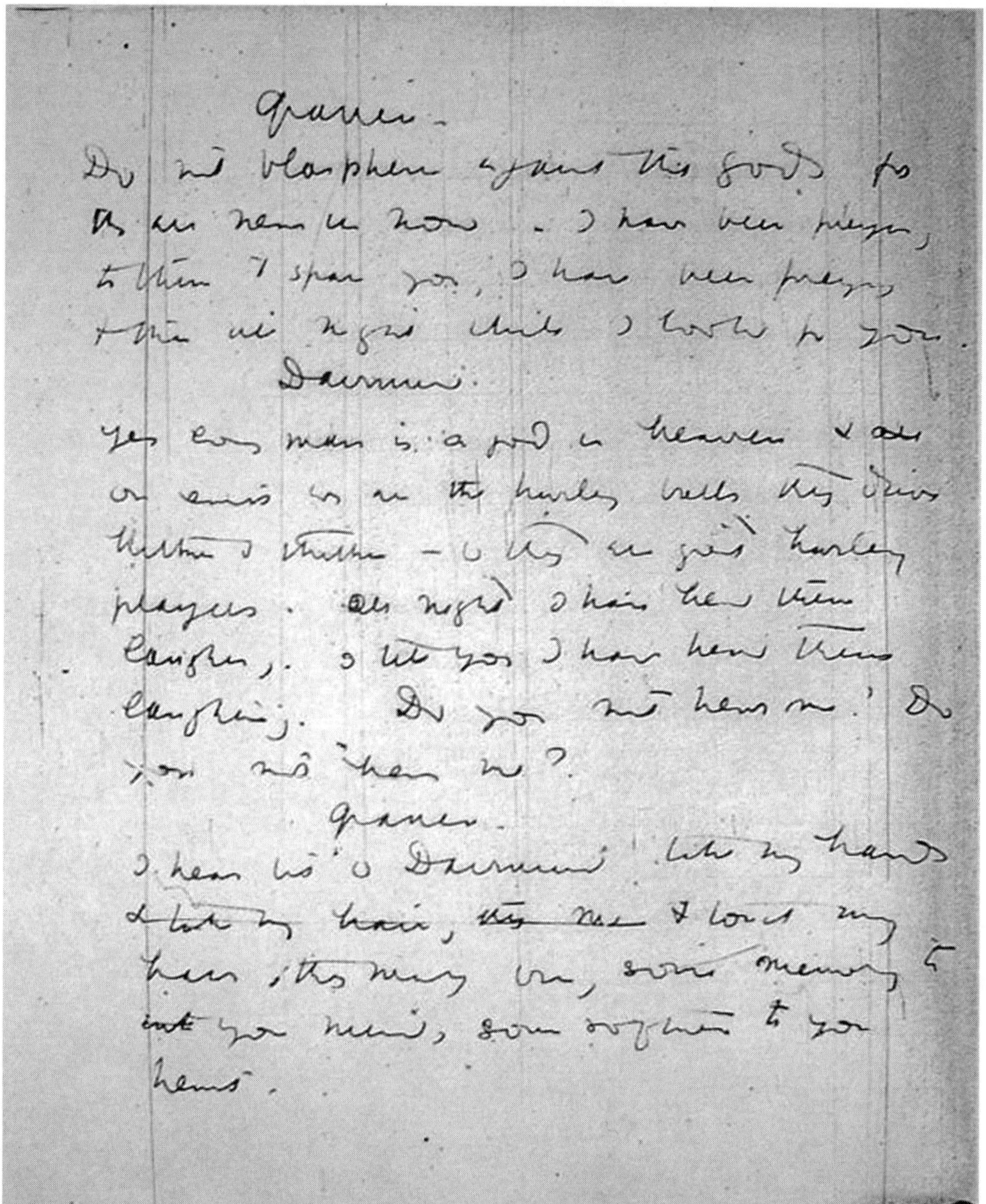
Grania.
Do not blaspheme against the gods for they are near us now. I have been praying to them & spare you, I have been praying there all night while I looked for you.
Diarmuid.
Yes every man is a god in heaven & all our enemies are there the hurley balls they drive thither & thither — O they are great hurley players. All night I have heard them laughing, I tell you I have heard them laughing. Do you not hear me? Do you not hear me?
Grania.
I hear not O Diarmuid I take my hands & take my hair, [illegible] & loosen my hair, that may bring some memory to into your mind, some softness to your heart.

[NLI 8777(5), 13r]

Grania –

Do not blaspheme against the gods for they are near us now – I have been preying to them to spare you, I hav been preyng to them all night while I looked for you.

Dairmuid.

Yes every man is a god in heaven & ~~all~~ on earth we are the hurley balls they drive hither & thither — O they are great hurley players . a[A]ll night I have heard them laughing. I tell you I have heard them laughing. Did you not hear me ? Do you not hear me ?

Grania.

I hear but O Dairmuid take my hands ~~& take my hair, they m~~ & touch my hair , they may bring some memory to ~~into~~ your mind, some softness to your heart.

[NLI 8777(5), 14r]

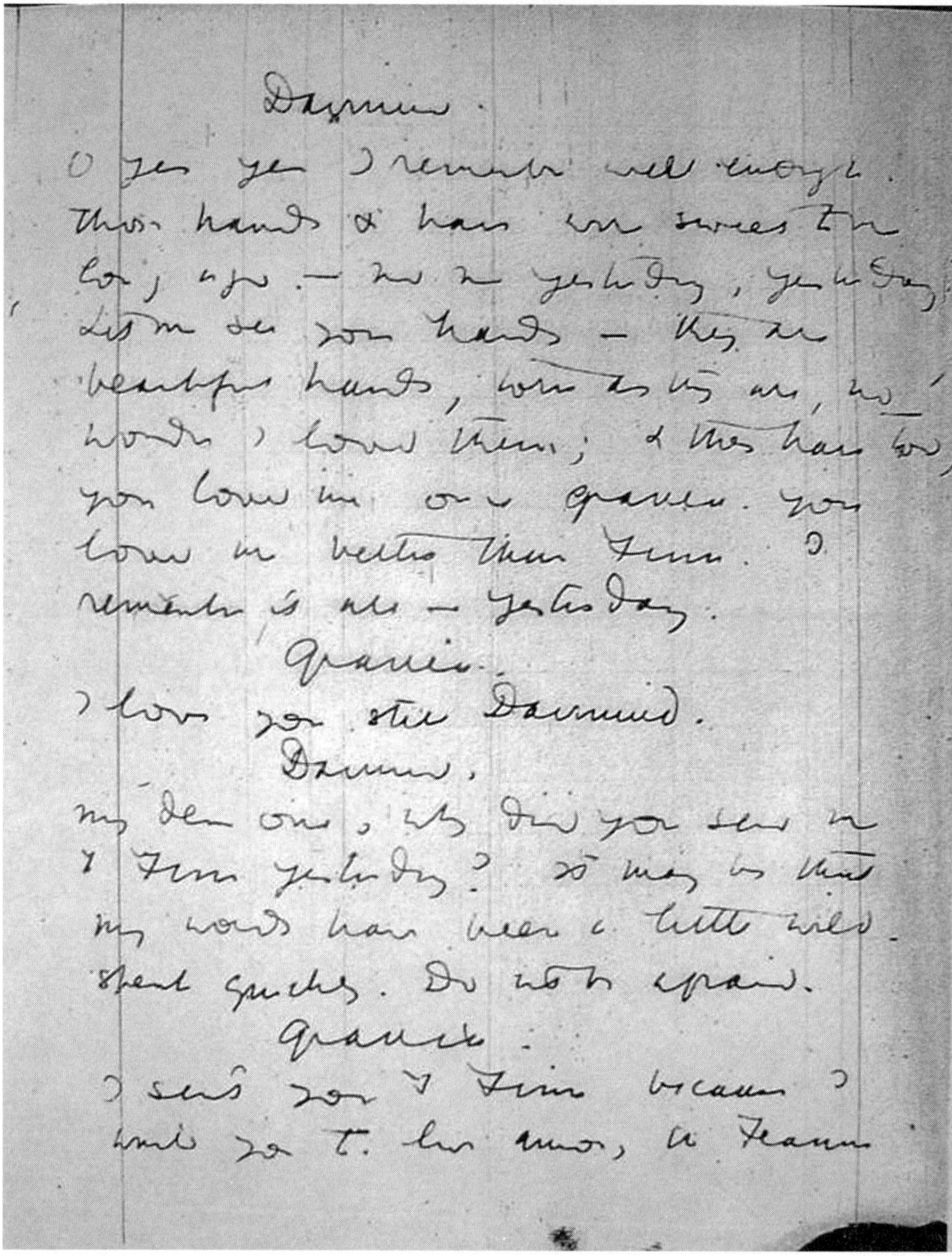
Dairmuid.
O yes yes I remember well enough
those hands I have not kissed since
long ago — not in yesterday, yesterday;
Let me see your hands — they are
beautiful hands, worn as they are, not
words I loved them; & these have loved,
you loved me once Grania. You
loved me better than Finn. I
remember it all — yesterday.
Grania.
I love you still Dairmuid.
Dairmuid.
My dear one, why did you send me
to Finn yesterday? It may be that
my words have been a little wild.
spent quickly. Do not be afraid.
Grania.
I sent you to Finn because I
wished you to be his [illegible], the Feanna

[NLI 8777(5), 14r]

Dairmuid.

O yes yes I remembr well enough. Those hands & hair were sweet to me long ago. — No no yesterday, yesterday. Let me see your hands — they are beautiful hands, torn as they are, no wonder I loved them; & this hair too{, .} you loved me once Grania – you loved me better than Finn. I remember it all — yesterday.

Grania.

I love you still Dairmuid.

Dairmud.

My dear one, why did you send me to Finn yesterday? It may be that my words have been a little wild – speak quickly. Do not be afraid.

Grania –

I sent you to Finn becaus I wantd you to live among th Feanni

[NLI 8777(5), 15r]

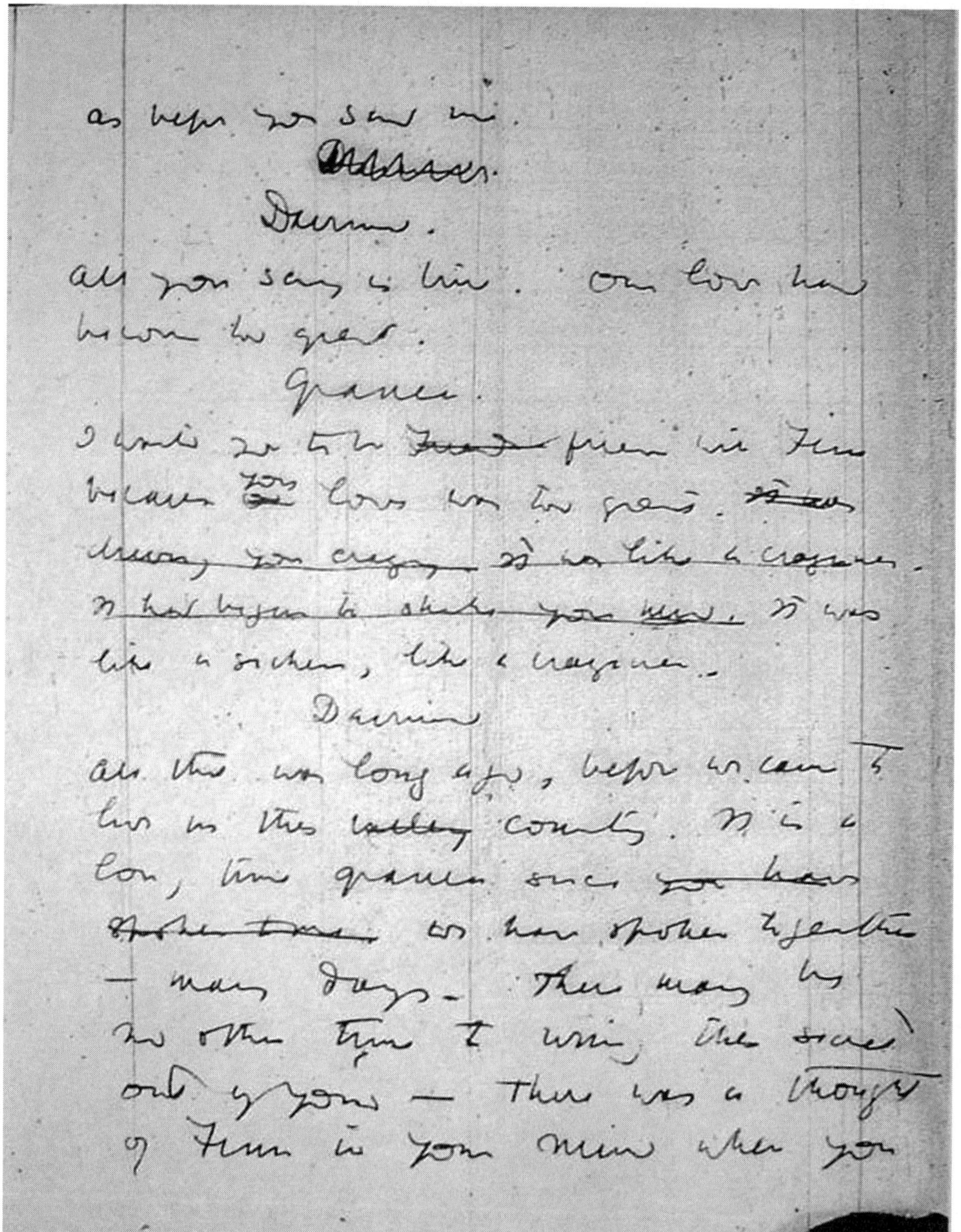

as before you saw me.

~~Diarmuid.~~

Diarmuid.

All you say is true. Our love has become too great.

Grania.

I would go to the ~~friend~~ friend with Finn because your love was too great. ~~It was~~ ~~meaning your crazy it was like a crazyness. It had begun to shake your mind.~~ It was like a sickness, like a crazyness.

Diarmuid

All this was long ago, before we came to live in this lonely country. It is a long time, Grania, since ~~we have spoken together~~ we have spoken together — many days. There may be no other thing to win the sickness out of you — there was a thought of Finn in your mind when you

[NLI 8777(5), 15r]

as before you saw me.

~~Dairmud.~~
Dairmud.

All you say is true. Our love had
become too great.

Grania.

I wanted you to be ~~Friends~~ frien with Finn
your
because ~~our~~ love was too great – ~~It was~~
~~driving you crazy – It was like a craziness~~ –
~~It had begun to shake your mind.~~ It was
like a sickness, like a craziness –

Dairmuid

All that was long ago, before we came to
live in this ~~valley~~ country. It is a
long time Grania since ~~you have~~
~~spoken to me.~~ We have spoken togeather
— many days – There may be
no other time to wring this secret
out of you — There was a thought
of Finn in your mind when you

[NLI 8777(5), 16r]

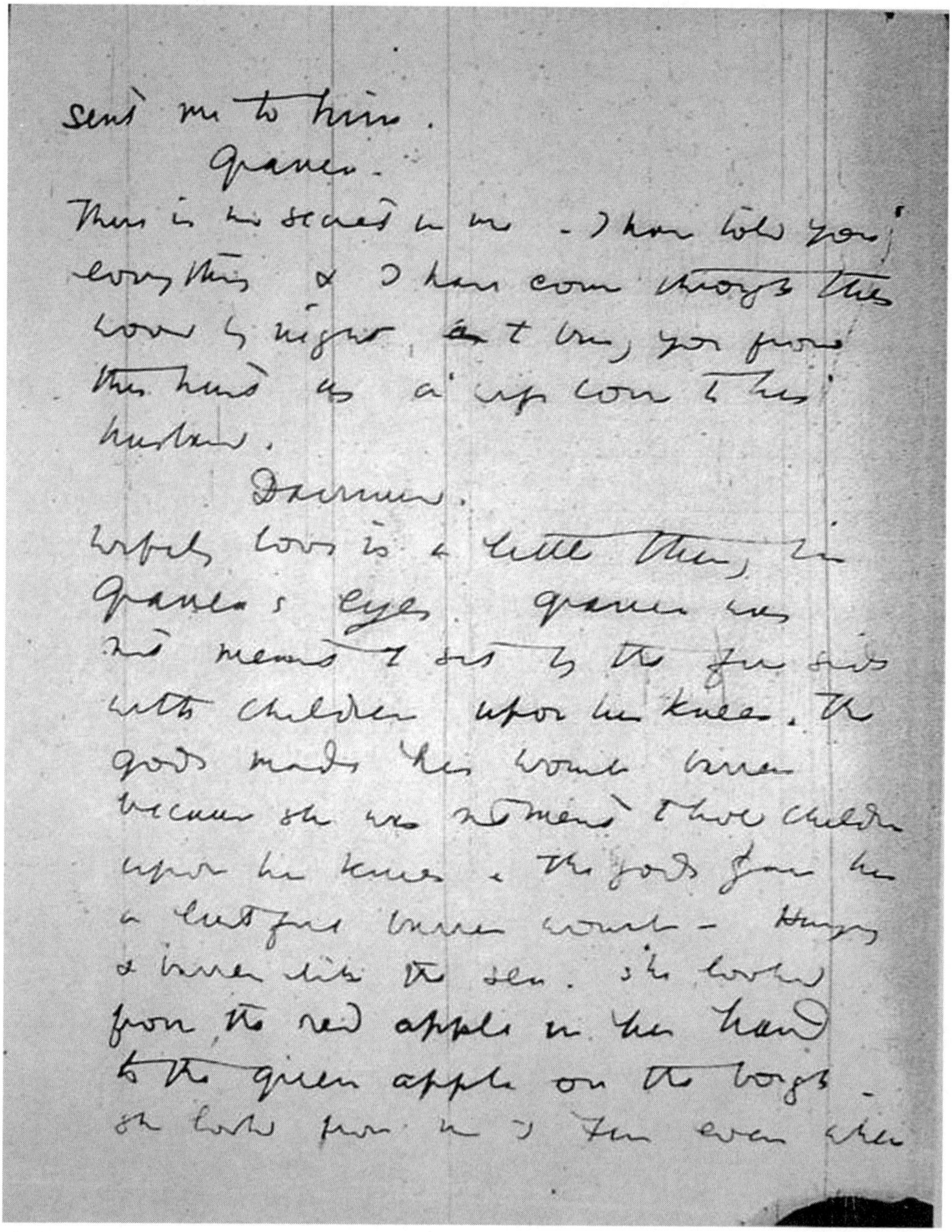
sent me to him.

Grania.

There is no secret in me — I have told you everything & I have come through the door by night [illegible] to bring you from this hand as a cup comes to her husband.

Diarmuid.

Nobody loves is a little thing in Grania's eyes. Grania was not meant to sit by the fire side with children upon her knees. The gods made her womb barren because she was not meant to have children upon her knees. The gods gave her a lustful barren womb — hungry & barren like the sea. She looked from the red apple in her hand to the green apple on the bough. She looked from me to Finn even when

[NLI 8777(5), 16^{r}]

sent me to him.

Grania –

There is no secret in me – I have told you every thing & I have come through this wood by night ~~as~~ to bring you from this hunt as a wife come to her husband.

Dairmuid.

Wifely love is a little thing in Grania s eyes. Grania was not meant to sit by the fire side with children upon her knees. The gods made her womb barren because she was not ment to [?have/?hold] childrn upon her knees – The gods gave her a lustful barren womb — Hungry & barren like the sea – she looked from the red apple in her hand to the green apple on the bough – she looked from me to Fin even when

[NLI 8777(5), 17[r]]

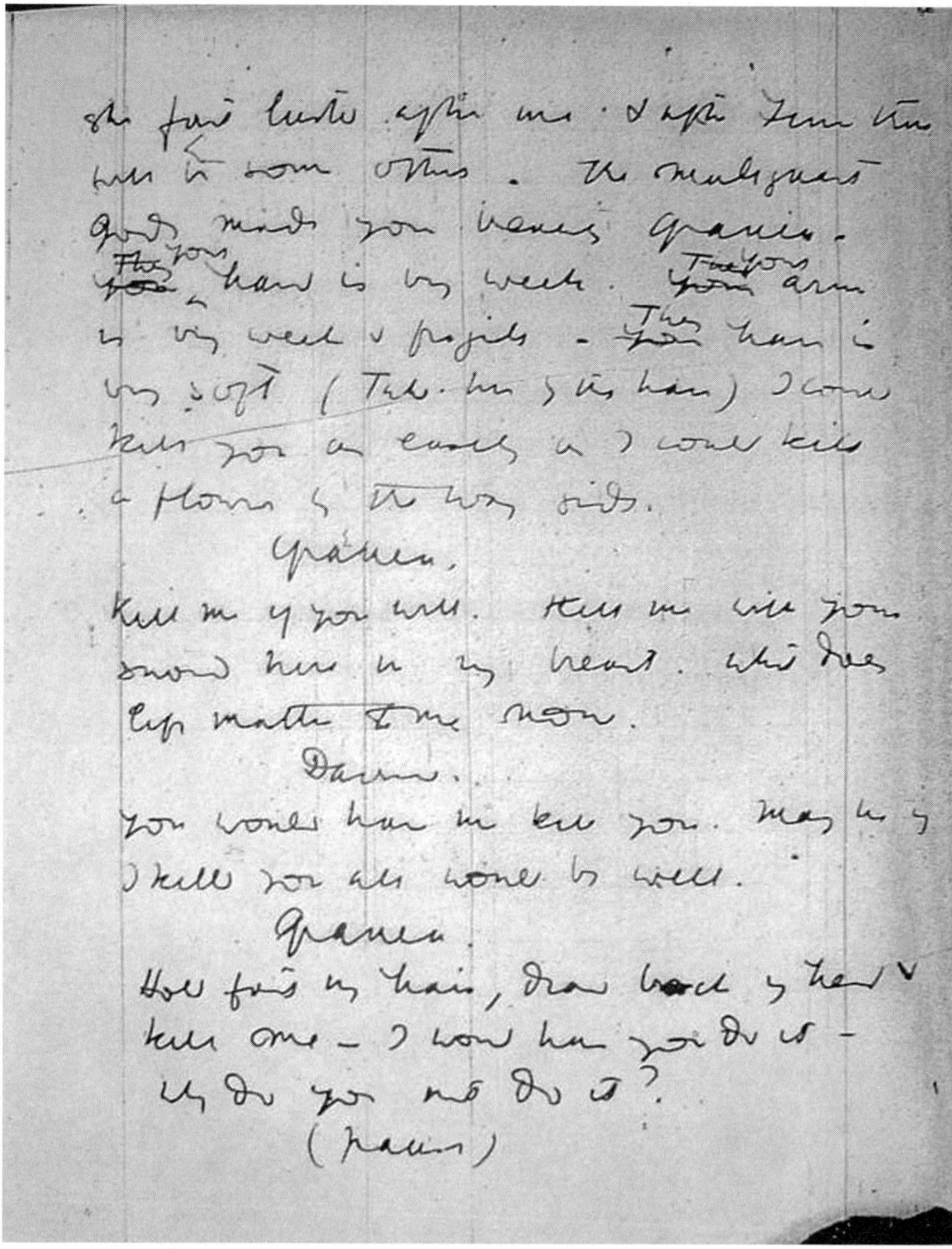
she first lusted after me & after Finn then
fell to some others. The malignant
gods made you beauty Grania.
~~Your~~ Thy your hand is very weak. ~~Your~~ Thy your arm
is very weak & fragile – ~~Your~~ Thy hair is
very soft (Takes him by the hair) I could
kill you as easily as I could kill
a flower by the way side.

Grania.

Kill me if you will. Kill me like your
sword here in my breast. What does
life matter to me now.

Diarmuid.

You would have me kill you. Maybe if
I kill you all would be well.

Grania.

Hold fast my hair, draw back my head &
kill me – I would have you do it –
why do you not do it?

(pause)

[NLI 8777(5), 17r]

she first lusted after me & after Finn there
will be som others – The malignant
Gods made your beauty Grania –
~~This~~ Your ~~The~~Your
~~Your~~ ^ hand is very week . ~~Your~~ arm
This
is very week & fragile – ~~Your~~ hair is
very soft (Takes her by the hair) I could
kill you as easily as I could kill
a flower by the way side.

Grania.
Kill me if you will. Kill me with your
sword here in my breast. What does
life matter to me now.

Darmud.
You would have me kill you. May be if
I kill you all would be well.

Grania.
Hold fast my hair, draw back my head &
kill me — I would have you do it —
why do you not do it ?
(pause)

[NLI 8777(5), 18r]

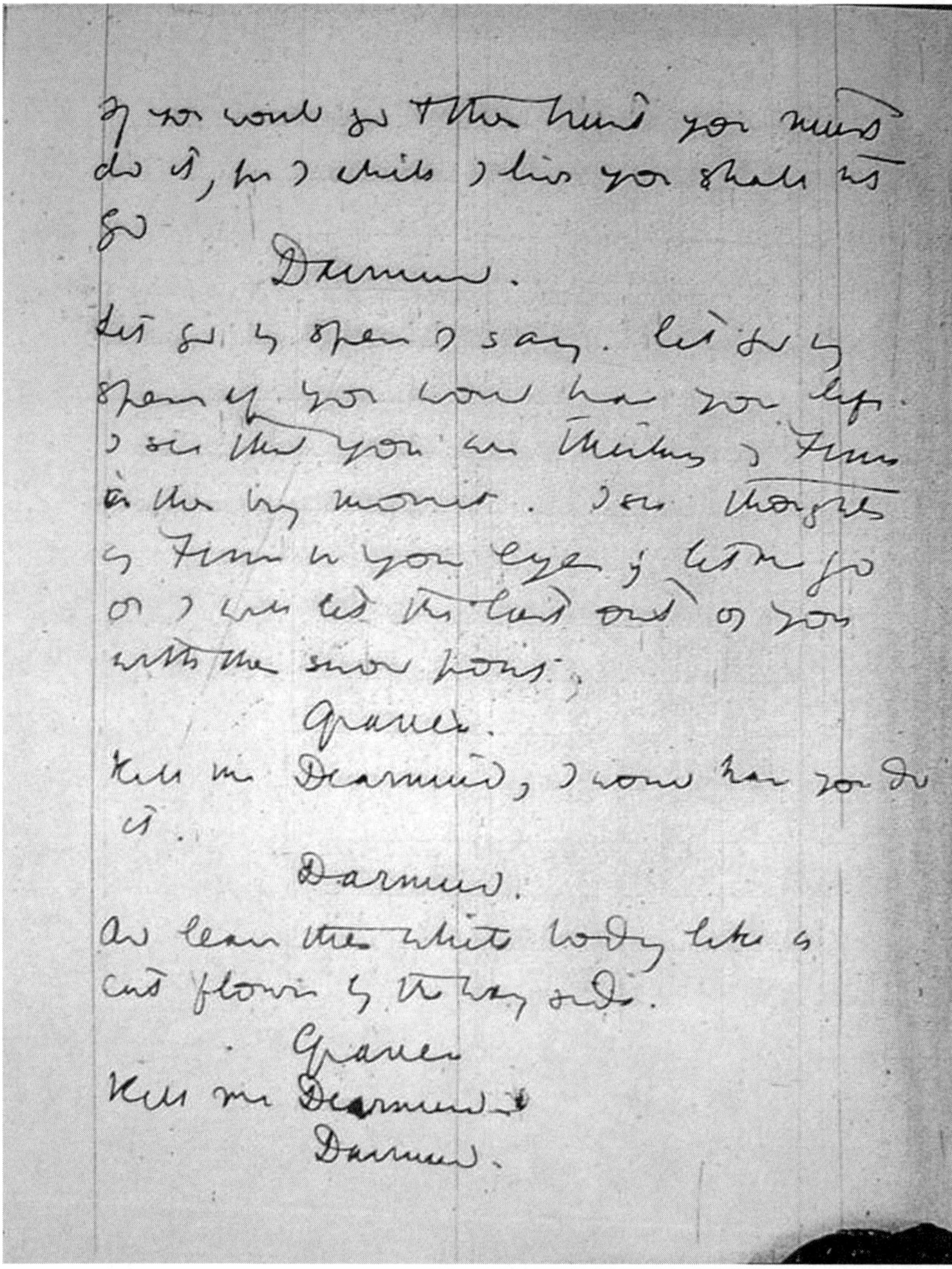

If you would go to the hunt you must
do it, for while I live you shall not
go

Diarmuid.

Let go my spear I say. Let go my
spear if you would have your life.
I see that you are thinking of Finn
in this very moment. I see thoughts
of Finn in your eyes, let me go
or I will let the life out of you
with the snow pons;

Grania.

Kill me Diarmuid, I would have you do
it.

Diarmuid.

And leave the white body like a
cut flower by the way side.

Grania

Kill me Diarmuid.

Diarmuid.

[NLI 8777(5), 18r]

If you would go to this hunt you must do it, for I while I live you shall not go

Dairmuid.

Let go my spear I say. let go my spear if you would have your life. I see that you are thinking of Finn
{at
{in this very moment . I see thoughts of Finn in your eyes ; let me go or I will let the lust out of you with this sword point.

Grania.

Kill me Diarmuid, I would hav you do it.

Darmuid.

And leave this white body like a cut flower by the way side.

Grania

Kill me Diarmuid –

Diarmuid –

[NLI 8777(5), 19r, 20r]

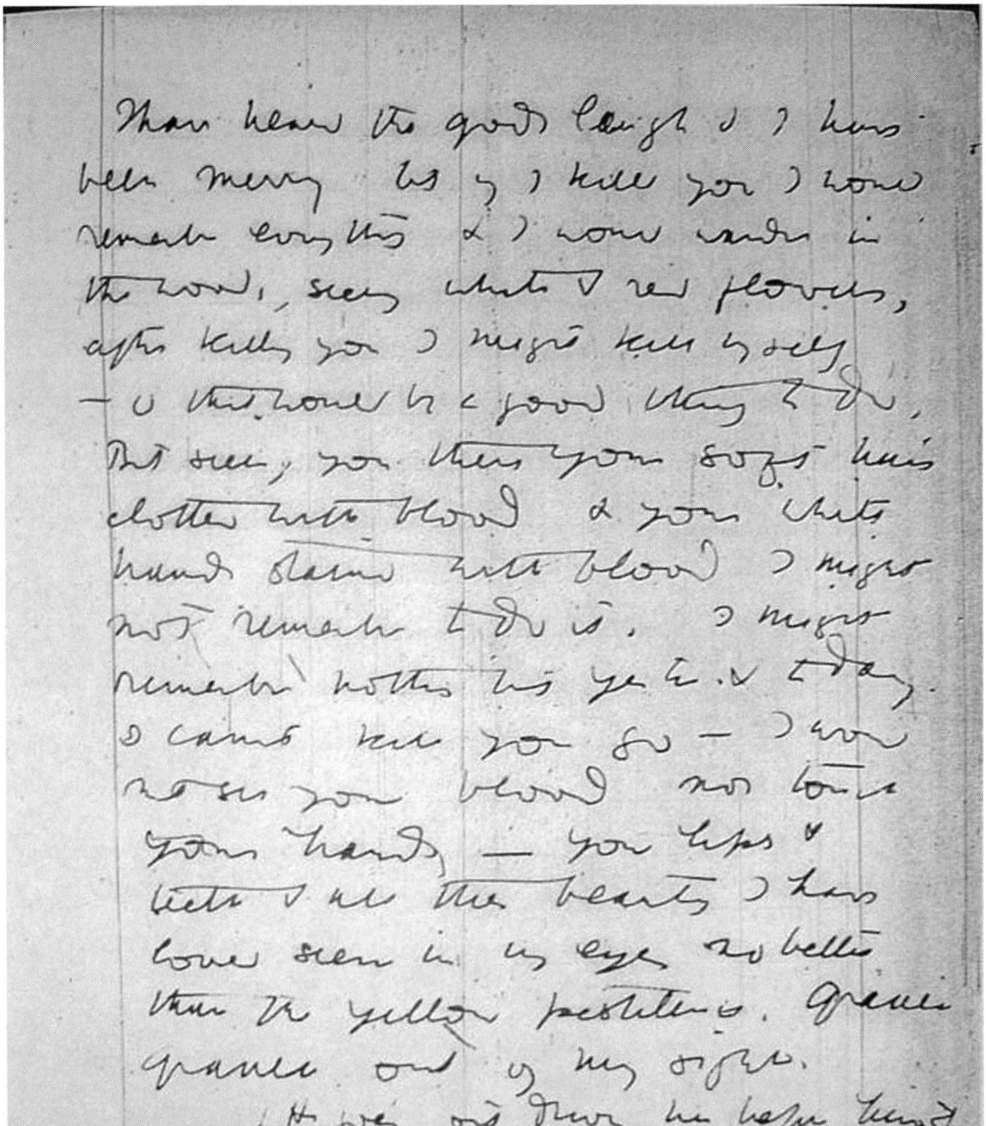

Thou hearst the gods laugh & I have been merry but if I kill you I would remember everything & I would wander in the woods, seeing white & red flowers, after killing you I might kill myself — & that would be a good thing to do, But seeing you there your soft hair clotted with blood & your white hands stained with blood I might not remember to do it. I might remember nothing but you to today. I cannot kill you so — I would not see your blood nor touch your hands — your lips & teeth & all the beauty I have loved seen in my eyes no better than the yellow pestilence. Go away go away out of my sight.
(He goes out through the little door & a moment after he returns)

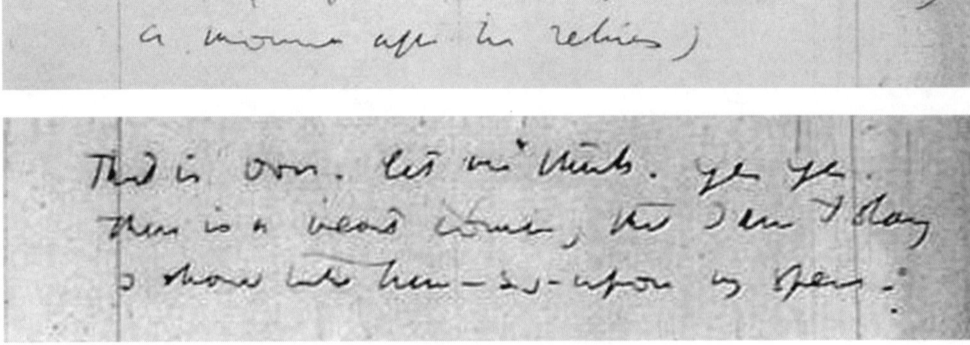

That is over. Let me think. Yes yes. There is a beast come, that I am to slay I should like him — so — upon my spear.

[NLI 8777(5), 19r]

I have heard the gods laugh & I have
been merry but if I killed you I would
remembr every thing & I would wander in
the wood, seeing white & red flowers,
after killing you I might kill my self
— O that would be a good thing to do,
But seeing you there your soft hair
clotted with blood & your white
hands staind with blood I might
not remembr to do it.   I might
remembr nothing but yester. & today.
I cannot kill you   go — I woud
not see your blood nor touch
your hands — your lips &
teeth & all this beauty I have
loved seem in my eyes no better
than the yellow pestilence.   Grania
Grania   out of my sight.

(He goes out drivng her before him~~)~~
a moment after he returns).

[NLI 8777(5), 20r]

That is over .   let me think.   Yes yes.
Their is a beast coming , that I am to slay
I should take him — so — upon my spear –

A –

the thicket.

~~grania~~ Grania.

It might be better for I have done mischief enough. I am weary of the world I do in the world. [Yes Finn there is no evil in me. ~~I wished that Finn &~~ ~~Diarmuid and all~~ I wished that Finn & Diarmuid should ~~nought~~ make peace be friends: and all might have been well had not this evil thing broke out of the earth.

Finn

~~and~~ Diarmuid & I could not be at peace: the peace he made was a false peace

(Hunting horn in distance)

The hounds are at the boars heels now I can hear my hounds — yes it is Bran, now it is Sgeolan, & now it is Lomair. They have found their courage & are driving him from cover to cover

[NLI 8777(5), 21r]

A —

the thicket.

~~Grani~~ Grania.

It might be better for I have done mischief
enough. I am weary of the work I do
in the world. Yet Fin there is no
evil in me. ~~I would that you &~~
~~Darmud~~ ~~and all~~ I wished that you &
should make peace
Dairmuid ~~might be friends~~ : and all
might have been well had not this
evil thing broken out of the earth.

Finn

~~I &~~ Dairmuid & I could not be at peace : the
peace we made was a false peace
(Hunting horns in distans)
The hounds are at the boars heels now
I can hear my hounds — yes it is
Bran, now it is Sgeolan & now it
is Lomair – They have found their
courage & ar driving him from cover
to cover

-1 The large "A" refers to the corrected typescript of which WBY's holograph is a revision; cf. Berg(14), fol. 3r.

[NLI 8777(5), 22r]

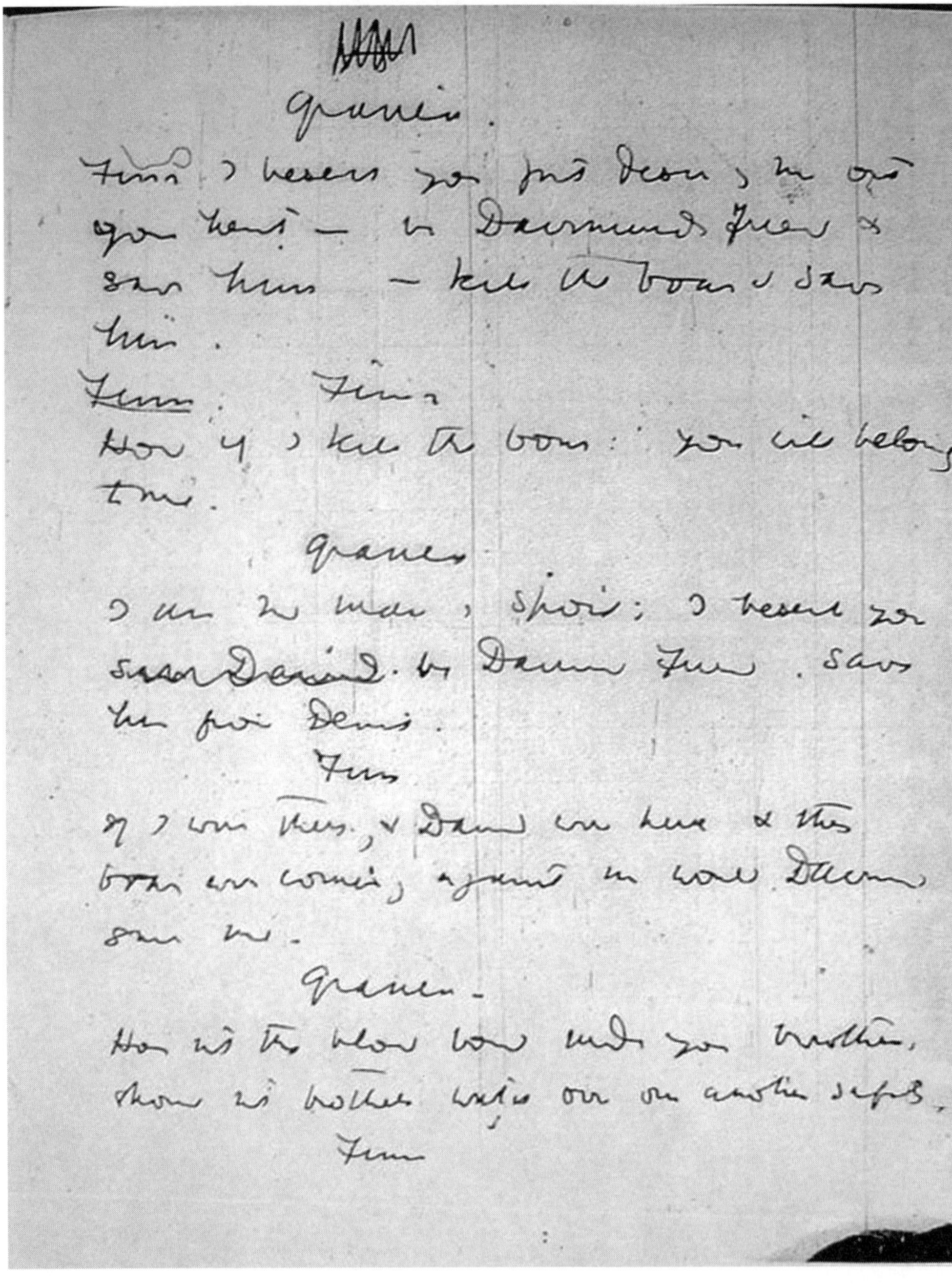

[NLI 8777(5), 22r]

~~A~~

Grania.

Finn I beseech you put the desire of me out your heart — be Dairmuids {f Friend & save him — kill the boar & save him.

~~Finn~~ Finn.

How if I kill the boar : you will belong to me.

Grania

I am no man s spoil : I besech you ~~save Dairmuid~~. be Dairmd Friend . Save him from Death.

Finn

If I were there, & Dairmd were here & this boar was coming against me would Dairmd save me –

Grania –

Has not the blood bond made you brothers, shoud not brothers watch over one another safety.

Finn

[NLI 8777(5), 23r]

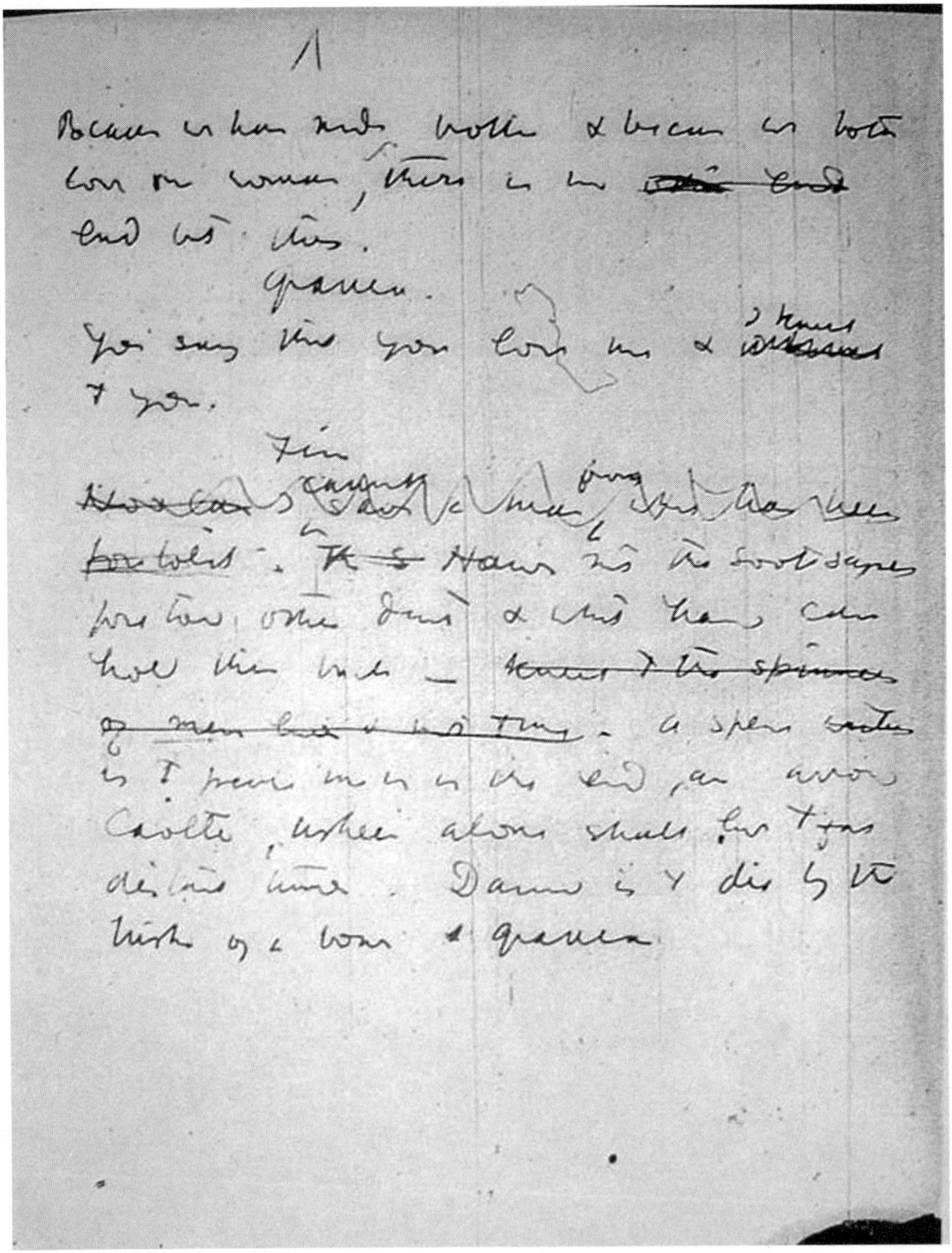

[NLI 8777(5), 23r]

⋀

Because we hav made brothers & becaus we both
love one woman, there is no ~~other end~~
end but this.

Grania.

I kneel
You say that you love me & ~~I kneel~~
to you.

Fin

cannot from
~~How can~~ I ^ save a man ^ ~~who has been~~
~~fore told~~ – ~~The S~~ Have not the sooth sayers
fore told other deat & what hand can
hold them back — Kneel to the spinners
of men luck & not to me – A spear ~~waiting~~
is to peirce me in in the end, an arrow
Caolte, Usheen alone shall live to far
distant times – Dairmd is to die by the
tusks of a boar & Grania

[NLI 8777(5), 24r]

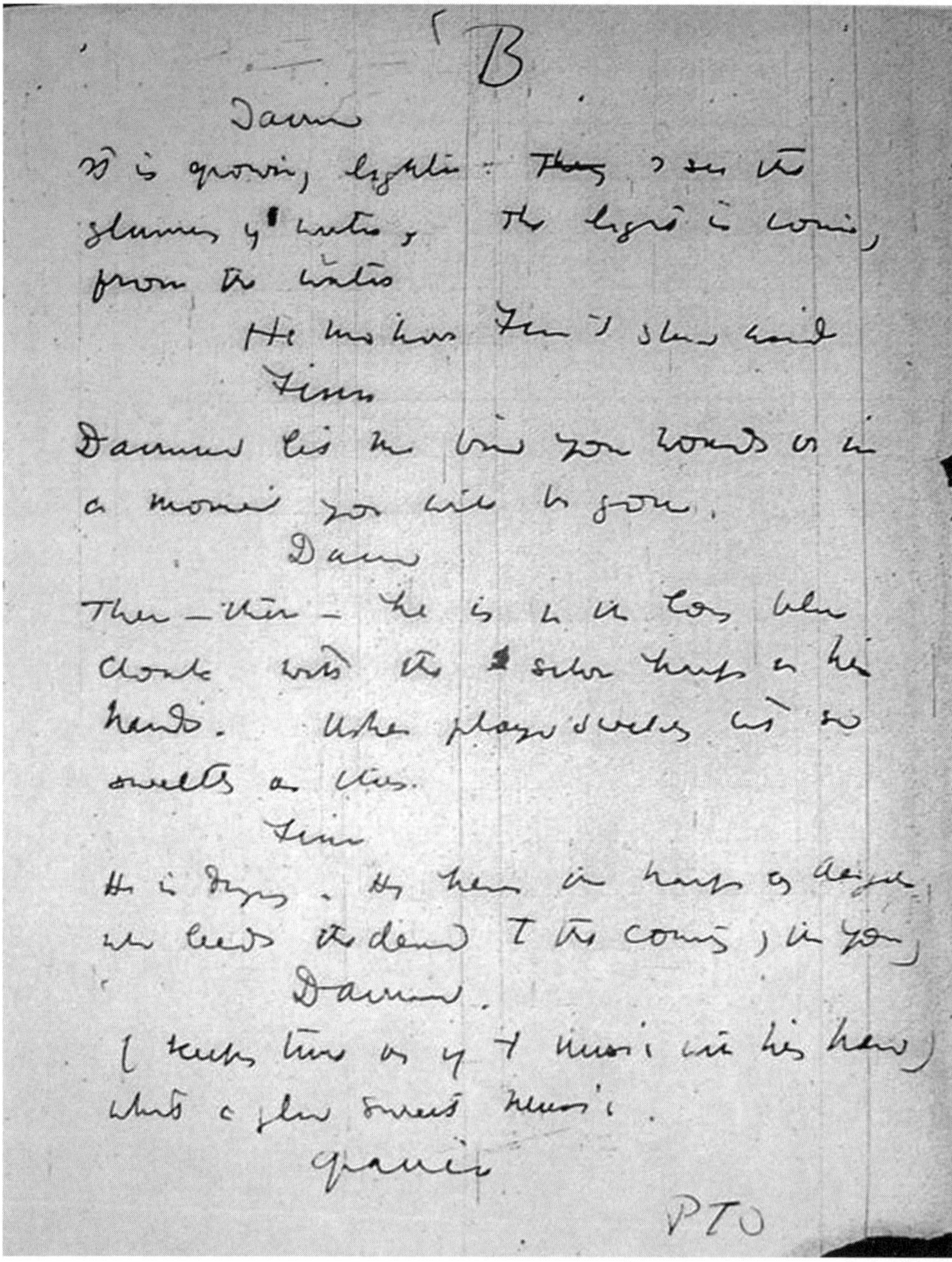
B

Dawn

It is growing lighter. ~~Thus~~ I see the glimmer of the waters, the light is coming from the waters

He has not seen I slew said

Finn

Darkness lies ... you would ... in a moment you will ... you.

Dawn

There — there — he is in the long blue cloak with the silver harp in his hands. When played sweetly ... so sweetly as this.

Finn

He is dying. His ... a harp of ... who leads the dead to the country of the young.

Dawn

(keeps time as if to music with his hand) What a plain sweet music.

Curtain

PTO

[NLI 8777(5), 24^{r}]

B.

Dairmd
It is growing lighter . ~~They~~ I see the
gleaming of watrs, The light is coming
from the waters
He motions Finn to stand aside

Finn
Dairmuid let me bind your wounds or in
a moment you will be gone.

Dairmd
There — there – he is in the long blue
cloak with the ~~h~~ silver harp in his
hands. Usheen playd sweetly [?but/?not] so
sweetly as this.

Finn
He is dying – He hears the harp of Aengus
who leads the dead to the country of the young

Dairmuid.
(Keepng time as if to music with his hand)
What a glad sweet music.

Grania

PTO

The page to which the present rewriting is keyed must be number 34 of the earliest continuous typescript of Act III, which, at this point, now exists only in a dispersed, fragmentary state: cf. Berg(08), fol. 2^{r}, and also Berg(14), fol. 5^{r}.

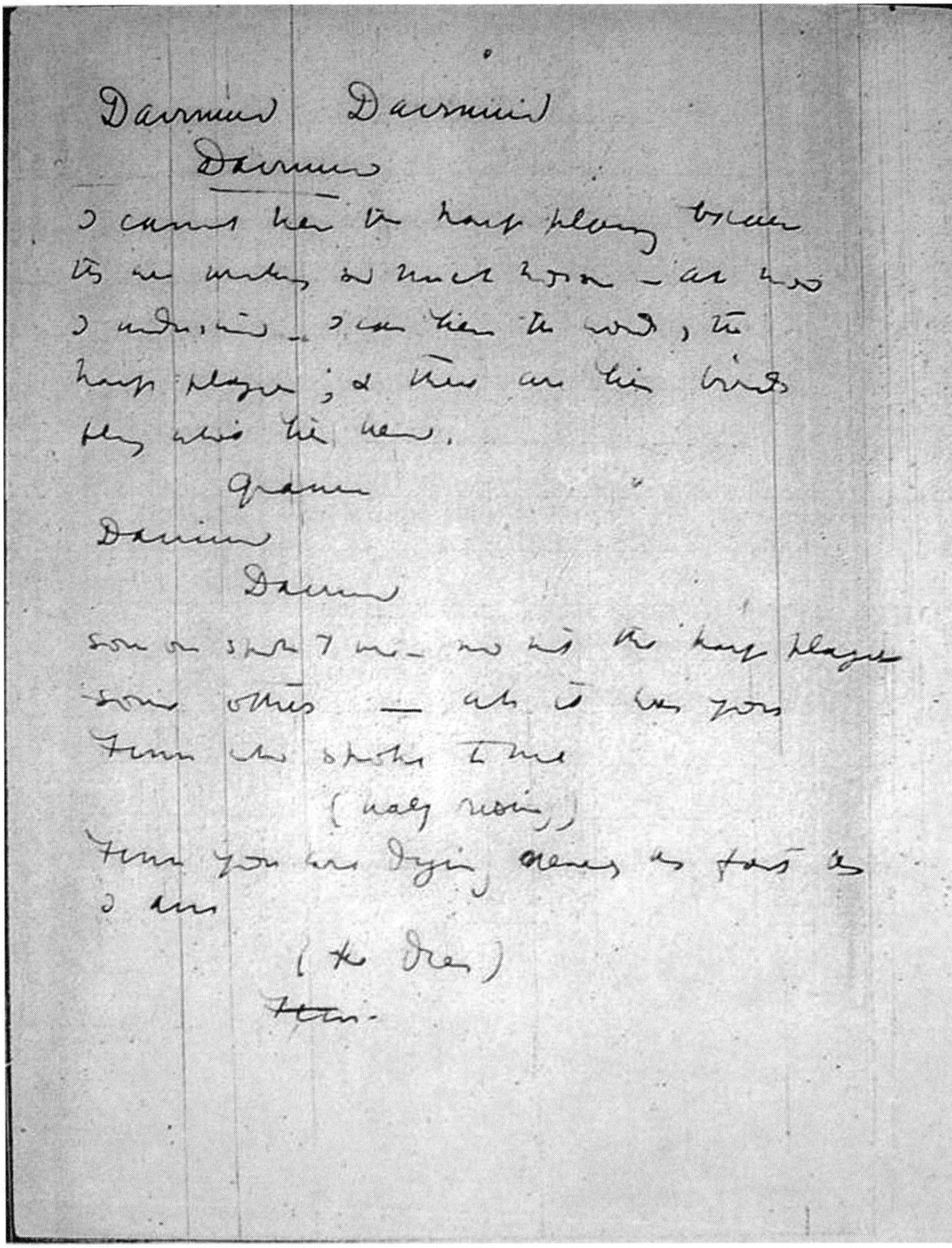

Dairmuid Dairmuid
Dairmuid
I cannot hear the harp playing because
they are walking so much [illegible] — as [illegible]
I understand — I can hear the words, the
harp player; & these are the birds
playing about his head.
Grania
Dairmuid
Dairmuid
Some one spoke to me — not with the harp player
some others — as it was yours
Finn who spoke to me
(half rising)
Finn you are dying already as fast as
I am
(he dies)
~~Finn~~

[NLI 8777(5), 24v]

Dairmaid Dairmuid

<u>Dairmuid</u>
I cannot her the harp playing becaus
they are making so much noise — ah now
I understand — I can hear the words of the
harp player; & there are his birds
flyng abov his head.

Grania
Darmuid

Dairmud
Some one spoke to me — no not the harp player —
some others — Ah it was you
Finn who spoke to me
(half rising)
Finn you are dying nearly as fast as
I am
(He dies)

~~Finn~~ –

[NLI 8777(8) e, 23r]

Act 111.

The woody slopes of Ben Bulben .Dermuid is sleeping under a tree. Two countrymen enter. One is young and one old. The young countryman:- Yes, I am telling you the truth. The woodcutter met an old woman in the woods before dawn. She had a spinning wheel in her arms and was laughing and weeping, and walked as the undying walk. She was going towards the heart of the woods where nobody goes because ~~ogf~~ of the gods and the evil spirits.

THE OLD MAN. That was the old woman who came yesterday to Dermuids house, from whemce nobody can tell. They say that she came out of the woods for the first time, many years ago . Some say that she was Granias nurse and taught her ~~to walk and and taught her~~ to spin, and no one knows what else. Nobody knows what evil she brought into Dermuids house yesterday and now that it is there she is going away again.

THE YOUNG COUNTRYMAN. Some evil is going to happen.

THE OLD MAN.

Her coming and her going are not the only signs that some evil is going to happen, for just now as I was going to the byre I met Finmole the herdsman .He heard fighting in the middle of the night and when he looked out of his door he saw many people fighting with swords. Presently they came quite near him, some flying and some following, and among those that were flying he saw Dermuid's father and grandfather who are dead these many years.

THE YOUNG MAN. It must have been ~~the friends of the living and of the dead fighting. Somebody of Dermuid's house is going to die, for the~~ The friends and enemies of the living that are among the dead who were fighting. Somebody of Dermuid's house is going to die, because the enemies of the living had the victory. It may be that Dermuid is

---

The corrections and emendations throughout the TS appear to be in the same hand and blue-black shade of ink as WBY's terminal instruction on 24r, but an element of doubt remains over the single-character overwritings, which may be by GM.

Rough Typescript Version of Opening of Act

[NLI 8777(8) e, 23ʳ]

Act 111.

The woody slopes of Ben Bulben .Dermuid is sleeping under a tree.

Two countrymen enter. One is young and one old. <u>The young countrym{an}na</u>: –

Yes, I am telling you the truth. {T}the woodcutter met an old woman in the woods before dawn. She had a spinning wheel in her arms and was laughing and weeping, and walked as the undying walk. She was going towards the heart of the woods where nobody goes because ~~egf~~ of the gods and the evil spirits.

THE OLD MAN. That was the old woman who came yesterday to {D}bermuids house , from whemce nob{o}idy can tell. They say that she came out of the woods for the first time, {m}M any years ago . Sr{o} me say that she was Grania's nurse and taught her ~~to walk and taught her~~ to spin, and no one knows what else. Nobody knows what evil she brought into Dermuids house yesterday and now that it is there she is go{i}ing away again.

THE YOUNG COUNTRYMAN. Some evil is going to happen

THE OLD MAN.

Her coming and her going are not the only signs that some evil is going to happen, for just now as I was going to thc byre I met Finmole the herdsman . {H}H e heard fighting in the middle of the night and when he looked out of his door he saw many people fighting with swords. Presently they came quite near him, some flying and some following, and among those that were flying he saw Dermuid's father and grandfather who are dead these many years.

THE YOUNG MAN. It must have been ~~the friends of the living and of the dead fighting. Somebody of Dermuid's house is going to die, for the .~~ The friends and enemies of the living that are among the dead who **were fighting. Somebody of Dermuid's house is going to die, because the enemies of the living had the victory. It may be that Dermuid is**

[NLI 8777(8) e, 24r]

going to die. (DIARMUID RISES ON HIS ELBOW AND LOOKS AT THEM AND THEN LIES DOWN AGAIN.)

The Old man. Likely enough. These great beauties never bring luck to any man. I myself have never had any luck since Grania came to Dermuid's house. I lost four sheep this year, three that died in lambing and one that fell from the side of the mountain.

THE YOUNG MAN. Hush, there is Dermuid, he is sleeping under that tree. Had we not better awake him and warn him ?

THE OLD MAN. Let him sleep on. What does it matter to us. These great people go here and there. They hunt and they feast and they kill one another nobody knows why. Nothing that they do makes the ground the fatter or the cows have more calves at a birth or the winter less cold and windy. Let him live or die as the gods please. Come to the sheepwashing. We have seen into the gods business and had best be silent.

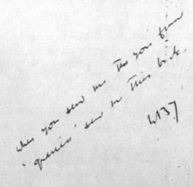

When you send me the new form 'Grania' send me this back.

WBY

[NLI 8777(8) e, 24r]

going to die. (DIARMUID RISES ON HIS ELBOW AND LOOKS AT THEM AND THEN LIES DOWN AGAIN.)

The Old man. Likely enough. These great beauties never bring luck to any man. I myself have never had any luck since Grania came to Dermuid's house. I lost four sheep this year, three that died in lambing and one that~~af~~ fell from the side of the mountain.

THE YOUNG NAN. Hush, there is Dermuid, he is sleeping under that tree. Had we not better awake him and warn him ?

THE OLD MAN. Let him sleep on. What does it matter to us. These great people go here an{d/e} there. They hunt and they feast and they kill one another nobody knows why. Nothing that that they do makes the ground the fatter or the cows have more calves at a birth or the winter be^ **less cold and windy{./,} {L/l}et him live or die as the gods please. Come to the sheepwashing. We have seen into the gods business and had best be silent.**

When you send me ~~the~~ your final 'Grania' send me this back.

W B. Y

-1-

DIARMUID & GRANIA.

ACT III.

SCENE: The wooded slopes of Ben Bulben. DIARMUID is sleeping under a tree. It is night, but the dawn is beginning to break – Enter two peasants.

OLD MAN What a storm, what a storm.

YOUNG MAN Maybe you have seen wilder nights.

OLD MAN There has been no such night ~~this~~ these fifty years. Many of the beasts broke out of their byres last night, and I met a shepherd just now who said that fifty had drowned themselves in the lake.

YOUNG MAN And a two-headed chicken was hatched ~~at~~ in Caibrie's barn last night.

OLD MAN Did you see it ?

YOUNG MAN They had burnt it before I came, but I saw what I saw, one host flying and one following, and among them the host flying DIARMUID'S father, and DIARMUID'S grandfather who have been dead these fifty years.

Typescript of Complete Act, Revised by W. B. Yeats Alone —George Moore's Copy?

[HRC(3), 1r]

–1–

DIARMUID & GRANIA.

ACT III.

SCENE: The wooded slopes of Ben Bulben. DIARMUID is sleeping under a tree. It is night, but the dawn is beginning to break – Enter two peasants.

OLD MAN **What a storm, what a storm.**

YOUNG MAN **Maybe you have seen wilder nights.**

these

OLD MAN **There has been no such night ~~this~~ fifty years. Many of the beasts broke out of their byres last night, and I met a shepherd just now who said that fifty had drowned themselves in the lake.**

in

YOUNG MAN **And a two-headed chicken was hatched ~~at~~ ^ Caibrie's barn last night.**

OLD MAN **Did you see it ?**

YOUNG MAN **They had burnt it before I came, but I saw what I saw,**

that were flying

one host flying and one following, and among them ^ DIARMUID'S father, and DIARMUID'S grandfather who have been dead these fifty years. ———

13 The pencil line was added so as to link with the first revision of the text on the next leaf (fol. 2r).

[HRC(3)]

[2^{r}]

stet

Yes *too, he saw them*

~~OLD MAN~~ **~~Yes~~, Lame Foot saw them ^ ~~clearly~~, though the moon was nearly gone.**

But

~~YOUNG MAN~~ **(In a half whisper.) ^ I too have seen something – I saw a gaunt, grey, ragged man, and he was driving this beast that the Fianna are hunting. He drove it along the top of the mountain, prodding it before him with a spear. (DIARMUID rouses himself to listen, but lies down again directly.)**

stet

~~OLD MAN~~ **That too means DIARMUID'S death. He will die in this hunting – Hush ! (He points to DIARMUID.)**

YOUNG MAN **If we do not waken him this beast may come upon him sleeping.**

OLD MAN **Better do nothing.**

YOUNG MAN **I would not have him die with no chance of life.**

OLD MAN **What are the misfortunes of these men to such men as we. These men put on fine clothes, and ride a-horseback with one another, or the swords are out and blood on the grass, and nobody knows what it is all about. The seasons are none the better. The cows have no more milk in their udders than before (The peasants go out).**

All the revisions and markings on this page are in pencil.

[3^r]

–3–

croak croak

They croak like raveven over carrion – ^

DIARMUID ~~**Croak, croak**~~ ^ ~~**! I saw a raven but now, and it put ravens into my head.**~~ **(Enter GRANIA).**

GRANIA **I have sought you all night. I have been wandering in the woods since the moon went down.**

DIARMUID **What have you come for ?**

GRANIA **I was afraid and have been running; give me time to draw my breath.**

DIARMUID **Your hair is down, and your hands are torn with brambles.**

GRANIA **Yes, look at my hands, and I am so weary, DIARMUID. I am so weary that I could lie down and die here.** | **That mossy bank is like a bed; lay me down there. Oh, I have come to beg you to give up this hunting.** | √ √

DIARMUID **And you show me torn hands, and you hold out to me wet hair, and would have me go home. You talk of dying too, and would have me lay you on this bank. But what good is there in all this, GRANIA, for I have no time to listen.**

GRANIA **DIARMUID, give up this hunting, for I have had warning that you will die if you do not turn back. Turn be-fore we lose ourselves in the darkness of the woods.** *e*

[4^r]

–4–

DIARMUID **I am in the little way that leads to darkness, but what does that matter to you, GRANIA ? Your way home winds along the hill, and down into the valley; my way is a different way, a shorter way, and the morrows**

3^r, ll. 10–12 The first of several such pencil markings to appear in the RH margin of this MS of Act III.
19 The faint pencil mark to the RH side of the line resembles a loosely formed "e".

[HRC(3)]

that men must live frighten me more than this short way. I have no heart for that crooked ~~way~~ road of morrows – my heart is all for yesterday.

GRANIA (Wringing her hands.) Come to our house, DIARMUID, come to our house.

DIARMUID All the roads, the straight road and the crooked road lead to blackness. Of blackness be the end, and there is no light beyond it. But what have such questions to do with me. Whatever road I am on I will walk firm– with my sword out – (He draws his sword.) But you have come to tell me something. What is it ? out with it quickly for the day is breaking, and when it is broken there will be hunting.

go *to*
GRANIA I have come to ask you to ~~come~~ back with me.

You would have me in the little straight road & so
DIARMUID ^You have come to tell me that I am in it. For it is certain that a man walks where he thinks he walks. The mind makes all; we will talk of that some day. I tell you that you are lying to me. I am not in the

[5r]

–5–

road that leads on and on, and then shatters under one's feet, and becomes flying bits of darkness.

GRANIA DIARMUID, you are going straight upon your death, if you do not come back with me.

DIARMUID What do you know of all this that you come like a sooth-sayer. Who has been whispering in your ear ? Who has sent you to me ?

GRANIA I had a warning last night.

DIARMUID From that old woman who spins ? I tell you I have had enough of her warnings. I saw her last night carrying a bundle of new flax through the woods.

GRANIA No, DIARMUID, I left her spinning.

DIARMUID I tell you I saw her . She is going somewhere on some evil work. I have heard that here are women who live seven hundred years in the depths of the sea, and seven hundred years in the woods , spinning the threads of the long lived people of the sea and of the woods, and then seven hundred years spinning for men. She is one of them. But where is she going with the new flax ? What have you come to tell me

[6r]

–6–

about her ?

GRANIA I have come to tell you of a dream that came to me last night.

DIARMUID Well, what did the dream tell you ?

GRANIA I dreamt I was sitting by FINN.

DIARMUID I do not think much of that dream, for I saw you yesterday walking with FINN and holding his hands.

GRANIA But I dreamed I was sitting by FINN, and that your shield was hanging among the shields of the slain over our heads.

DIARMUID Did you not say it was a bad dream ? I have heard worse dreams than that. Ah, foolish gods, can you find nothing better than the dreams of an unfaithful wife to vex and shake my will.

GRANIA Do not blaspheme against the gods, for they are near us now. I have been praying to them to spare you. I have been praying to them all night, while I looked for you.

DIARMUID Yes, every man is a god in heaven, and on earth we are the hurly balls they drive hither and thither –

[7r]

_7_

Oh, they are great hurly players. The canauns are

never out of their hands. All night I have heard them laughing. I tell you I have heard them laughing. Do you not hear me ? Do you not hear me ?

GRANIA I hear, but oh DIARMUID take my hands and touch my hair ; they may bring some memory to your mind, some softness to your heart.

DIARMUID Yes, yes, I remember well enough. Your hands and your hair were sweet to me long ago. No, no, yesterday, even yesterday. Let me see your hands. They are beautiful hands, torn as they are. No wonder I loved them; and this hair too. You loved me once, GRANIA, you loved me hetter than FINN. I remember it all , the day before yesterday.

GRANIA I love you still, DIARMUID.

DIARMUID My dear one, why did you send me to FINN ? It may be that my words have been a little wild. Speak quickly, do not be afraid.

GRANIA I sent you to FINN because I wanted you to live among the Fianna, as before you saw me.

[8r]

–8–

DIARMUID All you say is true. Our love had become too great.

GRANIA I wanted you to be a friends with FINN, because our love had become a sickness, a madness.

DIARMUID Yes, yes, it has become a madness. It is a long time, GRANIA, since we have been alone together.

GRANIA No, DIARMUID, not ~~for~~ long.

DIARMUID Yes, yes, many days, many months, many years. There √ may be no other time for wringing this secret out of you – There was nought of FINN in your mind when you sent me to him ?

8r, l. 6 The cancellation is in pencil.

GRANIA There is no secret in me; I have told you everything. And I have come through this wood by night, to bring you from this hunt, as a wife comes to her husband.

DIARMUID GRANIA was not meant to sit by the fireside with children on her knees. The gods made her womb barren because she was not meant to hold children on her knees. The gods gave her a barren womb, hungry and barren like the sea. She looked from the red apple in her hands to the green apple on the bough. She looked from me to FINN, even when she first lusted for me, and after FINN there will be some other. The

[9r]

–9–

malignant gods made your beauty GRANIA. Your hand is very weak, your arm is very weak and fragile. This hair is very soft – (He takes her by the hair.) I could kill you as easily as I could kill a flower by the wayside.

GRANIA Kill me if you will, kill me with your sword, here in my breast.

DIARMUID You would have me kill you. Maybe if I killed you all would be well.

GRANIA Hold fast my hair, draw back my head and kill me. I would have you do it – (Pause.) Why do you not do it. If you would go to this hunting you must do it, for while I live you shall not go.

DIARMUID Let go my spear I say, let go my spear if you would have your life. I see that you were thinking of FINN this very moment. I see thoughts of FINN in your eyes. Let me go, or I will let the lust out of you with this sword-point.

[HRC(3)]

GRANIA Kill me, DIARMUID, I would have you do it.

DIARMUID And leave this white body like a cut flower by the wayside.

[10r]

–10–

GRANIA Kill me DIARMUID.

DIARMUID I have heard the gods laugh and I have been merry, but if I killed you I would remember everything. And I should wander in the woods seeing white and red flowers – After killing you I might kill myself – Oh, that would be a good thing to do. But seeing you there, your soft hair spattered with blood, and your white hands stained with blood I might not remember to do it. I might remember nothing but yesterday and to-day. I cannot kill you. I would not see your blood nor touch your hands – Your lips and teeth, and all this beauty I have loved seem in my eyes no better than a yellow pestilence. GRANIA, GRANIA, out of my sight. (He goes out driving her before him; a moment after he returns alone.) That is over,let me think. Yes, yes, there is a beast coming that I am to kill. I should take him so, upon my spear. The spear will be my best weapon, but the hand must be steady beneath it. If the point slipped he would be upon me. Maybe it will be better to let him run upon my shield and kill him with my sword, while he digs his tusks into my shield. My danger will be the darkness, for the darkness makes the hand shake, and day breaks but slowly. Higher up in the woods there

[11r]

–11–

is a little more light – (He goes out – Enter CAOELTE and USHEEN.)

CAOELTE We have hardly escaped with our lives. The branches touched me as the tree fell.

USHEEN What made that great ash tree fall.

CAOELTE **The wind had lulled, and yet it crashed across our way, as if it would kill us.**

USHEEN **I heard a thud and a crackling of branches before it fell, as though a great ~~stone~~** *rock* **had been thrown against it, though I saw nothing, ^ and for some time I had heard crashing sounds in the woods. I think that hosts have been hurling rocks at one another. All night there has been fighting on the earth and in the air and in the water.**

CAOELTE **Never was there such a night before. As I came by the river I saw swans fighting in the [~~—?—~~] air, and three ~~flew~~** *fell* **screaming into the tree tops.**

USHEEN **Have you seen how FINN'S hounds whimper at his heels.**

CAOELTE **They whimper and cry till the touch of his hand gives them courage for a moment. They would not follow him**

[12r]

–12–

at all were they not afraid of being left alone: (they walk to and fro – (A pause.) That light must be the beginning of the day. A pale foolish light that makes the darkness worse. The sky and the earth and the √ **air would turn to their old works again, but they have been palsy struck. Let us put this darkness out of** √ **our mind. Find us something to talk of USHEEN. Where is DIARMUID ?**

DIARMUID **(Coming forward.) DIARMUID is here, waiting for whatever may befall him. Tell FINN that though the mountain arose like an ox from sleep, and came against me, and though the clouds came like eagles, and the sea upon its feet that are without number, I will not turn from this hunting.**

CAOELTE **We have been seeking you. We would have you leave**

11r, l. 15 The word erased in the ribbon copy makes "air," appear as if it had been canceled.

[HRC(3)]

this hunting.

DIARMUID It may be that you fear and that FINN fears because of the falling of trees and the screaming of swans; but I do not fear.

CAOELTE Turn from this hunting, DIARMUID.

DIARMUID I would not, had I nothing but a reason no bigger than a pea, and I have weighty reasons.

[13r]

–13–

CAOELTE It were no wonder if even we whose death at a hunt like this has not been foretold, should turn from this hunting. For we are following no common beast. A √ man who had been trapping otters followed the foot-marks last night, not knowing what they were, and as he followed they grew greater and greater and further and further apart.

DIARMUID The night was dark.

CAOELTE But the footmarks were deep. Deeper than any made by a mortal beast.

DIARMUID It came yesterday out of the woods like a blight, like a flood, like a toad-stool, and now it grows bigger and bigger. But so much the more need for hunters. Good-bye, comrades, goodbye – (Exit.)

CAOELTE I would not follow where he has gone. He is among those broken rocks where I heard screams, and sounds as of battle. They say that dwarfs and worse things have their homes among those rocks.

USHEEN He is the only one among us who has not been shaken by this night of terror. Look, look, something is coming up this way.

14r]

–14–

CAOELTE **A tall staff in his hand, and he moves noiselessly. And there is another following him.**

USHEEN **Draw your sword, CAOELTE.**

CAOELTE **It will not come out of its sheath. It is but a shepherd. We are craven and are no better than CONAN (Enter two peasants.)**

OLD MAN **Be of good heart great delivered of Eri. I am but a shepherd looking for his sheep, and not,as well might be,some bad thing out of the rocks.**

{s √

YOUNG MAN **Can you tell me noble Sir‸e of any strayed sheep, or what is troubling the water and the air over our heads.** √

OLD MAN **We must go, sirs, we must find our sheep or starve. (Exeunt peasants.)** √

USHEEN **Maybe he was laughing at us because we are afraid. We must wait here till we hear FINN'S horn. If we were to seek him we would lose him, and it maybe never come alive out of this wood.**

CAOELTE **We had better go further up the hill. Who is this coming ? Since dawn began the wood has been full~~er~~ of shadows and sounds. They are coming out of the**

14r, ll. 10–11 The pencil mark in the RH margin is not like the other ticks, but it is impossible to decide what else it is.

17 The cancellation is in pencil.

-15-

rocks; they rise up out of the rocks.

CAOELTE There is one who seems to be pushed along, and if it is but a shadow, it is a heavy one. It is CONAN. I can see the sheep skin. I am glad he has not seen our fear. (Enter GOLL and four spearmen and CONAN.)

GALL The night is over at last.

CONAN The night is over, the last day has begun. Give me a drink, for I can go no further without one.

CAOELTE We must go further up the hill. We must hurry on if we would find FINN again. Have you seen him. Have you heard his horn ?

GOLL No, he has not sounded it, but the beast will be stirring

1. SPEARMAN -The last time I saw FINN he was on the rock yonder. He stood facing the dawn and shouting to his hounds. When he saw us he shouted that we were to climb up to him. He bellowed like a bull for its heifer.

2. SPEARMAN But I had had climbing enough.

CONAN Sit down, I will go no further. When a man has got to die is it not better for him to die sitting down than

[HRC(3), 15r]

stet

–15–

rocks; they rise up out of the rocks.

CAOELTE **There is one who seems to be pushed along, and if it is but a shadow, it is a heavy one. It is CONAN. I can see the sheep skin. I am glad he has not seen our fear. (Enter G{O ALL and four spearmen and CONAN.)**

GALL **The night is over at last.**

CONAN **The night is over, the last day has begun. GIve me a drink, for I can go no further without one.**

CAOELTE **We must go further up the hill. We must hurry on if we would find FINN again. Have you seen him. Have you heard his horn ?**

GOLL **No, he has not sounded it, but the beast will be stirring**

1. SPEAR-MAN **The last time I saw FINN he was on the rock yonder. He stood facing the dawn and shouting to his hounds. When he saw us he shouted that we were to climb up to him. He bellowed like a bull for its heifer.**

2. SPEAR-MAN **But I had had climbing enough.**

CONAN **Sit down, I will go no further. When a man has got to die is it not better for him to die sitting down than**

15r, l. 5, etc. All the corrections on this page are in pencil.

[HRC(3)]

[16r]

–16–

walking about, and better to die on clean ground than in the mire, or up to his middle in water. Give me your ale skin, CAOELTE.

CAOELTE I will not, CONAN, you have been asking for it all night.

CONAN Give me your ale skin, USHEEN, it is the last drink I shall ever drink.

√√

USHEEN I will not CONAN.

CONAN Give me your ale skin, GOLL; you will give me your ale skin GOLL, you are the noblest and handsomest, and bravest of all the Fianna.

√√

USHEEN I will give him a drink; he will not move until we do. (USHEEN gives CONAN his ale skin.) Drink, and think no more of death.

CONAN All the disasters that have come to DIARMUID have come to him because of the spilling of the ale out of the flagon; but I have lost both ale and ale skin and must therefore die.

√√

CAOELTE (To one of the Spearman.) We might light a fire; there must be dry leaves under ~~some o~~ these rocks . (Two of the Spearmen go together to collect dry leaves

[17r]

–17–

and sticks and they return a moment after with them.)

CONAN We are shivering since we crossed that river; and it was in that river that I lost my ale skin; someone plucked it from me from behind.

CAOELTE I too am shivering; the day is bleaker than the night

CONAN Ah, be careful with the tinder, be careful, for the first leaves are the dry ones – Bring the fire a little nearer, I would die warm though I have to get cold after. Make room for me by the fire. Do you not understand that I am going to die – That CONAN is going to die – That CONAN THE BALD is going to die. You will never flout me for my big stomach again, CAOELTE. √

CAOELTE You are not going to die, CONAN. Here, I will give you a drink.

CONAN Yellow ale ~~is~~ bitter on the tongue, tasting a little of the vat of the red yew that it came from – The last drink CONAN will ever drink (CAOELTE and the others talk among themselves.) They think that all this hurly burly is for DIARMUID, but I know better; you are my friend and I will tell you about it.

CAOELTE Give me my ale skin CAOELTE.

[18r]

–18–

CONAN Not yet, I must drink a little more – And now this is the way it was – It was not the loss of the ale skin that told me I was going to die, that only showed me that some great evil was going to happen to me – It was a swan screaming in the trees that told me I was going to die. Before I was born, when yet my mother was carrying me, towards the seventh month, she was one day washing clothes in the river, and she saw three geese swimming, and while one was cackling and billing with its mate an otter caught it by the leg and dragged it under the water; so my mother knew something was under her belt happen to the child ~~she was carrying~~, and she told me never to cross a river when there were any geese about.

CAOELTE They were swans that screamed in the trees.

CONAN Are not swans a kind of geese; but how do I know it was not swans my mother saw.

17r, l. 15 The cancellation is in pencil.

[HRC(3)]

CAOELTE CONAN, give me ~~your~~ *my* ale skin.

CONAN Why did I keep FINN and DIARMUID from killing one another; they could have done it so easily in DIARMUID'S house – Why did I bring them to this hunt ? CONAN has brought his own death upon him. (Enter FINN.)

[19r]

–19–

FINN We have come upon the slot of the boar in the hills; he can only just have passed by; if we go to the bend of the stream we should come upon him – (To CONAN) Why are you lying there ? We want every man, get up, we will put you in the gap yonder, the boar shall not escape unless he escapes through you.

CAOELTE CONAN is in terror; he thinks he is going to die.

FINN CONAN get up, or you may have to face this beast alone.

CONAN Do not believe them; it is not DIARMUID this pig is looking for, it is looking for me.

FINN If CONAN will not go, let him stay there. Here is a handful more leaves to warm your shins (FINN throws some wet leaves on the fire and quenches it.)

CONAN You have thrown wet leaves on the fire; now I shall die of cold. But are you leaving me ? Is it not the oath of the Fianna to protect one another – CAOELTE, USHEEN, do you not hear me – (They go out laughing.) They are an evil, stony-hearted, proud race – Rot in the wheat ear, frogs spawn in the pool, yellow sickness in one's body, henbane in one's drink, lice in my beard, fleas in my sheep skin – A stony-hearted, evil, proud race. (Bellows this out – Enter GRANIA and FINN.) √

[20r]

–20–

FINN **You are cold and tired, GRANIA,and have stumbled through the wood, you are all bruised.**

GRANIA **I am bruised and full of wretchedness, and I am very cold; and the dawning of the day frightens me. However cold it is I do not wish to see the sun – But I am cold, oh, the cold !**

FINN **There has been a fire here; I will blow the ashes to a blaze.**

GRANIA **(SITTING DOWN) Why did you not leave me to die where I had chosen.**

FINN **The beast we are hunting might have run upon you and you would have been trampled and gored by it. I could not have left you there. The blaze is already beginning, hold your hands to it.**

GRANIA **I would that you had left me to be killed by it. You have planned that the death of this boar is to put me on one side or the other, to give me to DIARMUID or to give me to you. But I am not man's spoil. You have planned it all between you, your plans are not mine. Go from me FINN, go to this hunt and kill this boar, or make a fire here for me to warm myself by, it is all the same.**

20r, ll. 14–15 The marks in the RH margin are not exactly ticks, but nor are they anything else.

[HRC(3)]

[21^r]

–21–

FINN **Although I lose my chance of killing this beast I must stay with you. I must protect you.**

GRANIA **It does not matter. Leave me here or go to this hunt, so long as I have a fire I do not mind.**

FINN **I dare not leave you, if it were to spring upon you from the thicket.**

GRANIA **It might be better, for I have done mischief enough. I am weary of the work I do in the world. Yet, FINN there is no evil in me. I wished that you and DIARMUID could make peace, and all might have been well, had not this evil thing broken out of the earth.**

FINN **DIARMUID and I could not be at peace. The peace we made was a false peace. (Hunting horns in distance.) The hounds are at the boar's heels now. I can hear my hounds. Yes, it is Bran, now it is Skealon, and now it is Lomair. They have found their courage, and are driving him from cover to cover.**

GRANIA **FINN I beseech you put the desire of me out of your heart. Be DIARMUID'S friend and save him. Kill the boar and save him.**

FINN **If I kill the boar you will belong to me.**

[22r]

–22–

GRANIA **Not because you kill the boar. I beseech you be DIARMUID'S friend. Save him from death.**

FINN **If I were there and DIARMUID here and this boar coming against me would DIARMUID save me ?**

GRANIA **Has not the blood bond made you brothers, and should not brother watch over one another's safety ?**

FINN **Beacuse we have been made brothers and because we both love one woman there is no end but this.**

GRANIA **You say that you love me, and I kneel to you.**

FINN **But the soothsayers have foretold other deaths, and what hand can hold them back ? A spear is to pierce me, an arrow CAOELTE – USHEEN alone shall live to far distant times. DIARMUID is to die by the tusks of a boar, and GRANIA – (A cry is heard close by, FINN plunges into the thicket and returns with DIARMUID who has been mortally wounded by a boar – DIARMUID struggles to his feet and leans against a rock.)**

DIARMUID **Water, is there no water, my life is ebbing out with my blood. (FINN goes to a well and comes back with water in his hand, but as he hold up his hand the water drips through his fingers.)**

D Finn I am dying & whether you give me water or with hold it I shall still die.

[HRC(3)]

[23r]

GRANIA **FINN, bring him water in your helmet (DIARMUID looks from one to the other.)**

DIARMUID **GRANIA and FINN. (When FINN returns with his helmet filled with water he looks again from one to another, and then, whether by accident or design he overturns the helmet.)**

GRANIA **Why have you done this ? Why will you not drink the water that FINN brought you (She takes up the helmet and fetches the water herself – Again DIARMUID looks from one to another, and puts the water away.) For my sake, for the sake of GRANIA I beseech you drink of it, ~~let me go and fecth some water for you, DIARMUID.~~** √

DIARMUID **It is growing lighter. There is a light coming out of the hill.**

FINN **Let me bind up your wounds or in a moment you'll be gone.**

DIARMUID **They're about me, they're about me, they were always about me though I could not see them.**

FINN **He is dying, they are coming for him.**

23r The present page and the one following (fol. 24r) are the only two pages in HRC(3) on which text is set to wider (2.8 cm) margins). Whether or not this is significant is undetermined.

6–7 The deletion is in ink (the same color as WBY's on fol. 24r).

[24r]

DIARMUID There is somebody there by the tree –(He begins swaying his hands as if to music.)

FINN He hears the harp-playing of AOGNHUS – It is by music that he leads the dead.

GRANIA DIARMUID, Oh, DIARMUID. Do not look at them, if you do not look at them you will not die.

DIARMUID I cannot hear the harpplaying, there is so much noise about me.

FINN He has forgotten love~~s~~ and all that lives. Henceforth his business is with them.

GRANIA Oh, DIARMUID, oh DIARMUID, oh DIARMUID !

DIARMUID Someone spoke to me, no, not the harp-player, some other. It was you FINN who spoke to me. FINN you are dying almost as ~~fast~~ quickly as I am. (He falls back dead.)

FINN He is dead, he has died as the son of the gods should die. A friend against whom I have made war is dead. I warred against him for you GRANIA – (They stand looking at each other a moment, and then GRANIA goes away and weeps – Enter a young man.)

YOUNG MAN The beast you have been hunting is dead, killed by a spear thrust – Here is the spear.

FINN The spear is mine, give it to me – (Walking towards GRANIA) We must send for men to carry the body to

[HRC(3), 25r]

-25-

the house.

GRANIA (Trying to overcome her emotion.) What did you say ? What are you saying ? What is that spear with blood upon it that you hold in your hand ?

FINN It is the spear that killed the boar - a thrust behind the shoulder did it. We must send for help.

GRANIA Yes, we must send for help. (The hunters begin to come in from different sides.) Tell my father, KING CORMAC of the death of DIARMUID, and bid him come to me at once - (Acquiring command over herself)- My father, KING CORMAC will see that DIARMUID'S burning be worthy of him. It shall be the greatest burning that has been known in Eri; and I bid you make ready, it must last for many days . The pyre shall be built upon the mountain, and all the shepherds of the valley shall bring a tree to build it. There are birch trees on the mountain that the long summer has made ready for the flame. A thousand shall be cut down and built to the height of fifty feet, and upon them shall be laid a crimson cloth, and DIARMUID shall be laid upon it. His battle gear beside him, his heavy spear, and Broad-Edge his double-handed sword, and the short

[HRC(3), 25r]

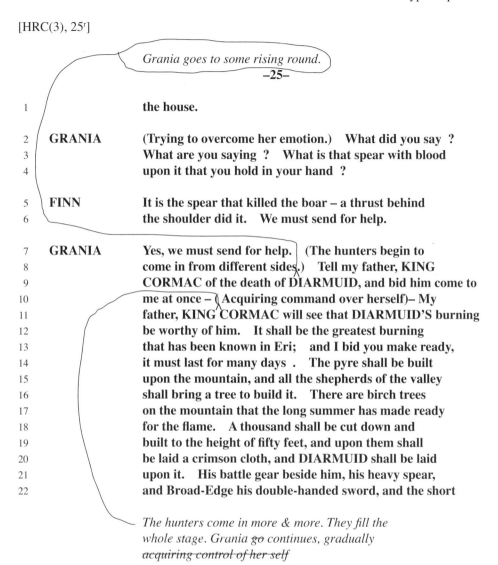

Grania goes to some rising round.

–25–

the house.

GRANIA **(Trying to overcome her emotion.) What did you say ? What are you saying ? What is that spear with blood upon it that you hold in your hand ?**

FINN **It is the spear that killed the boar – a thrust behind the shoulder did it. We must send for help.**

GRANIA **Yes, we must send for help. (The hunters begin to come in from different sides.) Tell my father, KING CORMAC of the death of DIARMUID, and bid him come to me at once – (Acquiring command over herself)– My father, KING CORMAC will see that DIARMUID'S burning be worthy of him. It shall be the greatest burning that has been known in Eri; and I bid you make ready, it must last for many days . The pyre shall be built upon the mountain, and all the shepherds of the valley shall bring a tree to build it. There are birch trees on the mountain that the long summer has made ready for the flame. A thousand shall be cut down and built to the height of fifty feet, and upon them shall be laid a crimson cloth, and DIARMUID shall be laid upon it. His battle gear beside him, his heavy spear, and Broad-Edge his double-handed sword, and the short**

The hunters come in more & more. They fill the whole stage. Grania ~~go~~ continues, gradually ~~acquiring control of her self~~

[HRC(3)]

[26r]

–26–

sword and light spear, that gave him little help, and all his casting spears, and his sheild with the flying heron upon it, that he may have all he needs when the immortals set   their battle host. The games in his honour shall last for three days, and men must be sent through the countries of Hebor and Hermon, and bring hither the flingers of the weight and the swift runner, and the skilful riders; and men must go hither and thither, and buy, or bring by force, two score of noble stallions, who shall be set to fight while the body burns. They shall beat one another with their hoofs, and tear one another with their teeth, till one half have been slain or wounded beyond help. The other half shall be taken and cast among the flames, so that DIARMUID may have noble horses when he awakes. KING CORMAC shall watch over his burning, but FINN the son of Cool, shall watch over it also, for though he warred against DIARMUID, DIARMUID was his friend many years. And bitterness is forgotten in death. All the Fianna shall watch over the burning, giving honour to DIARMUID, their companion and their friend. (The litter is brought in and DIARMUID'S body is laid upon it – USHEEN, CAOELTE and GOLL and FERGUS carry him up the path that ascends through the wood – CORMACK

26r, l. 4   Comparison with Berg(14), fol. 6r, line 8, suggests the gap should be filled with the words "him in", but note that the typist was not copying from Berg(14).

[27r]

–27–

Nial
and ~~FINMOLE~~ enter.)

Nial
~~FINMOLE~~ **CORMAC would speak with FINN and GRANIA – (FINN, CORMAC and GRANIA go up the stage talking together, and following the procession.)**

CONAN **GRANIA makes a great mourning for DIARMUID, but her welcome to FINN shall be greater.**

[NLI 8777(3) c, 81r, 81v/82r]

1.

DIARMID AND GRANIA.

Act. III.

Scene: The wooded slopes of Ben Bulben. Diarmid is sleeping under a tree. It is night, but the dawn is beginning to break – Enter two peasants.)

Old man!

There has been no such night as this these fifty years!

Young man.

How the wind rages, like the dragon or maybe it is the dragon himself. Listen, a tree has fallen.

Old man.

It is only the wind, I have seen wind like this before and then the sheep were lost in the ~~[illegible]~~ torrent

Young man.

I met a herdsman whose cattle broke out of their byres, and fifty drowned themselves in the lake.

Old man.

[illegible] then – the Fianna came into the forest at midnight sounding their horns.

XXXXX XXX.

Act III

That was the god Aengus. He watches over Diarmuid. The death of all these ~~[illegible]~~ men and the end of the Fianna has been foretold. Many will die in a great battle. Oscar who is but a child now will die in it, but Finn will die long after by a spearthrust, and Diarmuid by the tusk of a boar, and Usheen will go far away, and Caoilte storm the house of the gods at Ossory.

YOUNG MAN. Tell me that story, how Caolte will overcome the gods.

Typescript of Complete Act, Revised by W. B. Yeats and George Moore —W. B. Yeats's Copy?

[NLI 8777(3) c, 81^{r}]

1.

DIARMID AND GRANIA.

Act. III.

Scene: The wooded slopes of Ben Bulben. Diarmid is sleep ing under a tree. It is night, but the dawn is beginning to break – Enter two peasants.)

Old man'

There has been no such night as this these fifty years.

Young man.

How the wind rages, like the dragon or maybe it is the drag-on himself. Listen, a tree has fallen.

Old man.

It is only the wind , I have seen wind like this before and then the sheep were lost in the ~~forest~~. torrent

Young man.

I met a herdsman whose cattle broke out of their byres, and fifty drowned themselves in the lake.

Old man.

The Fianna frightened them – the Fianna came into the forest at midnight sounding their horns.

~~Young man~~.

[81^{v}/82^{r}]

Act III

That was the god Aengus. He watches over Diarmuid. The death of all **these ~~great~~ men and the end of the Fianna has been foretold. Many will die in a great battle. Oscar who is but a child now will die in it, but Finn will die long after by a spearthrust, and Diarmuid by the tusk of a boar, and Usheen will go far away, and Caoilte storm the house of the gods at Ossory.**

YOUNG MAN. Tell me that story, how Caolte will overcome the gods.

81^{v}/82^{r} The blue-ribbon TS text appears on a slip of paper measuring 7.6 by 20.0 cm, positioned between fols. 81 and 82, and is clearly meant to substitute for the canceled passage marked "E" on fol. 82^{r}. Cf. NLI 8777(3) d, fol. 112^{r} for another version of the same passage, in a similar typing format and on a similar kind of paper.

2 great] Canceled in ink, despite first appearances.

[NLI 8777(3) c]

[82r]

2

Young man.

fighting
And at midnight I saw the two hosts ~~flying~~, one host flying and one following, and among them that were flying an old one armed man.

Old man.

Grandfather
That was Diarmid's ~~father~~, he has been dead this fifty years.

Young man

But I saw something more.

Old man.

What did you see boy?

Young man.

A gaunt grey ragged man, and he was driving this beast the Fianna are hunting. He drove it along the edge of the mountain, prodding it before him with a spear.

Old Man.

That was the God Agonhus – he watches over Diarmid. The deaths of all these great men are foretold – Diarmid is to die by a boar tusk and a spear is to kill Finn but Caoelte will storm the house of the gods by the Red Torrent. E

Young man.

Tell me that story, how Caoelte will overcome the gods.

[83r]

3

Old man.

Not now, we must go in search of our sheep – If I have lost my ram my ewes will be useless to me. We must go now for at
They
day-break the Fianna will be sounding their horns. ~~Tehy~~ were
sounding
~~sending~~ them till the moon went down – It was they who frighten-

ed my sheep.

Young man.

But this hunting, will ~~be~~ the boar be killed?

Old man.

is no great *harm*

It matters ~~little~~ to us, maybe a little less ~~damage~~, to our fields, that is all. The seasons will be none the better, the cows will have no more milk in their udders – and my lambs , there will be no lambs next year.

Young man.

When the Fianna have killed the boar they will give us some parts of it.

Old man.

The Fianna have no thoughts for such as we, all that they do not eat of the boar they will throw to their dogs – they would
for us to
not think it well ~~that we should~~ taste meat. They beat back
more than
the invader when they can and it is ~~as much as~~ our lives are
from the
worth to pick up a dead hare ~~in the~~ path.

Young man.

Hush, there is a man sleeping under the tree – If we do not wake him the beast may come upon him sleeping.

[84r]

4.

Old man.

Better do nothing, we must not do anything against the gods. The god Aognhus will save him if it be pleasing to him to do so, or he may call him away. Let us begone boy, let us go find our sheep. (<u>Exit</u>)

Diarmid.

They croak like ravens over carrion – croak, croak, croak. (<u>Enter Grania</u>)

[NLI 8777(3) c]

Grania.

I have sought you all night. I have been wandering in the woods since the moon went down.

Diarmid.

What have you come for?

Grania.

I was afraid and have been running; give me time to draw my breath.

Diarmid.

Your hair is down and your hands are torn with brambles.

Grania.

tired

Yes, look at my hands, and I am so weary, Diarmid. I am so weary that I could lie down and die here. That mossy bank is like a bed; lay me down there. Oh I have come to ~~beg you to give up this hunting~~. bring you home with me.

[85r]

5.

{Diarmid
{**~~Grania~~.**

And you show me torn hands, and you hold out to me wet hair, and would have me go home. You talk of dying too, and would have me lay you on this bank. But what good is there in all this, Grania, for I have no time to listen.

Grania.

Give up this hunting for I have had warning that you will die if you do not turn back. Turn before we lose ourselves in the darkness of the woods.

Diarmid.

I am in a little way that leads to darkness, but what does that matter to you Grania? Your way home winds along the hill,

different

and down into the valley; my way is a ~~difficult~~ way, a shorter way, and the morrows that men ~~must~~ live frighten me more than this short way. I have no heart for that crooked road of

84r, l. 12 The overwritten word is largely erased.

morrows ~~my heart is all for yesterday~~.

Grania.

(Wringing her hands) Come to our house, Diarmid, come to our house.

Diarmid.

All the roads, the straight road and the crooked road, lead to blackness. {If. / Of} blackness be the end and there is no light beyond it. But what have such questions to do with me? What ever road I am on I will walk firmly with my sword out – (He

[86^{r}]

6.

draws his sword) But you have come to tell me something. What is it? Out with it quickly for the day is breaking, and when it is broken there will be hunting.

Grania.

I have come to ask you to go ~~back~~ home **with me.**

Diarmid.

You would have me in the straight road, and so you have come to tell me that I am in it. For it is certain that a man walks where he thinks he walks. The mind makes all; we will talk of that some day. I tell you that you are lying to me. I am not in the road that leads on and on, and then shatters under one's feet, and becomes flying bits of darkness.

Grania.

Diarmid, you are going straight upon your death, if you do not come back with me.

Diarmid.

What do you know of all this that you come like a soothsayer. Who has been whispering in your ear? Who has sent you to me?

Grania.

I had a warning last night.

[NLI 8777(3) c]

Diarmid.

From that old woman who spins? I tell you I have had

[87r]

7

enough of her warnings. I saw her last night carrying a bundle of new flax through the woods.

Grania.

No, Diarmid, I left her ~~spinning~~. in the house.

Diarmid.

I tell you I saw her. She is going somewhere on some
there
evil work, I have heard that ~~here~~ are women who live seven hundred years in the woods, spinning the threads of the long lived people ~~of the sea and~~ of the woods, and then seven hundred years spinning for men. She is one of them. But where is she going with the new flax? What have you come to tell me about her?

Grania.

I have come to tell you of a dream that came to me last night.

Diarmid.

Well what did the dream tell you?

Grania.

I dreamt I was sitting by Finn.

Diarmid.

I do not think much of that dream, for I saw you yesterday walking with Finn and holding his hands.

[88r]

8.

Grania.

But I dreamed I was sitting by Finn, and that your shield was hanging among the shields of the slain over our heads.

Diarmid.

Did you not say it was a bad dream? I have heard worse dreams than that. Ah, foolish gods, can you find nothing better than the dreams of an unfaithful wife to vex and shake my will.

Grania.

Do not blaspheme against the gods for they are near us now. I have been praying to them to spare you. I have been praying to them all night, while I looked for you,

Diarmid.

Yes, every man is a god in heaven, and on earth we are the hurly balls they drive hither and thither – Oh, they are great hurly players. The canauns are never out of their hands. All night I have heard them laughing. I tell you I have heard them laughing. Do you not hear me? Do you not hear me?

Grania.

I hear, but oh, Diarmid, take my hands and touch my hair; they may bring some memory to your mind, some softness to your heart.

Diarmid.

Yes, yes, I remember well,enough. Your hands and your

[89r]

9.

hair were sweet to me long ago. No, no yesterday, even yester-day. Let me see your hands. They are beautiful hands, torn as they are. No wonder I love them; and this hair too. You loved me once, Grania, you loved me better than Finn. I remem-ber it all the day before yesterday.

Grania.

I love you still, Diarmid.

Diarmid.

My dear one, why did you send me to Finn? It may be that my words have been a little wild. Speak quickly, do not be afrai d

Grania.

I sent you to Finn, because I wanted you to live among the Fianna as before you saw me.

[NLI 8777(3) c]

Diarmid.

All you say is true. ~~Our love has become too great.~~

Grania.

your

I wanted you to be friends with Finn, because ~~our~~ love had become a sickness, a madness.

Diarmid.

But i}

Yes, yes it has become a madness. I}t is a long ~~time~~ while **Grania since we were alone together.**

Grania.

No, Diarmid, not long.

[90ʳ]

10

Diarmid.

Yesterday is a long while and t}

~~yes, yes, many days, many months, many years.~~ ^ T}here may be no other time for wringing this secret from you – There was

a

~~no~~ thought of Finn in your mind when you sent me to him?

Grania.

There is no secret in me; I have told you everything. And I come through this wood by night, to bring you fromthis hunt, as a wife comesto her husband.

Diarmid.

Grania was not meant to sit by the fireside with children on her knees. The gods made her womb barren because she was not meant to hold children on her knees. The gods gave her a barren womb ~~because~~ hungry and barren like the sea. She looked from the red apple in her hand to the green apple on the bough. She looked from me to Finn, even when she first lusted for me, and after Finn there will be some other. The malignant gods made your beauty, Grania. Your hand is very weak, your arm is very weak and fragile. This hair is very soft – (<u>He</u> takes her by the hair). I could kill you as easily as I could kill a flower by the wayside.

90ʳ, l. 10 Type cancellation.

Grania.

Kill me if you will, kill me with your sword, here in my breast.

[91r]

11.

Diarmid.

You would have me kill you. Maybe if I killed you all would be well.

Grania.

Hold fast my hair, draw back my head and kill me. I would have you do it – (Pause) Why do you not do it? If you would go to this hunting you must do it, for while I live you shall not go.

Diarmid.

Let go my spear, I say, let go my spear, if you would have your life. I see that you are thinking of Finn this very moment. I see thoughts of Finn in your eyes. Let me go, or I will let the lust out of you with this sword-point.

Grania.

Kill me Diarmid, I would have you do it.

Diarmid.

And leave this white body like a cut flower on the wayside.

Grania.

Kill me, Diarmid.

[92r]

12.

Diarmid.

I have heard the gods laugh, and I have been merry, but if I killed you I would remember everything. And I should wander in the woods seeing white and red flowers – After killing you I might kill myself – Oh, that would be a good thing to do. But seeing you there, your soft hair spattered with blood, and your white hands stained with blood I might not remember to do it. I might remember nothing but yesterday and to-day. I cannot kill you. I would not see your blood nor touch your hands.

[NLI 8777(3) c]

Your lips and teeth, and all this beauty I have loved seem in my eyes no better than a yellow pestilence. Grania, Grania, out of my sight. – (<u>He goes out driving her before him; a moment after he returns alone</u>) That is over, let me think. Yes, yes, there is a beast coming that I am to kill. I should take him so, upon my spear. The spear will be my best weapon, but the hand must be steady beneath it. If the point slipped he would be upon me. Maybe it will be better ~~to~~ to let him run upon my shield and kill him with my sword, while he digs his tusks into my shield. My danger will be the darkness, for the darkness makes the hand shake, and day breaks but slowly. Higher up in the woods there is a little more light – (<u>He goes out – Enter Caoelte and Usheen</u>)

Caoelte.

We have hardly escaped with our lives. The branches touchme as the tree fell.

Usheen.

[93r]

13.

Usheen.

What made that great ash tree fall?

Caoelte.

The wind had lulled, and yet it crashed across our way, as if it would kill us.

Usheen.

I heard a thud and a crackling of branches before it fell, as though a great rock had been thrown against it, though I saw nothing, and for some time I had heard crashing s ~~sounds~~ in the woods. I think that hosts have been hurling rocks at one another. Al night there has been fighting on the earth, and in the air and in the water.

Caoelte.

Never was there sucha night before. As I came by the river I saw swans fighting in the air, and three fell screaming into the tree tops.

92r, l. 16 to] The word in canceled in pencil, probably by WBY.
93r, l. 3 The line is overtyped with a new ribbon.

Usheen.

Have you seen how Finn's nounds whimper at his heels?

Caoelte.

They whimper and cry till the touch of his hand gives them courage from a moment. They would not follow him at all were they not afraid of being left alone – (<u>They walk to and fro</u>– a <u>pause.)</u> That light must be the beginning of the day. A pale foolish

[94r]

14.

foolish light that makes the darkness worse. The sky and the earth would turn to their old works again but they have been palsy struck. Let us put this darkness out of our mind. Find us something to talk of Usheen – Where is Diarmid?

Diarmid.

(<u>Coming forward</u>) Diarmid is here, waiting whatever may befall him Tell Finn that though the mountain arose like an ox from sleep, and came against me, and though the clouds came like eagles, and the sea upon its feet that are without number,
would
I ~~will~~ not turn from this hunting.

Caoelte.

We have been seeking you. We would have you leave this hunting.

Diarmid.

that **of**
It may be that you fear ,and ~~the~~ Finn fears because the fallin g of trees and the screaming of swans, but I do not fear.

Caoelte.

Turn from this hunting, Diarmid.

Diarmid.

I would not, had I nothing but a reason no bigger than a pea, and I have weighty reasons.

94r, l. 12 The final letter in the line, "g", is inserted with a new ribbon.

[NLI 8777(3) c]

[95r]

15.

Caoelte.

It were no wonder if even we whose death at a hunt like this has not been foretold, should turn from this hunting. For we are following no ~~common~~ mortal beast. A man who had been trapping otters followed the footmarks last night, not knowing what they were, and as he followed they grew greater and greater and further and further apart.

Diarmid.

The night is dark.

Caoelte.

But the footmarks were deep. Deeper than any made by a mortal beast.

Diarmid.

It came yesterday out of the woods likea blight, like a flood, like a toad-stool, and now it grows bigger and bigger. But so much more the need for hunters. Goodbye comrades, goodbye. (Exit)

Caoelte.

I would not follow where he has gone. He is among those broken rocks where I heard screams, and sounds as of battle. They say that dwarfs and worse things have their homes among those rocks.

[96r]

16.

Usheen.

He is the only one among us who has not been shaken by this night of terror? Look, look, something is coming this way.

Caoelte.

A tall staff in his hand, and he moves noiselessly, and there is another following him.

Usheen.

Draw your sword, Caoelte.

95r, l. 1 "we whose d" is overtyped with a new ribbon.

Caoelte.

It will not come out of its sheath. It is but a shepherd. We are craven, and no better than Conan. (Enter two peasants.)

Old man.

Be of good heart great deliverer of Eri. I am but a shepherd looking for his sheep, and not, as well might be, some bad thing out of the rocks.

Young man.

Can you tell me noble sirs of any strayed sheep, or what is troubling the water and the air over our heads,

Caoelte

We have been wandering in the dark all night. We are as blind as you are.

Old man.

We must go sirs, we must find our sheep or starve. (Exit peasants.)

[97r]

17.

Usheen.

Maybe he was laughing at us because ~~he was~~ *we are* **afraid. We must wait here till we hear Finn's horn. If we were to seek him we would lose him, and it may be never come alive out of the wood.**

Caoelte.

We had better go further up the hill. Who is this coming? Since dawn began the wood has been full of shadows and sound. They are coming out of the rocks; they rise out of the rocks.

Usheen

There is one who seems to be pushed along, and if it is but a shadow, it is a heavy one. It is Conan. I can see the sheep skin. Iam glad he has not seen our fear. (Enter Goll, Creffan Fathna & two of the Fianna **Conan , ~~and four Spearmen.~~)**

Goll.

The night is over at last.

97r, l. -8 The part ascription, "Usheen", is overtyped with a new ribbon.

[NLI 8777(3) c]

Conan.

The night is over, the last day has begun. Give me a ~~d~~ drink for I can go no further without one.

Caoelte.

We must go further up the hill. We must hurry on if we would find Finn again. Have you seen him? Have you heard his horn?

[98r]

18.

Goll.

No, he has not sounded it, but the beast will be stirring.

Fathna
~~First Spearman~~. [?Creffan]

The last time I saw Finn he was on the rock yonder. He stood facing the dawn and shouting to his hounds. When he saw us he shouted that we were to climb up to ~~t~~him. He bellowed like a bull for its heifer.

~~Second Spearman~~. Creffan

But I had had climbing enough.

Conan.

Sit down I will go no further. When a man has got to die is it not better for him to die sitting down than walking about, and better to die on clean ground than in the mire, or up to his middle in water. Give me your ale skin, Caoelte.

Caoelte.

I will not, Conan, you have been asking for it all night.

Conan.

Give me your ale skin Usheen, it is the last drink I shall ever drink.

Usheen.

I will give him a drink; he will not move until we do.

97r, l. 13 Type deletion.

98r, l. -1 The page number is overtyped with a new ribbon.

4 Type deletion.

[99r]

19.

(Usheen gives Conan his ale skin) Drink and think no more of death.

Conan.

All the disasters tha have come to Diarmid have come to him because of the spilling of the ale out of the flagon; but I have lost both ale and ale skin and must therefore die.

Caoelte.

Fathna

(To ~~one of the Spearmen~~) We might light a fire; there

Fathna & Creffan

must be dry leaves under these rocks. (~~Two of the Spearmen~~ go together to collect dry leaves and sticks, and they return a moment after with them.)

Conan.

We are shivering since we crossed that river; and it was in that river I lost my ale skin; some one plucked it from ~~me~~

{d.

~~from~~ behin{f.

Caoelte.

I too am shivering; the day is bleaker than the night.

Conan.

A h, be careful with the tinder, be careful, for the first leaves are the dry ones – Bring the fire a little nearer, I would die warm though I have to get cold after. Make room fir me by the fire. Do you not understand that I am going to die –

[100r]

20.

That Conan is going to die – that Conan the Bald is going to

great belly

die. You will never flout me for my ~~big stomach~~ again, Caoelte.

99r, l. 11 The line is overtyped with a new ribbon.

[NLI 8777(3) c]

Caoelte.

You are not going to die, Conan. Here, I will give you
a drink.

Conan.

Yellow ale bitter on the tongue tasting a little of the
vat of ~~the~~ red yew that it came from – The last drink Conan will
ever drink – <u>(Caoelte and the others talk among themselves)</u>
They think that all this hurly burly is for Diarmid, but I know
better; you are my friend and I will tell you about it.

Caoelte.

Conan
Give me my ale skin, ~~Caoelte~~.

Conan.

Not yet, I must drink a little more – and now this is the
way it was – it was not the lossof the ale skin that told me
I was going to die, that only showed me that some great evil
was going to happen to me – It was a swan screaming in the trees
that told me I was going to die. Before I was born, and when
with
yet my mother was carrying me, towards the seventh month, she
was one day washing clothes in the river, and she saw three
one
geese swimming, and while ~~on~~ was cackling and billing with its
mate an otter caught it by the leg and dragged in under the

[101r]

21.

water; so my mother knew something was to happen to the child
a
under her belt, and she told me never to cross ~~the~~ river when
there were any geese about.

Caoelte.

They were swans that screamed in the trees.

Conan.

Are not swans a kind of geese; but how do I know it was
not swans my mother saw.

Caoelte.

Conan give me my ale skin.

Conan.

Why did I keep Finn and Diarmid from killing one another; they could have done it so easily in Diarmid's house – Why did I bringthem to this hunt? Conan has brought his own death upon him. (<u>Enter Finn</u>)

Finn.

We have come upon the slot of the boar in the hills; he

{ y just have

can onl{[? ? t] passed by; if we go to the bend of the stream we should come upon him – (<u>To Conan</u>) Why are you lying there? We want every man, get up, we will put you in the gap yonder the boar shall not escape unless he escapes through you.

Caoelte.

Conan is in terror; he thinks he is going to die.

[102r]

22.

Finn.

Conan, get up, or you may have to face this beast alone.

Conan.

Do not believe them; it is not Diarmid this pig is looking for it is for me.

Finn.

If Conan will not go, let him staythere. Here is a handful more leaves to warm your shins – (<u>Finn throws some wet leaves on the fire and quenches it.)</u>

Conan.

You have thrown wet leaves on the fire; now I shall die

They all go because Finn has bidden them

{?

of cold. But are you leaving me{. ^Is it not the oath of the

you leave me Goll yet some day Finn who has put out my fire will put out your life.

Fianna to protect one another – Caoelte, Usheen do you not hear

---

101r, l. 13 Revision over erasure. Traces of typed, different words ending with "t" are just visible beneath "have".

[NLI 8777(3).c]

me – (They go out laughing) They are an evil, stony-hearted, proud race – Rot in the (ear) wheat, ~~stony-hearted~~ frogs spawn in the pool, yellow sickness in one's body, henbane in one's drink, lice in my beard, fleas in my sheep skin – A stony-hearted, evil

follows them

proud race. (He ~~bellows this~~ out – Enter Grania and Finn.)

Finn.

You are cold and tired Grania, and have stumbled through the wood, you are all bruised,

Grania.

I am bruised and full of wretchedness, and I am very cold;

[103r]

23.

and the dawning of the day frightens me. However cold it is I do not wish to see the sun – But I am cold, oh the cold!

Finn.

There has been a fire here; I will blow the ashes to a blaze.

Grania.

(Sitting down.) Why did you not leave me to die where I had chosen.

Finnn.

The beast we are hunting might have run upon you and you would have been trampled and gored by it. I could not have left you there. The blaze is already beginning, hold your hands to it.

Grania.

I would that you had left me to be killed by it. You have planned that the death of this boar is to put me on one side or the other, to give me to Diarmid or to give me to you. But I

(Standing up)

am no man's spoil. You have planned it all between you, your plan are not mine. Go from me Finn, go to this hunt and kill

---

102r, l. 10 ear] The transposition is made in pencil (by WBY?).
stony-hearted] Type deletion.

the or go where you will
**the boar, ~~or~~ make ~~a~~ fire ~~for me here to warm myself by~~, ~~it is~~
~~all the same~~.**

Finn.

**Although I lose my chance of killing this beast I must stay
with you**

[104r]

24.

will
with you. I ~~must~~ protect you.

Grania.

Stay with me
It does not matter. ~~Leave me~~ here or go to this hunt.

Finn.

will
**I ~~dare~~ not leave you, if it were to spring upon you from
the thicket.**

Grania.

**It might be better for I have done mischief enough. ~~I
am weary of the work I do in the world~~. ~~Yet, Finn there is~~**
have made
~~no evil in me~~. I wished that you and Diarmid could ~~make~~ peace,
would
**and all ~~might~~ have been well, had not this evil thing broken
out of the earth.**

Finn.

**Diarmid and I could not be at peace. The peace we made
was a false peace. (<u>Hunting horns in the distance)</u> The hounds
are at the boar's heels now. I can hear my hounds. Yes, it
is Bran, now it is Skealon, ~~and now it is Lomair~~. They have**
{c
found their {tourage and are driving him from cover to cover. (<u>Going
up the stage</u>.) Listen — now it is Lomair

Grania.

**Finn I beseech you put the desire of me out of your heart.
Be Diarmid's friend and save him. Kill the boar and save him.**

[NLI 8777(3) c]

Finn.

If I kill the boar will you belong to me.

[105r]

25.

Grania.

Not because you kill the boar.

Finn.

If I were there and Diarmid here, and this boar coming against me would Diarmid save me?

Grania.

You have fought side by side. Will you let him die?

Finn.

Why do you wish me to do this?

Grania.

It was I who sent Diarmid to you: and the blood bond. You are brothers.

Finn.

Should not a woman's breast be more to me than a man's hand?

Grania,

But the blood bond, he who breaks it shall be cast out by God-kind and man-kind.

Finn.

I cannot save Diarmid, his end has been foretold. I cannot change it. A spear is to pierce me, ~~an arrow~~ Caoelte and **Usheen alone shall live to far distant times. Diarmid is to die by the tusks of a boar, and Grania – (A cry is heard close by, Finn plunges into the thicket and returns with Diarmid who has been mortally wounded by the boar – Diarmid struggles to his feet and**

105r The entire page is typed with a new ribbon.

12–13 The transposition and deletion are in the same shade of blue-black ink as WBY's insertion.

[106r]

26.

and leans against a rock.)

Diarmid.

Water, is there no water? My life is ebbing out with my blood. (Finn goes to a well and comes back with water in his hand but as he holds up his hand the water drips through his fingers.) If I had water I might not die.

Grania.

Finn, bring him water in your helmet – (Diarmid looks from one to the other.)

Diarmid.

Grania and Finn. (When Finn returns with his helmet filled with water ~~he~~ Diarmid **looks from one to the other, and then, whether by accidemt or design he overturns the helmet.)**

Grania.

Why have you done this? Why will you not drink the water that Finn brought you? (She takes up the helmet and fetches ~~the~~ water herself – Again Diarmid looks from one to another, and puts the water away,) For my sake for the sake of Grania I beseech you drink of it.

Diarmid.

It is growing lighter. There is a light coming out of the hill.

[107r]

27.

Finn

Let me bind up your wounds or in a moment you'll be gone.

Diarmid.

They're about me, they're about me, they were always about me though I could not see them.

106r, l. −1 The completion of the stage direction is in dark blue ribbon.

6+ Type deletion.

[NLI 8777(3) c]

Finn.

He is dying, they are coming for him.

Diarmid.

There is somebody there by the tree – move me a little that I may see him. (<u>Finn helps him and slightly changes his position. He begins swaying his hand as if to music.)</u>

Finn.

He hears the harp-playing of Aognhus – It is by music that he leads the dead.

Grania.

Diarmid, oh Diarmid! Do not look at them{. / ,} {I / **if**} **you do not look at them you will not die. Do not die**{. / } {Y / **you**} **said once that you would be lonely withoutnme among the immortals.**

Diarmid.

I cannot hear the harp playing; there is so much noise about me.

[108r]

28.

Grania.

He has forgotten me.

Finn.

Henceforth his business is with them.

Grania.

Oh Diarmid! Oh Diarmid! Oh Diarmid!

Diarmid.

Someone spoke to me; no not the harp player, some other. It was you Finn, who spoke to me. No, no, who was it who spoke to me? (He falls back dead.)

Finn.

He is dead; he has died as the son of the gods should die. A friend against whom I have made war is dead. I warred against him for you, Grania –(They stand looking at each other a moment and then Grania goes away and weeps. Enter a young man.)

Young man.

The beast you have been hunting is dead, killed by a spear thrust – Here is the spear.

Finn.

The spear is mine, give it to me – (Walking towards Grania) We must send for men to carry the body to the house. (To the young man) Go fetch King Cormac, bring him here. (Exit Shepherd)

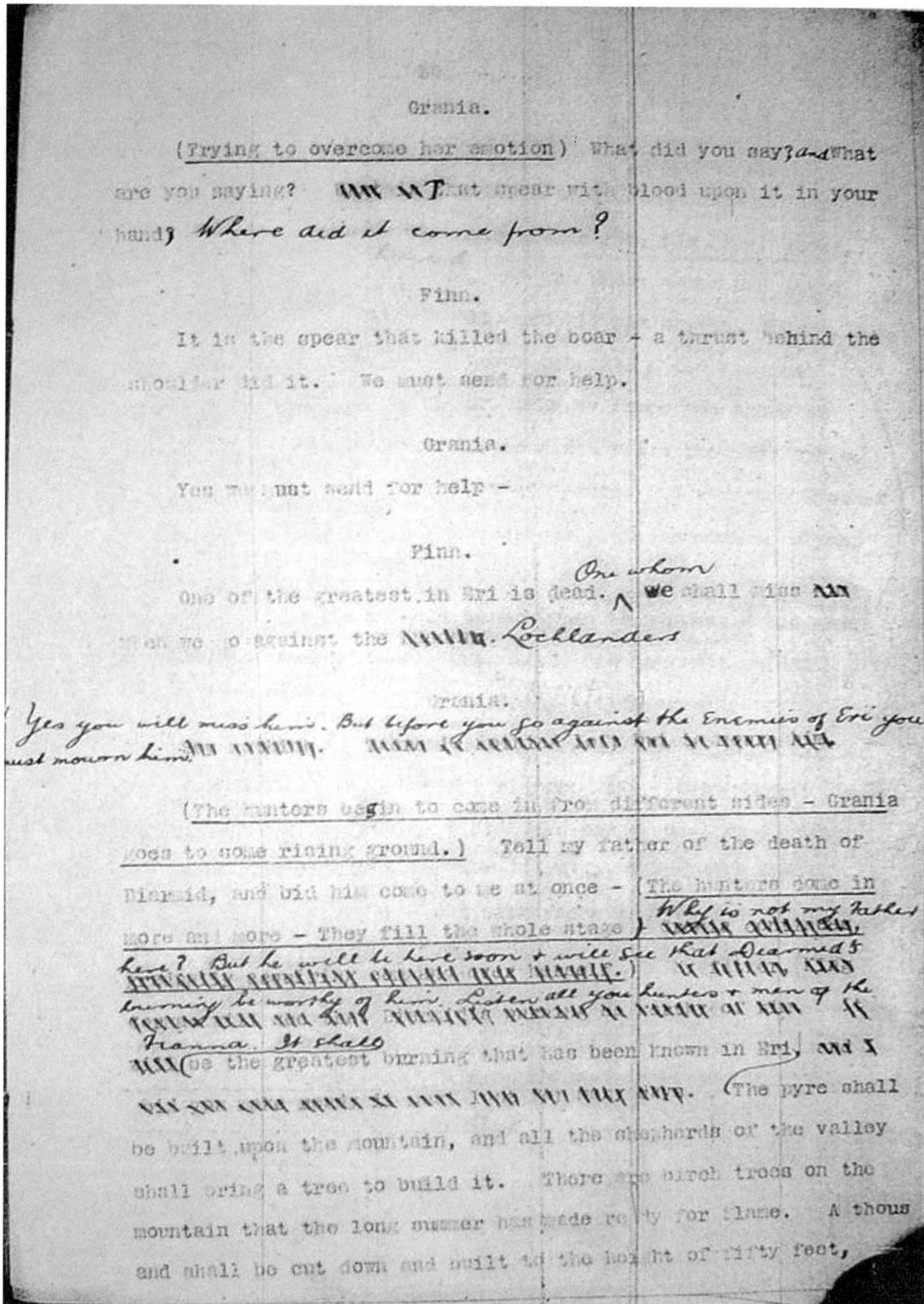

20

Grania.

(Trying to overcome her emotion) What did you say? and What are you saying? That spear with blood upon it in your hand? Where did it come from?

Finn.

It is the spear that killed the boar - a thrust behind the shoulder did it. We must send for help.

Grania.

You must send for help -

Finn.

One of the greatest in Eri is dead. One whom we shall miss when we go against the Lochlanders

Grania.

Yes you will miss him. But before you go against the Enemies of Eri you must mourn him.

(The hunters begin to come in from different sides - Grania goes to some rising ground.) Tell my father of the death of Diarmid, and bid him come to me at once - (The hunters come in more and more - They fill the whole stage) Why is not my father here? But he will be here soon & will see that Dearmed's burning be worthy of him. Listen all you hunters & men of the Fianna. It shall be the greatest burning that has been known in Eri, The pyre shall be built upon the mountain, and all the shepherds of the valley shall bring a tree to build it. There are birch trees on the mountain that the long summer has made ready for flame. A thousand shall be cut down and built to the height of fifty feet,

[NLI 8777(3) c, 109r]

Grania.

{,
(<u>Trying to overcome her emotion</u>) **What did you say**{? and **What**
{T
are you saying? ~~**What is**~~ **that**{**spear with blood upon it in your**
{,
hand{? Where did it come from?

Finn.

It is the spear that killed the boar – a thrust behind the shoulder did it. We must send for help.

Grania.

Yes we must send for help –

Finn.

One whom
{we
One of the greatest inEri is dead. ^{**We shall miss** ~~**him**~~
when we go against the ~~**Landers**~~**.** Lochlanders

Grania.

Yes you will miss him. But before you go against the enemies of Eri you must mourn him.

~~**Say nothing.**~~ ~~**There is nothing left but to mourn him.**~~

(<u>**The hunters be g in to come in from different sides – Grania goes to some rising ground.)**</u> **Tell my father of the death of Diarmid, and bid him come to me at once – (<u>The hunters come in</u>**
Why is not my Father
{)
<u>**more and more – They fill the whole stage**</u>{ ~~**– Grania continues,**~~
here? But he will be here soon & will see that Diarmid's
~~**gradually acquiring control over herself.**~~) ~~**My father, King**~~
burning be worthy of him. Listen all you hunters & men of the
~~**Cormac will see that Diarmid's burning be worthy of him.**~~ ~~**It**~~
Fianna. It shall
~~**will**~~ **be the greatest burning that has been known in Eri,** ~~**and I bid you make ready it must last for many days.**~~ **The pyre shall be built upon the mountain, and all the shepherds of the valley shall bring a tree to build it. There are birch trees on the mountain that the long summer has made ready for flame. A thous**
{,
and shall be cut down and built to the height of fifty feet{.

30

and upon them shall be laid a crimson cloth, and Diarmid shall
be laid upon it. His battle gear beside him, his heavy spear,
and Broad Edge his double *handed* sword, and the short sword and light
spear, that gave him little help, and all his casting spears,
and his shield with the flying heron upon it. And men must
go hither and thither, and buy or bring by force two score of
noble stallions, who shall be set to fight while the body burns.
They shall beat one another with their hoofs, and tear one another
with their teeth till one half have been slain or wounded beyond
help. The other half shall be taken and cast among the flames,
so that Diarmid may have noble horses when he awakes. The games
in his honour shall last for three days, and men must be sent
through the countries of Hebor[illegible] *to find* the casters of
the weight, and the casters of the spear, and the [illegible] and
the swift runner, and the skilful riders; King Cormac
shall watch over the games, but Finn the son of Cool shall watch
over them also, for though he warred against Diarmid, Diarmid
was his friend many years; and bitterness is forgotten in
death. All the Fianna shall watch over the games, giving honour to Diarmid their companion and their friend. (The litter
is brought in and Diarmid's body is laid upon it - Usheen, Caoelte and Goll and Fergus carry him up the path that ascends throug
the wood - Cormac and Niall enter.)

Niall.

Cormac would speak with Finn and Grania -

110r, l. -1 "30" has been typed in darker blue ribbon over an almost erased "29."
15 Type deletion.
111r, l. 4 (facing page) Type deletion.

[NLI 8777(3) c, 110r]

30

and upon them shall be laid a crimson cloth, and Diarmid shall be liad upon it. His battle gear beside him, his heavy spear,
handed
and Broad Edge his double^sword, and the short sword and light spear, that gave him little help, and all his casting spears, and his shield with the flying heron upon it./ And men must go hither and thither, and buy or bring by force two score of noble stallions, who shall be set to fight while the body burns. They shall beat one another with their hoofs, and tear one another with their teeth till one half have been slain or wounded beyond help. The other half shall be taken and cast among the flames, so that Diarmid may have noble horses when he awakes./ The games in his honour shall last for three days, and men must be sent
to find
through the countries of Hebor~~and bring~~ ~~hither~~ the casters of the weight, and the casters of the spear, and the boxers and the swift runner, and the skilful riders;/ ~~and~~ King Cormac shall watch over the games, but Finn the son of Cool shall watch over them also, for though he warred against Diarmid, Diarmid was his friend many years; and bitterness is forgotten in death. All the Fianna shall watch over the games, giving honour to Diarmid their companion and their friend. (The litter is brought in and Diarmid's body is laid upon it – Usheen, Caoelte and Goll and Fergus carry him up the path that ascends throug the wood – Cormac and Niall enter.)

Niall.

Cormac would speak with Finn and Grania –

[NLI 8777(3) c, 111r]

31.

Cormac.

Diarmid is dead but the Fianna are united and the Lochlanders shall be driven into the sea.

(Finn and Cormac and Grania go up the stage, talking together, and following the procession.)

Conan.

They have forgotten me, he has forgotten me though it was I who told ~~Grania~~ him that Grania shoul d be given to whomever killed the boar. An evil stony hearted proud race (turns to go up the stage, stops.) Grania makes a great mourning for Diarmid but her welcome to Finn shall be greater,

[NLI 8777(3) e, 113r; NLI 8777(3) d, 112r]

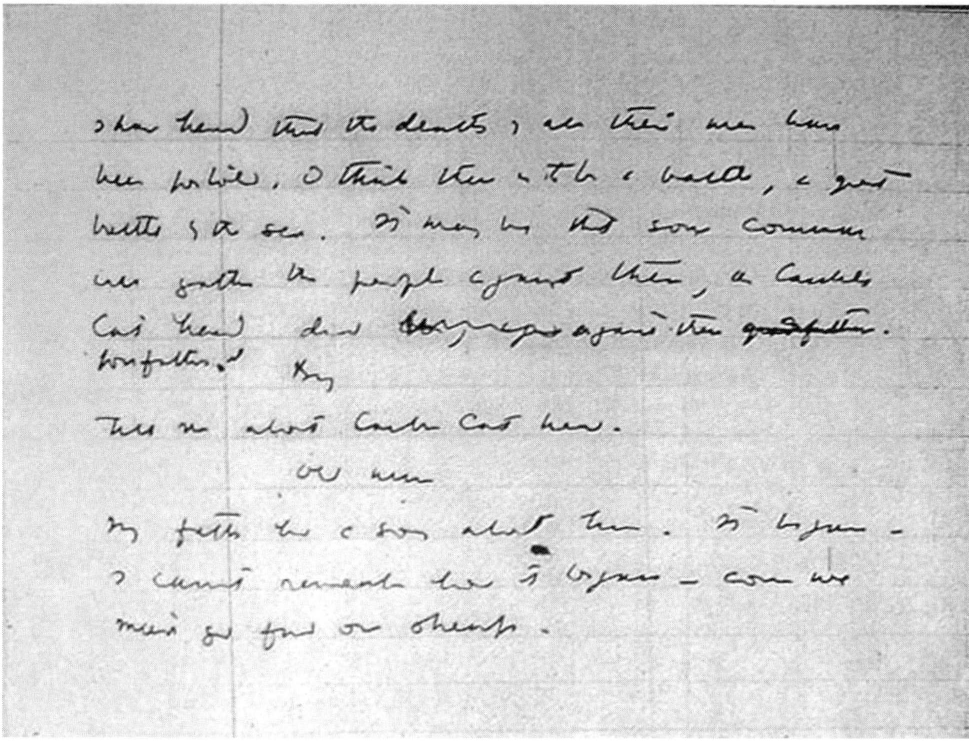

I have heard that the deaths of all these men have
been foretold. I think there is to be a battle, a great
battle of the sea. It may be that some common
man gather the people against them, as Cairbre
Cat head drove against their
forefathers."
Boy
Tell me about Cairbre Cat head.
Old man
My father had a song about him. It begins –
I cannot remember how it begins – come we
must go find our sheep.

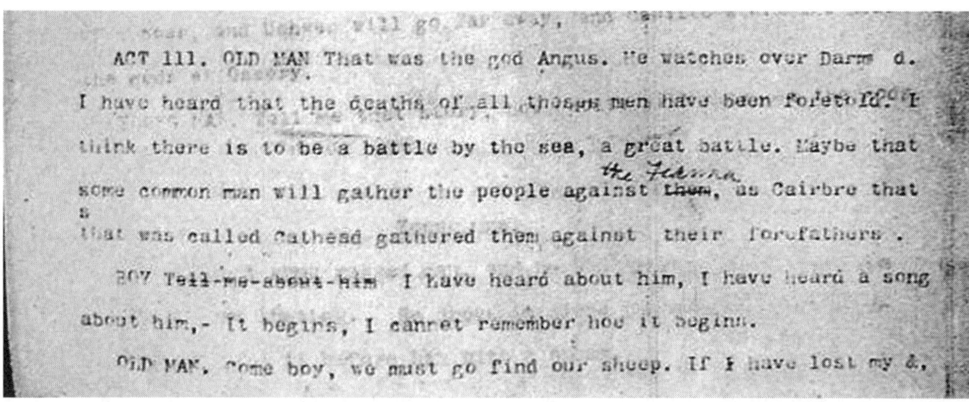

ACT 111. OLD MAN That was the god Angus. He watches over Darm d.

I have heard that the deaths of all thosgs men have been foretold. I

think there is to be a battle by the sea, a great battle. Maybe that

some common man will gather the people against ~~them~~ [the Fianna], as Cairbre that

that was called Cathead gathered them against their forefathers .

BOY ~~Tell-me-about-him~~ I have heard about him, I have heard a song

about him,- It begins, I cannot remember hoe it begins.

OLD MAN, Come boy, we must go find our sheep. If I have lost my &,

Single-Page Holograph Revision; Single-Page Typescript Containing Substitution

[NLI 8777(3) e, 113r]

I have heard that the deaths of all these men have
been for told, I think there is to be a battle, a great
battle by the sea. It may be that some [?comman]
will gather the people against them, as [?Cairbre]
Cat head did ~~long ago~~ against their ~~grandfather~~.
fore fathers?

Boy

Tell me about Cairbre Cat head.

Old man

My father had a sory about him. It began —
I cannot remember how it began — come we
must go find our sheap —

[NLI 8777(3) d, 112r]

ACT 111. OLD MAN That was the god Angus. He watches over Darmuid.
I have heard that the deaths of all theses men have been foretold. I
think there is to be a battle by the sea, a great battle. Maybe that
the Fianna
some common man will gather the people against ~~them~~, as Cairbre that
s
that was called Cathead gathered them against their forefathers .

BOY ~~Tell me about him~~ I have heard about him, I have heard a song
about him, – It begins, I cannet remember hoe it begins.

OLD MAN. Come boy, we must go find our sheep. If I have lost my &,

---

113r The substitution is evidently the basis of NLI 8777(3) d. Note that the paper is the same WBY used to rewrite the close of Act III in Berg(10).

112r This Act III substitution follows a nine-line substitution for Act I on the same sheet (see p. 207 above). It is closely related to Yeats's holograph draft on the next leaf in the leatherette folder (fol. 113r), and, like the versions of Act III which follow on fols. 114–117, it has a clear position in the evolving sequence. Cf. the earlier version represented by the loose leaf between fols. 81 and 82 in the folder. The incident at Inver Colpa in the Act I substitution on p. 207 above, on the other hand, is not developed in any other text. The typist was AG; cf. NLI 8777(11) and 8777(4) b.

[NLI 8777(3) f, 114r]

GRANIA.

A great man is dead. Ah, why did I send him to you, FINN. Because I thought that two such great men should be friends.

FINN.

The gods chose you GRANIA to give him love and death.

GRANIA.

(Wringing her hands) FINN, we must mourn for him. Now you have to go against the Lochlanders and the sweet chief that I took from you will be no longer by your side, and you may be overcome FINN. But before you go with your FIANNA against the Lochlanders we must mourn him, all his comrades must mourn him. (The hunters begin to come in from the O.P.) Yes, (turning to them) all the FIANNA must mourn him and all the shepherds of this valley.

[illegible].

We shall mourn him for many days and about a great pyre. There are birch trees on the mountain that the summer has made ready for flame. They shall be built up; each shepherd shall bring a tree, and the pyre shall be piled to the height of fifty feet, and upon it a crimson cloth shall be laid, and DIARMID shall be laid upon it, his sheild upon his breast and his spears beside him. (The hunters and the FIANNA have crowded round to hear her. She goes toward the body of DIARMID and they make way for her, and when

11 "O.P." is "opposite the prompter's side." In Ireland and Britain, the prompter occupies a position to the LH side of the actors; or at the RH side of the stage from the point of view of the audience.

13 Ink (WBY?) over type deletion.

Five-Page Typescript of Closing Sequence, Revised by W. B. Yeats and George Moore

[NLI 8777(3) f, 114r]

GRANIA.

A great man is dead. Ah, why did I send him to you,
who wer so
FINN. ~~Because~~ I thought that two ~~such~~ ^ great ~~men~~ should
be friends.

FINN.

The gods chose you GRANIA to give him love and death.

GRANIA.

(Wringing her hands) FINN, we must mourn for him.
one
~~Now~~ you have to go against the Lochlanders and the ~~great~~
that not be you had need of all
~~chief that~~ ^ I took from you will ~~be no longer~~ by your side, ^
the
~~and~~ you may be overcome FINN. ~~But~~ before ~~you go with your~~
go
FIANNA ^ against the Lochlanders we muct mourn him, all his
comrades must mourn him. (The hunters begin to come in
from the O.P.) Yes, (Turning to them) all the FIANNA
must mourn him and all the shepherds of this valley. ~~We~~
~~must mourn him, and all the shepherds of this valley~~.
shall build a great pyre for his burning & we shall
We ~~shall~~ ^ mourn him ~~for~~ many days ~~and about a great pyre.~~
that
There are birch trees on the mountain~~, that~~ the summer has
and
{; {t cut down every
made ready for flame{. {They shall be ~~built up~~; ~~each~~ shep-
they heaped up
herd shall bring a tree, and ~~the pyre~~ shall be ~~piled~~ ^ to
a
the height of fifty feet, and ~~upon it~~ crimson cloth shall
upon them, the cloth over
be laid, ^ and DIARMID shall be laid upon ~~it~~, his sheild ~~upon~~
his breast and his spears beside him. (The hunters and
the FIANNA have crowded round to hear her. She goes toward
the body of DIARMID and they make way for her, and when

she reaches DIARMID'S body a shepherd coming in from the back gives her DIARMID'S shield and his spear.) His shield with the flying white heron upon it shall be laid upon his breast and this light spear which I warned him against shall be laid by him. Where is my father? Where is KING CORMAC We shall see that DIARMID'S burning be worthy of him.

(Enter KING CORMAC) Here is my father (she goes straight to her father) Father he is dead, the greatest ... is dead and I am telling these people that you will see that his burning be worthy of him, the pyre shall be built high, ... and that this poor spear I warned him against shall lie beside him and that Broad Edge which I besought him to take and which would have saved him had he taken it.

CORMAC.

My daughter has lost a husband and Eri has lost a son and as she says there can but be mournin in the land.

The great pyre we shall build shall tell our people the great misfortune that has happened, and in the night its flames shall be seen for many many miles and the news of it shall reach even to the Northern Sea but before we go hence we must mourn him. There shall be great games and men shall be sent through the countries of Heber and Harmann to find skilful rimmers and casters of the wieght and skilful riders and on the last day twenty noble stallions

[NLI 8777(3) f, 116^r^]

<u>she reaches DIARMID'S body a shepherd coming in from the</u>
<u>back gives her DIARMID'S shield and his spear</u>.) His shield
over
~~with the flying~~ ' white heron ' ~~upon it~~ shall be laid ~~upon~~ his
I would not have had him take
breast and this light spear , ~~which I warned him against shall~~
~~besi~~ shall be laid beside
~~be laid by~~ him. Where is my father? Where is KING CORMAC
Let him of so great a one
~~He shall~~^see that DIARMUID'S burning be worthy ~~of him~~.
(<u>Enter KING CORMAC</u>) Here is my father (<u>she goes straight</u>
<u>to her father)</u> Father he is dead, the greatest ~~man in~~
all
~~Eri~~ is dead and I am telling^these ~~people~~ that you will look to
the that it **that**
~~see that his~~ burning^be worthy of him, the pyre shall be
built high, ~~that the cloth shall be crimson and gold~~, and
not to take
that this poor spear ~~that~~ I warned him ~~against~~ ~~shall~~ lie
~~that~~ that
beside him and ~~also~~^Broad Edge which I besought him to take
{d it may be lie beside him also
and which ~~would~~ ha{ve saved him ~~had he taken it~~.^

CORMAC.

Yes, yes there is a strong man
My daughter has lost a husband and ~~Eri has lost a son~~
less among the fiana – There must be a long mourning
~~and as she says there can but be mourning in the land~~.
^The great pyre we shall build shall tell our people the
{;
great misfortune that has happened{, ~~and in the night~~ its
flames shall be seen for many many miles and the news of
{. {B
it shall reach even to the Northern Sea{, {but before we go
The pyre must be built up high
hence we must mourn him. There shall be great games and
men shall be sent through the countries of Hebor and Harmann
to find skilful runners and casters of the wieght and
skilful riders and on the last day twenty noble stallions
and his arms & his wepons laid beside him, & men must

Note that fol. 116 is bound into the folder in the wrong sequence.

16–20 Canceled in two stages. The replacement text, "The pyre must be . . . & men must," is not canceled.

[NLI 8777(3) f, 115r]

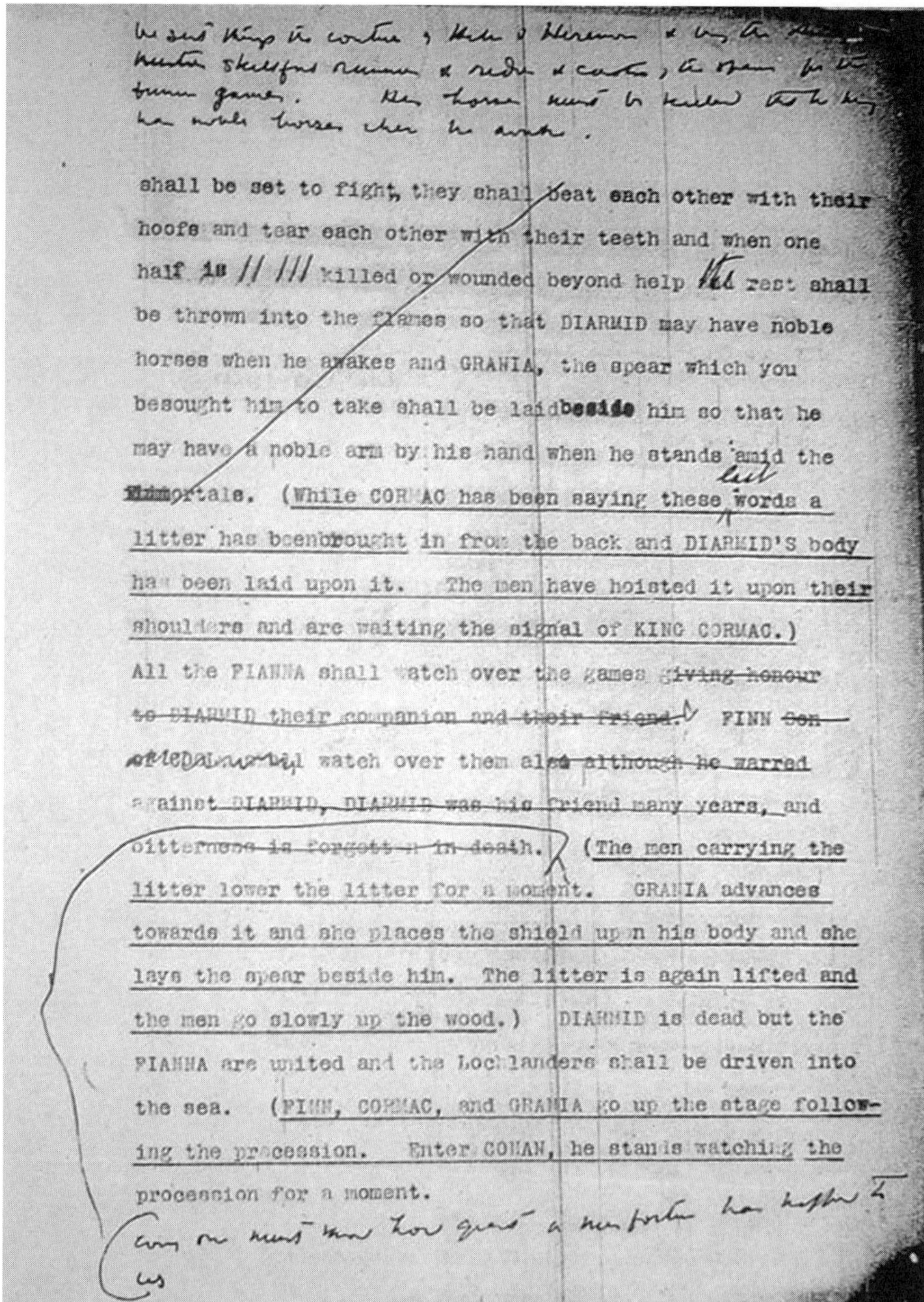

be set Kings the [illegible] of [illegible] & [illegible] & [illegible] huntsmen skillful runners & riders & [illegible], the [illegible] for the [illegible] games. His horses must be killed that he may have noble horses when he awake.

shall be set to fight, they shall beat each other with their hoofs and tear each other with their teeth and when one half is // /// killed or wounded beyond help the rest shall be thrown into the flames so that DIARMID may have noble horses when he awakes and GRANIA, the spear which you besought him to take shall be laid beside him so that he may have a noble arm by his hand when he stands amid the Immortals. (While CORMAC has been saying these last words a litter has been brought in from the back and DIARMID'S body has been laid upon it. The men have hoisted it upon their shoulders and are waiting the signal of KING CORMAC.) All the FIANNA shall watch over the games ~~giving honour to DIARMID their companion and their friend.~~ FINN ~~Son of~~ [illegible] will watch over them also ~~although he warred~~ against ~~DIARMID, DIARMID was his friend many years, and bitterness is forgotten in death.~~ (The men carrying the litter lower the litter for a moment. GRANIA advances towards it and she places the shield upon his body and she lays the spear beside him. The litter is again lifted and the men go slowly up the wood.) DIARMID is dead but the FIANNA are united and the Lochlanders shall be driven into the sea. (FINN, CORMAC, and GRANIA go up the stage following the procession. Enter CONAN, he stands watching the procession for a moment.

Conan [illegible] [illegible] [illegible] [illegible] [illegible] [illegible] [illegible] us

115r, l. 3 The final letter of "half", plus "is" and the following two sets of cancellations, are in darker blue ribbon.
6 beside] Overtyped in darker blue ribbon.

[NLI 8777(3) f, 115[r]]

be sent through the countries of Hebor & Heremon & bring the ~~skilful hunters~~ skillful runners & riders & casters of the spears for the funera games. His horses must be killed that he may have noble horses when he awakes.

1 **shall be set to fight, they shall beat each other with their**
2 **hoofs and tear each other with their teeth and when one**
the
3 **half is ~~or are~~ killed or wounded beyond help and rest shall**
4 **be thrown into the flames so that DIARMID may have noble**
5 **horses when he awakes and GRANIA, the spear which you**
6 **besought him to take shall be laidbeside him so that he**
7 **may have a noble arm by his hand when he stands amid the**
last
8 **immortals. (While CORMAC has been saying these words a**
litter has beenbrought in from the back and DIARMID'S body
has been laid upon it. The men have hoisted it upon their
shoulders and are waiting the signal of KING CORMAC.)
9 **All the FIANNA shall watch over the games ~~giving honour~~**
10 **~~to DIARMUID their companion and their friend.~~ FINN ~~Son~~**
11 **~~of COOL, shall~~ watch over them ~~also although he warred~~**
12 **~~against DIARMUID, DIARMUID was his friend many years,~~ and**
13 **~~bitterness is forgotten in death.~~ (The men carrying the**
litter lower the litter for a moment. GRANIA advances
towards it and she places the shield upon his body and she
lays the spear beside him. The litter is again lifted and
14 **the men go slowly up the wood.) DIARMID is dead but the**
15 **FIANNA are united and the Lochlanders shall be driven into**
16 **the sea. (FINN, CORMAC, and GRANIA go up the stage follow-**
ing the procession. Enter CONAN, he stands watching the
procession for a moment.

every one must know how great a misfortune has happend to us

[NLI 8777(3) f, 117[r]]

CONAN.

1 **They have forgotten me, and he has forgotten me, though**
2 **it was I who told him that GRANIA should be given to whom-**
3 **ever killed the boar. An evil stony-hearted proud race**
4 **(turns to go up the stage, stops) GRANIA makes great**
5 **mourning for DIARMUID, but her welcome to FINN shall be**
6 **greater.**

117[r] The subsequent, final leaf in the leatherette-bound folder contains a page relating to Act I (NLI 8777[3] g).

[Berg(10), 1r]

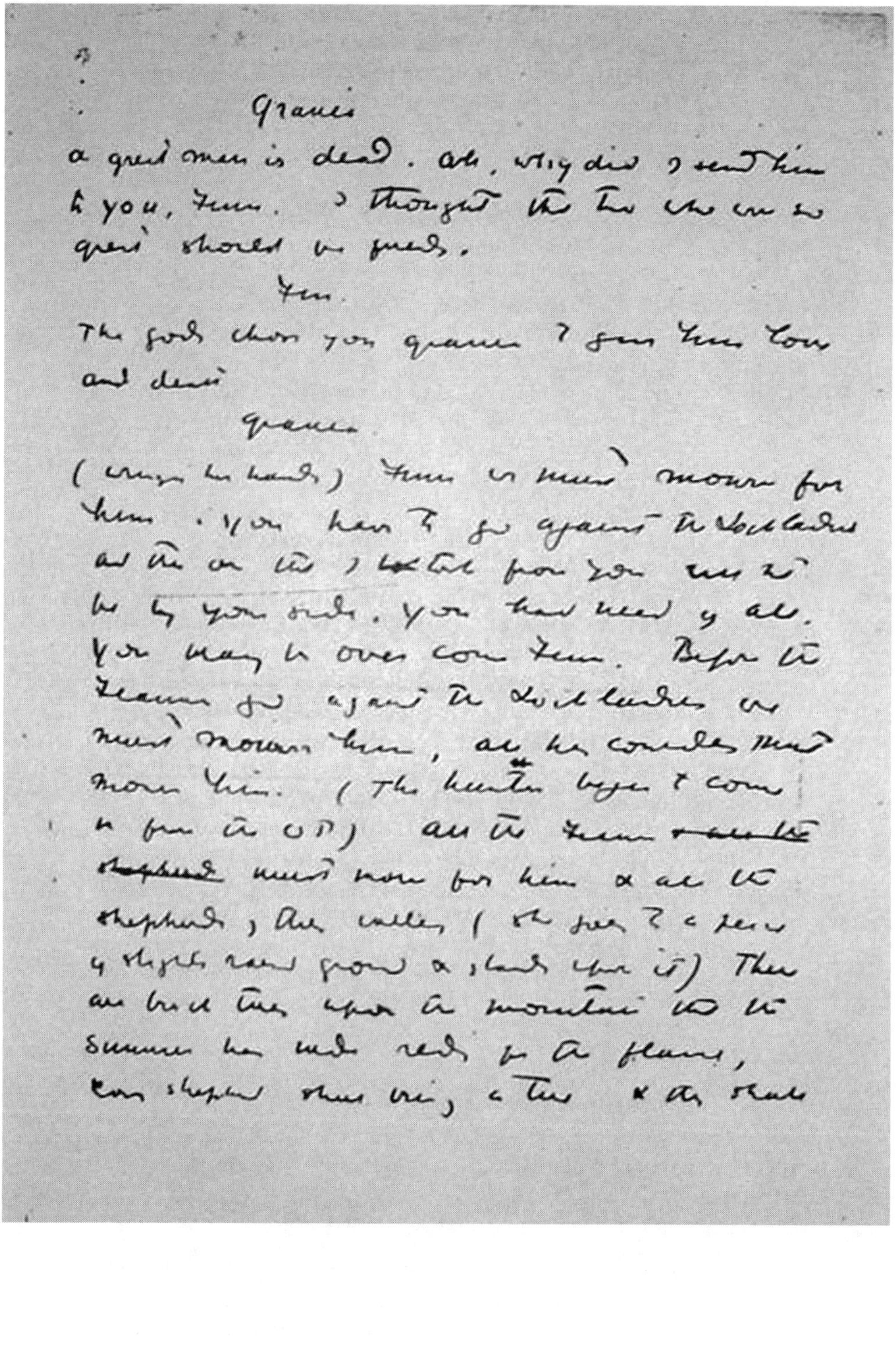

Grania

a great man is dead. ah, why did I send him to you, Finn. I thought that two who were so great should be friends.

Finn.

The gods chose you Grania to give him love and death

Grania

(wrings her hands) Finn we must mourn for him. You have to go against the Lochlanders and the [illegible] I looked for you [illegible] to be by your side. You have need of all. You may be overcome Finn. Before the Fianna go against the Lochlanders we must mourn him, all his comrades must mourn him. (The hunters begin to come in from the [illegible]) all the Fianna ~~[illegible]~~ ~~shepherds~~ must mourn for him & all the shepherds, all [illegible] (she goes to a piece of slightly raised ground & stands upon it) There are brick [illegible] upon the mountain that the summer has made ready for the flames, Every shepherd shall bring a tree & they shall

Four-Page Holograph by W. B. Yeats of Closing Sequence

[Berg(10), 1r]

Grania

A great man is dead . Ah, why did I send him to you, Finn. I thought that two who were so great should be friends.

Fin.

The gods chose you Grania to give him love and death

Grania.

(Wringing her hands) Finn we must mourn for him . You have to go against the Lochlanders and the one that I ~~ta~~ took from you will not be by your side . You hav need of all. You may be over come Finn. Before the Feanna go against the Lochlanders we must mourn him , all his comrades must mourn him. (The hunters begin to come in from the OP) All the Feann ~~& all the shepherds~~ must morn for him & all the shepherds of this valley (she goes to a peice of slighty raised ground & stands upon it) There are brich trees upon the mountain that the summer has made ready for the flame, evry shepherd shall bring a tree & they shall

[Berg(10), 2r]

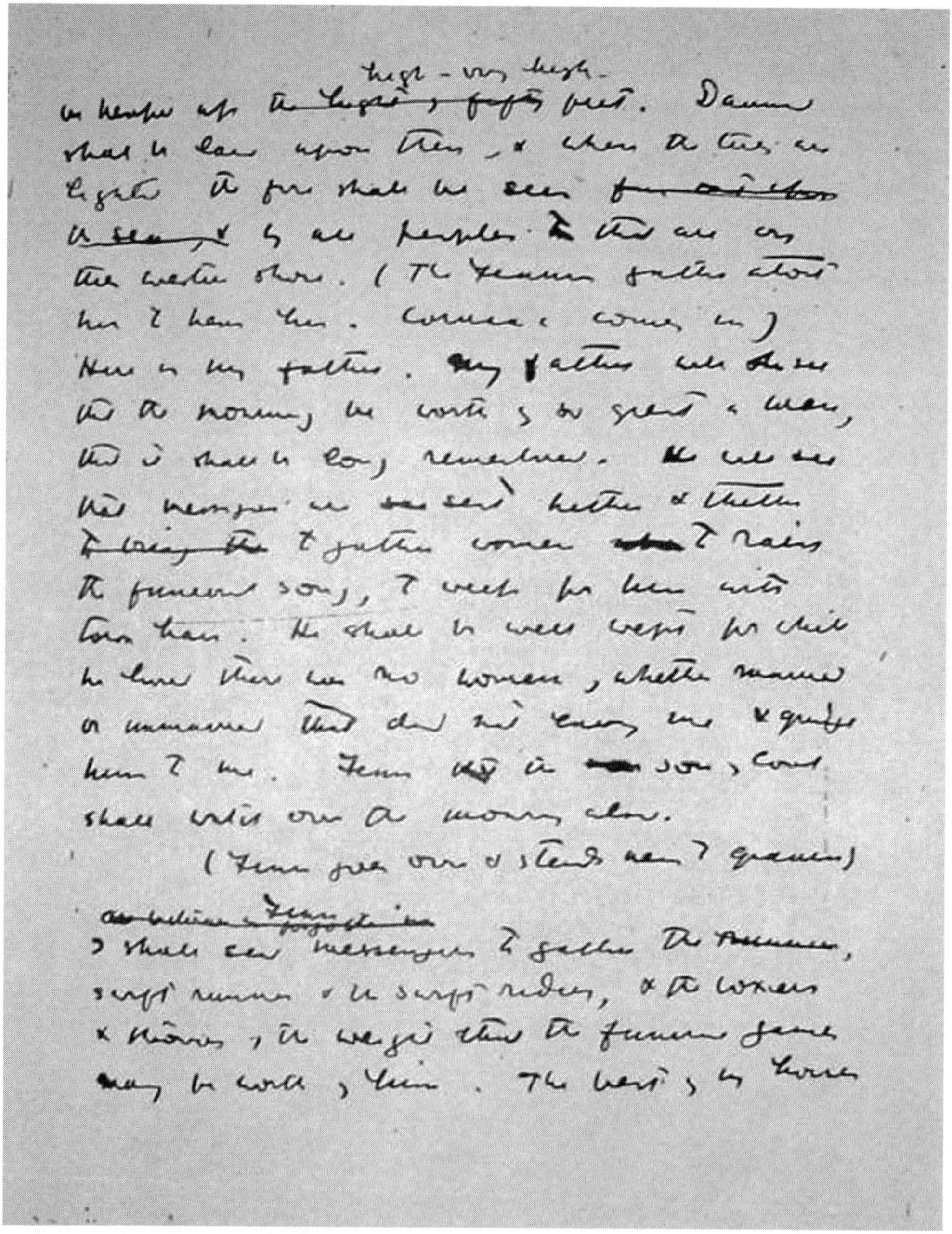

[Berg(10), 2^{r}]

high – very high –
be heaped up ~~the hight of fifty~~ feet. Darmud
shal be laid upon them – & when the trees are
lighted the fire shall be seen [?~~far/from~~] ~~out upon~~
~~th sea, &~~ by all peoples ~~to~~ that are on
the western shore . (The Feanna gather about
her to hear her . Cormac comes in)
Here is my father . My father will ~~sh~~ see
that the mourning be worth of so great a man,
that it shall be long remembred . He will see
that messngers are ~~sen~~ sent hither & thither
~~to bring the~~ to gather women ~~abou~~ to raise
the funeral song, to weep for him with
torn hair. He shall be well wept for while
he lived there was no women , whether married
or unmarried that did not envy me & grudge
him to me. Finn ~~that~~ is ~~son~~ son of Cool
shall watch over the mourng alone.

(Finn goes over & stands near to Grania)

Finn
~~all bitterness is forgottn in~~
I shall send messengers to gather the ~~runners~~,
swift runnes & th swift riders, and the boxers
& throwrs of the weight that the funeral games
may be worthy of him . The best of his horses

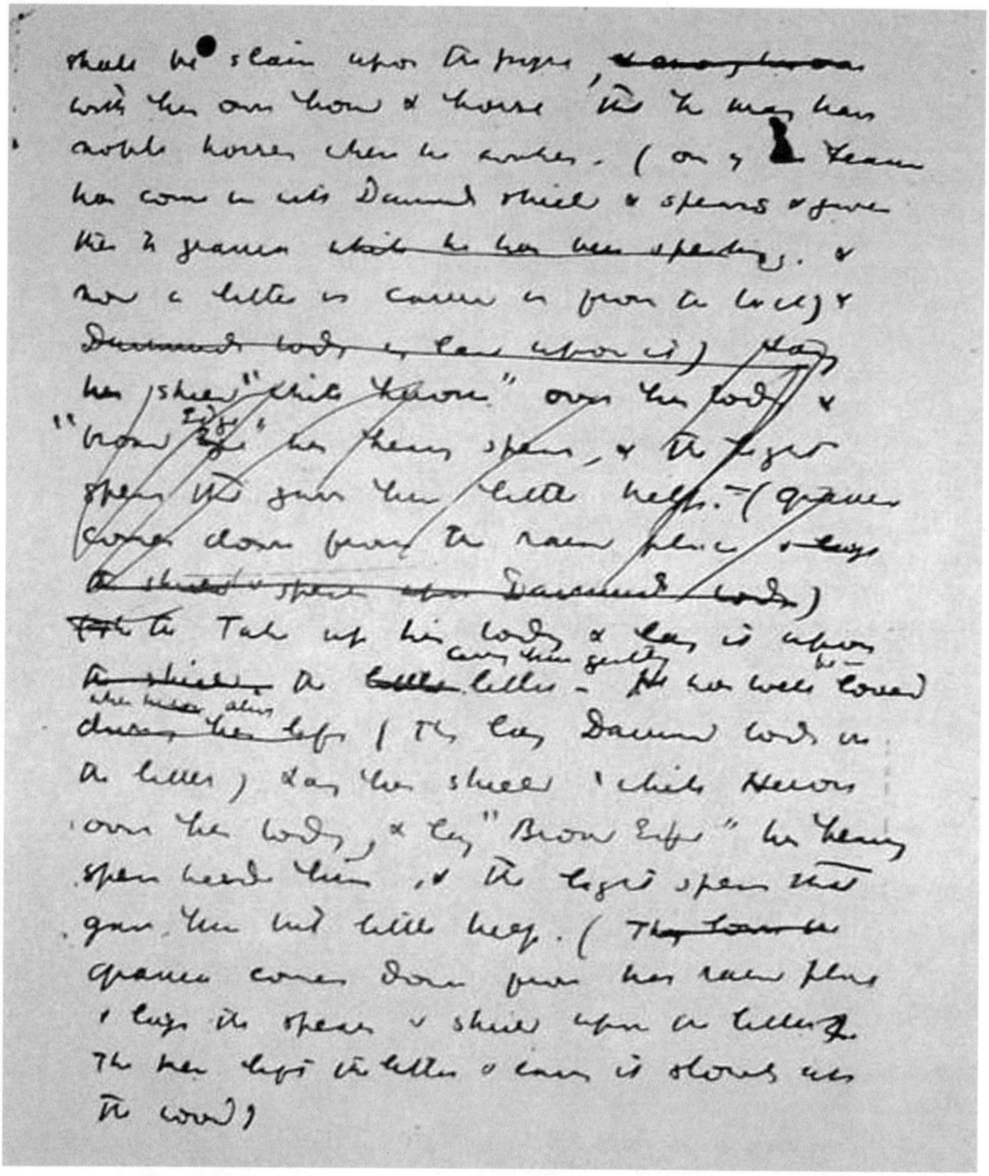

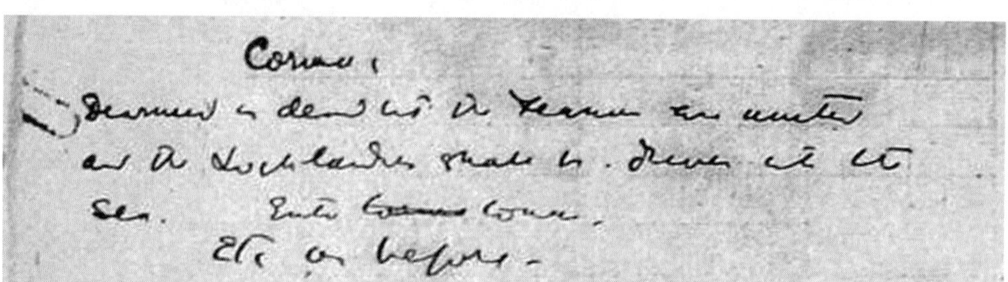

[Berg(10), 3r]

shall be slain upon the pyre, ~~& among his own~~
with his own hound & horse that he may have
noble horses when he awakes – (one of the Feana
has come in with Dairmuds shield & spears and gives
them to Grania ~~while he has been speaking~~. &
now a litter is carried in from the back) &
~~Dairmuids body is laid upon it) Lay~~
his shield "white heron" over his body &
Edge
"broad ~~Ege~~" his heavy spear, and the light
spear that gave him little help. — (Grania
comes down from the raisd place ~~& lays~~
~~the shield & spears upon Dairmuids body~~)
~~T The ta~~ Take up his body & lay it upon
carry him gently be-
~~the shield .~~ the ~~little~~ litter – He was well loved
when ~~he was~~ alive
~~during his life~~ (They lay Dairmud body on
the litter) Lay his shield 'white Heron
over his body , & lay "Broad Edge" his heavy
spear beside him , & the light spear that
gave him but little help . (~~They lower the~~
Grania comes down from her raisd place
& lays the spear & shield upon th litter ~~)~~
The men lift the litter & carry it slowly up
the wood)

[Berg(10), 4r]

Cormac
Dearmid is dead but the Feanna are united
and the Lochlanders shall be driven into the
sea.
Enter ~~Cormac~~ Conan –
Etc as before –

3r, l. 4 spears] The second "s" was inserted later (in the same ink).
4r, l. ‑4 Conan's entrance is written in a paler shade of the same ink, as if it was inserted later.

[Berg(11), 1r]

GRANIA.

A great man is dead. But why did I send him to you, FINN. Because I wished two great men should be friends.

FINN.

Our lives and our deaths are foretold, GRANIA, we cannot escape the net of the gods.

GRANIA.

(Wringing her hands) FINN, we must mourn for him. Now you haveto go against the Lochlanders and the great chief I have taken from you will not be by your side, and you may be overcome, FINN. But before you go with your FIANNA against the Lochlanders we must mourn him, all his comrades must mourn him. (The hunters begin to come in from the left) Yes, (turning to them) all the FIANNA must mourn him and all the shepherds of this valley. (The hunters and the FIANNA have crowded round to hear her. She goes towards the body of DIARMID they make way for her, and when she reaches DIARMID'S body a shepherd coming in from the back gives her DIARMID'S shield and his spear.) His shield with the flying white heron upon it shall be laid upon his breast and this broken spear which I warned him against shall be laid by him. Where is my father? Where is KING CORMAC? He shall see that DIARMID'S burning be worthy of

Three-Page Typescript of Closing Sequence, Revised by George Moore

[Berg(11), 1r]

GRANIA.

A great man is dead. But why did I send him to you, FINN. Because I wished two great men should be friends.

FINN.

Our lives and our deaths are foretold, GRANIA, we cannot escape the net of the gods.

GRANIA.

(Wringing her hands) FINN, we must mourn for him. Now you haveto go against the Lochlanders and the great chief I have taken from you will not be by your side, and you may be overcome, FINN. But before you go with your FIANNA against the Lochlanders we must mourn him, all his comrades must mourn him. (The hunters begin to come in from the left) Yes, (turning to them) all the FIANNA must mourn him and all the shepherds of this valley. (The hunters and the FIANNA have crowded round to hear her. She goes towards the body of DIARMID they make way for her, and when she reaches DIARMID'S body a shepherd coming in from the back gives her DIARMID'S shield and his spear.) His shield with the flying white heron upon it shall be laid upon his breast and this broken spear which I warned him against shall be laid by him. Where is my father? Where is KING CORMAC? He shall see that DIARMID'S burning be worthy of

---

2 The mark at the end of the line is a blue-black ink smudge.

3 The inserted comma is in blue-black ink, but not perhaps the same ink as the smudge in line 2 and the blots on Berg(15) c, fol. 6r (that is, GM's).

11 That is, left of the stage from the point of view of the actors; cf. NLI 8777(3) f, fol. 114r.

him. (Enter KING CORMAC) Here is my father (she goes straight to her father) Father he is dead, the greatest man in Eri is dead, and I am telling these people that you will see that his burning be worthy of him.

CORMAC.

My daughter has lost a husband and Eri has lost a son, and as she says there can but be mourning in the land. ~~And~~ But we shall build a great pyre and ^it shall tell ~~our~~ people the great misfortune that has happened. Its flames shall be seen for many miles and the news of DIARMID'S death shall reach all hearts. ~~There are [illegible]~~ It shall be built of the birch trees that the summer has made ready for flame, and every shepherd shall bring a tree and the pyre shall be built to the height of fifty feet. A crimson cloth shall be laid there and DIARMID shall be laid upon it. There shall be great games; ~~and~~ menshall be sent through the countries of Hebor and Hermann to find skilful riders and casters of the weight and ~~[illegible]~~ swift runners and noble stallions shall be set to fight and when one half are killed or wounded beyond help, the rest shall be thrown into the flames so that DIARMID may have noble horses when he awakes (turning to GRANIA). And, GRANIA, ~~that~~ the spear which you be[ought] him to take shall be laid beside him so that he may have noble ~~arm~~ by his hand when he stands amid the immortals. (While CORMAC has been saying these words a litter has been brought in from the back and DIARMID's body has been laid upon it. (The men

[Berg(15) c, 6r]

him. (Enter KING CORMAC) Here is my father (she goes
straight to her father) Father he is dead, the greatest
man in Eri is dead, and I am telling these people that you
will see that his burning be worthy of him.

CORMAC.

My daughter has lost a husband and Eri has lost a son,
and as she says there can but be mourning in the land.
But it
~~And~~ we shall build a great pyre and ^ shall tell our people
the great misfortune that has happened. Its flames shall
be seen for many miles and the news of DIARMID'S death shall
It shall be built of the birch trees.
reach all hearts. ~~There are birch trees in the mountain~~
that the summer has made ready for flame, and every shepherd
shall bring a tree and the pyre shall be built to the height
of fifty feet. A crimson cloth shall be laid there and
DIARMID shall be laid upon it. There shall be great games ;
~~and~~ menshall be sent through the countries of Hebor and
Hermann to find skilful riders and casters of the weight
swift
and ~~skilful~~ runners and noble stallions shall be set to
fight and when one half are killed or wounded beyond help,
the rest shall be thrown into the flames so that DIARMID
may have noble horses when he awakes (turning to GRANIA) .
{A the
{**and, GRANIA, ~~this~~ spear which you besought him to take shall**
be laid beside him so that he may have noble arm by his
hand when he stands amid the immortals. (While CORMAC has
been saying these words a litter has been brought in from
the back and DIARMID'S body has been laid upon it. (The men

[Berg(15) c]

[7r]

have hoisted it upon their shoulders and are waiting the signal of KING CORMAC) All the FIANNA shall watch over the games giving honour to DIARMID their companion and their friend. FINN son of COOL shall watch over them also although he warred against DIARMID, DIARMID was his friend many years, and bitterness is forgotten in death. (The men carrying the litter lower the litter for a moment. GRANIA advances towards it and she places the shield upon his body and she lays the spear beside him. The litter is again lifted and the men go slowly up the wood.) DIARMID is dead but the FIANNA are united and the Lochlanders shall be driven into the sea. (FINN, CORMAC, and GRANIA go up the stage following the procession. Enter CONAN, he stands watching the procession for a moment.)

CONAN.

They have forgotten me, and he has forgotten me, though it was I who told him that GRANIA should be given to whomever killed the boar. An evil stony hearted proud race (turns to go up the stage, stops) GRANIA makes great mourning for DIARMID, but her welcome to FINN shall be greater.

END.

Three-Page Typescript of Closing Sequence, Revised by W. B. Yeats

[Berg(15) a, 1r]

GRANIA.

**A great man is dead. Ah, why did I send him to you,
FINN? I thought that two who were so great should be
friends.**

FINN.

The gods chose you, GRANIA, to give him love and death.

GRANIA.

**(Wringing her hands) FINN, we must mourn him. You
have to go against the Lochlanders and this one that I
have taken from you will not be by your side. You had
need of all, you may be overcome, FINN. Before the FIANNA
go against the Lochlanders they must mourn him ; all his comrades must mourn him. (The hunters begin to come in from
the O'P.) All the FIANNA must mourn him and all the
shepherds of this valley. (She goes towards the body of
DIARMID. They make way for her and when she reaches
DIARMID'S body a shepherd coming in from the back gives her
DIARMID'S shield and his broken spear.) His shield with
the flying white heron upon it shall be laid upon his breast**
not to take
and not this spear ~~which~~ I warned him ~~against~~, but Broad
that ^
**Edge ~~which~~ I begged him to take ~~shall be laid by him~~.
Where is my father? Where is KING CORMAC? He shall see
that DIARMID'S burning be worthy of him. (Enter KING CORMAC)**

Here is my father, (She goes to her father) Father, he is dead, the greatest man in Eri is dead. I am telling these people that you will see that his burning shall be worthy of him.

CORMAC.

My daughter has lost a husband and Eri has lost a son and the FIANNA have lost a great chief and must mourn him, and all the shepherds of this valley, FINN son of COOL, you, too, shall watch over this mourning. (FINN goes over and stands by her)

FINN.

There are birch trees upon the mountain that the summer has made ready for the flame. Every shepherd shall bring a tree and they shall be heaped up high, DIARMID shall be laid upon them and when they are lighted the fire shall be seen by all people that are on this western shore.

CAOELTE.

I will send messengers to gather the swift runner and swift riders and the boxers and the throwers of the weight, that the funeral games be worthy of him.

USHEEN.

I shall send messengers through the country of Hebor and Hermann who will gather all the great harpers and the great singers and all Eri's most beautiful songs shall be

[Berg(15) a, 2r]

Here is my father. (<u>She goes to her father</u>) Father,
one of ~~th~~
he is dead, ^ the greatest ~~man~~ in Eri is dead. I am telling all
to that it may
these people , that you will see ~~that~~ his burning ^ ~~shall~~ be
worthy of him.

CORMAC.

a defender
My daughter has lost a husband and Eri ~~has lost a son~~
The Feanna ~~mus~~ ~~we~~
~~and the FIANNA have lost a great chief and~~ ^ must mourn him,
and all the shepherds of this valley, FINN son of COOL, you,
too, shall watch over this mourning. (<u>FINN goes over and stands by her</u>)

FINN.

There are birch trees upon the mountain that the summer
has made ready for the flame. Every shepherd shall bring
to a great height
a tree and they shall be heaped ^ ~~up high~~, DIARMID shall be
laid upon them and when they are lighted the fire shall
be seen by all people that are on this western shore.

CAOELTE.

I will send messengers to gather the swift runner and
swift riders and the boxers and the throwers of the weight,
that the funeral games be worthy of him.

USHEEN.

I shall send messengers through the country of Hebor
and Hermann who will gather all the great harpers and the
great singers and all Eri's most beautiful songs shall be

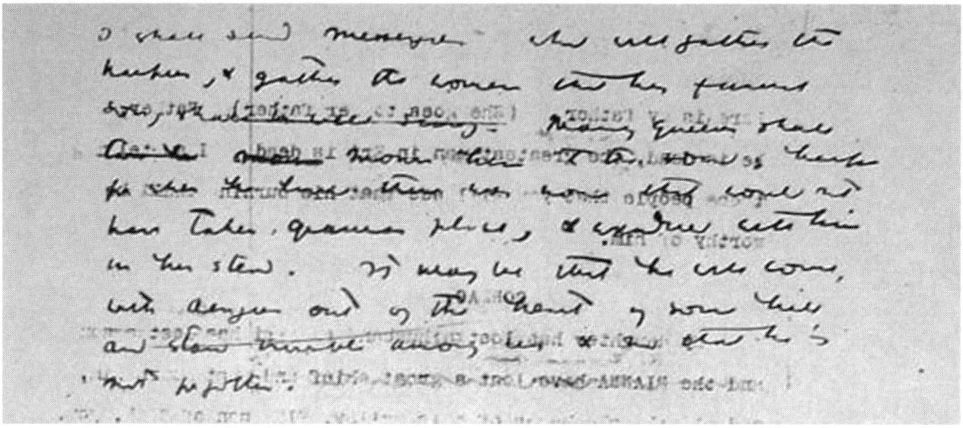

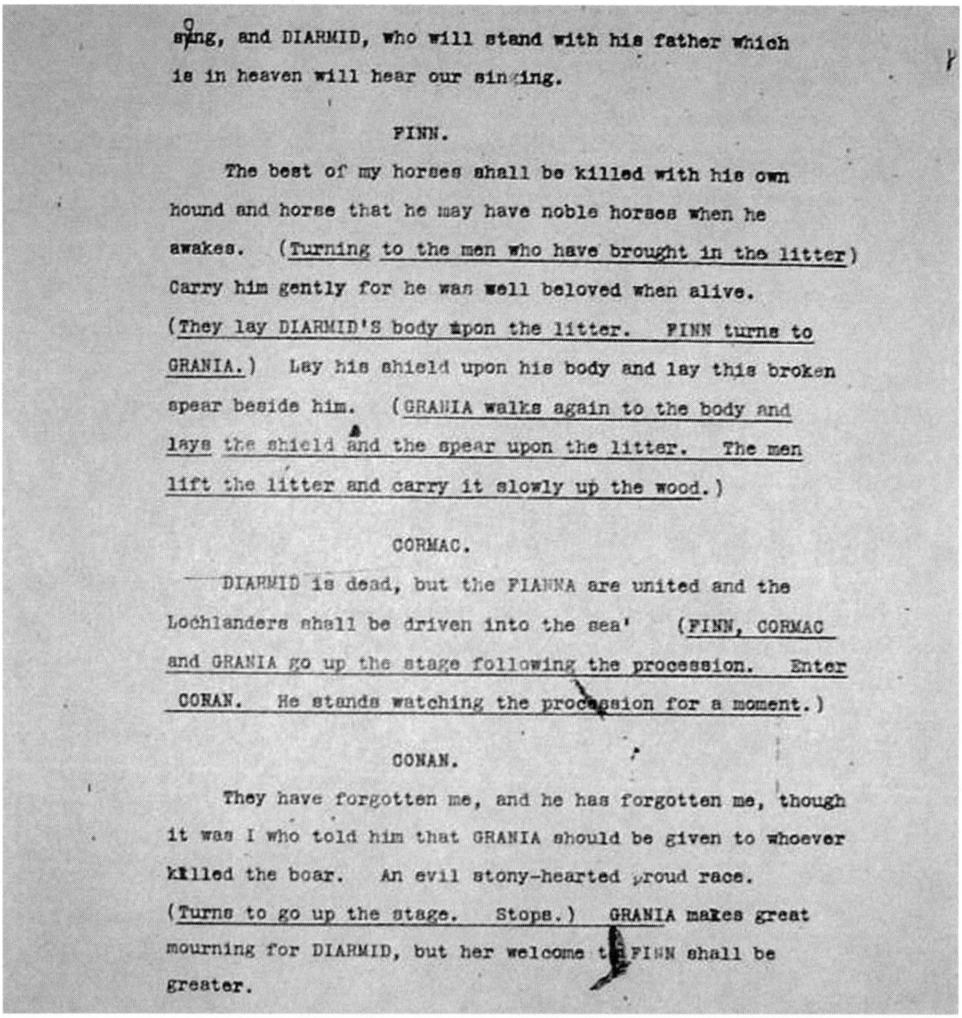

sing, and DIARMID, who will stand with his father which is in heaven will hear our singing.

FINN.

The best of my horses shall be killed with his own hound and horse that he may have noble horses when he awakes. (Turning to the men who have brought in the litter) Carry him gently for he was well beloved when alive. (They lay DIARMID'S body upon the litter. FINN turns to GRANIA.) Lay his shield upon his body and lay this broken spear beside him. (GRANIA walks again to the body and lays the shield and the spear upon the litter. The men lift the litter and carry it slowly up the wood.)

CORMAC.

DIARMID is dead, but the FIANNA are united and the Lochlanders shall be driven into the sea' (FINN, CORMAC and GRANIA go up the stage following the procession. Enter CONAN. He stands watching the procession for a moment.)

CONAN.

They have forgotten me, and he has forgotten me, though it was I who told him that GRANIA should be given to whoever killed the boar. An evil stony-hearted proud race. (Turns to go up the stage. Stops.) GRANIA makes great mourning for DIARMID, but her welcome to FINN shall be greater.

[Berg(15) a, 2v]

I shall send messengers who will gather the harpers, & gather the women that his funeral song ~~shall be well sung —~~ Many queens shall [?~~keen~~] ~~him mourn~~ mourn him to the sound of harps for when he lived there was none that would not have taken Granias place, & wandred with him in her stead. It may be that he will come, with Aengus out of the heart of some hill, and stand invisible among us & now that he is not forgotten

[Berg(11), 2r]

o

s~~u~~ng, and DIARMID, who will stand with his father which is in heaven will hear our singing.

FINN.

The best of my horses shall be killed with his own hound and horse that he may have noble horses when he awakes. (Turning to the men who have brought in the litter) Carry him gently for he was well beloved when alive. (They lay DIARMID'S body upon the litter. FINN turns to GRANIA.) Lay his shield upon his body and lay this broken spear beside him. (GRANIA walks again to the body and lays the shield and the spear upon the litter. The men lift the litter and carry it slowly up the wood.)

CORMAC.

DIARMID is dead, but the FIANNA are united and the Lochlanders shall be driven into the sea' (FINN, CORMAC and GRANIA go up the stage following the procession. Enter CONAN. He stands watching the procession for a moment.)

CONAN.

They have forgotten me, and he has forgotten me, though it was I who told him that GRANIA should be given to whoever killed the boar. An evil stony-hearted proud race. (Turns to go up the stage. Stops.) GRANIA makes great mourning for DIARMID, but her welcome to FINN shall be greater.

Berg(11), 2r, l. 1 sung] The authorship of the pencil revision is uncertain, though it looks more like GM's than WBY's. The other marks on the present page are blue-black ink smudges of the same shade as WBY's ink corrections on Berg(15) a.

[Berg(15) b, 3r]

GRANIA.

A great man is dead. Ah, why did I send him to you Finn. I thought that two who were so great should be friends.

FINN.

The gods chose you Grania to give him love and death.

GRANIA.

(Wringing her hands) Finn, we must mourn him. You have to go against the Lochlanders and this one that I have taken from you will not be by your side. Before the Fianna go against the Lochlanders they must ~~all~~ mourn him. All his comrades must mourn him. (The hunters begin to come in from the O.P.) All the Fianna must mourn him and the shepherds of this valley. (She goes towards the body of Diarmuid. They make way for her and when she r/eaches Diarmuid's body a shepherd coming in from the back gives her Diarmuid's shield and his broken spear). His shield with the flying white heron upon it shall be laid upon his breast and & under it ~~not~~ this spear I warned him not to take, I will lay beside him ~~[?]~~ broad edge that I bade him take. Where is my father ? Where is King Cormac ? He shall see that Diarmuid's burneng be worthy of him. (Enter King Cormac). Here is my father. (She goes to her father) Father, he is dead, one of the great men of Eri is dead. I am telling all these people that you will see to his burning that it may be worthy of him.

CORMAC. ~~My daughter~~

My daughter has lost a husband and Eri a defender. The Fianna must mourn him, and all the shepherds of this valley. Finn son of Cool, you too shall watch over this mourning. (Finn goes over and stands by her.)

FINN.

Berg(15) b, 3r, ll. 7, −18, etc. Ink deletions.

Three-Page Typescript of Closing Sequence, Revised by W. B. Yeats

[Berg(15) b, 3r]

~~F~~
GRANIA.

A great man is dead. Ah, why did I send him to you Finn. I thought
that two who were so great should be friends.

FINN.

The gods chose you Grania to give him love and death.

GRANIA.

(Wringing her hands) FINN, we must mourn him. You have to go against
the Lochlanders and this one that I have taken from you will not be
by your side. Before the Fianna go against the Lochlanders they must
~~all~~ mourn him, all his comrades must mourn him. (The hunters begin to
come in from the O.P.) All the Fianna must mourn him and the shepherds
{f
of this valley. (She goes towards the body o{d Diarmuid. They make way
for her and when she r‿eaches Diarmuid's body a shepherd coming in from
the back gives her Diarmuid's shield and his broken spear). His shield
with the flying white heron upon it shall be laid upon his breast and
I will lay beside him
& instead of {B {E
~~not~~ this spear I warned him not to take, ~~but~~‸{broad {edge that I bade
him take.‸ Where is my father ? Where is King Cormac ? He shall see
that Diarmuid's burning be worthy of him. (Enter King Cormac). Here is
my father. 'She goes to her father) Father, he is dead, one of the great
men of Eri is dead. I am telling all these people that you will see to
his burning that it may be worthy of him.

CORMAC. ~~My daughter~~

My daughter has lost a husband and Eri a defender. The Fianna must
mourn him, and all the shepherds of this valley. Finn son of Cool,
you too shall watch over this mourning.)Finn goes over and stands by
y
{)
her({.

FINN.

[4r]

FINN.

There are birch trees upon the mountain that the summer has made
ready for the flame. Every shepherd shall bring a tree and they shall
be heaped to a great height. DIARMUID shall be laid upon them and when

[Berg(15) b]

[4r continued]

they are lighted the fire shall be seen by all people that are on the western shore.

CAOLTE.

I will send messengers to gather the swift runner and the swift rides and the boxers and the throwers of the weight, that the funeral games be worthy of him.

USHEEN.

I shall send messengers t~~o gather~~ who will gather the harpers and go gather the women that h{is/er} funeral songs may be well sung. Many queens shall mourn him to the sound of harps, for when he lived there was none that would not have taken Grania's place, and wandered with him in her stead. It may be that he will come with Angus out of the heart of some hill and stand invisible among us and know that he is not forgotten.

FINN. The best of my horses shall be killed with his own horse and hound that he may have noble horses when he awakes.)Turning to the men who have brought in the litter.) Carry him gently for he was well beloved when alive. .(They lay Diarmuid's body upon the litter. Finn turns to Grania) Lay his s ield upon his body and lay this broken spear beside him. (Grania walkes again to the body and lays the shield and the spear upon the litter. The men lift the litter and carry it slowly to the wood).

CORMAC.

Diarmuid is dead, but the Fianna are united and the Lochlanders shall

[5r]

be driven into the sea. (Finn, Cormac and Granis go up the stage following the procession. Enter Conan. He stands watching the procession for a moment.)

CONANN CONAN.

They have forgotten me, and he has forgotten me, though it was I who told him that Grania should be given to whoever killed the boar. An evil stony hearted proud race. (Turns to go up the stage. Stops)

GRAnIA makes great mourn{nig/iag} for Diarmuid, but her welcome to Finn shall be greater.

Berg(15) b, 4r, l. 9 Type deletion.

Berg(15) b, 5r, l. 5 The correction, like other small corrections on this typescript, might be in the hand of AG—who might indeed have been the typist.

Continuously Paginated Texts

HRC: Composite Typescript, Revised by George Moore and W. B. Yeats—George Moore's Copy? Selectively Collated with Washington; Facing Berg(99)

[1^{r}]

DIARMID AND GRANIA.

[2^{r}]

DIARMID AND GRANIA.
A Play in Three Acts.
By George Moore

and

W. B. Yeats.

[3^{r}]

1	**KING CORMAC**		**The High King.**
2	**FINN MACCOOLE**		**The chief of the FIANNA.**
3	**DIARMID**	)	
4	**USHEEN**	)	**His chief men.**
5	**CAOELTE**	)	
6	**CONAN the Bald**		**One of the FIANNA.**
7	**NIALL**		**A head servant.**
8	**FERGUS**	)	
9	**FATHNA**	)	**Spearmen.**
10	**CRIFFAN**	)	
11	**GRANIA.**		**The king's daughter.**
12	**LABAN.**		**A Druidess.**
13	**An old man**	)	
14	**A boy**	)	
15	**A young man**	)	
16	**A shepherd.**	)	
17	**The four troops of the FIANNA.**		
18	**Serving Mem.**		

For an illustration of the typing style of this document, see the reproduction of 24^{r} on p. 852 below.

3^{r}, l. 10 CRIFFAN] Washington fol. 2^{r} gives as Griffan, here and in the majority of instances in Acts II and III.

Berg(99): Parallel Composite Typescript, Revised and Added to by George Moore and W. B. Yeats—W. B. Yeats's Copy; Facing HRC

[1^{r}]

DIARMUID and GRANIA.

A Play in Three Acts.

by

George Moore

and

W. B. Yeats.

[2^{r}]

KING CORMAC	**The High King.**
FINN MAC'COOLE	**The chief man of the FIANNA.**
DIARMUID)	
USHEEN)	**His chief men.**
CAOELTE)	
CONAN THE BALD.	**One of the FIANNA.**
NIALL.	**A head servant.**
FERGUS)	
FATHNA)	~~**Spearmen.**~~ Men of the Fianna.
CRIFFAN.)	
GRANIA.	**The King's daughter.**
LABAN	**A Druidess.**
An old man)	
A boy)	
A young man)	
A shepherd.)	
The four troops of the FIANNA.	
Serving Men.	

A preliminary leaf bears the title "DIARMUID and GRANIA." and is inscribed by WBY (blue-black ink) at the top LH corner, "From/W B Yeats/18 Woburn Buildings/Euston Road."

[HRC, 4r]

1

DIARMID AND GRANIA.

ACT I.

The banquetting hall in Tara - A table at the back of the stage on a dais - Pillars in front - There are doors to the right and left - A number of Serving Man are laying the table for the feast - NIALL is directing them. There is a spinning wheel to left.

NIALL.

Do not put the salmon there; put it in front of the chief man at the feast.

BOY.

Is not the KING the chief man at a feast.

NIALL.

Not at a wedding feast - the chief man at a wedding feast is the man come to be wed.

BOY.

Where shall I put the boar's head?

[Berg(99), 3r]

(1)

DIARMID and GRANIA.

ACT I.

The banqueting hall in Tara - A table at the back of the stage on a dais - Pillars in front - There are doors to the right and left - A number of Serving Men are laying the table for the feast - NIALL is directing them. There is a spinning wheel to left.

NIALL.

Do not put the salmon there: put it in front of the chief man at the feast.

BOY.

Is not the KING the chief man at a feast.

NIALL.

Not at a wedding feast - the chief man at a wedding feast is the man come to be wed.

BOY.

Where shall I put the boar's head?

NIALL.

Put it where the old King used to sit, ART, KING CORMAC'S father, ART the Melancholy they used to call him. He was deaf at the left ear, and he was always complaining that the meat was hard, and that the wind came under the door. Yes, BOY, under this roof a hundred kings have sat, right back to OLLAM FODLA that made the laws. What meals They have eaten! What ale they have drunk! Before

[4r]

1

DIARMID AND GRANIA.

ACT I.

<u>The banquetting hall in Tara – A table at the back of the stage on a dais – Pillars in front – There are doors to the right and left – A number of Serving Man are laying the table for the feast – NIALL is directing them. There is a spinning wheel to left</u>.

NIALL.

Do not put the salmon there; put it in front of the chief man at the feast.

BOY.

Is not the KING the chief man at a feast.

NIALL.

Not at a wedding feast – the chief man at a wedding feast is the man come to be wed.

BOY.

Where shall I put the boar's head?

[5r]

2

NIALL.

Put it where the old king used to sit, ART, KING CORMAC'S father, ART the Melancholy they used to call him. He was deaf at the left ear, and he was always complaining that the meat was hard, and that the wind came under the door. Yes, BOY, under this roof a hundred kings have sat, right back to OLLAM FODLA that made the laws. What meals they have eaten! What ale they have drunk! Before CORMAC there was ART, and before ART there was CONN.

[3r]

(1)

DIARMUID and GRANIA.

ACT I.

The banqueting hall in Tara – A table at the back of the stage on a dais – Pillars in front – There are doors to the right and left – A number of Serving Men are laying the table for the feast – NIALL is directing them. There is a spinning wheel to left.

NIALL.

Do not put the salmon there; put it in front of the chief man at the feast.

BOY.

Is not the KING the chief man at a feast.

NIALL.

Not at a wedding feast – the chief man at a wedding feast is the man come to be wed.

BOY.

Where shall I put the boar's head?

NIALL.

Put it where the old king used to sit, ART, KING CORMAC'S father, ART the Melancholy they used to call him. He was deaf at the left ear, and he was always complaining that the meat was hard, and that the wind came under the door. Yes, BOY, under this roof a hundred kings have sat, right back to OLLAM FODLA that made the laws. What meals They have eaten! What ale they have drunk! Before

[4r]

(2)

CORMAC there was ART, and before ART there was CONN.

4r The top half of the page has scribbled marks in red crayon.

BOY.

Was that CONN the hundred fighter?

NIALL.

Yes, CONN the hundred fighter they used to call him and he knew a hare was put before him if the fire had been bright behind it; and he knew if the swine's flesh had been dried in the smoke of a whitehorn tree. Put the curds over there; it is not the curds but the trotters and cow-heel that used to be put there, for that was the place of the king's fool. One day he flouted the FIANNA on the high road, and they hanged him on an apple tree.

BOY.

Did they hang the king's fool in time of peace?

[6r]

3

NIALL.

Fool, or wise man, war or peace, its all one to them when their pride is up. But they are great men, Bring the dishes quickly, it is time for their messenger to be here. Put the breadthere, ART'S wife, QUEEN MAIVE used to sit there, MAIVE THE HALF RUDDY they called her, and she liked thin barley cakes, and six men got their death because of her – Bring in the flagons (To the servants); put them here, where ART'S hound used to lie – (A knocking at the door) Here is the messenger of the FIANNA – I knew we should not get done in time. Bring in the flagons – (To the servants) Where are the drinking horns? (More knocking – he goes to the door and opens it – CONAN comes in; he is a fat rough man and is much out of breath. He is followed by three men, who carry bundles of shields on their backs.)

5r, l. 13 whitehorn] Berg(99) 2/fol. 4r repeats the error, but Washington 2/ fol. 4r correctly gives "whitethorn". See introduction, part v.

BOY.

Was that CONN the hundred fighter?

NIALL.

Yes, CONN the hundred fighter they used to call him and he knew a hare put before him if the fire had been bright behind it; and he knew if the swine's flesh had been dried in the smoke of a whitehorn tree. Put the curds over there; it is not the curds but the trotters and cow-heel that used to be put there, for that was the place of the king's fool. One day he flouted the FIANNA on the high road, and they hanged him on an apple tree.

BOY.

Did they hang the king's fool in time of peace?

NIALL.

Fool, or wise man, war or peace, its all one to them when their pride is up. But they are great men. Bring the dishes quickly, it~~i~~ is time for their messenger to be here. Put the bread there, ART'S wife, QUEEN MAIVE used to sit there, MAIVE THE HALF RUDDY they called her, and she liked thin barley cakes, and six men got their death because of her – Bring in the flagons (To the servants) put them here, where ART'S hound used to lie – (A knocking at the door) Here is the messenger of the FIANNA – I knew we should not get done in time. Bring in the flagons – (To the servants) Where are the drinking horns?

[5r]

(3)

(More knocking – he goes to the door and opens it – CONAN comes in; he is a fat rough man and is much out of breath. He is followed by three men, who carry bundles of shields on their backs.)

4r, l. 14 Type deletion.

CONAN.

This is the salmon, and this is the boar's head, and these are the barley cakes for the wedding feast of FINN, the son of COOL. Give me a horn full of ale – (<u>NIALL gives him a horn of ale</u>.) I have much trouble going messages for the FIANNA. Have I not legs to grow weary and body to sweat like another. I am hungry too! but I dare not put a knife in the meat till the FIANNA are here.

NIALL.

[6bis^{r}]

CONAN.

Well here are the shields, ~~you will hang FINN'S shield first~~ – I must tell you the order they have to be hung in; and you will want to know the deeds of all these boasters, that you may tell them to the horse boys and the scullions – But no, I have seen you before. Yes, now I remember, you have been in Tara fifty years and have hung them many a time. Come the sooner we bring the FIANNA the sonner we

[7^{r}]

4

NIALL.

There will be plenty and to spare when they are here.

CONAN.

Well, look to the hanging of the shields. I've seen you before, yes,now I remember: you have been in Tara fifty years and have hung them many a time – (<u>Turning to the men that are with him</u>.) Come, the sooner we bring FINN, the sooner we shall eat. (<u>They go out)</u>

6^{r}, ll. 12–18 The lines, together with the previous and following part ascriptions, are covered by a piece of paper—here fol. 6bis—measuring 7.6 by 18.8 cm. See below fol. 6bis^{r} for the overlay.

6bis^{r}, ll. 12–13 The blue-black ink of the cancellation is found elsewhere in this same TS in emendations by both GM and WBY. The revised text continues below on fols. 7bis^{r} and 7 tres^{r}. Cf. Berg(99) 3/ fol. 5^{r}.

7^{r}, ll. 1–6 The lines are covered by a pasted-in page made of two overlapping parts—here fol. 7bis and fol. 7tres—measuring 16.1 by 20.2 cm and 6.6 by 20.2 cm, respectively, and 21.7 by 20.2 cm when pasted together. The top edge of fol. 7bis is irregularly trimmed; that is, it might have contained abandoned text. When the composite page is imposed, lines 1–6 above expand to become lines 1–20 of the palimpsest text, and lines 7–14 above become palimpsest lines 21–28.

CONAN.

Well here are the shields – I must tell you the order they have to be hung in; and you will want to know the deeds of these boasters, that you may tell them to the horse-boys and the scullions – But no, I have seen you before Yes, now I remember, you have been in Tara fifty years and have hung them many a time. Come the sooner we bring the FIANNA the sooner we shall eat. (<u>He turns to go out, coming back</u>) Well there is good food on this table and all for the marriage of FINN and GRANIA. This boar was a fine beast, they fatten well on the acorns of Tara, and you have good big salmon in your river. Many a time I have had nothing but badger's flesh and otter's flesh when I have been in the woods with the FIANNA, and the war about us. Give me a horn of ale. (<u>He is given a horn of ale but the horn is not a big one and he flings it away in disgust. He is given a larger one)</u> Ah, you have a good life of it here,but I am tired running the messages of the FIANNA. Have I not legs to grow weary, and a body to sweat like another? I am hungry too, but I dare not put a knife in the meat till the FIANNA are here.

NIALL.

You are one of the FIANNA and have just left them.

[6r]

(4)

You will be able to tell us when they will be here.

CONAN.

I left them at the foot of the hill. A shepherd's wife followed DIARMUID and DIARMUID laughed at her. GOLL took her part, and FINN took DIARMUID'S part for FINN and DIARMUID always stand together. Well come let us go hurry them. I will tell them about the boar's head and the salmon Yes, you have fine salmon in Tara. (<u>They go out).</u>

BOY.

The FIANNA have a rough messenger.

NIALL.

I would have none say that I have said it, but he is a man of little account among them.

BOY.

Men wear sheep-skins in my country, but I had thought that the FIANNA wore fine clothes.

NIALL.

I will tell you why the FIANNA made him wear it one of these days, and why FINN made him one of the FIANNA. Would you be one of them?

[7bis^{r} and 7tres^{r}]

shall eat. (He turns to go out, coming back) Well there is good food on this table and all for the marriage of FINN and GRANIA. This boar'was a fine beast, they fatten well on the acorns of Tara, and you have good big salmon in your river. Many a time I have had nothing but badger's flesh and otters flesh when I have been in the woods with the FIANNA, and the war about us. Give me a horn of ale. (He is given a horn of ale but the horn is not a big one and he flings it away in disgust. He is given a larger one) Ah, you have a good life of it here, but I am tired running the messages of the FIANNA. Have I not legs to grow weary, and a body to sweat like another? I am hungry too, but I dare not put a knife in the meat till the FIANNA are here.

NIALL.

You are one of the FIANNA and have just left them. You will be able to tell us when they will be here.

CONAN.

I left them at the foot of the hill. A shepherd's wife followed DIARMUID and DIARMUID laughed at her. GOLL

7^{r}, ll. 7 In the revised version, line 7 follows after fols. 7bis^{r} and 7tres^{r}, line 20^{+}, below. See below, p. 5/fol. 8^{r}, for the continuation following line 14. Berg(99) 4/fol. 6^{r} clarifies the sequence; and the passage is seamlessly incorporated into Washington 4–5/fols. 6^{r}–7^{r}.

7bis^{r} Washington 3–4/fols. 5^{r}–6^{r}—together with Berg(99) 3/fol. 5^{r}—follows the revised palimpsest readings in the early pages of this act.

15–16 The division between the pasted-together portions of fols. 7bis and 7tres occurs here. Note that fol. 7tres has WBY's DIARMUID spelling. (Washington accurately reproduces the variations in spelling; Berg[99] spells Diarmuid throughout.)

BOY.

The FIANNA have a rough messenger.

NIALL.

I would have none say that I have said it, but he is a man of little account among them.

BOY.

Men wear sheep skins in my country, but I had thought that the FIANNA wore fine clothes.

NIALL.

I will tell you why the FIANNA made him wear it one of these days and why FINN made him one of the FIANNA. Would you be one of them?

took her part and FINN took took DIARMUID'S part for FINN and DIARMUID always stand together. Well come let us go hurry them. I will tell them about the boar's head and the salmon. Yes, you have fine salmon in Tara.

(They go out)

[8^{r}]

5

BOY.

Yes, if I might be FINN, or DIARMID, or CAOELTE.

NIALL.

They are famous for their battles; they are great men, but would you not be CONAN the BALD if you could?

BOY.

That man with the sheep skin?

NIALL.

Well he eats when he is hungry, and sleeps when he is sleepy and rails at whomever displeases him. Those great men have the best seats at the table, and the fairest women for their bed-fellows, and yet I would not -- (He rushes across the stage to keep oneof the men from hanging GOLL'S shield at the lower end of the table.) Would you put GOLL'Son of MORNA's shield below ALVIN'S and FERGUS'S; would you have the roof tree burnt over our heads. It is the third shield from FINN'S. Let me see now, let me think, it was COOL FINN'S father who made this custom of the hanging up of every man's shield above his place. No quarreling everything settled. I was going to tell you who made the FIANNA, BOY; it was COOL. He took a thousand men out of every kingdom, and made them into an army, and set them to watch the shores. No one is old enough but

[9^{r}]

6

myself to remember those times. The men of Lochland and the men of Mona, and the men of Alba carrying off women here and sheep there, and leaving smoke and fire behind

7bis^{r}, l. 20 The text continues with fol. 7^{r}, line 7. Cf. Berg(99) 4/ fol. 6^{r}.

BOY.

Yes, if I might be FINN or DIARMUID or CAOELTE.

NIALL.

They are famous for their battles; they are great men, but would you not be CONAN the BALD if you could?

BOY.

That man with the sheep-skin?

[7r]

(5)

NIALL.

Well he eats when he is hungry and sleeps when he is sleepy and rails at whomever displeases him. Those great men have the best seats at the table, and the fairest women for their bed-fellows, and yet I would not – –(He rushes across the stage to keep one of the men from hanging GOLL'S shield at the lower end of the table.) Would you put GOLL son of Morna's shield below ALVIN'S and FERGUS'S; would you have the roof tree burnt over our heads. It is the third shield from FINN'S. Let me see now, let me think, it was COOL, FINN'S father who made this custom of the hanging up of every man's shield above his place. No quarreling every thing settled. I was going to tell you who made the FIANNA BOY; it was COOL. He took a thousand men out of every king dom and made them into an army and set them to watch the shores. No one is old enough but myself to remember these times. The men of Lochland and the men of Mona and the men of Alba carrying off women here and sheep there and leaving smoke and fire behind them, and nobody to meet

7r, l. -1 The authorship of the inserted page numbering throughout this version is undecidable. It is in blue-black ink, like WBY's emendations, yet a slightly paler color; and the formation of numerals at times resembles GM's.

them, and nobody to meet them but men taken from the sheep-fold,and from the plough and from the smithy. Yes, that is where CAOELTE'S shield hangs. I told you its place last time and you remembered it – (<u>Returning to the BOY</u>) But I was telling you how the FIANNA saved the women and sheep. They fight well but they are proud – Ah they are very proud. I was telling you BOY, how they hanged the king's fool, and many and many a time they have made war on the king himself. FINN'S father, COOL, died fighting against CORMAC'S father, ART THE MELANCHOLY, and it was for that death FINN kept out of the battle CORMAC fought against the men of Mona. It has been this way always, and some-times Eri has been like a shaking sod between them; but this marriage mends all – (<u>Enter GRANIA and LABAN)</u>

BOY.

There is old Laban and the KING'S daughter.

NIALL.

Quick, quick put up the rest of the shields – Come

Page 86. {d

away, BOY. X **Ah, that ol{f woman she has come back after these many years an old witch; they say she has more shapes than one – (<u>NIALL and the BOY go out, and are followed by other Serving</u> Mem.)**

[10r]

7

GRANIA.

You cannot persuade me. I will not marry FINN.

LABAN.

Hush! Hush!

9r, l. 20 GM's transposition from p. 86/fol. 89r below is incorporated seamlessly into Washington 6–7/fols. 8r–9r. Berg(99) 6, 75/fols. 8r, 77r represent a transitional stage together with WBY's further thoughts.

them but men taken from the sheepfold and from the plough and from the smithy. Yes that is where CAOELTE'S shield hangs. I told you its place last time and you remembered it. (Returning to the BOY) But I was telling you how the FIANNA saved the women and sheep. They fight well but they are proud – Ah, they are very proud. I

[8r]

(6)

was telling you BOY how they hanged the king's fool, and many and many a time they have made war against CORMAC'S father, ART THE MELANCHOLY,and it was for that death FINN kept out of the battle CORMAC fought against the men of Mona. It has been this way always and sometimes Eri has been like a shaking sod between them; but this marriage mends all. (Enter GRANIA and LABAN)

BOY.

There is old LABAN and the KING'S daughter.

NIALL.

Quick, quick put up the rest of the shields – Come away BOY. I have heard that there are women who live seven hundred years in the woods spinning the threads of the long lived people of the woods, and then seven hundred years spinning for men. She is one of them. Ah, that old woman she has come back after these many years an old witch; they say she has more shapes than one (NIALL and the BOY go out, and are followed by Other Serving men)

[9r]

7
(6)

GRANIA.

You cannot persuade me. I will not marry FINN.

LABAN.

Hush! Hush!

8r, ll. 10–13, 16 The transposition lines are in pale blue-black ink (by WBY?). The transposed passage originally stood on p. 75/fol. 77r below, and cf. HRC 6, 86/ fols. 9r, 89r.

GRANIA.

But the FIANNA are coming too, you will tell me about them, about the young men. Yes, their shields are here already.

LABAN.

CONAN has brought them.

GRANIA.

You have promised to tell me about the FIANNA. If you will not NIALL will.

LABAN.

You have been in the woods with NIALL lately, and he has shown you where bees make their nests, and you have come home with honeycomb and flowers.

GRANIA.

But it was you who taught me the magic there is in the herbs. You took me to a place where Earth breathes out of a cave.

[11r]

8.

LABAN.

I am too old to go far now.

GRANIA.

MOTHER, there are some that say you will never be older than you are. And now we will go over to the shields because you will not refuse me anything I ask. NIALL would not refuse me anything.

LABAN.

Do not call him. Let nobody know what is in your mind.

GRANIA.

(<u>Going to the table)</u> My father sits here, FINN son of COOL sits next to him, and here is my place next to FINN – but it will be empty.

GRANIA.

But the FIANNA are coming too, you will tell me about them, about the young men. Yes, their shields are here already.

LABAN.

CONAN has brought them.

GRANIA.

You have promised to tell me about the FIANNA. If you will not NIALL will.

LABAN.

You have been in the woods with NIALL lately, and he has shown you where bees make their nests, and you have come home with honeycomb and flowers.

GRANIA.

But it was you who taught me the magic there is in the herbs. You took me to a place where Earth breathes out of a cave.

LABAN.

I am too old to go far now.

GRANIA.

MOTHER, there are some that say you will never be older than you are. And now we will go over to the shields because you will not refuse me anything I ask. NIALL

[10r]

{8
(7)

would not refuse me anything.

LABAN.

Do not call him. Let nobody know what is in your mind.

GRANIA.

(<u>Going to the table</u>) My father sits here, FINN son of COOL sits next to him, and here is my place next to FINN – but it will be empty.

LABAN.

HUSH! No man matters to you now but FINN.

GRANIA.

You told me his hair was grey.

LABAN.

You have always known that his hair was grey.

GRANIA.

Grey hair and brown hair were the same to me a month ago. A month ago I was in the woods –

[12r]

9

LABAN.

It was spring time when the young find many things among the woods.

GRANIA.

I had climbed a little path, and stood on the hill, where the trees grow sparer, looking into the mist.

LABAN.

And it was then that you thought about a young man.

GRANIA.

The mist was hanging on the brow of the hill, and something seemed to be moving over the world and to come out of the mist. It was beautiful mother. The world was singing and the singing came into my breasts, but come to the shields and tell me of the men who are to sit under them.

LABAN.

I dare not, I dare not.

GRANIA.

But you said that to-night would not be my marriage night.

LABAN.

Hush! No man matters to you now but FINN.

GRANIA.

You told me his hair was grey.

LABAN.

You have always known that his hair was grey.

GRANIA.

Grey hair and brown hair were the same to me a month ago– A month ago I was in the woods –

LABAN.

It was spring time when the young find many things among the woods.

GRANIA.

I had climbed a little path, and stood on the hill where the trees grow sparer looking into the mist.

LABAN.

And it was then that you thought about a young man.

[11r]

{9
(**8**)

GRANIA.

The mist was hanging on the brow of the hill, and something seemed to be moving over the world and to come out of the mist. It was beautiful, mother. The world was singing and the singing came into my breasts, but come to the shields and tell me of the men who are to sit under them.

LABAN.

I dare not. I dare not.

GRANIA.

But you said that to-night would not be my marriage night.

11r The page is bound into the sequence upside down.

LABAN.

No, no child I never said such a thing. Hush, lest

[13r]

10.

they should hear you.

GRANIA.

They who are wiser than you said it, MOTHER. The thread that you spun yesterday – the stars that we watched last night, the pebbles that we threw into the well this morning.

LABAN.

Hush, your father will be here; there is no time now. I saw you talking to KING CORMAC this morning, why did you not tell him of this change?.

GRANIA.

I took his hands in mine, and thought to tell him.

LABAN.

You should have told him.

GRANIA.

But he would have sent a messenger, and I should not have seen the FIANNA together.

LABAN.

So that you might pick a man who would carry you away. It will be long before men come to the end of this mischief. The FIANNA shall be broken in two because of it. Oh, why did CORMAC shut his ears to what I told him. There will be flights and battles ruin on ruin, and neither you

[14r]

11

nor I can do anything.

GRANIA.

I would not be a trouble if I could help it. I would not set FINN against any man. I would have FINN

LABAN.

No, no child I never said such a thing. Hush, lest they should hear you.

GRANIA.

They who are wiser than you said it, MOTHER. The thread that you spun yesterday — the stars that we watched last night, the pebbles that we threw into the well this morning.

LABAN.

Hush, your father will be here; there is no time now. I saw you talking to KING CORMAC this morning, why did you not tell him of this change?

GRANIA.

I took his hands in mine and thought to tell him.

[12^{r}]

{10
(**9**)

LABAN.

You should have told him.

GRANIA.

But he would have sent a messenger, and I should not have seen the FIANNA together.

LABAN.

So that you might pick a man who would carry you away. It will be long before men come to the end of this mischief. The FIANNA shall be broken in two because of it. Oh, why did CORMAC shut his ears to what I told him. There will be flights and battles, ruin on ruin, and neither you nor I can do anything.

GRANIA.

I would not be a trouble if I could help it. I would not set FINN against any man. I would have FINN and my

and my man friends. I would stand between them. I would hand them their ale. Whose shield is that,mother? That one with the red otter painted upon it.

LABAN.

That shield with the red otter is the shield of FERGUS. He is taller than all the others, his hair and his beard are brown, and he wears a crimson cloak over a white tunic.

GRANIA.

Is he strong and stately – would he make my heart beat?

LABAN.

He is strong and stately, but there is grey in his beard. That red shield with the white deer's head painted upon it is the shield of USHEEN. He has yellow hair, and he has long white hands, with fingers hard at the tips from plucking of harp strings, and they say that no woman has refused him her love.

GRANIA.

Is he young?

[15r]

12

LABAN.

There are younger than he. That grey shield with the raven painted upon it, is the shield of GOLL, the son of MORNA. He is a great hunter, and his arms and legs are as strong as the posts of a door.

GRANIA.

Is their mirth in his eyes?

LABAN.

He has the quiet of the woods in his eyes. But I see your mind is not set upon one that is strong, but one that is young. That white shield with the green fish is the shield of CAOELTE. They call him CAOELTE THE SWIFT-FOOTED, and he is young and a teller of battle tales. But that silver shield with the flying white heron upon it is the shield of DIARMID. He is the youngest and

---

15r, l. 5 their] Washington 12/fol. 14r adds a pencil query; but Berg(99) 11/fol. 13r repeats the mistake (for "there").

man friends. I would stand between them. I would hand them their ale. Whose shield is that mother? That one with the red otter painted upon it.

LABAN.

That shield with the red otter is the shield of FERGUS. He is taller than all the others, his hair and his beard are brown, and he wears a crimson cloak over a white tunic.

GRANIA.

Is he strong and stately – would he make my heart beat?

[13^{r}]

11
(10)

LABAN.

He is strong and stately, but there is grey in his beard. That red shield with the white'deer's head painted upon it is the shield of USHEEN. He has yellow hair, and he has long white hands, with fingers hard at the tips from plucking of harp strings, and they say that no woman has refused him her love.

GRANIA.

Is he young?

LABAN.

There are younger than he. That grey shield with the raven painted upon it is the shield of GOLL, the son of MORNA' He is a great hunter, and his arms and legs are as strong as the posts of a door.

GRANIA.

Is their mirth in his eyes?

LABAN.

He has the quiet of the woods in his eyes. But I see your mind is not set upon one that is strong but one that is young. That white shield with the green fish is the shield of CAOELTE. They call him CAOELTE THE SWIFT-FOOTED, and he is young and a teller of battle tales. But that silver shield with the flying white heron upon it is the shield of DIARMUID. He is the youngest and

brown

comeliest of all. He has ~~dark~~ hair and blue eyes, and light limbs, and his skin is white but for freckles. He is courteous and he is merry with women. It is said of him that he will not be remembered for deeds of arms but as a true lover, and that he will die young.

GRANIA.

DIARMID, DIARMID, a pleasant sounding name – DIARMID a sweet sounding name.

[16r]

13

LABAN.

But, child, how think you that these things will come about?

GRANIA.

I believe in your soothsaying, Mother,that a man as young as I am will come and carry me away.

LABAN.

No, no, DIARMID will not break his oath to FINN.
Dairmuid has saved Finn s life three times & Finn has saved Dairmuid s life once. ~~F~~ They always stand togeather.

GRANIA.

You said his hair was brown, and his eyes blue, and his limbs light; and his skin white but for freckles. It was for such a man that I looked into the mist. But thinking of love makes the brain ~~busy~~ giddy.

LABAN.

What can he do? He cannot overthrow FINN and his army.

GRANIA.

(<u>Waking from a reverie</u>) You must find a way, Mother it is for you to find a way.

15r, l. 13 dark/brown] Washington 13/ fol. 15r incorporates the substitution seamlessly. In Berg(99) 11/ fol. 13r, it is made with a different ribbon type, one word over the other.

16r, l. 5+ Washington 13/fol. 15r and Berg(99) 12/fol. 14r both incorporate the addition seamlessly.

9 Type deletion.

brown

comliest of all. He has ~~dark~~ hair and blue eyes, and is courteous and he is merry with women. It is said of him that he will not be remembered for deeds of arms but

[14r]

(12)

as a true lover and that he will die young.

GRANIA.

DIARMUID, DIARMUID a pleasant sounding name – DIARMUID a sweet sounding name.

LABAN.

But child how think you that these things will come about?

GRANIA.

I believe in your soothsaying MOTHER, that a man as young as I am will come and carry me away.

LABAN.

No, no DIARMUID will not break his oath to FINN. DIARMUID has saved FINN'S life three times and FINN has saved DIARMUID'S life once. They always stand together.

GRANIA.

You said his hair was brown, and his eyes blue, and his limbs light; and his skin white but for freckles. It was for such a man that I looked into the mist. But thinking of love makes the brain giddy.

LABAN.

What can he do? He cannot overthrow FINN and his army.

GRANIA.

(Waking from a reverie) You must find a way, MOTHER, it is for you to find a way.

13r, l. 20 Type deletion. This and the substitution are in bright blue ribbon type.

LABAN.

They would hang me from the rafters, child, they would hang me.

[17r]

14

GRANIA.

You would baffle them; it would not be difficult for you. But how shall I escape from FINN'S marriage bed? Shall I run into the woods?

LABAN.

The woods are full of wolves.

GRANIA.

I do not fear the wolves.

LABAN.

They would folloe you. You could not escape them. They would tear you to pieces.

GRANIA.

If you would not have me go into the woods, find a way of escape.

LABAN.

Why will you not marry FINN? You would be the great-est woman in Eri.

GRANIA.

I will not marry FINN; and you mother, who has taken care of me since you could carry me in your arms, you would not have me run alone into the woods.

LABAN.

The woods are lonely, GRANIA you must not go.

[18r]

15.

LABAN.

HUSH! (<u>Taking her aside</u>) Child love has made you wise as the bird in the wood that seeks a mate. There is a

LABAN.

They would hang me from the rafters, child, they would hang me.

[15r]

(13)
(12)

GRANIA.

You would baffle them; it would not be difficult for you. But how shall I escape from FINN's marriage bed? Shall I run into the woods?

LABAN.

The woods are full of wolves.

GRANIA.

I do not fear the wolves.

LABAN.

They would follow you. You could not escape them. They would tear you to pieces.

GRANIA.

If you would not have me go into the woods, find a way of escape.

LABAN.

Why will you not marry FINN? You would be the greatest woman in Eri.

GRANIA.

I will not marry FINN; and you mother, who has taken care of me since you could carry me in your arms, you would not have me run alone into the woods.

LABAN.

The woods are lonely, you must not go GRANIA. Hush! (Taking her aside) Child love has made you wise as the bird in the wood that seeks a mate. There is a way, listen!

way listen! The greatest among the FIANNA sit at table with CORMAC and FINN; And NIALL and another serving man will wait upon them. . . But do you say that you will pour out their ale for them, and let them not deny you this. You must say that there could be no denying you anything on your marriage night. Then come to me and I will find a way. Then I will betwitch the ale, and I will put a plae dust into it, and will make a spell over it. (Enter CORMAC with two Councillors) Hush here is your father. (LABAN sits down and begins to spin.)

CORMAC.

This is the wisest marriage, though I might have made a greater one – I might have married her to the King of Alba,but this marriage will keep our kingdom safe – (He turns and sees GRANIA) My dear daughter, I have been looking for you. Let us sit together and talk to one another. To-night you go away from me, but you go with the chief man in Eri. (The Councillors withdraw) Come, dear daughter, let us sit together. Why do you stand with fixed eyes, and I see you have not an ornament upon you.

[19r]

16

GRANIA.

I have forgotten them.

CORMAC.

I should have wished to have seen yourin your bracelets and your clasp with the emeralds – Will you wear them?

GRANIA'

I can send for them and wear them for you, but I am not minded to wear them.

18r, l. 10 plae] Washington 15/fol. 17r also has "plae". Berg(99) 14/fol. 16r gives the correct reading, "pale".
19r, l. 2 yourin] Washington 16/fol. 18r and Berg(99) 14/fol. 16r both have "you in".

The greatest among the FIANNA sit at table with CORMAC and FINN; and NIALL and another serving man will wait upon them

[16r]

(14)
(13)

. . . But do you say that you will pour out their ale for them, and let them not deny you this. You must say that there could be no denying you anything on your marriage night. Then come to me and I will find a way. Then I will bewitch the ale, and I will put a pale dust into it, and will make a spell over it. (Enter CORMAC with two Councillors) Hush, here is your father. (LABAN sits down and begins to spin.)

CORMAC.

This is the wisest marriage, though I might have made a greater one – I might have married her to the King of Alba, but this marriage will keep our kingdom safe – (He turns and sees GRANIA) My dear daughter, I have been looking for you. Let us sit together and talk to one another. To-night you go away from me, but you go with ~~another~~.the chief man in Eri. (The Councillors withdraw) Come, dear daughter, let us sit together. Why do you stand with fixed eyes, and I see you have not an ornament upon you.

GRANIA.

I have forgotten them.

CORMAC.

I should have wished to have seen you in your bracelets and your clasp with the emeralds. Will you wear them?

[17r]

(15)
(14)

GRANIA.

I can send for them and wear them for you, but I am not minded to wear them.

16r, l. 14 Type deletion.

CORMAC.

Why are you not minded to wear them? (<u>Pause</u>) What has LABAN told you? She was telling you something when I came in.

GRANIA.

Father you have often seen me wear my bracelets, and my clasp, and can love me without them, as can any other man. Father, listen, let us sit together, or let us talk as we walk hither and thither. I am going from this house where my mother lived and where I have always lived, with one you call the chief man in Eri, but whom I have never seen, so I have been questioning her spindle, and you know all that she find in her spindle is true.

[20r]

17

CORMAC.

And she has told you?

GRANIA.

Only that I am going away into the woods.

CORMAC.

You are troubled, my daughter, a woman is always troubled when her marriage is at hand. Maybe you think FINN too rough a man to marry – I might have married you to the King of Alba who is a man of peace; he sent messengers but FINN is more worthy to be your husband.

GRANIA.

I have not seen FINN.

CORMAC.

The enemies of Eri have seen him; you know how he has held its borders against them. FINN and his FIANNA have made Eri great, as when the Red Branch was at Eman of Macha.

GRANIA.

You wish me to marry as kings and queens marry – but I

19r, l. 16 find] Washington 17/fol. 19r and Berg(99) 15/fol. 17r both have "finds".

CORMAC.

Why are you not minded to wear them? <u>(Pause)</u> What has LABAN told you? She was telling you something when I came in.

GRANIA.

Father you have often seen me wear my bracelets, and my clasp, and can love me without them, as can any other man. Father, listen, let us sit together, or let us talk as we walk hither and thither. I am going from this house where my mother lived and where I have always lived, with one you call the chief man in Eri, but whom I have never seen, so I have been questioning her spindle, and you know all that she finds in her spindle is true.

CORMAC.

And she has told you?

GRANIA.

Only that I am going away into the woods.

CORMAC.

You are troubled, my daughter, a woman is always troubled when her marriage is at hand. Maybe you think FINN too rough a man to marry – I might have married you to the King of Alba who is a man of peace; he sent messengers but FINN is more worthy to be your husband.

[18r]

{ (16)
(15)

GRANIA.

I have not seen FINN.

CORMAC.

The enemies of Eri have seen him; you know how he has held its borders against them. FINN and his FIANNA have made Eri great, as when the Red Branch was at Eman of Macha.

GRANIA.

You wish me to marry as kings and queens marry – but I –

CORMAC.

(<u>Suspiciously</u>) You have set your heart upon some boy.

[21^{r}]

18

GRANIA.

The FIANNA are coming. I shall wed this night him who is the chief man among them in my eyes.

CORMAC.

That is well, FINN is the chief man of Eri after the high king. (<u>A sound of trumpets outside – The councillors of CORMAC and the servants enter – The servants open the door – NIALL stands by the door.</u>)

NIALL.

Way for FINN and his Council. (<u>Enter FINN, USHEEN, CAOELTE DIARMID, etc.</u>)

CORMAC.

FINN is welcome to my house.

FINN.

As the marriage law is, I declare the bride peace upon the threshold. I give my word to guard this kingdom against all cattle spoilers, that are of the kingdom of Eri, and to guard it before my own country from the men of Lochland and the men of Mona; and I give my word to overthrow all kings of Eri that raise their hand against the high king. I cannot give a king's gift for the FIANNA have neither sheep nor cattle, nor towns nor villages, nor great store of silver and gold.

[22^{r}]

19

CORMAC.

The bride price is worthy of FINN and of my daughter.

21^{r}, l. 7 peace] Thus also in Washington 18/fol. 20^{r} and Berg(99) 17/fol. 19^{r}. The word is "price" in the separate TSS of Act I; GM even corrected "peace" to "price" in NLI 8777(3) a, fol. 20^{r}/p. 16 (whose typist might indeed have been the same as for HRC).

CORMAC.

(Suspiciously) You have set your heart upon some boy.

GRANIA.

The FIANNA are coming. I shall wed this night him who is the chief man among them in my eyes.

CORMAC.

That is well, FINN is the chief man of Eri after the high king. (A sound of trumpets outside – The councillors of CORMAC and the servants enter – The servants open the door – NIALL stands by the door.)

NIALL.

Way for FINN and his Council. (Enter FINN, USHEEN, CAOELTE, DIARMUID, etc.,)

CORMAC.

FINN is welcome to my house.

[19r]

(17)
(16)

FINN.

As the marriage law is I declare the bride peace upon the threshold. I give my word to guard this kingdom against all cattle spoilers, that are of the kingdom of Eri, and to guard it before my own country from the men of Lochland and the men of Mona; and I give my word to overthrow all kings of Eri that raise their hand against the high king. I cannot give a king's gift for the FIANNA have neither sheep nor cattle nor towns nor villages, nor great store of silver and gold.

CORMAC.

The bride price is worthy of FINN and of my daughter.

(CORMAC takes FINN across the stage and presents him to GRANIA)

DIARMID.

(Atdthe door) And this is GRANIA.

USHEEN.

Do not look at her, DIARMID, king's daughters are not for us.

NIALL.

(In a loud voice) Let the hot meats be brought in way for the heads of the four troops of the FIANNA –
(Enter a number of men, they stand about the door, CORMAC leaves FINN and GRANIA and goes towards the door to welcome the FIANNA.)

GRANIA. X

There is a scar upon your cheek. That is the scar made by the sword of FORGAEL, when you overthrew the men X **of Aidne.**

FINN.

Has the tale of that battle come so far?

GRANIA.

[23^{r}]

20

GRANIA.

I have listened all my life to tales of your battles. (Taking his hand in both her hands) This hand has overthrown many kings.

FINN,

GRANIA must not praise me if she would not take my luck away.

GRANIA.

Some day you will tell me about your battles – (SHE

22^{r}, l. 2 Type deletion.

5–6 Washington 19/fol. 21^{r} adds a pencil query; Berg(99) 17/fol. 19^{r} types "in." with a period and begins a new sentence with "Way".

7, 8 The two pencil crosses might have been inserted by either author, or indeed anybody, and what they signify is a mystery—unless they are connected with the change made in Berg(99) 18/fol. 20^{r}, though not in Washington 20/fol. 22^{r}, from "Aidne" to "Lochland".

(CORMAC takes FINN across the stage and presents him to GRANIA)

DIARMUID.

(At the door) And this is GRANIA.

USHEEN

Do not look at her, DIARMUID, king'sdaughters are not for us.

NIALL.

(In a loud voice) Let the hot meats be brought in. Way for the heads of the four troops of the FIANNA – (Enter a number of men, they stand about the door, CORMAC leaves FINN and GRANIA and goes towards the door to welcome the FIANNA.)

GRANIA.

There is a scar upon your cheek. That is the scar

[20r]

{(18)
(17)

made by the sword of FORGAEL, when you overthrew the men of ~~Aidne.~~ Lochland.

FINN.

Has the tale of that battle come so far?

GRANIA.

I have listened all my life to tales of your battles. (Taking his hand in both her hands) This hand has overthrown many kings.

FINN.

GRANIA must not praise me if she would not take my luck away.

GRANIA.

Some day you will tell me about your battles – (She

20r, l. 2 The cancellation and substitution were made later, with bright blue ribbon type.

turns away as if already weary of him.)

FINN.

Are my battles more to you than my love? (CORMAC brings CAOELTE, USHEEN and DIARMID towards GRANIA – CORMAC and FINN go up the stage)

GRANIA.

Ah, this is USHEEN, I knew him by his harp of red yew. Will you sing us love songs to-night?

CAOELTE.

I am CAOELTE, and this is DIARMID.

GRANIA.

Welcome CAOELTE, teller of battle tales. There is a tale you tell – (She stands looking at DIARMID, forgetful of everything) And this is DIARMID.

[24r]

21

Has DIARMID nothing to say to me?

DIARMID.

~~I have much to say~~ ~~This is~~

~~What should I say to you~~ . . . ~~I see you on~~ your wedding night GRANIA. ~~could I but say it~~.

GRANIA.

~~There is the feast – the wedding feast~~

~~The wedding feast is spread~~ and Ishall be wedded and ^

before dawn, if

bedded ~~if~~ someone does not carry me away.
^

DIARMID.

If some one does not carry you away!

GRANIA.

I know your shield DIARMID. It has a flying white heron upon it, and this is your sword. (He gives her his sword and they stand looking at each other)

24r, ll. 2–4 GM's insertions are canceled in pencil, and the broken underlines of line 2 and line 4 are in pencil, also. They were not carried forward: cf. Washington 21/fol. 23r and Berg(99) 19/fol. 21r.

turns away as if already weary of him)

FINN.

Are my battles more to you than my love? (CORMAC brings CAOELTE, USHEEN and DIARMUID towards GRANIA – CORMAC and FINN go up the stage)

GRANIA.

Ah, this is USHEEN, I knew him by his harp of red yew. Will you sing us love songs to-night?

CAOELTE.

I am CAOELTE and this is DIARMUID.

GRANIA.

Welcome CAOELTE teller of battle~~s~~ tales. There is a tale you tell – (She stands looking at DIARMUID, forgetful of everything) And this is DIARMUID. Has DIARMUID nothing

[21r]

(19)
(18)

to say to me?

DIARMUID.

What should I say to you . . I see you on your wedding night GRANIA.

GRANIA.

The wedding feast is spread and I shall be wedded and bedded if someone does not carry me away.

DIARMUID.

If someone does not carry you away!

GRANIA.

I know your shield DIARMUID. It has a flying white heron upon it, and this is your sword. (He gives her his sword and they stand looking at each other)

20r, l. 14 Type deletion.

USHEEN.

DIARMID! (GRANIA gives back DIARMID'S sword.)

NIALL.

The king and FINN son of COOL are seated, the guests at this table are USHEEN, CAOELTE, GOLL son of MORNA, DIARMID FERGUS,FATHNA. The tables for the rest of the FIANNA are spread beyond the arras of the western hall. (The FIANNA and serving men withdraw leaving NIALL and one serving man to wait at the king's table.)

[25r]

22

CORMAC.

My daughter, why do you not take your place beside FINN son of COOL?

GRANIA.

Every night father I have poured out your ale, I would

HRC continues on p. 866.

USHEEN.

DIARMUID! (GRANIA gives back DIARMUID'S sword.)

NIALL.

The king and FINN son of COOL are seated, the guests at this table are USHEEN, CAOELTE, GOLL son of MORNA, DIARMUID,FERGUS and FATHNA. The tables for the rest of the FIANNA are spread beyond the arras of the western hall. (The FIANNA and serving men withdraw leaving NIALL and one serving man to wait at the king's/table)

CORMAC.

My daughter why do you not take your place beside FINN son of COOL?

GRANIA.

Every night father I have poured out your ale, I would

21r, l. 13 spread] The "s" is overwritten in ?dark pencil.
13+ The word separator is in black type.

[Berg(99), 21v]

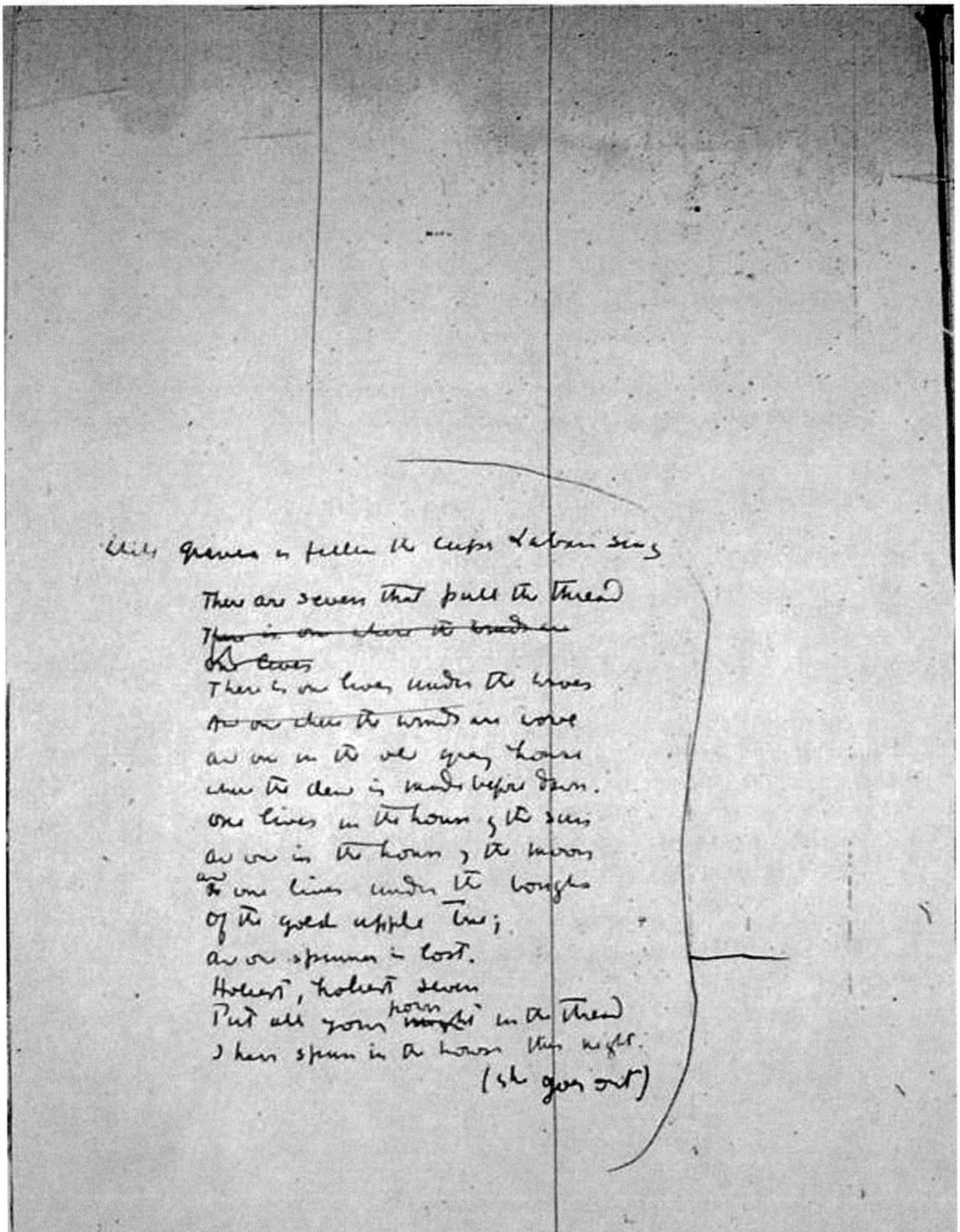
While Grania fills the cups & Laban sings

There are seven that pull the thread
~~There is one where the [illegible]~~
~~The trees~~
There is one lives under the waves
~~And one where the winds are wove~~
And one in the old gray house
Where the dew is made before dawn.
One lives in the house of the sun
And one in the house of the moon
And one lives under the boughs
Of the gold apple tree;
And one spinner is lost.
Holiest, holiest seven
Put all your ~~might~~ power in the thread
I have spun in the house this night.
(she goes out)

[Berg(99), 21v]

While Grania is filling the cups Laban sing
There are seven that pull the thread
~~There is one where the winds are~~
~~One lives~~
There is one lives under the waves
And one where the winds are wove
And one in the old grey house
Where the dew is made before dawn.
One lives in the house of the sun
And one in the house of the moon
And
[?~~Fo~~] one lives under the boughs
Of the goldn apple tree;
And one spinner is lost.
Holiest, holiest seven
power
Put all your ~~might~~ in the thread
I have spun in the house this night.
(she goes out)

21v The lines connect with the caret on the facing page (fol. 22r). For other versions of WBY's addition to Laban's charm, see Appendix I: Songs.

3 What appears to be a cancellation of "And . . . winds" is an imperfection in the film.

do so this the last time, and this night pour out my husband's for the first time.

CORMAC.

GRANIA must not pour out our ale.

FINN.

But if this be her wish?

GRANIA.

It is the first favour I have asked.

FINN.

All here will remember, this as a honour –(The king signs to the serving men to withdraw, GRANIA returns to LABAN.)

GRANIA.

Has this been done well? Give me the ale.

LABAN.

Here are two flagons that I have made sleepy – but no – I will make a spell over them.

[26^{r}]

23

DO all that I bid you
Pour sleep in the ale horns
That all that have drunk them
May sleep as on pillows
Till cock crow at morning.

Give them this ale and they will sleep till cockcrow. Give it to all but CAOELTE and USHEEN and DIARMID. (LABAN goes out – GRANIA passes along the table filling the cups and horns – CAOELTE and USHEEN are the last who should be served. When she comes to DIARMID she stands looking at him.)

25^{r}, l. 9 Thus in Washington 23/fol. 25^{r}; Berg(99) 20/fol. 22^{r} emends to "remember this as an honour –" etc.

26^{r}, l. 7^{+} Compare p. 24/fol. 27^{r} line $^{-}1$; that is, Laban's double exit. The double exit is repeated in Washington 23, 24/fols. 25^{r}, 26^{r}. The first exit was deleted by WBY in Berg(99) 20/fol. 22^{r}, but indirectly reinstated when he added to Laban's charm (on fol. 21^{v}). See introduction, part v.

[22r]

(20)
(19)

do so this last time, and this night pour out my husband's for the first time.

CORMAC.

GRANIA must not pour out our ale.

FINN.

But if this be her wish?

GRANIA.

It is the first favour I have asked.

FINN.

All here will remember this as an honour – (The king signs to the serving men to withdraw, GRANIA returns to LABAN)

GRANIA.

Has this been done well? Give me the ale.

LABAN.

Here are two flagons that I have made sleepy – but no – I will make a spell over them.

Do all that I bid you
Pour sleep in the ale horns
That all that have drunk them
May sleep as on pillows
Till cock crow at morning.

Give them this ale and they will sleep till cockcrow. Give it to all but CAOELTE and USHEEN and DIARMUID. (~~LABAN goes~~ out – GRANIA passes along the table filling the cups and horns – CAOELTE and USHEEN are the last who should be served. When she comes to DIARMUID she stands

22r, l. 16+ The cancellation was made with the same blue-black ink as the other emendations on this and the facing page (fol. 21v).

CORMAC.

Why do you not fill DIARMID'S cup? (GRANIA drops the flagon)

GRANIA.

The ale is all spilled; I will bring another flagon.

CORMAC.

Daughter, I do not like the spilling of ale at a marriage feast.

CONAN.

It never happens but it brings ill luck.

DIARMID.

[27r]

24

(Exeunt Laban)

DIARMID.

CONAN sees ill luck everywhere. When will FINN take away his favour from CONAN, and let the FIANNA give him his deserts?

FINN.

Tell us a story CAOELTE, and put the spilling of the ale out of our minds – (CAOELTE rises from his place, and takes his harp – He stands touching his harp as if uncertain what story he is going to tell.) Tell us the story of the house of the quicken trees.

CAOELTE.

Yes, I will tell you the story of the house of the quicken trees. (A pause) It is gone, it went out of my mind of a sudden – A new story is coming to me – It is coming to me – I see a man lying dead and his wife going

[23r]

{ (21)
(20)

looking at him)

CORMAC.

Why do you not fill DIARMUID'S cup? (GRANIA drops the flagon)

GRANIA.

The ale is all spilled; I will bring another flagon.

CORMAC.

Daughter I do not like the spilling of ale at a marriage feast.

CONAN.

It never happens but it brings ill luck.

(Exeunt LABAN)

DIARMUID.

CONAN sees ill luck everywhere. When will FINN take away his favour from CONAN, and let the FIANNA give him his deserts?

FINN.

Tell us a story CAOELTE and put the spilling of the ale out of our minds – (CAOELTE rises from his place, and takes his harp – He stands touching his harp as if uncertain what story he is going to tell.) Tell us ~~a~~ [the] story of the house with the quicken trees.

CAOELTE.

Yes, I will tell you the story of the ~~quicken~~ house of the quicken trees. (A pause) It is gone, it went out of my mind of a sudden. A new story is coming to me – It

[24r]

{ (22)
(21)

is coming to me – I see a man lying dead and his wife going

23r, ll. 11, 13 Type deletions.

away with another.

FINN.

What quarrel have you with me, that you should tell me such a story at my marriage?

USHEEN.

(STarting to his feet) FINN, FINN the gods are in the room, the ale has been spilled, and a strange tale has been put into CAOELTE'S mind. Our luck has been taken

[27bis^{r}]

FINN. What quarrel have you with me Caoilte, that you tell such a story at my marroage?

CAOILTE. There is fear on me Finn, for I saw beyond the world suddenly and clearly.

USHEEN Let us hear the story of the quicken trees ~~, and forget that the gods may be in the room.~~ Tell it to us Caoilte. Or shall we ask Goll to tell it to us. (He tries to rouse Goll). Goll is sleepy.

CONAN. You have no need to tell your stories to make men sleepy, The names of them are enough.

FINN. Let us drink and forget our thoughts of ill luck.

CONAN. The Fianna have had their share of good luck. To-day the ale has been spilt, and a strange tale put into Caoilte's mind.

DIARMUID. I am weary if Conan's bitter tongue, Finn. I would beat him from the table.

FINN. It would be worst of all for blows to be struck at my marriage feast. Conan and Diarmuid, I will have peace.

27^{r}, ll. 13–17 The lines are covered by a piece of paper—here fol. 27bis—measuring 16.4 by 20.1 cm and folded to tuck beneath the verso.

27bis^{r} NB the different spelling of Caoilte and Diarmuid and the different typing format on this overlay leaf (it is the same as on fol. 38bis^{r}).

13–19 There is firm pencil tick against these lines on the facing page (fol. 26^{v}). The continuation of the paste-in is folded over the page.

13–20 Washington 24–25/fol. 26^{r}–27^{r} and Berg(99) 22–23/fols. 24^{r}–25^{r} incorporate the emended reading here (and the cancellation on p. 25/fol. 27^{r}, lines 1–5).

15 fear] Thus also in Washington 25/fol. 27^{r}; Berg(99) 22/fol. 24^{r} has "a fear".

17–18 The blue-black ink of the cancellation is found elsewhere in this same TS in emendations by both GM and WBY.

away with another.

FINN.

What quarrel have you with me CAOELTE that you tell such a story at my marriage?

CAOELTE.

There is a fear on me FINN, for I saw beyond the world suddenly and clearly.

USHEEN.

Let us hear the story of the quicken trees. Tell it to us CAOELTE, or shall we ask GOLL to tell it to us. (He tries to rouse GOLL) GOLL is sleepy.

CONAN.

You have no need to tell your stories to make men sleepy,the names of them are enough.

FINN.

Let us drink and forget our thoughts of ill luck,

CONAN.

The FIANNA have had their share of good luck. To-day the ale has been spilt and a strange tale put into CAOELTE'S mind.

DIARMUID.

I am weary of CONAN'S bitter tongue, FINN. I would beat him from the table.

FINN.

It would be worst of all for blows to be struck at my marriage feast. DIARMUID and CONAN I will have peace.

CORMAC. (trying to rouse himself). Let Conan tell his story or let Usheen tell us a story; I am growing sleepy.

[28r]

25

away – (THEY all start to their feet)

FINN

Let us drink,and forget our thoughts of ill luck. (They all sit and drink except CAOELTE and USHEEN who re-main standing)

CORMAC.

(Suddenly sleepy and trying to rouse himself) Let somebody tell a story I am growing sleepy.

USHEEN.

I cannot remember any story – I too have had my thoughts taken away.

CONAN.

DIARMID, CAOELTE, and USHEEN have forgotten their boasting stories, but CONAN has many a pleasant story and no one asks him for one. I will tell a pleasant story I will tell of the death of DIARMID.

FINN.

I will have no tale of death at my marriage feast. To speak of DIARMID!S death may be to bring death upon him. Be silent or you may take his luck away.

[29r]

26

GRANIA.

(Coming nearer to the table) Will DIARMID die by sword or will he be made captive?

FINN.

I forbid this story.

DIARMID.

The story of my death is an old story, and it no longer makes me a'feards. Tell on.

29r, l. 5 Type deletion.

[25^{r}]

(23)
(22)

CORMAC.

(Trying to rouse himself) Let CONAN tell his story or let USHEEN tell us a story; I am growing sleepy.

USHEEN.

I cannot remember any story – I too have had my thoughts taken away.

CONAN.

DIARMUID, CAOELTE and USHEEN have forgotten their boasting stories, but CONAN has many a pleasant story and no one asks him for one. I will tell a pleasant story I will tell of the death of DIARMUID.

FINN.

I will have no tale of death at my marriage feast. To speak of DIARMUID'S death may be to bring death upon him. Be silent or you may take his luck away.

GRANIA.

(Coming nearer to the table) Will DIARMUID die by sword or will he be made captive?

FINN.

I forbid this story.

DIARMUID.

The story of my death is an old story, and it no longer makes me a'feard. Tell on.

CONAN.

(Obsequiously – Coming from the table) Oh, my beautiful GRANIA, this is the way it was – DIARMID was put out to foster with a shepherd, and no one was so beautiful as DIARMID when he was a child, except the shepherd's son. The shepherd's son was much more beautiful than DIARMID and his beauty made DIARMID'S father jealous and one day he crushed the shepherd's son to death between his knees.

GRANIA.

Tell me of DIARMID, tell me of DIARMID.

CONAN.

The shepherd wept – Oh, how he wept. And after a while he took his second son into the woods, and made a spell over him with a Druid hazel stick, and changed him into a black ~~boar~~ and bristless boar. And some day

[30r]

27

that boar is to break out of the woods and to kill many men and many women. All the FIANNA are to gather for the hunting of him; thcy arc to hunt him round Eri and through Eri and from kingdom to kingdom – Oh waht a hunting, Oh, what a hunting!

GRANIA.

Tell me more of DIARMID. Tell me quickly.

CONAN.

I must drink again, I am thirsty again – (He drinks) DIARMID must go out against that boar and must be killed. It was to kill him that the shepherd made the spell over his second son. He shall be torn by the tusks, and his face shall be foul, because it will be bloody. I would that the women of Eri could see him when he is foul and

---

29r, l. 17 Type deletion.

[26^{r}]

(24)
(23)

CONAN.

(Obsequiously – Coming from the table) Oh, my beautiful GRANIA, this is the way it was – DIARMUID was put out to foster with a shepherd, and no one was so beautiful as DIAR-MUID when he was a child, except the Shepherd's son. The shepherd's son was much more beautiful than DIARMUID and his beauty made DIARMUID'S father jealous and one day he crushed the shepherd's son to death between his knees.

GRANIA.

Tell me of DIARMUID, tell me of DIARMUID.

CONAN.

The shepherd wept and wept – Oh, how he wept. And after a while he took his second son into the woods, and made a spell over him with a Druid hazel stick, and changed him into a black and bristless boar. And some day that boar is to break out of the woods and to kill many men and many women. All the FIANNA are to gather for the hunting of him; they are to hunt him round Eri and through Eri and from kingdom to kingdom – Oh, what a hunting! Oh what a hunting!

GRANIA.

Tell me more of DIARMUID. Tell me quickly.

CONAN.

I must drink again, I am thirsty again – (He drinks) DIARMUID must go out against that boar and must be killed. It was to kill him that the shepherd made the spell over his second son. He shall be torn by the tusks, and his

[27^{r}]

(25)
(24)

face sh‿all be foul because it will be bloody. I would that the women of Eri could see him when he is foul and

27^{r}, l. 1 shall] The word join is made with pencil.

bloody. (He staggers) I am growing sleepy, because I have to run the messages of the FIANNA – (He recovers himself) I shall live to see him when the tusks have torn him, for it has been foretold of him also that he shall not live long. He shall not be remembered for thedeeds of arms but as a lover of women. He shall live as a lover of women, and his life will soon be over. Who has put witchcraft in my ale? Who among the FIANNA has done this? (He falls).

[31r]

28

USHEEN.

He said there was witchcraft in the ale, and look, they are all sleeping. Who was it that put witchcraft into the ale, GRANIA?

GRANIA.

LABAN, the DRUIDESS has done this for me. I had never a mind to marry FINN. But why does not DIARMID come to us? (DIARMID comes from the table) It was for you that I ordered witchcraft to be put into the ale.

DIARMID.

For me, GRANIA?

GRANIA.

I had never a mind to marry FINN; I am going away with you to-night, we shall be far away before they awake.

DIARMID.

You and I, and you did not see me before this night!

GRANIA.

I desired you and you were in my thoughts before I saw you, DIARMID. You were in my thoughts DIARMID. (She takes him in her arms.)

DIARMID.

I too desired you and you were in my thoughts – Oh

30r, l. 14 messages] Thus also in Washington 27/fol. 29r; Berg(99) 25/fol. 27r has "message".

bloody. (He staggers) I am growing sleepy, because I have to run the message of the FIANNA – (He recovers himself) I shall live to see him when the tusks have torn him, for it has been foretold of him also that he shall not live long. He shall not be remembered for the deeds of arms but as a lover of women. He shall live as a lover of women, and his life will soon be over. Who has put witchcraft in my ale? Who among the FIANNA has done this? (He falls)

USHEEN.

He said there was witchcraft in the ale, and look, they are all sleeping. Who was it that put witchcraft into the ale, GRANIA?

GRANIA.

LABAN, the DRUIDESS has done this for me. I had never a mind to marry FINN. But why does not DIARMUID come to us? (DIARMUID comes from the table) It was for you that I ordered witchcraft to be put into the ale.

DIARMUID.

For me, GRANIA!

GRANIA.

I had never a mind to marry FINN; I am going away with you to-night, we shall be far away before they awake.

[28r]

{(26)
(**25**)

DIARMUID.

You and I, ~~GRANIA~~– and you did not see me before this night!

GRANIA.

I desired you and you were in my thoughts before I saw you DIARMUID. You were in my thoughts DIARMUID. (She takes him in her arms)

DIARMUID.

I too desired you and you were in my thoughts – Oh,

28r, l. 1 Type deletion.

beautiful woman! You were in my thoughts, GRANIA –

[32^{r}]

29

Let me look at you – Let me put back your hair – Your eyes are grey, GRANIA, your eyes are grey and your hands – But FINN, but FINN, but FINN – GRANIA wife of FINN why have you played with me?

GRANIA.

I am not the wife of FINN (She goes towards DIARMID) And now I cannot be FINN'S wife for you have held me in your arms and you have kissed me.

DIARMID.

What is this madness, GRANIA? Here, here this night and FINN sleeping there.

GRANIA.

If he had loved me his love would have been stronger than witchcraft – (A pause) But why do you go away? Is not my hair soft, are not my cheeks red, is not my body shapely? You held my hair in your hands but now, and your lips were on my cheek and lips. Were not my lips soft? You see that he shrinks from me. It may be that no man will take me because he wants me, but only because I am a king's daughter. Would you shrink from me CAOELTE, if it were you I had asked to go away with me. Would you USHEEN?

CAOELTE.

Look GRANIA, at the sleeping man whose ale you have betwitched.

[33^{r}]

30

USHEEN.

If FINN were to wake he would take some terrible ven-genace for this.

32^{r}, ll. 5–7 There is firm pencil tick against these lines on the facing page (fol. 31^{v}).

10 The broken underline is in pencil.

19 the] Thus also in Washington 30/fol. 32^{r}; Berg(99) 27/fol. 29^{r} has "this".

20 Type deletion.

33^{r}, ll. 1–2 vengenace] So too in Berg(99) 27/fol. 29^{r}, which confirms the line of transmission; Washington 30/fol. 32^{r} gives "vengeance".

beautiful woman! You were in my thoughts, GRANIA – Let me look at you – Let me put back your hair – Your eyes are grey, GRANIA, your eyes are grey and your hands – But FINN, but FINN but FINN – GRANIA wife of FINN why have you played with me?

GRANIA.

I am not the wife of FINN. (She goes towards DIARMUID() And now I cannot be FINN'S wife for you have held me in your arms and you have kissed me.

DIARMUID.

What is this madness GRANIA? Here, here this night and FINN sleeping there.

GRANIA.

If he had loved me his love would have been stronger than witchcraft – (a pause) But why do you go away? Is not my hair soft, are not my cheeks red, is not my body shapely? You held my hair in your hands but now, and your lips were on my cheekaand lips. Were not my lips soft?

[29r]

(27)

You see that he shrinks from me. It may be that no man will take me because he wants me, but only because I am a king's daughter. Would you shrink from me CAOELTE if it were you I had asked to go away with me. Would you USHEEN?

CAOELTE.

Look, GRANIA at this sleeping man whose ale you have bewitched.

~~**FIN**~~ **USHEEN.**

If FINN were to wake he would take some terrible vengenace for this.

28r, l. 16 would] The word has a broken pencil underline in HRC 29/fol. 32r—though no underline of any sort in Washington 29/fol. 31r—so here, presumably, a query has been converted into a mistake.

29r, l. -7 Type deletion.

GRANIA.

What is his vengeance to me now. I will go into the woods and will wander alone there till I die

Finn (in his sleep)

Dairmuid Dairmuid –

DIARMID.

When I looked into your eyes, GRANIA, it was as though I had come out of a cave into the dawn. But I cannot, I cannot we have sworn an oath to FINN. We swore it upon the rock where the earth screamed under CON son of FILMY. If the oath were broken the earth would send famine, the corn would wither, the FIANNA would be devided, an enemy would come.

USHEEN.

Take down your shield and begone from,her DIARMID.

GRANIA.

He looks at me because it has been foretold.

DIARMID.

(Disengaging himself drom USHEEN and CAOELTE) What has been foretold? Who has foretold it?

USHEEN.

(Putting his hand on DIARMID'S shoulder) DIARMID!

[34r]

31

CAOELTE.

You will be the first of the FIANNA to break his oath.

DIARMID.

The fortune teller has lied, if she has said that I will break my oath to FINN. What did she tell you? What has she said? Has she said this?

GRANIA.

a

She spoke of a woman pledged to marry man whom she

33r, ll. 4–5 Washington 30/fol. 32r and Berg(99) 27/fol. 29r incorporate the insertion seamlessly.

GRANIA.

What is his vengeance to me now. I will go into the woods and will wander alone there till I die.

FINN.

(In his sleep) DIARMUID. DIARMUID.

DIARMUID.

When I looked into your eyes GRANIA, it was as though I had come out of a cave into the dawn. But I cannot, I cannot – we have sworn an oath to FINN. We swore it upon a rock where the earth screamed under CON son of FILMY. If the oath were broken the earth would send famine the corn would wither, the FIANNA would be divided, an enemy would come.

USHEEN.

Take down your shield and begone from her DIARMUID.

GRANIA.

He looks at me because it has been foretold.

[30r]

{(28)
(**27**)

DIARMUID.

(Disengaging himself from USHEEN and CAOELTE) What has been foretold? Who has foretold it?

USHEEN.

(Putting his hand on DIARMUID'S shoulder) DIARMUID!

CAOELTE.

You will be the first of the FIANNA to break his oath.

DIARMUID.

The fortune-teller has lied, if she has said that I will break my oath to FINN. What did she tell you? What has she said? Has she said this?

GRANIA.

She spoke of a woman pledged to marry a man whom she

did not love, and of a man who would come and take her away from that marriage bed. She foretold that the man would leave all things and that the woman would leave all things for love's sake. She foretold that they would go away in the middle of the marriage feast, and wander in the unpeopled woods, and be happy by the rushy margin of many streams.

DIARMID.

And the man is I, and the woman is you.

GRANIA.

She foretold that it shall seem as if all men had forgotten them, but the wild creatures shall not fly from them. They shall be happy under green boughs and become wise in all woodland wisdom, and as she spoke I too seemed to see them wandering on paths untrodden by the feet of the deer,where there are sudden odours of wild honey, and where

[35r]

32

they will often throw their arms about one another and kiss one another on the mouth. (<u>She goes nearer to him</u>) And she told me, DIARMID, that we should make our beds with the skins of deer under cromlechs and in caves, and awake from sleep we know not why, as though the dwarfs in the rocks had called to us, that we might see the starlight falling through the leaves. She told me the dwarfs of the rocks and the secret people of the trees should watch over us, and though all the men of Eri were our enemies they should not pluck us out of one's another's arms.

DIARMID.

I must not listen or I will take her in my arms. I will awake FINN – FINN, FINN awake!

GRANIA.

What would you tell him?

DIARMID.

That the world vanishes that I see nothing but you.

35r, l. 10 Type cancellation.

did not love, and of a man who would come and take her away from that marriage bed. She foretold that the man would leave all things and that the woman would leave all things for love's sake. She foretold that they would go away in the middle of the marriage feast and wander in the unpeopled woods, and be happy by the rushy margin of many streams.

DIARMUID.

And the man is I, and the woman is you?

GRANIA.

She foretold that it shall seem as if all men had forgotten them, but the wild creatures shall not fly from them. They shall be happy under green boughs and become wise in all woodland wisdom, and as she spoke I too seemed to see

[31r]

{(29)
(28)

them wandering on paths untrodden by the feet of the deer, where there are sudden odours of wild honey, and where they will often throw their arms about one another and kiss one another on the mouth. (She goes nearer to him) And she told DIARMUID that we should make our beds with the skins of deer under cromlechs and in caves, and awake from sleep we know not why, as though the dwarfs in the rocks had called to us, that we might see the starlight falling through the leaves. She told me the dwarfs of the rocks and the secret people of the trees should watch over us, and though all men of Eri were our enemies they should not pluck us out of one another's arms.

DIARMUID.

I must not listen or I will take her in my arms. I will awake FINN – FINN, FINN awake!

GRANIA.

What would you tell him?

DIARMUID.

That the world vanishes and that I see nothing but you.

GRANIA.

Is it not said that DIARMID never refused help to a woman and who is more helpless than I?

DIARMID.

Had you not told me that you loved me, I would have
he
helped you.

[36r]

33.

GRANIA.

Help me, DIARMID.

DIARMID.

CAOELTE and USHEEN have seen my trouble; they will tell FINN of my trouble. She has asked me for help and I must give it,

GRANIA.

(<u>Standing at the door which she has thrown open)</u>

Come, DIARMID to the woods, the birds of AOGNHUS, the birds of love, the birds that the eye cannot see, sing joyously, sing fiercely, they clap their wings and sing.

DIARMID.

She asks for my help and I must give it.

USHEEN.

From this night the FIANNA are broken in two.

CAOELTE.

And the kingdom that was to be made safe is in danger, and DIARMID'S oath is broken.

DIARMID.

My oath is not broken, tell FINN that – Tell him that this sword shall guard her by day, and will lie between us at night. Tell him I will send some messenger, some token that shall say to him – FINN I bring you word that so many

GRANIA.

Is it not said that DIARMUID never refused help to a woman and who is more helplessthan I?

DIARMUID.

Had you not told me that you loved me, I would have helped you.

[32r]

{ (30
{ **(29)**

GRANIA.

Help me, DIARMUID.

DIARMUID.

CAOELTE and USHEEN have seen my trouble; they will tell FINN of my trouble . She has asked me for help and I must give it.

GRANIA.

(Standing at the door which she has thrown open)
Come, DIARMUID to the woods, the birds of AOGNHUS the birds of love, the birds that the eye cannot see, sing joyously, sing fiercely they clap their wings and sing.

DIARMUID.

She asks for my help and I must give it

USHEEN.

From this night the FIANNA are broken in two.

CAOELTE.

And the kingdom that was to be made safe is in danger, and DIARMUID'S oath is broken.

DIARMUID.

My oath is not broken, tell FINN that – Tell him that this sword shall guard her by day and will lie between us at night. Tell him I will send some messenger, some token that shall say to him – FINN I bring you word that so many

[37r]

34.

hours or so many moons have passed by and that DIARMID'S oath is unbroken.

GRANIA.

The woods are sad with their summer sadness, and the birds of love have become silent, but they are not sleeping, their eyes are bright among the boughs – (She goes out)

DIARMID.

I must follow her. Upon whose face shall I after this lookin friendship again. (He takes his shield from the wall and goes out)

USHEEN.

(Goes to the door and looks after them) They have gone westward to the woods.

CAOELTE.

When FINN wakes, we must tell him that they have gone eastward towards the sea.

--

END ACT I.

--

hours or so many moons have passed by and that DIARMUID'S oath is unbroken.

GRANIA.

The woods are sad with their summer sadness, and the

[33r]

31
(**30**)

birds of love have become silent, but they are not sleeping, Their eyes are bright among the boughs – (She goes out)

DIARMUID.

I must follow her. Upon whose face shall I after this, look in friendship again. (He takes his shield from the wall and goes out)

USHEEN.

(Goes to the door and looks after them) They have gone westward to the woods.

CAOELTE.

When FINN wakes, we must tell him that they have gone eastward towards the sea.

END ACT I

[38^{r}]

35

DIARMID AND GRANIA.

ACT II.

Scene. DIARMID'S house. ~~A spinning wheel to left.~~ Walls made of roughly hewed timber. Laban ~~sitting before the~~ ~~is winding a~~ stet **~~spinning wheel.~~** ~~distaff~~ **~~The twilight is slowly deepening.~~** Cormac sitting near her

stet.

~~CORMAC enters.~~

~~Enter~~

m

CORMAC.

Every kind of sorrow has come upon this land: the Fianna are divided, and the galleys of our enemies are drawn up upon the shore. Our kingdom will be over-run by the Lochlanders and the hunting of DIARMID and GRANIA will begin again.

LABAN.

Have your long talks with Diarmid come to no better end than that?

CORMAC.

I talked with DIARMID late into the night and I could not persuade him. Old woman who has spoken nothing but lies, I told him that the kingdom I had given him would be taken from him, and that I could not save him from FINN, or Eri from the invader.

38^{r}, l. $^{-}$1 The broken underline beneath "Laban" (only) and the cancellation of "The twilight is slowly deepening." and of "Enter" are all in pencil. "Cormac sitting near her" is in GM's darker ink over (WBY's?) lighter ink. Some now-indecipherable pencil words—perhaps beginning "*Enter*"—have been erased in the space below "~~The twilight~~" etc.

Beneath "~~Enter~~", further to the LH side and connected by a diagonal short line, is the pencil character "*m*"—possibly registering GM's authorship—in what looks like the same later hand that appears on fol. 62^{r} and 77^{r} below and in the margins of HRC(1) and (2).

Washington 36/fol. 38^{r} omits "A spinning wheel to left." and "The twilight is slowly deepening.", and Berg(99) 32/fol. 34^{r} omits the second of these. Neither Washington nor Berg includes "Cormac sitting near her." Washington begins with Diarmuid's "We have not finished", Berg with "We have not yet finished", and both continue in tandem thereafter.

A half-page—here fol. 38bis—measuring 12.4 by 20.2 cm has been pasted onto the RH side of 38^{r} and folded over. If the unrevised insertion is included in the line count on this page, it adds nine extra lines at the beginning of the page; that is, lines 1–12 above become lines 10–21.

[34^{r}]

(32)

DIARMUID and GRANIA.

ACT II.

Scene. DIARMUID'S house. A spinning wheel to left. Walls made of roughly hewed timber. LABAN sitting before the spinning wheel. CORMAC sitting near her. Enter DIARMUID and a Shepherd carrying fleeces.

DIARMUID.

We have not yet finished our shearing. There are a few more sheep and we shall be done. (DIARMUID and Shepherd go out)

CORMAC.

Every kind of sorrow has come upon this land: the FIANNA are divided and the galleys of our enemies are drawn up upon the shore. Our kingdom will be over-run by the Lochlanders and the hunting of DIARMUID and GRANIA will begin again.

[35^{r}]

{33
(32)

LABAN.

Have your long talks with DIARMUID come to no better end than that?

CORMAC.

I talked with DIARMUID late into the night and I could not persuade.him. Old woman who has spoken nothing but lies, I told him that the kingdom I had given him would be taken from him, and that I could not save him from FINN, or Eri from the invader.

34^{r} The short page and its coincidence with a paste-over page at HRC 35/fol. 38bis^{r} suggest that 34^{r} may be a substitute page.

[38bis[r]]

Enter Diarmuid and a Shepherd. carrying fleeces.

~~**SHEPHERD. Mother we bring you wool for your winter spinning**~~**, plenty** ~~**of wool.**~~

~~**DIARMUID. She does not spin wool from a sheep, but only the**~~ **flax**
Has she told you anything Cormac
~~**that comes from the earth.... What has she told you Cormac? That Finn**~~
or is the thread still silent
~~**and I shall be friends again?**~~

~~**CORMAC. The thread breaks.**~~

DIARMUID. We have not finished our shearing. There are a few more sheep and we shall be done. (Diarmuid and Shepherd go out).

[39[r]]

36

LABAN.

I heard your voices, but I did not hear GRANIA'S voice.

CORMAC.

He said "Tell FINN to begone from my valley", "let the sod be blown into flame again and the pursuit of DIARMID and GRANIA begin again."

LABAN.

And GRANIA stood by the door post watching the moon shining down the valley; looking to where DIARMID'S cattle were feeding and towards the encampment of FINN.

CORMAC.

Yes, she stood there saying nothing. I turned to her often, saying "If I take this message to FINN you will have to fly into the woods again."

38bis[r] NB the different spelling of Diarmuid and the different typing format on this inserted page (the same as on fol. 27bis).

⁻1, 1–6 The underlining and the cancellations are in pencil. GM added his own ink cancellation when he made his insertion into lines 4–5.

LABAN.

I heard your voices, but I did not hear GRANIA'S voice.

CORMAC.

He said "Tell FINN to begone from my valley", "let the sod be blown into flame again and the pursuit of DIARMUID and GRANIA begin again."

LABAN.

And GRANIA stood by the door-post watching the moon shining down the valley;   looking to where DIARMUID'S cattle were feeding and towards the encampment of FINN.

CORMAC.

Yes, she stood there saying nothing.   I turned to her often, saying "If I take this message to FINN you will have to fly into the woods again."

LABAN.

And she answered nothing?

CORMAC.

Only this – "Where will Laban go if we are driven from this valley?" She said, "Father, you brought her here to be near me and if we are driven into the woods you will see that no harm comes to her." But remember how near the Fianna were to hanging you from a rafter that night at Tara,

[40^{r}]

37

and if I bring DIARMID'S message to FINN I may not know how to save you from them.

LABAN.

They did not dare. The rope fell out of GOLL'S hand; and CONAN told them, they could not hang me but with a rope that I had spun, and they tried to make me spin one.

CORMAC.

Yes, yes, but FINN has waited for three days. This sunset ends the third day (Going to the door). The horses are waiting and NIALL is at their heads. Speak if you have found any meaning in the thread.

LABAN.

distaff.

The thread keeps breaking as it runs from the ~~spindle~~.

CORMAC.

Then the end of somebody is near; the end of DIARMID or of GRANIA or of FINN – or the end of Eri. You must tell me before I go for I cannot wait any longer.

LABAN.

It may be a long while before I can tell you anything.

distaff

You must wait until the flax runs unbroken from the ~~spindle~~. Words will be put into my mouth.

40^{r}, ll. 10, 14–16 (+ p. 38/fol. 41^{r}, l. 10) Washington 38–39/fols. 40^{r}–41^{r} incorporates WBY's revisions and cancellations seamlessly; Berg(99) 34–35/fols. 36^{r}–37^{r} incorporates the revisions but makes the cancellations by overtyping.

LABAN.

And she answered nothing?

CORMAC.

Only this – "Where will LABAN go if we are driven from

[36r]

{34
(33)

this valley?" She said, "Father, you brought her here
to be near me and if we are driven into the woods you will
see that no harm comes to her." But remember how near
the FIANNA were to hanging you from a rafter that night
at Tara, and if I bring DIARMUID'S message to FINN I may
not know how to save you from them.

LABAN.

They did not dare. The rope fell out of GOLL'S hand;
and CONAN told them, they could not hang me but with a rope
that I had spun, and they tried to make me spin one.

CORMAC.

Yes, yes, but FINN has waited for three days. This
sunset ends the third day (Going to the door) The horses
are waiting and NIALL is at their heads. Speak if you
have found any meaning in the thread.

~~LABAN~~.

stet ~~The thread keeps breaking as it runs from~~ the distaff.

CORMAC.

Then the end of somebody is near; the end of DIARMUID
or of GRANIA or of FINN – or the end of Eri. You must
tell me before I go for I cannot wait any longer.

~~LABAN~~.

~~It may be a long while before I can tell you anything~~.
~~You must wait until the flax runs unbroken from the spindle~~.
~~Words will be put into my mouth.~~

36r, ll. ¯14–14, ¯18–20 Lines ¯14–14 were first typed with the predominant black ?ribbon and then largely erased. They were then overtyped and immediately canceled with bright blue ribbon. WBY at first began to cancel them once again (up to "The thread"), then queried them with broken underlining, and finally wrote "stet"—all in blue-black ink. The cancellations in lines ¯18–20 are bright blue ribbon over black.

[41r]

38

CORMAC.

Then spin, then spin.

LABAN.

The thread is breaking, I cannot find a whole thread in the flax.

CORMAC.

You have lied to me, old woman. You brought me this long way that you might be near GRANIA. (She gets up from the wheel. CORMAC puts her back again.) But spin since there is flax on the ~~spindle~~ distaff**, the earth knows all things and the flax comes out of the earth. ~~So spin while there is yet time~~.**

LABAN.

What would you know? If there be forgiveness in FINN'S heart?

CORMAC.

The men of Lochland have dragged up 70 galleys on to the beach of Rury.

LABAN.

You are troubled, being afraid that CAOELTE and USHEEN may not fight against the men of Lochland because they are angry with FINN. You are afraid that FINN may begin the hunting of DIARMID and GRANIA again? You are afraid that

[42r]

39

DIARMID and GRANIA – – – – –

CORMAC.

Old woman full of wisdom about everything but the

41r, ll. 7, 8–9 Washington 39/fol. 41r incorporates the revisions seamlessly; Berg(99) 35/fol. 37r makes them with a later type insertion.

[37r]

(~~34~~)
(35)

~~CORMAC~~.

~~Then spin~~. ~~Then spin~~!

LABAN.

The thread is breaking, I cannot find a whole thread in the flax.

CORMAC.

You have lied to me old woman. You brought me this long way that you might be near GRANIA. (She gets up from the wheel. CORMAC puts her back again) But spin since there is flax in the ~~spindle~~ distaff, the earth knows all things and the flax comes out of the earth. ~~So spin while there is yet time~~.

LABAN.

What would you know? If there be forgiveness in FINN'S heart?

CORMAC.

The men of Lochland have dragged up 70 galleys on to the beach of Rury.

LABAN.

You are troubled, being afraid that CAOELTE and USHEEN may not fight against the men of Lochland because they are angry with FINN. You are afraid that FINN may begin the hunting of DIARMUID and GRANIA again? You are afraid that DIARMUID and GRANIA – – – –

[38r]

(~~35~~)
(36)

CORMAC.

Old woman full of wisdom about everything but the

37r, ll. ⁻1–1, 7, 8–9 Type deletions. The cancellations in lines ⁻1–1 are made with bright blue ribbon, as are those in lines 7 and 8–9 and the replacement in line 7.

danger that waits us, I have to carry DIARMID'S answer to FINN and I would know what will happen to DIARMID and to my daughter. You sit silent. Will you answer me? (A long pause. The king walks up the stage slowly and when he turns LABAN rises from the wheel.)

LABAN.

I see DIARMID standing by FINN with his hand on FINN'S shoulder.

CORMAC.

Then they are friends.

LABAN.

I see DIARMID drawing his sword.

CORMAC.

Against whom, LABAN? And then – – – –

LABAN.

I can see FINN drawing his dagger.

[43r]

40

CORMAC.

His dagger – his sword – look again.

LABAN.

It is a dagger that I see.

CORMAC.

Now wind the thread tightly round the forefinger. Now hold the thread tightly and look,for the earth knows all and her knowledge is in the flax.

LABAN.

The vision has passed from me, I see nothing else.

CORMAC.

Spin again, spin another thread.

LABAN.

I cannot see more than once, and the thread is broken

danger that waits us, I have to carry DIARMUID'S answer to FINN and I would know what will happen to DIARMUID and to my daughter. You sit silent. Will you answer me?
(A long pause. The king walks up the stage slowly and when he turns LABAN rises from the wheel)

LABAN.

I see DIARMUID standing by FINN with his hand on FINN'S shoulder.

CORMAC.

Then they are friends.

LABAN.

I see DIARMUID drawing his sword.

CORMAC.

Against whom, LABAN? And then – – – –

LABAN.

I can see FINN drawing his dagger.

CORMAC.

His dagger – his sword – look again.

LABAN.

It is a dagger that I see.

CORMAC.

Now wind the thread tightly round the forefinger. Now hold the thread tightly and look, for the earth knows all and her knowledge is in the flax.

[39r]

{37
(36)

LABAN.

The vision has passed from me, I see nothing else.

CORMAC.

Then spin again, spin another thread.

LABAN.

I cannot see more than once, and the thread is broken

again,you have broken it.

CORMAC.

Then is ill luck in my hands. If the thread had not broken we should know all. You say you saw FINN pull out his dagger, but was not DIARMID standing by his side with his hand on FINN'S shoulder? What is the meaning of this? If you do not tell me I will have you beaten and your wheel thrown into the lake. (Enter GRANIA)

[44r]

41

GRANIA.

Ah, my father, she can tell you nothing if you speak so loud.

CORMAC.

She has told me strange things, things without meaning.

GRANIA.

You never believe her words, father, when she speaks them, but afterwards you find out that she had spoken truly.

CORMAC.

True or false it matters not since they do not help me. Where is DIARMID? ~~It is time that I were gone. I have not seen him all day~~. Does he speak to-day as he spoke last night?

GRANIA.

But a

He has said nothing to me, ~~and I would not speak to him of FINN. Nearly~~ a day and a night have gone since you have spoken to him. His mind may have changed. (Going up the stage.) This is the hour when the flock comes home DIARMID ~~has forgotten us all, he~~ is thinking of the folding of his sheep. You will find him with the shepherd, or shall I send LABAN to bring him? (LABAN gets up and goes out) The fold is not far from the house, it was brought

44r, ll. 7–8, 10–11, 14 The cancellations are in pencil, like GM's revision at lines 10–11. Washington 42/fol. 44r incorporates the changes seamlessly; Berg(99) 37–38/fols. 39r–40r cancels lines 7–8 with pencil and overtyping, and 10–11 and 14 with ink over pencil.

45r, ll. 8–10, 13, 14–17 (and p. 43/fol. 46r, ll. 1–10) The cancellations and revisions on this page are all in pencil. They are seamlessly incorporated into Washington 43/fol. 45r and Berg(99) 38–39/fols. 40r–41r.

again; you have broken it.

CORMAC'

Then is ill-luck in my hands. If the thread had not broken we should know all. You say you saw FINN pull out his dagger, but was not DIARMUID standing by his side with his hand on FINN's shoulder? What is the meaning of this? If you do not tell me I will have you beaten and your wheel thrown into the lake. (Enter GRANIA)

GRANIA.

Ah, my father, she can tell you nothing if you speak so loud.

CORMAC.

She told me strange things, things without meaning.

GRANIA.

You never believe her words, father, when she speaks them, but afterwards you find out that she had spoken truly.

CORMAC.

True or false it matters not since they do not help me. Where is DIARMUID? ~~It is time that I were gone. I have not seen him all day.~~ Does he speak to-day as he spoke last night?

[40r]

(38)

GRANIA.

He has said nothing to me, But a **~~and I would not speak to him of FINN. Nearly a~~ day and night have gone since you have spoken to him. His mind may have changed. (Going up the stage) (This is the hour when the flock comes home, DIARMUID ~~has forgotten us all, he~~ is thinking of the folding of his sheep. You will find him with the shepherd, or shall I send LABAN to bring him? (LABAN gets up and goes out) The fold is not far from the house,**

39r, ll. 17–18 The words are deleted in pencil as well as in bright blue ribbon type.

40r, ll. 1–2, 5 The corrections are all in ink over pencil (WBY over GM?).

nearer for the wolves carried off three of our sheep last

[45r]

42

week . . . . . AH, I see him coming up the path, LABAN is going to meet him. (GRANIA comes down the stage to CORMAC) But, dear father, three days are not a long while to see you in after seven years. You will come here again and forget the troubles that kingdoms bring. You are lonely at Tara. I used to sing for you. Shall I come to Tara and sing for you again?

CORMAC.

But Diarmuid & Finn — You cannot come to ~~**Our troubles grow greater as we grow older, and it may**~~ *Tara until they have made peace.* ~~**be that your singing could not make me forget my troubles now. These last troubles seem the worst.**~~ **I have persuaded FINN to make peace and I have brought him here . . . .But we go on saying this one thing again and again.**

GRANIA.

How will it all end? *What a broil it has been since that night at Tara.*

CORMAC.

~~**FINN has hunted you for seven years, he did not cease till the Fianna had deserted him.**~~

GRANIA.

~~**Do not pity me because of those years. The blood beats in my veins when I think of them.**~~

[46r]

43

~~**CORMAC.**~~

~~**There is a fire in your eyes, and your eyes were lighted like this when you poured out the enchanted ale at Tara.**~~

45r, ll. 8–10, 13, 14–17 (and p. 43/fol. 46r, ll. 1–10) The cancellations and revisions on this page are all in pencil. They are seamlessly incorporated into Washington 43/fol. 45r and Berg(99) 38–39/fols. 40r–41r.

it was brought nearer for the wolves carried off three of our sheep last week. . . . Ah, I see him coming up the path, LABAN is going to meet him. (GRANIA comes down the stage to CORMAC) But, dear father, three days are not a long while to see you in after seven years. You will come here and forget the troubles that kingdoms bring. You are lonely at Tara. I used to sing for you. Shall I come to Tara and sing for you again.

CORMAC.

But DIARMUID and FINN. You cannot come to Tara until

[41r]

(39)

they have made peace. I have persuaded FINN to make peace and I have brought him here. But we go on saying this one thing again and again.

GRANIA

How will it all end? What a broil it has been since that night at Tara.

41r Note the short page of text directly following a page that also bears holograph pagination: substitute pages? Cf. the revisions in HRC 42–43/fols. 45r–46r.

GRANIA.

~~**Seven years among the woods should have quenched those fires.**~~

CORMAC.

~~**What your heart was set on you would always have, you would always get it somehow. What other woman in Erie would have gone into the woods with a man she had never seen before?**~~

~~**GRANIA.**~~

~~**I think I had seen him many times. I saw him once on a hill when I stood looking into the mist.**~~

CORMAC.

Never did men sleep as we slept that night over our ale. We sat at that table like stones till the cock crew. We woke together at the crowing of the cock, and FINN cried out "Grania has been taken from me.

[47r]

44

GRANIA.

I thought that FINN did not love me, that you made the marriage that you mightbe stronger than any other king or than any invader.

CORMAC.

Ah, GRANIA, you have your mother's eyes. Your mother was very beautiful, GRANIA.

GRANIA.

I thought nothing but this – that a man should love me among the woods, far among the woods.

CORMAC,

And DIARMID has loved this fair face very dearly.

GRANIA.

But in this valley love has become terrible and we are sometimes afraid of one another. And now I would have

---

46r, ll. 1–10 The cancellations are all in pencil.

CORMAC.

Never did men sleep as we slept that night over our ale. We sat at that table ~~till~~ like stones till the cock crew. We woke together at the crowing of the cock and FINN cried out "GRANIA has been taken from me."

[42r]

(~~44~~)
(~~39~~)
(40)

GRANIA.

I thought that FINN did not love me, that you made the marriage that you might be stronger than any other king or than any invader.

CORMAC.

Ah, GRANIA, you have your mother's eyes. Your mother was very beautiful GRANIA.

GRANIA.

I thought nothing but this – that a man should love me among the woods, far among the woods.

CORMAC.

And DIARMUID has loved this fair face very dearly.

GRANIA.

But in this valley love has become terrible and we are sometimes afraid of one another. And now I would have

---

41r, l. 7 Type deletion.
42r, l. -1 The numeral typed first, "44", is canceled with a type deletion.

DIARMID arm the shepherds and lead them against the Lochlanders and drive them into their galleys.

CORMAC.

If you think like this why did you stand looking down the valley and saying nothing? DIARMID asked you, and I asked you.

[48r]

45

GRANIA.

If I had said "yes" to you, I should have said "no" to DIARMID. I would say nothing but leave things to work out whatever will may be in them.

(Enter NIALL and the King's Councillors. Councillors stand in the back ground. NIALL advances.)

CORMAC.

Yes, NIALL, I have delayed too long.

GRANIA.

(Going to NIALL) You are going now, NIALL, and I have had little time to speak with you, and I would have spoken to you about the days at Tara, when you were my only playfellow. How well I remember going with you, one spring morning to a little pool at the edge of the wood. We sat on the high bank fishing for roach. Have you forgotten?

~~NIALL.~~

stet.

~~No, PRINCESS, I have not forgotten. That same day I showed you a blackbird sitting on her nest. You had never seen a bird sitting on her nest before. But how many thing have happened since then; you know the woodland now better than I.~~

48r, l. 10 the] Thus in Washington 45/fol. 47r and earlier TSS; Berg(99) 41/fol. 43r has "a."

11–15 The style of cancellation is that of GM's typist. The underlining is in pencil and its wavy character appears to confirm that "*stet.*" is in GM's hand also. The lines are retained in Washington 45/fol. 47r and Berg(99) 41/fol. 43r.

DIARMUID arm the shepherds and lead them against the Lochlanders and drive them into their galleys.

CORMAC.

If you think like this why did you stand looking down the valley and saying nothing? DIARMUID asked you and I asked you.

GRANIA.

If I had said "yes" to you, I should have said "no" to DIARMUID. I would say nothing but leave things to work out whatever will may be in them.

[43^{r}]

(41)

(Enter NIALL and the King's Councillors. Councillors stand in the back-ground. NIALL advances)

CORMAC.

Yes, NIALL I have delayed too long.

GRANIA.

(Going to NIALL) You are going now NIALL and I ~~would~~ have had little time to speak with you, and I would have spoken to you about the days at Tara, when you were my only play-fellow, How well I remember going with you, one spring morning to a little pool at the edge of the wood. We sat on a high bank fishing for roach. Have you forgotten?

NIALL.

No, PRINCESS I have not forgotten. That same day I showed you a blackbird sitting on her nest. You had never seen a bird on her nest before. But how many things have happened since then; you know the woodland now better than I.

43^{r} Note that the text extends over an unusual extent of the page area (compared to surrounding pages, that is, not to later ones in the sequence) and that the page is numbered by hand: substitute page? It is possible that a preliminary version of the page omitted lines 9–12 (cf. HRC 45/fol. 48^{r}).

2 Type deletion.

[49r]

46

GRANIA.

Shall I ever see Tara again? I have wandered a long way.

CORMAC.

Five days' journey from here, GRANIA. We must hurry. Neither NIALL nor I can keep the saddle for many hours at a time; DIARMID'S cattle are coming this way and their sides are heavy with the rich grass of the valley which I have given you, and the rooks are flying home.

(Enter DIARMID.)

CORMAC.

I shall be with FINN in half an hour and I would not say to him the words you bade me say last night. Do not send me to the man you wronged with the words you spoke last night.

DIARMID.

Tell him to be gone out of my valley.

CORMAC.

Then farewell, dear daughter.

GRANIA.

Father stay with us, DIARMID do you not hear? Do you not understand?

[50r]

47

CORMAC.

DIARMID knows how great FINN'S anger will be when I bring him this answer.

DIARMID.

I have fought FINN and overthrown him. Did I not break out of the house with the seven doors when he had set

GRANIA.

Shall I ever see Tara again? I have wandered a long w way.

CORMAC.

Five day's journey from here GRANIA. We must hurry, neither NIALL nor I can keep the saddle for many hours at a time; DIARMUID'S cattle are coming this way and their sides are heavy with the rich grass of the valley which I have given you and the rooks are flying home. (Enter DIARMUID

CORMAC.

I shall be with FINN in half an hour and I would not say to him the words you bade me say last night. Do not sned me to the man you wronged with the words you spoke last night.

[44r]

{42
(41)

DIARMUID.

Tell him to be gone out of my valley.

CORMAC.

Then farewell, dear daughter.

GRANIA.

Father stay with us, DIARMUID do you not hear? Do you not understand?

CORMAC.

DIARMUID knows how great FINN'S anger will be when I bring him this answer.

DIARMUID.

I have fought FINN and overthrown him. Did I not break out of the house with the seven doors when he had

a watch at all doors? I went out of the door where he himself held the watch and my sword struck the sword out of his hand.

CORMAC.

If you will send me with this answer so be it – I can say no more – Farewell to all here.

(Exeunt CORMAC, NIALL and Councillors.)

DIARMID.

We thought we should wearyof the silence of this valley but it is of their voices that we weary. Why should we listen to anything except one another. Buththey are gone at last, and care is gone with them, and we are alone again with ourselves and our flocks and herds. Come to the door GRANIA and see my black bull in the meadow. (Coming down the stage to her) Do you not believe that care is gone with them.

[51r]

48

GRANIA.

You saw my father's face as he went out. His look has put a deep care into my heart.

DIARMID.

These northern raiders will not dare to move from their galleys, they will soon sail away and should we give up our happiness because we fear they may carry off a few score of cattle.

GRANIA.

Let it be as you wish it, DIARMID.

DIARMID.

But oath upon oath is broken. I broke my oath to FINN, and now I break the oath which binds me to take up arms against all invaders. GRANIA, you would like to see Tara again. You would like to see FINN again.

50r, l. 11 we weary] Thus in Washington 47/fol. 49r and earlier TSS; Berg(99) 42/fol. 44r inserts "should" after "we".

set ~~himself~~ a watch at all doors? I went out of the door where he himself held the watch and my sword struck the sword out of his hand.

CORMAC.

If you will send me with this answer so be it – I can say no more – Farewell to all here.

(Exeunt CORMAC, NIALL and Councillors)

DIARMUID.

We thought we should weary of the silence of this valley but it is of their voices that we should weary. Why~~s~~ should we listen to anything except one another. But they are gone at last and care is gone with them, and we are alone again with ourselves and our flocks and herds. Come to the door Grania and see my black bull in the meadow.

[45r]

(~~42~~)
43

(Coming down the stage to her) Do you not believe that care is gone with them.

GRANIA.

You saw my father's face as he went out. His look has put a deep care into my heart.

DIARMUID.

These northern raiders will not dare to move from their galleys, they will soon sail away and should we give up our happiness because we fear they may carry off a few score of cattle.

GRANIA.

Let it be as you wish it, DIARMUID.

DIARMUID.

But oath upon oath is broken. I broke my oath to FINN, and now I break the oath which binds me to take up arms against all invaders. GRANIA you would like to see Tara again? You would like to see FINN again.

44r, ll. 9, 15 Type deletions.

45r, l. 10 broken] The characters"ke" are overwritten with dark pencil.

GRANIA.

I gave up Tara for your sake, DIARMID, and that was easier than to live in this valley.

DIARMID.

Ah, you are weary of this valley. But FINN and I are divided, GRANIA, as by the sea and if the peace your father has made between us is not to be broken, FINN must leave my valley. It if for your sake, GRANIA, that he would have

[52r]

49

me among his FIANNA again.

GRANIA.

He has not seen me for seven years.

DIARMID.

To see you once is enough, GRANIA.

GRANIA.

I think that it is for Eri's sake he would have you among the FIANNA again. He does not think of women. Why should a woman think of him? Have I not loved you for seven years DIARMID? And my father has told you that FINN is bound by an oath and that he has said "DIARMID has his love let him keep her."

DIARMID.

He will not break his oath but he will find some way out of it. There is always treachery behind his peace-making.

GRANIA.

He made peace with GOLL and that peace is still unbroken Yet it was GOLL's father who plundered FINN'S country and murdered his people.

51r, l. 17 if] Given correctly as "is" in Washington 48/fol. 50r and Berg(99) 43/fol. 45r.

GRANIA.

I gave up Tara for your sake, DIARMUID, and that was easier than to live in this valley.

DIARMUID.

Ah, you are weary of this valley. But FINN and I are divided, GRANIA, as by the sea and if the peace your father has made between us is not to be broken, FINN must leave my valley. It is for your sake, GRANIA, that he would have me among his FIANNA again.

[46r]

(~~43~~)
44

GRANIA.

He has not seen me for seven years.

DIARMUID.

To see you once is enough GRANIA.

GRANIA.

I think that it is for Eri's sake he would have you among the FIANNA again. He does not think of women. Why should a woman think of him? Have I not loved you for seven years DIARMUID? And my father has told you that FINN is bound by an oath and that he has said "DIARMUID has her love let him keep her."

DIARMUID.

He will not break his oath but he will find some way out of it. There is always treachery behind his peace-m~~e~~aking.

GRANIA.

He made peace with GOLL and that peace is still unbroken; yet it was GOLL'S father who plundered FINN'S country and murdered his people.

46r, l. 11 Type deletion.

[53^{r}]

50

DIARMID.

GOLL does FINN'S bidding although he might be chief man himself. But FINN has not forgiven, USHEEN saw a look in his eyes at Tara.

GRANIA.

Ah, how well you remember. That was seven years ago.

DIARMID.

And when I am dead it will be GOLL'S turn.

GRANIA.

Unhappy brooding man you will neither believe in FINN'S oath nor in my love.

DIARMID.

Here we have everything we sought for. But in return for this kingdom your father would have me among the FIANNA again. I thought we should live and die here, I thought our children would grow up about us here, if the gods accept my offering and give us children. (He goes up the stage) Come, look at the sleepy evening. These evenings are better than the evenings of battle long ago, and were I among my old companions again, USHEEN, GOLL, CAOELTE,I should look back upon these quiet evenings when the flock came home and you gave me my supper in the dusk. (Comes down the stage)

[54^{r}]

51

If I were to die, GRANIA, would you be FINN'S wife?

GRANIA.

How did such a thought some into your mind?

DIARMID.

My life began with you and it ends with you. Oh, that these breasts should belong to another, and the usuage of this body. Life of my life I knew you before I was born,

54^{r}, l. 2 some] Given correctly as "come" in Washington 50/fol. 52^{r} and Berg(99) 45/fol. 47^{r}.

DIARMUID.

GOLL does FINN'S bidding although he might be chief man himself. But FINN has not forgiven, USHEEN saw a look in his eyes at Tara.

GRANIA.

Ah, how well you remember. That was seven years ago.

[47^r]

(~~44~~)

45

DIARMUID.

And when I am dead it will be GOLL'S turn.

GRANIA.

Unhappy brooding man you will neither believe in FINN'S oath nor in my love.

DIARMUID.

Here we have everything we sought for. But in return for this kingdom your father would have me among the FIANNA again. I thought we should live and die here, I thought our children would grow up about us here, if the gods accept my offering and give us children. (He goes up the stage) Come, look at the sleepy evening. These evenings are better than the evenings of battle long ago, and were I among my old companions again, USHEEN, GOLL and CAOELTE, I should look back upon these quiet evenings when the flock came home and you gave me my supper in the dusk. (Comes down the stage) If I were to die, GRANIA, would you be FINN'S wife?

GRANIA.

How did such a thought come into your mind?

DIARMUID.

My life began with you and it ends with you. Oh, that these breasts should belong to another, ~~and the usage of this body~~. Life of my life I knew you before I was

---

47^r, ll. 18–19 The cancellation is in blue-black ink.

I made a bargain with this brown hair before the beginning of time and it shall not be broken through unending time. And yet I shall sit alone upon that shore that is beyond the world – though all the gods are there the shore shall be empty because one is not there and I shall weep remembering how we wandered among the woods. But you say nothing, GRANIA. You are weary of the shadows of these mountains and of the smell of the fold. It is many day since you came to my bed and it is many weeks since I have seen an ornament upon you. Your love is slipping from me, It slips away like the water in the brook. You do not answer. These silences make me afraid.

GRANIA.

Then, DIARMID, go to your old companions.

[55^{r}]

52

DIARMID.

My old companions? What shall I say to them?

GRANIA.

You will fight shoulder to shoulder with FINN and CAOLT You will listen to USHEEN'S harp playing, and I shall love you better when you come to me with the reek of battle upon you.

DIARMID.

We shall be again what we were to one another. You are not that GRANIA I wandered with among the woods.

GRANIA.

You are no longer that DIARMID who overthrew Finn at the house of the seven doors.

DIARMID.

You speak the truth, GRANIA. I should have gone to the FIANNA. Now it is too late.

54^{r}, l. 13 day] Given correctly as "a day" in Washington 51/fol. 53^{r} and Berg(99) 46/fol. 48^{r}.

born, I made a bargain with this brown hair before the beginning of time and it shall not be broken through

[48r]

(~~45~~)
(46)

unending time. And yet I shall sit alone upon that shore that is beyond the world – though all the gods are there the shore shall be empty because one is not there and I shall weep remembering how we wandered among the woods. But you say nothing, GRANIA. You are weary of the shadows of these mountains and of the smell of the fold. It is many a day since you came to my bed and it is many weeks since I have seen an ornament upon you. Your love is slipping from me, it slips away like the water in the brook. You do not answer. These silences make me afraid.

GRANIA.

Then, DIARMUID go to your old companions.

DIARMUID.

My old companions? What shall I say to them?

GRANIA.

You will fight shoulder to shoulder with FINN and CAOELTE. You will listen to USHEEN'S harp playing, and I shall love you better when you come to me with the reek of battle upon you.

DIARMUID.

We shall be again what we were to one another. You are not that GRANIA I wandered with among the woods.

GRANIA.

You are no longer that DIARMUID who overthrew FINN at the house of the seven doors.

[49r]

(~~46~~)
(47)

DIARMUID.

You speak the truth, GRANIA. I should have gone to the FIANNA. Now it is too late.

GRANIA.

CORMAC cannot have reached the Ford, you will overtake him. (<u>She goes to her chest and takes out an ornament.</u>)

DIARMID.

Who is the shepherd, GRANIA? I have never seen him before. Where has he come from?

[56r]

53

GRANIA.

What shepherd do you speak of?

DIARMID.

There, there in the door way.

GRANIA.

There is nobody there.

DIARMID.

He beckons me – I must follow – (<u>He goes towards the door</u>) I see him no longer. A mist must have come in my eyes. I see clearer now and thereis no one. But I must follow.

GRANIA.

Whom would you follow?

DIARMID.

I see no one now and yet there was a sudden darkening of the light and a shepherd carrying a hazel stick came into the door-way and beckoned me.

GRANIA.

No, DIARMID, nobody has come into that door-way.

[57r]

54

DIARMID.

Nobody came for you, but one came for me. Let me go, GRANIA.

GRANIA.

CORMAC cannot have reached the Ford, you will overtake him. (She goes to the chest and takes out an ornament)

DIARMUID.

Who is the shepherd, GRANIA? I have never seen him before. Where has he come from?

GRANIA.

What shepherd do you speak of?

DIARMUID.

There there in the door-way.

GRANIA.

There is nobody there.

DIARMUID.

He beckons me – I must follow – (He goes towards the door) I see him no longer. A mist must have come in my eyes. I see clearer now and there is no one. But I must follow.

GRANIA.

Whom would you follow?

DIARMUID.

I see no one now and yet there was a sudden darkening of the light and a shepherd carrying a hazel stick came into the door-way and beckoned me.

[50r]

(~~47~~)

(48)

GRANIA.

No, DIARMUID, nobody has come into that door-way.

DIARMUID.

Nobody came for you, but one came for me. Let me go, GRANIA.

GRANIA.

No, no it is a warning that you must not go.

DIARMID.

That is not how I understand the warning. I am bidden to leave this valley. He beckoned me. I am bidden to the FIANNA. (They go out. Enter LABAN, who sits down at her wheel and begins to spin. GRANIA enters shortly after, she stands by the door looking after DIARMID.)

GRANIA.

He is like one whose mind is shaken. His thoughts are far away and I do no know what they are.

LABAN.

He is brooding over that story CONAN told him at Tara – it has been in his mind all day.

GRANIA.

And before he left me he saw a shepherd where there was nobody.

[58^{r}]

55

LABAN.

A shepherd with a Druid hazel stick.

GRANIA.

It is better that he should live among his old companions. He talks one moment of FINN'S crookedness; and at another of my love as if it were waning . . . . . Ina few minutes DIARMID and FINN will meet.

LABAN.

In a few minutes FINN will stand with his hand on DIARMID'S shoulder.

GRANIA.

Then I have done well in sending him to FINN. I did

57^{r}, l. 6 Inadvertent type deletion.

GRANIA.

No, no it i s a warning that you must not go.

DIARMUID.

That is not how I understand the warning. I am bidden to leave this valley. He beckoned me. I am bidden to the FIANNA. (<u>They go out. Enter LABAN, who sits down at her wheel and begins to spin. GRANIA enters shortly after she stands by the door ~~I~~ looking after DIARMUID</u>)

GRANIA.

He is like one whose mind is shaken. His thoughts are far away and I do not know what they are.

LABAN.

He is brooding over that story CONAN told him at Tara – it has been in his mind all day.

GRANIA.

And before he left me he saw a shepherd where there was nobody.

LABAN.

A shepherd with a Druid hazel stick.

GRANIA.

It is better that he should live among his old

[51r]

(~~48~~)
(49)

companions. He talks one moment of FINN'S crookedness; and at another of my love as if it were waning . . . . . In a few minutes DIARMUID ~~will~~ and FINN will meet.

LABAN.

In a few minutes FINN will stand with his hand on DIARMUID'S shoulder.

GRANIA.

Then I have done well in sending him to FINN. I did

50r, l. 7+ The redundant letter "I" is canceled with dark pencil.
51r, l. 3 Type deletion.

it for DIARMID'S sake, and for my father's sake and for the sake of my father's kingdom. I chose DIARMID because he was young and comely, but oh, how can I forget the greatness of FINN. He has gone to bring FINN to me. In a few minutes FINN and his FIANNA will stand under this roof.

LABAN.

That is true, my daughter, sit beside me here and tell me what happened to you when you left Tara.

[59r]

56

GRANIA.

When we left Tara we came to a little glade on the hill-side , and we heard there a sudden and a beautiful singing of birds, and we saw a red fox creeping in the grass.

LABAN.

And then?

GRANIA.

And then we saw a young man sitting in the long grass.

LABAN.

What did he say?

GRANIA.

He was but a herdsman's son seeking a master and so DIARMID took him into his service, and yet,Mother, I think that he was greater than DIARMID or I, for he gave us such good service,and so much good counsel. He never put us in a cave that had not two mouths, or let us take refuge in an island that had not two harbours, nor eat our food where we had cooked it, nor sleep where we had eaten it. He never let us lie for many hours in one place, and he often changed our sleeping places in the middle of the night.

LABAN.

What name did he bid you call him?

it for DIARMUID'S sake, and for my father's sake and for the sake of my father's kingdom. I chose DIARMUID because he was young and comely, but oh, how can I forget the greatness of FINN. He has gone to bring FINN to me. In a few minutes FINN and his FIANNA will stand under this roof.

LABAN.

That is true, my daughter, sit beside me here and tell me what happened to you when you left Tara.

GRANIA.

When we left Tara we came to a little glade on the hill-side, and we heard there a sudden and a beautiful singing of birds, and we saw a red fox creeping in the grass.

LABAN.

And then?

GRANIA.

And then we saw a young man sitting in the long grass.

LABAN.

What did he say?

[52^{r}]

(~~49~~)
(50)

GRANIA.

He was but a herdsman's son seeking a master and so DIARMUID took him into his service, and yet, Mother, I ~~t~~ think that he was greater than DIARMUID or I, ~~did~~ for he gave us such good service and so much good counsel. He never put us in a cave that had not two mouths, or let us take refuge in an island that had not two harbours, nor eat our food where we had cooked it, nor sleep where we had eaten it. He never let us lie for many hours i n one place, and he often changed our sleeping places in the middle of the night.

LABAN.

What name did he bid you call him?

52^{r}, ll. 2, 3 Type deletions.

[60^{r}]

57

GRANIA.

He bid us call him, MUDHAM. But I think he had some great and beautiful name did webut know it. Have you ever seen him, MOTHER?

LABAN.

It is said that none who have seen him have been long content with any mortal lover.

GRANIA.

I have been content with DIARMID nigh on seven years.

LABAN.

Did you ever hear that beautiful singing of birds again?

GRANIA.

Yes, I heard them sing by the banks of a river; I heard them when DIARMID broke his oath to FINN. We had wandered by the banks of s river nine days, and MUDHAM fished for us, and every day we hung an uncooked salmon,on a tree as a token to FINN. On the tenth day we hung a cooked salmon, for on the ninth night a sword had not lain between us – But MOTHER,I can tell you no more. I would have you tell me, you who knows all things, what is passing in the valley. Have FINN and DIARMID made friends? Has DIARMID passed the fires of the FIANNA without speaking?

[61^{r}]

58

LABAN.

They have spoken,and they are on their way hither, so forget them for a while, and tell me if you are happy in this valley.

GRANIA.

I stand by the door of this house, seeing the hours wane, waiting for DIARMID to come home from his hunting. Nothing has happened until~~l~~ to-day, and now DIARMID and FINN

60^{r}, l. 10 s river] Washington 56/fol. 58^{r} and Berg(99) 51/fol. 53^{r} both correctly give "a river".
61^{r}, l. 6 Type deletion.

GRANIA.

He bid us call him MUDHAM. But I think he had some great and beautiful name did we but know it. Have you ever seen him Mother?

LABAN.

It is said that none who have seen him have been long content with any mortal lover.

GRANIA.

I have been content with DIARMUID nigh on seven years.

LABAN.

Did you ever hear that beautiful singing of birds again?

[53r]

(5~~0~~)
(51)

GRANIA.

Yes, I heard them sing by the banks of a river; I heard them when DIARMUID broke his oath to FINN. We had wandered by the banks of a river nine days, and MUDHAM fished for us, and every day we hung an uncooked salmon on a tree as a token to FINN. On the tenth day we hung a cooked salmon, for on the ninth night a sword had not lain between us – But MOTHER, I can tell you no more. I would have you tell me, you who knows all things, what is passing in the valley. Have FINN and DIARMUID made friends? Has DIARMUID passed the fires of the FIANNA without speaking?

LABAN.

They have spoken and they are on their way hither, so forget them for a while, and tell me if you are happy in this valley.

GRANIA.

I stand by the door of this house, seeing the hours wane, waiting for DIARMUID to come home from his hunting. Nothing has happened until to-day, and now DIARMUID and

are walking up the valley together, reconciled at last. I had come to think I should never look on a stirring day again, and I had thought to send all the thread you would spin to be woven into a grass green web on which to embroider my wanderings with DIARMID among the woods. I should have been many years embroidering it, but when it was done and hung round this room, I should have seen birds, beasts and leaves which ever way I turned and DIARMID and myself wandering among them.

LABAN.

But now you have thrown the doors wide open and the days are streaming in upon you again.

[62^{r}]

59

GRANIA.

Yes, yes, haveII done rightly? Had I not sent DIARMID to FINN the broil would have begun again . . . . I must put on my jewels. The FIANNA will be here in a moment, and FINN has never seen me in my jewels. ~~Spin for me. MOTHER, spin for me;~~ tell me I have done rightly. But no, they are coming I can hear their footsteps. Go to the serving men and bid them take the drinking horns and the flagons from the cup-board. (Exit LABAN, GRANIA stands before a long brazen mirrow that hangs upon the wall, and puts the gold circlet about her head and the heavy bracelets upon her arm, and the great many-coloured cloak upon her which she fastens with an emerald clasp – she puts a gold girdle about her waist ENTER CORMAC, FINN, CAOELTE, DIARMID and others of the FIANNA DIARMID is talking to FINN – Enter servants with flagons of ale, drinking horns and torches.) Welcome USHEEN, Welcome CAOELTE, Welcome GOLL and all the noble FIANNA into my house. I am happytthat such men shall stand under my roof. The shepherds of Ben Bulben will tell each other many years after

---

62^{r}, ll. 4–5 The cancellation is in ink. A later hand has written, in pencil, above the end of line 4: "*(in 1st state)*". Cf. fols. 38^{r} above and 77^{r} below. Washington 58/fol. 60^{r} incorporates the revision seamlessly; Berg(99) 52/fol. 54^{r} employs a later type cancellation.

8 The same later hand has written in pencil above the end of the line: "*(stet)*".

FINN are walking up the valley together, reconciled at last. I had come to think I should never look on a stirring day again, and I had thought to send all the thread you would spin to be woven into a grass-green web on which to embroider my wanderings with DIARMUID among the woods.

[54r]

(~~51~~)
(52)

I should have been many years embroidering it, but when it was done and hung round this room, I should have seen birds, beasts and leaves which ever way I turned and DIARMUID and myself wandering among them.

LABAN.

But now you have thrown the doors wide open and the days are streaming in upon you again.

GRANIA.

Yes, yes, have I done rightly? Had I not sent DIARMUID to FINN the broil would have begun again. . . .I must put on my jewels. The FIANNA will be here in a moment, and FINN has never seen me in my jewels. ~~Spin for me~~, ~~Mother, spin for me~~; tell me I have done rightly. But, no they are coming, I can hear their footsteps. Go to the serving men and bid them take the drinking horns and the flagons from the cup-board. (Exit LABAN, GRANIA stands before a long brazen mirror that hangs upon the wall, and puts the gold circlet about her head and the heavy bracelets upon her arm, and the great many-coloured cloak upon her which she fastens with an emerald clasp – She puts a gold girdle about her waist. Enter CORMAC, FINN, CAOELTE DIARMUID and others of the FIANNA. DIARMUID is talking to FINN – Enter servants with flagons of ale, drinking horns, and torches.) Welcome, USHEEN, welcome CAOELTE, welcome GOLL and all the noble FIANNA into my house. I am happy that such men shall stand under my roof. The shepherds of Ben Bulben will tell each other many years after we dead

54r, ll. 10–11 Type deletion in bright blue ribbon.

we are dead that FINN, USHEEN, CAOELTE,and GOLL stood under this roof, (GRANIA goes to her father and leads him to a high seat.) You cannot go from us now,for I am too glad for leave taking.

[63r]

60

CORMAC.

I will stay a little while, and will drinka horn of ale with this noble company who will defend Eri against the men of Lochland.

DIARMID.

We have been here but three moons and have not had time to build a house great enoughfor ourselves and for our peo-ple. This winter we shall build a house of oak wood great enough for two hundred people to sleep under its pillars. All the FIANNA who come shall sleep under our roof.

GRANIA.

When you speak of their coming you make us think of their leave-taking, and I would forget that they shall ever leave us.

CORMAC.

Eri is safe now that her great men are united.

CAOELTE.

For a long while when we lighted out fires at night there was no fire at which some did not side with FINN some with DIARMID – But al last those that were of FINN'S party and those that were of DIARMID'S party gathered about differ-ent fires. And this year the fires were lighted far apart.

[64r]

61

USHEEN.

And time wore on until one day the swords were out and the earth|red underfoot.

62r, l. 13 are] Washington 58/fol. 60r and earlier TSS include; Berg(99) 52/fol. 54r omits.
63r, l. 15 al] Washington 59/fol. 61r and Berg(99) 53/fol. 55r correctly give "at".
64r, l. 2 A faint (later?) pencil line separates the two joined words; cf. fol. 90r below.

[55r]

(5~~2~~)
53

that FINN, USHEEN, CAOELTE and GOLL stood under this roof.
(GRANIA goes to her father and leads him to a high seat)
You cannot go from us now, for I am too glad for leave-taking.

CORMAC.

I will stay a little while, and will drink a horn of ale with this noble company who will defend Eri against the men of Lochland.

DIARMUID.

We have been here but three moons and have not had time to build a house great enough for ourselves and for out people. This winter we shall build a house of oak wood great enough for two hundred people to sleep under its pillars. All the FIANNA who come shall sleep under our roof.

GRANIA.

When you speak of their coming you make us think of their leave-taking, and I would forget that they shall ever leave us.

CORMAC.

Eri is safe not that her great men are united.

CAOELTE.

For a long while when we lighted our fires at night there was no fire at which some did not side with FINN some with DIARMUID – But at last those that were of FINN'S party and those that were of DIARMUID's party gathered about different fires; and this year the fires were lighted far apart.

[56r]

(5~~3~~)
(54)

USHEEN'

And time wore on until one day the swords were out and the earth red underfoot.

55r, l. 21 apart] Inserted with bright blue ribbon.

FINN.

If all Eri were red under foot, it was but GRANIA'S due that men in coming times might know of the love she had put into men's hearts. (He puts his hand on DIARMID'S shoulder – Two serving men go round with ale, GRANIA stops them and takes the flagons from them.)

GRANIA.

It is right that I should derve the ale on such a day as this.

CORMAC.

My daughter must not pour out the ale.

USHEEN.

If GRANIA pours out the ale we shall sleep sound to-night.

CORMAC.

You have spoken folly, USHEEN – I, I spoke out of a dream. GRANIA since you have taken the flagons from your serving men serve us, But I would youhad not done this. (GRANIA goes round filling each one's horn with ale – DIARMID and FINN are still standing together on the right – she pauses, considering,)for an instant,and then fills Finn's

[65r]

62

horn).

CAOELTE.

DIARMID, we have not spoken to you nor seen you these seven years.

GOLL.

Have you no word for us?

USHEEN.

We would drink with you (DIARMID goes up the stage and joins the group who are standing half way up the stage, near to where the king is sitting.)

64r, l. 12+ Type deletion.

FINN.

If all Eri were red under-foot it was but GRANIA'S due that men in coming times might know of the love she had put into men's hearts. (He puts his hand on DIARMUID'S shoulder – Two serving men go round with ale, GRANIA stops them and takes the flagons from them)

GRANIA.

It is right that I should serve the ale on such a day as this.

CORMAC.

My daughter must not pour out the ale.

USHEEN.

If GRANIA pours out the ale we shall sleep sound to-night.

CORMAC.

You have spoken folly USHEEN, I – I spoke out of a dream. GRANIA since you have taken the flagons from your serving men serve us. But I would you had not done this. (GRANIA goes round filling each one's horn with ale – DIARMUID and FINN are still standing together on the right – she pauses, considering for an instant and then fills FINN'S horn)

CAOELTE.

DIARMUID we have not spoken to you nor seen you these seven years.

[57r]

(~~54~~)

(53)

GOLL.

Have you no word for us?

USHEEN.

We would drink with you. (DIARMUID goes up the stage and joins the group who are standing half-way up the stage, near to where the king is sitting)

GRANIA.

In this ale you will not drink sleep but you will drink forgetfulness of me, and friendship for DIARMID.

FINN.

Had I known that you would speak like this I would not have come to your house.

GRANIA.

But you have come here for this.

USHEEN.

It is not enough for FINN and DIARMID to drink together they must be bound together by the blood bond. They must be made brothers before the gods – They must be bound together.

[66r]

63

CAOELTE'

Yes, yes, one of you there by the door – you FINMOLE– cut a sod of grass with your sword. They must be bound together.

DIARMID.

(As he comes down the stage he draws his sword.) FINN draw blood out of your hand as I draw blood out of mine. (FINN pricks his hand with his dagger and goes towards DIARMID and lets blood from his hand drop into DIARMID'S cup. DIARMID lets the blood from his hand drop into the cup also. He gives the cup to FINN.) Speak the holy words, FINN.

FINN

(Having drunk out of the cup)

This bond has bound us
Like brother to brother
Like son to father
Let him who breaks it
Be driven from the thresholds
Of God-kind and man-kind.

~~DIARMUID~~
GRANIA.

In this ale you will not drink sleep but you will drink forgetfulness of me and friendship for DIARMUID.

FINN.

Had I known that you would speak like this I would not have come to your house.

GRANIA.

But you have come here for this.

USHEEN.

It is not enough for FINN and DIARMUID to drink together they must be bound together by the blood-bond. They must be made brothers before the gods – they must be bound together.

CAOELTE.

Yes, yes one of you there by the door– you FINMOLE cut a sod of grass with your sword. They must be bound together.

[58r]

(~~**55**~~)
(56)

DIARMUID.

(As he comes down the stage he draws his sword)
FINN draw blood out of your hand as I draw blood out of mine. (FINN pricks his hand with his dagger and goes towards DIARMUID and lets blood from his hand drop into DIARMUID'S cup. DIARMUID lets the blood from his hand drop into the cup also. He gives the cup to FINN) Speak the holy words FINN.

FINN.

(Having drunk out of the cup)
This bond has bound us
Like brother to brother
Like son to father
Let him who breaks it
Be driven from the thresholds
Of God-kind and man-kind.

57r, l. -3 Type deletion.

[67r]

64

(DIARMID takes the cup and drinks.)

DIARMID.

Let the sea bear witness,
Let the wind bear witness,
Let the earth bear witness,
Let the fire bear witness,
Let the dew bear witness,
Let the stars bear witness.

(FINN takes the cup and drinks.)

FINN.

Six that are deathless
Six holy creatures
Have witnessed the binding.

(A sod of grass is handed in through the door and from man to man till it comes to USHEEN and CAOELTE who hold it up one on each side. First FINN and then DIARMID pass under it.)

CAOELTE.

They are of one blood.

USHEEN.

They have been born again out of the womb of the earth.

[68r]

65

CAOELTE.

Give back the sod to the ground. Give the holy sod to the Goddess. (The FIANNA pass the sod from one to another and out through the door, each one speaking these words over it in a monotonous and half audible muttering "Blessed is the Goddess. May the ground be blessed.")

GOLL.

This bond has snown that FINN can forgive. It has been said falsely that he never forgives although he has forgiven

68r, l. 3 snown] Washington 63/fol. 65r and Berg(99) 57/fol. 59r correctly give "shown".

(DIARMUID takes the cup and drinks)

Let the sea bear witness,
Let the wind bear witness,
Let the earth bear witness,
Let the fire bear witness,
Let the dew bear witness,
Let the stars bear witness.

(FINN takes the cup and drinks)

FINN

[59r]

(~~56~~)
57

FINN.

Six that are deathless
Six holy creatures
Have witnessed the binding.

(A sod of grass is handed in through the door and from man to man till it comes to USHEEN and CAOELTE who hold it up one on each side. First FINN and then DIAR÷MUID pass under it)

CAOELTE.

They are of one blood.

USHEEN.

They have been born again out of the womb of the earth.

CAOELTE.

Give back the sod to the ground. Give the holy sod to the Goddess. (The FIANNA pass the sod from one to another and out through the door, each one speaking these words over it in a monotonous and half-audible muttering "Blessed is the Goddess. May the ground be blessed.")

GOLL.

This bond has shown that FINN can forgive. It has been said falsely that he never forgives although he has
Finn has forgiven Goll.
forgiven me. ^ **(FINN turns to GOLL effusively)**

has
Finn ~~have~~ forgiven Goll.

me.^ (FINN turns to GOLL effusively.)

CORMAC.

Now my errand is done and I shall bid GRANIA and DIARMID and all this goodly company farewell. (He rises but lingers talking with certain of his councillors.)

DIARMID.

I have done this though you have followed me and hunted me through the woods of Eri for seven years.

FINN.

I forgave you because we had need of you, DIARMID. (Turning away) Although you left the FIANNA for a woman.

[69^{r}]

66

DIARMID.

GRANIA pour out the ale for FINN.

FINN.

It is right for a man to have a time for love but now you are with your old companions again.

DIARMID.

I did not acceptnthe peace you offered me at once, because I had taken GRANIA from you.

FINN.

(Looking at GRANIA) It seems a long while ago, GRANIA you should have been my wife seven years ago.

GRANIA.

Then it was not for me that you followed DIARMID so many years. Why did you follow him? What reason could you have had, if it all seems so long ago.

FINN.

Our marriage was to have mended an old crack in theland.

68^{r}, l. 5 Washington 64/fol. 66^{r} incorporates the revision seamlessly; WBY again inserted it by hand into Berg(99) 57/fol. 69^{r}.

CORMAC.

Now my errand is done and I shall bid GRANIA and DIARMUID and all this goodly company farewell. (He rises but lingers talking with certain of his councillors)

[60^{r}]

(58()

DIARMUID.

I have done this though you have followed me and hunted me through the woods of Eri for seven years.

FINN.

I forgave you because we had need of you DIARMUID. (Turning away) Although you left the FIANNA for a woman.

DIARMUID.

GRANIA pour out the ale for FINN.

FINN.

It is right for a man to have a time for love but now you are with your old companions again.

DIARMUID.

I did not accept the peace you offered me at once, because I had taken GRANIA from you.

FINN.

(Looking at GRANIA) It seems a long while ago, GRANIA you should have been my wife seven years ago.

GRANIA.

Then it was not for me that you followed DIARMUID so many years. Why did you follow him? What reason could you have had if at all seems so long ago.

FINN.

Our marriage was to have mended an old crack in the

It was to have joined the FIANNA to the high king for ever, but it was not for this marriage sake that I followed DIARMID I followed him because he had broken his oath.

[70[r]]

67

DIARMID.

I shall make atonement for the breaking of my oath with fifty heads of cattle, and I will give you my black bull. Come to the door, and you will see him in the valley. He is grazing on the edge of the herd and you will see what a noble stride he has. But who is this with two of the FIANNA this fat man in the sheep skin. It is my enemy CONAN. I shall be glad to drink a horn of ale with him to the forgetfulness of all enemity (to the others) I have not seen you for seven years and seven years have changed some here a little. I would drink with every one of you. I would that you had but a single hand that I might hold it this day this happy day. (Enter CONAN with CRIFFAN and FERGUS and a shepherd.)

CONAN.

Keep your spears in your hands. We are only just in time – a great beast – come – come – we will be in front of him before he can run into the wood. (Exeunt CONAN and all the FIANNA except FINN.)

DIARMID.

I thought I had driven off the last of the wolves. (DIARMID goes out. ~~(~~There are only ~~CORMAC~~, FINN, GRANIA and a Shepherd on the stage)

[71[r]]

68

SHEPHERD.

He is not wolf! He is not a wolf! He has gored twenty of my sheep. He broke out by the stepping stones. (He goes out)

70[r], l. 16[+] The second parenthesis is deleted in type. The name "CORMAC" is deleted in ink. Washington 66/fol. 68[r] incorporates the deletions seamlessly; Berg(99) 59/fol. 61[r] cancels the name in type.

land. It was to have joined the FIANNA to the high king for ever, but it was not for this marriage sake that I followed DIARMUID, I followed him because he had broken his oath.

[61^{r}]

(59)

DIARMUID.

I shall make atonement for the breaking of my oath with fifty heads of cattle, and I will give you my black bull. Come to the door, and you will see him in the valley. He is grazing on the edge of the herd and you will see what a noble stride he has. But who is this with two of the FIANNA this fat man in the sheep skin. It is my enemy CONAN. I shall be glad to drink a horn of ale with him to the forgetfulness of all enemity. (To the others) I have not seen you for seven years and seven years have changed some here a little. I would d drink with every one of you. I would that you had but a single hand that I might hold it this day this happy day.
(Enter CONAN with CRIFFAN and FERGUS and a shepherd)

CONAN.

Keep your spears in your hands. We are only just in time – a great beast – come – come – we will be in front of him before he can run into the wood. (Exeunt CONAN and all the FIANNA except FINN)

DIARMUID.

I thought I had driven off the last of the wolves.
(DIARMUID goes out. There are only ~~CORMAC~~, FINN, GRANIA and a shepherd on the stage)

SHEPHERD.

He is not a wolf – He is not a wolf! He has gored twenty of my sheep. He broke out by the stepping stones.
(He goes out)

61^{r}, l. 16^{+} Type deletion in bright blue ribbon.

GRANIA.

The shepherd said it was not a wolf,ask him.

FINN.

He said it has gored twenty of his sheep. It must be the boar I heard of as I came hither. It has come out of a dark wood to the east ward – A wood men are afraid of.

GRANIA.

Then DIARMID must not go to this hunting. I will call him (she goes to the door) He is standing on the hillside He is coming towards us. That is well. (Coming down the stage to FINN.) So it was not for my sake that you followed DIARMID. This flight and this pursuit for seven years were for no better reason than the breaking of an oath.

FINN.

I followed DIARMID because I hated him.

[72^r]

69

GRANIA.

But now you have forgiven him. You are friends again. Yes, FINN, I would have you friends but my wish can be nothing to you. I was proud to think you followed DIARMID for me, but you have said it was to avenge the breaking of an oath. This is a man's broil. No woman has part in it.

FINN.

CORMAC told me that it was you who persuaded DIARMID to bring me to this house, and, but for this I would not have come.

GRANIA.

It was well that you came. Men who are so great as FINN and DIARMID must be friends. My father fears a landing of the men of Lochlann, and I am weary of this valley where

---

72^r, l. 11 Lochlann] Washington 68/fol. 70^r and Berg(99) 61/fol. 63^r both have "Lochland".

[62^{r}]

(60)

GRANIA.

The shepherd said it was not a wolf, ask him.

FINN.

He said it has gored twenty of his sheep. It must be the boar I heard of as I came hither. It has come out of a dark wood to the east ward – A wood men are afraid of.

GRANIA.

Then DIARMUID must not go to this hunting. Itwill call him (She goes to the door) He is standing on the hill-side. He is coming towards us. That is well. (Coming down the stage to FINN) So it was not for my sake that you followed DIARMUID. This flight and this pursuit for seven years were for no better reason than the breaking of an oath.

FINN.

I followed DIARMUID because I hated him.

GRANIA.

But now you have forgiven him. You are friends again. Yes, FINN, I would have you friends but my wish can be nothing to you. I was proud to think you followed DIARMUID for me, but you have said it was to avenge the breaking of an oath. This is a man's broil. No woman has part in it.

[63^{r}]

(61)

FINN.

CORMAC told me that it was you who persuaded DIARMUID to bring me to this house, and, but for this I would not have come.

GRANIA.

It was well that you came. Men who are so great as FINN and DIARMUID must be friends. My father fears a landing of the men of Lochland, and I am weary of this

there is nothing but the rising and the setting of the sun and the grazing of flocks and herds.

FINN.

Did you send for me because you are weary of this valley.

GRANIA.

I wanted to see you because of your greatness. I loved DIARMID – he was young and comely and you seemed to me tobe old, you were grey.

[73^{r}]

70

FINN.

I am seven years older now, and my hair is greyer – I must seem very old to you know.

GRANIA.

No, you seem younger, as you stand there as you lean upon your spear you seem to me a young man. I do not think of your grey hair any longer.

FINN.

That day in Tara you would not wear your ornaments, but now you wear them.

~~GRANIA~~.

(DIARMID comes slowly down the stage)

DIARMID.

What have you to say to one another; what were you saying to GRANIA, FINN, I can see by GRANIA'S face that she is but little pleased to see me again.

GRANIA.

Why do you say this? What has happened, DIARMID? That shepherd said the wolf had killed twenty sheep.

73^{r}, l. 2 know] Washington 68/fol. 70^{r} and Berg(99) 61/fol. 63^{r} both give "now", correctly.

7–8 An attempt to erase the type-deleted part ascription has smudged onto the word "slowly" beneath.

valley where there is nothing but the rising and the setting of the sun and the grazing of flocks and herds.

FINN.

Did you send for me because you are weary of this valley?

GRANIA.

I wanted to see you because of your greatness. I loved DIARMUID – he was young and comely and you seemed to me to be old, you were grey.

FINN.

I am seven years older now, and my hair is greyer – I must seem very old to you now.

GRANIA.

No, you seem younger, as you stand there as you lean upon your spear you seem to me a young man. I do not think of your grey hair any longer.

FINN.

That day in Tara you would not wear your ornaments, but now you wear them.

[64r]

(62)

(DIARMUID comes slowly down the stage)

DIARMUID.

What have you to say to one another; what were you saying to GRANIA, FINN, I can see be GRANIA'S face that she is but little pleased to see me again.

GRANIA.

Why do you say this? What has happened, DIARMUID? That shepherd said the wolf had killed twenty sheep.

[74^{r}]

71

DIARMID.

There is no wolf in the thicket; they do not know what they are hunting. (Enter CONAN.) No matter whether it be a wolf or a boar that is hiding there, I have come in to find you and FINN talking together in a way that is not to my liking. (Cormac & the Feanna enter)

FINN.

Was it to watch me, DIARMID, that you came back again? And would you not have me speak to GRANIA? As you will then. (Turning to CONAN) CONAN is listening. What has he to say about this beast that has gored twenty sheep?

CONAN.

And DIARMID has come back again because he saw it was a boar and not a wolf, and he remembered that day in Tara, when I told him he is to go out hunting a boar and be killed by it, and DIARMID is to be torn by the tusks, he is to be bloody. his face shall be foul because it shall be bloody. I told him these things in Tara, and he remembers them, that is why he has not gone out hunting.

DIARMID.

FINN has contrived the trap for me, but I shall not fall into it. There can be no peace between FINN and me'

[75^{r}]

72

FINN.

(Who draws his sword) By the drawing of his sword, DIARMID has broken the peace I gave him, and the sight of GRANIA has brought to mind all the wrongs he has done me.

GRANIA.

To you, FINN, I say that I would not have sent for you had I thought that the broil would begin again – To you, DIARMID, I say that I will speak to what man I please, that no man shall thwart me – Where is my father? (Turning

---

74^{r}, l. 5 The insertion is seamlessly incorporated into Washington 69/fol. 71^{r}. It is made with a later type insertion in Berg(99) 62/fol. 64^{r}.

DIARMUID.

There is no wolf in the thicket; they do not know what they are hunting. (Enter CONAN) No matter whether it be a wolf or a boar that is hiding there, I have come in~~t~~ to find you and FINN talking together in a way that is not to my liking. (CORMAC and the FIANNA enter)

FINN.

Was it to watch me, DIARMUID,that you came back again? And would you not have me speak to GRANIA? As you will then. (Turning to CONAN CONAN is listening. What has he to say about this beast that has gored twenty sheep?

CONAN.

And DIARMUID has come back again because he saw it was a boar and not a wolf, and he remembered that day in Tara, when I told him he is to go out hunting a boar and be killed by it, and DIARMUID is to be torn by the tusks, he is to be bloody, his face shall be foul because it shall be bloody. I told him these things in Tara, and he remembers them, that is why he has not gone out hunting.

[65r]

(63)

DIARMUID.

FINN has contrived the trap for me, but I shall not fall into it? There can be no peace between FINN and me.

FINN.

(Who draws his sword) By the drawing of his sword DIARMUID has broken the peace I gave him, and the sight of GRANIA has brought to mind all the wrongs he has done me.

GRANIA.

To you, FINN, I say that I would not have sent for you had I thoughttthat the broil would begin again – To you, DIARMUID, I say that I will speak to what man I please, that no man shall thwart me – Where is my father? (Turning

---

64r, l. 9 Type deletion.

10 The stage direction is inserted with bright blue ribbon.

suddenly towards them) No, I will not have you fight for me, forbid them, father. (She goes to CORMAC.)

DIARMID.

Our swords shall decide between us, I shall slay you, FINN.

FINN.

One of us two shall die – (They draw their swords, and the FIANNA rush between them)

GOLL.

FINN and DIARMID cannot fight – fling up their swords, thrust the spear between them. Has FINN forgotten the blood bond? He who raises his hand against the blood bond raises his hand against the gods.

[76r]

73

CONAN.

(Coming towards them) If FINN and DIARMID cannot fight with one another, let them hunt the boar, and let GRANIA be given to him who kills it – AOGNHUS, who watches over lovers and hunters shall decide between them– (DIARMID lifts his sword to strike. Leaving her father GRANIA comes forward.)

GRANIA.

He is not worthy enough for you to strike him – give me your sword.

FINN.

(Standing in front of CONAN) No, GRANIA, he shall not die, he has spoken the truth – FINN and DIARMID love the one woman.

CONAN.

A tale I once told him has given him no stomach for the hunting of a boar.

FERGUS.

The boar is bigger than any beast I ever saw.

CRIFFAN.

It is certainly no mortal beast.

suddenly towards them) No, I will not have you fight for me, forbid them, father. (She goes to CORMAC)

DIARMUID.

Our swords shall decide between us. I shall slay you, FINN.

FINN.

One of us two shall die – (They draw their swords and the FIANNA rush between them)

GOLL.

FINN and DIARMUID cannot fight – fling up their swords, thrust the spear between them. Has FINN forgotten the blood-bond? He who raises his hand against the blood-bond raises his hand against the gods.

[66^{r}]

(64)

CONAN.

(Coming towards them) If FINN and DIARMUID cannot fight with one another, let them hunt the boar, and let GRANIA be given to him who kills it – AOGNHUS who watches over lovers and hunters shall decide between them – (DIARMUID lifts his sword to strike. Leaving her father GRANIA comes forward)

GRANIA.

He is not worthy enough for you to strike him – give me your sword.

FINN.

(Standing in front of CONAN) No, GRANIA, he shall not die, he has spoken the truth – FINN and DIARMUID love the one woman.

CONAN.

A tale I once told him has given him no stomach for the hunting of a boar.

FERGUS.

The boar is bigger than any beast I ever saw.

CRIFFAN.

It is certainly no mortal beast.

[77ʳ]

74

DIARMID.

What was its colour, was it covered with bristles?

CONAN.

I saw it; it was black and bristless – (He goes over and stands by DIARMID) FINN, CAOELTE,USHEEN look at us; there is one terror in the heart of DIARMID and CONAN.

CRIFFAN.

I saw it too, it was dark like the sea, and it made a noise like the sea in a storm.

FINN.

We listen to the idle tales of Spearmen – whatever the colour of the beast may be we shall slay it – (The FIANNA move up the stage) CONAN has spoken well. DIARMID has little stomach for this hunting. Why did he ask for the blood bond? It was not √ I who went to him – it was he who came to me with his hand pricked with his dagger. These *16* **are the only wounds he will dare. This blood bond keeps him from my sword and he speaks of an old tale that he may not go to the hunt – DIARMID is craven.**

[78ʳ]

75

DIARMID.

FINN lies; he knows why I will not go to this hunt. He seeks my death because he loves GRANIA.

FERGUS.

If DIARMID does not go to this hunt DIARMID is craven.

CRIFFAN.

FINN has said it, he is craven.

CAOELTE.

DIARMID must not go to this hunt. You have done wickedly this day, CONAN, and after your kind.

77ʳ, l. 12 The significance of the pencil tick and numeral is undetermined. They might be later additions.

DIARMUID.

What was its colour, was it covered with bristles?

[67r]

(65)

CONAN.

I saw it; it was black and bristless – (He goes over and stands by DIARMUID) FINN, CAOELTE, USHEEN look at us; there is one terror in the heart of DIARMUID and CONAN.

CRIFFAN.

I saw it too; it was dark like the sea, and it made a noise like the sea in a storm.

FINN.

We listen to the idle tales of Spearmen – whatever the colour of the beast may be we shall slay it – (The FIANNA move up the stage) CONAN has spoken well. DIARMUID has little stomach for this hunting. Why did he ask for the blood bond? It was not I who went to him it was he who came to me with his hand pricked with his dagger. These are the only wounds he will dare. This blood bond keeps him from my sword and he speaks of an old tale that he may not go to the hunt. DIARMUID is craven.

DIARMUID.

FINN lies; he knows ahy I will not go to this hunt. He seeks my death because he loves GRANIA.

FERGUS,

If DIARMUID does not go to this hunt DIARMUID is ~~craven~~ a coward**.**

CRIFFAN.

FINN has said it, he is ~~craven~~ a coward**.**

CAOELTE.

DIARMUID must not go to this hunt. You have done wickedly this day, CONAN, and after your kind.

FATHNA.

He has a hare's heart. The gods have given him a hare's heart.

FINN.

Take up your spears we will go against this beast, let him who will stay behind.

DIARMID.

Go against the boar, but it shall be as if you hunted the sea or the wind. Your spears shall break, and your hounds fly and whimper at your heels – (Exeunt all except GRANIA, CORMAC and DIARMID – after a moment's pause a horn is heard in the distance – DIARMID takes a spear from the wall.

[79r]

76

GRANIA.

Why do you take your spear – you will not go to this hunt hunt?

DIARMID.

This beast came to slay us. This hunt will sweep over us. It is coming through the woods, and I shall be caught up like a leaf. (They bar the door and stand listening.)

GRANIA.

They said the boar ran into the woods – it will have gone into the mountain before this.

DIARMID.

The things to come are like the wind; they could sweep this house away. This image of death is coming like the wind – who knows what enchantment has called it out of the earth? It was no here yesterday; it was not here at noon. I have hunted deer in these woods and have not seen the slot of natural or unatural swine – No, it will not bear thinking of. I am caught in this valley like a wolf in a

---

79r, l. 11 no] Correctly given as "not" in Washington 74/fol. 76r and Berg(99) 67/fol. 69r.

[68r]

(66)

FATHNA.

He has a hare's heart. The gods have given him a hare's heart.

FINN.

Take up your spears we will go against this beast let him who will stay behind.

DIARMUID.

Go against the boar, but it shall be as if you hunted the sea or the wind. Your spears shall break and your hounds fly and whimper at your heels – (Exeunt all except GRANIA, CORMAC and DIARMUID – after a moment's pause a horn is heard in the distance – DIARMUID takes a spear from the wall.)

GRANIA.

Why do you take your spear – you will not go to this hunt?

DIARMUID.

This beast came to slay us. This hunt will sweep over us. It is coming through the woods,and I shall be caught up like a leaf. (They bar the door and stand listening)

GRANIA.

They said the boar ran into the woods – it will have gone into the mountain before this.

[69r]

(67)

DIARMUID.

The things to come are like the wind; they could sweep this house away. This image of death is coming like the wind – who knows what enchantment has called it out of the earth? It was not here yesterday; it was not here at noon. I have hunted deer in these woods and have not seen the slot of natural or unnatural swine, No, it will not bear thinking of. I am caught in this

pit – (<u>Pause</u>) CORMAC you sit there like a stone, why did you do this? You came here with a tale about the men of Lochlann but you were on the gods business.

[80^{r}]

77

CORMAC.

I gave you this valley to be happy in.

DIARMID.

When we are about to die the gods give us more than we ask, There has been too much happiness here for our hunger, and I would roll up the broken meats in a sack for you to carry them away.

GRANIA.

That tale has shaken your mind.

DIARMID.

Then you do not believe in it.

GRANIA.

Wc bclievc, wc disbclievc, and there is a time when we do not what we think.

DIARMID.

We are always on the gods business. CORMAC in crafti-ness, you in lust; they put lust into women's bodies that men may not defy the gods who made them – I too, shall be on their business in this hunting.

[81^{r}]

78

GRANIA.

You are not going to this hunting.

DIARMID.

I see many ornaments upon you – How long is it since you have worn them for me? – You have not worn them . . …. we are common to one another night and day.

79^{r}, l. 17 Lochlann] Washington 74/fol. 76^{r} gives "Lochland"; Berg(99) 67/fol. 69^{r} mistakenly repeats HRC.

valley like a wolf in a pit – (Pause) CORMAC you sit there like a stone, why did you do this? You came here with a tale about the men of Lochlann but you were on the gods business.

CORMAC.

I gave you this valley to be happy in.

DIARMUID.

When we are about to die the gods give us more than we ask. There has been too much happiness here for our hunger, and I would rool up the broken meats in a sack for you to carry them away.

GRANIA.

That tale has shaken your mind.

DIARMUID.

Then you do not believe it?

GRANIA.

We believe, we disbelieve, and there is a time when we do not what we think.

[70r]

(68)

DIARMUID.

We are always on the gods business. CORMAC in craftiness, you in lust; they put lust into women's bodies that men may not defy the gods who made them – I too, shall be on their business in this hunting.

GRANIA.

You are not going to this hunting.

DIARMUID.

I see many ornaments upon you – How long is it since you have worn them for me? – You have not worn them . . . we are common to one another night and day.

GRANIA.

Take your Broad Edge, your heavy spear – Take your heavy shield.

DIARMID.

No man shall say DIARMID went to this hunting with his battle gear upon him. (Exit)

GRANIA.

He is gone to this hunting – he is gone that he may give me to FINN – (She turns her face towards the wall and weeps.)

CORMAC.

Have you ceased to love him? (GRANIA walks a few steps towards her father as if she were going to speak but her emotion overpowers her, and she returns to the same place.) If you have not ceased to love him follow him and bring him back.

[82^r]

79

GRANIA.

I will folow him in the woods; he will take the path under the oak trees. (Exit GRANIA)

CORMAC.

(Coming down the stage) LABAN, LABAN. (He goes towards the wheel and takes the ~~spindle~~ distaff **in his hand.) There is no more flax in the ~~spindle~~** distaff **– ~~LABAN, LABAN~~! (Going to the door at the side) They have all followed the hunters – there is nobody in the house – But LABAN must be here – LABAN! LABAN! (Exit and Curtain.)**

82^r, ll. 3–8 Both Washington 75/fol. 77^r and Berg(99) 69/fol. 71^r seamlessly incorporate the revisions.

GRANIA.

Take your Broad Edge, your heavy spear – take your heavy shield.

DIARMUID.

No man shall say DIARMUID went to this hunting with his battle gear upon him. (Exit)

GRANIA.

He is gone to this hunting – he is gone that he may give me to FINN – (She turns her face towards the wall and weeps)

CORMAC.

Have you ceased to love him? (GRANIA walks a few steps towards her father as if she were going to speak, but her emotion over-powers her, and she returns to the same place.) If you have not ceased to love him follow him and bring him back.

[71r]

(69)

GRANIA.

I will follow him in the woods; he will take the path under the oak trees. (Exit GRANIA)

CORMAC.

(Coming down the stage) LABAN! LABAN! (Going to the door at the side) They have all followed the hunters – there is nobody in the house – but LABAN must be here – LABAN! LABAN! (He goes towards the wheel and takes the distaff in his hand) There is no more flax in the distaff.

----------- ---------------

END ACT II.

71r The only page with holograph numbering following the continuous sequence up to p. 58/fol. 60r. It is impossible to know if it is a substitution, but note that it rewrites the corresponding passage in HRC (p. 79/ fol. 82r).

[83r]

80

DIARMID AND GRANIA.

ACT III.

Scene. The wooded slopes of Ben Bulben. DIARMID is sleeping under a tree. It is night, but the dawn is beginning to break – Enter two peasants.

OLD MAN.

There has been no such night as this these fifty years.

YOUNG MAN.

How the wind rages, like the dragon or maybe it is the dragon himself. Listen, a tree has fallen.

OLD MAN.

It is only the wind, I have seen sind like this before, and then the sheep were lost in the torrent.

YOUNG MAN.

I met a herdsman whose cattle had broken out of their byres, and fifty drowned themselves in the lake.

OLD MAN.

The FIANNA frightened them – the FIANNA came into the forest at midnight sounding their horns.

[84r]

81

YOUNG MAN.

And at midnight I saw two hosts fighting, one host flying and one following, and among them that were flying an old one armed man.

OLD MAN.

That was Diarmid's grandfather he has been dead this fifty years.

[72r]

(70)

DIARMUID and GRANIA.

ACT III.

Scene: The wooded slopes of Ben Bulben. DIARMUID is sleeping under a tree. It is night, but the dawn is beginning to break – Enter two peasants.

OLD MAN.

There has been no such night as this these fifty years.

YOUNG MAN.

How the wind rages, like the dragon or maybe it is the dragon himself. Listen, a tree has fallen.

OLD MAN.

It is only the wind, I have seen wind like this before, and then the sheep were lost in the torrent.

YOUNG MAN.

I met a herdsman whose cattle had broken out of their byres, and fifty drowned themselves in the lake.

OLD MAN.

The FIANNA frightened them – the FIANNA came into the forest at midnight sounding their horns.

YOUNG MAN.

And at midnight I saw two hosts fighting, one host flying and one following and among them that were flying an old one-armed man.

OLD MAN.

That was DIARMUID'S grandfather he has been dead this fifty years.

YOUNG MAN.

But I saw something more.

OLD MAN.

What did you see boy?

YOUNG MAN.

A gaunt grey ragged man, and he was driving this beast the FIANNA are hunting. He drove it along the edge of the mountain prodding it before him with a spear.

OLD MAN.

That was the god AOGNHUS – He watches over DIARMID. the deaths of all these great men are foretold, and the end of the FIANNA. They will perish as their forefathers did when CAIRBRE CATHEAD called the folk together and broke their power for two hundred years.

[85^{r}]

82

YOUNG MAN.

Tell me about CAIRBRE CATHEAD.

OLD MAN.

Not now we must go in search for our sheep – If I have lost my ram my ewes will be useless to me. We must go now for at day-break the FIANNA will be sounding their horns. They were sounding them till the moon went down – It was they who frightened my sheep.

YOUNG MAN.

But this hunting, will the boar be killed?

OLD MAN.

It is no great matter to us, maybe a little less damage, to our fields that is all. The seasons will be none the better, the cows will have no more milk in their udders – and my lambs there will be no lambs next year.

85^{r}, l. 2 for] Washington 78/fol. 80^{r} has "of"—like NLI 8777(3) c 3/fol. 83^{r}. Berg(99) 71/fol. 73^{r} has "for".

[73r]

(71)

YOUNG MAN.

But I saw something more.

OLD MAN.

What did you~~s~~ see boy?

YOUNG MAN.

A gaunt grey ragged man, and he was driving this beast the FIANNA are hunting. He drove it along the edge of the mountain prodding it before him with a spear.

OLD MAN.

That was the god AOGNHUS – He watches over DIARMUID. The deaths of all these great men are foretold, and the end of the FIANNA. They will perish as their forefathers did when CAIRBRE CATHEAD called the folk together and broke their power for two hundred years.

YOUNG MAN.

Tell me about CAIRBRE CATHEAD.

OLD MAN.

Not now we must go in search for our sheep – If I have lost my ram my ewes will be useless to me. We must go now for at day-break the FIANNA will be sounding their horns They were sounding them till the moon went down – It was they who frightened my sheep.

YOUNG MAN.

But this hunting, will the boar be killed?

OLD MAN.

It is no great metter to us, maybe a little less damage to our fields that is all. The seasons will be none the

[74r]

(72)

better, the cows will have no more milk in their udders – and my lambs there will be no lambs next year.

73r, l. 2 Type deletion.

YOUNG MAN.

When the FIANNA have killed the boar they will give us some parts of it.

OLD MAN.

The FIANNA have no thoughts for such as we, all thatthey do not eat of the boar they will throw to their dogs – they would not think it well for us to taste meat. They beat back the invader when they can and it is more than our lives

[86r]

83

are worth to pick up a dead hare from the path.

YOUNG MAN.

Hush, there is a man sleeping under the tree – If we do not wake him the beast may come upon him sleeping.

OLD MAN.

Better do nothing, we must not do anything against the gods. The god AOGNHUS will save him if it be pleasing to him to do so, or he may call him away. Let us begone, boy let us find our sheep. (Exit)

DIARMID.

They croak like ravens over carrion – croak, croak, croak. (Enter GRANIA)

GRANIA.

I have sought you all night. I have been wandering in the woods since the moon went down.

DIARMID.

What have you come for?

GRANIA.

I was afraid and have been running; give me time to draw my breath.

YOUNG MAN.

When the FIANNA have killed the boar they will give us some parts of it.

OLD MAN.

The FIANNA have no thoughts for such as we, all that they do not eat of the boar they will throw to their dogs – they would not think it well for us to taste meat. They beat back the invader when they can, and it is more than our lives ~~as~~ are worth to pick up a dead hare from the path.

YOUNG MAN.

Hush, there is a man sleeping under the tree– If we do not wake him the beast may come upon him sleeping.

OLD MAN.

Better do nothing, we must do nothing against the gods. The god AOGNHUS will save him if it be pleasing to him to do so, or he may call him away. Let us begone, boy, let us find our sheep. (Exit)

DIARMUID.

They croak like ravens over carrion – croak, croak, croak, (Enter GRANIA)

GRANIA.

I have sought you all night. I have been wandering in the woods since the moon went down.

DIARMUID.

What have you come for?

[75r]

(73)

GRANIA.

I was afraid and have been running; give me time to draw my breath.

74r, l. 9 Type deletion.

[87^{r}]

84

DIARMID.

Your hair is down and your hands are torn with brambles.

GRANIA.

Yes, look st my hands, and I am so weary, DIARMID. I am so weary that I could lie down and die here. That mossy bank is like a bed; lay me down there. Oh, I have come to bring you home with me.

DIARMID.

And you show me torn hands, and you hold out to me wet hair, and would have me go home. You talk of dying, too, and would have me lay you on this bank. But what good is there in all this, GRANIA, for I have no time to listen.

GRANIA.

Give up this hunting for I have had warning that you will die if you do not turn back. Turn before we lose ourselves in the darkness of the woods.

DIARMID.

I am in a little way that leads to darkness, but what does that matter to you, GRANIA? Your way home winds along the hill, and down into the valley; my way is a different way, a shorter way, and the morrows that men live frighten me more than this short way. I have no heart for that crook ed road of morrows.

[88^{r}]

85

GRANIA.

(Wringing her hands) Come to our home, DIARMID, come to our house.

DIARMID.

All the roads, the straight road and the crooked road, lead to blackness. If blackness be the end and there isno light beyond it? But what have such questions to do with me? Whatever road I am on I will walk firmly with my sword

---

87^{r}, l. 2 st] Washington 80/fol. 82^{r} and Berg(99) 73/fol. 75^{r} have "at".

DIARMUID.

Your hair is down and your hands are torn with brambles.

GRANIA.

Yes, look at my hands, and I am so weary DIARMUID. I am so weary that I could lie down and die here. That mossy bank is like a bed; lay me down there. Oh, I have come to bring you home with me.

DIARMUID.

And you show me your torn hands, and you hold out to me wet hair, and would have me go home. You talk of dying, too, and would have me lay you on this bank. But what good is there in all this, GRANIA, for I have no time to listen.

GRANIA.

Give up this hunting for I have had warning that you will die if you do not turn back. Turn before we lose ourselves in the darkness of the woods.

DIARMUID.

I am in a little way that leads to darkness, but what does that matter to you, GRANIA? Your way home winds along the hill, and down into the valley; my way is a different way, a shorter way, and the morrows that men live frighten me more than this short way. I have no heart for that crooked road of morrows.

[76r]

(74)

GRANIA.

(Wringing her hands) Come to our home, DIARMUID, come to our house.

DIARMUID.

All the roads, the straight road and the crooked road, lead to blackness. If blackness be the end and there is no light beyond it? But what have such questions to do with me? Whatever road I am on I will walk firmly with

out – (He draws his sword) But you have come to tell me something. What is it? Out with it quickly for the day is breaking, and when it is broken there will be hunting.

GRANIA.

I have come to ask you to go home with me.

DIARMID.

You would have me in the straight road, and so you have come to tell me that I am in it. For it is certain that a man walks where he thinks he walks. The mind makes all; we will talk of that some day. I tell you that you are lying to me. I am not in the road that leads on and on, and then shatters under one's feet, and becomes flying bits of darkness.

[89r]

86

GRANIA.

DIARMID, you are going straight upon your death, if you do not come back with me.

DIARMID.

What do you know of all this that you come like a soothsayer? Who has been whispering in your ear? Who has sent you to me?

GRANIA.

I had a warning last night.

DIARMID.

From that old woman who spins? I tell you I have had enough of her warnings. I saw her last night carrying a bundle of new flax through the woods.

GRANIA.

No, DIARMID, I left her in the house.

DIARMID.

I tell you I saw her. She is going somewhere on

my sword out – (<u>He draws his sword</u>) But you have come to tell me something. What is it? Out with it quickly for the day is breaking, and when it is broken there will be hunting.

GRANIA.

I have cometo ask you to go home with me.

DIARMUID.

You would have me in the straight road, and so you have come to tell me that I am in it. For it is certain that man walks where he thinks he walks. The mind makes all; we will talk of that some day. I tell you that you are lying to me. I am not in the road that leads on and on, and then shatters under one's feet, and becomes flying bits of darkness.

GRANIA.

DIARMUID you are going straight upon your death, If you do not come back with me.

DIARMUID.

What do you know of all this that you come like a

[77r]

(75)

soothsayer? Who has been whispering in your ear? Who has sent you to me?

GRANIA.

I had a warning last night.

DIARMUID.

From that old woman who spins? I tell you I have had enough of her warnings. I saw her last night carrying a bundle of new flax through the woods.

GRANIA.

No, DIARMUID, I left her in the house,

DIARMUID.

I tell you I saw her. She is going somewhere on

Transferred to page 6.

some evil work. X I have heard that there are women who live seven hundred years in the woods, spinning the threads of the long lived people of the woods, and then seven hundred years spinning for men. She is one of them. X But where is she going with the new flax? What have you come to tell me about her?

[90r]

87

GRANIA.

I have come to tell you of a dream that came to me last night,

DIARMID.

Well, what did the dream tell you?

GRANIA.

I dreamt I was sitting by FINN.

DIARMID.

I do not think muchof that dream, for I saw you yesterday walking with FINN and holding his hands.

GRANIA.

But I dreamed I was sitting by FINN, and that your shield was hanging among the shields of the slain over our heads.

DIARMID.

Did you not say it was a bad dream? I have heard worse dreams than that. Ah, foolish gods, can you find nothing better than the dreams of an unfaithful wife to vex and shake my will.

[91r]

88

GRANIA.

Do not blaspheme against the gods for they are near

89r, ll. 12–15 The words are encircled in pencil. Washington 82/fol. 84r incorporates the change seamlessly; Berg(99) 75/fol. 77r gives the lines as here—but type deleted afterward—as well as incorporating them on what is probably a replacement page (p. 6/fol. 8r).

90r, l. 5 A pencil separator has been inserted between the two joined words; cf. fol. 64r above.

some evil work. ~~I have heard that there are women who live several hundred years in the woods, spinning the threads of the long lived people of the woods, and then seven hundred years spinning for men. She is one of them~~. But where is she going with the new flax? What have you come to tell me about her?

GRANIA.

I have come to tell you of a dream that came to me last night.

DIARMUID.

Well, what did the dream tell you?

GRANIA.

I dreamt I was sitting by FINN.

[78^{r}]

(76)

DIARMUID.

I do not think much of that dream, for I saw you yesterday walking with FINN and holding his hands.

GRANIA.

But I dreamed I was sitting by FINN, and that your shield was hanging among the shields of the slain over our heads.

DIARMUID.

Did you ~~tel~~ not say it was a bad dream? I have heard worst dreams than that. Ah, foolish gods, can you find nothing better than the dreams of an unfaithful wife to vex and shake my will.

GRANIA.

Do not blaspheme against the gods for they are near

77^{r}, ll. 9–12 Type deletions in bright blue ribbon. These are the lines GM transferred to Berg(99) 6/fol. 8^{r}: cf. HRC 6, 86/fols. 9^{r}, 89^{r}.

78^{r}, l. 6 Type deletion.

to us now. I have been praying to them to spare you. I have been praying to them all night, while I looked for you.

DIARMID.

Yes every man is a god in heaven, and on earth we are the hurly balls they drive hither and thither – Oh, they are great hurly players. The canauns are never out of their hands. All night I have heard them laughing. I tell you I have heard them laughing. Do you not hear me? Do you not hear me?

GRANIA.

I heard, but oh, DIARMID, take my hands and touch my hair, they may bring some memory to your mind, some softness to your heart.

DIARMID.

Yes, yes, I remember well enough. Your hands and your hair were sweet to me long ago. No, no yesterday, even yesterday. Let me see your hands. They are beautiful hands, torn as they are. No wonder I love them; and this hair too. You loved me once, GRANIA, you loved me better than FINN. I remember it all the day before yesterday.

[92^{r}]

89

GRANIA.

I love you still, DIARMID.

DIARMID.

My dear one, why did you send me to FINN? It may be that my words have been a little wild. Speak quickly do not be afraid.

GRANIA.

I sent you to FINN, because I wanted you to live among the FIANNA as before you saw me.

91^{r}, l. 11 heard] Washington 83/fol. 85^{r} has "hear"—like NLI 8777(3) c 8/ fol. 88^{r}. Berg(99) 76/fol. 78^{r} has "heard you".

to us now. I have been praying to them to spare you. I have been praying to them all night, while I looked for you.

DIARMUID.

Yes, every man is a god in heaven, and one earth we are the hurly balls they drive hither and thither – Oh, they are great hurly players. The canauns are never out of their hands. All night I have heard them laughing. I tell you I have heard them laughing. Do you not hear me? Do you not hear me?

GRANIA.

I heard you, but oh, DIARMUID, take my hands and touch my hair, they may bring some memory to your mind, some soft-

[79^r]

(77)

softness to your heart.

DIARMUID.

Yes, yes I remember well enough. Your hands and your hair were sweet to me long ago. No, no yesterday, even yesterday. Let me see your hands. They are beautiful hands, torn as they are. No wonder I love them; and this hair too, You loved me once, GRANIA, you loved me better than FINN. I remember it all the day before yesterday.

GRANIA.

I love you still DIARMUID.

DIARMUID.

My dear one, why did you send me to FINN? It may be that my words have been a little wild. Speak quickly do not be afraid.

GRANIA.

I sent you to FINN because I wanted you to live among the FIANNA as before yous saw me.

78^r, l. 14 Type deletion.
79^r, l. 14 Type deletion.

DIARMID.

All you say is true'

GRANIA.

I wanted you to be friends with FINN, because your love had become a sickness, a madness.

DIARMID.

Yes, yes it has become a madness. But it is a l long while GRANIA, since we were alone together.

GRANIA.

No, DIARMID not long.

[93^{r}]

90

DIARMID.

Yesterday is a long while and there may be no other time for wringing this secret from you – There was a thought of FINN in your mind when you sent me to him.

GRANIA.

There is no secret in me; I have told you every-thing. And I come through this wood by night, to bring you from this hunt, as a wife comes to her hus-band.

DIARMID.

GRANIA was not meant to sit by the fireside with children on her knees. The gods made her womb bar-ren because she was not meant to hold children on her knees. The gods gave her a barren womb hungry and barren like the sea. She looked from the red apple in her hand to the green apple on the bough. She looked from me to FINN, even shen she first lusted for me, and after FINN there will be come other. The malignant gods made your beauty, GRANIA, Your hand is very weak, your arm is weak and fragile.

93^{r}, l. 15 shen] Washington 85/fol. 87^{r} has "then"; Berg(99) 78/fol. 80^{r} has "when"—like NLI 8777(3) c, fol. 90^{r}.

16 be come other.] Berg(99) 78/fol. 80^{r} also has "be come other". Washington 85/fol. 87^{r} has "be others" and earlier texts have "some other"—which is probably intended. See introduction, part v.

DIARMUID.

All you say is true.

GRANIA.

I wanted you to be friends with FINN because your love had become a sickness, a madness.

DIARMUID.

Yes, yes, I has become a madness. But it is a long while GRANIA since we were alone together.

[80r]

(78)

GRANIA.

No, DIARMUID not long.

DIARMUID.

Yesterday is a long while, and there may be no other time for wringing this secret from you – There was a thought of FINN in your mind when you sent me to him.

GRANIA.

There is no secret in me: I have told you every-thing. And I come through this wood by night to bring you from this hunt as a wife comes to her husband.

DIARMUID.

GRANIA was not meant to sit by the fireside with child-ren on her knees. The gods made her womb barren because she was not meant to hold children on her knees. The gods gave her a barren womb hungry and barren like the sea. The looked from the red apple in her hand to the green apple on the bough. She looked from me to FINN, even when she first lusted for me, and after FINN there will be come other. The malignant gods made your beauty, GRANIA, your hand is very weak, your arm is weak and fragile. Your

Your hair is very soft, (He takes her by the hair) I could kill you as easily as I could kill a flower by the wayside.

[94^{r}]

91

GRANIA.

Kill me if you will, kill me with your sword, here in my breast.

DIARMID.

You would have me kill you. Maybe if I killed you all would be well.

GRANIA.

Hold fast my hair, draw back my head and kill me. I would have you do it – (Pause) Why do you not do it? If you would go to this hunting you must do it, for while I live you shall not go.

DIARMID.

Let go my spear I say, let go my spear, if you would have your life. I see that you are thinking of FINN this very moment. I see thoughts of FINN in your eyes. Let me go, or I will let the lust out of you with this sword point.

GRANIA.

Kill me, DIARMID, I would have you do it.

DIARMID.

And leave this white body like a cut flower on the wayside.

[95^{r}]

92

GRANIA.

Kill me, DIARMID.

DIARMID.

I have heard the gods laugh, and I have been merry, but if I killed you I would remember everything. And I

94^{r}, l. 2 breast] So too in Washington 85/fol. 87^{r}. Berg(99) 78/fol. 80^{r} has "breasts".

hair is very soft. (He takes her by the hair) I could kill you as easily as I could kill a flower by the wayside.

GRANIA.

Kill me if you will, kill me with your sword, here in my breasts.

DIARMUID.

You would have me kill you. Maybe if I killed you all would be well.

[81r]

(79)

GRANIA.

Hold fast my hair, draw back my head and kill me. I would have you do it – (Pause) Why do you not do it? If you would go to this hunting you must do it, for ~~a~~ while I live you shall not go.

DIARMID.

Let go my spear, let go my spear, if you would have your life. I see that you are thinking of FINN this very moment. I see thoughts of FINN in your eyes. Let me go or I will let the lust out of you with this sword point.

GRANIA.

Kill me DIARMUID, I would have you do it.

DIARMUID.

And leave this body like a cut flower on the wayside.

GRANIA.

Kill me DIARMUID.

DIARMUID.

I have heard the gods laugh, and I have been merry, but if I killed you I would remember everything. And I

81r, l. 3 Type deletion.

should wander in the woods seeing white and red flowers – After killing you I might kill myself – Oh, that would be a good thing to do. But seeing you there, your soft hair spattered with blood, and your white hands stained with blood I might not remember to do it. I might remember nothing but yesterday and to-day. I cannot kill you. I would not see your blood nor touch your hands. Your lips and teeth, and all this beauty I have loved seem in my eyes no better than a yellow pestilence. GRANIA, GRANIA, out of my sight – (He goes out driving her before him – a moment after he returns alone.) That is over, let me think. Yes, yes, there is a beast coming that I am to kill. I should take him so,upon my spear. The spear will be my best weapon, but the hand must be steady beneath it. If the point slipped he would be upon me. Maybe it will be better to let him run upon my shield and kill him with my sword, while he digs his tusks into my shield. My danger will be the darkness, for the darkness makes the hand shake, and day breaks but slowly. Higher up in the woods there is a little more light – (He goes out –

[96r]

93

(Enter CAOELTE and USHEEN.)

CAOELTE.

We have hardly escaped with our lives. The branches touched me as the tree fell.

USHEEN.

What made that great ash tree fall?

CAOELTE'

The wind had lulled and yet it crashed across our way as if it would kill us.

USHEEN.

I heard a thud and a crackling of branches before it fell, as though a great rock had been thrown against it, though I saw nothing, and for some time I had heard crashings in the woods. I think that hosts have been hurling rocks at one another. All night there has been fighting

should wander in the woods seeing white and red flowers. After killing you I might kill myself – Oh, that would be a good thing to do. But seeing you there, your soft hair spattered with blood, and your white hands stained with blood I might not remember to do it. I might remember nothing but yesterday and to-day. I cannot kill you. I would not see your blood nor touch your hands. Your lips and teeth, and all this beauty I have loved seem in

[82r]

(80)

my eyes no better than a yellow pestilence. GRANIA, GRANIA out of my sight – (He goes out driving her before him – a moment after he returns alone.) That is over, let me think. Yes, yes there is a beast coming that I am to kill. I should take him so, upon my spear. The spear will be my best weapon, but the hand must be steady beneath it. If the point slipped he would be upon me. Maybe it will be better to let him run upon my shield and kill him with my sword, while he digs his tusks into my shield. My danger will be the darkness, for the darkness makes the hand shake and day breaks but slowly. Higher up in the woods there is a little more light – (He goes out – Enter CAOELTE and USHEEN)

CAOELTE.

We have hardly escaped with our lives. The branches touched me as the tree fell.

USHEEN.

What made that great ash tree fall?

CAOELTE.

The wind had lulled and yet it crashed across our way as if it would kill us.

USHEEN.

I heard a thud and a crackling of branches before it fell, as though a great rock had been thrown against it, though I saw nothing and for some time I heard crashing in the woods. I think that hosts have been hurling rocks at one another. All night there has been fighting on

on the earth, andin the air, and in the water.

CAOELTE.

Never was there such a night before. As I came by the river I saw swans fighting in the air, and three fell screaming into the tree tops.

USHEEN.

Have you seen how FINN'S hounds whimper at his heels.

[97r]

94

CAOELTE.

They whimper and cry till the touch of his hand gives them courage for a moment. They would not follow him at all were they not afraid of being left alone – (They walk to and fro – apause) That light must be the beginning of the day. A pale foolish light that makes the darkness worse. The sky and earth would turn to their old works again but they have been palsy struck. Let us put this darkness out of our mind. Find us something to talk of, USHEEN. Where is DIARMID?

DIARMID.

(Coming forward) DIARMID is here, waiting whatever may befall him. Tell FINN that though the mountain arose like an ox from sleep, and came against me, and though the clouds came like eagles, and the sea upon its feet that are without number, I would not turn from this hunting.

CAOELTE.

We have been seeking you. We would have you leave this hunting.

DIARMID.

It may be that you fear, and that FINN fears because of the falling of trees, and the screaming of swans, but I do not fear.

[83r]

(81)

the earth and in the air and in the water.

CAOELTE.

Never was there such a night before. As I came by the river I saw swans fighting in the air and three fell screaming into the tree tops.

USHEEN.

Have you seen how FINN'S hounds whimper at his heels.

CAOELTE.

They whimper and cry till the touch of his hand gives them courage for a moment. They would not follow him at all were they not afraid of being left alone – (They walk to and fro – A pause) That light must be the bginning of the day. A pale foolish light that makes the darkness worse. The sky and earth would turn to their old works again but they have been palsy struck. Let us put this darkness out of our mind. Find us something to talk of USHEEN. Where is DIARMUID?

DIARMUID.

(Coming forward) DIARMUID is here waiting whatever may befall him. Tell FINN that though the mountain arose like an ox from sleep and came against me and though the clouds came like eagles and the sea upon its feet that are without number, I would not turn from this hunting.

CAOELTE.

We have been seeking you. We would have you leave this hunting.

[84r]

(82)

DIARMUID.

It may be that you fear and that FINN fears because of the falling of trees and the screaming of swans but ~~I~~ do not fear.

84r, l. 2 The deletion is made with dark pencil.

[98^{r}]

95

CAOELTE.

Turn from this hunting, DIARMID.

DIARMID.

I would not, had I nothing but a reason no bigger than a pea, and I have weighty reasons.

CAOELTE.

It were no wonder if eve$\{^{n}_{r}$ we whose death at a hunt like this has not been foretold, should turn from this hunting. For we are following no mortal beast. A man who had been trapping otters followed the footmarks last night, not knowing what they were, and as he followed they grew greater and greater and further and further apart.

DIARMID.

The night is dark.

CAOELTE.

But thc footmarks were deep. Deeper than any made by a nortal beast.

DIARMID.

It came yesterday out of the woods like a blight, like a flood, like a toad stool, and now it grows bigger and bigger. But so much more the need for hunters. Goodbye, Comrades, goodbye. (Exit)

[99^{r}]

96

CAOELTE.

I would not follow where he has gone. He is among those broken rocks where I heard screams, and sounds as of battle. They say that dwarfs and worse things have their homes among those rocks.

98^{r}, l. 4 ever/n] The tail of the "r" has been extended downward to form an "n", with blue-black ink or perhaps pencil. Washington 89/fol. 91^{r} and Berg(99) 82/fol. 84^{r} both read "even".

CAOELTE.

Turn from this hunting DIARMUID.

DIARMUID.

I would not had I nothing but a reason no bigger than a pea and I have weighty reasons.

CAOELTE.

It were no wonder if even we whose death at a hunt like this has not been foretold, should turn from this hunting. For we are following no mortal beast. A man who had been trapping otters followed the footmarks last night no knowing what they were and as he followed they grew greater and greater and further and further apart.

DIARMUID.

The night is dark,

CAOELTE.

But the footmarks ~~are~~ were deep. Deeper than any made be a mortal beast.

DIARMUID.

It came yesterday out of the woods like a blight, like a flood, like a toad-stool and now it grows bigger and ~~higher~~ bigger. And so much more the need for hunters. Good-bye Comrades, goodbye.(Exit)

[85r]

(83)

CAOELTE.

I would not follow where he has gone. He is among those broken rocks where I heard screams and sounds as of battle. They say that dwarfs and worse things have their homes among those rocks.

84r, ll. 14, 18 Type deletions. In line 18, the typist made the substitution over what she had typed before canceling both and typing the revision afresh.

USHEEN.

He is.the only one among us who has not been shaken by this night of terror. Look, look something is coming this way.

CAOELTE.

A tall staff in his hand, and he moves noiselessly, and there is another following him.

USHEEN.

Draw your sword, CAOELTE.

CAOELTE.

It will not come out of its sheath. It is but a shepherd. We are craven and no better than CONAN. (Enter two peasants)

OLD MAN.

Be of good heart great deliverer of Eri. I am but a shepherd looking for his sheep, and not,as well might be, some bad thing out of the rocks.

[100r]

97

YOUNG MAN.

Can you tell me noble sirs of any strayed sheep, or what is troubling the water and the air over our heads?

CAOELTE.

We have been wandering in the dark all night. We are as blind as you are.

OLD MAN.

We must go, sirs, we must find our sheep or starve. (Exit peasants)

USHEEN.

Maybe he was laughing at us because he was afraid. We must wait here till we hear FINN'S horn. If we were to seek him we would lose him, and it may be never come alive out of the woods.

99r, l. 5 The first two words in the line are smudged, as if an erasure might have been made in the top (ribbon) copy.

USHEEN.

He is the only one among us who has not been shaken by this night of terror. Look, look something is coming this way.

CAOELTE.

A tall staff in his hand and he moves noiselessly and there is another following him.

USHEEN.

Draw your sword CAOELTE.

CAOELTE.

It will not come out of its sheath. It is but a shepherd. We are craven and no better than CONAN.
(<u>Enter two peasants</u>)

OLD MAN.

Be of good heart great deliverer of Eri. I am but a shepherd looking for his sheep, and not, as well might be some bad thing out of the rocks.

YOUNG MAN.

Can you tell me noble sirs, of any strayed sheep, or
and
what is troubling the water ~~in~~ the air over our heads?

CAOELTE.

We have been wandering in the dark all night, we are

[86^{r}]

(84)

as blind as you are.

OLD MAN.

We must go,sirs, we must find out sheep or starve.
(<u>Exit peasants</u>)

USHEEN.

Maybe he was laughing at us because he was afraid. We must wait here till we hear FINN'S horn. If we were to seek him we would lose him, and it may be never come alive out of the woods.

85^{r}, l. 17 Type deletion.

CAOELTE.

We had better go further up the hill, Who is this coming? Since dawn began the wood has been full of shadows and sound. They are coming out of the rocks; they rise out of the rocks.

USHEEN.

There is one who seems to be pushed along, and if it is but a shadow it is a heavy one. It is CONAN. I can see the sheep-skin. I am glad he has not seen our fear.

[101r]

98

(<u>Enter GOLL, CONAN, CRIFFAN, FATHNA and two of the FIANNA</u>)

GOLL.

The night is over at last.

CONAN.

The night is over, and the last day has begun. Give me a drink for I can go no further without one.

CAOELTE.

We must go further up the hill, We must hurry on if we would find FINN again. Have you seen him? Have you heard his horn?

GOLL.

No, he has not sounded it, but the beast will be stirring.

FATHNA.

The last time I saw FINN he was standing on the rock yonder. He stood facing the dawn and shouting to his hounds When he saw us he shouted that we were to climb up to him. He bellowed like a bull for its heifer.

CRIFFAN.

But I had had climbing enough.

CAOELTE.

We had better go further up the hill. Who is this coming? Since dawn began the wood has been full of shadows and sounds. They are coming out of the rocks; they rise out of the rocks.

USHEEN.

There is one who seems to be pushed along, and if it is but a shadow it is a heavy one. It is CONAN. I can see the sheep-skin. I am glad he has not seen our fear.
(Enter GOLL, CONAN, CRIFFAN, FATHNA and two of the FIANNA)

GOLL.

The night is over at last.

CONAN.

The night is over and the last day has begun. Give
no
me a drink for I can go further without one.

CAOELTE.

We must go further up the hill. We must hurry on if we are to find FINN again. Have you seen him? Have

[87^{r}]

(85)

you heard his horn?

GOLL.

No, he has not sounded it, but the beast will be stir-ring.

FATHNA.

The last time I saw FINN he was standing on the rock yonder. He stood facing the dawn and shouting to his hounds. When he saw us he shouted that we were to climb up to him – He bellowed like a bull for its heifer.

CRIFFAN.

have
But I ~~had~~ had climbing enough.

87^{r}, l. 8 Type deletion.

[102r]

99

CONAN.

Sit down I will go no further. When a man has got to die is it not better for him to die sitting down than walking about, and better to die on clean ground than in the mire, or up to his middle in water. Give me your ale skin, CAOELTE.

CAOELTE.

I will not CONAN you have been asking for it all night.

CONAN.

Give me your ale skin USHEEN, it is the last drink I shall ever drink.

USHEEN.

I will give him a drink; he will not move until we do. (USHEEN gives CONAN his ale skin) Drink and think no more of death.

CONAN.

All the disasters that have come to DIARMID have come to him because of the spilling of the ale out of the flagon; but I have lost both ale and ale skin and must therefore die.

CAOELTE.

(To FATHNA) We might light a fire, there must be dry

[103r]

100

leaves under these rocks. (FATHNA and CRIFFAN go together to collect dry leaves and sticks, and they return a moment after with them)

CONAN.

We are shivering since we crossed that river; and it was in that river I lost my ale skin; some one plucked it from behind.

CONAN.

Sit down I will go no further. When a man has got to die is it not better for him to die sitting down than walking about, and better to die on clean ground than in the mire or up to his middle in water. Give me your ale skin CAOELTE.

CAOELTE.

I will not CONAN you have been asking for it all night.

CONAN.

Give me your ale skin USHEEN, it is the last drink I shall ever drink.

USHEEN.

I will give him a drink, he will not move until we do. (USHEEN gives CONAN his ale skin) Drink and think no more of death.

[88^r]

(86)

CONAN.

All the disasters that have come to DIARMUID have come to him because of the spilling of the ale out of the flagon; but I have lost both ale and ale skin and must therefore die.

CAOELTE.

(To FATHNA) We might light a fire, there must be dry leaves under these rocks. (FATHNA and CRIFFAN go together to collect dry leaves and sticks, and they return a moment after with them)

CONAN.

We are shivering since we crossed that river; and it was in that river I lost my ale skin; someone plucked it from behind.

CAOELTE.

I too am shivering; the day is bleaker than the night.

CONAN.

Ah, be careful with the tinder, be careful,for the first leaves are the dry ones – Bring the fire a little nearer, I would die warm though I have to get cold after. Make room for me by the fire. Do you not understand that I am going to die – that CONAN the BALD is going to die – You will never flout me for my great belly again, CAOELTE.

CAOELTE.

You are not going to die, CONAN. Here I will give you a drink.

[104r]

101

CONAN.

Yellow ale bitter on the tongue tasting a little of the vat of red yew that it came from – The last drink CONAN will ever drink – (CAOELTE and the others talk among themselves) They think that all this hurly burly is for DIARMID, but I know better; you are my friends and I will tell you about it.

CAOELTE.

Give me my ale skin, CONAN.

CONAN,

Not yet, I must drink a little more – and now this is the way it was – it was not the loss of the ale skin that told me I was going to die, that only showed me that some great evil was going to happen – it was a swan screaming in the trees that told me I was going to die. Before I was born, and when yet my mother was carrying with me, towards the seventh month she was one day washing clothes

104r, l. 13 with me] So too in Washington 95/fol. 97r. Berg(99) 87/fol. 89r omits the word "with" (it had been inserted into the NLI 8777(3) c, fol. 100r, TS by GM).

CAOELTE.

I too am shivering; the day is bleaker than the night.

CONAN.

Ah, be careful with the tinder, be careful, for the first leaves are the dry ones – Bring the fire a little nearer, I would die warm though I have to get cold after. Make room for me by the fire. Do you not understand that I am going to die – that CONAN THE BALD is going to die – You will never flout me for my great belly again, CAOELTE.

CAOELTE.

You are not going to die CONAN, here I will give you a drink.

[89^{r}]

(87)

CONAN.

Yellow ale bitter on the tongue tasting a little of the vat of red yew that it came from – The last drink CONAN will ever drink – (CAOELTE and the others talk among them-selves) They think that all this hurly burly is for DIAR-MUID but I know better; you are my friends and I will tell you about it.

CAOELTE.

Give me my ale skin CONAN.

CONAN.

Not yet, I must drink a little more – and now this is the way it was – it was not the loss of the ale skin that told me I was going to die, that only showed me that some great evil was going to happen – it was a swan screaming in the trees that told me I was going to die. Before I was born, and when yet my mother was carrying me, towards the seventh month she was one day washing clothes

in the river, and she saw three geese swimming and while one was cackling and billing with its mate an otter caught it by the leg and dragged it under the water; so my mother knew something was to happen to the child under her belt, and she told me never to cross a river when there were geese about.

[105^{r}]

102

CAOELTE.

They were swans that screamed in the trees.

CONAN.

Are not swans a kind of geese; but how do I know it was not swans my mother saw.

CAOELTE.

CONAN give me my ale skin.

CONAN.

Why did I keep FINN and DIARMID from killing one another; they could have done it so easily in DIARMID'S house – Why did I bring them to this hunt? CONAN has brought his own death upon him. (Enter FINN)

FINN.

We have come across the slot of a boar in the hills; he can only just have passed by; if we go to the bend of the stream we should come upon him (To CONAN) Why are you lying there? We want every man, get up, we will put you in the gap yonder the boar shall not escape unless he escapes through you.

CAOELTE.

CONAN is in terror; he thinks he is going to die.

FINN.

CONAN, get up or you may have to face this beast alone.

105^{r}, l. 10 just have] Thus in Washington 95/fol. 97^{r}; Berg(99) 88/fol. 90^{r} reverses the words ("have just"). Traces of the same mistake are visible in NLI 8777(3) c, fol. 101^{r}.

in the river, and she saw three geese swimming and while one was cackling and billing with its mate an otter caught it by the leg and dragged it under the water;   so my mother knew something was to happen to the child under her belt, and she told me never to cross a river when there were geese about.

CAOELTE.

They were swans that screamed in the trees.

[90r]

(88)

CONAN.

Are not swans a kind of geese;   but how do I know it was not swans my mother saw.

CAOELTE.

CONAN give me[y] ale skin.

CONAN.

Why did I keep FINN and DIARMUID from killing one another;   they could have done it so easily in DIARMUID'S house – Why did I bring them to this hunt?   CONAN has brought his own death upon him.   (Enter FINN)

FINN.

We have come upon the slot of a boar in the hills; he can only have just passed by;   if we go to the bend of the stream we should come upon him.   (To CONAN)   Why are you lying there?   We want every man, get up, we will put you in the gap yonder the boar shall not escape unless he escapes through you.

CAOELTE.

CONAN is in terror;   he thinks he is going to die.

FINN.

CONAN get up, or you may have to face this beast alone.

90r, l. 3   Sensing an error, the typist changed "me" to "my" without correcting the omission.

[106r]

103

CONAN.

Do not believe them; it is not DIARMID this pig is looking for, it is for me.

FINN.

If CONAN will not go let him stay there. Here is a handful more leaves to warm your shins – (FINN throws some wet leaves on the fire and quenches it.)

CONAN.

You have thrown wet leaves on the fire; now Ishall die of cold. But are you leaving me? They all go because FINN has bidden them. You leave me, GOLL, yet some day FINN who has put out my fire will put out your life. ~~IsI~~ Is it not the oath of the FIANNA to protect one another? CAOELTE USHEEN do you not hear me (They go out laughing) They are an evil stony-hearted proud race – Rot in the ear wheat, frogs spawn in the pool, yellow sickness in one's body, henbane in one's drink,lice in my beatd, fleas in my sheep skin – A stony-hearted proud race. (He follows them out – Enter GRANIA and FINN.)

FINN.

You are cold and tired, GRANIA, and have stumbled through the wood, you are all bruised.

[107r]

104

GRANIA.

I am bruised and full of wretchedness, and I am very cold; and the dawning of the day frightens me. However, cold it is I do not wish to see the sun – But I am cold oh, the cold!

FINN.

There has been a fire here; I will blow the ashes

106r, l. 8 Type deletion.

13 beatd] Washington 97/fol. 99r has "head"; Berg(99) 89/fol. 91r has "beard" (like earlier TSS of Act III).

CONAN.

Do not believe them; ~~DIARMUID~~ it is not DIARMUID this pig is looking for, it is for me,

[91[r]]

~~FINN~~.

(89)

FINN.

If CONAN will not go let him stay there. Here is a handful more leaves to warm your shins – (<u>FINN throws some wet leaves on the fireaand quenches it</u>)

CONAN.

You have thrown wet leaves on the fire; now I shall die of cold. But are you leaving me? They all go because FINN has bidden them. You leave me, GOLL, yet some day FINN ~~will~~ who has put out my fire will put out your life. Is it not the oath of the FIANNA to protect one another? CAOELTE, USHEEN do you not hear me – (<u>They go out laughing</u>) They are an evil stony-hearted proud race – Rot in ~~on~~ the ear wheat, frogs spawn in the pool, yellow sickness in one's body, henbane in one's drink, lice in my beard, fleas in my sheep skin – A stony-hearted proud race. (<u>He follows them out – Enter GRANIA and FINN</u>)

[92[r]]

(90)

FINN.

You are cold and tired, GRANIA, and have stumbled through the wood, you are all bruised.

GRANIA.

I am bruised and full of wretchedness, and I am very cold; and the dawning of the day frightens me. However cold it is I do not wish to see the sun – But I am cold, oh, the cold.

FINN.

90[r], l. 16 Type deletion.

91[r] Note that the typing on this page is double-spaced, uniquely in this version. This might suggest another substitute: the corresponding passage at HRC 103/fol. 106[r] is unrevised, but see NLI 8777(3) c, fol. 102[r].

-1, 6, 9 Type deletions.

to a blaze.

GRANIA.

(Sitting down) Why did you not leave me to die where I had chosen.

FINN.

The beast we are hunting might have run upon you and you would have been trampled and gored by it. I could not have left you there. The blaze is already beginning hold your hands to it.

GRANIA.

I would that you had left me to be killed by it. You have planned that the death of this boar is to put me on one side or the other, to give me to DIARMID or to give me to you. But I am no man's spoil. (Standing up) You have planned it all between you, your plans are not mine. Go from me, FINN go to this hunt and kill the boar, make the fire or go where you will.

[108r]

105

FINN.

Although I lose my chance of killing this beast I must stay with you. I will protect you.

GRANIA.

It does not matter. Stay with me here or go to this hunt.

FINN.

I will not leave you, if it were to spring upon you from the thicket.

GRANIA.

It might be better for I have done mischief enough. I wished that you and DIARMID could have made peace and all would have been well, had not this evil thing broken out of the earth.

There has been a fire here; I will blow the ashes to a blaze.

GRANIA.

(Sitting down) Why did you not leave me to lie where I had chosen.

FINN.

The beast we are hunting might have run upon you and you would have been trampled and gored by it. I could not have left you there. The blaze is already beginning hold your hands to it.

GRANIA.

I would that you had left me to be killed by it. You have planned that the death of this boar is to put me on one side or the other, to give me to DIARMUID or to give ~~yo~~ me to you. But I am no man's spoil. (Standing up) You have planned it all between you, your plans are not mine. Go from me, FINN, go to this hunt and kill the boar or make the fire or go where you will.

[93r]

(91)

FINN.

Although I lose my chance of killing this beast I must stay with you. I will protect you.

GRANIA.

It does not matter. Stay with me here or go to this hunt.

FINN.

I will not leave you, if it were to spring upon you from the thicket.

GRANIA.

It might be better for I have done mischief enough. I ~~y~~wished that you and DIARMUID could have made peace and alll would have been well, had not this evil thing broken out of the earth.

92r, l. 18 Type deletion.
93r, l. 9 Type deletion.

FINN.

DIARMID and I could not be at peace. The peace we made was a false peace. (Hunting horns heard in the distance) The hounds are at the boar's heels now. I can hear my hounds,Yes it is Bran, Now it is Skealon. They have found their courage and are driving him from cover to cover. (Going up the stage) Listen – now it is Lomair.

[109r]

106

GRANIA.

FINN, I beseech you to put the desireof me out of your heart. Be DIARMID'S friend and save him. Kill the boar and save him.

FINN.

If I kill the boar will you belong to me?

GRANIA.

Not because you kill the boar.

FINN.

If I were there, and DIARMID here, and this boar coming against me, would DIARMID save me?

GRANIA.

You have fought side by side. Will you let him die?

FINN.

Why do you wish me to do this.

GRANIA.

It was I who sent DIARMID to you; and the blood bond you are brothers.

FINN.

Should not a woman's breast be more to me than a man's hand?

[110r]

107

GRANIA.

But the blood bond, he who breaks it shall be cast

FINN.

DIARMUID and I could not be at peace. The peace we made was a false peace. (Hunting horns heard in the distance) The hounds are at the boar's heels now. I can hear my hounds, yes it is Bran, now it is Skealon. They have found their courage and are driving him from cover to cover. (GOING up the stage) Listen – now it is Lomair.

GRANIA.

FINN I beseech you to put the desire of me out of your heart. Be DIARMUID'S friend and save him. Kill the boar and save him.

FINN.

If I kill the boar will you belong to me?

[94r]

(92)

GRANIA.

Not because you kill the boar.

FINN.

If I were there, and DIARMUID here, and this boar coming against me, would DIARMUID save me?

GRANIA.

You have fought side by side. Will you let him die?

FINN.

Why do you wish me to do this?

GRANIA.

It was I who sent DIARMUID to you; and the blood-bond – you are brothers.

FINN.

Should not a woman's breast be more to me than a man's hand?

GRANIA.

out by God-kind and man-kind.

FINN.

I cannot save DIARMID, his end has been foretold. I cannot change it. The deaths of every one of us and the end of the FIANNA have been foretold. Many will die in a great battle, OSCAR who is but a child will die in it, but I shall die long after by a spear thrust, and DIARMD by the tusk of a boar, and USHEEN will go far away, and CAOELTE storm the house of the gods at ~~Ossory~~ *Assaroe*. **(A cry is heard close by, FINN plunges into the thicket and returns with DIARMID who has been mortally wounded by the boar – DIARMID struggles to his feet, and leans against a rock.)**

DIARMID.

Water, is there no water? My life is ebbing out with my blood. (FINN goes to a well and comes back with water in his hand, but as he holds up his hand the water drips through his fingers.) If I had water I might not die.

GRANIA.

FINN, bring him water in your helmet. (DIARMID looks from one to the other) **and then whether by accident or design he overturns the helmet.)**

[111^{r}]

108

DIARMID.

GRANIA and FINN. (When FINN returns with his helmet filled with water, DIARMID looks from one to the other, and then whether by accident or design he overturns the helmet.)

GRANIA.

Why have you done this? Why will you not drink the water that FINNbrought you? (She takes up the helmet and

110^{r}, l. 9 The pencil emendation is not certainly in WBY's hand. The neat, light formation of the word is similar to that of the marks that appear on fols. 38, 62, 77 above. The emendation is seamlessly incorporated into Washington 100/fol. 102^{r} and Berg(99) 92/fol. 94^{r}.

14^{+} A bracket was inserted in pencil, and the underline beneath "other" firmed up, following an attempt to erase the remainder of the stage direction. The curtailed stage direction—ending with "the other)"—appears in Washington 101/fol. 103^{r} and Berg(99) 93/fol. 95^{r}.

But the blood bond, he who breaks it shall be cast out by God-kind and man-kind.

FINN.

I cannot save DIARMUID, his end has been foretold. I cannot change it. The deaths of every one of us and the end of the FIANNA have been foretold. Many will die in a great battle, OSCAR who is but a child will die in it, but I shall die long after by a spear thrust, and DIARMUID by the tusk of a boar, and USHEEN will go far away and CAOELTE storm the house of the gods at Assaroe. (A cry

[95r]

(93)

is heard close by, FINN plunges into the thicket and returns with DIARMUID who has been mortally wounded by the boar – DIARMUID struggles to his feet, and leans against a rock)

DIARMUID.

Water, is there no water? My life is ebbing out with my blood. (FINN goes to the well and comes back with water in his hand, but as he holds up his hand the water drips through his fingers) If I had water I might not die.

GRANIA.

FINN, bring him water in your helmet. (DIARMUID looks from one to the other)

DIARMUID.

GRANIA and FINN. (When FINN returns with his helmet filled with water,DIARMUID looks from one to the other and then whether by accident or design he overturns the helmet)

GRANIA.

Why have you done this? Why will you not drink the

fetches the water herself – Again DIARMID looks from one to another and puts the water away.) For my sake, for the sake of GRANIA I beseech you to drink it.

DIARMID.

It is growing lighter. There is a light coming out of the hill.

FINN.

Let me bind up your wounds or in a moment you'll be gone.

DIARMID.

They're about me, they're about me. they were ~~w~~always about me though I could not see them.

FINN.

He is dying, they are coming for him.

[112r]

109

DIARMID.

There is somebody there by the treev – move me a little that I may see him. (FINN helps ^Diarmud^ and slightly changes his position. He begins swaying his hand as if to music.)

FINN.

He hears the harp-playing of AOGNHUS – It is by music that he leads the dead.

GRANIA.

DIARMID, oh,DIARMID! Do not look at them. If you do not look at them you will not die. Do not die. You said once that you would be lonely without me among the immortals.

DIARMID.

I cannot hear the harp playing; there is so much noise about me.

111r, l. 10 Type deletion.

112r, l. 2 Diarmud] Washington 102/fol. 104r and Berg(99) 94/fol. 96r seamlessly incorporate the insertion.

8 water that FINN brought you? (She takes up the helmet and
fetches the water herself – Again DIARMUID looks from one
9 to another and puts the water away) For my sake, for the
10 sake of GRANIA I beseech you to drink it.

DIARMUID.

11 It is growing lighter. There is a light coming out
12 of the hill.

[96r]

(94)

FINN.

1 Let me bind up your wounds or in a moment you'll be
2 gone.

DIARMUID.

3 They're about me, they're about me, they were always
4 about me though I could not see them.

FINN.

5 He is dying they are coming for him.

DIARMUID.

6 There is somebody there by the tree – move me a little
7 that I may see him. (FINN helps DIARMUID and slightly
changes his position. He begins swaying his hand as if
to music)

FINN.

8 He hears the harp-playing of AOGNHUS - It is by music
9 that he leads the dead.

GRANIA.

10 DIARMUID oh, DIARMUID! Do not look at them. If
11 you do not look at them you will not die. Do not die.
12 You said once that you would be lonely without me among
13 the immortals.

DIARMUID.

14 I cannot hear the harp-playing; there is so much
15 noise about me.

96r, l. -1 The same number "94" appears at the head of the verso, in bright blue ribbon, and shows through.

GRANIA.

He has forgotten me.

FINN.

Henceforth his business is with them.

GRANIA.

Oh, DIARMID! Oh, DIARMID! Oh, DIARMID!

[113r]

110

DIARMID.

Someone spole to me; no not the harp player, some other. It was you FINN, who spoke to me. No, no, who was it who spoke to me? (<u>He falls back dead)</u>

FINN.

He is dead; he has died as the son of the gods should die. A friend against whom I have made war is dead. I warred against him for you, GRANIA. (<u>They stand looking at each other for a moment and then GRANIA goesaway and weeps. Enter a young man</u>.)

YOUNG MAN.

The beast you have been hunting is dead, killed by a spear thrust ~~I~~ here is the spear.

FINN.

The spear is mine, give it to me – (<u>Walking towards GRANIA</u>) We must send for me *n* to carry the body to the house. (<u>To the YOUNG MAN</u>) Go fetch KING CORMAC, bring him here. (<u>Exit Shepherd</u>.)

GRANIA.

(<u>Trying to overcome her emotion</u>) What did you say, and what are you saying? That spear with the blood upon it ~~where~~ in your hand, where did it come from?

113r, l. 15 Type deletion.

GRANIA.

He has forgotten me.

[97^{r}]

(95)

FINN.

Henceforth his business is with them.

GRANIA.

Oh, DIARMUID! Oh DIARMUID! Oh, DIARMUID!

DIARMUID.

Some one spoke to me;no not the harp player, some~~one~~ other. It was you~~n~~ FINN who spoke to me. No, no who was it spoke to me? (He falls back dead)

FINN.

He is dead; he has died as the son of the gods should die. A friend against whom I have made war is dead. I warred against him for you GRANIA. (They stand looking at each other for a moment and then GRANIA goes away and weeps. Enter a young man)

YOUNG MAN.

The beast you have been hunting is dead, killed by a spear thrust – here is the spear.

FINN.

The spear is mine, give it to me – (Walking towards GRANIA) We must send for men to carry the body to the house. (To the YOUNG MAN) Go fetch KING CORMAC, bring him here. (Exit Shepherd)

GRANIA.

(Trying to overcome her emotion) What did you say, and what are you saying? That spear with the blood upon it in your hand, where did it come from?

97^{r}, ll. 3, 4 Type deletions.

[114^{r}]

111

X

FINN.

It is the spear that killed the boar – a thrust behind the shoulder did it. We must send for help.

GRANIA.

Yes, we must send for help.

FINN.

One of the greatest in Eri is dead. One whom we shall miss when we go against the Lochlanders.

GRANIA.

Yes, you will miss him. But before you go against the enemies of Eri you must mourn him. (The hunters begin to come in from different sides – GRANIA goes to some rising ground) Tell my father of the death of DIARMID, bid him come to me ay once – (The hunters come in more and more – they fill the whole stage) Why is not my father here? But he will be here soon and will sea that DIARMID'S burning be worthy of him. Listen all you hunters and men of the FIANNA. It shall be the greatest burning that has been known in Eri. The pyre shall be built upon the mountain, and all the shepherds of the valley shall bring a tree to build it. There are birch trees on the mountain that the long summer has made ready for flame. A thousand shall be cut down and built to the height of fifty feet,

[114bis^{r}]

GRANIA.

A great man is dead. Ah, why did I send him to you Finn. I thought that two who were so great should befriends.

FINN.

The gods chose you Grania to give him love and death.

GRANIA.

/Wringing her hands/ FINN, we must mourn him. You have

114^{r}, ll. 3–18 The lines are covered by a piece of paper (here fol. 114bis, measuring 20.5 by 17.6 cm), this being the first page of the three-page revised ending.

114bis^{r}, ll. 3 et seq. Washington 104/fol. 106^{r} and Berg(99) 96/fol. 98^{r} follow the superimposed TS to the close of the play.

[98r]

(96)

FINN.

It is the spear that killed the boar – a thrust behind the shoulder did it. We must send for help.

GRANIA.

A great man is dead. Ah, why did I send him to you FINN. I thought that two who were so great should be friends.

FINN.

The gods chose you GRANIA to give him love and death.

GRANIA.

to go against the Lochlanders and this one that I have taken from you will not be by your side. Before the Fianna go against the Lochlanders they must mourn him, all his comrades must mourn him. /The hunters begin to come in from the O.P./ All the Fianna must mourn him and the shepherds ofthis valley. /She goes towards the body of Diarmuid. They make way for her and when she reaches Diarmuid's body a shepherd coming in from the back gives her Diarmuid's shield and his broken spear/. His shield with the flying white heron upon it shall be laid upon his breast and I will lay beside him "Broad Edge' that I bade him take instead of this spear I warned him not to take. Where is my father? Where is King Cormac? He shall see that Diarmuid's burning be worthy of him. /Enter King Cormac/ Here is my father. /She goes to her father/ Father, he is dead, one of the great men of Eri is dead. I am telling all these people that you will see to his burning that it may be worthy of him.

[115^{r}]

112

and upon them shall be laid a crimson cloth, and DIARMID shall be laid upon it. His battle gear beside him, his heavy spear, and Broad Edge, his double handed sword, and the short sword and light spear that gave him little help, and all his casting spears and his shield with the flying heron upon it. The games in his honour shall last for three days, and men must be sent through the country of Hebor to find the casters of the weight, and the casters of the spear, and the boxers and the swift runner, and t he skilful riders. And men must go hither and thither, and buy or bring by force two score of noble stallions, who shall be set to fight while the body burns. They shall beat one another with their hoofs, and tear one another with their teeth till the half have been slain or wounded beyond help. The other half shall be taken and cast among the flames so that DIARMID may have noble horses when he awakes. KING CORMAC shall watch over the games, but FINN son of Cool shall watch over them also, for though he warred against DIARMID, DIARMID was his friend for years; and bitterness is forgotten in death. All the FIANNA shall watch over the games giving honour to DIARMID their companion and their friend.

114bis^{r}, l. 20+ The superimposed text continues below with fol. 115bis^{r}.

115^{r} The whole page is covered by a piece of paper (here fol. 115bis, measuring 25.4 by 18.2 cm) numbered "–2–", this being the second page of the three-page revised ending.

(Wringing her hands) FINN we must mourn him. You have to go against the Lochlanders and this one that I have taken from you will not be by your side. Before the FIANNA go against the Lochlanders they must mourn him, all his comrades must mourn him.a (The hunters begin to come in from the O.P.) All the FIANNA must mourn him and the shepherds of this valley. (She goes towards the body of ~~this valley~~.DIARMUID. They make way for her and when she reaches DIARMUID'S body a shepherd coming in from the back gives her DIARMUID'S shield and his broken spear) His shield with the flying white heron upon it shall be laid upon his breast and I will lay beside him Broad Edge that I bade him to take instead of this spear which I warned him not to take. Where is my father? Where is King CORMAC? He shall see that DIARMUID'S burning be worthy of him. (Enter KING CORMAC) Here is my father. (She

[99r]

(97)

goes to her father) Father he is dead, one of the great men of Eri is dead. I am telling these people that you will see to his burning that it may be worthy of him.

98r, l. 13+ Type deletions—note, in a style unique in this TS.

[115bis^r]

–2–

Fianna must mourn him, and all the shepherds of this valley. Finn son of Cool, you too shall watch over this mourning.
/Finn goes over and stands by her./

GRANIA.

There are birch trees upon the mountain that the summer has made ready for the flame. Everyshepherd shall bring a tree and they shall be heaped to a great height. Diarmuid shall be laid upon them and when they are lighted all people that are on the western shore shall see the blaze.

CAOLTE.

I will send messengers to gather the swift runner and the swift riders and the ~~swift~~ boxers and the throwers of the weight, that the funeral games be worthy fo him.

USHEEN.

I shall send messengers who will gather the harpers and gather the women that his funeral songs may be well sung. Many queens shall mourn him to the sound of harps, for when he lived there was none that would not have taken Grania's placc, and wandered with himin her stead. It may be that he will come with Angus out of the heart of some hill and stand invisible among us and know that he is not forgotten.

FINN.

The best of my horses shall be killed with his own horse that he may have noble horses when he awakes. /Turning to the men who have brought him in the litter/. Carry him gently

---

115bis^r, l. $^-1$ A slip measuring 2.8 by 17.7 cm, comprising a TS fragment of the same paper, using the same carbon ribbon as the paste-in, is now tucked into the HRC bound volume following fol. 116bis and supplies the omission here. It was probably not pasted in at the head of the page because so doing would mask the page number. It reads:

CORMAC.

My daughter has lost a husband and Eri a defender. The

The text contained on the slip is incorporated seamlessly into Washington 105/fol. 107^r and Berg(99) 97/fol. 99^r.

2$^+$ her.] Thus in Washington 105/fol. 107^r. Berg(99) 87/fol. 99^r has "GRANIA."

3 A pencil cross has been drawn at the LH side of the facing page (fol. 114^v), 6.5 cm from the top.

9 Type deletion.

16 Angus] Washington 106/fol. 108^r repeats this spelling—confirming its close reliance on the revised HRC—although Berg(99) 97/fol. 99^r normalizes it.

20$^+$ The superimposed text continues below with fol. 116bis^r.

CORMAC.

My daughter has lost a husband and Eri a defender. The FIANNA must mourn him and all the shepherds of this valley. FINN son of COLL you too shall watch over this mourning. (FINN goes over and stands by GRANIA)

GRANIA.

There are birch trees upon the mountain that the summer has made ready for the flame. Every shepherd shall bring a tree and they shall be heaped to a great height. DIAR-MUID shall be laid upon them and when they are lighted all the people that are on the western shore shall see the blaze.

CAOELTE.

I will send messengers to gather the swift runnera and the swift riders and the boxers and the throwers of the weight that the funeral games be worthy of him.

USHEEN.

I shall send messengers who will gather the harpers and gather the women that his funeral songs may be well sung. Many queens shall mourn him to the sound of harps, for when he lived there was none that would not have taken GRANIA'S place and wandered with him in her stead. It may be that he will come with AOGNHUS out of the heart of some hill and will stand invisible among us and know that he is

[100r]

(98)

is not forgotten.

FINN.

The best of my horses shall be killed with his own horse that he may have noble horses when he awakes. (Turning to the men who have brought in the litter)

[116r]

113

(The litter is brought in and DIARMID'S body is laid upon it – USHEEN, CAOELTE, and GOLL and FERGUS carry him up the path that ascends through the wood – CORMAC and NIALL enter)

NIALL.

CORMAC would speak with FINN and GRANIA.

CORMAC.

DIARMID is dead, but the FIANNA are united and the Lochlanders shall be driven into the sea.

(FINN CORMAC and GRANIA go up the stage, talking together,and following the procession.)

CONAN.

They have forgotten me, He has forgotten me though it was I who told him that GRANIA should be given to whom-ever killed the boar. An evil stony hearted proud race (turns to go up the stage, stops) GRANIA made a great mourning for DIARMID but her welcome to FINN shall be greater.

END.

116r The whole page is covered by a piece of paper (here fol. 116bis, measuring 25.3 by 18.9 cm) numbered "–3–", this being the third page of the three-page revised ending.

4 Carry him gently for he was well-beloved when alive. (
(They lay DIARMUID'S body upon the litter. FINN turns to
5 GRANIA) Lay his shield upon his breast. (GRANIA walks
again to the body and lays the shield upon DIARMUID. The
men lift the litter and carry it slowly to the wood)

CORMAC.

6 DIARMUID is dead but the FIANNA are united and the
7 Lochlanders shall be driven into the sea. (FINN CORMAC
and GRANIA go up the stage following the procession.
remains warming his shins by the fire)
~~Enter~~ CONAN ~~he stands watching the procession for a moment~~)

CONAN.

8 ~~They have forgotten me and he has forgotten me, though~~
9 ~~it was I who told him that GRANIA should be given to who-~~
10 ~~ever killed the boar. An evil stony hearted proud race.~~
11 ~~(Turns to go up the stage. Stops.)~~ GRANIA makes great
12 mourning for DIARMUID but her welcome to FINN shall be
13 greater.

END.

100r, ll. 7+–11 Type deletions. The cancellations and substitution are all in bright blue ribbon type.

[116bis^{r}]

–3–

for he was well-beloved when alive. /They lay Diarmuid's body upon the litter. Finn turns to Grania/. Lay his shield ypon his breast. /Grania walks again to the body and lays the shield upon Diarmuid. The men lift the litter and carry it slowly to the wood/.

CORMAC.

Diarmuid is dead, but the Fianna are united and the Lch-landers shall be driven into the sea. /Finn, Cormac and Grania go up the stage following the procession. ~~Enter~~ Conan, ~~He stands watching the procession for a moment.~~ remains warming his shins by the fire.

Conan.

~~They have forgotten me and and he has forgotten me, though it was I who told him that Grania should be given to whoever killed the boar. An evil stony hearted proud race. /Turns to go up the stage. Stops/~~ Grania makes great mourning for Diarmuid, but her welcome to FINN shall be greater.

116bis^{r}, ll. 5–9 Washington 106/fol. 108^{r} incorporates the revisions seamlessly; Berg(99) 98/fol. 100^{r} takes them in later with type corrections.

Appendixes

[Berg(04), 1r]

(While GRANIA is pouring out the enchanted ale in the first act LABAN stelas up the stage watching her all the while, and while watching her LABAN half murmurs half sings:-

THE FIANNA are drinking
The enchanted ale,
And DIARMUID will carry
GRANIA away.
A fountain is flowing
In the deeps of the sea,
And no man's bonds
Can stay the waters
Of the life-giving fountain,
Of the fountain that brings
The nuts of the hazel,
Of the fountain whose waters
Cast the nuts of the hazel
On the shores of the world.

Now CORMAC has drunken
And he nods in his chair,
His wisdom is drowned
In the ale, in the ale,
And the white head is nodding . . .
The ale works well.
Now GRANIA is filling
FINN's ale-cup with ale.

I: Songs

The way in which Yeats wrote the songs to bolster the part of Lucy Franklein, who played Laban, is described at the close of part ii of the introduction. Further notes on Elgar's involvement are provided in Appendix IV, which reprints the printed text that accompanied Elgar's setting of the spinning song, which may or may not have separate authority.

Preliminary Two-Page Typescript Version of Spinning Song in Act I

[Berg(04), 1^{r}]

(While GRANIA is pouring out the enchanted ale in the first act LABAN stelas up the stage watching her all the while, and while watching her LABAN half murmurs half sings: –

THE FIANNA are drinking
The enchanted ale,
And DIARMUID will carry
GRANIA away.
A fountain is flowing
In the deeps of the sea,
And no man's bonds
Can stay the waters
Of the life-giving fountain,
Of the fountain that brings
The nuts of the hazel,
Of the fountain whose waters
Cast the nuts of the hazel
On the shores of the world.

Now CORMAC has drunken
And he nods in his chair,
His wisdom is drowned
In the ale, in the ale,
And the white head is nodding . . .
The ale works well.
Now GRANIA is filling
FINN's ale-cup with ale.

This singular trial version of a song appears to have been drafted following the revision of Laban's charm found in the complete HRC and Berg(99) versions (fols. 25^{r}–26^{r} and 22^{r} respectively), before Yeats substituted the first version of a spinning song in Berg(99), fol. 21^{v}. The description in the heading ("While . . . in the first act") registers its semi-independent status.

5–14 Pencil cancellation—possibly by GM (on grounds of the style of cancellation alone).

(FINN lifts up the cup)

He has drunken and lost her
For seven long years,
The others are holding
Their ale-cups for ale.
Now GOLL has drunken.
All soon will be sleeping
And the lovers will fly
Through woods and through mountain
And FINN'S sword shall never,
Cut the thread I am weaving
The long, long thread
That a Boar's tusk shall break.

(She takes a thread from her distaff)

FINN will pursue them
Year after year,
This is their thread
The thread on my distaff.

(She goes out)

[Berg(04), 2r]

(FINN lifts up the cup)

He has drunken and lost her
For seven long years,
The others are holding
Their ale-cups for ale.
Now GOLL has drunken.
All soon will be sleeping
And the lovers will fly
Through woods and through mountain
And FINN'S sword shall never,
Cut the thread I am weaving
The long, long thread
That a Boar's tusk shall break.

(She takes a thread from her distaff)

FINN will pursue them
Year after year,
This is their thread
The thread in my distaff.

(She goes out)

[Emory, 1ᵛ]

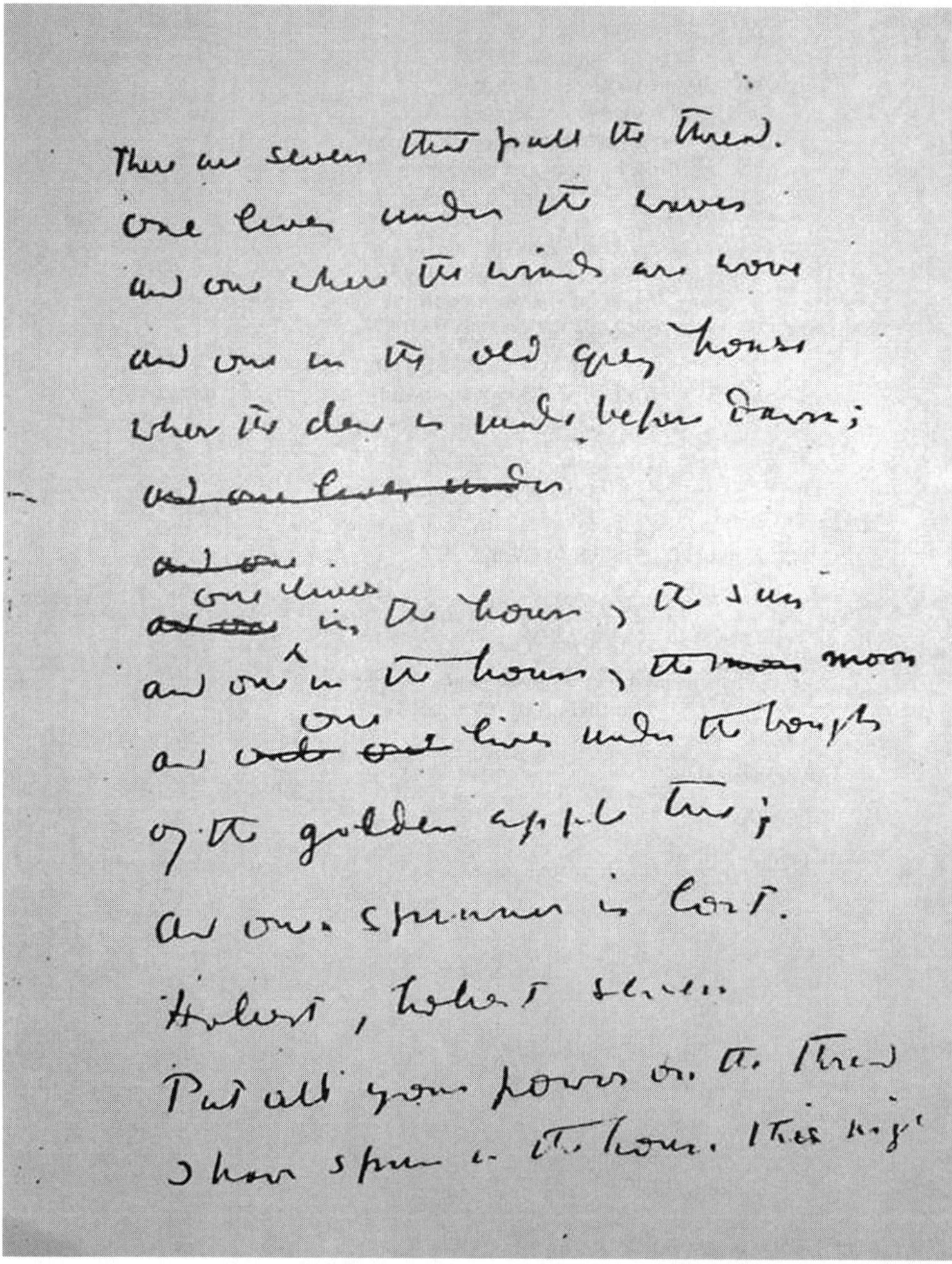

There are seven that pull the thread.
One lives under the waves
and one where the winds are wove
and one in the old grey house
where the dew is made before dawn;
~~and one lives under~~
~~and one~~
~~and one~~ one lives in the house of the sun
and one in the house of the ~~moon~~ moon
and ~~under~~ ~~one~~ one lives under the boughs
of the golden apple tree;
and one spinner is lost.
Holiest, holiest shadow
Put all your power on the thread
I have spun in the house this night

W. B. Yeats's Holograph Fair Copies of Laban's Spinning Song in Act I and the Blood Bond in Act II

[Emory, 1^{v}]

There are seven that pull the thread
One lives under the waves
And one where the winds are wove
And one in the old grey house
Where the dew is made before dawn;
~~And one lives under~~
~~And one~~
    One lives
~~And one~~^ in the house of the sun
And one in the house of the ~~moon~~ moon
        one
And ~~onl~~ ~~one~~ lives under the boughs
Of the golden apple tree;
And one spinner is lost.
Holiest, holiest seven
Put all your power in the thread
I have spun in the house this night

A revised fair copy of the holograph version inserted into Berg(99), fol. 21^{v}, made for Edward Elgar in October 1901.

[Emory, 1^{r}]

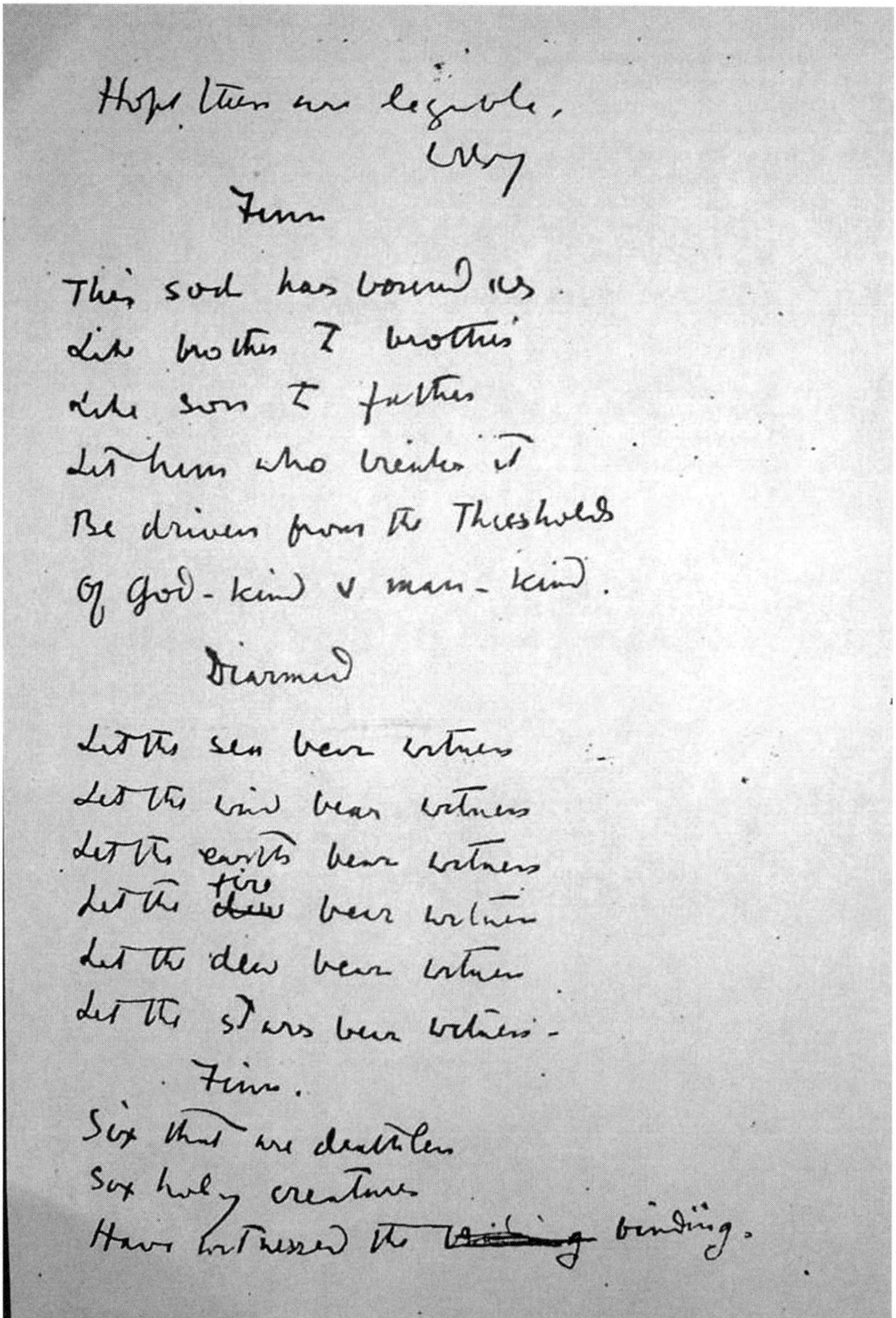

Hope these are legible.
WBY

Finn

This sod has bound us
Like brother to brother
Like son to father
Let him who breaks it
Be driven from the Threshold
Of God-kind & man-kind.

Diarmuid

Let the sea bear witness
Let the wind bear witness
Let the earth bear witness
Let the ~~dew~~ fire bear witness
Let the dew bear witness
Let the stars bear witness—

Finn.

Six that are deathless
Six holy creatures
Have witnessed the ~~[illegible]~~ binding.

[Emory, 1^{r}]

Hope these are legible,
WBY

Finn
This sod has bound us
Like brother to brother
Like son to father
Let him who breaks it
Be driven from the Threshold
Of God-kind & man-kind.

Diarmid
Let the sea bear witness
Let the wind bear witness
Let the earth bear witness
fire
Let the ~~dew~~ bear witness
Let the dew bear witness
Let the stars bear witness –

Finn.
Six that are deathless
Six holy creatures
Have witnessed the ~~braiding~~ binding.

WBY improved the first line in the course of making his fair copy for Elgar.

[Berg(3–4), 1v]

There are seven that pull the thread
There is one that is
~~One lives~~ ^ under the waves,
And one where the winds are wove
And one in the old grey house
Where the dew is made before dawn,
And one ~~lives~~
~~One~~ ~~And~~ ^ in the house of the sun
And one in the house of the moon
And one lives under the boughs
Of the golden apple tree,
And one spinner is lost.
Holiest, holiest, holiest seven
Put all your power on the thread
I have spun in the house this night.

W B Yeats.

W. B. Yeats's Holograph Fair Copy of the Spinning Song in Augusta Gregory's Copy of *Samhain*

[Berg(3–4), 1^{v}]

1 There are seven that pull the thread
There is one that is
2 ~~One lives~~ under the wave~~s~~,
3 And one ^ where the winds are wove
4 And one in the old grey house
5 Where the dew is made before dawn,
And one ~~lives~~
6 ~~One~~ ~~And~~ ^ in the house of the sun
7 And one in the house of the moon
8 And one lives under the boughs
9 Of the golden apple tree,
10 And one spinner is lost.
11 Holiest, holiest, holiest seven
12 Put all your power on the thread
13 I have spun in the house this night.

W B Yeats.

Written on the verso of the title page of Augusta Gregory's copy of *Samhain*.

[*Broad Sheet*, p. 1]

A BROAD SHEET

JANUARY, 1902.

FINN.
This rod has bound us
Like brother to brother,
Like son to father.
Let him who breaks it
Be driven from the threshold
Of God-kind and man-kind.

DIARMID.
Let the sea bear witness,
Let the wind bear witness,
Let the earth bear witness,
Let the fire bear witness,
Let the dew bear witness,
Let the stars bear witness!

FINN.
Ye that are deathless,
Ye holy creatures,
Have witnessed the binding.

The Blood Bond, from "GRANIA," by George Moore and W. B. Yeats.

SPINNING SONG.

There are seven that pull the thread.
One lives under the waves,
And one where the winds are wove,
And one in the old gray house
Where the dew is made before dawn;
One lives in the house of the sun,
And one in the house of the moon,
And one lives under the boughs
Of the golden apple tree;
And one spinner is lost.
Holiest, holiest seven,
Put all your power on the thread
I have spun in the house this night!

W. B. Yeats.

THE POOKA! THE POOKA!

Printer. Croydon

Printed Versions of Spinning Song and Blood Bond

[*Broad Sheet*, p. 1]

SPINNING SONG.

There are seven that pull the thread.
One lives under the waves,
And one where the winds are wove,
And one in the old gray house
Where the dew is made before dawn;
One lives in the house of the sun,
And one in the house of the moon,
And one lives under the boughs
Of the golden apple tree;
And one spinner is lost.
Holiest, holiest seven,
Put all your power on the thread
I have spun in the house this night!

W. B. Yeats.

FINN.

This sod has bound us
Like brother to brother,
Like son to father.
Let him who breaks it
Be driven from the threshold
Of God-kind and man-kind.

DIARMID.

Let the sea bear witness,
Let the wind bear witness,
Let the earth bear witness,
Let the fire bear witness,
Let the dew bear witness,
Let the stars bear witness!

FINN.

Six that are deathless,
Six holy creatures,
Have witnessed the binding.

The Blood Bond, from
"GRANIA," by George Moore
and W. B. Yeats.

II: Experimental Redrafting of Act II

Yeats's reservations concerning Act II as he and Moore had written it, which became evident even as the play went into production, have been described in the introduction, part iii (p. xli above). They concentrated on the first half of the act, the last half having "proved itself powerful and exciting upon the stage" (memorandum for Horace Plunket, July 1904: *CL* III 621). The two authors agreed the act should be recast and Yeats went to work without delay.

No preliminary material in Moore's hand is extant; there is indeed no suggestion that he provided such material, but he is the first to describe a new act in detail. His description is worth giving here because it differs from the version drafted by Yeats in several particulars. It is contained in a letter to Elgar from Ely Place, dated February 26, 1902 (Kennedy 181–182), which opens with a request for the *Grania* music to be performed in Dublin by an Irish orchestra, and continues:

> Now about another matter which interests me more. The play of "Diarmuid and Grania" was not liked as much as I thought it would be liked, but it was so badly acted that it was impossible to judge it. It looked very well on the stage but the audience missed something and I have been trying to think what that was, and I think I have discovered what they missed. What has kept this legend alive for thousand years [*sic*] is the romantic flight of the lovers, the forest scenes and I omitted this part of the legend.
>
> I am thinking of adding an act, an act that would contain the forest scenes. It would come immediately after the first act, and would be divided into three scenes. In the first scene would be a wood with Diarmuid and Grania immediately after their escape from Tara. They would naturally speak of those who still slept in the banqueting hall, and Grania would endeavour to persuade Diarmuid to forego his oath. They meet Mudham, and Mudham says he will guide them through the forest. A back cloth is lifted and a larger part of the forest is disclosed. Diarmuid and Grania enter. They speak to an old man, a hermit in the wood, but they have not said much when Mudham tells them that Finn is on their track and he takes them into a cave. Finn comes in with all his followers, and questions the old man and he departs hearing they have gone towards the west. No sooner has he gone than they return and the old man shares the fish he has caught with the lovers, and they lie down on the mossy bank, Mudham keeping watch. Suddenly Mudham tells them that Finn is coming back and they must prepare again for flight. The scene closes. Another back cloth is raised and we see Diarmuid at the house of the seven doors overthrowing Finn, breaking through the lines, and carrying Grania away. This act

> would enable me to curtail the next act. There need be no account of the wandering in the forest. What do you think?

Moore's summary leaves open how the replacement scenes were to be stitched into the fabric of the play. Both his description and Yeats's sample typescript do not specify whether the new material would form a separate Act II in a four-act play, or how the present Act II would be curtailed to avoid repeating material, or how it would be linked with the insertion (one new longer Act II, or a pair of shorter medial Acts II and III). Equally important, Moore's summary leaves open the question of how it relates to the revision Yeats had been working on during the previous several months. Perhaps Moore, eager to encourage Elgar to think of the musical opportunities of a loosened-up libretto, was working with a different end in mind, little concerned with how his suggestion connected with the existing stage play.

The fitful holograph revisions of the typescript Yeats dictated to Moore's "type writer" bear out the impression that the experiment was not pursued much further. The two authors may indeed have abandoned it before their open quarrel over *Where There Is Nothing*.

Twenty-nine-Page Continuous Typescript of Three Scenes for a New Act II, Revised by George Moore and W. B. Yeats

[NLI 8777(12), 1ʳ]

(1)

ACT II

(A cave. GRANIA lying upon a bear skin. She awakes suddenly and sits up)

GRANIA.

I heard something moving. Something moves in the shadows of these rocks. . . DIARMUID.

(Enter DIARMUID. He holds an apple branch in his hand. There are apples upon it.

DIARMUID.

Did my steps frighten you.
~~**I have brought you apples**~~**.**

GRANIA

But
{B
~~**Apples**~~**!** *No. {O what do you bring me? What is that golden fruit?*

DIARMUID.

You sent me in search of apples{. / !
~~**You said you wished t o eat apples**~~**. Have you forgotten?**

GRANIA.

But where did you find such apples as these?
No. ~~**This fruit is like gold**~~**.**

DIARMUID.

at the end of a desolate valley
I came upon an apple tree~~.~~ ^ It must be the apple tree that
These must be the apples that
the shepherd spoke to us about. ~~**He said one grew at thee end**~~

NLI 8777(12) and its continuation, Berg(12) (pp. 1046–1055 below), were originally a single typescript that was later divided between two archives; they are discussed in Chronology of Manuscripts, p. lxi above.

1ʳ, l. 8 "thee" is corrected to "the" with a type deletion.

~~of a desolate valley and it was there I found it.~~ **(He gives the branch to Grania)**

GRANIA.

[2r]

(2)

GRANIA.

These apples are beautiful. They are like gold. (She hides an apple in her bodice) It is strange that none come to gather them{. , ~~they are so beautiful~~. ~~But~~ none ventures here. The solitude saves us as it saves ~~the sacred apple tree.~~ ^*them.* Such beautiful apples as these should be sign of some great ill or perhaps, DIARMUID, of some great joy . . . But now DIARMUID I hear steps among the rocks. (She listens) DIARMUID draw your sword.

DIARMUID.

You hear nothing. We are far from all pursuit. (DIARMUID listens) It is but the footstep of some animal. . . or the wind blowing through these old rocks. . . GRANIA you were right. Men are about us. (He takes his shield and draws|his sword. He goes up the stage) Who are you? Where did you come from? Why did you come here? (Enter two young men)

FIRST YOUNG MAN

We come from FINN.

DIARMUID.

Why has he sent you?
~~And you come here to kill me.~~

FIRST YOUNG MAN.

~~Yes.~~ *He has sent us to kill you.*

GRANIA.

What ill have we done you? We are here in the unknown wastes and if we are not dead it is because the forest has saved

---

2r, l. 3, etc. All the cancellations on this page are in pencil (by GM).

7 The opening parenthesis has been overtraced in pencil.

12 Pencil word separation

[NLI 8777(12), 3r]

(3)

us. The forest shelters lovers. What have we done that you should come here to kill eus?

SECOND YOUNG MAN.

We wish to enter the FIANNA and we have passed all the tests which were demanded of us.

FIRST YOUNG MAN.

We have proved equal to the swordsmen of FINN in swordsplay.

SECOND YOUNG MAN.

We have proved ourselves with the heavy as well as with the light spear, we have thrown them well.

FIRST YOUNG MAN.

Our skill was greeted with acclamations. That is why FINN sent us here.

DIARMUID.

To prove your skill in a last test.

FIRST YOUNG MAN.

Before being admitted into the FIANNA we must bring FINN your head.

GRANIA.

But are not all the FIANNA friends of DIARMUID except FINN?

FIRST YOUNG MAN.

DIARMUID has still some friends among the FIANNA,but the

[NLI 8777(12), 3r]

[3r]

(3)

us. T he forest shelters lovers. What have we done that you should come here to kill ~~e~~us?

SECOND YOUNG MAN.

We wish to enter the FIANNA and we have passed all the tests which were demanded of us.

FIRST YOUNG MAN.

We have proved equal to the swordsmen of FINN in swordsplay.

SECOND YOUNG MAN.

We have proved ourselves with the heavy as well as with the light spear, we have thrown them well.

FIRST YOUNG MAN.

Our skill was greeted with acclamations. This is why FINN sent us here.

DIARMUID.

To prove your skill in a last test.

FIRST YOUNG MAN.

Before being admitted into the FIANNA we must bring FINN your head.

GRANIA.

But are not all the FIANNA friends of DIARMUID except FINN?

FIRST YOUNG MAN.

DIARMUID has still some friends among the FIANNA, but the

3r, l. 2 Type deletion.

(4)

many are against him.

SECOND YOUNG MAN.

They say that DIARMUID has broken his oath and that he deserves death.

DIARMUID.

I have not broken any oath. ~~You come to take my head my head in fair fight. Be it so.~~ (see back)

GRANIA.

Which of you will be the first to attack DIARMUID.

SECOND YOUNG MAN.

Wehave not come here to make sword play with DIARMUID. We have come here to kill him as quickly as we can.

GRANIA.

Then ~~two~~ may be two murderers will be chosen to
And these are the ~~terms whereby~~ you ~~are to~~ enter the FIANNA.

DIARMUID.

~~GRANIA away~~. The wild beasts do not make terms with their prey, and they come here as wild beasts to get it as best they may.

GRANIA.

They will drag me back to FINN if they kill you DIARMUID.

FIRST YOUNG MAN.

Yes, GRANIA, we shall bring you back to FINN.

[NLI 8777(12), 4r]

(4)

many are against him.

SECOND YOUNG MAN.

They say that DIARMUID has broken his oath and that he deserves death.

DIARMUID.

I have not broken any oath. ~~You come to take my head my head in fair fight. Be it so~~. X *(see back)*

GRANIA.

Which of you will be the first to attack DIARMUID.

SECOND YOUNG MAN.

Wehave not come here to make sword play with DIARMUID. We have come here to kill him as quickly as we can.

GRANIA.

Then ~~two~~ maybe two murderers will be chosen to
~~And these are the terms whereby you are to~~ enter the FIANNA.

DIARMUID.

~~GRANIA away~~. The wild beasts do not make terms with their prey, and they come here as wild beasts to get it as best they may .

GRANIA.

They will drag me back to FINN if they kill you DIARMUID.

FIRST YOUNG MAN.

Yes, GRANIA, we shall bring you back to FINN.

4r, ll. 4–5, 9, 10 All the cancellations and emendations on this page are in pencil.

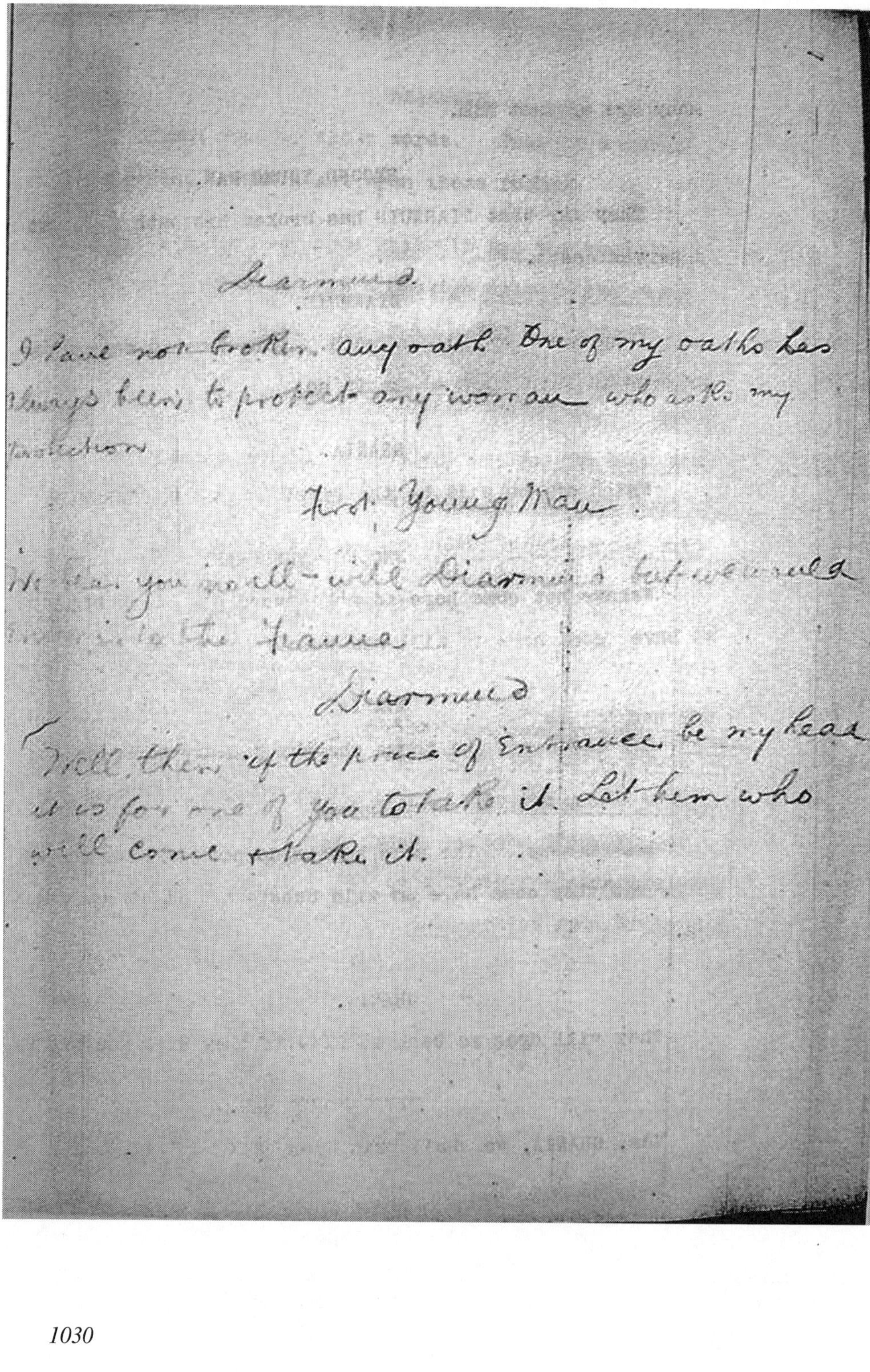

Diarmuid

I have not broken any oath. One of my oaths has always been to protect any woman who asks my protection.

First Young Man

We hear you well-will Diarmuid but we would enter in to the Fianna.

Diarmuid

Well then if the price of Entrance be my head it is for one of you to take it. Let him who will come & take it.

[NLI 8777(12), 4^{v}]

Diarmuid.

I have not broken any oath One of my oaths has always been to protect any woman who asks my protection

First Young Man.

We bear you no ill-will Diarmuid but we would enter into the Fianna

Diarmuid

Well, then, if the price of entrance be my head it is for one of you to take it. Let him who will come & take it.

4^{v} GM's draft here is to be inserted into fol. 4^{r}/p. 4 at line 4.

2–3 "who asks my protection" was added later.

-4 "First" was inserted later.

[NLI 8777(12)]

[5ʳ]

(5)

DIARMUID.

Thank you for those words. They have made me strong~~er~~ as seven. GRANIA get upon those rocks{! .}

(GRANIA moves away from DIARMUID and the young men attack him. DIARMUID retreats into a passage between the rocks. One of the young men rushes forward. DIARMUID wounds him. He falls. DIARMUID passes over his body, and fights with the other. He pursues him up the stage and overthrows him. But before he has time to kill him the other one who has been wounded in the right arm advances,~~and~~ his sword in his left hand and is about to stab DIARMUID in the back when GRANIA cries out)

GRANIA.

DIARMUID look back!

(DIARMUID looks back in time and leaving the man who is upon the ground he begins to fight with the first young man. GRANIA draws a dagger and by putting it to the man's throat prevents him from rising. The combat between DIARMUID and the young man who fights with his left hand lasts for some time and during this while the other young man escapes from GRANIA through the rocks and is pursued by her. DIARMUID at length succeeds in knocking the sword out of his enemy's hand. The first young man retreats into a corner and awaits death. Diarmuid looks around and not seeing GRANIA nor the second young man forgets all about his last enemy)

5ʳ, ll. 1, 2+ Type deletions.

[6r]

(6)

DIARMUID.

GRANIA! GRANIA! (Enter GRANIA) You are not hurt GRANIA?

GRANIA.

No. I am not hurt.

DIARMUID.

But he has escaped.

GRANIA.

No. He has not escaped. He fell over a rock and I stabbed him.

DIARMUID.

And then?

GRANIA.

Then he crawled a little way and I followed him and stabbed him as I followed him. I hated him DIARMUID for he would have

& I struck him again & again

killed you. ~~I stabbed him many times, little quick stabs where I thought the pain would be quickest~~. (She wipes the dagger upon DIARMUID'S ~~sleev~~ cloak) ~~I would have stabbed him many more times if you had not called me~~. I would have cut off the ear that listened to Finn, and I would have stabbed him in the mouth that said he would kill you, and I would have stabbed out his murderous eyes, and I would have stabbed the fingers

of the hand

and palm, ^ and I would have had him live a while to see he would never hold a sword again.

6r, ll. 10–11 WBY's ink cancellation(s).

12 Type deletion, followed by WBY's ink cancellation in lines 12–13.

[NLI 8777(12)]

[7r]

(7)

DIARMUID.

And this soft hand did this.

GRANIA.

The paw of the wild cat is likewise soft. There was a fever in my blood when I stabbed him, and I liked the feel of the iron as it plumped into his body. You know that feel, you have known it in battle.

DIARMUID.

You said he was dead.

GRANIA.

Yes, ~~he is dead now~~. But it was hard to kill him. He would not die. ~~I see you have not killed~~ the other. I see no blood on the ground. He has not escaped you DIARMUID?

DIARMUID.

No. ~~He is among these rocks~~.

GRANIA.

Why have you not killed him? ~~Let me see you kill him~~.

~~**DIARMUID.**~~

~~**No.**~~

~~**GRANIA.**~~

You would not have him escape. You would not have him go back to FINN.

7r, ll. 1–5, 11 The two cancel lines are in dark blue ink, that is, drawn by WBY. All other emendations on this page are in pencil, that is, by GM.

[8r]

(8)

DIARMUID. ×

I cannot kill a man who has no arms in his hand~~,~~ and I would not see you kill him. ~~It was FINN who sent him here.~~ ~~He will tell FINN that I have not broken my oath.~~

GRANIA.

~~You can turn your head, I'll kill him.~~ ~~(DIARMUID detains her)~~ ~~He will hate you for giving him his life and will go back~~ to FINN and betray us. (Turning to the man) You say nothing. DIARMUID you see he does not answer.

DIARMUID. See back

What should he answer?

GRANIA.

~~Let him come here, let him die at our feet.~~ (To the man) Come here. Now say whether you will die by the dagger or by the sword. (The man does not answer) I would here you speak.

DIARMUID.

I never struck but the man that faced me in battle. And when he fell I ~~fo~~ ~~often lifted him and I often tore away a piece of my scarf to bind~~ have often bound up his wounds ~~with~~. (He cuts a piece off his dress and tires it about the arm of the young man)

GRANIA.

He will betray our hiding place to FINN.

8r, l. 1 The comma is deleted in pencil, that is, by GM. All the other emendations on 8r, apart from at lines 13–14, are also in pencil.

13–14 "fo" is a type deletion. The passage "often . . . bind" and the word "with" are canceled in ink (by WBY).

14+ Type deletion.

[NLI 8777(12), 8v]

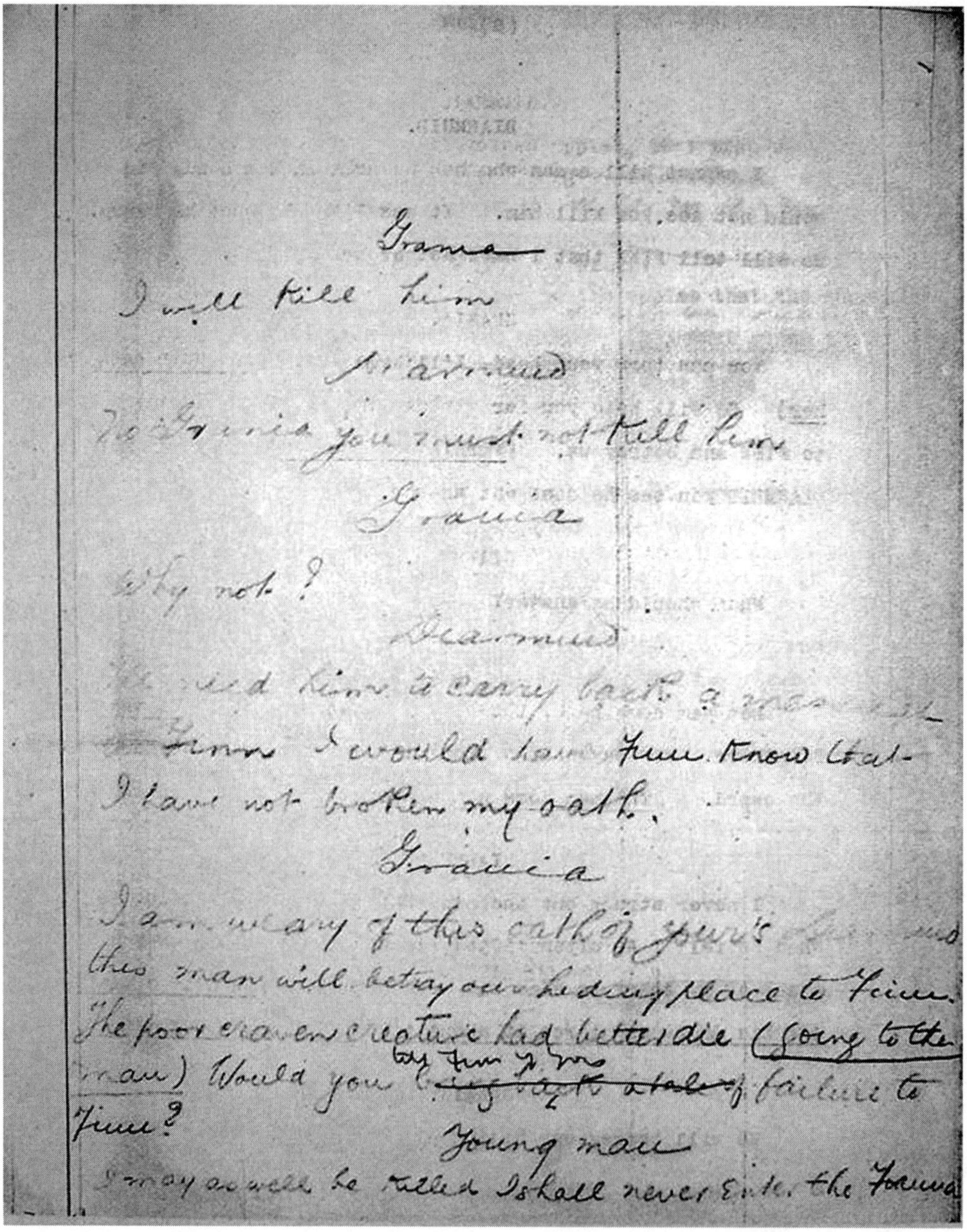

Grania

I will kill him

Diarmuid

No Grania you must not kill him

Grania

Why not?

Diarmuid

I need him to carry back a message to Finn I would have Finn know that I have not broken my oath.

Grania

I am weary of this oath of yours and this man will betray our hiding place to Finn. The poor craven creature had better die (going to the man) Would you ~~carry back a tale~~ of failure to Finn?

Young man

I may as well be killed I shall never enter the Fianna

[NLI 8777(12), 8^{v}]

Grania

I will kill him

Diarmuid

{ *r*
No G{[?*r*]*ania you must not Kill him*

Grania

Why not?

Diarmuid

We need him to carry back a message
to Finn I would have Finn know that
I have not broken my oath.

Grania

I am weary of this oath of your's Diarmuid
this man will betray our hiding place to Finn.
The poor craven creature had better die (<u>going to the</u>
tell Finn of your
<u>man)</u> Would you ~~bring back a tale of~~ failure to
^
Finn?

Young Man

I may as well be killed I shall never enter the Fianna

8^{v} GM's draft here is to be inserted into fol. 8^{r}/p. 8, line 1.

[9r]

(9)

DIARMUID.

I will give him these golden apples{. , ~~they will be a sign that I have kept my troth.~~ let him give them Finn & perhaps Finn ~~he~~ will take him int th Feann.

GRANIA.

~~or~~ or it may be they will vanish

are

They will wither.^**If they ~~be~~ the apples that the shepherd**

~~The~~ ^The cannot be seen but in th wilderness.

has spoken to us of they will vanish.^**<u>(DIARMUID gives the branch to the man. The man gets up and goes out)</u>**

GRANIA.

You have done a foolish thing DIARMUID{, , ~~that man will betray us. I read betrayal in his eyes~~.

DIARMUID.

We must go from hence, we must seek some unknown forest, lest that man should betray us, lest he should be overcome.

GRANIA.

Lest I should be taken back to FINN.

DIARMUID.

Ah *!* for some peaceful valley where love would be enough.

GRANIA.

And what DIARMUID will happen between us if we should find that valley?

DIARMUID.

Those beautiful hands soft and as cruel as the paws of the wild cat make me tremble, ~~make me forget my oath~~.

9r, ll. 1–2 The deletion of the end of the sentence, and the substitution of a period for a comma, were made by GM in pencil before WBY added his revision in ink.

4–4+ Both parentheses have been overwritten in pencil.

5–6 Pencil cancellation (by GM).

10 The exclamation point was inserted in pencil.

14 Ink cancellation (by WBY).

[10r]

(10)

GRANIA.

But your oath to FINN does not follow you into the forest.
The gods you have called to witness are absent.

DIARMUID.

Here we are amid new divinities – the divinities of the
woods – will they protect us from the divinities that I have
broken faith with?

GRANIA.

~~We must follow this winding cave.~~ DIARMUID I think of
is as a wasting fire.
you night and day and my desire ~~leaves me without strength~~.
DIARMUID are not the apples that you found in the desolate valley
the sign that my mouth is for you mouth?

DIARMUID.

T}
~~The twilight of the cavern frightens me,and~~ t}here is blood
smell
here and an ~~odour~~ of blood.

GRANIA.

DIARMUID you are a great warrior and you have overcome
two men before my eyes, but the apple I have hidden in my breasts
is more venturesome than you.

DIARMUID.

FINN is my brother in arms, and my captain. How often
have we fought shoulder to shoulder. No, GRANIA, no. (<u>He</u>
<u>takes her in his arms and the stage darkens</u>)

10r. ll. 6, 7, 10, 11 Pencil cancellations.

[NLI 8777(12)]

[11r]

(11)

GRANIA.

The day is for battle and for perils, for pursuit and for flight, but the night and the silence are for lovers who have nothing except themselves.

(The scene changes. We are in a stony valley at the mouth of a cave. At the left is a wood. The sun is sinking. A stream passes the cave. There is an old man dressed in grey fishing in the stream with a net which is fastened to the end of a long pole. While he is fishing DIARMUID and GRANIA come out of the cave. He does not see them at first being busy with his fishing)

GRANIA.

There is a man under that tree.

DIARMUID.

I can see no one.

GRANIA.

Yes, DIARMUID, under that tree there is a man sitting by the stream. He sits there quiet as a stone. But just now I saw him leane forward a little. I think he is fishing in the stream.

DIARMUID.

He may be one of FINN'S watchers. We have come so far

[12r]

(12)

underground that we may have wandered back to Tara.

GRANIA.

I do not think he is one of FINN'S watchers. He seems to have been here a long while, so long that he has become grey like a rock, and may have forgotten speech. Listen! He murmurs to himself as a tree does.

DIARMUID.

He will remember some speech and we must ask him for one of his fish, for he is fishing as you said GRANIA. (Going towards the old man) Old man we have not eaten for a long time. The old man gets up and seeing DIARMUID and GRANIA he falls on his knees)

OLD MAN.

Great spirits of the hills do not do me any harm . . . I have not forgotten to pray to the people of the hills,every night I leave a portion of my food outside my door to be taken by the passer-by.

DIARMUID.

Old man we are not spirits,we are DIARMUID and GRANIA, the lovers that FINN pursues through Erie. Have you not heard of our flights. (The old man shakes his head)

GRANIA.

I am the King's daughter, she who was to marry FINN son of COOL, but who poured enchanted ale into the wine cups and fled

[13r]

(13)

with DIARMUID.

OLD MAN.

I know nothing of these things, I have been here so long. The world's stories do not reach me here, and I have forgotten the old stories.

GRANIA.

Do men and women never pass~~es~~ by?

OLD MAN.

I have lived amid these rocks for many years and have seen no man nor woman, that is why I knelt to you believing you to be the spirits of the hills. You say you are not of these. It is well;I have no means of knowing.

13r, l. 5 Type deletion.

[NLI 8777(12)]

DIARMUID.

We are the lovers we told you of, and we have wandered here underground. We seem to have wandered many miles,the cave seems of measureless length. Seeing you we thought that it had brought us back to Tara, but the cave has brought us far into the wilds and where we shall have to remain many years.

GRANIA.

We have been underground a long while old man, we have wandered far and are very hungry .

OLD MAN.

My food is the fish that I take from the stream. I will

[14r]

(14)

cook some of these for you. I had lost myself in dreams before you came and as I dreamed I fished and have taken more than I have need for. Here are three and these I will cook for you. The largest I will give to DIARMUID for he is a man and a warrior the second largest I will give to GRANIA for she is a woman, and the smallest I will keep for myself for I am an old man and have need of little food. GRANIA here is a mossy place for you to sit upon, and you will wait a little while I gather twigs for the fire.

DIARMUID.

May I help you? We have been so long underground that we shall be glad to see a fire again, and while we are eating your fish you will tell us who you are and how you came here.

OLD MAN.

I will tell you as much as I remember of my story but that is very little. You will let me share your meal with you, you will let me sit with you and eat among you.

DIARMUID.

We shall be glad to have you sit by us and to hear who you are and how you came here.

OLD MAN.

This much I will tell you at once, that you do well to let me sit among you and eat my food in your company for I was once a king and shall not cause offence by my manners. I have

forgotten much but I remember enough manners to sit with you.

[15r]

(15)

GRANIA.

So you were once a king, old man. Maybe you once had a queen.And what unhappiness drove you out here into this wilderness?

OLD MAN.

Like many another king I was worsted in war and there is no place on earth for conquered kings except the wilderness. . . no one minds them . . . and seeing I was no use to my people, many were murdered and many dispersed I came among the rocks to be near the spirits of the hills. (He moves away and gathers twigs, DIARMUID and GRANIA watch him)

GRANIA.

And have you ever met here any of the strange women who sit among the rocks and spin the threads of men's lives?

OLD MAN.

Yes, indeed, Princess, I have met those women at eventide, and they throw their distaffs to each other across the great open clefts. Oh, Princess if you are a PRINCESS and not as I still think a spirit of these hills – –

(The horn of FINN is heard among the hills quite close)

DIARMUID.

That is FINN'S horn.

[16r]

(16)

GRANIA.

The young man whom you refused to kill has guided FINN hither. DIARMUID! DIARMUID!

DIARMUID.

That he should be so craven . . . In that cave I can defend you. I know its windings. Come GRANIA, we will fight them

in its secret passages and many men will get their death suddenly out of the shadows. But maybe FINN will not search the cave, they will not dare. (To the old man) Our enemy is coming upon us. We are going back into the cave. They will question you but you will not betray us.

(Exit DIARMUID and GRANIA into the cave. Enter FINN and the FIANNA)

FINN.

(To the young man) Is that the hole you entered? Is that the den? You should know it. (The young man examines the cave) Is that the cave you entered when you and -------- followed DIARMUID amid the rocks as a dog follows a wild cat. The wild cat's claws are strong and makes short work of curs.

CONAN.

Two curs are not equal to one wild cat.

YOUNG MAN.

The cat was not alone, the she was with him. Had we not

[17r]

(17)

been afraid ~~of~~ to kill her we could have killed DIARMUID.

FINN.

Had you killed her you would have died more cruelly than your friend died. Is this the den you found them in? (The young man looks round and examines the rocks again) For two whole days we have been scraping amid stones as dogs scrape for animals that lie underground. Three of my men have had their legs broken and one was drowned in a dark hole. We heard him far away in the water but had to leave him to the rats and nutes. I have had enough of this underground hunting. I am neither a rat nor a badger nor a fox. Now, CONAN into that cave and bring youe enemy out.

17r, l. 1 Type deletion.

CONAN.

Like you FINN I have not taste for burrowing. We have done nothing for two whole days but search in holes. I think this fool has been dreaming. He lost his friend amid the woods, he left him fighting with some cat or badger, some squirrel or some rat and dreamed a boasting tale. You see he knows not if that be the cave. We waste time here, those we seek are in the woods but – – (Turning CONAN sees the old man) There is one who will tell us. (He goes to the old man who has resumed his fishing and brings him to FINN)

FINN.

Have you met a man and woman wandering in these woods.

[Berg(12), 1r]

(18)

What do you here? Who are you? You seem as melancholy as the place itself.

OLD MAN'

I have lived here a long while and have seen no one. None comes here for this is a haunted place.

GOLL.

Do the spirits of the woods meet here?

OLD MAN.

I sometimes see them sitting at even-tide amid those rocks, a circle of women sit there spinning.

GOLL.

Let us away FINN, I would not stay in a haunted place,

FINN.

Old man tell me if you have met lovers wandering in these woods.

OLD MAN.

I have lived here so long, sir, that if I had seen lovers I should have thought that they were spirits. The place is so lonesome that there is little mortality in it.

GOLL.

He speaks well. Only those on the edge of life as he himself is could live here. FINN we must go. There is no one

[Berg(12), 1^{r}]

(18)

What do you here? Who are you? You seem as melancholy as the place itself.

OLD MAN'

I have lived here a long while and have seen no one. None comes here for this is a haunted place.

GOLL.

Do the spirits of the woods meet here?

OLD MAN.

I sometimes see them sitting at even-tide amid those rocks, a circle of women sit there spinning.

GOLL.

Let us away~~m~~ FINN, I would not stay in a haunted place,

FINN.

Old man tell me if you have met lovers wandering in these woods.

OLD MAN.

I have lived here so long, sir, that if I had seen lovers I should have thought that they were spirits. The place is so lonesome that there is little mortality in it.

GOLL.

He speaks well. Only those on the edge of life as he himself is could live here. FINN we must go. There is no one

---

1^{r} Note that the typescript is described as part of Act III by the Berg cataloguer. The pages follow directly on NLI 8777(12), fol. 17^{r}.

8 Type deletion.

[Berg(12)]

[2r]

(19)

in that cave. Who would dare to enter it?

FINN.

It is likely ~~enough~~ that we shall find them higher up among the hills. If they were in that cave they would have to leave it in search of food.

(FINN and the FIANNA go out. The old man continues to gather sticks. Presently he lights a fire. He goes to the mouth of the cave)

OLD MAN.

All is well now. Your enemy has gone and I have laid the fish upon the fire.

(Enter DIARMUID and GRANIA)

DIARMUID.

I was not far from the mouth of the cave, I heard. The FIANNA fear no man but tremble before the Gods. I would that FINN had come into that cave for sooner or later FINN and I must meet. But that meeting is distant since it was not to-day it will not be for many days. GRANIA would eat some of your fish, oh, King. (They sit about the fire) I would have come out of that cave and asked FINN to fight with me, but FINN would not have met me in single fight,he would have contrived some trap, some pitfall, he would have sent someone to stab me in the back. I was forced to stay quiet and listen to him speaking of me as a badger, as a fox, as a weasel, as a rat, he only

[3r]

(20)

forgot to say a mole. I think he spoke of all the animals that burrow underground. It was not FINN I feard but FINN'S treachery. Has he been alone I should have sprung upon him as a wild cat springs.

GRANIA.

DIARMUID think no more of FINN. Wee shall not find food

2r, l. 2 Type deletion.
3r, l. 5 Type deletion.

again for many hours. Come and eat your fish. (Suddenly the horn of FINN is heard again)

DIARMUID.

FINN is coming back. We must go into the cave.

OLD MAN.

No. He is coming back to search the cave. Better get you into the wood. (Exit DIARMUID and GRANIA. Enter FINN and the FIANNA. There is a shepherd with FINN)

FINN.

The shepherd says that the cave winds for miles underground. It must be the other end of the cave in which the two young men ~~cma e~~ came upon DIARMUID. Now you will carry the torch and I will go into the cave, and when DIARMUID comes to the fight you will run forward so that I may see him well.

(The FIANNA prepare a torch)

YOUNG MAN.

If I do this well shall I be admitted into the FIANNA.

[4r]

(21)

FINN.

No you will not be admitted into the FIANNA, but if you do it ill you will join your comrade who is now in the cave.

(FINN takes the torch, gives it to the young man and enters the cave)

GOLL.

If FINN meets DIARMUID in the cave the fight will last many hours before one gets the better of the other.

CONAN.

It will be a fight that the FIANNA will boast of for many years, and though none of you has seen the fight everyone will tell of the great blows struck. (Turning towards the FIANNA) I see you all now gaping like owlets in a nest thinking of the great deeds of the parent birds, of the mice they are catching and will bring home for supper, and the mice soon to grow to the size of rats in the minds of owlets talking of father and mother.

3r, l. 12 Type deletion.

[Berg(12)]

The fish are spoiling, they have lain already too long on the fire. I will eat the fish.

OLD MAN.

You will not eat my fish. You will not take my fish from me. This is my supper for to-night, and if you take it I shall go supperless to bed.

CONAN.

You would not eat three fish, old man. Why a re you cookin g

[5r]

(22)

three fish?

OLD MAN.

I lay fish outside my door so that the ever-living ones may have food should they pass my way.

CONAN'

Come GOLL, I will divide the fish between you. Let the FIANNA sit down and think of the tales they will tell of the great fight that is now being fought underground.

GOLL.

I will not eat the fish he lays outside his door for the everliving ones, nor will any of the FIANNA do this except yourself CONAN.

(The scene changes. A barren mountain top. LABAN dressed in grey is sitting among the stones with her distaff in her hand.)

LABAN.

The FIANNA have waked
From their sleep in Tara
The FIANNA are hunting
The lovers of Erie
Through forest and fell.
FINN has sworn an oath
That his hate will abide *and his limbs*

[6r]

(23)

~~That his limbs~~ will never grow weary
Till his vengeance is sated.
And ^**DIARMUID has found the apple**
That grows in the waste
That grows at the end
Of a desolate valley.
And GRANIA has hidden the apple
And DIARMUID has sent the branch
To FINN as a token
That his oath is unbroken.
But GRANIA has hidden
The apple for DIARMUID,
And this apple they will eat
Year after year,
And this apple will never grow less
Though they eat it year after year,
It will never grow less till they have come
To the end of the waste
To the peaceful valley of rest.
Where no
~~The sacred~~^**apple grows –**
~~In no peaceful valley~~ *(The sacred apple grows*
It grows in the waste.
(She begins to spin a thread)
They will lose this apple

[7r]

(24)

DIARMUID will lose it
In a peaceful valley.
The thread I am spinning
Is a long long thread,
And I know no more
Of the end than this
That DIARMUID will lose the apple
DIARMUID will lose it.
(DIARMUID and GRANIA come out of the wood)

6r, ll. 1, 20, 21 Pencil cancellations.

[Berg(12)]

DIARMUID.

What is that light yonder. Dawn is breaking about the fell. ~~GRANIA there is an~~ *That* **old woman spinning among the rock~~s~~ { , . } ~~She~~ must be one of the spirits of the hills that the old man spoke to us about,**

GRANIA.

It is like LABAN.

DIARMUID.

But we could not find LABAN here.

GRANIA.

She may have learned that we would pass this way, that our way led through this valley at dawn.

DIARMUID.

But we are many miles from Tara. LABAN could not be here.

[8r]

(25)

GRANIA I cannot pass that woman sitting there.

GRANIA,

DIARMUID it is LABAN, she is waiting for us.

DIARMUID.

How could she escape from Tara?

GRANIA.

When I asked her to put enchantment upon the ale she said that FINN would hang her from a rafter. Do you remember she went out singing, she went out singing while I filled the ale-cups.~~wit~~ I will thank the Gods if it be LABAN. DIARMUID go forward for me heart tells me it is LABAN.

(<u>They go forward together</u>)

DIARMUID.

Yes, GRANIA it is LABAN.

7r, ll. 10, 11 Pencil cancellations (including the "s" at the end of line 10).

8r, l. 7 Type deletion.

(The stage grows a little lighter. LABAN comes down from the rocks)

LABAN.

I have been waiting for you since mid-night.

DIARMUID.

How did you know that we would comes this way?

[9r]

(26)

LABAN.

I know the shepherds and they know all the passes and then the Gods tell me what the shepherds do not know.

DIARMUID.

~~But old woman~~ we have escaped a great peril ~~and many perils~~
had
~~await us~~. We ~~have~~ wandered through caves and men came to kill us in the caves and then we wandered until we came to an opening in the cave and there we found an old man fishing. He saved us from FINN but FINN'S horn resounds through these woods. Only an hour ago his hound Bran who knows me as well as he knows FINN came and put his head in my bosom.while we slept, and then we hastened away and so we came here pursued by friends who had become enemies and saved only from them by an old man
world
who had forgotten the ~~wodls~~ and by the simple friendship of a dog.

LABAN.

DIARMUID was always greatly known for his courage among the FIANNA. But greater courage is required of him than any he has shown in battle for Erie will be against him. He
from to
will be hunted ~~through~~ forest ~~and~~ forest, through mountain and morass but he must not lose heart.

DIARMUID.

But old woman how shall I save GRANIA against so many enemies?

9r, ll. 3–4 Pencil deletions.
12, 17 Type deletions.

[Berg(12)]

[10^{r}]

(27)

LABAN.

You must save GRANIA, you must conquer every enemy who comes to attack you for all will come to rob you of GRANIA.

DIARMUID.

~~So I am to be an out cast from the FIANNA~~ – GOLL, CAOELTE, USHEEN, all my brothers in arms know me no longer. In the wastes GRANIA and I must live. Is this your prophecying old woman?

LABAN.

GRANIA has the golden apple in her bosom. It must console you.

DIARMUID.

GRANIA is a sweet woman . But why should all me men be against me?

LABAN.

All men are against the man who possesses GRANIA.

DIARMUID.

Will there be peace in the end? Shall we never come upon some peaceful valley where I may love GRANIA in peace?

LABAN.

You will come upon some peaceful valley.

DIARMUID.

And there I shall live in love and peace?

[11^{r}]

(28)

LABAN.

You will come upon some peaceful valley.

DIARMUID.

And there we will plant the seed of the apple we have

10^{r}, l. 3 Pencil cancellation.

gathered in the waste and there it shall flourish and bear morebeautiful apples.

GRANIA.

We must find some new hiding place.

DIARMUID.

There is a steep path up ~~these~~ this mountain, it will lead us across the mountain and we can place rocks in the path that will conceal it from FINN. (He goes up the path~~)~~ GRANIA returning to LABAN) Will FINN pursue us always? Will FINN love me always?

LABAN.

The followed shall turn and follow and the end shall be the same as the beginning.
(GRANIA withdraws, the old woman chants: –

FINN and DIARMUID
Shall be friends again
And the murderedbrother
Shall be 'venged by the brother,
The second son that the shepherd

[12ʳ]

(30)

Changed to a boar, a black
And bristless boar in the forest
With a Druid hazel stick{ *,* **.**
~~This boar~~ shall come out of the forest *;*
And DIARMUID must go to the hunting
And be killed as the story tells
And the cunning of FINN
Shall wind and un~~wind~~ *ravel* **the story.**
I sing for good and ill,
I sit and spin.
(The scene closes)

11ʳ, ll. 6, 8 Type deletions.
12ʳ, l. ⁻1 The page number is a mistake for "29": a page has not been lost.
3, 4, 8 All the emendations on this page are in pencil.

III: Ulick's Scenario

The scenario was published in *The Musician* November 17, 1897, p. 24, and is given here literatim. It appears to have been excerpted from an early draft of *Evelyn Innes,* chapter 23 (first edition published in May 1898): see pp. 304–305 of the first edition, where Ulick tells stories of Mongan and Fin and some phrases overlap. Note that the spellings Diarmid, Dermont, and Caolte recur in Moore-derived versions of the play.

A SCENARIO FOR AN OPERA.

DEAR SIR,—

I send you a scenario—a suggestion for the book of an opera. Perhaps Wagner has made the musical setting of legends so much his own that any continuation on this line is at present impossible. However, some musicians do not take this view, for we have Vincent d'Indy's *Fervaal*, and Hamish MacCunn's *Diarmid.* The new music is probably waiting for thc ncw librcttist who must introducc a new class of subject suitable to a musical interpretation.

Yours, etc.,

GEORGE MOORE.

FIN MACCOOL, the great chieftain, who two hundred years later became, by reincarnation, Mongan—there is another legend telling how Mongan and the Bard fell into dispute concerning the exact spot where a certain king had been slain. It is Caolte, one of Fin's most famous warriors, who appears to confirm Mongan's statement. Mongan, being Fin MacCool, knows the exact spot, for Fin was present when the King was slain. Caolte is another subject for an opera.

Ulick looked forward to writing it, and as the vision of the glory of Caolte increased in distinctness within him, he seemed to forget Evelyn and Fin MacCool. But his absorption in the legends and the gods, and the names and deeds she heard, carried her over the rim of natural existence. The atmosphere grew denser, and she saw spears and spear-heads and the dying attitudes of fallen warriors. Her ear caught the sound of distant battle, and to the top of high rocks prophets had climbed, and their prophecying was borne away on the colours of lurid sunsets. At last the evening appears when Fin MacCool is to marry Grania, the most beautiful woman in all Ireland. The lake shines in the last rays, and the tribesmen are building a raft on which they will cross the lake at daybreak

to raid the kingdom of Dermont, a former vassal and friend of Fin MacCool's. For his love of Grania, Dermont has left Fin's court, and has fortified himself in his own castle, in his own country. But a harper comes, and tells the tribesmen that they may cross the lake, but that they may not capture or kill Dermont. A different fate is his. Only the boar shall kill Dermont, and none but Dermont shall kill the boar. Dermont's father, he tells, was jealous of a shepherd's son, the shepherd's son being more beautiful that Dermont, so he took the boy between his knees and crushed him to death. The shepherd in his grief went into the woods with his other son, whom he changed into a boar, which should ravage the country, invulnerable to all weapons till it should mortally wound Dermont. Then Dermont should kill it and free the country from its destruction. The barbarians are alarmed by the prophesying, and in the midst of their alarm trumpets call them into the encampment for the wedding festival. But Grania has heard of Dermont, who is dying of love of the mere fame of her beauty—Dermont and Grania have never seen each other. She comes down the stage to watch the lights of his castle, and Dermont lands from a boat with three companions who endeavour to dissuade him. But he must see Grania, and at first sight she falls so violently in love with Dermont that she begs him to carry her off. The barbarians throw spears and shoot arrows after the fugitives; and so ends the first act.

The Second Act opens with an account of the pursuit. For seven years battles, pursuits and flights have been the order of their lives, but Dermont has no fear of Fin. He knows that the mighty Fin cannot reach him, but his forebodings have not been assuaged by the fact that Fin had relaxed his pursuits; has apparently acquiesced in his possession of Grania, for a boar has been heard of in the neighbourhood and Dermont fears it may be the boar on which his fate hangs. At that moment the folk enter with account of the ravages committed by the boar, and Dermont's companions cannot understand how it is that one so brave, one who has defied even the mighty Fin, should stand in mortal dread of a boar. It is believed that none but a great chief can kill the boar, and the folk in their despair at Dermont's indecision have sent for Fin MacCool. The news of Fin MacCool's arrival is brought in, and Grania seems taken by an uncontrollable desire to see Fin. She begs Dermont to send him a welcome, urging that perhaps as he, Dermont, may not hunt the boar Fin may rid the country of the pestilence. Dermont's shame of his own cowardice begets suspicion of Grania. But there is no escape from his destiny; the arrival of Fin at his gates is announced, and he consents to receive his former rival. Fin comes in chanting the song of the boar. He holds out a hand of friendship to the man who has withstood him for seven years, and to celebrate their peace he proposes that they shall hunt the boar together. Grania declares that this is the one thing Dermont may not do, she goes to Fin and begs of him to withdraw his challenge to Dermont. With magnificent arrogance Fin declares his willingness to hunt the boar himself, and in the midst of the dilemma the harper says that the death of the boar shall unite the greatest man in Ireland to the most beautiful woman in Ireland. So no choice is left to Dermont but to accept the ordeal, and in answer to Grania's entreaty he says that whatever a man's fate may be, he had better meet it valiantly in the open field that that it should seek him out in a corner.

The Third Act is laid in the forest. Wrapt in a skin Dermont sleeps under a tree. The dawn is breaking. Grania, who has been consulting the oracles, arrives in haste and begs him to abandon the hunt; but he doubts her oracles, for he can see that she is casting covetous eyes on Fin. The strains of the horns are heard, and Dermont starts in pursuit of the boar. Then Fin and his vassals arrive, telling various narratives how the boar has

escaped their spears and arrows; they are about to start again in pursuit, when the harper warns them that pursuit is useless. What must happen had better be allowed to happen; and they had better betake themselves to pursuit of other game. Fin remains behind. He hears a cry and goes in the direction of the cry, and returns with Dermont, who, as has been predicted, has been mortally wounded by the boar. He begs for water, but the water that Fin carries in his hands runs through his fingers, and Dermont dies before he has tasted a drop. At that moment Grania appears at the top of the rocks. Fin hurries after her, tribesmen enter from both sides, and a battle is about to begin when Grania, leaning on Fin's shoulder, bids them cease.

The tribesmen burst into laughter and tears, for they at last understand that Grania has loved Fin all the while, and the body of Dermont is borne away, and a bridal procession is formed.

IV: Elgar's Musical Accompaniment

The way in which Moore involved Elgar and afterward pressed him to write an opera on the same subject is told in Moore's words in Kennedy and also in the introduction, parts ii and iii, above. Even as the stage play went into production, Moore's mind had returned to earlier hopes for a full-length operatic score; and his retrospective narrative involves Elgar in his earliest thoughts for musical accompaniment, remembering "some music I had heard long ago at Leeds" (*Salve, H&F* 313). Given Moore's habitual deviousness, it is possible that he approached Henry Wood in Bayreuth in the hope that that Wood, in turn, would introduce him to his more talented friend. Thus, his first letter to Elgar requests the music for the death of Diarmuid that he had just learned Augusta Holmes could not supply and, without ado, broaches the topic of an opera, which his subsequent letters return to with flattering insistence.

At this point (August 22, 1901), the funeral march and some incidental horn music was all he wanted for the stage play: "I don't want music in the first or second acts" (Kennedy 171). It is also important to note that the question of Laban's song did not arise until the play went into rehearsal: Moore did not send Elgar the words until October 9 (Kennedy 176–177; cf. *Salve, H&F* 315–316). Nonetheless, despite the almost accidental background of Elgar's contribution to the stage play, the result was that "*Diarmuid and Grania* was the first of the [Irish Literary Theatre's] plays to use music in any integral fashion" (Hogan 115).

For comments on the finished music, from a compositional point of view, see Jerrold Northrop Moore, *Edward Elgar: A Creative Life* (Oxford: Oxford University Press, 1984), pp. 354–355. For the records of Elgar's compositional process, for the most part in the British Library and demonstrating that he began work on September 28, 1901, see Christopher Kent, *Edward Elgar: A Guide to Research* (New York: Garland, 1993), pp. 185–186. Kent also lists contemporary and later references to the music.

Following the performances of the play in Dublin in October 1901, the "Funeral March" was performed on January 18, 1902, in London. The full score, comprising three pieces of incidental music for orchestra, was published by Novello and Company as Elgar's opus 42 later in the same year. It was dedicated, appropriately, to Henry Wood. The three parts of opus 42 comprise (1) incidental music, (2) funeral march, and (3) song: "There are Seven that Pull the Thread," and they all together last for approximately twelve minutes. The full score for the song alone is reproduced below. Novello also published a score of the same for voice and piano in 1902. The other two parts of opus 42 were also published separately.

It is difficult to determine the authority of the text that accompanies Elgar's music. Variations such as the repetition of lines 5 and 11, the stanza break, and the contraction in line 11 derive from musical exigency, but other variations, such as the grammatical formula in lines 2 and 3, could be argued to derive from a version intermediate between the one inserted into

Berg(99), folio 21^{v}, and the two extant fair copies. To make comparison easier with the versions recorded in Appendix I, the words are transcribed separately below:

There are seven that pull the thread
There is one under the waves,
There is one where the winds are wove,
There is one in the old grey house
Where the dew, where the dew is made before dawn

One lives in the house of the sun,
And one in the house of the moon,
And one lies under the boughs
Of the golden apple tree,
And one spinner is lost.
Holiest, holiest seven
Put all your pow'r on the thread
That I've spun in the house to night.

There are seven that pull the thread.
SONG in ACT I.
W. B. Yeats.
Edward Elgar.
Andante.
Flauto.
Clarinetto in A.
Fagotto.
Corni in F.
Arpa.
Violini I.
Violini II.
Viole.
Voce.
Violoncelli.
Bassi.
con sordini
pp subito
dim.
div.
Quasi Recit.
There are seven that pull the thread
rit.
a tempo
cresc.
colla parte
ad lib
There is one un-der the waves, There is one where the winds are wove, There is
Copyright 1902 by Novello & Co Limited

rit.
a tempo
colla parte
dolciss.
one in the old grey house Where the dew, where the dew is made before dawn.
One lives in the house of the sun, And one in the house of the moon, And one lies under the
espress.
div.
pizz
arco
dim.

Adagio.
Fl.
Cl.
Fag.
Cor.
Arpa.
Vic I.
Vic II.
Viole
Voce
Vcl.
B.
dim.
Recit.
pizz.
con espress.
boughs Of the golden ap-ple tree,
And one spinner is lost.
Ho-li-est, ho-li-est seven
Adagio.
rit.
div.
pp ad lib.
Put all your pow'r on the thread ___ That I've spun in the house to night.___
rit.

V: Staging

(1) Cast, etc

Diarmuid and Grania produced at the Gaiety Theatre by the F. R. Benson Company for the Irish Literary Theatre. Music for the play was specially composed by Edward Elgar and the cast was as follows:

King Cormac	Alfred Brydone
Finn MacCoole	Frank Rodney
Diarmuid	F. R. (Frank) Benson
Goll	Charles Bibby
Usheen	Henry Ainley
Caoelte	E. Harcourt Williams
Fergus	G. Wallace Johnstone
Fathna	Walter Hampden
Criffan	Stuart Edgar
Niall	Matheson Lang
Conan the Bald	Arthur Whitby
An Old Man	H. O. Nicholson
A Shepherd	Mr Owen
A Boy	Ella Tarrant
A Young Man	Joan Mackinlay
Grania	Mrs F. R. (Constance) Benson
Laban	Lucy Franklein

The companion-piece was Douglas Hyde's *Casadh an tSugáin*, with Hyde in the main role and supporting parts played by members of the Keating Branch of the Gaelic League.

The first night was on October 21, 1901. Evening performances followed on Tuesday and Wednesday, and there was a matinee on Wednesday. Benson continued in Dublin and the company was persuaded to substitute *Grania* and *Sugáin* for an evening performance of *King Lear* on Friday. There were therefore five performance of the double-bill in all. Details and references are supplied in part iii of the introduction.

(2) Scenes and Costuming

Augusta Gregory's grangerized copy of *Samhain* (no. 1, 1901; Berg[3–4]) contains sketches of some of the people who attended the first and second nights (of J. M. Synge, W. B. Yeats "The Lecturer," and John O'Leary, all by John Butler Yeats); of other sketches by John Butler Yeats, Jack B. Yeats, Pamela Colman ("Pixie") Smith [dated October 22, 1901], and ?Alice Milligan; and autographs by Augusta Gregory, Constance Benson, Frank R. Benson, Edward Dowden, John O' Leary, and ?Alice Milligan.

In particular, it contains six pencil and wash sketches, with ink outlining, of scenes and characters, from Act I (figs. *a–e, h*); and five similar sketches by the same artist of characters in *Casadh an tSugáin*, together with an illustration of Dr. Hyde speaking after the performance. They are executed on a small artist's drawing tablet, with double holes on the left, some on leaves that have been trimmed or divided; they are unsigned, although the view across the heads of the audience in figure *a* and the portrait of Dr. Hyde speaking in particular resemble the manner of Jack B. Yeats, who habitually used the same kind of drawing tablet.

It also contains ink sketches of ?Cormac and ?Niall in a very different style by AE (George Russell) (figs. *f* and *g*); a cartoon by, or of, "R.M."; and what appears to be a joint cartoon that combines an ink sketch by Alice Milligan with another by Jack B. Yeats (fig. *i*).

Finally, a line illustration from a newspaper, "Scene from 'The Twisting of the Rope'" (signed "PB") is pasted onto the rear inside cover, and a cartoon of Moore plucking W. B. Yeats in the shape of an Irish harp, together balanced on the dome of St. Paul's, (signed "Max"), is pasted on rear outside cover. (The cartoon had been published in *World*, Christmas 1900, untitled: see Rupert Hart-Davis, compiler, *A Catalogue of the Caricatures of Max Beerbohm* [London: Macmillan, 1972], #1045.)

The illustrations that bear on *Diarmuid and Grania* are, in more detail, as follows:

(*a*) Pencil and wash, with ink outlining; 8.7 by 12.6 cm; unsigned; pasted onto inside front cover. Grania in a red dress, listening to Laban dressed in blue.

(*b*) Pencil and wash, with ink outlining; 8.7 by 12.6 cm; unsigned; pasted onto inside front cover. Grania in a red dress, leaving with Diarmuid dressed in brown.

(*c*) Pencil and wash, with ink outlining; 8.7 by 12.0 cm; unsigned; pasted onto verso of title page. The drugged Fenians, Cormac presiding over them (blue robe), and Usheen (red tunic, green trousers) and Caoelte (blue tunic) standing alongside.

(*d*) Pencil and wash, with ink outlining; 11.9 by 6.5 cm; unsigned; pasted onto page 10. Usheen, holding his harp (red tunic, green trousers).

(*e*) Pencil and wash, with ink outlining; 9.3 by 5.0 cm; unsigned; pasted onto page 10. Conan, wearing dove gray sheepskins. These first five sketches, figures *a–e*, together with figure *h*, are tentatively ascribed to JBY.

(*f*) Ink; approx 9.0 by 6.5 cm; signed AE (George Russell); sketched directly onto top LH side of page 3 and partly across text. Stocky figure with winged helmet, moustache, and spear, one arm akimbo, perhaps Diarmuid.

(*g*) Pencil and wash, with ink outlining; 15.0 by 5.2 cm; unsigned, but in the manner of figure *f*; sketched directly onto top RH side of page 3 and partly across text. Suppliant figure holding ?goblet, perhaps Niall.

(*h*) Pencil and wash, with ink outlining; 11.3 by 3.9 cm; unsigned; pasted onto page 14. Usheen (red tunic, green trousers). An illegible name might have been written in pencil across the bottom of the sketch; I suppose the character is Usheen because of the coincident color scheme with figure *d*.

(*i*) In bottom half of page [38], on the LH side of a total area approximately 10.5 by 14.5 cm, is an ink sketch of Hanrahan/Dr Hyde twisting a rope, over which is written, in unpracticed Irish script, "Elis ni Macleageán". An inserted slip says "Drawing on left, bottom of last page, is by Eric Maclagan", but the script spells an approximate version of Alice Milligan's name that she used, alongside other versions, on other occasions. On Eric R. Maclagan, see *CL* III 185n. Meanwhile, Milligan had taught herself enough Irish to write a short play, *Diarmuid agus Grania*, which she and Anna Johnston had staged on a tour of Donegal in autumn 1898; her short play in English, *The Last of the Fianna*, had been performed alongside Edward Martyn's *Maeve* by the Irish Literary Theatre on February 19, 1900; and she was a friend not only of Yeats and Russell but of the Fay brothers, who produced Hyde's *Sugáin*.

Adjacent to this, on the right side of the area, is a sketch marked off by an encircling line and signed below with JBY's distinctive monogram. It delineates a character isolated on stage, wearing a winged helmet like the one Russell pictured in figure *f*, nervously peering out of a barrel: it is Diarmuid preparing to suffer the brickbats of the audience. Milligan's and JBY's sketches together construct a comment on the different reception of the two plays. That is, while sketches *a–h* (along with the other sketches of *Sugáin*) record the extreme simplicity of the theatrical arrangements, figure *i* conjoins Irish Hyde weaving his own popular success with the luckless Benson as fairground Barrel Man (cf. the illustration of the same in JBY's *Life in the West of Ireland* [Dublin: Maunsel, 1912], p. 61).

In addition to the above, Declan Kiely recently discovered a ring-bound sketchbook belonging to Jack B. Yeats in the Berg Collection ("Sketch books [v.p.] 1900–1908, 6 v.", no. 4) that contains further illustrations of the play. Paper and page size (respectively, 12.9 by 8.9 cm. and 12.7 by 8.8 cm.) prove it to be the source for the sketches in AG's *Samhain*, although those left in the sketchbook are in a less finished state. The following illustrations have most bearing on *Diarmuid and Grania*. They appear on the opening sequence of pages, the intervening and subsequent pages being either blank or filled with other material.

(*j*) The upper cover carries the description "DUBLIN / 1901" in large caps, along with "Diarmid / and Grania", with JBY's logo at bottom RH corner.

Inside, the front paste down (not reproduced) is inscribed in ink "Jack . B Yeats / Diamid and Grania / and of / the Twisting of the Rope". An arrow, the purpose of which can only be guessed at, points toward the bottom RH corner of a (facing?) page. The present facing page (1^r; not reproduced) has "Dublin / 1901 / Diarmid / and Grania" written in pencil over what appears to be an erased list of words, beneath which is (LH side) an erased male figure and (RH side) another list of erased words.

(*k*) Folio 2^r is headed "DIARMID AND GRANIA" and described beneath as "King looking into shield 1901", with JBY's logo at bottom RH corner. Pencil and wash, with ink outlining. The seated figure's clothing is blue, like Cormac's robe in figure *c*; the tunic of the dozing guard in the foreground is uncolored.

This piece of business is not recorded in the extant texts; and the figure on the throne wears a flattened wimple and dependent collar, not a conical headdress as the white-bearded Cormac does elsewhere (in figs. *m* and *o*). It is indeed likely that the figure is Laban, whose clothing is also blue (see figs. *m* and *n*), sitting on the king's throne and explaining the shields to Grania in Act I. If this is the case, the mistake confirms one's impression that the headings and descriptions were added some time after the sketches were made.

(*l*) Folio 2^{v} carries the barely legible description at the bottom LH corner, on the colored border, "DIARMID / AND GRANIA" above JBY's logo and the date "1901". Pencil and wash, with ink outlining. The sketch most likely depicts a scene from near the end of Act II, with Grania lying on the ground (in a red dress) in the forest, as Diarmuid (dressed in brown), in a helmet and carrying a light spear, prepares to pursue the boar.

(*m*) Folio 3^{r} is headed "DIARMID and GRANIA", and at the bottom carries the date "1901" (LH side) and JBY's logo (RH side). Pencil and wash, with ink outlining. The sketch depicts the moment in Act I when Laban prepares the drink Grania will serve. Both women are depicted in dresses of the same light blue color.

(*n*) Folio 5^{r}, pencil and wash, depicting Laban in a light blue dress and described as "THE SPINNER".

(*o*) Folio 6^{r}, pencil and wash, with ink outlining, depicting Cormac, described as "KING". While his throne and cushion are painted in (brown and blue, respectively), his robe remains uncolored (as in fig. *m*). The verso carries the pencil memo "Audience at Grania / sang the Men of the West". For the singing by Gaelic League members of the audience who came to support Hyde's play, see introduction, page xxxvii.

(*p*) Folio 8^{r}, pencil and wash, with ink outlining, carries an untitled depiction of Conan in gray-colored sheepskins. Compare figure *e*, where the dress is belted and he is wearing thonged shoes.

(*q*) Folio 9^{v}. An incomplete pencil and wash sketch of a scene in Act II or III that could represent an abandoned beginning of figure *l*, before the figures were inserted, or the beginning of a reworking of the same. The color wash representing shadow is the same shade of gray in both sketches.

Note that the illustrations accompanying the Act I spinning song and Act II blood bond in *A Broad Sheet* (January 1902; see Appendix I) were by the joint editor (with Jack Yeats) of that journal, Pamela Colman Smith, who attended the second performance. Despite their statuesque idealism, therefore, they possess particular interest. On Colman Smith, see *CL* III 251n.

(3) Performances

The memoirs and reviews cited in the introduction, part iii, contain some references to individual performances. Other reviews containing additional details are conveniently available in Hogan 102–117.

Illustration (*a*)

Illustration (*b*)

Illustrations (*c*), above; (*d*), left; (*e*), below

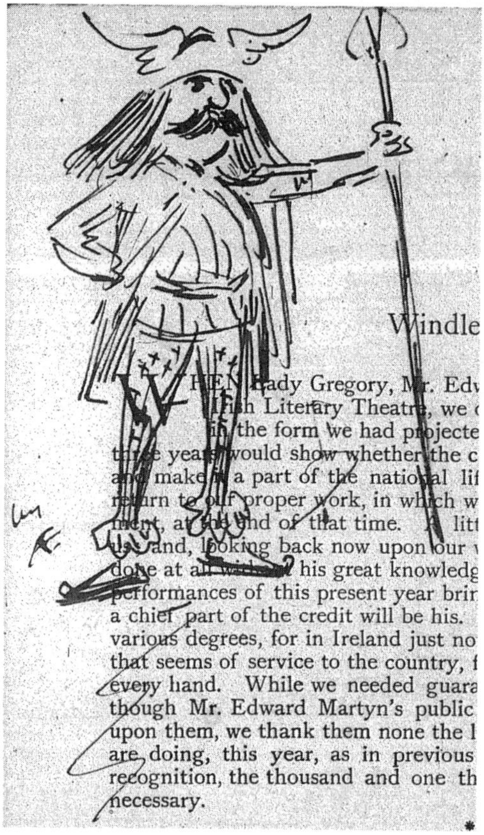

Illustration (*f*)

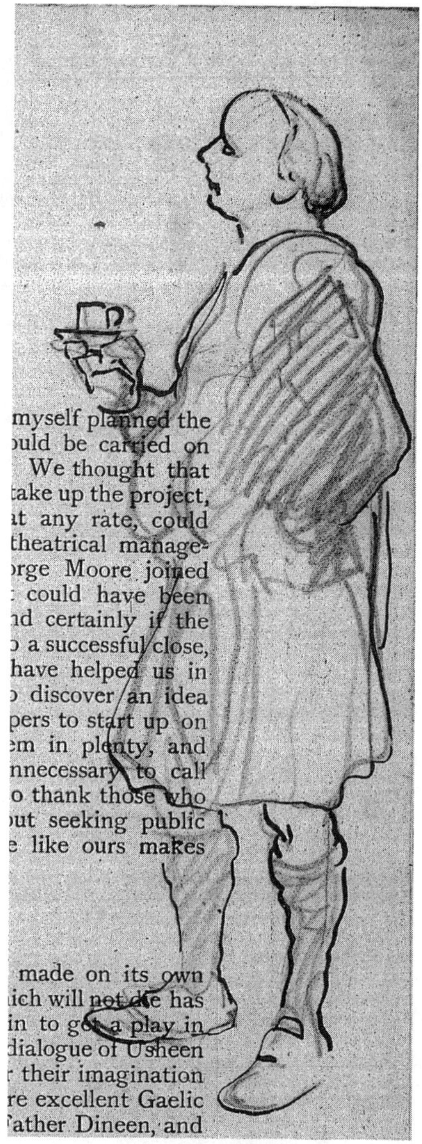

Illustration (*g*)

Illustration (*h*), right

Illustration (*i*), below

Illustration (*j*)

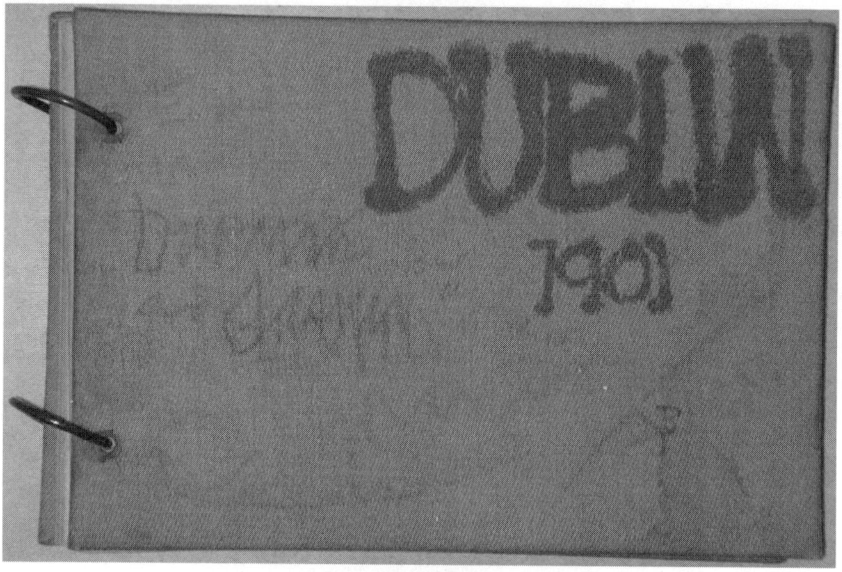

Illustration (*k*)

Illustration (*l*)

Illustration (*m*)

Illustration (*n*)

Illustration (*o*)

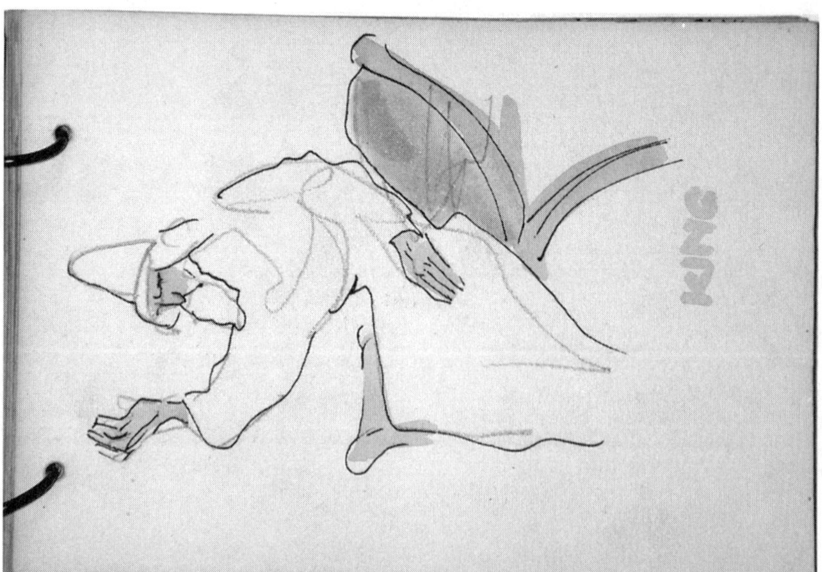

Illustration (*p*)

Illustration (*q*)

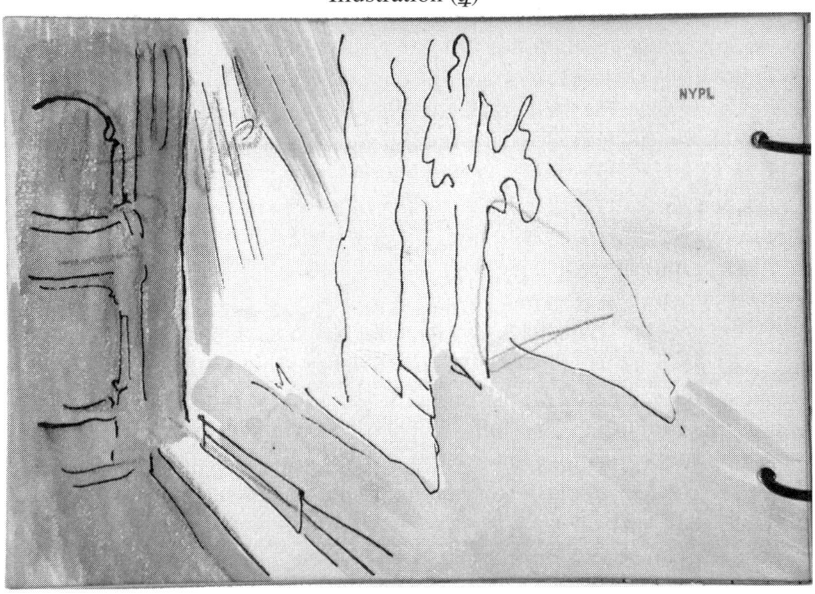

VI: Moore's French Translation of the Redrafted Act II

In Moore's *Hail and Farewell* account of the composition of the play, he suggests he began to write a version of Act II in French following an argument with Lady Gregory and Yeats at Coole Park. The argument over an appropriate style was supposedly resolved by an agreement for Moore to compose a text in French, which Gregory would translate into English, which Taidgh O'Donoghue would translate into Irish, which Gregory would translate into English; and this circuitously derived English text, finally, would have style put upon it by Yeats. James Joyce mocked the procedure by adding a footnote to some text in French: "Translout that gaswind into turfish, Teague, that's a good bog and you, Thady, poliss it off, there's a nateswipe, on to your blottom pulper" (*Finnegans Wake*, 3d ed. [London: Faber and Faber, 1964], p. 281n). Moore supplies the present example, and describes it as written at a French hotel (*Ave, H&F* 246–255; cf. also Hone 238–239).

If one disregards the claim that the hotel was in France, one must suppose the scenes were written at the Shelbourne Hotel between September 17 and 28, 1900; in other words, at the beginning of the first intense period of work on the play and previous to the open quarrel that nearly wrecked the collaboration during October–November. However, Moore's account is at variance with the scenarios he printed in 1897 and drafted for Yeats at Tillyra in 1899–1900, as well as contrary to what we know he was working on during September 1900. Further evidence confirms that the language of original composition was never French but always English, that the present version is a translation based on a scenario that came from Yeats and was in turn developed, in English, by Moore; in short, that the English original dates from after the production of the play and before the final breakdown between the collaborators; also that the present French translation contributes to Moore's rewriting of events again later, perhaps several years later, when he revisited the quarrel.

Moore's account is therefore faction-fiction, not history. He blames Gregory and Yeats for the "insulting proposal" that a first version of the play should be composed by him in French (*Ave, H&F* 255), despite his proposals of similar translation schemes with respect to *The Shadowy Waters* and his own *The Untilled Field.* He uses a 1902 revision to bolster his beginning position in a dispute about style that began in 1900. He pretends a translated text is an original composition, and the example in French is allowed to be as ruinous as he protested Yeats's revisions made his adequate English. Here, by a process of mirror clowning, Kiltartan romance is made to appear zany and banal. The contextual narrative supplied by *Hail and Farewell* thrives on muddling strands of chronology, on exchanging details from analogous situations, and most of all on Moore's's particular kind of storytelling. We enjoy evident distortions to the extent that we must be churlish to wish them otherwise.

Moore retained a choice of versions of the complete text of the play, and it remains uncertain why he translated the March 1902 substitution for Act II, not something else. Did he reckon that it lent itself especially to pastiche in "Stratford atté Bowe" French? Or did he settle on the revision because, unusually, the scenario for the substitution originated not from himself but from Yeats (*Aut* 330; cf *CL* III 167)? Yeats claimed the decision to revise the act was by mutual agreement and, unusually, he bothers to mention that his correspondence with Moore bears this out (*Aut* 322). However, significantly, no surviving letters refer to the matter from either side. It is possible that Yeats was rewriting history in his turn, just as Moore took the opportunity to caricature a scenario he felt he had accepted too readily.

Part iv of the introduction describes how, at the time Yeats began to construct his substitute Act II, Moore simultaneously began to frame a strikingly different treatment of the golden apple motif that threads through the opening dialogue; and how Yeats's use of the same emblem, brimming with mythological and hermetic significance in poems like "The Man Who Dreamed of Fairyland" and "The Song of Wandering Aengus" onward, also appears in Gregory's writing. In short, Moore's cod-French translation concentrates an area of disagreement that opened up at Coole and neatly apportions blame within it.

The text that follows is from the first printing in *Hail and Farewell: Ave* (London: William Heinemann, 1911), pp. 355–360. It may be observed that the same pages—indeed Moore's entire account of the *Diarmuid and Grania* saga—remain unrevised in his annotated copy of the 1925 Appleton (New York) edition, now NLI 19,697.

Une caverne.* GRANIA *est couchée sur une peau d'ours; se réveillant en sursaut.

GRANIA.

J'ai entendu un bruit. Quelqu'un passe dans la nuit des rochers. Diarmuid!

DIARMUID.

Je t'ai fait peur.

GRANIA.

Non. Mais qu'est ce que tu m'apportes? Quels sont ces fruits d'or?

DIARMUID.

Je t'apporte des pommes, j'ai trouvé un pommier dans ces landes, très loin dans une vallée désolée. Cela doit être le pommier dont le berger nous a parlé. Regarde le fruit! Comme ces pommes sont belles! Cela doit être le pommier des admirables vertus. Le berger l'a dit.

(*Il donne la branche à* GRANIA.)

GRANIA.

Ces pommes sont vraiment belles, elles sont comme de l'or. (*Elle fait glisser une pomme dans sa robe.*) Les solitudes de ces landes nous ont sauvegardés de toute poursuite. N'est-ce pas, Diarmuid? Ici nous sommes sauvegardés. C'est la solitude qui nous sauvegarde, et ce pommier sacré dont le berger nous a parlé. Mais les pommes si belles doivent être le signe d'un grand malheur ou peut-être bien, Diarmuid, d'une grand joie. Diarmuid! j'entends des pas. Écoute! Cherche tes armes!

DIARMUID.

Non, Grania, tu n'entends rien. Nous sommes loin de toute poursuite. (*On écoute et alors* DIARMUID *reprend le bouclier qu'il a jeté par terre; avançant d'un pas.*) Oui, Grania, quelqu'un passe dans la nuit des rochers. . . . Qui êtes-vous? D'où venez-vous? Pourquoi venez vous ici?

Entrent deux **Jeunes Hommes.**

1er JEUNE HOMME.

Nous venons de Finn.

DIARMUID.

Et vous venez pour me tuer?

1er JEUNE HOMME.

Oui.

GRANIA.

Vous êtes donc venus ici en assassins! Pourquoi cherchez-vous à tuer deux amants? Quel mal vous avons-nous donc fait? Nous sommes ici dans les landes inconnues, et si nous ne sommes pas morts c'est parce que la Nature nous a sauvegardés. La Nature aime les amants et les protège. Qu'avons nous donc fait pour que vous veniez aussi loin nous tuer?

2ème JEUNE HOMME.

Nous avons voulu faire partie du Fianna, et nous avons passé par toutes les épreuves de la prouesse que l'on nous a demandée.

1er JEUNE HOMME.

Nous avons fait des armes avec les guerriers de Finn.

2ème JEUNE HOMME.

La lance lourde et la lance légère, nous avons couru et sauté avec eux.

1er JEUNE HOMME.

Nous somme sortis acclamés de toutes les épreuves.

DIARMUID.

Et vous êtes venus chercher la dernière épreuve. Finn vous a demandé ma tête?

1er JEUNE HOMME.

Avant d'être admis au Fianna il faut que nous apportions la tête de Diarmuid à Finn.

GRANIA.

Et ne savez-vous pas que tout le Fianna est l'ami de Diarmuid excepté Finn?

DIARMUID.

Ils veulent ma tête? Eh, bien! qu'ils la prennent s'ils le peuvent.

GRANIA.

Qui de vous attaquera Diarmuid le premier?

1er JEUNE HOMME.

Nous l'attaquerons tous les deux à la fois.

2ème JEUNE HOMME.

Nous ne venons pas ici faire des prouesses d'armes.

DIARMUID.

Ils ont raison, Grania, ils ne viennent pas ici faire des prouesses d'armes, ils viennent commes des bêtes cherchant leur proie; cela leur est égal comment.

(*Ils commencent l'attaque; l'un est plus impétueux que l'autre, et il se met en avant.* DIARMUID *se recule dans un étroit passage entre les rochers. Soudain il blesse son adversaire qui tombe.* DIARMUID *passe par dessus son corps et s'engage avec l'autre. Bien vite il le jette par terre et il commence à lui lier les mains, mais l'autre se lève et s'avance l'épée à la main gauche.* DIARMUID *donne son poignard à* GRANIA, *laissant à la charge de* GRANIA *l'adversaire qui est par terre, il attaque l'autre et dans quelques ripostes fait sauter l'épée de sa main. Pendant ce combat* GRANIA *est restée assise le poignard en main. Tout de suite, l'homme ayant voulu se relever, elle le poignarde, et avance nonchalamment vers* DIARMUID.)

DIARMUID.

Ne le quitte pas.

GRANIA.

Il est mort.

DIARMUID.

Tu l'as tué?

GRANIA.

Oui, je l'ai tué. Et maintenant tue celui-ci, ce sont des lâches qui n'auraient osé t'attaquer un par un.

DIARMUID.

Je ne peux pas tuer un homme qui est sans armes. Regarde-le! Son regard me trouble, pourtant c'est Finn qui l'a envoyé. Laisse le partir.

GRANIA.

Les malfaiteurs restent les malfaiteurs. Il retournerait à Finn et il lui dirait que nous

sommes ici. (*S'adressant a l'homme.*) Tu ne dis rien, tourne-toi pour que le coup soit plus sûr. Mets-toi contre le rocher. (*L'homme obéit.*)

DIARMUID.

Dans la bataille je n'ai jamais frappé que mon adversaire et je n'ai jamais frappé quand il n'était pas sur ses gardes. Et quand je le fis tomber, souvent je lui donnai la main, et j'ai souvent déchiré une écharpe pour étancher le sang de ses blessures. (*Il coupe un lambeau de son vêtement et l'attache autour du bras du jeune homme.*)

GRANIA.

Qu'est ce qu'il dira à Finn?

DIARMUID.

Je lui donne ces pommes d'or et Finn saura que ce n'est pas lui qui les a trouvées. Oui, je lui donnerai cette branche, et Finn saura que je tiens mon serment.

GRANIA.

Entre ses mains les pommes seront flétries, elles n'arriveraient pas à Finn si elles sont les pommes dont le berger nous a parlé, elles disparaîtraient comme une poussière légère. (DIARMUID *donne la branche à l'homme, et l'homme s'en va traînant le cadavre de son compagnon.*) Tu aurais dû le tuer, il conduira Fina à cette caverne. Il faut que nous cherchions des landes plus désertes, plus inconnues.

DIARMUID.

Peut-être au bout de ces landes où il faut que nous nous cachions des années, peut-être trouverons nous une douce vallée paisible.

GRANIA.

Et alors, Diarmuid, dans cette vallée que se passerait-il entre nous?

DIARMUID.

Grania, j'ai prêté serment à Finn.

GRANIA.

Oui, mais le serment que tu as prêté à Finn ne te poursuit pas dans la forêt: les dieux à qui tu as fait appel ne régnent pas ici. Ici les divinités sont autres.

DIARMUID.

Si cet homme nous trahit, il y a deux sorties à cette caverne et comme tu dis il ne faut pas attendre ici, il faut que nous nous en allions très loin.

GRANIA.

Je ne puis vous suivre. Je pense à toi, Diarmuid, nuit et jour, et mon désir me laisse sans force; je t'aime, Diarmuid, et les pommes que tu as trouvées dans cette vallée désolée ne sont-elles pas un signe que ma bouche est pour ta bouche?

DIARMUID.

Je ne puis t'écouter . . . nous trouverons un asile quelque part. Viens au jour. La caverne te fait peur et elle me fait peur aussi. II y a du sang ici et une odeur de sang.

GRANIA.

Restons, Diarmuid; tu es un guerrier renommé, et tu as vaincu deux hommes devant mes yeux. Mais, Diarmuid, la pomme qui est tombée dans ma robe . . . regarde-la; elle ose plus que toi. Nous avons des périls à traverser ensemble, les serments que tu as prêtés à Tara ne te regardent plus. Notre monde sera autre et nos divinités seront autres.

DIARMUID.

Mais j'ai prêté serment à Finn. Finn c'est mon frère d'armes, mon capitaine. Combien de fois nous avons été contre l'ennemi ensemble! -- non, Grania, je ne puis.

(*Il la prend dans ses bras. La scène s'obscurçit.*)

GRANIA.

Le jour est pour la bataille et pour les périls, pour la poursuite et pour la fuite; mais la nuit est le silence pour les amants qui n'ont plus rien qu'eux-mêmes. (*Un changement de scène; maintenant on est dans une vallée pierreuse à l'entrée d'une caveme, à gauche un bois et le soleil commence à baisser.*)